DICTIONARY OF AMERICAN HISTORY

DICTIONARY
OF
AMERICAN HISTORY

DICTIONARY
OF
AMERICAN
HISTORY

REVISED EDITION

VOLUME VI

Quebec, Capture of–Tariff

CHARLES SCRIBNER'S SONS
MACMILLAN LIBRARY REFERENCE USA
Simon & Schuster Macmillan
NEW YORK

Simon & Schuster and Prentice Hall International
LONDON · MEXICO CITY · NEW DELHI · SINGAPORE · SYDNEY · TORONTO

An Imprint of Simon & Schuster Macmillan
1633 Broadway
New York, NY 10019-6785

15 17 19 AG/H 20 18 16

Printed in the United States of America
Library of Congress Catalog Card Number 76-6735
ISBN 0-684-13856-5 (set)

ISBN 0-684-15071-9 (vol. 1)   ISBN 0-684-15075-1 (vol. 5)
ISBN 0-684-15072-7 (vol. 2)   ISBN 0-684-15076-X (vol. 6)
ISBN 0-684-15073-5 (vol. 3)   ISBN 0-684-15077-8 (vol. 7)
ISBN 0-684-15074-3 (vol. 4)   ISBN 0-684-15078-6 (Index)

EDITORIAL STAFF

DICTIONARY OF AMERICAN HISTORY

Quebec, Capture of–Tariff

QUEBEC, CAPTURE OF. In 1759, the year after the fall of Louisburg, Nova Scotia, British Gen. James Wolfe was given command of 9,280 men, mostly regulars, with which, supplemented by naval aid, he was ordered to capture Quebec. Assembled at Louisburg in May 1759, steadily drilled and trained, Wolfe's force sailed June 4, 1759, for the Saint Lawrence River. On June 27 he landed on the Île d'Orléans below Quebec and for two months, while the fleet dominated the river, made many abortive attempts against the city.

The French under Marquis Louis Joseph de Montcalm defended the north bank of the Saint Lawrence from the city to the Montmorency River, a distance of seven miles. Wolfe went ashore east of this stream and, thus partially encircling Quebec with soldiers on the east, batteries on the south bank, and the fleet upstream, conducted a long-range bombardment and siege. On July 31 he aimed a powerful but unsuccessful stroke by land and water at the Montmorency end of the French shore entrenchments. Attacks in August were also unsuccessful.

On Sept. 3 the British skillfully abandoned the Montmorency camp. Wolfe secretly moved 3,000 soldiers to the ships upstream, where his fleet threatened several well-entrenched landing places. On the calm, cloudy night of Sept. 12, he slipped a strong force downstream in small boats, effected a surprise landing at a small cove near the city, overpowered a small guard, captured an adjacent battery, and made it possible for about 5,000 troops, rowed over from the south shore and brought downstream by the ships

themselves, to land safely and climb to the heights of the Plains of Abraham by six in the morning.

In this position, Wolfe threatened Quebec's communications with Montreal and inner Canada and the bridge across the Saint Charles. Montcalm thus had to assemble and fight for the possession of Quebec from the outside. In the formal 18th-century manner, Wolfe had his force arrayed by eight o'clock. Although skirmishing intervened, it was ten o'clock before Montcalm formed for a conventional assault. This was met by formal volleys from the British battalions. Shots were exchanged for a few moments only, then the French wavered. The British charged, and the French fled. Wolfe was killed on the field, and Montcalm was carried off mortally wounded. Wolfe's successor entrenched and closed in, and the surrender of Quebec on Sept. 18 made inevitable British hegemony in Canada and the close of the French and Indian War, with the capture of Montreal, the following year.

[J. C. Long, *Lord Jeffrey Amherst*; F. Parkman, *Montcalm and Wolfe*; W. T. Waugh, *James Wolfe*.]

ELBRIDGE COLBY

QUEBEC, PHIPS'S ATTACK ON (1690). In retaliation for French depredations, the New England colonies and New York formed an expedition to capture Canada for England (*see* King William's War). On Aug. 9 Sir William Phips sailed from Massachusetts with a fleet of thirty ships, 2,000 men, and provisions for four months, bound for Quebec. Phips, who several months earlier had easily captured Port Royal, the outpost in Acadia, expected another swift victory, but Canadian Gov. Louis Frontenac, who had been advised of the expedition, did his best to strengthen his position. When the English fleet appeared before Quebec, on Oct. 16, the fortress was garrisoned by 2,700 French regulars and militia. A demand for surrender was answered by a curt refusal. The English landing party was repulsed, and, bombardment failing, Phips realized the futility of his enterprise and within a week sailed for home.

[Gilbert Parker, *Old Quebec*.]

ROBERT W. BINGHAM

QUEBEC ACT (one of the Intolerable Acts), passed by Parliament on May 20, 1774, was intended to pacify the French-Canadians by granting the free exercise of the Roman Catholic religion and reestablishing French civil law in Quebec. Much to the consternation of many American colonists, the boundaries of Quebec were extended to the Ohio River on the south and to the Mississippi on the west, the city to be governed by an appointive governor and council without benefit of a representative legislative body, and all acts were subject to royal veto. The interior was thereby closed to the expansion of the free institutions of the seaboard, and the hopes of colonial land speculators were blasted. Colonial propagandists effectively used the Quebec Act to widen the breach between Great Britain and colonies by declaring that the British government intended to employ the "Popish slaves" of Quebec to establish the doctrines of royal absolutism and Roman Catholicism throughout the American colonies.

[Victor Coffin, *Province of Quebec and the Early American Revolution*.]

JOHN C. MILLER

QUEEN ANNE'S WAR (1702–13) was the American counterpart of the War of the Spanish Succession, which was fought in Europe from 1701 to 1714. Fundamental issues, including the rivalry of France and England in America, had been left unsolved by the Treaty of Ryswick (1697). They were revived upon the acceptance of the Spanish throne by a grandson of Louis XIV of France in November 1700. The threat of Bourbon domination in Europe and in French and Spanish America caused William III of England and the Dutch Netherlands to ally (Sept. 7, 1701) with Holy Roman Emperor Leopold I, a member of whose Hapsburg family claimed the Spanish throne. On May

4, 1702, two months after Anne had succeeded William as sovereign of England, the three allied powers jointly declared formal war on France.

In America the war was fought in the West Indies and on the Carolina and New England frontiers. In the summer of 1702 the English captured the West Indies island of Saint Christopher, but Adm. John Benbow's action against a French squadron along the Spanish Main was indecisive. After the English failure to take Guadeloupe in 1703, military activity in the West Indies was restricted to privateering, from which English colonial trade suffered. In December 1702 South Carolinians destroyed the town, not the fort, of Spanish Saint Augustine; and in 1706 a Franco-Spanish fleet was repulsed from the harbor of Charleston.

In the North, New England bore the brunt of the war against the French in Canada. Until 1709 neither New York nor England rendered material assistance. English settlements, including those at Wells and Saco (Maine) and Deerfield, Reading, Sudbury, and Haverhill (Massachusetts), became the victims of barbarous French and Indian raids. After retaliatory attacks on Port Royal, led in 1704 by Col. Benjamin Church and in 1707 by John March, had failed, the English colonists secured, in 1709, Great Britain's promise of aid for expeditions against Quebec and Montreal. These projected campaigns under Samuel Vetch and Francis Nicholson were abandoned in October 1709, after the promised British force had been diverted to Portugal. In the following year a British contingent arrived, secured by Nicholson and Peter Schuyler in London. With that support, colonial troops, led by Nicholson and Sir Charles Hobby took Port Royal in October 1710. The capture of Port Royal, renamed Annapolis Royal, signified the fall of Acadia to Great Britain.

The new Tory government in England, dominated by Robert Harley and Henry St. John and interested in obtaining the asiento (a license from Spain to sell slaves in its colonies) for the projected South Sea Company, disavowed the contention of John Churchill, Duke of Marlborough, that the European fronts were alone decisive, and dispatched an expedition to support colonial troops in attacks on Quebec and Montreal. However, on Aug. 23, 1711, ten of the expedition's ships were wrecked with the loss of nearly 750 men on the rocks above Anticosti Island in the Saint Lawrence, and the rest of the expedition returned to England.

Meanwhile, in 1711, peace negotiations had begun in Europe. In October 1712, American colonial governors received a royal proclamation of an armistice, and on Apr. 11, 1713, Queen Anne's War was concluded by the Treaty of Utrecht.

[E. B. Greene, *Provincial America;* F. Parkman, *A Half-Century of Conflict;* G. M. Trevelyan, *England Under Queen Anne.*]

E. B. GRAVES

QUEENSTON HEIGHTS, BATTLE OF (Oct. 13, 1812), the second serious reversal sustained by American arms in the disastrous campaign of 1812, arose out of the attempt of Maj. Gen. Stephen Van Rensselaer to invade Canada across the Niagara River. The advanced units of the American force (which amounted in all to about 3,100 men) successfully established themselves upon the steep escarpment overlooking the village of Queenston, Ontario, and defeated the first attempts of the British forces to dislodge them. In one of these attempts the British commander, Maj. Gen. Isaac Brock, was killed. American hopes of victory were dispelled by the refusal of the main body of the New York militia to cross the river to support the troops already engaged on the grounds that their military duty did not require them to leave the state. Later in the day Maj. Gen. Roger Sheaffe, upon whom the British command had devolved, collected a force of about 1,000 men, gained the summit of the heights by a flanking movement, and enveloped and captured the whole force that had crossed the Niagara. The British reported the capture of 925 prisoners, of whom 417 were regulars; among them was Lt. Col. Winfield Scott. American casualties numbered 90 men killed; the British had 14 killed, 77 wounded, and 21 missing.

[Henry Adams, *History of the United States of America During the First Administration of James Madison;* Sir C. P. Lucas, *The Canadian War of 1812.*]

C. P. STACEY

QUIDS. Adapted from *tertium quid* ("third something"), the term "quid" was used in the early 19th century in the United States to refer to a member of a third political party or faction composed of disaffected Jeffersonian (or Democratic) Republicans who attracted Federalist support with varying success. Quids were most commonly so called in Pennsylvania and New York, although the term was occasionally used in other states. "Quid" was generally applied reproachfully by political opponents and was rarely used in self-designation.

In Pennsylvania the Quids, a Republican faction, officially called themselves the Society of Constitutional Republicans. In 1805 the Pennsylvania Quids, with Federalist support, reelected Gov. Thomas McKean, who had lost the support of the majority wing of the Pennsylvania Republican party after his election in 1802. In New York the Quids were the Republicans who remained loyal to Gov. Morgan Lewis after he was repudiated by the Republican majority led by De Witt Clinton. Like the Pennsylvania supporters of McKean, the Lewisites of New York recruited Federalist support, but they failed to reelect Lewis in 1807. In 1806 Virginia Rep. John Randolph broke with President Thomas Jefferson, creating the most serious schism in the Republican party on the national level during Jefferson's presidency; Randolph's supporters were also labeled Quids. Historians have sometimes implied that all Quids were supporters of Randolph and that the Quids represented something of a national third-party movement, but contemporary records show that there was no connection between the Pennsylvania and the New York Quids and that neither faction was aligned with Randolph. While Randolph supported James Monroe for the Republican nomination for the presidency in 1808, there was no similar support by Quids in New York or Pennsylvania. No national Quid party ever developed, and most Quids continued to regard themselves as Jeffersonian Republicans.

[Noble E. Cunningham, Jr., *The Jeffersonian Republicans in Power: Party Operation, 1801–1809,* and "Who Were the Quids," *Mississippi Valley Historical Review,* vol. 50 (1963).]

NOBLE E. CUNNINGHAM, JR.

QUINTEROS BAY EPISODE (Aug. 20, 1891), one of the factors that caused the anti-U.S. feeling among the rebel Chilean forces, known as Congressionalists, following the overthrow of President José Manuel Balmaceda. The Valparaíso press charged that the captain of a U.S. ship broke neutrality laws when, after observing the landing of rebel forces at Quinteros Bay, he was said to have reported what he had seen to officials of the Balmaceda government. Subsequent investigations failed to show any impropriety in the captain's actions, but the anger of the Congressionalists finally expressed itself in the attack on American sailors from the U.S.S. *Baltimore* in Valparaíso in October.

[H. C. Evans, *Chile and Its Relations With the United States.*]

OSGOOD HARDY

QUITRENTS

QUITRENTS originated in England from the commutation into a fixed money equivalent of the annual food and labor payments due the lord of the manor. By the period of colonization the quitrents had become firmly established and were being enforced by distraint upon personal property and in extreme cases by forfeiture of the land. As it was transplanted to the American colonies, the quitrent was a feudal due payable by freeholders to the proprietaries to whom the land had been granted. Later, after the proprietary rights were taken over, as in Virginia and the Carolinas, it became a crown revenue in the royal colonies.

Customarily, the right to charge quitrents was included in all the early charters, but in Plymouth and Massachusetts Bay the title to the land was soon vested in the freeholders, and this system of free tenure soon spread to the other New England colonies. So firmly did it become one of the "liberties of New England," that an attempt to exact quitrents was one of the chief grievances in the overthrow of Gov. Edmund Andros in 1689 (see New England, Dominion of). Quitrents were nominally due in all the American colonies outside of New England, but they were more effectively enforced in Pennsylvania and the colonies to the south. Also, they were proposed, but not always collected, in the West Indies, the Floridas, Nova Scotia, and other outlying colonies, and were included in the several schemes to set up British colonies west of the Appalachians.

The annual amount of the quitrent was nominal, varying in individual colonies from two to four shillings per 100 acres, with occasionally one pence per acre, yet collection became a frequent source of irritation. Distraint was the usual means of enforcement, and efforts to secure forfeiture of the land, where necessary, met with determined opposition. The medium of payment, likewise, stirred up much controversy. With specie scarce, it was necessary to use commodities, such as wheat, tobacco, and other native products. Consequently, many disputes arose between the assemblies and the representatives of the proprietaries or the crown over the rate of exchange, grading, the cost of transportation, and the place of payment. Actually, the quitrents produced a sizable revenue in the colonies in which they were enforced. In Pennsylvania, by 1776, nominally £10,204 was annually due, of which about a third was collected. In Maryland, in 1774, practically the entire rent roll of more than £8,518 was collected. In South Carolina, toward the close of the colonial period, the annual return averaged between £2,000 and £3,000.

In both the proprietary and royal colonies the quitrents constituted an independent revenue for which there was no public accounting. But, especially as the revolutionary period approached, they were collected with much less friction in the royal than in the proprietary colonies. After the outbreak of the American Revolution the assemblies summarily ended these feudal dues upon the land, notably in Maryland where the Act of Abolition showed how galling this sign of perpetual dependence upon an absentee landlord had become.

[B. W. Bond, Jr., *The Quit Rent System in the American Colonies.*]

BEVERLEY W. BOND, JR.

QUIVIRA. *See* **Coronado's Expedition; Gran Quivira.**

QUO WARRANTO, in its broadest sense, is a writ to determine the right to the use or exercise of a franchise, public office, or liberty. This ancient writ was used to initiate proceedings for the forfeiture of the Massachusetts Bay charter in 1684 though the actual forfeiture resulted from a suit on a writ of *scire facias.* The writ has given way to the speedier "information in the nature of a *quo warranto*" that has been used in many cases to determine the right of individuals to hold offices or of corporations to enjoy privileges under franchises. Generally, *quo warranto* proceedings are not employed if other legal remedies are available, and, since about 1775, they have been civil in character.

[C. M. Andrews, *Colonial Self-Government.*]

ERIK MCKINLEY ERIKSSON

QUOTA SYSTEM. There were no numerical restrictions on immigration into the United States until 1921. In that year a law was passed, purportedly as a temporary measure, specifying that annual immigration from any country outside the Western Hemisphere and Asia was limited to 3 percent of those born in that country who resided in the United States in 1910. A permanent quota system was enacted by the Immigration Act of 1924, which allocated immigration quotas for each country outside the Western Hemisphere. The quotas were fixed on a "national origins" basis, related to the national origins of the U.S. population in 1929, with a maximum total allocation of approximately 150,000. The national origins system was criticized as discriminatory, particularly against immigrants from southern and eastern Europe, but it was retained in the McCarran-Walter Act of 1952. The national origins system of quota allocation was abandoned in 1965, when new legislation was adopted establishing a total annual allocation of 170,000 for all countries outside the Western Hemisphere. Certain close relatives of American citizens were exempted from these numerical restrictions, and designated preferences were established for other relatives of American citizens and resident aliens and for aliens with certain occupational skills. Since 1965 visas have been allocated under the Eastern Hemisphere quota on a first-come, first-served basis, without regard to race or national origin. In addition the 1965 act established an annual allocation of 120,000 for immigrants from the Western Hemisphere, also to be selected on a first-come, first-served basis, but also with the qualification that certain close relatives of American citizens were to be exempted from this numerical restriction.

[C. Gordon and H. N. Rosenfield, *Immigration Law and Procedure.*]

CHARLES GORDON

RABAUL, AIR CAMPAIGN AGAINST (1943–44). In August 1943 the World War II Allies decided to drop earlier plans to capture the key Japanese base of Rabaul, on New Britain, just east of New Guinea, and instead to neutralize and bypass it, leaving its ultimate reduction to air attacks. By fall, indeed, Allied advances in New Guinea to the west and in the Solomons to the south had all but isolated Rabaul. Beginning in October, Allied air power, both land- and sea-based, struck repeatedly with increasing intensity at the enemy base, concentrating on eliminating Japanese air strength there. Within a month Rabaul was no longer an offensive threat. By the end of 1943 the line of Allied air bases had advanced close enough to permit the initiation of a sustained air offensive aimed at knocking out the Japanese base completely. This offensive, combined with continuing Allied advances in the central and southwest Pacific, soon rendered Rabaul useless to the enemy as a strategic base. Under almost daily attack, the Japanese in Rabaul began evacuating aircraft and shipping. By March 1944, when the great Allied air offensive came to an end, roughly 20,000 tons of bombs had been dropped. The nearly 100,000 Japanese troops still defending Rabaul were isolated and impotent, no longer factors in the war.

[Wesley Frank Craven and James Lea Cate, eds., *The Army Air Forces in World War II,* vol. IV; John Miller, Jr.,

Cartwheel: The Reduction of Rabaul, United States Army in World War II.]

STANLEY L. FALK

RACE RELATIONS in complex societies, such as that of the United States, involve patterns of behavior between members of large categories of human beings classified on the basis of similar phenotypic or observable physical traits, particularly skin color. Race is a social status that individuals occupy along with other statuses, such as ethnicity, occupation, religion, age, and sex. In the United States racial status has often been paramount, transcending all other statuses in affecting human relations.

Although there have been numerous instances of friendly and egalitarian relationships across racial lines in American history, the major pattern of race relations has been one characterized by (1) extreme dominant-subordinate relationships between whites and nonwhites, as indicated by the control by whites of the major positions of policymaking in government, the existence of formal and informal rules restricting nonwhite membership in the most remunerative and prestigious occupations, the often forcible imposition of the culture of white Americans on nonwhites, the control by whites of the major positions and organizations in the economic sector, and the disproportionate membership of nonwhites in the lower-income categories; and (2) extreme social distance between whites and nonwhites, as indicated by long-existent legal restrictions on racial intermarriage, racial restrictions in immigration laws, spatial segregation, the existence of racially homogeneous voluntary associations, extensive incidents of racially motivated conflict, and the presence of numerous forms of racial antipathy and stereotyping in literature, the press, and legal records. This pattern has varied by regions and in particular periods of time; it began diminishing in some measure after World War II.

The Colonial Period. Race relations in America began when the first Europeans labeled all the diverse indigenous ethnic groups they encountered "Indians"; when members of a number of ethnic groups forcibly brought from Africa became "Negroes"; and when Europeans conceived of themselves as a distinct group, as "Whites." There were at least 1 million Indians in North America before the arrival of Europeans, divided into hundreds of tribes and bands and speaking at least 200 mutually unintelligible languages. In a pattern that was repeated until 1871, treaties were signed with Indian groups conceived of as "nations"; whites infiltrated their territories; conflict and war ensued; and the Indian groups were driven from their territory in violation of treaty agreements.

In 1619 the first blacks arrived in the English colonies, probably as indentured servants. Between 1660 and 1770 black chattel slavery was institutionalized into the legal system, creating a status that ran counter to English law. The rudiments of English culture were forcibly imposed on diverse black ethnic groups, eliminating in time most of their African heritage.

1783–1900. After the American Revolution white Americans increased their migration into Indian territories to the west and into the Spanish empire (and after 1821, Mexico). The policy of the federal government toward Indians before the Civil War was the removal of Indians to then unwanted territories west of the Mississippi River. By 1821 the tribes in the Great Lakes region had been forcibly relocated, and the Indians of the Southeast were forcibly removed between 1817 and 1835. In 1862 Indians were designated wards of the Bureau of Indian Affairs rather than enemies, and in 1871 Congress declared an end to the policy of signing treaties with Indian nations. Numerous conflicts took place during the 19th century as Indians resisted the invasion of their territories and their placement on reservations. Of the Indians in California 70,000 were killed by war and disease between 1849 and 1859, and other groups were similarly devastated. The defeat of the Plains Indians was made possible, in part, by the reduction of the bison herds from an estimated 13 million in 1867 to 200 in 1883. With the defeat of the Apache in 1886, the Indian wars came to an end; the Indian population had been reduced to about 200,000 and was forced into impoverishment on reservations under the paternalistic and often corrupt control of the Bureau of Indian Affairs. From 1887 to 1934 federal policy toward Indians was governed by the General Allotment Act (Dawes Severalty Act) of 1887, under which Indians were to be transformed into individualistic and responsible farmers on family-owned plots. The policy reduced reservation acreage from 139 million acres in 1887 to 47 million acres by 1933.

By 1804 all the northern states had either eliminated slavery or passed laws for its gradual abolition. But the humanitarian motives behind the antislavery laws were not sufficient to prevent the imposition of a system of severe discrimination and segregation on the 10 percent of the black population that resided in the North. Before the Civil War blacks in the North were restricted from entering various states, were given inadequate and segregated schooling, were barred from most public facilities, were excluded from jury service and denied the vote, and were nursed in segregated hospitals and buried in segregated graveyards.

In the South slavery became more profitable and more widespread after the invention of the cotton gin in 1793, and the number of black slaves increased from 697,624 in 1790 to 3,953,760 by 1860 as the system spread from the Southeast to the Southwest. Although only 350,000 slaveholders existed and 90 percent of these owned fewer than twenty slaves, the large slaveholders set the standards and policies for the antebellum South. A few slave uprisings occurred, but the most common forms of resistance to the slave system consisted of theft; day-to-day acts of sabotage, such as tool-breaking; individual acts of overt aggression; and efforts to escape.

After the Civil War, blacks improved their economic status as a whole, engaged in civil rights efforts to enforce new antidiscrimination laws, and became politically active. However, between 1877, when the federal troops were withdrawn from the South, and 1910, a new system of segregation and discrimination was imposed on blacks. With each depression in the later 19th century blacks lost their hard-won gains, were deserted by liberals, and saw a number of rights eliminated or curtailed by Supreme Court decisions in 1873, 1883, and 1896. With the passage of numerous state and local ordinances dealing with segregation, the disfranchisement of the black voter, and the economic relegation of blacks to the lowest menial occupations, the apartheid system was complete, not to be seriously challenged by white liberals or blacks until after World War II. In the North between 1865 and 1945, blacks could vote and segregation was never formalized into the legal code; but *de facto* segregation and a disproportionate placement in the less desirable occupations were still a social reality for blacks in the North.

With the end of the Mexican War in 1848, half of Mexico was annexed to the United States, and the estimated 150,000 Mexicans who lived in the territory rapidly became a numerical minority as Americans inundated the area. Most of this Mexican population was reduced to landless menial labor by 1900, through discriminatory property taxes and title laws. As the economic status of Mexicans was reduced, those of Spanish and of Indian-Spanish, or mestizo, descent were lumped together by Americans and viewed as a single, distinct, and inferior race—a view intensified by the entrance of over 700,000 legal immigrants from rural Mexico into the United States between 1900 and 1930. (In 1930 the U.S. Census Bureau, for the first and only time, divided Mexican-Americans into 4.6 percent white and 95.4 percent colored.)

During the same period European and Asian immigrants arrived in the United States in increasing numbers to meet the demands of an expanding economy. Between 1820 and 1920 some 30 million Europeans entered the United States. Being white, most of them entered the American mainstream within two or three generations, the rate of assimilation being affected primarily by the degree to which their cultures approximated that of Americans of British descent. Asians, however, met increasing resistance by white workers and West Coast legislatures. The peak decades for the Chinese immigration were 1861–90 (249,213) and 1891–1920 (239,576) for the Japanese. The Chinese were barred from voting in California in 1848, from testifying in court between 1854 and 1872, and from employment in corporations and the government by the constitution of California; were forced to pay discriminatory taxes and fees; and were subjected to numerous acts of violence made possible by the lawless conditions in the West at this time. By arriving in a more stable period, the Japanese avoided this "frontier" situation but were excluded from white unions and denied ownership of land by a number of western states (a practice declared constitutional by the U.S. Supreme Court in 1923). Further Chinese and Japanese immigration was almost terminated by congressional acts in 1902 and 1924.

1900–45. By the beginning of the 20th century almost all nonwhites were in the lowest occupation and income categories in the United States and were attempting to accommodate themselves to this status within segregated areas—barrios, ghettoes, reservations. The great majority of whites, including major educators and scientists, justified this condition on the ground that nonwhites were biologically inferior to whites. Although the period was largely characterized by the accommodation of nonwhites to subordination, a number of major incidents of racial conflict did occur: the mutiny and rioting of a number of black soldiers in Houston, Tex., in 1917; black-white conflict in twenty-five cities in the summer of 1919; and the destruction of white businesses in Harlem in New York City in 1935 and in Detroit in 1943. A major racist policy of the federal government was the forc-ible evacuation and internment of 110,000 Japanese living on the West Coast in 1942—a practice not utilized in Hawaii, and not utilized against Italians and German-Americans.

1945–75. Following World War II major changes occurred in the pattern of white dominance, segregation, and nonwhite accommodation that had been highly structured in the first half of the 20th century. After the war a number of new nonwhite organizations were formed and, with the older organizations, sought changes in American race relations as varied as integration, sociocultural pluralism, and political independence. The government and the courts, largely reacting to the activities of these groups, ended the legality of segregation and discrimination in schools, public accommodations, the armed forces, housing, employment practices, eligibility for union membership, and marriage and voting laws. In addition the federal government in March 1961 (by Executive Order 10925) began a program of affirmative action in the hiring of minorities and committed itself to a policy of improving the economic basis of Indian reservations and promoting Indian self-determination within the reservation framework (1969).

Although government efforts to enforce the new laws and court decisions were, at least at the outset, sporadic and inadequate, most overt forms of discrimination had been eliminated by the mid-1970's, and racial minorities were becoming proportionally represented within the middle occupational and income levels. Changes in dominance and social distance were accompanied by white resistance at the local level, leading to considerable racial conflict in the postwar period. The Mississippi Summer Project to register black voters in Lowndes County in 1965 resulted in the burning of 35 black churches, 35 shootings, 30 bombings of buildings, 1,000 arrests, 80 beatings of black and white workers, and 6 murders. Between 1964 and 1968 there were 239 cases of hostile black protest and outbursts in 215 cities, lasting overall 523 days, with 49,607 arrested, 7,942 wounded, and 191 killed. In 1972 Indian groups occupied Alcatraz, set up road blocks in Washington, D.C., and occupied and damaged the offices of the Bureau of Indian Affairs in Washington, D.C. The Alianza movement of Chicanos in New Mexico in 1967 attempted to reclaim Rio Arriba County as an independent republic by storming the courthouse in Tierra Amarilla. Mexican-American students walked out of high schools in Los Angeles in 1968, and a number of Chicano organizations boycotted the Coors

RACE RIOTS

Brewery in Colorado between 1968 and 1972. During the 1970's Chinese youth organizations in San Francisco staged a protest and engaged in violence, claiming the right to armed self-defense against the police and the release of all Asians in American prisons.

The major developments in the 1970's were the increased efforts on the part of federal agencies to enforce the civil rights laws of the 1960's; a greater implementation of affirmative-action programs, involving efforts to direct employers to take positive actions to redress employment imbalances (through the use of quotas in some cases); and the resistance in numerous communities to busing as a device to achieve racial integration in the public schools.

[Harry H. L. Kitano, *Japanese Americans*; Charles F. Marden and Gladys Meyer, *Minorities in American Society*; Joan W. Moore, *Mexican Americans*; Alphonso Pinkney, *Black Americans*; Benjamin Quarles, *The Negro in the Making of America*; George Eaton Simpson and J. Milton Yinger, *Racial and Culture Minorities*; Murray L. Wax, *Indian Americans*.]

RICHARD M. BURKEY

RACE RIOTS. The violent conflicts between groups having different racial or cultural backgrounds have shown themselves in the United States from time to time in the form of riots, commonly referred to as race riots even when involving hostile ethnic groups, rather than hostile races, in the anthropological sense of the term. But outbreaks between blacks and whites have been most common. If slave revolts are excluded, there were relatively few such riots in the colonies or in the United States prior to the 1960's, considering the prevalence of racism and ethnocentrism and racial and ethnic discrimination. Lynchings were far more common as an expression of the hostility of the white majority toward racial or ethnic minorities. The most serious race riots of the period were between Irish and other whites in Boston in 1837, between blacks and whites in Philadelphia in 1838, between Chinese and whites in San Francisco in 1877, between Italians and other whites in New Orleans in 1891. In the 20th century riots took place between blacks and whites in East Saint Louis in 1917, Chicago in 1919, and Detroit and Harlem in New York City in 1943. Characteristic of these conflicts was resentment of members of the majority group toward the real or imagined attempts of those considered socially inferior to gain greater rights. Typically a local incident led to the gathering of a crowd, which became a mob that indiscriminately attacked minority group members, and local law enforcement authori-

ties did little or nothing to halt the conflict. East Saint Louis in 1917 is a classic example. In this case a strike at an aluminum plant resulted in the company's hiring other workers. As was often the case, the potential labor force of unemployed persons seeking work was largely black. A delegation of white men from one of the unions called on the mayor to protest the migration of black workers into East Saint Louis. As they left the meeting they heard that a black man had shot a white man in a holdup. Rumors spread quickly, and a mob formed to avenge the shooting. Blacks were beaten indiscriminately, and shots were fired into the homes of blacks. They began arming for self-defense; shots were fired at a police car; and more violence erupted. Homes of blacks were set afire, and a number of blacks were shot, some after being beaten. The police did little more than take the injured to a hospital and disarm the blacks. When order was restored by the National Guard, forty-eight people (thirty-nine blacks and nine whites) were dead; hundreds were wounded; and over 300 buildings had been destroyed.

In the 1960's the most serious and most widespread series of race riots in the history of the United States occurred as part of a more general period of racial disturbance, which involved demonstrations by civil rights activists against segregation and discrimination. Some of the conflicts in the early part of the decade occurred when whites attacked nonviolent demonstrators or when demonstrators were attacked by police. Over 250 disturbances occurred during the period, more than 50 of which are considered full-fledged riots. Unlike the riots of earlier periods these arose largely from the minority group's striking out against racial oppression or symbols of it. Whereas all involved blacks and whites, these riots were atypical in that most of the physical conflict occurred between blacks and the police or the National Guard. Characteristically, a local incident or an event in some other area (as was the case with the assassination of Martin Luther King, Jr., in 1968 when violence erupted in 125 cities) led to the gathering of a crowd, which turned into mobs that set fires, looted stores, and fought with police. Whereas earlier race riots were for the most part characterized by white violence against the persons of blacks or other minorities, the 1960 riots were largely characterized by black violence against property. In both periods the vast majority of the casualties were blacks, killed by rioters in the first instance and by policemen or guardsmen in the second. Major riots of the period occurred in Birmingham, Ala., in 1963; New York in 1964; Watts in

8

Los Angeles in 1965; and Chicago in 1966. In 1967 alone Tampa, Fla.; Cincinnati; Atlanta; Newark, Plainfield, and New Brunswick, N.J.; and Detroit all experienced riots.

As an example of the riots of the 1960's, conflict in Newark started on July 12, 1967, when a black cabdriver was arrested and beaten by police. A crowd formed at the station house to protest the incident. The crowd became unruly and ignored requests to disperse. When police used force to clear the area, some stores were looted. The next day a rally was held to protest police brutality. When police again used force to disperse the crowd, looting began again and fires were set. Mobs roamed through some areas of the city burning, looting, and fighting with police. On July 14 the National Guard was brought in to help restore order. By the time the National Guard was withdrawn on July 17, twenty-three persons (twenty-one blacks and two whites) had been killed and $10.25 million in damage had been done.

The widespread disorders of the 1960's led President Lyndon B. Johnson to establish a National Advisory Commission on Civil Disorders on July 29, 1967. Under the chairmanship of Gov. Otto Kerner of Illinois the commission made its report in the spring of 1968. The report reviewed the history of the riots, examined the causes, and made recommendations. It identified white racism as the main cause. Specifically mentioned were pervasive discrimination and segregation, black migration to the cities and white exodus, ghetto life in the cities, frustration of hopes aroused by judicial and legislative civil rights victories, legitimatization of violence, and a feeling of powerlessness on the part of many blacks. There is little evidence of serious efforts to implement the recommendations of the commission.

[Hugh Davis and Ted Gurr, eds., *Violence in America: Historical and Comparative Perspectives;* Richard Hofstadter and Michael Wallace, eds., *American Violence: A Documentary History; Report of the National Advisory Commission on Civil Disorders.*]

HENRY N. DREWRY

RACING. *See* **Automobile; Horse Racing; Yacht Racing.**

RADAR, an acronym for "radio detection and ranging," is a method of locating distant targets by measurements made on electromagnetic radiation reflected from them. In the most common method regular brief bursts of ultrashort radio waves are beamed toward the target by a scanning antenna. The resulting echoes (which arrive in the intervals between successive bursts) are then displayed on a cathode-ray tube by means of a scanning signal synchronized with the antenna, so that the echo from each target appears as an illuminated dot in the appropriate direction and at a proportional distance and a map of the entire area being scanned is created. In other versions continuous waves are used; in some, only moving targets are detected (for example, in police sets used to detect speeding vehicles) by changes in the reflected signal relative to the transmitted signal.

Radar goes back to observations, in the 1920's, of the unintentional perturbations caused by obstacles moving in a radio field. (The phenomenon is familiar to television viewers from the disturbances caused in the picture by overflying aircraft.) Such perturbations were familiar to both amateurs and professionals in many countries and were at first freely discussed in engineering journals. As the military significance of locating enemy vessels or aircraft dawned on researchers in government laboratories in the 1930's, such references grew rarer. Among those acknowledged as having been particularly significant were two American reports, perhaps owing to the broad distribution of the journals in which they were published: a 1933 report (by C. R. Englund and others in the *Proceedings of the Institute of Radio Engineers*) describing a systematic investigation of the interferences caused by overflying aircraft and a 1936 report (by C. W. Rice in the *General Electric Review*) on the uses of ultrahigh-frequency equipment, among which was listed "radio-echo location for navigation." Throughout the 1930's commercial developments on related topics took place, for instance, on radio altimeters and on attempts to prevent collisions at sea; among the latter, experimental equipment installed on the French Line's giant ship *Normandie* received considerable publicity but achieved only moderate success. During the same period radio methods of locating storms, of measuring the height of the ionosphere, and of surveying the countryside in rugged terrain began to evolve, as did such subsequently essential technical developments as ultrahigh-frequency (microwave) tubes, circuits, and antennas; cathode-ray (picture) display tubes; and wide-band receivers capable of amplifying and resolving extremely short pulses, of the order of one-millionth of one second (microsecond) or less.

As World War II approached, parallel developments took place in government (mainly military) laboratories in several countries, primarily concerned with locating unseen enemy ships and aircraft. Such development is well documented in at least six countries (the United States, Great Britain, France, Germany, Italy, and Japan), but there were doubtless others, including Canada, the Netherlands, and the Soviet Union. The nation that made the greatest progress before the outbreak of the war was Great Britain, where a team assembled by the engineer Robert Watson-Watt devised a system of radar stations operating at metric wavelengths and of backup information-processing centers. This complex was partly in place when the war broke out in September 1939 and was rapidly extended to cover most of the eastern and southern coasts of England; by the time of the air Battle of Britain a year later, the system was fully operational and is credited with swinging the balance in the defenders' favor by enabling them to optimize deployment of their dwindling air reserves.

American military developments had started even earlier, in the early 1930's, and were carried on at fairly low priority at the Naval Research Laboratory under R. M. Page and at the army's Signal Corps laboratories under W. D. Hershberger. By the time the United States was drawn into the war, radar had been installed on several capital warships and in a number of critical shore installations, including Pearl Harbor; although the attack on Pearl Harbor in December 1941 was detected by radar, the backup system was not in place and the warning did not reach the defending forces in time. This situation was quickly corrected, and radar played a significant role in the U.S. victory over a Japanese naval force at Midway Island six months later, a battle that proved to be a turning point of the war in the Pacific.

British radar developments had not stood still in the meantime, and Great Britain made a great step forward with the invention of a high-power magnetron, a vacuum tube that made operation at the even shorter centimetric wavelengths feasible for the first time, with resulting improvements in resolution and compactness of equipment. Even before the attack on Pearl Harbor, a British delegation led by Sir Henry Tizard had brought a number of devices, including the centimetric magnetron, to the United States in an effort to enroll U.S. industry in the war effort, since British industry was already strained to full capacity. The resulting agreement was not entirely one-sided, since it placed some American developments at the Allies' disposal, for instance, the transmit-receive (TR) tube, a switching device that made it possible for a single antenna to be used alternately for radar transmission and reception. From then on until the

end of the war, British and U.S. radar developments were combined, and the resulting equipment was largely interchangeable between the forces of the two nations.

The principal U.S. radar research laboratories were the Radiation Laboratory at the Massachusetts Institute of Technology (MIT), directed by Lee Du Bridge, where major contributions to the development of centimetric radar (including quite sophisticated airborne equipment) were made; and the smaller Radio Research Laboratory at Harvard University, directed by F. E. Terman, which specialized in electronic countermeasures (that is, methods of rendering the enemy's radar ineffective and overcoming its countermeasures). The MIT group produced an elaborate and detailed twenty-eight-volume series of books during the late 1940's that constituted an invaluable basis for worldwide radar developments for several decades.

Wartime industrial advances gave U.S. manufacturers a head start over foreign competitors, notably in the defeated nations, where war-related industries remained shut down for several years. Postwar developments were enhanced by commercial demand (there was soon scarcely an airport or harbor anywhere that was not equipped with radar) and by the exigencies of the space age, including astrophysics. Many of the basic inventions of World War II remained fundamental to new developments, but additional refinements were introduced by research workers in many countries; among them, the contributions of Americans were perhaps the most numerous and ensured that American-made radar equipment could hold its own in world markets despite high production costs.

[C. R. Englund, A. B. Crawford, and W. W. Mumford, "Some Results of a Study of Ultra-Short-Wave Transmission Phenomena," *Proceedings of the Institute of Radio Engineers,* vol. 21 (1966); R. M. Page, *The Origin of Radar;* C. W. Rice, "Transmission and Reception of Centimeter Radio Waves," *General Electric Review,* vol. 39 (1936); L. N. Ridenour, *MIT Radiation Laboratory Series;* C. Susskind, *Birth of the Golden Cockerel: The History of Radar;* Sir Robert Watson-Watt, *Three Steps to Victory.*]
CHARLES SÜSSKIND

RADICAL REPUBLICANS, the determined antislavery wing of the Republican party during the first twenty years of its existence, beginning in the mid-1850's. Opposed to further compromises with slaveholders before the Civil War, they became the most persistent advocates of the emancipation of slaves during the conflict and of the elevation and enfranchisement of blacks afterward.

Veterans of the free-soil and antislavery movements, the radical Republicans played an important role in the founding of the Republican party as an organization committed to the restriction of slavery. Successful in keeping the party true to the free-soil principle, radical Republicans blocked concessions to retain the southern states' loyalty during the secession crisis and cooperated with President-elect Abraham Lincoln in defeating the Crittenden Compromise. They also demanded the retention of Fort Sumter and strongly supported the president in his refusal to evacuate it.

When the Civil War broke out, the radicals insisted on its vigorous prosecution. For this purpose they helped organize and dominated the Joint Committee on the Conduct of the War and agitated for the dismissal of conservative generals, notably George B. McClellan. They favored the confiscation of enemy property, the establishment of the state of West Virginia, and the raising of black troops. Above all, they never ceased to work for the liberation of the slaves.

The radicals' emphasis on speedy emancipation often brought them into conflict with Lincoln. They deplored his reversal of John C. Frémont's order to end slavery in Missouri, criticized his failure to oust conservative cabinet members, and demanded that he take immediate steps to abolish servitude. Their clashes with the president were formerly considered proof of their irreconcilable differences with him, but mid-20th-century historians stress the essential similarities between Lincoln and his radical critics. In many respects he tended to sympathize with their aims, if not with their methods, and he was thus able to make use of their energy and zeal to achieve the essential racial progress that he gradually came to favor.

In the controversy about Reconstruction the radicals were the main proponents of the protection of black rights in the South. Instrumental in the passage of the Wade-Davis Bill (1864), which would have freed all remaining slaves and set forth a stringent plan of reconstruction, they mercilessly denounced Lincoln when he vetoed it. Nevertheless, the president later not only cooperated with them in effecting the passage of the Thirteenth Amendment but also in his last speech endorsed at least in part their demand for black suffrage in Louisiana.

The radical Republicans at first welcomed President Andrew Johnson's accession. As a southern Unionist who had been a member of the Committee on the Conduct of the War, he was considered sufficiently stern to impose rigorous conditions on the defeated insurgents. But when he insisted on his mild plan of Reconstruction, the radicals took the lead in the congressional struggle against him. Their tireless agitation induced the moderates to cooperate in passing various measures for the protection of the blacks: the Fourteenth Amendment, the Freedmen's Bureau, and the civil rights acts may be cited as examples. The group was also responsible for the inauguration of radical Reconstruction. Because of the president's interference with Republican policies in the South, the radicals provided the impetus for his impeachment, although they suffered a severe blow in their failure to secure his conviction.

During the administration of President Ulysses S. Grant, their influence gradually waned, although they were able to maintain enough enthusiasm to enable the party to pass the Fifteenth Amendment, implement Reconstruction, and enact enforcement bills as well as one last civil rights measure. But the weakening of the reform spirit, the death and retirement of leading radicals, and the emergence of new issues contributed to their decline. Then came the panic of 1873, and when the Democrats recaptured the House of Representatives in 1874, the end of radicalism was in sight.

Because they never possessed a cohesive organization, the exact identification of individual radicals is difficult. Some Republicans were always radicals; others cooperated only at certain times. Among the most consistent radicals were Charles Sumner, Thaddeus Stevens, Benjamin F. Wade, Zachariah Chandler, and George W. Julian. Benjamin F. Butler, John A. Logan, and Henry Winter Davis were identified with the group after 1862; Lyman Trumbull collaborated only before that time. The test of radicalism was always the degree of commitment to reform in race relations; on all other issues, individual radicals differed. Protection and free trade, inflation and hard money, woman's rights and labor reform—all had their advocates and opponents. The only issues that held them together were those of opposition to slavery and insistence on fair treatment of the freedmen.

Just as different radicals had conflicting views on many economic and social questions, so were they also motivated by widely disparate incentives. While some were undoubtedly conscious of the party advantages of black suffrage in the South, many were sincerely devoted to the ideal of racial justice. Often accused of vindictiveness, they were not primarily interested in revenge and failed to punish severely any of the prominent Confederates. Because practical and ideological considerations did not necessarily conflict, such leaders as Stevens could publicly admit the influence of both. The radical Republicans' importance lies in their successful pressure for reform as evidenced in emancipation and the passage of the Thirteenth, Fourteenth, and Fifteenth amendments.

[Harold M. Hyman, ed., *The Radical Republicans and Reconstruction, 1861–1870;* Grady McWhiney, ed., *Grant, Lee, Lincoln and the Radicals;* David Montgomery, *Beyond Equality: Labor and the Radical Republicans, 1862–1872;* Hans L. Trefousse, *The Radical Republicans: Lincoln's Vanguard for Racial Justice;* T. Harry Williams, *Lincoln and the Radicals.*]

HANS L. TREFOUSSE

RADICAL RIGHT, a term applied in the United States to sociopolitical movements and groups and political factions and parties that constitute a backlash in response to supposed threats against the values and interests of their supporters. Such backlashes usually stem from rapid social or economic change: for example, sharp economic growth or decline; urbanization; immigration or migration; or acute shifts in the status of religious, ethnic, or racial groups. The protesting groups seek to maintain or narrow lines of power and privilege. And they are seen as radical or extremist because they often violate democratic political norms, and sometimes the law. They justify their actions by discounting the legitimacy of their opponents, seeing them as agents of an un-American conspiracy not deserving of political respect or constitutional protection.

Threats to the religious values of the most traditional evangelical groups gave rise in the late 1790's and again in the late 1820's to efforts to eliminate what they considered to be irreligious elements and liberal forces. In the first instance the backlash was directed against the Illuminati, a society supposedly responsible for the French Revolution and other upheavals, which worked largely through Masonic lodges in the United States; in the second instance, against the Masons themselves, culminating in the formation of the Anti-Masonic party in 1830. For the next century the most important source of rightist backlash in politics was anti-Catholicism, particularly among the Methodists and Baptists, who had become the dominant religious groups in terms of numbers.

The same deep streak of anti-Catholic feeling was seized on at different times in American history to sustain nativist movements that sought to preserve existing institutions and traditional values against the threat of change—a threat that was attributed to the increased number of immigrant Catholics, and even to conspiracies directed by the Vatican. Such groups include the Native Americans of the 1840's, the Know-Nothings of the 1850's, the American Protective Association of the 1890's, and the multimillion-member Ku Klux Klan of the 1920's.

The decade of the 1930's—with its massive depression, unemployment, and political pressures linked to events in Europe—witnessed many extremist movements. The most potent on the right was that led by a Catholic priest, Charles E. Coughlin, which was anti-Semitic and increasingly pro-Fascist.

After World War II the anti-Catholicism and anti-Semitism of the radical right were supplanted by concern with the supposed threats of Communists and blacks to national security and social institutions. The most prominent movement of the early 1950's followed the line of Sen. Joseph R. McCarthy's investigations into alleged Communist infiltration of the government and the key opinion-forming and policy-controlling institutions. Efforts to resist the changing position and the demands of the black population with respect to greater equality in the schools and the economy were first centered in the postwar South in white citizens councils. Subsequently the largest and most important rightist movement linked to racial concerns was particularly manifested in the presidential campaigns of Gov. George Wallace of Alabama, which produced large votes in primary and general elections from 1964 to 1972, as Wallace effected a coalition of disparate right-wing forces in support of the American Independent party.

Characteristically, radical-right movements, from the Anti-Masonic party to the American Independent party, have drawn their major support from the poorer, less educated, more provincial (rural and small town), and more religiously traditional elements of American society. Lacking a power center, they have generally been taken over by the conservative elite, as when the Anti-Masons merged with the Whigs after the election of 1836. Thus, most of the mass-based, radical-right groups have been short-lived, generally lasting about five years. Inability to compromise, intense factional struggles, propensities to become more extreme and thus alienate moderate supporters, gradual solidification of opposition to their extremism, and, not infrequently, policy concessions in their direction by more established forces all reduce their capacity to maintain their strength.

[Daniel Bell, ed., *The Radical Right;* R. A. Billington, *The Protestant Crusade 1800–1860;* D. B. Davis, ed., *The*

Fear of Conspiracy: Images of Un-American Subversion From the Revolution to the Present; John Higham, *Strangers in the Land: Pattern of American Nativism 1860–1925;* Earl Latham, ed., *The Meaning of McCarthyism;* S. M. Lipset and E. Raab, *The Politics of Unreason: Right-Wing Extremism in America 1790–1970;* R. A. Schoenberger, ed., *The American Right Wing;* Edward Shils, *The Torment of Secrecy.*]

SEYMOUR MARTIN LIPSET

RADICALS AND RADICALISM. The derivation of the word ''radical'' from the Latin *radix* (''root'') gives only a vague clue to its meaning in modern thought and history. It is, of course, a significant term in mathematics. But the word has also been used in a number of other fields and in a variety of contexts. Thus, one can speak of radical views in philosophy, science, art, or architecture (Frank Lloyd Wright, for example, was once thought of as a radical in architecture). The term is often used to designate a person who wishes to alter drastically any existing practice, institution, or pattern of conduct. It may be used to designate any outlook or person appearing to be unorthodox or atypical and in this sense connotes opposition to whatever is regarded as accepted or established. Thus, it is sometimes used derogatorily to discredit the views of opponents.

''Radical'' and ''radicalism'' are words used frequently in politics and fields related to politics. The radical is sometimes seen as the individual or position reflecting the most ''leftward'' view. It is therefore common to designate points on the political spectrum as radical, liberal, conservative, and reactionary. In the 20th century the term is sometimes employed to designate any view considered extreme, whether of the ''left'' or of the ''right'': hence, during the presidential campaign of 1964 candidate Barry Goldwater was not infrequently called a ''radical of the Right.'' But some view radicalism as any outlook, proposal, or program seeking basic change in the direction of greater economic, social, or political equality.

Whatever the precise meaning attached to such words as ''radical'' and ''radicalism,'' it seems they are designations that can be understood best in relation to the contexts within which they are used. They are relative terms: a position is radical in comparison with other positions that may be taken, and what is regarded as radical in one generation may be orthodox or nonradical in another. For example, Victoria Claflin was a radical in the feminist movement of the late 19th century in her advocacy not only of woman's suffrage but also of free love, but she might be regarded as less radical in the context of the feminist movement of the 1970's.

The 18th- and early 19th-century advocates of reform in the British Parliament were seen as radical, as were the utilitarians and Chartists. In pre–Civil War America many of the utopian community experiments could be described in similar terms (the Oneida Community of John Humphrey Noyes, for instance, which stressed communism in material and sexual spheres and advocated fundamental changes in the status of women). The Workies, a political party organized in 1829, was radical, as were William Lloyd Garrison and other abolitionists. The abolitionist movement as a whole was sometimes described as having conservative, moderate, and radical wings; and somewhat similarly the 19th-century peace movement was said to consist of conservatives (who thought that while war in general must be opposed, defensive wars were permissible) and radicals (who viewed all war, including so-called defensive war, as morally wrong and impermissible).

Immediately after the Civil War the label Radical Republican came to be attached to Republican party leaders who, in the manner of Thaddeus Stevens and Charles Sumner, pressed more aggressively than most Republicans for guarantees of social and political equality for newly emancipated slaves and advocated somewhat harsh measures against the former Confederacy.

Radicalism in politics from 1865 to World War I was centrally associated with proposals to alter fundamentally the ''capitalist'' economic and social system. In varying ways radicals demanded far-reaching changes in property relations, in distribution of wealth and income, or in the status of labor. The Knights of Labor were originally thought of as radical, as were the members of the Greenback Labor party, the Free Silver men, the Single Taxers of Henry George, and many leaders of the so-called Populist revolt. There were several types of so-called agrarian radicals, who advocated drastic change in the agricultural economy and society. Then there were the Socialist groups, such as the Socialist Labor Party, established in 1877, and the American Socialist Party, founded in 1901. The anarchists should also be mentioned, and their leaders, Emma Goldman and Alexander Berkman, for example. American syndicalism was represented by the Industrial Workers of the World, founded in 1905, which from its birth until the end of World War I symbolized for many all that was supposedly iniquitous in radicalism as a whole.

With the decline of socialism and anarchism after

RADIO

World War I, the center of much radicalism in the public mind came to be concentrated in the so-called Communist movement and its "front" groups. "Bolshevist," "Communist," "Red," "subversive," and "radical" were often used interchangeably, both by citizens and by congressional and state legislative investigating committees. During the 1950's "Communist radicals" became the targets of Sen. Joseph McCarthy's campaigns, and "McCarthyism" became a kind of shorthand for "antiradicalism." In the heyday of McCarthyism fundamental criticism in any area of American life was at an ebb and new radical movements were correspondingly rare.

During the 1960's many leaders and movements appeared that were called radical either by themselves or by their critics. Students for a Democratic Society (SDS) was one such group, with its criticism both of the Old Left (the Marxists) and of orthodox American politics. The student protest movement, centering in such institutions as the University of California, Berkeley, was variously described as being radical in general or as having a radical wing. Many thought of the civil rights movement as an exemplification of radicalism, and many held that Martin Luther King, Jr., advocated radical solutions. Before his assassination in 1968 King was regarded by many as nonradical, the mantle of radicalism having passed to such leaders as Stokely Carmichael and H. Rap Brown. The peace movement of the 1960's, which concentrated on ending the Vietnam War, produced a number of self-styled radicals and leaders who were seen by others as radical. The veteran peace leader A. J. Muste described himself as a radical pacifist, and several of his associates, including David Dellinger, saw themselves in a similar light. Nonregistrants under the Selective Service law were viewed by many as radicals.

It is highly characteristic of the American experience that many proposals that at one time were described as radical, and even as unthinkable, should later be adopted as public policy. The list is a long one, including federal income taxes (originally described by many opponents as a kind of communism), collective bargaining, and Social Security. Some of the immediate demands included in the Socialist party platform of 1912—radical in their day—came to be embodied in New Deal legislation enacted after 1933.

The functions of American radicalism, viewed as sharp social criticism and pleas for fundamental changes in society, have been described as manyfold: to challenge an ever-present and strong tendency to social complacency; to emphasize the proneness of a society to fall away from its professed ideals; to point out the frequently gross inadequacy of moderate remedies; and to provide the drastically unorthodox paradigms seemingly so essential for stimulation of creative public discussion.

[Benjamin R. Epstein, *The Radical Right;* Christopher Lasch, *The New Radicalism in America;* Sidney Lens, *Radicalism in America;* Staughton Lynd, *Intellectual Origins of American Radicalism.*]

MULFORD Q. SIBLEY

RADIO. Although in a broad sense the technology of radio broadcasting is usually associated with the early experimental work of Heinrich Hertz and Guglielmo Marconi, the growth of the medium as a means of broadcasting entertainment and news bears a curious relationship to the development of the telephone. As early as the fall of 1876 experimental "concerts" were transmitted by Alexander Graham Bell from Paris to Brantford, Ontario, Canada, utilizing a voice transmitter designed to accommodate several soloists. The following two decades witnessed considerable experimental work relating to the conveying of concerts and entertainments over wire line, although the commercial phase of these ventures was more successful in Europe than in the United States. In 1893 the Telefon-Hirmondo ("Telephonic Newsteller") began operation in Budapest, Hungary, with a sophisticated schedule of news and music programming up to twelve hours per day. In the following year the Electrophone Company started a similar service in London.

These "wire service" broadcasts had limited application in comparison with the conventional use of the telephone for business and personal communication. Tonal fidelity was an obvious consideration, and the vacuum tube amplifier had yet to be invented. Innovation, however, was not lacking, and as early as 1881 a stereophonic arrangement was installed by French engineer Clément Ader to broadcast Paris Opera performances to a listening salon at the nearby Electrical Exposition Center. Even loudspeaker devices were employed to distribute sound over a wider area.

Marconi's investigations and those of other radiotelegraph pioneers were concerned primarily with the transmission of Morse Code intelligence via radio. The feasibility of implanting voice or music signals on a radio wave developed from experimental work in this new branch of physics, but not always in a manner that indicated full understanding of the scientific principles involved. The person most responsible for initiating a viable system of radiotelephony was Reginald Fessenden, who developed the high frequency alternator for radio work and whose radiotelephone transmissions from Brant Rock, Mass., in November and December 1906 provided crucial tests for the new technology in its embryonic stage. Lee De Forest proceeded along similar lines of investigation but employed the modulated high frequency arc as the transmission device. In January 1910, De Forest broadcast *Cavalleria Rusticana* and *I Pagliacci* from the stage of the Metropolitan Opera in New York City with several famous soloists participating, including Enrico Caruso.

By 1914 the triode vacuum tube, a De Forest invention, gave promise of providing some outstanding improvements in performance for radio technology. Improvements in the physical operation of the device were contributed by both the Bell Telephone Laboratories and the General Electric Company. De Forest and Edwin H. Armstrong designed further circuit innovations to make the tube practical for radio receivers and transmitters. In 1915 the Bell System conducted tests in transatlantic radiotelephony employing the antenna of Navy Station NAA, Arlington, Va. Vacuum tubes were used exclusively in the transmission system.

By 1915 it was evident to both telephone and radio engineers that the cooperation between their respective technologies could provide entertainment and news transmissions via wireless. De Forest was perhaps most active in these endeavors, but the period 1915–20, the last phase of radio's prehistory, saw a rapid increase in experimentation by radiotelephone enthusiasts. Although the Radio Act of 1912 provided only marginal regulation over the new medium, the Department of Commerce saw fit to issue Special Land Station designations to many amateurs and to college experimental stations, thus stimulating interest in the technology of voice and music transmission.

In 1919 the Radio Corporation of America (RCA) was formed as an effort to preserve U.S. initiatives in the wireless field. The new company absorbed the assets of the Marconi Wireless Telegraph Company of America and entered into manufacturing agreements with both the Westinghouse Electric Corporation and the General Electric Company. A sizable percentage of radio receiver production over the following decade was made under this cross-licensing structure, and crucial circuit innovations, such as the superheterodyne, were introduced.

Although it is impossible to pinpoint the beginning of news and entertainment broadcasting as an industry, it is considered to have originated with the transmission of the returns of the Harding-Cox presidential election over station KDKA, Pittsburgh, on Nov. 2, 1920. An industrial giant was seemingly born overnight, and urgent matters of financing, regulation, and engineering required immediate attention.

The first broadcasting stations were assigned to either 360 or 400 meters (833 or 750 kilocycles per second [kHz]), but the Department of Commerce was faced with critical regulatory problems under the Radio Act of 1912, which did not envision the rapid growth of such service. Four major industry-government conferences were held under the aegis of Secretary of Commerce Herbert Hoover. Out of many committee meetings arose the modern AM (amplitude modulation) broadcast structure, covering the band of frequencies from 550 to 1600 kHz. And stations were assigned frequencies in accordance with a predetermined allocation program.

Although engineering developments were significant during the decade 1920–30, certain unique problems developed that had no precedents in other technological areas. Principally, the expansion of the medium was limited in that only so many broadcast stations could be assigned within the allowable spectrum space without serious interstation interference. This problem was alleviated in some measure through more selective design in receivers (particularly the superheterodyne), but the 700-odd stations in existence by 1927 seemed the maximum that could be tolerated. To complicate the problem, the authority of the Department of Commerce to regulate radio communication was gradually eroded by court decisions until a final blow was struck in 1926, when a federal district judge ruled that the secretary of commerce had no power to establish regulations under terms of the Radio Act of 1912.

New legislation was needed. On Feb. 23, 1927, President Calvin Coolidge signed the Radio Act of 1927 into law, creating the five-member Federal Radio Commission to regulate radio communication according to "public interest, convenience, and necessity." The new legislation proved to have far-reaching implications, for given the limited expansion possible, the government was often forced to choose one among several applicants for a single channel, generally on the basis of programming.

Owing to the rapid growth of the entire field of telecommunications, President Franklin D. Roosevelt recommended that a single agency be created to cover the many facets of the new developments in electronics, and Congress passed the Communications

Act of 1934, which established the Federal Communications Commission (FCC).

The creation of the FCC came at a time when engineering developments were about to have a wide-ranging effect on radio broadcasting. The design of directive antenna arrays for broadcast stations, in conjunction with a revised allocation structure, greatly extended the capability of the AM spectrum. From the 700-odd stations in existence in 1927 arose a system capacity in excess of 4,000 stations by the early 1970's. But the 1930's foreshadowed even greater things for broadcasting. The low frequencies in use and the conventional method used to put voice and music on the radio carrier (amplitude modulation) made the system intrinsically susceptible to noise—both atmospheric and man-made. Owing largely to the efforts of one person, Armstrong, the technique of frequency modulation (FM) was introduced. It not only freed the system of static but also allowed efficient use of the higher frequency spectrum (generally above 40 megacycles per second [MHz]) to permit wide-range high-fidelity broadcasting. Extensive field tests conducted from a transmission site at the Empire State Building in New York City proved the viability of the medium as a unique broadcast service. But FM had to suffer through another twenty years of growing pains before the industry adopted it as the broadcast service Armstrong envisioned. The reasons for the delay (as opposed to the quick introduction of AM) involved several crucial factors—political, economic, and engineering. The AM interests were firmly entrenched and could not envision any significant improvement in service by changing to FM. Television was "just around the corner," and the principal industrial group involved in the area, RCA, chose to put its research and development task force to work in what seemed a more exciting and promising electronic area. From the technical point of view, many AM engineers did not understand FM, which was based on a more complex circuit structure. Armstrong persisted in his developmental work, financed largely with funds available from his other radio inventions. The period 1939–41 saw expansion of FM broadcast station licenses and manufacture of receivers under the Armstrong FM patents. A victory for Armstrong was the adoption of FM for the television sound channel, under FCC regulations, adopted for the commercial introduction of television, July 1, 1941.

Following World War II, FM broadcasting held to a precarious existence. In 1945 the FCC moved the spectrum allocation from the band of frequencies between 42 and 50 MHz to that between 88 and 108 MHz. Considerable controversy developed over this frequency shift; in addition, Armstrong had protracted litigation with RCA and other industry members over basic FM patents.

The spectacular rise of FM broadcasting after 1960 can be traced to several developments in sound engineering technology. In 1947 Harry Olson of RCA proved that a type of distortion termed harmonic must be extremely low in electronic reproducers for the listener to enjoy high-fidelity broadcasting. In 1957–58 a major breakthrough occurred with the commercial introduction of stereophonic recordings and, experimentally, with the design of several stereo broadcast systems. In 1960 the FCC examined a number of stereo-FM methods in tests conducted over station KDKA-FM and received at Uniontown, Pa. The following year stereo FM was in commercial service, using a system designed by the Zenith Radio Corporation and the General Electric Company. The stereo technique that was adopted also permitted room in the spectrum for an additional channel. Termed SCA (subsidiary communication authorization), FM stations were able to offer a background music service to stores and businesses, thus ensuring a stronger economic base.

Much of the systems study for the 1960 FM achievements was performed by the National Stereophonic Radio Committee. A similar group was established in the early 1970's for examination of four-channel broadcasting; as the National Quadraphonic Radio Committee it established technical panels to examine methods of improving FM radio capability for the listener. In the mid-1970's it appeared that the future of radio broadcasting might hinge on innovative technology connected with direct broadcasting from communications satellites or as adjunct channels in closed-circuit community television systems.

[Erik Barnouw, *History of Broadcasting in the U.S.;* Frank J. Kahn, ed., *Documents of American Broadcasting.*]

ELLIOT N. SIVOWITCH

RADIO ASTRONOMY orginated in 1930 when Karl G. Jansky of the Bell Telephone Laboratory in New Jersey set out to investigate the annoying problem of high-frequency radio disturbances in the atmosphere. Using a sensitive shortwave radio receiving system to which he had connected an automatic signal intensity recorder, Jansky noticed that there was a residual "noise" in his equipment that showed a daily variation. Although his equipment had poor directivity (except in the horizontal plane), Jansky was able to establish that the radio noise was most intense in the direction of the center of the Milky Way. From this he concluded that the stars themselves must be emitting radio waves.

Jansky's discovery did not attract much attention among astronomers. Although Fred Whipple and Jesse Greenstein of the Harvard Observatory presented a theoretical discussion of his results, most astronomers took little interest in his work; some were not acquainted with the highly technical aspects of radio engineering, and others did not perceive the revolutionary implications of the new discovery. Jansky himself took up other duties at his laboratory, and his work in radio astronomy came to an end.

During the middle 1930's, Grote Reber, a radio engineer and amateur astronomer, built the world's first parabolic radio antenna in the garden of his home in Wheaton, Ill.; it was 31 feet in diameter and could be pointed to any part of the sky. Although Reber confirmed Jansky's general finding, he was unable to find any radio emission from individual stars, nebulas, or other well-known astronomical objects, and he concluded that the radio waves must originate in the ionized interstellar hydrogen gas.

The publication of Reber's first results in 1940 was the beginning of a concerted effort on the part of astronomers and radio engineers to explain the source of the radio radiation. After World War II radio astronomy developed rapidly—in part because of advances in electronic devices made during the war that resulted in highly refined receivers for radio observations and in part because of the publication of the findings of the English radio astronomer J. S. Hey. Working with radar equipment in connection with his duties as a member of the Army Operational Research Group, Hey and his colleagues discovered the existence of radio radiation originating from the sun, which was related to solar activity, and the existence of a "discrete radio source" in the direction of the constellation Cygnus. This latter finding stimulated great interest in the search for other discrete radio sources and in the determination of more-accurate positions for them in order to identify them with optically observed objects.

Important research along these lines was undertaken first in England and Australia and then somewhat later in the Netherlands, France, Canada, and the Soviet Union. The serious development of radio astronomy in the United States, where the initial discoveries had been made, did not occur until the 1950's, and during the next two decades Americans

contributed importantly to a succession of discoveries that revolutionized man's understanding of the universe: for example, radio galaxies, quasars, pulsars, and the spectral line emission from neutral hydrogen and the hydroxyl radical (OH).

[R. D. Davies and H. P. Palmer, *Radio Studies of the Universe*; J. S. Hey, *The Evolution of Radio Astronomy*; J. L. Pawsey and R. N. Bracewell, *Radio Astronomy*; C. H. Van de Hulst, ed., *Radio Astronomy*.]

HOWARD PLOTKIN

RADIOCARBON DATING is the measurement of the age of dead matter by comparing the radiocarbon content with that in living matter. It was discovered at the University of Chicago in the 1940's, but research on it had to wait until the end of World War II. In 1960 Willard F. Libby was awarded the Nobel Prize in Chemistry for his development of the radiocarbon dating method.

Radiocarbon, or radioactive carbon (C-14), is produced by the cosmic rays in the atmosphere and is assimilated only by living beings. At death the assimilation process stops, and thereafter the immutable radioactive loss through decay is no longer compensated by the intake of food. The average life of a radiocarbon atom is 8,300 years; so ample time for thorough mixing throughout the earth and through its atmosphere and oceans and the biosphere ensures that living matter, wherever found on earth, always has the same radiocarbon concentration—that is, the same ratio of radioactive carbon to ordinary carbon. This ratio is very small—about one in a trillion atoms—but it is enough to be measured by sensitive instruments to somewhat more than 1 percent accuracy.

The law of radioactive decay is that a given fraction is always lost in a given time. The half-life of radiocarbon, 5,730 years, is the time for 50 percent loss. Thus, 5,730 years after a tree has fallen, it will have half the radiocarbon content of a living tree. For any other ratio, larger or smaller, the age is less or greater. If the content is 25 percent of that of living material, the age is twice 5,730 years. This progression continues until it reaches an immeasurably low figure at about 50,000 years. Thus, radiocarbon dating applies only to materials that have not been dead longer than 50,000 years, but since most of human history falls in this span, radiocarbon dating covers the great reaches of time most important to human history.

The assumption that the concentration of radiocarbon in living matter remains constant over all of time is a bold one. It appears to be nearly correct, although deviations of a few percentage points do occur. These are determined by the measurement of radiocarbon in the wood in trees dated by the number of rings found, of which the bristlecone pine is the most useful. It has been possible to determine the accuracy of the basic assumption back some 8,000 years, and a correction curve has been produced that allows absolute dating by radiocarbon back 8,000 years. The deviation is about 8 percent, at maximum, although it is not entirely clear that the 8,000-year deviation is decreasing from its maximum at about 6,000 years ago.

The discovery of the radiocarbon dating method has given a much firmer base to archaeology and anthropology. For example, man first came to the Americas in substantial numbers apparently only 12,000 years ago, much later than animals. On the other hand, the magnificent color paintings of the Lascaux Cave in France are 16,000 years old, made 4,000 years before the first substantial number of human beings came to the Americas. Of course, evidences of older man may be found in America, but by the mid-1970's firm radiocarbon dates for human occupation had never exceeded 12,000 years, whereas in Europe and Asia Minor they reached back to the limits of the radiocarbon method and well beyond, according to other dating methods. Radiocarbon dates are a measure of simultaneous events, for the radiocarbon mixes quickly throughout the atmosphere and oceans. Thus, if the cosmic rays do vary by a few percentage points, so long as they are calibrated at any one place, the calibration applies worldwide.

The radiocarbon dating technique is somewhat demanding, requiring about a total time of one week and equipment that in the 1970's cost about $30,000.

[Willard F. Libby, *Radiocarbon Dating*.]

WILLARD F. LIBBY

RADISSON'S *VOYAGES*. Pierre Esprit Radisson was long thought to have been one of the two traders sent by Gov. Jean de Lauson of New France in 1654 to establish trade with the Huron, Ottawa, and other western tribes scattered by the Iroquois in the late 1640's and early 1650's. It is now certain that he was in Quebec in 1655, since a document of that date, a deed of sale signed by him there, has been found. He could not have been on the trade expedition, therefore, since it lasted for two years. His brother-in-law, Médard Chouart, Sieur de Groseilliers, does appear to have been one of the governor's two traders. It is probably Groseilliers' story that Radisson has given in his *Voyages*, derived in all likelihood from Groseil-

liers' oral accounts of his trip into and about Lake Huron and Lake Michigan. The book was printed from a manuscript, written about the year 1669, which is a defective, contemporary translation of an original French document now lost. The translation is among the papers of Samuel Pepys in the Bodleian Library at the University of Oxford.

Radisson's account of the trip is inaccurate, confused, and ambiguous, but it does give an inkling of the culture of the Indians and of the trading methods used in the West at a very early date. Other parts of the same manuscript are the narratives of two of Radisson's sojourns among the Iroquois in the 1650's while in his early teens and a trip made by Radisson and Groseilliers in 1659 and 1660 from their homes in Trois Rivières on the lower Saint Lawrence River to the end of Lake Superior and even a little south and west of that lake. This account is fairly detailed, exact, and explicit. Its chief value lies in its descriptions of Indians before they were influenced by white men. On this trip the two men learned from the Indians of an easy route for fur trading from Hudson Bay to the great beaver country northwest of Lake Superior, and of the supposed Northwest Passage in that area. It was these ideas that led the two men successively to France, New England, and London in an effort to obtain financial aid to explore the possibilities of Hudson Bay, both for trade and for finding a route to Asia. In England they succeeded. After many disappointments, the Hudson's Bay Company was founded on May 2, 1670, after Groseilliers' return from a successful trip to Hudson Bay in 1668 and 1669.

[Gideon D. Scull, ed., *Voyages of Peter Esprit Radisson*.]

GRACE LEE NUTE

RAFTING, EARLY. In the period before the Civil War, and chiefly on the rivers of the Mississippi Valley, rafts with crude lean-tos were used as a means of transportation downstream by the poorer immigrants. They were steered by long sweeps and appear to have been a perennial menace to navigation. Some immigrants built rafts of sawlogs with the intention of selling them to the sawmills downriver; other such rafts were used to transport cattle, forage, and lumber products for sale, together with the logs, in the cities downriver. When the rafts reached their destination they were usually broken up and sold as lumber.

[Leland D. Baldwin, *Keelboat Age on Western Waters*.]

LELAND D. BALDWIN

RAIL FENCES. For many years following the first settlement in America, rail fences were common. Easily split tree trunks were abundant, and an ax was the only tool necessary to make rails and fence. Pine, oak, and chestnut were favorite woods for rails, the tree trunks being cut into 11-foot lengths about 4 or 5 inches thick. A 10- or 12-inch log would make five or six rails, all three-cornered; a 20- or 24-inch log would turn out twelve to eighteen rails, those next to the heart of the log three-cornered, those outside four-cornered. In a snake, or worm, fence, the ground rails, laid zigzag, were the "worm"; the top rails were the "riders." The worm zigzagged across the line 2 feet or more on each side, the fence thus covering a strip of land 5 feet wide. If stakes were dug in at the corners to support the riders, they toed out still farther. In a cap fence, upright stakes (posts) clamped each corner, and the worm was more nearly straight. The caps were short clapboards, with an auger hole in each end, fitted down over the tops of the posts, holding them together. The best rail fences were straight on the line, with the ends of the rails mortised into heavy posts. Soldiers in the Revolution, the War of 1812, and the Civil War found old dry fence rails handy for campfires and burned millions of them.

JOHN W. WAYLAND

RAILROAD ADMINISTRATION, U.S. In April 1917 railroad executives formed the Railroads' War Board to achieve a coordinated "railway system" for the World War I emergency. There resulted some pooling of freight cars and coal supplies, but without governmental intervention it was difficult to unify other transportation resources and almost impossible to obtain adequate financial assistance. Therefore, in December 1917 President Woodrow Wilson, in a proclamation authorized by an act of Aug. 29, 1916, established the Railroad Administration to control and operate all rail transport for the duration of the war. These facilities were "leased" by the government and eventually comprised 532 properties with 366,000 miles of track, valued at $18 billion. Terminal companies, an express company, and certain coastal and inland waterways and piers were included, but not street cars, interurban lines, or industrial railroads. In general, the personnel and administrative machinery of each property were retained, under the direct charge of a federal manager, usually an officer of the corporation. Operations were coordinated by regional directors, who in turn were under the director general (William Gibbs McAdoo, former

secretary of the Treasury, and, later, railroad lawyer Walker D. Hines) and a central administration at Washington, D.C.

This episode of government enterprise was intended to be an emergency military measure to help win the war and was not regarded as a Socialist experiment. Certain efficiencies and economies did result, and competitive wastes were eliminated by centralization and standardization. Unified terminals were organized, notably at Chicago, and a "permit system" prevented loading until assurances for unloading were given by shippers. Locomotives and freight cars were standardized, and the purchasing of equipment and supplies was centralized. Repair shops and maintenance were pooled. A coal zoning plan helped to eliminate fuel wastes (*see* Fuel Administration). Passenger service, while discouraged because of the war, was unified by such devices as consolidated ticket offices, the universal mileage book, and standard ticket forms and baggage rules. Finally, advertising was eliminated and statistics were standardized. Expenditures totaling $1.12 billion were made by the government, mostly for additions, betterments, and equipment. By the act of Mar. 21, 1918, stockholders and bondholders were guaranteed compensation equal to the average annual net operating income during the preceding three years, 1914–17. Wages were generally increased, and the administration formally recognized the eight-hour day for 2 million railroad employees. In March 1920, sixteen months after the armistice, the railroads were returned to private management under the supervision of the Interstate Commerce Commission and in accordance with the Transportation Act of 1920.

[F. H. Dixon, *Railroads and Government, 1910–1921;* W. D. Hines, *War History of American Railroads.*]

MARTIN P. CLAUSSEN

RAILROAD BROTHERHOODS. The traditional pattern of union organization in the railroad industry has been along multiple craft-union lines. As late as 1970 there were more than thirty separate unions representing the approximately 800,000 railway workers of the nation. Historically, the unions have been divided into two groupings: the operating employees, who are involved in the physical movement of trains, and nonoperating employees, an amorphous group composed of workers who fall into numerous classifications.

The five major brotherhoods of the industry (the "Big Five") have been the operating unions: locomotive engineers (founded in 1863), railroad conductors

(1868), locomotive firemen and enginemen (1873), railway trainmen (1883), and switchmen (1894). Early efforts by Eugene V. Debs to unify the separate crafts into a single body, the American Railway Union, were aborted by the Pullman strike of 1894. Until the 1960's each union largely went its separate way. With the introduction of major technological changes into railroad operations, the extensive consolidation of once-competing lines, and the increasing use of other modes of transportation by travelers and by freight shippers, railroad employment began a secular decline after World War II. To overcome their weaker bargaining structure and to reduce the numerous jurisdictional disputes that were the inevitable result of employment contraction, four of the operating brotherhoods departed from their past pattern by merging on July 1, 1969, into the United Transportation Union. With only the locomotive engineers remaining aloof, the new union represented about 87 percent of the operating employees of the industry.

The original impetus for collective organization was the establishment of mutual life insurance and accident benefit programs. The inordinately high frequency of job-related deaths and injuries that plagued railway operations—especially in the early years—made such protective arrangements naturally attractive to large numbers of workers. Regular commercial companies, because of the high risk factor, offered such insurance only at high rates, if at all. Subsequently, the brotherhoods became more fraternal in purpose and, ultimately, assumed the character of business unions, focusing on wages, hours, and working conditions.

Once touted as the aristocracy of the American union movement, the operating brotherhoods earned a well-deserved reputation for militancy. Aside from the bitter conflicts between them, the militancy derived from the industry's history of making wage cuts during depressions, the use of militia to quell strikes, the frequent issuance of labor injunctions by courts, and the pervasive hostility of railroad management toward worker organizations.

[Jacob J. Kaufman, *Collective Bargaining in the Railroad Industry;* Reed C. Richardson, *The Locomotive Engineer 1863–1963: A Century of Railway Labor Relations.*]

VERNON M. BRIGGS, JR.

RAILROAD CONSPIRACY (1849–50) was directed against the Michigan Central Railroad, the first built in that state, by certain persons angered by such issues as disputes over rights of way, the location of

stations, and the killing of cattle by locomotives. The conspirators stoned and shot at trains, destroyed culverts, removed rails, and burned stations. The freight depot at Detroit was burned, and when rebuilt, was burned again. Twelve participants were tried in 1851 and given prison sentences ranging from five to ten years.

ALVIN F. HARLOW

RAILROAD CONVENTIONS were phenomena of the early years of railroad promotion. They were held before the railroads were built rather than after their completion, and they were composed not only of railway builders but also, and principally, of the public-spirited citizens of their vicinities.

The conventions served as a vent for popular enthusiasm for better means of transportation, which they helped to generate. They probably did not greatly stimulate private investment in railroad securities, but they undoubtedly did yeoman service in the numerous campaigns for state or local aid. It was hoped in many cases that they would serve to reconcile conflicting interests and aspirations as to routes and termini; in the nature of things they could only demonstrate or promote popular interest in particular projects.

Railroad conventions were innumerable. Perhaps the most notable were the three great Pacific Railroad conventions in Saint Louis and Memphis, October 1849, and in Philadelphia, April 1850. They were held to demonstrate the strength of the popular demand for federal aid for a railroad to the Pacific coast, to formulate a practicable plan of financing it, and to assert claims for the eastern terminus—the Philadelphia convention supported the pretensions of the Saint Louis convention. But Congress gave their resolutions scant courtesy. One of the most influential gatherings of the sort ever held was the Southwestern Railroad Convention in New Orleans, January 1852. It helped to launch Louisiana and New Orleans on ambitious programs of state and municipal aid and to make clear the broad outlines of a proper railroad system for the whole Southwest. The Pacific Railroad conventions in Sacramento, September 1859 and February 1860, sought to unite the Pacific coast in support of a central route and to persuade the legislatures of California, Oregon, and Washington Territory to make provision for getting the western leg of the proposed railroad started. The Southwestern Convention in Memphis, November 1845, was interested primarily in the improvement of western rivers; but it also endorsed the major railroad projects of the Southwest and broached the subject of a southern route for a Pacific railroad. Similarly the Chicago Rivers and Harbors Convention, July 1847, gave secondary concern to railroad projects for connecting the East and the West.

[F. A. Cleveland and F. W. Powell, *Railroad Promotion and Capitalization in the United States;* R. S. Cotterill, "Early Agitation for a Pacific Railroad, 1845–1850," *Mississippi Valley Historical Review,* vol. 4; R. E. Riegel, *The Story of the Western Railroads.*]

R. R. RUSSEL

RAILROAD LAND GRANTS. *See* Land Grants for Railways.

RAILROAD MEDIATION ACTS.

The federal government began in the 1890's to try to devise machinery to avoid railroad strikes and assure uninterrupted transportation service without denying the rights of workers to organize. In the Erdman Act of 1898 and the Newlands Act of 1913 Congress created mediation procedures, and in the Adamson Act of 1916 it established the eight-hour day on the railroads. The Transportation Act of 1920 founded the Railroad Labor Board. After the board failed to prevent the shopmen's strike of 1922, Congress passed the Railway Labor Act of 1926. As amended in 1934, it continues to be the basic legislation in the field.

The amended law provides several procedures designed both to prevent and to resolve labor-management disputes. It established the thirty-six-member National Railroad Adjustment Board to act in a quasi-judicial capacity over rates of pay, working conditions, and work rules in case of the failure of ordinary collective bargaining. It set up the three-member National Mediation Board to assist labor and management in resolving differences. In case of the failure of all other procedures, including voluntary arbitration, the president was empowered to appoint an impartial emergency board to avoid strikes and the government was empowered to enforce a sixty-day cooling-off period to forestall a strike. The law also provided for the enforcement of the workers' right to organize unions of their own choosing.

In the 1960's major strikes concerning work rules threatened railroad service. Congress enacted legislation to settle individual disputes that endangered the national economy, and it reviewed the idea of enforcing compulsory arbitration in labor disputes affecting transportation.

[Merle Fainsod and Lincoln Gordon, *Government and the American Economy;* Robert H. Zieger, *The Republicans and Labor, 1919–1929.*]

K. AUSTIN KERR

RAILROAD POOLS. *See* Pools, Railroad.

RAILROAD RATE LAW.

Attempts to regulate railroad rates by law began at the state level. The so-called Granger laws of the 1870's were passed by the states in response to demands by farmers for lower rates on agricultural products from the Midwest to the eastern seaboard and by midwestern river towns (which had been hurt when river transport was displaced by the new East-West trunklines) that rates be based on mileage. The first demand was satisfied, not by laws but by the striking twenty-five-year decline in all railroad rates after 1873. The second demand was submerged in the economic boom after 1877, but it survived in the durable issue of discrimination in rates between long and short hauls. The Supreme Court in *Munn* v. *Illinois* (1877) declared for the right of states to fix interstate rates so long as the federal government did not act. Anticipating the decision in *Wabash, Saint Louis and Pacific Railroad Company* v. *Illinois* (1886), which reversed *Munn,* Congress began studies that culminated in the Interstate Commerce Act of 1887. Support by business groups was broad, including some railroad men who sought the right to enter into legally enforceable agreements— that is, cartels—to pool revenues and/or freights.

The traditional view of the failure of the act of 1887 is that the Interstate Commerce Commission (ICC) was intended to fix specific maximum rates and energetically abolish discrimination between long and short hauls, powers of which it was deprived by two 1897 decisions of the Supreme Court. But neither Congress nor the affected interests had wanted the ICC to fix specific rates, nor did many want a literal application of the clause that prohibited discrimination between long and short hauls. (Although energetic attempts were made under subsequent legislation to abolish this ratemaking practice, they failed because the United States, a vast area in which trade is carried on free of regional barriers, was devoted to a tradition of low through rates arrived at under competitive conditions.) The fatal weakness of the act of 1887 was that it prohibited pooling, even under ICC supervision, an anomaly that led contemporary experts to predict correctly that the only other antidote to rate chaos—consolidation of the railroads into a few systems—would be adopted.

While the Elkins Act of 1903 enhanced the ICC's powers to deal with rebates as criminal acts, it was the overloading of the American railroad system after 1898 that effectively killed rate cutting. Reaction to a stable and moderately rising rate structure resulted in the Hepburn Act of 1906, which gave the ICC power to fix specific maximum rates and broadened its jurisdiction. Before it was fully operative the Hepburn Act was overshadowed by the Mann-Elkins Act of 1910, which enabled the ICC effectively to freeze rates at levels pervasive in the 1890's throughout the great inflation of the Progressive era, despite repeated concerted efforts by the railroads to raise rates. When the government took over the railroad system in December 1917, the ICC was as far from developing a criterion of "reasonableness" of rates as ever, and literal application of the Sherman Antitrust Act of 1890 had rendered the carriers impotent to operate the system in a unified manner as a war measure. Without consulting either the ICC or the state commissions, the U.S. Railroad Administration raised rates by almost 60 percent, thereby returning them to about the level of the 1890's in real dollars. Meanwhile, in the *Shreveport* case (1914) the Supreme Court had completed the reversal of the *Munn* decision by giving the ICC power to set intrastate rates, on the ground that they are economically linked to interstate rates.

Neither the power to pool revenues nor the encouragement of consolidation, both features of the Transportation Act of 1920, was germane to postwar regulatory problems. But the power to fix specific minimum rates operated in a totally unforeseen manner. By 1933 the emergence of competition by trucks, which were not federally regulated until 1935, had become the crucial problem. Despite repeated declarations in the acts passed in 1940 and 1958 in favor of a balanced transportation system based on the "inherent advantages" of rail and highway modes, both the ICC and lawmakers shrank from giving railroads freedom to compete through lowering rates, and the Supreme Court failed consistently to enunciate a rule of ratemaking based on cost. As a result the railroads lost most of their profitable, high-class freight and came to be operated at a fraction of capacity; 60 percent of highway freight came to be carried by unregulated private carriers because, under the ICC's policy of high rates for railroads and regulated motor carriers, it was advantageous for the shippers; and the nation's transportation costs thus rose. Despite widespread belief among transportation economists that

rate laws had failed, by late 1975 it seemed likely that Congress would seek to solve the problem by a system of guaranteed loans, or quasi subsidies, or limited nationalization of the railroads, or perhaps all three.

[Albro Martin, "The Troubled Subject of Railroad Regulation in the 'Gilded Age': A Reappraisal," *Journal of American History* (September 1974); Charles F. Phillips, Jr., *The Economics of Regulation*.]

ALBRO MARTIN

RAILROAD RATE WARS. The rapid expansion of railroads following the close of the Civil War added greatly to the number of communities, large and small, served by two or more railroads competing for the traffic between these communities and markets. The fact that many of the points served by competitive railroads were ports intensified competition by bringing into the competitive struggle the water carriers serving the ports.

Competition led to rate cutting by the railroads and water carriers and caused widespread use of rebates. Competition among railroads and between railroads and water lines, the cutting of rates, and the payment of rebates were not unknown prior to this period, but heretofore they had been sporadic and intermittent; in the post–Civil War period they were widespread and regular and became a public scandal.

In the competitive struggle for traffic, freight rates and passenger fares were cut by rival railroads and steamship lines between competitive points, while the rates and fares between, to, or from noncompetitive points served by only one railroad, or where railroad and water competition did not exist, were not reduced. In other cases, rates on the traffic of certain preferred shippers were reduced, while the rates and fares charged those whose patronage was not so ardently sought were not reduced. Rates on certain types of traffic moving in large quantities and with regularity—desirable traffic to the hard-pressed competitors—were slashed, while rates on traffic moving in smaller quantities and with less regularity were not reduced. These conditions resulted in widespread public complaints against the relatively high "local," or noncompetitive, rates and the lower "through," or competitive, rates.

Railroad competition became particularly severe when, after 1869, the trunk line railroads, especially the Pennsylvania Railroad and the New York Central, reached the large cities of the Middle West. Recurrent rate wars in the period following 1869 caused freight rates and passenger fares between principal competitive centers to fall to absurdly low prices, while rates to and from the less-favored points where competition was absent did not follow the same trend. The excesses of the competitive orgy resulted in sharp fluctuations in rates and in the bankruptcy of many railroads. The disastrous panic of 1873, caused in part by unbridled railroad competition and an attendant fall in railroad earning capacity, did not check the rate wars. In fact, they were intensified. In 1874 the Baltimore and Ohio Railroad was extended to Chicago, and the Grand Trunk Railroad was opened to Milwaukee. The following two years witnessed one of the most disastrous railroad rate wars in history, that between the Baltimore and Ohio, Erie, Grand Trunk, New York Central, and Pennsylvania railroads, all serving the same points between the Middle West and the Atlantic seaboard. The rates between competitive points served by these railroads were demoralized and often, it has been said, were not sufficient to defray direct train operating expenses. The impaired financial position of the roads as a result of this ruthless competition led to a temporary truce and a traffic-sharing arrangement in 1877.

Competition among railroads serving the northern Atlantic ports—Boston, New York, Philadelphia, and Baltimore—resulted in rate wars among the railroads and between the railroads and the Erie Canal. In like manner, competition among southern railroads was intensified as several railroads reached inland points, such as Atlanta. Severe competition occurred between railroads and water carriers at the principal ports on the Atlantic Ocean, Gulf of Mexico, Mississippi River, and Ohio River. Rate wars indeed threatened to demoralize the financial structures of rail and water carriers.

In the West rate wars resulted from the multiplication of railroads and the struggle between the railroads and steamboat lines for freight at important traffic centers, such as Saint Louis, Kansas City, and Omaha.

The overbuilding of railroads and the unregulated competition among railroads and between railroads and waterlines, accompanied by the speculative management of some of these carriers and by the inability of the railroads to temporarily suspend service until the excessive competition had abated, accounted for the severity and destructiveness of rate wars. Another interesting commentary on rate wars was the peculiar ability of railroads or other carriers in impaired financial condition to cause and exaggerate the effects of the rate-cutting contests. These carriers were usually bankrupt and had no interest charges to pay. They were not earning enough to pay these charges or divi-

dends on capital stock. Freed of the burden of such charges they were able to reduce rates in the hope of attracting traffic from their solvent rivals, which were meeting interest charges and sometimes paying dividends. They had little to lose and much to gain either through increasing their traffic and gross earnings or forcing their more vulnerable competitors to yield and divide traffic or earnings.

Railroad rate wars, accompanied by unjust and unreasonable discriminations among persons, communities, and kinds of traffic, led to the development of popular antagonism to railroads in the period following 1870. One result of this popular protest was the enactment by a number of states, particularly the western Granger states, of severe and often restrictive and punitive railroad regulatory legislation and the organization of state regulatory commissions (*see* Granger Cases).

Another result of rate wars and their attendant abuses was the demand for federal railroad regulation. The Cullom Committee, headed by Illinois Sen. Shelby M. Cullom, recommended in 1886 federal legislation to regulate railroad transportation and the formation of a federal regulatory commission to correct the paramount evils of unjust discrimination. Congress in 1887 enacted the Interstate Commerce Act, which established the Interstate Commerce Commission in order to correct these evils.

[A. T. Hadley, *Railroad Transportation;* E. R. Johnson, *American Railway Transportation;* L. G. McPherson, *Railroad Freight Rates;* W. Z. Ripley, *Railroads: Rates and Regulations.*]

G. LLOYD WILSON

RAILROAD REBATES. *See* **Rebates, Railroad.**

RAILROAD RETIREMENT ACTS. A railroad retirement act was approved by President Franklin D. Roosevelt, June 27, 1934, with the comment that it was "crudely drawn" and would require revision. Under the act retirement allowances were provided for certain categories of employees, two-thirds of the cost to be borne by employers and the balance by the employees. A federal board of three members was created to administer the system. No adequate actuarial studies had been made, and it was freely predicted that benefit payments would soon exhaust available funds, while the carriers claimed that their share would prove a crushing load on the finances of most railroads. In March 1935 the U.S. Supreme Court, in *Railroad Retirement Board* v. *Alton*

Railroad Company, declared the act unconstitutional. New legislation was promptly introduced, and two bills were passed the following August, the first (Wagner-Crosser Railroad Retirement Act) providing a retirement plan and the second imposing special taxes for its support. These acts retained several features that the Supreme Court had found objectionable in the earlier enactment, and the railroads renewed the contest on its constitutionality in the court of the District of Columbia, which issued an injunction against its enforcement on June 30, 1936. Efforts to find a satisfactory solution by conference of railroad managements and the employee organizations were now begun. In May 1937 new legislation approved by both parties was introduced in Congress and carried with little opposition a month later. Sen. Bennett Champ Clark of Missouri declared, on passage of the Railroad Retirement Act of 1937, that "it was the most hopeful thing that has happened in the United States in a great many years with regard to the relationship between employer and employee."

W. A. ROBINSON

RAILROAD RETIREMENT BOARD. *See* **Federal Agencies.**

RAILROAD RETIREMENT BOARD V. ALTON RAILROAD COMPANY, 295 U.S. 330 (1935), a case in which the Supreme Court, divided five to four, invalidated the Railroad Pension Act of 1934. The majority opinion declared the act contrary to the due process clause of the Fifth Amendment because of a long series of arbitrary impositions on the carriers and, furthermore, because "the pension plan thus imposed is in no proper sense a regulation of the activity of interstate transportation." The minority opinion, while agreeing that the retroactive feature of the law violated the Fifth Amendment, declared that the establishment of a pension system was entirely within the power of Congress to regulate interstate commerce.

W. A. ROBINSON

RAILROADS. The earliest railroads in the United States were short wooden tramways connecting mines or quarries with nearby streams, upon which horses could draw heavier loads than on the common roads. The idea of the railroad as it came to be, tracks on which trains of cars are pulled by mechanical power

in common-carrier service, was first expounded by Col. John Stevens of Hoboken, N.J., who in 1812 published his *Documents Tending to Prove the Superior Advantages of Rail-Ways and Steam Carriages Over Canal Navigation.* On Feb. 6, 1815, he secured a charter from the New Jersey legislature authorizing the building of a railroad across the state, but he was unable to enlist the capital necessary for construction.

The first charter under which a railroad was built in the United States was that of the Granite Railway of Massachusetts, a three-mile line built in 1826, which used horses to haul stone for the building of the Bunker Hill monument from quarries at Quincy.

The first railroad incorporated as a common carrier of passengers and freight, the Baltimore and Ohio, was chartered by the state of Maryland on Feb. 28, 1827. Construction was started with due ceremony on July 4, 1828, and the first passengers were carried in January 1830 in single cars drawn by horses.

Experiments with steam locomotion were already under way. Stevens had built a tiny locomotive that ran on a circular track on his estate in 1825. More significant was the *Stourbridge Lion,* imported from England by the Delaware and Hudson Canal and Railroad for use on the line of rails connecting its mines with its canal. On its one trial trip on Aug. 8, 1829, the *Lion* proved to be too heavy for the track and was not used again as a locomotive. In August 1830 the Baltimore and Ohio experimented with the *Tom Thumb,* an engine whose diminutive size was indicated by its name. It was built and operated by Peter Cooper.

The essential elements of a railroad in the modern sense—track, trains of cars, mechanical locomotive power, and public service as a common carrier—were first combined on the South Carolina Canal and Rail Road Company (later included in the Southern Railway system) when, on Dec. 25, 1830, it inaugurated scheduled service on the first six miles of its line out of Charleston with the steam locomotive *Best Friend,* the first to pull a train of cars on the American continent. Three years later the line was opened to Hamburg, a terminus across the river from Augusta, Ga., 136 miles away, making it at the time the longest railway in the world.

Railroads opened for operation by steam power in the early 1830's included the Mohawk and Hudson, earliest link in the future New York Central system, over which the locomotive *DeWitt Clinton* pulled a train of cars between Albany and Schenectady on Aug. 9, 1831; the Camden and Amboy, later part of the Pennsylvania system, on which the British-built

John Bull was placed in service at Bordentown, N.J., also in 1831; the Philadelphia, Germantown and Norristown, later part of the Reading, on which *Old Ironsides*, built by Matthias Baldwin, first ran in 1832; and the railroad connecting New Orleans with Lake Pontchartrain, afterward part of the Louisville and Nashville, on which the first locomotive in the Mississippi Valley made its initial scheduled run on Sept. 17, 1832.

By 1835 railroads ran from Boston to Lowell, the beginnings of the future Boston and Maine; to Worcester, first link in the Boston and Albany; and to Providence, the genesis of the New York, New Haven and Hartford. The Petersburg Railroad, later part of the Atlantic Coast Line, ran from the Virginia city whose name it bore south into North Carolina. The Baltimore and Ohio had built a branch to Washington, D.C., and had pushed its main line westward to the Blue Ridge. Countering this effort by Baltimore to reach out for the trade of the West, several New York businessmen had started the New York and Erie, headed westward for Lake Erie through the southern tier of counties of the state. The state of Pennsylvania, not to be outdone, had opened a hybrid route between Philadelphia and Pittsburgh, using two stretches of canals, a railroad operated with both locomotives and horses, and a series of inclined planes by which cars were raised and lowered over the Alleghenies.

Pennsylvania was not the only state to undertake the building of a railroad. North Carolina, acting through corporations in which the state was a majority stockholder, built and owns lines that came to constitute a substantial segment of the Southern Railway, which operates them under lease. Georgia, acting directly, built, and later leased to the Louisville and Nashville, an important link between Georgia and Tennessee. Virginia became a large stockholder in the Richmond, Fredericksburg and Potomac. Less fortunate were the railroad ventures of the states of Michigan and Illinois, which embarked prematurely on ambitious state transportation schemes that failed and were sold to private companies. One of the most successful ventures in public ownership was the Cincinnati Southern, a line built and owned by the city and operated under lease by the Southern Railway system.

1840–60. By 1840, the end of the first decade of the railroad era, 2,800 miles of railroad were in operation in the United States, with mileage in every seacoast state and in Kentucky, Ohio, Indiana, Michigan, and Illinois. In the second decade of railroad development, mileage more than trebled, reaching a total of 9,000 miles. Lines had been opened in Vermont and Wisconsin, and missing links had been supplied, so that by 1850 it was possible to travel by rail between Boston and Buffalo, with numerous changes of cars, and between Boston and Wilmington, N.C., with occasional gaps covered by steamboat.

By 1850, also, there had been developed a standard American-type locomotive, with a four-wheel swivel leading truck and four driving wheels, coupled. The design was simple, powerful, and easy on the track. It became the ancestor of a variety of heavier and more powerful types for freight and passenger service, but itself remained the backbone of the locomotive fleet until almost the end of the century.

In the decade of the 1850's railway mileage again more than trebled, as the ambitious efforts of the Atlantic seaports to reach the West were fulfilled. New York was connected with the Great Lakes, both by the Erie Railroad and by way of Albany and the New York Central, formed in 1853 by the consolidation of a dozen small railroads between the Hudson River and Buffalo. Philadelphia established an all-rail connection with Pittsburgh, and Baltimore reached the Ohio at Wheeling early in the 1850's.

Before these lines reached their trans-Allegheny goals, other lines were being built across the more open and level country of the Middle West. Chicago was entered from the East in 1852 almost simultaneously by two lines, the Michigan Central and the Michigan Southern, both of which were later included in the New York Central system. Already, lines were building west from Chicago—the Galena and Chicago Union (later the Chicago and North Western), which brought the first locomotive to the future rail center on a Great Lakes sailing vessel, and the Chicago and Rock Island, which reached the Mississippi River in February 1854. Only a year later a route between Chicago and East Saint Louis afforded another rail connection between the East and the Mississippi, while in 1857 two such connections were added—the direct route from Baltimore via Cincinnati and, to the south, a route between Charleston and Savannah, on the Atlantic, and Memphis, on the Mississippi.

But before the rails reached the great river from the East, railroads had started from the west bank. The first locomotive to turn a wheel beyond the Mississippi ran on Dec. 9, 1852, on the Pacific Railroad of Missouri (later the Missouri Pacific) from Saint Louis five miles westward. In 1856 the Iron Horse crossed the Mississippi on the first railroad bridge, that of the

Rock Island line, later called the Chicago, Rock Island and Pacific. Before the end of the decade, the railroad had reached the Missouri on the tracks of the Hannibal and Saint Joseph (later part of the Burlington lines).

For the most part these routes had been built as separate local lines, in many instances lacking the physical connections without which through movement of freight and passengers was impossible. One road built as a unit was the Illinois Central, a north-south line connecting East Dubuque and Cairo, with a "branch" from Centralia to Chicago. Chartered in 1851, the line of more than 700 miles was completed in 1857.

One factor in the successful building of the Illinois Central was the grant by the federal government to the state of Illinois, and through that state to the railroad corporation, of vacant lands from the public domain in Illinois as an aid to financing the construction of the line. This grant, and a like grant of lands in Alabama and Mississippi to the Mobile and Ohio Railroad, which was to be built northward, was the beginning of a policy of making such grants-in-aid for railroad building, following an earlier precedent of such grants-in-aid for canals and wagon roads. Lands were granted to railroads in alternate sections of one mile square, for distances of from six to twenty miles on either side of the line. The government retained title to alternate sections, making a checkerboard pattern of private and government ownership. The purposes of the grants were to use vacant and unsalable lands lacking transportation and to encourage the building of railroads into undeveloped regions, thereby attracting settlers, adding value to the lands retained by the government, increasing production and taxable wealth, and unifying the nation.

During the twenty-one years the policy was in effect, from 1850 to 1871, federal land grants were made to aid in the building of less than 10 percent of the railroad mileage of the United States, by which some 131 million of the approximately 1.4 billion acres of public lands owned in 1850 were transferred to private ownership. The value of the lands granted as of the time of the grants was approximately $125 million. In return for the grants the railroads carried government freight, mail, and troops at reduced rates until 1946, when the arrangement was ended by act of Congress. By that time land grant rate deductions for the government amounted to a total of more than $1 billion.

In the 1850's, railroad building was started in newly annexed Texas, where the Buffalo Bayou, Brazos and Colorado was opened from present-day Houston westward toward Richmond, Tex., in 1853, and in the new state of California, where the Sacramento Valley was opened in 1856 from navigable waters at Sacramento to Folsom (both later part of the Southern Pacific system).

1861–65. With the coming of the Civil War, the building of new railroads was slowed down somewhat, but the existing railroads were called upon to play essential roles in the struggle. Even before war started, the east-west railroads, tying the Northwest to the Northeast rather than to the lower Mississippi Valley, had been largely decisive in determining the attitude of the interior states of the North. More than two-thirds of the 1861 mileage and an even greater proportion of railroad transportation capacity lay in the states that adhered to the Union. Invasion of the South soon reduced even the small percentage of the railroad mileage in Confederate hands. It is not too much to say that relative railroad strength was a decisive factor in the "first railroad war."

On the railroads of both sides there were remarkable transportation achievements. The outcome of the first Battle of Bull Run was determined by troops shifted by rail from the Shenandoah Valley to the vicinity of Manassas, Va. A major rail movement was the transfer of the Confederate Army of Tennessee from Tupelo, Miss., to Chattanooga, via Mobile, Ala., and Atlanta, preparatory to the launching of Gen. Braxton Bragg's Kentucky campaign. A more remarkable accomplishment was the movement of Gen. James Longstreet's army corps from Virginia through the Carolinas and Georgia, just in time to win the Confederate victory of Chickamauga, Ga. Most remarkable of all was the movement of Gen. Joseph Hooker's two corps of 22,000 men over a distance of 1,200 miles from Virginia to the vicinity of Chattanooga, via Columbus, Indianapolis, Louisville, and Nashville.

More important even than these spectacular shifts of large army units from one strategic field to another was the part played by the railroads in the day-to-day movement of men, food, ammunition, matériel, and supplies from distant sources to the combat forces. Movements of this sort reached a climax in Gen. William Tecumseh Sherman's campaign for the capture of Atlanta in the summer of 1864, when his army of 100,000 men and 35,000 animals was kept supplied and in fighting trim by a single-track railroad extending nearly 500 miles from its base on the Ohio River at Louisville.

1865–1916. There had been agitation for a transcontinental railroad since 1848 at least, and during the 1850's the topographical engineers of the army had explored five routes. Ultimately railroads were built on all those routes, but sectional jealousies and the immensity of the task prevented such an undertaking until the Civil War removed the southern routes from consideration and, at the same time, made imperative the need for better communication with the Pacific coast. Congress accordingly passed, and President Abraham Lincoln signed on July 1, 1862, a bill authorizing a railroad between the Missouri River and California, to be built on the central, or "overland," route.

The president designated Council Bluffs, Iowa, as the starting point. Construction was undertaken by the Union Pacific, building westward from Omaha, and by the Central Pacific (later part of the Southern Pacific), building eastward from Sacramento, Calif. On May 10, 1869, the construction crews met and joined tracks at Promontory, Utah, in the mountains north of the Great Salt Lake. The junction was celebrated by the ceremony of driving a golden spike, as the telegraph instruments clicked out to the waiting and rejoicing United States the message "The last rail is laid . . . the last spike driven. . . . The Pacific Railroad is completed."

The first transcontinental route was built as a "great military highway," in the words of Sherman, and was not expected to be self-supporting. Construction was aided by land grants and by government loans, frequently and erroneously described as gifts, despite the fact that the loans were repaid in full with interest. Later transcontinental routes were not aided by loans but in most instances received grants of land, in return for which they carried government traffic at reduced rates.

The second transcontinental connection was supplied in 1881 when the Atchison, Topeka and Santa Fe, building westward, met the Southern Pacific, building eastward, at Deming, N.Mex. The Southern Pacific continuing to build eastward, met the Texas and Pacific at Sierra Blanca, Tex., in 1882 and, by further construction and acquisition of lines, established a through route to New Orleans in 1883. In the same year California was reached by a line built by the Santa Fe westward from Albuquerque, N.Mex., forming still another transcontinental route.

The first route to reach the Pacific Northwest was opened in 1883 by the Northern Pacific, built through the northernmost tier of states. A second route to the Northwest was opened a year later when the Oregon Short Line, built from a junction with the Union Pacific, joined tracks with the Oregon Railway and Navigation Company (both later part of the Union Pacific system).

In 1893 a third route to the Pacific Northwest, and the first to be built without the aid of land grants, was completed by the Great Northern. The extension to the coast of the Chicago, Milwaukee and Saint Paul, which added "Pacific" to its name, was completed in 1909, also without the aid of land grants.

The Union Pacific route to southern California was completed in 1905 by the San Pedro, Los Angeles and Salt Lake, while another route to northern California was opened in 1910 when the Western Pacific effected a junction at Salt Lake City with the Denver and Rio Grande Western.

Meanwhile, railroad construction continued in the older portions of the United States, closing the gaps in the rail net. Between 1860 and 1870, despite the interruption of the Civil War, total mileage increased from 31,000 to 53,000 miles. This rate of growth was exceeded in the 1870's when 40,000 miles of new line were built.

The decade of the 1880's recorded the greatest growth in railway mileage, with an average of more than 7,000 miles of new line built each year. By the end of the decade the conversion from iron rail to the stronger, more durable, and safer steel rail was largely completed. The same decade also saw the standardization of track gauge, of car couplers, of train brakes, and of time, all essential steps toward a continent-wide commerce by rail.

The earlier railroads were built to serve the interests of particular points and, for the most part, without thought of future interconnection with other lines. Under such circumstances the question of gauge, or the width of track between rails, was of small importance. Altogether twenty-four different gauges have been used in the United States, ranging from 2 feet to 6 feet. By the 1880's gradual adjustment had brought about general agreement on two gauges. One of 5 feet predominated in the South. The other, predominant in the rest of the country, was 4 feet, 8.5 inches, a width originally used in England by George Stephenson, which had spread to the United States through the importation by early railroads of English-built locomotives. In 1886 the railroads of the South changed their gauge to conform, and the odd figure of 4–8.5 became "standard gauge" for all but a limited mileage of narrow-gauge railroads.

Along with standardization of track gauge, cars and locomotives had to be standardized to make it possible for the cars of any railroad to run on the tracks and in the trains of every other railroad. Car couplers, for example, had to work not only with other couplers of like design but also, as cars went from road to road, with those on other lines. As new models of couplers were introduced, they had to work with those already in use. As early as 1869, the Master Car Builders' Association, one of the ancestors of the Association of American Railroads, had begun tests of various types of couplers designed to replace the simple but unsafe and unsatisfactory link-and-pin device. Altogether more than 3,000 patents were issued for various forms of safety couplers. Forty-two were considered practical enough to warrant consideration in a series of tests at Buffalo beginning in 1885, which resulted in the adoption, in 1887, of the design of Eli H. Janney as standard. Vastly modified and improved, the basic principle remained standard in the 1970's.

As in the case of couplers, interchange of freight cars between railroads required standardization of brakes. Early trains were stopped by hand brakes, set on each car by brakemen. Efforts to control the setting of brakes from the locomotive were unsuccessful until, in 1869, George Westinghouse devised his first air brake for passenger trains. Three years later he developed an improved system in which the brakes would be applied automatically if the train was accidentally separated. These brakes were installed on most passenger cars within the next decade, but the problem of a satisfactory brake for freight trains remained. In 1886 and 1887 exhaustive tests were conducted on the Chicago, Burlington and Quincy at Burlington, Iowa, which resulted in the adoption of a quick-acting brake for freight trains. With further improvements, especially those adopted in 1933 after exhaustive laboratory and road tests, the air brake remained fundamental in train operation.

Another feature of railroad operation standardized in the 1880's was time. Previously, each locality had used its own sun time, while each railroad had its own standard, usually the local time of its headquarters or of some important city on the line. There were altogether nearly a hundred different railroad times, bringing about unimaginable confusion. On Nov. 18, 1883, under an arrangement put into effect by the General Time Convention (another predecessor organization of the Association of American Railroads), all railroad clocks and watches were set on a new standard time with four zones one hour apart. Within a short time most localities abandoned their particular times and conformed to the system of Eastern, Central, Mountain, and Pacific time zones set up by the railroads. The system of standard time continued under railroad auspices until 1918, when by act of Congress it was placed under control of the Interstate Commerce Commission (ICC).

The ICC itself dates from the 1880's. Early attempts to regulate railroad rates and practices by action of the states had been only partially successful, although in 1876 the so-called Granger laws had been upheld by the U.S. Supreme Court for intrastate application. In 1886, however, the Court held, in *Wabash, Saint Louis and Pacific Railroad Company* v. *Illinois,* that Congress had exclusive jurisdiction over interstate commerce and that a state could not regulate even the intrastate portion of an interstate movement. Efforts had been made for a dozen years before to have Congress enact regulatory legislation. The decision in the *Wabash* case brought these efforts to a head and resulted in passage on Feb. 4, 1887, of the Interstate Commerce Act, which created the ICC. Subsequent enactments, notably those of 1903, 1906, 1910, 1920, 1933, 1940, and 1958, broadened the commission's jurisdiction and responsibilities, increased its powers, and strengthened its organization.

In 1888 the first federal legislation dealing with relations between railroads and their employees was passed. This enactment applied only to employees in train and engine service, who were the first railway employees to form successful unions—the Brotherhood of Locomotive Engineers in 1863, the Order of Railway Conductors in 1868, the Brotherhood of Locomotive Firemen and Enginemen in 1873, and the Brotherhood of Railroad Trainmen in 1883. These, with the Switchmen's Union of North America, organized in 1894, constitute the "operating" group of unions. "Nonoperating" crafts formed organizations at various dates—the telegraphers (1886), the six shop-craft unions (1888–93), the maintenance-of-way employees (1891), the clerks and station employees (1898), the signalmen (1901). Nevertheless, the Erdman Act (1898) and the Newlands Act (1913), providing various measures of mediation, conciliation, arbitration, and fact-finding in connection with railway labor disputes, dealt with train service cases only.

Between 1890 and 1900 another 40,000 miles were added to the railroad net, which by the turn of the century had assumed its main outline. After 1900, still another 60,000 miles of line were built, to bring the total of first main track to its peak of 254,000 miles in 1916. Mileage of all tracks, including additional main tracks, passing tracks, sidings, and yards reached its maximum of 430,000 miles in 1930. By 1960, mileage of line declined to approximately 220,000, and miles of tracks of all sorts had declined to 390,000.

This reduction in mileage was the result of many factors, including the exhaustion of the mines, forests, and other natural resources that were the reason for being of many branch lines; intensified water and highway competition; and the coordinations and consolidations that made many lines unnecessary. In 1916 more than 1,400 companies operated 254,000 miles of line; in 1960, fewer than 600 companies operated 220,000 miles of line—but the reduced mileage had more than double the effective carrying capacity of the more extensive network.

1917–41. Railroad mileage was at its peak when, in April 1917, the United States entered World War I. Immediately the railroads established the Railroads' War Board to coordinate their work in meeting increased transportation demands. Increased service was achieved, but by December it was apparent that a voluntary organization of this kind could not cope with all the many difficulties: congestion arose from abuse by government organizations of the privilege of demanding priority and preference for cars, loading them even when they could not be unloaded promptly at destination, and further complications arose from the failure to suspend for the emergency the application of the antitrust laws and the antipooling provisions of the Interstate Commerce Act. On Dec. 26, 1917, President Woodrow Wilson issued his proclamation taking over the railroads for operation by the government, to start Jan. 1, 1918.

Operation of the railroads by the U.S. Railroad Administration lasted for twenty-six months, until Mar. 1, 1920. From the standpoint of meeting the transportation demands of the war, the operation was creditable. From a financial point of view, it resulted in losses, largely because of increased wages and prices not compensated for by increases in rates and fares, which amounted to an average of nearly $2 million a day for the period of government operation.

Congress voted to return the railroads to private operation and set up the terms of such operation in the Transportation Act of 1920. Among the changes in government policy was recognition of a measure of responsibility for financial results, found in the direction to the ICC to fix rates at such a level as would enable the railroads, as a whole or in groups, to earn a fair return on the value of the properties devoted to public service. This provision was frequently described as a government guarantee of railroad profits, although there was no guarantee of earnings. Commercial conditions and competitive forces kept railway earnings well below the contemplated level, and the government was not called on to make up the deficiency.

Another shift in government policy related to consolidation of railroads, previously frowned upon but encouraged by the Transportation Act of 1920. The change in policy stemmed from the fact that consolidation in one form or another had been from early times the way of growth of the major systems, some of which included properties originally built by a hundred or more companies. Accordingly the 1920 law directed the ICC to work out a scheme of consolidation for the railroads, a requirement of which the commission was relieved at its own request in 1933.

The 1920 act also set up the U.S. Railroad Labor Board, with jurisdiction extending to all crafts of employees and with power to determine wage rates and working conditions, although without power to enforce its decisions otherwise than by the force of public opinion. The first nationwide strike on the railroads took place in 1922, when the shopmen struck against a Labor Board decision reducing wages. The strike failed, but its aftereffects were such that in the Railway Labor Act of 1926, agreed to by the unions and the railroads, the Labor Board was abolished and the principles of the earlier labor legislation, with their reliance on mediation and conciliation, were restored, with improved machinery for making them more effective. The 1926 law was amended in important particulars in 1934, at the instance of the Railway Labor Executives Association, an organization of the "standard" railway unions formed in 1929.

In 1934, also, the Railroad Retirement Act was passed as the first of the Social Security measures of the New Deal period. This legislation was declared unconstitutional, but in 1937 a retirement and unemployment insurance system was set up under legislation agreed upon by the Railway Labor Executives Association and the Association of American Railroads, an organization of the industry formed in 1934.

While railway mileage was shrinking in the two decades between World War I and World War II, the same years saw the introduction of numerous innovations in railroad plant, equipment, and methods, which greatly increased capacity and efficiency. The wooden car virtually disappeared. The steam locomotive became more powerful and more efficient. The diesel locomotive was introduced in passenger service in 1934 and in freight service in 1941. Passenger car air conditioning was introduced in 1929, and the first all air-conditioned train was operated in 1931. Streamlining was added to passenger train service, beginning in 1934. Passenger train speeds were increased, and overnight merchandise freight service for distances of more than 400 miles was inaugurated.

Centralized traffic control and train operation by signal indication multiplied the capacity of single-track lines and even made it possible to take up trackage that was no longer required. Car retarders increased the speed and capacity, as well as the economy, of handling trains in terminal yards. Methods of operation, including car supply and distribution, particularly through the operations of the Car Service Division of the Association of American Railroads, were so improved that periodic general car shortages were no longer experienced.

1942–60. The combined effect of these and other improvements in plant, methods, and organization was such that the railroads, continuing under private operation, were able to meet all transportation demands during World War II. With one-fourth fewer cars, one-third fewer locomotives, and nearly one-third fewer men than they had in World War I, the railroads handled double the traffic of the first war and did so without congestion or delay.

In spite of wartime increases in wages and the prices of materials and supplies, railway rates and fares were no higher at the end of the war than they were when war began. As a result of postwar increases in wages average hourly earnings of employees went up from approximately $1 an hour to more than $2.50 an hour, and the level of prices paid for materials and supplies more than doubled in fifteen postwar years. In the same period the average revenue received for hauling a ton of freight one mile went up from about 1 cent to 1.5 cents, and the average charge for carrying a passenger one mile went up from about 2 cents to a little less than 3 cents. At the same time competitive forces reduced the railroads' share of the total transportation movement.

In May 1946, President Harry S. Truman, acting under his war powers, seized the railroads as a means of dealing with a nationwide strike by the engineers and trainmen, which had paralyzed the railroads for two days. Similar strike threats by other groups of unions brought similar seizures by the government in 1948 and again in 1950, the latter lasting nearly two years. In 1951 Congress amended the 1934 Railway Labor Act by removing the prohibition against compulsory union membership as a condition of holding a job on the railroads, thereby permitting the establishment of the union shop by negotiation, and such agreements were negotiated on most railroads.

Throughout the postwar years the railroads carried forward a program of capital improvements, with expenditures for such purposes averaging more than $1 billion yearly. The most striking and significant change was the displacement of the steam locomotive by the diesel-electric. Other major developments included the wider use of continuous welded rail in lengths of a quarter-mile, a half-mile, and even longer; the wide use of off-track equipment in maintenance-of-way work; the development of new designs of freight cars to make them ride more smoothly; the introduction of container or trailer-on-flat-car service, commonly called piggybacking; and the development of the automatic terminal with electronic controls, known as the push-button yard.

In passing the Transportation Act of 1958 Congress somewhat relaxed regulatory requirements on the railroads, providing, in effect, that competitive cost factors be given greater consideration in determining the lawfulness of rates, so long as the rates proposed were compensatory to the carrier and not discriminatory, as they were among shippers.

In 1959 Congress amended the Railroad Retirement Act and the Unemployment Insurance Act, increasing the benefits and the taxes levied to pay them: the measures provided for the financing of retirement by taxes on both companies and employees, half and half, and of unemployment insurance by taxes on the companies alone, without contribution from the employees.

As 1959 ended, railroads and employees were engaged in negotiations over wages and working conditions. The companies were seeking changes in rules that, it was charged, compelled payment for work not done and not needed. The operating unions denied the charge, maintaining that the rules under criticism were necessary for safety and the protection of the right of employees. Besides the dispute over featherbedding, with the operating unions only, negotiations over wages were in progress with all the employee organizations.

1961–74. In the seventh decade of the 20th century American railroads achieved some technical gains, but in other areas they suffered both real and relative losses. Total mileage operated declined from 216,000 miles in 1961 to 202,000 miles in 1973. In those twelve years total operating revenues for the industry climbed from $9.2 billion in 1961 to an all-time high of about $14.8 billion in 1973, but much of the increase was caused by inflation. Freight revenue increased in importance, climbing from 84 percent to 93 percent of the total operating revenue. While freight carloading declined, because of the use of larger and larger cars, there was a significant increase in total ton-mileage, and the 852 billion ton-miles reached in 1973 was a record high. However, the railroads' share of total intercity commercial freight was still declining, dropping from 43 percent in 1961 to about 38 percent in 1973. The discontinuance of hundreds of passenger trains and the growing popularity of jet air travel caused an even greater decline in rail passenger service. The 10.3 billion passenger-miles in 1974 was only about 50 percent of the 1961 figure, and the railroads' share of all passenger traffic declined from 26 percent in 1961 to less than 6 percent in 1973. By the early 1970's a major portion of the remaining rail passenger mileage was urban commuter traffic.

During the 1960's and early 1970's rises in freight rates and passenger fares roughly matched the growing inflation. Between 1961 and 1974 average freight rates increased from 1.37 cents to 1.85 cents per ton-mile, while average passenger fares climbed from 3.08 cents to 5.22 cents a mile. The total investment in the railroad industry grew but modestly in these years, increasing from $35.1 billion in 1961 to $37.4 billion in 1972. Nor was there much favorable news on the profit front, since the rate of return for the entire industry ranged from a low of 1.73 percent to a high of 3.90 percent, averaging only 2.46 percent for the period, significantly lower than the average rate of 3.45 percent for the 1950's and 4.25 percent for the 1940's.

The rather bleak financial picture was in part relieved by the achievement of modest technological advances. Innovation was especially notable in freight service. There was a slight drop in the number of freight cars in service, but the average capacity per car increased by nearly 25 percent. This factor plus greater daily car mileage resulted in a significant gain in the net ton-miles per freight-train hour.

A major reduction in "hot boxes" (overheated journal bearings) was achieved during the 1960's. Improved lubrication plus infrared detection devices placed trackside reduced the number of set-out freight cars (those left on a siding because of a hot box) by more than 90 percent. Started in the late 1960's a program of automatic car identification (ACI) began providing the industry with a nationwide computer car-locating system. By the late 1960's many railroads were using sophisticated computers to help handle the mountains of paperwork that go with nearly every railroad operation. Almost 10,000 miles of Centralized Traffic Control (CTC) was installed during the decade, and CTC signaling was in use on about 40,000 miles of road by 1972.

New types of freight service were also appearing or being expanded. Piggyback freight service, introduced in the 1950's, continued to grow: such carloadings more than doubled between 1961 and 1968 and in the latter year amounted to almost 5 percent of the total carloadings for the year. A great increase was achieved in the railroad movement of new motor vehicles: in the late 1950's such traffic was about 90 percent by highway rack truck; in the early 1960's specially built railroad trilevel rack cars carried more and more of this traffic, and between 1969 and 1972 railroads delivered more than 50 percent of all automobiles produced. The railroads also rebuilt a declining coal traffic by introducing "unit trains"— whole trains of permanently coupled cars that carry bulk tonnage to a single destination on a regular schedule—thus reducing rates. The unit coal trains were so popular that the idea was soon extended to the shipment of grain, ore, pulpwood, and even trash and garbage.

Passenger service dropped off sharply in the 1960's. In 1961 passenger service was offered on more than 40 percent of the nation's rail network, whereas by 1971 passenger trains were running on less than 20 percent of the national mileage. Early in 1969 a government-sponsored project for high-speed passenger service in the Northeast Corridor was started when Metroliner service was provided between New York City and Washington, D.C. In May 1971 most railroad passenger service was taken over by the federally sponsored National Railroad Passenger Corporation, soon to be known as Amtrak. Amtrak provided passenger service consisting of about 1,300 trains a week, running over 20,000 miles of track on twenty-two different railroads, and serving 340 American cities. The financial support provided by the government assured at least some continuing rail passenger service for the immediate future.

In these years the railroad labor picture was marked by a continued drop in the work force accompanied by a marked increase in wages and salaries. Increased productivity plus the loss of some traditional rail traffic in the 1960's caused the total number of rail workers to drop from 717,000 in 1961 to 525,000 in 1974, a decline of more than 25 percent.

Wage rates and pay scales for railroad workers climbed rapidly. Between 1961 and 1974 average annual earnings per employee climbed from $6,444 to $14,235. The average straight time hourly rate rose from $2.72 to $5.84, more than doubling over the thirteen-year period. In general terms, railroad wages were climbing twice as fast as the cost of living. As it had for some time, the total cost of railroad labor, including fringe benefits and payroll taxes, continued to total just over 50 percent of all railway operating revenues.

The featherbedding issue, which railroad management had first raised in 1959, continued to color all railroad labor relations. One of the most difficult aspects of this problem, the issue of the employment of firemen in freight diesels, was finally resolved during 1972. Also by 1972 "full crew" laws had been eliminated in nearly all the states of the union. As in the case of the settlement concerning diesel firemen, fairly generous employment-security provisions were provided for those workers employed at the time of the repeal of the "full crew" laws.

A major development was the trend toward merger or consolidation: in the late 1950's there were 116 Class I railroads operating in the nation, and by 1973 this number had been reduced to just over 60. Between 1959 and 1964 the Norfolk and Western expanded by taking over the Virginian, the Wabash, and the Nickel Plate. During the same years the Chesapeake and Ohio gained control of the larger Baltimore and Ohio. Farther south the Atlantic Coast Line and the Seaboard Air Line merged in 1967 to become the Seaboard Coast Line. Between 1962 and 1968 long involved proceedings between the New York Central and the Pennsylvania resulted in a new consolidated 21,000-mile system, the Penn Central, which included the New York, New Haven and Hartford. And in 1970 approval was given for the mammoth 23,500-mile Burlington Northern system, a merger of the Great Northern, the Northern Pacific, and the Chicago, Burlington and Quincy.

Extensive operational savings were projected and claimed for nearly every proposed railroad merger, and often such economies were realized, when the consolidation was orderly and well planned. The merger problems facing the Penn Central in the first two years of its corporate existence were so difficult that the railroad was forced into bankruptcy in the summer of 1970. Part of the Penn Central's problem was that it was operating hundreds of miles of route-mileage that generated very little profitable traffic. This same condition was largely responsible for the bankruptcy of several other eastern railroads in the early 1970's.

Throughout these years the role of government in railroad affairs continued to be a dominant one. While federal controls had been somewhat lessened by the Transportation Act of 1958, most railroad managers still believed their industry to be overregulated. Nor did they feel that any significant improvement came

with the establishment, in 1966, of the new Department of Transportation. When the newly merged Penn Central went into bankruptcy in 1970, Congress did pass legislation that provided some indirect financial support. But in the early 1970's the continuing low rate of return on the investment, the increased concern over railroad safety, and the threat of additional bankruptcy for eastern lines all tended to deepen the sense of crisis within the industry. In some quarters a renewed consideration of possible nationalization of the nation's railways was favored, while in others it was believed that the federal government might, through new legislation, achieve some solution to the problems facing American railroads.

RAILROADS, SKETCHES OF PRINCIPAL LINES

Atchison, Topeka and Santa Fe. Chartered in 1859 to connect Atchison and Topeka, Kans., the Atchison, Topeka and Santa Fe expanded rapidly. Through a combination of construction, purchases, and leases the road by 1889 had become a 7,000-mile system stretching from Chicago westward to the Pacific coast and southward to the Gulf of Mexico. It was a pioneer in the use of diesel locomotives, especially in freight service. The system of just under 13,000 miles made the Santa Fe first in mileage in the middle decades of the 20th century.

Boston and Maine. The first of the 111 companies absorbed into the Boston and Maine was the Boston and Lowell, chartered in 1830. The name "Boston and Maine" dates from 1835. In the early 1970's the railroad operated 1,500 miles of line in Massachusetts, New Hampshire, Maine, Vermont, and New York.

Burlington Northern. In 1970 the ICC approved the merger of the Chicago, Burlington and Quincy, the Great Northern, and the Northern Pacific into the Burlington Northern. The combined trackage of 23,500 miles made it the longest railroad system in the nation.

Chicago, Burlington and Quincy. The original unit of the Burlington system was the Aurora Branch Railroad, a 12-mile line chartered in Illinois in 1849. It expanded through the amalgamation of some 200 railroads into a system that in the early 1970's extended from Chicago and Saint Louis to Minneapolis–Saint Paul and thence to Montana, Wyoming, Colorado, and the Gulf coast of Texas. The Burlington pioneered in the development of streamline passenger equipment with the introduction of the first Zephyr in 1934.

Great Northern. The original line included in the Great Northern was the Saint Paul and Pacific, which started in 1862 to build northward and westward from Saint Paul. After James J. Hill secured control, the emphasis was on building to the west, although the line was built north to Winnipeg, Manitoba, Canada. The transcontinental line was opened in 1893. In the early 1970's the company operated 8,200 miles of road, extending from Minneapolis–Saint Paul and the head of the Great Lakes to Vancouver, British Columbia; Seattle; and Portland, Oreg.

Northern Pacific. The first of the northern transcontinental lines, the Northern Pacific, was chartered by an act of Congress signed by President Abraham Lincoln on July 2, 1864. Construction of the line to connect the head of the Great Lakes with Portland, Oreg., was started in 1870 and completed in 1883. In the early 1970's the company operated 6,700 miles of line, extending from Minneapolis–Saint Paul and Duluth-Superior, on Lake Superior, to Seattle and Tacoma, Wash., and Portland.

Central of Georgia. Chartered in 1833 as the Central Railroad and Banking Company of Georgia to build a railroad from Savannah to Macon, the Central of Georgia operated 2,000 miles of line in Georgia, Alabama, and Tennessee in the early 1970's. It should not be confused with the Georgia Railroad between Augusta and Atlanta, built and owned by the Georgia Railroad and Banking Company, also incorporated in 1833, and operated under lease after 1882. Nor should it be confused with the Western and Atlantic Railroad, under which name the state of Georgia built a line between Atlanta and Chattanooga, still owned by the state and operated under lease by the Louisville and Nashville.

Chesapeake and Ohio. The 22-mile Louisa Railroad, chartered in Virginia in 1837, had grown into the 5,100-mile Chesapeake and Ohio system by the early 1970's, extending from Hampton Roads, Va., and Washington, D.C., to Louisville, Ky., Chicago, the Straits of Mackinac, and the western shore of Lake Michigan (by car ferry). In 1947 the railroad absorbed into its system the Père Marquette. Between 1960 and 1963 it took over the larger Baltimore and Ohio, when that line was in financial trouble.

Baltimore and Ohio. Chartered in 1827 (the oldest charter under which a railroad operated in the early 1970's), the Baltimore and Ohio was built to Wheel-

ing on the Ohio River by late 1852. Later through construction and the acquisition of other lines it expanded northward to Philadelphia and New York City and westward to Saint Louis and Chicago, extending its mileage to 5,500.

Chicago and North Western. Chartered in 1848, the Galena and Chicago Union was the first railroad to serve Chicago. It became the Chicago and North Western in 1859. Eight years later it was the first line to reach the Missouri River at Omaha, where it connected with the Union Pacific. In 1910 the Chicago and North Western was the first railroad to sponsor the "Safety First" movement. Serving the region between the Great Lakes and the Rockies, it acquired the Chicago Great Western in 1968, thus extending its system to 10,700 miles.

Chicago, Milwaukee, Saint Paul and Pacific. The earliest "ancestor" of the Chicago, Milwaukee, Saint Paul and Pacific was chartered in 1847 to build a line across Wisconsin to the Mississippi River. By 1900 the Chicago, Milwaukee and Saint Paul operated between the Great Lakes and the Missouri River. Between 1905 and 1909 the line was extended to the Pacific coast, and during the next decade some of the mountain route was electrified. In 1921 the line was extended into Indiana. With more than 150 companies consolidated in the system, the Milwaukee operated about 10,200 miles in 1973. Early in that year the line decided to shift to diesel power on its two mountain electrified divisions.

Chicago, Rock Island and Pacific. Incorporated in 1847 to build from Rock Island to LaSalle, Ill., but built from Chicago under an amended charter, the Chicago, Rock Island and Pacific was the first railroad to bridge the Mississippi, in 1856. It operated 7,500 miles of line in the early 1970's, extending from Chicago, Saint Louis, and Memphis on the east, to Minneapolis–Saint Paul on the north, Colorado and New Mexico on the west, and the Texas and the Louisiana Gulf coast on the south.

Delaware and Hudson. The original company, the Delaware and Hudson Canal Company, chartered in 1823, built a canal and a railroad to bring out coal from Carbondale, Pa., to Rondout, N.Y., on the Hudson River. On this line, in 1829, the first steam locomotive to turn a wheel on an American railroad made its first, and only, run. The original canal was abandoned in 1898. The system, extending through upstate New York to Montreal, Quebec, Canada, was built up by acquisition and construction to over 700 miles.

Denver and Rio Grande Western. Chartered in 1870 by Denver interests, the Denver and Rio Grande Western built a narrow-gauge line that reached a large part of southern and western Colorado and extended to Salt Lake City. By 1890 main lines had been converted to standard gauge. Consolidation with the Denver and Salt Lake, with its Moffatt Tunnel through the crest of the Rocky Mountains, and construction of a new cutoff connection with the original main line shortened the distance between terminals by 175 miles. In the early 1970's the road operated 1,900 miles, of which some was narrow gauge.

Erie Lackawanna. A 2,900-mile road, the Erie Lackawanna was formed in 1960 out of two lines, the Delaware, Lackawanna and Western and the Erie.

Delaware, Lackawanna and Western. Chartered in 1851 to build an outlet for the coal of the Lackawanna Valley in Pennsylvania, the Liggitt's Gap Railroad was extended west to Buffalo, north to Lake Ontario, and east to New York via Hoboken, N.J., becoming the Delaware, Lackawanna and Western.

Erie. Chartered as the New York and Erie, in 1832, to build from Piermont, N.Y., on the Hudson, to Dunkirk, on Lake Erie, the Erie completed a 6-foot-gauge track in 1851. The financial and corporate history of the road was checkered in the extreme, but after a reorganization in 1941, it began a career of solid success. Before merging with the Lackawanna in 1960, the Erie operated 2,300 miles, extending from New York City to Buffalo, Cleveland, and Chicago.

Florida East Coast. The railroad that extends from Jacksonville to Miami, the Florida East Coast, is the result of the vision and determination of one man, Henry M. Flagler. Retiring from the Standard Oil Company at the age of fifty-three, he went to Saint Augustine, then reached only by a narrow-gauge railroad from the Saint Johns River. Acquiring the railroad in 1885, he steadily pushed it southward, reaching Miami in 1896. The overseas extension, built across the Florida keys and stretches of open sea, reached Key West in 1912, the year before Flagler's death. In 1935 the extension suffered severe hurricane damage and was abandoned as a railroad, to become the overseas highway to Key West.

Grand Trunk Western. A subsidiary of the Canadian National Railways, the Grand Trunk Western was built from Port Huron and Detroit across Michigan, Indiana, and Illinois, reaching Chicago in 1881, and then extended to Milwaukee, via cross-lake car ferry. The tunnel under the Saint Clair River, connecting the western extension with the parent Grand

Trunk, was completed in 1891. In the early 1970's the Grand Trunk Western operated nearly 1,000 miles. Other Canadian National subsidiaries in the United States include the Grand Trunk to Portland, Maine, opened in 1853, and the Central Vermont, acquired in 1899.

Illinois Central Gulf. A 9,500-mile-line, the Illinois Central Gulf was the result of the 1972 merger of the Gulf, Mobile and Ohio and the Illinois Central.

Gulf, Mobile and Ohio. The Gulf, Mobile and Ohio dates from 1940, when the corporation was formed by the consolidation of the Gulf, Mobile and Northern (itself a 1917 consolidation of earlier small railroads) with the Mobile and Ohio, which in the decade before the Civil War built a through line from Mobile, Ala., to Columbus, Ky., and afterward extended it to Saint Louis. In 1947 the firm absorbed the Alton, originally the Chicago and Alton, which dated from 1847. At the time of its merger with the Illinois Central the Gulf, Mobile and Ohio had a 2,700-mile system extending from Chicago and Kansas City, Mo., to Mobile and New Orleans.

Illinois Central. Incorporated in 1851, the Illinois Central was still operating in the early 1970's under its original charter, which called for a 705-mile railroad within the state of Illinois. Along with the Mobile and Ohio, the Illinois Central received the first railroad land grant provided by the federal government. After the Civil War a southern line to the Gulf was acquired. At the time of the 1972 merger the Illinois Central operated a 6,700-mile system in fourteen states, extending from Chicago west to the Missouri River and south to New Orleans and Birmingham, Ala.

Lehigh Valley. Originally chartered as the Delaware, Lehigh, Schuylkill and Susquehanna for the purpose of hauling coal from the vicinity of Mauch Chunk, Pa., the Lehigh Valley adopted its present name in 1853. The line expanded to 925 miles, reaching the Niagara frontier on the west and New York on the east. In the process it acquired numerous other lines, some dating back to 1836.

Louisville and Nashville. Chartered in 1850, the Louisville and Nashville completed its line between the cities whose names it bears in 1859. Continuing to operate under its original charter, the railroad constructed and acquired some seventy-five other lines and by the early 1970's had created a 6,300-mile system extending from Chicago, Cincinnati, and Saint Louis to Memphis, Atlanta, and New Orleans. The oldest existing part of the railroad was the line between Lexington and Frankfort, Ky., chartered in

1830, opened for traffic in 1834, and acquired by the Louisville and Nashville in 1881.

Missouri, Kansas and Texas. The Union Pacific, Southern Branch, a road chartered in 1865, was the first of several short roads to make up the Missouri, Kansas and Texas, organized in 1870. A line from Junction City, Kans., was built southward to the southern border of Kansas by 1870, and to the Texas line by 1872. Subsequent expansion by the end of the century created a system of 2,600 miles extending from Saint Louis and Kansas City, Mo., to San Antonio and Houston.

Missouri Pacific. The Pacific Railroad of Missouri, the earliest part of the Missouri Pacific, was chartered on July 4, 1851, to build a line of 5.5-foot gauge from Saint Louis to the West Coast. The first locomotive west of the Mississippi ran on the first 5 miles of this road in December 1852. By construction and consolidation, the road extended from Saint Louis, Memphis, and New Orleans to Omaha; Pueblo, Colo.; Laredo, Tex.; and the Gulf coast, operating nearly 9,000 miles.

Norfolk and Western. The City Point Railway, a 9-mile line between Petersburg, Va., and the James River, chartered in 1836, is the oldest part of the Norfolk and Western. It grew into the Southside Railroad, which, with connections, stretched across southern Virginia from tidewater to Tennessee and with extensions westward into the coal fields, and became the basis of the Norfolk and Western. The railroad grew to 2,700 miles with the addition of the Virginian in 1959. In 1964 two other roads, the Nickel Plate and the Wabash, were added, creating a system of 7,600 miles.

New York, Chicago and Saint Louis. The Nickel Plate Road, as the New York, Chicago and Saint Louis is usually called, was opened for operation between Buffalo and Chicago in 1882; the last spike, driven at Bellevue, Ohio, was nickel plated. Control soon passed to the New York Central, which acquired the road rather than have it fall into unfriendly hands. In 1916 control was sold to Mantis James Van Sweringen and Oris Paxton Van Sweringen, two brothers interested in Cleveland real estate. They later added the Lake Erie and Western and the Toledo, Peoria and Western to the Nickel Plate; subsequently the Wheeling and Lake Erie was added. In the early 1970's the system operated 2,200 miles, extending from Buffalo and Wheeling to Chicago and Peoria, Ill., and Saint Louis.

Wabash. The Northern Cross, 12 miles long, built in 1838, was the first railroad in Illinois and the earliest part of the Wabash. It became a system of nearly 3,000 miles, one of the few operating in both the East and the West, stretching from Buffalo and Toledo to Saint Louis, Kansas City, Mo., Omaha, and Des Moines. A separately operated subsidiary, the Ann Arbor Railroad, with car ferries across Lake Michigan, extended the system.

Penn Central. After long years of negotiation the Pennsylvania New York Central Transportation Company was created in 1968 out of the New York Central, the Pennsylvania, and the New York, New Haven and Hartford. The problems facing the 21,000-mile Penn Central in the first two years of its corporate existence were so great that the line was forced into bankruptcy in the summer of 1970. Congress passed legislation that provided some indirect financial aid, but after nearly three years of receivership the Penn Central was still operating hundreds of miles of excess track that produced very little profitable traffic.

New York Central. The Mohawk and Hudson, the oldest of the many companies that made up the New York Central, was incorporated in 1826 and ran its first train in 1831. The Hudson River Railroad was added to the New York Central (organized in 1853) in 1869, to be followed in the course of time by the Lake Shore and Michigan Southern, the Michigan Central, the Big Four, the Boston and Albany, the West Shore, the Toledo and Ohio Central, and other railroads, including the separately operated Pittsburgh and Lake Erie. The system grew to more than 10,000 miles, extending from Montreal, Boston, and New York to the Straits of Mackinac, Chicago, and Saint Louis.

New York, New Haven and Hartford. Earliest of the approximately 125 companies that made up the New York, New Haven and Hartford was the Boston and Providence, chartered in 1831 and in operation by 1834. The Hartford and New Haven, incorporated in 1833, connected New Haven with Springfield, Mass., by 1844, the year in which a railroad was chartered to connect New Haven with New York. This line, providing the first all-rail service between Boston and New York via Springfield, was opened in 1848. The Shore Line, operating between New Haven and Providence, was leased in 1870. The New York, New Haven and Hartford thus came to operate 1,800 miles, serving southern New England and New York. Between 1907 and 1914 the railroad installed the first railroad electrification using high-voltage alternating-current transmission between New York and New Haven.

Pennsylvania. Long known as the "standard" railroad, because of the high quality of its property and operation, the Pennsylvania for decades took pride in its unbroken record of dividend payments. It was chartered in 1846 to build a line between Harrisburg and Pittsburgh, paralleling the state's canal and inclined-plane system. By purchase, lease, and construction the line was expanded to a system of 10,000 miles, extending eastward to Philadelphia, New York, Washington, D.C., and Norfolk, Va., and westward to Chicago and Saint Louis. The oldest segment of the system was the pioneer Camden and Amboy, chartered by New Jersey in 1830 and completed in 1834. The first "T" rail was rolled in a design whittled out by Robert Stevens, son of Col. John Stevens, while on a voyage to England to purchase rail for the Camden and Amboy. The design became the basis of rail used throughout the world.

Pullman Company. George M. Pullman built his first sleeping cars (rebuilt coaches of the Chicago and Alton) in 1858. His first completely Pullman-built car was finished in 1864. By the end of the century the name "Pullman" was substantially synonymous with the sleeping-car business, although the company also manufactured passenger and freight cars. As a result of an antitrust suit, the enterprise was required to divest itself of either the car-manufacturing or the car-operating business. In 1947 the latter was taken over by fifty-seven railroads.

Reading. The Reading Company, which operated 1,200 miles of line in Pennsylvania, New York, and Delaware in the early 1970's, was a successor company to the Philadelphia and Reading Railroad, incorporated in 1833, although parts of the line had been built by still earlier companies. It was on one of these predecessor lines, the Philadelphia, Germantown and Norristown, that *Old Ironsides,* the first locomotive built by Matthias Baldwin, ran in 1832. In the 1970's the Reading owned a majority of the stock of the Jersey Central Lines.

Saint Louis–San Francisco. The Saint Louis–San Francisco, started in 1866, was planned to run from Springfield, Ill., to the Pacific coast; but its point of origin was changed to Saint Louis, and it never reached the California city whose name it bears. It developed as a system of some 4,800 miles, stretching from Saint Louis and Kansas City, Mo., to Oklahoma and northern Texas, on the southwest, and to Alabama and Florida, on the southeast. The "Frisco" is one of the few systems to operate in both the West and the Southeast.

Saint Louis–Southwestern. The "Cotton Belt," as the Saint Louis–Southwestern is commonly called, started as the Tyler Tap Railroad, chartered in 1871, to build a connection from Tyler, Tex., to a main-line railroad. The enterprise expanded to a system of 1,500 miles, connecting Saint Louis and Memphis with Fort Worth, Dallas, and Waco, Tex. The present name of the company dates from 1891.

Seaboard Coast Line. In 1967 two major southern railroads, the Atlantic Coast Line and the Seaboard Air Line, merged to form the Seaboard Coast Line.

Atlantic Coast Line. The Richmond and Petersburg was chartered in 1836 to connect those two Virginia cities. The Atlantic Coast Line was created out of the Richmond and Petersburg and dozens of other southern railways. Service south of Virginia was possible with the acquisition of lines serving the Carolinas, Georgia, Alabama, and Florida. It became the Atlantic Coast Line in 1900, when the parent company absorbed its southern connections. In the early 1970's the railroad operated 5,600 miles of line and had substantial interests in the Louisville and Nashville, the Clinchfield, and other roads.

Seaboard Air Line. The name "Seaboard Air Line" was first applied in 1889 to a loose operating association of a half a dozen separate connecting railroads in Virginia and the Carolinas. The oldest line was the Portsmouth and Roanoke, chartered in 1832, which was built from Portsmouth, Va., to Weldon, N.C. In 1900 the several railroads were consolidated and, by acquisition and construction, they grew into a system of 4,000 miles extending from Norfolk and Richmond through the Carolinas and Georgia to Birmingham and Montgomery, Ala., and to both coasts of Florida.

Soo Line (Minneapolis, Saint Paul and Sault Sainte Marie). Chartered in 1873 by businessmen of Minneapolis to build a line eastward to the Canadian border at Sault Sainte Marie, the Soo Line reached the sault in 1887. By the same time it had extended westward into the Dakotas, finally building to a western connection with the Canadian Pacific at Portal, N.Dak. After 1909 the Soo Line operated the Wisconsin Central, effecting an entrance into Chicago. The 4,600-mile system became a separately operated subsidiary of the Canadian Pacific in the 1940's.

Southern Pacific. The beginnings of the Southern Pacific were in Louisiana, Texas, and California. In Louisiana the New Orleans, Opelousas and Great Western Railroad was chartered in 1850 to build from New Orleans westward. In the same year, in Texas, the Buffalo Bayou, Brazos and Colorado was chartered; it was in operation by 1852. The Sacramento Valley Railroad also was started in 1852 in California. The Central Pacific, incorporated in California in 1861, undertook the task of building a railroad eastward over the Sierra Nevada and, in 1862, was selected to build the western leg of the first transcontinental route. The Southern Pacific, incorporated in California in 1865, built south and east, to become part of the second transcontinental route. The interests of the Central Pacific and the Southern Pacific were closely linked as early as 1870. In 1934 the twelve companies making up the Southern Pacific interests in Texas and Louisiana were consolidated into the Texas and New Orleans Railroad. In the early 1970's the Southern Pacific system operated more than 13,000 miles of line.

Southern Railway. The Southern Railway was formed in 1894, when the purchasers of the Richmond and Danville were authorized to acquire the East Tennessee, Virginia and Georgia, and other lines, among them the pioneer South Carolina Railroad. The system came to include the separately operated Cincinnati, New Orleans and Texas Pacific; Alabama Great Southern; New Orleans and Northeastern; Georgia, Southern and Florida; and Carolina and Northwestern railroads. A total mileage of 8,000 in the early 1970's extended from Washington, D.C., Cincinnati, and Saint Louis to New Orleans, Mobile, and Florida.

Texas and Pacific. Chartered by act of Congress in 1871, the Texas and Pacific took over the barely started projects of the Southern Pacific (a company in no way related to the later company of that name), formed in 1856; the Memphis, El Paso and Pacific, also formed in 1856; and the Southern Transcontinental, organized in 1870. From northeast Texas, at Marshall and Texarkana, lines were built westward toward El Paso and eastward to New Orleans. In 1882, at Sierra Blanca, Tex., 90 miles east of El Paso, the Texas and Pacific met the crews of the Galveston, Harrisburg and San Antonio, building the Southern Pacific line eastward. Joint trackage was arranged, effecting an entrance into El Paso for the Texas and Pacific. The line to New Orleans was completed in 1882, with full service starting early in 1883. In the early 1970's the company operated 2,100 miles of line.

Union Pacific. The Union Pacific was incorporated by act of Congress in 1862, to build westward from the Missouri River to meet the Central Pacific of Cali-

fornia, building eastward. To the approximately 1,000 miles of the original main line, the company added the Kansas Pacific; Denver Pacific; Oregon Short Line; Oregon-Washington Railway and Navigation Company; San Pedro, Los Angeles and Salt Lake; and other railroads. The property was extensively improved after it came under the control of Edward H. Harriman in 1897. In the early 1970's it operated nearly 9,500 miles of line, extending from Council Bluffs, Iowa, Omaha, Nebr., Saint Joseph, Mo., and Kansas City, Mo., to Portland, Oreg., Seattle and Spokane, Wash., and Los Angeles.

Western Pacific. The latest of the transcontinental connections in the United States to be formed was the Western Pacific, organized in 1903 and opened for service between Salt Lake City and Oakland–San Francisco, Calif., in 1909. A branch line connecting with the Great Northern, opened in 1931, added a north-south route to the original east-west line of the railroad. Total mileage, including the subsidiary Sacramento Northern, was approximately 1,500 in the early 1970's.

[Association of American Railroads, *Yearbook of Railroad Facts;* Stewart H. Holbrook, *The Story of American Railroads;* Robert G. Lewis, *Handbook of American Railroads;* John F. Stover, *The Life and Decline of the American Railroad.*]

ROBERT S. HENRY
JOHN F. STOVER

RAILROADS IN THE CIVIL WAR. The Civil War was the first great armed conflict in which railroads were an important factor. Because of the nature of the war and the vast area of operations, railroad transportation was essential. The line of separation between the rival forces was fully 2,000 miles long; great portions of the region were thinly settled; in many localities it was difficult for large bodies of troops to live off the country; supplies and munitions frequently had to be transported long distances; and it was often necessary or advisable to transfer troops quickly from one area to another.

Northern railroad building westward into the Ohio and Mississippi valleys had insured the adherence of these sections to the Union. Southern construction was mainly east and west between the Atlantic seaboard and the Mississippi River, and from Richmond to the Carolinas and Georgia, although in 1861 lines connecting the lower South and the Tennessee River valley to the Ohio at Louisville and Cincinnati were projected or under way. For military purposes perhaps the most important lines were those from the Gulf states to Richmond via Chattanooga enabling shipment of supplies and munitions to Virginia and the transfer of troops on interior lines.

The North, bent on invasion and conquest of the seceded states, necessarily took the offensive; the South stood mostly on the defensive. As early as Mar. 31, 1861, the federal government began to use important strategic roads, and on Jan. 31, 1862, President Abraham Lincoln was authorized "to take possession of [certain] railroad and telegraph lines." On Feb. 11, 1862, a military director and superintendent of railroads were appointed. The Confederate government, from necessity becoming more federalistic as the war progressed, was restricted to "supervision and control." Although government work practically monopolized the transportation system of the Confederacy, it was not until February 1865 that authorization was given to take over the southern railroads. Of a total mileage of 31,256 in the United States in 1861, less than 30 percent, or 9,283 miles, was in the Confederate states, and this was soon reduced by Union captures to about 6,000 miles. In general the northern railroads were better built, better equipped, and better run. There were no southern trunk lines, most of the railroads being essentially local in character and purpose. Intercommunication with other lines was by transfer, both because of lack of physical connection and differences in track gauge. Southern roads were also handicapped by disrepair, inferior track and roadbed, worn-out rolling stock and bridges that could neither be replaced nor properly repaired, all of which resulted in long delays, frequent accidents, and limited traffic. In the North the east-west lines constantly transported men and supplies to the Virginia battlefront. Reinforcements to the Tennessee Valley and Gulf states came down the Ohio and Mississippi rivers to western terminals at Memphis, Saint Louis, and Vicksburg, to be transported eastward.

Inability of the Confederate government, at first, to appreciate the proper use of railroads and later states' rights opposition to government control and operation of the roads as an auxiliary to southern defense were in no small measure responsible for the final collapse of the Confederacy. The superior northern railroads, both as to condition and location; prompt federal control where necessary; and greater means made the railroads an effective military auxiliary.

[Edward Channing, *History of the United States*, vol. VI; J. C. Schwab, *The Confederate States of America*.]

THOMAS ROBSON HAY

RAILROAD STRIKE OF 1877. The depression of the 1870's reached its lowest point in 1877, a year that was marked by repeated wage reductions, particularly in the railroad industry. Militant feeling among trainmen expressed itself in spontaneous outbreaks. On July 17, 1877, after a new 10 percent wage reduction went into effect, trainmen halted freight cars of the Baltimore and Ohio Railroad at Martinsburg, W. Va. When the local militia proved sympathetic, President Rutherford B. Hayes, upon request of the governor, sent Gen. Winfield S. Hancock and 200 federal soldiers to the scene, and the strike ended there, but not before it had begun spreading over the nation. At Baltimore, a mob surrounded the state armory, fought with the soldiers, and attempted unsuccessfully to burn the building. At Pittsburgh, where popular feeling was strongly against the railroads, militia, ordered from Philadelphia, was besieged in a roundhouse and narrowly escaped the flames of a fire begun at the shops. Sympathetic strikes in other cities brought further news of rioting. A wave of reaction followed as courts and legislators revived the obsolete doctrines of conspiracy. The precedent of federal troops in industrial disputes became an active one, and the states strengthened their policing activities. Radical labor parties found expression in a new rift between classes.

[Samuel Yellen, *American Labor Struggles*.]

HARVEY WISH

RAILROAD STRIKES OF 1886. During 1884–85, the Knights of Labor succeeded in winning four of the five major railroad strikes. Although Jay Gould, whose railway system had fought the Knights, expressly agreed to show no antiunion discrimination, he secretly prepared to break the power of the order. The Knights, encouraged by their victories, pressed for full observance of the agreement, and when the Texas and Pacific Railroad office at Marshall, Tex., discharged its union foreman, a general strike was ordered for Mar. 1, 1886, on the issue of union recognition and a daily wage of $1.50 for the unskilled. Under the leadership of Martin Irons, 900 men struck, tying up 5,000 miles of railway in the central states, and the struggle soon took on the aspect of a crusade against capital. Gould would neither arbitrate unless the workers first returned to work nor would he reinstate discharged strikers. After two months, marked by occasional violence and the employment of federal troops, the strike collapsed on May 3. This defeat discredited industrial unionism and its proponent, the Knights of Labor, assuring the subsequent victory of the craft unions as exemplified by the American Federation of Labor.

[J. R. Commons and others, *History of Labor in the United States,* vol. II.]

HARVEY WISH

RAILROAD SURVEYS, GOVERNMENT. Interest in a railroad to the Pacific coast, already aroused by the writings and activities of John Plumbe, Asa Whitney, and others, became keen and widespread after the territorial expansion resulting from the Mexican cession of 1848. The question of the best route became the subject of a great deal of discussion, especially since each state along the Mississippi and most midwestern cities evinced a direct and active interest in the selection.

In 1853 Congress added the sum of $150,000 to an army appropriation bill to defray the expenses of surveying feasible routes to the Pacific. Under the direction of Jefferson Davis, secretary of war, parties were sent into the field and five routes were surveyed. The northernmost survey, between the forty-seventh and forty-ninth parallels from Saint Paul to the mouth of the Columbia River, received widespread publicity because of the enthusiasm of Isaac I. Stevens, governor of Washington Territory. Data regarding a route in general along the emigrant trail to California were secured by a party under Lt. E. G. Beckwith. A difficult route between the thirty-eighth and thirty-ninth parallels was surveyed by Capt. John W. Gunnison, who was killed in an Indian ambush. A survey following the thirty-fifth parallel as closely as possible from Fort Smith, in western Arkansas, to Los Angeles was conducted by Lt. Amiel W. Whipple. Finally parties under Capt. John Pope, Lt. John G. Parke, and others explored a far southern route along the thirty-second parallel.

The reports of these surveys, later published in copiously illustrated volumes, contributed greatly to geographical and scientific knowledge concerning the Far West. But the surveys themselves did not bring agreement as to a route. Davis championed the southernmost survey (*see* Gadsden Purchase), but sectional rivalry was too great to permit the choice of a route until after the southern states had seceded from the Union. When the Pacific Railroad Bill was adopted in 1862, the central route from the western border of Iowa to the California-Nevada line was chosen for the construction of the transcontinental railroad.

[George L. Albright, *Official Explorations for a Pacific Railroad;* William H. Goetzmann, "The Grand Reconnaissance," *American Heritage,* vol. 23 (October 1972).]

DAN E. CLARK

RAILS. The first railroads in the United States were short tramways built to haul heavy materials in and from quarries and mines, the motive power usually being horse, mule, or gravity. The earliest steam railroads used wooden rails, called "strap" rails, with flat strips of bar iron secured to the upper surface. Because they were light and especially because of the danger of the strap rails coming loose and causing accidents, heavy rolled iron rails were imported from England. Until 1844 the rails used in the United States, except most of the strap rails and a small amount of cast-iron rails, were imported. The rolling of heavy iron rails in the United States was begun in 1844 at the Mount Savage Rolling Mill in Maryland. Rails of the inverted U, or Evans, type and of the T type—designed in 1830 by Robert L. Stevens, an engineer and president of the Camden and Amboy Railroad—were manufactured. Other rolling mills began producing heavy rails, but much railroad iron was secured abroad.

A few imported steel rails were laid in 1864, but the manufacture of Bessemer steel rails did not begin in the United States until 1867. The greater uniformity, strength, and hardness of these rails gave them such excellent wearing qualities that the amount of iron rails produced after 1883 was relatively small. By 1912 the manufacture of open-hearth steel rails had surpassed Bessemer rails. During the 20th century rails have been made of greater and greater strength and hardness to keep pace with the increasing weight, speed, and frequency of railroad trains.

The use of rail welded into strips up to one-half mile in length first began in 1933 but did not become common in the United States until the 1950's. Welded rail requires less maintenance and provides greater comfort for railroad passengers. With the introduction of high-speed trains, especially between New York and Washington, D.C., in the late 1960's, the need for stronger and more easily maintained rails became even more apparent; by the early 1970's all new and most relaid rail in the United States was of the welded type.

[G. P. Raidabaugh, "Origin and Development of the Railway Rail in England and America," *Journal of the Iron and Steel Institute,* vol. 95; James M. Swank, *History of the Manufacture of Iron in All Ages.*]

ARTHUR C. BINING

"RAIL SPLITTER," a nickname for Abraham Lincoln, originated in the Illinois State Republican Convention at Decatur, May 9, 1860, when Richard J. Oglesby, later governor of Illinois, and John Hanks, who had lived with the Lincolns, marched into the convention hall with two fence rails placarded, "Abraham Lincoln, The Rail Candidate for President in 1860." The sobriquet caught on at the national convention at Chicago, spread quickly over the North, and became a valuable campaign asset.

[W. E. Baringer, *Lincoln's Rise to Power.*]
PAUL M. ANGLE

RAILWAY ADMINISTRATION ACT. *See* **Railroad Administration, U.S.**

RAILWAY LABOR ACTS. *See* **Railroad Mediation Acts.**

RAILWAYS, ELECTRIC. Thomas Davenport of Vermont in 1836 and Robert Davidson of Scotland in 1838 devised electrically propelled cars, both using current from voltaic batteries on the car. Other models were produced in England in 1840 and in America in 1851. Sir William Siemens and Johann Halske's third-rail electric railway was shown in Berlin in 1879. Stephen D. Field and Thomas A. Edison exhibited an electric locomotive at the Chicago Railway Exposition in 1883, and Charles J. Van Depoele demonstrated also in Chicago, 1883, a car taking power from a wire laid in a trough. Short electric street railways were built in Providence and Kansas City in 1884. Frank J. Sprague brought electric street transportation to practicability when he installed the trolley-car system of Richmond, Va., in 1888, now recognized as a pioneer in commercial electric traction. By 1890 there were 1,200 miles of electric street railway in the United States, and by 1895, 10,863 miles. In 1896–97 Chicago elevated lines began to be electrically operated, followed in 1901 by those of New York and Boston. In 1895 a railroad tunnel, 7,300 feet long, under Baltimore was given electric traction, and other railroads presently began using electricity for tunnels and short distances. The Chicago, Milwaukee and Saint Paul's 645-mile electrification through the Western Mountains (constructed 1914–18) was an epochal achievement in this category. (*See also* Interurban Electric Lines; Subways.)

[Edwin J. Houston and A. E. Kennelly, *Electric Street Railways.*]
ALVIN F. HARLOW

RAILWAY SHOPMEN'S STRIKE. The Railway Employees Department of the American Federation of Labor (AFL), representing 400,000 members, struck July 1, 1922, protesting the unfavorable decisions of the Federal Labor Board (*see* Railroad Mediation Acts) and the unpunished violations of the Transportation Act by the carriers. Faced with the most extensive railroad strike in American history, President Warren G. Harding issued a warning against interference with the mails and attempted unsuccessfully to mediate the strike. Attorney General Harry M. Daugherty gave powerful aid to the carriers by obtaining an exceptionally sweeping injunction against the strikers, which prohibited union officers from encouraging union members to leave their jobs. Finally, a settlement was effected largely in favor of the carriers by the Baltimore Agreement on Oct. 27, although both sides claimed victory.

[Margaret Gadsby, "Strike of the Railroad Shopmen," *Monthly Labor Review,* vol. 15.]
HARVEY WISH

RAINES LAW, a New York State liquor tax law of 1896, devised by John Raines, Republican state senator, which prohibited Sunday and all-night sales by the retail liquor trade, but exempted hotels. As a result the number of hotels in the state increased rapidly, especially in New York City, where many minor hostelries became resorts of prostitution, known as "Raines Law hotels."

[J. P. Peters, "The Story of the Committee of Fourteen of New York," *Social Hygiene* (July 1918).]
STANLEY R. PILLSBURY

RAINFALL. The United States has moisture conditions more favorable to agriculture than most other countries of the world. The vast expanse of comparatively level and fertile country extending from the Great Plains on the west to the Atlantic Ocean on the east and from Canada to the Gulf of Mexico receives, as a rule, adequate rainfall, and temperatures are mostly favorable for crop growth. There are, however, large areas in the western half of the country that, because of scanty moisture, are unsuited for intensive crop growth unless irrigated.

On the basis of effective rainfall, the United States may be divided into an eastern and a western part, the dividing line roughly coinciding with the one-hundredth meridian, in the vicinity of which the annual rainfall is about 20 inches. In general, there is usually enough moisture east of this line for crop production by ordinary methods, but it is insufficient in large areas of the West, where much of the land is better suited for grazing than for crops. Variations in rainfall from year to year are important. Less than the normal amount of rain falls in slightly more than half the years, and there is a well-recognized tendency for several successive years of comparatively heavy rains to be followed by a group of years with deficient moisture.

Weather is the farmers' working partner, and the most important phase of weather in its relation to agriculture is the occurrence of droughts. Droughts in the United States fall into two general classes. One is of a transitory nature, usually affecting a comparatively small area or lasting for a single season, to be followed quickly by enough rainfall for current needs. In the other and more important class rainfall is abnormally low for several years, as in the decade 1930–40. Transitory droughts may be expected every year in some parts of the country, but "families" of droughts, where there is a tendency to dryness over a long period of time, are infrequent.

A few rainfall records are available for the United States for nearly 200 years. These show that there was an extended drought in the midwestern area that culminated in the 1840's, after which there was more abundant precipitation, reaching a maximum phase in the 1870's and 1880's. Again, in the period between 1886 and 1895 an extensive drought prevailed, somewhat comparable to the dryness of the 1930's, followed by a number of years of comparatively abundant rainfall. Not every year, of course, was wet. There were short droughts, but generally there was enough rain. For the interior agricultural sections 1915 was the wettest year of the 20th century (through 1975), and 1934 and 1936 were the driest.

Another dry phase began about 1930 and continued, with few interspersions of fairly good years, such as 1935, up through the summer of 1941. Within this period there were three extremely dry years—1930, 1934, and 1936—the first being most pronounced in the central-eastern portion of the country and the other two affecting most extensively the interior valleys and Great Plains.

The two longest and worst droughts in U.S. history up to 1975 were both suddenly terminated by con-tinued torrential rains throughout the Great Plains and the Southwest—that of the 1930's, in late September and October of 1941, and that of 1950–57, in the summer of 1957. In both cases rainfall was 15 to 20 inches above normal the first year the drought ended, and in some states (Oklahoma in 1941 and Arkansas in 1957) all-time records for monthly or annual rainfall were set.

The year the drought ended in the Southwest (1957), a long period of drought began in the Atlantic coast states, and by the mid-1960's water tables, rivers, and reservoirs reached dangerously low levels. A series of hurricanes and deep cyclones from the Gulf of Mexico raked the Appalachians during 1967–72 (especially in 1972), bringing rivers and water tables back to the above-normal stages of the predrought years, while inflicting tremendous losses from floods. The dilemma of those who would suppress hurricanes is that these disastrous natural phenomena (from $500 million to $2 billion in economic losses each year during that period) are also the lifeblood for water resources and even agriculture from Florida to New England. Dust storms can be alleviated in some measure during drought conditions by employing proper agricultural practices—learned during the 1930's and 1940's—even though artificial rainfall stimulation is not, and may never be, sufficient to prevent or end a drought. But to prevent or divert the tropical storms that produce one kind of disaster might merely bring on another and worse disaster for the populous areas east of the Mississippi.

When deficiencies in rainfall (with reference to the normal) are discussed, the enormous quantities of water represented in such shortages is seldom grasped. They should be a matter of study for all who contend that man can make it rain or who advocate certain practices on a large scale, such as constructing ponds, to change natural climatic conditions. One inch of rainfall represents 113 tons of water for one acre of land. Ohio in 1934 had only about 70 percent of normal rainfall. Based on normal rainfall, the state was short of an average of some 1,270 tons of water per acre of land, or a state total of some 33 billion tons. For each acre of land within its borders the state had about 2,000 more tons of rainfall in 1937 than in 1934.

[Environmental Science Service Administration, *Climatic Atlas of the United States;* U.S. Department of Agriculture, "Precipitation and Humidity," *Atlas of American Agriculture,* part II, and *Yearbook of Agriculture* (1941).]

J. B. KINCER
MALCOLM RIGBY

RAINMAKING ON THE GREAT PLAINS

RAINMAKING ON THE GREAT PLAINS was an effort during the 19th century to supplement the natural rainfall that was often deficient. The need was so acute and persistent that various methods, some possessing a smattering of scientific value and others offered by quack rainmakers, were given frequent, hopeful, and unsuccessful trials. Conspicuous among the first was the tree-planting plan, based on the principle that trees would serve as windbreaks and retard evaporation on the leeward side. Another plan involved constructing ponds to increase humidity. High explosives were also given trials by the U.S. Department of Agriculture. A little rain fell on the occasion of both official trials, but it was not deemed sufficient to justify the effort and expense. Officials of trans-Plains railroads who stood to gain by rainmaking successes were frequent dupes of quacks. Prayer was offered both in local communities and, in times of great need, in statewide efforts to secure Divine mercy. Frequently such prayers were offered simultaneously in a concerted effort to placate Providence. In the drier states camp meetings and revivals were held in the summer, when drought was most threatening.

In the 1940's attempts to induce increased rainfall by means of seeding clouds with silver iodide or salt failed to make a significant change in the amount of precipitation, except in areas where natural rainfall was most likely anyway.

[W. P. Webb, *The Great Plains.*]

CARL L. CANNON

RAISIN RIVER MASSACRE (Jan. 22, 1813). Following Gen. William Hull's surrender of Detroit to the British in August 1812, the Americans raised two new armies to recover the post. Late December found Gen. James Winchester encamped at Maumee Rapids (above Toledo), facing the British Gen. Henry A. Proctor at Amherstburg on the Detroit River in what is now southeast Ontario. On Jan. 14, 1813, Winchester sent 650 Kentuckians to recover Frenchtown (modern Monroe), at the mouth of the Raisin River, from a British-Indian force. Shortly afterward he himself led 300 more to the support of his force. Proctor advanced from Amherstburg and at dawn, Jan. 22, assailed the American army. Winchester was captured and one wing of the army cut to pieces, whereupon the other surrendered under promise of protection from Proctor's Indian allies. This pledge was disregarded and a frightful massacre followed. The Americans suffered a loss of some 900 killed or taken prisoner. The affair stirred American opinion deeply and "Remember the River Raisin" became a rallying cry throughout the war. A capable British official, castigating Proctor's conduct, wrote: "Within my hearing protection was promised for those poor people, be assured we have not heard the last of this shameful transaction. I wish to God it could be contradicted."

[A. C. Casselman, ed., *Richardson's War of 1812*; Silas Farmer, *History of Detroit.*]

M. M. QUAIFE

RALEIGH CONFERENCE OF SOUTHERN GOVERNORS (Oct. 13, 1856) was called by Virginia Gov. Henry A. Wise—a proslavery Democrat largely responsible for James Buchanan's nomination for the presidency in 1856—to formulate a policy in the event that the Republican, antislavery candidate, John C. Frémont, was elected. Only the governors of Virginia, North Carolina, and South Carolina attended, and they were unable to adopt a program. Although Wise failed in his efforts to bring together all the southern governors, his opposition to Frémont and the Republican's antislavery program and the fear of secession possibly influenced northern voters to elect Buchanan.

[B. H. Wise, *The Life of Henry A. Wise.*]

HENRY T. SHANKS

RALEIGH LETTER, a letter written Apr. 17, 1844, by Henry Clay, Whig presidential candidate in 1844, to explain his position on the proposed annexation of Texas. Since this letter indicated Clay's opposition to annexation, condemning it as both inexpedient and dishonorable, it displeased many southern voters and contributed to his defeat.

[Carl Schurz, *Life of Henry Clay*, vol. II.]

RICHARD E. YATES

RALEIGH'S LOST COLONY. The group usually designated as the Lost Colony cleared from Plymouth, England, in three small ships on May 8, 1587, and reached Roanoke Island in the Albemarle region of the present state of North Carolina on July 22. The region then was known as Virginia. The colony was composed of 91 men, 17 women, and 9 boys, a total of 117 persons. Sir Walter Raleigh named John White, who led the expedition, governor of the colony, which was incorporated as "the Governour and Assistants of the Citie of Ralegh in Virginia." White, an artist, had been a member of the Ralph Lane colony of 1585–86, as had several other members of his colony.

The colonists had not intended to stop permanently on Roanoke Island; they had been instructed by Raleigh to pick up fifteen men left there by Sir Richard Grenville and to proceed on to the Chesapeake region, where a more suitable English base for action against the Spanish might be established. They were frustrated in this plan by the pilot of the expedition, who set them ashore, where they occupied the houses and fort abandoned the previous year by Lane's unsuccessful colony.

From the first the Roanoke colonists, inheriting the enmity Lane had provoked, encountered the hostility of Indians on the mainland opposite the island, although they enjoyed the friendship of Manteo and his kinsmen from the island of Croatoan (probably present-day Hatteras) to the south. On Aug. 18 Ellinor (or Elyoner) White Dare, daughter of Gov. John White and wife of Ananias Dare, gave birth to a daughter, Virginia, the first English child born in America. Soon thereafter controversy arose about who should return to England for supplies. It was decided that White should go, and on Aug. 27 he reluctantly sailed. When White reached England the danger of the threatened Spanish armada overshadowed all else. White was not able to come back to Roanoke Island until August 1590. He discovered no trace of the colony except the letters "C R O" carved on a tree and the word "CROATOAN" cut on the doorpost of the palisade. The colonists had agreed to leave a sign if they moved from Fort Raleigh.

The fate of Raleigh's colony remains a mystery. It has usually been assumed that the colonists went to the friendly Croatoans, but it has also been suggested that they were victims of the Spanish. Settlers at Jamestown after 1607 were told by Indians that some of the colonists from Roanoke Island, apparently trying to make their way to Chesapeake Bay, were caught between two warring bodies of Indians not far from their destination and slaughtered. Chief Powhatan had been present and had some utensils that he said had been in the possession of the colonists. Rumors circulated in Virginia that a few had escaped and were held by Indians to engage in metalwork, but attempts to find them failed.

In England in 1594, seven years after the sailing of the colonists, relatives of a youth, John Dare, natural son of Ananias Dare of the Parish of Saint Bride's, Fleet Street, London, petitioned the court that he be awarded his father's property. Under the common law of England an unaccounted-for absence of seven

years was necessary for a ruling of presumed death. In 1597 the petition was granted and the Lost Colony legally recognized as lost.

[William S. Powell, "Roanoke Colonists and Explorers: An Attempt at Identification," *North Carolina Historical Review*, vol. 34; David B. Quinn, *The Roanoke Voyages*.]

WILLIAM S. POWELL

RALEIGH'S PATENT AND FIRST COLONY. On Mar. 25, 1584, Queen Elizabeth renewed Sir Humphrey Gilbert's patent of 1578 in the name of Gilbert's half-brother, Walter Raleigh, giving him and his heirs and assigns the right to explore, colonize, and govern "such remote, heathen, and barbarous lands not actually possessed of any Christian prince, nor inhabited by Christian people." The settlers planted within this grant were to have "all the privileges of free Denizens, and persons native of England," and all laws passed must be in harmony with the laws of England.

On Apr. 27, 1584, Raleigh sent out an expedition led by Philip Amadas and Arthur Barlowe, who were instructed to explore the country and decide on the site for a future colony. Coming via the West Indies, they reached the North Carolina coast early in July. They entered Albemarle Sound, took possession of the country in the name of the queen, and a few days later landed at Roanoke Island where they feasted as guests of the Indians at a small village. After two months spent in exploring and trading with the Indians, they returned to England with reports of the beautiful country, the friendly Indians, the abundance of game and fish, and the soil that was "the most plentiful, sweete, fruitfull and wholsome of all the worlde." Queen Elizabeth was pleased; she named the new land "Virginia" and knighted Raleigh.

In April 1585 Raleigh sent out a colony, consisting of 108 men, with Ralph Lane as governor and Sir Richard Grenville in command of the fleet. This colony landed at Roanoke Island on July 27. About a month later, Grenville returned to England, leaving behind the first English colony in America. Lane built a fort and "sundry necessary and decent dwelling houses," and from this "new Fort in Virginia," Sept. 3, 1585, he wrote Richard Hakluyt in London the "first letter in the English language written from the New World." The Lane colony spent most of its time in a vain quest for gold. Soon supplies began to run low and had to be obtained from the Indians, who were becoming more and more unfriendly. War finally broke out in the spring of 1586. Lane won an easy victory, but unrest and distress continued to increase. When Sir Francis Drake's fleet appeared along the coast and offered to take the colony back to England, Lane consented and they departed after having been on Roanoke Island for about ten months.

About two weeks later, Grenville arrived with supplies, finding the colonists gone. He soon returned to England, but being "unwilling to loose possession of the countrey which Englishmen had so long held," he left fifteen men on Roanoke Island, "furnished plentifully with all manner of provisions for two years." When the next Raleigh colony (*see* Raleigh's Lost Colony), headed by John White, arrived at Roanoke in July 1587, they found only the bones of one of the men Grenville had left and the fort and houses in ruins.

[C. W. Sams, *The First Conquest of Virginia.*]
HUGH T. LEFLER

RALEIGH TAVERN, in Williamsburg, Va., existed as early as 1742. Twice, in 1769 and 1774, the house of burgesses, dissolved by the governor, met in rebellious session at this hostelry. Both George Washington and Thomas Jefferson frequently stopped there. Tradition has it that Phi Beta Kappa was organized in Raleigh Tavern in 1776; certainly the annual meetings of the fraternity from 1777 to 1781 were held there. In 1854 the building became a young ladies' seminary, and in 1859 it was destroyed by fire. The present building came into being as part of the Williamsburg restoration, which began in 1926.

[Lyon Gardner Tyler, *Williamsburg, the Old Colonial Capital.*]
ALVIN F. HARLOW

RALSTON'S RING, a group of San Francisco financiers headed by William C. Ralston, that, in the early 1860's, sought to capitalize for their benefit the profits of the big bonanza of the Comstock Lode in Nevada. The ring organized the Bank of California in 1864 and supported the efforts of Adolph Sutro to build a tunnel to mine the lode. They pushed through Congress an act that granted the right of way to public lands that the Sutro tunnel would cross. In 1866 Ralston's ring made an unsuccessful attempt to take over the still incomplete tunnel. In the early 1870's, as president of the bank, Ralston engaged in unwarranted speculation with the bank's funds, deceiving directors and examiners as to the extent of the losses incurred. The panic of 1873 almost overthrew the ring and the bank, but both survived until a second crash in 1875. Ralston, with a deficit of more than $1.5

million, was ousted from the bank on Aug. 27, 1875. He drowned under mysterious circumstances the following day.

[C. B. Glasscock, *The Big Bonanza;* G. D. Lyman, *Ralston's Ring.*]

RAMBOUILLET DECREE. *See* **Napoleon's Decrees.**

RAMS, CONFEDERATE. The distinguishing feature of the rams built by the Confederate forces was a massively constructed bow carrying an iron beak or ram, which enabled them to revive the smashing tactics of the ancient galleys. The novelty of their design was the armor-plated casemate constructed amidship to house the artillery. The sides of this citadel were sloped to cause the enemy's cannonballs and projectiles to ricochet. The *Virginia,* first and most famous of this type, was designed by a board consisting of chief engineer William P. Williamson, Lt. John M. Brooke, and naval constructor John L. Porter and appointed by the Confederate Navy Department on June 23, 1861. It was constructed on the salvaged hull of the U.S. frigate *Merrimack,* which had been partly burned and sunk at the evacuation of the Norfolk Navy Yard (*see Monitor* and *Merrimack,* Battle of). The rams were used with much success by the Confederates, who put in service or had under construction forty-four ironclad (armor 4 to 8 inches), fourteen partially protected, and six cottonclad vessels of this general type.

WILLIAM M. ROBINSON, JR.

RANCH, an extent of land on which cattle, sheep, or horses are raised and pastured. In the United States most ranching is carried out west of the Mississippi River. Ranches vary greatly in size, although several thousand acres are generally required to qualify a unit as a ranch (chicken ranches, mink ranches, and dude ranches notwithstanding). The King Ranch in Texas is the largest in the country, comprising about 1 million acres. The larger ranches are almost self-sufficient economic units. In addition to the grazing lands, they include farmlands, where grain and silage are grown for the stock, deep-well irrigation systems, power plants that generate electricity, and a ranch-wide communication system. Traditionally, ranches were family-run affairs, but the modern ranch, as often as not, is owned by a corporation.

Ranching began in the United States in Texas in the

early 19th century. The early settlers in west Texas became ranchers by collecting into herds the wild cattle that had escaped from Mexican herds and migrated north. Since the land on which these cattle grazed was public, the "ranch" consisted of the temporary campsite that the foremen and cowboys pitched wherever the cattle halted in their search for pasture and water. As the Southwest became more densely settled in the late 19th century, much of the vast public lands was homesteaded, crops were planted on them, and the farms and ranches were fenced. Fencing ended the free movement of the cattle herds, and fenced, self-contained ranches became common.

As the railroads moved westward, so did ranches; the railroad opened a vast eastern market for western beef. Texas cattlemen drove their herds north annually to railheads in the Midwest. Abilene and Wichita, Kans., were the termini of the Chisholm Trail, first used in 1866, the most celebrated of the routes by which Texas beef went to market. As the railroads continued westward, vast ranches were established in Nebraska, Wyoming, Montana, the Dakotas, and eventually in California (where limited ranching had begun under Mexican rule). The long-distance cattle drives to the railroads continued until networks of feeder lines to the rail trunks created a more efficient way of getting beef to market. By the beginning of the 20th century, the legendary cattle drives were mostly a thing of the past.

The wild cattle that the American settlers tamed were the type known as Spanish Longhorn (now generally called Texas Longhorn). Eastern settlers also brought their own breeds of cattle with them, and in time Hereford, Shorthorn, and Aberdeen Angus herds became more common than the Longhorn. Beginning about 1900, western cattlemen developed special breeds that would prosper in the climate and terrain of the West, thereby producing the most beef per acre of grazing land. The hump-backed Brahma, especially conditioned to hot climates and impervious to flies and other pests, was introduced from India and crossbred with so-called native breeds. The first purely American breed of cattle, the Santa Gertrudis, was developed at the King Ranch about 1910; it is a cross between the Brahma and the Shorthorn. The Charolais, a sturdy French breed, was introduced about 1936 and crossbred with American beef cattle.

Sheep ranching (for both mutton and wool) developed somewhat later than cattle ranching. As long as both cattle and sheep roamed openly on public lands, there was bitter enmity between cattlemen and sheep raisers; cattle raisers claimed that the sheep permanently ruined pastures for cattle grazing. Bloody warfare often erupted; it ended only when both cattle and sheep herds became fenced onto private ranches.

Horse ranches were also a later phenomenon. Like the early cattle ranchers who tamed wild cattle, horsemen tamed the wild herds of Spanish horses that roamed the Southwest. They tamed and broke the horses and sold them as cowhorses or shipped them east as dray animals. Horse ranching, as an important economic factor, was short-lived; the invention of the automobile quickly diminished the huge demand for horses in the East; the demand for cow horses in the West diminished more slowly. At any rate, the economic base of horse ranching—the herds of wild horses—was being quickly eroded. The steady supply of cheap horses to the East would have had to come to an end shortly after the turn of the century regardless of the automobile.

[Lewis Eldon Atherton, *The Cattle Kings;* J. Frank Dobie, *Cow People;* George Wilkins Kendall, *Letters From a Texas Sheep Ranch.*]

DONALD W. HUNT

RANCHOS DEL REY (royal ranches) were established under the Spanish regime in California during the 18th century at San Diego, San Francisco, and Monterey. In 1800 they possessed 18,000 head of sheep. The California presidios, which were fortified posts and sometimes seats of government, were supplied from the royal ranches. The secularization of the California missions in 1825 resulted in the San Diego ranch passing into private hands. Gov. Juan Bautista Alvarado gave the *rancho* of Monterey to his brother-in-law, and the other *ranchos* passed into private possession.

[K. Coman, *Economic Beginnings of the Far West.*]

CARL L. CANNON

RANDOLPH, FORT, originally Fort Blair, was built by the British at Point Pleasant, near the junction of the Ohio and Kanawha rivers, in what is now western West Virginia. After a battle with the Shawnee in 1774, it was abandoned. The fort was destroyed at the beginning of the revolutionary war in 1775. The Americans rebuilt it early in 1776, naming it Fort Randolph. Cornstalk, a friendly Shawnee chief, was murdered there by militiamen in 1777. The fort withstood an attack by Indians in 1778.

[Thomas C. Miller and Hu Maxwell, *West Virginia and Its People.*]

ALVIN F. HARLOW

RANDOLPH PLAN. *See* **Constitution of the United States.**

RANDOLPH'S COMMISSION. In 1676 Edward Randolph was commissioned as the special agent of the king to carry to Massachusetts Bay Colony the king's orders that agents be sent to England authorized to act for the colony concerning the boundary disputes with Robert Mason and the heirs of Sir Ferdinando Gorges. As with the royal commission of 1664 (*see* Nicolls' Commission), he was also commanded to investigate conditions there, by which it was apparent that the real matter at issue was the king's decision to face the problem of the uncertainty and confusion as to the relationship between Massachusetts and England. During Randolph's month in New England he was to make a complete investigation concerning the governments of the colonies; their methods of defense, finance, religion, and trade; the character of their laws; and their attitude in general toward each other and toward England. Needless to say, Randolph did not meet with a cordial reception. The government of Massachusetts personally affronted Randolph and ignored the king's demands, although agents were actually dispatched after Randolph's departure. On his return to England he made a comprehensive report, adverse as far as Massachusetts was concerned. Many people had complained to him of religious and political discriminations, and neighboring colonies resented the arrogant attitude of Massachusetts toward them. Most serious of all offenses listed were the flagrant breaches of the Navigation Acts and the denial of parliamentary legislative authority over the colony. Randolph's report caused grave concern at court and was chiefly responsible for the reopening of the fifty-year-old question as to the legal position of the Massachusetts Bay Company, which ended in the annulment of the charter in 1684.

[H. L. Osgood, *The American Colonies in the Seventeenth Century*, vol. III.]

VIOLA F. BARNES

RANGE CATTLE INDUSTRY. *See* **Open Range Cattle Period.**

RANGER-DRAKE **ENGAGEMENT.** On Apr. 24, 1778, the Continental sloop *Ranger* (eighteen 6-pounders and 123 men), Capt. John Paul Jones commanding, sighted the British ship *Drake* (twenty 4-pounders and 175 men) anchored at Carrickfergus, Ireland. The *Drake,* there expressly to capture Jones, after losing a reconnoitering boat, came out to give battle. Waiting until it came within close range, Jones opened fire. For over an hour he raked the *Drake.* Then with guns silenced it called for quarter. The *Drake* lost forty-two men, including its principal officers; the *Ranger* had but eight casualties. With much trouble Jones succeeded in working it around Ireland to Brest, France, on May 8.

[Mrs. Reginald de Koven, *Life and Letters of John Paul Jones.*]

MARION V. BREWINGTON

RANGERS, specially trained infantry capable of acting in small groups to make rapid attacks into enemy territory and withdrawing without major engagement. Traditionally, rangers are traced back before the American Revolution, when groups of specialized infantry were used by the British to cope with the French and Indians. Made up of skilled marksmen who understood woodlore and the ways of the Indians, they gathered intelligence and harassed the enemy. They were so successful that in 1756 British Gen. John Campbell, Earl of Loudoun, stated, "It is impossible for an Army to act in this Country without Rangers." Most notable of the organizations of this period was Rogers' Rangers, commanded by Maj. Robert Rogers. Other ranger groups were organized throughout the colonies to 1775.

Rangers were found on both sides during the Revolution; John Butler's Rangers and the Queen's American Rangers fought for the British, while George Washington often referred to Daniel Morgan's riflemen as "rangers." Other units, such as Thomas Knowlton's Connecticut Rangers, also served in the Continental army.

Ranger units fought in the War of 1812, in the Black Hawk War, and in the Mexican War. In the Civil War many units of both the North and South adopted the name. Col. John S. Mosby's Rangers and Gen. Alfred H. Terry's Texas Rangers are the best known of this period.

Rangers were not used again until World War II. During 1942–44, six ranger battalions were organized and saw action in Africa, Europe, and the Pacific. Col. William O. Darby is the most famous of the wartime ranger commanders. Other units such as Merrill's Marauders, led by Brig. Gen. Frank D. Merrill, and the First Special Service Force employed ranger philosophy and tactics in their operations. By the end of 1945 all these units were inactivated. After the invasion of Korea, sixteen ranger companies were organized, seven of them fighting in Korea. In 1951 it was decided that ranger-trained personnel would be better utilized if they were spread among standard infantry units, and the ranger companies were inactivated. Since that time, selected officers and enlisted men have taken intensive training at Fort Benning, Ga., before being awarded the "Ranger tab," worn as a part of their uniform. They are then assigned to units throughout the army.

In Vietnam, infantry long-range patrol units were designated ranger companies (1969) and made the descendants of Merrill's Marauders, while the World War II ranger battalions, the First Special Service Force, and the Korean War ranger companies were still perpetuated in the U.S. Army's Special Forces in the 1970's.

[James J. Altieri, *Darby's Rangers;* John K. Mahon and Romana M. Danysh, *Infantry,* part I; Richard J. Stillman, *The U.S. Infantry.*]

JOHN E. JESSUP, JR.

RAPPAHANNOCK STATION, BATTLE AT (Nov. 7, 1863). Union Gen. George G. Meade's army, following Gen. Robert E. Lee after the latter's abortive Bristoe campaign in October 1863, reached Rappahannock Station, Va., where Gen. Harry T. Hays's Confederate division was found holding two formidable redoubts on the north bank of the Rappahannock River. Meade ordered an attack. Artillery fire proving ineffective, the Union troops assaulted, sweeping over the works with slight loss and capturing two brigades (more than 1,600 men). Next day other Union troops, crossing the Rappahannock at Kelly's Ford, turned Lee's right, and he retired behind the Rapidan River.

[R. U. Johnson and C. C. Buel, eds., *Battles and Leaders of the Civil War,* vol. IV; Douglas S. Freeman, *R. E. Lee,* vol. III.]

JOSEPH MILLS HANSON

RAPPIST COMMUNITY. *See* **Harmony Society.**

RATE BASE. *See* **Public Utilities.**

RATON PASS through the Raton Mountains, on the Colorado–New Mexico boundary, is located just north of Raton, N.Mex. During the 18th and 19th centuries it was an important gateway between the upper Arkansas basin and eastern New Mexico. It was used by the Spanish expedition under Don Pedro de Villasur against the French in 1720, and the Spanish-Mexican expedition to intercept Lt. Zebulon M. Pike in 1806. Later a branch of the Santa Fe Trail passed through it.

[LeRoy R. Hafen, "Raton Pass, An Historic Highway," *The Colorado Magazine,* vol. 7.]

RUPERT N. RICHARDSON

RATTLESNAKE FLAG, having a yellow field bearing a coiled rattlesnake and the motto "Don't Tread on Me," was used during the French and Indian War (1754–63) as a colonial symbol. It was presented to the Continental Congress by Col. Christopher Gadsden of South Carolina and unofficially adopted by Capt. Esek Hopkins as a commodore's flag.

[G. H. Preble, *History of the Flag of the United States.*]

MARION V. BREWINGTON

RATTLESNAKES, a venomous snake of the pit viper family, found from southern Canada to Argentina, but associated mainly with the United States. The largest, the eastern diamondback, is found in the southeastern states. So characteristic is the rattlesnake of the United States that tradition credits Benjamin Franklin with having proposed it as the national emblem. No creature of the wilds has entered more into common talk and lore: the plant rattlesnake master, a weed used as a remedy for snakebite; the virtue of rattlesnake oil for rheumatism; legendary dilemmas like that of the lone man on the prairie who crawled into a dry buffalo carcass to hide from Indians, and then when an Indian sat down on the carcass to rest heard a rattler begin singing next to him; the cleverness of the roadrunner—which really does kill rattlesnakes—in corralling a sleeping rattler with cactus joints and then making him bite himself to death; the way rattlesnakes "guard" certain caves—in which great numbers hibernate; certain rattlesnake monsters, rivaling sea serpents in size; and thousands of authentic anecdotes.

A few people die from bites annually; but the spread of civilization and man's instinctive objection to rattlers are steadily diminishing the snake population.

[Raymond L. Ditmars, *Snakes of the World.*]

J. FRANK DOBIE

RATTLETRAP. See **Willing Expedition.**

RAW MATERIALS, RESOURCES OF. The raw material needs of the modern U.S. technological society are provided by the primary industries of agriculture, mining, forestry, and fisheries. To a large extent the prosperity of a materials culture lies in the ability to exploit these resources for human welfare.

The United States is especially well endowed with a wide variety of subtropical and middle latitude agricultural products. In the 1970's it was the world's largest producer of soybeans, corn, cotton, citrus fruits, cattle, meat, eggs, and cheese. It ranked high in pigs, oats, potatoes, barley, beet sugar, and tobacco. In 1973 its farms produced 46.1 percent of the world's corn, 21.8 percent of the world's cotton, and 12.1 percent of the world's wheat.

The United States had 2,821,000 farms in 1974, containing a total of 1,087,000,000 acres. Of the farm acreage about 38 percent was used to grow crops. Nearly 10 million people lived on American farms, but agricultural workers numbered only 3,437,000. Output per farm worker more than doubled between 1930 and 1970. In 1800 three out of every four workers in the nation were required to produce the food needed for domestic consumption; in 1973 only one worker out of every twenty-five was required.

Minerals played a significant role in the development of the economy of the United States throughout the 19th and 20th centuries. The industrial and military strength and high standard of living in America became increasingly dependent on an adequate supply of such materials. Man's release from the drudgery of labor began when he started to devise schemes to utilize mechanical energy, for when minerals are converted into tools and machines, man can produce the goods he needs more abundantly and efficiently. In the mid-19th century the United States became the world's largest producer and consumer of minerals. Of the world's annual mineral production of over $100 billion in the 1970's the United States produced about 30 percent, and Americans consumed about $160 worth of minerals per person in comparison with an average of only about $17 per person for the rest of the world.

Within the United States fuels are the most important minerals. From the 1830's to the early 20th century coal was the most important energy source, but after that time petroleum assumed first place. In 1972 the energy minerals made up 69 percent of U.S. mineral production; the metallic minerals, such as iron, copper, lead, and zinc, about 11 percent; and the nonmetallic minerals, which include salt, sulfur, common rock, and others, nearly 20 percent.

Although the United States was the world's leader in mineral output in the 1970's, it was not self-sufficient in all its mineral needs. Of the thirty-eight important industrial minerals, the United States was essentially self-sufficient in only thirteen—bituminous coal, anthracite, sulfur, molybdenum, vanadium, cadmium, salt, magnesium, phosphate, potash, helium, natural gas, and nitrogen. The nation had large reserves of iron ore and petroleum, but it was particularly deficient in such ferrous alloys as manganese, tungsten, and nickel. Large quantities of lead, zinc, copper, tin, aluminum, and mercury ores and metals were imported.

Water has become one of the nation's most precious resources. In 1970 about 370 billion gallons of fresh water were used every day in homes, factories, and power-generating plants or for irrigation. The demands for water were rising rapidly not only for industry but also for the growing urban population.

Forest land occupied about one-third of the United States in 1970. There were about 785 species of trees, of which twenty-nine were widely used for lumber production. The most important are southern pine, Douglas fir, oak, hemlock, gum, maple, spruce, cypress, and redwood. The total volume consumption of forest products remained virtually unchanged from the 1930's to the 1970's.

[Ronald G. Redker, ed., *Population, Resources and the Environment;* Sam H. Schurr, *Energy, Economic Growth, and the Environment.*]

E. WILLARD MILLER

RAYMOND, BATTLE OF (May 12, 1863). Having crossed the Mississippi River below Vicksburg and captured Port Gibson, Gen. Ulysses S. Grant's army moved to cut the railroad between Vicksburg and Jackson. His right corps, that of Gen. James B. McPherson, advanced toward Jackson, where it encountered Confederate Gen. John Gregg's brigade, of Gen. John C. Pemberton's army, deployed across the road at Raymond. Union Gen. John A. Logan's division, later supported by Gen. Marcellus M. Crocker, attacked Gregg and after a stubborn fight drove him toward Jackson. Next day McPherson reached Clinton, on the railroad, and thus separated Confederate Gen. Joseph E. Johnston's army at Jackson from Pemberton's army, which was defending Vicksburg.

[R. U. Johnson and C. C. Buel, eds., *Battles and Leaders of the Civil War,* vol. III.]

JOSEPH MILLS HANSON

RAYSTOWN PATH derives its name from Robert Ray, an Indian trader who settled sometime before 1750 at Raystown (now Bedford, Pa.). It led from a point near Carlisle, Pa., in the Susquehanna Valley to Shannopin's Town (now within Pittsburgh) and Logstown, eighteen miles below Pittsburgh. The trail, in terms of present-day towns, went from Carlisle through Shippensburg, Chambersburg, Fort Loudon, Fort Lyttleton, Bedford, and Ligonier; then north toward Latrobe, Harrison, Trafford, and Shannopin's Town. This route in the main was the same as that followed by Gen. John Forbes in 1758 and by Col. Henry Bouquet in 1763. Much of it today parallels closely the Lincoln Highway west from Chambersburg to Pittsburgh.

[George P. Donehoo, *A History of the Indian Villages and Place Names in Pennsylvania.*]

R. J. FERGUSON

RAZORBACK HOGS, half-wild mongrel descendants of domestic hogs, once common all over the South. Derived from European importation, many of them were as wild and fierce as the wild boars of the Old World, and hunting them was a great sport. Every settler had his "hog claim," although it often took guns, dogs, and canebrake fire to make it good. The animal is distinguished by snout, tail, tusk, skin, and sinew rather than by fat and flesh. The animal remains the subject of a cycle of folk jokes and tales.

[Lewis C. Gray, *History of Agriculture in the Southern United States to 1860.*]

J. FRANK DOBIE

REACTORS. *See* **Atomic Power Reactors.**

READING RAILROAD. *See* **Railroads, Sketches.**

READJUSTER MOVEMENT in Virginia had its inception in the contention of Rev. John E. Massey, Col. Frank G. Ruffin, and a few others that the antebellum state debt, which had been funded in 1871, ought to be readjusted so that it could be met without ruin to farmer taxpayers (already hard pressed by economic conditions) or the neglect of public schools and charities. Gen. William Mahone, seeking the Democratic gubernatorial nomination, endorsed the idea in 1877, swung the *Richmond Whig* to its support, and in 1879 organized the Readjuster party. Winning the legislature in 1879 with the help of the disorganized Republican voters, and gaining the governorship in

1881 with William E. Cameron as their candidate, the new party scaled the debt by the Riddleberger Bill of 1882, enacted laws in the economic and social interest of the masses, and, carefully guided by Mahone, apportioned the offices among its leaders. Elected to the Senate in 1880 (where he was soon joined by H. H. Riddleberger), Mahone cooperated with the Republicans and received the federal patronage on the theory that he stood for anti-Bourbonism and a fair vote. Thus supported, blacks rallied unanimously to his standard, while many of the whites continued faithful. His machine now seemed invincible. But the regular Democrats, led by John S. Barbour and John W. Daniel, accepted the debt settlement; welcomed back such sincere Readjusters as Massey and Ruffin, who would not brook Mahone's "bossism"; drew the color line; and won in 1883 and thereafter, although sometimes very narrowly. Perhaps the most lasting result of the movement, aside from the debt settlement, was the fixed belief among the white masses that, while the blacks could vote, white men must not be divided, however important the issues on which they differed and however "rotten" the Democratic machine.

[N. M. Blake, *William Mahone;* C. C. Pearson, *The Readjuster Movement in Virginia.*]

C. C. PEARSON

REAPER. *See* **Agricultural Machinery; McCormick Reaper.**

REAPPORTIONMENT, CONGRESSIONAL. *See* **Apportionment, Congressional.**

REBATES, RAILROAD, in the 19th century were special low rates that a railroad carrier charged its favored customers. This form of rebate has been defined by the Interstate Commerce Commission as "transportation at a less rate in dollars and cents than the published rate which the shipping public are charged." The intent of a carrier in granting a rebate was usually to discriminate in favor of a particular shipper by giving him a secret rate that was less than that charged his competitors. This practice developed in the mid-1850's and continued because of the spectacular railroad rate wars that took place during the second half of the 19th century and that often proved disastrous to carriers and public alike. These costly rate wars led carriers to avoid general rate cuts and to develop the practice of making secret agreements with certain shippers, whereby the shipper would get some form of rate reduction in exchange for his promise to ship his goods over the line offering the concession. Such concessions enabled the favored shippers to undersell their competitors and thus increase their business and the business of the railroad offering the rebates.

The public objected bitterly to the practice of rebating because of its obvious unfairness and because the process of building up one shipper at the expense of others promoted the development of monopolies, with all of their attendant evils. Rebating also proved objectionable to those carriers who practiced it because it did not take long for competing carriers to realize what was going on and attempt to make secret arrangements of their own with other shippers, and if they were successful, none of the carriers enjoyed an increase in traffic. If a carrier did succeed in building up a shipper to a monopolistic position, that carrier was at the mercy of the shipper, and such shippers sometimes secured enormous concessions by playing one carrier off against another.

The outstanding recipient of railroad rebates was the Standard Oil Company, and much of its early success may be traced to the advantages it enjoyed in the way of rate concessions. In one case the published rate on oil between two points was 35 cents a barrel, but on each barrel shipped the Standard received a 25 cent rebate, making its rate 10 cents, while its competitors paid 35 cents. Not only did the Standard receive the 25 cent refund on all the oil it shipped, but it also received 25 cents for every barrel shipped by its competitors. This type of rebate in which a particular shipper is given a part of the rate paid by his competitors is known as a drawback. The packers were also notorious recipients of rate concessions.

The Interstate Commerce Act (1887) prohibited rate discrimination and established a fine of $5,000 for each violation, and two years later violation of the law was made a penitentiary offense. But it was necessary to prove that a rebate actually resulted in discrimination, and this was difficult to do. Furthermore, juries were reluctant to send men to prison for civil offenses even if proven guilty. Hence the act did not stop the practice of discrimination, and further legislation was necessary. Under the Elkins Act (1903) any departure from a printed rate was considered an offense, thus eliminating the necessity of proving that discrimination existed. At the same time, the penalty of imprisonment was dropped, the maximum fine raised to $20,000, and the law applied to shippers who received rebates as well as to carriers who

granted them. The Hepburn Act (1906) restored the penalty of imprisonment and subjected the receiver of a rebate to a fine equal to three times the value of the rebates received during the preceding six years. Subsequent acts brought a further tightening of the law.

[W. Z. Ripley, *Railroads, Rates and Regulation.*]
R. E. WESTMEYER

REBELLION, RIGHT OF. Rebellion is defined as open or determined defiance of, or organized armed resistance to, the ruler or government of one's country. According to generally accepted political theory, a law is a command, a general rule of human action enforced by a sovereign political authority (T. E. Holland). Hence, disobedience to authority or rebellion can never be legal, and the right of rebellion can exist only on moral grounds. But according to the theory of John Locke, government powers are fiduciary, and the right of revolution exists when a government abuses or ill-uses this authority or oppresses its people. The community of citizens is the judge when this oppressive or unjust administration exists and when rebellion actually is justified. It was largely on this basis that the American patriots justified their rebellion against Great Britain and issued the Declaration of Independence. Also, the leaders of the Confederate States of America in great measure justified their secession from the Union on the same theoretical grounds.

[T. E. Holland, *Jurisprudence;* C. E. Merriam, *American Political Theories.*]
WILLIAM STARR MYERS

REBELLIONS. *See* **Insurrections, Domestic.**

REBEL YELL was the description given by Union soldiers and the general public to the high-pitched shout used by the Confederates in spirited charges and violent clashes on the battlefields of the Civil War. With passing generations, the once familiar "hy-eeee" of the men in gray was used rarely and recorded mainly in reminiscences.

ALFRED P. JAMES

RECALL, an electoral process for determining whether or not the voters wish to retain a public official in public office before his term comes to an end. This remedy to remove an official who allegedly no longer retains the public's confidence or support can be invoked through a special election upon the filing of a petition signed by a stipulated number of qualified electors who seek a ballot determination of the issue.

Originally provided for in the Los Angeles city charter (1903) and in the Oregon state constitution (1908), the concept of the recall—along with the initiative, the referendum, and the direct primary—found wide acceptance among the electoral reform proposals of early 20th-century American progressivism. Recall provisions were incorporated into the constitutions of nearly a dozen states—Arizona, California, Colorado, Idaho, Kansas, Louisiana, Michigan, Nevada, North Dakota, Washington, and Wisconsin—although elective judicial officials were exempted constitutionally from recall in Alaska, Idaho, Louisiana, Michigan, and Washington, and three states—Kansas, Nevada, and Oregon—made the recall applicable to all public officials, elective or appointed.

Despite its potential for a more immediate and demanding insistence on direct public satisfaction, the recall never did become as radical a tool of direct democracy as its critics so seriously feared when first proposed. The recall has rarely been invoked on a statewide basis. By the 1970's, for example, two public utilities commissioners had been recalled in Oregon and a governor and two state officials in North Dakota. Although a few local governmental officials have been threatened with the recall, by 1975 only three mayors actually had their tenure so terminated—one each in Los Angeles, Seattle, and Detroit.

A resurgence of interest in the use of the recall developed in the 1960's and 1970's in connection with the issue of school integration and mandatory busing. While a Pasadena, Calif., attempt to recall school board members failed in 1970, it succeeded in Detroit the same year and was the subject of a special election in Seattle in 1973.

As might be expected in the inevitable controversy surrounding the possible application of the recall, recourse to the courts and to judicial intervention is often attempted by one or the other of the parties involved. In the absence of a clear showing of constitutional or statutory violations, courts generally have been disinclined to probe beyond the procedural aspects of the recall election. If the petitions have been filed properly, the signatures correctly entered, the required number of qualified voters reached (most frequently a fixed percentage of either the total vote cast for the office at the preceding election or a fixed percentage of the voters residing in the district), the

courts usually let the electorate decide whether or not the official is to retain title to his office.

If the charges are specific enough to permit public debate on the merits of the dispute, the voters, not the courts, determine the "truth" or "falsity" of the charges. Voters weigh the motivations of the petition seekers and wrongful or improper performance of duty (which may not necessarily be criminal in nature). In its essential character, the recall election charging an official with substantial misconduct substitutes for the jury box the tribunal of the ballot box.

Recall elections are at best a procedurally complex and difficult option available when all else seems to fail to assure public accountability and confidence, especially in a society characterized by highly competitive politics, periodic public audits, wide and nearly instant communication, and elaborate governmental investigative mechanisms and institutions.

G. Theodore Mitau

RECESSION OF 1937, a short but severe business slump that began in the middle of 1937 and lasted ten months. After the settlement of the banking crisis of 1933, business staged one of the most rapid recoveries in the history of the country. *The Annalist* index of business activity rose approximately 50 percent between March and July 1933. Then a reaction set in and business activity fell off about 25 percent between the latter month and October 1934. Thereafter it increased irregularly by more than 50 percent up to the close of 1936. This level was fairly well maintained through August 1937. Then a decline set in that was as rapid as the recovery of 1933 had been, and that resulted in a 27 percent reduction of business activity by the end of the year. A further sharp decline in activity occurred in the first six months of 1938, after which *The Annalist* index turned sharply upward to the end of the year. Stock prices followed a course similar to that of business activity, rising rapidly from the beginning of 1935 to 1937, and then falling sharply until the spring of 1938, when they again turned upward. Although the recession of 1937 was unusually severe, no panic ensued either in the stock market or in business.

[Board of Governors of the Federal Reserve System, *Bulletins* (1937–38).]

Frederick A. Bradford

RECIPROCAL TRADE AGREEMENTS. In the election of 1932 the Democrats came to power on a program involving "a competitive tariff" for revenue

RECIPROCAL TRADE AGREEMENTS

and "reciprocal trade agreements with other nations." Cordell Hull, President Franklin D. Roosevelt's secretary of state, was the driving force behind congressional action in getting the Trade Agreements Act made law on June 12, 1934. The new act, in form an amendment to the 1930 Tariff Act, delegated to the president the power to make foreign-trade agreements with other nations on the basis of a mutual reduction of duties, without any specific congressional approval of such reductions. The act limited reduction to 50 percent of the rates of duty existing then and stipulated that commodities could not be transferred between the dutiable and free lists. The power to negotiate was to run for three years, but this power was renewed for either two or three years periodically until replaced by the Trade Expansion Act of 1962.

Although Congress gave the State Department the primary responsibility for negotiating with other nations, it instructed the Tariff Commission and other government agencies to participate in developing a list of concessions that could be made to foreign countries or demanded from them in return. Each trade agreement was to incorporate the principle of "unconditional most-favored-nation treatment." This requirement was necessary to avoid a great multiplicity of rates.

After 1945 Congress increased the power of the president by authorizing him to reduce tariffs by 50 percent of the rate in effect on Jan. 1, 1945, instead of 1934, as the original act provided. Thus, duties that had been reduced by 50 percent prior to 1945 could be reduced by another 50 percent, or 75 percent below the rates that were in effect in 1934. But in 1955 further duty reductions were limited to 15 percent, at the rate of 5 percent a year over a three-year period, and in 1958 to 20 percent, effective over a four-year period, with a maximum of 10 percent in any one year.

In negotiating agreements under the Trade Agreements Act, the United States usually proceeded by making direct concessions only to so-called chief suppliers—namely, countries that were, or probably would become, the main source, or a major source, of supply of the commodity under discussion. This approach seemed favorable to the United States, since no concessions were extended to minor supplying countries that would benefit the chief supplying countries (through unconditional most-favored-nation treatment) without the latter countries' first having granted a concession. The United States used its bargaining power by granting concessions in return for openings to foreign markets for American exports.

Between 1934 and 1947 the United States made separate trade agreements with twenty-nine foreign countries. The Tariff Commission found that when it used dutiable imports in 1939 as its basis for comparison, U.S. tariffs were reduced from an average of 48 percent to an average of 25 percent during the thirteen-year period, the imports on which the duties were reduced having been valued at over $700 million in 1939.

During World War II the State Department and other government agencies worked on plans for the reconstruction of world trade and payments. They discovered important defects in the trade agreements program, and they concluded that they could make better headway through simultaneous multilateral negotiations. American authorities in 1945 made some far-reaching proposals for the expansion of world trade and employment. Twenty-three separate countries then conducted tariff negotiations bilaterally on a product-by-product basis, with each country negotiating its concessions on each import commodity with the principal supplier of that commodity. The various bilateral understandings were combined to form the General Agreement on Tariffs and Trade (GATT), referred to as the Geneva Agreement, which was signed in Geneva on Oct. 30, 1947. This agreement did not have to be submitted to the U.S. Senate for approval because the president was already specifically empowered to reduce tariffs under the authority conferred by the Trade Agreements Extension Act of 1945.

From the original membership of twenty-three countries, GATT had expanded by the mid-1970's to include more than seventy countries, a membership responsible for about four-fifths of all the world trade. During the numerous tariff negotiations carried on under the auspices of GATT, concessions covering over 60,000 items had been agreed on. These constituted more than two-thirds of the total import trade of the participating countries and more than one-half the total number of commodities involved in world trade.

With the expiration on July 30, 1962, of the eleventh renewal of the Reciprocal Trade Agreements Act, the United States was faced with a major decision on its future foreign trade policy: to choose between continuing the program as it had evolved over the previous twenty-eight years or to replace it with a new and expanded program. The second alternative was chosen by President John F. Kennedy when, on Jan. 25, 1962, he asked Congress for unprecedented authority to negotiate with the European Common Market for reciprocal trade agreements. The European Common Market had been established in 1957 to eliminate all trade barriers in six key countries of Western Europe: France, West Germany, Italy, Belgium, the Netherlands, and Luxembourg. Their economic strength, the increasing pressure on American balance of payments, and the threat of a Communist aid and trade offensive led Congress to pass the Trade Expansion Act of 1962. This act granted the president far greater authority to lower or eliminate American import duties than had ever been granted before, and it replaced the negative policy of preventing dislocation by the positive one of promoting and facilitating adjustment to the domestic dislocation caused by foreign competition. The president was authorized, through trade agreements with foreign countries, to reduce any duty by 50 percent of the rate in effect on July 1, 1962. Whereas the United States had negotiated in the past on an item-by-item, rate-by-rate basis, in the future the president could decide to cut tariffs on an industry, or across-the-board, basis for all products, in exchange for similar reductions by the other countries. In order to deal with the tariff problems created by the European Common Market, the president was empowered to reduce tariffs on industrial products by more than 50 percent, or to eliminate them completely when the United States and the Common Market together accounted for 80 percent or more of the world export value. The president could also reduce the duty by more than 50 percent or eliminate it on an agricultural commodity, if he decided such action would help to maintain or expand American agricultural exports.

After Kennedy's death, President Lyndon B. Johnson pushed through a new round of tariff bargaining that culminated in a multilateral trade negotiation known as the Kennedy Round. The agreement reached on June 30, 1967, reduced tariff duties an average of about 35 percent on some 60,000 items representing an estimated $40 billion in world trade, based on 1964 figures, the base year for the negotiations. As a result of the tariff-reduction installments of the Kennedy Round, by 1973 the average height of tariffs in the major industrial countries, it is estimated, had come down to about 8 or 9 percent.

Although both Johnson and President Richard M. Nixon exerted pressure on Congress to carry some of the trade expansion movements of the Kennedy Round further, Congress resisted all proposals. The crisis in foreign trade that developed in 1971–72 was the result of stagnation as well as of an unprecedented deficit in the U.S. balance of payments. Some pressure groups from both industry and labor tried to

revive the protectionism that had flourished before 1934, but they had had small success except on petroleum imports by the mid-1970's.

[Grace Beckett, *The Reciprocal Trade Agreements Program;* Sidney Ratner, *The Tariff in American History.*]

SIDNEY RATNER

RECIPROCITY. *See* **Reciprocal Trade Agreements; Tariff.**

RECLAMATION. Federal assistance in the reclamation of arid lands by means of irrigation began when Congress enacted the Desert Land Act of 1877. This law encouraged reclamation by offering 640 acres at $1.25 per acre to those citizens who would irrigate one-eighth of their newly purchased holdings within three years. Although 10 million acres passed from government ownership under the provisions of the act, widespread fraud limited its effectiveness. Somewhat more positive were the results of the Carey Act of 1894, which granted 1 million acres of the public domain to each of the western states on condition that they irrigate them and sell them to settlers in maximum tracts of 160 acres. Under the provisions of that act 1,067,635 acres were reclaimed, 75 percent of them in the states of Idaho and Wyoming.

By the middle of the 1890's it was becoming apparent to westerners that more positive assistance from the federal government was needed to construct larger reservoirs and canals. In 1896 Congress appropriated $5,000 for a survey by the Corps of Engineers of reservoir sites in Colorado and Wyoming. Capt. Hiram M. Chittenden was placed in charge, and when he recommended the following year that the federal government construct the reservoirs, westerners under the leadership of George H. Maxwell organized the National Irrigation Association to champion the recommendation. On Jan. 26, 1901, Rep. Francis G. Newlands of Nevada introduced a bill into Congress to provide for federal reclamation. With the support of President Theodore Roosevelt it passed in a revised form and became law on June 17, 1902.

The Reclamation Act of 1902 authorized the secretary of the interior to construct irrigation works in the sixteen western states and to pay for them from a revolving reclamation fund accumulated from the sales of public lands in those states. It stipulated that the reclaimable lands were to be disposed of under the Homestead Act of 1862 in tracts of 160 acres or less and that the settlers repay within ten years the costs of constructing the irrigation dams and canals. Ethan

Allen Hitchcock, the secretary of the interior, did not delay implementation of the act. He created the Reclamation Service, with Frederick H. Newell of the Geological Survey in charge, and within one year had authorized the construction of three projects—the Newlands in Nevada, the Salt River in Arizona, and the Uncompahgre in Colorado.

As water became available to these and other projects, problems appeared. Construction and land-acquisition costs were higher than anticipated, as were the expenses of settlement and the preparation of farms for irrigation. Consequently, settlers began to complain that they were unable to make their payments and petitioned the government for relief. Congress responded with the Reclamation Extension Act of 1914, which extended the repayment time from ten to twenty years.

When the postwar depression hit the settlers in 1920, they renewed their appeals, and Secretary of the Interior Hubert Work replied by appointing a fact-finding committee in 1923 under the chairmanship of Thomas E. Campbell of Arizona. It studied the situation and recommended reforms. In 1926 Congress extended the repayment period to forty years, and later it allowed even longer periods of time for some projects.

On June 20, 1923, Work renamed the Reclamation Service the Bureau of Reclamation and the next year appointed Elwood Mead its second commissioner. Under Mead's leadership the bureau began to design multipurpose projects to provide—in addition to water for irrigation—flood control, hydroelectric power, municipal water, and recreational opportunities. The first of these projects was the Boulder Canyon project, with its 726-foot Hoover Dam and Lake Mead reservoir, designed to provide water for crops in Arizona and California and 1,344,800 kilowatts of electric power. Its authorization by Congress in 1928 was followed by authorizations of the Columbia Basin (1935), Central Valley (1935), Colorado-Big Thompson (1937), and Colorado River Storage (1956) projects, to name four of the larger ones.

By 1970 the bureau and its predecessor had built 276 storage reservoirs, which provided water for 8.5 million acres, producing nearly $2 billion worth of crops a year, as well as water for an expanding urban population. In addition, they had constructed forty-nine hydroelectric power plants with 16,000 miles of high-voltage transmission lines to provide electric power for the industrialization of the western states, including the defense industries of California.

Another government agency involved in reclamation is the Bureau of Indian Affairs, which in 1962 supervised projects irrigating 837,000 acres and producing crops valued at $67.3 million. Reclamation by this agency began with a congressional appropriation of $30,000 in 1891 for use on reservations in Arizona, Montana, and Nevada.

[Paul W. Gates, *History of Public Land Law Development;* Alfred R. Golzé, *Reclamation in the United States;* U.S. Department of the Interior, Bureau of Reclamation, *Reclamation Project Data* (1961); William E. Warne, *The Bureau of Reclamation.*]

ROBERT G. DUNBAR

RECOGNITION, POLICY OF. The U.S. Constitution is silent on the matter of recognition of new states and new governments and thus gives no indication which organ of government is charged with that responsibility. In practice, the executive has discharged that function, and it has been generally accepted that the power of the president to recognize any country is absolute. Congress has never seriously challenged the presidential prerogative.

There are several modes of recognition. Most common is an express declaration embodied in a message by the president to the head of the state or government to be recognized. Or the president may send or receive a minister or ambassador, grant or accept an exequatur, or acknowledge a letter from the head of the new state or government announcing his assumption of authority. Or Congress may enter into a bilateral treaty comprehensively regulating relations between the two states. There must be an intent to recognize. The mere entry into relations with a new state or government does not imply recognition if there is no intent. Similarly, a communication addressed to the head of a new state or government or the signing of a multilateral treaty to which the new state or government is also a party does not, of itself, imply recognition.

The criteria for recognition were established by Secretary of State Thomas Jefferson in 1792 in an instruction to the American minister to France. The occasion was the extension of recognition to the new republican government in France, which replaced the Bourbon monarchy. Jefferson said, "It accords with our principles to acknowledge any Government to be rightful which is formed by the will of the nation, substantially declared. . . . we surely cannot deny to any nation that right whereon our own Government is founded—that every one may govern itself according to whatever form it pleases, and change these forms at its own will." Thus, if a new government possessed the machinery of state, if it governed with the assent of a majority of the people, and if it met with no substantial resistance, American recognition followed. Jefferson did not look behind the facts to determine how the new government came to power or whether its form or the conduct of its leaders was agreeable to the United States: recognition was not a moral act and did not imply approval.

The Jeffersonian policy on recognition has been followed, with one additional criterion and several aberrations, throughout U.S. history. The additional criterion was the new state's or new government's capacity and willingness to carry out its international obligations. One aberration was contributed by Woodrow Wilson, who, as president, withheld recognition from governments that came into power unconstitutionally and in defiance of fundamental local laws. Regarding a change in government in Costa Rica in 1917, Wilson said that the United States "will not give recognition or support to any government which may be established unless it is clearly proven that it is elected by legal and constitutional means." The Republican administration that followed soon returned to the traditional policy. Faced with a new government in Chile, Secretary of State Charles Evans Hughes in 1924 extended recognition as quickly as the new regime demonstrated its capacity to discharge its international obligations, its ability to maintain order, and the acquiescence of the people of the country.

No state is obliged to accord recognition. It is voluntary, not compulsory. Recognition may be conditional, but once granted, it is not normally withdrawn. Severance of diplomatic relations does not necessarily affect recognition.

The refusal of the United States to recognize the Soviet Union (from 1917 to 1933), the People's Republic of China, and Fidel Castro's regime in Cuba constitutes a clear departure from America's traditional recognition policy. The reason for the departure seems clear enough: the antipathy toward the Communist regimes in those countries was greater than the devotion to historic principles. Recognition was accorded the Soviet Union only because of the harsh realities of the Great Depression. The prospect of a large volume of trade with the Soviets caused the animosity toward communism to subside. Similarly, the international political situation in 1971 accounted for the beginning by the administration of Richard M. Nixon of eventual recognition of China. In casting about for a makeweight against the Soviet Union, China appeared to be the most likely prospect. As for

Cuba, in the 1970's demands by many of the nations in the Americas that Cuba take its proper place in the hemisphere and the visits of U.S. congressmen to Cuba indicated that recognition would be accorded the Castro regime.

[Taylor Cole, *The Recognition Policy of the United States, 1901;* Julius Goebel, Jr., *The Recognition Policy of the United States;* Green Hackworth, "The Policy of the United States in Recognizing New Governments During the Past 25 Years," *Proceedings of the American Society of International Law* (1931).]

ARMIN RAPPAPORT

RECOLLECTS. *See* **Franciscans.**

RECONSTRUCTION. The question of the restoration of the seceded states to the Union became an issue long before the surrender at Appomattox, Va., on Apr. 6, 1865. According to the Crittenden-Johnson Resolutions of July 1861, the object of the war was to restore the Union with "all the dignity, equality, and rights of the several States unimpaired." But as the conflict progressed, it became evident that this objective was impossible to achieve. Congress refused to reaffirm its policy; President Abraham Lincoln appointed military governors for partially reconquered states; and radicals and moderates debated the exact status of the insurgent communities.

The president viewed the process of wartime reconstruction as a weapon to detach southerners from their allegiance to the Confederacy and thus shorten the war. Consequently, on Dec. 8, 1863, he issued a proclamation of amnesty that promised full pardon to all but a select group of disloyal citizens. Wherever 10 percent of the voters had taken the oath of allegiance, they were authorized to inaugurate new governments. All Lincoln required was their submission to the Union and their acceptance of the Emancipation Proclamation.

The president's plan encountered resistance in Congress. Perturbed by his failure to leave Reconstruction to the lawmakers and anxious to protect Republican interests in the South, Congress, on July 2, 1864, passed the Wade-Davis bill, a more stringent measure than the "10 percent plan." Requiring an oath of allegiance from 50, rather than 10, percent of the electorate before new governments could be set up, the bill prescribed further conditions for prospective voters. Only those able to take an "ironclad oath" of past loyalty were to be enfranchised, and slavery was to be abolished. When Lincoln pocket-vetoed the measure, its authors bitterly attacked him in the Wade-Davis Manifesto. After the president's reelection, efforts to revive the Wade-Davis bill in modified form failed. Congress refused to recognize the "free-state" governments established in accordance with Lincoln's plan in Louisiana and Arkansas, and so Lincoln's assassination on Apr. 14, 1865, left the future of Reconstruction in doubt.

What Lincoln would have done if he had lived is difficult to establish. It is known that as soon as Gen. Ulysses S. Grant had forced Gen. Robert E. Lee to surrender, the president withdrew his invitation to members of the Confederate legislature of Virginia to reassemble: his wartime plans are evidently not necessarily a guide to his peacetime intentions. It is also clear that he was not averse to the enfranchisement of qualified blacks. He wrote to this effect to the governor of Louisiana and touched on the subject in his last public address, on Apr. 11, 1865. But his larger policy had not yet fully matured.

With the end of war the problem of Reconstruction became more acute. If the seceded states were to be restored without any conditions, local whites would soon reestablish Democratic rule. They would seek to reverse the verdict of the sword and, by combining with their northern associates, challenge Republican supremacy. Moreover, before long, because of the end of slavery and the lapse of the Three-fifths Compromise, the South would obtain a larger influence in the councils of the nation than before the war.

The easiest way of solving this problem would have been to extend the suffrage to the freedmen. But in spite of an increasing radical commitment to votes for blacks, the majority of the party hesitated. Popular prejudice, not all of it in the South, was too strong, and many doubted the feasibility of enfranchising newly liberated slaves. Nevertheless, the integration of the blacks into American life became one of the principal issues of Reconstruction.

Lincoln's successor, Andrew Johnson, was wholly out of sympathy with black suffrage. A southerner and former slaveholder, Johnson held deep prejudices against blacks, who, he believed, should occupy an inferior place in society. He was willing to concede the vote to the very few educated or propertied blacks, if only to stop radical agitation, but he did not even insist on this minimum. Based on his Jacksonian convictions of an indestructible Union of indestructible states, his Reconstruction policies in time of peace resembled those of his predecessor in time of war. But they were no longer appropriate.

Johnson's plan, published on May 29, 1865, called for the speedy restoration of southern governments based on the (white) electorate of 1860. High Confederate officials and all those owning property valued at more than $20,000 were excluded from his offer of amnesty, but they were eligible for individual pardons. Appointing provisional governors who were to call constitutional conventions, Johnson expected the restored states to ratify the Thirteenth Amendment abolishing slavery, nullify the secession ordinances, and repudiate the Confederate debt.

In operation the president's plan revealed that little had changed in the South. Not one of the states enfranchised even literate blacks. Some balked at nullifying the secession ordinances; others hesitated or failed to repudiate the Confederate debt; and Mississippi refused to ratify the Thirteenth Amendment. Former insurgent leaders, including Alexander H. Stephens, the vice-president of the Confederacy, were elected to Congress. Several states even passed black codes that in effect remanded the blacks to a condition not far removed from slavery.

The reaction of northerners to these developments was not favorable. When Congress met in December, it refused to admit any of the representatives from the seceded states. All matters pertaining to the restoration of the South were to be referred to the newly created Joint Committee of Fifteen on Reconstruction.

Johnson had to make a choice. Either he could cooperate with the moderate center of the party or, by opposing it, break with the overwhelming majority of Republicans and rely on the small minority of conservatives and the Democrats. When Lyman Trumbull, the moderate chairman of the Senate Judiciary Committee, framed the Freedmen's Bureau and civil rights bills largely for the protection of the blacks, the president, unwilling to compromise on the subject of race and federal relations, refused to sign them. As a result, the moderates cooperated increasingly with the radicals, and the civil rights bill veto was overridden on Apr. 9, 1866.

Congress then developed a Reconstruction plan of its own: the Fourteenth Amendment. Moderate in tone, it neither conferred suffrage on the blacks nor exacted heavy penalties from the whites. Clearly defining American citizenship, it made blacks part of the body politic, sought to protect them from state interference, and provided for reduced representation for states disfranchising prospective voters. If Johnson had been willing to accept it, the struggle over Reconstruction might have been at an end. But the president was wholly opposed to the measure. Believing the amendment subversive of the Constitution and of white supremacy, he used his influence to procure its defeat in the southern states, an effort that succeeded everywhere except in Tennessee, which was admitted on July 24, 1866. At the same time, he sought to build up a new party. The rival plans of Reconstruction thus became an issue in the midterm elections of 1866, during which four national conventions met, and Johnson on his "swing around the circle" actively campaigned for his program. His claims of having established peace in the South were weakened by serious riots in Memphis and New Orleans.

The elections resulted in a triumph for the Republican majority. Since the president was still unwilling to cooperate, Congress proceeded to shackle him by restricting his powers of removal (Tenure of Office Act) and of military control ("Command of the Army" Act). In addition, it passed a series of measures known as the Reconstruction Acts, which inaugurated the congressional or "radical" phase of Reconstruction.

The first two Reconstruction Acts divided the South (except for Tennessee) into five military districts, enfranchised blacks, and required southern states to draw up constitutions safeguarding black suffrage. The new legislatures were expected to ratify the Fourteenth Amendment, and certain Confederate officeholders were for a time barred from voting and from officeholding.

The president refused to concede defeat. After his vetoes of the Reconstruction Acts were not sustained, he sought to lessen their effect as much as possible. His lenient interpretation of the law led to the more stringent third Reconstruction Act (July 19, 1867), which only spurred him to further resistance. On Aug. 12 he suspended Edwin M. Stanton, his radical secretary of war. After appointing Grant secretary ad interim, he also removed several radical major generals in the South. Democratic successes in the fall elections greatly encouraged him.

Johnson's intransigence resulted in a complete break with Congress. Because the radicals lacked a majority, their first attempt to impeach him failed, on Dec. 7, 1867. But when the Senate reinstated Stanton and the president dismissed him a second time, the House acted. Passing a resolution of impeachment on Feb. 24, 1868, it put Johnson on trial before the Senate. Because of moderate defections and the weakness of the case, he was acquitted by one vote, on May 16 and 26. His narrow escape once more encouraged southern conservatives, so that it was difficult for Grant, elected president in November 1868, to carry congressional Reconstruction to a successful conclusion.

During 1867 and 1868 radical Reconstruction had been gradually initiated. Despite conservative opposition—Congress had to pass a fourth Reconstruction Act easing requirements before the constitution of Alabama was accepted; the electorate ratified the new charters in all but three states—Mississippi, Texas, and Virginia. Accordingly, in the summer of 1868 the compliant states were readmitted and the Fourteenth Amendment declared in force. Because Georgia later excluded blacks from its legislature and because Mississippi, Texas, and Virginia, for various local reasons, did not ratify their constitutions on time, those four states were subjected to additional requirements. These included the ratification of the Fifteenth Amendment, prohibiting the denial of suffrage on account of race. After complying with the new demands, these states too were restored to their places in the Union in 1870, and the amendment was added to the Constitution.

Historians have long argued about the nature of the radical governments. According to William A. Dunning and his school, they were characterized by vindictiveness, corruption, inefficiency, and ruthless exploitation of southern whites. Northern carpetbaggers, local scalawags, and their alleged black tools supposedly trampled white civilization underfoot. Some scholars have questioned these assumptions. Pointing out that the radical governments succeeded in establishing systems of public education, eleemosynary institutions, and lasting constitutions, modern experts have discarded the concept of "black Reconstruction." Black legislators were in a majority only in South Carolina, and even there their white allies wielded considerable influence. Conceding the presence of corruption in the South, these historians have emphasized its nationwide scope. They have tended to show that the new governments deserved credit for making the first efforts to establish racial democracy in the South and that many radical officeholders, black and white alike, did not compare unfavorably with their conservative colleagues.

But the experiment could not last. The rapid disappearance, by death or retirement, of radical Republicans, the granting of amnesty to former Confederates, the conservatives' resort to terror, and a gradual loss of interest by the North would have made Reconstruction difficult in any case. These problems were complicated by the blacks' lack of economic power—Johnson had gone so far as to return to whites lands already occupied by freedmen. Factionalism within the dominant party increased with the rise of the Liberal Republicans in 1872, and the panic of 1873 eroded Republican majorities in the House. The Supreme Court, which had refused to interfere with Reconstruction in *Mississippi* v. *Johnson* (1867) and *Georgia* v. *Stanton* (1867), began to interpret the Fourteenth Amendment very narrowly, as in the Slaughterhouse Cases (1873). Such a tendency foreshadowed the Court's further weakening of not only the Fourteenth Amendment but also the Fifteenth Amendment, in *United States* v. *Cruikshank* (1876) and *United States* v. *Reese* (1876) and its invalidation in 1883 of the Civil Rights Act of 1875 in the Civil Rights Cases.

The end of Reconstruction came at different times in the several states. Despite the passage of three Federal Force Acts during 1870 and 1871, the gradual collapse of the radical regimes could not be arrested. In some cases terror instigated by the Ku Klux Klan and its successors overthrew Republican administrations; in others, conservatives regained control by more conventional means. By 1876 Republican administrations survived only in Florida, Louisiana, and South Carolina, all of which returned disputed election results in the fall. After a series of economic and political bargains enabled Rutherford B. Hayes, the Republican candidate, to be inaugurated president, he promptly withdrew federal troops, and Reconstruction in those states also came to an end. For a time blacks continued to vote, although in decreasing numbers, but by the turn of the century they had been almost eliminated from southern politics.

Reconstruction thus seemed to end in failure, and the myth of radical misrule embittered relations between the sections. But in spite of their apparent lack of accomplishment, the radicals had succeeded in embedding the postwar amendments in the Constitution, amendments that were the foundation for the struggle for racial equality in the 20th century.

[Herman Belz, *Reconstructing the Union: Theory and Policy During the Civil War;* Michael Les Benedict, *A Compromise of Principle;* William R. Brock, *An American Crisis: Congress and Reconstruction, 1865–1867;* La-Wanda Cox and John H. Cox, *Politics, Principle, and Prejudice, 1865–1866;* John Hope Franklin, *Reconstruction After the Civil War;* Eric L. McKitrick, *Andrew Johnson and Reconstruction;* Rembert W. Patrick, *The Reconstruction of the Nation;* J. G. Randall and David Donald, *The Civil War and Reconstruction;* Kenneth P. Stampp, *The Era of Reconstruction.*]

HANS L. TREFOUSSE

RECONSTRUCTION, LINCOLN'S PLAN OF. In his proclamation of Dec. 8, 1863, President Abraham Lincoln offered pardon, with certain exceptions, to those southerners who would take an oath to support the U.S. Constitution and abide by federal laws and proclamations concerning slaves. When oath-takers equal in number to one-tenth of the state's voters in 1860 should "reestablish" a government in a seceded commonwealth, Lincoln promised executive recognition to such government without commitment as to congressional recognition. Both the plan and the whole southern policy of Lincoln were denounced as far too lenient, and there followed a storm of controversy with the Radical Republicans, who by their control of Congress prevented any settlement of this vital problem during Lincoln's life. The hopeless deadlock between president and Congress was seen in the radical Wade-Davis bill that Lincoln killed by a pocket veto. Afterwards Lincoln issued a proclamation (July 8, 1864) explaining that he could not accept the radical plan as the only method of reconstruction, and he was promptly answered by Sen. Benjamin F. Wade of Ohio and Rep. Henry W. Davis of Maryland in a truculent manifesto. No state was actually restored in accordance with Lincoln's plan, although he considered his terms fulfilled in Tennessee, Arkansas, and Louisiana. In Virginia he considered that a loyal government already existed. Lincoln's private secretary, John Hay, was sent to assist in the reorganization of Florida, and the president's policy became entangled with intraparty rows concerning delegates' votes for 1864. In his last public speech Lincoln urged generosity in restoring the states, and in his last cabinet meeting (Apr. 14, 1865) he advised leniency toward the defeated South.

[Charles H. McCarthy, *Lincoln's Plan of Reconstruction;* Eben G. Scott, *Reconstruction During the Civil War;* J. G. Randall, *The Civil War and Reconstruction.*]

J. G. RANDALL

RECONSTRUCTION ACTS, a series of laws designed to carry out the congressional program of Reconstruction. The first Reconstruction Act (Mar. 2, 1867) divided all southern states except Tennessee into five military districts to be commanded by general officers. Conventions chosen by universal male suffrage were to frame constitutions, which would then have to be accepted by the electorate. After completing these steps and ratifying the Fourteenth Amendment, the southern states would be deemed ready for readmission as full-fledged members of the Union. Insurgents disfranchised for their participation in rebellion were denied the right to vote.

When southerners refused to take steps to call conventions, a supplementary Reconstruction Act (Mar.

23, 1867) provided that the commanding generals initiate the voting process. Registrars were required to take an "ironclad oath," and the electorate was to vote on the question of holding a convention. Because Attorney General Henry Stanbery interpreted the law in such a way as to favor the conservatives, a second supplementary Reconstruction Act (July 19, 1867) declared that the state governments were strictly subordinate to the military commanders, broadly defined the disfranchising clauses, and spelled out the generals' right to remove state officers. After the conservatives in Alabama had defeated the radical state constitution by registering but not voting, a third supplementary Reconstruction Act (Mar. 11, 1868) enabled a majority of the actual voters, rather than of the registrants, to ratify. The first three of these measures were passed over President Andrew Johnson's veto; the last became law without his signature.

The Reconstruction Acts were the result of Johnson's refusal to modify his policies in conformity with the wishes of the majority of the Republican party. His own plan of Reconstruction was so mild as to fail to protect either the freedmen in the South or the interests of the Republican party in the country. Consequently, when the voters rejected his policies in the fall of 1866 and all southern states except Tennessee refused to ratify the Fourteenth Amendment, the radicals demanded more stringent legislation. Thaddeus Stevens, who had originally advocated a more comprehensive measure, then reported a bill remanding the South to military rule, but the pressure of moderates forced him to agree reluctantly to Sen. John Sherman's amendments providing for a possible method of restoration.

Although the purposes of the acts were ostensibly achieved with the inauguration of radical governments in the South, in the long run they must be deemed a failure. In state after state conservative rule was eventually restored and blacks once more subordinated to whites. The revolutionary effect often ascribed to the acts because of their emphasis on black suffrage has been exaggerated. While modern historians have criticized them for ambiguities and imperfections, they are no longer considered unprovoked examples of vindictive radicalism. Their principal importance lies in their hastening the ratification of the Fourteenth Amendment.

[John Hope Franklin, *Reconstruction After the Civil War;* Eric L. McKitrick, *Andrew Johnson and Reconstruction;* J. G. Randall and David Donald, *The Civil War and Reconstruction;* Kenneth M. Stampp, *The Era of Reconstruction, 1865–1877.*]

HANS L. TREFOUSSE

RECONSTRUCTION AND THE CHURCHES. Religious bodies in the United States were particularly concerned with public affairs during and following the Civil War. Most of the major northern churches had entered the South during the war, having won the consent of the War Department to take over church buildings abandoned by southern ministers. Their refusal to return them to their owners at the close of the war led in some instances to court action and recriminations on the part of the southern church leaders. The northern churches generally looked upon the South, at the close of the war, as a new mission field, and new organizations were formed to carry on work in the South, especially among the freedmen. Numerous northern ministers found employment in the Freedmen's Bureau, some of whom became involved in carpetbag and Afro-American politics. The great exodus of southern blacks from the churches of their former masters and the large influx of northern blacks into the South, together with the activity of the northern white and black churches, soon created an entirely new religious situation in the former slave states. The former slaves were gathered into independent congregations all over the South, a great majority being Methodists and Baptists. The Afro-American's religion at this time, quite naturally, was tinged with politics, and Afro-American churches were used by unscrupulous carpetbag and black politicians to gain control of the black ballot. Generally speaking, the black ministers were the first recognized leaders of the freedmen and under their direction they took their first steps as American citizens.

[P. H. Douglas, *Christian Reconstruction in the South;* W. W. Sweet, "Negro Churches in the South: A Phase of Reconstruction," *Methodist Review* (1921); A. A. Taylor, *The Negro in the Reconstruction of Virginia.*]

WILLIAM W. SWEET

RECONSTRUCTION FINANCE CORPORATION. The stock market crash of 1929 and the subsequent severe depression resulted in a gradually increasing crisis for the banking system. The steep decline in the value of assets combined with the insistent demand of depositors for their money produced a situation in which a large number of banks whose solvency would have been unquestioned in normal times could attempt to achieve liquidity only at ruinous cost to themselves and to their customers with loans outstanding. In this emergency, President Herbert Hoover recommended, and Congress created, the Reconstruction Finance Corporation (RFC) on Jan. 22, 1932, to make loans not only to banks but also to insurance companies and railroads and, by the Emergency Relief and Construction Act of July 21, 1932, to states and to farmers. The immediate aim was to restore faith in financial institutions generally, prevent ruinous liquidation, and revive the economy through the restoration of credit.

The corporation was capitalized at $500 million, which was entirely subscribed by the federal government, and it was empowered to sell $3.3 billion of debentures. Through the end of the Hoover administration $2.2 billion was actually loaned to authorized borrowers. The RFC undoubtedly saved many railroads, banks, insurance companies, and farmers, but its effectiveness was limited by overly stringent security requirements for loans and by the decision of Congress to require public disclosure of borrowers, a stipulation that aggravated the liquidity problem of many banks.

In the New Deal years the RFC was vigorously utilized and its lending powers increased. In the banking crisis of 1933 its purchase of $1.3 billion of bank stock was especially effective. Loans were made to a great variety of institutions, both public and private, for a variety of projects. The loans included, for example, $73 million for the San Francisco Golden Gate Bridge, $208 million for an aqueduct from Arizona to southern California, and a sum to the city of Chicago for back pay for schoolteachers. From January 1932 through February 1939 the corporation loaned $7.2 billion, of which $5.4 billion was repaid. From a business standpoint the RFC was a success in that its operating expenses were low and a high percentage of loans were eventually repaid.

During World War II the RFC proved useful in expanding defense production. Through the Defense Plant Corporation, a subsidiary, the RFC invested some $7 billion in various defense-related industries.

It was an objective of the administration of President Dwight D. Eisenhower to remove the government from competition with private business. Accordingly, on July 30, 1953, the president signed a bill ending the Reconstruction Finance Corporation. It had loaned out $12 billion, of which all but $800 million was repaid. Its successor was the Small Business Administration, established with a revolving fund of $300 million.

[Jesse H. Jones, *Fifty Billion Dollars: My Thirteen Years With R.F.C.;* Paul Studenski and Herman E. Krooss, *Financial History of the United States.*]

ROBERT P. SHARKEY

RECOVERY, FORT, was built in what is now west central Ohio near the Indiana line in December 1793 by a detachment of Gen. Anthony Wayne's army under Capt. Alexander Gibson. The fort was erected on the site of Gen. Arthur St. Clair's defeat, Nov. 4, 1791, by the Indians along the Wabash and Maumee rivers. One of the soldiers' first duties was to inter the bones of the 600 slain on the field two years earlier. On June 30, 1794, the garrison of 150 men under Maj. William McMahon was subjected to attacks for two days by more than 1,000 Indians, apparently under British leadership (this was Wayne's opinion), with Simon Girty conspicuous among them. Twenty-two soldiers were killed and several wounded, but the attackers were unable to take the fort. After this it had little importance except as a supply base and as an important identification point for the Indian boundary delineated in the Treaty of Greenville (Aug. 3, 1795). A small village grew up around the site of the fort, which in 1970 had a population of 1,348.

[E. O. Randall and D. J. Ryan, *History of Ohio,* vol. II.]

EUGENE H. ROSEBOOM

RECOVERY ADMINISTRATION, NATIONAL. *See* **New Deal.**

RECRUITMENT. Since the reorganization of the armed forces for peacetime service in 1787, and aside from volunteer and drafted troops, the U.S. armed services have depended for the greatest number of their troops on recruitment by voluntary enlistment. In the 1970's the strength of the armed forces was still determined by the National Defense Act of 1916—but throughout the history of the armed services the number of recruits at any given time has varied greatly.

Because the given strength of the armed forces has generally been limited by law, recruitment has occasionally been suspended. Such action is usually of short duration, because the rate of attrition in armed forces personnel is so high that recruits are almost constantly needed.

During the Mexican War (1846–48), most of the organized fighting was carried out by the standing army. The only recruitment was of mounted ranger companies to protect the outlying districts of the new Republic of Texas from the Mexicans and the Indians. During the war itself, companies of Texas Rangers, the law enforcement body of the territory, were formed into regiments and mustered into the federal service for the duration of the war, but they operated primarily on what was termed "detached duty" on scouting, patrol, and raiding missions. They were more paramilitary than military.

During the Civil War (1861–65), Union recruitment involved, in many instances, the paying of recruits a sum of money for joining, the amount of which varied. This was ineffective, especially since many people collected the money and then paid others only a small portion of it to take their places on the rolls. Because of the emotionally charged issues of slavery and states' rights, much of the armies on both sides consisted of volunteer forces.

In the Spanish-American War (1898) the recruitment issues were again emotional, for not only was the suffering of the Cuban people an important factor, but the sinking of the *Maine* in Havana harbor caused many Americans to volunteer. The best-known volunteer force of this war was Theodore Roosevelt's Rough Riders. Most of the fighting and the decisive battles of the war were carried out by the standing navy.

Recruiting for all branches of the armed forces proceeds in about the same manner, although methods have changed greatly over the years. The armed forces have had to develop means of interesting men and women in joining the services, especially since the elimination of the draft in 1973. Recruitment posters of World War I style—bearing the legend "Uncle Sam Wants You!"—were no longer effective by the time World War II began. And by the 1970's recruitment posters had come full circle in approach, bearing the slogan "Today's Army Wants to Join You." The new slogan was designed to avoid the impersonality of the old-style recruitment as well as the feeling of authority, which many contemporary young people found objectionable.

In addition to changing their recruitment approach, the various branches of the armed forces initiated a great number of training programs for recruits in many job fields. In 1972 the navy offered training in fifteen occupational categories and had sixty-six schools and courses. The air force offered four major fields of study and guaranteed the availability of assignments in any field in which the recruit qualified on the aptitude exams. An army recruit in the 1970's could also choose from among four specialized fields of study. Many specialized technical courses and job opportunities were available in all branches of the service.

American dissatisfaction with the Vietnam War and with U.S. involvement in other areas of Southeast Asia caused such problems with the draft that volunteer forces and recruitment of regular forces became an important factor in retaining a powerful standing army. Job opportunities proved a greater attraction in the midst of the depressed economic conditions of the 1970's than the appeals to patriotism that had attracted recruits throughout the earlier history of the United States. In addition, the opposition to the Vietnam War in the late 1960's and early 1970's caused much expatriation of young men seeking to avoid conscription. Conscription thus became a highly emotional issue, and with public support of the military falling off, conscription was abolished in favor of an all-volunteer army. This action alleviated the feelings of resentment on the part of those who opposed foreign wars, and the army's "new look," especially in the field of job training, proved highly successful in raising an effective standing army consisting entirely of volunteers.

[Melvin R. Laird, *Final Report to the Congress;* Walter Millis, *American Military Thought;* U.S. Department of Defense, *Pathways to Military Service.*]

LORING D. WILSON

RED CLOUD'S WAR. *See* **Sioux Wars.**

RED CROSS, AMERICAN, was founded May 21, 1881, by Clara Barton to provide care to ill and wounded soldiers in wartime even though the United States was then at peace. The first official act of the new society was to send assistance to the victims of the Michigan forest fires of September 1881. Disaster relief became a major program of the Red Cross in the United States and is still known internationally as the "American Amendment." Urged by Barton, Congress ratified the 1864 Geneva Convention in 1882. Services to the armed forces began in Cuba during the Spanish-American War (1898). Congress granted the American Red Cross its first charter in 1900, and it now operates under a second congressional charter, granted in 1905. The charter obliges it to serve the armed forces, veterans, and their families and to assist victims of natural disasters. Other programs and services have been developed to meet existing community needs.

Between 1906 and 1914 the Red Cross established its first aid, public health nursing, and water safety training programs. It did not become a nationwide organization until the United States entered World War I. The Red Cross set up and staffed fifty-eight base hospitals and forty-seven ambulance companies overseas to care for the wounded. Nearly 20,000 registered nurses were recruited to serve in military establishments. The field staff on military posts in the United States and overseas and the Home Service (later Service to Military Families) in the chapters maintained communications between servicemen and their families and provided assistance to both. Volunteers manned canteens, provided motor service, and made millions of surgical dressings. The Junior Red Cross (later Red Cross Youth Service Programs) was organized in 1917 to give youths and educators a way to serve their communities. Extensive civilian war relief activities were carried on overseas. After the war Red Cross safety training, home care of the sick, accident prevention, and nutrition education gained in popularity. Major disasters, particularly the Mississippi River floods of 1927, called for large-scale relief and rehabilitation programs.

In World War II the Red Cross carried on civilian relief operations that helped more than 75 million persons in sixty countries. With U.S. entry into the war the Red Cross recruited more than 71,000 registered nurses for military duty and trained more than 200,000 nurse's aides to care for civilian patients. The Red Cross established worldwide welfare and recreation programs to serve U.S. troops. The first nationwide blood program was organized, and more than 13 million units of blood were collected for the armed forces from volunteer donors. Red Cross volunteers numbered in the millions and carried out myriad assignments, including packing food and medical parcels for prisoners of war. During the war years approximately 12 million people were trained in first aid, home nursing, and water safety. When hostilities ceased, there was a marked increase in services to veterans and their dependents. In 1948 the Red Cross established a program to provide blood and its components to civilians without charge, and this program produces nearly half the blood collected in the United States.

The volunteer board of governors of the Red Cross has fifty members, thirty of whom are elected by chapter delegates to the national convention; it replaced the central committee on May 8, 1947. The Red Cross is a membership organization deriving its main support from the American citizenry. By the mid-1970's there were 3,142 chapters and 30,660,438 members who contributed $1 or more annually. A member of the international League of Red Cross Societies, which it helped to found in 1919, the American Red Cross was cooperating with 122 other societies in program development and in bringing aid to victims of disasters overseas by the mid-1970's. Its aim is to involve and serve the entire American community in peacetime with needed services that can be expanded rapidly in time of national emergency.

[Foster Rhea Dulles, *The American Red Cross: A History;* Charles Hurd, *The Compact History of the American Red Cross;* Ishbel Ross, *Angel of the Battlefield.*]

HERBERT V. CARMAN

REDEMPTIONERS, white immigrants who, in return for their passage to America from Europe, sold their services for a period varying from two to seven years. Upon arrival in port, captains of vessels having redemptioners aboard advertised in newspapers the sale of their services to persons who should advance the cost of their passage. From 1681 until after the Revolution, these indentured servants migrated to America primarily to settle after working off their debt. Scarcity of slaves in Pennsylvania created a brisk demand for this type of labor, and farm laborers, skilled craftsmen, and domestic servants were included in their lists. Until 1730 this traffic emanated chiefly from England; after that date, the majority were Germans and Scotch-Irish.

[C. A. Herrick, *White Servitude in Pennsylvania.*]

JULIAN P. BOYD

RED LEGS, so called because of their red leggings, were members of a secret military society organized in Kansas in 1862 under command of George W. Hoyt. They numbered from fifty to one hundred; their predatory activities rivaled depredations committed by Missouri guerrillas; and they served as federal scouts in border conflicts.

[L. W. Spring, *Kansas, The Prelude to the War for the Union.*]

WENDELL H. STEPHENSON

RED LINE MAP. Soon after the signing of the preliminary articles of peace and independence with Great Britain in 1782, Benjamin Franklin, as one of the American plenipotentiaries, marked the boundary of the United States for the reference of Charles Gravier, Comte de Vergennes, French foreign minister, in a "strong red line" on a copy of John Mitchell's *Map of British and French Dominions in North America,* which copy has never since been located in the French archives despite its vital relationship to American boundary disputes, notably the northeast boundary. In 1932 a transcript of the map, red line and all, was discovered in the Spanish archives.

[Lawrence Martin and Samuel Flagg Bemis, "Franklin's Red-Line Map Was a Mitchell," *The New England Quarterly,* vol. 10.]

SAMUEL FLAGG BEMIS

RED RIVER BOUNDARY DISPUTE. *See* **Greer County Dispute.**

RED RIVER CAMPAIGN (1864). Early in 1864 Union Gen. Henry W. Halleck ordered an invasion of the great cotton-growing sections of Louisiana, Arkansas, and Texas. The thrust, to be under the command of Gen. Nathaniel P. Banks, was to move up the Red River. The advance of the expedition was begun in March to take advantage of the spring rise in the river, which that year did not take place.

Banks's command and a force from Mississippi under Union Gen. Andrew Jackson Smith, together with a river fleet, were to converge on Alexandria, La., after which the combined force would move on to a junction with troops under Gen. Frederick Steele coming southward from Arkansas. The two armies would then sweep up the Red River valley to Shreveport, the Confederate headquarters, and on into eastern Texas. Scattered Confederate troops of half the Union strength, under Gen. Edmund Kirby-Smith, were available to oppose the invasion.

By the middle of March the fleet and Banks's army had taken Fort DeRussy (Mar. 14) and occupied Alexandria (Mar. 16), there to await the arrival of reinforcements marching overland from the Mississippi River. The retreating Confederate troops under Gen. Richard Taylor, receiving reinforcements as they retired, halted at Mansfield, south of Shreveport. Posted in good defensive positions, Taylor, on Apr. 8, with less than half his opponents' numbers, sustained Banks's attack. The Union forces were defeated and driven back in confusion (*see* Sabine Crossroads, Battle at). The next day Taylor's troops advanced against Banks's army posted in a strong position at Pleasant Hill, southeast of Mansfield, and in their turn were repulsed. Banks failed to follow up his success. During the night the Union army retreated to Grand Ecore near Natchitoches, and thence to Alexandria. The withdrawal of the army placed the Union fleet in jeopardy. On account of continued low water it was uncertain if the ships could pass the rapids at Grand Ecore. Engineering skill and resourcefulness got them safely through in time to escape capture or destruction.

When the threat of Banks's advance was removed, Kirby-Smith, at Shreveport, undertook both to pursue Banks and to crush Steele. He attacked at Jenkins Ferry, Ark., on the Saline River, on Apr. 30. Steele retreated to Little Rock. Kirby-Smith then turned southward to join Taylor for a final blow against Banks. He was too late. Banks had reembarked and started on his way back to the Mississippi, where the troops were dispersed.

The defeat of Banks's expedition ended important operations in the trans-Mississippi. The Confederate forces held out until May 26, 1865, when Kirby-Smith surrendered, thus ending the war in that area.

[R. U. Johnson and C. C. Buel, eds., *Battles and Leaders of the Civil War*, vol. IV.]

THOMAS ROBSON HAY

RED RIVER CART TRAFFIC. The Red River cart was a two-wheeled vehicle developed from the primitive cart used by Alexander Henry, Jr., at Pembina, in present northeastern North Dakota, in 1801. It had wheels made from sections of tree trunks, some 3 feet in diameter. The carts were made entirely of wood and carried a maximum load of 1,000 pounds. They were each drawn by an ox or Indian pony with a rude harness of rawhide.

The traffic began as early as 1822 with the founding of Fort Snelling (built 1820–23) at what is now Saint Paul, Minn. A train of Red River carts a mile in length was not at all infrequent. The carts were loaded at Fort Garry (Winnipeg) or Pembina with buffalo robes, pemmican, dried meat, and furs. These products were exchanged at Fort Snelling for the trade goods needed at the fur trade posts tributary to Fort Garry. Two trips during the season was the limit, since the carts were unable to travel more than twenty miles a day. In 1843 the American Fur Company established a post at Pembina under Norman W. Kittson, and thereafter the traffic from this point grew rapidly in volume.

The Red River cart trails most used were on the west side of the river, their location being dependent on the season. In the early summer, when the tributaries of the Red River were swollen by floods, the trails ran along the western edge of the ancient Lake Agassiz, following the western beach line. In late summer and fall these trails followed closer to the river at a distance depending on the contour of the country. Streams were crossed, where necessary, by the use of hastily improvised rafts. The transport animals swam the streams and were used to pull the rafts across the water. The Red River fords, or crossings, as they were called, were well known. The most used of these fords was Graham's Crossing about five miles north of Wahpeton, N.Dak. On the east side of the Red River the trail ran southeast to Fort Snelling. Later the trails crossed the Mississippi River at Sauk Rapids and reached Saint Paul on the east side of the river. The Lake Traverse route ran southeast to the crossing of the Minnesota River at Bois de Sioux and then to Mendota, at its junction with the Mississippi. After 1850 ferries connected Fort Snelling with Mendota and Saint Paul.

RED RIVER INDIAN WAR

The low cost of this form of transportation explains its popularity. The oxen and horses were pastured on the prairie grasses and the drivers found abundant game along the entire route. One serious drawback arose from the fact that these trails traversed the area that was the battleground of two Indian tribes, the Chippewa and the Dakota. This forced the traders to travel in large trains and to be ready to form a corral of the carts to meet either siege or attack anywhere along the route. The trails on the east side of the river were also used to avoid the attacks of the hostile Indians.

Gradually cart traffic gave way to the cheaper form of flatboat and steamboat traffic of the early 1850's, and the coming of the railroads the following decade completed the transformation.

O. G. Libby

RED RIVER INDIAN WAR (1874–75). As a result of the Treaty of Medicine Lodge (Barber County, Kans.), in October 1867, the Comanche, Kiowa, and Kataka were put on a reservation about the Wichita Mountains and the Arapaho and Cheyenne on another farther north (both within western Oklahoma). The Indians, not content to accept a sedentary life, again and again slipped away to raid the borders of Kansas, Colorado, New Mexico, and Texas. During the summer of 1874, Gen. Philip H. Sheridan was ordered to conduct a punitive campaign against the refractory Indians. Soon thereafter both cavalry and infantry under the command of colonels Nelson A. Miles, George Buell, John W. Davidson, and Ranald S. Mackenzie and Maj. William Price advanced from their posts in Texas, New Mexico, and Indian Territory against the hostile Indians who were encamped along the Red River, its tributaries, and the canyons of the Staked Plain (Llano Estacado) in west Texas and southeastern New Mexico. More than fourteen pitched battles were fought before the Indians submitted and returned to their reservations. Seventy-five of their leaders were sent to Florida for confinement.

[W. S. Nye, *Carbine and Lance;* C. C. Rister, *The Southwestern Frontier, 1865–1881.*]

C. C. Rister

RED RIVER OF THE NORTH, so called to distinguish it from the Red River of the South, forms the boundary between Minnesota and North Dakota and flows through Manitoba, Canada, into Lake Winnipeg. It was discovered by Pierre Gaultier de Varennes,

Sieur de La Vérendrye, French explorer and fur trader, in 1733. In that and the ensuing decades, the French built several posts in the Red River country, and by the middle of the century it was the center of a profitable fur trade. With the defeat of France in North America in 1763, British fur traders occupied the western country beyond the Red River, and in time it again became the scene of great trade activity. In the 1780's and 1790's it was the battleground of rival Canadian fur traders' organizations; and from 1800 to 1820 the Hudson's Bay and North West companies waged bitter warfare for its control.

American fur traders did not push into the Red River country until after the War of 1812. The Columbia Fur Company, in 1822, established itself advantageously on Lake Traverse. Six years earlier the American Fur Company built a post on Red Lake and in the following decade extended down the river into the Hudson's Bay Company's Winnipeg and Red River districts. In the 1840's American and British traders fought hard for the trade of the country; but it was a losing fight for all fur-trade interests—for by the middle of the century American farmers were advancing into the region.

The first permanent settlements on the Red River were begun by Thomas Douglas, Earl of Selkirk, at "the Forks" and Pembina in 1812. For many years these were the only real settlements in the country, although many of the fur trade posts after 1850 became the centers of thriving farming communities, for example, Grand Forks, N.Dak. During the decades of the 1870's, 1880's, and 1890's, thousands of settlers—mostly northern Europeans and eastern Americans—poured into the Red River valley south of the international boundary. At the same time Canadians were rapidly settling the lower reaches of the river. Before the close of the century, the Red River country ranked first among the wheat-producing regions of North America.

[John L. Coulter, "Industrial History of the Valley of the Red River of the North," *Collections of the State Historical Society of North Dakota,* vol. III; John Perry Pritchett, "Some Red River Fur Trade Activities," *Minnesota Historical Bulletin,* vol. 6.]

John Perry Pritchett

RED RIVER POST. French encroachments into Texas after 1685 aroused the Spaniards to establish missions and military posts in the region. In 1691 Don Domingo de Teran, governor of Coahuila (Mexico) and Texas, established a post among the Caddo on the Red River, near the northwestern corner of modern Louisiana. The post was supplied with cattle and seeds for planting, but the cattle died, the crops failed, the Indians were hostile, and the French menace disappeared. The post was abandoned in 1693.

[H. Yoakum, *History of Texas From Its First Settlement in 1685 to Its Annexation to the United States in 1846*, vol. I.]

WALTER PRICHARD

RED RIVER RAFT. An obstruction of logs and other debris, accumulating for many years, had become lodged and fastened together so as to form an almost solid mass that blocked the channel of the Red River of the South for a distance of 180 miles above Coushatta Bayou, stopping steamboat navigation at Natchitoches, La. About 1830 the War Department complained of the heavy expense of transporting supplies from Natchitoches to Fort Towson in Indian Country, and Congress made an appropriation for removing the Red River raft and improving the river's navigation. Capt. Henry Miller Shreve, who had succeeded in removing obstructions to navigation on the Ohio and Mississippi rivers, was placed in charge of the work, and between 1833 and 1839 he entirely removed the raft, leaving the river navigable for more than 1,000 miles. Shreveport, named in honor of Shreve, arose as the commercial center of the region thus opened to settlement. After the removal of the original raft, new obstructions formed from time to time at different points in the channel, and Congress made additional appropriations for their removal in almost every decade from 1840 to 1890, when railroads superseded steamboats as the chief transportation agencies in the Red River valley. The removal of the Red River raft was one of the most important internal improvement projects undertaken by the federal government in the antebellum South. Total congressional appropriations for that project approximated $1 million, but the value of the lands thus opened to settlement amounted to many times that sum.

[J. Fair Hardin, "The First Great Western River Captain: A Sketch of the Career of Captain Henry Miller Shreve, Founder of Shreveport," *Louisiana Historical Quarterly*, vol. 10.]

WALTER PRICHARD

RED SHIRTS, the most widely accepted designation of the bands of armed horsemen who overthrew Radical Republican rule in South Carolina. Beginning in 1870, whites, without official sanction, organized themselves in groups for protection against the black

militia, and, as the crucial political campaign of 1876 got under way, they converted white sentiment to a policy of no compromise with the Radical Republicans by bloody work at the Hamburg Riot of July 8. Within two months of that event a Garibaldian uniform was adopted, and thousands of red-shirted whites rode about encouraging the Wade Hampton canvass for governor, disturbing Radical Republican meetings, and terrorizing blacks. There were 290 companies composed of 14,350 men. By intimidation the Red Shirts secured a majority for Hampton in the November election and forced the flight of Radical Republican officeholders when the federal troops were withdrawn from the state in April 1877.

[F. B. Simkins and R. H. Woody, *South Carolina During Reconstruction*.]

FRANCIS B. SIMKINS

REDSTONE OLD FORT, the pioneers' name for a Mound Builder entrenchment at the confluence of Dunlap's Creek with the Monongahela River in southwestern Pennsylvania. A focus of conflict in the preliminary expeditions of the French and Indian War, Fort Burd was erected at the site in 1759 by Col. James Burd of the Pennsylvania militia. It served as a refuge from Indian alarms, a rallying point for scouts and rangers, and a depot for military stores until the close of the revolutionary war. "Redstone Old Fort" persisted as the common appellation for the fort and for the village of boat builders and traders that grew about it. In 1785 the site passed into private ownership and was rechristened Brownsville.

[James Veech, *The Monongahela of Old*.]

E. DOUGLAS BRANCH

REED RULES, adopted by the House of Representatives on Feb. 14, 1890, marked the successful conclusion of Speaker of the House Thomas B. Reed's long-continued fight for more efficient procedure in that body. The new rules permitted the suppression of dilatory tactics, substituted a "present" for a "voting" quorum, reduced the size of the Committee of the Whole, and provided sundry changes in the order of business. They brought an immediate increase in efficiency but greatly increased the power of the speaker; and the title of "Czar" was promptly bestowed upon their author. A contemporary opponent declared that the speaker and committee chairmen would henceforth constitute "a petty oligarchy with absolute control of the business of the House," and twenty years later the rules were considerably modified in this particular. Many of them, however, proved their worth and are still in effect. (*See also* Cannonism.*)

[De Alva S. Alexander, *History and Procedure of the House of Representatives;* W. A. Robinson, *Thomas B. Reed, Parliamentarian.*]

WILLIAM A. ROBINSON

REED TREATY, also known as the U.S. Treaty of Tientsin. Following the defeat of China in the Anglo-French War (1857–58), the victorious allies imposed peace terms by the Treaties of Tientsin in 1858, which opened up eleven more treaty ports to foreign trade and residence and provided for extraterritorial protection of foreign nationals traveling and trading throughout all China. The British Treaty of Tientsin further stipulated the right of a diplomatic representative to appear at Peking; the toleration of the Christian religion, missionaries, and converts; and fixed tariff charges, collected by British officials under Chinese sovereignty at a general level of 5 percent. Despite the fact that the United States had remained neutral during the war, William B. Reed, the American minister, simultaneously negotiated a treaty, signed June 18, securing for citizens of the United States equality of treatment extended to other foreigners, thus securing the same privileges from China without having participated in hostilities.

[Samuel Flagg Bemis, *A Diplomatic History of the United States.*]

SAMUEL FLAGG BEMIS

REFERENDUM. There are many ways of classifying or categorizing a referendum, but one prime characteristic is common to all its various manifestations: a referendum generally involves the submission of a public-policy measure or question directly to the people at a formal election for their approval or disapproval. Such referenda may be compulsory or advisory, constitutional or legislative, local or statewide in nature. Questions posed to the public on a referendum ballot may deal with proposed changes in state constitutional provisions, in city charters, in state laws, or in levels of school taxes or bonding.

In terms of mere volume, the public referendum no doubt finds its heaviest use among the thousands of local governmental units where state constitutions or state laws stipulate voter approval before public resources may be either sought or spent or before certain governmental functions may be either added or abolished.

The Massachusetts constitution of 1780 is usually credited with introducing the use in the United States of statewide constitutional referenda on the adoption or rejection of new constitutions or on the adoption or rejection of amendments to existing constitutions. Use of the statewide legislative referendum came somewhat later. After an early beginning in Texas (1840's) major impetus for legislatures to submit measures to the voters for their approval before they could become law did not develop until the end of the 19th century and the first two decades of the 20th century.

The Progressive movement viewed the legislative referendum—along with the initiative, the recall, and the primary—as part and parcel of urgently needed governmental reforms through wider and more direct forms of citizen participation.

By 1975 provision for the use of the legislative referendum could be found in the constitutions of at least twelve states—Colorado, Georgia, Maine, Michigan, Missouri, Montana, New Jersey, North Carolina, Oklahoma, Oregon, Vermont, and Washington. An even larger number of states permitted a citizen-initiated legislative referendum on the filing of a petition (containing a specified number of signatures) with the secretary of state. This group of twenty-three states includes Alaska, Arizona, Arkansas, California, Colorado, Idaho, Kentucky, Maine, Maryland, Massachusetts, Michigan, Missouri, Montana, Nebraska, Nevada, New Mexico, North Dakota, Ohio, Oklahoma, Oregon, South Dakota, Utah, and Washington.

Although infrequently called into operation when compared with the hundreds of constitutional amendments and thousands of local issues, the approximately half-a-dozen legislative referenda voted on annually have been employed to ascertain the public will on a wide variety of legislative subject matters. Two major categories appear frequently: referenda dealing with changes in governmental machinery or organization and those addressing themselves to fiscal or financial matters. Since many of these issues included proposals for higher taxes or for the establishment of additional governmental agencies or departments, the electoral responses to such referenda not surprisingly have more often been negative than positive.

Voters who view the extension of public services as socially desirable and therefore consider it proper for state or local governments to enhance their functions and operations have become more and more disenchanted with the usefulness of the referendum as an instrument for change. Such disillusionment with "plebiscitary democracy" has been reinforced when the usual low voter-turnout at referendum elections (averaging about 30 percent or less in most communities) quite often accrued to the distinct advantage of individuals and groups with ample resources to strengthen and favor the cause of the status quo. The referendum has also come under increasing criticism for inviting campaign strategies that tend to exacerbate racial antagonisms in legislative issues affecting changes in the development of housing, urban renewal, and neighborhood school patterns.

In theory at least, the referendum, whether initiated by the action of citizens or of the legislature, remains a viable "populist" device in the arsenal of direct democracy whenever the instrumentalities of representative democracy fail to function in the interest of the general public.

[Penelope J. Gazey, "Direct Democracy: A Study of the American Referendum," *Parliamentary Affairs* (Spring 1971); Howard D. Hamilton, "Direct Legislation: Some Implications of Open-Housing Referenda," *American Political Science Review* (March 1970).]

G. THEODORE MITAU

REFORESTATION. Although artificial regeneration of forests by tree planting dates back to the colonial period in the United States, general and successful reforestation did not occur until the 20th century. Nineteenth-century attempts under the Timber Culture Act of 1873 (repealed 1891) and by the transcontinental railroads were generally unsuccessful. In 1905 the Forest Service began a program of reforesting the national forests, and by 1914 nearly 10,000 acres a year were being reforested.

The Forest Service gradually expanded its program, and a few states developed programs after World War I, principally to reforest state-owned abandoned farmlands and to furnish trees for planting on privately owned lands. The Clarke-McNary Act of 1924, which provided federal subsidies for tree planting and nursery establishment, appreciably enhanced the state programs, although before 1933 the effort in relation to the need remained insignificant, with never more than 140,000 acres reforested in any one year.

Establishment of the Civilian Conservation Corps (CCC) in 1933 made a rapid increase in tree planting possible. More than 519,000 acres were reforested in 1940, principally in the national forests and on private lands that needed wind and erosion control. World

War II brought the CCC program to an end in July 1942 and greatly reduced the total reforestation effort. By 1945 annual reforesting again covered less than 140,000 acres.

After World War II, efforts expanded slowly but steadily. Timber sales from the national forests increased rapidly, resulting in greater utilization of the Knutson-Vandenberg Act of 1930, which provided for timber purchasers to make deposits for reforestation and other betterment work in the sale area. Many industrial timberland owners also developed and expanded reforestation efforts. The Soil Conservation and Domestic Allotment Act of 1936 provided substantial federal subsidies for reforestation on private lands. Development of reliable direct-seeding techniques at reduced costs per acre also resulted in substantial increases in total acreage reforested. In 1960 more than 2.1 million acres were reforested. When the soil bank program ended, reforesting dropped to about 1.4 million acres a year during the period 1962–67. The trend reversed itself after that, however, and reforestation covered nearly 2 million acres in 1973.

WALKER NEWMAN

REFORMATORIES, institutions designed primarily for youthful offenders of the law, had their origin in part in the experience of the United States in the operation of its first prisons between 1825 and 1850. During that period a lively debate was carried on between the advocates of the Pennsylvania and the Auburn systems of prison management. Other voices were raised to question the basic assumption upon which both systems rested—namely, that the principal purpose of imprisonment was punishment. Out of the controversy grew the idea of the reformatory as an institution designed to rehabilitate young offenders through the provision of programs of education and vocational training and through systems of positive incentives to encourage good behavior. The length of a youth's stay in the institution was to be determined in large part by his response to the program. Initially, the child-saving institutions, the houses of refuge for juvenile offenders, were designated as reformatory in character. In 1876 a new institutional program was established at Elmira, N.Y., at what was to become the first reformatory for young men. It was directed by Zebulon R. Brockway, a 19th-century prison reformer who was strongly supported in his efforts by Frank Sanborn, Enoch C. Wines, and Gaylord Hubbell.

Many of the seminal ideas that led to the creation of the reformatory emerged from the discussions of English reformers in the 1830's and 1840's. These men began to advance the notion that a prison should be a "moral hospital" designed to retain offenders, not for a fixed period, but until they were "cured of their bad habits." The early implementation of these ideas came with the assignment of Capt. Alexander Maconochie to a prison colony on Norfolk Island, 1,000 miles east of Australia, in 1840. At the Norfolk Prison Colony, to which convicts were transported from England, Maconochie established a system through which offenders might earn earlier release as a result of hard work and good conduct. Maconochie's ideas had a strong influence on the establishment of the Irish prison system by Sir Joshua Jebb and Sir Walter Crofton in the mid-19th century.

The Irish system introduced the concept of the indeterminate sentence and release on "ticket of leave," the predecessor of modern parole systems. In addition, the Irish system provided for the grading of offenders according to the degree of their reformation; the use of religion, education, and labor as reformatory agents; and a system of positive incentives to good behavior. The Irish system became the focus of widespread discussion in the United States; it received special attention at the first American prison congress, the National Congress on Penitentiary and Reformatory Discipline, at Cincinnati in 1870, as well as at the International Prison Congress in London in 1872.

The reformatory program initiated by Brockway included elementary education for illiterates, designated library hours, lectures by faculty of the local Elmira College, and vocational training. The cost to the state of the institution's operation was to be held to a minimum. At Elmira, inmates limited to a sixteen-to-thirty-year age group were divided into three classes or grades. When an offender entered the institution he was ordinarily placed in the second grade. After six months of good behavior he was placed in the first or top grade, where six months more of good behavior entitled him to release on parole. Serious misconduct resulted in his demotion to the third or bottom grade, where a month of good behavior was necessary before he could be promoted to the second grade and then earn release by a year of good behavior from that point.

Despite the enthusiasm of the reformers and the construction of many reformatories designed on the Elmira model, the reformatory system did not produce the results expected. One of the greatest handicaps to the system was that physical plant was not compatible with rehabilitative program; in particular, experts agree, the Elmira institution was perhaps three times as large as was desirable for the conduct of a good reformatory program. In addition, the classification program and segregation system projected in the Elmira plan were not maintained, and many institutions designated as reformatories housed populations not significantly different from those of other prisons. Thus, it appears that the greatest significance of Brockway's reform may be found in his having injected a new degree of humanitarianism into the industrial prison of his day. The Brockway innovations, however, were to have a profound impact on correctional reforms introduced in the 20th century.

Beginning with the establishment of the U.S. Bureau of Prisons in 1930, the concept of diversification of adult correctional institutions to meet the varying needs of individual offenders gained significant headway. There has been general acceptance of the idea that the use of the walled, maximum-security prison should be limited to persons known to be dangerous. The number of medium- and minimum-security camps, farms, and other semiopen or open facilities has grown steadily since the beginning of the 20th century. Special attention has been given to the differential treatment of offenders who have common needs. Particular emphasis has been placed on the development of specialized programs for youthful offenders and young adults as well as for other offenders who have identifiable treatment needs, including the aging. As a consequence many types of prisoners who in the latter part of the 19th century would have served their sentences in walled prisons may now be found in smaller, more open facilities, which are believed to provide a better climate for delivery of correctional services.

[Harry E. Barnes and Neagley Teeters, *New Horizons in Criminology;* Vernon Fox, *Introduction to Corrections;* Joint Commission on Correctional Manpower and Training, *Perspectives on Correctional Manpower and Training;* Blake McKelvey, *Prisons in America.*]

HERMAN G. MOELLER

REFORMED CHURCHES are the American representatives of Dutch Calvinism. Their first American congregation, the Collegiate church in New York City, was established in 1628 and was still functioning in 1975. The church was divided by the Great Awakening over the issue of evangelism and its relationship to the church in the Netherlands. The church was reunited in 1771 under the ultimate authority of the home church, but it declared itself independent in 1819. The largest schism in the history of the movement occurred in 1822 when the Christian Reformed Church left the parent body. Although the early strength of the church was concentrated in the New York–New Jersey area, migrations to Michigan and Iowa in the 1850's gave the church a firm midwestern basis. The principal Reformed denominations in 1974 were the Christian Reformed Church, 287,114 members; Reformed Church in America, 366,381; Protestant Reformed Church in America, 3,000; and Reformed Church in the United States, 4,008.

[Herman Hoeksema, *The Protestant Reformed Churches in America: Their Origin, Early History and Doctrine;* Diedrich Kromminga, *The Christian Reformed Church: A Study in Orthodoxy;* Frederick James Zwierlein, *Religion in New Netherland 1623–1664.*]

GLENN T. MILLER

REFRIGERATION. The preservation of winter ice, principally for cooling drinks in summer, was practiced from antiquity, when ice was stored in insulated caves. Ice cooling was so popular in America that within a decade of the Revolution the United States led the world in both the production and consumption of ice. As the use of ice was extended to the preservation of fish, meat, and dairy products, ice production became a major industry in the northern states, and ice was shipped not only to the southern states but to the West Indies and South America. By 1880 the demand in New York City exceeded the capacity of 160 large commercial icehouses on the Hudson River. This industry reached its peak in 1886, when 25 million pounds were "harvested" by cutting lake and river ice with horse-drawn saws. The subsequent decline was caused by the development of mechanical refrigeration, but it was slow, and the natural ice industry did not expire until about 1920.

A method of making ice artificially, lowering the temperature of water by accelerating its evaporation, had long been practiced in India, where water in porous clay dishes laid on straw evaporated at night so rapidly as to cause ice to form on the surface of the remaining water. This method enjoyed a long life; as late as 1871 the principle was applied in a U.S. patent on a refrigerator that depended on the evaporation of water from the porous lining of the food compartment. But long before that, scientific discoveries had suggested more efficient methods of cooling—through the construction of appropriate machines.

Several types of refrigeration machine were developed in the 19th century. All depended on the absorp-

tion of heat by expanding gases, which had been a subject of scientific research in the previous century. It had been observed in the 18th century that the release of humid compressed air was accompanied by a stream of pellets of ice and snow. This phenomenon, the cooling effect of expanding air, was to lead to the development of the Gorrie ice machine in the 1840's. John Gorrie was a physician of Apalachicola, Fla., who was concerned with relieving the sufferings of malaria victims in the southern summer climate. In Gorrie's machine water was injected into a cylinder in which air was compressed by a steam engine. This cooled the air. The air was allowed to expand in contact with coils containing brine, which was then used to freeze water. Gorrie's machine was scarcely used (although at least one was built—in England), but his 1851 patent, the first in the United States for an ice machine, was a model for others, including the first large machines that in the 1880's began to compete with lakes and rivers as a source of ice.

More important were "absorption" machines, based on the observation, made by Sir John Leslie in 1810, that concentrated sulfuric acid, which absorbs water, could accelerate the evaporation of water in a dish to such a degree as to freeze the remaining water. This method of artificial ice production was patented in England in 1834; but it was to be less successful than another, identical in principle but using ammonia as the evaporating fluid and water as the absorbing fluid. The first important example was developed in France, by Ferdinand Carré, about 1858. In this machine a vessel containing a solution of ammonia in water was connected by a tube to a second vessel. When the former was heated and the latter cooled (by immersing it in cold water), the ammonia was evaporated from the first vessel and condensed in the second. Heating was then terminated and the ammonia allowed to reevaporate, producing a refrigerating effect on the surface of the second (ammonia-containing) chamber. Such a "machine" was no automatic refrigerator, but it was inexpensive and simple and well suited for use in isolated areas. One of them, the Crosley "Icyball," was manufactured in large numbers in the United States in the 1930's. Supplied with a handle, the dumbbell-shaped apparatus had occasionally to be set on a kerosine burner, where the "hot ball" was warmed and then moved to the "ice box," where the "cold ball" exercised its cooling effect (the hot ball being allowed to hang outside).

The machines that have been mentioned were ultimately replaced by another, simpler in principle but more difficult to construct and maintain. In this machine, called the vapor compression machine, a volatile fluid is circulated while being alternately condensed (with the evolution of heat) and evaporated (with the absorption of heat). This is the principle of the modern refrigeration machine. Oliver Evans, an ingenious American mechanic, had proposed in 1805 to use ether in such a machine, and in 1834 Jacob Perkins, an American living in London, actually built one, using a volatile "ether" obtained by distilling rubber. Perkins built only one machine, but improved versions were developed and actually manufactured from the 1850's; one of the most important was based on the patents of Alexander C. Twining of New Haven, Conn.

The earliest demand for refrigeration machines seems to have come from breweries, from the Australian meat industry, and from southern states that wanted artificial ice. Only when the operation of such machinery could be made reliably automatic could it serve the now familiar purpose of household refrigeration, a step that was successfully taken by E. J. Copeland of Detroit in 1918. Just slightly less crucial to this step was the use of less hazardous fluids than the ethers common in commercial refrigerators. Ammonia replaced the ethers in a few machines from the 1860's and became the most common refrigerating fluid by 1900. But it was only relatively less hazardous. The problem was to be solved through a research program remarkable for its basis in theoretical science. In the 1920's Thomas Midgley, Jr., with the support of the General Motors Corporation, studied the relevant characteristics (volatility, toxicity, specific heat, and so on) of a large number of substances. The result was a description of an "ideal" refrigerating fluid, and a prediction of what its chemical composition would be. Midgley then proceeded to synthesize several hitherto unknown substances that his theory indicated would possess these ideal characteristics. In 1930 he announced his success with the compound dichlorodifluoromethane. Under the commercial name Freon 12, it became the most widely used refrigerant.

The most noteworthy subsequent development in the use of refrigeration has been the introduction of frozen foods. It began in 1924 with an apparatus in which prepared fish were carried through a freezing compartment on an endless belt, developed by Clarence Birdseye of Gloucester, Mass. By 1929 Birdseye had modified the apparatus to freeze fresh fruit, and in 1934 frozen foods were introduced commercially.

[Oscar Anderson, *Refrigeration in America.*]

R. P. MULTHAUF

REFUGEE TRACT, established by the Act of Feb. 18, 1801, consisted of the fractional townships of the public domain, Ranges XVI–XXII inclusive (*see* Public Lands, Survey of), just below the U.S. Military Tract. This narrow strip of 103,527 acres extending forty-two miles eastward from the Scioto River at Columbus, Ohio, was set aside for Canadians who had aided the American cause during the Revolution and had become refugees. By various acts, 58,080 acres were granted to sixty-seven claimants, the rest of the tract being thrown open to public sale.

[W. E. Peters, *Ohio Lands and Their History.*]

EUGENE H. ROSEBOOM

REGICIDES. When the members of the High Court of Justice that condemned Charles I (Jan. 27, 1649) were exempted from amnesty at the Restoration in 1660, three of them, variously called the Colonels, the Judges, or the Regicides, escaped to New England. Lt. Gen. Edward Whalley, a cousin of Oliver Cromwell, and Maj. Gen. William Goffe, Whalley's son-in-law, arrived in Boston on July 26, 1660. After a sojourn with Maj. Daniel Gookin in nearby Cambridge, safety required them to move to New Haven in March 1661, where they were sheltered by the Rev. John Davenport and his neighbor, William Jones. In May, agents in pursuit of them were cleverly delayed and thrown off the scent by Gov. William Leete and the other magistrates. Meanwhile Whalley and Goffe made their escape and seem to have lived for some time in what is still known as the "Judges' cave" on West Rock, near New Haven, receiving succor from a nearby farmer, Richard Sperry.

From June 1661 they lived at Milford, on Long Island Sound, southwest of New Haven, with Micah, or Michael, Tomkins. As circumstances rendered their further stay dangerous, they took refuge with the Rev. John Russell at Hadley, Mass., in October 1664. Whalley appears to have died there late in 1674 or early in 1675. During King Philip's War Hadley was one of the centers of military operations, and, when attacked one day, a strange and venerable person, presumably Goffe, suddenly appeared and assumed leadership of the defenders and as promptly disappeared. Since further residence there seemed too perilous, Goffe moved to Hartford not later than September 1676, where he lived with Capt. Thomas Bull or his son, Jonathan, perhaps until his death in the latter part of 1679, although he may have spent his last days at either New Haven or Hadley.

The third regicide to seek refuge in New England

70

was John Dixwell, who had had a distinguished but less prominent career in England and whose life in New England was less romantic. He escaped to Germany in 1660 and appeared at Hadley in February 1665. The next record of him is at New Haven in 1673 under the name of James Davids. There he was twice married and lived quietly until his death on Mar. 18, 1689. His grave is still pointed out in the rear of Center Church.

During their residence in New England all three of the judges maintained correspondence with their relatives in England through the Rev. Increase Mather of Boston.

[Lemuel A. Welles, *The History of the Regicides in New England*.]

GEORGE MATTHEW DUTCHER

REGISTRATION OF VOTERS. Because of widespread election fraud in the 19th century by the use of such devices as "repeaters" and "tombstone" voters, almost every state requires that a person register in order to vote. The first voter registration law was enacted in Massachusetts in 1800, and similar laws were soon enacted in other New England states. Most large cities initiated registration laws between 1850 and 1900, but many laws were inadequate and election fraud was common. Since 1900 reform legislation has made registration laws more effective.

To register, the voter appears before county or city election officials during a set period and establishes his or her right to vote. In most states the individual must be at least eighteen years old; be an American citizen; and have lived in the state thirty days. Once the person is registered, his or her name appears on registration lists and is checked off when he or she votes. The registration lists are public documents and are available for inspection to check the qualifications of voters or for use in campaigning. Registration may be either permanent or periodic. Under permanent registration the voter's name stays on the list as long as the voter resides at the same address. In a few states a person is dropped from the list if he or she fails to vote in two successive elections. Periodic registration requires voters to reregister at certain times. This practice keeps the registration lists current but is often inconvenient for voters.

Unnecessarily restrictive registration laws have kept many persons from voting. In 1970 Congress passed a voting rights act that replaced the confusing pattern of state residency requirements with a uniform national law for presidential elections. The law also permits absentee registration and voting. The Supreme Court ruled in 1972 (*Dunn* v. *Blumstein*) that

states may not require residency of more than thirty days in federal elections. By contrast, in 1973 the Court ruled that states may have a residency requirement of fifty days for state and local elections.

The nature of voter registration and the high mobility of the American people are major factors leading to low voter-turnout. Nationwide approximately 75 percent of those eligible to vote are registered. In 1972 nearly 62 million Americans of voting age did not vote in the presidential election, and in the 1974 congressional elections there was only a 38 percent nationwide turnout. In many Western European countries the government takes the initiative in registering voters, and in some countries there are compulsory registration laws. The result is high rates of voter turnout. The U.S. Senate in 1973 passed a bill to allow all potential voters in federal elections to register by postcard, but the bill was not approved by the House of Representatives.

[Joseph P. Harris, *Model Voter Registration System*, and *Registration of Voters in the United States*.]

DAVID C. SAFFELL

REGULATING ACT. *See* **Massachusetts Government Act.**

REGULATORS, irregular armed combinations, organized in numerous southern communities after the Civil War to obstruct the welfare activities of the Freedmen's Bureau. These local self-appointed committees of vigilantes, known also as "Black-Horse Cavalry" and "Jayhawkers" in Georgia and Louisiana, generally rode at night, in disguise, employing arson, murder, and mutilation to terrorize the freedmen and prevent the exercise of their rights to make labor contracts and to migrate. The Regulators resembled the Ku Klux Klan (organized 1866) in the methods employed, but they lacked the hierarchical organization and the political aims of the Klan.

MARTIN P. CLAUSSEN

REGULATORS OF NORTH CAROLINA. A long struggle of the settlers in the 18th-century back counties of North Carolina against the oppressive administration of the laws by corrupt officials, and excessive fees charged by them and by attorneys, began in 1764 in Anson, Orange, and Granville counties. Serious disturbances led to the issuance by Gov. Arthur Dobbs of a proclamation forbidding the taking of illegal fees. This action for a time measurably allayed the discontent; not until the spring of 1768 was there any further organized resistance to the official class. The protesters then organized what they termed the "Regulation," the center being Orange County. The new governor, William Tryon, was in the western counties in July and August 1768 and assembled at Hillsboro a body of militia to suppress a threatened uprising and protect the courts. Before this show of force the Regulators wilted and agitation subsided.

The second phase of the Regulation covered the years of 1769–71. Suits brought against extortioning officials failed to afford adequate relief; consequently the movement took the form of driving local justices from the bench and threatening the officials of the courts with violence. At the September 1770 session of the superior court at Hillsboro the Regulators presented a petition to the presiding judge, Richard Henderson, demanding unprejudiced juries and a public accounting of taxes by sheriffs, and concluding, "Though there are a few men who have the gift and art of reasoning, yet every man has a feeling and knows when he has justice done him, as well as the most learned." The court had hardly convened when 150 Regulators, equipped with sticks, switches, and cudgels, crowded into the courtroom and insisted that one of their number be permitted to speak. Jeremiah Fields, in their behalf, demanded that their cases, based on extortion, be tried at that term and by jurors newly chosen. A leading lawyer, John Williams, starting into the courthouse, was given a severe thrashing. Peaceful methods cast aside, the crowd rushed upon Edmund Fanning, who was, in their eyes, their chief oppressor, and whipped him and three others. Fanning's house was looted and demolished. Judge Henderson had promised to comply with the demands the following day, but at night he mounted his horse and rode away to his home in Granville County. The following November Henderson's home, barn, and stables went up in flames.

Tryon ordered the arrest of the leaders concerned in these outbreaks. Energetic preparations were made for a military expedition to Orange County, and there resulted the Battle of Alamance (May 16, 1771) between about 1,000 militia and 2,000 Regulators, which ended in disaster for the latter. A large majority of North Carolina historians vindicate the Regulators.

[John S. Bassett, "The Regulators of North Carolina," *American Historical Association Report* (1894).]

SAMUEL C. WILLIAMS

REGULATORS OF SOUTH CAROLINA, irregular and sporadic organizations of backcountry settlers formed 1767–69 for the purpose of breaking up bands of horse thieves and their accomplices, which had established a reign of terror in the new settlements. Proceeding with efficiency but with self-restraint, they purged the country of the vicious and lawless. The lack of courts in the interior of the province, the cause of the evil, was corrected by the assembly in 1769, and the movement came to an end.

[Edward McCrady, *History of South Carolina Under the Royal Government.*]

R. L. MERIWETHER

RELIEF. The English concept of poor relief dominated the philosophy and operation of poor relief in the colonies and the United States into the 20th century. It branded a poor man as shiftless. Poverty was a disgrace.

In colonial America local governments provided relief for the needy. Under the prevailing system, called outdoor relief, individuals were farmed out to the lowest bidder or a contract was given for the care of all paupers in a local community. Indentured service was also used. Direct aid, when given, was in kind—that is, in goods or food, not cash. The able-bodied were expected to work for the aid provided. In the 18th century the continued pressure to keep relief costs low, the increase in population density, and the increase in the movement of people caused county governments to assist in the care of the needy.

Advancing industrialism combined with the economic depressions of the 1830's, 1850's, 1870's, and 1890's, plus natural disasters, convinced many state officials that the state must assume a major role in relief and public assistance; therefore, in the 19th century the number of almshouses, county poor farms, and state institutions for the insane, blind, and crippled grew. State charity boards or a state agency supervised many of these institutions directly or indirectly. Inefficiency and graft in the giving of contracts to operate county and state almshouses and institutions were fairly common, and the inmates were often cruelly treated, although conditions did improve by the early 20th century.

Private charity, usually more humane than public relief, was an important part of relief in most towns and cities, but as more and more people needed relief, the percentage receiving aid from private charities decreased. In 1928, of all relief in fifteen major cities, 71 percent was public.

The Great Depression had a tremendous impact on the philosophy behind, and the practice of, providing relief or giving public assistance. Shortly after the stock market crash of 1929, President Herbert Hoover encouraged private, local, and state relief agencies to expand their activities. He then used the resources of the federal government by establishing the President's Emergency Relief Organization and later the President's Emergency Employment Committee. The first organization stimulated relief activity, while the second stressed employment efforts to be made by private business and industry and work relief for the able-bodied.

In 1932 Congress created the Reconstruction Finance Corporation, which was authorized to lend $300 million in relief funds directly to the states. It also had funds available to finance loans to private businesses and federal, state, and local governments to initiate activities that would increase employment.

In the spring of 1933, with nearly 14 million workers unemployed, President Franklin D. Roosevelt initiated the nation's first direct federal relief program with the establishment of the Federal Emergency Relief Administration (FERA). Harry L. Hopkins, a dynamic administrator, administered the relief programs for the next four-and-a-half years. The FERA provided funds by three procedures: First, direct cash grants were made to state governments for the needy. Second, FERA distributed funds on a matching basis, forcing state governments to provide funds. (The direct grants to states became more common later, since some states lacked matching funds.) Third, funds were provided for work projects. Thus, work relief projects were common, plus cash grants or in-kind aid (food and shelter). The states administered most of the direct aid; the federal government supervised most of the work projects.

In the early fall of 1933 Roosevelt and Hopkins launched the Civil Works Administration (CWA). The federal government financed 90 percent of CWA's cost; localities financed 10 percent. The CWA spent over $900 million during the winter of 1933–34. Local officials initiated most projects. The CWA employed over 2.5 million people during much of the winter of 1933–34, and there were over 4 million on CWA rolls in early February 1934. Most CWA workers repaired roads and schools, laid sewer pipes, and built small airports. The CWA employed 50,000 schoolteachers to keep schools open.

Operating concurrently with the FERA and the CWA were the Civilian Conservation Corps (CCC) and the Public Works Administration (PWA). The CCC provided work for several hundred thousand young men, mostly from relief families. They contributed greatly to the nation's conservation and to the development of outdoor recreation facilities. The PWA provided funds, along with matching funds of local and state governments, for a great variety of construction projects, which in turn stimulated manufacturing; among the projects was the construction of many public buildings. The PWA employed several hundred thousand skilled workers, many of whom were not on relief.

The Roosevelt administration carried out a variety of programs during 1934–35. The FERA remained in existence through 1935, providing relief funds for the sick, the crippled, dependent mothers and their children, and the elderly. The Federal Surplus Relief Corporation provided means for the distribution of large amounts of surplus foods and meats to the needy. The FERA extended aid and established camps for 300,000 transients. Work relief projects were set up for women and white-collar workers, and efforts were made to upgrade the skills of workers. The FERA funded a few housing projects, and the Rural Rehabilitation Division assisted many farmers in obtaining livestock, grain, and tools.

The Social Security Act of 1935 provided for unemployment compensation for a set number of weeks; old-age assistance payments for millions of Americans aged sixty-five and over; and economic aid for the blind, the crippled, and dependent mothers and children. The act provided that these be administered by the states under the supervision of a federal Social Security board.

In 1935 the Roosevelt administration, by an act of Congress, launched the Works Progress Administration (WPA). The WPA provided work for over 5 million Americans between July 1935 and December 1938, most of whom came from the public relief rolls. Since they had a great variety of skills and backgrounds, WPA workers labored on many different kinds of projects, including construction, research, writing, and recreation facilities. The projects developed had to be suited mostly for unskilled and semiskilled workers since a higher percentage of this part of the nation's labor force was unemployed.

The hourly wage scale system, coupled with delays in projects and bad weather, often meant that WPA workers did not earn per month the basic security wage anticipated, but the WPA encouraged workers to take part-time jobs in the private sector as a means of developing skills or of making contacts that might lead to private employment on a full-time basis. But many people found the WPA a haven from private employment, since their advanced age or limited skills prevented them from successfully competing for jobs. Even so, the WPA always had a sizable turnover as people found private employment.

A popular operation within the WPA was the National Youth Administration (NYA). Providing aid on the basis of need, its major objectives were to provide funds for part-time employment of high school and college students and nonemployed school-age youths and additional apprentice-type training. NYA funds kept thousands in schools and colleges who otherwise would have been on direct-relief rolls. Less popular, but of significant social, cultural, and historical value, were the arts and writers projects of the WPA.

Federal relief programs in the 1930's cost the nation over $11 billion; however, the preservation of faith in democracy, skills maintained or improved for individuals, and the maintenance of national morale may have had value considerably beyond that amount. There was on occasion favoritism in the selection of projects, but there was little actual graft or corruption.

In the post–World War II era the federal and state governments continued to assume the major financial and program role in areas of unemployment insurance and categorical assistance for the blind, aged, crippled, deaf, mentally disturbed, and mothers with dependent children. Local and state governments assumed most of the responsibility for relief for the temporarily unemployed needy not provided for by federal-state programs.

Principal changes and advancements in public assistance beginning in 1950 include aid to the permanently and totally disabled (1950); federal financial participation in vendor payments for medical care (1950); medical assistance for the aged (1960); extension of aid to families of dependent children (AFDC) to include, at the option of the state, children of the unemployed (1961); increased federal sharing in the cost of providing social services and establishing improved programs of rehabilitation, self-support, and self-care (1962); replacement of medical assistance for the aged by a broader program of medical assistance, permitting states to extend medical aid to the medically needy (1965); work-study grants for needy college students (1965); emphasis on work by the able-bodied as a component in public assistance by the inclusion of mothers as eligible for training and education for employment (1965); and the provision of work experience and training programs for employable adults (1965 and 1967). The last two programs have necessitated the establishment of day-care centers.

By 1969 these programs and others were providing aid to more than 10.2 million persons at an annual cost in excess of $10.6 billion in federal and state funds. Costs continued to increase into the 1970's, in part because of inflation but also because the number of AFDC recipients continued to increase. Desertion of families by husbands and fathers has contributed significantly to the increase in costs. In addition, court interpretation of federal and state acts, plus a continued emphasis on humaneness in the provision of relief, increased the number of persons eligible for aid through categorical public assistance programs.

One of the important developments in public assistance in the 1960's was the Neighborhood Legal Service, established in 1965. Legal aids assisted many thousands of families in securing public assistance for which they were eligible and in securing court decisions favorable to the needy (such as the elimination of durational residence as a requirement for the receipt of public assistance).

In the 1970's the system was still plagued by a significant variation in the level of aid from state to state, by state-imposed eligibility rules, by meager financing in some states, and by exclusion of the working poor from some federally aided programs. President Richard M. Nixon in 1969 suggested a family-assistance program to replace the AFDC, by which each family in need would have been guaranteed a basic annual income. The reason for the need of assistance was not to be a factor, only low income as identified below a specific level; therefore, the number of families and children receiving aid would have been increased. Incentive to work was to be encouraged, and the able-bodied were to be required to work or to educate themselves for work and then seek it. Categorical assistance programs for such persons as the blind were to be continued. By the mid-1970's Congress had failed to enact legislation based on such an approach. Even if a guaranteed-income system were enacted and implemented, the welfare agencies in the states would continue to have responsibility for providing social services; some public assistance would be needed from local government; and federal-state categorical assistance would continue.

[Arthur J. Altmeyer, *The Formative Years of Social Security;* Jules H. Berman, ''Public Assistance,'' *Encyclopedia of Social Work,* vol. II; Josephine C. Brown, *Public Relief, 1929–1939;* Eveline M. Burns, *Social Security and Public Policy;* Harry L. Hopkins, *Spending to Save: The Complete Story of Relief;* Donald S. Howard, *The WPA and Federal Relief Policy;* A. W. Macmahon, J. D. Millett, and Gladys Ogden, *The Administration of*

Federal Work Relief; President's Commission on Income Maintenance Programs, *Poverty and Plenty—The American Paradox;* Edward A. Williams, *Federal Aid for Relief.*]

SEARLE F. CHARLES

RELIEF ACT OF 1821. Between 1806 and 1820 fully a dozen acts were passed granting extensions of time to settlers who either could not or deliberately did not complete the payments on public land purchased by them under the credit system laid down in the Harrison Land Act of 1800. When the credit system was abolished by the Land Act of 1820, delinquent land purchasers owed the government more than $21 million. In order to aid settlers in completing their payments, Congress passed another relief act, dated Mar. 2, 1821, remitting accrued interest, offering a liberal discount for prompt payment, granting a further extension of time, and permitting purchasers to cancel their debt by relinquishing a portion of their land.

[Benjamin H. Hibbard, *A History of the Public Land Policies.*]

DAN E. CLARK

RELIGION. When Europeans arrived in America, they hoped to reestablish the patterns of ecclesiastical life that had sustained them in the Old World. They envisioned the new land in terms of the traditional parish system, in which a settled minister represented both civil and religious order. Changing patterns of territorial ownership, Old World religious controversies, and the vastness of the country conspired to defeat these initial attempts to recreate European Christendom.

Two groups, the Anglicans in Virginia and the Puritans in New England, are examples of the effects of the new situation on the older pattern of organization.

The Anglicans hoped to establish the church in Virginia as it existed in England. Under the authority of the bishop of London, the colony was divided into parishes and laws were passed to secure religious and moral order. But almost as soon as the colony was founded, the settlers began to devise their own pattern of church life. By means of the vestry system, the leading laymen were able to control both the tenure and the salary of the local clergy. In addition, the young church did not always attract the best clergymen, and it was further depressed by frequent salary disputes. With regularity these disputes were settled in favor of the laity.

The commissaries sent by the bishop of London were charged with improving the standard both of the ministry and of ecclesiastical discipline. Thomas Bray, appointed in 1696, established the Society for the Promotion of Christian Knowledge (SPCK) and the Society for the Propagation of the Gospel (SPG) to accomplish these ends by supplying funds and libraries. The SPG was unable to avoid denominational quarrels and was often accused of being as concerned with the conversion of Puritans as with the conversion of sinners.

The Glorious Revolution in England (1688) resulted in a number of new Anglican establishments: Maryland (1702), South Carolina (1706), and North Carolina (1715). The establishment in New York, erected under the Ministries Act of 1693, provided for an orthodox clergyman in each parish but did not specify denomination. While these new establishments strengthened Anglicanism on paper, the church prospered to a greater degree in New England, where it was not supported by law. Sparked by the defection of Timothy Cutler, another tutor at Yale, and three neighboring ministers in 1722, the New England Anglicans assumed a High Church posture.

Although challenged by dissent in those areas where it was established—especially Virginia, where the more evangelical Presbyterians and Baptists were advancing—American Anglicanism was maturing. When disestablishment came after the American Revolution, the Broad Church tradition of the South combined with the High Church tradition of New England to produce a church that was democratic in its government and yet preserved the values of an episcopal organization.

The New England Puritans, with the exception of the Plymouth settlers, were nonseparating Congregationalists who hoped to reform, but not replace, traditional ecclesiastical structures. Their basic theological position was derived from the Reformed (Calvinist) tradition as interpreted by a succession of pastor-theologians centered at the University of Cambridge. It stressed the importance of Scripture for all areas of human life.

Although the Puritans had been reformers in England, their understanding of the church was partially the product of their American experience, and by the time of the Cambridge Platform (1648) the basic outline of Congregationalism had been established. The local parishes were independent congregations that owed cooperation to each other. Each member of a church was to have had an experience of conversion, which he would relate to the congregation as a

RELIGION

whole. Although such visible saints were the core of the Holy Commonwealth that the Puritans hoped to establish, all the residents of the area were expected to attend services and live Christian lives.

Three significant concepts sustained the New England way. First, the Puritans believed that God's election was manifest in a subjective religious experience; much of their theology was a careful delineation of the stages of conversion. Second, the Puritans believed that it was God's usual way to covenant with men, making an agreement in which each side accepted certain conditions. In Puritan theory a covenant was the basis of salvation, the church, and the community. The divines used this doctrine in a characteristic form of preaching, the jeremiad, which cataloged New England's sins and proposed repentance as the cure for the evils that had befallen the people. Third, the divines were fascinated by the predictions of the Revelation, especially the millennium. Their vision of the future gradually became more this-worldly and is one of the sources of American patriotism.

The history of religion in colonial New England was turbulent. Puritanism generated dissent, and the problem of religious diversity was the center of many disputes. In the first generation, Anne Hutchinson shocked the Massachusetts Bay Colony with her emphasis on the indwelling of the Holy Spirit and was banished. Roger Williams, perhaps the region's greatest heretic, challenged the union of church and state on biblical grounds and, following his expulsion from Massachusetts, went to Rhode Island, where he founded a colony based on complete religious toleration. He was also instrumental in gathering the First Baptist Church in Providence, but he quickly changed his position and became a Seeker. Other disputes stayed within Congregational orthodoxy and included controversies over baptism in the 1660's, over the charter in the 1690's, and over the infamous Salem witch trials of the same decade.

The pattern of religious development in the Middle Colonies was different from that of either New England or the South. From its beginnings the region experienced the religious diversity that was to become the national norm. Pennsylvania is an example of this pattern. It was established by William Penn as a colony of refuge for the Society of Friends, and the proprietor encouraged immigration by any group that desired to come. His active recruitment policies attracted many German groups. The Mennonites, followers of the 16th-century religious reformer Menno Simons, established themselves in the southern part of the colony. Other German groups also came: the Church of the Brethren, a radical pietist sect founded by Alexander Mack, and the Moravian Brethren, who had been reconstituted by Count Nikolaus Ludwig von Zinzendorf at his estate in Saxony.

Lutheran and Presbyterian churches were first organized in America in the Middle Colonies. Although both had been established in Europe, they had to learn to exist as denominations in the New World. Henry Melchior Mühlenberg, who arrived in 1742, helped the Lutherans to make this adjustment. After a struggle with Zinzendorf, who wanted the church to be assimilated by the Moravians, he guided the church in its formation of synodal government and church discipline.

The history of colonial Presbyterianism was complicated by the fact that two streams fed the young church: a New England tradition that was influenced by Puritanism and a Scotch-Irish tradition that was more confessional in its beliefs. The two parties struggled throughout the colonial period for control. The church split in 1741 over the issue of evangelism, and although it was reunited in 1758, the tension between the two parties was a continuing problem.

The Great Awakening, an explosion of the revivalist impulse, was not confined to any particular denomination or region. It is impossible to date its origins, but clearly the revivals of Theodore J. Frelinghuysen in the 1720's in New Jersey and Solomon Stoddard in the late 17th century in Massachusetts set the pattern. Frelinghuysen's work inspired the graduates of William Tennent's Log College (1726–42), who led a revival of major proportions in New Jersey. Jonathan Edwards, Stoddard's grandson and successor in Northampton, Mass., led his congregation in a revival in 1732–33. This revival spread to most of the towns of the Connecticut Valley.

These early revivals were dying down when George Whitefield reignited the country during his first evangelistic tour (1739–42). Whitefield, an Anglican clergyman, preached an emotionally charged version of Calvinism that stressed the imminence of death and judgment. A man of tremendous charisma, he is said to have been able to bring tears to an audience simply by pronouncing the word "Mesopotamia."

The religious experience characteristic of the revival was a deep awareness of sin, followed by a personal sense of the forgiving presence of God. The emotionalism of the revival raised theological questions that were discussed by both clergy and laity.

One such debate between the revivalist Edwards and his rationalist opponent Charles Chauncy is a classic of American theology. For Chauncy, the revival was a purely natural work that played on human weaknesses; it not only deprived men of their reason, he thought, but made them overly censorious of others. By contrast, Edwards maintained that the revival was a manifestation of the Spirit of God that would in time lead to the Kingdom of Heaven. Although he condemned the excesses of the revival, he argued that emotions are a necessary part of any religion based on love.

The Great Awakening influenced the development of the nation in a variety of ways. It brought the colonists together as no earlier event had done and created a feeling of intercolonial solidarity. Its radical emphasis on the individual and the sanctity of his own experience contributed to the emerging sense of democracy that was to sustain the Revolution.

The crisis of the Revolution led American religion to reorganize itself along denominational lines similar to those in colonial Pennsylvania, as the various Christian churches competed with one another for membership and prestige. Although the last vestige of establishment was not removed until 1833, when Massachusetts disestablished Congregationalism, the denominational system was fully operative by 1800. The Revolution increased the visibility of rational religion and revealed a lack of vitality in the churches. To many, it seemed that the country might become de-Christianized or, at a minimum, that the western areas might be lost to Protestantism. The response to this crisis was twofold: a return to the revivalist tradition of the Awakening and the formation of interdenominational voluntary societies to work for moral and social betterment.

The second Great Awakening in the East was a relatively mild renewal movement. Led by such moderates as Lyman Beecher, Ashahel Nettleton, and Timothy Dwight, it brought men to a warm faith without the excesses of the earlier movement. The western clergyman Charles G. Finney, who was the first great urban revivalist, introduced an element of the older enthusiasm in the 1820's. According to Finney's reinterpretation of revivalism, revivals operated in accord with philosophical or psychological laws; consequently, one had only to find the right technique to convert the world. His own program, "the new measures," included the protracted meeting; unseasonable hours, or hours at which service was not ordinarily held; harsh language; the anxious bench; and prayer for particular individuals.

The revivals in the West were more dynamic. Based on the camp meeting, a gathering of people who camped out during a series of services usually lasting several days, the typical western revival was marked by extreme emotionalism, including such phenomena as the jerks, holy laughter and dancing, and barking. The revival at Cane Ridge, Ky., in August 1801 attracted a crowd of between 10,000 and 25,000 people.

Western revivalism generated a number of peculiarly American denominations. Western New York, known as the "burned over district" because of its revivalistic fervor, produced two influential movements. The Latter-Day Saints (Mormons) were organized by Joseph Smith on the basis of a revelation that combined many evangelical elements with a belief in the special place of America in God's plan. Adventism, which survives in a number of denominations, was a response to the failure of the prophecies of William Miller, who taught that the world would end in 1843. Farther south the western revival generated an interest in restorationism, or the belief that the apostolic pattern of Christianity could be recreated. The Christian Churches, or Disciples of Christ, which had their origins in the preaching of Alexander Campbell and Barton W. Stone, institutionalized this thrust.

Although Methodism had been founded by John Wesley in England, its American form was ideally suited to frontier conditions. Based on the circuit rider or traveling preacher, Methodism spread a revivalist theology that stressed the possibility of a holy life—entire sanctification or holiness—and each man's responsibility before God. Growing rapidly, it was the largest Protestant denomination by 1850.

The voluntary societies were the second response to the postrevolutionary crisis of faith. Often called the righteous empire, various societies sought to reform morals, to raise money for domestic and foreign missions, to work with the urban poor, to end or modify slavery, and to distribute Bibles and tracts. The societies were interdenominational in membership. Although much of their leadership was provided by the Presbyterian and Congregational clergy, the role of women in these societies cannot be overlooked. Many women received their first experience outside the home as workers in the societies, and their participation was a major step toward their emancipation. It was a setback for American ecumenism when the denominations asserted their authority in many of the spheres that had been served by the societies, especially foreign and domestic missions.

Although revivalism was the most influential element in early 19th-century religion in the United States, it was not unopposed. On the religious left, the Unitarians broke away from Congregationalism to advocate a theology based on the Enlightenment. In 1819 William Ellery Channing preached Unitarian Christianity, which set forth the principles of the movement: an emphasis on the unity of God; a belief in the revelation by Christ, but not in His divinity; and a denial of the doctrines of limited atonement and election. Unitarianism could not maintain even such a limited creed and—to the horror of its conservative members—generated its own radicals: the transcendentalists. Heavily influenced by German idealism, Eastern mysticism, and Puritan individualism, Ralph Waldo Emerson, Theodore Parker, and others of their conviction stressed man's immediate relationship to the divine force in the world and man's duty to humanity.

From the right, the Mercersberg theologians John W. Nevin and Philip Schaff used German idealism to defend the confessions against revivalist erosion. A stricter confessional movement, led by Charles Hodge of Princeton Seminary, sought to return Presbyterianism to the Westminster Standard of 1646, the most widely accepted summary of Presbyterian doctrine in English-speaking countries. This theology, which drew heavily on Scottish common-sense philosophy, legitimized Presbyterian withdrawal from the voluntary societies and was a source of later fundamentalism.

Episcopalianism benefited from the Oxford movement in England throughout the 19th century. Centered in New York, where Bishop John Henry Hobart had founded General Theological Seminary, the new movement generated dissent within the church, causing some priests to defect to Roman Catholicism.

The most effective critic of revivalism, Horace Bushnell, was a product of evangelical Christianity. As pastor of a Congregational church in Hartford, Conn., he realized that the evangelical tradition was not meeting the needs of his upper-class congregation. Using categories derived from European romanticism, he argued in *Christian Nurture* (1847) that Christian faith develops within an individual parallel to the development of the whole personality and that it is thus possible for some men never to need an experience of conversion. He acted as a mediating theologian, and his idea of the role of religious sensitivity as the foundation of doctrine had an important influence on later liberalism.

Immigration was the central event in 19th-century American social history, and it had begun to reshape American religious life before the Civil War. Succes-

sive waves of Irish, German, and Scandinavian immigrants in the early part of the century gave way to immigration from southern and eastern Europe as the century progressed. By 1850 immigration had made the Roman Catholic church the largest single religious body in America. Immigration changed the direction of American Lutheranism. Many immigrants formed their own synods, and their confessional heritage contributed to the weaning of Lutheranism from its earlier participation in the Evangelical consensus.

The Civil War marked a turning point in American religious history. Before the conflict the churches were divided over the issue of slavery. Many northern Evangelicals, such as Theodore D. Weld, preached against slavery as part of the Protestant crusade, and southern churchmen often took the lead in building up the proslavery sentiment of that region. As a consequence, many denominations split before the war, notably the Baptists and Methodists (1844–45). After the war the religious development of the two regions followed separate paths.

Even before the war American blacks had been forming their religious tradition. Starting from Evangelical Protestantism, they transformed that tradition into a witness for human freedom. After the war they organized their own churches, free from white domination, and continued the development of their own religious practices. The black churches, while often nonpolitical, have been important in maintaining black solidarity and hope.

After the Civil War the churches were confronted with the questions raised by modern scientific, evolutionary, and historical thinking. While many Americans continued to think in the older Evangelical pattern, other Christians sought new expressions of Christian faith. Notable leaders in the rise of this new liberalism were biblical scholar Charles A. Briggs, preacher Phillips Brooks, and theologian William Newton Clarke.

The social problems of the new age necessitated a rethinking of Christian social ethics. Building on the older evangelicalism and the new liberalism, the Social Gospel was recovered. Although Congregational pastor Washington Gladden is considered the father of the movement, its most powerful advocate was Walter Rauschenbusch. His books *Christianity and the Social Crisis* (1907), *Christianizing the Social Order* (1912), and *A Theology for the Social Gospel* (1917) had an abiding influence among northern Baptists, Methodists, and Presbyterians.

The opponents of the new thought consolidated their position around the turn of the century. Finding inspiration in the dispensational premillennialism taught by the Plymouth Brethren, they saw history as a succession of periods leading to the end of the age. Cyrus Ingerson Scofield elaborated this position in the notes to his *Scofield Reference Bible,* a best-seller since its publication in 1909. Fundamentalists frequently combined this perspective with the Princeton theology to produce a new version of Evangelical Christianity.

The publication of the Fundamentals (1910–13), a series of conservative tracts, heralded the beginning of the fundamentalist-modernist controversy, which was to grow in intensity after a hiatus provided by World War I. The fundamentalists, supported by such traveling evangelists as Billy (William Ashley) Sunday hoped to expel the liberals from their positions of influence in seminaries and denominational hierarchies. The controversy faded into the background with the advent of the Great Depression, but it remained an undercurrent in Protestant life. In the 1970's fundamentalist churches, separated from the major denominations, were the fastest-growing segment of American Protestantism.

The late 19th and early 20th centuries saw an increase in the number of Jews in the United States. The earliest American Jews had been Sephardic (Spanish and Portuguese); these later immigrants were either Ashkenazic (German) or eastern European. American Judaism has been a dynamic movement in its Reformed, Conservative, and Orthodox branches and has established a religious community second only to that in Israel (*see* Judaism).

World War I was preached as a crusade by almost all American religious groups. The churches were so sure of the righteousness of the American position that there was little criticism of the government or its policies. Although this tended to strengthen the churches in the short run, it raised serious questions for them in the 1930's, when the ambiguities of America's participation in the struggle became common knowledge. Many clergy and laity believed that the government had manipulated them into unqualified support of an unjust war.

The period between the Civil War and the Great Depression was also characterized by the formation of small religious movements called sects or cults. While some of these were merely modifications of evangelicalism, others attempted a synthesis of modern philosophy and faith. The most successful of these has been Christian Science, founded by Mary Baker Eddy, whose *Science and Health With a Key to the Scriptures* (1875) has been widely read.

The most significant religious movement since World War I has been the quest for Christian unity.

As the churches became aware of the futility of competition and of the changing nature of modern theological questions, many sought to promote cooperation. The first institutional expression of this search was the Federal Council of Churches of Christ (1908), which coordinated church work in World War I and World War II and led the churches' involvement in social questions. It was succeeded in 1950 by the National Council of Churches, which includes interdenominational agencies for missions and education.

The search for unity also found expression in the merger of many denominations. The United Lutheran Church was formed in 1918 and the American Lutheran Church in 1930; the Methodists ended their North-South schism in 1939. On a more adventuresome level, the Congregational Christian and the Evangelical and Reformed churches, both the product of earlier mergers, joined in 1957 to form the United Church of Christ. The Consultation on Church Unity (COCU), convened in 1962, attempted to unite nine major denominations. Talks continued in the 1970's, although not as hopefully as in the 1960's.

The most important ecumenical event in the 20th century was the rapprochement between Protestantism and Catholicism begun by Pope John XXIII's calling of the Ecumenical Council. Although a union of the two Christian camps remained distant, a new atmosphere of cooperation and trust largely replaced the long-standing polemics on both sides.

The period after World War I saw a renewal of Reformation theology in both Europe and America. Influenced by such European thinkers as Karl Barth, Emil Brunner, and the early Rudolf Bultmann, American theologians recovered many insights lost in the 19th century. The most creative theologian of this movement was H. Richard Niebuhr, who was able to blend the best of European thought with native elements. The new theology also led to a rethinking—but not a repudiation—of the Social Gospel. Reinhold Niebuhr, his brother, set a new trend in American social ethics by focusing on limitations he felt to be imposed by the radical evil within man.

In the late 1950's the theological consensus associated with neo-orthodoxy began to disintegrate. The problems of modernity that provoked the earlier liberal movement reemerged as catalysts for new directions. Some theologians, turning to the thought of Paul Tillich and the later Rudolf Bultmann, sought to use existentialism to find nonmythological ways of speaking about God. Others, notably Daniel Day Williams, found Alfred North Whitehead's process philosophy congenial in their struggle with the problem of the relationship between science and religion.

RELIGIOUS LIBERTY

The decade of the 1960's saw a continuation of this basic questioning as some theologians wondered if theistic doctrines were not themselves antiquated.

The decade of the 1960's also saw American Christians struggling with a host of social questions. The problem of racial discrimination was the subject of long debate as believers sought to understand their role in the civil rights movement. Such social struggles had theological, as well as practical, implications, and theologians began to appreciate the depth of insight present among minority groups. The war in Vietnam also provoked theological and institutional controversy.

Despite a superficial religious revival in the 1950's, religion steadily lost influence in the United States after World War I. The reasons for this decline are by no means self-evident, but some tentative suggestions may be made. Sociologically, changing patterns of American life, especially increased mobility and leisure, weakened traditional loyalties. The participation of the churches in public questions also alienated many: the Left felt that the churches were too slow to act, while the Right resented the direction the churches took. In addition, the rise of the so-called "civil religion," an amorphous blend of American religiosity and patriotism, displaced traditional religion for some. Although the churches attempted to find new religious forms, the future seemed to hold less of a place for organized religion than the past.

[Sidney Ahlstrom, *A Religious History of the American People;* Winthrop S. Hudson, *Religion in America;* Sidney Mead, *The Lively Experiment: The Shaping of Christianity in America;* H. Shelton Smith, Robert T. Handy, and Lefferts A. Loetscher, *American Christianity: An Historical Interpretation With Representative Documents.*]

GLENN T. MILLER

RELIGIOUS LIBERTY is perhaps the greatest contribution America has made both in the realm of politics and of religion. At the time of the establishment of the American colonies there was no country in Europe without a state church, and everywhere, with the possible exception of Holland, unity of religion was considered essential to the unity of the state. There is a mistaken notion, widely held, that the Reformation more or less automatically brought about religious liberty, but nothing is farther from the truth. The Reformation resulted in the establishment of numerous national churches, as in England, Scotland, Holland, and the Scandinavian countries, which were as intolerant of Roman Catholicism and the small dissenting sects as Roman Catholicism was intolerant of them.

Besides the national churches that arose out of the religious and political upheaval of the Reformation, there also developed numerous small sects, generally poor and despised, most of them taking as their pattern the primitive church of the first three centuries. These small minority bodies generally stood for the separation of church and state and for complete religious liberty. It is an important fact to bear in mind that religious liberty and the separation of church and state have been principally advocated by the small minority sects and never by the great state churches. The English Baptists, a small despised sect, took over the principles of the Anabaptists of the continent and held to religious liberty as their first and greatest principle. The Quakers also became the advocates of freedom of conscience. Another source of the principle of religious liberty is found in the work of such 16th- and 17th-century political philosophers as Sir Thomas More, who pictured in his ideal state one where there was complete religious liberty, and John Locke, who wrote an important series of essays on religious toleration.

The American colonies became the first place in the world where complete religious liberty was actually tried in a political state. Roger Williams, the founder of Rhode Island, had become thoroughly imbued with this idea, and when he established Rhode Island the principle was there put into operation. Another factor that made the American colonies a fruitful place for the growth of this principle was the fact that a majority of the colonies were begun as proprietary grants, where the governments as well as the land were controlled by the same person or groups of persons. This meant that, in order to attract settlers to buy and settle the land, persecuted religious groups from almost every country in western Europe were invited to come to these colonies. Thus, William Penn; Cecilius Calvert, Lord Baltimore; and the proprietors of the Carolinas and Georgia welcomed the persecuted sectaries. Still another factor creating an environment in America favorable to religious liberty was the fact that, by the end of the colonial period, a great majority of the population throughout the colonies was unchurched, and unchurched people generally are opposed to granting special privileges to any one religious body. It is an interesting and significant fact that the political leaders who led in the movement to separate church and state with the establishment of independence, such as James Madison and Thomas Jefferson, were nonchurch members. Of all the colonial religious bodies the Baptists were the most tenacious in their advocacy of religious liberty and as a whole made the largest contribution toward its achievement.

In the colonies south of Pennsylvania the Anglican church was established by law, but only in Maryland and Virginia was it a factor of significance. In Massachusetts, Connecticut, and New Hampshire the Congregational church was the privileged body, but by the end of the colonial period the factors noted above had considerably relaxed control. The great colonial awakenings had strengthened the dissenting bodies especially in the middle and southern colonies and the coming of the Revolution gave them an opportunity to bargain for greater privileges.

Although there were no direct religious issues involved in the revolutionary war, the disturbed political and social situation that it created, together with the necessity for the formation of new governments, gave opportunity for the new principle, religious liberty, to be incorporated in the new constitutions as they were adopted. Thus, the new state and federal constitutions simply took over, in this respect, what already was to a large degree in practical operation.

[Sanford H. Cobb, *Rise of Religious Liberty in America;* M. L. Greene, *The Development of Religious Liberty in Connecticut;* E. F. Humphrey, *Nationalism and Religion in America;* H. R. McIlwaine, *Struggle of the Protestant Dissenters for Religous Toleration in Virginia.*]

WILLIAM W. SWEET

RELIGIOUS THOUGHT AND WRITINGS. Most American theologians in the colonial period were influenced by the Reformed (Calvinist) tradition as it had been interpreted by a succession of pastor-theologians connected with the University of Cambridge. It was a practical theology, emphasizing religious experience and Scripture, that was expressed in sermons, spiritual autobiographies, and tracts. Although Samuel Willard attempted a systematic exposition of the faith in his *Compleat Body of Divinity* (1726), Cotton Mather was America's first great theological mind. In works dealing with church history (*Magnalia Christi Americana*, 1702), ethics (*Bonifacius,* or *Essays to Do Good,* 1710), and science (*The Christian Philosopher,* 1721), he sought to show the harmony between traditional faith and the emerging Enlightenment.

Jonathan Edwards, working from an idealist philosophical stance, attempted to justify the Evangelical Calvinism of the Great Awakening with categories drawn from John Locke. In *A Treatise Concerning Religious Affections* (1746), perhaps his greatest work, he maintained that since emotion was the root of human action, religious emotions were the building blocks of a faith that sought to express itself in love. On a more speculative level, he attempted to refute the "rational religion," or Arminianism, that was threatening Calvinism, by showing that its presuppositions logically led to the orthodox position. He set forth these views in *Freedom of the Will* (1754), *The Great Christian Doctrine of Original Sin Defended* (1758), and *The Nature of True Virtue* (1765). In some of his later works and his unpublished notes, Edwards also set forth a vision of being that has inspired theologians down through the years.

Edwards' thought inspired America's first theological school, the New England theology, which was to dominate American religious thought for almost a century. As in the case of many schools, each member developed a characteristic element of the master's thought without any of the successors grasping the whole. Samuel Hopkins stressed the concept of disinterested benevolence derived from *True Virtue;* Nathanael Emmons, the divine sovereignty; Jonathan Edwards, Jr., the doctrine of atonement and original sin; and Timothy Dwight, the revivalist and practical elements. Edwardseanism gradually decayed into a morass of pietism and moralism, and by the time Nathaniel W. Taylor redefined the doctrine of original sin in his *Concio ad Clerum* ("Advice to the Clergy"), the rigor of its Calvinist base was gone. It survived for a while at Andover Seminary under Edwards Amasa Park, but its heart was gone.

The second Great Awakening, although influenced by late Edwardseanism, did not produce a theological harvest comparable to that of the earlier revival. Charles G. Finney, the first great urban evangelist, illustrates the direction theology was taking. In his *Lectures on Revivals of Religion* (1835), he argued that conversion should be understood in philosophical or psychological terms and, thus, that it could be produced by the use of the right means or measures. His *Lectures on Systematic Theology* (1846–47) stressed the power of man to cooperate with the divine will, the religious value of democracy, and the possibility of avoiding willful sin (perfectionism).

Two reactions against the dominant revivalist theology of the 19th century should be noted. Unitarianism, which initially drew its inspiration from the Enlightenment, gradually broadened into transcendentalism. Ralph Waldo Emerson, blending themes drawn from Puritanism and European romanticism, challenged the young clergymen of Harvard in his "Divinity School Address" (1838) to experience the divine within nature and themselves. Theodore Parker exposed the full radicalism of the movement in his sermon "The Transient and Permanent in Christianity" (1841), in which he denied the supernatural and urged Christians to move beyond Christ and stand for the truths He had taught. Christianity is not true because Jesus taught it, but rather Jesus taught it because it is true. Parker was also one of the men who first introduced German biblical criticism into America, especially the Old Testament studies of Wilhelm M. L. De Wette.

The response of Horace Bushnell was more moderate. In *Christian Nurture* (1847), he argued that the error of revivalism was in its demand that every man pass through a violent conversion experience. He asserted that such conversions are unusual, since the faith of the average man develops along with the other aspects of his personality and that there are, consequently, faiths appropriate to childhood, adolescence, and adulthood. Bushnell was deeply concerned with the controversies that periodically swept New England, and he sought to develop a method, Christian comprehension, that could mediate between conflicting perceptions of the truth. In *God and Christ* (1849) he put forth a theory of language that stressed its symbolic nature and suggested that many religious disputes were the product of a confusion of the levels of discourse—that both the Unitarians and the Congregationalists had erred by attempting to translate indirect language about Christ into scientific propositions about His nature. In *Nature and the Supernatural* (1858) he attempted to resolve the controversy between the transcendentalists and the orthodox by suggesting that God's transcendence was best understood by means of an analogy with man's natural transcendence over his environment.

Although the Mercersberg theologians Philip Schaff—later to be prominent as a church historian—and John W. Nevin articulated an orthodox theology based on romantic motifs, the more stringent conservatism of Charles Hodge was more influential. Despite his boast that "a new idea never originated in this [Princeton] seminary," his *Systematic Theology* (1871–75) was based as much on the Scottish Enlightenment as it was on the Reformed tradition. Princeton conservatism, as his school was called, contributed to Presbyterian resistance to interdenominational cooperation and was one of the sources of later fundamentalism.

During the post–Civil War period theologians and pastors began to struggle with the issues raised by modern science and historical criticism. George A. Gordon, Theodore T. Munger, and Newman Smyth, pastor-theologians, adapted Bushnell's insights to the problems of modern life, especially the question of evolution, and were able to aid many in reconciling science and religion. William Newton Clarke, a Baptist professor at Colgate Seminary, built both on their work and on the work of German theologians in his *Outline of Christian Theology* (1898), which was the first comprehensive statement of American liberalism. Clarke based his position on research into the teachings of the historical Jesus and on religious experience. Borden P. Bowne, a professor at Boston University, attempted to provide the new theology with a sound philosophical base with his doctrine of personalism. According to Bowne, human personality is the generator of all categories of thought and life, and religious experience is the root of personality.

Industrialization raised theological, as well as practical, questions for American theologians. Although many of the themes of the Social Gospel movement had appeared earlier, the movement did not become influential until the publication of *The Christian Way* by Washington Gladden in 1877. Basically the Social Gospel stressed the need for a Christian business ethic to replace laissez-faire capitalism, a concern for justice instead of subsistence charity, and the social element in both sin and salvation. Theologically, its program emphasized the Kingdom of God as the distinguishing mark of Christianity. Although many men contributed to the Social Gospel, including theologian Shailer Mathews, economist Richard T. Ely, and preacher Newman Smyth, its greatest proponent was Walter Rauschenbusch. In his major works, *Christianity and the Social Crisis* (1907) and *A Theology for the Social Gospel* (1917), he argued for a realistic understanding of social evil in contrast to the sentimental view of many of his co-workers.

These new directions evoked a conservative reaction. Benjamin B. Warfield published a series of articles critical of the new theology in the *Presbyterian and Reformed Review,* which he edited from 1890 to 1903. J. Gresham Machen was the most militant defender of the old orthodoxy. In his *Christianity and Liberalism* (1923) and *The Virgin Birth of Christ* (1930) he charged the liberals with teaching a new religion. These heirs of Princeton orthodoxy were joined on the right by the premillennial dispensationists, who interpreted the Bible as the account of a series of epochs or dispensations leading up to the imminent end of the world. The *Scofield Reference Bible* (1909), annotated by Cyrus I. Scofield, has been the most popular vehicle of this new conservatism.

The period following the Great Depression saw a general repudiation of the most optimistic aspects of liberalism. American theologians, taking a lead from such European thinkers as Karl Barth, Emil Brunner, and the early Rudolf Bultmann, turned to existentialism and the Reformation for guidance. Two brothers, Reinhold and H. Richard Niebuhr, were the most sophisticated theologians of this movement, called realism or neo-orthodoxy. H. Richard Niebuhr began his career as a student of Douglas Clyde MacIntosh, a Yale liberal, whose influence is present in Niebuhr's first major work, *The Social Sources of Denominationalism* (1929). His movement beyond this early liberalism is evident in his great theological history, *The Kingdom of God in America* (1937), in which he argued that the doctrine of the divine sovereignty is at the heart of American theology. His mature views are most characteristically expressed in *The Meaning of Revelation* (1941), which maintained that the church could find itself only as a confessing community. Significantly, his last major work, *Radical Monotheism in Western Culture* (1960), was the signal for the beginning of the new theology of the 1960's.

In contrast to his brother's theoretical approach, Reinhold Niebuhr directed his attention to a revision of the Social Gospel. In *Moral Man and Immoral Society* (1932), he maintained that while individuals are capable of moral development, such collective entities as nations, corporations, and labor unions are incapable of altruistic conduct. He developed his anthropology more completely in *The Nature and Destiny of Man* (1941–43), which stressed the depths of human sinfulness on both individual and corporate levels.

Neo-orthodoxy was not unopposed, and many liberals continued to develop their own paradigms. Henry Nelson Wieman, a religious naturalist at the University of Chicago, developed his own distinctive position based on his understanding of the good. His best-known works are *Religious Experience and Scientific Method* (1926), *Methods of Religious Living* (1929), and the *Source of Human Good* (1949).

The neo-orthodox consensus began to weaken in the late 1950's when the questions raised by the older liberalism reoccupied center stage. In many ways, Gabriel Vahanian's *Death of God: The Culture of Our Post-Christian Era* (1961) set the stage for a decade of debate. His emphasis on the question of culture was prophetic, as the central problems of the 1960's turned out to be as much social as intellectual. Despite the optimism of such neo–Social Gospel works as Harvey Cox's *Secular City* (1965), theologians seemed unable to find either traditional or innovative ways to deal with a mounting sense of social crisis. The minor gains made by a reevaluation of the religious experience of minority groups by such men as James H. Cone did little to improve the situation. Despite the vigor of theological debate, theologians entered the 1970's with the sense that little had been accomplished.

[Sidney Ahlstrom, *Theology in America: The Major Protestant Voices From Puritanism to Neo-Orthodoxy;* Lloyd James Averill, *American Theology in the Liberal Tradition;* Barbara M. Cross, *Horace Bushnell: Minister to a Changing America;* Frank Hugh Foster, *A Genetic History of the New England Theology;* Daniel Day Williams, *What Present-Day Theologians Are Thinking.*]

GLENN T. MILLER

RELOCATION PROGRAM, VOLUNTARY, was started in 1952 for the resettlement of reservation Indians in selected urban areas, with government assistance. The reservations generally had inadequate resources and were economically underdeveloped, at the same time that the Indian population was increasing rapidly. Some Indians had been moving into the cities on their own initiative for many years, and over 40,000 Indians had been attracted to urban areas during World War II for work in war-related industries. Under the new relocation program Indians were assisted in moving to such cities as Chicago, Los Angeles, Oakland, and Denver, being provided with money for transportation and moving costs; once in the cities they were aided in finding employment and housing. In 1956 the program was enlarged to include adult vocational training for prospective migrants, with the objective of improving their potential for employment. By 1960 a dozen relocation centers had been opened in various cities. In 1962 the name of the program was changed to the Employment Assistance Program, and services to Indians were expanded to include job placement on or near the reservations. By 1973 more than 100,000 Indians had been resettled in thirteen cities, although at least a third of them moved back to the reservations. The resettlement was continuing in the mid-1970's with centers to aid the migrants functioning in Los Angeles, Oakland, and San Jose, Calif.; Seattle; Dallas; Denver; Oklahoma City and Tulsa, Okla.; Chicago; and Cleveland.

[Howard M. Bahr, Bruce A. Chadwick, and Robert C. Day, *Native Americans Today: Sociological Perspectives;* La Verne Madigan, *The American Indian Relocation Program;* Jack O. Waddell and O. Michael Watson, *The American Indian in Urban Society.*]

KENNETH M. STEWART

REMAGEN, a German town on the Rhine River upstream from, and south of, Cologne, was the site of a railroad bridge that American troops captured in one of World War II's more astonishing events. Against faltering German resistance, contingents of Combat Command B, Ninth Armored Division, arrived on Mar. 7, 1945, on a bluff overlooking the Rhine at Remagen. In disbelief, the men saw that the bridge, named after Germany's first quartermaster general in World War I, Erich F. W. Ludendorff, still stood. Although crossing the Rhine was not the division's objective, the commander, Maj. Gen. John W. Leonard, ordered a swift attack to seize the bridge. As American troops drew near, the Germans set off demolitions designed to destroy the bridge. The bridge appeared to lift from its foundations, but when the smoke cleared, men on both sides saw with amazement that the bridge, although damaged, still stood. Infantrymen led by Sgt. Alexander Drabik and First Lt. Karl Timmerman raced across under heavy fire. A minuscule bridgehead established, the First U.S. Army commander, Lt. Gen. Courtney H. Hodges, rushed reinforcements across. Because of difficult terrain, the Allied high command planned no immediate exploitation of the bridgehead, but it served to attract German reserves and thus facilitate Rhine crossings at other points. With planes, artillery, and rockets, the Germans tried without success to destroy the bridge. On Mar. 17, as American engineers worked to repair damage, the bridge nevertheless collapsed, killing twenty-eight Americans. By that time, a number of tactical bridges were in place, so that the loss of the bridge had little effect on troops beyond the Rhine. Breakout of the bridgehead as part of a general advance across Germany occurred on Mar. 25. It was impossible to determine with certainty either why the German demolitions failed to destroy the bridge or why the bridge eventually collapsed.

[Ken Hechler, *The Bridge at Remagen.*]
CHARLES B. MACDONALD

"REMEMBER THE ALAMO," a battle cry in which the bitterness of the Texans over the massacres by Mexican forces at the Alamo in San Antonio (Mar. 6, 1836) and at Goliad (Mar. 27) found expression. Use of the phrase has been attributed both to Gen. Sam Houston, who supposedly used the words in a stirring address to his men on Apr. 19, 1836, two days before the Battle of San Jacinto, and to Col. Sidney Sherman, who fought in the battle.

C. T. NEU

"REMEMBER THE *MAINE*," a popular slogan current just before and during the Spanish-American War (1898). Popular opinion, led by such "yellow" journals as the *New York Journal* and *New York World*, held Spain responsible for the destruction of the battleship *Maine* in Havana harbor on Feb. 15, 1898. The *Journal* boasted that its readers had known "immediately after the destruction of the *Maine* that she was blown up by a Spanish mine." The *World*, by Feb. 20, declared it had "proved" destruction by a mine, and when the report of a naval court of inquiry sustained this position, announced: *"It is in itself a cause of war* if not atoned for. . . . If Spain will not punish her miscreants, we must punish Spain." This sentiment was echoed in the service journals, the *Army and Navy Register* and *Army and Navy Journal*, and in Congress, where one senator declared, "The battle cry on sea and land will be 'Remember the *Maine!*' " The resentment embodied in the phrase contributed immeasurably to the war spirit.

[Joseph E. Wisan, *The Cuban Crisis as Reflected in the New York Press.*]
JULIUS W. PRATT

REMOVAL, EXECUTIVE POWER OF. The power to effect removals is the logical complement of the appointive power of chief executives. Although the U.S. Constitution is silent on the matter, the First Congress, in legislation establishing executive departments, gave recognition to the proposition advanced by James Madison that the president's power of removal is inherent in the general grant of executive power and in the duty to "take care that the laws be faithfully executed."

This "Decision of 1789" prevailed unchallenged until the administration of President Andrew Jackson, when Sen. Henry Clay tried unsuccessfully to secure adoption of four resolutions designed to curb Jackson's assertion of an unqualified power of removal beyond the scope of congressional authority. Thirty years later Congress imposed drastic limits on the removal power in the Tenure of Office Act of 1867, which was passed over President Andrew Johnson's veto. This statute provided that all executive officers appointed by the president and confirmed by the Senate could not be removed without senatorial consent. Johnson's removal of Secretary of War Edwin McMasters Stanton, in violation of the act, led to the filing of impeachment charges by the House of Representatives. Johnson's acquittal by a one-vote margin in the Senate left the question of the nature of the removal power unresolved. The courts did not pass on the constitutionality of the Tenure of Office Act prior to its repeal in 1887.

The Supreme Court did not attempt to make a definitive ruling regarding the president's removal power until 1926. In *Myers* v. *United States* (1926) the Court upheld President Woodrow Wilson's 1920 removal of Postmaster Frank S. Myers of Portland, Oreg., in violation of a rider to an 1876 appropriation bill. The statute had fixed a four-year term for first-, second-, and third-class postmasters and specified that they could be removed only with senatorial consent. In a sweeping decision the Court held invalid any congressional limitation of the president's power to remove any of his appointees.

Less than ten years later, in *Humphrey's Executor* v. *United States* (1935), the Supreme Court confined the scope of the *Myers* case to include only ''all purely executive officers.'' In apparent reliance on the *Myers* precedent, President Franklin D. Roosevelt had removed William E. Humphrey as a member of the Federal Trade Commission because of policy differences, whereas in establishing the agency, Congress had provided for removal only for inefficiency, neglect of duty, or malfeasance in office. In a unanimous decision the Court invalidated Roosevelt's action and upheld the authority of Congress to limit the president's power to remove officials performing quasi-judicial and quasi-legislative functions.

The doctrine of the *Humphrey* case has generally prevailed, as in *Wiener* v. *United States* (1958). However, the decision in *Morgan* v. *Tennessee Valley Authority* (1940), *certiorari denied* (1941), indicates that the courts will examine the president's purpose in using the removal power even when it involves an independent agency. In that case the U.S. Court of Appeals upheld removal of a Tennessee Valley Authority director who had refused to cooperate in a presidential investigation of a policy controversy that had seriously impaired the activities of the agency. The court held that statutory language limiting removal to specific causes did not deny the president the power of summary removal as part of his duty to execute the laws.

In an operational sense the most effective limits to the president's removal power are neither constitutional nor statutory, but political. The influence of key congressional leaders and of powerful interest groups and the support for particular officials in the mass public imposes informal constraints on the president's capacity to dispose of unwanted subordinates that far transcend any formal restrictions.

Generally speaking, the power of state governors to make removals is even more limited than that of the president. The power tends to be specifically confined by state constitutions or statutes, and in only a few states are governors powerful enough to exercise broad summary powers of removal over executive officials.

[Edward S. Corwin, *The President: Office and Powers;* Joseph E. Kallenbach, *The American Chief Executive: The Presidency and the Governorship.*]

NORMAN C. THOMAS

REMOVAL ACT OF 1830. In his first annual message to Congress on Dec. 8, 1829, President Andrew Jackson recommended legislation looking to the removal of the Indians from east of the Mississippi River. A bill was introduced in the House of Representatives, Feb. 24, to carry this recommendation into effect. Although bitterly opposed in and out of Congress, it was enacted by a close vote, May 28, 1830. It authorized the president to cause territory west of the Mississippi to be divided into districts suitable for exchange with Indians living within any state or territory of the United States for lands there claimed and occupied by them and authorized the president to make such exchange.

[Grant Foreman, *Indian Removal.*]

GRANT FOREMAN

REMOVAL OF DEPOSITS. As early as Sept. 19, 1832, the *Washington Globe,* President Andrew Jackson's official organ, began hinting that the veto of the bill rechartering the second Bank of the United States would be followed by the removal of the government deposits from the institution and their placement in state banks. Later, the *Globe* prepared the public for the action by attacking the bank's handling of government funds. In July 1833 Amos Kendall was sent to arrange with various state banks to receive the deposits. Jackson then called his cabinet together on Sept. 18, 1833, and, after explaining his purpose, assumed responsibility for the removal policy. Two days later, the *Globe* officially announced that the removals would be made. Since Secretary of the Treasury William J. Duane refused to order the removal he was dismissed (Sept. 23) and replaced by Roger B. Taney, who carried out the president's program. Later, both Jackson and Taney were censured by the Senate for their parts in the episode.

[R. C. H. Catterall, *The Second Bank of the United States.*]

ERIK MCKINLEY ERIKSSON

RENDEZVOUS. *See* **Trappers' Rendezvous.**

RENEGOTIATION BOARD. *See* **Federal Agencies.**

RENEWAL, URBAN, the sum of the processes of building, clearing, rebuilding, modernizing, and renovating, by which cities evolve, change, and are rebuilt. Attributable to Miles L. Colean, an urban economist, the term first came into general use in the 1950's, succeeding "urban redevelopment," referring to similar processes, in common use in the 1940's. Lewis Mumford's broader, but less specific, writings on human renewal and urban renewal in the 1920's and 1930's can be cited as a more generic source.

Since the late 19th century American cities have grown with unprecedented rapidity, sometimes passing through stages of new building, deterioration, and rebuilding within a single generation. Inner areas of almost every American city of substantial size have been built, cleared, and rebuilt at least once. In dramatic cases a ten- or twenty-story building may be demolished to make way for a thirty- or forty-story building. Such market-generated renewal usually changes areas one building at a time. American cities have also seen large-scale public and private renewal, particularly in the reconstruction of railroad terminal or port areas in major cities; commercial development, such as Rockefeller Center in New York City; or residential renewal of historic, but deteriorated, areas, such as Beacon Hill in Boston or Georgetown in Washington, D.C.

During the 1930's the federal government sponsored about a hundred public housing projects to clear slums and replace them with housing for low-income families. Other federal agencies holding several million foreclosed mortgages experimented with programs of neighborhood rehabilitation to improve the value of deteriorating properties. During the years 1940 to 1945 these experiments were reviewed and reformulated and were expressed in the urban redevelopment title of the Wagner-Ellender-Taft bill, the first comprehensive piece of national housing legislation, finally enacted as the Housing Act of 1949. Under that legislation the federal government offered loans to local governments to enable them to plan for, acquire, and clear slum areas for urban redevelopment; install needed public improvements; and sell the resulting sites to private or public agencies for the ultimate planned reconstruction. Under amendments enacted in 1954 greater emphasis was given to renovation and rehabilitation of areas as opposed to clearance and reconstruction, and the term "urban renewal" was substituted for "urban redevelopment."

With the assistance provided by the Housing Act, 1,100 municipalities in the United States had undertaken 2,800 urban renewal projects involving federal-grant contracts of $10 billion by 1972. All metropolitan cities had engaged in the program, as had 600 smaller cities. Involving residential, commercial, civic, and industrial land uses, the projects included 200,000 acres of urban land, 80,000 of which were marked for clearance. Overall, the projects completed and committed by 1972 involved the relocation of 530,000 people, the provision of new homes for 630,000, and the rehabilitation of 149,000 structures containing 300,000 dwelling units. The reconstruction phases of the program were larger in cost but smaller in area than the rehabilitation phases.

Very large areas (for example, Golden Gate in San Francisco; Lake Meadows in Chicago; the southwest Washington, D.C., area) have been cleared for residential reconstruction in all major cities. Perhaps more numerous have been projects for the development of central business districts, civic centers, and university complexes, such as Constitution Plaza in Hartford, the University Center and Penn Center in Philadelphia, and Lincoln Center in New York City. Less well known are many projects for industrial development. Under the Housing Act of 1975 all federal aids for community development were lumped into a block grant composition in which every city shares with the anticipation that the revised program would enable cities to move more expeditiously and broadly on rehabilitation types of efforts.

Despite the large number of publicly sponsored projects, private renewal is considerably greater in volume and area, although no systematic records are available to compare its relative impact. Overall private market processes predominate in the massive process of urban renewal that changes the character of cities in some way at a rate of between 3 and 10 percent per year. The lower figure covers the bare level of maintenance required for continued functioning; the upper figure would mean the replacement of an entire city or its doubling or total disappearance in a decade. There are frequent examples of such phenomena.

[Jewel Bellush and Murray Hausknecht, eds., *Urban Renewal: People, Politics and Planning;* U.S. National Commission on Urban Problems, *Building the American City.*]

WILLIAM L. C. WHEATON

RENO, FORT (Oklahoma), a post established in Indian Territory in 1874, near the present town of El Reno. In 1876 it was named in honor of Gen. Jesse L. Reno. It was garrisoned continuously until 1908, when it became a remount depot and later a quartermaster's intermediate depot.

[Charles J. Sullivan, *Army Posts and Towns.*]
ALVIN F. HARLOW

RENO, FORT (Wyoming). Fort Connor, a stockade built on Powder River in 1865, was enlarged in 1866 by Col. Henry B. Carrington and named Fort Reno, for Gen. Jesse L. Reno, killed in the Civil War. As demanded by the Indians, the fort was abandoned in 1868, but was temporarily reestablished in 1876.

[G. R. Hebard and E. A. Brininstool, *The Bozeman Trail.*]
LEROY R. HAFEN

REORGANIZED CHURCH OF JESUS CHRIST OF LATTER-DAY SAINTS claims to be the continuation of and successor to the Church of Jesus Christ of Latter-Day Saints, organized by Joseph Smith, Jr., on Apr. 6, 1830, at Fayette, N.Y. (*see* Latter-Day Saints, Church of Jesus Christ of). After Smith and his brother Hyrum were killed by a mob in Carthage, Ill., June 27, 1844, many factions were formed among church members. The main body eventually followed Brigham Young to Utah; another group followed Sidney Rigdon to Pennsylvania; and a third followed James J. Strang to Wisconsin and Michigan. A number, including Joseph Smith III, Smith's eldest son, and other members of Smith's family, finally formed a new group in 1852, still under the name of the Church of Jesus Christ of Latter-Day Saints. In October 1869, for legal reasons, the word "Reorganized" was added to the name. Independence, Mo., was named as the central place for the establishment of the church, and there followed a suit in the U.S. Circuit Court, decided in 1894, for possession of the temple lot there. In this case, in which the three principal factions of the Church of the Latter-Day Saints were involved, the court decided that the reorganized church was the true successor, with doctrines and practices identical with those of the original church. The pleadings put in issue the question of polygamy, and Judge John F. Philips held it was no part of the teaching or practice of the original church, thereby exonerating Joseph Smith, Jr., of responsibility for the teaching. The members of the reorganized church reject the name Mormon because of the association of the name in the popular mind with doctrines and practices that they have always repudiated.

S. A. BURGESS

REPARATION COMMISSION (1920–30) was directed by articles 231–235 of part VIII of the Treaty of Versailles to estimate damage done by Germany to Allied civilians and their property during World War I and to formulate methods of collecting assessments, since the Paris conferees had become deadlocked on the issue. In June 1920 the Supreme Council decided that Germany should pay at least 3 billion gold marks for thirty-five years, the total not to exceed 269 billion marks. Within this frame, and after sanctions had been applied because of German defaults, the commission, on advice of a committee of experts, reported to the Supreme Council in April 1921 that damages amounted to 132 billion marks and recommended annual payments of 2 billion marks and 26 percent of German exports, with a cash payment of 1 billion marks by Sept. 1. Economic and monetary chaos in Germany coupled with resentment at the reparations scheme brought a Franco-Belgian force into the Ruhr. By the time of complete collapse of the German mark in 1923, accompanied by dislocation of world trade, there had been paid in cash, commodities, and services an amount that was estimated by the commission at approximately 10.5 billion gold marks, by the Germans at something over 42 billion marks, and by various economists at sums somewhere between these extremes. Of this indeterminate amount the United States received nothing of the reparations per se, although considerable sums had been paid to reimburse expenses of the Army of Occupation, damage in the United States, and the like.

In 1922 Secretary of State Charles E. Hughes had suggested, although the United States not being a party to the Treaty of Versailles technically had nothing to do with the matter, that the whole issue be taken out of politics and adjusted on economic principles, and intimated that the services of American experts might be available. Accordingly, a committee set up to study German finances, with Charles G. Dawes as chairman, worked out a plan to go into effect on Sept. 1, 1924, with a sliding scale of annuities in cash and kind, together with suggestions how revenues should be raised and payments distributed. In the opinion of competent economists the plan worked fairly well, at least in the short run, providing for the payment of nearly 10 billion marks to the creditors and at the same time allowing stabilization of German currency and an upward trend in German economic life, even though no definite aggregate total had been fixed. Desire on the part of the creditor powers to arrange a definitive settlement and to have turned into marketable bonds Germany's future obligations brought a second committee of experts, even though Germans were afraid of the effect such an arrangement would have on them. The conference, meeting under the chairmanship of Owen D. Young in the spring of 1929, produced a new plan that, somewhat modified by the Reparation Commission especially on the insistence of Great Britain, arranged for annuities running until 1988 and aggregating with interest 121 billion marks. On May 17, 1930, the Young Plan went into operation and on that day the Reparation Commission ceased operations. In barely two years, however, payments stopped with the moratorium proposed by President Herbert Hoover, effective June 30, 1931, after a sum of 2.871 billion marks had been turned over to the creditor nations. Thenceforward, to all intents and purposes reparations were suspended regardless of the Lausanne Agreement (July 9, 1932), which attempted to replace the Young Plan with a set of new and reduced obligations.

In American popular estimation reparations were tied to debts owed the United States by various governments that had been ranged against Germany in World War I or had been advanced loans subsequently. The U.S. government, however, never acknowledged any such relationship even though such payments as had been made on these debts actually had been derived from Germany. (*See also* War Claims Act.)

[David Felix, *Walter Rathenau and the Weimar Republic: The Politics of Reparations.*]

L. B. SHIPPEE

REPEATING, a corrupt election practice in which persons cast ballots in more than one precinct during the same election, or vote under different names more than once in the same precinct. The practice, at one time notorious in large cities, has disappeared with the adoption of adequate personal registration laws (including signature tests) and the appointment of honest and vigilant election officials.

[F. R. Kent, *The Great Game of Politics.*]

P. ORMAN RAY

REPRESENTATION. Alexander Hamilton, in *The Federalist,* called representation a principle, imper-

fectly known to the ancients, which has made most of its progress toward perfection in modern times, and a powerful means by which the excellencies of republican government may be retained and its imperfections lessened or avoided. The idea of representation is absent from Aristotle's *Politics,* partly because a state so large that it required representation would have seemed too large for political excellence to classical political theorists.

The democracy of the modern world has generally been representative democracy. Pure democracy, in which the politically qualified members of the community meet together to discuss and decide public questions, is suitable only for small communities with simple collective needs. All the members of modern democratic communities cannot personally assemble to make laws in one gigantic town meeting. Rather the community is represented by individuals who can legislate for the people more effectively than the people can legislate directly themselves.

A representative is someone who will be held responsible by those for whom he acts, who must account for his actions. If the representative's actions bear no relation to his constituents' needs or interests, he is not representing his constituents. Should a representative act on his own judgment of what is in the national interest, or should he be a faithful servant of his constituency's expressed will? There are those who argue that the representative must act independently, on his own judgment, and that his job is to adapt the constituent's separate interests into the national interest. Others stress the popular mandate given a representative by those for whom he acts and say he has an obligation to do what they expect of him, to act as if they were acting themselves.

A representative, said Thomas Hobbes, is a man who acts in the name of another, who has been given authority to act by that other, so that whatever the representative does is considered the act of the represented. Representation is authority, the right to make commitments for another. Within limits, the representative is free to do as he pleases, at least insofar as his constituents are concerned. According to Hobbes, every government is a representative government in that it represents its subjects. Edmund Burke thought of a representative essentially as representing, not individuals, but the large, stable interests that constitute the national interest. The duty of each representative is to determine the good of the whole, and the selfish wishes of parts of the nation or the wills of individual voters are irrelevant. The representative must discover the national interest. Since the relation of each representative is to the nation as a whole, he stands in no special relation to his constituency. He represents the nation, not merely those who elected him. Therefore the representative is like a trustee: his obligation is to look after his constituents, not to consult or obey them. John Stuart Mill said that what distinguishes a representative assembly from any other collection of people is its accurate correspondence to the larger population for which it stands. To be representative, a legislature must be a mirror that accurately reflects the various parts of the populace. According to Mill, every man needs to have his vote count equally because no one can know or defend his particular interest as well as he. Mill was much more inclined to think of the representative as an agent than as a trustee.

[J. Roland Pennock and John W. Chapman, eds., *Representation (Nomos X)*; Hannah F. Pitkin, *The Concept of Representation*.]

MORTON J. FRISCH

REPRESENTATIVE GOVERNMENT, government that represents all the people, giving effect to their opinions and interests, not imposing on them the opinions and interests of their rulers. Representative government, which emerged in the 17th century, had come to be virtually universal by the mid-20th century in the sense that most governments claimed to be representative, for much of world opinion condemns governments that rule contrary to popular opinions and interests. Representative government in its present form, moreover, is democratic government. The ancient democracies lacked the representative principle, having neither the geographic extent nor the large populations that later called the principle into play.

According to the modern theory of representative government, democratic government deals with its problems most competently and protects the liberties of the people most effectively when assemblies are composed of representatives of the citizenry rather than of the citizens themselves en masse. The presumption is that representatives will be capable men who will deliberate wisely in the interests of the people and not misrepresent their interests. Representative government can be made less democratic either through suffrage limitations (limiting voters) or representative qualifications (limiting those who may be elected).

Since the practice of politics and government requires the exercise of discretion in variable circumstances, direct democracy is practicable only in a small country in which the populace can meet as a body often enough to consider new circumstances. The theorists of modern representative government—notably Edmund Burke; Alexander Hamilton, James Madison, and John Jay, the authors of *The Federalist* (1788); and John Stuart Mill—preferred a large country as more favorable to liberty and more powerful and insisted upon representative government allowing discretion to representatives to deal with changing circumstances. The authors of *The Federalist* hoped and intended that the representatives of the American people would "refine and enlarge" the views of their constituents and that they would be governed not by temporary and partial considerations, but by the true interests of the country.

Mill, in *Representative Government* (1861), argued that representatives should have the responsibility of thinking about and discussing public issues in the interest of the whole, that they should not merely reflect the views of their constituencies. But he also argued that they should not actually govern. The functions of government, he believed, require highly skilled, experienced, well-trained individuals. He advocated that experts should govern, while being controlled by representatives of the people; the representatives would not constitute the government, but act for the people to control the government. And he warned that effective representative government would require that a balance be maintained between the representative assembly and the government.

Jean-Jacques Rousseau, on the other hand, contended that representative government is undesirable, because responsibility is removed from the hands of the citizens, that there is no way to institutionalize or guarantee that the representative's vote will always coincide with the will of those he represents. But confronted with nations too large to allow all citizens to meet in a common body, representation becomes an unfortunate necessity. Rousseau proposed that the representatives should be elected by local assemblies of all the citizens and be given complete instructions. Opposing the use of independent judgment by the representatives, he further proposed that every new question should be referred back to the electors, to ensure an expression of the general will.

The problem of modern representative government—of which Rousseau was well aware—is how to govern the people without instructing or educating them. The people must be governed; but if they are instructed or educated, they are no longer simply represented. They are ruled. A representative is supposed to act on behalf of others, in their place, in their name, for their sake, in accordance with their opinions and interests, in order to please or satisfy them, as they would have acted themselves. But it is difficult, if not impossible, to have a democratic government that governs the populace without imposing any views or opinions on it.

[Benjamin Fletcher Wright, "Direct and Representative Democracy," in Wright, ed., *The Federalist*.]

MORTON J. FRISCH

REPRESENTATIVES, HOUSE OF. *See* **Congress, United States.**

REPRISAL, LETTERS OF. *See* **Marque and Reprisal, Letters of.**

REPTILES. Contributions to the study of American reptiles prior to 1800 were made primarily by travelers and have had little impact. Notable among the earliest contributors were the Englishman Mark Catesby, who published *The Natural History of Carolina, Florida, and the Bahama Islands* (1731–43), and the Philadelphian William Bartram, who traveled throughout the southeastern United States making natural history observations on many organisms, including the alligator, which he published in his *Travels Through North and South Carolina, Georgia, East and West Florida* (1791). Some American reptiles were described by Carolus Linnaeus in his *Systema Naturae* (1758). He described only a fraction of the total reptile fauna, and then inadequately.

In the late 1700's and early 1800's, foreign naturalists such as Constantine S. Rafinesque, Charles A. Lesueur, and Prince Maximilian zu Wied traveled in America and described the reptiles they saw. European scientists such as Arend F. A. Wiegmann, Johann David Schoepff, and Pierre André Latreille worked on American reptiles that had been sent to them, thereby adding to the knowledge of existing forms. Additions to the growing list of American reptiles were also made by John Eaton LeConte of the U.S. Army; Thomas Say, who traveled with the Stephen H. Long expedition to the Rocky Mountains (1820); and Richard Harlan, a practicing physician. Harlan attempted to draw together the body of information on American reptiles with his *Genera of North American Reptiles and a Synopsis of the Species* (1826–27) and *American Herpetology* (1827), but these contributions only partly alleviated some of the confusion regarding taxonomic matters that had developed by that time.

John Edwards Holbrook, a Charleston, S.C., physician, produced the first major contribution to U.S. knowledge of American reptiles. Holbrook's *North American Herpetology* (1836, 1842) was a milestone in herpetology. His work was almost exclusively oriented to species known in the East, as the West was largely unexplored at that time. The success and influence of his work probably related to its completeness for the time and to the superb color lithographs drawn from living examples by talented artists. His work caught the attention of European scientists and brought a measure of recognition to the rise of science in America. Only nine years after its appearance he was proclaimed "father of American herpetology."

In the period immediately after the appearance of Holbrook's *North American Herpetology,* a number of expeditions sponsored by the U.S. government were organized to explore the American West. Notable among these were Charles Wilkes's expedition to the Pacific Northwest, Howard Stansbury's expedition to the Great Salt Lake, George M. Wheeler's explorations west of the 100th meridian, Maj. William H. Emory's Mexican boundary survey, Capt. Randolph B. Marcy's exploration of the Red River, Capt. Lorenzo Sitgreaves' expedition down the Zuni and Colorado rivers, and the Pacific Railroad surveys. It was to the credit of Spencer Fullerton Baird that large collections of reptiles were brought back to museums, in particular the U.S. National Museum, which he helped establish in 1857. The reptiles collected by the U.S. exploring teams were studied by a number of scientists, including Baird, Charles F. Girard, Henry C. Yarrow, and Charles Pickering. By 1880 most of the expeditions to the West had been completed and the results published, providing a first glimpse of the diversity and extent of the American reptile fauna.

Concomitant with the work on western reptiles, contributions were being made on eastern forms. Several state herpetofaunal surveys were published, including those by David Humphreys Storer for Massachusetts (1839) and James E. DeKay for New York (1842–44). Louis Agassiz of the Museum of Comparative Zoology at Harvard added much to the knowledge of the embryology of the turtle in his *Contributions to the Natural History of the United States of America* (1857).

From the 1880's to the early 1900's a number of individuals made important contributions to the study of American reptiles. Samuel Garman of the Museum of Comparative Zoology put together an important treatise on American snakes, bringing together much of the information that had been published in the scattered reports of various U.S. exploring expeditions. His work, *North American Reptilia, Part I, Ophidia* (1883), remained of considerable value to scientists until outdated by the appearance of *The Crocodilians, Lizards, and Snakes of North America* (1900) by Edward Drinker Cope. Cope made many contributions in the field of herpetology, but was equally well known in the fields of ichthyology and paleontology. Leonhard Hess Stejneger of the U.S. National Museum introduced the careful designation of type specimens and type localities into the description of new species, produced an important treatise entitled *The Poisonous Snakes of North America* (1895), and later produced under coauthorship with Thomas Barbour five editions of *A Check List of North American Amphibians and Reptiles* (1917). These checklists provided a concise synopsis of the known species of reptiles and amphibians and reference for other workers. John Van Denburgh of the California Academy of Sciences described new species of western reptiles and provided information on geographic distributions, most of which he later summarized in his work *The Reptiles of Western North America* (1922). Alexander G. Ruthven of the Museum of Zoology, University of Michigan, influenced subsequent herpetological studies by the introduction of the use of biometric methods in his monograph on garter snakes (1908).

Since the 1920's scientific investigations have been made on every conceivable aspect of the biology of reptiles. American universities have become the primary centers for these studies. Some of the more important contributors have been Frank N. Blanchard, who pioneered in field studies of reptiles and developed marking techniques, and Henry Fitch, who subsequently produced some of the most complete field studies of reptiles to date. Clifford H. Pope published *The Turtles of North America* (1939), which was a welcome treatise on a neglected group. Archie Carr greatly expanded the knowledge of North American turtles with shorter papers and his *Handbook of Turtles* (1952); he later made pioneering contributions on sea turtles and their conservation. Hobart M. Smith provided an excellent summary of the North American lizard fauna with his *Handbook of Lizards* (1946). Alfred S. Romer contributed to the work on fossil reptiles; his *Osteology of the Reptiles* (1956) was still the standard reference for that field of research twenty years later. Albert Hazen Wright coauthored with his wife Anna the scholarly *Handbook of Snakes of the United States and Canada* (1957), which drew together all the information prior to that date.

Laurence M. Klauber made many contributions on western reptiles and introduced refined statistical techniques. His book *Rattlesnakes* (1956) remained the most complete herpetological monograph produced by the mid-1970's. Detailed lizard population studies were published by W. Frank Blair, in *The Rusty Lizard* (1960), and Donald W. Tinkle, in *The Life and Demography of the Side-blotched Lizard* (1967). Albert M. Reese published widely on the development and anatomy of the American alligator, including his book *The Alligator and Its Allies* (1915). James A. Oliver, in his book *The Natural History of North American Amphibians and Reptiles* (1955), summarized much of what was known about the life history of amphibians and reptiles.

The role of the scientist in presenting technical information in a form that can be understood by amateurs and laymen has often been neglected. During the 20th century several scientists produced semipopular works that served to generate wide interest in reptiles. Raymond Lee Ditmars probably did more to stimulate interest in the study of reptiles than any other individual. He routinely lectured to a wide variety of audiences and published many books, but his *Reptile Book,* first appearing in 1907, was one of the most stimulating to young naturalists. Karl P. Schmidt produced the *Field Book of Snakes* (1941) in coauthorship with D. Dwight Davis. Roger Conant wrote the first of the newest type of field guides, *A Field Guide to Reptiles and Amphibians* (1958), that contained range maps, color illustrations, and synoptic information about the organisms. Robert C. Stebbins further improved the field guide format with his *Field Guide to Western Reptiles and Amphibians* (1966). In addition to field guides, herpetofaunal surveys have been written for most of the states and have stimulated interest. Some of the better state surveys are those by Paul Anderson, *The Reptiles of Missouri* (1965), and Philip W. Smith, *The Amphibians and Reptiles of Illinois* (1961).

Three major societies sponsor periodicals to handle the great increase in the number of scholarly contributions within the field of herpetology: *Copeia* (1913–) is published by the American Society of Ichthyologists and Herpetologists, *Herpetologica* (1936–) is published by the Herpetologists' League, and the *Journal of Herpetology* (1968–) is published by the Society for the Study of Amphibians and Reptiles.

[E. L. Kessel, *A Century of Progress in the Natural Sciences, 1853–1953.*]

RICHARD D. WORTHINGTON

REPUBLIC

REPUBLIC derives from the Latin *res publica; res* means "thing" or "affair," and *publica* means "public," as against "private." The word thus denotes government in which politics is a public affair and not the personal prerogative of a single ruler. There have been aristocratic republics, oligarchic republics, and democratic republics. But *The Federalist* (1788), the authoritative commentary on the American Constitution, written by Alexander Hamilton, James Madison, and John Jay, uses the word to mean only a democratic republic; that is, it construes a republic to be a particular kind of democracy.

The Federalist distinguishes a republic from a pure democracy, describing the latter as "a society consisting of a small number of citizens, who assemble and administer the government in person." In the context of *The Federalist*, a republic differs from a pure democracy only in that it is "a government in which the scheme of representation takes place." According to this interpretation "republic" is synonymous with "representative democracy," although the principle of representation introduces an impurity into the republican form vis-à-vis the pure form of democracy. At the same time, it is pointed out, the representative principle militates against the irresponsible exercise of majority power, for it makes a large republic possible, and it is difficult in a large republic for any faction to become a majority. From the perspective of the authors of *The Federalist*, a large republic fosters the formation of a large number of factions, and this sheer multiplicity of factions hinders the formation of an oppressive or irresponsible majority. They believed that because of its size, the republic of the United States would contain a great variety of factions, no one of which would constitute a majority of the whole. Majorities would have to be formed by coalition, a deliberate coalescing of smaller factions, and the process of coalition would moderate majorities and thus rule out the possibility of a tyrannical or irresponsible majority.

Europeans had established partly or wholly representative governments before the American Revolution, but none was both wholly representative and wholly democratic. The republic of the United States achieved that novel combination. A danger remained, however, according to Alexis de Tocqueville, in its representative institutions: if representatives are little better than their constituents, the hoped-for improvement in the government of democracy may come to nothing.

[Martin Diamond, "The Federalist," in Morton J. Frisch and Richard G. Stevens, eds., *American Political Thought;*

Paul Eidelberg, *The Philosophy of the American Constitution.*]

MORTON J. FRISCH

REPUBLICAN PARTY. Failure of the established American political parties to contain sectional conflict over the status of slavery in the new territories stimulated organizations of protest throughout the free states in the two decades before the Civil War. The sentiment of northern farmers and workingmen was crystallized by the Kansas-Nebraska Act of 1854, which repealed the Missouri Compromise.

The Republican name was first adopted at a protest meeting in Ripon, Wis., on Feb. 28, 1854, and the first convention of a Republican state party was held "under the oaks" at Jackson, Mich., on July 6, 1854. Local and congressional election victories followed in several states. The new party included politicians and voters who had previously given their allegiance to the northern (or "Conscience") Whigs, the Free Soil party, the free Democrats, and the nativist American (or "Know-Nothing") party. The name "Republican" was taken from that of the Jeffersonian Republicans, the party of Thomas Jefferson, who was recognized as the spiritual leader of the 1854 protests. Jefferson was seen as an opponent of slavery (or at least of its expansion), champion of the concept of a nation of small landholders, and leader of radical opposition to the established aristocracy.

The sentiments of the new party were firmly agrarian and radical. Opposition to the slavocracy was coupled with support for new railroads, free homesteads, and the opening of the West by free labor. Support for the protective tariff was added in an appeal to the manufacturing (as opposed to the plantation) interest.

The 1856 Republican National Convention nominated John C. Frémont of California as its candidate for the presidency. Frémont was defeated, but he carried eleven states, establishing the organizational base of the new party. Winning every free state in 1860, Abraham Lincoln moved to consolidate his political support, but he could not deter the southern secessionists. Lincoln selected the preservation of the Union as the issue of broadest appeal, emancipating the slaves only when the political time was ripe. The party was known as the Union party for Lincoln's reelection campaign of 1864, for which Andrew Johnson of Tennessee was nominated as vice-president to attract future southern support.

After Lincoln's assassination, Radical Republicans

in Congress asserted party leadership. They did not regard Johnson as a Republican, and the Tennessean's efforts to enact Lincoln's policies of reconciliation with the South led only to his impeachment. Reconstruction policies drove the southern Whigs into the Democratic party and created the Solid South. Republicans demonstrated their party's sectional nature by nominating former Union soldiers, as long as any were available—Ulysses S. Grant, Rutherford B. Hayes, James A. Garfield, Benjamin Harrison, and William McKinley—and Republicans occupied the White House for all but eight of the thirty-two years following Lincoln's first election. But the national strength of the two parties was remarkably equal; in the popular vote the majority alternated between them. Resolving the contested election of 1876 between Hayes and Samuel J. Tilden, Republicans abandoned the freedman to the mercies of the southern whites in return for a renewed lease on the White House.

McKinley's election in 1896 constituted the defeat of radical, lower-class reform as personified by populism and William Jennings Bryan. It established the Republicans as the normal majority party, representing industrial progress, northern farmers, middle-class respectability, eastern urban labor, and even college presidents. McKinley was assassinated during his second term, and Theodore Roosevelt became president. After reelection in his own right in 1904, Roosevelt assumed leadership of the Progressive movement, making the Republicans also the party of conservation and reform. Only a feud between Roosevelt and his successor, William Howard Taft, brought about the Democratic victory that installed Woodrow Wilson in the White House in 1913—the only break in thirty-six years of Republican domination.

With the exception of Roosevelt, Republican presidents followed the pattern imposed on Andrew Johnson into the 20th century. Warren G. Harding and Calvin Coolidge personified this Whig tradition, which subordinated executive leadership to the legislature. Although a Progressive by background, Herbert Hoover shared this limited concept of presidential power, and it proved inadequate to the demands of the Great Depression. Hoover's defeat for a second term by Franklin D. Roosevelt was followed by the stunning defeat of Alfred M. Landon, the Kansas Progressive, in 1936. The Republicans were cast in a long-term minority role.

As the New Deal forged a majority by adding organized labor, urban minorities, and intellectuals to the base of the South, the Republicans came to be regarded as the party of eastern big business and midwestern farmers. Conservative (and some isolationist) Republicans predominated in Congress, while presidential nominations were controlled by the eastern, liberal, internationalist wing of the party. The era's defeated Republican candidates were Wendell L. Willkie in 1940 and Thomas E. Dewey in 1944 and 1948. Dwight D. Eisenhower's phenomenal personal popularity made inroads even into southern Democratic allegiances and won him the presidency in 1952 and 1956, but little of his popularity was transferred to the Republican party. "Ike" had a Republican Congress for only two of his eight years in office, and his vice-president, Richard M. Nixon, lost narrowly to John F. Kennedy in 1960. Four years later, Republican delegates from the South and West repudiated the eastern leadership by nominating Barry Goldwater, an avowed conservative. Goldwater carried only his native Arizona and five states of the Deep South against Lyndon B. Johnson.

In 1968 Nixon claimed the moderate position between liberal and conservative Republicans and won the nomination easily. In a three-way contest, George C. Wallace won 13 percent of the vote, and Nixon edged out Hubert H. Humphrey for a plurality, while the Democrats recaptured Congress. Winding down American involvement in the Vietnam War, Nixon visited the Soviet Union and China, striving for a "generation of peace." In 1972 he defeated Sen. George McGovern in a historic personal landslide, failing to carry only Massachusetts and the District of Columbia. But Nixon offered little support to other Republican candidates, and the Democrats retained control of Congress.

The Watergate burglary was raised as an issue in the 1972 campaign but received little public attention. Beginning in 1973, press exposures, congressional investigations, and court proceedings revealed the complicity of Nixon administration officials in that crime and others. Tainted by an unrelated Maryland scandal, Vice-President Spiro T. Agnew resigned in October 1973 rather than face indictment. Invoking the Constitution's Twenty-fifth Amendment for the first time, Nixon appointed House Minority Leader Gerald R. Ford to replace Agnew. When Nixon was forced by a Supreme Court decision to release tape recordings that proved he had known of his leading aides' involvement in Watergate, he resigned his office (August 1974) rather than face impeachment proceedings, which had been voted by the House Judiciary Committee.

REPUBLICANS, JEFFERSONIAN

Gerald Ford's accession to the presidency was greeted with relief because of his apparent honesty and plain-spokenness. But this image was immediately tarnished when he pardoned Richard Nixon, and conservative Republicans were affronted when Ford appointed Nelson Rockefeller as vice-president. Ford retained the foreign policy leadership of Henry Kissinger, who had served Nixon, and frequently used the veto power in domestic matters. During 1975, the Democratic majority in Congress did not present a coherent opposition. Ford's chief political problem as 1976 began was a conservative challenge for the Republican presidential nomination from former Gov. Ronald Reagan of California.

[George H. Mayer, *The Republican Party, 1854–1966;* Malcolm Moos, *The Republicans.*]

KARL A. LAMB

REPUBLICANS, JEFFERSONIAN, or **Demo-cratic-Republicans.** The Jeffersonian Republican party was the first opposition party under the new national government. Its elements appeared in the first two congresses when the vigorous leadership of Alexander Hamilton and his Federalist party associates aroused the fear and hostility of various members who disliked the funding system, the revenue acts, the first Bank of the United States, and the general tendency to create a powerful national authority by liberal construction of the Constitution. The frank reliance of the Federalists on "the wise and good and rich," their liking for forms and ceremonies that smacked of the aristocratic, and particularly their horror of the French Revolution and all its works, tended to make the opposition the party of the common man and gave it its title of "Republican."

Thomas Jefferson supplied the necessary leadership and philosophy for the party. Organization spread throughout the country, at least in rudimentary form, and the Democratic Clubs played an important part. Its leaders realized the importance of propaganda, and a number of important newspapers were acquired or founded at strategic points. Jefferson won the presidency in 1800, carried out a series of mild reforms and innovations, and was reelected by a large majority (162 of 176 electoral votes) four years later. The Federalists henceforth declined to the position of a factious and intransigent minority largely centered in New England (*see* Essex Junto). With the election of James Madison to the presidency in 1808, there ensued a period of twenty years when the Democratic-Republican party, nominally in power, was in

reality a collection of sectional and personal factions rather than a genuine cohesive party. Under its auspices there was a gradual broadening of the suffrage, an increasing democratizing of local life, a perceptible emphasis on humanitarian reform, and, after the War of 1812, the development of a nationalist spirit in striking contrast to the divisions of the Federalist era. Nevertheless, new issues were appearing. The tariff, the second Bank of the United States, and internal improvements caused a cleavage comparable to that of 1790–1800 and, with the election of Andrew Jackson in 1828, a new and more logical alignment of "National" and "Democratic" Republicans was well established, to evolve, a few years later, into the Whig and Democratic parties respectively.

[C. A. Beard, *The Economic Origins of Jeffersonian Democracy;* E. Channing, *The Jeffersonian System;* Noble E. Cunningham, Jr., *Jeffersonian Republicans in Power;* C. M. Wiltse, *The Jeffersonian Tradition in American Democracy.*]

W. A. ROBINSON

REPUDIATION OF PUBLIC DEBT. When an individual goes bankrupt he pays, say, one cent on the dollar, but when a nation goes bankrupt it inflates its currency and pays in a one-cent dollar. That is approximately what the United States and many states did in the 1780's. To guard against a repetition, the Constitution provides that "no State shall . . . coin Money; emit Bills of Credit; make any Thing but gold and silver Coin a Tender in Payment of Debts; pass any . . . Law impairing the Obligation of Contracts. . . ." Only Congress is empowered to coin money, and nothing is said about issuing bills of credit (the 18th-century name for legal-tender Treasury notes). The implication was that only gold and silver coins could be legal tender. This rule was observed until the exigencies of the Civil War produced, on Feb. 25, 1862, the first of several issues of U.S. notes, familiarly known as "greenbacks" or "legal tenders." They were legal tender for all payments except import duties and interest on the public debt. On July 11, 1864, the value of $100 of these reached a low of $35 in gold. The constitutionality of the Legal Tender Acts was questioned in a series of cases known as the Legal Tender Cases. On Feb. 7, 1870, in the first of these, the case of *Hepburn* v. *Griswold,* the Supreme Court decided, by a vote of four to three, that the acts were unconstitutional. This decision was reversed May 1, 1871, in *Knox* v. *Lee* and *Parker* v. *Davis* on the grounds that the acts were a valid exercise of the war powers of Congress. In 1884 the Court upheld, in

Juilliard v. *Greenman,* the right of Congress to make Treasury notes legal tender in peacetime. There were several interesting exceptions to the new general rule. In one especially, *Bronson* v. *Rodes,* decided in December 1868, the Court held that the Legal Tender Acts did not apply to obligations specifically calling for payment in gold and silver coin. Accordingly the custom spread of inserting in many kinds of debt contracts, government as well as industrial, the so-called gold clause, one form of which stated that the debt was "payable in gold coin of the United States of the present standard weight and fineness." The practice increased decidedly after the Sherman Silver Purchase Act of 1890.

Early in March 1933 the government temporarily abandoned the gold-coin standard; on Apr. 19 it did so definitely, and gold went to a considerable premium. On June 5 President Franklin D. Roosevelt signed a joint resolution of Congress declaring all specific gold contracts inoperative. This was necessary as a practical matter if the United States was to devalue, and devaluation was an important instrument of the administration's price-raising policy. On Jan. 31, 1934, the government ordained a new and smaller gold dollar of 13.71 grains of fine gold. It was nearly 41 percent smaller than the old gold dollar of 23.22 grains of fine gold, which means that the old gold dollar was worth 1.69 times as much as the new.

Four cases, known collectively as the Gold Clause Cases, were brought before the Supreme Court questioning the constitutionality of the resolution of June 5, 1933, and claiming for the creditors, on the basis of the gold clause, $1.69 for each $1 owed. Two plaintiffs held railroad bonds, and a third, gold certificates. The fourth case, *Perry* v. *United States,* is most pertinent because it involved a Liberty bond. The decisions were of vital importance, since they affected about $100 billion of debt bearing the gold clause, $21 billion of it federal. Hearings were begun Jan. 8, 1935, and the decisions rendered Feb. 18, 1935. The Supreme Court unanimously held the resolution of June 5, 1933, unconstitutional, stating that Congress was vested with power "to authorize the issue of definite obligations for the payment of money borrowed" but not "with authority to alter or destroy those obligations." On the other hand, the Supreme Court refused, five to four, to award damages, on the ground that the "plaintiff has not shown or attempted to show that in relation to buying power he had sustained any loss whatsoever."

The buying-power theory was precedent breaking; "value" under the Constitution had theretofore meant weight of gold, not purchasing power. This decision left the way open for suits against the government as soon as anyone could demonstrate loss in purchasing power, which presumably would be easy after prices had risen appreciably. On Aug. 27, 1935, the president signed a joint resolution of Congress closing the Court of Claims to such suits (the government may refuse to be sued if it chooses) but granting bondholders the privilege, until Jan. 1, 1936, of receiving cash payment for the par value of the bonds plus accrued interest. This was done to eliminate the financial confusion that would have resulted from the success of such suits, but according to many critics, it was done at the expense of the national honor, since the administration admitted by its action that the courts would probably judge the bondholders deserving of further indemnity.

To the extent that a nation allows its currency to depreciate in value and pays its borrowings in that currency, it is also repudiating part of its public debt. It is not doing so as openly as the United States did in 1933–34, but it is still doing so. Admittedly all nations have at some time inflated their currency, some more often or at a faster rate than others, but it nevertheless remains a form of repudiation. Since March 1933 individuals have not had the right to demand gold coin for paper dollars, and on Aug. 15, 1971, President Richard M. Nixon informed foreign central banks and treasuries, who did have that right, that they had lost it too. Between March 1933 and March 1973 the dollar lost 71 percent of its buying power. Between 1939 and 1952 the dollar depreciated at an annual rate of 5 percent a year on the average and lost half its buying power. A person who bought a U.S. government bond in 1939 and held it to maturity in 1952 would have got back dollars with only half the purchasing power of those he paid in.

[Federal Reserve Board, *Federal Reserve Bulletins;* E. W. Kemmerer, *Money;* P. Studenski and H. Krooss, *Financial History of the United States;* U.S. Department of Commerce, *Historical Statistics of the United States, Colonial Times to 1957;* Charles Warren, *The Supreme Court in United States History;* R. B. Westerfield, *Money, Credit and Banking.*]

DONALD L. KEMMERER

REPUDIATION OF STATE DEBTS was the subject of agitated discussion in the United States and abroad during the 1840's and the 1870's. In the 1830's various American states incurred heavy debts in the construction of canals and railroads and in the creation of banks. By 1839 the public indebtedness of

REPUDIATION OF STATE DEBTS

American states amounted to $170 million. Frequently, in authorizing these loans, the faith of the state was pledged for the payment of the interest and the redemption of the principal. In many cases the laws specified that the bonds should not be sold below par. In negotiating these loans authorized agents of the states violated the state statutes and American bankers aided and abetted them. In London, Baring Brothers and Company and other English banking houses sold the bonds to their clients; in Amsterdam, Hope and Company did the same. Foreign investors bought these securities with avidity because of the guaranty of the states, the high rate of interest they carried, the high standing of the national credit, and the confidence of foreign bankers in the Bank of the United States. The aggressive salesmanship of American agents abroad somewhat accounts for the lack of caution and prudence on the part of the European bankers. By 1839 it was estimated that British subjects held between $110 million and $165 million of American securities. When the American financial structure collapsed in the panic of 1837, European bankers tactlessly suggested that the U.S. government assume the state debts. Whatever merit the scheme might have possessed was lost by the hostility created by its supposedly foreign origin and the scramble for votes in the presidential election of 1840.

Between 1841 and 1842 eight states and one territory defaulted on their interest payments (*see* State Debts). Mississippi repudiated $5 million of Union Bank bonds in 1842 on the ground that the law providing for their issuance was unconstitutional and that the bonds had been sold on credit to the Bank of the United States in violation of the state statute. Ten years later the people of Mississippi defeated a tax levy for the purpose of paying the interest on $2 million of Planters' Bank bonds; and in 1875 an amendment to the state constitution was ratified by the voters prohibiting the state from redeeming or paying the Union Bank bonds and the Planters' Bank bonds. In 1842 Florida disavowed its responsibility for $3.9 million of bank bonds on the ground that the territorial legislature was not empowered to issue them. In 1842 Michigan repudiated a portion of a $5 million loan on the ground that the state had not received payment for the bonds obtained by the Bank of the United States.

There were many reasons for the growth of repudiation sentiment at this time. The sneers and jeers of the foreign press at American integrity fanned the flames of national prejudices, while the universal indebtedness gave an impetus to the movement in favor of repudiation. Repudiation resulted from a series or combination of forces—speculative mania, ignorance of sound banking, a ruinous depression, blatantly demagogic leadership, and the stupidity of the bondholders in refusing to consider propositions that might have resulted in partial payments of their holdings. While it is true that the meager resources of the American people at that time made it impossible for them to meet their obligations when they fell due, an inability to pay was no justification for refusal to pay.

The second attack of the disease of state repudiation came with the funding of the state debts incurred during the Reconstruction era. These bonds were issued by governments that were not representative of the southern states. Foreign investors were warned not to purchase them. The forced repudiation of the Confederate war debts by the Fourteenth Amendment strengthened the southerner's opposition to the payment of the "bayonet bonds," especially since a large proportion of these securities were held by the "conquerors of the north" who had foisted and maintained the hated Reconstruction governments in the South. The ravages of the Civil War, the misrule of the Reconstruction period, and the hard times following the panic of 1873 increased the heavy burdens of the southern people; but in no case were the debts scaled or repudiated until it was apparently impossible to discharge them. In 1876 Alabama repudiated $4,705,000 of railroad bonds. In 1884 Arkansas, after a long dispute, repudiated $500,000 of bonds held by James Holford of London along with other obligations incurred during the carpetbag regime. In 1876 the Florida Supreme Court declared unconstitutional and void $4 million of railroad bonds. In 1876 Georgia repudiated railroad bonds whose minimum face value amounted to $9,352,000; and the following year the legislature approved a constitutional amendment confirming the repudiation statutes. The total amount of Louisiana's repudiations between 1875 and 1884 was approximately $22 million. In 1879 North Carolina scaled its debt and repudiated more than $12 million of bonds. In 1873 South Carolina repudiated $5,965,000 of "conversion bonds."

Foreign creditors had been prevented by the Eleventh Amendment to the U.S. Constitution from seeking redress. In December 1933 the principality of Monaco, which had come into possession of some of the repudiated Mississippi bonds, asked leave to bring suit in the U.S. Supreme Court against the state of Mississippi; but on May 21, 1934, the Court unanimously held that the principality could not sue the state of Mississippi.

[Robert Trescott Patterson, *Federal Debt-Management Policies, 1865–1879;* Benjamin U. Ratchford, *American State Debts.*]

REGINALD C. MCGRANE

RESACA DE LA PALMA, BATTLE OF (May 9, 1846). The day following Gen. Zachary Taylor's minor triumph at Palo Alto, Texas, the Mexican army under Mariano Arista fell back five miles to the Resaca de Guerrero, where natural defenses offset the effectiveness of superior American cannon and necessitated reliance on infantry and cavalry. In these branches Arista had a numerical advantage, and when Taylor attacked in mid-afternoon the Mexicans at first held firm. After a fierce hand-to-hand combat in the underbrush and chaparral, the Mexican left gave way before the insistent hammering of Taylor's troops. Arista's flank was turned, and his army crumbled under the American assault. A precipitant flight ensued, Taylor's men pursuing the Mexicans to the bank of the Rio Grande, which the latter crossed with difficulty and without order. Mexican losses were 547 killed, wounded, or missing. The American losses were 33 killed, 89 wounded. Taylor wrote his report at the Resaca de la Palma, which gave the battle its name.

[J. H. Smith, *The War With Mexico.*]

HOLMAN HAMILTON

RESERVATIONS, INDIAN. *See* **Indian Reservations.**

RESERVATION SYSTEM, TERMINATION OF. After World War II there were strong pressures in Congress to terminate the Indian reservation system and accelerate the liquidation of the government's responsibilities to the Indians. In 1953 the House of Representatives passed Concurrent Resolution 108, providing for a speedy end to federal supervision of the Indians of five designated states and of seven other tribes. Termination laws were enacted for the Menomini of Wisconsin, the Klamath of Oregon, and a few other small groups, despite intense opposition by Indians throughout the country. The effects of the laws on the Menomini and Klamath were disastrous, and many members of the tribes were soon on the public assistance rolls. President John F. Kennedy in 1961 halted further termination, and the administrations of President Lyndon B. Johnson and President Richard M. Nixon also recognized that the policy had

been in error and that it should be replaced by a policy of encouraging Indian self-determination, with continuing government assistance and services.

[Vine Deloria, Jr., *Custer Died for Your Sins;* D'Arcy McNickle, *Native American Tribalism: Indian Survivals and Renewals.*]

KENNETH M. STEWART

RESERVED POWERS OF STATES. The Constitution of the United States created a government of enumerated powers. The framers intended that all powers not conferred on the national government by the Constitution nor denied by that document to the states should be retained by the states. In the ratifying conventions questions were raised as to why such an important matter had been left to inference. The First Congress reflected this feeling of uneasiness in proposing a series of amendments. Ten of these were ratified by the states. The Tenth Amendment states, "The powers not delegated to the United States by the Constitution, nor prohibited by it to the States, are reserved to the States respectively, or to the people." This amendment securely established the United States as a federal state composed of a central government and a number of constituent state governments, each possessing powers independent of the other.

In Article I, Section 8, of the Constitution, in seventeen clauses, the powers of Congress are set forth. Except in a few instances no state may exercise any of these. To the powers expressly conferred on the national government by the Constitution, the U.S. Supreme Court has, by a consistent policy of broad construction, added many implied powers. It has also pointed out that the national government possesses certain inherent powers by virtue of its sovereign character. No state may invade these fields. These are the powers delegated to the United States that are referred to in the Tenth Amendment.

The powers prohibited to the states by the Constitution are found principally in Article I, Section 10, and in the Fourteenth, Fifteenth, Nineteenth, Twenty-fourth, and Twenty-sixth amendments. By Article I, Section 10, the states are forbidden absolutely to enter into treaties, alliances, or confederations; to grant letters of marque; to coin money; to emit bills of credit; to make anything but gold or silver coin tender in payment of debts; to pass bills of attainder, ex post facto laws, or laws impairing the obligation of contracts; and to grant titles of nobility. They are also prohibited, except with the consent of Congress, from laying duties on imports or exports (with certain exceptions), from laying duties of tonnage, keeping troops or ships of war in time of peace, entering into agreements or compacts, and engaging in war. The Fourteenth Amendment forbids the making or enforcing of any state law that shall abridge the privileges and immunities of citizens of the United States; the deprivation of any person of life, liberty, or property without due process of law; or the denial of equal protection of the laws. The Fifteenth Amendment restrains the power of the states to define the qualifications of electors by forbidding discrimination on the grounds of race, color, or previous condition of servitude; the Nineteenth, on the basis of sex; the Twenty-fourth, by reason of failure to pay any poll tax or other tax; and the Twenty-sixth, on the grounds of age. All of these things states may not do except upon the conditions specified in the Constitution. But all remaining powers of government are theirs.

The Supreme Court of the United States is the final arbiter in case of conflict between a state and the national government over the right to exercise a governmental power. On occasion, as in the Child Labor Cases, the Court has declared acts of Congress invalid because they invaded the reserved powers of the states. On many other occasions state statutes have been declared void as invasions of the power of the national government.

[J. M. Mathews, *The American Constitutional System;* Samuel P. Orth and Robert E. Cushman, *American National Government.*]

HARVEY WALKER

RESERVED POWERS OF THE PEOPLE. The Tenth Amendment reserves all powers not granted to the United States by the Constitution, nor prohibited by it to the states, to the states respectively or the people. It seems clear that the people referred to were the people of the several states, not the people of the United States. Thus viewed, the phrase "to the people" is a pronouncement of a political theory of popular sovereignty—a recognition of the right of the people to create and alter their state governments at will.

If the people of a state merely established a government, placing no limitations upon its powers, the legislative branch would possess all of the authority implied by the Tenth Amendment. But state constitutions commonly go much further than this. Bills of rights to protect the citizen of the state from his state government are found in every state constitution (*see* Bills of Rights, State). In many states the people have reserved to themselves the power to propose new laws through the initiative or to require the submission to

popular vote of laws passed by the legislature through the referendum. As state constitutions grow longer, more and more subjects are removed from legislative competence and are made subject to alteration only by popular vote. Such reservations of power as these give content to the final phrase of the Tenth Amendment.

In another sense it may be said that the effect of the amendment was to guarantee to the citizens of the states the continuation of the legal rights and duties that had been built up by the courts in the common law. Or from still another point of view it is an embodiment in legal phraseology of the right of revolution asserted in the Declaration of Independence. Thus it may be interpreted as an effort on the part of the First Congress to suggest that each citizen might possess a sphere of privacy that should be inviolate from interference by his government.

HARVEY WALKER

RESERVE OFFICERS' TRAINING CORPS. The Morrill Act of 1862 required land grant colleges to provide military training for male students, and these schools predominated among the many American colleges and universities that offered military training before World War I. The U.S. Army contributed officers and equipment, with the aim of obtaining educated officers for the National Guard, and in several states college military units were integrated with the guard. As World War I raged in Europe the National Defense Act of 1916 provided for the establishment of the Reserve Officers' Training Corps (ROTC) designed to bring greater order and new purpose to college military training. Fully trained graduates were assured commissions in an Officers' Reserve Corps that would become available for active duty in a major war. In World War I the land grant schools alone had 30,000 officer-graduates in action.

Between World War I and World War II the army gave even stronger support than before to military training on college campuses, and the navy began similar training in 1925. Military training in secondary schools in the Junior Reserve Officers' Training Corps, begun on a sizable scale by the 1890's, also flourished after World War I. Some opposition to college military training arose, focused on its compulsory character for freshmen and sophomores, but it had no real effect on reserve officer production. At the outset of World War II the army's college units furnished more than 100,000 officers for active duty with the army itself; an additional 7,000 served with the navy and Marine Corps. Their availability at the beginning of the war has been generally recognized as vital to its successful prosecution.

After 1945 the air force joined the army and navy in reviving campus military training. The results were as fortunate for the armed services in the Korean War as in the preceding conflict. During the cold war the substantial and seemingly permanent enlargement of the American military establishment changed the primary objective of college military training from reserve to active duty service; the bulk of military graduates after 1953 were required to serve two years or more of active duty. Then, from 1961 through the decade of conflict in Southeast Asia, almost all college military graduates were called to active duty, and only the cessation of American ground action promised a partial return to the reserve concept.

The unpopularity of the prolonged Vietnam War led to widespread and sometimes violent opposition to military training on civilian campuses, which overshadowed efforts to improve its academic quality and deemphasize its martial characteristics. Some colleges abandoned military activity altogether, and most of them discontinued compulsory training. Even before the truce of January 1973, enrollments had dropped by two-thirds, but more schools than ever, about 375, had military units. All three services had adopted the navy's method of providing scholarships and other inducements designed to assure a steady supply of college graduates for active duty despite reduced enrollments, since they regarded the ROTC as their principal source of junior officers.

[Gene M. Lyons and John W. Masland, *Education and Military Leadership: A Study of the ROTC;* Ira L. Reeves, *Military Education in the United States.*]

STETSON CONN

RESETTLEMENT ADMINISTRATION. Before 1933 agricultural economists had deplored the wasteful and destructive use to which much land was being put in the United States and had urged the adoption of certain controls in land use and the retirement from cultivation of badly eroded and submarginal lands. The conservation-minded New Deal undertook to retire submarginal land as part of its agricultural adjustment program. The Resettlement Administration was created in May 1935 to administer the land retirement program and to resettle the displaced farmers on other areas. It was also given responsibility for the efforts being made to enable tenants to become homeowners.

In 1937 the Resettlement Administration was transferred to the Department of Agriculture, where it became the Farm Security Administration.

PAUL W. GATES

RESIDENCY REQUIREMENTS FOR VOTING. Early in the history of the United States it was established that only residents of a given jurisdiction might vote in its elections. This rule reflects the democratic idea that while it is well to have and consider the views of transients and other nonresidents, a community (be it national, state, or local) is entitled to self-government. More immediately pragmatic justifications—generally and judicially recognized—are problems of fraud, voter identification, and opportunity to acquire knowledge of community affairs.

Until 1970 typical requirements called for one year of residence in the state, six months in the county, and thirty days in the precinct in which one wished to vote. Because of the growing mobility of the population, such restrictions are reported to have barred from the polls some 8 million otherwise qualified voters in the 1960 elections. Congress responded to such reports in 1970 with legislation (upheld by the Supreme Court in *Oregon* v. *Mitchell,* 400 U.S. 112 [1970]) that fixed thirty days as the maximum durational residence requirement for voting in presidential elections. In 1972 in *Dunn* v. *Blumstein* (405 U.S. 330) the Supreme Court struck down a typical state durational residence requirement and indicated that all legitimate state interests could be protected adequately by a thirty-day requirement for voting in state and local elections. The Court, however, emphasized the difference between a requirement of bona fide residence and a durational residence requirement: "An appropriately defined and uniformly applied requirement of bona fide residence may be necessary to preserve the basic conception of a political community, and therefore could withstand close constitutional scrutiny." In this context the Court mentioned approvingly the state's test of bona fide residence: "(1) an intention to stay indefinitely [in the community] . . . , joined with (2) some objective indication consistent with that intent." This or similar tests are appropriate, according to the Court, for determining residence, for example, of college students and military personnel who "leave home" and live for more than thirty days in communities that may resent political "intrusion" by masses of "transient outsiders."

WALLACE MENDELSON

RESOLUTIONS, LEGISLATIVE. Three classes of resolutions are used by Congress. The simplest resolution is one by which one house deals with its own affairs, and such a resolution is not called to the attention of the chief executive or the other house. It may be used, for example, to create an investigating committee, to authorize the printing of special reports, to allow committees to increase their staffs, or to amend its own rules of procedure. Since 1932 some legislation empowering the president to reorganize executive bureaus and to set salaries for federal executives, judges, and members of Congress has provided that the presidential proposals would go into effect unless either house, by a simple resolution, disapproved within a limited time.

Concurrent resolutions involve action by both houses. They are without force and effect beyond the confines of the Capitol; they do not go to the president for approval or disapproval. They may be used to express an opinion or purpose of Congress, as in the case of the 1962 Berlin Resolution declaring it to be the sense of Congress that all necessary means were to be used to prevent Soviet violation of Allied rights in Berlin. More often, they are used to make corrections in bills passed by both houses, to amend conference reports, to fix a time for a joint session to hear an address by the president, or to fix a time for adjournment, for example.

Joint resolutions must be approved by both houses and the chief executive, who may also veto them, with the exception of joint resolutions proposing amendments to the Constitution, which are not submitted to the president. Joint resolutions have the force and effect of law, but they are ordinarily used for minor legislative purposes, such as invitations to foreign governments, extensions of existing laws, or corrections of errors in bills that have already been signed into law by the president. Joint resolutions have been employed for important foreign policy actions—for example, the annexation of Texas (1845) and the delegation to the president of broad powers in the conduct of the Vietnam War, by the Gulf of Tonkin Resolution (1964).

[Clarence Cannon, *Cannon's Procedure in the House of Representatives;* Congressional Quarterly, *Guide to the Congress of the United States;* George B. Galloway, *The Legislative Process in Congress.*]

D. B. HARDEMAN

RESORTS AND SPAS. An interest in mineral springs began in the American colonies in the 17th century. In the years following the French and Indian War the springs became as much a vogue in America as they were in England, both because of their therapeutic promise (drinking and bathing were recommended for a variety of rheumatic, liver, kidney, alimentary, and other complaints) and because they had become a "fashionable indulgence" of the colonial gentry. Stafford Springs, Conn. (with 17th-century roots), Berkeley Warm Springs, Va., and many others conceded preeminence to Saratoga Springs, N.Y., in the 19th century.

As the country moved west new spas attracted the visitor. Early in the 19th century numerous "temporary retreats" sprang up throughout the Mississippi Valley, among them Hot Springs, Ark. (1804), and Blue Licks, Ky. (1818). Later, the presence of springs coupled with the promise of salubrious climate helped bring health seekers to such spas as Colorado Springs, Colo.; Las Vegas Hot Springs, N.Mex.; and Napa Valley and Santa Barbara Hot Springs, Calif.

The seashore also offered some hope to the sick, but the attraction was more often recreational. Long Branch, N.J., claimed prerevolutionary roots, but by mid-19th century the Atlantic coast (and to a lesser extent, the Gulf coast) was dotted with resorts. "Bathing" rather than "swimming" describes the activity in the surf, and by 1871 it could be said that "the etiquette of American sea-beaches permits the two sexes to bathe in company, and a gentleman may escort a lady into the surf, at mid-day with . . . propriety and grace." Long Branch and Cape May, N.J., catering between them to the gentry from New York, Philadelphia, and the South, lost their fashionable position at the end of the century to Newport, R.I., the most exclusive resort of them all, where only the wealthiest could build their "castles."

Steamships, railroads, stages, and eventually trolley cars brought excursionists even to the most exclusive resorts, and with the two-week vacation becoming more commonplace, the shore was no longer the domain of the elite. "Its very proximity to the city," it was said of Coney Island in 1871, "soon made it so popular with the multitude, that its more fashionable frequenters departed to other less accessible regions." In the late 1800's Atlantic City, N.J., had begun to flourish; by the 1950's it boasted 1,200 hotels and 12 million visitors a year.

Still a third type of resort—the "mountain" house—attracted easterners, and the late 19th century, often under the stimulation of the railroads, saw the White Mountains, the Berkshires, the Adirondacks, and much of the Appalachian chain studded with resort hotels, some very large and very fashionable.

In the settlement of the American West the search for good health was turned into a business of immense proportions. Railroaders, real estate operators, and public officials (often with the help of the medical profession) puffed as virtually miraculous the climate of the Great Plains, the deserts, the Rocky Mountains, and southern California—in that order. Hotels and sanitariums, often indistinguishable, catering especially to the tubercular and asthmatic, played a significant role in the growth of such cities as Denver and Colorado Springs in Colorado; San Diego, Pasadena, Los Angeles, and Santa Barbara in California; Phoenix and Tucson in Arizona; and San Antonio and El Paso in Texas in the last three decades of the 19th century. For the most part only the well-to-do could afford the accommodations provided; but in Texas, Arizona, and New Mexico a substantial "invalid traffic" of people who were of modest means, and even indigent, existed. By the 1890's bitter experience and new medical knowledge brought disillusionment. Resorts and hotels, no longer dependent on the sick, began to discourage their patronage.

The railroads, which had made it possible for easterners to winter in California, made Florida even more accessible. Florida, too, had had an appeal to health seekers going back to antebellum days, but its buildup as a winter resort was the work of entrepreneurs who mixed railroading and the hotel business, speculators, promoters, and developers. The culmination came with the creation of Miami Beach out of the jungle in ten years (1913–22). The automobile and then the airplane helped turn all of Florida into a winter haven for many easterners and midwesterners.

One other type of winter resort was to flourish—that devoted to winter sports, especially skiing. Although skiing was not unknown earlier, it was not until the Olympic Winter Games of 1932 at Lake Placid, N.Y., that American interest in skiing began to skyrocket.

Ski resorts first became popular in the East in northern New York and New England. The introduction of uphill transportation—the first rope tow was built at Woodstock, Vt., in 1933; the Franconia Aerial Tramway at Cannon Mountain, N.H., was built in 1938; North Conway, N.H., offered a "ski-mobile"; Pico Peak near Rutland, Vt., copied the European T-bar lift—turned skiing into a downhill sport. The resorts flourished, fed at first by the weekend ski and snow trains from the seaboard cities and later by the ease of automobile transportation.

Colorado, with its ideal climate for skiing and its more than fifty peaks of over 14,000 feet, was not far behind in developing ski resort areas, among them Steamboat Springs, where there has been a winter carnival since 1902; Aspen, which built its first runs in 1935 and which, after World War II, built a 14,000-foot chair lift; and Estes Park, where the first national downhill race was run in 1934. In Idaho the Union Pacific Railroad turned the town of Ketchum into a magnificent resort area, complete with chair lift, hotels, and heated swimming pools; called Sun Valley, it began operating in 1936.

Skiing, with its health as well as its recreational aspects, kept flourishing. In California Yosemite National Park, Lake Tahoe, and Donner Summit were among the early ski areas. In the Northwest ski lodges appeared in the vicinity of Mount Rainier and Mount Hood, the latter built by the Works Progress Administration after the fashion of Sun Valley. From Butte, Mont., to San Diego, Calif., to Flagstaff, Ariz., ski resorts appeared. For the winter of 1974–75 Aspen, with runs on three mountains, could boast of ninety-nine lodges and condominiums for its guests. An inn at Steamboat Springs had a "pillow count" of 728. At Sun Valley two "villages" under the same management had a pillow count of 1,500. Lake Tahoe, in California and Nevada, found itself surrounded by skiing resorts—Squaw Valley, Northstar-at-Tahoe, and a half dozen others.

This popularity of the Rocky and Sierra regions reflected the ease of air travel and the promotion of "package deals" by the airlines. One added feature was the development of the ski resort as a family vacation spot, as evidenced by the ready availability of children's rates, nurseries, and baby-sitters. In the East ingenuity was to meet the competition of the West: the snow-making machine was to turn every sizable hill within driving distance of any populous area into a ski resort.

[C. Amory, *The Last Resorts;* B. M. Jones, *Health-Seekers in the Southwest, 1817–1900;* J. Jay, *Skiing the Americas.*]

DAVID L. COWEN

"RESTOOK WAR." *See* **Aroostook War.**

RESTRAINING ACTS. *See* **Coercion Acts.**

RESTRAINT OF TRADE. The 20th-century importance of the legal doctrine relating to restraint of trade stems from its statutory recognition by the antitrust laws of the United States, although its origins can be traced to the rulings of medieval tribunals. Seeking to protect the public weal, these early judgments found that measures preventing journeymen from opening shops in competition with their former masters were illegal, since the effect was to deny to society the beneficial services of some of its members.

Incorporated into the common law by the 17th century, restraints of trade were characterized by the English courts as either general or partial. Following historical precedent, general restraints were held illegal, since their broad impact was deemed injurious both to the public good and to the well-being of the rising national state. Partial restraints, which arose principally as covenants subordinate to a primary contract for the sale of a business, were permitted, since they customarily restrained the seller from competing with the buyer either for a limited time or in a local area. Such restraints, when otherwise reasonable and therefore enforceable, were judged legal, since their adverse effect on the public good was assumed to be minimal. In so ruling, the courts also avoided conflict with the rights of free contract, as in *Mitchel* v. *Reynolds* (Court of King's Bench, 1711).

In the United States, judicial interpretation of the English common-law heritage varied greatly. As a result the federal courts were obliged to clarify restraint of trade concepts in dealing with section 1 of the Sherman Antitrust Act (1890), which declared every contract, combination, or conspiracy in restraint of trade or commerce to be illegal. Drawing on his view of the common law, Judge William Howard Taft, in *United States* v. *Addyston Pipe and Steel Company* (1898), divided restraints into those ancillary or subordinate to the main purpose of the agreement and those nonancillary, constituting its core. He further held that ancillary restraints alone were to be assessed for reasonableness, depending on their impact on third parties or on the public, while those deemed nonancillary were judged unlawful per se. Upheld by the Supreme Court in *Addyston Pipe and Steel Company* v. *United States* (1899), this decision declared an agreement between Addyston Pipe and other firms to rig price bids and divide markets illegal and, in effect, rendered cartel agreements in the United States unlawful.

Using a different approach in *Standard Oil Company of New Jersey* v. *United States* (1911), Chief Justice Edward D. White applied the test of reasonableness to all restraints, taking the view that only an unreasonable agreement constituted a restraint under the law. This construction semantically avoided conflict between the law of contract and section 1 of the Sherman Antitrust Act, which states that every agreement in restraint of trade is illegal, and thus established a "rule of reason" standard for judging restraints. In practice courts continued to find agreements directly restricting market competition both unreasonable and illegal, rejecting the defense that a restraint with adverse market effects is ancillary to an otherwise legitimate contract, as in *United States* v. *Trenton Potteries Company* (1927) and *United States* v. *National Lead* (1947).

The general terms of the Sherman Act were supplemented by subsequent legislation that sought to deal more specifically with abuses in restraint of trade. The Clayton Antitrust Act (1914) not only declared price discrimination illegal when it undermined competition but also outlawed other restraints, such as tying and exclusive dealing arrangements. The Federal Trade Commission Act of 1914 established a commission, according it the responsibility of maintaining fair competition and the power to bring charges of illegality under the provisions of both the Federal Trade Commission Act and the Clayton Antitrust Act. The Robinson-Patman Act (1936) expanded the area of illegal price actions and, although controversial in some respects, was used successfully in attacking regional (basing point) price systems. The illegality of resale price agreements was measurably lessened by the Miller-Tydings and Maguire-Keogh acts (1937 and 1952), which exempted such agreements from antitrust prosecution in states in which fair trade laws obtained. Although "the rule of reason" remained residual to court interpretation, a trend initiated by the Clayton Act toward holding specific restraints illegal per se has continued, as in *Klors* v. *Broadway Hale Stores* (1959) on refusals to deal and commercial boycotts and in *White Motor Company* v. *United States* (1963) and *United States* v. *Arnold Schwinn and Company* (1967) on exclusive dealing.

Application of restraint of trade concepts to business activity has been uneven in the United States. The trustbusting era at the turn of the century was succeeded by a more strictly legalistic period in the 1920's. An official retreat from earlier positions marked the years of economic crisis in the 1930's, as market agreements, legal under the National Industrial Recovery Act and other governmental programs, were condoned by law. Court decisions also followed the tenor of the times, although deviations from precedent were again reversed in a few years, as in

Appalachian Coals v. *United States* (1933) and *Socony Vacuum Oil Company* v. *United States* (1940). Subsequently the definition of combinations in restraint of trade was extended, and the search for factual proof of market effects was sharpened. In *American Tobacco Company* v. *United States* (1946), the court moved against oligopoly by accepting evidence of parallel price movement as proof of conspiracy in restraint of trade. This doctrine of "conscious parallelism" did not result in meaningful action, although it served to warn oligopolistic firms that their behavior is subject to scrutiny. The courts also interpreted the law more broadly, finding that the mandate of the Federal Trade Commission includes the power to stop "incipient" violations: *Federal Trade Commission* v. *Cement Institute* (1948) and *Federal Trade Commission* v. *Brown Shoe Company* (1966). The Clayton Antitrust Act phrase "may be to lessen competition" has also been construed as bringing the future market effects of restraints within the purview of the law. Most frequently invoked in merger actions, this broader interpretation brought the courts to consider market foreclosure and the elimination of potential competition to be restraints of trade.

With a history of failure in their efforts to use the Clayton Act to block mergers, federal authorities turned to the restraint of trade clause of the Sherman Act in prosecuting merger cases, as in *United States* v. *Columbia Steel Company* (1948). In the 1950's, both the Sherman Act and section 7 of the Clayton Act, as amended by the Celler-Kefauver Act of 1950, began to be invoked. This amendment, closing loopholes in the original law and adding the words "substantially to lessen competition," established the first significant preventive antitrust measure designed to treat monopolistic restraints in their "incipiency," upheld in *United States* v. *Brown Shoe Company* (1962) and *United States* v. *Philadelphia National Bank* (1963). By the 1960's the court was enjoining mergers in markets that evidenced increasing concentration or in which the possibility of market foreclosure was thought to exist. At the same time attention was also being directed toward the reciprocity effects of merger and toward joint ventures between firms. The "incipient restraints" policy has dealt successfully with horizontal and vertical mergers; its application to conglomerate acquisitions was still uncertain in the mid-1970's.

In practice, then, both evolving court interpretation and the enactment of statutes have broadened the application of the restraint of trade doctrine. Many specific market actions came to be held illegal per se

and others to be held illegal depending on the court's assessment of market effects and the type of restraint involved.

Aside from its application to restrictive market agreements, the restraint of trade doctrine under common law precedent was sometimes employed by the courts to prohibit labor from organizing, finding that such activity violated contract rights. For example, in the *Philadelphia Cordwainers'* case (1806), a society of workingmen seeking to raise wages was held to be an illegal conspiracy by the Mayor's Court, which contended that its efforts would result in higher prices for the public and in injury to workers not members of the group. By the 1840's judicial interpretation had changed, and a Massachusetts court limited its legal obligation to the assessment of the lawfulness of the tactics employed, finding that union organization in itself was legal (*Commonwealth of Massachusetts* v. *Hunt*, 1842).

Union activity was at first considered subject to the restraint of trade clause of the Sherman Act, and injunctions were issued against strikes as early as 1893. The public reaction to the Supreme Court's ruling in *Loewe* v. *Lawler* (1908) on the plight of the Danbury, Conn., hatters—who were individually fined for damages resulting from a labor dispute—led Congress to pass the labor exemption provisions of the Clayton Act. While these provisions were hailed as freeing labor from antitrust prosecution, the widespread use of injunctions in labor disputes was not effectively limited until the Norris–La Guardia Act in 1932. In the *Coronado Coal* cases (1919–25) and *Duplex Printing Press Company* v. *Deering* (1921) the Court found against the unions; in *United States* v. *Hutcheson* (1941) the Court reversed its stand.

Union activity was exempt from antitrust prosecution in the mid-1970's except for restraints involving third parties, although the final disposition of agreements between unions and multiemployer associations remained uncertain. Some labor practices involving restraints such as secondary boycotts had been put under the jurisdiction of the National Labor Relations Board (NLRB) by the provisions of the Taft-Hartley Act (1947). Court decisions in *United Mine Workers* v. *Pennington* (1965) and *Amalgamated Meat Cutters* v. *Jewel Tea Company* (1965) suggest that the NLRB may have to consider the antitrust implications before ruling on some cases coming before it.

[J. R. Commons et al., *History of Labor in the United States;* D. J. Dewey, *Monopoly in Economics and Law;* Carl Kaysen and Donald Turner, *Antitrust Policy;* H. H.

RESUMPTION ACT

Liebhafsky, *American Government and Business;* S. C. Oppenheim and G. E. Weston, *Federal Antitrust Laws;* C. Wilcox, *Public Policies Toward Business.*]

OLIVE E. VAUGHAN

RESUMPTION ACT. Late in 1861, owing to conditions produced by the Civil War, specie payments were suspended in the United States. Shortly afterwards, early in 1862, the first issue of legal-tender notes, called greenbacks, was authorized (*see* Legal Tender Act). Before the end of the war, a total of $431 million in greenbacks had been issued, and authorization had been given for another $50 million in small denominations, known as fractional currency or "shin plasters."

During the period of Reconstruction, a political struggle took place between the inflationists and the "sound money" men, thus preventing the early resumption of specie payments and retirement of the greenbacks. At the end of 1874 a total of $382 million of these notes was still in circulation. As a result of the panic of 1873 the Republicans were defeated in the congressional elections of 1874. While they still had the necessary votes they hastened to pass the Resumption Act on Jan. 14, 1875. This law provided for the replacement, "as rapidly as practicable," of the Civil War fractional currency by silver coins. Provision was also made for reducing the greenback total to $300 million. Most important of all, the secretary of the Treasury was directed to "redeem, in coin" legal-tender notes presented for redemption on and after Jan. 1, 1879.

The inflationists in 1878 succeeded in modifying this law by securing the enactment of a measure stopping the destruction of greenbacks when the total outstanding was $346,681,000. The actual resumption of specie payments was carried out under the direction of Secretary of the Treasury John Sherman during the presidency of Rutherford B. Hayes. Aided by the return of prosperity, Sherman was able to accumulate gold to carry out the intent of the Resumption Act. But when people found greenbacks to be on a par with gold, they lost their desire for redemption, thus making possible complete success for the legislation. (*See also* Bland-Allison Act.)

[D. R. Dewey, *Financial History of the United States.*]

ERIK MCKINLEY ERIKSSON

RETALIATION IN INTERNATIONAL LAW. Re-
taliation is a nonamicable action short of war taken by one state against another in response to conduct that the retaliating state considers injurious or unfriendly.

It may be forcible or peaceful. The retaliation is generally in kind when in response to a legal act, such as discrimination in tariffs, restriction of immigration, closure of ports, or legislation against aliens; such action is called retortion. Reprisal, on the other hand, is a retaliatory action that seeks redress for an illegal act, such as refusal to arbitrate or to satisfy claims, confiscation or seizure of property, or injury to citizens of the retaliating state. Reprisal is generally not limited to retaliation in kind and need not be proportioned to the offense that prompted it. Reprisal may take one of several forms: withdrawal or severance of diplomatic relations, display of force, pacific blockade, embargo, nonintercourse, bombardment, or seizure and occupation of property.

Historically the United States has taken reprisals in an effort to seek redress for injuries or wrongs after exhausting diplomatic channels for settlement. In 1807 President Thomas Jefferson, with congressional approval, placed an embargo on all American vessels as a reply to the illegal treatment of American merchant vessels on the high seas by France and England. That measure having failed after a year, the president tried nonintercourse as a means of forcing the two offending nations to mend their ways. In 1834 President Andrew Jackson threatened France with seizure of the property of France or of its citizens in America if the French government persisted in refusing to pay an installment due in the settlement of claims of American citizens. In 1914 an incident involving the unjust arrest of three American seamen by Mexican authorities in Tampico led to the bombardment of the port of Veracruz by warships of the U.S. Navy and to the occupation of that port for several months by U.S. Marines. The reprisal was a response to the failure by Mexico to make adequate amends for the arrest of the sailors. An example of retortion taken by the United States occurred in 1818 when, in response to restrictions placed on American vessels trading with British colonies in the Western Hemisphere, American ports were closed to British ships.

Retaliation takes place in wartime, too, by the belligerents who respond to the introduction by the enemy of measures deemed illegal. Such actions as extending the contraband list, sowing mines, using submarines, bombing unfortified cities, invoking the doctrine of continuous voyage or ultimate destination, or blockading from long range are typical forms of retaliation. During the French revolution the British declared foodstuffs contraband in retaliation for the French policy of placing the whole nation under arms. During the Napoleonic Wars the prodigious system of economic warfare that reached its climax in the Napoleonic Berlin and Milan decrees and in the British Orders in Council was erected by a series of retaliatory measures undertaken by each belligerent in response to the other's actions. Finally, it may be said that fear of retaliation has played a role in determining the weapons used in warfare, as evidenced by the failure by both sides in World War II to use biological and chemical warfare.

[C. C. Hyde, *International Law Chiefly as Interpreted and Applied by the United States.*]

ARMIN RAPPAPORT

REUNION, a French colony established under the leadership of Victor Prosper Considérant in April 1855 near Dallas, Tex., by French Socialists who were followers of Charles Fourier. Considérant explained that Reunion would serve as a center from which would radiate numerous lines leading to other colonies to be established by people who had imbibed the doctrines of Fourier. Some attempts were made to organize colonies in Houston, Tex., and, by the purchase of 50,000 acres, at Uvalde, Tex., but, like Reunion, they were never successful. Some writers estimate that the population of Reunion reached 500, but a more probable estimate would be approximately 300. The colony continued with varying degrees of success and failure until 1867, when it was disbanded and its assets were distributed.

[Victor Prosper Considérant, *Au Texas, le premier rapport à mes amis;* W. J. Hammond, "La Reunion, A French Colony in Texas," *Southwestern Social Science Quarterly,* vol. 17.]

WILLIAM J. HAMMOND

REVENUE, PUBLIC, has been derived from a changing array of tax sources in the United States. Before 1913 customs duties on imports and proceeds from the sale of public lands constituted the major part of the revenue of the federal government. Thereafter taxes on the income of individuals and corporations became the dominant source of government income.

Excise taxes on the sale of selected commodities—notably alcohol, tobacco, and automobiles—provide an important, but lesser, source of revenue. After the 1930's a rapid expansion occurred in social security taxes and other employment-related "contributions" that are, in turn, dedicated to financing specific social insurance benefits.

In the fiscal year 1972 the federal government received about $86 billion, or 43 percent of its total revenue of $198 billion, from the progressive personal income tax. Another $30 billion, or 15 percent, came from the corporate income tax. Social insurance taxes and contributions accounted for $54 billion, or 28 percent. Excise, estate, and gift taxes; customs duties; and miscellaneous receipts produced a total of $28 billion, or 14 percent.

State governments, in contrast, have generally depended most heavily on sales taxes, although most have adopted personal and/or corporate income taxes as sources of supplementary revenue. Through grants-in-aid, the federal government has financed major shares of state expenditures for highways and public assistance.

Cities, counties, and other local governments raise the bulk of their income from the traditional taxes on property values. The larger cities, particularly, have levied payroll taxes in an effort to obtain revenue from commuters who work in the central city but live in adjacent suburbs. State and federal governments have financed rising proportions of education and other local activities, in response to the slow growth in the yield of fixed-rate property taxation.

Overall, revenues raised by state and local governments rose from $18.8 billion in 1951 to $114.8 billion in 1971. These funds were supplemented by $2.3 billion of federal grants in 1951 and $26.9 billion in 1971.

The following table shows the growth of federal revenue, by ten-year periods (in millions):

1791	$ 4.4
1801	12.9
1811	14.4
1821	14.6
1831	28.5
1841	16.9
1851	52.6
1861	41.5
1871	383.3
1881	360.8
1891	392.6
1901	587.7
1911	701.8
1921	5,624.9
1931	3,189.6
1941	7,995.6
1951	53,368.6
1961	94,371.0
1971	$188,392.0

MURRAY L. WEIDENBAUM

REVENUE SHARING

REVENUE SHARING. *See* **Grants-in-Aid.**

REVERE'S RIDE. Paul Revere, a Boston silversmith and a trusted messenger of the Massachusetts Committee of Safety, had foreseen an attempt by the British troops in Boston to seize the military stores collected in Concord, and had arranged to signal a warning to the Whigs in Charlestown. In the late evening of Apr. 18, 1775, he was told by Joseph Warren, chairman of the Committee of Safety, that the British were about to cross the river to begin their march to Concord. Revere signaled the fact by two lanterns (Henry Wadsworth Longfellow's "two if by sea") hung by a friend from the tower of the Old North Church in Boston. Then, using a secreted boat, he managed to cross the river in spite of British patrols and, borrowing a horse in Charlestown, started for Concord. Blocked by British officers from the Cambridge road, he rode via Medford, alarming the country as he went. About midnight he arrived in Lexington, and at the house of the Rev. Jonas Clark roused John Hancock and Samuel Adams, who were thus enabled to seek safety. Joined by William Dawes (sent by Warren via Roxbury) and by young Samuel Prescott of Concord, Revere then set forward with his news, only to be intercepted, a few miles farther on, by a patrol of British officers. Prescott leaped a fence and escaped, carrying the alarm to Lincoln and Concord. Dawes fled back toward Lexington; but Revere was taken. Assuring his captors that the country was roused against them, he so alarmed them that they set him free. He returned to Lexington, helped to save Hancock's papers, and saw the first shot fired on the green. Revere did not reach "the bridge in Concord town," but his feat was of quite as great importance as Longfellow supposed.

[Allen French, *The Day of Concord and Lexington;* Elbridge H. Goss, *Life of Col. Paul Revere.*]

ALLEN FRENCH

REVIVALS. *See* **Evangelism, Evangelicalism, and Revivalism.**

REVOLUTION, AMERICAN. A special place in the national consciousness is reserved for the American Revolution. Its "sanctifying power" arises from the virtual unanimity with which all shades of American political opinion, from Left to Right, regard it as the seedbed of the subsequent development of the nation. Unlike other wars in American history, the Revolu-

tion was not followed by a lengthy period of recrimination and self-doubt by participants, nor did it become the object of revisionism by historians seeking to explain away the country's participation or criticizing the leadership that precipitated it. The Loyalist critics of the event had virtually no audience either in America or in Great Britain for a century thereafter. The lost cause of the Loyalists aroused none of the sentimental affection that southerners managed to excite for their cause after the Civil War. Despite such unanimity there is considerable disagreement among historians about the causes, nature, and consequences of the Revolution. Some aspects of the event remain undisputed: it changed the colonies into independent states, replaced monarchy with republicanism, and welded thirteen separate polities into a union based on the unique principle of divided sovereignty—that is, federalism. While an American nationalism did not precede the rupture with England, the end of the war saw the emergence of characteristics uniquely American: a sense of optimism arising from the relative ease with which the war was won; a belief in the superiority of "militia" soldiers and amateur diplomats over professionals; a rejection of Europe as the home of monarchies, war, and political corruption; and a commitment, however inchoate in the revolutionary era, to the principle that good government is republican government, without the privileges and inequalities of the European order.

The view that the new American nation personified a novel social and political ethic and was not merely a transplanted fragment of the Old World was expressed by contemporaries on both sides of the Atlantic. Thomas Paine, the propagandist of independence, was convinced that by 1783 Americans had become so transformed by the Revolution that their very "style and manner of thinking" were different; and a French observer, Brissot de Warville, was astounded to find how deeply the new Americans believed that "all men are born free and equal." In the 20th century, historians have come to perceive in the American Revolution the first of a whole wave of such phenomena in the Western world, an age of democratic revolutions, expressive of the near-universal aspiration for popular government and of the principle that public power must arise from those over whom it is exercised. In short, then, the American Revolution was more than a colonial revolt against a mother country: it was the beginning of the assault on the ideas and institutions of the "old regime," both in the New World and in the Old World; and its course has not yet been run. Critics on the American Left in the

20th century cavil largely over the incompleteness of the Revolution, the missed opportunities during that upheaval for improving the lot of women, blacks, servants, and children and for restructuring the social, as well as the political, order. Whatever the angle of vision, however, the American Revolution is understood as a momentous event for the history of the world as well as for the future United States.

Background. Years afterward John Adams declared that the Revolution was not synonymous with the War for Independence—that the latter began at Lexington and Concord, but the former occurred long before "in the minds and hearts of the people." The real revolution was the radical change in the colonists' principles and opinions, and this could be traced back to "the history of the country from the first plantation in America." The statement is both true and untrue. The preconditions for the separation from the mother country were surely rooted in the colonial past, but their existence in no way foretold the inevitability of the rupture of the British Empire. Two months after the Battle of Concord, Thomas Jefferson affirmed his cordial affection for continued union with Britain, a view restated officially by the Continental Congress in its Declaration of Causes of Taking up Arms (July 6, 1775): "We mean not to dissolve that union which has so long and so happily subsisted between us. . . . We have not raised armies with ambitious designs of separating from Great Britain." And yet the Revolution arose from a set of conditions that made many, perhaps most, Americans receptive to the idea of independence by 1776. These conditions, of long-standing development, included (1) a system of imperial regulation that subordinated the colonial polity to the administrative direction of officials in London; (2) a web of economic controls, generally designated as the mercantile system, that restricted colonial trade, manufacturing, and fiscal policy by parliamentary legislation; (3) the laxity of enforcement of both the political and the economic controls, permitting the colonies to develop, in effect, a wide degree of autonomy in the years before 1763; (4) the conceptualization in the American mind during the years of "salutary neglect" of the rights to self-government as arising not from royal favor but from the intrinsic character of the British constitution and from those natural laws that the European Enlightenment professed to be the normative feature of the political world in the same sense that Newtonian mechanics determined the shape of the physical universe; (5) the series of British measures, beginning in the mid-18th

century, designed to tighten the bonds between colonies and mother country and to reassert the primacy of imperial over colonial interests; and (6) the colonial response to these "triggers of rebellion," which assumed the character not merely of specific reactions to British measures but of an American world view that saw in the combination of imperial regulations a generalized threat to the liberties of the colonists and a conspiracy to reduce them to political vassalage.

English Mercantilism. Historians writing in the century following independence were wont to attribute primary responsibility for the Revolution to the British mercantile system. Thus, the 19th-century historian George Bancroft solemnly asserted that although there were many sources of the torrent that became the Revolution, "the headspring which colored all the stream was the Navigation Act." Bancroft was referring to the cluster of regulatory acts passed by Parliament between 1660 and 1696 and generally designated as the Acts of Trade and Navigation. Originally intended to bar the Dutch from the imperial carrying trade, the laws came to constitute a comprehensive pattern of regulation of Anglo-American commerce. They confined trade between America and England to ships that were manufactured and manned by Englishmen (or Americans); enumerated a variety of American natural products that must be shipped to or through English ports; required goods of European or Asian origin to be imported into the colonies via England; and levied high duties on non-English sugar and molasses imported into the colonies (the latter by an act of 1733). To prevent colonial exporters from evading English duties by first shipping their products to other colonial ports, these taxes were collected at the port of shipment. Complementing the commercial regulations were laws limiting colonial manufacturing and export of woolens (1699), hats (1732), sailcloth (1736), and finished iron (1750); and a series of acts prohibiting the minting of colonial coins, the establishment of banks, and the issue of paper money except under the most extraordinary (usually wartime) circumstances.

Superficially these laws appeared to place the colonies in an economic straitjacket, compelling them to concentrate their labors on the production of raw materials needed in England and making them dependent on the mother country for their finished products. As in most colonial economies the consequence was to create heavy and increasing trade deficits in the colonies and an imbalance of payments in Britain's favor. In the absence of accurate and complete statistics, the extent of this imbalance can only be estimated. It was greatest in New England and the Middle Colonies, which raised few products for export to Great Britain, and smallest in the southern colonies, which could use their exports of tobacco, rice, indigo, and naval stores to pay for their British imports. Overall the colonial trade deficit with England ranged from £67,000 annually during the decade 1721–30 to almost £900,000 annually during the years 1751–60. There is little evidence, however, that these deficits were major causes of colonial complaint. Further, they were offset by colonial profits earned in trade with southern Europe and the West Indies, funds brought to America by immigrants, and expenditures by the British government for the defense and administration of the colonies. The view of some modern economic historians is that no actual deficits were incurred by the colonies throughout the 18th century and that the benefits of membership in the British Empire (protection of the British navy, favorable insurance and shipping rates, bounties, and preferential tariffs) offset the costs to such a degree that the net burden imposed on the colonists by the Navigation Acts was no more than 25 cents per capita annually, or between 1 and 2 percent of national income.

The restrictive character of the regulations on manufacturing and currency may have been exaggerated as well. It is unlikely that a large-scale woolen industry would have developed in America in any case, given the superiority of British woolens; the hat industry expanded despite British restrictions; and some colonial industries actually profited from British regulatory legislation. There were more forges and furnaces in America than in England and Wales, and by 1775 one-seventh of the world's iron was being produced in British North America. American shipyards contributed one-third of all the vessels in the empire trade, and three-quarters of the ships in the colonial carrying trade were American. British legislation did not prevent the development of active distilling, glass, stoneware, milling, and meat-packing industries in the colonies or of the profitable fur business. Despite British currency restrictions, the colonies appear to have acquired enough specie from their international trade and enough paper money from periodic local emissions to meet their needs; in the Middle Colonies, particularly, the paper money was neither largely inflated nor badly managed. The observations of European travelers about the well-being of Americans, the rise of colonial fortunes, the high rate of wages, and the relatively high economic growth rate all attest to the general prosperity of colonial America

as adequately as a statistical estimate that, in 1967 dollars, the per capita physical wealth of the free population in 1774 (excluding cash, servants, and slaves) was $1,086, making colonial Americans better off than most Europeans at the time and as well off as 19th-century Americans. Clearly, the American Revolution was not the product of economic privation.

On the other hand, neither the benefits nor the burdens of English mercantilism were evenly distributed within the colonies, nor can statistical evidence document the frustrations, irritations, and personal hardships created by British economic restrictions. It is impossible to calculate how much more colonial energy and capital would have been invested in manufacturing had obstructive legislation not acted as a deterrent. Surely the price of imports was raised by the inability of Americans to purchase under competitive conditions from other than English sources, and the price of exports was correspondingly depressed by being confined to English outlets. The merchants of New England and the Middle Colonies were often able to meet their trade balances with Great Britain only by illicit trade with the West Indies, and smuggling everywhere eased somewhat the burdens of lawful observance of the Navigation Acts. Southern planters traded so exclusively with the mother country and were so dependent on its credits that they found themselves saddled, by 1776, with a huge debt, prompting Jefferson to quip wryly that Virginians were ''a species of property annexed to certain mercantile houses in London.'' The condition reflected the extravagance of the Virginia aristocrats and the limitations of a one-crop economy as much as involuntary participation in the British mercantile system. Perhaps the most important explanation for the ability of Americans to prosper within British mercantilism was the failure of the mother country before 1763 to make the system fully operative and of the colonies to observe all its strictures.

Old Colonial System. Britain's colonies in North America were not settled according to any comprehensive plan, and during most of the 17th century they received little direction from the imperial government. Although the crown after 1625 asserted its jurisdiction over all the colonies, it developed no overall administration for them. In 1675 a committee of the Privy Council, designated the Lords of Trade, was given general responsibility for the political and economic direction of the colonies, but during its ten-year life it failed to construct a system for ensuring colonial subordination to royal authority. In 1696 a new body, the Board of Trade, was established to handle colonial affairs. Although having an advisory function only, its eight permanent members became the crown's and Parliament's experts on colonial matters, reviewing all colonial legislation, writing instructions for colonial governors, hearing complaints from colonial assemblies and royal officials, and recommending appropriate action to the king and Parliament. Not until 1768 was a secretary of state for American affairs created as a separate cabinet post. Above the Board of Trade sat the Privy Council, which disallowed colonial laws, heard appeals from colonial courts, and appointed colonial governors and approved their instructions.

A host of other officials assisted in administering the empire: the bishop of London, with ecclesiastical jurisdiction over the colonies; the treasury and the customs board, with responsibility for the collection of duties and revenues; and the Admiralty and the War Office, supervising the army and navy in America. But the linchpin of empire was the royal governor, who sat in all the colonies except Connecticut and Rhode Island, where by charter right the governor was elected. With wide powers to appoint local officials, to grant land, to hand down pardons, to hear lawsuits on appeal, to command the militia, to veto legislation, and to convene and dismiss the provincial assembly, the governor possessed in theory all the majesty of the crown itself within the colony over which he held sway as "captain general and governor in chief."

But practice did not comport with theory, and in the divergence between the two lay both the strength and the weakness of the imperial system. In America the governor's extensive prerogatives were effectively weakened by the rising power of the assemblies, controlled by local elites, who by 1776 dominated the political, social, and economic life of their colonies. Using as levers their power to levy taxes and to disburse funds, the assemblies wrested a variety of other powers from the chief executive simply by threatening to withhold the grant of his annual salary unless he complied with their legislative wishes. Without permanent salaries guaranteed from England, governors became complaisant, even if this meant a rebuke from the authorities in London. By 1776 the assemblies not only possessed fiscal power but, through it, controlled the appointment of local officials whose salaries they determined. In addition, they largely set the qualifications for membership in the house, established franchise requirements, and

denied the governor's council the right to amend money bills—and they claimed such rights by virtue of the status of each as a miniature House of Commons.

Governors were generally unequal to the contest with the assemblies. Largely English-born, serving short terms in their colonial posts, they never acquired enough familiarity with local politics to learn to manage the assembly or to build political machines of their own. The patronage powers through which they might have created countervailing forces were undermined by the absence of an independent gubernatorial purse and by the failure of the home authorities to honor gubernatorial nominations. As early as 1670 one chief executive complained that the assembly's fiscal powers had "left his Majesty but a small share of the Sovereignty." A strong governor was likely to arouse complaints to London from the colonists about his "uneasy administration." A compliant governor would be admonished by the Board of Trade for his weakness. The problem, as described by Gov. Jonathan Belcher of Massachusetts, was to "steer between Scylla and Charybdis; to please the king's ministers at home, and a touchy people here." Only the most extraordinary of chief executives was capable of resolving the dilemma, and the men sent to administer the American colonies were far from extraordinary. They may not have been the "decayed courtiers and abandoned, worn-out dependents" that one colonist complained of, but even friends of the crown, such as New York merchant John Watts, were convinced that "better men must be sent from home to fill offices or all will end in anarchy."

The shortcomings of imperial administration in the colonies were paralleled by weaknesses in the machinery of government in London. The Board of Trade possessed only recommendatory powers; it shared responsibility for the colonies with too many other official agencies. The most important single office in colonial administration before 1768 was that of secretary of state for the Southern Department—and the post was held by no fewer than twenty-three men between 1696 and 1768. The damage created by such instability was acute. Colonial problems received only short-term attention in London, while the colonial governors, who might have provided the needed strength and stability for imperial administration, had their authority undermined by inadequate support in England and by the challenge of powerful assemblies in America. In cases of conflict between provincial assemblies and royal governors, the inclination of

British officials was to concede to the American legislatures, especially during wartime, when the colonies were relied on as reservoirs of men and money. The objective, in the words of the Board of Trade, was to make government in the colonies "as easy and mild as possible."

The relationship between colonies and mother country by 1763 has been described as an "uneasy connection." The colonies had achieved a wide measure of political competence. They had their own political institutions, controlled by the local elites who governed with the support and even the participation of a relatively broadly based constituency. The economic prosperity of the colonies added to their sense of self-importance. That this *de facto* autonomy existed within a theoretical framework that held the colonies to be inferior polities within the empire troubled Americans not at all so long as no real effort was made by Britain to have practice conform to theory. When after 1763 Great Britain undertook to do just that, the crisis was precipitated.

Crisis of Empire. The old British Empire was set on the road to disruption when authorities in London decided to end the policy of accommodation, or salutary neglect, that had characterized colonial administration throughout much of the 18th century and to bring the American provinces under stricter control. The need for a less "slovenly and chaotic" system of governance was evident in the late 1740's, as governors deluged the Board of Trade with complaints about the intractability of their assemblies and the perpetual encroachments of local legislatures on the royal prerogative. One consequence was the establishment of a regular packet service in 1755 between England and America to speed up the process of decisionmaking. Another was instructions to all governors to enforce the Navigation Acts rigorously, to secure permanent salaries for royal officials, and to disapprove any fiscal legislation that permitted the assemblies to spend money without the order of the governor. The outbreak of the French and Indian War (or the Great War for Empire) in 1754 temporarily halted the campaign to reduce the autonomy of the colonies, but the war itself emphasized the need for the effort.

The cost of the conflict with France doubled the British national debt and added £8 million to the British annual budget. For this expenditure on their behalf, the American colonies appeared to show little gratitude. Colonial manpower contributed minimally to the military effort; colonial assemblies had only grudgingly met their financial obligations to support the troops engaged in their own defense; and, worse, colonial merchants engaged in illicit private trade with the enemy in the midst of the armed contest. The acquisition from France and Spain of the tramontane West, Canada, and Florida enlarged the task of imperial government considerably. The new territories had to be administered; the Indian tribes that had aided Britain during the war had to be assured against spoliation of their hunting grounds by covetous settlers; a permanent army of regulars had to be stationed in the American colonies for their defense and for keeping the peace with the Indians. As a matter of equity no less than of financial necessity, the colonies were to be required to share the new burdens of empire. More, the weak links in the commercial connection between Britain and the colonies had to be strengthened. A system of customs collection that required an outlay of from £7,000 to £8,000 a year to produce a return of under £2,000 appeared ridiculous to British officials. In a comprehensive report to the Privy Council in October 1763, the Board of Trade warned that the proper regulation of colonial commerce was "of immediate Necessity, lest the continuance and extent of the dangerous Evils . . . render all Attempts to remedy them hereafter more difficult, if not impracticable."

Under the leadership of George Grenville and Charles Townshend the British ministry took steps between 1763 and 1767 to ward off the threatened evils. A royal proclamation in 1763 placed a temporary limit on further western settlement and established stricter regulations for carrying on the fur trade in Indian territory. Customs collectors formerly living at ease in Britain while deputies in America did their work were ordered to their colonial posts. An American board of customs commissioners was established at Boston, and a new system of vice-admiralty courts was created to try offenses under the Acts of Trade—in juryless courts. The Quartering Act (1765) required the colonies to defray the cost of housing a 10,000-man standing American army. The Currency Act (1764) strictly enjoined the colonial assemblies from emitting any further paper money as legal tender. And to defray at least half the cost of the new American military establishment and to provide funds for a permanent civil list in the colonies, a whole range of new taxes and duties was mandated: a tax on newspapers and legal and commercial documents (Stamp Act, 1765); lower but strictly enforced duties on the importation of foreign molasses (Revenue Act, 1764); and new duties on imported lead, glass, paint, paper, and tea (Townshend Acts, 1767).

However defensible and propitious from the British point of view, the efforts at tightening the reins of imperial administration could scarcely have come at a less opportune time in America. Flushed with the victory over the French, the colonists saw themselves as the saviors of the British Empire in America. The removal of the enemy in Canada decreased their military dependence on England, and their heightened sense of independence and self-confidence led them to expect a more important, not less important, role in the empire. Colonial assemblies, already in the ascendancy before the war began, increased their powers during the conflict as they successfully appealed over the heads of the governors to William Pitt as war minister; and the governors had many of their own powers usurped by the British army and navy commanders in America. Finally, the economic climate was insalubrious for new British taxes, for the artificial prosperity of wartime was followed by a recession, reflected in a shortage of specie, declining land values, and the end of the French West Indian trade.

The introduction into this volatile situation of a range of unaccustomed impositions appearing to alter the traditional relationship between the colonies and England produced almost predictable results. The new imperial program was denounced not only as unjust and burdensome but also as unconstitutional; and the heart of the American objection in the long run was that whatever the logic or necessity of the program, it lacked the essential element of colonial consent. For Americans, whose conception of empire had become that of a greater England in which the colonies functioned as partners rather than as subordinates, the Grenville-Townshend measures bore the marks of insult and illegitimacy.

The colonists may well have been able to afford the new taxes. The rum industry probably would not have been ruined by the higher duties on French sugar and the more strictly enforced duties on French molasses. The Stamp Act would not have drained the colonies of specie: the monies collected would have been spent in America to support the British military establishment there. The new customs duties would have been passed on by importers to American consumers, whose tax burden was some fifty times less than that of English taxpayers. But whatever the economic basis of their dissent, the Americans framed their protests during the next decade in the context of their "ancient, legal, and constitutional rights" not to be taxed without their own consent. "The question is not of the expediency of the Stamp Act," the British commander in Boston, Gen. Thomas Gage, informed

the secretary of state, "or of the inability of the colonists to pay the tax; but that it is unconstitutional, and contrary to their rights." When the British denied the charge on the grounds that the colonists were "virtually" represented in Parliament, as were all other Englishmen, whether they participated directly in the election of representatives or not, Americans responded that the interests of the colonists could never be adequately represented in a body 3,000 miles away. When one American publicist, Daniel Dulany, objected to the stamp tax as a novel "internal tax" intended for revenue purposes exclusively, Parliament countered with "external" duties designed to regulate trade. The New York Assembly thereupon responded for the colonies that "all impositions, whether they be internal taxes, or duties paid for what we consume, equally diminish the estates upon which they are charged"; and John Dickinson, in his enormously influential *Letters From a Farmer in Pennsylvania to the Inhabitants of the British Colonies* (1767–68), enlarged the grounds of colonial opposition by insisting that any "Act of Parliament commanding us to do a certain thing . . . is a tax upon us for the expence that accrues in complying with it."

As they argued their case, the colonists came to formulate a well-rounded constitutional theory representing an American consensus: The British constitution fixed the powers of Parliament and protected the liberties of the citizen; such a constitution could not be changed by the stroke of a pen; the powers of Parliament were limited; and those powers were specifically limited with regard to the American colonies by their immutable right to legislate for themselves in matters of internal concern. No objection was raised to Parliament's exercise of broad general authority in imperial affairs, but the demand was made that the line between imperial and American concerns be clearly defined and scrupulously observed. Just as a delicate and proper balance existed between the elements of the British government—king, lords, and commons—so the division needed to be observed in the colonies between the prerogative power of the crown and the lawful rights of the provincial assemblies. When Britain taxed the colonies, authorized searches of private homes without specific warrant through writs of assistance, tried Americans in juryless courts, and placed American judges at the mercy of the executive by appointments "at the pleasure of the Crown" rather than "during good behavior," it denied Americans rights that Englishmen at home possessed. If Americans were indeed entitled to the "rights of Englishmen," then such rights implied equality of treatment for Britons wherever they resided. By stressing the constitutionality of their own position, American leaders sought to legitimize their cause and to place Britain on the defensive. As Richard Dana put the matter on the occasion of the Revolution's first centennial, "We were not the revolutionists. The King and Parliament were . . . the radical innovators. We were the conservators of existing institutions."

The heavy emphasis that Americans placed on constitutional forms of protest bespoke the essential conservatism of the colonial leadership—lawyers, merchants, and planters. But the protesters were not unwilling to employ more forcible means of expression to achieve their ends. These other "necessary ingredients" in the American opposition were economic coercion by the boycott of British imports, a technique used against both the Stamp Act and the Townshend Acts; mob violence, such as the intimidation of stamp distributors, the public humiliation of customs informers, street rioting, and effigy burning; and outright defiance of the law, including the refusal to do business with stamped documents, the publication of newspapers on unstamped paper, and the refusal of the New York Assembly to vote the funds required for troop support under the Quartering Act. That the violence was more tempered in America than in Europe's popular disturbances is explained not only by the reluctance of the American leadership to resort to force except under the most disciplined controls but also by the absence of the kind of official constabulary that might have interposed counterforce and thus produced heightened violence. To conservatives there was obvious danger in enlisting the mob, both because of the ease with which violence could be shifted from imperial to local objects of hostility and because of the opening that would be provided for the politically inarticulate to become part of the body politic.

The furious American protests engendered by the Grenville-Townshend program took British officialdom by surprise. All the new imperial measures had been approved by large parliamentary majorities, and little attention had been given to the consequences. Horace Walpole's classic statement about the passage of the Stamp Act stands as testimony to the state of British insouciance: "Nothing of note in Parliament but one slight day on American taxes." In the face of the colonial onslaught, Parliament retreated: it repealed the Stamp Act in 1766 and the Townshend Acts in 1770; and it modified the Proclamation of 1763 so as to permit gradual movement of settlers and

fur traders to the West. The retreat was prompted by the damage done to British economic interests by the colonial boycotts. British exports dropped 20 to 40 percent during the protest movements of 1765–66 and 1767–70; the Townshend duties were estimated to have produced £3,500 in revenue at a cost to British business of £7.25 million. On the issue of its right to tax the colonies, Parliament did not retreat at all. In the Declaratory Act (1766), which accompanied the repeal of the stamp duties, it asserted unequivocally its power "to make laws and statutes . . . to bind the colonies and people of America . . . in all cases whatsoever"; and when it repealed the Townshend duties, it retained a tax on tea to reaffirm that power.

Between 1770 and 1773, incidents in the colonies maintained and even escalated the mutual suspicions already generated between representatives of British authority and spokesmen of the colonial position: a clash between some of New York City's citizens and British soldiers over the destruction of a liberty pole on Jan. 19, 1770 (the Battle of Golden Hill); the encounter between Bostonians and English soldiers on Mar. 5, 1770, resulting in the death of five Americans (the Boston Massacre); the destruction of a British customs schooner, the *Gaspée,* by the irate citizens of Rhode Island on June 9, 1772; and a protracted controversy that continued throughout these years between the South Carolina Assembly and the governor over the legislature's right to disburse funds without the approval of the chief executive or his council (the Wilkes Fund controversy). In Massachusetts such radicals as Samuel Adams used each anniversary of the Boston Massacre to remind Bostonians of the need for eternal vigilance to prevent the utter extinction of American liberties by British armies. In all the northern colonies the period witnessed a wave of fear on the part of dissenting religious sects over the proposal initiated by some Anglican clergymen, notably Samuel Seabury and Thomas Bradbury Chandler, to strengthen the Church of England in the colonies by appointing a resident bishop. Overly suspicious colonists saw in the proposal a move to enlarge the encroachments of British temporal power by adding to it ecclesiastical suzerainty.

Underneath all the specific irritants in the Anglo-American relationship was the overriding constitutional-legal question of how the claims of two contending centers of political power could be reconciled. Disclaiming independence, the colonists came to conceive of the empire as a divided sovereignty, part being exercised by the English Parliament and part inhering in the respective colonial assemblies. To

English Whigs, whose Glorious Revolution had in 1688 wrested independent powers from the crown and vested them in the "King *in* Parliament," it seemed that any diminution of parliamentary sovereignty would only enhance that of the crown. The idea of a commonwealth of autonomous sovereignties seemed chimerical: either Parliament had all power to govern the colonies or none at all. Americans gradually came to prefer the second alternative. Their reluctant acceptance of the idea of separation from the British Empire was given emotional support by the conviction that Britain had lost its ancient virtue, corrupted its constitution, and abandoned the liberties of its citizens. America must not go the way of Britain. The example of classical antiquity was cited as proof of the ease with which republics could become captured by despots when a free people failed to resist encroachments on their liberties by power-hungry officials. The writings of English radical thinkers of the early 18th century, particularly Thomas Gordon and John Trenchard, provided evidence of the dangers to liberty even in Whig England, in the form of standing armies, patronage-ridden parliaments, corrupt ministers, controlled elections, and grasping priests and bishops. The republication of these writings—*Cato's Letters* and the *Independent Whig*—in American newspapers and pamphlets revealed the readiness of the colonists to accept the reality of such danger and, at the same time, heightened their fears of its imminence. The spirit of Puritanism was summoned up to warn Americans of the threat to their souls if they failed to purge themselves of the evil of political, as well as moral, corruption. And John Locke's familiar compact theory of government provided theoretical justification for the last resort of a free people whose liberties were infringed by an arbitrary government: dissolution of the original compact.

For such modern historians as Bernard Bailyn, the emergence of this American ideology—integrating constitutional theory, legal abstractions, political grievances, and economic and social discontent into a comprehensive set of values, beliefs, and attitudes—explains the outbreak of the Revolution and makes understandable its character and consequences. America's response to British measures, in this view, was less the result of economic despair, social unrest, or religious oppression than of fear that traditional colonial liberties were being deliberately destroyed by acts of British power. The mood evoked by these fears was not merely a defensive adherence to a cherished past when American liberties were secure, but a buoyantly optimistic vision of the future; for the

obligation now imposed on Americans was not merely to preserve their own virtue and freedom but also to "rouse the dormant spirit of liberty in England"—that it was a "great and glorious cause." Colonial leaders felt that the eyes of all Europe were upon them: "If we fail, Liberty no longer continues an inhabitant of this Globe," James Allen, a Philadelphian, confided to his diary on July 26, 1775. And Paine gave the idea consummate expression in *Common Sense:* "Every spot of the old world is over-run with oppression. Freedom hath been hunted round the Globe. . . . O! receive the fugitive and prepare an asylum for mankind."

By 1776, Americans possessed the machinery for revolution as well as the ideology. At the local level, militants had organized groups called Sons of Liberty to carry on the agitation against the Stamp Act. While the Sons engaged in intercolonial correspondence with each other, no real union was effected. A more serious instrumentality of intercolonial action was the system of committees of correspondence initiated by the Virginia legislature in 1773. Other colonial assemblies took up the idea, and a network of official legislative committees was soon in existence to concert uniform efforts against British measures. In 1773 Great Britain unwittingly put the system to the test by the enactment of the Tea Act, a blunder of the most momentous consequence. The act aimed to save the East India Company from bankruptcy by permitting it to sell its large tea surpluses directly in America, without payment of the usual British reexport duties. The measure threatened to undercut the business not only of colonial smugglers but also of lawful merchants who usually acted as consignees of the company's tea. Tea "parties" in a number of colonies destroyed the company's product before it could be distributed. The most famous act of destruction was the dumping of 90,000 pounds of tea in Boston harbor on Dec. 16, 1773. When Parliament in 1774 punished Massachusetts by a series of acts—the so-called Intolerable Acts—that included the suspension of the province's charter of government and the closing of the port of Boston, the intercolonial apparatus of committees of correspondence went into action. Relief supplies were sent from everywhere to the beleaguered city, and a congress of the colonies convened in Philadelphia on Sept. 5, 1774.

"No one circumstance could have taken place more effectively to unite the colonies than this manoeuvre of the tea," John Hancock noted. The issue debated in Philadelphia at the Continental Congress was not the East India Company's monopoly, or even the tea tax, but the larger issue of the rights of the colonies and their constitutional relationship with Great Britain. The Declaration of Colonial Rights and Grievances reaffirmed the colonists' right to "a free and exclusive power of legislation in their several provincial legislatures"; a conservative proposal of reconciliation by Joseph Galloway of Pennsylvania, hinging on an American parliament as an "inferior and distinct branch of the British legislature," was rejected; and a comprehensive nonimportation, nonexportation, and nonconsumption agreement was adopted. By the meeting of the Second Continental Congress on May 10, 1775, hostilities had already commenced. Blood had been shed at Lexington and Concord on Apr. 19, and in all the colonies militia units were being organized and armed. With the appointment on June 15 of George Washington to command an American army, the colonies were ready for civil war. The Revolution had begun, but its objectives were not yet clearly defined.

Conciliation or Independence. Americans of all shades of political opinion in 1775 were prepared to fight for their rights, but not all favored a separation from Britain. Only a minority of the Second Continental Congress agreed with John Adams that "the cancer is too deeply rooted and too far spread to be cured by anything short of cutting it out entire." Congress was controlled by moderates, sentimentally attached to the empire, admiring of its institutions, and deeply respectful of the virtues of the British constitution. They feared the consequences of a total rupture: the danger to their persons and property as rebels should their challenge to authority fail, and the equal danger that success would bring social upheaval and mob rule. Could an independent America, shorn of British protection, prevent a foreign invasion? The mood of the moderates was perhaps best expressed by Thomas Jefferson's cautionary note in the later Declaration of Independence: "All experience hath shewn, that mankind are more disposed to suffer, while evils are sufferable, than to right themselves by abolishing the forms to which they are accustomed."

Many conservatives clung to the hope that friends of America in Great Britain would bring about a change in the ministry and thereby end colonial grievances. These hopes were shattered by the failure of every plan of accommodation that emanated from Britain before 1776. A proposal by William Pitt the Younger that Parliament renounce taxation of the colonies in return for American acceptance of parliamentary sovereignty was overwhelmingly beaten in the House of Lords. A conciliatory resolution sponsored by the prime minister, Frederick North, known by courtesy as Lord North, to forbear taxing any colony that made adequate voluntary contributions for the support of the empire was rejected by the Continental Congress as unduly vague. A scheme offered by a Scottish nobleman, Thomas Lundin, the titular Lord Drummond, going further than North's plan in promising a "formal Relinquishment" of all future parliamentary claims to colonial taxes and a permanent imperial constitution, failed when Drummond could not produce an official stamp of approval.

Colonial militants were content to allow the force of events to dash the hopes of the conciliationists, and Britain contributed effectively to this end. The king rejected the so-called Olive Branch Petition of the Continental Congress in August 1775 and declared the colonies to be in open rebellion. A few months later a royal proclamation interdicted all trade with the colonies. Sentiment for independence was increasingly aired in the press and was given its clearest expression in Paine's pamphlet *Common Sense,* which appeared in January 1776. Its sale was extraordinary and its impact enormous. In their extralegal associations, Americans had already come to accept the republican idea that all power stemmed from the people. Paine articulated the idea in more uncompromising language: Monarchy was an "exceedingly ridiculous" invention of the devil; the king of Great Britain was a "royal brute"; America gained nothing by its connection with Britain; the tie was a liability, involving America in Europe's wars; and it was time to part. Less logical than emotional, Paine's pamphlet summed up in fervid language all the deep-seated fears and hopes that had been latent in the American mind for a half-century: colonial resentment of inferior status; the New World's rejection of the Old World; the child's demand for recognition as an adult; and America's optimism that it represented the opportunity of creating a political Zion for all mankind in the New World, just as the Puritans had sought to build in Massachusetts a model for wayward England. Paine reassured Americans that they need not fear the separation from Englishmen abroad: they were indeed a different people, not Britons transplanted but new men in a new world. A few years later the Frenchman M. G. J. de Crèvecoeur, who became a naturalized American, summed up the sentiment in *Letters From an American Farmer* (1782): "He is an American, who leaving behind him all his ancient prejudices and manners, receives new ones from the new mode of life he has embraced, the new government he obeys, and the new rank he holds.

. . . Here individuals of all nations are melted into a new race of men."

Declaration of Independence. On June 7, 1776, Richard Henry Lee of Virginia introduced into Congress a resolution declaring the colonies "free and independent states." On July 2, it was adopted. The negative phase of the Revolution was thus ended. Americans gave up the hope of restoring the past and of reconstituting their former relationship with Britain. In the Declaration of Independence, adopted on July 4, they voiced their aspirations for the future as well as their rejection of the past. The Declaration's lengthy indictment of George III and its detailed enumeration of colonial grievances were history; the almost incidental preamble, expounding the principles of equality and popular government, was prophecy. It is unlikely that the conservative signers of the document fully recognized its revolutionary implications. Fifty years later Americans came to appreciate how quintessentially it expressed the primal truths of democratic government; a hundred years later President Abraham Lincoln recognized how perfectly the principles of the declaration served as a "standard maxim" for all free societies, "familiar to all, and revered by all; constantly looked to . . . and augmenting the happiness and value of life to all people of all colors everywhere." The invocation of the declaration by South Americans and Hungarians in the 19th century and by black militants in the United States and emerging nations of Asia and Africa in the 20th century attests the validity of Carl Becker's observation that the philosophy of human rights imbedded in Jefferson's preamble is applicable "if at all, not for Americans only, but for all men." Thus, what was intended as a timely public vindication of the revolt of a single people became a timeless universal political testament.

Loyalists. A substantial minority of Americans declined to opt for independence, and for their refusal they suffered historical neglect for almost two centuries. To the patriots, the Loyalists were traitors to the American cause. Those Loyalists who adhered to their position even after the war ended fled to other parts of the empire, where their voices were not heard by the citizens of the new United States. Other Loyalists remained quietly in their former homes, not daring to call attention to their earlier stand. For republican America the Loyalists were the un-Americans, and they passed from the collective memory.

Estimates of their number vary. Loyalists themselves assured the British government at the outset of the conflict that the majority of colonists were loyal to the mother country. John Adams, some forty years after the event, noted that one-third of the colonial population opposed the Revolution. Both figures are undoubtedly high. More recent estimates suggest that between 15 and 30 percent of the population was loyal to Britain. From 15,000 to 30,000 served in British regular or militia units during the war, and about 60,000 to 100,000 went into exile after the Revolution ended. Some 5,000 eventually made claims to the British government for losses incurred by their loyalty to the crown. Geographically the centers of Loyalist strength were those areas occupied by British troops, either because it was unhealthy to be a rebel in those places or because Loyalists gravitated to garrison towns for protection. New York, Georgia, South Carolina, and North Carolina produced the largest number of Loyalists; Virginia, Maryland, and Delaware, probably the fewest.

Early patriot historians tended to denigrate the Loyalists by characterizing them as the old, the cowardly, the rich and wellborn, and the political reactionaries, but later research has discounted all such categorization. Loyalists came from every segment of the population and from all social and occupational groups and represented every shade of political opinion. Most were probably small farmers, as were most Americans at the time. Obviously, most high officeholders under the crown remained loyal, as did most Anglican ministers in the northern colonies; for the latter, the king was head of the Church of England and was thereby owed spiritual as well as temporal obedience. Yet in the South, most Anglican ministers joined the patriot ranks. Wealthy merchants and landowners, fearful of social instability and the political democracy of republican government, elected to remain with monarchical Britain; but Charles Carroll of Maryland, reputedly the wealthiest man in the colonies, became a rebel. So did many other prominent merchants and landholders. One historian has suggested that loyalism enlisted the support of cultural minorities, such as the Quakers and Highland Scots, because they felt threatened by the drive to cultural uniformity that might be expected of an independent United States; they felt more secure under British rule. Another historian views loyalism as essentially a matter of temperament and disposition, engaging men of timid character who feared the dangers ahead more than the disabilities of the present. Still another has mustered evidence that loyalism was the choice of older elites and established families, patriots comprising the rising and ambitious political and social leadership.

It is unlikely that the friends of Britain deserved the appellation "Tory," with which they were often branded. Their political beliefs, like those of the patriots, were largely Whig. They objected to parliamentary taxation, defended the right of the colonists to govern themselves, and were as suspicious of corruption in the British ministry as were their rebellious neighbors. They were not absolute monarchists but rather "good Whigs" and devotees of the principles of John Locke. What differentiated them from the patriots was that they did not think British provocations extreme enough or the alleged conspiracy against American liberties imminent enough to warrant political parricide. Their inability to feel the moral indignation of other Americans explains their failure to publicize their case more vigorously in print. Many were sure the crisis of 1774–76 would pass, as had the earlier crises. They saw no need for an intercolonial organization to combat the Sons of Liberty, no need to present a lengthy exposition of the merits of loyalty. The prospective rebels, in their view, were the ones who had to make a case. When the Loyalists realized how well the rebels were succeeding, it was too late for the king's friends to make their own bid for public support.

The ultimate tragedy of the Loyalists is illustrated by the fate of the 7,000 who exiled themselves to Great Britain. They returned "home" because they felt more British than American, but they soon discovered that they were not welcomed by Englishmen and that they were not at home in Britain. Those Loyalists who remained in America during the Revolution suffered harassment, physical assault, incarceration, banishment, and confiscation of property. In some regions, such as New York, the civil war fought between Loyalists and patriots assumed bloody proportions. Yet when the war ended, many Loyalists were permitted to resume their old places in their native states and to become quietly reintegrated into the life of the American republic.

Diplomacy. Although the Declaration of Independence represented America's rejection of the Old World, the Revolution was from its inception pursued in an international context. The revolutionary crisis was itself an outcome of the great war between France and Britain for supremacy of North America. In weighing the decision for independence, European considerations were never far from the minds of the American leadership. Some opposed independence precisely because an America standing alone would be prey to foreign foes; others opposed independence until there was assurance of foreign support for the new republic. Still others urged independence out of fear that Great Britain would partition North America with France and Spain in return for their aid in suppressing the rebellious colonies. One purpose of the Declaration of Independence was to enlist the sympathetic ear of "a candid world" and to state the causes of separation in such a way as to ensure the "decent respect" of the "opinions of mankind." Few Americans believed that they could fight a successful war without aid from abroad. Thus, the United States entered nationhood with the same diplomatic ambivalence it was to exhibit thereafter: a desire to be free of the intrigues and politics of Europe, mixed with the conviction that the fate of the New World was indissolubly linked with that of Europe. Testifying to this ambivalence was America's dualistic stand: isolationism in separating from Great Britain, accompanied by involvement in European politics through a binding alliance with Britain's traditional foe, France, as an essential ingredient in the success of that separation.

The alliance with France of 1778 reflected the colonies' desperate need for men, money, arms, and recognition, not any emergent affection for the Bourbon monarchy. France, in turn, found the alliance a useful tool in its long-range diplomatic struggle to reduce the power of Great Britain; it did not have any enthusiasm for colonial uprisings or republican government. France began sending supplies to the colonies secretly even before independence was declared and unofficially from 1776 to 1778. It required the American victory at Saratoga in October 1777 to convince the French that an open and official alliance could be risked. A commercial treaty assured each signatory of "most favored treatment" in its trade with the other; a political compact united the two countries in the war against Britain, each agreeing not to make peace without the consent of the other.

The French liaison was enormously useful to the colonists. French gunpowder made possible the victory at Saratoga, and the presence of the French fleet off the Virginia coast assured the defeat of Gen. Charles Cornwallis at Yorktown in 1781. French monetary aid amounting to $7 million constituted a substantial contribution to the precarious war chest of the American states; French seaports provided refuge for American privateers; and French recognition lifted American morale. On the negative side, the entry of Spain into the war in 1779 as an ally of France confused the objectives of the conflict, for Spain was interested in recapturing Gibraltar from Britain and was assured of French assistance, thus linking the American cause to Spain's European interests. The French alliance proved even more embarrassing to the new United States when it sought in the years after the Revolution to pursue an independent diplomatic course. It was not until 1800 that the vexatious treaties were canceled, during the administration of President John Adams.

That the alliance with France was a mixed blessing was made evident during the peace negotiations with Great Britain. Technically, the American peace commissioners—Benjamin Franklin, John Adams, and John Jay—were barred from undertaking negotiations without the consent of the French ally; but there is ample evidence that French officials were prepared to terminate the war early without American consent and on terms that would have left the British in possession of considerable American territory. The boldness of America's "militia" diplomats in negotiating a treaty and then presenting it as a *fait accompli* to their French ally was rewarded by extraordinarily favorable terms. By the Treaty of Paris of 1783, to which France ultimately acceded, the United States secured recognition, all of the trans-Appalachian West to the Mississippi River, and the liberty of fishing off the Newfoundland banks. In return the United States promised to place no lawful impediments in the way of the collection of private British prewar debts in the United States and to recommend to the states the restoration of confiscated Loyalist property. The concessions were a small price to pay for two crucial gains: independence and a continental domain for thirteen seaboard states.

Home Front. The two major problems confronting the united colonies in the Revolution were manpower and money; and both stemmed from the absence of any effective centralized political authority through which concerted action by all thirteen commonwealths could be achieved. The problem of effective authority was solved only in 1781 by the ratification of the Articles of Confederation, creating "a firm league of friendship." But by then, the war was virtually over. The political instrumentality by which the states acted at the national level throughout the war was the Continental Congress. It functioned without specific constitutional authority and operated on the principle of government by supplication. Its decisions were not laws but requests to the sovereign states. In securing supplies and military services, the Congress in effect borrowed on the security of the good faith of the United States and its future ability to honor its wartime commitments to suppliers and soldiers.

Both the Congress and the states relied heavily on

paper money or bills of credit to finance the war, the former issuing over $200 million worth and the states about as much. By 1780 the acceptability of national currency had dropped to 2.5 percent of its face value, giving rise to the phrase "not worth a continental." Price inflation was correspondingly fierce; Philadelphia prices, for example, increased 100 percent in three weeks during May 1779. The effect was to impose an enforced tax on most of the public, which by modern standards is a harsh, but not uncustomary, way of financing a war. State price-fixing failed to curb the inflationary spiral, and workers struck for higher pay in several states, including New York, Pennsylvania, and North Carolina; merchants made huge profits from the artificial war-boom economy, and so did farmers, who made up 90 percent of the population, as the demands of both armies for foodstuffs provided them with a ready market for their produce. Congress issued bonds, or loan-office certificates, bearing 4 and 6 percent interest; borrowed abroad, largely from France but also from Holland and Spain; made requisitions for money and commodities directly on the individual states; and secured some funds through the sale of confiscated ships and other enemy property. By early 1781 the whole system was so chaotic that Robert Morris was appointed superintendent of finance to reorganize it. Morris succeeded in rationalizing the various forms of paper credit and in issuing new bank notes through the medium of the quasi-public Bank of North America. Redemption of its notes was expected to come from a variety of excise taxes and customs duties, but Congress never approved the tax program upon which the Morris fiscal plan was structured.

Manpower was in as short supply as money, again resulting from the absence of a centralized political authority possessing coercive powers. The American forces consisted of two basic types, the Continental Line, or regulars, and the state militia. Altogether, almost 400,000 men served in one or the other, but the figure is deceptive. Few of the 230,000 men who were in the Continental army were long-term enlistees. Some served for terms as brief as three months, and Washington never had more than 20,000 men in his command at any one time. The militia, totaling some 165,000 men, were not much more useful in major campaigns than the short-term regulars. At the critical Battle of Yorktown, almost half of Washington's command consisted of French troops. Regulars served by enlistment, having been attracted by numerous bounties in cash and land. Frequently state recruiters competed with Continental recruiters for men. Militiamen were conscripted, with the option of providing substitutes or paying fines for not serving. Deserters were not uncommon, being estimated at half of the militia and one-third of the Continentals during the course of the war. The most spectacular of the many mutinies in the ranks was that of the Pennsylvania Line in January 1781. Whatever the causes of their disaffection, virtually none of the deserters or the mutineers went over to the British; neither did many of the American prisoners who were incarcerated in miserable British prison ships in New York harbor.

An estimated 5,000 blacks served in the American forces; the largest source was the New England states. At first, only free blacks were accepted in the army, but as manpower became short, slaves were drafted for military service in all states except South Carolina and Georgia. Blacks also served as spies, messengers, guides, naval pilots, and construction workers. They were not organized in segregated units but fought side by side with white soldiers. The recruitment, voluntarily and involuntarily, of white servants, vagrants, and convicts, along with free and bonded blacks, lent substance to the British denigration of the American forces as a "rabble in arms." But it was something else, something the British could not appreciate: a citizen army, with high morale and extraordinary powers of survival, which provided almost a half-million Americans with a political education in the merits of republican government. The highest tribute paid to this "rag, tag, and bobtail" army was the contrast made by the Marquis de Lafayette, Marie Joseph du Motier, between American and European soldiery: "No European army would suffer the tenth part of what the Americans suffer. It takes citizens to support hunger, nakedness, toil, and the total want of pay." Paine offered still another explanation of the victory of America's citizen soldiers: "It is not a field . . . but a cause that we are defending."

Results of the Revolution. The American Revolution began as a quest for political independence on the part of thirteen British colonies in North America. The patriot leaders of 1776 did not intend to make a social revolution as well, nor did they mean their war for independence to be a clarion call to colonial peoples everywhere to take up arms against their own imperial masters. The mystery and enduring fascination of the Revolution is that it overflowed its narrow banks and produced consequences greater than intended. The war disrupted existing social institutions, enlarged the body politic, and established new standards by which to measure social progress. The suspicion of power and privilege and the assumption that men had "a common and an equal right to liberty, to property, and to safety; to justice, government, laws, religion, and freedom" became the yardsticks by which institutions in the new republic were tested, immediately and in the distant future. The specific evidences of change were not always spectacular. Bills of personal rights were included in the constitutions of the new states; governors were made elective and often shorn of traditional executive powers; the state legislatures were less dominated by wealthy elites than before. Blacks were freed in some northern states; provision for their future emancipation was made in others; and antislavery sentiments spread even in southern states. Official churches disappeared in all but three of the states, and religious freedom was guaranteed in all of them. Confiscated Loyalist estates were broken up, and some of the property found its way into the hands of small farmers.

But the optimism engendered by the Revolution constitutes the real measure of its transforming character. Slavery did continue; the new men in politics were neither libertarian nor proletarian; the new state governments were still controlled by elites; discrimination against religious minorities did not cease; and women remained second-class citizens in a male society. But there was universal expectation that the road to improvement had been opened. To liberal thinkers in Europe as well as in America, the success of the American Revolution gave hope of a roseate future. An Englishman, Richard Price, viewed events in the New World as opening up "a new prospect in human affairs" and "a new era in the history of mankind." The old regime had been assaulted and its defenses breached. The French philosopher Anne Robert Jacques Turgot, Baron de l'Aulne, agreed with Price: America was "the hope of the human race," and he speculated that it might become the model. Fifty years after writing the Declaration of Independence, Jefferson was confident that its liberal principles would be the signal for arousing men everywhere to burst the chains of bondage that kept them in vassalage to the old order. For these men the American Revolution was the fruition of the European Enlightenment. The Old World through its philosophers had imagined the Enlightenment; the New World in the American Revolution had institutionalized it. It was for later generations of Americans to perfect the design of those institutions and to spell out more fully the implications of the democratic ideology to which the Revolution had given birth.

[John Alden, *The American Revolution,* and *A History of the American Revolution;* Charles M. Andrews, *The Colonial Background of the American Revolution;* Bernard Bailyn, *The Ideological Origins of the American Revolution;* Carl Becker, *The Declaration of Independence;* Samuel F. Bemis, *Diplomacy of the American Revolution;* William A. Benton, *Whig-Loyalism;* Carl Bridenbaugh, *The Spirit of '76: The Growth of American Patriotism Before Independence;* Wallace Brown, *The Good Americans;* Weldon A. Brown, *Empire or Independence;* Edmund C. Burnett, *The Continental Congress;* Robert M. Calhoon, *The Loyalists in Revolutionary America;* Ian R. Christie, *Crisis of Empire: Great Britain and the American Colonies, 1754–1783;* Elisha P. Douglass, *Rebels and Democrats;* Joseph A. Ernst, *Money and Politics in America, 1755–1775;* E. James Ferguson, *The American Revolution;* Lawrence H. Gipson, *The Coming of the Revolution;* Everts B. Greene, *The Revolutionary Generation;* David Hawke, *A Transaction of Free Men;* John Head, *A Time to Rend;* Don Higginbotham, *The War of American Independence;* J. Franklin Jameson, *The American Revolution Considered as a Social Movement;* Merill Jensen, *The American Revolution Within America,* and *The Founding of a Nation: A History of the American Revolution;* Lawrence S. Kaplan, *Colonies Into Nation;* Bernard Knollenberg, *Growth of the American Revolution,* and *Origin of the American Revolution;* Stephen G. Kurtz and James H. Hutson, eds., *Essays on the American Revolution;* Benjamin Labaree, *The Boston Tea Party;* Piers Mackesy, *The War for America;* Pauline Maier, *From Resistance to Revolution;* John C. Miller, *Origins of the American Revolution,* and *Triumph of Freedom;* Broadus Mitchell, *The Price of Independence: A Realistic View of the American Revolution;* Edmund S. Morgan, *The Birth of the Republic;* Edmund S. Morgan and Helen M. Morgan, *The Stamp Act Crisis;* Richard B. Morris, *The American Revolution Reconsidered,* and *The Peacemakers;* William H. Nelson, *The American Tory;* Allan Nevins, *The American States During and After the American Revolution;* Mary Beth Norton, *The British-Americas;* Howard H. Peckham, *The War for Independence;* Benjamin Quarles, *The Negro in the American Revolution;* Arthur M. Schlesinger, *The Colonial Merchants and the American Revolution,* and *Prelude to Independence: The Newspaper War on Britain;* Marshall Smelser, *The Winning of Independence;* Paul H. Smith, *Loyalists and Redcoats;* William C. Stinchcombe, *The American Revolution and the French Alliance;* Carl Van Doren, *Secret History of the American Revolution;* Claude H. Van Tyne, *The Loyalists in the American Revolution;* Willard M. Wallace, *Appeal to Arms: A Military History of the American Revolution;* Esmond Wright, *Fabric of Freedom;* Arthur Zilversmit, *The First Emancipation;* Hiller Zobel, *The Boston Massacre.*]

MILTON M. KLEIN

REVOLUTION, DIPLOMACY OF THE. The revolt of the British colonies in North America became almost instantly a factor in the European international situation. France, prostrated by Great Britain in the French and Indian War, had been compelled at the Peace of Paris (1763) to give up its colonial ambitions and to accept a secondary role in European affairs. The revolt of the colonies was France's opportunity to intervene on the side of the insurrectionists—at first secretly, then openly by treaty—in order to split apart the British Empire, and, by abasing the power of Great Britain, proportionately to raise that of France. Before any agent of the rebel colonies set foot in France, the government of that monarchy, acting under the direction of Charles Gravier, Comte de Vergennes, minister of foreign affairs, and the impulsion of the playwright-courtier Pierre Augustin Caron de Beaumarchais, had adopted a policy of secret assistance in munitions and money (*see* Franco-American Alliance of 1778). The colonies, on their side, hoped for intervention by France without having to pledge themselves as allies.

Before the Declaration of Independence, the Continental Congress sent Silas Deane to France to seek secret assistance. After independence was proclaimed, an American diplomatic commission, composed of Benjamin Franklin, Deane, and Arthur Lee, was sent to France. Vergennes received them informally but not officially. He continued a policy of watchful waiting and secret assistance through 1777, until, following Gen. John Burgoyne's surrender at Saratoga, N.Y., Great Britain made peace overtures on the basis of home rule within the empire (*see* Peace Commission of 1778). To prevent a reconciliation, France made the alliance and treaties of Feb. 6, 1778, which brought it openly into the war. France wanted a triple alliance with Spain; but Spain preferred to enter the war in 1779 on the basis of a separate alliance with France alone (*see* Aranjuez, Convention of). The Spanish government feared the example on its own American colonies of recognition of the independence of the United States.

The Netherlands became involved in the war over the question of neutral rights, and most of the neutral states of Europe joined the Armed Neutrality of 1780 as at least an expression of protest against British naval practice on the high seas. Great Britain thus found itself isolated diplomatically and, after Gen. Charles Cornwallis' surrender at Yorktown, Va., in 1781, confronted by military disaster in America. Opposition in Parliament to further prosecution of the war forced a salvaging of the empire on the basis of American independence, precisely the object of the Franco-American alliance (*see* Definitive Treaty of Peace).

[Samuel Flagg Bemis, *Diplomacy of the American Revolution;* Claude-Anne Lopez, *Mon Cher Papa: Franklin and the Ladies of Paris;* Richard B. Morris, *The Peacemakers;*

REVOLUTION, FINANCING OF THE

Max Sevelle, *The Origins of American Diplomacy;* William C. Stinchcombe, *The American Revolution and the French Alliance;* Richard W. Van Alstyne, *Empire and Independence.*]

SAMUEL FLAGG BEMIS

REVOLUTION, FINANCING OF THE. Because of colonial hatred of any form of taxation, one of the most difficult tasks that faced the Continental Congress was raising money to finance the revolutionary war. Following hostilities at Bunker Hill (June 17, 1775) an issue of $2 million in bills of credit was voted, based on the credit of the states. Unsatisfactory as this method proved, Congress continued until Nov. 29, 1779, to emit paper money to the amount of $241,552,380, to be redeemed by the states. Depreciation set in shortly, and by March 1780, in spite of legal-tender laws and an attempt to fix prices, the value of continental currency in silver had fallen to forty to one. Debtors pursued their creditors and "paid them without mercy," according to a contemporary sufferer; prices rose to unheard of heights; while excessive speculation and counterfeiting demoralized the whole financial structure of the struggling colonies. "Not worth a continental" became a phrase of derision and stark reality.

A system of direct requisitions on the states for corn, beef, pork, and other supplies was resorted to in 1780 but proved equally discouraging, for it lacked an efficient plan of assessment and record. Other means used to obtain funds included domestic and foreign loans; quartermaster, commissary, and purchasing agent certificates; lotteries; and prize money received from the sale of captured enemy vessels. Domestic loans were offered for sale from time to time at high rates of interest, and although $63,289,000 was subscribed, its real value was but a small percentage of that amount. Certificates of purchasing agents were used extensively in payment for supplies to be used by the army, and Alexander Hamilton estimated in 1790 that they were outstanding to the amount of $16,708,000. Foreign loans secured from France, Spain, and Holland through the influence of Benjamin Franklin and John Adams proved invaluable. French loans from 1777 to 1783 amounted to $6,352,500; Spanish loans, to $174,017; and Dutch loans, to $1,304,000—making a total of $7,830,517. These, and an outright gift from France made largely through the agency of Pierre Augustin Caron de Beaumarchais in the first years of the war, did much to strengthen colonial morale and finance (*see* Franco-American Alliance of 1778).

On Feb. 20, 1781, Robert Morris was appointed by Congress to the new Office of Superintendent of Finance. He brought some order out of the existing chaos, but was hampered by local jealousies, by continued state refusal to levy taxes, and by inadequate financial provisions of the Articles of Confederation. It remained for the new Constitution and the financial genius of Hamilton (*see* Assumption and Funding of Revolutionary War Debts) to place the United States on a firm national and international credit basis. The cost of the Revolution in gold has been estimated at:

Paper money	$ 41,000,000
Certificates of indebtedness	16,708,000
Loan-office certificates	11,585,000
Foreign loans	7,830,000
Taxes (requisitions on states)	5,795,000
Gifts from abroad	1,996,000
Miscellaneous receipts	856,000
State debts	18,272,000
Total	$104,042,000

[Davis R. Dewey, *Financial History of the United States;* E. James Ferguson, *The Power of the Purse;* Curtis P. Nettles, *The Emergence of a National Economy, 1775–1815.*]

ELIZABETH WARREN

REVOLUTION, PROFITEERING IN THE, was the result of many merchants taking advantage of the colonies' straits during the crisis. When the Revolution began, the colonies had neither a specie reserve nor a large manufacturing base. The hostilities left them without hard currency and cut off European trade. The only backing of the money issued by the Continental Congress was a promise to pay in metal at some future date. So easy and successful were such issues and so long did Congress delay creating a firm financial base that inflation destroyed the system. When circulation amounted to $30 million, prices rose rapidly. In 1777 wages doubled but prices quadrupled, and two years later the currency collapsed. Prices continued to rise throughout the Revolution. Facing increased risks and costs, importers raised their prices, and retailers followed suit. Food and manufactured items were in short supply and demand overwhelming, in part because the Continental army and state armed forces—as well as the British—were competing on the open market with civilian consumers. Fortunes were made overnight from speculation in commodities. Profiteers bought all available goods, held them until prices rose, and then sold for profits of double or more. The Continental army suffered throughout the war from profiteers. Although many merchants tried to be fair, this was ruinously expensive under the circumstances, and to stay in business they were forced to raise their prices also. Robert Morris, known as the financier of the Revolution because of his financial activities in behalf of the Continental Congress, was also one of the biggest profiteers. Both the national and state governments tried, through taxation, embargo, and price-fixing, to halt the profiteering, but the governments were too weak to enforce regulations. Profiteering continued through the Revolution and afterward. Although the Constitutional Convention of 1787 resolved to protect public securities, speculators anticipated the resolve by buying up great amounts of the paper money that was almost worthless during the Revolution and gained fortunes when it was redeemed at face value.

[John C. Miller, *Triumph of Freedom, 1775–1783.*]
WARNER STARK

REVOLUTION, RIGHT OF, made its first appearance in America as part of the philosophy of natural rights. The power of the New England congregations to discipline and depose their officers and ministers had earlier been asserted in the church platforms. At the same time the philosophy of the theocrats was so permeated with the dogma of divine right that this power was denied in practice. But the newer currents of thought that crossed the Atlantic after 1688 brought the idea of John Locke that a dissolution of government takes place not by any hostile act of the people but by the usurpations of those to whom authority has been delegated. It is the legislature or the executive acting contrary to the trust imposed in them that brings about the dissolution of government. Then and there arises the right of revolution whereby the people repossess themselves of their powers in order to delegate them into other hands. Locke thought that the right of revolution ought not to be exercised for light and transient causes, and that all changes should require the assent of a majority of the people. But, like all the natural-rights philosophers, he left a fruitful source of debate in the unanswered question who should judge between the people and the government. By the time of the American Revolution the theory of popular sovereignty embraced clearly the idea that the people have the right to alter their government. The right of revolution was identified with civil liberty, as "a power existing in the people at large, at any time, for any cause, or for no cause but their own sovereign

pleasure, to alter or annihilate both the mode and essence of any former government, and adopt a new one in its stead." Thomas Jefferson regarded with composure the prospect of frequent recourse to the right of revolution in order that the free spirit of the people might not be suppressed. But the U.S. Constitution provides an orderly means of change in the government. Hence revolution is now applied to the process of effecting changes outside the Constitution. An example of this is secession, which was described by Robert E. Lee as "nothing but revolution." The terms constitutional and revolutionary are mutually exclusive; a political act cannot be revolutionary and at the same time be within the Constitution.

[C. E. Merriam, *History of American Political Theories.*]
WILLIAM S. CARPENTER

REVOLUTIONARY COMMITTEES. The American Revolution was fomented by committees, organized by committees, and, in great measure, conducted by committees. At the first sign of trouble with England committees sprang up everywhere to give voice to the general protest; and, by the time the break came with Great Britain in the spring of 1775, the whole country, from the colonial capital to the remotest community, was afire with committees.

First in the procession of these laborers in the revolutionary cause were the committees of correspondence, so called because they were chiefly engaged in gathering information and propagandizing their doctrines by means of the quill. There followed another group, generally known as the committees of safety (quite as often called councils of safety), whose function was to keep the revolutionary spirit alive and assist in its formulation. In some instances these colonial committees, of whatever name, were instrumental in establishing provincial congresses, which constituted the revolutionary governments of the colonies for the time being. They were also the chief agencies, either directly or through the provincial congresses, in calling together a convention of colonial committees, the First Continental Congress, which met in September 1774.

The First Continental Congress, in its turn, gave a new impetus to committees, for in the boycott of British goods that it proposed, called the "Association," it recommended that committees be chosen in every county, city, and town, "whose business it shall be attentively to observe the conduct of all persons touching this association"; that is, to enforce the Association. Such committees (usually called committees of observation and inspection, committees of inquiry, and the like) were set up; and they not only observed, inspected, and inquired, they took action, usually as courts both of first and last resort. When the Second Continental Congress met in May 1775, it soon became the head and center of the Revolution, and with its aid and comfort there presently began a new era both in provincial congresses and in committees. As a first essential step in the collapse of the old colonial governments the timid and hesitant Congress advised the colonies to appoint committees of safety to serve as *de facto* governments, "in the recess of their assemblies and conventions." Only when Congress had grown bolder did it urge the completion of the revolutionary process.

The committees that were created in this period varied widely from colony to colony in constitution and powers, but in general the central committee was appointed by the provincial congress, with designated powers to be exercised between sitting of the provincial congress or convention, and with some degree of authority over the local committees. This authority did not always subsist. The local committees were much disposed to act independently. In fact, these local committees became, in great measure, the effective agencies of the Revolution. It was they chiefly that dealt with the Tories, just as in many other matters they promoted the cause of the Revolution in ways that to them seemed good. They have had their later versions in the frontier vigilante committees, but, unlike the vigilantes, they chose to implement their authority by such means as tar and feathers rather than the noose. In short, reform, not execution, was their main objective.

Other revolutionary committees were councils of war or boards of war, which might or might not act independently of the committee of safety. There were also, occasionally, various other committees designed to aid in the prosecution of the war, as, for instance, committees of supplies. There were also organizations quite outside any official enclosure, such as the Sons of Liberty, that played a significant part in the Revolution.

There were some committees that survived the organization of state governments, but for the most part committees of the sort described simply vanished from the picture. At the same time the shifting of the revolutionary center of gravity to the Continental Congress gave rise to the development of another type of committee that had an important part in the conduct of the Revolution and likewise in the development of the American system of government. Like every other legislative body, Congress had to do much of its work through committees of its own members; and such were the importance and the permanence of the tasks devolving upon some of these committees that they came to be called "standing committees." Because of the fluctuating membership of Congress it frequently came about that the personnel of these committees became depleted, and their business fell into neglect accordingly. The first serious effort by Congress to remedy this state of affairs was in the creation of mixed boards, composed partly of members and partly of outsiders, the latter to constitute a sort of permanent staff. The next step was to erect these boards into executive departments, composed entirely of nonmembers, or with single executive heads. This last step was not taken until 1781, when the war was approaching an end. Several of these executive departments, still functioning when the Constitution was adopted, passed over to the new government intact and became departments in the so-called cabinet. What was first a committee of secret correspondence, then a committee for foreign affairs, later a department of foreign affairs, became the Department of State. What was the Board of War developed into the Department of War. The business of the treasury, beginning with a committee and developing into a board, passed for a time into the hands of a single executive, the superintendent of finance, then back into the board form, thence into the Treasury Department under the new government. The Navy Department similarly had its origin in the Marine, or Naval, Committee, which became for a time a department of marine. The most important of the standing committees of the Continental Congress that did not become one of the early cabinet departments was the Committee of Commerce, or Commercial Committee, of which the earliest progenitor was the Secret Committee (not to be confused with the Committee of Secret Correspondence).

[Richard D. Brown, *Revolutionary Politics in Massachusetts: The Boston Committee of Correspondence and the Towns, 1772–1774;* Agnes Hunt, *The Provincial Committees of Safety of the American Revolution.*]

EDMUND C. BURNETT

REVOLUTIONARY WAR (1775–83) lasted eight and a half years and was America's longest conflict before the Vietnam War. It was fought over a huge area, from Canada to Florida, from the Atlantic to the Mississippi. It marked the first time in modern history that a colonial people had fought a successful revolutionary war for their freedom and independence. The Americans did so by employing citizen soldiers, not long-term professionals drawn from the opposite ends of the social spectrum in the European fashion—officers from the aristocracy and gentry and enlisted men from the lower social orders, particularly from the nonproductive, even criminal and pauper, elements.

For Britain, despite obvious advantages as the most powerful nation in Europe, the struggle posed formidable problems. Men, supplies, and ships had to be dispatched 3,000 miles, and British strategists and troops, accustomed to an entirely different terrain, had to contend with the vastness of America, with its innumerable forests, mountains, and rivers. In fact, given Britain's logistical problems and the depth of American feeling, it is highly doubtful that Britain could ever have achieved a total military victory, even if France and Spain had not entered the conflict and turned it into a world war.

The war began in Massachusetts, where British troops had been stationed for some time because of that colony's role in leading opposition to British imperial reorganization. Gen. Thomas Gage, on orders from London to take action, sent troops through Lexington to Concord to seize provincial military stores. American armed resistance on Apr. 19, 1775, was followed by the arrival outside Boston of an army of New England militia, which fought the king's regulars in the bloody Battle of Bunker Hill on June 17. The Continental Congress, then meeting at Philadelphia, adopted the New England forces—the nucleus of the U.S. Continental Army, as it was known after Congress declared independence on July 2, 1776. George Washington, a prominent member of that body and a Virginia officer in the French and Indian War, was named commander in chief.

In 1776 the major scenes of action shifted to the middle states after British Gen. William Howe, Gage's successor, evacuated Boston. British strategy called for dividing the colonies along the Lake Champlain–Hudson River waterway. An army under Gen. Guy Carleton, governor of Quebec, threw a small American invasionary force out of Canada and proceeded southward in order to link up with Howe on the Hudson, from which point the two commanders were to overwhelm New England. A temporary setback at the hands of a tiny American fleet on Lake Champlain and the lateness of the season resulted in Carleton's return to Canada.

Howe, too, was unable to carry out all of his part of the scheme, for it took the general and his brother Adm. Richard Howe from August until November to clear Washington from New York City and its environs. The Howes found Washington stubborn, even though they defeated him on Long Island and narrowly missed trapping him on Manhattan and on the mainland to the north.

Washington, an aggressive fighter, was frequently down but never out. After escaping through New Jersey and over the Delaware River, he struck back at the unsuspecting British already settled in winter quarters, picking off their garrisons at Trenton on Dec. 26, 1776, and at Princeton on Jan. 3, 1777. Despite the greatest British military effort in history to that time (and not to be exceeded for many years)—the sending of more than 30,000 soldiers and more than 40 percent of the Royal Navy to America—the campaign of 1776 had failed to throttle the rebellion.

The following year once more saw operations conducted by two British armies. The Canadian-based army under Gen. John Burgoyne had no assurances of help from Howe as it pressed down the Lake Champlain–Hudson River trough. Howe, after much indecision, decided to leave Sir Henry Clinton with a garrison force at New York City and lead the bulk of his army by sea in a move against Philadelphia. (The colonial secretary, Lord George Sackville-Germain, was at fault in not insisting that the two generals coordinate their operations.)

Burgoyne managed to take Fort Ticonderoga on July 5, 1777, but his overconfidence and the dense wilderness of upper New York led to his downfall. Initially, he lost valuable days by proceeding at a leisurely pace, thus giving the Americans time to raise guerrilla forces and to destroy his road southward. Eventually Burgoyne advanced to rugged Bemis Heights, near Saratoga, N.Y., where Gen. Horatio Gates's American northern army was securely dug in. In two major battles, on Sept. 19 and Oct. 7, 1777, Burgoyne lost heavily in men, and he surrendered at Saratoga on Oct. 17.

Howe, meanwhile, pursued a strategy that made little sense. His subordinates felt that he should have advanced up the Hudson to meet Burgoyne or at least marched on Philadelphia by land so as to remain in touch with the Canadian army. As it was, he landed at the head of the Chesapeake, more than fifty miles from Philadelphia, which Washington raced southward to defend. At Brandywine Creek, just northwest of Wilmington, Washington, on Sept. 11, 1777, failed to halt Howe in several hours of fighting; soon after the British general entered Philadelphia, Washington assaulted Howe's advance base at Germantown, Pa., on Oct. 4, but the Americans were again driven off.

The year 1778 was a transitional period in the war. The American forces not only survived the cruel winter at Valley Forge but emerged a more formidable threat than ever, owing to the labors of Prussian drillmaster Baron Friedrich Wilhelm von Steuben and to increasing aid from France, which culminated in the Franco-American alliance of February 1778. As for the Howe brothers, they will probably always be enigmas because of their failure to press the war more vigorously. Interpretations of their conduct range from incompetence to deliberate leniency, since they were known to have expressed hopes that the contest might be ended by negotiations. (They held titles as peace commissioners as well as commanders in chief.)

In any event, they resigned their American positions, and Clinton became the military commander. His orders were to evacuate his army from Philadelphia, concentrate his forces at New York City, and send several thousand men to help cope with French threats in the West Indies. Clinton made good his withdrawal, although at Monmouth Courthouse in New Jersey he was overtaken on June 28, 1778, and fought to a standstill by Washington, who then also moved northward and spent the next three years watching the British from outside New York City.

Just as the war in the North was indecisive, so too the conflict in the West saw neither side gaining the upper hand. George Rogers Clark in 1778 eased the pressure on the new settlements in Kentucky and Tennessee by taking several British-controlled villages in the Illinois Country and capturing the hated Col. Henry Hamilton, the so-called "hair-buyer." But neither Clark nor American commanders at Fort Pitt (Pittsburgh) were strong enough to destroy the anchor points of British power in the interior, Detroit and Niagara, from which Loyalists and Indians continued to hit the frontier communities along the Ohio and in the valleys of western New York.

The South was different. A theater long neglected except for a half-hearted British naval stab at Charleston, S.C., in 1776, it became after 1778 the principal area of operations and the scene of the war's climax. Unable to win in the North, British strategists believed that the thinly settled South, with a reputedly Loyalist-leaning majority, could be easily overrun; and Washington could not come to the assistance of southern rebels as long as Clinton maintained a strong detachment at New York.

From 1778 to 1781 the southern campaign was a catalog of American reversals. Georgia fell in 1779; South Carolina, in 1780. Two American armies were erased in the latter state—at Charleston in May, when besieged Gen. Benjamin Lincoln surrendered the American southern army, and at Camden in August,

when Gates, after hastily assembling a new army, was crushed by Gen. Charles Cornwallis, whom Clinton had placed in command in the South. And yet, under still another commander, Gen. Nathanael Greene, still another southern force took the field. It was a crucial truism about the revolutionary war that manpower was always available to Washington or Greene and always in short supply to Howe or Cornwallis. Although suffering the loss of two strong detachments in encounters at King's Mountain on Oct. 7, 1780, and Cowpens on Jan. 17, 1781, Cornwallis pursued Greene into North Carolina, where, after a bloody contest at Guilford Courthouse on Mar. 15, 1781, the British army limped eastward and then northward to the Virginia coast.

While Greene returned southward and brilliantly cut off every British post save Charleston and Savannah, Ga., Cornwallis united with a British raiding party in Virginia and soon dug in at Yorktown. His superior, Clinton, and Washington as well, saw that Cornwallis was vulnerable to a land and sea blockade. Consequently, Franco-American army and navy operations—previously unsuccessful at Newport, Va., and Savannah—proved decisive. Joined in Rhode Island by French troops under the command of Jean Baptiste Donatien de Vimeur, Comte de Rochambeau, Washington raced southward and prepared to open siege operations before Yorktown on Sept. 28, while a French fleet from the West Indies under Comte François Joseph de Grasse sealed off a sea escape. Cornwallis capitulated on Oct. 19, 1781. British strategy in the South had failed because of an exaggerated notion of Loyalist numbers, an inadequate program of pacification, an inability to recognize the significance of seapower, and friction between Clinton and Cornwallis.

Yorktown, for all practical purposes, brought the Revolution to an end, although France and its ally Spain—which entered the contest in 1779—continued to duel the British in India, the Caribbean, and elsewhere until the Definitive Treaty of Peace was signed in 1783.

[Don Higginbotham, *The War of American Independence;* Piers Mackesy, *The War for America;* Paul Smith, *Loyalists and Redcoats;* Willard M. Wallace, *Appeal to Arms;* Christopher Ward, *The War of the Revolution;* William B. Willcox, *Portrait of a General: Sir Henry Clinton.*]

DON HIGGINBOTHAM

REVOLUTIONARY WAR, AMERICAN ARMY IN THE. The American army of the Revolution came into existence almost by accident, and it developed gradually. It stemmed from the various local minutemen, alarm companies, and volunteers who had sprung to arms to meet the British expedition against Lexington and Concord and pursued the redcoats back to Boston on Apr. 19, 1775. Many of these men remained to besiege the city, and they were joined by volunteers from other New England colonies in the weeks that followed. At first there was no overall command, no definite enlistments, and only such discipline as the natural decency of the men provided. Some colonies, especially Massachusetts and Connecticut, attempted to meet the crisis by appointing officers and enlisting volunteers for the rest of the year. They even organized expeditions such as the one against Fort Ticonderoga in May 1775, but still confusion reigned. Finally the Massachusetts Provincial Congress sent an urgent appeal to the Continental Congress in Philadelphia asking it to adopt the new army and provide direction. The Congress responded. On June 14 it authorized the raising of ten companies of riflemen in Virginia, Maryland, and Pennsylvania as the nucleus of a new national army, and on June 15 it appointed George Washington of Virginia commander in chief. By July 3 Washington had arrived in Cambridge, Mass., to take command, and a few weeks later the rifle regiments joined him.

The new commander immediately set out to bring order from chaos. Appealing to patriotism to maintain discipline and hold men in camp, he developed in conjunction with a congressional committee a plan of organization that was ready by September. This plan called for a Continental army of twenty-six regiments or battalions of infantry with a strength of 728 men each, one regiment of riflemen, and one of artillery, for a total of 20,372 men. Each of the infantry regiments was to consist of eight companies of 86 men, 4 officers, and 8 regimental staff officers. All were to be enlisted until the end of 1776 and responsible only to the Continental Congress. The effective date for the new organization was to be Jan. 1, 1776, but when that day arrived, arrangements were far from complete. Many men considered the enlistment period too long. Others hesitated to serve under new officers whom they had not selected themselves. Officers who had achieved high rank in the existing thirty-eight volunteer regiments were reluctant to accept lower ranks in the Continental army. By March, when the spring campaign began, only 9,170 men had joined the ranks. This was less than half the desired number, and Washington had to rely on help from local militia units in order to obtain an adequate operating force.

Congress authorized additional regiments. The rifle and artillery regiments became a corps and a brigade, respectively. Cavalry, light infantry, and artificer regiments were added, as well as special mixed units called legions. Still the Continental army, or Continental line as it was sometimes called, remained throughout inadequate to conduct a campaign entirely by itself. Before the end of the war, Congress had authorized eighty-eight battalions totaling 80,000 men, but the quota was never met. Some of the regiments were never raised; others were always under strength. The actual number of men under arms varied, but the best estimates indicate that Washington never had as many as 15,000 able-bodied Continentals under his command at any one time; the usual number was about 10,000. To muster an adequate force, he had to rely on state regiments and on local militia organizations called out for short-term emergencies in their local areas. Almost all major actions and campaigns were fought with a mixture of these three types of troops, even after 1776 when Congress began to recruit soldiers for longer periods—usually three years or the duration of the war.

In its recruiting, Congress relied almost entirely on volunteers. Some states used a quota system requiring either men or money. There were offers of bounties in money or land to induce enlistment or to make it financially possible for a man to sign up. After much discussion it was agreed that all free men regardless of color were welcome, and many regiments numbered blacks among their veterans. By the end of the war, in fact, the Rhode Island regiment was almost entirely black because of that state's policy of purchasing the freedom of any slave willing to enlist.

The basic weapon of the Continental infantryman was the smoothbore flintlock musket. It was an inaccurate weapon at best. A good marksman could only expect to hit a target the size of a man at 100 yards, but this lack of precision was not important in 18th-century warfare. In the tactics followed by all armies, the important thing was to lay down a field of fire and saturate it with bullets through volley firing; thus, speed of loading was critical, and a well-trained soldier could be expected to load and fire four times a minute, using a paper cartridge. The rifle, a much more accurate firearm, took considerably longer to load, and so it was used primarily for sniping, long-range shooting, and other special tasks. The rifleman, whose weapon did not have a bayonet, was useless in the hand-to-hand combat that decided many actions; at close quarters only the infantryman with his musket and bayonet could perform satisfactorily. Cavalrymen carried either pistols, musketoons, or carbines but generally scorned them; they considered the saber the only really useful weapon for a horseman.

In order to perform properly with any of these arms, it was necessary to establish a uniform drill. The older veterans at Boston had for the most part followed the manual first published by British Gen. Humphrey Bland in 1727, entitled *A Treatise of Military Discipline*. About 1768 there was a general shift, at least in New England, to a simplified drill prepared for the militia of Norfolk in 1759. Timothy Pickering of Salem, Mass., further simplified the ''Norfolk Discipline,'' as it was called, in *An Easy Plan of Discipline for a Militia,* published in 1775. Some colonies adopted the regular British army manual of 1764. Thus, there were at least three different systems of discipline in use during the early years of the war. They were generally similar, but there were minor differences that could cause confusion in a crisis.

The man who providentially arrived to correct this potential hazard was Baron Friedrich Wilhelm von Steuben. A born teacher and drillmaster, von Steuben hammered the Continental soldiers into well-trained and disciplined units during the bleak winter of 1778 at Valley Forge. As part of his program he prepared a new drill manual with ideas borrowed freely from British, German, and French sources. He simplified and sharpened commands; reduced the number of motions required for firings and maneuvers; and, most important of all, changed the line of battle from three ranks to two, achieving more maneuverability. The first edition of his manual, *Regulations for the Order and Discipline of the Troops of the United States,* was published in 1779, and it remained the basic manual for American soldiers for more than twenty-five years.

Under von Steuben's guidance the Continental became a first-class soldier in the approved European tradition. Contrary to popular belief, he did not hide behind trees and fences to snipe at enemy troops. Such tactics were sometimes used by militiamen, as at King's Mountain, but the American regular met the British army on its own terms, in open fields, drawn up in line of battle. He learned to make and receive fierce bayonet charges, and in such notable attacks as at Stony Point and the assault on the British redoubt at Yorktown, he charged with unloaded musket, relying solely on cold steel.

A major general in the Continental army, von Steuben was only one of a number of foreign officers who offered their services to the Americans. American representatives in Europe, such as Silas Deane and Benjamin Franklin, were besieged with offers. Some of these volunteers made outstanding contributions, notably Marie Joseph du Motier, Marquis de La-fayette; Johann Kalb; Casimir Pulaski; and Thaddeus Kosciusko. Others, such as Philippe Tronson du Coudray, were either arrogant or incompetent or both and nearly produced a revolt by American officers who found themselves being superseded. The situation became so bad, in fact, that Washington and Congress soon reversed the policy of welcoming foreign officers and began actively to discourage them.

With rare exceptions, notably the Battle of King's Mountain, the militia and state line units that supplemented the Continental army were ineffective by themselves. When used for delaying tactics and backed by Continentals, as at Guilford Courthouse and Cowpens, they performed useful service. Among the state line regiments, the outstanding unit was the Illinois Regiment of the Virginia State Army. Under its commander, George Rogers Clark, it captured Cahokia, Kaskaskia, and Vincennes and thus established American claims to the Middle West.

[Fred Anderson Berg, *Encyclopedia of Continental Army Units;* Francis B. Heitman, *Historical Register of Officers of the Continental Army;* Harold L. Peterson, *The Book of the Continental Soldier;* Hugh F. Rankin, *The North Carolina Continentals.*]

HAROLD L. PETERSON

REVOLUTIONARY WAR, BRITISH ARMY IN THE. Although in April 1775 the authorized strength of the British army was 48,647, the army numbered only about 32,000 men, of whom 6,991 were in America. By March 1782, through desperate recruiting and impressment and the hiring of German regiments, the total had risen to 113,000 effectives, exclusive of regulars in Ireland, armies of the East India Company, and paid militia. That total included 8,756 in the West Indies and 46,000 in North America, and of the latter, two-thirds were Germans or American provincials.

The Western Hemisphere contained four independent commands: (1) the Lesser Antilles, (2) Jamaica, (3) the new province of Quebec, and (4) the sprawling mass composed of Nova Scotia, the thirteen colonies on the Atlantic seaboard, and the Floridas, Bahamas, and Bermudas. The rich islands of the two West Indian commands were imperiled when France, Spain, and the Netherlands joined in America's struggle, and Great Britain was therefore induced to divert into that theater armament critically needed along the North American coasts. More than any other factor, it was the predicament of the West Indies that hastened British defeat. But patriot leaders, naturally, were preoccupied with the Quebec command and the other North

American command, whose headquarters lay in New York between 1776 and 1783. As War Office and Admiralty functions were purely administrative, operation control over these four commands (but only these) lay with the secretary of state for the American department, who, between 1775 and 1782, was Lord George Sackville-Germain. Because the prime minister, Lord Frederick North, chose to wage parliamentary politics rather than war, the final arbiter of domestic and global priorities could only be the king. Satisfactory distribution of operational responsibilities never emerged, because of lack of comity among the cabinet and the services, and because global communications lay at the mercy of wind and weather; the army was considered of only secondary importance in comparison with the navy, and empire had spread too far for communication to be maintained by preindustrial technology.

Socially the army was, along with an established church, a form of outdoor relief for disinherited brothers of rural landlords, a price the nation paid to maintain primogeniture. In all about 2,000 British officers served in America during the war. Commonly they were promoted gratis to fill vacancies caused by death, or else, with permission, they bought commissions from previous holders and could sell out at any time; in 1783 most of those still serving reverted to the reserve on half pay for life. A few were members of Parliament, a dozen were baronets, and at least seventy-eight were peers or sons of peers; these and scores of others possessed such political connections as to make a travesty of discipline.

By contrast, private soldiers represented strictly nonpolitical Britain. Those serving in 1775 had largely enlisted for life or according to regimental contract; others, later, for three years or until the "rebellion" ended, at the crown's option. Voluntary enlistment, highly unpopular, was stimulated by bounties; by acceptance of Roman Catholics, previously excluded; and by the creation of dozens of new regiments, whose cadres recruited partly at private expense in order to obtain commissions. Also convicts were pardoned on condition of enlistment: in Britain, it has been said, "every gaol became a recruiting depot." After the Revolution merged with foreign war, press acts of May 1778 and February 1779 provided for conscripting the unemployed poor—but not voters—for service of five years or the duration of war. Although a latent purpose was certainly control of the poor, the fear of riots permitted only casual conscription. Given a base pay of eight pence per day minus deductions for food, clothing,

repair of arms, and Chelsea Hospital (a pension fund), the rank and file seldom saw money except as proceeds of crime. Until July 1778 all supplies and provisions for the American theater, except fresh meat, came from Europe; after France intervened, shipments were often delayed and damaged or spoiled. For bachelors the horrors of service were avoided by simple desertion—in Ireland one-sixth of the soldiers deserted each year—and for married men they were tempered by the presence of wives and children, for whom they drew rations; bad as it was, the regiment was literally the soldier's home. Yet discipline was ferocious; severe floggings were administered as well to women (100 lashes) as to men (1,000 lashes). Nevertheless, death sentences were seldom carried out. Difficulties of recruitment and transport made conservation of men the paramount concern; major engagements had to be avoided, and no commander dared exploit an advantage if he would thereby diminish compactness and facilitate desertion. In brief, although the background explanations differ, the redcoats and the ragged Continentals were remarkably similar in character and circumstances. Patriotic assumptions that the Continental rank and file were superior in spirit, because they were free citizens of a threatened land, have not yet been validated by intensive research in the rosters of both armies, to compare them in social composition and in the statistical indices of morale.

Disease took a heavy toll of all ranks in southern campaigns and West Indian service. Battle casualties were also higher than had been usual, because of American emphasis on marksmanship. Reared in an open country less rich in game, the British relied less on the musket than on the bayonet. Rather than aim the piece, they pointed it, fired hit-or-miss, and then endeavored to rout the enemy with a bayonet charge. It was estimated in 1776 that 1,400 shots were fired by the British for each American killed. Accustomed to meager risk and to substantial cavalry support, redcoats at first maintained their usual solidity, but American conditions gradually forced on them new conceptions of looseness, flexibility, and firepower. Even before 1775 an "Americanization" of the army had begun, and the Revolution broadened and sealed the shift.

[John Adlum, *Memoirs of the Life of John Adlum in the Revolutionary War;* Henry Belcher, *The First American Civil War,* vol. I; Edward E. Curtis, *The Organization of the British Army in the American Revolution;* J. W. Fortescue, *The History of the British Army,* vol. III; Piers Mackesy, *The War for America, 1775–1783;* John Shy, *Toward Lexington: The Role of the British Army in the Coming of* the American Revolution; Christopher Ward, *The War of the Revolution*, vol. I.]

HENRY J. YOUNG

REVOLUTIONARY WAR, CONTINENTAL NAVY IN THE. On Oct. 13, 1775, the Continental Congress appointed Silas Deane, Christopher Gadsden, and John Langdon to be a committee charged with founding a modest navy. Seventeen days later the committee was expanded by the inclusion of John Adams, Stephen Hopkins, Joseph Hewes, and Richard Henry Lee. Originally called the Naval Committee and then the Marine Committee, in 1779 it became the Board of Admiralty.

Effective colonial naval power actually commenced with the initiative of Gen. George Washington. As the commander besieging Boston in the spring of 1775, he commissioned six schooners and a brigantine to make a tiny naval force. On Sept. 7, 1775, Nicholas Broughton in the *Hannah* recaptured the colonial ship *Unity* from a British prize crew, the first of fifty-five captures made by the flotilla. The most appreciated occurred on Nov. 28 with the taking of the brig *Nancy,* stuffed with 2,000 muskets, a 13-inch brass mortar, and plentiful equipment, by John Manley of the *Lee.* After the formation of the Continental service, many of Washington's seamen joined, as did Manley, who became a commodore.

Although in December 1775 Congress voted to build thirteen frigates, the first of the twenty-seven men-of-war of the Continental navy were converted from merchant vessels at Philadelphia, under the direction of John Barry, assisted by such masterbuilders as Joshua Humphreys. Esek Hopkins was the first commodore to go to sea, aboard the *Alfred,* carrying thirty guns, under the command of Capt. Dudley Saltonstall, and leading the *Columbus,* twenty-eight guns, under Abraham Whipple; *Andrew Doria,* fourteen guns, under Nicholas Biddle; *Cabot,* fourteen guns, under John B. Hopkins (eldest son of the commodore); *Providence,* twelve guns, under John Hazard; *Hornet,* ten guns, under William Stone; *Wasp,* eight guns, under William Hallock; and *Fly,* tender, under Hoystead Hacker. Smallpox infected the squadron before Mar. 4, 1776, when its 200 marines and 50 seamen under Capt. Samuel Nicholas seized the forts of Nassau to capture eighty-eight cannon, fifteen mortars, and considerable military stores. En route to deliver the loot to Washington's needy army, the squadron took six small prizes, had an indecisive engagement with an elusive British frigate, and so had 9

killed, 16 wounded, and 164 sick upon reaching New London, Conn. Fortuitously, Washington was near there; the munitions were thus expeditiously transferred, and in addition the small naval force was able to screen Long Island Sound for the water passage of the army to Manhattan.

Congress next employed the navy as dependable bearers of American products to French and Dutch ports in the West Indies to be exchanged for military supplies. At the same time, against the Royal Navy on the American coast, Continental cruisers strove to slow the buildup of the king's strength. As an outstanding example, in May, June, and July of 1776, Biddle (who as a British midshipman had been a shipmate of Horatio Nelson on a polar expedition), commanding the *Doria,* took ten prizes, while John Paul Jones in the *Alfred* in the months following captured sixteen.

The coast of Britain was not immune. Lambert Wickes, in the *Reprisal,* carrying eighteen guns, delivered Benjamin Franklin to France in 1776 and then in Irish waters took or sank eighteen British vessels and outsailed pursuit by the seventy-four-gun *Burford* to slip safely into French Saint-Malo. That cruise, begun in company with the *Lexington,* sixteen guns, commanded by Henry Johnson, and the *Dolphin,* ten guns, under Samuel Nicholson, startled Britons into increasing the costs of shipping insurance. The North Sea was raided by Gustavus Conyngham in the ten-gun *Surprise.* All such ventures were covertly supported by the French.

The British response was more than mere augmentation of the blockade: it was a thrust in the autumn of 1777 at the supposed heart of the rebellion, Philadelphia. The loss of the city was a heavy blow to the Continental navy, costing its main base, three new frigates, and six smaller units. Most of the sizable Pennsylvania navy was also wiped out. (Only Delaware and New Jersey lacked a state navy.)

The open advent of France into the war probably averted the extinction of the Continental navy. In July 1778, when Adm. Jean Baptiste d'Estaing and the Brest fleet sailed for New York, British ships-of-the-line could no longer be penny-packeted in scattered support of the blockade but had to concentrate to offer formal battle. Under the wing of the strong French, the Continentals had a new lease on life and again prospered. French regularization of supplies abated the securing of munitions via the West Indies, and the navy could embark on offensives. In the spring of 1779, for example, John B. Hopkins in the *Warren,* thirty-two guns, with the *Queen of France,* twenty-eight guns, under Joseph Olney, and the *Ranger,* eighteen guns, under Thomas Simpson, captured eight rich prizes near the Chesapeake Bay entrance. Out of Boston in July, Whipple in the twenty-eight-gun *Providence,* with the *Queen of France,* under John P. Rathbun, and the *Ranger,* under Simpson, swept eleven prizes from a large convoy. Overall, the aggressiveness was epitomized by Jones and his statement "I have not yet begun to fight!" when the forty-two-gun *Bonhomme Richard* defeated the forty-four-gun *Serapis* in the North Sea, Sept. 23, 1779.

Only the *Alliance,* carrying thirty-two guns, survived the hostilities, and it was sold in 1785.

[G. W. Allen, *A Naval History of the American Revolution;* William James, *The British Navy in Adversity;* D. W. Knox, *The Naval Genius of George Washington;* A. T. Mahan, *The Influence of Sea Power Upon History, 1660–1783;* W. J. Morgan, *Captains to the Northward;* C. O. Paullin, ed., *Out-letters of the Continental Marine Committee and Board of Admiralty.*]

R. W. DALY

REVOLUTIONARY WAR, FOREIGN VOLUNTEERS IN.

The ideal of human liberty actuating the colonies in 1776 found response in the hearts of many Europeans, especially in France. A small proportion of those who wrote Benjamin Franklin offering their services actually reached America. The first secret aid ships of Pierre Augustin Caron de Beaumarchais, the *Mercure* and the *Amphitrite,* landed about thirty volunteers in March and April 1777 at Portsmouth, Va. A few stragglers and four royal engineers, the latter sent for by Congress, reached Philadelphia in June from the West Indies, while Marie Joseph du Motier, Marquis de Lafayette, and his eleven officers, making their way over intolerable roads from Charleston, arrived in July. More than half of these men were rejected by Congress and had their expenses paid back to France.

Among the most notable of those commissioned were: Charles Armand, Marquis de la Rouërie; Pierre Charles l'Enfant, later designer of the insignia of the national capital; Philippe Tronson du Coudray, drowned in September in the Schuylkill River; Thaddeus Kosciusko, a Lithuanian, who arrived in 1776 and built the fortifications at West Point; Louis Lebegue DuPortail, who fortified Valley Forge; and Casimir Pulaski, a Polish count, who was killed at Savannah, Ga., in 1779. Only two of Lafayette's officers were retained by Congress: Johann Kalb (Baron de Kalb), killed at Camden, S.C., in 1780, and the latter's aide Paul Dubuisson, wounded and made prisoner there.

The last secret aid volunteers to arrive came on the *Flamand* in December 1777, sent by Beaumarchais: among them were Baron Friedrich von Steuben and his interpreter, Pierre Étienne Du Ponceau, the latter of whom remained in America and became a noted lawyer in Philadelphia.

[Thomas Balch, *The French in America;* E. S. Kite, *Duportail and the French Engineers.*]

ELIZABETH S. KITE

REVOLUTIONARY WAR, LOYALIST TROOPS IN THE.

Britain had to tap American manpower during the American Revolution. There were difficulties in recruiting at home and staggering problems of ocean transport, whereas in America loyal subjects were fleeing to British posts, ready for revenge and exerting a moral claim on the royal bounty. To relieve their destitution most efficiently, military organization was needed; moreover, in military guise a costly relief program might prove more acceptable to British taxpayers. At no time between the Battle of Bunker Hill and peace in 1783 were refugees not recruited. At times, especially 1780–82, Loyalists under arms may have exceeded patriot troops.

Americans were to be found in British sea and land forces. As in preceding decades, New York and New England provided scores of officers, midshipmen, and seamen for the Royal Navy. From New York between 6,000 and 16,000 Loyalists went out in privateers; privateers sailed from Quebec; Halifax; Bermuda; Saint Augustine, Fla.; and West Indian ports as well. Refugees nevertheless made their greatest contribution to the British cause on land.

The regular army had already been somewhat Americanized by intermarriage and land investment, as well as by recruiting and purchases of commissions for Americans, and throughout the war it attracted Loyalist refugees. But the term of enlistment was long, the supply of free commissions was limited, and indigent refugees could not buy commissions. Temporary provincial regiments were created, therefore, specifically for Loyalists, who would serve only in America or in the West Indies. They ranked just below the regulars, but ahead of the militia, in command and privileges; many commissions were offered to them gratis and others were offered at low cost. Headquarters authorized suitable provincial candidates to earn their commissions by enlisting specific quotas. Within the limited areas under British control, competition became intense, and recruiters slipped behind the American lines at the risk of their lives to bring in new parties of refugees. Eventually they also recruited among deserters from the Continental army, civil prisoners, and prisoners of war. Because simple desertion was only a venial offense and battle and disease took a heavy toll, recruiting could not keep pace with attrition. Provincial regiments were chronically undermanned; about sixty-eight corps were started; many were disbanded and their manpower reconstituted; only half a dozen attained full strength. Before peace came, however, about 19,000 had served as provincials.

Provincials did duty in garrison and under fire, wherever regulars served and in other places as well: from Saint Augustine to Natchez on the Mississippi and from Detroit to Quebec, Prince Edward Island, and Newfoundland. The Prince of Wales American Volunteers, New Jersey Volunteers, Oliver De Lancey's Second and Third battalions, and the Volunteers of Ireland engaged heavily in the South. John Graves Simcoe's Queen's Rangers distinguished themselves from New York to Virginia; Banastre Tarleton's British Legion became a dark legend in the Carolinas. Maryland and Pennsylvania units helped defend Pensacola, Fla., unsuccessfully, against a vastly superior Spanish fleet and army. East Florida Rangers fought nine actions in defense of the Florida boundary. John Stuart's Loyal Refugees, the South Carolina Royalists, and the King's Carolina Rangers were continually engaged in the backcountry of the South, while, along with the Iroquois, John Butler's Rangers and the Royal New Yorkers ranged the northern frontier. Fresh from stinking prison hulks Lord George Montagu's Duke of Cumberland's Regiment sailed to defend Jamaica, and William Odell's Loyal American Rangers sailed to attack the Spanish Main. In one of the most stirring episodes of the war Col. Andrew Deveaux embarked from Saint Augustine with a motley force of provincials and five privateers and recaptured the Bahamas from Spain. Without seeing much action, the Black Pioneers, recruited from refugee blacks, exhibited perhaps the highest death rate and the lowest desertion rate in either of the opposing armies. The Black Carolina Corps, similarly raised in Charleston, S.C., served in the West Indies for many years after the peace.

But the provincials were not the only Loyalists in land service. Between 10,000 and 20,000 royal militiamen enrolled and chose their own officers during British occupations in Georgia, the Carolinas, New York, and Maine; heavily dependent on the army, those in the South experienced the bitterest fighting of the war. Elsewhere, notably in Pennsylvania, Loyalist guerrillas seriously annoyed the patriots, although they were not of major help to the British.

Materials for social analysis of the provincials are abundant. Less than 10 percent of the officers had ever served as regulars. As 1750 was the average year of birth for 197 officers ranking above lieutenant, few could have served in the French and Indian War even as provincials; the experience before 1775 of the great majority must have consisted of peacetime militia musters. Since refugees lacked opportunities for civil employment, the proportion of college graduates probably stood higher in provincial corps than in the Continental army or among the regulars. Well over 200 refugees qualified as surgeon or surgeon's mate. More than 100 were chaplains, although most treated chaplaincies as unemployment relief, generally neglecting their duty. As the average year of birth of 584 officers was 1752, it is likely that they were younger than their peers in Gen. George Washington's army, who were probably put to sterner tests of experience and merit. British policy held that sixteen years was the proper age to begin service as an ensign, but Loyalist colonels sometimes exerted their right of nomination to obtain commissions prematurely for sons of Loyalist friends. Instead of being mustered, these overly young ensigns were furloughed to school; although unpaid, they were entitled to half pay on demobilization, as were other officers, a lifelong supplement to the income of impoverished families. In three extreme cases ensigns were commissioned at the ages of ten, eight, and two, but only twenty-four officers were commissioned when under the age of sixteen, and so the abuse did little military harm.

In 1783–84 a total of 1,014 officers were disbanded, to receive half pay or a similar military allowance for life. These constituted an army reserve from which hundreds returned to active duty during the Anglo-French wars of 1793–1815, serving in every part of the empire. A number of them resettled after a time in the United States, and during the Franco-American crisis of 1798 the crown even authorized them to accept U.S. commissions. Loyalist veterans were conspicuous in the forces opposing the United States in the War of 1812, but failure to serve did not impair half-pay rights of officers living quietly in the United States; indeed, the heirs of Capt. Philip Barton Key collected arrears due him for the years 1807–13, when he held a seat in Congress. The Napoleonic Wars founded prominent careers for numerous

Loyalist veterans, including a vice admiral, an admiral, three major generals, four lieutenant generals, and five generals.

Both British and patriot leaders supposed that American sympathies were closely correlated with American nativity, but the assumption wants verification. Rosters describing 754 provincial officers indicate that 58.9 percent were born in America; 14.3 percent in Ireland; 14.6 percent in Scotland; 9.2 percent in England; and 2.2 percent in Germany. Such a mix clearly differed from that of rank and file, as Irishmen had poorer chances of obtaining commissions. The makeup of the 520 rank and file of the Queen's Rangers in 1780 was probably near the average for provincials: 27.1 percent, natives of America; 37.7 per cent, of Ireland; 7.1 percent, of Scotland; 23 percent, of England (probably higher than the average); and 4.8 percent, of Germany. Random indicators suggest that the Continental army was similar—unsurprising, since the opposing armies tended to recruit from each other.

Although provincial veterans scattered widely, they settled principally where their regiments disbanded, in present-day Ontario and Quebec, the Maritime Provinces, and the Bahamas. In these places they received free grants of crown land. Substantial numbers later retired to the less fashionable parts of the British Isles, to Jamaica, and to the United States. The Black Pioneers, disbanded at Halifax, Nova Scotia, were largely resettled in Sierra Leone, where they prospered. Loyalist half-pay officers became a distinct caste and sociopolitical force, and they seemed likely to live forever (the last one died in 1860). As their land grants proved unprofitable and their half-pay status deterred them from commerce, they endured lives of genteel poverty, begetting enormous families of portionless daughters and half-educated sons. They begged for civil and military appointments for themselves, ensigncies in old regiments for their sons, pensions for widows, and annuities for indigent daughters of comrades, looking to great men for influence and to government for succor; they behaved, in short, much like younger sons of the English gentry. In the politics of British North America they consequently played a conservatizing role: a bulwark of empire, a bastion of agrarian influence, perhaps at times a roadblock in the way of commercial and industrial development.

[Robert M. Calhoon, *The Loyalists in Revolutionary America, 1760–1781;* Paul H. Smith, *Loyalists and Redcoats: A Study in British Revolutionary Policy,* and "The

American Loyalists: Notes on Their Organization and Numerical Strength," *William and Mary Quarterly,* vol. 25 (1968); Esther C. Wright, *The Loyalists of New Brunswick.*]
HENRY J. YOUNG

RHEA LETTER. On Jan. 6, 1818, Gen. Andrew Jackson wrote to President James Monroe, offering to conquer the Floridas if approval was signified "through any channel (say Mr. J. Rhea)." Monroe, ill at the time, left the passage unread. Subsequently, Jackson received a letter from his friend Rep. John Rhea of Tennessee, which he construed as giving Monroe's sanction to the plan. On this basis Jackson later claimed Monroe's authorization for his campaign in Florida, despite the president's denial (*see* Arbuthnot and Ambrister, Case of).

[John S. Bassett, *The Life of Andrew Jackson,* vol. I.]
HARVEY WISH

RHODE ISLAND. Smallest in size of the United States, Rhode Island is approximately forty-eight miles long and thirty-seven miles wide. The state comprehends nearly 1,500 square miles, of which almost 200 are constituted of Narragansett Bay, providing about 400 miles of coastline. The relatively poor agricultural potential made the colony dependent for surplus wealth on commerce, and in its early years on waterpowered industry.

Rhode Island was founded in 1636 by colonists who accompanied Roger Williams to Providence after his banishment from Massachusetts in 1635. The Providence exiles signed a covenant on Aug. 20, 1636, to live together in a society regulated by majority rule, agreeing that their government applied "only in civill things." Thus they set a precedent for the separation of church and state and for religious freedom. Others fled Massachusetts during the Antinomian controversy (1637) under the leadership of William Coddington, a merchant, and John Clarke, a physician, and settled Portsmouth in 1638, on the island of Aquidneck in Narragansett Bay—after 1644 known as Rhode Island, because of Giovanni da Verrazano's 1524 description of it as resembling the isle of Rhodes. Dissatisfaction in Portsmouth prompted Coddington to found Newport, in 1639, on the southern end of Aquidneck. The fourth original settlement is associated with Samuel Gorton, a religious mystic, who was banished from Plymouth, Mass., and later founded Warwick, in 1648. Each of the plantations, following the example of Williams, purchased their lands from the Indians, who numbered perhaps 30,000 in 1511.

The union of these settlements started in 1644, when Williams went to England and obtained a parliamentary charter. The first legislature met on May 19, 1647; John Coggeshall, a Newport resident, was the first president. The restoration of Charles II in 1660 invalidated the parliamentary charter uniting the colony, and in 1663 Clarke obtained a new royal charter that gave Rhode Island virtual autonomy. All officials were annually elected or appointed, including the governor and judges, and the governor exercised no veto; the general assembly of popularly elected deputies and assistants was dominant. The royal charter, acknowledging Rhode Island's ''livelie experiment'' in religious freedom, remained in force until 1842.

Rhode Island's liberal policies attracted minorities, especially Baptists and Quakers and some Jews. Although farming was the principal occupation, the carrying trade, re-exports, and the slave trade were vital to the colonial economy. The population grew from 7,181 in 1708 to 17,935 in 1730, and to 59,678 in 1774; the number of towns increased from the original four to thirty by 1781. Rhode Island took part in ten wars from 1675 to 1763, benefiting from privateering and commercial opportunities. An exception was the devastation caused by the Indian uprising known as King Philip's War (1675–76). A decisive battle, the Great Swamp Fight, took place near North Kingstown on Dec. 19, 1675, in which the Narraganset were defeated; King Philip, the Wampanoag chief, was killed at Mount Hope on Aug. 12, 1676. One by-product of these wars was the use of paper money, beginning with the first of eight colonial issues in 1710. Depreciation often led to conflicts and alarmed English creditors. In 1751, responding to the Rhode Island emissions, Parliament prohibited paper money in New England.

Commercial wealth generated the growth of Newport and Providence. Newport expanded, from 2,203 inhabitants in 1708 to 9,209 in 1774; Providence increased, from 1,446 to 4,321. The merchants patronized prominent local artists, including John Smibert, Robert Feke, and Gilbert Stuart; supported the Redwood Library, founded in 1747 in Newport; and built elegant homes. The Nicholas Browns of Providence, a leading mercantile family, founded Rhode Island College (Brown University) in 1764, but the colony did not develop an effective system of public education.

Resistance to British policies after 1763 was consistent with Rhode Island's colonial experience. Passage of the Sugar Act in 1764 brought the first important protest that presaged the American Revolution, ''An Essay on the Trade of the Northern Colonies'' (1764), a pamphlet of Gov. Stephen Hopkins. The episode in Rhode Island of greatest intercolonial impact was the destruction of the British warship *Gaspée* by Providence men on June 22, 1772. The general assembly deposed Gov. Joseph Wanton on Oct. 31, 1775, because he refused to prepare for war following the Battle of Lexington. On May 4, 1776, Rhode Island renounced its allegiance to the British crown.

At first Rhode Island supported interstate unity as needed to win colonial independence. The state quickly ratified the Articles of Confederation on Dec. 20, 1778, and contributed disproportionately to the costs of the Revolution. Former governors Hopkins and Samuel Ward attended the First Continental Congress in 1774; Esek Hopkins became the first head of the Continental navy, while Gen. Nathanael Greene was instrumental in the Revolution's military success. But after the victory at Yorktown in October 1782, Rhode Island reverted to an independent course in its relations with the other states.

A signal of Rhode Island's rejection of the Union came on Nov. 1, 1782, when the legislature vetoed the congressional impost of 1781. Underlying Rhode Island's united opposition was a desire to maintain state sovereignty, local control over revenue, and support of the state's own debt. Internal political harmony dissolved under the pressure of the commercial depression of 1785–87. Rhode Islanders demanded paper money to ameliorate deepening hardship. A paper money country party won overwhelmingly in the elections of April 1786. In May 1786 the legislature issued £100,000 in paper bills, which could be used to pay off any debt, public or private, under the threat of cancellation should the money be refused. Between 1787 and 1789 Rhode Island redeemed its debt; the largest creditors, mostly merchants, refused payments in depreciated money. A paper money law that did not provide for trial by jury led to the famous decision in the case of *Trevett* v. *Weeden* (1786), which set a pattern for the practice of judicial review.

Reorganization of the federal system in 1787 posed a serious problem. The country party was determined to concentrate on domestic affairs and refused over the merchants' objections to allow Rhode Island to participate in the federal convention. Symptomatic of the state's recalcitrance was a popular referendum on Mar. 24, 1788, rejecting the federal constitution,

2,708 to 237. Only after the state debt had been redeemed did the country leaders calculate the dangers of economic sanctions from the United States and secession of the maritime towns if Rhode Island left the Union. The general assembly authorized a ratifying convention on Jan. 16, 1790; the upper house approved by a single vote. At a reconvened session in Newport on May 29, 1790, the convention ratified the federal constitution, thirty-four to thirty-two. Rhode Island rejoined the United States after more than a year of separation. Political stability characterized the period just after Rhode Island reentered the Union. Arthur Fenner and his son James served as governor for twenty-six of the forty-one years between 1791 and 1831. This internal political unity provided the basis for the state's economic and social transformation.

Taking initial advantage of available sources of waterpower, Rhode Island entrepreneurs shifted their venture capital from declining mercantile opportunities to the manufacture of cotton and woolen textiles. In the 19th century the hinterland surrounding Providence became the most heavily industrialized and densely populated region of the nation. The first successful cotton factory was established by Samuel Slater in 1790 at Pawtucket Falls, a project initiated and funded by Moses Brown, an enterprising merchant and entrepreneur. By 1809 the number of cotton spindles had expanded to 14,000, leaping ahead to almost 80,000 in 1815, with the added spur of President Thomas Jefferson's embargoes and the Napoleonic Wars. Before the Civil War, Rhode Island cotton manufacturing was among the most important industries in the country, employing nearly 16,000 people and producing over $20 million in cotton goods.

Massive expansion of cotton manufacture also encouraged other industries. Slater and George Corliss experimented with the adaptation of the steam engine to industrial production. Then the invention of the vernier caliper by Joseph Bow in 1848 helped ensure Rhode Island's prominence as a metal trades center; the state also became a leader in the silver and costume jewelry industries. The dominance of manufacturing is clearly indicated in 1860, when 80 percent of all capital investments was concentrated in textiles and base metals, and only 28 percent of the work force was employed in agriculture, commerce, and the maritime trade.

The impact of industrialization was manifest by 1840. Growth of the northern centers of manufacturing created disparities of economy, population, and political interests between the industrial communities and dormant agricultural towns. Providence grew to be Rhode Island's largest city, containing 50,000 of the state's 174,000 inhabitants in 1860; more than two-thirds of the population lived in the northern Blackstone-Pawtucket region. Equally dramatic was the change in the ethnic composition of the industrial cities. The foreign-born population increased markedly, from 1 percent in 1830 to almost 20 percent in 1860, mostly congregated in the manufacturing areas. Apart from ethnic conflicts, other strains resulted from the inflexibility of Rhode Island's constitution, the royal charter of 1663, which took no account of the size or wealth of a town in distributing representation in the general assembly, disfranchised the mass of industrial workers who did not own land, and failed to provide a bill of rights or to guarantee an independent judiciary. Political and sectional discontent gave rise to the organization of the People's Convention in 1841 under the leadership of Thomas Wilson Dorr, a Providence attorney. The struggle for constitutional changes resulted in the bloodless Dorr War of 1842, in which armed forces commanded by Dorr tried to seize control of the state government under the claim of legitimization by right of extralegal elections and republican principles. (Dorr was subsequently imprisoned, and the constitutional issues he raised were rejected by the Supreme Court in the case of *Luther* v. *Borden* [1848].) Concessions by the incumbent government in 1843 led to partial reforms in representation and voting. More substantial reform of the state government was achieved in 1909–11 and in 1935, at which time the complete reorganization of the state government was achieved, including an equitable mode of distributing seats in the state legislature, manhood suffrage, biennial elections, a vote for the governor, and an independent judiciary.

Just as industrial growth dominated Rhode Island history in the 19th century, so industrial decline and diversification characterized its experience in the 20th century. Highly industrialized, with disproportionate investments in textiles, Rhode Island's unbalanced economy was severely affected by the movement of cotton and woolen manufactures to the South. This movement was already evident in 1875, when employment in the cotton mills increased at only half the rate of other industries, but the recession after World War I and the Great Depression disrupted the state's textile industry and ended its central place in the economy. Unemployment and social dislocation gave rise to control of the state government by the Democratic party, under the reform leadership of governors Theodore Francis Greene and John Pastore, the latter being the first person of Italian origin to serve in the U.S. Senate. Democratic political victories in Rhode Island reflected national political developments and Franklin D. Roosevelt's electoral success in 1932.

Since World War II Rhode Island has adjusted to its latest economic and social transformation by less concentration of employment in textiles and by economic diversification, especially reliance on small, technologically innovative industries, particularly electronics; tourism; expansion of government and military employment; small dairy, fishing, and poultry businesses; and a large and successful program of urban renewal.

Rhode Island's population in 1970 was 949,723.

[Samuel G. Arnold, *History of the State of Rhode Island and Providence Plantations;* Charles Carroll, *Rhode Island: Three Centuries of Democracy;* Peter J. Coleman, *The Transformation of Rhode Island, 1790–1860;* Marvin Gettleman, *The Dorr Rebellion: A Study in American Radicalism, 1833–1849;* James B. Hedges, *The Browns of Providence Plantations;* Erwin L. Levine, *Theodore Francis Greene;* David S. Lovejoy, *Rhode Island Politics and the American Revolution, 1760–1776;* B. Mayer and Sidney Goldstein, *Migration and Economic Development in Rhode Island;* Irwin H. Polishook, *Rhode Island and the Union, 1774–1795.*]

IRWIN H. POLISHOOK

RHODE ISLAND, COLONIAL CHARTERS OF.
Roger Williams secured the first Rhode Island charter in March 1644 from a parliamentary commission headed by Robert Rich, Earl of Warwick. It provided for an elected president, assistants, and general court and guaranteed liberty of conscience. The first assembly, with John Coggeshall of Newport as president, met at Portsmouth, May 19–21, 1647.

The restoration of Charles II in 1660 made necessary a royal charter, which was secured July 8, 1663, by John Clarke. It provided for an elected governor, deputy-governor, assistants, and general assembly. Separation of church and state was maintained; suffrage was left to colonial control.

[F. N. Thrope, *The Federal and State Constitutions, Colonial Charters, and Other Organic Laws of the States, Territories, and Colonies,* vol. VI.]

JARVIS M. MORSE

RHODE ISLAND IN THE DUTCH WAR OF 1653.
The council of state having authorized the colony to take warlike action against the Dutch, the Rhode Island assembly in May 1653 issued privateer commissions to John Underhill, William Dyer, and Edward Hull, and subsequently to Thomas Baxter and to the vessel *Debora.* Underhill and Dyer captured the Dutch House of Hope, or Fort Good Hope, on the south bank of the Little River at its junction with the Connecticut River. Underhill raided Southold, L.I., and destroyed the fort near Islip. Hull captured a Dutch pinnace in the Connecticut River, a Dutch trading boat at Milford, and a French frigate. His lieutenant raided Block Island, at the eastern approach to Long Island Sound. Baxter captured three small vessels and seized some horses. He caused disturbances in Stamford and Milford, Conn., was blockaded by a Dutch fleet, and arrested by Connecticut authorities. Rhode Island was the only New England colony actively to engage against the Dutch in this war.

[Howard M. Chapin, *Privateer Ships and Sailors.*]

HOWARD M. CHAPIN

RHODES SCHOLARSHIPS,
established by the will of Cecil J. Rhodes, English-born South African statesman and financier, who died in 1902, provide appointments for study in the University of Oxford to students drawn from eighteen countries. Thirty-two students from the United States are selected annually. Rhodes Scholars are also chosen from Australia, Bermuda, the British Caribbean, Jamaica, Canada, Ceylon, Germany, Ghana, India, Malaysia, Malta, Nigeria, New Zealand, Pakistan, Rhodesia, South Africa, and Zambia.

Candidates for the Rhodes Scholarships in the United States should be unmarried citizens between the ages of eighteen and twenty-four, and they should have achieved at least junior standing in a recognized degree-granting university or college. Competitions are held annually in each of the fifty states. Appointments to the scholarship are for a period of two years in the first instance, with the possibility of renewal for a third. The stipend is calculated to cover all tuition expenses and to provide an allowance adequate to cover a student's living requirements.

Intellectual distinction is a necessary, but not a sufficient, condition for election to a Rhodes Scholarship. In keeping with the instructions of Rhodes's will, Rhodes Scholars are also expected to demonstrate qualities of character that promise potential service to others. Although less important than the other criteria for selection, Rhodes Scholars are further expected to possess physical vigor. The will further specifies that "no student shall be qualified or disqualified for election to a Scholarship on account of his race or religious opinions."

Between 1904, when the first American delegation arrived at Oxford, and 1975, 2,086 students drawn from more than 240 American colleges and universities had been designated Rhodes Scholars. As Rhodes Scholars are free to pursue any field of study available in the University of Oxford, so also have they chosen to enter a wide variety of professional careers.

Until 1975 the competition for the Rhodes Scholarships was restricted, by the terms of Rhodes's will, to male students. Changes in British law permitted the opening of the competition to women, beginning in 1976.

WILLIAM J. BARBER

RHYOLITE, the chief town of the Bullfrog Mining District, in southern Nye County, Nev., during the active period, 1904–14. Permanent stone and concrete buildings were erected at this site on the railroad connecting Las Vegas and Goldfield. Water and electric light systems, churches, schools, and newspapers served several thousand citizens. Mining decline was followed by abandonment of the railroad in 1914, leaving Rhyolite a ghost town.

[Francis C. Lincoln, *Mining Districts and Mineral Resources of Nevada.*]

JEANNE ELIZABETH WIER

RIBBON FARMS, a name given by the American settlers at Detroit and elsewhere to the narrow riverfront farms of French feudal origin. A typical farm might be one or more arpents (192.24 English feet) wide and either 40 or 80 arpents (1.5 to 3 miles) deep.

M. M. QUAIFE

RICE, FORT, was established in Dakota Territory on July 11, 1864, and the military reservation at this point was authorized by President Abraham Lincoln on Sept. 2, 1864. It was situated on the west bank of the Missouri River, ten miles north of the mouth of the Cannonball River and twenty-eight miles south of the later site of Fort Abraham Lincoln. The fort was named for Henry M. Rice, first territorial delegate to Congress and later first U.S. senator from Minnesota.

The fort was first occupied by Gen. Alfred Sully as a base of supplies in his operations against the Dakota Indians west of the Missouri River (1864–65). When he started on his campaign to the northwest in the summer of 1864, he left Col. Daniel H. Dill of the Thirtieth Regiment of the Wisconsin Volunteer Infan-

try, with five companies, to construct the buildings at the fort. In 1871 a force consisting of 1,000 soldiers, scouts, and surveyors was sent from Fort Rice, under Gen. Garland Whistler, to act as guard for the Northern Pacific Railway Company survey party west of the Missouri River.

The fort was abandoned Nov. 25, 1878, and the garrison was transferred to Fort Lincoln. The military reservation was vacated by order of President Chester A. Arthur, July 22, 1884.

O. G. LIBBY

RICE-CAMPBELL DEBATES, between Nathan Lewis Rice, an Old-School Presbyterian, and Alexander Campbell, a founder of the Disciples of Christ, took place in Lexington, Ky., from Nov. 15 to Dec. 2, 1843, before large crowds. Henry Clay lent prestige to the debates by his presence as moderator. The propositions debated were the nature, purpose, and regulation of baptism and its relation to church creeds. The debates fixed public attention on the Disciples of Christ as a denomination, consolidated their doctrines of primitive Christianity around the ordinance of baptism, clarified the differences between them and the Presbyterians and Baptists, and emphasized the Disciples' plea for Christian union.

[A. Campbell and N. L. Rice, *Debate on Christian Baptism;* W. E. Garrison, *Religion Follows the Frontier.*]

HAROLD E. DAVIS

RICE CULTURE AND TRADE. Before 1860 the growing of rice on American soil was confined largely to a narrow band of land along the banks of the slow-moving creeks, inlets, and substantial rivers located along the Atlantic coastline from Virginia to Florida. The plentiful supply of water produced by the operation of the tides at the mouths of these streams altered their levels and made possible the flooding and drainage of the nearby low-lying rice fields. The Carolina coast, especially the Charleston area, was the scene of the earliest attempts at rice culture during the last decade of the 17th century. By the early 18th century rice had become a major export crop, as a growing surplus was produced. The regions engaged in this enterprise continued to expand, and by 1840 other areas—such as Georgetown and Beaufort, S.C., Wilmington, N.C., and Savannah, Ga., as well as the entire hundred-mile seacoast of Georgia— offered competition to Charleston. As the once rich lands of South Carolina wore out from continuous planting and the destruction of the tree and bush cover on the upper reaches of its rivers, the comparatively new lands of Georgia and even some river localities in Alabama, Mississippi, and Louisiana expanded their productivity. After the Civil War, especially after the introduction of steam and, later, gasoline pumps, the bulk of American rice came to be produced in the prairie regions of Texas, Arkansas, and Louisiana.

The requirements for the successful growing of rice in antebellum years included a slave labor force of at least fifty field hands and from 300 to 1,000 acres of level, cleared swampland, located above the saltwater line on a river. Medium or heavy surface soil, such as clay and swamp muck, was best. The fields were crisscrossed by a network of banks, canals, ditches, and drains; the flow of water in and out was controlled by flood gates and trunks. A succession of from three to five flowings covered the fields, which were drained periodically. A mean temperature of 70 degrees during the growing season and yearly rainfall of from 50 to 60 inches were also necessary. Planting was timed with the new and full moons so as to have high tides available on schedule. A bare minimum of farm machinery was adequate, although some plantations had their own milling facilities.

The sheaves were harvested from late August to November, dried, and then threshed by hand with a flail. Coastal sloops from nearby marketing centers came to plantation wharves and transported the crop to factorage houses that had extended operating credit to the planters. During the colonial period the bulk of the crop was then sent to the West Indies and Europe, subject to varying English tariff restrictions on rice. In the 19th century 20 percent of the rice harvest was marketed in the West Indies; 5 percent, directly to Europe; and the remainder to commerce centers in the North for domestic consumption or transshipment to Europe.

The antebellum rice coast nurtured a closely knit, nonmobile, elite plantation society that could not respond fully to the forces of western expansion and other social, political, and economic changes, because it was yoked to the tide-flow banks of coastal rivers. By 1860 it had become largely separated from the mainstream of southern life and interests.

[D. C. Heyward, *Seed From Madagascar;* A. V. House, ed., *Planter Management and Capitalism in Ante-Bellum Georgia.*]

ALBERT V. HOUSE

"RICH, AND GOOD AND WISE." *See* **"Wise, and Good and Rich."**

RICHELIEU RIVER, a Canadian river flowing northward from Lake Champlain into the Saint Lawrence River, was discovered by Samuel de Champlain in 1609. It was first known to the French as the Rivière des Iroquois, as it was the route between the Iroquois country and Quebec. Afterward it was the recognized thoroughfare, in peace and war, between New England and New France. French Gen. Louis Joseph de Montcalm sent François Gaston de Lévis up the Richelieu in 1756 to defend the frontier; and the following year took the same route to capture Fort William Henry in northeastern New York; and in 1758 to win the Battle of Ticonderoga. Brig. Gen. Richard Montgomery, in 1775, led an expedition against Canada (*see* Canada and the American Revolution) and captured forts Saint Johns and Chambly on the Richelieu in Quebec. In more recent and peaceful times, the Richelieu has borne a moderate volume of commerce between the United States and Canada. A canal was built (1833–43) between Saint Johns and Chambly to circumvent the rapids at Saint-Ours and allow navigation from the Saint Lawrence to Lake Champlain and the Hudson River. The Chambly canal, 11.8 miles long and with nine locks, enabled the Richelieu River to remain an important shipping route between Montreal and New York City.

[Edward P. Hamilton, *The French and Indian Wars;* F. F. Vanderwater, *Lake Champlain and Lake George.*]

LAWRENCE J. BURPEE

RICHMOND, a city in Virginia on the James River, ninety miles from the Atlantic Ocean, and capital of Virginia since 1779. Soon after Jamestown was founded in May 1607, Capt. Christopher Newport led an expedition up the James River to the fall line. There on June 10, 1607, on a hill north of the river, he erected a cross dedicated to James I. This was the future site of Richmond. One of the earliest settlers in the vicinity was a farmer and trader named Thomas Stegg. In 1671 his landholdings descended to his nephew, William Byrd, whose son, William Byrd II, laid off the town of Richmond in 1737. The general assembly granted an act of incorporation in 1742, at which time Richmond was a mere hamlet of perhaps 300 people. The continuing westward shift of population together with the town's strategic location at the head of navigation made Richmond a commercial center of growing importance. In 1764–65, for example, 20,000 hogsheads of tobacco, large quantities of wheat and corn, and 4,900 bushels of coal were shipped to England.

As the Revolution approached, considerations of security led many to regard Richmond rather than Williamsburg as the proper political center of Virginia. The famous convention of 1775 was held there, and in 1779 Richmond became the capital of the new state. Capture by the British in 1780 resulted in some damage, although a village of some 300 structures offered little scope for the incendiary's torch.

Within a generation after the war, Richmond was the social, cultural, and economic hub of the state. Numerous stage lines intersected there. The first steamboat from Norfolk arrived in 1815, and by 1830 the city was connected with Lynchburg via the James River and Kanawha Canal. In 1860, with a population nearing 40,000, Richmond was the terminus for five railroads and was ranked thirteenth in manufacturing among American cities.

In May 1861, after the outbreak of the Civil War and the secession of Virginia, the capital of the Confederate states was moved from Montgomery, Ala., to Richmond. Because of its political, economic, and strategic importance, the city was the object of repeated Union offensives. It was closely beleaguered in 1862 but was relieved by Gen. Robert E. Lee's offensive in the Seven Days' Battle. Two years later federal forces under Gen. Ulysses S. Grant began a long siege that ended with the fall of Richmond on Apr. 2, 1865. The city was greatly damaged in the fire that broke out during the evacuation.

Postwar recovery was relatively rapid, thanks largely to the vitality of the tobacco industry, which also would later help to soften the effects of the Great Depression, and by 1890 the population was more than double that of 1860. The city inevitably became the chief repository of the Confederate legend. The numerous historical sites include Saint John's Church, where Patrick Henry delivered his "liberty or death" speech; the Capitol, designed by Thomas Jefferson and containing Jean Antoine Houdon's statue of George Washington; the White House of the Confederacy; the Lee House; Battle Abbey; and other memorials to the Revolution and the "Lost Cause." Richmond's population in 1970 was 249,430.

[J. P. Little, *History of Richmond;* Samuel Mordecai, *Richmond in By-gone Days;* M. N. Stanard, *Richmond: Its People and Its Story.*]

LUDWELL H. JOHNSON III

RICHMOND, BATTLE OF (Aug. 29–31, 1862). In the late summer of 1862, Confederate Brig. Gen. Edmund Kirby-Smith, with some 16,000 troops, in-

vaded Kentucky in the direction of Lexington. His first skirmish with Union troops occurred on Aug. 29 near Rogersville, south of Richmond in Madison County. Here the Confederates were repulsed, but the next day Kirby-Smith drove the raw Union force of about 7,000 men, under Maj. Gen. William Nelson and Brig. Gen. Mahlon D. Manson, along the highway, over the meadows and cornfields, and even into the cemetery and through the streets of Richmond. The Union troops made two or three desperate attempts to stop the enemy but were defeated, with losses of 1,050 killed and wounded, 4,303 prisoners, and a great quantity of supplies.

[J. T. Dorris, *Old Cane Springs: A Story of the War Between the States in Madison County, Kentucky.*]

JONATHAN T. DORRIS

RICHMOND, BURNING AND EVACUATION OF, in the first days of April 1865, was the dramatic and tragic end of the Confederate capital. On Sunday, Apr. 2, Union forces captured the outer works around Petersburg, Va. On notice from Gen. Robert E. Lee, Confederate President Jefferson Davis and his cabinet left Richmond. Mobs temporarily took control, looting shops and warehouses. By military order of the Confederates, bridges and warehouses, along with shipping, were fired. Once started, the fire, driven by high winds, spread to the business district. On their arrival, Union troops were used to extinguish the fire and restore law and order. The burning and evacuation of Richmond signalized the overthrow of the Confederacy.

[A. H. Bill, *The Beleaguered City: Richmond, 1861–1865;* Rembert W. Patrick, *The Fall of Richmond.*]

ALFRED P. JAMES

RICHMOND, CAMPAIGN AGAINST (1864–65). Strictly speaking, the campaigns against Richmond began under Union Gen. Irvin McDowell in July 1861 (*see* Bull Run, First Battle of) and continued throughout the war, but the final campaign is usually the one referred to as the campaign against Richmond. It began early in May 1864 when Gen. Ulysses S. Grant crossed the Rapidan River and entered the Wilderness, a dense forest in northeastern Orange and northwestern Spotsylvania counties, in command of an army of 122,000 men. His military objectives were to destroy Gen. Robert E. Lee's army and capture Richmond. With a much smaller force Lee contested Grant's purpose for eleven months. A terrific but fruitless two-day struggle (May 5–6) in the Battle of the Wilderness was followed by a flanking march to Spotsylvania Courthouse, eleven miles southwest of Fredericksburg, where another bloody and indecisive conflict took place (May 8–21). Another move to his left by Grant brought the two armies together on the North Anna River (May 23–25), but Grant declined battle and, by a flanking march, reached Cold Harbor, where on June 3, in sight of Richmond, his troops were devastated in direct attack on Confederate entrenchments. Stalled north of the James River, Grant, by another flanking move late in June, crossed the river and sought to force the Confederates out of Richmond by cutting its railway connections with the lower Confederacy. Failures before Petersburg in June and in the Battle of the Crater on July 30 reduced operations to a long drawn-out siege of Petersburg, which lasted nine months. By the following spring the strength of the Confederacy was sapped, and the forces defending Petersburg and Richmond were no longer adequate. It was necessary for Lee's army to evacuate Petersburg and abandon further defense of Richmond, Apr. 2, 1865. In attempted withdrawal to southwestern Virginia, Lee's troops were surrounded at Appomattox and compelled to surrender on Apr. 9.

This final campaign against Richmond was a feature of a more extensive strategy involving both Gen. Benjamin Franklin Butler's expedition up the James River and Gen. William Tecumseh Sherman's marches in Georgia and the Carolinas.

[D. S. Freeman, *R. E. Lee.*]

ALFRED P. JAMES

RICHMOND JUNTO, a group headed by Thomas Ritchie, editor and publisher (1804–45) of the *Richmond Enquirer*, that controlled Virginia Democratic politics for more than a quarter century. Spencer Roane and John Brockenbrough, cousins of Ritchie, were also members of the junto. Strongly states' rights in tone, the Richmond junto exercised much influence on the Democratic-Republican party's national policies and played a large part in defeating Martin Van Buren for the Democratic presidential nomination in 1844. It was first called the junto about 1820.

[C. H. Ambler, *Thomas Ritchie: A Study in Virginia Politics.*]

ALVIN F. HARLOW

RICH MOUNTAIN, BATTLE OF (July 11, 1861). Planning to seize western Virginia for the Confederacy, Gen. Robert S. Garnett fortified the roads to

Wheeling and Parkersburg at Laurel Mountain and Rich Mountain. Union Gen. George B. McClellan, advancing from Grafton, held the Confederates while Gen. William S. Rosecrans led a column around the left of those on Rich Mountain and cut off the Confederate retreat. Confederate Lt. Col. John Pegram, commanding there, surrendered. Garnett, retreating hastily from Laurel Mountain, was killed during the retirement.

[R. U. Johnson and C. C. Buel, eds., *Battles and Leaders of the Civil War,* vol. I.]

JOSEPH MILLS HANSON

RICKERT RICE MILLS, INC. V. FONTENOT, 297 U.S. 110 (1936), a case in which the Supreme Court, on Jan. 13, 1936, invalidated a statute amendatory to the Agricultural Adjustment Act of 1933. The statute, approved Aug. 24, 1935, had attempted to clarify the provisions of the original enactment. Relative to this amendment, Justice Owen J. Roberts ruled, without dissent, that it "remains a means for effectuating the regulation of agricultural production, a matter not within the powers of Congress." Funds impounded during the proceedings were returned to the Rickert Rice Mills and companion complainants, but the Court refused to discuss the procedure of recovering money previously paid under the unconstitutional processing tax provisions.

BENJAMIN F. SHAMBAUGH

RIDERS, LEGISLATIVE, are sections or clauses not germane to the subject matter of a bill that are added by amendment before passage. This is done with the expectation that the sentiment favorable to the bill will be sufficient to sweep the whole enactment through the final vote and secure executive approval even though the proposal would probably be defeated by vote or vetoed if submitted separately. Where the executive has power to veto sections of acts this device may not be used to escape his disapproval (*see* Item Veto). In many states constitutional provisions restrict each bill to a single subject, which must be clearly expressed in its title. In such cases riders would invalidate the whole law.

Riders are most commonly used in the federal government and in connection with appropriation acts. In 1913 Congress attached to an appropriation act a rider exempting labor unions from the Sherman Antitrust Act. President William Howard Taft had to veto the whole bill to annul this provision. Similarly, a rider repealing daylight saving time was attached to an appropriation bill in 1919. President Woodrow Wilson vetoed the bill, and the rider was then made a separate act, which he vetoed, Congress repassing it over his veto.

[Robert Luce, *Legislative Procedure*.]
HARVEY WALKER

RIDGEFIELD, BATTLE OF (Apr. 27, 1777). On Apr. 25, 1777, a detachment of British troops, under the command of the last colonial governor of New York, William Tryon, disembarked at Compo Point (present Westport, Conn.) and, scattering a small group of patriots who tried to stop them, marched rapidly inland to Danbury, Conn. The following day they burned the American supplies stored there. Retreating by way of Ridgefield on Apr. 27, they were followed by Maj. Gen. David Wooster with 200 men and attacked twice. On the second attack, just outside Ridgefield, Wooster was mortally wounded. At Ridgefield the retreating British found the way blocked by generals Gold Selleck Silliman and Benedict Arnold with 500 Connecticut militia. The Americans had hastily built a barricade across the village street. After a frontal attack, which failed, Tryon ordered an attack on the left flank. Arnold was unhorsed, the barricade forced, and the British, hurrying forward, reached their boats with difficulty the following day.

[G. L. Rockwell, *The History of Ridgefield*.]
A. C. FLICK

RIDGELY, FORT. The sale of their Minnesota lands by the Sioux, under the Treaty of Traverse des Sioux, July 23, 1851, and the concentration of these Indians on small upper Minnesota River reservations brought about the establishment of Fort Ridgely, Apr. 29, 1853, on the north bank of that river in Nicollet County, Minn. On Aug. 20 and 22, 1862, it was successfully defended against powerful Sioux attacks (*see* Sioux Uprising in Minnesota). After serving as a base for Henry H. Sibley's expedition in 1863, the post became obsolete and was abandoned on May 22, 1867.

[Willoughby M. Babcock, ed., "Up the Minnesota Valley to Fort Ridgely in 1853," *Minnesota History*, vol. 11.]
WILLOUGHBY M. BABCOCK

RIFLE. Early in the 16th century, central European gunsmiths began developing the process of rifling gun barrels. This was accomplished by cutting spiral grooves from the breech to the muzzle, inside the gun barrel. The spiral grooves caused the ball to spin when leaving the barrel and imparted stability to the projectile. In America, German gunsmiths working in Pennsylvania and other Middle Atlantic states modified the short, large-caliber, German "Jaeger" rifle into the long, graceful, and accurate American rifle. Originally, no particular name was assigned to these uniquely American weapons; they were simply called "rifles" to differentiate them from the more common smoothbore muskets and shotguns. During the American Revolution they were often referred to as "long rifles," and the term "Kentucky rifle" was probably not used until the end of the War of 1812. Later the name "Pennsylvania rifle" came into limited usage to denote the place of manufacture of the majority of the weapons. American riflemen rendered significant service during the revolutionary war, although their exploits have been somewhat exaggerated over the years. Most American soldiers were armed with the smoothbore musket and fought in line of battle, like their British counterparts.

The first official U.S. Army rifle was the model of 1803. This weapon was produced at the federal arsenal at Harpers Ferry, Va., and was used to arm soldiers of the special rifle regiments. Although various models of rifles were adopted by the U.S. Army, the musket continued to dominate the battlefield until the introduction of the U.S. rifle-musket, Model 1855. This weapon fired the lead hollow-base Minié bullet invented by a French army officer, Claude Étienne Minié, in 1849. Since the Minié bullet was smaller than the bore diameter, it allowed the soldier to load and fire a rifle at the same rate as the smoothbore musket.

During the American Civil War many types of breech-loading rifles and carbines were developed and issued. Some of these early breechloaders, such as the Henry and Spencer rifles, used metallic cartridges with a self-contained, rim-fire primer, which eliminated the need for a separate priming cap required by all percussion weapons. In the years immediately after the war, large quantities of muzzle-loading rifle-muskets were converted to breechloaders firing a rim-fire cartridge. A modification of this conversion resulted in the adoption of the U.S. Rifle, Model 1873. This simple and dependable single-shot rifle, firing the powerful 45–70 cartridge, became the first U.S. martial arm to utilize the center fire primer in the cartridge. It was the weapon used by the army during the Indian wars and was not replaced until the adoption of the Krag-Jörgensen rifle in 1892. The latter, an excellent five-shot, bolt-action rifle, was based on a Danish design and was known officially as the U.S. Rifle, Model 1892. Although the Krag rifle proved adequate for the needs of the army, improvements in cartridges, loading systems, and general design created the need for an improved bolt-action rifle. The U.S. Rifle, Model 1903, based on the Mauser bolt-action principle, was adopted to replace the Krag rifle. This model, with only slight modifications, was to be the standard arm of the U.S. armed forces until World War II, when it was replaced by the semiautomatic M1 Garand rifle. The dependable, eight-shot Garand rifle was perhaps the best infantry rifle of World War II. It was retained by the government until 1957, when it was replaced by the M14 rifle, 7.62-mm caliber, to comply with standards set up by the North Atlantic Treaty Organization. The design of the M14 was based on the Garand, but the new rifle was fitted with a twenty-round detachable magazine and a selector switch for fully automatic fire. The M14 rifle was gradually phased out of service during the Vietnam War and was replaced with the experimental AR-15 rifle, which was easier to control during fully automatic fire. This weapon, which fired a 5.56-mm cartridge, initially created some controversy because of alleged jamming of the action. Modifications in the rifle and improvements in ammunition eliminated most of the problems, and the weapon was officially adopted under the designation of U.S. Rifle M16 A1 in 1967.

[Arcadi Gluckman, *United States Muskets, Rifles and Carbines;* Harold L. Peterson and Robert Elman, *The Great Guns;* Joseph E. Smith, *Small Arms of the World.*]

PHILIP M. CAVANAUGH

RIFLE, RECOILLESS, is a lightweight, air-cooled, manually operated, breech-loading, single-shot, direct-fire weapon used primarily for defense against tanks and secondarily against fortifications and personnel. Unlike the obsolete 3.5-inch Rocket Launcher (bazooka) and its replacement, the Rocket 66-mm M72 (Light Antitank Weapon—in reality a round of ammunition), both of which use a self-propelled rocket round, the recoilless rifle uses fixed ammunition. The cartridge is perforated so that the expanding gases exert equal pressure in all directions within the chamber. The pressure to the front, against the chamber's sloping wall, equals the force to the rear, against the breech's closed portion. The remaining gases are permitted to escape to the rear through openings in the breech, so that the rifle remains motionless when

fired. The gases escaping rearward, called the backblast, create a danger space to the rear of the weapon.

First developed by the German army in World War II, the weapon saw further refinement as a form of antitank artillery for airborne units in the U.S. Army. The 57-mm M18 and 75-mm M20 were used in limited numbers in the closing months of the war. After the Korean War, advances in armor indicated a need for heavier antitank weapons. The 90-mm M67 and the 106-mm M40 A1 (the 106-mm is actually a 105-mm weapon but is so classified to forestall accidental use of its ammunition in tube artillery) were introduced. Two heavier indirect fire rifles were subsequently developed, the 120-mm M28 and the 155-mm M29 "Davy Crockett," both of which fire the same 279-mm light nuclear round using the "spigot principle," whereby the round fits over the tube but the propellant chamber fits inside the tube and utilizes the weapon's reaction chamber.

[G. M. Barnes, *Weapons of World War II;* U.S. Department of the Army, "Crew Served Weapons and Gunnery," Pamphlet ROTCM 145-41.]

WARNER STARK

RIGHT OF SEARCH. *See* **Visit and Search.**

RIGHT OF WAY LAW OF 1852 gave to all railroad, plank road, and turnpike companies chartered by the public-land states before 1862 a right of way of 100 feet through the public lands, with station sites and the right to take timber and stone from adjoining lands for construction purposes. In 1855 the act was amended to make it apply to the territories.

[L. H. Haney, *Congressional History of Railways in the United States, 1850–1887.*]

PAUL W. GATES

RIGHTS OF ENGLISHMEN came to America with the first royal charters, but throughout the greater part of the 17th century local regulations, particularly in New England, prevailed. The struggle against the arbitrary government of Gov. Edmund Andros (*see* New England, Dominion of) did more than anything else to introduce a knowledge of these rights, which came to be identified with the common law, into New England. A genuine admiration for the system sprang up when it was realized that its principles contained safeguards against governmental tyranny both at home and abroad. "Let an Englishman go where he will," said the Board of Trade in 1720, "he carries as much of law and liberty with him, as the nature of things will bear." Henry Care's *English Liberties, or the Free-born Subject's Inheritance,* was reprinted at Boston (1721), and British liberties came to be defined in terms of laws that stood above both king and Parliament, and of which the colonists could not therefore be deprived. Applied to the relations between the home government and the colonies after 1761, the colonists claimed the right of Englishmen to be taxed only in case they were represented (*see* Taxation Without Representation). Since the colonists were not represented in Parliament, it followed, so they held, that they were not liable to internal taxation by that body. In its final and boldest form the doctrine appeared in 1774 to the effect that the colonists "are entitled to life, liberty and property, and they have never ceded to any sovereign power whatever a right to dispose of either without their consent."

[C. E. Merriam, *History of American Political Theories.*]
WILLIAM S. CARPENTER

RIGHTS OF MAN, a defense of the French Revolution written by Thomas Paine in reply to Edmund Burke's *Reflections on the Revolution in France* (1790). The work, which was dedicated to George Washington, appeared in two parts, the first in 1791 and the second in 1792. Its circulation was very great, both in the United States and abroad, the number of copies sold in England alone being estimated at 1.5 million. To Paine the rights of man were indefeasible:

A man, by natural right, has a right to judge his own cause, and so far as the right of the mind is concerned, he never surrenders it. But what availeth it him to judge if he has not the power to redress? He therefore deposits his right in the common stock of society, and takes the arm of society, of which he is a part, in preference and in addition to his own. Society grants him nothing. Every man is a proprietor in society, and draws on the capital as a matter of right.

Only when it could be said in any country in the world that its people were happy, then might that country boast of its constitution and government. (*See also* Natural Rights.)

[Mary Agnes Best, *Thomas Paine.*]
J. HARLEY NICHOLS

RIGHTS OF THE BRITISH COLONIES AS-SERTED AND PROVED, a tract written by James Otis in 1764 that denied the authority of Parliament to tax the colonies, drawing analogy between the colonies and Ireland. At the same time it favored representation in Parliament for the colonies. By way of appendix, Otis declared that acts of Parliament against natural equity or the British constitution were void.

[C. F. Mullett, "Some Political Writings of James Otis," *University of Missouri Studies,* vol. 4.]
RICHARD B. MORRIS

RILEY, FORT, named for Maj. Gen. Bennet Riley, is located on the north bank of the Kansas River, just east of the mouth of the Republican River, in Geary County, Kans. In 1852 Col. Thomas T. Fauntleroy, commanding officer at Fort Leavenworth, recommended its erection as a station and supply depot for frontier troops. Next year Congress appropriated $65,000 for its construction, and Maj. Edmund A. Ogden was placed in charge of the work, which began immediately. It soon became important in frontier defense. Cholera attacked it in 1855, killing Ogden and many of his men. Its troops aided in restoring order during the days of civil war in Kansas (1856) and helped to protect emigrants and the overland mail during the Civil War. On Jan. 29, 1887, Congress authorized the establishment of a school of instruction for cavalry and light artillery, which was located at Fort Riley on Mar. 14, 1892. In 1917 Fort Riley was converted to a U.S. Army staging and training center. By 1975 the fort occupied 5,760 acres.

[E. Hunt, *History of Fort Leavenworth.*]
IDA PARKER BIEBER

RINGGOLD GAP, BATTLE OF (Nov. 27, 1863). After Confederate Gen. Braxton Bragg's defeat on Missionary Ridge in Tennessee, the Confederate Army of Tennessee retreated southward into northwestern Georgia. Gen. Ulysses S. Grant sent Union Gen. Joseph Hooker in pursuit (*see* Chattanooga Campaign). Confederate Gen. Patrick R. Cleburne, in command of Bragg's rear guard, halted at Ringgold Gap to insure the safe withdrawal of the army and trains. Hooker attacked repeatedly but each time was repulsed. After dark, Cleburne withdrew, and Hooker's pursuit ended.

[R. U. Johnson and C. C. Buel, eds., *Battles and Leaders of the Civil War.*]
THOMAS ROBSON HAY

RINGGOLD-RODGERS EXPLORING EXPEDI-TION, or the North Pacific Exploring and Surveying

Expedition, consisting of five naval vessels—*Vincennes, John Hancock, Porpoise, John P. Kennedy,* and *Fenimore Cooper*—under Comdr. Cadwalader Ringgold, sailed from Norfolk, Va., in June 1853. In the interests of the U.S. whaling industry and to correct naval charts, it surveyed in the western Pacific from Tasmania northward to Herald Island in the Arctic Ocean. During the first year of the expedition, numerous shoals and islands were charted. When the ships reached China in 1854, Ringgold fell ill, and the expedition was turned over to the second-in-rank, Comdr. John Rodgers. The expedition continued to cruise the Pacific, surveying the Hawaiian and Society islands and the coast of Japan. It reached the Arctic Ocean in August 1855, some vessels continuing work until 1859.

[James R. Soley, "Rear-Admiral John Rodgers," *Naval Institute Proceedings* (1882).]

DUDLEY W. KNOX

RINGS, POLITICAL. A political ring is a comparatively small group of persons, usually headed by a political boss, organized to control a city, county, or state, and primarily interested in deriving therefrom large personal monetary profit. Political rings have been found here and there throughout the country periodically as far back as colonial days, but they occupy a particularly colorful position in American history of the second half of the 19th century.

William Marcy Tweed did more to bring political rings into the limelight than any other person. As a young man on the New York Board of Aldermen, in 1851 he joined a ring, known as the "Forty Thieves," whose purpose it was to gain personal profit from the improper granting of franchises. As a member of the Board of Supervisors, Tweed belonged to several short-lived rings that stole rather moderately from the public. The famous political ring that bears his name, and that for boldness has probably never been surpassed, was organized in 1869 and composed of Tweed, Mayor A. Oakey ("O.K.") Hall, Comptroller Richard ("Slippery Dick") Connolly, and ("Brains") Peter B. Sweeny.

Although less notorious than the Tweed Ring, the Philadelphia Gas Ring actually exerted greater political influence but indulged in less peculation. Whereas the Tweed Ring came to grief within three years of its founding (although Tweed himself had been profiting from his political offices and influence for a decade), the Gas Ring wielded great political power from 1865 until 1887.

Less well known than either the Tweed or Gas rings were the Butler Ring, the Ames Ring, and the Ruef Ring. "Colonel" Edward Butler built a political ring in Saint Louis in the 1890's with himself as mastermind and a select group of members of the two houses of the city council as members. This ring disposed of valuable franchises to the highest bribers. About 1900 the "genial doctor," A. A. Ames, constructed a ring around the Minneapolis Police Department, which preyed upon thieves, gamblers, and other crooks. The "Curly Boss" Abraham Ruef used members of the San Francisco Board of Supervisors as associates and sold numerous official favors to public utilities during the first decade of the 20th century until his trial for bribery, conviction, and imprisonment in 1911.

The designation "political ring" is not used currently to the extent that it has been in the past, largely because the phrase "political machine" has been expanded to include what at an earlier period was meant by political ring. At an earlier time the top men in such machines as those operating in Chicago and Kansas City during the 20th century would have been designated a political ring. (*See also* Bosses and Bossism, Political.)

[Walton Bean, *Boss Ruef's San Francisco: The Story of the Union Labor Party, Big Business, and the Graft Prosecution;* Alexander B. Callow, Jr., *The Tweed Ring;* Lyle W. Dorsett, *The Pendergast Machine;* Seymour J. Mandelbaum, *Boss Tweed's New York;* Zane L. Miller, *Boss Cox's Cincinnati: Urban Politics in the Progressive Era;* Alfred Steinberg, *The Bosses;* Joel Arthur Tarr, *A Study in Boss Politics: William Lorimer of Chicago.*]

HAROLD ZINK

RIO DE JANEIRO CONFERENCE (Aug. 15–Sept. 2, 1947), a meeting of nineteen American republics (Nicaragua and Ecuador did not take part), was in line with the long-standing U.S. practice, as exemplified in Pan-Americanism, of encouraging cooperation among the twenty-one republics. Wishing to give permanent form to principles of hemispheric solidarity embodied in the Act of Chapultepec (March 1945), the participating countries signed the Inter-American Treaty of Reciprocal Assistance (Sept. 2, 1947), also known as the Pact of Rio. The treaty had great significance because it was the first regional collective security agreement as authorized by Article 51 of the United Nations Charter. Under the treaty it became the duty of each member of the pact to assist in meeting an armed attack by a country against an American country, pending action by the United Nations; or if an American country were threatened by a situation not involving an armed attack by another country (for example, a revolution), the members would immediately meet to decide on what measures should be taken. The importance attached to the conference by the United States was indicated by President Harry S. Truman's journey to Brazil to address the final session.

CHARLES S. CAMPBELL

RIO GRANDE, a North American river, 1,300 miles of which form the boundary separating the United States and Mexico. The Rio Grande—known in Mexico as the Río Bravo del Norte—is 1,885 miles long, making it the fifth longest river in North America. It rises in the San Juan Mountains in southwestern Colorado and flows generally southward through New Mexico until it reaches El Paso, Tex. It then flows generally to the southeast until it empties into the Gulf of Mexico at Brownsville, Tex., and Matamoros, Mexico.

After the Louisiana Purchase (1803), American expansionists claimed the Rio Grande as the southern and western border of the territory covered by that purchase. By the Adams-Onís Treaty (1819) the United States recognized Spain's rights to Texas by accepting the Sabine River (which separates Louisiana and Texas) as the western limit of the United States. American colonizers and filibusters continued to covet the lands north of the Rio Grande, but Spain discouraged all such designs. After Mexican independence from Spain (1821), American colonizers fared better, and numerous American colonies sprang up in Texas. The American colonists in Texas always looked on the Rio Grande as the border separating them from Mexico proper; the Mexican government ignored that boundary when it annexed Texas to the state of Coahuila (1830), which action was one of the main causes of the Texas Revolution (1835–36).

The Texas Republic maintained and never surrendered the principle that the Rio Grande, from its westernmost headsprings to the Gulf of Mexico, constituted its southern and western boundaries. The United States inherited those claims with the annexation of Texas in 1845, but Mexico's unwillingness to accept the river as the boundary was an immediate cause of the Mexican War (1846–48). The Treaty of Guadalupe Hidalgo (1848), which ended the war, recognized the river as an international border; this has not been questioned seriously since then.

Seasonal flooding causes the Rio Grande to change its course from time to time. The International Boundary Commission was established by Mexico and the United States to settle disputes arising from such changes. The longest lasting dispute concerned 630 acres, known as El Chamizal, near El Paso. When the Rio Grande flooded and changed course in 1864, El Chamizal, formerly in Mexico, found itself on the U.S. side of the river. Finally in 1963 the two governments agreed to build a 4.5-mile concrete channel to the north of El Chamizal, thereby ceding it permanently to Mexico. In 1966 the federal government established the Chamizal National Memorial, commemorating the peaceful settlement of the boundary dispute. On Dec. 13, 1968, President Lyndon B. Johnson and Mexican President Gustavo Díaz Ordaz met at El Paso and set off a blast that shifted the Rio Grande permanently through the new channel.

The Rio Grande is not important as a trade route—it is navigable only for a short distance from its mouth—but its waters have long been important for irrigation in the arid Southwest. In prehistoric times the Pueblo of New Mexico built elaborate irrigation systems. In modern times, irrigation water from the Rio Grande supports the commercially important citrus and truck farm regions in the Rio Grande Valley in both Texas and Mexico. Cooperation between the two countries has resulted in various irrigation and flood-control projects, the most spectacular being the vast Amistad Dam (completed 1969) at Del Rio, Tex., just below the confluence of the Rio Grande and the Devils River.

[Harvey Fergusson, *The Rio Grande;* Laura Gilpin, *The Rio Grande: River of Destiny;* Paul Horgan, *Great River: The Rio Grande in North American History;* Norris Hundley, *Dividing the Waters.*]

DONALD W. HUNT

RIO GRANDE, ENGLISH COLONY ON. From 1832 to 1834 John Charles Beales (an Englishman), in league with other empresarios, secured colonization grants from the Mexican state of Coahuila-Texas embracing much of present western Texas and eastern New Mexico. By transfer, most of the other empresarios left their interests to Beales. Not having money to promote the venture, he organized in New York a joint-stock company, composed of such well-known men as Silas M. Stilwell, Charles Edwards, Samuel Swartwout, and James Watson Webb. The colony was recruited largely in England, Ireland, and the Continent.

On Nov. 11, 1833, the *Amos Wright* brought the immigrants and supplies from New York to the Gulf of Mexico. They landed at Copano Bay, near Saint Joseph's Island and above the present city of Corpus Christi, and traveled to Beales's Rio Grande grant via La Bahia and San Antonio. The site selected was on Las Moras Creek, about six miles above its confluence with the Rio Grande. Here, on Mar. 16, 1834, a small town was built and named Dolores in honor of Beales's wife. Beales made two other attempts to bring additional immigrants, but the colony was doomed to failure, for it was in a semiarid land, quite remote from any well-settled area. Therefore, when Antonio López de Santa Anna crossed the Rio Grande in early 1836 to suppress the Texas Revolution, the colonists abandoned their homes and started in ox-drawn wagons for Matamoros. But while they were camping beside a lake on the San Patricio trail, all but two women and three children were massacred by a war party of Comanche. The two women were ransomed several months later by the Comancheros (New Mexican traders), and the children died in captivity.

[William Kennedy, *Texas: The Rise, Progress and Prospects of the Republic of Texas.*]

C. C. RISTER

RIO GRANDE, SIBLEY'S OPERATIONS ON

(1861–62). In June 1861 Maj. Henry H. Sibley resigned his commission with the U.S. Army and received permission from the Confederacy to raise a force to drive the Union soldiers from New Mexico. A regiment made up mostly of Texans was raised at San Antonio and marched to Fort Bliss, near El Paso, which had recently fallen into the hands of the South. From here Sibley, now a general, moved up the Rio Grande toward Fort Craig, where Union Col. Edward R. Canby, in command of the department of New Mexico, made his headquarters. A severe fight occurred on Feb. 21, 1862, known as the Battle of Valverde, in which Canby was driven across the river into the fort. Sibley continued on up the river and took Albuquerque without a fight, but all the stores had been destroyed by the Union troops on their evacuation. Desperate for provisions for his men and their horses, Sibley continued on toward Santa Fe. He was met, Mar. 28, by Union Col. John P. Slough, from Fort Union, and at Glorieta, in a terrific hand-to-hand battle, Sibley was stopped. He began his retreat back down the Rio Grande. Finding himself caught between the armies of Canby on the south and Slough on the north, he made a 100-mile circuit around Fort Craig through the pathless mountains. Forced to abandon

his wagons, he was soon without food, water, and supplies, and much suffering occurred. On July 6, 1862, the unfortunate army crossed back into Texas. They had lost over 500 men, killed, dead from disease, or prisoners, and the Union forces still held New Mexico.

J. G. SMITH

RIPLEY, FORT,

a one-company army post, first called Fort Gaines, was established, Apr. 13, 1849, on the west bank of the Mississippi near the Crow Wing River, in what is now central Minnesota. The fort was built to control the Winnebago Long Prairie Reservation. Chippewa unrest in August 1862 brought an increased garrison. The fort was abandoned about 1877.

[George C. Tanner, "History of Fort Ripley, 1849 to 1859," *Minnesota Historical Collections,* vol. 10; Louis B. Kinder, "The Story of Old Fort Ripley," *Minnesota History,* vol. 9.]

WILLOUGHBY M. BABCOCK

RIPPER LEGISLATION,

the name given to acts of state legislatures, motivated by partisan considerations, whereby local (usually city) officials of one party are turned out of office and replaced with political opponents. The New Hampshire legislature in 1921 transferred the administration of streets, highways, and sewers from the city authorities in Manchester to commissions appointed by the governor. The New Jersey legislature in 1927 passed over the governor's veto bills designed to strip the Democratic majority in the common council of Union City of its control over appointments made by the Republican mayor and empowered the mayor to remove all officials in office at the time of his election. Pennsylvania's Democratic legislature in 1937 sought to weaken Republican influence in local government by passing, among others, bills abolishing the Philadelphia civil service commission and municipal court. These measures were later held unconstitutional by the state supreme court.

Legislatures can forego frontal attacks on undesired employees by cutting an agency's budget drastically and thereby forcing the layoff of staff. This is known as "riffing," from RIF (reduction in force). Civil service commissions that enforce the merit system have been starved into impotence to hide patronage firings and hirings. And compulsory retirement ages can be manipulated to trigger early departures and thereby open new slots for the majority party's minions.

[S. Frazer, "The New Jersey Ripper Bills—A Review of the Decision of the Court of Errors and Appeals in McCarthy v. Walker," *National Municipal Review*, vol. 21; D. D. McKean, *Party and Pressure Politics*.]

CHARLES H. BACKSTROM

RIP RAPS CONTRACT-SCANDAL. In 1818, under Secretary of War John C. Calhoun, a contract was made with Elijah Mix for 150,000 perches of stone to strengthen the fortification on the Rip Raps, a small island at Old Point Comfort on the Virginia coast, near Hampton Roads. Calhoun's enemies associated his name and that of his chief clerk, Maj. Christopher Van Deventer, a brother-in-law of Mix, with scandals growing out of this contract, and forced its cancellation in 1822. In 1827 a committee of the House of Representatives, after a prolonged investigation, exonerated Calhoun, but ordered Van Deventer dismissed from his position in the War Department.

A. C. FLICK

RIP VAN WINKLE. The story of the ne'er-do-well Rip Van Winkle, who wandered off with his dog and gun into the Catskill Mountains, slept for twenty years, and returned only to find what his creator, Washington Irving, calls "the dilapidations of time," has a complex and ancient lineage. Perhaps Irving, when he offered this tale in *The Sketch Book of Geoffrey Crayon, Gent.* (serialized 1819–20), had heard its equivalent from one of the Dutch families in New York or in the regions of the Hudson River. Yet it is equally certain that he was dependent upon a German version of the tale. In essence the story belongs to the lore of many peoples, for versions of it are to be found in writers as various as Herodotus, Thomas the Rhymer (a 13th-century Scottish poet), and historians of the Moors. Yet the legend of the magic slumber, the dwarfs and their bowling, and the return from the hills along the blue Hudson has for more than a century continued to delight the imaginations of Americans. Irving had made articulate a myth that seemed to be wholly American, and had made the Catskills blossom with an unforgettable legend. Moreover, as the years passed, the meaning of the old tale seemed to deepen into a symbolic representation of the inevitable changes in American life, and of the passage of time itself, a tragedy for human beings that the whimsical, wistful story of Rip but thinly veils.

[Stanley T. Williams, *The Life of Washington Irving*, vol. I.]

STANLEY T. WILLIAMS

RIVER AND HARBOR IMPROVEMENTS. Referring in 1783 to his country's extensive natural waterways, George Washington wrote, "Would to God we may have the wisdom to improve them." In colonial times rivers and lakes were principal avenues of transit and schemes for their development abounded, but scarcities of money and engineering skills precluded large undertakings. With the formation of the federal government in 1789, the outlook brightened. The First Congress enacted legislation for "the establishment and support of the Lighthouses, Beacons, Buoys, and Public Piers"; and in 1790, with congressional assent, states began levying tonnage duties to be used for deepening harbors and removing sunken vessels.

The administration of Thomas Jefferson pointed the way toward greater federal involvement. The founding of the U.S. Military Academy at West Point, N.Y., in 1802 was auspicious. The first school of technology in the New World, the academy made possible a technically competent corps of engineers within the army. In 1808, at the behest of Congress, Secretary of the Treasury Albert Gallatin produced a farsighted plan that envisaged a grand network of water routes binding together the seaboard states and linking the East Coast with the interior and the Great Lakes. The estimated cost was $20 million. Although the plan captured public interest, financial considerations, debate over the federal role in internal improvements, and the War of 1812 combined to forestall action.

The decade that followed the Treaty of Ghent (1814) witnessed signal changes. The War of 1812 had taught the value of interior lines of communication, and nationalism fostered by the war fired enthusiasm for public works. Navigation projects became important features both of Henry Clay's "American system" and of Secretary of War John C. Calhoun's plans for an adequate defense. Presidential vetoes, based on constitutional scruples, curbed the will of Congress for a time and left the initiative largely to the states. Construction of the Erie Canal, the greatest undertaking of this period, began in 1817 under state auspices. At length, in March 1824, the historic decision of the Supreme Court in *Gibbons* v. *Ogden* cleared the way for prompt enactment of two important laws. The first, the General Survey Act of Apr. 30, authorized planning for roads and canals "of national importance in a commercial or military point of view" and empowered the president to employ army engineers in this work. The second, an appropriation act of May 24, provided $75,000 for naviga-

RIVER AND HARBOR IMPROVEMENTS

tion improvements on the Ohio and Mississippi rivers. These acts marked the real beginning of the federal program for waterway development.

Over the next thirty-five years, programs evolved and work went forward. Between 1824 and 1831, the War Department Board of Engineers for Internal Improvements outlined a comprehensive plan, segments of which were swiftly implemented. With federal subsidies and technical aid from army engineers, states and chartered companies soon began construction of such important canals as the Chesapeake and Delaware, the Chesapeake and Ohio, and the Louisville and Portland. At the same time the U.S. Army Corps of Engineers launched a nationwide endeavor that has continued to this day. Snagging on the Mississippi, opening up the log-choked Red River, deepening the Ohio, preserving Saint Louis as a river port, and clearing harbors all along the Atlantic and Gulf coasts were among its early activities. In 1857 the Corps of Engineers introduced the seagoing hopper dredge at Charleston, S.C. During this same period the corps entered the field of lighthouse construction, completing the famous Minots Ledge off the Massachusetts coast and many other lights. The Topographical Engineers, an independent branch from 1838 until the Civil War, also rendered impressive service. The Great Lakes survey, inaugurated in 1841, provided accurate information for shippers; and the Humphreys-Abbot study of the Mississippi, completed in 1861, was a major contribution to the science of hydraulics. Minuscule by latter-day standards (the total cost was less than $20 million), the antebellum program nevertheless had a decided impact on commercial growth.

A great upsurge of activity followed Appomattox. During the last third of the 19th century, the Corps of Engineers expended nearly $333 million on rivers and harbors. To meet its enlarged responsibilities, the corps established a permanent, nationwide system of districts and divisions staffed by military and civilian engineers. Meanwhile, Congress created special organizations designed to meet special needs: the Mississippi River Commission (1879); the Missouri River Commission (1884–1902); the office of the supervisor, New York harbor (1888); and the California Debris Commission (1893). Among major projects of the period were improvement of the Mississippi River by wing dams, revetments, and levees and construction of the Eads Jetties that opened the river's South Pass to ocean traffic; canalization of the Ohio; provision of a ship channel to connect the waters of the Great Lakes between Buffalo, N.Y., Chicago, and

Duluth, Minn.; erection of Tillamook (Oregon) and Stannard Rock (Michigan) lighthouses; and completion of the Muscle Shoals Canal in the Tennessee River and the "Soo" locks at Sault Sainte Marie, Mich., both engineering marvels of the day. Virtually every major harbor on the oceans, the Great Lakes, the Mississippi, and the Ohio was improved for shipping. A time of great accomplishment, these years were also the heyday of the pork barrel, when many schemes of marginal value won legislative sanction. Mark Twain's fictional Columbus River, alias Goose Run, which if "widened, and deepened, and straightened, and made long enough . . . would be one of the finest rivers in the western country" had many a real life counterpart.

By the turn of the century, a trend toward comprehensive planning and multiple-purpose projects was discernible. In 1902 Congress created the Board of Engineers for Rivers and Harbors, composed of officers of the corps, to review proposals for waterway development. Over the next seventy years the board turned down 57 percent of the proposals laid before it. Minor streams received progressively less attention; to win approval, projects generally had to promise far-reaching benefits. Symbolic of the new era was the Intracoastal Waterway, authorized in 1909, to connect all ports from Boston to the Rio Grande. The act of Mar. 3, 1909, that created the National Waterways Commission contained a little known, but highly significant, section directing the chief of engineers to aim in the future for multipurpose projects. Hence, the way was open to marry navigation improvement with hydropower development and flood protection. In 1917 flood control work on the Mississippi, which had been carried on by the federal government since 1882 under the guise of navigation improvement, was formally recognized by Congress as a national responsibility. At the same time, the corps was authorized to undertake such work on the Sacramento River in California. The following year the Corps of Engineers began construction of their first multipurpose dam at Muscle Shoals, Ala.

Noteworthy advances took place in the period between World War I and World War II. In 1927 Congress instructed the army to make a comprehensive survey of the multiple-use potentialities of the nation's rivers. During the next decade, the Corps of Engineers prepared some 200 reports, known as "308 reports," outlining possible development of major river basins for navigation, flood control, irrigation, and power generation. These reports furnished basic guides for many valuable public works projects launched under the New Deal, among them such well-known dams as Bonneville (Oregon), Fort Peck (Montana), Norris (Tennessee), and Shasta (California); and, in fact, these same reports furnished basic guides for all subsequent river-basin development. At the same time, federal programs for flood control expanded. In 1928 Congress adopted an extensive project for flood protection on the Mississippi, commonly called the Jadwin Plan. A year later, the Corps of Engineers established the U.S. Waterways Experiment Station at Vicksburg, Miss., to further the sciences of hydraulics and hydrology. In 1936 nationwide flood-control activities became a function of the corps. From this time forward, goals steadily widened to encompass water supply, recreation, fish and wildlife conservation, pollution abatement, and flood plain management.

The quarter century after World War II was a period of great accomplishment. Programs increased in both size and scope. From a curtailed wartime level of $100 million in 1945, annual expenditures rose sharply to $1.8 billion in 1973. In these years comprehensive planning attained full maturity. Authorization of the Pick-Sloan Plan for the Missouri River Basin, proposed jointly by the Corps of Engineers and the Bureau of Reclamation, launched the nation's first postwar attempt at comprehensive basin development. Constructed under the plan was a series of dams and reservoirs, the largest being Garrison in North Dakota and Oahe, Big Bend, Fort Randall, and Gavins Point in South Dakota; extensive systems of levees and floodwalls; and a 9-foot channel upstream on the Missouri to Sioux City, Iowa. Similar developments followed in the Columbia River and Arkansas River basins. Other projects of special importance in this period were construction of the Saint Lawrence Seaway, recanalization of the Ohio, and modernization of the Black Warrior–Tombigbee Waterway in Alabama. Growing numbers of supertankers and giant cargo vessels spurred efforts to improve harbors and channels and called forth plans for superports. From the mid-1960's onward, environmental protection became an increasingly weighty factor in the concept and execution of all projects.

An effort spanning nearly a century and a half, embracing 3,600 projects, and costing $20.3 billion produced far-reaching benefits. Contributing materially to national defense as well as to national prosperity (as of 1973) were more than 250 deep-draft harbors, which handled more than 750 million tons per year; 22,000 miles of inland waterways, which car-

ried roughly one-sixth of the nation's interurban commerce, mostly in bulk cargo; 334 reservoir sites, with a total storage capacity of 237 million acre-feet; 62 hydropower dams, with installed capacity of 14.3 million kilowatts; and more than 700 flood control projects, which have prevented approximately $3 worth of flood damage for every dollar spent.

[Carter Goodrich, *Government Promotion of American Canals and Railroads, 1800–1890;* Forest G. Hill, *Roads, Rails and Waterways: The Army Engineers and Early Transportation;* W. Stull Holt, *The Office of the Chief of Engineers of the Army;* Frank E. Smith, *The Politics of Conservation;* U.S. Army Chief of Engineers, *Annual Reports.*]

LENORE FINE
JESSE A. REMINGTON

RIVERMEN OF THE OHIO. The American Indians were the first rivermen of the Ohio. As the Indian canoes were well suited to the needs of white explorers and early traders, they were taken over by them. When white immigrants began to push into the Ohio Valley, larger and more substantial craft than canoes were needed for the transportation of the ever-increasing numbers of people, their household and kitchen furnishings, and their livestock. This led to the building of flatboats and keelboats and their numerous modifications. The operators of these craft were known as rivermen, of whom Mike Fink and others were notorious. In time such rivermen gave place to the rousters, gamblers, and bullies of the passenger packets of Ohio River navigation. While the rousters were making a place for themselves in verse and song, gamblers in the cloistered retreats of the passenger packets lay in wait for "gullible folk," whom they gamed out of their cash and in some instances of their clothing and their slaves. Meanwhile, bullies kept alive the traditions of the keelboatmen; others, for instance Enoch Enochs, became notorious for petty pilfering; and the bargemen developed a class of rivermen all their own.

The best human products of the heyday of the passenger packet on the Ohio, a period that extended from about 1840 to about 1855, were its gentlemen captains. In dress and bearing they rivaled the ocean captains of that day, and many of them were very popular. Following the Civil War the passenger packet captains recovered a measure of their former elegance.

Rivermen of the Ohio in the 20th century are a less colorful lot. Hauling heavy freight by 150-foot tugboats that pull as many as twenty barges each, these captains, pilots, and engineers are products of the machine age.

[C. H. Ambler, *A History of Transportation in the Ohio Valley*; A. B. Hulbert, *The Ohio River, A Course of Empire*.]

C. H. AMBLER

RIVER NAVIGATION. The native Americans' means of navigating American rivers was by bullboats (coracles), bark canoes, and pirogues; and the whites added to these bateaux, keelboats, and barges. Where the nature of the river permitted, sailing craft were utilized, as on the Hudson, Delaware, and Potomac rivers; and it was often possible for ships to ascend far upstream. On such streams as the Connecticut and most of the western rivers, the bateau and keelboat were preferred because rowing or poling were more feasible than sailing.

Boatbuilding was among the earliest activities of the colonists, especially in New England and New Amsterdam and on Delaware Bay. Flatboats, known also as arks and Kentucky boats, were built at the headwaters of eastern and western rivers for the transportation of produce, coal, cattle, and immigrants and continued in use until after the Civil War. Their number is incalculable, and so are the amount of freight they carried and the number of immigrants they transported, but they were certainly a vital factor in the development and peopling of the West, particularly by way of the Ohio and Tennessee rivers.

Regular packet boats were rare in the keelboat age on the western rivers, and their services were not long continued, but in the East they existed on the Hudson and Delaware rivers. The Spanish maintained a fleet of galleys on the Mississippi for military purposes, and the United States built a number of gunboats during the Revolution and the following years. Gunboats and keelboats were used by the army against the Indians on the western rivers as late as the War of 1812, and thereafter steamboats took their place. A steam gunboat was an important factor in the victory of Bad Axe in 1832. From about 1792 to about 1817 there were built on the western rivers approximately sixty ships, which were floated downstream and put into ocean service. The practice did not prove economical and was discontinued. A second spurt of ocean vessel building came in the 1840's, and many wooden and iron ships were built at Pittsburgh, Pa., Marietta, Ohio, and other points for use in world commerce.

Robert Fulton's *Clermont* was launched on the Hudson in 1807, and a battle royal was soon initiated between river and coastwise steamboats and sailing packets, with the former destined to eventual victory. Fulton's *Orleans,* or *New Orleans,* was put into operation on the Mississippi between Natchez and New Orleans in 1811 and was of some assistance to Andrew Jackson's army in 1814 and 1815 (*see* New Orleans, Battle of). Fulton's boats were built with deep hulls, which were unsuited to the shallow western rivers, and it was not until Henry Shreve's *Washington* was launched in 1816, with its boilers on the deck, that a craft was found suitable for western river navigation. The title "packet" as applied to the western passenger steamboat was a misnomer, as they rarely operated on schedule. The eastern river steamboats were more reliable. The use of high-pressure boilers resulted in so many explosions that in 1852 Congress set up a system of licensing and inspection. The average life of a western steamboat was about four years.

By 1850 the railroads had begun to sap the trade from the steamboats and from the canals both in the East and West. The tremendous volume of transport needed during the Civil War gave the steamboats a new lease on life, and this continued for a couple of decades since most railroads crossed rather than paralleled the rivers. Barges (the modern form of flatboat) came into general use for carrying coal, oil, and other heavy goods and were towed by steamboats. During this second great age of the steamboat, lines of packets were formed and schedules became more honored by observance. "Low water boats" were even developed to cater to mail and passenger needs during the summer. By the 1880's, however, the competition of the railroads parallel to the rivers was rapidly displacing steamboats in the West and had won a victory in the East. It was partially in a desperate sectional effort to block the railroads that the federal government was pushed into western river improvements after 1879. A magnificent system of dams and other water controls have made the rivers of the Mississippi Basin important highways for heavy freight, carried chiefly in barges. The Mississippi system is connected with the Saint Lawrence Seaway and the Great Lakes by the Great Lakes-to-Mississippi waterway (Illinois Waterway, completed 1933) and the Ohio River system and extends to the Gulf of Mexico and the Gulf Intracoastal Waterway. This system, including the Ohio, Missouri, and Illinois rivers, saw a great increase in commercial traffic during the 1960's and early 1970's.

On the Atlantic coast, the Hudson, Delaware, and Savannah rivers were linked to the Atlantic Intracoastal Waterway, which connected Boston and New

York City with Key West, Fla. This system was especially important during World War II, since it enabled navigation to continue to and from Florida and Massachusetts unmenaced by German submarines. Commercial traffic on the Atlantic coastal rivers and canals increased more than 340 percent from 1950 to 1971, but only slightly over 7 percent between 1960 and 1971. (*See also* River and Harbor Improvements.)

[C. H. Ambler, *Transportation in the Ohio Valley;* L. D. Baldwin, *Keelboat Age on Western Waters;* E. W. Gould, *Fifty Years on the Mississippi;* G. B. Merrick, *Old Times on the Upper Mississippi;* Mississippi River Commission, *Mississippi River Navigation.*]

LELAND D. BALDWIN

RIVERS. The rivers of eastern America played a major part in the settlement and early development of the country. First, they were avenues of exploration. Even where a river was not navigable, its valley or gorge frequently offered the best route for travel on foot or horseback, and it was a thread or clue by which one might find one's way to the outer world. Settlement followed river courses into the interior, and for a long time there was scarcely a hamlet or a trading post that did not have water connection with the coast. The rivers soon became great arteries of traffic, carrying the products of the backcountry down to the cities and seaports. From the vast forests of Maine the Saint Croix, Penobscot, Kennebec, Androscoggin, Saco, and Piscataqua (where there was a sawmill as early as 1631, making lumber, shingles, and barrel staves) through the better part of three centuries bore millions of logs downstream until the forests were depleted. The Merrimack River, until the coming of the railroads, bore a goodly portion of New Hampshire's products, principally timber and granite, to towns below, and especially to its nearest large market, Boston. Parts of New Hampshire and Vermont depended upon the Connecticut River. Northwestern Vermont and northern New York traded via the Richelieu and Saint Lawrence rivers with Quebec and Montreal.

Up the western tributaries of the Susquehanna and Potomac rivers thousands of emigrants during the 18th century toiled, crossed the watershed, and followed the Youghiogheny, Monongahela, Conemaugh, and Allegheny rivers downward to populate the Ohio Valley. Thereafter, the mountains behind them became a wall that shut them off from the Atlantic coast. The great Mississippi River system became their highway; their natural markets were the French towns, Saint Louis and New Orleans. They favored the War of 1812 because they dreamed of a conquest of Canada and a new commercial outlet to the east through control of the Saint Lawrence River. George Washington and others warned that if better connections were not established with them, their allegiance might follow the emigrants' trade down the Mississippi to the Spaniards. That river system influenced all their thinking until the railroads began cutting across the natural trade routes.

Farther southward, emigrants from Virginia and the Carolinas pushed up the James, Dan, Yadkin, and Catawba rivers, through the mountains, to populate southwestern Virginia and northeastern Tennessee. The men of that region, in signifying their allegiance to the Revolution, spoke of themselves as "Men of the settlements beyond the Alleghenies, where the Watauga and the Holston flow to the Tennessee." Some of the earliest settlers of Nashville left a fort on the Holston River on Dec. 22, 1779, journeyed down the Holston and the Tennessee in flatboats to the mouth of the latter, worked up to the mouth of the Cumberland River and traveled up the Cumberland to the site of Nashville, which they reached, on Apr. 24, 1780, after a journey of some 1,300 miles (*see* Cumberland Settlements).

Down the lower Atlantic coast were many broad rivers, really estuaries, having tidewater far upstream from their mouths—Patuxent, Chester, Choptank, Nanticoke, Potomac, Rappahannock, York, James, Chowan, Roanoke, Pamlico, Cape Fear, Pee Dee, Santee, Cooper, Saint Johns, and others—on which sailing vessels carried much traffic in early days. Great plantations were located on them, the mansions fronting on the river, which was often the chief highway for travel as well as for freight traffic. A number of these fine old manor houses still survive.

Rivers wholly impossible for steamboat travel carried vast quantities of pioneer products down to market in arks and flatboats on the spring freshets. With the coming of steam and before railroads conquered the river traffic, steamboats were placed on small, swift rivers, especially in the Middle West and South, where such navigation was later considered impracticable, and where the boat must be of such light draft that it could, as was jokingly said, "run on a heavy dew." It is a fact that steamboats traveled where channels were so narrow that they could not turn around save by backing into the mouth of a tributary stream. Such boats could operate only in parts of the winter and spring, when the water was high and there was not too much ice. Such a river is the Cumberland, where boats once ran 150 miles or more above Nashville, and the stream was so tortuous that it was said a town might hear a boat whistle across a bend in the early morning and not see the craft until late afternoon.

In California, when the Gold Rush began in 1849, the Sacramento and San Joaquin rivers were almost the only feasible highways of travel from San Francisco to the mining regions. There were no steamboats, and many goldseekers paid high fees for passage upstream in a skiff or yawl, with the understanding that they were to help with the rowing. Others traveled in slow-moving sailing vessels. A steamer built in New York for the Atlantic coast trade went safely around Cape Horn and began operating on the Sacramento River; and until another one followed it four months later, its rates were so high that it earned $20,000 or more on a round trip. The Columbia River likewise became the highway after 1855 to and from the Pacific coast for the mining regions of Idaho and northeastern Washington.

Rivers have played an important part in the nation's warfare. The French and Indian War was fought almost entirely along rivers or intervening lakes. The French came down the Allegheny to seize the forks of the Ohio and build Fort Duquesne. Washington marched by the Potomac, Wills Creek, and the Youghiogheny on his ill-fated expedition of 1754 (see Great Meadows), and Maj. Gen. Edward Braddock, a year later, traversed the same route to his death. The Ohio River was perhaps the most noted pathway of Indian warfare in American history. The upper Missouri River was for decades the scene of frequent Indian attacks upon white trappers, traders, and settlers. Much of the fighting of the revolutionary war in New York State was done on, or immediately near, the Hudson and Mohawk rivers (see Burgoyne's Invasion). Washington heavily fortified and blocked the Hudson at West Point to prevent British penetration of its upper reaches; Maj. John André went up the stream on a British vessel to his fatal conference with Benedict Arnold, and the latter escaped downstream on the same vessel. In the Civil War the Potomac, the Rapidan, Rappahannock, North Anna, Chickahominy, and James rivers were important strategic barriers in the East, along which armies aligned themselves or fought. The division of Union Gen. George B. McClellan's army by the Chickahominy in the Seven Days' Battles came near being its ruin. The Potomac below Washington, D.C., was a highway by which the North could move armies quickly to block the mouth of the James. In the Midwest and South the

Mississippi and its tributaries were among the chief objects of strategy. The Confederate forts Henry and Donelson were built to block the Tennessee and Cumberland rivers respectively, and when they fell, early in 1862, the South had received a penetrating blow. The seizure of the Mississippi in 1863 split the Confederacy in twain and presaged its downfall. The Tennessee River was the route by which Gen. Ulysses S. Grant's army was provisioned when it reached Chattanooga in the autumn of 1863, and the Battle of Wauhatchie was fought to keep it open. The Red River (southern) was the scene of an important but unsuccessful Union expedition in 1864 aimed at Texas. Meanwhile, the white settlements strung along the Minnesota River had been the victims of the terrible Sioux uprising of 1862.

[Esther Singleton, ed., *Great Rivers of the World.*]
ALVIN F. HARLOW

RIVERS IN AMERICAN DIPLOMACY. The drainage system of North America, and the territorial expansion of the United States westward across it, have given to the great rivers (notably the Mississippi, Rio Grande, and Columbia) an important geographic role in American diplomacy.

The Mississippi Question was one of the first major diplomatic issues. Spain denied that the United States (after 1783) extended to that river, at least below the Ohio River, and refused to admit any right of the citizens of the United States to free navigation of the stream through Spanish territory. Spain's distresses in Europe impelled it in 1795 to concede the imperfect American claims in Pinckney's Treaty. After the retrocession of New Orleans and Louisiana by Spain to France in 1800 (see San Ildefonso, Treaty of), Spain in 1802 revoked the right of deposit established in this treaty, and the consequent alarm of American western citizens, who saw in the revocation an augury of the character of future French control of the river, induced President Thomas Jefferson to send Robert R. Livingston to Paris to try to buy New Orleans, with the astonishing result of the procurement of all Louisiana. Jay's Treaty of 1794 had guaranteed to British subjects and American citizens the free navigation of the river, a provision that was not renewed after the War of 1812 put an end to it.

The Rio Grande was claimed, somewhat expansively, by the Republic of Texas as its boundary with Mexico. Mexico's refusal to negotiate a settlement of this boundary after the annexation of Texas by the United States precipitated war. Hostilities began when Mexican forces crossed the Rio Grande on Apr. 25. The Treaty of Guadalupe Hidalgo (1848), which ended the Mexican War, fixed the boundary at the Rio Grande as far north as El Paso. The changing course of the river bed subsequently caused boundary controversies, such as that of the Chamizal Tract at El Paso (settled in 1963 and formalized in 1967 by the Chamizal Treaty). A convention of 1889 provided an international boundary commission of one Mexican and one American representative to assist the peaceful regulation of such controversies arising by "natural causes" along the Rio Grande or Colorado rivers.

The Columbia River played an epochal part in the exploration, settlement, and territorial claims of the Pacific Northwest (*see* Oregon Question). The British government contended that the Columbia River from its intersection with forty-nine degrees north latitude to the sea was the boundary of British North America, but in the Oregon Treaty of 1846 it abandoned this position and accepted the line of forty-nine degrees to the sea, with the provision, however, that British subjects trading with the Hudson's Bay Company were to enjoy the free navigation of the entire river. (This provision, now archaic, has never caused any serious discussion between the two governments.) Other rivers flowing through both British and American territory, the Saint John (between Maine and New Brunswick), the Stikine (from British Columbia into Alaska), the Yukon and Porcupine (both from the Yukon into Alaska), and the Saint Lawrence rivers have been opened to joint navigation by treaty arrangement.

[Samuel Flagg Bemis, *A Diplomatic History of the United States;* Eugene Schuyler, *American Diplomacy and the Furtherance of Commerce.*]

SAMUEL FLAGG BEMIS

RIVER TOWNS OF CONNECTICUT were Windsor, Hartford, and Wethersfield, together with Springfield until it was discovered that the latter lay within the boundaries of Massachusetts. The settlement of these towns represented a group migration from the Massachusetts Bay Colony, which began in the summer of 1635 and continued through 1636. Thus, practically the whole of the Bay town of Dorchester removed to Windsor; Newtown (Cambridge) removed to Hartford; and Watertown removed to Wethersfield. For a short time the original Massachusetts town names were applied to the new settlements on the Connecticut River.

Various reasons were given for the removals, but probably the motivating reason lay in the urge that

during the next two and a half centuries drew Americans ever westward. With this migration from the Bay to the Connecticut River the westward movement began.

Interestingly enough, these Massachusetts pioneers found themselves in a situation that came to be a commonplace in western settlement: they were squatters on land to which no clear title was available. The legal title lay with the Council for New England, which, at a series of meetings held in London from February to April 1635, had voted to surrender its patent to the king and had divided its domain between its eight active members. To James Hay, Earl of Carlisle, had gone the parcel on which the three river towns of Windsor, Hartford, and Wethersfield were established. There is no evidence that the settlers of these towns asked, or received, any authorization from the council or from Carlisle.

Simultaneously with the migration of the settlers from Massachusetts and the legal activities of the council in London, a group of Puritan "lords and gentlemen" in England put forth a claim to the Connecticut country through a deed or patent allegedly derived from Robert Rich, Earl of Warwick (*see* Connecticut, Old Patent of), and in the summer of 1635 sent over young John Winthrop as governor, with orders to build a fort at Saybrook. The settlers of the river towns made no objection to the fort but promptly ejected a party that attempted to take up land where Windsor was to be founded. Nor were the agents of the Plymouth trading post, which had been established in the same neighborhood some two years earlier, treated with more consideration. The Massachusetts people had come to take the land; they had the manpower to do it; and neither legal title nor claims of title nor incidental prior occupation was to stand in their way.

Possession of the land was promptly followed by the establishment of a federated form of government under a general court, the first meeting of which, on Apr. 26, 1636, was presided over by Roger Ludlow, former deputy governor of Massachusetts Bay and the leader of the migration.

With the growth of the original settlements, the founding of new towns, and the adoption of the Fundamental Orders of Connecticut, the river towns evolved into the commonwealth of Connecticut.

[R. V. Coleman, *The Old Patent of Connecticut.*]

R. V. COLEMAN

RIVINGTON'S GAZETTE, published in New York City from 1773 to 1783, was one of the more important colonial newspapers, with a circulation that extended into several colonies. James Rivington named his paper *Rivington's New-York Gazetteer; or the Connecticut, New Jersey, Hudson's River, and Quebec Weekly Advertiser,* but this title was soon shortened. It was a strongly partisan sheet, favoring the Tories during the Revolution. A group of armed patriots destroyed Rivington's press in November 1775 and forced suspension of the paper until October 1777, when it was revived under the patronage of the king's government. The *Gazette* was useful to the English in publishing proclamations, revealing the misrepresentations of patriot newspapers, and perpetrating misrepresentations to aid the Loyalists. Rivington remained in New York City at the end of the war, trying to continue publication, but the last issue printed was Dec. 31, 1783. Thereafter he continued business only as a bookseller.

[Isaiah Thomas, *History of Printing in America.*]
CHARLES MARION THOMAS

ROAD IMPROVEMENT MOVEMENT. Organized groups of bicycle riders furnished the first popular demand for good roads in the United States. With the development of low-priced automobiles, the demand for improved roads greatly increased, and after the first decade of the 20th century state aid for road construction became practically nationwide. The first national legislation to aid roadbuilding, the Federal Aid Road Act, was passed in 1916. Initially, road construction funds came from poll taxes, general property taxes, and bond issues. Automobile license fees, at first designed merely to cover the cost of registration, and gasoline taxes, started in 1919 in four states, eventually came to supply the bulk of construction and maintenance funds. By an act of Congress, 1921, the federal government began giving, through the U.S. Bureau of Public Roads, financial assistance to the states for the construction of highways connecting principal cities and other populated areas. By 1937 more than $1 billion in federal aid had been distributed. By the Interstate Highway Act of 1956 Congress authorized the construction of a 42,500-mile nationwide network of limited-access highways, 90 percent of which would be paid for by the federal government, 10 percent by the states. By 1975 more than 36,000 miles of the Interstate Highway System had been completed, at a total cost of almost $100 billion.

[Charles L. Dearing, *American Highway Policy.*]
NATHAN C. ROCKWOOD

ROADS. America's first roadmakers were the ruminant bison. Centuries before the white man came, these creatures had made traces throughout the Mississippi Valley and through parts of the Rocky and Appalachian mountains. The buffalo traces were not only the first roads in America but also, for the early period of American history, the best. As road engineers the buffalo were unexcelled. They invariably selected the easiest and most practical routes to the watersheds.

Popular fancy associates the pre-Columbian travel with canoes, whereas in reality most American Indians had to walk. At one time a network of Indian trails spread over America, distinct from the buffalo traces, although they were not infrequently used by the native Americans. Indians, like buffalo, followed the lines of least resistance, and they too cut through important mountain passes, wound over portages, followed the watersheds, and blazed trails for white traders, trappers, and missionaries that became the wagon roads of a later era.

England's first colonists established a tidewater and river civilization, but before long a nonriparian element emerged, which brought about distinct changes in existing modes of travel and transportation. The trodden paths of the Indians were soon widened by the extensive use the colonists made of ox sledges and of packhorses. As early as 1639 the Massachusetts Bay Colony court ordered that roads be laid out so as to provide "ease and safety for travelers"; it added, "For this end every town shall choose two or three men, who shall join with two or three of the next town, and these shall have power to lay out the highways in each town where they may be most convenient." The New England township system also specified the construction of roads. With the establishment of government in other colonies—particularly in New York and Pennsylvania—similar official steps were taken for the construction of roads and bridges. Even the Virginia statutes at large for the period 1619–60 stated that highways should be "layd out" and that "surveyors of highwaies and maintenance for bridges be yearly kept and appointed in each countie court respectively." Colonial laws pertaining to roads should not be taken too seriously. As the result of official action, precious little was done toward actual improvement in the means of overland transportation, with the exception of occasional tree and stump clearings.

The inauguration of stagecoach passenger and mail service and the introduction (particularly in Pennsylvania) of the Conestoga wagon freight business during the 18th century provided the necessary inducement for road improvements. So extensive were these improvements that at the time of the revolutionary war dirt and corduroy roads existed throughout the more thickly settled areas of the northern and central colonies. Land companies were not without their effect on early road building; it was under the auspices of the Ohio and Transylvania companies that the first trails were blazed into the Old Northwest and Kentucky, respectively. In March 1775, under the direction of the Transylvania Company, Daniel Boone and his party left the Watauga to cut a wagon trail into Kentucky. This route was fittingly called the Wilderness Road; in view of the thousands of settlers who jolted their way over it, it ranks among the historic highways of the land.

The rapid development of civilization in the trans-Appalachian region at the opening of the national period was accompanied by an acute transportation problem. Heavy goods were floated on the rivers, but Spanish possession of the mouth of the Mississippi River created a potentially dangerous national situation. Partly to overcome this hazard and partly to establish faster means of communication between the East and the West, the new U.S. government took steps toward the construction of roads under federal auspices. In the Enabling Act of 1802, which granted statehood to Ohio, provision was made for an East-West road—a road that, when extended, was destined to become the National (or Cumberland) Road.

Early roads, except for some in the larger cities, were generally dirt roads—quagmires in the wet season, which made them impassable, sometimes for extended periods. On occasion little more was done than to clear a roadway. Streams generally had to be forded or crossed by ferry. Corduroy roads made of logs laid transversely or plank roads were sometimes employed, especially across swampy ground. But such roads presented a very rough surface, did not last long, and were rarely well maintained. During 1792–94 the Philadelphia and Lancaster Turn Pike Company constructed a sixty-six-mile macadamized toll road. It "is a masterpiece of its kind," wrote Francis Baily, a traveler; "it is paved with stone the whole way, and overlaid with gravel, so that it is never obstructed during the most severe season."

The immense flow of freighters, stagecoaches, and ordinary vehicles over the Lancaster Turnpike demonstrated the volume of traffic that would accompany the construction of well-built roads through populous areas. In 1806 the decision was reached to expand the Cumberland Road into a national toll road to extend from the Atlantic Ocean to the Mississippi River at Saint Louis, and actual construction was begun two years later. Constitutional questions were raised, and because of political obstructionism the road did not reach Wheeling until 1819. Thereafter the National Road continued to be a political football. New surveys and constructions were occasionally made, but it never got beyond Vandalia, Ill., which it reached in 1852. As far as Terre Haute, Ind., the road was superbly built, but from that point westward it remained a dirt road. Its success from a social and economic point was unquestioned. "As many as twenty four-horse coaches have been counted in line at one time on the road," wrote one of the early historians of the National Road, "and large broad-wheeled wagons, . . . laden with merchandise and drawn by six Conestoga horses were visible all the day at every point, . . . besides innumerable caravans of horses, mules, cattle, hogs and sheep." The financial burden that this enterprise entailed and the protracted fight over the constitutionality of internal improvements contributed to a reduction of federal aid for roads by President Andrew Jackson's time. Ultimately the National Road was completely abandoned by Congress and was ceded to the states through which it passed. Such also appears to have been the fate of other federal or pseudofederal roads that had been built for military or social purposes during the early decades of the 19th century.

Roads in all parts of the country were allowed to fall into disrepair as the rail network was extended, but the blazing of trails and the construction of some sort of passable roadways were still essential preliminary steps to railway development. By the mid-1850's most principal points east of the Mississippi River were served by rail, and the frontier of railroad construction was moving westward. Roads ceased to be major intercity arteries where canal or rail transport was available and, instead, served merely to provide access to the nearest canal wharf or rail station. During construction of the Cumberland Road the Far West was still a land of Indian trails. Before long, fur traders and missionaries were headed for the Oregon Country, and they marked out what by 1841 became widely known as the Oregon Trail—a route extending from Saint Joseph, Mo., to the Willamette Valley, Oreg., that roughly followed the south bank of the Platte River, went through South Pass, and moved along the Green and Snake rivers and then over Immigrants Pass to the banks of the Columbia. By following or floating down this river gorge the immigrants could reach their destination. In 1843 nearly

1,000 pioneers moved westward over the Oregon Trail, and for many succeeding years the number remained large. Less permanent, but nevertheless of historical significance, were such routes as the Santa Fe and Mormon trails.

With the discovery of gold in California in 1848 migration westward took on greater magnitude. Many preferred either a five-month sea voyage or the fever-ridden Isthmus of Panama route to overland travel. But most of the travelers from the Middle West used the Oregon Trail to a point slightly west of Fort Hall, Idaho. From there they turned southward and continued over the Carson Sink, across the High Sierras south of Lake Tahoe, and on to Hangtown, Calif. Within a decade after the discovery of gold California's population rose from 15,000 to almost 380,000; half of the newcomers are believed to have passed over the seemingly endless stretches of the Oregon-California Trail. Before long, some trails were converted into passable roadways, and as early as the autumn of 1849 teamsters, using horses, mules, or oxen, were able to haul supplies to some of the more accessible mining towns. Despite the efforts of local and private agencies in the construction of roads, bridges, and ferries, the routes they provided were far from smooth: British traveler Frank Marryat claimed that "no one knows what a wagon will undergo until he has mastered California trails and gulches."

Shortly after the settlers and miners came to the Pacific coast they began to clamor for a transcontinental railroad and for an immediate, safe, and practical overland route to serve until a railroad could be built. In 1857 the Overland California Mail Bill became law. This measure did not prescribe federal aid in road construction, but it did empower the postmaster general to provide a liberal subsidy to a firm that he might select "for the conveyance of the entire letter mail from . . . the Mississippi River . . . to San Francisco." The route selected ran from Saint Louis to Little Rock, Ark., then through El Paso, Tex., and Yuma, Ariz., to its western terminus. It became popularly known as the Butterfield, or Southern Overland, route, and between 1858 and 1861 a semi-weekly passenger and mail service was maintained over it. In 1860 this stage road was extended northward from San Francisco to Portland, Oreg.—making a total length of 3,600 miles. The outbreak of the Civil War necessitated switching the Butterfield route into northern territory, and thereafter it followed in a general way the old Oregon-California Trail. Not until May 10, 1869, when the first transcontinental railroad was completed by the meeting of Union Pacific and Central Pacific in Utah, did this important stage road lose its economic significance and popularity.

The great expansion and the excellence of the American railway system account in part for the protracted lull in good roadbuilding during the last part of the 19th century. But the federal government was once again to become interested in roads both in an effort to reduce the farmer's isolation and in response to the demands of the growing number of bicyclists. In 1893 Congress appropriated $10,000 for an inquiry into good road management. With the advent and use of the automobile after 1900, interest increased in view of the inadequacy of state and county roads for motor travel. As late as 1908 there was not a single mile of concrete highway in the entire United States and only 650 miles of macadam. For directions to go from Albuquerque to Los Angeles in 1908 the secretary of an automobile club was told to "follow this mountain range eighty miles south to a stick in the fork of a road, with a paper tied at the top. Take the rut that leads off to the right."

In 1912 a plan was proposed for the construction of a direct transcontinental road to be called the Lincoln Highway. This enterprise was not completed until 1930, but it marked the beginning of widespread federal and state aid for highway construction, much of which was for hard-surfaced roads. By the outbreak of World War I, highway construction was getting under way on a national scale.

The Federal Aid Road Act of 1916 marked the real beginning of a national policy designed to secure a nationwide system of roads through stimulation by the federal government. By then few entertained doubts on the constitutional issues that had dogged the National Road in the previous century. The Congressional Joint Committee on Federal Aid asserted that "federal aid to good roads will accomplish several of the objects indicated by the framers of the Constitution—establish post-roads, regulate commerce, provide for the common defense, and promote the general welfare. Above all, it will promote the general welfare." Consistent with this view it was the intent of Congress to secure a system of self-contained roads that would provide routes for communication between various parts of the country and between centers of population. The system was not to be designed as a feeder system to the rail and water routes, nor was it to produce routes primarily for pleasure travel.

The new policy was exactly what its name implied—an aid policy. The federal government would assist with funding, would play a role in the planning of a national highway network, and would influence design and construction standards, since approval would be required prior to financing. Actual construction and maintenance would be left to the states and localities. Stimulated by the new policy, all states had state highway agencies by 1924, with authority over main routes classified as state systems. Engineering capability rapidly developed, and the new state agencies gradually garnered political power over highway programs and funding. A steady shift from local to state responsibility for highways occurred, the state proportion of nonfederal highway expenditures growing from 32 percent in 1921 to 65 percent in 1939.

Total highway expenditures by all levels of government grew from just under $1 billion in 1921 to $2.4 billion in 1939, $4.2 billion in 1949, $10.9 billion in 1959, and $23.4 billion in 1972. Between 1921 and 1972 a total of $352 billion was spent for the provision of highways. The federal portion was but 6 percent in 1921; by 1958 it reached about 25 percent of the total, and it continued in about that proportion into the mid-1970's. Although the mileage of roads and streets increased by only about 40 percent in the sixty years following 1914, the portion provided with all-weather surface grew from 12 percent in the earlier year to some 80 percent of the nearly 4 million miles in service in the mid-1970's.

Federal appropriations in the late 1930's were considerably swollen by emergency funds as a part of the public works program designed to assist the nation's economic recovery from the Great Depression. The period was also marked by the first steps in recognition of the desirability of extending federal aid to urban, as well as rural, portions of the highway network. In subsequent years such participation increased. Deferral of construction and reduction of maintenance during World War II left the nation with a large backlog of highway work to do in the early postwar years when motor vehicle use resumed its upward trend. Congestion had occurred on many parts of the system before the war and was considerably exacerbated afterward. In addition rapid growth in the size and speed of motor vehicles had not been matched by an equivalent upgrading of the roads. A wide range of deficiencies was noted—bridges too weak for modern trucks, narrow bridges and pavements, sharp curves, and inadequate sighting distances, among others. The conventional federal aid system with its spread of funds nationwide over vast mileages of primary and secondary roads, on a fifty-fifty matching basis, appeared to require reconsideration.

In 1954 President Dwight D. Eisenhower appointed a high-level commission headed by Gen. Lucius D. Clay to undertake such a review. The result was the Highway Act of 1956, which gave official recognition to the commission's concept of a 41,000-mile interstate system of limited-access highways and established the Highway Trust Fund as a means of financing such a system. Registration fees, gasoline taxes, and other excises falling on highway users had long been the principal sources of highway funding. Other old and new federal excises were dedicated to the trust fund.

The tremendous American highway program that followed from the act made the nation extraordinarily dependent on motor transport. By the mid-1970's some 100 million motor vehicles were traveling U.S. highways; nearly 20 percent of all freight ton-miles were being generated by trucks, and more than 85 percent of all passenger miles were being accounted for by private automobiles. But even before that time —by the late 1960's—serious questions were being raised about the national devotion to highways. Accelerated highway building seemed to increase rather than relieve congestion. Public transit in the nation's cities was gradually being killed as urban bus companies collapsed or curtailed service. Urban extensions of the interstate system cut broad swaths across cities, involved enormous property destruction, and disrupted community life. Annual highway fatalities moved above the 50,000 mark. And the automotive vehicle was recognized as the primary source of air pollution. In the mid-1970's a more balanced approach to transport planning was being counseled, and diversion of some highway revenues to mass transit and other nonhighway transport purposes was being advocated.

[Philip H. Burch, Jr., *Highway Revenue and Expenditure Policy;* Charles L. Dearing, *American Highway Policy;* Seymour Dunbar, *A History of Travel in America;* Archer Butler Hulbert, *Historic Highways of America.*]

ERNEST W. WILLIAMS, JR.

ROADS, MILITARY. From the colonial period to the beginning of the 20th century, many notable achievements were made in the construction of military roads: the Braddock Road, cut through the wilderness to Fort Duquesne in 1755; the backbreaking labors of Continental troops struggling to clear a path for guns captured at Fort Ticonderoga in the first year of the American Revolution; George Rogers Clark's road to Kaskaskia and Vincennes, built in 1778 and 1779; supply routes to the forts of the Old Northwest; the long stretches of corduroy road laid by the engineer battalion in the Civil War; the blazing of jungle trails in the Philippines during the insurrection of 1899–1902; and the road constructed in 1916 by engineers of the punitive expedition to Mexico, which made possible the first motorized movement by an army.

World War I and World War II called forth prodigious efforts. In 1918 engineers of the American Expeditionary Forces repaired war-torn French highways and rebuilt and maintained roads across no-man's-land and beyond. The first conflict to require construction of substantial hard-surfaced roads, World War I witnessed the debut of army engineer units trained especially for roadbuilding. In World War II, U.S. Army engineers completed more than 10,000 miles of road in the southwest Pacific area alone; and two projects of that war—the Ledo Road, linking India with China, and the Alcan, or Alaska, Highway, stretching across northwestern Canada and southeastern Alaska—rank among the greatest military roads of all times. The largest engineering project undertaken by the U.S. armed forces in a foreign country involved reconstruction of highways in the Republic of Vietnam. Owing to this effort, the major towns of that country were linked by some 3,000 miles of modern high-speed asphalt-surfaced roads capable of bearing heavy loads.

The term "military roads" also has broader connotations. Since ancient times, roads have served a dual purpose. The great Roman highway system was designed both for military movements and for trade. Similarly, the first large roadbuilding project undertaken in the United States, the National, or Cumberland, Road, was intended not only as a postal and commercial route but also as a military route. As one congressional sponsor emphasized, its utility "in time of war for the transportation of the munitions of war, and the means of defense from one point of the country to another . . . must be palpable and plain to every reflecting mind." Later the myriad wagon roads built by the army in the trans-Mississippi West carried both military supply trains and caravans of prairie schooners. During the 20th century the vast interstate highway system was planned and built with both military and commercial ends in view.

Experience gained by the army on military projects was turned to good account in civil works. The systems of scenic roads in Yellowstone and Crater Lake national parks and the initial highway network in Alaska were designed and constructed by the U.S. Army Corps of Engineers. And it was by no means coincidental that an army engineer, Francis V.

Greene, perfected asphalt as a street-paving material and adapted it for use in the North American climate.

[Karl C. Dod, *The Corps of Engineers: The War Against Japan;* Forest G. Hill, *Roads, Rails and Waterways: The Army Engineers and Early Transportation;* W. Turrentine Jackson, *Wagon Roads West: A Study of Federal Road Surveys and Construction in the Trans-Mississippi West;* Joseph E. Morse and R. Duff Green, eds., *Thomas B. Searight's The Old Pike.*]

LENORE FINE
JESSE A. REMINGTON

ROAD SURVEY BILL. *See* **Survey Act.**

ROAD WORKING DAYS. Until the development of modern highways, rural Americans often paid road taxes by working on road construction jobs. A regular scale of payment was set up for men, horses, and equipment, and work was overseen by township or road district supervisors. Road working days were usually fixed at a time when farm work was not pressing and were more often occasions for socializing and exchanging neighborhood gossip than for hard work. Construction was almost always unsatisfactory, and abolition of the system was one of the first recommendations of the "good roads" movement. The increasing technical demands of road construction and the rigid requirements of state and federal aid statutes served to eliminate the system in most localities.

[G. R. Chatburn, *Highways and Highway Transportation.*]

W. A. ROBINSON

ROANOKE, SETTLEMENT AT. *See* **Raleigh's Patent and First Colony; Raleigh's Lost Colony.**

ROANOKE ISLAND, CAPTURE OF. On Feb. 8, 1862, Union Gen. A. E. Burnside, with an overwhelming force of vessels and men, overran the weakly fortified Confederate positions on Roanoke Island, N.C. The capture of this strategic island enabled Union troops to occupy Elizabeth City and to overrun many North Carolina counties bordering on Albemarle Sound.

[S. A. Ashe, *History of North Carolina,* vol. II.]

RICHARD E. YATES

ROBBER BARONS, a term that is widely used in describing big businessmen of the late 19th century. It implies that entrepreneurial policies and practices during the Gilded Age, as Mark Twain first called it, were characterized by a ruthless and unscrupulous drive for monopoly and economic power. The origins of the term are not precise. Edwin L. Godkin, editor of the *Nation,* used it in 1869; at about the same time Sen. Carl Schurz of Missouri used the phrase in a speech. Contemporaries Charles Francis Adams, Jr., and Henry Demarest Lloyd contributed strongly to the image by denouncing the activities of the new moguls.

During the Progressive period of the early 20th century various muckraking writers, such as Ida M. Tarbell and Gustavus Myers, did much to crystallize the stereotype of the businessman as a destructive agent in society. The 1920's witnessed a dramatic swing of the pendulum to the other side as the nation enjoyed apparent prosperity and the businessman reached the zenith of his popularity. Even Tarbell, who in the Progressive years had scathingly attacked the Standard Oil Company, produced a laudatory biography of Judge Elbert H. Gary of the United States Steel Corporation.

Then came October of 1929. The businessman came crashing from his pedestal of popular acclaim as the nation sank deeper and deeper into the despair accompanying the economic frustrations of the 1930's. The term "robber barons" became a permanent part of the historian's vocabulary with the publication in 1934 of Matthew Josephson's *The Robber Barons: The Great American Capitalists, 1861–1901.* Numerous volumes during the 1930's echoed the view of big business as decadent.

As World War II approached and the economy rebounded, the businessman received his reprieve and historians began viewing the "robber baron" from a more positive vantage point. A school of historians known as revisionists was led by Allan Nevins, in a biography of John D. Rockefeller (1940); Louis M. Hacker, in the *Triumph of American Capitalism* (1940); and Thomas C. Cochran and William Miller, in the *Age of Enterprise* (1942). After World War II this ever-increasing number of historians and economists attempted to evaluate the late-19th-century businessman in a less emotional, more objective way. Rather than concentrate on the destructive characteristics of the moguls, the revisionists examined their creative contributions and attempted to ascertain the reasons for the growth of big business in the evolution of American society more clearly.

THOMAS BREWER

ROBINSON, FORT, was located on White River at the Red Cloud agency in Nebraska. It was built by the U.S. Army in 1874 after most of the Indian campaigns were over and was used, for the most part, to maintain order among the Sioux warriors recently settled on the Red Cloud agency. It was also a distribution point for rations and a remount depot. Most of the famous Sioux chiefs were at some time located at the fort, and Crazy Horse was killed there.

[J. S. Morton, *Illustrated History of Nebraska.*]

CARL L. CANNON

ROBINSON-PATMAN ACT, or the Federal Anti-Price Discrimination Act, was passed by Congress in 1936 primarily to protect independent merchants against the preferential wholesale prices chain stores were able to command because of their great purchasing volume. The act, sponsored by Sen. Joseph T. Robinson and Rep. Wright Patman, prohibited discrimination in price or terms of sale between purchases of commodities of like grade or quality, prohibited questionable brokerage or advertising allowances, and attempted to prevent the setting of unreasonably low prices for the purpose of destroying competition.

ALVIN F. HARLOW

ROCHESTER RAPPINGS, the name given to spiritual manifestations reported by Margaret and Kate Fox; the women claimed that rappings on walls and furniture had occurred at their home in Hydesville, N.Y., in 1848 and at their sister's home in Rochester the following year. The credence given to these claims marked the beginning of spiritualism in the United States. Although the Fox sisters subsequently confessed to faking, the spiritualism movement continued.

AUGUSTUS H. SHEARER

ROCKEFELLER FOUNDATION was established by John D. Rockefeller and chartered on May 14, 1913, under the laws of the state of New York, "to promote the well-being of mankind throughout the world." Within a few years after its organization, Rockefeller had given the foundation approximately $182 million. By the end of 1974 the foundation had paid out close to $1.18 billion from income and principal.

During its first fifteen years the foundation devoted itself almost entirely to public health and the medical sciences. The foundation's field staff extended campaigns against hookworm from the American South into many lands and undertook control measures against other communicable diseases, particularly malaria and yellow fever. The need for trained people led to the support of medical education and to the development of strategically placed schools of public health. The development of the vaccine against yellow fever in 1937, a joint effort of foundation field staff and laboratory investigators, culminated two decades of worldwide health activities. By 1929 the work of the foundation had been rounded out to include support of the natural sciences, the social sciences, and the arts and humanities. From support of investigations of basic physiological processes that were then little understood came, many years later, great advances in such fields as biochemistry, molecular biology, and human genetics; much demonstrably valuable work was supported at the same time in international relations, economics, and cross-cultural research and teaching.

About 1952 the foundation began to reduce the support of science and scholarship in the West, by then well funded from other sources, to help apply existing knowledge to the solution of the overwhelming problems of the developing world. The foundation's pioneering operating programs in agriculture, initiated in Mexico in 1943, led to greater per-unit production of food crops in many countries. These programs, as well as population stabilization efforts and the strengthening of selected universities.to serve the needs of their regions, were being continued in the 1970's with a greater emphasis on their economic and social consequences. In the United States, grantmaking efforts to bring about equality of opportunity, a renewed emphasis on America's cultural identities, and a concern for the technological impact on the environment became the foundation's main thrusts. A modest program in international relations sought to resolve conflict inherent in transnational issues.

Although the foundation is both an operating and a grantmaking organization, much of its program lies in the support of other agencies and in the training, through fellowships, of competent people in its fields of interest. Between 1915 and 1975 more than 10,000 men and women—primarily from the developing countries—received study awards. Awards are now also available for competition among American scientists and scholars in the fields of agriculture, the humanities, and population, as well as the environment, minority-group education, conflict resolution, and the arts.

[Rockefeller Foundation, *Annual Report.*]
JOHN H. KNOWLES

ROCKEFELLER UNIVERSITY was founded in 1901 by John D. Rockefeller as the Rockefeller Institute for Medical Research. At the time there were no research centers in the United States comparable with those founded decades earlier in Europe by Louis Pasteur, Robert Koch, Ivan P. Pavlov, and other noted investigators. Only a few American universities maintained laboratories. Most students who wanted postgraduate training in medical research had to go abroad. Significantly, the institute's first mission was the support by grants-in-aid of young men preparing for research careers in universities.

Simon Flexner was elected director in 1902. In 1904 temporary laboratories were set up in rented quarters in New York City. Soon thereafter the institute acquired the site overlooking the East River that became the university campus. The first permanent buildings were dedicated in 1906. Flexner played a major role in setting the institutional pattern of individual freedom to formulate experimental projects and of a flexible organization based on laboratory groups rather than departments. A pathologist and a bacteriologist, he regarded the investigation of disease as the institute's central purpose. He was succeeded in 1935 by Herbert Spencer Gasser, whose field was electrophysiology, and under his direction greater emphasis was placed on the study of life processes at the level of the cell and its constituents. By 1953, when Gasser retired, the research ideals pioneered by the institute were well established in the United States, and there were scores of research centers, some of them founded and staffed largely by Rockefeller-trained scientists. In the universities the importance of laboratory research was taken for granted.

A special committee, chaired by Detlev W. Bronk, president of the Johns Hopkins University, recommended that the institute's scope be extended to include graduate education in the natural sciences. A reorganization was effected, and Bronk was named the first president of the institute. In 1954 it became a graduate university—part of the University of the State of New York—with authority to grant the advanced degrees of doctor of philosophy and doctor of medical science. In 1959 degrees were conferred on the first graduates. The name "The Rockefeller University" was adopted in 1965. Frederick Seitz, a physicist and president of the National Academy of Sciences, succeeded Bronk as president of the university in 1968. The life and medical sciences remained the predominant areas of research and study, but new fields were added: the behavioral sciences, physics, mathematics, and philosophy.

[George W. Corner, *A History of The Rockefeller Institute: 1901–1953 Origins and Growth;* John Kobler, *The Rockefeller University Story.*]

FULVIO BARDOSSI

ROCKETS have been prominent in American history from "the rockets' red glare" in 1814 and traditional Fourth of July skyrockets to the global "balance of terror" with intercontinental ballistic missiles (ICBM's) in the 1960's and man's "one small step" on the moon by Neil A. Armstrong on July 20, 1969, and beyond. Generically speaking, rockets include a wide variety of military missiles, research and space flight vehicles (unmanned and manned), and fireworks using reactive thrust for locomotion. For hundreds of years all rockets used gunpowder. Rockets carry their own oxidizer for fuel combustion, in contrast to jet aircraft, whose engines use atmospheric oxygen. In the 1950's, liquid- and solid-fueled chemical rocket propulsion was under intensive development for military missiles (from small tactical ones to intercontinental-range nuclear-tipped weapons) and for both unmanned earth satellites and planetary probes and manned spacecraft (Mercury, Gemini, and Apollo). Nuclear, ion, and electric rocketry have also proven feasible.

On Aug. 20, 1814, British forces fired Congreve metal-cased rockets at Bladensburg, Md., assisting in the capture of Washington, D.C. Three weeks later Fort McHenry, Md., was bombarded. Hale 16-pound rockets were adopted by the U.S. Army in the 1840's. Rockets were adapted to whaling in the mid-1850's and also were used for signal flares and shore-to-ship lifeline rescue. On Nov. 9, 1918, Robert H. Goddard of Clark University demonstrated a small solid-fuel rocket, the genesis of the hand-held antitank "bazooka" of World War II fame. Preoccupied with scientific sounding of the upper atmosphere and interplanetary navigation, Goddard tested the world's first liquid-fuel rocket (gasoline and liquid oxygen) at Auburn, Mass., on Mar. 16, 1926. In 1944 the first rocket-carrying German fighter aircraft appeared (the Me 163), and on Oct. 14, 1947, the U.S. rocket research aircraft known as the Bell X-1 first exceeded the speed of sound.

The German V-2 liquid-fuel ballistic rocket was a major innovation during World War II (200-mile range, 1-ton TNT warhead, over 3,000 fired on London and Antwerp in 1944). German engineers with their designs of V-2 rockets and key documents were transferred to the United States in 1945. Lacking an atomic bomb or long-range aircraft, the Soviet Union first began intensive rocket development in 1947. By 1954 the feasibility of thermonuclear warheads and Soviet rocket progress had created a crisis, and President Dwight D. Eisenhower approved an urgent ICBM development program. In 1955 he also approved the first U.S. space satellite program, to contribute to the International Geophysical Year (1957–58). Then, on Oct. 4, 1957, the Soviet Sputnik I, the first man-made earth satellite, was launched. It demonstrated that the Soviet Union had an ICBM-size rocket and triggered a race in space achievement.

Priority development of long-range ballistic missiles (Atlas, Titan, Polaris), as well as of passive military satellites, was pressed by the U.S. Department of Defense. In the 1960's thousands of silo-sited (Titan II, Minuteman) or nuclear-submarine-based missiles (Polaris, Poseidon), as well as observation satellites and numerous tactical missiles, became a reality. Rockets were also harnessed for space. Created in response to Sputnik, the civilian National Aeronautics and Space Administration (NASA) undertook, after Oct. 1, 1958, the development of rocket carriers for all classes of space missions. It launched hundreds of unmanned satellites for scientific and practical uses, plus interplanetary probes, observatories, and manned space flights. After the Soviet Union placed the first man (Yuri A. Gagarin) in earth orbit on Apr. 12, 1961, President John F. Kennedy called for a manned lunar landing by 1970. The Apollo program was launched, and the Apollo 8 crew were the first men to fly around the moon (Christmas eve, 1968). Within fifteen years after Sputnik, advances in rockets and their associated technologies had revolutionized American concerns about national security and world peace as well as about man's place in universal nature.

[E. M. Emme, *The History of Rocket Technology;* W. Ley, *Rockets, Missiles, and Space Travel;* W. von Braun and F. I. Ordway, *History of Rocketry and Space Travel.*]

EUGENE M. EMME

ROCK ISLAND BRIDGE CASE (1857), also known as the *Effie Afton* case (officially, *Hurd* v. *Railroad Bridge Company*), was a suit for damages that grew out of the collision, in 1856, of the steamer *Effie Afton* with the newly erected railroad bridge connecting Rock Island, Ill., and Davenport, Iowa. Basically, the case was a contest between river and rail transportation and their respective interests. The trial, held in the U.S. Circuit Court at Chicago, was made notable not only by the issues involved but also by the

ROCKY MOUNTAIN FUR COMPANY

participation of Abraham Lincoln and other prominent lawyers. The jury failed to reach a verdict.

[A. J. Beveridge, *Abraham Lincoln, 1809–58.*]

PAUL M. ANGLE

ROCKY MOUNTAIN FUR COMPANY, a partnership of fur traders established in 1822. An announcement published in Saint Louis on behalf of William H. Ashley on Mar. 20, 1822, asked for the enlistment of "one hundred young men to ascend the Missouri River to its source, there to be employed for one, two, or three years" (*see* Ashley Expeditions). The company was later under the control of other partners, of whom Jedediah S. Smith, David E. Jackson, and William L. Sublette were the best known.

The Rocky Mountain Fur Company opened up the wealthiest fur sections of the West. It was the first fur trading company to depend primarily on directly trapping beaver rather than securing the skins by trading with the Indians. Knowledge of the geography of the West was greatly increased by the explorations incidental to the activities of its members. The regions of the Platte, Green, Yellowstone, and Snake rivers were explored by them. Trapping also was done in the region around the Great Salt Lake, and Smith made his way from there into California, and then along the coast into Oregon; he was the first white person known to have covered most of this great distance. Guides for later fur trade and settlement enterprises received their training with this company. The company was dissolved in 1834.

[Hiram M. Chittenden, *The American Fur Trade of the Far West.*]

ROBERT MOULTON GATKE

ROCKY MOUNTAINS, a vast mountain system that extends from northern Mexico to northwest Alaska, a distance of more than 3,000 miles, and forms the continental divide. Spanish pioneers in Mexico were the first white men to see the Rocky Mountains. Francisco Vásquez de Coronado, in 1540, was the first to see the U.S. Rockies. The presence of precious metals in the region of the mountains induced the earliest exploration and first settlements, by Spaniards in the southern portion of the Rockies.

From the east, via the Great Lakes, came the French. As early as 1743, members of the La Vérendrye family saw the "shining mountains" in the Wyoming region. Frenchmen and then Englishmen, hunting furs, followed Canadian streams to the western mountains. Then came the pelt-hungry Americans up the Missouri River and its tributaries. The trappers and traders, first gathering beaver skins and later buffalo hides, became the mountain men, who were the real trailblazers of the central Rockies. Their pack trains and wagons broke the practicable trails into and over the mountains.

The Louisiana Purchase (1803) was without definite boundaries, but the original French claim to the drainage area of the Mississippi River indicated the crest of the Rockies as the western boundary. Meriwether Lewis and William Clark, in the Northwest (1804–06), and Zebulon M. Pike, in the Southwest (1806–07), led the first official expeditions for the United States into the Rocky Mountains. Their reports were more favorable than that of Maj. Stephen H. Long, who, in 1820, came to the base of the mountains and labeled the adjoining high plains the "Great American Desert." To the westward-moving flood of homeseekers, these plains, the Rocky Mountains, and intervening plateaus were uninviting for settlement, and the homesteaders traveled another 1,000 miles to the Pacific coast, over trails determined by mountain topography. In southern Wyoming, where the Rockies flatten to a high plain, South Pass became the gateway to Oregon. Participants in the Mormon trek of 1847 and the California gold rush of 1849 used this same crossing of the continental divide. Gold discoveries during the 1850's and 1860's led to permanent settlement in the Rockies and eventually to the formation of the mountain states (*see* Pikes Peak Gold Rush).

The agriculture that followed mining in the West was determined by the mountains. The high regions catch the snows that make the rivers, and these feed the irrigation canals that make farming possible in the semiarid country east of the Rockies. These same geographical factors later inspired reservoir construction and reclamation and tramontane water diversion projects. The vital importance of mountain watershed protection led to national forest conservation, as lumbering became an important industry in the more heavily wooded areas of the Rockies.

The locations of cities and towns were fixed by the mountain geography, as were the routes of the transcontinental railroads. The automobile highways were also similarly directed.

The federal government has established four national parks in the Rocky Mountain region: Yellowstone National Park in Wyoming, Montana, and Idaho (Mar. 1, 1872), which is the world's greatest geyser area; Glacier National Park in Montana (May 11, 1910); Rocky Mountain National Park in Colorado (Jan. 26, 1915), which includes 410 square miles of the Rockies' Front Range; and Grand Teton National Park in Wyoming (Feb. 26, 1929), which includes the winter feeding ground of the largest American elk herd.

[W. A. Atwood, *The Rocky Mountains;* R. G. Thwaites, *A Brief History of Rocky Mountain Exploration.*]

LeRoy R. Hafen

RODEOS, or roundups, were an essential aspect of open-range ranching and later became entertainment events.

The first ranching in America (by Spanish settlers) was done on the open range, and open-range conditions existed throughout a long period of expansion of the industry by English-speaking rangemen. (Such ranching ended after the advent of barbed wire.) Cattle and horses on the open range always drift, fences not altogether confining them. As a result, the working of stock on any unfenced range concerned neighboring—and even far distant—stockmen as much as the immediate controller of that range. While Texas and California were still Mexican territory, laws were added to custom to regulate the gatherings of stock. Riders from far and near participated in these rodeos. A *juez de campo*—judge of the plains—presided with full authority. Cattle were selected for slaughter (their only value on the Pacific slope until in the late 1840's was the worth of the hides and tallow); colts, calves, and unbranded animals were branded; young horses were caught for breaking; *manadas* (bands of mares, each kept in charge by a stallion) were "shaped up"; and animals belonging on distant ranges were separated, or cut out.

During the 1870's and 1880's, when the Great Plains and adjacent territory developed into a major cattle-raising area, roundups that dwarfed the original rodeos became systematized. Their times, limits, and manner of procedure were, during their heyday, regulated by cattle associations of Texas, Colorado, Wyoming, and other states. As many as 200 to 300 riders—though lesser roundups were far more common—representing scores of brands, fed by dozens of chuck wagons, and having in their remudas from six to ten horses for each rider, would gather by some natural boundary, mountain, or stream. The general roundup boss would then direct various units as to each day's work. Daily, a big piece of country was "combed," and out of the cattle brought together calves would be branded, beefs would be held for shipping, and strays to be returned to their proper ranges would be cut out. The "cuts" were kept under

herd, were daily driven to each new roundup ground, and thus were constantly augmented. The roundup might end more than 100 miles from where it started.

Rodeos and roundups alike brought together socially men leading isolated lives; they were festivals of a kind. Horse-racing and betting were inevitable. Fancy riding and expert roping were displayed by horsemen, who were proud of their occupation and their expertise. Poker and other card games were played on blankets spread out in the firelight. Cowboys exchanged songs, and occasionally there was an "augering match"—a contest in storytelling. Long before the range was all fenced in the Southwest, riding and roping contests became popular features of fairs and barbecues.

Buffalo Bill's Wild West Show proved the popular interest in a dramatization of the skills involved in roundup work. Around 1900, Booger Red and other "stove-up" cowpunchers put together bronco-riding exhibitions for which they charged admission. In 1908 the Millers of Oklahoma put their 101 Ranch exhibition on the road. In 1897 Cheyenne, Wyo., began its annual exhibition, which became famous all over the continent as Frontier Days. The Calgary Stampede and the Pendleton Roundup, both of which started later, became equally famous. Rodeos now draw millions of spectators annually. Professionals follow the big rodeos; but all over the range country there are held, each summer and fall, rodeos in which only local talent—ranch people—participate. The rodeo—with its steer and bronco riding, wild-cow milking, bulldogging, calf-roping, and other features—has become as much an American institution as bullfighting is a Spanish one.

[Ellsworth Collings and Alma Miller England, *The 101 Ranch;* Chas. W. Furlong, *Let 'Er Buck;* Charles Simpson, *El Rodeo.*]

J. Frank Dobie

RODNEY'S RIDE. After Richard Henry Lee's resolution for independence was debated in the Continental Congress on July 1, 1776, a preliminary vote was taken. One of Delaware's delegates, Thomas McKean, voted for the resolution; another, George Read, voted against it; and the third, Cæsar Rodney, was absent on official business in his home state. According to a letter later written by McKean, he sent a messenger to Rodney urging him to hurry to Philadelphia to break the tie vote of the Delaware delegation. Rodney promptly mounted a fleet horse and, changing to fresh horses at various intervals, covered a distance of some eighty miles during the night and morning of

July 1–2. He arrived in Philadelphia in time to join McKean in casting Delaware's vote for independence when the formal vote of Congress was taken on July 2. Read joined McKean and Rodney in signing the Declaration of Independence on behalf of Delaware on Aug. 2.

[George H. Ryden, ed., *Letters to and From Cæsar Rodney.*]

GEORGE H. RYDEN

RODRIGUEZ-CHAMUSCADO EXPEDITION. In 1580, the Spaniards having occupied northern Mexico, Augustin Rodríguez, a Franciscan lay brother, obtained permission to cross the Rio Grande and found a mission among the Pueblo. Two Franciscan priests, Francisco López and Juan de Santa Maria, joined him. They were accompanied by nine soldiers and sixteen Mexican Indian converts under the command of Francisco Sánchez Chamuscado. Leaving Santa Bárbara (Chihuahua) on June 5, 1581, they proceeded northward and entered a region near present-day Bernalillo (N.Mex.). The friars then visited the Indian towns, while Chamuscado led his followers on a tour westward to Pecos, Acoma, and Zuni. The enterprise was soon abandoned, owing to the extravagant conduct of Chamuscado. His domineering policy vexed the soldiers, alienated the peaceful natives, and nullified the work of the friars. On his way to Mexico with a report for the viceroy, Juan de Santa Maria was murdered by hostile Indians. In the end, Chamuscado ordered a return to Mexico, leaving the friars without military protection. Both Rodríguez and López were soon after killed by the Indians. Although itself a failure, the expedition paved the way for the permanent occupation of New Mexico by Juan de Oñate in 1598.

[H. E. Bolton, *Spanish Exploration in the Southwest*, and *The Spanish Borderlands*.]

FRANCIS BORGIA STECK

ROGERENES, also known as Rogerene Baptists and Rogerene Quakers, were members of a nonconformist sect founded about 1675–77 by John Rogers; subsequently the sect was led by members of the Rogers family and other influential and prosperous families of New London, Conn., and vicinity. Among the Rogerenes' beliefs, which were based on a literal interpretation of the New Testament, were separation of church and state, nonviolence, baptism of believers only, no medical care for the sick, and no observance of a special Sabbath. However, until about 1705 they did observe a seventh-day Sabbath, holding worship on Saturday and working on Sunday. This and other nonconformist religious practices brought upon the Rogerenes fines, whippings, imprisonment, and confiscation of property by Connecticut authorities. Their retaliation consisted of entering the churches of their persecutors during meetings and making public protests. Aside from being extremely zealous in their chosen faith, the Rogerenes were good workers and excellent businessmen, respected by most of the townspeople. Under the Connecticut constitution of 1818, separation of church and state (and thus religious liberty) was finally established. Because the main purpose of the Rogerenes' existence was realized and because of much westward emigration, the sect dwindled in influence and numbers.

[J. R. Bolles and A. B. Williams, *The Rogerenes.*]

MARJORIE E. CASE

ROGERS' RANGERS, the most colorful corps in the British-American army during the French and Indian War. It was commanded by Maj. Robert Rogers, with such capable soldiers as John Stark, Israel Putnam, and James Dalyell as lieutenants. The unit of 600 frontiersmen, which served as the eyes of Gen. James Abercromby's and Gen. Jeffrey Amherst's armies, conducted scores of raids, scouting enemy forces and positions and capturing prisoners.

On Jan. 21, 1757, the rangers cleverly escaped extermination by a greatly superior French force between Crown Point and Ticonderoga, N.Y. The Battle of Snowshoes, fought to the south of Ticonderoga on Mar. 13, 1758, did not end so well for Rogers, who lost 130 of his 180 men and barely escaped himself. (He did so, according to tradition, by making the Indians believe he had descended the steep promontory on Lake George now known as Rogers' Rock.) In 1759 the rangers boldly wiped out the village of the Saint Francis Indians, and during the next year Rogers journeyed as far west as Detroit, where he received the surrender of the French posts.

The great strength of the rangers came from their adoption of the best features of Indian warfare. Each ranger was extremely mobile and highly self-sufficient. He was clad in buckskin and carried a smoothbore firelock, sixty rounds of powder and ball, a heavy hatchet, and a small supply of dried meat and biscuit. Extremely vigilant, the rangers marched through the forest silently in single file with skirmishers spread out to the front and sides. In battle they fought from behind the heavy covert of shrubs and bushes. If outnumbered, they retired with slow, withering fire and, under cover of night, melted away in a hundred directions, reassembling at the appointed rendezvous many miles away. Their dashing courage, incredible hardihood, and humorous pranks made them famous both in Great Britain and in the colonies.

[Allan Nevins, ed., *Ponteach, or the Savages of America . . . by Robert Rogers;* Kenneth Roberts, *Northwest Passage.*]

EDWARD P. ALEXANDER

ROMAN CATHOLIC CHURCH. *See* **Catholicism.**

ROORBACK, a term originating in the presidential campaign of 1844, when, in order to injure the candidacy of James K. Polk, the *Ithaca* (N.Y.) *Chronicle* published a defamatory falsehood that was said to be an extract from Baron von Roorback's *Tour Through the Western and Southern States in 1836.* The word has come to mean any defamatory falsehood or forgery published for political effect.

P. ORMAN RAY

ROOSEVELT COROLLARY to the Monroe Doctrine was a policy of action by the United States in certain unstable Latin-American republics to forestall intervention by European creditor nations. Such action was allegedly a responsibility derived from the Monroe Doctrine. The corollary was first set forth by President Theodore Roosevelt in May 1904 and was repeated in his annual message of Dec. 6, 1904, and his special message of Feb. 15, 1905. In the 1905 message the corollary was invoked to justify U.S. establishment of customs control over the Dominican Republic. Financial controls and interventions in Honduras, the Dominican Republic, Haiti, and Nicaragua during the administrations of William Howard Taft and Woodrow Wilson were also defended on the basis of the Roosevelt Corollary. (*See also* Good Neighbor Policy; Monroe Doctrine.)

[J. Reuben Clark, *Memorandum on the Monroe Doctrine.*]

BENJAMIN H. WILLIAMS

ROOT ARBITRATION TREATIES, a series of twenty-five bilateral pacts concluded in 1908 and 1909 during the tenure of Elihu Root as U.S. secretary of state. (At least three similar documents were

signed subsequently.) The pacts remained the chief bipartite nonaggression treaties to which the United States was a signatory until 1928, when Secretary of State Frank Kellogg negotiated with France the first pact of a new type (*see* Kellogg-Briand Pact). In general, the Root treaties obligated the parties to arbitrate differences of a legal nature and those relating to the interpretation of a treaty. Following the model of the Anglo-French Arbitration Treaty of 1904, they contained the sweeping exception of all questions involving the vital interests, independence, or national honor of the parties or the interests of third parties. They generally provided that controversies to be arbitrated under the treaty should be submitted to a tribunal of the Permanent Court of Arbitration. The expiration dates of the treaties varied.

The U.S. Senate ratified the treaties subject to a reservation requiring the consent of the Senate for the arbitration of every individual case under each treaty. The Senate's insistence on this reservation in 1905 had prevented the ratification of four substantially identical arbitration treaties negotiated by Secretary of State John M. Hay. Root, convinced that the Senate would not recede from its position, persuaded President Theodore Roosevelt to accept the reservation.

[H. M. Cory, *Compulsory Arbitration.*]

PHILIP C. JESSUP

"ROOT, HOG OR DIE," an expression originating in the mid-19th century or earlier, based on the hog's habit of digging for food. It was a typically American pioneer way of saying, "Work or starve." Its grimly humorous meaning was that there was no place for the idler of limited means in a new, frontier country.

ALVIN F. HARLOW

ROOT MISSION TO RUSSIA. In April 1917, President Woodrow Wilson appointed a mission to go to Russia, chiefly for the purpose of ascertaining whether Russia's active participation in World War I could be continued after the March revolution. The mission was headed by Elihu Root and included Charles Edward Russell, James Duncan, John R. Mott, Charles R. Crane, Cyrus H. McCormick, S. R. Bertron, Gen. Hugh L. Scott, and Rear Adm. James H. Glennon. A separate railroad commission to Russia, under John F. Stevens, had already been appointed, and the Root mission was specifically excluded from dealing with that vital problem. The Root mission was in Petrograd (now Leningrad) from June 13 to July 9, 1917. The strength of Nikolai Lenin and his Bolshevik party was not then appreciated by the diplomatic corps in Petrograd or by the Root mission, and their contacts were chiefly with the moderate parties of Prince Georgi Evgenievich Lvov and Aleksandr Kerenski. The mission reached the conclusion that the most effective action the United States could take was to spend a large sum on propaganda to offset the strenuous German efforts to stimulate Russian peace sentiment. The mission's recommendations were practically ignored by the administration in Washington.

[P. C. Jessup, *Elihu Root*.]

PHILIP C. JESSUP

ROOT-TAKAHIRA AGREEMENT, an accord concluded on Nov. 30, 1908, by U.S. Secretary of State Elihu Root and the Japanese ambassador, Baron Kogoro Takahira. It declared the wish of the two governments to develop their commerce in the Pacific; their intention to defend the Open Door policy and the independence and integrity of China; their resolve to respect each other's territorial possessions in the Pacific; and their willingness to communicate with each other if these principles were threatened. (An earlier proposal for such an arrangement in October 1907 had been repudiated by the Japanese government, but the suggestion was renewed when Count Katsura became premier of Japan.) The proposal was welcomed by the United States as helpful in quieting the widely held belief that war between the two countries was imminent, a belief stimulated by the disputes over Japanese immigration and the anti-Japanese measures in California (*see* Japanese Exclusion Acts). The agreement was enthusiastically received in European capitals but did not please the Chinese, who feared that it would strengthen Japan's position in China.

[P. C. Jessup, *Elihu Root*.]

PHILIP C. JESSUP

ROSALIE, FORT, was erected by the French under Jean Baptiste Le Moyne, Sieur de Bienville, in 1716, on the site of present-day Natchez, Miss., to protect their trading post and settlement against the surrounding Natchez Indians. In 1722 it became the administrative center of the civil and military district of Natchez. The original fort was destroyed by the Indians during the Natchez massacre in 1729, but a new fort was constructed soon thereafter. It remained

an important French post until 1763, when Great Britain gained possession of Louisiana east of the Mississippi. In 1764 British troops occupied and repaired the dilapidated fort, which was renamed Fort Panmure.

[Charles Gayarré, *History of Louisiana,* vol. I.]

WALTER PRICHARD

ROSEBUD INDIAN RESERVATION, established in 1890, is located in southwestern South Dakota and is the home of the Brulé Sioux. In the 1970's the reservation became one of the centers of activity of the American Indian Movement, which sought to publicize and change the living conditions of reservation Indians and what it considered historical and current discrimination against Indians. The reservation's population in 1972 was 7,488.

ROSE INTRIGUE, an 1808 conspiracy involving British minister Sir George Rose and a group of New England Federalists. Strong pro-British sentiment had developed in New England as a result of Democratic-Republican President Thomas Jefferson's embargo on British goods and his Francophile tendencies. Rose, early in 1808, entered into an intrigue with Timothy Pickering and the Essex Junto to secure repeal of the embargo and to ensure peaceful relations between the United States and Great Britain—and thereby give new life and power to the Federalists. The embargo remained in effect until March 1809. (*See also* Henry Letters.)

[Henry Adams, *History of the United States,* vol. V; J. T. Adams, *New England in the Republic.*]

THOMAS ROBSON HAY

ROSENBERG CASE. On Apr. 5, 1951, Julius Rosenberg and his wife Ethel, natives of New York City, were sentenced to death after being found guilty of furnishing vital information on the atomic bomb to Soviet agents in 1944 and 1945. Julius Rosenberg had been an electrical engineer. Evidence against the pair was supplied by Ethel Rosenberg's brother, David Greenglass, who was himself sentenced to fifteen years' imprisonment. Also involved was Morton Sobel, sentenced to thirty years. Despite worldwide appeals to President Dwight D. Eisenhower to commute their sentences, the Rosenbergs were executed at Sing Sing Prison on June 19, 1953.

Controversy continued over the tactics used by government agencies during the trial; in particular, charges were made that the Federal Bureau of Investigation tampered with the evidence. In 1975 Michael and Robert Meeropol, the sons of the Rosenbergs (who had taken the surname of their adoptive parents), won a court battle forcing the government to release hitherto secret documents relating to the case.

[Louis Nizer, *The Implosion Conspiracy;* Walter Schneir and Miriam Schneir, *Invitation to an Inquest.*]

ROSS, IN RE, 140 U.S. 453 (1891), a case in which the Supreme Court clearly stated three principles related to imperial growth: (1) the United States has jurisdiction over aliens on U.S. ships in foreign waters; (2) the United States may exercise extraterritorial rights under treaty provisions; and (3) constitutional guarantees do not extend beyond U.S. shores.

[M. O. Hudson, *Cases on International Law.*]
THEODORE M. WHITFIELD

ROTATION IN OFFICE, the theory of public employment that maintains short terms of office and frequent changes in personnel are desirable. It is based on the premise that long continuance in office leads incumbents to become arrogant and unmindful of their obligations as public servants. Historically, a permanent civil service has often been opposed on this basis.

President Andrew Jackson, in his first annual message (1829), said, "The duties of all public officers are, or at least admit of being made, so plain and simple that men of intelligence may readily qualify themselves for their performance; and I cannot but believe that more is lost by the long continuance of men in office than is generally to be gained by their experience." Whether this statement arose out of sincere conviction or was merely a rationalization of Jackson's attitude toward political patronage is difficult to establish. It seems clear that the requirements of the public service in a technological age cannot be met adequately by any scheme that would deny the need for special preparation of employees and for conserving the advantages to be gained from their experience.

[W. E. Mosher and J. D. Kingsley, *Public Personnel Administration.*]
HARVEY WALKER

ROUGH RIDERS, officially the First U.S. Cavalry Volunteers, was the most widely publicized single regiment in American military history. It was recruited for the Spanish-American War, its members coming from the cattle ranges and mining camps and from the law enforcement agencies of the Southwest. Such personnel offered brilliant copy for the flamboyant and unrestrained war correspondents of the era, and the unit's commanding officers further enhanced its image. Leonard Wood, of the Army Medical Corps, left his post as White House physician to accept the colonelcy; Theodore Roosevelt became lieutenant colonel. Neither was trained for line command, but both had exceptionally colorful personalities.

The Rough Riders had a brief training period at San Antonio in the spring of 1898 and then entrained for Tampa, Fla. There the unit's horses were abandoned, and in the chaos of embarkation, only slightly more than half the regiment left Florida. The fragment that did reach Cuba lived up to its advance publicity. From Las Guásimas, after which Wood was promoted to a brigade commander, to San Juan Hill, the Rough Riders' attacks were often unconventional but usually successful.

[Theodore Roosevelt, *The Rough Riders.*]
JIM DAN HILL

ROUNDUP. *See* **Rodeo.**

ROUSE'S POINT BOUNDARY CONTROVERSY, a dispute between the United States and Great Britain over the New York–Canadian border. The Proclamation of 1763 set the forty-fifth parallel as the New York–Quebec boundary. Three years later Gov. Henry Moore of New York and Gen. Guy Carleton of Quebec, assisted by Prof. Robert Harpur of King's College, determined where the line should run. Gov. William Tryon of New York had it surveyed in 1771–74. The Definitive Treaty of Peace, 1783, retained the forty-fifth parallel as the United States–Canadian boundary between the Connecticut and Saint Lawrence rivers, and in 1816 the United States commenced to build a fort near the border just north of Rouse's Point.

A new survey of the boundary, made in 1818–19 under the Treaty of Ghent, found that the true parallel was far south of Tryon's line. "Fort Blunder," as the U.S. fortification came to be known, was clearly on Canadian soil if the forty-fifth parallel was the boundary. In 1831 the king of Holland (*see* Netherlands Award), acting as arbitrator of the dispute, suggested that the boundary should extend far enough north to include the fort, but this solution was not ratified by the U.S. Senate. The Webster-Ashburton Treaty, 1842, retained the line of 1774, so that the site of "Fort Blunder" was within the American boundary. In 1843 a new fort, named Montgomery, was begun, but it was never completed or garrisoned. The ruined works were sold in 1926 and have since been demolished.

[D. H. Hurd, *History of Clinton and Franklin Counties*.]
EDWARD P. ALEXANDER

ROUSSEAU'S RAID (July 10–22, 1864). To assist Union Gen. William Tecumseh Sherman's advance to Atlanta, Gen. L. H. Rousseau was directed to assemble 2,500 cavalry and destroy the West Point and Montgomery Railroad in Alabama from a point opposite Tuskegee to Opelika. Rousseau left Decatur, Ala., on July 10 and in the following twelve days completely accomplished his mission.

[R. U. Johnson and C. C. Buel, eds., *Battles and Leaders of the Civil War*, vol. IV.]
ROBERT S. THOMAS

ROYAL COLONIES. Except for Connecticut and Rhode Island, all of the original thirteen colonies began as chartered, or proprietary, provinces—and the two exceptions shortly came to be chartered colonies as well. But governmental problems eventually caused most proprietors to surrender their charters to the crown. The new form of government was known as a royal province, and it began first in Virginia in 1624 (*see* Virginia Company of London). At the time of the Revolution only Connecticut, Maryland, Pennsylvania, and Rhode Island retained the earlier forms of government. Thus, the royal province became the standard type of colonial government in America.

In the royal province no legal limitations stood between the king and the people. The king was represented by a royal governor (*see* Colonial Governors), appointed and removable at will, whose authority rested upon a commission and a set of instructions. The first conferred authority, the latter directed how the authority was to be exercised. Together these documents comprised a written constitution, subject to change by the crown. The governor was assisted by a council of twelve, appointed by the crown (*see* Colonial Councils).

Each colony had an elected assembly (*see* Colonial Assemblies) representing the people, and until shortly before the Revolution, the assemblies had complete control over lawmaking, taxation, and the handling of public revenues (although all laws were subject to

royal veto). Most royal governors were dependent upon the assembly for financial support. This reliance opened the way for extensive popular control of government in America by the assemblies, and by 1764 the royal provinces were, essentially, self-governing commonwealths. Georgia was the only original colony supported directly by parliamentary appropriations. By an act of Parliament in 1767 the royal governors and other civil officers were made independent of the assemblies and began to be paid directly from revenues raised in America.

Judges were appointed by the crown, usually for life terms (contingent on good behavior). After 1760 they could be removed by the crown just as governors could, and under the act of 1767 (*see* Colonial Judiciary) they were no longer paid by the assemblies.

All unsold public land belonged to the crown and could be granted by the governor. The colonial governments' communications with British authority in London were with the Board of Trade, in ordinary civil matters; with the secretary of state for the Southern Department, in major political affairs; with the Treasury Department, in matters of customs duties; and with the Admiralty office, in matters of admiralty.

[Leonard Woods Labaree, *Royal Government in America*.]
O. M. DICKERSON

ROYAL DISALLOWANCE. In addition to possessing authority to review cases on appeal from colonial courts (*see* Appeals From Colonial Courts), the Privy Council had the power to approve or disallow colonial legislation. By 1730 this power applied to all the colonies except Connecticut and Rhode Island. Laws contrary to English common or statute law, to a colonial charter, or to a governor's instructions, as well as laws manifestly inequitable or badly drafted, were principal targets of the disallowance procedure. Although only a very small percentage of colonial laws were disallowed, the practice helped to tighten the mercantilist vise on the colonies, as frequent objects of royal disapproval were laws affecting English trade and shipping interests, establishing debt moratoriums and inflation, and fostering colonial manufactures.

[C. M. Andrews, "The Royal Disallowance," *American Antiquarian Society Proceedings*, new series, vol. 24.]
RICHARD B. MORRIS

RUBBER. Although rubber-yielding plants are native to Africa and Asia as well as to the Americas, the first mention of rubber in the West was made by Pietro Martire d'Anghiera, the Italian representative to the court of Spain (*De Rebus Oceanicis et Novo Orbe*, 1516). In the early 17th century Juan de Torquemada (*Monarquía Indiana*, 1615) described how the Mexican Indians—besides using it for religious rites and sport—made crude footwear, waterproof bottles, and garments from a milklike fluid drawn from a tree. Although a little rubber was used in Europe in the 18th century to make erasers (it was named for its property of erasing, or rubbing out, pencil marks), elastic thread, surgical tubes, and experimental balloons, the rubber manufacturing industry was not established until the 19th century.

The first record of rubber in the United States is a patent for gum elastic varnish for footwear issued to Jacob F. Hummel in 1813. This was followed by a patent for a grinding and mixing machine granted to John J. Howe in 1820. Prompting these first steps was the profitable trade being done in crude rubber shoes imported into Boston and New York City from Brazil. By 1833 America's pioneering rubber factory had been established at Roxbury, Mass. Other rubber shoe and clothing factories soon appeared elsewhere in Massachusetts, as well as in New Jersey, Rhode Island, Connecticut, New York, and Pennsylvania. By 1840 the infant industry had experienced a speculative boom (about $2 million in stock was issued) and a disastrous collapse. The primary cause for the loss of confidence was the fact that rubber products had not proved reliable (they softened in the heat and stiffened in the cold), but the downturn in general business conditions that began in the fall of 1837 only added to the industry's distress. So great was the distress that in 1843 the Roxbury Rubber Company sold for $525 the "monster" spreading machine (built by Edwin Marcus Chaffee in 1837) that it had bought for $30,000.

The basic technical problem of early rubber manufacture was solved by Charles Goodyear's discovery in 1839, at Woburn, Mass., of the vulcanization process, which gives rubber a durable quality. Goodyear treated rubber with sulfur and white lead at a high temperature. His samples of "cured" rubber, with which he tried to raise funds in England, prompted the English inventor Thomas Hancock to make his own "discovery" of vulcanization. The "elastic metal" provided by these two inventors (actually, experiments to cure rubber have been ascribed to the 18th-century Swedish physician and pharmacist Petter-Jonas Bergius) would soon prove indispensable to the Western world.

Nowhere was this more marked than in the development of the automobile industry. Yet long before the automobile appeared at the end of the 19th century, America's consumption of raw rubber had grown twentyfold, from 1,120 short tons in 1850 to 23,000 tons in 1900 (two-fifths the world total of 59,000 short tons). Wherever elastic, shock-absorbing, water-resistant, insulating, and air- and steam-tight properties were required, vulcanized rubber was used. Most of the raw rubber came from Brazil, with Africa the second most important source. The problem was not to find rubber but to find the labor to collect it in the almost inaccessible forests and ship it to the factories of the Northern Hemisphere. Until the systematic development of plantation rubber in Southeast Asia in the 20th century made collection and transportation a comparatively easy task, the growing demand for crude rubber could only be met at increased cost. In 1830 Para rubber was 20 cents a pound; in 1900 the annual average wholesale price had risen to about a dollar.

Between 1849 and 1900 the industry's output of manufactured goods—chiefly footwear, mechanicals (for use with machinery), proofed and elastic goods, surgical goods, bicycle tires, and toys—increased in value from $3 million to $53 million. In the same years, the work force grew from 2,500 to 22,000. Because of the economies of scale and the absence of product differentiation, the market for rubber products was fiercely competitive—hence the tendency for the early rubber manufacturers to band together. Before the Civil War, marketing arrangements were already in existence to control the sale of footwear and other products. By the eve of World War I production had come to be dominated by the "Big Four": Goodyear Tire and Rubber Company, United States Rubber Company, B. F. Goodrich Company, and Firestone Tire and Rubber Company. Partly to be close to the carriage-making industry, the center of rubber manufacture had shifted from the towns of New England to Akron, Ohio. The industry's first branch factories were established in western Europe in the 1850's.

The most dramatic phase of the industry's growth followed the introduction in the early 1900's of the internal combustion engine, cheap petroleum, and the widespread use of the pneumatic tire. Between 1900 and 1920, consumption of raw rubber increased tenfold to 231,000 short tons. Even the world depression of the early 1930's only halted the industry's rapid expansion temporarily. By 1940 the United States was consuming 726,000 tons out of a world total of

1,243,000 tons of crude rubber. Between 1900 (when the first 4 tons of Southeast Asia plantation rubber had reached the market) and 1910, the annual average wholesale price of a pound of crude rubber doubled from $1 to $2. By 1915 more than twice as much rubber was coming from the plantations of Southeast Asia than from America and Africa combined, and prices had fallen to a quarter of their 1910 level; on June 2, 1932, the price was 3 cents a pound.

Partly because of the great fluctuations in the price of crude rubber and partly because the plantation industry of the Far East was largely in British hands, the industry began a search for rubber substitutes in the 1920's. In the next decade a few hundred tons a year of a special type of synthetic rubber were produced. As Japan seized the rubber lands of Southeast Asia during World War II, U.S. production of synthetic rubber was increased a hundredfold, from 9,000 short tons in 1941 to 919,000 tons in 1945. Four-fifths of America's needs were being met by synthetic rubber. By 1973, of a world output of 6.3 million metric tons, the United States produced about 40 percent, almost three times more than the next greatest producer, Japan. That year, the United States had consumed only 696,000 metric tons of a world output of approximately 3.5 million tons of natural rubber.

Chemists not only succeeded in synthesizing rubber by making a wide range of elastomers and plastomers available; they changed the character of the industry until it was no longer possible to distinguish between rubber and rubber-substitutes. The price of the synthetic compared favorably with that of the natural product, and for some uses synthetic rubber was preferred.

The rise of other industrialized nations in the 20th century lessened America's domination of the industry; still, its output in 1970 (including plastics) was worth about $15 billion; the labor force employed exceeded half a million. Although rubber was used in thousands of ways, automobile tires—with which the major technical developments in manufacture have been associated—continued to account for more than one-half the industry's consumption of raw materials in the mid-1970's. The overwhelming size of the major rubber corporations (a fifth giant was added to the "Big Four" in 1915 when the General Tire and Rubber Corporation was formed at Akron) did not lessen the industry's competitive nature. After World War II, the tendency toward global expansion increased, and in 1975 the major rubber manufacturers were worldwide in scope and operation.

[P. W. Allen, *Natural Rubber and the Synthetics*; W. C. Geer, *The Reign of Rubber*; F. A. Howard, *Buna Rubber: The Birth of an Industry*; P. Schidrowitz and T. R. Dawson, eds., *History of the Rubber Industry*; W. Woodruff, "Growth of the Rubber Industry of Great Britain and the United States," *Journal of Economic History*, vol. 15 (1955).]

WILLIAM WOODRUFF

RUBÍ'S TOUR. In accordance with Charles III's comprehensive program of revitalizing Spanish colonial defense, the Marqués de Rubí was commissioned in 1765 to inspect the northern military posts of New Spain. During 1766–68, he traversed the entire northern border, from Texas to Sonora, and found it subject to chronic Indian attack, especially by the Apache and the Comanche. In his report Rubí suggested a realignment of the presidios (border settlements populated by military personnel), the abandonment of the Louisiana border posts, and an exterminatory war against the eastern Apache. Most of Rubí's recommendations were adopted in 1772, in the form of the New Regulation of Presidios.

[C. E. Chapman, *The Founding of Spanish California*; H. E. Bolton and T. M. Marshall, *The Colonization of North America*.]

CHARLES EDWARD CHAPMAN
ROBERT HALE SHIELDS

RUFFNER PAMPHLET, an 1847 publication that included the antislavery address before the Franklin Literary Society given by Henry Ruffner, president of Washington College, in Lexington, Va. Endorsed by prominent leaders, the pamphlet was widely circulated and much discussed. Ruffner, although not an abolitionist, contended that slavery retarded the industrial and commercial development of the South and should be gradually ended. Frequently a subject of political controversy, the pamphlet was used in the Virginia gubernatorial campaign of 1859 to discredit John Letcher, who had originally endorsed it.

[C. H. Ambler, *Sectionalism in Virginia*.]

HENRY T. SHANKS

RULE OF REASON, a judicial principle applicable to the interpretation of legislation whose purpose and intent are open to serious question. In practice, application of the principle has been largely restricted to the interpretation of the Sherman Antitrust Act of 1890.

This measure, either by accident or by design, was so poorly drawn that if taken literally, it would be unenforceable, socially and economically unsound, and probably unconstitutional as well. In an effort to evade the issue of the law's constitutionality, the Supreme Court, in the 1911 cases *Standard Oil Company* v. *United States* and *United States* v. *American Tobacco Company,* enunciated the rule of reason and used it to conclude that the statutory prohibition of "all combinations in restraint of trade" set forth in the act, actually meant "all unreasonable combinations in restraint of trade." The next year the Court developed and elaborated on the rule-of-reason concept (which essentially enabled judicial amendment of the antitrust act) in *United States* v. *Saint Louis Terminal Railway Association.*

[John G. Hervey, *The Anti-Trust Laws of the United States;* Charles W. Needham, ed., *Cases on Foreign and Interstate Commerce;* William H. Taft, *The Anti-Trust Act and the Supreme Court.*]

W. BROOKE GRAVES

RULE OF THE WAR OF 1756. In 1756, while France and Great Britain were at war, the French, because of British maritime supremacy, opened their colonial trade to the neutral Dutch. This action resulted in a notification by Great Britain to the Netherlands that Great Britain in the future would not allow neutrals to engage in time of war in a trade from which they were excluded in time of peace. The British prize courts enforced this dictum, since known as the Rule of the War of 1756.

During the wars of the French Revolution and the Napoleonic Wars, the shipping industry of the neutral United States endeavored to circumvent the rule by taking French colonial goods to American ports and reexporting them as American goods. In the case of the *Polly,* decided by British prize courts in 1802 (during an interval of peace), it was held that this circuitous voyage, broken at a neutral port, did not constitute a violation of the Rule of the War of 1756. In making this decision the court did not consider the question of whether the payment of drawbacks (or refunds) of import tariff charges when the imported goods were reexported nullified the Americanization and made the exports subject to capture under the Rule of the War of 1756. In the case of the *Essex,* decided in 1805, after the renewal of the war, the British prize courts decided that payment of drawbacks on colonial goods reexported by way of neutral countries nullified the neutralization of those goods

and subjected them to capture and condemnation under the Rule of the War of 1756. The 1805 ruling was the cause of much diplomatic dispute between Great Britain and the United States.

[Samuel Flagg Bemis, *A Diplomatic History of the United States;* John Bassett Moore, *Digest of International Law,* vol. VII.]

SAMUEL FLAGG BEMIS

RULES OF THE HOUSE. The rules of the U.S. House of Representatives and the ever-increasing thousands of precedents that influence their interpretation constitute one of the most complete bodies of parliamentary law in the world, rivaled, perhaps, only by that of the British House of Commons. The size of the House (since 1912, fixed at 435 members) and its immense volume of proposed legislation require strict regulation of the actions of members while in session. The Constitution gives the House the right to make its own rules, which are adopted anew by each Congress, usually with few or no changes. Overall revisions have occurred several times, notably in 1860, 1880, and 1890. In addition, legislative reorganization acts such as those of 1946 and 1970 made extensive changes in House rules. The 1970 act, for example, allowed radio and television coverage of committee hearings, required that all committee roll-call votes be made public, and strengthened the rights of the minority party.

Congressional rules are the product of centuries of parliamentary experience in Great Britain, the colonies, and, since 1789, the United States. The speaker (or presiding officer), often with the counsel of his parliamentarian, rules on points of order. Such rulings may provide new interpretations or set new precedents, which then become part of the regulations guiding the internal conduct of the House. The objectives of the rules are complex and hard to reconcile: to enable the majority to work its will while protecting the rights of the minority and to legislate expeditiously while avoiding reckless haste. The 1936 compilation of the House rules and precedents (Asher C. Hinds and Clarence Cannon, eds., *Precedents of the House of Representatives*) filled eleven volumes and was still being used in the mid-1970's.

[Lewis Deschler, ed., *Deschler's Procedure;* Randall B. Ripley, *Congress—Process and Policy.*]

D. B. HARDEMAN

RULES OF WAR. *See* **War, Laws of.**

RUMBOUT'S PATENT was a tract of 85,000 acres located in Dutchess County near the present-day town of Fishkill, N.Y. License to purchase from the Indians was given to Francis Rumbout and Gulian Verplanck by Gov. Thomas Dongan in 1682. Before the patent was issued Verplanck died (Oct. 17, 1685), and Stephanus Van Cortlandt became associated with Rumbout, Jacobus Kipp representing Verplanck's minor children.

[Frank Hasbrouck, *The History of Dutchess County.*]

A. C. FLICK

"RUM, ROMANISM AND REBELLION." *See* **Burchard Incident.**

RUM ROW. Soon after the beginning of the Prohibition era in 1919, quantities of liquor began to be smuggled into the United States by sea, most of it along the eastern and southern coasts. The boats, which stole into city harbors at night or landed their cargoes in lonely inlets, were called rumrunners. In the South, they operated directly from the West Indies; but farther north, along the New Jersey, New York, and lower New England coasts, the larger vessels anchored, or lay to, outside the three-mile jurisdictional limit, waiting for smaller, faster boats—their agents or customers—to transship portions of the cargo and make a run for shore. This chain of loitering vessels—which included former fishing boats, freighters, private yachts, and even an old Spanish cruiser—came to be known as Rum Row. Speedy government gunboats, called rum chasers, watched for the smugglers who tried to steal ashore, and some wild pursuits and bloody battles took place.

[Roy A. Haynes, *Prohibition Inside Out.*]

ALVIN F. HARLOW

RUMSEY'S STEAMBOAT. On Dec. 3, 1787, James Rumsey exhibited at Shepherdstown (then in Virginia, now in West Virginia), in the presence of a crowd of spectators, a boat that was propelled by water forced out through the stern by a pump operated by a steam engine. Gen. Horatio Gates, Maj. Henry Bedinger, and other prominent men who were present gave Rumsey certificates stating that they had had the pleasure of seeing his boat ''get on her way, with near half her burthen on board and move against the current at the rate of three miles per hour by the force of steam, without any external application whatever.''

On Dec. 11, at another trial, a speed of four miles an hour against the current was attained. Being without funds to carry on further experiments, Rumsey went to Philadelphia where, shortly after his arrival, the Rumseian Society was formed. In May 1788 that organization provided funds for him to go to England to carry on his steamboat experiments. There, after suffering numerous disappointments and hardships, he died Dec. 20, 1792, a few days before he was to make a public trial of his boat. The following February his boat made a successful trip on the Thames at the rate of four knots. In 1785 Rumsey had invented a watertube boiler of the type employed in the 20th century by the U.S. and British navies and in various steam plants where high pressure was required.

[James Rumsey, *A Plan Wherein the Power of Steam Is Fully Shewn;* Ella M. Turner, *James Rumsey.*]

ELLA M. TURNER

RUM TRADE began in the New England colonies in the 17th century and soon became vital to the existence of a people unable to produce staple crops on their land. The climate of Massachusetts and Rhode Island being unsuitable to such large staples as tobacco, which maintained the southern colonies, agriculture was confined in much of New England to the subsistence farms. Since the lumber and fishing industries of New England were unable to find markets in England large enough to produce revenue sufficient to pay for the manufactured goods imported from the mother country, the New England colonies were forced to seek a market in the West Indies. There, lumber and fish were paid for by molasses, the main product of the islands. The manufacture of rum from the imported molasses thus became one of the earliest of the New England industries. The rapidity with which this industry grew is evident from the fact that in 1731, 1.25 million gallons of rum were manufactured in Boston from molasses brought in from the French West Indies.

It was presently understood by the Yankee traders that the most pressing need of the island planters was for slaves. The more adventurous of the New England sea captains thus became familiar with the African Gold Coast before the end of the 17th century, engaging in triangular trade: molasses to New England, rum to Africa, slaves to the West Indies. This commerce maintained the prosperity of the northern colonies through the 18th century.

These colonies soon came into conflict with Great Britain over the rum trade. Yankee traders found it more profitable to deal with the French, Dutch, and Spanish islands than with the English. First, the Roman Catholic populations constituted a market for New England fish; second, the supply of sugar (from which molasses is extracted) was inadequate in the English islands; and third, the sugar of the English colonies was more expensive. In France, legislation designed to protect native brandy forebade importation of rum from its colonies, so that most of the molasses supply of the French islands was available to the Yankees. The British Parliament attempted, through the Molasses Act of 1733, to limit this trade by imposing high duties on non-British molasses imported into New England. This legislation was consistently evaded; smuggling became an accepted practice and reached an enormous scale. It has been estimated that of 15,000 hogsheads of molasses imported into Massachusetts in 1763, the duty (nine pence per gallon) was paid on only 1,000 hogsheads.

Also in 1763 the conflict over molasses imports reached crisis proportions, largely because of the war between Great Britain and France. Parliament passed the Sugar Act, a stronger version of the Molasses Act, and attempted to enforce it by the use of the British navy, by the appointment of customs commissioners, and by the issuance of writs of assistance, actions that are recognized as causes of the American Revolution. By 1763 smuggling was regarded by New Englanders as a patriotic exercise.

The rum trade was an important factor in the development of colonial shipping; it was partly responsible for the design of fast ships and for the skill of Yankee skippers.

[R. Burlingame, *March of the Iron Men;* W. B. Weeden, *Economic History of New England.*]

ROGER BURLINGAME

RUNIC INSCRIPTIONS. *See* **Kensington Stone; Norsemen in America.**

RURAL DEVELOPMENT means many things— improving the quality of rural life, eliminating poverty in rural areas, attracting capital and industry to rural areas, and achieving rural-urban balance in population and resources. In the United States the emphasis has shifted from one to another of these factors with changes in the national economy and in national goals.

President Theodore Roosevelt appointed the Country Life Commission in 1908 to report on the condition of country life. When the report was sub-

mitted to Congress in 1909, the president stressed as one of the chief problems the failure of country life to satisfy the "higher social and intellectual aspirations of country people." This deficiency and superior urban business opportunities, the president stated, were contributing to the movement of rural people to the cities.

Congress expressed concern about the "overbalance of population in industrial centers" in a section of the National Industrial Recovery Act of June 16, 1933, which authorized an expenditure of $25 million to bring about a better balance of population. Rural homestead projects were initiated in 1933 to enable industrial workers, subject to seasonal unemployment, to raise a considerable part of their own food supply. A number of programs were initiated during the 1930's to help destitute farm families retain their farms or move from submarginal to more productive lands.

Since farmers constituted more than 50 percent of the rural population, and others living in rural areas were mostly retired farmers or small business people who served the economic needs of farmers, government programs during the 1930's were focused on helping individual farmers. The balance of farm to nonfarm population in rural areas began to shift after 1940. By 1970 farm people constituted less than 20 percent of the total rural population. As a result, during the 1960's and early 1970's government programs shifted much of their emphasis from helping individual farmers to providing assistance for rural communities.

The Department of Agriculture's rural development program was not formalized until 1954. In a Jan. 11 message to Congress President Dwight D. Eisenhower asked that particular attention be given to the problems peculiar to low-income farmers. A report was prepared within the department on the development of agriculture's human resources. In addition to increasing productivity in agriculture, the report recommended improving job prospects in part-time farming and nonfarm work, increasing opportunities for training in trades and industrial skills, improving the health of poor farm families using available medical and nutrition education resources, and encouraging decentralization of the defense industry to provide more jobs in rural areas. The work on the new rural development program was largely decentralized, emphasizing the development of state and county programs in pilot counties.

The Economic Opportunity Act of 1964 expanded the scope of the department's rural development pro-

171

gram and provided funds to reach farm people in rural areas who had insufficient financial resources to benefit from government loan and price programs. It also provided funds to reach people in rural areas who were not living on farms. The act provided for the establishment of a job corps, for community action programs, and for loans to low-income rural families when such loans had a reasonable prospect of increasing family income. The 1965 Housing and Urban Development Act authorized the Farmers Home Administration to make personal loans for the purchase of previously occupied homes and farms or for improvements in farm buildings. Although progress was made during the 1960's, the rural development program was limited by substantial cuts in funds that resulted from a drive to cut expenditures on domestic programs during 1964 and 1965.

In his first State of the Union message, Jan. 22, 1970, President Richard M. Nixon said "We must create a new rural environment that will not only stem the migration to urban centers but reverse it. If we seize our growth as a challenge, we can make the 1970's an historic period when by conscious choice we transform our land into what we want it to become."

Congress, in the Agricultural Act of 1970, committed itself to the goal of achieving a sound balance between rural and urban America and to giving the highest priority to the revitalization and development of rural areas. The funding of the principal rural development programs was substantially increased from 1.369 billion for fiscal year 1969 to 2.668 billion for fiscal year 1971.

Nixon approved the Rural Development Act of 1972 on Aug. 17, 1972. This legislation expanded the basic statutory missions of the Department of Agriculture to include rural development and empowered the secretary of agriculture to coordinate the rural development work of all departments and agencies of the federal government and to focus their programs on rural development. The purpose of the legislation was "to encourage and speed up economic growth in rural areas, to provide the jobs and income required to support better community facilities and services, to improve the quality of rural life, and to do so on a self-earned, self-sustaining basis." The Rural Development Act of 1972 established, for the first time, a framework for the organization of a comprehensive the rural population, and others living in rural areas made by the mid-1970's, neither adequate leadership nor funds had been provided to fully implement the law.

[Wayne D. Rasmussen and Gladys L. Baker, *The Department of Agriculture;* U.S. Country Life Commission, *Report;* U.S. Department of Agriculture, *Yearbooks* (1940, 1963, 1970, 1971).]

GLADYS L. BAKER

RURAL ELECTRIFICATION ADMINISTRATION. *See* **New Deal.**

RURAL FREE DELIVERY, a service designed to bring mail directly to rural people, was initiated on an experimental basis in 1896. Cities had had a similar service as of July 1, 1863. The need to extend free delivery service in the interest of equity and of making daily newspapers available to the majority of the nation's citizens who lived in rural areas was recognized. The problems were cost and feasibility of constructing a large network through sparsely settled areas. Opposition from local merchants and local postmasters, who feared the loss of business or of jobs, was a factor in the delay. Rep. Thomas E. Watson of Georgia was the author of the first free rural delivery legislation, enacted in 1893 and providing $10,000 for an experiment, but he was not the first to promote the extension of the city delivery system to rural areas. An earlier bill had been introduced by Rep. James O'Donnell of Michigan that embodied the proposal of Postmaster General John Wanamaker. The O'Donnell bill would have provided $6 million, a sum suggested by the postmaster general. The House Committee on Post Offices and Post Roads had refused to report out the O'Donnell bill because of the cost. Although Watson's bill was enacted in 1893, service was not started until 1896 because of the opposition of Postmaster General Wilson S. Bissell, who succeeded Wanamaker in 1893.

Congress had added $20,000 in 1894 and directed the postmaster general to make a report. Initiation had to await the appointment of a postmaster general who was willing to start the experiment. In the meantime, petitions were pouring in to Congress from local and state organizations of the National Grange, which had called for rural free delivery (RFD) during 1891, and from other organizations of farmers. Charges of favoritism and discrimination were made. In 1896 Congress added another $10,000 appropriation, and Postmaster General William L. Wilson, who had succeeded Bissell, decided to experiment with five rural routes in his home state of West Virginia. Between the autumn of 1896 and the spring of 1897, eighty-two pioneer routes were started, scattered through twenty-eight states and the territory of Arizona. In testing the cost, Wilson laid the pioneer routes in areas having a sparse population and no roads as well as in more favorable areas. He estimated that extending the service nationally would cost between $40 million and $50 million.

After Wilson left office, Perry S. Heath, the first assistant postmaster general, and August W. Machen, superintendent of free delivery, adroit politicians who favored extension of the system, began active promotion of RFD. Securing an appropriation of $150,000 in 1898, they announced that any group of farmers wanting a mail route need only petition their congressman for it, sending a description of their communities and their roads. Congressmen were overwhelmed with petitions they could not resist. In 1902 there were not more than 8,000 routes in the nation. Three years later there were 32,000.

By 1915 the number of rural mail carriers was 43,718, as against 33,062 city mail carriers. Routes continued to be organized until the mid-1920's, and in 1925 the number of rural mail carriers reached 45,315. Afterward consolidation of routes based on the use of automobiles brought sharp declines. In 1970 there were 31,346 rural routes extending 2,044,335 miles, or an average of about 65 miles per route.

Rural free delivery, by bringing daily delivery of newspapers with news of national and world events, changing fashions, and market quotations and by delivering mail-order catalogs, was of major importance in breaking down rural isolation. The rural free delivery system was probably the most important factor in the development of a parcel post system. It also played an important part in the good roads movement. Rural free delivery ranks as one of the great accomplishments of the Post Office, but it could not have occurred without strong pressure from farmers and their organizations.

[Gerald Cullinan, *The Post Office Department;* Wayne E. Fuller, *RFD: The Changing Face of Rural America.*]

GLADYS L. BAKER

RURAL HEALTH. Since public health prior to the 20th century was conceived largely in terms of epidemic diseases, the health of the rural population of America, which faced neither large-scale sanitary problems nor major epidemics, received little consideration. Leaving out the frontier, where life was both dangerous and full of drudgery, rural Americans for most of history enjoyed better health than their urban

counterparts. Relative isolation enabled them to avoid many communicable diseases, and their waste products were absorbed into the natural environment. The rising standard of living, which proved of chief benefit to urbanites, and the creation of effective city health departments swung the balance in favor of city-dwellers during the 20th century. Dependent on rural areas for water, milk, and other supplies, municipalities, at the turn of the century, began promoting health activities beyond their boundaries for their own protection. For example, in the late 19th century New York City secured the passage of state laws requiring residents and communities in the Croton watershed to make adequate provision for sewage disposal. The city also began sending its milk inspectors out to farms and dairies to safeguard its milk supplies.

At about the same time state health departments were set up. Although theoretically responsible for the state as a whole, their chief concern was with towns and incorporated areas; they had little direct effect on rural health. Initiative for public health action has traditionally come from local communities, and rural areas had neither the interest nor the financial base to establish effective health units. The first three county health departments in America grew out of the needs of their urban centers. In 1908 the city of Louisville, Ky., extended its health services into the surrounding county of Jefferson; in 1911 Greensboro, N.C., turned its health department into a county unit; and in the same year a major typhoid epidemic in Yakima, Wash., led to the appointment of a full-time health officer for all of Yakima County.

The Rockefeller Foundation gave a sharp impetus to the rural health movement in 1910 when it allocated $1 million to eradicate hookworm in the rural South. Within a few years county health departments began springing up throughout the region. Meanwhile, the U.S. Public Health Service became interested in pellagra and typhoid fever, two diseases plaguing many rural areas. Through health demonstrations in disease control and the encouragement of state health officers, the Public Health Service played an important role in building county health units.

During the 1920's progress toward providing health services for rural areas was slow. As of 1934, when 44 percent of the population lived in communities of less than 2,500, only about 27 percent was provided with full-time county or district health services. The Social Security Act in 1935 opened up a new era in public health. Under Title VI of the act relatively large sums of money were made available for grants-in-aid to promote health work at state and local levels. As a result, by 1942 about 75 percent of the American population was served by health agencies. The majority of the remaining 25 percent lived in small communities and rural areas.

The rising standard of living during World War II and the succeeding years was reflected in improved health for all Americans. Mortality rates declined generally, and the death rates for rural and urban Americans steadily converged. By 1959 the mortality rates and life-expectancy statistics showed virtually no difference between the general level of health in urban and rural areas. Geographic differentials became more important than rural-urban ones as determinants of the level of health, but even they were not significant. The explanation lies in the changing mode of rural life, for by the mid-1970's rural isolation had disappeared in large measure, and over half the rural population no longer lived on farms. In addition, improved health services and access to health facilities in urban centers had steadily contributed to improving rural, as well as urban, health.

[M. Lerner and O. W. Anderson, *Health Progress in the United States, 1900–1960;* Harry S. Mustard, *Rural Health Practice;* Wilson G. Smillie, *Public Health Administration in the United States;* C.-E. A. Winslow, *Health on the Farm and in the Village.*]

JOHN DUFFY

RURAL LIFE, CHANGES IN. Rural life meant farm life in colonial America, and this meaning continued for more than a hundred years after the Declaration of Independence. By 1910 approximately two out of every three rural residents still lived on farms. Although the proportion of farm residents declined after 1920, it was more than one-half of all rural residents in 1940. Not only did farm life set the pattern for rural life in the early days of the country; it also set the pattern for national life.

The first settlers in colonial America were forced into a subsistence level of farming during their early years as colonists, but their food problems were solved within a few years through the adoption of Indian practices and the adaptation of European methods. By the mid-1600's farming methods and farm life were generally fixed, with small subsistence farms in the North and substantial plantations in much of the South.

The self-sufficient farm family in the North produced its own food, clothing, house furnishings, and farm implements, and most of its other needs. Water usually had to be hauled by hand from a spring or well. The Saturday evening bath was taken in the kitchen in the same wooden tub that served for the laundry. Women were responsible for the gardens, and many had to help in the fields. Fireplaces were used for heating and cooking, and chimney flues were the chief source of ventilation in the winter. There was no indoor plumbing, only outdoor privies—and well and spring water were often contaminated by their proximity. Added to the backbreaking drudgery of the farmer and his family were the isolation and lack of adequate communication and social life. After the home, the rural school and church played the largest role in the social life of farm families. The school term of the one-room school was adjusted to fit the needs of youthful labor and also adjusted to the amount of money available to pay the teacher. The school year was frequently limited to four or five months. Classes were often ungraded, progress being based on the completion of graded readers. Since all members of the family participated in the farm work as soon as they were old enough to carry out simple chores, families were close knit. In addition to the common sharing of work, the limited social life was shared.

Farm life in the South before the Civil War differed from that in the North because of the development of staple cash crops, large plantations, and slave labor. The plantation system dominated the economy, and the planters dominated the colonial governments. Yet the small farmers far outnumbered the planters, and the economy of that vast group was largely one of self-sufficiency. Life on the plantation for the planter and his family was sharply different from that of the small-scale farmer. Living in a spacious house and served by slaves, the planter did not depend on the local community for his social life or for the education of his children. His slaves lived in cabins about 16 to 18 feet wide, with lean-to roofs. In rare instances, the cabins had brick fireplaces. The hours of field hands were sometimes limited by colonies and states to sixteen hours. Nearly all states had regulations prohibiting teaching slaves to read and write.

After the Civil War many of the plantations were broken up, but the planters who retained their old estates and the newcomers who acquired many of the plantations devised a new labor system that gave the former slave no more economic security than he had had in slavery. The sharecropper was hired before the spring planting season to grow a crop of cotton or tobacco, the number of acres varying with the number of his children able to work. The owner gave close supervision to everything the sharecropper did. At the end of the season the whole crop was taken by the landlord, who assessed its value, deducted what the cropper owed him from his share, and paid for the remainder, if any.

The rise of manufacturing with its resulting concentration of population in towns and cities after 1820, providing a market for farmers, brought about important changes in farming and in rural life. With cash for their crops, farmers could turn to the factories to obtain the clothes, tools, and furniture they had formerly made for themselves. Sons and daughters of farmers began migrating to mill towns to take up a new way of life. Those who remained behind began developing a taste for urban standards of living. Changes took place slowly, but by 1900 the movement of farm people to towns and cities, the decline in the rural church, the lag in rural education, and the loss of farm ownership led to the fear that rural culture would be lost. As a result, the first studies of rural life began to be made, in the early 1900's, and rural sociology was organized as a field of study.

Concern over migration to the cities and the deficiencies of rural life led President Theodore Roosevelt to appoint the Country Life Commission in 1908. In its assessment of agricultural conditions the commission stated that taken altogether farmers were prosperous when measured by the past but that the progress of agriculture was not satisfactory when compared with that of business.

Commercialization of agriculture after the Civil War contributed to the improvement of rural life. The development of organizations and agricultural fairs for the improvement of agriculture expanded the social life of farm people and contributed to their education. The first important national organization of farmers, the National Grange, was started in 1867 by Oliver Hudson Kelley, a clerk in the U.S. Department of Agriculture who felt a national fraternal organization devoted to the improvement of education and social and cultural life would contribute to the improvement of farming and rural life. Although the Grange soon began to emphasize the economic interest of farmers, it continued to provide a program of education and social life for the entire family. The National Farmers' Alliance and Industrial Union and other farm organizations that followed the Grange also helped to break down the isolation of rural life.

Improvements in methods of communication and their extension to rural areas were other factors of major importance. Rural free delivery to bring mail directly to rural people was initiated in 1896, and the parcel post system in 1913, making it possible for rural families to order not only clothes and farm equipment but also toys and other nonessentials from catalogs.

The development of telephone lines in rural areas and their general availability after 1949 and the introduction of radio and motion pictures in the 1920's and television in the 1950's had important roles in breaking down isolation and in eliminating rural-urban differences in customs and habits. Improvements in methods of transportation, particularly the introduction of the automobile, made it possible for farm people as well as city people to travel to distant areas. Farm people were no longer limited for shopping and entertainment to the immediate community. The organization on a nationwide basis in 1914 of the Federal-State Cooperative Extension Service, with its county agricultural agents, home demonstration agents, and 4-H clubs contributed to social life as well as education.

The disastrous depression in agriculture that began in 1920 led to intense pressure from farmers and farm organizations for government to raise farm prices and to increase the standard of living of farm people. Beginning in 1933 many new government programs were instituted that, with modifications, remained in effect in the mid-1970's—price support and adjustment, rehabilitation and development, and rural electrification.

The widespread extension of electrification to rural areas after 1935 made it possible for the farm family to enjoy many of the conveniences of the city and to automate some farm operations. And rural electrification was one of the factors that enabled farmers to increase production greatly during World War II. The great wartime demand for food and the doubling of farm prices led to the adoption of many technological improvements that revolutionized agricultural production. The number of persons supplied with food and fiber by one farm worker increased from 9.75 in 1930 to 15.50 in 1950. Production efficiency continued to increase until, by 1971, one farm worker was producing enough for 49.2 people.

The result of such a great increase in the efficiency of farm production was a decline in the farm population from 30.5 million in 1940 to less than 10 million in 1970. As a total of the U.S. population the percentage of farm population fell from 23.2 in 1940 to 4.8 in 1970. About one-fifth of the rural population was constituted of farm people in 1970, as against three-fifths in 1920. The percentage of farm operators who were tenants was 25.6 in 1880 and 35.3 in 1900. It reached a high of 42 in the 1930's, but by 1954 had fallen to 24.4, and by 1969, to 12.9.

RURAL POST ROADS ACT

Some rural residents who are not engaged in farming supply goods, services, machinery, feed, fuel, fertilizer, or labor to farmers. Some provide financing, marketing services, or primary processing of agricultural products. Others perform the many activities that are related to farming but generally are no longer done on farms, such as hatching chickens, making butter and cheese, and slaughtering poultry and meat animals.

Rural residents receive less than their national share of income, health services, education, and government services for the disadvantaged. Of the rural population of the United States in the mid-1970's, one person out of every four is poor as compared with one person in eight in the cities and one person in fifteen in the metropolitan areas. Furthermore, the incidence of poverty in most rural counties, those not in commuting distance of urban employment centers, was double that in nonrural counties. With 12 percent of the nation's population, these rural counties had 24 percent of the nation's poor, but only about 2 percent of federal outlays for basic adult education, 6 percent of health services, and 17 percent of appropriations for elementary and secondary education.

Statistical measures of income and standard of living showed rural people at a national disadvantage in the mid-1970's, but on the basis of less tangible standards and values many rural people preferred to remain in nonurban areas. Many rural people believed that the uncrowded environment was beneficial in the rearing of children, and farm people in particular believed in family enterprise as salutary. Many farm people cherish traditional rural values: dedication to independence; belief that agriculture is man's fundamental employment, upon which other economic activities depend; and conviction that farming is a natural life and therefore a good life.

[L. C. Gray, *History of Agriculture in the Southern United States to 1860;* U.S. Country Life Commission, *Report;* U.S. Department of Agriculture, *Agricultural Statistics* (1957, 1973), *Century of Service: The First Hundred Years of the United States Department of Agriculture,* and *Yearbooks of Agriculture* (1940, 1963, 1970, 1971).]

GLADYS L. BAKER

RURAL POST ROADS ACT was passed in 1916 to provide for aid to the states by the federal government in the construction of rural post roads. Under the provisions of this measure, the secretary of agriculture was authorized to cooperate with the states in the construction of such roads. The term ''rural post road'' was construed, with certain limitations, to mean any public road over which the U.S. mails were then, or thereafter might be, transported. The measure carried with it an appropriation for the current fiscal year of $5 million, which was to be increased annually until, for the fifth year, the amount available would be $25 million. (*See also* Rural Free Delivery.)

I. HOWELL KANE

RUSH-BAGOT AGREEMENT. *See* **Great Lakes Disarmament Agreement.**

RUSSELL, MAJORS, AND WADDELL. William H. Russell of Missouri and Alexander Majors, a Kentuckian, formed a partnership on Dec. 28, 1854, and procured a contract for carrying government supplies from Fort Leavenworth, Kans., to the Plains and mountain army posts, for which work they used about 350 wagons. The sending of an army force to Utah in 1857 brought them a greatly increased business; they took in another partner, William B. Waddell, and in 1858 they carried 16 million pounds of government freight. To achieve this, they increased their equipment to 4,000 men, 3,500 wagons, 1,000 mules, and 40,000 oxen. When the Pikes Peak gold rush began, Russell, against his partners' wishes, formed a partnership in May 1859 with John S. Jones as the Leavenworth and Pikes Peak Express. The new company was soon in financial difficulties, and Russell, Majors, and Waddell took it over. They also absorbed Hockaday and Liggett's stage line from Saint Joseph, Mo., to Salt Lake City, reorganized as the Central Overland California and Pikes Peak Express. In 1860–61 they operated the Pony Express. Their losses in these ventures were so heavy that they were forced out of business. On Mar. 21, 1862, Ben Holladay took over the Salt Lake stage line on foreclosure, and soon afterward the partnership of Russell, Majors, and Waddell was dissolved.

[Alexander Majors, *Seventy Years on the Frontier.*]

ALVIN F. HARLOW

RUSSELL SAGE FOUNDATION, one of America's oldest general-purpose foundations, was established in 1907 by Margaret Olivia Sage (Mrs. Russell Sage) for the improvement of social and living conditions in the United States. She originally provided a principal of $10 million and later added another $5 million.

The foundation was created at a time when money for the study of social science problems was scarce.

In its early years the foundation sought to investigate the causes of adverse social conditions and bring these conditions to the attention of the public. The foundation was influential in helping to effect change in a number of areas; for example, child welfare, working conditions for women, education, and social work.

In later years the foundation funded social science research, giving primary attention to the application of this research to policy formation in the areas of social change, law, education, human resources, mass media, and biology. The foundation maintains a professional staff of social scientists who conduct their own research and advise on a wide range of projects.

In addition to funding research, the foundation assures dissemination of the results of its research findings by supporting an active publications program. By 1975 the foundation had published more than 250 books and 300 pamphlets. The books are sold commercially, and the income from their sale is used to help finance additional publications. Headquartered in New York City, the foundation employed a support staff of approximately thirty-five people in 1975.

[John M. Glenn, Lilian Brandt, and F. Emerson Andrews, *Russell Sage Foundation, 1907–1946.*]

JEAN C. YODER

RUSSIA, U.S. RELATIONS WITH. Ever-shifting European alliances found Russia a British ally during the American Revolution. It is probable that Russia did not send troops to aid England because of the more immediate threats posed by Sweden and Poland and because of the irksome comments of England's George III that Russia was a "half-barbarian nation." Although furious at these slights and England's inability to control its colonies, Catherine II promised to withhold recognition so long as England considered the Americans rebels. Catherine had successfully kept Russia out of the European war that followed and was in part spawned by the American Revolution. Her formation of the Armed Neutrality of the North (1780), however, was directed specifically at England. Even so, Russia did not extend diplomatic recognition to the newly formed American nation. In the interim, a backdoor diplomacy existed from December 1780, when Francis Dana was sent to Russia. While the American minister's mission to Saint Petersburg was unsuccessful insofar as recognition was concerned, his efforts in commercial areas brought an increase in Russo-American trade. At the same time

American ideas found their way into Russian intellectual circles. The Bill of Rights, criminal law, and freedom of printing were eulogized by such political thinkers as Aleksandr N. Radishchev.

When the Franco-Russian alliance (1807) brought war with England, Alexander I formally recognized the United States (1809). Russia's expression of friendship was as much tied to its aims in North America as to problems with England. In return for a U.S. prohibition of arms sales to the Indians of the Pacific Northwest, Russia offered to limit its expansion to north of the Columbia River. The Russians also offered to restrict trade with their settlements in Alaska to American ships if the United States would let Russia into the China trade.

Although the United States refused these offers, the issues remained important. The Anglo-American War of 1812 proved inconvenient for Russia in its struggle against Napoleon Bonaparte, but it was the czar's ukase of 1821 warning all foreign vessels to stay outside 100 miles of the Pacific coast north of the fifty-first parallel and Russia's claim of exclusive trading right in the North Pacific that proved to be the significant events of the next two decades. A series of American warnings culminated in the Monroe Doctrine (1823), indirectly aimed at Russia. Through negotiation a treaty was signed (Apr. 17, 1824) limiting Russian influence to the region north of 54°40′. This became the first formal Russo-American agreement.

Although Americans generally abhorred Russian suppression of the Polish rebellion (1830) and czarist support of Austria during the revolt led by Lajos Kossuth in Hungary (1848–49), relations between the two nations continued on a friendly course into the period of the American Civil War. When Russia refused to be drawn into European schemes to meddle in the war it received assurances of American friendship over any other European power. The arrival of Russian warships in Union ports in 1863 caused speculation of a military alliance. In actuality, Russia, fearing war in Europe, had simply moved its fleet to safer waters. Because this fact was not made known for many years, the event marked a high point in friendship and had a direct influence on the purchase of Alaska. Since America had made overtures concerning Alaska, Russia saw the opportunity to unload a burdensome liability at a profit and at the same time deal a blow to British ambitions in the Pacific. Hints of a willingness to sell were eagerly accepted and the agreement was signed on Mar. 30, 1867. The ensuing uproar in Congress abated only when Alaska's potential was realized; some even visualized the acquisition as a stepping-stone to the annexation of Canada. Although relations remained friendly and a number of treaties were negotiated, points of friction began to develop by the turn of the century.

There had been a general agreement among the nations sending troops to China during the Boxer Rebellion (1900) to withdraw immediately, but Russia still occupied Manchuria in 1903, with the intent of annexation. Realizing the challenge to its own plans for the region, Japan attacked the Russian base at Port Arthur in northeast China (Feb. 8, 1904). The ensuing war saw the United States side with Japan, as much because of unhappiness with Russian excesses in the Siberian exile system and its treatment of Jews as in the naive hope that Japan was acting within the framework of the Open Door policy. At the Portsmouth (N.H.) Conference, Theodore Roosevelt, acting as mediator, hammered out an agreement (Sept. 5, 1905) unfavorable to Russia. As a result, Japan became the dominant power in the Far East.

With the fall of the Romanov dynasty in March 1917, the United States saw its impending entry into World War I as a struggle against autocracy. The provisional government that replaced the czarist regime was immediately recognized and, after the United States entered the war, $325 million was allocated to bolster Russian determination to stay in the fight. The weakness of the government of Aleksandr F. Kerenski and increased German pressure on the battlefield set the stage for the Bolshevik seizure of power in November.

Almost at once, the Bolsheviks announced a "decree for peace," declaring the U.S. role in the war as nothing more than a means of exploiting the American arms industry. The publication of secret agreements with the czarist government infuriated the Allies; but the desire to keep Russia in the war was paramount, and little could be done to stop the propaganda except to withhold acceptance of the Soviet government. This led to the unusual situation of Allied embassies continuing to operate in a state none of them recognized.

The American mission in Petrograd was in a precarious position; members of the staff, including the ambassador, were threatened or arrested. All discussions with Soviet officials were immediately broadcast to the world as either statements of formal U.S. recognition or as American apologies for past misdeeds. Even Woodrow Wilson's Fourteen Points statement (Jan. 8, 1918) concerning noninterference in Russian internal affairs failed to dissuade the Bolsheviks in their quest for immediate peace and world

revolution. The subsequent signing of the Treaty of Brest-Litovsk (Mar. 3, 1918) set into motion reactions felt around the world.

Russia, suffering from grievous losses against the Germans, now found itself in a civil war involving a number of factions. In early 1919 three "governments" claimed *de facto* status: the Bolshevik government and the rival groups led by Aleksandr V. Kolchak and by Anton I. Denikin. The end of the war in France found the Allies divided but adamant that Russia would not sit at Versailles if it could not find a legitimate government. Bolshevik appeals for revolution in Europe and Red Army expansion into the Ukraine so infuriated the Allies that any prospect of seating the Soviet delegation disappeared. Kolchak and the others who attempted to rally anti-Communist forces all failed, and by November 1920 the Bolsheviks remained as the only viable government. Although the Allied intervention had ended (January 1920) and the blockade of Soviet-controlled ports was lifted, Russia found itself isolated, especially from America. In 1921 the United States preemptorily excluded Soviet participation in the Washington Conference on the Limitation of Armaments but at the same time sent the Hoover mission to aid in Russian famine relief.

Although most European powers and China had granted diplomatic recognition to the Soviet Union in 1924, the United States still refused, seeing in Soviet activities at home and abroad the same manifestations of tyranny that had led to America's disavowal of friendship in late czarist times. But, as happened before Russia's recognition of the United States in 1809, backdoor relations existed, as American businessmen extended their interests into the Soviet Union. When the Great Depression hit, the opportunity of compounding America's economic problems was not overlooked by the Soviet Union: it dumped huge quantities of wheat and other commodities on the market. America's retaliatory embargoes, coupled with embitterment over U.S. support of Japan during the conflict of 1929, created great animosity in Moscow, but in 1933 the realization of the potential of the Russian market, a new American administration, and a more Western-oriented Soviet foreign policy finally brought American recognition (Nov. 16). By the end of 1939 the Soviet agreements with Nazi Germany, the attack on Finland, and the seizure of the Baltic states again strained relations between Washington and Moscow. There were hopes in 1940 that the Soviet Union would break away from Germany, but the signing of the Russo-Japanese Neutrality Pact (Apr.

13, 1941) and the Soviet rejection of U.S. warnings of an imminent German invasion negated any hope of improving relations at the moment.

When Germany invaded the Soviet Union on June 22, 1941, Britain immediately announced support of the USSR. The United States followed suit two days later, offering support on a cash-and-carry basis. Within a week the Soviets had requested $1.8 billion in aid. The provisions of lend-lease were not extended to the Soviet Union until Nov. 7. By the end of the war, $9.5 billion in aid had been furnished.

America's entry into the war in December ended all debate on "measures short of war," and a joint effort against the common enemy began. Joseph Stalin received Franklin D. Roosevelt's assurances that a second front would be opened in France before the end of 1942. By August it had become obvious that the promise could not be kept, and Winston Churchill's explanation of the facts to Stalin laid seeds of distrust of Western intentions that have remained to this day. Russia stoically continued its fight, bearing the brunt of the German onslaught until the Allied invasions on June 6, 1944, forced the enemy to face two opponents on the Continent.

Important points affecting future U.S.-Soviet relations arose at all the major wartime allied conferences. In October 1943 the initial steps were taken at Moscow toward forming the United Nations, and Stalin promised that after Germany's defeat, Soviet support would be given to the Allied fight in the Pacific. At Tehran, Iran (November-December 1943), Stalin subscribed to the provisions of the Atlantic Charter even though he was convinced that the United States would withdraw from the Continent once Germany was defeated. At the Yalta Conference (February 1945) numerous Western concessions were made in return for Stalin's reaffirmation of the pledge of assistance against Japan. The subsequent American use of the atomic bomb, along with Japan's loss of will to continue the war, were to change the situation drastically, but not before the Russians had gained much that had been lost at Portsmouth four decades earlier.

At Yalta and the subsequent meetings at Potsdam, Germany (July 1945), and Moscow (December 1945), the Russians demanded that their needs be given priority in the determination of German reparations, so that Russia could rebuild its own economic base. It was the U.S. and British positions that nothing be done to Germany that would further the economic problems of the Allies. Although there was no resolution of the issue and the Soviets systematically stripped the industrial potential in their areas of oc-

cupation, they have consistently held the refusal of the Allies to grant this demand as an indication of the West's desire to see the collapse of the Soviet Union.

The creation of the United Nations after the Dumbarton Oaks Conference (August-September 1944), held near Washington, D.C., and the inaugural meeting at San Francisco (April-June 1945) saw the United States and the Soviet Union both seated as permanent members of the Security Council. In drafting the UN Charter, the Soviet Union sponsored a position of unanimity on all decisions. This position has brought the two nations into a number of confrontations over the years.

While the immediate postwar period saw attention drawn to problems at home, disagreement between the Allies, already developing during the war, led to an almost complete collapse of East-West cooperation. Some accounts hold that the cold war began as early as 1944, when the Soviets coined the new slogan "The war on Fascism ends, the war on capitalism begins." By August 1945, when Michael I. Kalinin, the titular chief of state of the USSR, stated that many of Russia's enemies still existed, the lines had been drawn. Stalin's reiteration in February 1946 that war was inevitable so long as capitalism existed left little doubt in anyone's mind that a state of ideological warfare existed with the United States. Conferences held in Europe did settle most of the issues relating to the former Axis powers but left the question of what to do about Germany and Austria unresolved. When the United States offered to support Greece and Turkey and began economic aid to Europe (1947), the Soviet Union refused to cooperate and established its own recovery program in Eastern Europe. In effect, the result was the formulation of two spheres separated by "an iron curtain."

The next decade saw the failure of the Soviet attempt to blockade Berlin (1948), the creation of the North Atlantic Treaty Organization (NATO, 1949), and the belated countercoalition, the Warsaw Pact (1955). In 1950 the attack on South Korea led the United States into armed conflict with Soviet-supported powers. Even so, it was Soviet initiatives in 1951 that helped bring about an armistice in 1953. A period of lessening tension followed Stalin's death (Mar. 5, 1953) that culminated in Nikita S. Khrushchev's visit to the United States in September 1959. The spirit of the Camp David summit meeting was destroyed eight months later when the Soviet Union shot down an American U-2 spyplane (May 1, 1960) near Sverdlovsk in central Russia. Wnen Khrushchev demanded an apology from the United States, President Dwight D. Eisenhower refused and the summit conference just beginning in Paris to settle the Berlin question collapsed. The Vienna conference (June 1961) between Khrushchev and President John F. Kennedy also failed to reach agreement on Berlin. In retaliation, the Communists cut off east-west access in the city by constructing the Berlin Wall. Although this led to a confrontation, it did not reach the magnitude of the Cuban missile crisis, which brought the Soviet Union and the United States to the brink of war. Kennedy's announcement in late October 1962 that Soviet-manned offensive missile emplacements had been discovered in Cuba brought an irate American reaction. Kennedy saw the Soviet move as a violation of the Monroe Doctrine, one that would require the use of armed force to remedy if the Soviet Union failed to heed a series of warnings. At the eleventh hour, Khrushchev relented and agreed to withdraw the weapons.

The following year (Aug. 5, 1963) a nuclear test-ban treaty was signed and much of the antagonism of the preceding decade abated. The assassination of Kennedy saw the Soviet Union make unprecedented gestures of goodwill.

Since 1963 the Soviet Union and the United States have taken a number of steps toward rapprochement. While much of the Soviet cooperativeness may have been a reaction to Communist China's growing independence, it is also evident that both nations fully appreciated the warmaking potential of the other and were actively seeking other means to settle their differences. The beginning of the 1970's showed even more promise in spite of the problems posed by Vietnam. Signs of détente became evident in such areas as space exploration and cultural exchanges, and President Richard Nixon visited the Soviet Union. A controversial sale of grain to Russia illustrated a certain naiveté in American dealings with the Soviets that manifested itself in a slackening of U.S. confidence in dealing with the Soviets. Other problems, such as the Middle East situation, Jewish emigration from the Soviet Union, and an undiminishing arms competition tended to lessen the effects of Russo-American cooperation. (*See also* Cold War.)

[Samuel Flagg Bemis, *Diplomatic History of the United States;* Basil Dmytryshyn, *USSR: A Concise History;* William Hayter, *Russia and the World;* Oliver Jensen, ed., *America and Russia: A Century and a Half of Dramatic Encounters;* Marx M. Laserson, *The American Impact on Russia, 1784–1917;* Alexander Tarsaidze, *Czars and Presidents.*]

JOHN E. JESSUP, JR.

RUSSIAN-AMERICAN COMPANY. *See* **Russian Claims.**

RUSSIAN CLAIMS. The creation of the Russian-American Company in 1799, with Aleksandr A. Baranov as manager, was the first occasion for Russia to define its claims to North American lands. The charter, granted by Czar Paul I, established a monopoly of Russian-American trade and, of necessity, gave some indication of the territorial limits within which the trade could be carried on. These extended from the fifty-fifth parallel to the Bering Strait and included the "Aleutian, Kurile, and other islands situated in the northeastern ocean."

The company was also empowered to make new discoveries to the south as well as to the north of the fifty-fifth parallel, a privilege the company soon began to exercise, as well as an additional privilege of attempting trade with neighboring or attainable peoples, such as the Japanese. It was soon learned that the great market for furs was at Canton, China, so the statesmen of the company, notably Count Nikolai Petrovich Rezanov, planned a great trade route that would embrace the Asian islands and tie all in with the Alaska fur trade with Canton.

The problem of securing supplies for the Alaskan establishments caused the Russians to look toward the Spanish settlements far to the South. Rezanov himself made a voyage to Spanish California in order to procure food for the Alaskans; and he was interested in making a farming settlement in the valley of the Columbia, but failed to enter the river. Finally, it was decided to plant a colony on the California coast above the Spanish settlements. Fort Ross, begun in 1809 at Bodega Bay in what is now Marin County, was intended as a supply station for meat and grain. No agreement was ever made with the Spaniards in regard to the California lands thus occupied; and finally, in 1841, the Fort Ross settlement was abandoned as no longer useful.

In 1821, on renewing the charter of the Russian-American Company, the Russian government declared its authority would extend as far down the coast as fifty-one degrees north latitude. The ukase setting forth that claim alarmed Great Britain and the United States, both of whose governments were by that time (1821) claiming territory on the northwest coast. In consequence, both these governments protested successfully, and each succeeded in limiting Russia's exclusive claim to the southern line of 54°40′ north latitude. The British-Russian treaty of

1825 also delimited the Russian claims from the coast inland, thus establishing the basis for the boundary of Alaska as granted by Russia to the United States in 1867. (*See also* Alaska Boundary Question.)

[Frank A. Golder, *Bering's Voyages;* J. Schafer, *The Pacific Slope and Alaska.*]

JOSEPH SCHAFER

RUSSIAN FLEETS, VISIT OF. In September 1863, during the Civil War, six Russian warships under Rear Adm. Stepan S. Lesovsky arrived at New York, and, in October, six more warships under Rear Adm. Andrei A. Popov anchored off San Francisco. The northern states warmly welcomed both fleets, believing that they came as possible allies. Popov, indeed, when a threatened attack on San Francisco by the Confederate raiders *Alabama* and *Sumter* was reported, ordered his ships to "clear for action." On Apr. 25, 1864, both fleets were ordered home. The Russians had not come as northern allies, but, fearing war with Great Britain and probable blockade, both fleets had been ordered to neutral ports, from which, if war were declared, they might make raids on British merchant shipping.

[F. A. Golder, "The Russian Fleet and the Civil War," *American Historical Review* (1915); W. F. Johnson, *America's Foreign Relations.*]

LOUIS H. BOLANDER

RUSSIAN RECOGNITION. On Nov. 7, 1917, the government of Aleksandr F. Kerenski in Russia was overthrown by the Bolsheviks who, the following February, annulled all state debts. Because of this and because of Communist propaganda in the United States, the administrations of Woodrow Wilson, Warren G. Harding, Calvin Coolidge, and Herbert Hoover refused to recognize the Soviet government. President Franklin D. Roosevelt, believing that recognition would stimulate trade, invited the Soviet Union to send a representative to discuss the matter. As a result, he accorded recognition on Nov. 16, 1933.

[Samuel Flagg Bemis, *A Diplomatic History of the United States.*]

ERIK MCKINLEY ERIKSSON

RUSTLERS. *See* **Cattle Rustlers.**

RUSTLER WAR, a conflict centering in Johnson County, Wyo., between ranchmen and a large group of alleged cattle rustlers, and their friends. Finding it

impossible to stop cattle stealing or to secure convictions in the local courts, owing to the fact that jurors and county officials were either intimidated by the rustlers or sympathized with them, the cattlemen resolved to take matters into their own hands. In April 1892 they brought in a group of hired gunmen from Texas and organized an expedition of about forty-five men to hunt down and kill some seventy men who they claimed were known to be cattle thieves. The expedition first visited the K. C. Ranch, where two men, alleged to be thieves, were killed. The cattlemen soon met resistance and took refuge in the buildings of the T A Ranch, where they were besieged for three days by a force of some 200 men. On the request of the governor of Wyoming, President Benjamin Harrison sent U.S. troops commanded by Col. James Van Horn from Fort McKinney to the scene of disorder. The cattlemen, whose situation had grown desperate, gladly surrendered. They were delivered over to the civil courts for trial, but were all eventually acquitted. (*See also* Cattle Associations.)

[Frank Canton, *Frontier Trails;* Robert B. David, *Malcolm Campbell, Sheriff.*]

EDWARD EVERETT DALE

RUTGERS UNIVERSITY was chartered as Queens College in 1766 and began operations in New Brunswick, N.J., in 1771. The eighth of nine colleges founded in the colonial period, it owed its origin to the Dutch Reformed church, with which it remained affiliated for nearly a century. In 1825 its name was changed to Rutgers College to honor a benefactor, Col. Henry Rutgers of New York City. It became the land-grant college of New Jersey in 1864. In 1945 Rutgers achieved legal recognition as the state university, and in 1956 management of the institution was vested in a board of governors, a majority of whose members were state appointees. The university grew rapidly after 1945. A Newark campus was established in 1946 and a Camden campus in 1952. By 1974 Rutgers had eleven undergraduate and six graduate divisions, enrolling 36,000 students.

[Richard P. McCormick, *Rutgers: A Bicentennial History.*]

RICHARD P. MCCORMICK

RUTGERS V. WADDINGTON. *See* **Trespass Act.**

RYSWICK, PEACE OF, signed Sept. 30, 1697, ended King William's War between the English and

French and the Iroquois and French. By its provisions all conquests made during the war were to be mutually restored. But the ownership of the lands lying around Hudson Bay was to be decided by an Anglo-French joint commission. Such a commission met in 1699 but failed to reach a decision.

[F. G. Davenport, ed., *European Treaties Bearing on the History of the United States and Its Dependencies*, vol. II.]
MAX SAVELLE

SABBATH-DAY HOUSES were small buildings where members of a congregation who had come from a distance would take refuge between the morning and afternoon church services. Considered typical of colonial New England, somewhat similar conditions saw their revival in the West where, at least in Texas, they lasted into the 20th century.

[A. M. Earle, *The Sabbath in Puritan New England.*]
FREDERICK L. BRONNER

SABINE CROSSROADS, BATTLE AT (Apr. 8, 1864). During his raid up the Red River Valley in Louisiana, in the spring of 1864, Union Gen. Nathaniel P. Banks was unable to get his fleet above Grand Ecore, near Natchitoches. He then marched overland toward Shreveport, but was met and defeated by Confederate forces under Gen. Richard Taylor in the Battle of Sabine Crossroads, about forty miles south of Shreveport, thus ending the Union advance on Shreveport and causing the abandonment of the campaign.

[C. A. Evans, ed., *Confederate Military History.*]
WALTER PRICHARD

SABINE RIVER BOUNDARY. *See* **Louisiana Purchase, Boundaries of; Neutral Ground.**

SABLE ISLAND, about 150 miles east of Halifax, Nova Scotia, was of interest to colonial New Englanders and Acadians as a place to obtain walrus, seal, wild horses, and black foxes. Attempts to make settlements there failed because of the danger to navigation—more than 200 recorded shipwrecks having taken place near the island.

[Harold St. John, "Sable Island," *Boston Society of Natural History Proceedings*, vol. 36, no. 1.]
ROBERT E. MOODY

SABOTAGE, a term that first came into general use in the United States early in the 20th century. It was bor-

rowed from the syndicalist movement of southern Europe and introduced in the United States by the Industrial Workers of the World (IWW) to describe one phase of its fundamental strategy of direct action. This strategy, having a class-struggle animus and a revolutionary aim, involved repudiation of political action and disdain for collective bargaining. Sabotage tactics represented a means of harassing the avowed class enemy—capitalist employers—without forgoing wage income as in strikes.

The practice of sabotage involves injury, in some way, of the employer's property, as by surreptitiously mixing a little sand in lubricating oil. While the methods of sabotage are myriad and need not in all cases involve violence or destruction of plant equipment, the aim is invariably vexation and pecuniary loss to the employer. Methods of somewhat similar import, such as "soldiering on the job" (pretending to work but getting little done), had long been familiar and are still regularly practiced by conservative unionists simply as an incident of effective bargaining procedure: giving as little as need be for as much as can be obtained. But the general terrorist strategy of the IWW made little appeal to American labor, and sabotage never became established in the United States as a concerted, persistent tactic in the labor struggle.

[S. B. Mathewson, *Restriction of Output Among Unorganized Workers*; T. Veblen, *Absentee Ownership.*]
MYRON W. WATKINS

SACCO-VANZETTI CASE. Nicola Sacco, a skilled shoeworker born in 1881, and Bartolomeo Vanzetti, a fish peddler born in 1888, were arrested on May 5, 1920, for a payroll holdup and murder in South Braintree, Mass.; a jury, sitting under Judge Webster Thayer, found the men guilty on July 14, 1921. Complex motions relating to old and new evidence, and to the conduct of the trial, were argued before Thayer, the Massachusetts supreme court, and a special advisory commission serving the governor; the accused did not prevail and were executed on Aug. 23, 1927.

Among the legal issues were these: prejudicial behavior by the prosecutor, complemented by an often inept defense; profane and violent prejudice by the judge against the defendants, expressed outside the courtroom and possibly implicit in his behavior on the bench; possible perjury by a state police captain; refusal to deal with a set of circumstances pointing more exactly to a group of professional criminals; inexpert presentation of ballistics evidence; and failure of the evidence as a whole to remove "reasonable doubt." Throughout the trial the men were disadvantaged by their declared philosophical anarchism, their status as unassimilated alien workers, and the general "Red baiting" atmosphere of the times. Scholarly legal opinion overwhelmingly holds that apart from the question of guilt or innocence, the case is an extremely serious instance of failure in the administration of justice.

Within the United States, Sacco and Vanzetti received from the start the help of compatriots, fellow anarchists, and scattered labor groups. By 1927 they had the support in money, action, and words of major liberal figures, concerned men of law, numerous writers, and, increasingly, organized labor and the Communist party leadership. Nevertheless, it is clear that the majority of persons in the United States who held an opinion, and they were in the millions, believed the verdict sound and approved of the death penalty. By 1927 the case had become a worldwide issue, with many demonstrations against U.S. embassies.

By 1970 the case had inspired 7 novels, 7 plays, 3 television presentations, and 150 poems. Important are Upton Sinclair's novel *Boston* (1928) and Maxwell Anderson's play *Winterset* (1935). Ben Shahn, the artist, produced a notable series of gouaches on Sacco and Vanzetti. The letters written by the men themselves, during their seven years in prison, are regarded by many as the most profoundly human and genuinely literary commentary on the case.

[*The Sacco-Vanzetti Case: Transcript of the Record;* Herbert B. Ehrmann, *The Case That Will Not Die;* Osmond K. Fraenkel, *The Sacco-Vanzetti Case;* G. Louis Joughin and Edmund M. Morgan, *The Legacy of Sacco and Vanzetti;* Robert H. Montgomery, *Sacco-Vanzetti: The Murder and the Myth;* Nicola Sacco and Bartolomeo Vanzetti, *Letters.*]

LOUIS JOUGHIN

SACHEM. The native federation of the Iroquois, the five original tribes of the league, rooted its political organization in a council of fifty sachems. These chiefs represented their respective tribes in deliberations of "peace." The sachem offices were named, and to some degree ranked, and passed to the officeholder through the female line, a reflection of the strong Iroquois emphasis on maternal descent. The component tribes of the Iroquois league were allowed varying numbers of sachems. Thus, the Onondaga, although smallest in numbers, had fourteen sachems, the Mohawk and Oneida nine each, the Cayuga ten, and the Seneca eight. The great council deliberated on

all external affairs affecting the tribes of the federation.

Despite the association with the Iroquois, the term "sachem" is drawn from an Algonkin stem. Among the various Algonkin-speakers of New England, chieftainships were designated as sachemships if a federation was involved, both as a result of Iroquois influence and as a defense against the imperialistic Iroquois. First used in English about 1625 in the sense of any Indian chief, the term was adopted to refer to the ranked officialdom of the Tammany Hall organization in New York City.

[Harold E. Driver, *Indians of North America.*]

ROBERT F. SPENCER

SACKETS HARBOR, OPERATIONS AT. In the War of 1812 the importance of naval control of Lake Ontario made the Sackets Harbor naval base, near its foot, in northern New York, a hive of shipbuilding activity. There seamen, shipwrights, and stores were assembled for Commodore Isaac Chauncey's flotilla, and in 1814 some 600 workers were building two immense three-deckers of more than 100 guns. The base underwent two British attacks, the first, July 19, 1812, being limited to an ineffective two-hour naval bombardment. The second, May 27–29, 1813, was a combined operation by Commodore James Lucas Yeo's squadron and more than 1,000 British regulars and Indians under Gen. George Prevost. Although the base was well fortified and manned by equal forces, the New York militia fled at the first landing of British troops. But as the British approached the blockhouse and barracks, they were held up by sharp fire from regulars and artillery. Gen. Jacob Brown, in chief command, rallied the militia, and at this reinforcement the British retreated to their boats. Losses were: for the British, 52 killed and 211 wounded; and for the Americans, 23 killed and 114 wounded. Stores valued at $500,000 were burned to prevent capture, but two ships on the stocks escaped with slight damage.

[Theodore Roosevelt, *The Naval War of 1812.*]

ALLAN WESTCOTT

SACKVILLE-WEST INCIDENT. In September 1888 Lord Lionel Sackville-West, the British minister at Washington, D.C., received a letter, signed Charles F. Murchison, saying that the writer was a naturalized Englishman who desired advice as to how he should vote in the coming election. The letter was actually written by George Osgoodby, a fruit grower and a Republican. Without suspecting that the letter was only a decoy and that he was being made the victim of a hoax, the minister replied that he thought the incumbent, President Grover Cleveland, more friendly to England than Benjamin Harrison. The Republicans promptly published the correspondence, expecting that the incident would turn the Irish vote away from Cleveland. Sackville-West's explanations only made matters worse. When Prime Minister Robert Gascoyne-Cecil, Marquis of Salisbury, refused to call him home, he was dismissed by Cleveland.

[Allan Nevins, *Grover Cleveland, A Study in Courage.*]

THOMAS L. HARRIS

SACO BAY, SETTLEMENT OF, proceeded from various grants made by the Council for New England. In 1630 Richard Vines, by a grant of Feb. 23, 1629, to John Oldham and himself, began a settlement on the south side of the Saco River, in southwestern Maine; and in 1631 Thomas Lewis and Richard Bonython, by a grant of the same date, began a settlement north of the river. Farther east Thomas Cammock, in 1633, took possession of 1,500 acres granted Nov. 1, 1631; and beyond that was the land granted to Robert Trelawney and Moses Goodyear (Dec. 1, 1631), of which John Winter took possession in 1632, driving out George Cleeve and his partner, Richard Tucker. The majority of the settlers came as employees of, or as settlers under, the proprietors. The settlements were contemporaneously known as Winter Harbor (Biddeford Pool); Saco (Saco and Biddeford), about four miles up the river where Vines, Lewis, and Bonython had their dwellings; Blue Point (Pine Point); Black Point (Prout's Neck); Spurwink (Cape Elizabeth); and Richmond's Island, the main seat of the Trelawney plantation. Andrew Alger, who came with his brother Arthur and Winter, settled Dunstan (the village of Scarboro), claiming under Indian deed. Fishing, farming, lumbering, and trading were the means of livelihood. All the Saco Bay settlements were abandoned during King Philip's War in 1675.

[W. D. Spencer, *Pioneers on Maine Rivers.*]

ROBERT E. MOODY

SACRAMENTO, BATTLE OF (Feb. 28, 1847). During the Mexican War, in order to defend the city of Chihuahua, the Mexicans under Gen. José A. Heredia erected fortifications on the Sacramento River, fifteen miles north. Although superior in number, they were routed with heavy losses by Col. Alex-

ander W. Doniphan's Missouri mounted volunteers, whose casualties were only two killed and seven wounded.

[G. R. Gibson, *Journal of a Soldier Under Kearny and Doniphan.*]

RALPH P. BIEBER

SADDLEBAG BANKS. Under the free bank laws passed by middle western states in 1851–53, anyone purchasing state bonds up to a given amount or higher might start a bank and issue notes in a commensurate sum. Smart promoters "organized" many such banks, giving as their location remote, unknown (sometimes purely imaginary) hamlets, the object being to keep the notes in circulation and make it difficult for any noteholder to collect their face value from the "bank of issue"—often just a crossroads merchant or blacksmith acting as the promoter's agent and holding a small sum in cash to take care of any notes that might come in.

[William Graham Sumner, *A History of Banking in the United States.*]

ALVIN F. HARLOW

SADDLES. Saddles have been of three principal types: (1) the English saddle—a flat tree with low pommel and cantle, introduced into America during the early colonial period; (2) the army saddle—first fully developed during the Civil War and, in its initial form (the McClellan), an English tree modified by heightening pommel and cantle, dishing the seat, and lengthening the stirrup leathers; and (3) the stock saddle—interchangeably termed "cowboy," "cow," "Mexican," "western," and "range" saddle.

The progenitor of the stock saddle was brought to Mexico by Hernando Cortes in 1519. Of the same pattern as that which the Moors carried into Spain during their 8th-century invasion, it was a deeply dished tree with wall-like pommel and cantle. The rider sat in it, rather than on it. On the pommel of the Cortes saddle Mexican vaqueros attached a vertical protuberance (the horn) to which the lariat could be fastened. This Mexican saddle was adopted by western Americans in the 1820's. It became the standard saddle of the West. By facilitating the throwing of a lariat from horseback, riding of bucking broncos, and traveling great distances, it hastened the spread of civilization throughout the Plains.

At the outset of the colonial period women used a pillion (a pad fastened behind the saddle occupied by a rider) on which they sat facing sideways. Soon the pillion was supplanted by the sidesaddle—in its ultimate form, a copy of the man's English tree altered by omitting the right-hand stirrup and adding hooked-shaped pommels that imprisoned the horizontally bent right knee and prevented the left foot from losing its stirrup. Once eastern women began riding astride, about 1900, the sidesaddle gradually disappeared.

Packsaddles for conveyance of goods were of two sorts, the wooden crossbuck and the leathern aparejo. They originated in Spain and came, without change of form, by way of Mexico into the United States.

[S. Dunbar, *History of Travel in America;* J. A. Garland, *The Private Stable;* P. A. Rollins, *The Cowboy.*]

PHILIP ASHTON ROLLINS

SAFETY FIRST MOVEMENT. Massachusetts pioneered, in 1877, in the establishment of factory safeguards and, in 1886, in the reporting of accidents. Voluntary efforts of leading corporations, particularly those of the steel industry in 1907, accelerated the efforts to reduce accidents, partly as a result of the high rate of industrial injury during 1907–08. The greatest incentive came with the passage of thirty workmen's compensation laws between 1910 and 1915. By 1948 all the states plus Alaska, Hawaii, and Puerto Rico had enacted workmen's compensation laws. Many national and international organizations, as well as governmental agencies, rendered valuable service in promoting safety in industry. The Iron and Steel Engineers' Association studied the safety problem in 1911 and in 1913 organized the National Safety Council, chartered by Congress in 1953, which carries on research in the development and standardization of safety methods and devices and collects and disseminates data pertaining to safety activities. The American Standards Association promulgates safety codes that are used by increasing numbers of administrative bodies.

At first the safety movement emphasized adequate mechanical safeguards, but gradually the personal or human factor received more careful consideration. Leading companies employ safety engineers to educate and supervise the superintendents, foremen, and employees in safety work.

[John R. Commons and John B. Andrews, *Principles of Labor Legislation;* W. H. Heinrich, *Industrial Accident Prevention.*]

JOSEPH H. FOTH

SAFETY FUND SYSTEM. By way of abating some of the abuses that prevailed in the field of banking in New York State in the early 19th century, a plan was formulated and incorporated in the Safety Fund Act (passed in 1829) for the mutual insurance of the debts of banks. This plan came to be called the Safety Fund System. Each bank incorporated in New York was required to contribute each year to a common fund—the safety fund, administered by the state comptroller—an amount equal to one-half of 1 percent of its capital stock, until such contributions aggregated 3 percent of its capital stock. Whenever a bank failed, after its assets had been fully utilized, this fund was to be used in settlement of its debts. Should this safety fund be drained by a succession of bank failures, the state comptroller was empowered to levy on the banks for additional contributions. As experience with bank failures accumulated, the need became clear for giving the holders of the notes (somewhat similar in form and appearance to national bank notes) of a defunct bank priority in the distribution of its assets, and the state laws were changed accordingly.

[Robert E. Chaddock, *The Safety-Fund Banking System in New York State, 1829–1866.*]

FRANK PARKER

SAGADAHOC, the alternative ancient Indian name for the Kennebec region and river in Maine, especially that stretch of the river from Merrymeeting Bay south to the Atlantic Ocean. The first recorded English settlement in New England was made at the mouth of the Sagadahoc by George Popham in 1607. The region was remarkably rich in fish and furs, and many of the first settlers were fishermen or traders with the Indians. Settlements were established along this waterway on Georgetown and Arrowsic islands and at Merrymeeting Bay and Bath about the middle of the 17th century. The river was also the scene of bitter fighting with the Indians in the 18th century.

[Wilbur D. Spencer, *Pioneers on Maine Rivers.*]

ROBERT P. TRISTRAM COFFIN

SAGE PLAINS were encountered by California-bound emigrants turning south at Fort Boise, Idaho, to the Malheur and Pitt rivers, after which the Sage Plains intervened on the way to Sacramento. The journey was so disastrous that after 1844 it was given the name of Death Route.

[K. Coman, *Economic Beginnings of the Far West.*]

CARL L. CANNON

SAG HARBOR, a village at the eastern end of Long Island, was one of the leading whaling ports during the colonial period and until the mid-19th century. During the Revolution it was, for a time, used by the

British as a depot for military stores. In the spring of 1777 the Americans, angered by the destruction of Danbury, Conn., by Gov. William Tryon, planned a raid on Sag Harbor. Lt. Col. Return Jonathan Meigs with 234 men in thirteen whale boats crossed Long Island Sound from Connecticut on May 23, made a surprise attack, destroyed the military supplies at Sag Harbor, and took ninety prisoners.

By the middle of the 19th century the increasing use of petroleum began seriously to affect the whaling industry. The fleet of Sag Harbor dwindled, and it is said that the last whaling ship, the *Myra,* sailed out of the harbor in 1871. Sag Harbor then developed as a yachting and resort community.

[B. F. Thompson, *History of Long Island.*]

A. C. FLICK

SAGINAW, FORT. In 1822 soldiers from Fort Howard on the Fox River in Wisconsin, led by Maj. Daniel Baker, established Fort Saginaw on the west bank of the Saginaw River in Michigan. An epidemic of fever the following summer utterly prostrated the garrison; the survivors were taken to Detroit in October; and the fort was permanently abandoned. Despite this a small community grew up around the abandoned fort and developed into the city of Saginaw, first chartered in 1857.

[James C. Mills, *History of Saginaw County, Michigan.*]

M. M. QUAIFE

SAGINAW'S GIG, CRUISE OF THE, was undertaken to rescue the officers and seamen of the U.S.S. *Saginaw,* commanded by Lt. Comdr. Montgomery Sicard, and wrecked by a reef near Ocean Island in the mid-Pacific on Oct. 29, 1870. A party of five men volunteered to navigate the ship's gig to Honolulu and secure relief. The party consisted of Lt. John G. Talbot, the *Saginaw*'s executive officer; William Halford, coxswain; Peter Francis, quartermaster; and John Andrews and James Muir, seamen. They left Ocean Island on Nov. 18, 1870. After thirty-one days of danger, privation, and suffering, they arrived on Dec. 19 off the island of Kauai, one of the Hawaiian group. They had previously lost their oars in a storm, and in attempting to land without them they upset the gig. William Halford alone survived to reach the shore with Sicard's dispatches. The Hawaiian government immediately sent a steamer, the *Kilauea,* with supplies to rescue the men left on Ocean Island. The *Kilauea* reached them Jan. 4, 1871. The American

minister to Hawaii, Henry A. Pierce, also chartered a schooner, the *Kona Packet,* to assist in the rescue; it reached the island Jan. 5. The *Saginaw*'s gig is now permanently on display at the U.S. Naval Academy.

[G. H. Read, *Last Cruise of the Saginaw.*]

LOUIS H. BOLANDER

SAGINAW TREATY. On Sept. 24, 1819, Gov. Lewis Cass of the Michigan Territory negotiated a treaty with the Chippewa at Saginaw, in which a large land cession, located chiefly in Michigan Territory, was obtained from the tribe. There were sixteen reservations established for the tribe within the lands ceded and several other smaller reserves for specified individuals. For the cession the United States agreed to pay annually $1,000 in silver and to convert all previously promised annuities into payments in silver. The United States promised to furnish the Indians with a blacksmith, cattle, farm tools, and persons to aid them in agriculture, in return for the privilege of building roads through their country.

[C. J. Kappler, *Indian Affairs, Laws, and Treaties,* vol. II.]

GEORGE D. HARMON

SAILOR'S CREEK, BATTLES AT (Apr. 6, 1865). After the Battle of Five Forks, Gen. Robert E. Lee abandoned Petersburg and Richmond, Va., eluded Union Gen. George Meade at Jetersville, and fled westward, his remnant of an army sleepless, fatigued, and hungry. Near Sailor's Creek, Union pursuers overtook Gen. John Brown Gordon, Gen. Richard H. Anderson, and Gen. Richard Stoddert Ewell, protecting the trains. Union Gen. Andrew A. Humphreys' II Corps drove Gordon toward the Appomattox River. Union Gen. Philip H. Sheridan's cavalry corps struck from the south and demolished Anderson on the road from Rice's Station. In the center at Sailor's Creek, Union Gen. Horatio G. Wright's VI Corps charged Ewell's ridge position, outflanking left and rear from the northeast as Sheridan sent cavalry against its right. Ewell surrendered. Anderson's and Gordon's reduced commands escaped toward Appomattox Courthouse.

[A. A. Humphreys, *The Virginia Campaign of 1864 and 1865.*]

ELBRIDGE COLBY

SAILORS' SNUG HARBOR, a home for retired seamen on Staten Island, N.Y., was created by the estate of Robert R. Randall, a New York merchant, in 1801, but its beginning was delayed by litigation until 1831. Randall's farm in mid-Manhattan was the nucleus of the trust, and the ground rents from the land have made it one of the world's wealthiest charities. During the 1970's the home's buildings were landmarked, and plans were developed to turn them into a cultural center. Sailors' Snug Harbor moved in 1976 to a new $6 million facility, which accommodates 120 retired mariners, at Sea Level, N.C.

[I. N. Phelps Stokes, *Iconography of Manhattan Island*.]

ALVIN F. HARLOW

SAINT ALBANS RAID (Oct. 19 1864), in northwestern Vermont, was led by Confederate Lt. Bennett H. Young, with about thirty men not in uniform, from Canada. The raid was in retaliation for the depredations of Union Gen. Philip H. Sheridan in Virginia (*see* Shenandoah Campaign). Three banks were looted of over $200,000, but an attempt to burn the town failed. One citizen was killed. The raiders escaped into Canada pursued by an American posse. Young and twelve of his men were captured and held by the Canadian authorities, who released them Dec. 13 but later rearrested five of them.

[J. B. McMaster, *A History of the People of the United States During Lincoln's Administration*.]

CHARLES H. COLEMAN

SAINT ANTHONY, FALLS OF, a waterfall in the Mississippi River in Minneapolis, were named after Saint Anthony of Padua by Father Louis Hennepin, the first white man known to arrive there (1680). Later Jonathan Carver, Zebulon M. Pike, and other explorers came to the area of the falls. Attracted by their water power, settlements grew up on either side of the falls, Saint Anthony and Minneapolis, beginning in 1837 and uniting under the latter name in 1872. First lumber and then flour industries were developed. Threatened with destruction in 1869, the falls were saved with emergency cofferdams. Later a great dike and apron preserved the falls permanently, allowing them to remain the seat of world-famous flour mills.

[Father Louis Hennepin, *A New Discovery of a Vast Country in America;* W. W. Folwell, *A History of Minnesota*.]

RUTH THOMPSON

SAINT ANTOINE, FORT, a French military post built by Nicolas Perrot, in 1686, on the southeast shore of Lake Pepin (a widening of the Mississippi River on the Minnesota-Wisconsin border) and named for Antoine Le Febvre de La Barre, governor of New France. There, in May 1689, Perrot staged a ceremony of annexation in which he took possession for France of the upper Mississippi and the Sioux country. The fort was abandoned in 1690.

[L. P. Kellogg, *French Régime in Wisconsin and the Northwest*.]

LOUISE PHELPS KELLOGG

SAINT AUGUSTINE, a city in northeastern Florida and the oldest settlement in North America, was founded by Pedro Menéndez de Avilés in September 1565 near the site of Juan Ponce de León's landing in 1513. Saint Augustine was founded to establish Spanish authority on the mainland, protect shipping in the Bahama Channel, and demolish the French settlement at Fort Caroline. Menéndez hoped to make Saint Augustine the center of an ambitious expansion, a dream never realized, but it remained the garrisoned settlement, generally poor and needy, from which radiated mission enterprise to the south, west, and north. As the colonial rivalry of England and Spain developed, it was attacked by British corsairs and by expeditions from the southern colonies. It was defended by Castillo de San Marcos (Fort Marion), which was begun in 1672 and completed in 1756.

When Florida was ceded to the British in 1763, Saint Augustine was the government seat of East Florida, and although most of the inhabitants left, the town shared the plantation prosperity of the region. Restoration to Spain in 1783 turned it into a sleepy and unprogressive garrison town, for Spain's interests lay elsewhere; but Saint Augustine remained the administrative seat of East Florida. It was also one of three Spanish forts in East Florida when the United States acquired the region through purchase in 1819 (*see* Adams-Onís Treaty).

During early territorial days, Saint Augustine was the leading eastern town connected with Pensacola by the new national road. It developed a reputation as the leading winter resort, a position it held until the opening of south Florida. During the 1820's the orange industry, first fostered by the British, became important, and by 1834 the harbor of Saint Augustine was filled with fruit boats trading with northern markets. The great freeze of 1835 and the purple scale sent the groves farther south; the second Seminole War (1835–43) frightened away many settlers; and Jacksonville, to the north, proved a successful rival. Between 1830 and 1839 the population dropped nearly

50 percent. The city was occupied by Union troops from March 1862 until the end of the Civil War.

In 1937 a program of historical restoration was begun under the auspices of the Carnegie Institution of Washington and other research organizations. The restoration of many of Saint Augustine's 17th- and 18th-century buildings revitalized its tourist industry and the city once again became a popular resort area. Both Castillo de San Marcos and Fort Matanzas, built in 1740–42 by the Spanish, have been declared national monuments. The city's population in 1970 was 12,352.

[George R. Fairbanks, *St. Augustine;* Charles B. Reynolds, *Old St. Augustine;* Charlton Tebeau, *A History of Florida.*]

KATHRYN T. ABBEY

SAINT-CASTIN'S TRADING HOUSE was situated at the French fort at Pentegoet, the present town of Castine, Maine. Jean-Vincent d'Abbadie de Saint-Castin, gentleman adventurer, came to the Penobscot Bay region about 1667 and adopted the habits of the Indians, one of whom he married. He amassed a fortune in trade, particularly after Fort Pentegoet came into his hands (1676). Anxious to remain neutral, he was alternately in difficulties with both the French and the English. The seizure of his trading house in 1688 by New England Gov. Edmund Andros was believed by the people of New England to have been the cause of King William's War, which began in 1689. Saint-Castin returned to France at the end of 1701, leaving the trade in the charge of his son.

ROBERT E. MOODY

SAINT CHARLES, FORT, was established in 1732 by Pierre Gaultier de Varennes, Sieur de La Vérendrye, on the southern shore of the Northwest Angle inlet of the Lake of the Woods, in what is now Minnesota. It served as a base for the earlier explorations of the Northwest made by La Vérendrye, his sons, and his nephew Christophe Dufrost de La Jemerais; and it was occupied by the French for more than two decades. In 1908 Jesuits from Saint Boniface College discovered its ruins.

[T. C. Blegen, "Fort St. Charles and the Northwest Angle," *Minnesota History* (1937).]

T. C. BLEGEN

SAINT CLAIR, FORT, a stockade for storage purposes, was built by American troops (1791–92) during the expeditions against the northwestern Indians. Constructed by a detachment of James Wilkinson's

troops a mile north of the present village of Eaton, in southwestern Ohio, it constituted a lesser link in the chain of communications erected between Fort Washington (Cincinnati), built 1789, and the Lake Erie region.

[E. O. Randall, "Fort St. Clair," *Ohio Archaeological and Historical Society Publications,* vol. 11.]

FRANCIS PHELPS WEISENBURGER

SAINT CLAIR'S DEFEAT (Nov. 4, 1791). Gen. Josiah Harmar's failure to subdue the Indians on the Ohio frontier (1785–90) compelled the American government to send a second army against them. President George Washington obtained from Congress authority to raise an army of 3,000 men and appointed Arthur Saint Clair, governor of the Northwest Territory, to command it.

Plans were made to have the army in readiness at Fort Washington (Cincinnati) by July 10, whence it was to march to Fort Wayne and conquer the hostile Indian confederacy (six bands of the Miami). From beginning to end, however, everything went wrong. October had arrived before as many as 2,000 men could be assembled. Considered as an army, their quality was deplorable. The supplies provided were poor; the commissary department was both corrupt and incompetent; the commander was sick and incapable; the soldiers themselves (apart from two small regular regiments) were "wretched stuff," consisting of raw militia and six-months' levies "purchased from prisons, wheel-barrows and brothels at two dollars a month."

Thus composed, the army stumbled northward through the Ohio wilderness; about sunrise of Nov. 4 it was furiously assailed in its camp at present-day Fort Recovery, and after two hours the survivors fled to Fort Jefferson, twenty-two miles away. Two-thirds of the army—900 men—had been killed or wounded. Efforts to make Saint Clair a scapegoat for the sins of others proved unavailing; responsibility for the disaster rested squarely on the government and the American public in general, which entered upon a difficult war without troubling to undertake the preparations essential for success. Saint Clair resigned from the army and resumed his duties as territorial governor.

[Elmore Barce, *The Land of the Miamis;* B. J. Griswold, *The Pictorial History of Fort Wayne;* W. H. Smith, ed., *The St. Clair Papers.*]

M. M. QUAIFE

SAINT CROIX, a river forming the southern section of the Maine–New Brunswick boundary. After the extinction of the short-lived Saint Croix Island settlement (1605–06), the precise location of the Saint Croix River was lost sight of. Two sizable rivers, known locally as the Schoodiac and the Magaguadavic, were alternately claimed by 17th- and 18th-century mapmakers as the true Saint Croix without knowing which was the river discovered and named by Samuel de Champlain shortly before establishing the Saint Croix Island settlement. The British and American negotiators of the preliminary articles of the Definitive Treaty of Peace (1783) used John Mitchell's map of North America (1755), which designates the Magaguadavic as the Saint Croix; and the treaty placed the boundary of the United States and Canada at that river. After the treaty was ratified, the British and American governments disputed the identity of the Saint Croix. Great Britain claimed it was the Schoodiac; the United States contended for the Magaguadavic. Some 2 million acres of coastal land were involved. By Jay's Treaty of 1794 the identity of the true Saint Croix River was left to a mixed commission, which in 1798 fixed on the Schoodiac, traced through its northeastern branch, and placed a monument there.

[Hunter Miller, *Treaties and Other International Acts of the United States,* vols. I, IV; John Bassett Moore, *International Adjudications,* vols. I, II.]

SAMUEL FLAGG BEMIS

SAINT CROIX SETTLEMENT.

In March 1604 Pierre du Guast, Sieur de Monts, sailed with two vessels to Acadia to establish a fur trading monopoly and settlements in "Acadia, Canada and other places in New France," privileges granted him the previous year. With more than 100 settlers, Samuel de Champlain, a Catholic priest, and a Protestant minister, de Monts "entered a river almost half a league in breadth at its mouth," and came to an island, which he and Champlain named Saint Croix Island. During the long and severe winter, with a scarcity of fresh food and water, scurvy developed among the settlers, and thirty-five perished. Finding the island unsuited for permanent settlement, the survivors moved in the summer of 1605 to Port Royal (now Annapolis Royal, Nova Scotia). While de Monts returned to France, Champlain explored the Atlantic coast. Two years later the remaining settlers returned to France, and their buildings were completely destroyed in 1613 by the English from Virginia.

[W. D. Williamson, *The History of the State of Maine.*]

THOMAS MORGAN GRIFFITHS

SAINT-DENIS' EXPEDITION.

In 1714 Louis Juchereau de Saint-Denis led a French expedition from the present Natchitoches, La., into Spanish Texas. Although captured by Spaniards and sent to Mexico City, he secured his release by winning the friendship of the Spanish viceroy. Saint-Denis' 1714 expedition, and another made in 1716, resulted in establishing a profitable trade between the French post of Natchitoches, of which he was commandant from 1722 to 1744, and the Spanish territory to the southwest.

[Charles Gayarré, *History of Louisiana.*]

WALTER PRICHARD

SAINTE GENEVIEVE LEAD MINING DISTRICT.

One of the earliest references to lead in Missouri was made by Father Jacques Gravier in an account of his trip in 1700. Later in the same year, an expedition headed by Pierre Le Sueur was sent up the Mississippi River from its mouth for the special purpose of investigating minerals in the valley. The report was inadequate, but it mentioned that the Indians in the Merrimac River (Mo.) area had lead mines.

Pierre Lemoyne, Sieur d'Iberville, was interested in the report to the extent that he asked the French government in 1701 for the exclusive right of lead mining and fur trading in the Missouri area, but he died (1706) before the petition was granted. The French authorities gave a similar but enlarged grant to the wealthy entrepreneur Antoine Crozat in 1712. Crozat's governor, Sieur Antoine de la Mothe Cadillac, investigated the lead producing area, but little was done in the way of developing lead production until Crozat's successor to the grant of the monopoly, the financier John Law of the Company of the Indies, commissioned Philip Renault in 1723 as director general of mining operations. A rapid development followed, and lead was carried to Kaskaskia (Ill.) to be shipped down the Mississippi. By 1735 the activities of the lead miners and fur traders had become so great on the west side of the river that Sainte Genevieve was established above Kaskaskia in what is now eastern Missouri and became the shipping point for the lead mining district of the hills a few miles to its west.

The French, like the Indians, continued to use the primitive shallow-pit method of mining until Moses Austin moved to the district in 1798 and developed shaft mining and other tendencies toward modern methods. With the building of a railroad connecting the "lead belt" with Saint Louis, Sainte Genevieve lost its lead shipping industry. Flat River, about fifty-five miles south southwest of Saint Louis, became the most important of a number of mining towns in Saint François County, which continues to be one of the greatest lead-producing areas in the world.

[Louis Houck, *History of Missouri;* Ruby Johnson Swartzlow, "Early History of Lead Mining in Missouri," *Missouri Historical Review,* vols. 28, 29.]

W. J. HAMILTON

SAINT FRANCIS, ROGERS' EXPEDITION AGAINST. Having been driven from their New England lands by the British, the Indians of the Saint Francis mission village in Quebec (mostly Abnaki) made several retaliatory raids into New England during the early years of the French and Indian War. In September 1759, because of attacks against Gen. Jeffrey Amherst's army at Crown Point (on the western shore of Lake Champlain in New York), Maj. Robert Rogers, commander of Rogers' Rangers, proposed to Amherst that he be allowed to attack and destroy the Saint Francis village. Amherst agreed, and Rogers left Crown Point on Sept. 13, 1759, with seventeen whaleboats and a force of 220 rangers, among them several Mohawk and Stockbridge. Two days later forty members of the expedition returned to Crown Point, ostensibly because of sickness. The remainder rowed on, arriving in Missisquoi Bay, at the northern end of Lake Champlain, on Sept. 23. The detachment hid its boats and set off through the forest for Saint Francis. On Sept. 25 the boats were discovered and burned by the French and Indians, leaving Rogers without a base. He sent a messenger to Amherst asking that supplies be deposited at the juncture of the lower Ammonoosuc and Connecticut rivers and then went on. For nine days Rogers and his men marched through a spruce bog, sleeping at night in the branches of felled trees. On Oct. 5 the detachment, reduced to 142 men, sighted Saint Francis; and at dawn on Oct. 6 Rogers attacked, burning the town, killing 200 Indians, releasing 5 whites who had been held captive, and keeping 5 Indian children as prisoners. An hour after the attack he commenced his homeward trip with no provisions but dried corn. His second-in-command, Capt. Amos Ogden, was wounded but contrived to keep up. On Oct. 14, near Lake Memphremagog, the detachment ran short of food. Rogers divided his force into small companies, so that they might live off the country, and ordered them to rendezvous at the mouth of the Ammonoosuc. On Oct. 16 one of the companies was am-

bushed by French and Indians and destroyed. Several days later Rogers arrived at the mouth of the lower Ammonoosuc to find that Amherst had sent provisions as requested, but that they had been taken away a few hours before his arrival. He built a raft and on Oct. 27 set off down the Connecticut to get supplies for his starving men. With him went Ogden, another ranger, and one of the Indian boys captured at Saint Francis. On Oct. 28 the raft was wrecked at White River Falls. Too weak to swing a hatchet, Rogers obtained logs for another raft by burning down trees, saved it from destruction at Wattoquitchey Falls with his last reserve of strength, and on Oct. 31 arrived at the fort at Number 4 (Charlestown, N.H.). He returned at once to the mouth of the Ammonoosuc with food for the survivors of the expedition. Lt. Samuel Stephens, the ranger officer who had gone with provisions to the mouth of the Ammonoosuc but failed to wait, was court-martialed and found guilty of neglect of duty. Of the 142 men who attacked Saint Francis, 93 returned to Crown Point.

[J. R. Cuneo, *Robert Rogers;* Kenneth Roberts, *Northwest Passage.*]

KENNETH ROBERTS

SAINT FRANÇOIS XAVIER, FORT. *See* **Green Bay.**

SAINT GERMAIN-EN-LAYE, TREATY OF, signed Mar. 29, 1632, was the general settlement between England and France that followed the Treaty of Susa (1629). Its American section provided for the return by England to France of all places occupied by England in New France, Acadia, and Canada—including Port Royal, Quebec, and Cape Breton Island. The following summer Quebec was restored to the United Company, and Port Royal to the Company of New France.

[F. G. Davenport, ed., *European Treaties Bearing on the History of the United States and Its Dependencies to 1648.*]

ROBERT E. MOODY

SAINT IGNACE MISSION. Father Claude Dablon, superior of the Jesuit missions of the Upper Lakes, began on Mackinac Island in the winter of 1670–71 a mission named for Saint Ignatius. In the spring of 1671 Father Jacques Marquette arrived with his Huron flock from the upper end of Lake Superior. Whether they settled at once on the island or on the promontory on the mainland north of the Straits of

Mackinac is not known; in any case Dablon's Saint Ignace Mission was soon, very probably in 1672, being conducted at the latter location with Father Marquette in charge. There the mission, surrounded by a fort, a French village, a village of Huron, and one of the Ottawa, was maintained until 1706, when difficulties occasioned by the brandy trade and the withdrawal of most of the Indians to Detroit or elsewhere caused its suspension. Reopened about 1712, it was moved, probably in 1741, to a site on the mainland south of the island, where Jesuits were in charge until 1765.

[A. I. Rezek, *History of the Diocese of Sault Ste. Marie and Marquette;* E. O. Wood, *Historic Mackinac.*]

GILBERT J. GARRAGHAN

SAINT JOHN, FORT, also called Fort Saint Jean, Fort San Juan, and Spanish Fort, was built by France on Lake Pontchartrain, at the mouth of Bayou Saint John, to protect New Orleans from the rear. It was occasionally garrisoned by Spaniards between 1776 and 1803; held by American troops during the British attack on New Orleans in 1814–15; occupied by Confederate forces at the outbreak of the Civil War; and since abandoned.

[J. S. Kendall, *History of New Orleans.*]

WALTER PRICHARD

SAINT JOHNS, SIEGE OF (1775). The newly fortified position of Saint Johns, on the Richelieu River in Quebec, was the first important obstacle encountered in the American invasion of Canada in 1775. Fort Saint John was held by a garrison of about 650 men, chiefly regulars. After two initial movements made against it by Gen. Philip Schuyler had failed, the post was invested on Sept. 17, 1775, and bombardment began on Sept. 25. The American guns were few and small, supplies were short, and the besieging army was depleted by sickness; there were probably never more than 2,000 effectives before Saint Johns. The surrender of Fort Chambly (Oct. 20), however, provided the Americans with ammunition and provisions; new batteries were established; and on Nov. 2, the commander of the fort, with food running short in the fort, signed a capitulation providing for the surrender of his force with the honors of war to Gen. Richard Montgomery (who had replaced Schuyler on Sept. 13). With this surrender, the majority of the British regulars in Canada fell into American hands, and the way to Montreal and Quebec was open; nevertheless, the delay of seven weeks oc-

casioned by the siege of Fort Saint Johns had been of great value to the defenders of Canada.

[A. L. Burt, *The Old Province of Quebec;* Justin H. Smith, *Our Struggle for the Fourteenth Colony.*]

C. P. STACEY

SAINT JOSEPH, a city on the Missouri River in northwestern Missouri, was founded by Joseph Robidoux as a trading post called Blacksnake Hills in 1826. The town was platted in 1843 and incorporated in 1845; the city of Saint Joseph was incorporated in 1851. The population increased from 964 in 1846 to 4,257 in 1853. Saint Joseph's economic growth, particularly in grain and livestock, was stimulated by the outfitting of Oregon and California immigrants and furnishing of supplies to military posts. In 1859 the Hannibal and Saint Joseph Railroad was completed; in 1860 Saint Joseph became the eastern terminus of the Pony Express, linking the city with California. During the 1860's the population increased from 8,932 to 19,565. Thereafter, the construction of stockyards, the completion of the Missouri River bridge, and the extension of the railroad accelerated Saint Joseph's growth as a grain and cattle mart. By the 20th century Saint Joseph had become a major transportation terminus for such additional railroads as the Atchison, Topeka and Santa Fe; the Chicago Great Western; and the Union Pacific. Meat-packing, flour milling, and cereal manufacture became the city's major industries. The population had reached 72,961 by 1970.

[Edwin C. Reynolds, *Missouri: A History of the Crossroads State.*]

WILLIAM J. PETERSEN

SAINT JOSEPH, FORT, near present-day Niles, Mich. (close by the Saint Joseph–Kankakee rivers portage), was one of the earliest centers of French activity in the Great Lakes area. Precise dates for the establishment of both the fort and Saint Joseph Mission are unknown, and it was not until the 20th century that the true location of the fort was determined. It is known that Robert Cavelier, Sieur de La Salle, passed near the site of the fort in 1679, and Father Claude Jean Allouez labored and died (1689) at the Saint Joseph Mission. The fort was garrisoned by French soldiers from about 1700 to 1760; a British troop then took over the fort, but was destroyed in 1763 during Pontiac's War. Although the fort remained ungarrisoned until 1779, it was under constant British control, exercised from Detroit and Mackinac. In July and August 1779 a British force occupied it for several weeks, awaiting a threatened rebel invasion, which did not materialize. In December 1780 a band of raiders from Cahokia (Illinois) plundered the place and, retreating, was itself overtaken and destroyed near Michigan City. In January 1781 the Spanish governor at Saint Louis dispatched a small army against Fort Saint Joseph. It ascended the Illinois River to Peoria in boats and from there made a midwinter march across 300 miles of wilderness. Fort Saint Joseph was occupied on Feb. 12, and for twenty-four hours the flag of Spain flew over it. The Spanish army then retired, having laid the foundation for the claim, advanced by Spain in the peace negotiations at Paris in 1783, to the ownership of the Old Northwest. After the Revolution, British and American traders dominated the life of the settlement until the arrival of American settlers in the 1830's.

[Francis P. Prucha, S.J., *A Guide to the Military Posts of the United States, 1789–1895.*]

M. M. QUAIFE

SAINT LAWRENCE RIVER, the largest river in North America, was explored by the French explorer Jacques Cartier in 1535 as far as the island of Montreal, Cartier having discovered the Gulf of Saint Lawrence in his voyage of the previous year. The name "Saint Lawrence" was first given by the explorer to a bay on the gulf and later extended to the gulf and river. In 1541 Cartier carried his exploration to the second rapid above Montreal. It is not certain who first ascended the river from there to Lake Ontario, but it is known that the missionary Simon Le Moyne traveled to the villages of the Onondaga south of Lake Ontario in 1653 and returned the following year by way of the upper Saint Lawrence. The Saint Lawrence—with, its tributary, the Ottawa River, and with the Great Lakes, which geographically are part of the same river system—formed the main water thoroughfare from the sea to the interior of the continent during the 17th and 18th centuries. From Quebec or Montreal set forth explorers and missionaries bound for the west or the southwest: Samuel de Champlain up the Richelieu to Lake Champlain and by the Ottawa to Lake Huron; Robert Cavelier, Sieur de La Salle, Father Jacques Marquette, and Louis Jolliet to the Mississippi; Pierre Esprit Radisson, Daniel Greysolon, Sieur Duluth, and Father Claude Jean Allouez to Lake Superior and the country south of it; Pierre Gaultier de Varennes, Sieur de La Vérendrye, to the plains of Manitoba, the Missouri, and the

Yellowstone. Fur trading brigades of the North West Company left Montreal bound for Mackinac, Grand Portage, Lake Winnipeg, and the Saskatchewan and Columbia rivers. Trading goods came from overseas up the Saint Lawrence to Montreal and thence in canoes to the west; and furs came down to Montreal and over to the London market. The combatants in the colonial wars, the American Revolution, and the War of 1812 each found the use or mastery of the Saint Lawrence waterways a factor to be striven for.

During the 19th century shipping developed on the Great Lakes as communities grew up about their shores and beyond; canals were built and channels deepened in the connecting rivers and the Saint Lawrence; and grain and other commodities were brought down to Montreal from both the Canadian and American West for shipment to Europe and elsewhere. Ocean vessels of limited draft made their way up from the sea through the Saint Lawrence and the Great Lakes to Toronto, Cleveland, Detroit, and Chicago. With the completion of a deep channel from the head of the lakes down to Lake Ontario, and from Montreal to the sea, a movement grew in the first half of the 20th century, in both the United States and Canada, for the removal of the only remaining barrier—the 182-mile extent between Lake Ontario and Montreal. The result was the Saint Lawrence Seaway, begun in 1954 and opened in 1959.

[Henry Besten, *The Saint Lawrence;* Doneight Creighton, *The Commercial Empire of the Saint Lawrence, 1760–1850.*]

LAWRENCE J. BURPEE

SAINT LAWRENCE SEAWAY. Stretching 2,342 miles (3,768 kilometers) from Lake Superior to the Atlantic, the Saint Lawrence Seaway opens the industrial and agricultural heart of North America to deep-draft ocean vessels. Via the seaway and the great circle route, Detroit is 400 miles closer to Amsterdam than New York is.

The entire Great Lakes–Saint Lawrence Seaway system comprises 9,500 square miles of navigable waters, linked by three series of locks, at Sault Sainte Marie, at the Welland Canal, and at the head of the Saint Lawrence River. A ship entering at Montreal is lifted to more than 600 feet above sea level at Lake Superior. The waterway accommodates vessels 730 feet long, with a 76-foot beam and a draft of 26 feet.

The present seaway, opened to deep-draft navigation in 1959, evolved from the engineering efforts of several centuries. The Lachine Rapids above Montreal turned back the ships of Jacques Cartier in 1534. They were bypassed in 1783 by a canal that afforded passage to flat-bottomed bateaux. By 1798 a small canal had been built around the Sault Sainte Marie, on the Canadian side. In 1829 William Hamilton Merritt completed a chain of forty wooden locks across the Niagara peninsula. By 1861 ships were sailing regularly between the Great Lakes and Europe.

Increasing ship sizes and the rapidly growing economy of the Midwest created pressures for further improvements. Between 1913 and 1932, Canada built the Welland Canal to lift deep-draft ships from Lake Ontario to Lake Erie. Strong opposition from sectional interests blocked U.S. participation in proposals to develop the power-generating and navigation potential of the International Rapids. The Wiley-Dondero Act of 1954 authorized the Saint Lawrence Seaway Development Corporation to construct that part of the seaway in the United States, and construction began under agreement with Canada.

Three initiatives in public policy distinguish the Saint Lawrence Seaway: It is international in character, with navigation facilities in both the United States and Canada; it is operated by entities of two governments—each with authority to negotiate with the other; and its operating expenses are met from tolls assessed on shippers. The Saint Lawrence Seaway Authority borrowed $340 million from the Canadian government to build the Canadian sections. Revenue bonds totaling $144.8 million were issued to the U.S. Treasury by the Saint Lawrence Seaway Development Corporation to finance construction of the American locks at Massena, N.Y.

The Dwight D. Eisenhower Lock and the Bertrand H. Snell Lock are operated and maintained by the Saint Lawrence Seaway Development Corporation with an administrator appointed by the president of the United States, serving under the direction of the secretary of transportation.

More than 6,000 commercial vessels transited the Seaway each year between 1959 and 1973. Each year from 1970 through 1973, they carried more than 50 million tons of bulk and general cargo: grain, ores, coal, petroleum, steel, and manufactured products. In the early 1970's the Seaway was open from April to mid-December. Beginning in 1972 government agencies carried out a congressionally authorized demonstration program to assess the practicability of winter navigation for the Saint Lawrence–Great Lakes Seaway system.

D. W. OBERLIN

SAINT-LÔ. A town in France of about 10,000 people during World War II, and the capital of the Department of Manche in Normandy, Saint-Lô marked the culminating act of the Battle of the Hedgerows (so called because of the hedgerows that lined the Normandy roads) and the opening event of American troops breaking out of Normandy. Gen. Omar N. Bradley's First U.S. Army started the battle in the Cotentin peninsula on July 4, 1944, and closed it, after taking 40,000 casualties, on July 18, with the capture of Saint-Lô. Holding the Lessay-Périers-Saint-Lô road, Bradley, on July 25, launched Operation Cobra with the support of heavy bombers and broke the German defenses in Normandy. The subsequent exploitation of this victory by all the Allied forces resulted in the pursuit of the defeated German forces to the Siegfried Line, which was reached in September.

[Martin Blumenson, *The Duel for France.*]
MARTIN BLUMENSON

SAINT LOUIS, a city on the west bank of the Mississippi River in eastern Missouri, was founded Feb. 15, 1764, by the French trader Pierre Laclède Ligueste. Laclède was the commander of an armed force and commercial enterprise organized in New Orleans to take over, for a period of eight years, the exclusive privilege to "trade with the savages of the Missouri and all nations residing west of the Mississippi River." This monopoly was granted in 1762 by the French director-general of Louisiana. When placed at the head of his "considerable armament," Laclède moved his outfit, containing a large quantity of merchandise and supplies, up the Mississippi River to Sainte Genevieve, in what is now eastern Missouri, and thence across the river to Fort de Chartres (Ill.), where he found temporary housing. After searching the west bank of the Mississippi above this point to the mouth of the Missouri River for a suitable place to build his establishment, Laclède found, in December 1763, the best location at the present site of Saint Louis: perched on a limestone bluff forty feet high and two miles long, backed up by terraces of higher ground around which the river flowed in the shape of a bow. Here he blazed with his own hands a number of trees to mark the place, and returned to Fort de Chartres. There he announced that he had chosen a spot that, on account of its many natural advantages, would become one of the finest cities in America. The following February Laclède sent a party of thirty, including "two dependable men," with René Auguste Chouteau to clear off the trees and begin necessary buildings on the chosen ground. In April 1764 Laclède followed, selected the spot for his own dwelling, and laid out the exact plan of the village, which he named Saint Louis in honor of the patron saint of Louis XV, reigning king of France. Saint Louis early became the center of the fur trade and the starting point of most expeditions and trails into the western country. There explorers and settlers outfitted and gathered supplies for their journeys, and from there voyageurs, trappers, traders, and soldiers plied their labored way along the streams into the wilderness.

In 1762 in the secret Treaty of Fontainebleau, France ceded New Orleans and all the territory of Louisiana west of the Mississippi River to Spain, but it was several years before local authorities knew of the transaction and the first Spanish governor was driven away. Even after 1770 when Spanish Lt. Gov. Pedro Piernas came into command at Saint Louis, the village continued to be predominantly French. Soon after the purchase of Louisiana from France by the United States in 1803, the town was overrun by a large number of speculative New Englanders, who launched a very considerable boom. In course of time a new town grew up beside the old one. An almost imperceptible line of cleavage began between the new industrial speculators and the old conservatives, which ultimately divided the city into two groups of different social and political caste. Racial changes in the course of time greatly altered the character of the population. Many Virginians, Kentuckians, and North Carolinians moved into Missouri in the Spanish days and also after the purchase. These settled largely in rural districts, but a goodly number settled in Saint Louis and participated in the early fur trade, Santa Fe and Oregon expeditions, as well as in local merchandising. These people mixed well with the French, were accustomed to slavery, and found no antagonism in the native trend. In the early days the slaves numbered about one-third of the total population.

In 1808 Saint Louis was incorporated as a town, and in 1822 it was chartered as a city. A new city charter in 1876 separated the city from Saint Louis County; the city is still independent from any of the Missouri counties.

With the advent of the steamboat Saint Louis rose very rapidly in both population and wealth. From 1811 to 1882 the assessed valuation of real estate was multiplied about fifteen hundredfold. With a great river at its feet, and near to the outlets of many other rivers, there came to its wharf rivercraft of every shape and kind from the many navigable tributaries of the Mississippi. Iron, lead, and zinc from nearby mines; bituminous coal from across the river; farm and garden products from rich valleys nearby; hemp, cotton, and sugar from the South—all contributed to make Saint Louis the great river capital of the West and, with the coming of the railroads in the 1850's, the second largest railroad center of the United States.

In the late 1820's a German by the name of Duden wrote many letters and stimulated considerable immigration from his native land. This influx was followed by another and larger German immigration in 1848–49. Most of these German immigrants were industrialists and became strongly allied with the New Englanders. They opposed slave labor as a kind of aristocratic paternalism, a menace to free labor, and a phase of social life to which they had never been accustomed. When the sectional war excited by the abolitionists was seen to be approaching, large numbers of privately drilled, unofficial German military bodies early joined in a movement to suppress the militia and block the legislative and executive departments of the state. Thus identified with the Union cause and constituting a large portion of the victorious element in the Civil War, the German population of Saint Louis increased rapidly in numbers and political power.

The Louisiana Purchase Exposition, held in Saint Louis in 1904, highlighted the city's rapid industrial expansion. Although slowed by the depression of the 1930's, the expansion was revived during World War II, particularly in aircraft production. Other major manufactures include chemicals, electrical equipment, and iron and steel products.

Saint Louis is also a noted cultural center, housing one of the oldest symphony orchestras in the nation, the Missouri Botanical Garden, the Saint Louis Municipal Theater, and many institutions of higher learning. The Jefferson National Expansion Memorial (forty city blocks) is a national historic site and has as its central feature the Gateway Arch, 630 feet high, which was designed by Eero Saarinen.

The city's population peaked in 1950 at 856,976, and by 1970 had declined to 622,236. The decrease is accounted for by the fact that Saint Louis' boundaries have been constitutionally fixed since 1876, and the city, therefore, has been unable to include in its population the people of the surrounding, densely populated, Saint Louis County.

[E. M. Coyle, *Saint Louis: Portrait of a River City;* William Hyde and Howard L. Conard, *Encyclopedia of the History of St. Louis;* M. Quigley, *Saint Louis: The First Two Hundred Years.*]

STELLA M. DRUMM

SAINT LOUIS, BRITISH ATTACK ON

SAINT LOUIS, BRITISH ATTACK ON (May 26, 1780), was part of the British strategy of the revolutionary war, and the successful defense of this village is generally accounted a victory for the Americans. It shared with King's Mountain the sum total of victories over the British in 1780. Instructions had been received by British Gen. Frederick Haldimand, governor of Canada, on June 16, 1779, to reduce the Spanish and Illinois posts. In consequence he organized a force of Indian bands, including Menomini, Sauk, Fox, Winnebago, and Sioux, under Emmanuel Hesse, together with some Canadians, traders, and their servants. Sent by various routes, these combined into a body of about 1,200 for a surprise attack on Saint Louis. It was generally supposed that Cahokia, a village about five miles farther south and across the Mississippi, was the first British objective, but the garrison at Saint Louis had some warning the previous day that they would be first attacked. In consequence the British, who had planned a surprise attack, were themselves astonished. The village was successfully defended by 50 soldiers and 280 townsmen, including a small reinforcement from Sainte Genevieve, with a loss of 104 men. The attackers were so badly demoralized and delayed that the whole expedition collapsed and the British menace from the West was entirely removed.

[Stella M. Drumm, "The British-Indian Attack on Pain Court (St. Louis)," *Journal of the Illinois State Historical Society,* vol. 23.]

STELLA M. DRUMM

SAINT LOUIS, FORT

SAINT LOUIS, FORT, in Illinois, was intended to be the principal defense of the colony established by Robert Cavelier, Sieur de La Salle. An enclosure of palisades and log houses, it was built on Starved Rock in the winter of 1682–83 by La Salle and Henry de Tonti. Nine years later it was abandoned in favor of Fort Pimitoui (now Peoria), but Tonti and others used it intermittently for a decade. The priest Jean-François Buisson de Saint-Cosme found it deserted in 1699, and Pierre François de Charlevoix saw only its ruins in 1721.

[Francis Parkman, *LaSalle and the Discovery of the Great West.*]

PAUL M. ANGLE

SAINT LOUIS, FORT, in Texas, was first a temporary fort built by Robert Cavelier, Sieur de La Salle, in 1685 near the shore of Matagorda Bay and the mouth of a river that he called La Vaca (since identified as Garcitas Creek) to house his colony of more than 180 persons. The location was unsuitable, and the fort was moved five or six miles up the river where a permanent fort was built. Named Saint Louis, in honor of the French king, the fort consisted of one large building and several smaller ones, the whole being surrounded by a palisade with cannon mounted at the corners. La Salle set out from Fort Saint Louis on his three futile attempts between 1685 and 1687 to reach the Mississippi. Sickness, accidents, and desertions reduced the number of La Salle's colonists until there were only about thirty left after he departed on his last journey in 1687. Most of the remaining colonists were massacred by Indians early in 1689. A few months later, the Spanish searches for La Salle, who had been murdered by his crew, came to an end when Alonso de León, governor of Coahuila, found the ruins of the fort. On his next expedition in 1690, de León burned the buildings that remained.

[H. E. Bolton, "The Location of LaSalle's Colony on the Gulf of Mexico, *Southwestern Historical Quarterly,* vol. 27; C. E. Castañeda, *The Finding of Texas.*]

C. T. NEU

SAINT LOUIS MISSOURI FUR COMPANY

SAINT LOUIS MISSOURI FUR COMPANY should not be confused with the Missouri Fur Company. Manuel Lisa, one of the more famous fur traders, persistently spoke of the former as the "Missouri Fur Company," and historians have thus been led astray. The Saint Louis Missouri Fur Company was formally organized through articles of copartnership dated Mar. 7, 1809. Its purpose was to launch and conduct hunting and trading expeditions on the upper Missouri River and tributaries for a term of three years. A subordinate enterprise was the safe conduct of the Mandan chief Shahaka and his family from Saint Louis to their village on the upper Missouri. Two years earlier Shahaka, who had visited President Thomas Jefferson, and his party had been attacked by Arikara near Saint Louis, thereby delaying their return home. The federal government paid the company $10,000 for escorting the Indian party on the last part of their journey.

The partners in the company were Lisa, Benjamin Wilkinson, Pierre Chouteau, Auguste P. Chouteau, Reuben Lewis, William Clark, Sylvester Labadie, Pierre Menard, William Morrison, and Andrew Henry. Clark was detailed to manage the headquarters at Saint Louis. The first expedition left Saint Louis in June 1809 with 172 men and nine barges loaded with goods worth $4,269, including $165 worth of whiskey. Because of desertions and sickness, only 153 men remained when the expedition left Fort Osage on the south bank of the Missouri (present-day Kansas) on July 10, 1809. The main party reached the Bighorn River about Nov. 1, where they built a trading post. A profitable trading and trapping campaign ensued, but two of the partners suffered severe losses through treachery of the Blackfoot, when they set out in the spring for the Three Forks of the Missouri (in southwest Montana). Many of the men were killed and all of their horses, guns, traps, and furs were taken (*see* Manuel's Fort). In spite of these losses, the returns from the posts that were not attacked saved the original capital and a small profit besides. A relief expedition was launched Sept. 10, 1810, with Lisa (who returned with Menard in July 1810) in charge. The other partners and some of the men did not return until the following summer. The company was reorganized Jan. 14, 1812, with the surviving partners except Morrison. The capital was fixed at $50,000 and the time limitation at 1818. Clark was made president and Lisa and Labadie directors. An expedition with two barges, leaving in May 1812, yielded a profit of $9,000. Fort Manuel (not to be confused with Manuel's Fort), near the present-day Kenel, S.D., and probably Fort Lisa, near Omaha, were established on this expedition. After six months' liquidation the company was dissolved Jan. 17, 1814.

The Missouri Fur Company, as distinguished from the Saint Louis Missouri Fur Company, was a partnership formed by Lisa and Theodore Hunt in July 1814. For this company Lisa conducted expeditions up the Missouri River from 1814 to 1817. On June 14, 1817, the cargo of fur brought in was valued at $35,000. This company expired by limitation the following month, and another Missouri Fur Company was organized by Lisa in April 1819. The new partners were Joshua Pilcher, Thomas Hempstead, Joseph Perkins, Andrew Woods, Moses B. Carson, John B. Zenoni, Andrew Drips, and Robert Jones. Their principal establishment, like those of the former companies from 1813 on, was at Fort Lisa. Lisa died in 1820, and Pilcher was made president of the company. Lucien Fontenelle, William Vanderburg, and Charles Brent were added to the partnership, and the firm continued in business until about 1830.

[Thomas James, *Three Years Among the Indians and Mexicans;* John C. Luttig, *Journal of a Fur Trading Expedition on the Upper Missouri, 1812–1813.*]

STELLA M. DRUMM

SAINT LOUIS–SAN FRANCISCO. *See* **Railroads, Sketches.**

SAINT LOUIS–SOUTHWESTERN. *See* **Railroads, Sketches.**

SAINT LOUIS WORLD'S FAIR. *See* **Louisiana Purchase Exposition.**

SAINT MARKS, FORT, on Apalachee Bay in Florida, was fortified by the English early in the 18th century and also served as a trading post. When the Treaty of Paris (1763) fixed the western boundary of British Florida at the Apalachicola River, British troops occupied Saint Marks. By the Definitive Treaty of Peace (1783) it was transferred to Spain, the British trading firm of Panton, Leslie and Company being permitted to remain. In 1788 William Augustus Bowles, agent of the trading firm of Miller, Bonnamy and Company, threatened an attack, and in 1792, and again in 1800, he burned the Panton Leslie store. In 1818 Gen. Andrew Jackson occupied the post (*see* Arbuthnot and Ambrister, Case of). After the Florida cession (*see* Adams-Onís Treaty) Saint Marks became U.S. territory (*see* Forbes Purchase). During the Civil War it was used by the Confederates as a blockade-running and saltmaking center. The fort was destroyed by a Union naval raiding party, June 15, 1862, but was rebuilt. The salt works were destroyed on Feb. 17, 1864.

[M. F. Boyd, ''The Fortification at San Marcos de Apalache,'' *Florida Historical Quarterly,* vol. 15; H. G. Cutler, *History of Florida.*]

THOMAS ROBSON HAY

ST. MARTIN'S STOMACH. When Alexis St. Martin, a nineteen-year-old French-Canadian voyageur, was wounded accidentally in the stomach by a gunshot on Mackinac Island, June 6, 1822, he was cared for by William Beaumont, the post surgeon. Miraculously the patient recovered, but the hole in his stomach would not close. At length a fold of the stomach's coats filled the orifice, forming a lid that could be pushed aside by a finger.

The invitation to experiment actuated Beaumont in May 1825 to begin testing the time particular foods required to digest by introducing pieces tied to threads into the stomach and withdrawing them at intervals. He continued making other experiments, with interruptions and changes of locality, until the end of 1833. His observations and conclusions were published in *Experiments and Observations on the Gastric Juice and the Physiology of Digestion* (1833) and have been called the "greatest contribution ever made to the knowledge of gastric digestion."

Beaumont left army service in 1839 and practiced successfully in Saint Louis until his death in 1853. St. Martin, who had married, became the father of seventeen children, farmed a little, "hired" out his stomach to at least one other physician for experiments, and exhibited himself to the public. He died at Saint Thomas, Quebec, in 1880.

[J. S. Myer, *Life and Letters of Dr. William Beaumont.*]
HOWARD H. PECKHAM

SAINT MARYS, the first settlement in Maryland, was founded, Mar. 27, 1634, on the north bank of the Potomac River not far from its mouth, in accordance with instructions from Cecilius Calvert, Lord Baltimore, proprietor and founder of Maryland. Saint Marys was the capital of Maryland until 1694 and was later renamed Saint Marys City. The village rapidly declined during the 18th century until little remained of the original settlement. Interest in Saint Marys was revived during Maryland's Tercentenary Celebration in 1934, and the site is now maintained by the state.

[B. C. Steiner, *Beginnings of Maryland and Other Maryland Studies.*]
RAPHAEL SEMMES

SAINT MARYS, TREATY OF, negotiated with the Chippewa by Lewis Cass, territorial governor of Michigan, was signed June 16, 1820. The Indians ceded to the United States a four-mile-square tract at the Sault (present-day Sault Sainte Marie) on which Fort Brady was erected in 1822. The treaty, negotiated under dramatic circumstances, marks the first real assertion of American authority in the Lake Superior area.

[M. M. Quaife, "From Detroit to the Mississippi in 1820," *Burton Historical Collection Leaflet,* vol. 8.]
M. M. QUAIFE

SAINT MARYS FALLS SHIP CANAL. *See* **Sault Sainte Marie Canals.**

SAINT-MIHIEL, OPERATIONS AT (Sept. 12–16, 1918). The front between the Moselle River and the Argonne Forest in France having been selected as the field for American operations against German forces, after the successful Aisne-Marne offensive in which many American divisions participated, the American First Army was organized, Aug. 10, and immediately

began gathering its troops between the Moselle and Verdun. Marshal Ferdinand Foch and Gen. John J. Pershing planned that this army should direct its first blow against the German salient at Saint-Mihiel. Nine American divisions, numbering 550,000 men, and four French divisions under Pershing's command, numbering 70,000, were assembled. Seven American divisions were placed on the south face of the salient, two American and two French divisions on the west face, and two French divisions around its tip. The Germans held this front with nine divisions of the Gallwitz Army Group (about 60,000 men).

On the morning of Sept. 12, after a violent artillery bombardment, the First Army advanced into the salient, and by midnight the southern attack had penetrated to an average depth of five miles. Just after daylight, Sept. 13, the First Division from the south and the Twenty-sixth Division from the west met at Vigneulles-les-Hattonchatel, trapping 16,000 Germans in the point of the salient. Altogether 443 guns were captured. By Sept. 16 the salient was entirely obliterated. The Americans suffered 7,000 casualties.

[Richard M. Coffman, *The War to End All Wars: The American Military Experience in World War I.*]
JOSEPH MILLS HANSON

SAINT PAUL. *See* **Twin Cities.**

SAINT PHILIP, FORT, SURRENDER OF. *See* **Mississippi River, Opening of the.**

SAINT STEPHENS, in Washington County, Ala., was begun about 1789 as a fortification on the site of a former French post at the head of navigation on the Tombigbee River by the Spaniards after their conquest of West Florida. It was a severe blow to Spain when this outpost was found to be on the American side of the demarcation line of 1798 (*see* Southern Boundary, Survey of the). The settlement was surrendered to Lt. John McClary, who marched from Natchez in 1799, but who moved his troops south to Fort Stoddert, near the junction of the Alabama and Tombigbee rivers, which was closer to the international boundary. Saint Stephens survived as a town and became the seat of the government trading house established by Joseph Chambers in 1803 and made famous by George Strother Gaines. For twenty-five years it remained the center of American influence among the Choctaw.

[Dunbar Rowland, *Mississippi.*]
JAMES W. SILVER

SAINT-VITH, a town in Belgium where for six days during World War II American troops denied critical roads to German forces attacking in the Battle of the Bulge. On Dec. 16, 1944, with the 106th Infantry Division under heavy attack on the Schnee Eifel Ridge near Saint-Vith, the 7th Armored Division tried without success to gain the ridge. On Dec. 19 two regiments of the 106th Division surrendered; meanwhile, the armored division, aided by a surviving regiment of the 106th Division, a regiment of the 28th Division, and a combat command of the 9th Armored Division, fashioned a horseshoe-shaped defense about Saint-Vith. Although the Germans took the town late on Dec. 21, the defenders held nearby for another day until authorized to withdraw. The Americans lost 6,000 of 22,000 men, plus 8,000 captured on the Schnee Eifel, but delayed the Germans long enough for a new line to form ten miles to the rear.

[H. M. Cole, *The Ardennes: Battle of the Bulge.*]
CHARLES B. MACDONALD

SAIPAN (June 15–July 9, 1944). Measuring about fourteen miles by five miles, Saipan is the northernmost of the southern Mariana Islands and lies 3,350 nautical miles west of Honolulu and 1,270 south of Tokyo. In June 1944, when it was invaded by American forces, it was the most heavily fortified of the entire Marianas chain. Three major strategic considerations pointed to the American invasion. Saipan was close enough to Tokyo to be within flying range of the new Army Air Force B-29 very-long-range bomber. To defend the island, the Japanese were expected to dispatch a major fleet and thereby precipitate a sea battle with the U.S. fleet. Also, the island's capture would expedite further U.S. amphibious operations in the central Pacific area.

Overall command of the operation was given to Adm. Chester W. Nimitz, commander in chief of the U.S. Pacific Fleet and Pacific Ocean areas. Under him was Vice Adm. Raymond A. Spruance, commander of the U.S. Fifth Fleet; next in command was Vice Adm. Richmond Kelly Turner, commander of the Joint Expeditionary Force. Tactical command of the invading troops devolved upon Lt. Gen. Holland M. Smith of the U.S. Marine Corps. These consisted mainly of the Second and Fourth Marine divisions, reinforced by the Twenty-seventh Infantry Division. After two days of intense preliminary bombardment by naval guns and aircraft, the two marine divisions landed at dawn on June 15, 1944, on the eastern coast of the island and by nightfall had established a defensible beachhead. While the U.S. Fifth Fleet defeated a Japanese carrier task force in the adjacent Philippine Sea on June 18–19, Marine and Army units pushed rapidly to the western coast of Saipan, then deployed northward on a three-division front with the army in the center. The subsequent slow progress of the Twenty-seventh Infantry Division led to the relief of its commander, Maj. Gen. Ralph C. Smith. By July 9, however, the attacking troops reached the northernmost point of the island, which was then declared secured.

Total American casualties came to an estimated 14,111 killed and wounded. In exchange almost the entire Japanese garrison of about 30,000 men was wiped out. The inner defense line of the Japanese empire had been cracked. Premier Hideki Tojo and his entire war cabinet resigned forthwith. The American forces were at last within bombing range of the enemy homeland.

[Philip A. Crowl, *Campaign in the Marianas;* Carl W. Hoffman, *Saipan: The Beginning of the End;* Jeter A. Isely and Philip A. Crowl, *The U.S. Marines and Amphibious War;* Samuel E. Morison, *History of United States Naval Operations in World War II,* vol. VIII.]
PHILIP A. CROWL

SALARIES. *See* **Wages and Salaries, Regulation of.**

SALARY GRAB was the popular name for a congressional act for boosting specified federal salaries. It was originally designed to benefit the president only, whose compensation was considered too small. As finally passed during the closing hours of the Forty-second Congress, Mar. 3, 1873, the bill provided increases of salary for the president from $25,000 to $50,000, for the chief justice from $8,500 to $10,500, for the vice-president, cabinet members, associate justices, and speaker of the House from $8,000 to $10,000, and for senators and representatives from $5,000 to $7,500. A last-minute amendment made the advance for the members of Congress retroactive for the preceding biennium, thus enabling them to return home with a bonus in back pay of $5,000 each. Coming at a time when Congress was in disfavor because of the Crédit Mobilier and the exposure of other scandals, the "salary grab" and the "back pay steal" became issues in all the elections of that year. In most of the state platforms both parties denounced the act openly. Consequently, most congressmen, for political or other reasons, either refused to accept the increased compensation or, having received it, returned it to the U.S. Treasury or donated it to charity. In January 1874 the Forty-third Congress repealed the legislation except for those provisions affecting the salaries of the president and the justices.

[E. P. Oberholtzer, *A History of the United States Since the Civil War*, vol. III.]

ASA E. MARTIN

SALEM, a seaport in northeastern Massachusetts. In 1626 Roger Conant and a few settlers of the defunct Dorchester Company had moved up from Cape Ann and built some huts on the peninsula of Salem. In 1628 John Endecott and the colonists sent out by the Massachusetts Bay Company in the ship *Abigail* reached Salem on Sept. 6 with a copy of the charter that superseded the rights of the Dorchester Company. In 1629 the ministers Samuel Skelton and Francis Higginson arrived in Salem and founded, on Aug. 6, the first Puritan Congregational church, modeled to a large extent on the Separatist church at Plymouth. Roger Williams was minister of the church from 1633 to 1635, but was forced out by the magistrates of Boston over the protests of the Salem people for political reasons. Hugh Peter replaced Williams and was instrumental in starting the fisheries through which trade with Spain, Portugal, and the West Indies was built up and that largely accounted for the prosperity of Salem for the next 150 years. John Winthrop and his fleet (*see* Great Migration) landed at Salem on June 12, 1630, and then proceeded to Boston Bay, around which they settled in the summer. In the same year Salem was incorporated as a town.

In 1692 a wave of witchcraft hysteria, which had spread all over Europe, reached Salem, and an outburst of accusations occurred, chiefly at Salem Village (now Danvers). Those accused of witchcraft were tried in Salem, and eighteen persons were hanged. All the convictions and executions occurred between June and September 1692. The jury and most of the judges not long afterward made public confessions of their error.

Salem aided vigorously in all the colonial wars, and Benjamin Pickman was a dominant figure in promoting the crusade against the French settlement at Louisburg on Cape Breton Island in 1745. The capital of Massachusetts was twice transferred to Salem: under Gov. William Burnet in 1728 and under Gov. Thomas Gage in 1774. The first provincial congress was organized there in October 1774, and the first armed resistance to the British troops occurred at the North Bridge on Feb. 26, 1775. A Salem ship, the *Quero,* carried the first news of the Battle of Lexington to England, and another, the *Astrea,* brought the first news of the treaty of peace to America. About one-tenth of the privateers of the Revolution, about 200, were sent out of Salem Bay.

After the Revolution for forty years Salem ships sought out trade in every corner of the world and actually began trade with more different foreign ports than all other American ports combined. By the second quarter of the 19th century, Salem had lost much of its shipping to the larger ports of Boston and New York. Since then the economy has been based on such diverse industries as the manufacture of shoes and other leather goods, textiles, and games and the tourist industry. Tourists are attracted to the city by many of the fine old buildings that remain, including Nathaniel Hawthorne's birthplace and the John Turner House, which dates from 1668 and was made famous by Hawthorne's *House of the Seven Gables*. The Salem Maritime Historic Site preserves the old wharves, and the Peabody Museum (1868) houses the exhibits of a museum organized in 1799 by the Salem East India Marine Society. Pioneer Village is a 20th-century reproduction of the 1630 settlement. Salem's population in 1970 was 40,556.

[J. B. Felt, *Annals of Salem;* J. B. F. Osgood and H. M. Bachelder, *Sketch of Salem;* J. D. Phillips, *Salem in the 17th and 18th Centuries.*]

JAMES DUNCAN PHILLIPS

SALERNO, a seaport of over 100,000 people in Campania, Italy, where Anglo-American forces in World War II came ashore against German opposition on Sept. 9, 1943. The invasion came the morning after the Italian government of Marshal Pietro Badoglio announced its surrender to the Allies. Surprised by the capitulation of their ally, the Germans defended Salerno from strong positions in the high ground ringing the shore. Lt. Gen. Mark W. Clark's Fifth U.S. Army made the amphibious landings with three divisions, a relatively small force. The Germans under Field Marshal Albert Kesselring offered resistance primarily to insure the safe withdrawal from the Italian toe of two divisions blocking Lt. Gen. Bernard L. Montgomery's British Eighth Army, which had crossed the Strait of Messina on Sept. 3. The defense at Salerno was so effective that a German counterattack on Sept. 13–14 came close to reaching the beaches and splitting the British and American components at the Sele River. Although the Allies gave some thought to evacuating their beachhead, a determined stand averted crisis. The arrival of Allied follow-up units, intensified air strikes, and increased naval gunfire support turned the tide. On Sept. 20, with all German forces brought out of the toe, Kesselring started withdrawing slowly to the north. On Oct. 1 Allied troops entered Naples and gained the objective of the operation.

[Martin Blumenson, *Salerno to Cassino*.]
MARTIN BLUMENSON

SALESMAN, TRAVELING. *See* **Traveling Salesmen.**

SALES TAXES consist of two types: excise taxes and general sales taxes. The excise tax is placed on specified commodities and may be at specific rates or on an ad valorem basis. The general sales tax can be a manufacturers' excise tax; a retail sales tax paid by consumers; a "gross income" tax applied to sales of goods and provision of services; or a "gross sales" tax applied to all sales of manufacturers and merchants.

During the 19th century several states adopted tax levies resembling sales taxes. The sales tax in its modern form was first adopted by West Virginia in a gross sales tax in 1921. During the 1930's many states adopted the sales tax in its various forms as a replacement for the general property tax that had been their chief source of income.

The adoption of sales taxation slowed somewhat during the 1940's but became more popular in the post–World War II period. At the end of 1971 forty-five states and the District of Columbia levied a sales tax in some form.

A corollary of the sales tax is the use tax. This is a charge levied on taxable items bought in a state other than the state of residence of the purchaser for the privilege of using the item in the state of residence. The rate structure is the same as that of the sales tax. Automotive vehicles are the most significant item in the yield of use taxes.

The rate structure used in the general sales tax is proportional; that is, the rate is constant as the base increases. For ease of administration and determination of the tax due, bracketing systems have been adopted by nearly all states. The rates in use in the mid-1970's varied from 2 percent to a high of 7 percent; 4 percent was the most common rate. A combination of state and local rates may exceed 7 percent. A selective sales tax applying to a single commodity

may have much higher rates. At the time of initial adoption of many of the sales taxes in the 1930's, tokens were used for the collection of the tax on small sales where the tax was less than one cent. Ohio used stamps to show that the tax had been collected. Nearly all these systems have been abandoned in favor of collection of the tax in full cent increments.

Several forms of sales taxes have been used abroad. Canada has used a manufacturers' excise, in the belief that a levy at that level of the distribution process offers fewer administrative problems because of the small number of business units with which to deal. The value-added tax has been extensively used in Europe and has been adopted by the European Economic Community nations as a major revenue source with the goal of uniform rates within each member nation. During the 1950's and early 1960's Michigan used a business receipts tax that was an adaptation of the value-added tax. This was the only experience with such a tax in the United States, as of the mid-1970's.

Specific sales taxes on selected commodities have long been used by the states. Selective sales taxes were used in the colonial period, with liquor being the most frequently taxed commodity. Gasoline was selectively taxed by Oregon in 1919. The disadvantage of specific sales taxes is that they do not produce the revenues a general sales tax does. During World War II a national sales tax was proposed, but no action was taken by Congress. The proposal has been revived periodically, but changes in personal and corporate income taxes have been preferred over a national sales tax.

A great deal of attention is given to the regressive effect of the sales tax. Admittedly, an individual with a low income spends a greater portion of his income on consumption goods that are taxed than do those with higher incomes. When the necessities of food and clothing are excluded from the sales tax base, the regressive effect is reduced.

The impact of sales taxes is on the seller, for in nearly all cases, he makes the payment to the state. However, the incidence, or final resting place of the tax burden, is on the purchaser of the taxed commodity or service as the price is increased or the price is constant but the tax is stated separately on the sales slip and added to the sum collected from the purchaser. In fact, the laws of some states require forward shifting of the tax to the consumer.

[John F. Due, *State and Local Sales Taxes;* Clinton V. Oster, *Retail Sales Taxation*.]
CHALMERS A. MONTEITH

SALK VACCINE. *See* **Poliomyelitis.**

SALMON FALLS, ATTACK ON (Mar. 18, 1690). Louis de Buade, Comte de Frontenac, governor of New France, sent out three expeditions against the English settlements in the winter of 1690. The smallest, of about fifty men, half French and half Abnaki, led by François Hertel, reached Salmon Falls, N.H., after a hard winter journey of two months from Three Rivers, Quebec. At daybreak they attacked the fortified house and two stockades, completely surprising the settlers and finding no opposition. The buildings and nearby farms were burned, and at least thirty persons were killed. Fifty-four were made prisoners, of whom several were later murdered, and the others taken to Canada. A force from Portsmouth, N.H., caught up with the raiders but was repulsed.

[Jeremy Belknap, *History of New Hampshire;* Francis Parkman, *Frontenac and New France.*]

HERBERT W. HILL

SALMON FISHERIES along the northern New England coast had been fished out or otherwise destroyed by 1850. On the Pacific coast six varieties of salmon were found from Monterey, Calif., north to Alaska and had been taken by the American Indians before the arrival of Europeans. In the 1820's the Hudson's Bay Company failed to develop an English market for barreled salmon from the Columbia River but did create a modest trade with California, South America, and Hawaii. Extensive development of the West Coast salmon industry began in 1864, when William, John, and George Hume and Andrew S. Hapgood, all from Maine, built a salmon cannery on the Sacramento River. In the first season they produced 2,000 cases (one case equals 48 pounds). In 1866 they moved to the Columbia River and in 1867 packed 18,000 cases. The abundance of fish; the relative ease of taking them with improved and enlarged nets, seines, traps, and fish wheels; the rapid advance of canning technology; and the constantly growing market induced enormous expansion. The salmon business spread to the coastal rivers, to the Puget Sound, to British Columbia, and, before 1890, to Alaska. After 1890 Alaska became the dominant producer. In 1883 total U.S. production surpassed 1 million cases; in 1901, 5 million; and in 1918, 10 million. Since 1918, with wide seasonal fluctuations, the production trend has been downward. In 1972, for example, the total pack was a little over 1.9 million cases.

Attempts to regulate fishing periods and to establish hatcheries had begun by the 1880's. Competition between American and Canadian fishermen for Fraser River fish brought about the establishment of the International Pacific Salmon Fisheries Commission in May 1930. High-seas salmon fishing by the Japanese led to friction and the North Pacific Fisheries Convention of 1953 (signed by Canada, Japan, and the United States), but regulation and management of the North Pacific salmon fisheries embrace many issues—loss of spawning grounds, pollution, overfishing—that still were not resolved twenty years later.

[V. Carstensen, "The Fisherman's Frontier on the Pacific Coast," in J. G. Clark, ed., *The Frontier Challenge;* J. A. Crutchfield, *The Pacific Salmon Fisheries: A Study of Irrational Conservation.*]

VERNON CARSTENSEN

SALOONS. During the heyday of the saloon, 1870 to 1900, one could be found on nearly any corner. Its windows were heavily curtained, but once inside the swinging doors of the front entrance one crossed the sawdust-covered floor to a long hardwood bar. In front of this was a brass footrail, behind it a huge gilded mirror usually topped by the image of a nude Venus or a brawny John L. Sullivan. Although reputedly the home of "demon rum," the standard drinks were straight corn or rye whiskey and beer. Fancier drinks were on display but seldom sold. Cocktails were known but not shaken until Prohibition. The free lunch consisted of salty foods to stimulate thirst. The saloon's alliance with gambling and prostitution contributed to its downfall. In 1880 the ratio of saloons to population in the United States was 1 to 735; by 1910 it was 1 to 1,350. Many towns, for example Lafayette, Ind., in the 1880's, had one saloon for every 200 people; as local option grew many had none. Elegant bars like the Sazerac in New Orleans, the Waldorf in New York, or Righeimer's in Chicago, and the wild, wide-open saloons of mining boomtowns like Deadwood and Tombstone will be best remembered in American social history.

[George Ade, *The Old Time Saloon.*]

HARVEY L. CARTER

SALT. As a commodity of universal demand, common salt (sodium chloride) has been produced and traded on a large scale since the dawn of civilization. As a national industry, it appears to have gone through three stages in most countries, including the United

States: (1) a drive for self-sufficiency in salt, (2) the discovery of rock salt by deep drilling, and (3) the development, through the application of science, of a large chemical industry based on salt.

Salt can be obtained through the evaporation of seawater or of inland brine springs, or mined as rock salt. The British colonies in America were well situated for the production of sea salt, and there were saltworks at the Jamestown and Plymouth colonies. But they were dependencies of what became in the 18th century the greatest salt-producing country in Europe, and were to be largely importers of salt. During the American Revolution there was a frantic, and largely successful, attempt to produce salt on the American coast, either by the solar evaporation of seawater in lagoons laid out along the shore or (more usually) by boiling it down in cast-iron pots. With the end of the war these establishments became too uneconomical to compete with salt imported from England or from the West Indies, and the United States again became an importer of salt. It was still an importer in the last half of the 19th century.

Interior America possessed many brine springs, known as "licks" because wild animals, especially buffalo, congregated around them to lick the salt deposits. Buffalo trails to these licks became some of the first roads beyond the Appalachians. Many of the licks were known to the French, who largely controlled that region; the first to which the British settlers appear to have paid any attention was in the Onondaga country of central New York. French travelers had reported the Indians to be making a little salt there in the mid-18th century, and in 1788 the Anglo-Americans began to manufacture salt at Salina (now part of Syracuse), N.Y. A little later buffalo licks gave rise to salt production from brine at two other localities, both in Virginia, at what are now Saltville, Va., and Charleston, W.Va. As late as the 1870's salt was produced from buffalo licks in Kansas.

As in Europe, salt was regarded as important enough in the United States to justify government intervention, and most salt-producing lands were reserved to the states, which leased them to private producers. The state of New York provided brine to producers and applied a tax (which was a major source of funds for construction of the Erie Canal). Salt production from brine began on the Scioto River in Jackson County, Ohio, before 1800, and when the state was organized in 1803 the area was set aside as a state reservation. On the Wabash, near Shawneetown, Ill., the federal government actually took on the operation of a saline works in the early 19th century. But as salt proved to be plentiful the interests of governments waned. Salt exploration in Michigan was begun in 1838 under state auspices, but the actual production (1860) was entirely private.

Salt became plentiful in consequence of the discovery of rich sources at great depths. Very deep holes were drilled for salt in China before the Christian era, but the corresponding development in Europe and America only occurred in the 19th century. Salt production appears to have succeeded slightly earlier in the United States, through the effort of two brothers, David and Joseph Ruffner, in the Kanawha country, near present-day Charleston, W.Va., in 1806–08. Their success in finding strong brine at 98 feet made Kanawha a leading salt-producing region. Many other wells followed. By 1835 there were forty furnaces in the region for boiling down brine, and by 1845 one well there had reached 1,500 feet in depth.

Drilling ultimately led to the decline of Kanawha and Onondaga, for production was even greater elsewhere. After reaching a level of 2 million bushels (1 bushel = 56 pounds) a year, by 1850 Kanawha's output declined. Onondaga reached 9 million bushels in 1862, after which its output also declined, drastically after 1883 when salt production began at Wyoming County, N.Y., from a deep well that had been made in search of oil. Rock salt had been found and was produced at various places in New York from 1886. The first discovery of deep rock salt in the United States is thought to have been made in 1841 near Abingdon, Va.

Rock salt was not always deep, and it is now known that the Indians mined salt at several shallow deposits in the Far West. Salt had been made at a spring on Avery Island, La., in 1791, and sporadically thereafter. In the Civil War emergency the Confederate government began to work the spring again, and in 1862 rock salt was found at a depth of only 16 feet. Large-scale mining was begun, only to be terminated by the destruction of the works by Union troops in April 1863. Mining has been continuous at Avery Island since 1883.

Deep salt strata can either be mined or, often more economically, made sources of brine by adding water. Michigan's salt production began in 1860, with a 636-foot well at East Saginaw. In Kansas rock salt was found in 1887, by drilling to 800 feet, near Hutchinson. Drilling has also uncovered salt deposits in many other states, so many that salt has lost its status as a precious commodity.

Since the 1850's one of the most important sources of salt in the United States has been the tidelands of

San Francisco Bay. Here solar salt production was successfully accomplished by a method practiced in France since the Middle Ages. Seawater is admitted to enclosed rectangular basins and transferred to smaller and smaller enclosures as the sun reduces its volume; ultimately, salt is deposited.

Up to the mid-19th century nearly all salt was produced for human (and some animal) consumption, although about half of it was for an indirect use, in meat-packing. In England large quantities were used in making artificial soda (sodium carbonate); this industry came to the United States in 1882, and by 1900 consumed about half of the salt used in the country. By 1957 nearly 80 percent of the salt consumed in the United States went to the chemical industry, and the artificial soda industry had been replaced as the primary user by industries based on the elemental constituents of salt—sodium and chlorine. The primary uses of sodium are in the manufacture of caustic soda (sodium hydroxide), which is in turn used to make the artificial fiber rayon; in the process for producing aluminum; and in the plastics and detergents industries, which were developed during the two decades after 1890. The chlorine-consuming industries are even newer, although they depend on the mid-19th-century discoveries of the chlorinated hydrocarbons, organic compounds in which one or more carbon atoms have been replaced by chlorine. By the 1970's over half the salt used in the United States was converted to chlorine (and sodium), the chlorine ultimately being converted into the chlorinated hydrocarbons used in plastics (for example, vinyl chloride), solvents (for dry cleaning), automotive fluids (antifreeze and leaded gasolines), and pesticides (such as DDT).

Most of these uses date from about 1940. But despite the growing chemical industry, its share of American salt had dropped by 1974 to 63 percent, because of an even newer application. Beginning in the 1950's the salting of highways for snow and ice removal increased continuously, until by 1974, 17 percent of the salt consumed was for this purpose. Since the automobile also accounts for the salt used in making automotive fluids and uses much of the plastics, it has clearly become the largest consumer of salt.

American salt production in 1974 was over 46 million tons, by far the world's largest. And yet to meet demand, 3 million tons were imported, an amount equal to the entire consumption of the country in 1900.

[G. W. Atkinson, *History of Kanawha Company, W.Va.;* G. Bathe, "The Onondaga Salt Works of New York State,"

Transactions of the Newcomen Society, vol. 25 (1945–47); Ella Lonn, *Salt as a Factor in the Confederacy;* D. C. McMurtrie, "Negotiations for the Illinois Salt Springs, 1802–03," *Bulletin of the Chicago Historical Society* (March 1937); E. W. Parker, "History of Salt Making in the United States," *Eighteenth Annual Report of the U.S. Geological Survey,* part 5 (1897); H. B. Weiss and G. M. Weiss, *The Revolutionary Saltworks of the New Jersey Coast.*]

ROBERT P. MULTHAUF

SALT LAKE CITY, capital and largest city of Utah, located on the Jordan River thirteen miles east of the Great Salt Lake, was founded by Brigham Young and his Mormon followers in 1847. It was originally laid out in ten-acre squares with streets 132 feet wide after the plan of the City of Zion prepared in 1833 by Joseph Smith and was called Great Salt Lake City until 1868. It has been the headquarters of the Church of Jesus Christ of Latter-Day Saints (Mormons) since its founding. For a brief period Salt Lake City was the capital of the State of Deseret, and in 1856 it became the capital of Utah Territory; in 1896 it became the state capital. Salt Lake City remained entirely Mormon in population until the Utah War of 1857–58.

The city is in an area of great mineral wealth, but mining did not begin until 1862. With the completion of the Utah Central Railroad in 1870, Salt Lake City became an important commercial and transportation center. Industries include oil refining, food processing, and the manufacture of textiles and electronic equipment. Among the many fine structures in the city are the Mormon Tabernacle (1867) and the Temple. The latter is of gray granite from the nearby Wasatch Mountains and was under construction from 1853 to 1893. The population of Salt Lake City in 1970 was 175,885.

[Richard F. Burton, *The City of the Saints;* William Chandless, *A Visit to Salt Lake City;* O. F. Whitney, *History of Utah.*]

"SALT RIVER," or "up Salt River," is a term used to describe political defeat. It originated in an incident occurring during the presidential campaign of 1832 on the Salt River, a Kentucky branch of the Ohio River. Henry Clay, as the National Republican candidate against President Andrew Jackson, a Democrat, hired a boatman to row him up the Ohio to Louisville, where he was to make a speech; but the boatman, said to be a Jackson man, rowed Clay, by mistake or by design, up the Salt River instead, and Clay failed to reach Louisville in time for his speech.

His defeat for the presidency brought later derisive references to this incident, and Rep. Alexander Duncan of Ohio, gifted in coining apt terms, probably first used the expression, "they have been rowing up Salt River," in a speech in the House of Representatives in 1839 to describe the futility of the opposition party.

CLARENCE A. BERDAHL

SALT SPRINGS TRACT consisted of 24,000 acres of land along the Mahoning River, near Niles, Ohio, granted (1788) by Connecticut (*see* Western Reserve) to Gen. Samuel H. Parsons. Parsons visited his lands but, returning home in 1789, was drowned in the Beaver River. At first the Parsons claim was disregarded by the Connecticut Land Company, but later parts of two townships were given to his heirs and assigns. The springs, used by the Indians for salt-making, were known to pioneers at least by 1755, as is evident from the Lewis Evans Map, and were visited by Pennsylvania's saltmakers during the Revolution. The springs were used, later, by settlers in the region, but were never developed commercially.

[C. L. Shepard, *Connecticut Land Company and Accompanying Papers.*]

HAROLD E. DAVIS

SALT WAR (1877), a disturbance in El Paso County, Texas, over the free use of the salt lakes east of San Elizario, a town on the Rio Grande. The salt question became involved in politics, and a feud developed between Louis Cardis, who was backed by the Mexicans, and Charles H. Howard, supported by the Americans. Howard killed Cardis, and the bitter feeling that followed culminated in a riot at San Elizario, in which Howard and two other men were slain by a mob of Mexicans from both sides of the Rio Grande. Later some Mexicans were killed by Texas rangers and a sheriff's posse, but most of the rioters escaped to Mexico.

[H. H. Bancroft, *North Mexican States and Texas;* W. P. Webb, *The Texas Rangers.*]

C. T. NEU

SALVATION ARMY, an evangelistic organization created in 1865 by William Booth, a former Methodist, to work among the poor of London. His book *In Darkest England and the Way Out* (1890) not only won popular support for his movement but was instrumental in awakening public opinion to conditions in the world's richest city. The present military for-

mat dates from the publication of *The Orders and Regulations for the Salvation Army* in 1878. Booth became known as General Booth. The uniforms, designed by his wife, Catherine Mumford Booth, were adopted in the early 1880's. A branch of the army was formed in the United States in 1880 and received leadership from Evangeline Cory Booth, the general's daughter, from 1904 to 1934. The group has been noted for the vigor of its preaching, its energetic use of music, and its crusades on behalf of the poor and oppressed. It has considered itself to have a special mission to alcoholics. The U.S. membership in 1975 was 361,571.

[Sallie Chreham, *Born to Battle: The Salvation Army in America.*]

GLENN T. MILLER

SALZBURGERS IN GEORGIA. In 1734 a group of seventy-eight Protestants, who had been driven out of Salzburg, Austria, by the bishop of Salzburg, landed in the new colony of Georgia. They were settled by James Oglethorpe up the Savannah River at a place that they called Ebenezer. Being dissatisfied with their original location, they were moved to a more convenient spot on the river itself, bringing the name Ebenezer with them. By 1741, 1,200 Salzburgers were living in Georgia, mostly in Ebenezer and the surrounding territory, but a few had settled on Saint Simon Island. Lutheran in religion and German in language, they were largely ruled over by their ministers.

[C. C. Jones, Jr., *The History of Georgia,* and *The Dead Towns of Georgia;* P. A. Strobel, *The Salzburgers and Their Descendants.*]

E. MERTON COULTER

SAM HOUSTON, FORT, a U.S. Army post located in San Antonio, Tex., originally the mission of San Antonio de Valero, established by the Spanish in 1718. Known as the Alamo, the mission was secularized in 1794 and became a Spanish military post, and from the close of the Mexican War in 1848 it was used as an American troop garrison. Construction of a permanent post began in the late 1870's, and in 1890 it was redesignated Fort Sam Houston to honor the leader and hero of the Texas Revolution.

Fort Sam Houston is now the home of the Fourth Army and the Brooke Army Medical Center, the major training center for army medics.

[Mary O. Handy, *History of Fort Sam Houston;* Francis P. Prucha, *A Guide to the Military Posts of the United States, 1789–1895.*]

SAMOA, AMERICAN. The only territory of the United States lying south of the equator, American Samoa was the subject of international interest and tension for most of the last half of the 19th century. After several abortive efforts to settle its fate, the United States, Germany, and England agreed in 1899 to divide the islands of the Samoa group at the 171st meridian, with Germany acquiring the islands of Western Samoa (which later became a mandate of New Zealand under the League of Nations, then a trusteeship under the United Nations, and still later an independent state) and with the United States acquiring the six eastern islands, thereafter known as American Samoa. In 1900 and 1904, respectively, the principal chiefs of Tutuila and the three Manua islands, the major islands of the American Samoa group, executed voluntary acts of cession of their islands to the United States. In 1925 a seventh island, Swains Island, was acquired by the United States.

The Samoan population, numbering about 27,000 in 1970, is largely Polynesian. Although increasingly westernized, the Samoans continued to cling to a strong local clan system, known as the matai system. The seven principal islands that constitute American Samoa have a total land area of seventy-six square miles. The seat of government is on the island of Tutuila, which has 80 percent of the population and 55 percent of the land, and where the superb port of Pago Pago is located.

Until July 1, 1951, American Samoa was administered by the U.S. Navy, pursuant to executive orders of the president. An act of Congress of Feb. 20, 1929, which remained the basis of government in Samoa in the mid-1970's, states merely that until the Congress further provides ''all civil, judicial, and military powers shall be vested in such person or persons and shall be exercised in such manner as the President of the United States shall direct.'' Administration was transferred from the navy to the Department of the Interior by executive order in 1951, and governors of Samoa have since been civilians, appointed by the secretary of the interior. In 1960 the interior secretary, acting pursuant to his authorization from the president, approved a constitution for the territory that had been drafted and approved by a constitutional convention elected by the Samoans. Subsequent amendments have been ratified by the Samoan electorate. The constitution of American Samoa contains a bill of rights somewhat similar to that of the U.S. Constitution. It grants extensive legislative authority to a bicameral legislature; the lower house is popularly elected and the upper house is composed largely of Samoan

chiefs. The judicial branch includes the High Court of American Samoa and lesser courts. There is no appeal to the U.S. federal judicial system.

The people of Samoa are nationals but generally not citizens of the United States. Some have achieved citizenship status through individual naturalization, often as a result of service in the U.S. armed forces. The processing of fish, caught by foreign fishing fleets, and, increasingly, tourism represent Samoa's principal economic activities.

[J. A. C. Gray, *Amerika Samoa and its Naval Administration.*]

RUTH G. VAN CLEVE

SAMPLERS originated as a means of keeping samples of stitches used in embroidering tablecloths, napkins, towels, pillowcases, and other household articles before books of patterns existed.

The earliest known mention of a sampler occurred in 1505, when Elizabeth of York paid 8 pence for ''an elne of lynnyn for a sampler for the queen.'' The will of Mary Thompson, dated 1546, reads: ''I gyve to Alys Pinchebeck my sampler with semes.'' By the middle of the century samplers had become the fashion in England, and in the early part of the next century English women were making them in New England.

What is believed to be the earliest example of a sampler in the United States (now in the Essex Institute, Salem, Mass.) was worked by Anne Gower in 1610 and brought by her to America. The first sampler known to have been made in America (now in Pilgrim Hall, Plymouth, Mass.) was the work of Laura Standish, daughter of Myles Standish.

Not infrequently the creation of children as young as age five, the American samplers surpass all others in originality, inventiveness, and decorative quality. In the mid-18th century Adam and Eve were popular subjects for samplers. Later, family trees, shepherds, the maker's house, and sometimes whole villages were depicted, the designs becoming increasingly freer. In the early 19th century the American eagle often appeared. After 1830 the art of sampler making declined but did not completely disappear.

[Ethel S. Bolton and Eva J. Coe, *American Samplers.*]

KATHARINE METCALF ROOF

SAMPLING METHODS AND PROCEDURES. Sampling is another name for statistical work, in which the aim is rational conclusions from statistical data, with the aid of the theory of probability, and for planning quantitative studies to achieve maximum reliability at lowest cost.

A statistical study requires (1) specification of the frame, a list of units that comprise the whole aggregate of material subject to observation (for example, all the manufactured product turned out last week by a production line; all the adults of some specified age, occupation, or sex within a specified area, as in studies of unemployment, nutrition, or ailment; the patients in a hospital with a specified ailment; all the business establishments of a specified kind and size in a region; the crop of wheat or of rice in a country); (2) specification of the method of selection from the frame of a sample of units for investigation (in modern practice, this step requires use of random numbers); (3) the estimator, or formula by which to prepare estimates of characteristics of the whole frame or of the process; (4) formulas for the calculation of the standard errors of the estimates; (5) controls to detect, reduce, and evaluate the effects of contamination (errors, illegible entries, nonresponse, investigation of wrong units, spoilage, and so on); and (6) a statement of inferences or conclusions drawn from the investigation, together with the limitations of these inferences, which will be based on the standard error and the contaminations detected.

A study of the cause of change or of difference (called an analytic study), such as a study of medical treatments, manufacturing processes, or agricultural treatment, requires, besides the frame, a statement of the environmental conditions under which the study was, or will be, conducted, such as economic conditions, soil, climate, rainfall, types of patients studied, duration of the test, range of voltage, temperature, and speed. In an analytic study, the sample is often 100 percent of the frame. Even if the sample is a 100 percent sample of the frame, the theory of probability is necessary for valid statistical inference in respect to the cause-system or production process.

Sampling covers a wide range of application. For example, the aim of a study might be to estimate the total number of inhabitants of a city or of a region or the number of persons unemployed. The aim might be to estimate from records of the flow of a certain river the minimum flow or the maximum flood to be expected in the next century. Other applications are in tests of drugs, medical treatments, safety devices, or complex apparatus and prototypes; numerical evaluation of complex functions that defy mathematical integration; creation of models of the economy or of population growth; and determination of trajectories of spacecraft.

The chief characteristic of modern statistical practice is that every estimate is accompanied by a practical limit of uncertainty.

Mathematicians and scientists in many lands have made contributions, one age-old application being the calculation of odds in playing with dice or cards. Use of least squares by Carl Friedrich Gauss, around 1815, for the calculation of orbits of planets and comets is an example. The work of Karl Pearson in the theory of heredity and evolution, mainly between 1900 and 1930, is another. The kinetic theory of gases, Brownian motion, osmosis, and filtering are further contributions.

Arthur L. Bowley of England, beginning about 1900, laid the foundation for the design and analysis of experiments and for the use of small samples for estimation of demographic characteristics of the population. Morris H. Hansen in America, beginning in 1934, led the modern foundation for sampling for demographic data: his initial activity was to estimate the proportion of people unemployed during the Great Depression. P. C. Mahalanobis made parallel advances in agricultural censuses and experimentation in India. Sir Ronald Fisher, at Rothamsted, later at Cambridge, between 1923 and 1950 laid the foundation for analytic studies, with applications mainly to agricultural science. Harold F. Dodge and Harry Romig of the Bell Telephone Laboratories in New York published in 1926 the theory of acceptance sampling of manufactured product, together with tables, now used worldwide. Walter A. Shewhart of America opened up the field of statistical control of quality for economy in production. L. C. H. Tippett and Egon Pearson of England contributed heavily from 1931 onward to the theory and application of statistical methods in industry.

[W. G. Cochran, *Sampling Techniques;* W. Edwards Deming, *Sample Design in Business Research;* Morris H. Hansen, William Hurwitz, and William G. Madow, *Sample Survey Methods and Theory;* Leslie Kish, *Survey Sampling.*]

W. Edwards Deming

SAMPSON-SCHLEY CONTROVERSY arose primarily from the fact that when the Battle of Santiago began, July 3, 1898, Adm. William T. Sampson in his flagship *New York* was seven miles to the east, in distant signal range but unable to participate effectively against the Spanish ships fleeing the Cuban harbor. Sampson had signaled that the other ships should disregard the movement of the flagship, but did not turn over command to Commodore Winfield S.

Schley, second in command. Largely because of his more affable treatment of press correspondents, Schley—actually Sampson's senior in rank—received popular credit for the victory. The resultant controversy raged bitterly in press and Congress, halted promotion of both officers, and raised criticism of Schley's conduct earlier in the campaign. In 1901 a court of inquiry requested by Schley condemned the much-discussed outward turn of his flagship *Brooklyn* at Santiago and his "dilatoriness" earlier while commanding the Flying Squadron. Upon final appeal, President Theodore Roosevelt declared Santiago "a captains' battle," in which "technically Sampson commanded" and movements followed standing orders. Both officers received routine promotion to permanent rear admiral in 1899.

ALLAN WESTCOTT

SAM SLICK, a literary character created by Thomas Chandler Haliburton (1796–1865), a Canadian humorist. Although a native of Nova Scotia, Haliburton achieved his fame as a portrayer of the typical New England Yankee. In several volumes of sketches Haliburton carried Sam Slick, a Yankee clock peddler, through numerous adventures in America and England.

[V. L. O. Chittick, *Thomas Chandler Haliburton, Sam Slick: A Study in Provincial Toryism.*]

E. H. O'NEILL

SAN ANTONIO, a city and port of entry in south central Texas, was founded in 1718 by a Spanish military expedition that established a mission and presidio. Some of the soldiers were married, and their families formed the nucleus of a village, or civil settlement. Several years later a chain of missions was established in the valley below San Antonio, and in 1731 the village was reinforced by a small colony from the Canary Islands. The settlement thus became the civil and military capital of Texas during the Spanish-Mexican regime.

The prominence of San Antonio in state and regional life and literature is derived chiefly from its historic past. During the Texas Revolution, it was first captured from its strong Mexican garrison by siege (December 1835) and later recaptured by Gen. Antonio López de Santa Anna in the tragic assault on the Alamo (March 1836), only to be regained by the Texans as a result of their victory at San Jacinto (April 1836), which practically established the in-

dependence of the Republic of Texas. As the largest settlement on the southern and western frontier, San Antonio was exposed to raids from Mexicans and Indians. During 1842 it was twice occupied by Mexican raiders and was the scene of desperate fighting in which a considerable proportion of the Comanche leaders who had assembled for a council to discuss terms of peace were massacred. Soon after the annexation of Texas by the United States in 1845, San Antonio became the chief military post in a line of forts that the federal government established to guard the southern and western frontiers.

Prior to the development of ranching on the west Texas plains in the early 1880's, San Antonio, the starting point of the Chisholm Trail, was the headquarters of the Texas cattle industry. The establishment of Fort Sam Houston, the headquarters of the Fourth Army, in the late 1870's marks the beginning of San Antonio's development as a military center. The city is also the home of four air bases, including Kelly Air Force Base (established 1917), which in 1943 was converted to a vast industrial complex, manufacturing aircraft and serving as a supply base. The population of San Antonio in 1970 was 654,153.

[Gerald Ashford, *Spanish Texas: Yesterday and Today;* Clayton Williams, *Never Again: Texas B.C. to Eighteen Twenty-One,* 3 vols.]

E. C. BARKER

SAN ANTONIO MISSIONS, so named because they lie in and near San Antonio, Tex., were founded by the Spanish Franciscans between 1718 and 1731 and formed the center of activity in Texas during the 18th century. San Antonio de Valero in San Antonio, the present much-visited Alamo, is the oldest. Best known of the other four missions along the San Antonio River are Purísima Concepción and, the most beautiful of all, San José, which was founded in 1720 by Antonio Margil and designated a national historic site in 1941.

[C. E. Castañeda, *Our Catholic Heritage in Texas.*]

FRANCIS BORGIA STECK

SANBORN CONTRACTS. President Ulysses S. Grant's secretary of the Treasury, W. A. Richardson, in collusion with Rep. Benjamin F. Butler of Massachusetts, gave to John D. Sanborn of Boston contracts to collect large sums of overdue federal internal revenue taxes. Since little effort had been made to secure payment, Sanborn easily collected $427,000 at a commission of 50 percent. On May 4, 1874, the

SAND CREEK MASSACRE

House Ways and Means Committee exposed the fraud. The committee privately asked Grant to remove Richardson from the cabinet, and the following month Richardson was appointed to the U.S. Court of Claims. Butler was defeated for reelection.

GEORGE D. HARMON

SAND CREEK MASSACRE. On Nov. 29, 1864, Colorado militiamen descended upon an encampment of Southern Cheyenne at Sand Creek, thirty miles northeast of Fort Lyon in southeastern Colorado Territory, killing about a third of a band of 500, most of whom were women and children. The chief of the Cheyenne, Black Kettle, had tried to keep peace with the whites, but there had been a number of incidents and clashes between white gold miners and the Indians of the area. Indian activity had endangered lines of communication between Denver and the Missouri River. Chief Black Kettle, following instructions after a conference with the governor and having been guaranteed safe conduct, had brought his band to Sand Creek and had placed them under the protection of the fort. Despite the peaceful intentions of the Cheyenne, they were the object of a vicious attack by the Colorado volunteers under Col. J. M. Chivington and were slaughtered, mutilated, and tortured, although the militiamen were so undisciplined that many of the Indians managed to escape. The wanton massacre was a cause of further Indian warfare in the Plains, as the Cheyenne warriors, most of whom had been away hunting at the time of the massacre, joined with the Sioux and Arapaho in new attacks on the settlers.

[Stan Hoig, *The Sand Creek Massacre.*]
KENNETH M. STEWART

SAN DIEGO, a California city located about twelve miles from the Mexican border. It was named San Diego de Alcalá de Henares, after a Spanish monk, by Sebastián Vizcaíno in 1602. A presidio was founded in 1769 by Gaspar de Portolá, governor of Baja (Lower) California. A military post until 1835, it occupied the site known today as Old Town. Being a seaport and close to the Mexican border, San Diego loomed large in the disturbances following Mexico's emancipation from Spain and in the later conflict between Mexico and the United States. Although a civil government was established in 1835, the town had in 1840 only 150 inhabitants. It was practically extinct when ten years later California became a state. The present metropolis, three miles below Old Town, was founded in 1867 by Alonzo E. Horton, a merchant prospector of San Francisco. At San Diego in 1846 the U.S. flag was raised officially, though prematurely, for the first time on California soil.

San Diego was incorporated in 1872, and its favorable climate drew many settlers. The population and real estate values boomed after the arrival of the Santa Fe Railway in 1884. The rapid growth of the city led to the development in the 20th century of the aerospace, electronics, and shipbuilding industries. San Diego is headquarters for the Eleventh Naval District and home of a number of army, navy, and Coast Guard installations. Balboa Park, center of the city's cultural activities, also houses the San Diego Zoo, one of the largest in the world. The city's population in 1970 was 697,027.

[H. H. Bancroft, *History of California.*]
FRANCIS BORGIA STECK

SANDUSKY, from the Huron *Otsaandosti,* meaning "cool water," was a name applied to the river, bay, and Indian villages in northern Ohio. The Wyandot (Huron) from Detroit occupied the region by 1740 and permitted English traders to erect a post on the northern side of the bay in 1745. The French displaced the English and built "Fort Sandoski" (1751), but soon evacuated it and erected Fort Junandot (1754) on the east side of the mouth of the Sandusky River, retaining it until the fall of Fort Duquesne. An English blockhouse was built and occupied in 1761 by Ensign Paulli and fifteen men, but the garrison, except Paulli, was wiped out in Pontiac's War in 1763. Col. John Bradstreet's expedition later encamped up the river at present-day Fremont to treat with the Indians. Both Lower Sandusky (Fremont) and Upper Sandusky were important Indian centers during the American Revolution. By the Treaty of Greenville the former became a government military reservation, two miles square. In the War of 1812 Fort Stephenson, located there, was attacked unsuccessfully by the British and Indians. In 1816 an act of Congress created the town of Croghansville in the reservation. Later they were united and became Lower Sandusky, which was renamed Fremont. The present city of Sandusky on the bay was settled in 1817.

[E. O. Randall and D. J. Ryan, *History of Ohio;* Lucy E. Keeler, "Old Fort Sandoski of 1745," and "The Sandusky Country," *Ohio Archaeological and Historical Society Publications,* vol. 17.]

EUGENE H. ROSEBOOM

SANDWICH ISLANDS. *See* **Hawaii.**

SANDY CREEK, BATTLE OF (May 30, 1814). Driven into Sandy Creek, on the New York shore of Lake Ontario, while transporting guns and cables from Oswego to Sackets Harbor, U.S. Capt. Melancthon Woolsey ordered 120 riflemen to wait in ambush for six pursuing British boats. The riflemen captured all the boats, inflicting a loss of 18 killed, 40 wounded, and about 130 captured. One American was wounded.

[E. S. Maclay, *A History of the United States Navy.*]
ALLAN F. WESTCOTT

SAN FELIPE–CORREO **AFFAIR.** The *Correo de Méjico,* a Mexican revenue cutter, on Sept. 1, 1835, attempted to capture the *San Felipe,* which was allegedly laden with munitions for the coming Texan revolt. The Texans not only resisted capture but attacked and captured the cutter, thus stirring Mexico City to punitive action that committed the Texans to war.

[Jim Dan Hill, *The Texas Navy.*]
JIM DAN HILL

SAN FRANCISCO, a seaport city in California commanding one of the world's best harbors. In 1769 during the course of Spain's settlement of Upper (Alta) California, Gaspar de Portolá, while exploring northward from the first Spanish settlement of San Diego, discovered San Francisco Bay. Subsequent expeditions revealed the landlocked harbor's great size, safety, and strategic value, and in 1776 Spain occupied the peninsula site of the present city. On Sept. 17 settlers brought from Sonora by Juan Bautista de Anza founded a presidio, and the mission San Francisco de Asís was dedicated on Oct. 9. Following California's transfer to Mexico with the latter's independence from Spain in 1821, the village of Dolores was formed near the mission. Three miles away, the small trading settlement of Yerba Buena (changed to San Francisco in 1848) grew up on the beach, beginning in 1835.

U.S. interest in the region began in the early 19th century. New England whalers used the bay as a provisioning and refitting station, and American traders largely dominated Yerba Buena, except for a short period of control by the Hudson's Bay Company. After vain endeavors by President John Tyler to purchase the bay region, Capt. John B. Montgomery of the U.S. Navy at length established American rule on July 9, 1846, during the Mexican War.

With the discovery of gold on the American River in 1848, San Francisco mushroomed from a quiet village of about 900 people to a bustling cosmopolitan town of at least 10,000 by September 1849. In 1850 San Francisco was incorporated as a city. Six great fires between December 1849 and May 1851 swept away the community's makeshift tents and buildings, causing damage estimated at nearly $25 million, uninsured, but resulting in the building of a new city on a more substantial basis. Lawlessness was an even greater problem. The government's failure to deal effectively with the large criminal element led in 1851 and 1856 to the organization of citizens' vigilance committees, which rid the city of many lawbreakers. Politics largely continued to be corrupt until 1906, when a sweeping graft investigation, halted temporarily by the great earthquake and fire of that year, brought about the victory of a reform party.

Following the decline of gold production and the resultant depression of the late 1850's, San Francisco developed rapidly as a center of industry, finance, and world trade. Threatened in the 1870's by a severe financial crash, largely the product of overspeculation in Nevada mining stocks, the city's position was assured by the completion of the transcontinental railroad in 1869 and the Panama Canal in 1914.

During the 20th century San Francisco became the financial capital of the West, being the home of the Bank of America, the nation's largest bank since 1945, and the Pacific Coast Stock Exchange. A culinary capital as well, and physically one of the most beautiful cities in the world, San Francisco also became an important cultural center. Its War Memorial Opera House (1934) was the first major opera house in the United States to be municipally built and owned. Important innovations in public transportation include the cable cars, first installed in 1873, the San Francisco–Oakland Bay Bridge (1936), the Golden Gate Bridge (1937), and the Bay Area Rapid Transit (BART) system (opened 1972), the first major urban transit system to be planned and built in the United States since World War II. San Francisco draws a great many tourists each year to see such sights as Fisherman's Wharf, Ghirardelli Square, Nob Hill, and Alcatraz. In 1970 the city's population was 715,674.

[C. C. Dobie, *San Francisco: A Pageant;* Z. S. Eldridge, *The Beginnings of San Francisco;* Oscar Lewis, *San Francisco: Mission to Metropolis.*]
CHARLES EDWARD CHAPMAN
ROBERT HALE SHIELDS

SAN FRANCISCO DE LOS TEJAS, the first Spanish mission established in eastern Texas, was founded in 1690 west of the Neches River, near the present village of Weches. Pestilence and Indian hostility led to its abandonment in 1693. In 1716 it was refounded farther inland near the present town of Alto, where it was called San Francisco de los Neches. Three years later it was again abandoned, but Marquis San Miguelde Aguayo, governor of the province of Tejas, reestablished it in 1721. It was never successful because the Indians could not be induced to accept mission life. It was moved from eastern Texas in 1730 and refounded the next year at San Antonio, under the name of San Francisco de la Espada.

[F. W. Hodge, *Handbook of American Indians.*]

C. T. NEU

SAN FRANCISCO EARTHQUAKE (Apr. 18, 1906). San Francisco had experienced several earthquakes and major fires prior to 1906, but none approached the catastrophe of that year. The first and heaviest shocks came early on the morning of Apr. 18 and were followed by minor tremors for the next three days. Serious damage was produced in an area about 450 miles long and 50 miles wide. In San Francisco, buildings crumbled, streets on filled ground buckled, and gas and water mains ruptured. Fire, however, caused the heaviest damage, raging through the central business and residential districts for three days before being controlled. Some 497 city blocks were razed, or about one-third of the city. Because the water-supply system was disrupted, dynamite and artillery were used to check the holocaust.

The property loss has been estimated at between $350 million and $500 million. There were about 700 deaths, and some 250,000 homeless refugees flooded the streets, the Presidio, and Golden Gate Park or went to neighboring cities. To meet the emergency, martial law was declared.

The tragedy excited nationwide and international sympathy and, through the medium of the Red Cross, money and supplies poured in from American, Asian, and European contributors. Under stringent building regulations, reconstruction progressed rapidly and within three years a new city arose upon the ruins of the old.

[F. W. Aitken and E. Hilton, *A History of the Fire and Earthquake in San Francisco.*]

CHARLES EDWARD CHAPMAN
ROBERT HALE SHIELDS

SAN GABRIEL, BATTLE OF (Jan. 8–9, 1847), a conflict between about 600 American soldiers, sailors, and volunteers, commanded by Commodore Robert F. Stockton and Gen. Stephen W. Kearny, and 500 Mexicans under Col. José María Flores, Andrés Pico, and José Antonio Carrillo, at Paso de Bartolo on the San Gabriel River, a little north of present-day Whittier, Calif. The Mexicans were dislodged from their position on Jan. 8, after about two hours of fighting. As the American forces continued their advance toward Los Angeles the next day, the Mexicans, reduced in numbers, attacked them on both flanks, near the Los Angeles River. This action, known also as the Battle of La Mesa, resulted in the retreat of Flores' command. On Jan. 10 the Americans reoccupied Los Angeles, and three days later the remnants of the Mexican forces surrendered to Lt. Col. John C. Frémont at Rancho Cahuenga, ending hostilities in California.

[R. G. Cleland, *A History of California: The American Period.*]

RUFUS KAY WYLLYS

SANGRE DE CRISTO GRANT. In 1844 the Mexican government deeded to Narcisco Beaubien and Stephen Louis Lee a parcel of land totaling 1,038,195 acres in the San Luis Valley of southern Colorado and northern New Mexico. The grant included the main waters of the Costilla, Trinchera, and Culebra rivers and extended from the Rio Grande on the west to the summit of the Sangre de Cristo range on the east. Beaubien, a boy in his teens, held title as surrogate for his father, Carlos, already co-owner of a large adjacent grant. Narcisco Beaubien and Lee died in New Mexico in the Taos massacre of 1847. The former's claim passed to his father, who purchased Lee's share from his estate for $100. The Sangre de Cristo became American territory after the Mexican War (1848), and in 1860 Congress confirmed the original charter. The first successful attempt to colonize the area was made in 1851, north of the present town of San Luis, Colo. In 1864, after Charles Beaubien's death, William Gilpin, Colorado's first territorial governor, and some associates purchased the grant. It was later divided and passed through the hands of various land developers, but the northern quarter, 240,000 acres, remained intact as the Trinchera Ranch, one of the largest private estates in Colorado.

[L. R. Hafen, "Mexican Land Grants in Colorado," *Colorado Magazine* (1927); R. C. Taylor, *Colorado South of the Border.*]

DAVID C. BAILEY

SAN ILDEFONSO, TREATY OF, a secret treaty, executed in preliminary form on Oct. 1, 1800, and made effective on Oct. 15, 1802, by which Spain retroceded Louisiana to France in return for the newly created Italian kingdom of Etruria.

Sovereign over Louisiana since the French and Indian War (1754–63), Spain had developed neither economic profit from nor colonial attachment to the region, but in surrendering the province the king of Spain ignored vital issues of strategy and national prestige. He negotiated without the knowledge of his chief minister, Manuel de Godoy, who, on learning the facts, was shocked by the levity with which an empire had been alienated. Godoy's chagrin equaled the elation of Lucien Bonaparte, Napoleon's brother, who assumed much credit for the French success. While Spain was losing a vast but unprofitable domain beyond the Mississippi, Napoleon believed himself restorer of the colonial empire lost so ignominiously by his Bourbon predecessors.

Rumors of the pending transfer rekindled President Thomas Jefferson's interest in the Mississippi Valley, which he had hoped the United States would eventually acquire from Spain. Pressure from the Federalists led to Jefferson's dispatching James Monroe to France in March 1803 and the purchase of Louisiana the following month.

[Edward Channing, *A History of the United States,* vol. IV; Charles E. Hill, *Leading American Treaties.*]
LOUIS MARTIN SEARS

SANITARY COMMISSION, UNITED STATES, was created by the federal government in June 1861 under the presidency of Rev. Henry W. Bellows, a noted Unitarian divine, who had been active in organizing war-relief work. Its purpose was to assist in the care of sick and wounded soldiers and their dependent families during the Civil War. It was supported mainly by private contributions. Most of the local aid societies, active since the very first days of the war, immediately affiliated as branches of the national organization. (*See also* Christian Commission.)

The commission developed an elaborate organization and at times employed as many as 500 agents. Its work covered almost every conceivable form of aid, including field and hospital medical inspection, field ambulance and hospital service, and hospital cars and steamers. It also maintained feeding stations and soldiers' lodges and supplied assistance to dependent families. Funds were raised by churches, private contributions, and especially by fairs. Camp life during the Civil War was much improved by its work.

[E. D. Fite, *Social and Industrial Conditions in the North;* C. J. Stillé, *History of the U.S. Sanitary Commission.*]
JOHN COLBERT COCHRANE

SANITATION, ENVIRONMENTAL. To the first settlers the fresh clean air and sparkling waters of the New World contrasted sharply with the ingrained dirt and filth of ancient European cities, and the vast reaches of the new continent made it difficult for them to contemplate the possibility of dirt and crowding. But man's unhappy faculty for befouling his environment soon made governmental action necessary. Shortly after the establishment of the Dutch colony of New Amsterdam a law in 1644 forbade its residents from urinating and depositing filth within the fort. In 1657 other ordinances prohibited throwing dead animals, rubbish, and filth into the streets and canals of the town, and the following year another ordinance decreed that certain privies that were causing an outrageous stench should be torn down. In Boston and other early colonial towns similar sanitary measures were soon enacted. As early as 1634 Boston prohibited depositing garbage or dead fish in the vicinity of the common landing place and passed other measures seeking to eliminate the "loathsome smells" arising from privies, slaughterhouses, and the so-called nuisance trades.

The connection between filth and disease had been made early in history, and informed American colonists argued for sanitary measures on both aesthetic and health grounds. In the 18th century, yellow fever, which struck most heavily in the crowded and dirty dock areas, gave emphasis to the prevailing miasmatic thesis, the theory that disease was caused by a mysterious and invisible gas or miasma emanating from putrefying organic substances. Cadwallader Colden, a physician best known for his political activities and historical writings, warned in 1743 that New York City, because of its deleterious atmosphere and unsanitary condition, was in grave danger of yellow fever, and he urged a massive drainage and sanitary program to restore the city to a healthful state.

The pleas of Colden and other intelligent observers went unheeded, and as the colonial settlements grew, their sanitary problems intensified at an even faster rate. The records are full of complaints about the deplorable condition of the streets and the offensive stenches arising from slaughterhouses, tanners, fat and bone boilers, and other trades. Despite a series of ordinances prohibiting the practice, drainage ditches, canals, docks, gutters, and vacant lots continued to be repositories for garbage, offal, carrion, rubbish, and human waste products. Municipal authorities began assuming some responsibility for street cleaning and sewage removal, but their efforts rarely achieved more than temporary success.

The first tentative steps in the direction of sewer

systems arose from the offensive condition of the drainage ditches and canals. In despair, local residents began demanding that these ditches be covered. In one response to a petition in 1703, a "Common Sewer," approximately 1,200 feet long, was constructed along Broad Street in New York City. In the succeeding years New York and other colonial towns gradually built more of these sewers. These structures were originally meant to be conduits for draining surface water, but so much sewage flowed into the gutters that they were in actuality sewers. Since they poured their contents into the docks or onto the shores and banks of adjacent bodies of water, they created almost as much of a nuisance as the one they sought to remedy.

Water supplies were an equally grave problem. The more fortunate towns in the colonial period drew their water from fast-flowing streams or large rivers, but the majority of colonists relied on public and private wells. With the contents of privies and cesspools constantly seeping into the ground and overflowing into the gutters, these wells seldom ran dry; the consequence was endemic enteric diseases that affected all segments of the population but took their heaviest toll among infants and young children. By the 1790's Boston, Philadelphia, New York, and other cities were developing elementary water systems. By use of wooden pipes and primitive steam engines, water was supplied to the homes of the well-to-do and occasional hydrants appeared in the poorer neighborhoods. Unfortunately the water sources were often polluted and, even when they were safe, the frequent loss of pressure combined with leaking pipe connections led to contamination.

The 19th century saw sanitary conditions, particularly in towns and cities, grow steadily worse. The twin movements of industrialization and urbanization crowded the working poor into squalid warrens and created an ideal environment for Asiatic cholera and other enteric disorders. During the first half of the century temporary health boards emerged. Although they functioned only when epidemics threatened, they occasionally initiated massive sanitary programs. These programs involved removing garbage and dead animals from the streets and lots, emptying privies and cesspools, and draining the many stagnant pools. In addition, quicklime and other substances were spread in the gutters, graveyards, and all possible sources of noxious miasmas.

Despite the efforts of these health boards, the sheer size of the garbage and human waste problems made the fight for a cleaner environment a losing battle.

Municipal governments were ineffective; the prevailing technology was inadequate; the upper classes were reluctant to pay for large-scale sanitary programs; and the degradation of the poor was such that they made few protests. Not until the diseases that were so rampant among the poor were perceived as a threat to the more affluent were serious efforts made to improve the situation. The two dramatic epidemic diseases already noted, Asiatic cholera and yellow fever, provided the chief impetus to sanitary reform.

Agitation for sanitary reform resulted in the formation of the Louisiana State Board of Health and a series of national sanitary conventions in the 1850's, but the Civil War cut short these promising developments. With New York City leading the way in the postwar years, municipal health departments and state boards of health rapidly began to appear. Although the bacteriological revolution was under way during these years, health boards still conceived their major task to be that of improving the physical environment.

During the later years of the 19th century, water systems were improved and extended, sewer systems began replacing the haphazard construction of individual conduits, street paving improved drainage and facilitated the collection of garbage and rubbish, and technological improvements eliminated many of the former nuisances that had outraged sensibilities and threatened health.

By the advent of the 20th century, the discovery of pathogenic organisms had provided health authorities with a better rationale; they no longer concentrated their attacks on dirt per se but rather on pathogenic organisms and disease-producing conditions. The old fears of miasmas and sewer gas were replaced by equally grave apprehensions about germs. While dirt was no longer the bête noire of health authorities, environmental sanitation benefited from the rising standard of living that brought higher standards of personal and public hygiene.

During the 20th century, technology solved the problem of safe water supplies through the introduction of rapid sand filtration and chlorination and made possible effective sewer systems in the major cities. It eliminated horses and dairy cows from built-up areas and supplanted noisy, dirty steam engines with electric trolley cars. It facilitated garbage collection and street cleaning and brought profound changes in the food-processing industry. On the other hand, technology also resulted in food adulteration through dangerous chemical additives and led to new forms of air and water pollution. The internal combustion engine and the electric motor combined to eliminate the stench and flies that characterized 19th-century towns; but they, along with other technological developments, helped raise noise to dangerous levels and posed both immediate and more subtle threats to man's environment.

Among the subtle threats to health are carcinogens spewed forth by petrochemical and other industries; pollution of air and water by trace elements of lead, mercury, arsenicals, and asbestos; and the residues from tons of insecticides and herbicides that annually drench the landscape. Two new potential hazards to world health are high-flying jets and the widespread use of Freon compounds in aerosol cans, both of which may be capable of reducing or destroying the protective blanket of ozone surrounding the earth. This layer of ozone limits the effect of ultraviolet rays, and any damage to it would at least result in a major increase in skin cancer. The scientific community has long been aware of most of these problems, but research has been piecemeal and haphazard. A growing public awareness of the need for a concerted attack on environmental dangers led Congress, on Dec. 2, 1970, to establish the Environmental Protection Agency (EPA). The major purpose of the agency is to coordinate the work of the many government and private institutions and agencies involved in studying, monitoring, and enforcing antipollution activities. Affirmative action by EPA inevitably brought it into sharp conflict with strong vested interests, and by 1975 it had had only limited success.

[John B. Blake, *Public Health in the Town of Boston, 1630–1822;* J. J. Cosgrove, *History of Sanitation;* John Duffy, *A History of Public Health in New York City, 1625–1866;* Mazyck P. Ravenel, *A Half Century of Public Health.*]

JOHN DUFFY

SAN JACINTO, BATTLE OF (Apr. 21, 1836). On Mar. 11, 1836, five days after the defeat of the Texas revolutionaries at the Alamo, Gen. Sam Houston took command of 374 men at Gonzales and two days later began his retreat from Mexican Gen. Antonio López de Santa Anna's advance. Extermination of forces under Capt. James Fannin left Houston's band the sole body under arms in the republic. Difficulties were increased by the flight of the government and of the civil population toward the United States border and the Gulf ports. For thirty-seven days Houston retreated, adding to the force he held together by the exercise of personal authority, while Santa Anna divided his army in pursuit. On Apr. 20, with about 800 men, Houston intercepted Santa Anna, with about

900 troops, at a ferry over the San Jacinto River. Brushing aside a Mexican reconnaissance in force, Houston waited for between 400 and 600 men under Gen. Martín Perfecto de Cos to join Santa Anna the following morning, in order, he later said, not "to take two bites of a cherry." Then, cutting down a bridge protecting his own as well as the Mexicans' avenue of retreat, Houston formed up under a screen of trees and attacked. Santa Anna's surprise was complete. A thinly held barricade protecting his camp was quickly overrun, and organized resistance ended within twenty minutes. The rest was slaughter. Texan figures on enemy casualties—630 killed, 208 wounded, 730 prisoners—are inexact, the total probably representing more men than Santa Anna had on the field. Texan losses were 16 killed, 24 wounded including Houston. Santa Anna, a prisoner, signed armistice terms under which the other divisions of his army immediately evacuated Texas.

[Marquis James, *The Raven, A Biography of Sam Houston.*]

MARQUIS JAMES

SAN JUAN COUNTRY in southwestern Colorado includes rich ranching land, the Mesa Verde National Park, and the famous gold and silver mines around Creede, Durango, Ouray, Rico, Silverton, and Telluride. After discovery of rich ore in the San Juan Mountains in 1870 and 1871 the region flourished until the silver collapse in 1893, although mining for gold and other minerals has steadily continued. The region includes such famous mines as Camp Bird (opened by Thomas F. Walsh), Smuggler-Union, American Nettie, Silver Lake, and Liberty Bell.

[Robert L. Brown, *An Empire of Silver: A History of the San Juan Silver Rush.*]

MALCOLM G. WYER

SAN JUAN HILL AND EL CANEY, BATTLES OF. After the withdrawal of Spanish outposts from Las Guásimas, Cuba, the key points defending Santiago de Cuba against U.S. Gen. William Shafter's advance, June 1898, were along a line from San Juan Hill northeast to El Caney. The former was directly in the path of the American advance; the latter protected the city from envelopment by the American right wing.

On July 1 the Americans attacked along the entire line. Gen. Henry Lawton's division, on the right, carried El Caney. The attack against San Juan Hill was not so well timed. One division and Col. Theodore Roosevelt's dismounted Rough Riders, advancing as much from desperation as by design, captured San Juan. This placed the American army in control of high ground overlooking Santiago and in position to isolate the city. Adm. Pascual Cervera y Topete, alarmed by possibilities of American artillery on hills overlooking the bay in which his fleet was anchored, sought safety, July 3, in a dash to the open sea. He and the Spanish fleet were overwhelmed by the superior firepower of the U.S. Navy, under Adm. William T. Sampson, which had been blockading the harbor. Santiago surrendered on July 17.

[Walter Millis, *The Martial Spirit.*]

JIM DAN HILL

SAN JUAN ISLAND, SEIZURE OF (July 1859). San Juan Island, important for its position midway in the Juan de Fuca Strait, became the object of rivalry between American settlers in Washington Territory and the Hudson's Bay Company, with headquarters at Victoria, British Columbia. Americans colonized the island in 1854, although the company had previously established a stock ranch there. In 1859 the alleged shooting of a pig by an American and his threatened removal to Victoria for trial provided the necessary "incident." Within a month 500 American soldiers invaded the island and two British warships took up a menacing position. The American and British governments temporarily settled the dispute in March 1860 by arranging for joint occupation, which continued until 1872. In the latter year William I of Germany arbitrated the matter and settled the boundary line through the Haro Strait, thus giving San Juan Island to the United States. The San Juan Island National Park was established in 1966 to commemorate the peaceful relations between Great Britain and the United States since the settlement of the dispute.

[Hugh L. Keenleyside, *Canada and the United States.*]

RICHARD W. VAN ALSTYNE

SAN LORENZO, TREATY OF. *See* **Pinckney's Treaty.**

SAN MARCO, FORT. *See* **Marion, Fort.**

SAN PASQUAL, BATTLE OF (Dec. 6, 1846). Eighty mounted Mexicans, under the command of Capt. Andrés Pico, attempted to halt the advance of Gen. Stephen Kearny's 160 U.S. cavalrymen coming from Santa Fe, N.Mex., at San Pasqual, forty miles northeast of San Diego, Calif. Kearny had been reinforced by Capt. Archibald Gillespie's relief party of forty men from San Diego, but his men, worn by their long journey, found themselves at a disadvantage. The Mexicans broke through their lines. Nineteen Americans were killed and an equal number were wounded, while the Californian loss is said to have been only twelve wounded. Pico received no reinforcements and had to give way, so that Kearny, with the aid of 200 of Commodore Robert F. Stockton's marines, reached San Diego safely on Dec. 12.

[H. H. Bancroft, *History of California*, vol. V; I. B. Richman, *California Under Spain and Mexico, 1535–1847.*]

RUFUS KAY WYLLYS

SAN SALVADOR. *See* **Watlings Island.**

SANTA ELENA. *See* **Port Royal.**

SANTA FE, capital city of New Mexico, located in the north central section of the state.

Abandoning their first settlement in New Mexico, on the Rio Chama, the Spaniards selected for their capital a more suitable site twenty-five miles to the southeast. Here in 1609 Gov. Pedro de Peralta founded the present city of Santa Fe. In 1630 the town numbered about 1,050 inhabitants, of whom 250 were Spaniards. It suffered severely during the Pueblo revolt in 1680 when it was abandoned by the Spaniards, not to be recovered until 1692. After the Spanish reconquest and during the first half of the 18th century, Santa Fe with its 1,500 inhabitants was the objective of Mexican traders from Chihuahua and of French traders from the Mississippi Valley, whose activities after 1800 were continued by the Americans over the famous Santa Fe Trail. During the first decades of the 19th century and the war between the United States and Mexico, Santa Fe was often the scene of political disturbances. Gen. Stephen W. Kearny occupied the city in 1846 and suppressed the revolt that broke out the next year. Santa Fe remained the capital when, in 1850, Congress organized New Mexico into a territory and in 1912 made it a state. The second oldest European settlement in the United States, Santa Fe has retained a special attraction for historians and antiquarians, as well as for artists, musicians, and writers, who have come there to live and who have helped make the city a cultural center of the Southwest. Without major industries, Santa Fe has depended on tourism for its economic well-being. In 1970 its population was 41,167.

[H. H. Bancroft, *Arizona and New Mexico;* F. W. Hodge in *The Memorial of Fray Alonso de Benavides,* Ayer translation with Notes.]

FRANCIS BORGIA STECK

SANTA FE RAILROAD. *See* **Railroads, Sketches: Atchison, Topeka and Santa Fe.**

SANTA FE TRAIL, famed in history and fiction, was an important commerce route from 1821 to 1880. Since the greater extent of its 780 miles from Missouri to Santa Fe, N.Mex., lay across the Plains and avoided the rivers, wagons could easily traverse it. As the trail was extended south from Santa Fe for an additional thousand miles through El Paso to the Mexican towns of Chihuahua and Durango, wagon masters continued to find natural roads the entire distance.

Prior to the opening of the trail, the city of Santa Fe was supplied with goods brought by mule at great expense from the Mexican seaport of Veracruz over a roundabout path, the last 500 miles of which were infested with Apache. Thus, while Santa Fe was rich in silver, wool, and mules, it lacked the simplest manufactured articles. News of this condition came to Pierre and Paul Mallet of Canada, who crossed the Plains to Santa Fe in 1739. In succeeding years more Frenchmen passed at intervals from the Missouri River or from Arkansas Post to the Rio Grande. Zebulon M. Pike, American army lieutenant, arriving in 1807, met two Americans, Baptiste LaLande and James Purcell, who had preceded him to Santa Fe in 1804 and 1805 respectively.

American attempts at Santa Fe trade met with summary action by Spanish authorities, who arrested twelve men from Saint Louis in 1812 and imprisoned them for nine years and arrested Auguste Pierre Chouteau's Saint Louis fur brigade in 1815 for trapping on the Upper Arkansas. Chouteau's property, valued at $30,000, was confiscated, but he was released after forty-eight days. Information that Mexico had overthrown Spanish rule and that traders were welcome in Santa Fe came to three Indian traders on the Plains late in 1821. First of the three to arrive was William Becknell of Arrow Rock, Mo., who reached Santa Fe on Nov. 16 and sold his Indian trade goods at from ten to twenty times higher than Saint Louis prices. Thomas James of Saint Louis, who reached Santa Fe Dec. 1, and Hugh Glenn, an Osage Indian

trader who arrived in June 1822, were also welcomed. There was no well-defined Santa Fe Trail prior to Becknell's journey. The Mallets, LaLande, and Purcell followed the Platte River partway to the mountains. Chouteau and Glenn traversed the Osage Trail from southwest Missouri to the Arkansas River. James crossed the present states of Oklahoma and Arkansas from the Mississippi River.

Becknell, father of the trail, started from the steamboat landing of Franklin, Mo., followed the prairie divide between the tributaries of the Kansas and Arkansas rivers to the Great Bend of the Arkansas, then followed the Arkansas almost to the mountains before turning south to New Mexico. His route became the Santa Fe Trail of history. All early travelers transported their goods by packhorse, but in 1822 Becknell, on his second journey, carried part of his merchandise in wagons. After that wagons were generally employed. The Missouri River terminus was first Franklin, then Independence, and finally Westport (now Kansas City). At the western end the trail turned south to Santa Fe from the Arkansas by three different ways. The Taos Trail diverged from the Arkansas at the Huerfano River, in what is now south central Colorado. A middle course branched from the Arkansas west of the mouth of Purgatory River to cross Raton Pass on the present Colorado–New Mexico border. The shortest and in later times the most-traveled route was the Cimarron Cutoff, leaving the Arkansas near the present city of Cimarron, Kans. (this crossing varied), and proceeding southwest across the Cimarron Valley.

Merchants traveled in caravans, the wagons moving in parallel columns so that they might be quickly formed into a circular corral, with livestock inside, to repel Indian attacks. Indians seldom risked battle with well-organized caravans. Up to 1843 Josiah Gregg reported that the Indians killed but eleven men on the trail. Losses were greatest from 1864 to 1869, the bloodiest year being 1868, when seventeen stagecoach passengers were captured and burned at Cimarron Crossing. In that year Gen. George Custer's *My Life on the Plains* lists forty-five deaths on or near the trail.

Santa Fe trade brought to the United States much-needed silver, gave America the Missouri mule, and led to the conquest of New Mexico in the Mexican War. The heavy volume of westward-bound traffic on the trail has been shown by various reports: Gregg reported that 350 persons transported $450,000 worth of goods at Saint Louis prices in 1843, the largest year up to that time; Lt. Col. William Gilpin's register shows 3,000 wagons, 12,000 persons, and 50,000 animals in twelve months of 1848–49, a large part of the number being bound for California; and the register at Council Grove, Kans., in 1860 showed 3,514 persons with 2,567 wagons, 61 carriages and stagecoaches, 5,819 mules, 478 horses, and 22,738 oxen. Federal mail service by stagecoach was instituted in 1849. Completion of the last section of the Atchison, Topeka and Santa Fe Railroad in 1880 ended the importance of the wagon road.

[Herbert E. Bolton, ''French Intrusions Into New Mexico,'' in H. Norse Stephens, ed., *The Pacific Ocean in History;* R. L. Duffus, *The Santa Fe Trail;* Josiah Gregg, *Commerce of the Prairies.*]

BLISS ISELY

SANTA MARIA, the flagship of Christopher Columbus, headed the fleet of three vessels that reached the New World on Oct. 12, 1492 (*see* America, Discovery of). Two months later, on Christmas Eve, it ran aground off the coast of Hispaniola. From the wreckage Columbus had a fort erected at La Navidad before he left for Spain. He found it destroyed and its garrison murdered when he returned in November 1493.

[John Fiske, *The Discovery of America;* R. H. Major, *Select Letters of Christopher Columbus.*]

FRANCIS BORGIA STECK

SANTA ROSA ISLAND, BATTLE ON (Oct. 8–9, 1861). On Jan. 10, 1861, Lt. Adam J. Slemmer withdrew Union troops from Pensacola, Fla., to Fort Pickens on Santa Rosa Island in the Gulf of Mexico, leaving the navy yard and mainland forts to the Confederates. By Apr. 13 reinforcements reached Pickens, and two months later volunteer forces arrived (*see* Powhatan Incident). By midsummer 1861 Pensacola was blockaded. In September Union soldiers burned the dry docks and the schooner *Judah.* Confederates under Gen. Richard H. Anderson retaliated by a night attack (Oct. 8–9, 1861) on Santa Rosa. They surprised and burned the Union camp, driving the troops to the fort. At daylight Anderson withdrew to the mainland. Both sides claimed victory.

[William Watson Davis, *The Civil War and Reconstruction in Florida.*]

KATHRYN T. ABBEY

SANTEE CANAL, connecting the head of navigation on the Cooper River with the Santee River in South Carolina, was a work of private enterprise, begun in 1792 and completed in 1800 at a cost of about $750,000. The channel was 22 miles long, 35 feet wide, and 4 feet deep, containing thirteen locks and capable of carrying vessels of 22 tons burden. Projected as a means of cheapening the transportation of foodstuffs from the interior of the state to the low-country plantations, the enterprise was never a financial success, especially after the introduction of cotton into the up-country. With the building of railroads its business gradually declined and it was abandoned about 1858.

[U. B. Phillips, *History of Transportation in the Eastern Cotton Belt;* F. A. Porcher, *History of the Santee Canal.*]

JAMES W. PATTON

SANTIAGO, BLOCKADE AND BATTLE OF. Ten days after four armored cruisers commanded by Spanish Adm. Pascual Cervera y Topete arrived at the harbor of Santiago de Cuba on May 19, 1898, they were blockaded by Adm. William T. Sampson and Commodore Winfield S. Schley with the battleships *Massachusetts, Iowa, Indiana, Oregon,* and *Texas* and the armored cruisers *New York* and *Brooklyn.* At nine o'clock on the morning of July 3 Cervera dashed out to avoid being caught in a trap by the army encircling the city (*see* San Juan Hill and El Caney, Battles of). As the flagship *Infanta Maria Teresa* headed westward, followed by the *Vizcaya, Colon,* and *Oquendo,* the blockaders quickly closed in and concentrated on the *Teresa,* which within fifteen minutes was set on fire and three-quarters of an hour later driven ashore, as was also the *Oquendo.* By eleven o'clock the *Vizcaya* was crippled and beached, and at one o'clock the *Colon,* a new and fast ship, already under fire from the 13-inch guns of the *Oregon,* lowered its colors and turned shorewards. Meanwhile the *Gloucester* had forced the Spanish destroyer *Pluton* ashore, where it soon blew up. Another Spanish destroyer, the *Furor,* was sent to the bottom by a heavy shell from the *New York.*

The greater Spanish loss, about 400 killed, as compared with one American killed and one seriously wounded, was due primarily to the American rapid-fire guns, which swept the decks, ignited the woodwork, and drove the gunners from their stations. The victory removed all chance of Spanish naval resistance in the Western Hemisphere and greatly increased the respect that Europe held for the American navy.

Schley, second in command, had been on the *Brooklyn* in the very forefront of the engagement, so close indeed that when the *Teresa* turned toward the *Brooklyn* as if to ram, Schley circled back and narrowly avoided a collision with the other ships. As Sampson was not within firing distance during most of the fight, having gone in the *New York* for a conference with Gen. William R. Shafter, a controversy arose as to who should receive the chief credit for the victory (*see* Sampson-Schley Controversy).

[Philip S. Foner, *The Spanish-Cuban War;* Frank Freidel, *The Splendid Little War.*]

WALTER B. NORRIS

SANTIAGO DE CHILE INTER-AMERICAN CONGRESS. The fifth Inter-American Congress was held at Santiago, Chile, from Mar. 25 to May 3, 1923. Mexico, unrecognized by the United States, was absent. Peru, at odds with Chile over the Tacna-Arica dispute, did not attend, nor did Bolivia, involved in the same controversy. The principal achievements of the conference were the adoption of the Gondra Convention and a projected reform of the Pan American Union at Washington, D.C. The Gondra Convention for international conciliation was a multilateral cooling-off device for the preservation of peace similar to the bilateral conventions previously negotiated by Secretary of State William Jennings Bryan for the United States.

SAMUEL FLAGG BEMIS

SANTO DOMINGO. *See* **Dominican Republic.**

SANTO DOMINGO, SECRET MISSION TO. Soon after the Republic of Santo Domingo separated from Haiti in 1844, it became necessary for Secretary of State James Buchanan to investigate its social stability and resources, preliminary to according recognition. In May and June 1846, two navy lieutenants, David D. Porter and William E. Hunt, accomplished the work on a secret mission. Porter traveled through the little-known interior of the island while Hunt in the brig *Porpoise* surveyed its coast. The reports being favorable, friendly relations between the United States and Santo Domingo were shortly established.

[R. S. West, Jr., *The Second Admiral.*]

RICHARD S. WEST, JR.

SARATOGA, SURRENDER AT (Oct. 17, 1777). After his defeat at the second Battle of Freeman's Farm on Oct. 7, British Gen. John Burgoyne with his

4,500 men slowly retreated northward. He neglected to crush a detachment of 1,300 Continental militia commanded by Gen. John Fellows, which had been posted to block his retreat, but instead took up a strong position near Old Saratoga (now Schuylerville, N.Y.). The British troops were exhausted and their supplies were running low. The American forces under Gen. Horatio Gates now consisted of about 5,000 regulars and more than 12,000 militia. Gates almost made a fatal mistake by ordering an attack against the British position on Oct. 11 under the misconception that it was defended only by a rear guard, but he finally changed his mind, perhaps at the suggestion of Col. James Wilkinson.

Burgoyne could not decide what to do, although a prompt and complete retreat was the only logical course left open to him. While he hesitated, Gates surrounded his position. Burgoyne finally asked for terms on Oct. 13. Gates at first demanded an unconditional surrender but on Oct. 15 weakly accepted Burgoyne's "convention," which provided that the British troops should be returned to England on condition that they would take no further part in the war (*see* Convention Army). Burgoyne, having heard that Sir Henry Clinton had captured the Continental forts near West Point (*see* Highlands of the Hudson) and was sending an expedition against Albany, now tried to delay the surrender. The negotiations came to resemble a comic opera, but on the afternoon of Oct. 16 Burgoyne accepted the inevitable, and the formal laying down of arms took place on the next day. Burgoyne, with a graceful bow, said, "The fortune of war, General Gates, has made me your prisoner," and Gates courteously replied, "I shall always be ready to testify that it has not been through any fault of your Excellency." This event marked the turning point of the American Revolution, since France now decided to enter the war as an ally of the Americans (*see* Franco-American Alliance of 1778).

[Rupert Furneaux, *The Battle of Saratoga;* Hoffman Nickerson, *The Turning Point of the Revolution.*]

EDWARD P. ALEXANDER

SARATOGA SPRINGS, a city in east central New York, west of the Hudson River, that has more than 100 natural mineral springs. In the summer of 1767 Sir William Johnson, suffering from a wound received in the French and Indian War, was taken by the Mohawk to bathe in the healing waters of High Rock Spring. George Washington, as a result of a visit in 1783, considered the purchase of a tract of land to include "the mineral spring at Saratoga." At first little or no attempt was made to exploit the springs. Accommodations were scarce and many visitors came in wagons equipped with beds in which they slept. In 1789 Gideon Putnam, called the founder of Saratoga Springs, settled in the area, and in 1802 he began construction of the Grand Union Hotel. Other hotels were built, including the United States Hotel, and the popularity of the springs increased rapidly. An English visitor in 1828 stated that "1,500 visitors have been known to arrive in a week." Incorporated as a village in 1826, Saratoga was declared to be a "resort of wealth, intelligence and fashion—a political observatory." Madam Eliza Bowen Jumel, Martin Van Buren, Stephen Douglas, De Witt Clinton, Daniel Webster, and Joseph Bonaparte were frequent visitors. Lavish display became the order of the day. The size and number of the trunks of the visitors became a fashionable feature. The medicinal properties of the springs, which contain bicarbonates of lime, sodium, magnesium, chloride of sodium, and other minerals and are heavily charged with carbonic acid gas, ceased to be important to the thousands of pleasure-seekers. During the decade of the 1860's Civil War profiteers discovered Saratoga Springs. Drilling was started on six new springs; several new hotels were opened; and the first horse races were run at the Travers track. In 1863 the Saratoga Association for the Improvement of the Breed of Horses was organized, and its annual races continue to draw large crowds.

Throughout the last quarter of the 19th century, Saratoga Springs was the most fashionable spa in the United States. Commercial bottling of the waters nearly depleted the springs, but the state intervened. In 1909 New York State acquired the property and in 1916 the springs were placed in the charge of a conservation commission. Saratoga Springs has continued as a popular tourist resort, mainly for the horse racing every summer and the historical sites in the area.

[Cleveland Amory, *The Last Resorts;* W. L. Stone, *Reminiscences of Saratoga.*]

A. C. FLICK

SAUGUS FURNACE was erected on Saugus Creek near Lynn, Mass., in 1646 by British and colonial proprietors, including John Winthrop and James Leader, to smelt bog ores found in the vicinity. This furnace, which had a capacity of 7 or 8 tons a week, cast cannon and hollow ware directly from the ore as well as pig iron. A finery and forge attached to the works refined the latter into bars "as good as Spanish." The enterprise was not very profitable but remained in operation with interruptions for more than 100 years until neighboring ore and timber were exhausted. The ironworks were restored by the Steel Institute in 1954, and specimens of its castings are preserved. (*See also* Bog Iron Mining; Iron and Steel Manufacture.)

[E. N. Hartley, *Ironworks on the Saugus.*]

VICTOR S. CLARK

SAUK PRAIRIE, a large and fertile prairie that stretches along the Wisconsin River, rimmed by the bluffs of the Baraboo Range, in Sauk County, Wis. On this prairie the Sauk settled about the middle of the 18th century, after having been driven from the shores of Green Bay by the French. The first British officer in Wisconsin, who occupied Fort Edward Augustus at Green Bay, 1761–63, made a treaty of alliance with the Sauk chiefs, who professed their friendship for the British newcomers. When the explorer Jonathan Carver in 1766 passed along the Fox-Wisconsin waterway, he found a large and prosperous village of the Sauk on the prairie, and noted that the loss of the friendship of this large tribe would be disastrous for the British cause in the West. This was tested after the outbreak of the American Revolution, when in 1777 Capt. Charles Michel de Langlade, of the British Indian department, sent his nephew, Charles Gautier de Verville, to arouse the Wisconsin Indians for auxiliaries in Canada to assist in repelling the American invasion. Gautier arrived at the Sauk village in Sauk Prairie in May 1778, only to find that he had been preceded by a "rebel belt," that is, by a messenger from the tribes of the eastern United States, to engage the western Indians to come to the support of Gen. George Washington's army. At the same time a Spanish messenger from Saint Louis arrived bidding for the Sauk trade and alliance.

Thus in the heart of Wisconsin was heard the repercussion of the contest being waged between the British and the colonies, with the outlying support of the Spanish officials. Gautier succeeded in securing a number of Sauk for Langlade's party; but the tribe began moving to the Mississippi near the mouth of Rock River, in what is now northwest Illinois, in order to approach the Spanish and the Americans of the Illinois settlements, which were captured by George Rogers Clark in July 1778. Thereafter, the Sauk forsook for a time their British alliance for that of Clark and the Americans.

[L. P. Kellogg, *British Régime in Wisconsin and the Northwest.*]
LOUISE PHELPS KELLOGG

SAULT SAINTE MARIE, GREAT PAGEANT AT.

Jean Talon, Canada's "great intendant," cherished a dream of French imperial expansion into midcontinental North America. His first step toward realizing it was to annex the illimitable and altogether unknown "country of the West" (*pays de l'Ouest*) to the French crown by proclamation, and this he did by staging, through his agent, Simon François Daumont, Sieur de St. Lusson, a dramatic ceremony at Sault Sainte Marie, June 14, 1671. The French colors were displayed and St. Lusson thrice cried aloud that he took possession, in the name of Louis XIV, of Sault Sainte Marie, lakes Huron and Superior, Caientoton (Manitoulin) Island, and "of all other countries, streams, lakes and rivers contiguous and adjacent, as well discovered as to be discovered which are bounded on one side by the seas of the North and of the West, and on the other side by the South Sea, and in all their length and breadth." An official record of the proceedings was drawn up, signed by nineteen of the witnesses present, and affixed with the French arms to a tree, while Father Claude Jean Allouez, a Jesuit, made an address to the Indians who had been summoned in numbers from far and near for the historic occasion. St. Lusson's *prise de possession* ignored standing Spanish and English claims to parts or all of the territory in question.

[F. Parkman, *La Salle and the Discovery of the Great West;* R. G. Thwaites, ed., *Jesuit Relations,* vol. LV; J. Winsor, *The Pageant of St. Lusson.*]
GILBERT J. GARRAGHAN

SAULT SAINTE MARIE CANALS, or Soo Canals,

two U.S. canals and one Canadian canal, connecting Lake Superior with Lake Huron. The first U.S. canal, completed in 1855, is an artificial waterway on the Saint Marys River and was originally known as the Saint Marys Falls Ship Canal.

In 1797 the North West Company of Montreal constructed a small canal and lock on the north shore of the rapids of Saint Marys River, where the water of Lake Superior descends some 21 feet to the level of Lake Huron. An American canal was projected by Michigan in 1837, and it became imperative after the commencement of copper and iron mining in the next decade. Congressional aid was sought, and in 1852 a land grant of 750,000 acres was provided for this pur-

pose. The state contracted with an eastern corporation to construct the works, and the canal was ready for use in June 1855. Tolls were charged, but they were inadequate for the maintenance and necessary improvement of the waterway. In 1869 the legislature invited federal operation. This was effected in 1881 when the state ceded the canal to the United States, which abolished tolls and assumed maintenance and control. The U.S. Army Corps of Engineers operates the canals and has enlarged both the canals and locks (the first or southern part completed 1896; the second or northern, 1919). The largest of these locks, the Davis Lock, is 1,350 feet long. A new lock was built on the site of the earlier Poe Lock in the early 1960's after the opening of the Saint Lawrence Seaway to provide for the increased shipping in the Great Lakes.

[Paul Fatan, *Indiana Canals;* Madeline S. Waggoner, *The Long Haul West: The Great Canal Era, 1817–1850.*]
L. A. CHASE

SAULT SAINTE MARIE MISSION AND TRADING POST.

The sault or rapids of Saint Marys River, which discharges the waters of Lake Superior into Lake Huron, were a favorite rendezvous in colonial days for Indians and traders. The limitless supply of excellent whitefish found in the rapids was a lure to the Indians. Moreover, if they came from the North, the Indians had to pass through this locality on their trading trips to the lower Saint Lawrence River. The designation Sault Sainte Marie (Saint Marys Falls) originated with the Jesuit missionaries. The first white man to reach the sault appears to have been Étienne Brulé sometime during 1621–23, followed in 1634 by Jean Nicolet and in 1641 by the Jesuits Saint Isaac Jogues and Father Charles Raymbaut, who gave the place its first distinct mention in the records. In 1668 Father Jacques Marquette opened a mission post on the south (American) side of the rapids, at their foot, around which grew up the earliest settlement of whites in Michigan. Marquette is generally taken to be the founder, as he was the first chronicler, of Sault Sainte Marie.

By 1670 the Jesuit mission was a square enclosure of cedar posts 12 feet high with chapel and residence within. The Indian population of the sault numbered some 2,000, among them the Chippewa, called Saulters by the whites because their customary habitat was at the rapids. As a trading center and crossroads the settlement began early to decline, owing, among other causes, to the enterprise of the Hudson's Bay Company, which directed much trade to the North, and to Antoine de la Mothe Cadillac's policy of concentrating the Indians at Detroit. Later came a revival; the North West Company, and afterward the American Fur Company, maintained important posts at the sault. The mission declined toward the end of the 17th century, the last resident pastor, Father Charles Albanel, dying in 1696. Afterward, there was no resident clergyman of any denomination at Sault Sainte Marie until 1831.

[L. P. Kellogg, *The French Régime in Wisconsin and the Northwest;* Stanley Newton, *The Story of Sault Ste. Marie.*]
GILBERT J. GARRAGHAN

SAVAGE'S STATION, BATTLE AT (June 29, 1862). Union Gen. George B. McClellan, having abandoned his base on the Pamunkey River in Virginia (*see* Stuart's Ride), left Gen. Edwin V. Sumner's and Gen. William B. Franklin's corps to guard a temporary issue depot at Savage's Station while the rest of the army retreated across White Oak Swamp. Confederate Gen. John B. Magruder pursued and attacked the Union forces during the afternoon, momentarily expecting Gen. Thomas "Stonewall" Jackson to assail them from the north. Jackson did not arrive, and Sumner repulsed Magruder's attacks. After destroying vast quantities of supplies and leaving 2,500 sick and wounded in field hospitals, the Union troops retired unmolested after nightfall.

[Matthew F. Steele, *American Campaigns.*]
JOSEPH MILLS HANSON

SAVANNAH, a city in Georgia, located on a plateau overlooking the Savannah River, eighteen miles from the Atlantic Ocean. It was settled in 1733 under the leadership of Gen. James E. Oglethorpe as the first community in the Georgia colony and was Georgia's capital until 1786.

In 1734 the town consisted of forty houses. Each settler's family had a house and garden lot and a fifty-acre farm. George Whitefield in 1740 organized the first Anglican communion in Georgia, known as Christ Church, in Savannah. One of the early rectors was John Wesley. At the end of the colonial period Savannah had fewer than 500 houses and was surrounded by a pine forest, but luxuriant rice fields and savannas stretched northward and eastward from the town. A promising export trade in rice, indigo, lumber, potash, and skins had begun.

Savannah was the state's earliest center of resis-

tance to British authority. The royal governor, Sir James Wright, was forced to flee in 1776, but he returned and restored British authority there in 1779. An attempt to recapture the town with a combined force of over 6,000 French and Americans in October 1779 failed, and the British remained in possession until July 11, 1783.

Incorporated as a city in 1789, Savannah was the first planned city in the United States. Its original ground plan featured broad streets in checkerboard design and numerous public squares. In time the squares were filled with monuments, live oaks, and flowers. These, combined with modern restoration achievements, express unusual grace and beauty. But at the opening of the 19th century Savannah had few public improvements. Paving was unknown. There was no street lighting and no systematic garbage disposal. Water came from wells sunk in the public squares. Serious yellow fever epidemics occurred in 1820, 1854, and 1876, each resulting in heavy mortality and paralysis of business. Cholera swept the city in 1834, hitting the slave population most heavily. A hurricane in 1804 destroyed considerable property and took more than 100 lives. Disastrous fires occurred in 1796 and 1820; the latter destroyed 500 buildings.

Commercial rivalry with Charleston and Augusta caused Savannah citizens to promote the Central of Georgia Railroad, which reached Macon in 1843. By 1860 the Atlantic and Gulf road connected the city with points in southern Georgia. Early in the Civil War Savannah was blockaded by federal gunboats, and Fort Pulaski, commanding the mouth of the Savannah River, was captured by Union forces. The city itself fell to Gen. William Tecumseh Sherman in December 1864. After the war the river channel was choked with obstructions that were difficult and expensive to clear away. The years 1880–1900 saw economic recovery and some growth. The population increased from 30,709 to 54,244, and the total value of Savannah's commerce increased threefold. Extensive drainage reduced the incidence of traditional diseases, and artesian wells provided pure drinking water.

In the early 20th century Savannah became one of the world's largest cotton and naval stores markets. At mid-century these activities had declined, but manufactures included sugar, plywood, lumber, fertilizer, paper, paint, roofing, steel products, and gypsum materials. Savannah's fisheries also remained important. The old rice and cotton plantations of its hinterland had largely reverted to forest. The population had grown slowly but steadily to 149,245 in 1960 but had declined to 118,349 by 1970.

[Thomas Gamble, Jr., "History of the Municipal Government of Savannah From 1790 to 1901," in Herman Myers, *Report . . . of the City of Savannah for the Year Ending Dec. 31, 1900;* William Harden, *A History of Savannah and South Georgia;* O. F. Vedder and F. Welden, *History of Savannah.*]

JAMES C. BONNER

SAVANNAH, the first ship to cross the Atlantic Ocean propelled or aided by steam. Built in New York as a 300-ton sailing ship with auxiliary steam power, the *Savannah* was bought by a shipping company in Savannah, Ga., whence it sailed for Liverpool on May 24, 1819, arriving on June 20.

[M. S. Anderson and others, *Georgia: A Pageant of Years;* J. F. Reigart, *The Life of Robert Fulton.*]

E. MERTON COULTER

SAVANNAH, SIEGE OF (September 1779). Comte Jean Baptiste Hector d'Estaing with about 4,500 soldiers, joined by Benjamin Lincoln with about 2,100 Americans, sought to wrest Savannah from the British, who had about 2,500 defenders. After a siege of three weeks, on Oct. 9 a general assault was made that resulted in a disastrous failure. More than 1,000 of the attacking forces were killed, including Count Casimir Pulaski and Sergeant William Jasper of Fort Moultrie fame. Lack of coordination and understanding between the French and Americans was held responsible for the defeat.

[C. C. Jones, Jr., *The Siege of Savannah in 1779, as Described in Two Contemporaneous Journals of French Officers in the Fleet of d'Estaing.*]

E. MERTON COULTER

SAVANNAH, SIEGE OF (December 1864). On Dec. 10, Union Gen. William Tecumseh Sherman began to invest Savannah (*see* Sherman's March to the Sea). A skillful Confederate defense at Honey Hill kept the railroad open to Charleston, S.C. But Fort McAllister, eighteen miles southwest of Savannah and commanding the southern water approach, was captured, and connection was established with the Union supply fleet. Greatly outnumbered, but his line of escape still open, Gen. William J. Hardee, the Confederate commander, after a brief defense on the night of Dec. 20, withdrew into South Carolina (*see* Carolinas, Sherman's March Through the). Sherman telegraphed President Abraham Lincoln: "I beg to present you, as a Christmas gift, the City of Savannah" with "plenty" of guns, ammunition, and cotton.

[R. U. Johnson and C. C. Buel, eds., *Battles and Leaders of the Civil War,* vol. IV.]

THOMAS ROBSON HAY

SAVINGS AND LOAN ASSOCIATIONS began with the Oxford Provident Building Association, founded in 1831 in a suburb of Philadelphia. Early associations were simply cooperative clubs, usually created by working-class people of limited resources to build themselves homes. Gradually they became more formal, opened offices, and sought members who did not plan to build. The number grew rapidly after the Civil War, reaching 5,800 by 1893. They were usually called building and loan associations, but they were also known as cooperative banks in New England and as homestead associations in Louisiana. Since the 1930's they have favored the name savings and loan association. Lenders and borrowers both are voting members of these mutual organizations. Persons placing savings with them are, strictly speaking, shareholders, not depositors, and receive dividends, not interest.

Bank failures and withdrawals of bank savings in the depressed early 1930's limited mortgage loans, held back home building, and thus blocked an important route to economic recovery. The Hoover administration by act of July 22, 1932, set up the Federal Home Loan System with eleven regional banks and a Home Loan Bank Board in Washington to facilitate again the flow of mortgage funds. Anyone familiar with the American dual banking system of state and nationally chartered banks and the Federal Reserve System will recognize much the same pattern in the savings and loan world. The Home Owners Loan Act of June 13, 1933, provided for the first time for nationally chartered federal savings and loan associations. These had to belong to the Federal Home Loan Bank System, but state associations might also become members. Member associations' purchases of stock and their deposits in Federal Home Loan banks provide those institutions with much of their capital. The Home Loan Bank Board also directs the Federal Savings and Loan Insurance Corporation, created by law of June 27, 1934, to insure savings accounts. State member associations are not obliged to belong to it, although most large ones do.

Between 1933 and 1971 the total number of savings and loan associations declined from 10,956 to 5,544. Of the latter, 2,049 were federal and 4,271 were insured, these last accounting for 96.9 percent of the assets of all associations. Initially accounts were insured up to $5,000; but in 1950 this amount was raised to $10,000; in late 1966, to $15,000; and in 1969, to $20,000. Savings and loan associations were among the fastest-growing of savings institutions during this period. Their accounts grew from a modest $4.8 billion in 1933 to $235 billion in May 1974—putting their "deposits" in much the same class as commercial banks' time deposits, life insurance companies' paid-up policies, and U.S. Savings Bond issues.

Associations normally invest about 80 to 85 percent of their funds in mortgages. In 1890, 48 percent of American families owned their own homes; the economy was still 65 percent rural. The rural home was often a productive unit serving as a farm as well as a residence. As urbanization grew, it broke the productive tie, and the rate of home ownership fell off slightly for forty years. During the prosperous 1920's urban dwellers began buying homes, and by 1930 the rate of home ownership was again 48 percent. The Great Depression drove it to an all-time low of 43.6 percent in 1940. Then the home ownership rate rose sharply, reaching 61.9 percent in 1960 and creeping up to 62.9 percent in 1970. During the 1950's and 1960's saving and loan associations supplied between 22 and 38 percent a year of all monies lent to finance nonfarm homes and were thus in considerable measure responsible for the fact that home ownership grew so fast during this period. They had about $239 billion so invested in 1974.

[American Savings and Loan Institute, *Savings and Loan Principles;* H. Prochnow, *American Financial Institutions.*]

DONALD L. KEMMERER

SAVINGS BANKS. *See* **Banks, Savings.**

SAVINGS BONDS. After the discontinuation of "liberty loans"—U.S. Treasury bonds sold to the public in small denominations during World War I—no similar offering was made by the federal government until 1935. Between March 1935 and April 1941, $3.95 billion worth of "baby bonds," as they were called, were issued in denominations of from $25 to $1,000. The "baby bonds" were taken off the market on Apr. 30, 1941, and the following day the first of the defense savings bonds, in the same denominations and bearing the same 2.9 percent interest, were issued. The first bond ($100) was sold to President

Franklin D. Roosevelt by Secretary of the Treasury Henry Morgenthau, Jr. In December, when the United States entered World War II, defense savings bonds became known as war savings bonds. After the war they were once again known as defense bonds; after the Korean War they were simply called savings bonds.

Interest rates on savings bonds were raised periodically to reflect rising rates in the general market, but they were always lower than prevailing interest rates. Between 1952 and 1956, $10,000-denomination bonds were also sold to the general public; beginning in 1954, trustees of employee savings plans were able to buy $100,000 bonds.

Savings stamps, introduced during World War I, were revived in a different form in April 1941. They were sold in denominations of from 10 cents to $5. They bore no interest, but could be exchanged for bonds in units of $18.75—the price of a bond redeemable at maturity for $25. The purpose of the stamp program, which was discontinued on June 30, 1970, was to foster patriotism and thrift in schoolchildren.

In December 1941 the federal government established the payroll savings plan, whereby employees voluntarily arrange for regular deductions from their salaries for the purchase of savings bonds. The plan became the major source for sales of $25 to $1,000 bonds both during and after World War II. By the end of 1975 almost $68 billion worth of bonds had been sold.

NORMA FRANKEL

SAWMILLS. By 1634 a sawmill was in operation on the Piscataqua River (forming part of the border of the present states of Maine and New Hampshire); by 1706 there were seventy. A primitive type had a single sash saw pulled downward by a waterwheel and upward by an elastic pole, but more usually the saw was moved both up and down by waterpower. A few colonial mills already had gangs, or parallel saws, set in one frame so as to cut several boards simultaneously. Muley saws, with a lighter guiding mechanism, were also used. Sawmills multiplied but were not greatly improved in colonial times. They handled principally soft timber of moderate dimensions and were considered satisfactory if they cut 1,000 board feet a day.

Shortly before 1810 Oliver Evans' wood-burning high-pressure steam engines began to be installed in sawmills. These engines made it possible to manufacture lumber where waterpower was not available, as in the forested flatlands of the South. Indeed, the portable engine owes its development in America partly to its usefulness for sawing timber. Circular saws, introduced about the middle of the 19th century, increased mill capacity on account of their higher speed, but they were wasteful in that they turned too much of the log into sawdust. Band saws, though invented earlier, were not introduced in America until after the Civil War. They are now used extensively because they are faster, create less sawdust and more usable wood with their narrower kerf, or cut, and can handle logs of the largest size.

The giant sawmills developed for the most part in the great forest regions west of the Appalachians: in the white-pine belt of the Great Lakes Basin, in the yellow-pine area of the South, and in the fir and redwood forests of the Pacific Northwest. (*See also* Lumber Industry.)

[Ralph Andrews, *This Was Sawmilling.*]
VICTOR S. CLARK

SAYBROOK, or **Old Saybrook,** a town in southern Connecticut, located on Long Island Sound and the west bank of the Connecticut River. On the basis of the Warwick Patent (*see* Connecticut, Old Patent of), John Winthrop, Jr., was appointed on July 7, 1635, ''governor of the river Connecticut'' for one year and commissioned to establish a settlement and fort there. He arrived in Boston on Oct. 6 and sent out a party of about twenty men, who began the settlement of Saybrook on Nov. 24, on land claimed by the Dutch, who had settled there in 1623. They were soon joined by Capt. Lion Gardiner, an expert in fortifications. Thus a Dutch undertaking to occupy the place was forestalled by a few days.

After entering into an agreement in March 1636 with the settlers of the River Towns—Windsor, Hartford, and Wethersfield—Winthrop reached Saybrook in late spring. About the same time George Fenwick, now one of the patentees, appeared. Neither stayed long, so Gardiner was in charge until Fenwick returned in 1639, bringing his wife. Meanwhile Saybrook had been the center of the Pequot War. In 1643 Fenwick became a magistrate of the Connecticut colony and on Dec. 5, 1644, sold the fort and land at Saybrook to Connecticut. Saybrook has remained a small residential community and was incorporated as a town in 1854. In 1970 its population was 8,468.

[C. M. Andrews, *Colonial Period of American History,* vol. II; G. C. Gates, *Saybrook.*]
GEORGE MATTHEW DUTCHER

SAYBROOK PLATFORM, a revision of the ecclesiastical polity of the colony of Connecticut, drawn up by a synod meeting at the call of the legislature in Saybrook, Sept. 9, 1708. Its chief feature was an accentuation of the principle of ''consociation,'' or rule by councils, away from the independency of early Congregationalism. The platform was the outcome of a wide feeling in conservative circles that the Cambridge Platform (1648), which gave to synods a right merely to advise individual churches, did not furnish adequate authority for keeping all churches in line. At Saybrook the churches were organized into county associations ruled by a council of ministers and lay delegates, which was given extensive disciplinary powers over erring congregations and supervision over the choice of new pastors; county associations then sent delegates to an annual assembly that regulated the whole colony. A similar movement in Massachusetts, resulting in the ministerial proposals of 1705 initiated by Increase Mather and others, failed because of a lack of legislative support and the attacks of John Wise, a Congregational minister at Ipswich, Mass. In Connecticut governmental support of the platform effectively transformed the polity of the 18th century into a centrally administered unit, making the church practically a form of presbyterianism.

[Williston Walker, *The Creeds and Platforms of Congregationalism.*]
PERRY MILLER

SCAB, a term of opprobrium applied to one who takes the job of a union worker during a strike. The word was used in 1806 at a trial in Philadelphia of eight workingmen for intimidation of nonunion men. A journeyman shoemaker testified that when he came to America from England in 1794, he was notified that he must either join the shoemakers' union or be considered a ''scab'' and be forbidden to work with union men (*see* Philadelphia Cordwainers' Case). The word ''scab'' did not come into public notice until about 1885–86, when unions were coalescing into great national organizations. Its meaning had to be explained to a congressional committee in the latter year.

[Mary Ritter Beard, *The American Labor Movement.*]
ALVIN F. HARLOW

SCALAWAG, the term of opprobrium applied by conservative southerners to those native whites who joined with the freedmen and the carpetbaggers in support of Republican policies during Radical Reconstruction. The word, originally used to describe runty or diseased cattle, came to be a synonym in the antebellum period for a "mean fellow, a scape grace," and acquired its political connotations after the war.

Scalawags came from all elements of southern society. In the states of the upper South, where they were most numerous, white Republicans were generally hill-country farmers characterized by their Unionist sympathies. In contrast, those in the Deep South came from elements of the planter-business aristocracy with Whig antecedents. The role of the scalawags in Reconstruction has generally been underrated. Comprising approximately 20 percent of the white electorate, they often provided the crucial margin of victory for the Republicans. In the constitutional conventions of 1867–68 and the subsequent state governments they exerted leadership disproportionate to their popular strength.

[Warren A. Ellem, "Who Were the Mississippi Scalawags?" *Journal of Southern History,* vol. 38 (May 1972); John Hope Franklin, *Reconstruction After the Civil War;* Allen W. Trelease, "Who Were the Scalawags?" *Journal of Southern History,* vol. 29 (November 1963).]

WILLIAM G. SHADE

SCALPING. Some modern apologists for the American Indian have argued that the custom of taking scalps from slain or captive enemies was introduced from Europe. Some frontier settlements where there was continuing conflict with various Indian tribes did offer bounties for Indian scalps, but although scalps were honorable trophies in the view of many native peoples, to the European settler they represented all that was savage and hostile. Viewed objectively, the practice of scalping is too widely spread in native America to be other than aboriginal. Gonzalo de las Casas, writing of the Chichimec of northeastern Mexico in 1574, indicated that the taking of scalps and other physical trophies, such as arm and leg bones, was deeply rooted in the native culture. Variations on the theme of scalping may be traced from Alaska to Mexico, then sporadically southward as far as the Gran Chaco in Paraguay-Argentina.

Given this distribution of an apparent pre-Columbian complex, the question of origins and meaning may be raised. Perhaps more deeply rooted in time is the concept of the head trophy, the notion that by taking the head of an enemy one assimilates his vital force or courage or nullifies his potential for spiritual vengeance. The scalping complex is probably related to the taking of heads and may simply be a more economical way of achieving the same magical or mys-

tical result. Head and skull trophies are known for a very few North American tribes; this pattern tended to cluster in Mesoamerica and tropical South America. Shrinking human heads by removing the bone material and subjecting the remaining skin to a tanning process was a purely local development among the Jivaro of eastern Peru. Just as the different New World cultures might variously rationalize the taking of heads, the prevailingly North American practice of scalping had its own variations.

The Indians of the North American Plains and their neighbors to the east, those of the Great Lakes, the Eastern Woodlands, and the Gulf, had stressed war as a major social institution. All took scalps in the course of warfare, although how the scalp was taken and handled reflected various local customs. Plains Indians generally took scalps from the center of a victim's head, pulling hair and a silver dollar-sized piece of skin away after a circular incision. There are numerous instances of survival after such treatment, a reflection of the point that Plains Indian warfare was less directed to killing the enemy and more toward touching him, that is, counting "coup." Only the Teton Dakota regarded killing and scalping as the coup of highest worth.

But even tribes that were not drawn to war took scalps. Natives of California, the Plateau, and segments of the Northwest Coast practiced scalping, although it began to fade in the latter area, where, as among the Tlingit, head trophies appeared. Scalping was not known to the Eskimo. Some Plateau and California tribes took the entire scalp with ears and eyebrows. A larger scalp was also taken by the Pima-Papago and the warrior societies of the Pueblo. The Pima-Papago took scalps with great reluctance, having an inordinate fear of the dead, while the Pueblo Indians kept enemy scalps, usually those of Navaho and Apache, in the ceremonial chambers, "feeding" them corn pollen in solemn fertility rituals.

The variations in custom were extensive: scalps might be braided together, as among some Plains tribes; stretched on frames and painted, as among the Pueblo; or, as with the South American Guaycurú, used as drinking vessels.

[Harold E. Driver, *Indians of North America;* Gabriel Nadeau, "Indian Scalping," *Bulletin of the History of Medicine,* vol. 10 (1941); Gabriel Nadeau, "Indian Scalping Techniques in Different Tribes," *Ciba Symposia,* vol. 5 (1944).]

ROBERT F. SPENCER

SCANDINAVIAN IMMIGRATION. See Immigration.

SCHECHTER POULTRY CORPORATION V. *UNITED STATES*, 295 U.S. 495 (1935), also known as the "Sick Chicken Case," led to a unanimous Supreme Court decision that declared the National Industrial Recovery Act (NIRA) of June 16, 1933, unconstitutional. The case, and that of *United States* v. *Schechter*, arose out of alleged violations of the Code of Fair Competition for the Live Poultry Industry of metropolitan New York, which had been established under provisions of the NIRA. The Schechters, who owned a wholesale poultry business with a plant in Manhattan and one in Brooklyn, were indicted and convicted in a federal district court on nineteen counts for violation of the code. The circuit court of appeals reversed the lower court on two counts, holding that the federal government had no constitutional right to regulate hours of work and wages. The conviction on the other seventeen counts was sustained.

Both the government and the Schechters then appealed to the Supreme Court, which on May 27, 1935, unanimously ruled the code to be unconstitutional. Rejecting the emergency justification, the Court declared that the codemaking authority conferred on the president by section III of the NIRA was "an unconstitutional delegation of legislative power."

While granting that Congress had authority to regulate not only interstate commerce but also those intrastate activities that directly affected such commerce, the highest tribunal insisted that codes could not regulate activities that only indirectly affected commerce among the states.

[T. R. Powell, "Would the Supreme Court Block a Planned Economy?" *Fortune*, vol. 12.]

ERIK MCKINLEY ERIKSSON

SCHENCK V. *UNITED STATES*, 249 U.S. 47 (1919), a unanimous Supreme Court decision that upheld the Espionage Act of 1917. The act, which penalized any attempt to cause disloyalty in the army or navy or to obstruct recruiting, was used to prosecute Charles T. Schenck, secretary of the Socialist party, who circulated leaflets encouraging resistance to the draft. He was convicted and appealed to the Supreme Court on the grounds that the act violated the First Amendment. The Court sustained the act. In his opinion Justice Oliver Wendell Holmes made his famous statement that absolute freedom of speech may be curtailed if "the words used . . . create a clear and present danger" of substantive

evils, which Congress has a right to prevent. In the 1930's and 1940's this doctrine was often employed in bringing about convictions of members of the Communist party and other persons considered politically subversive.

[William Preston, Jr., *Aliens and Dissenters: Suppression of Radicals, 1903–1933.*]

HARVEY PINNEY

SCHENECTADY, a city in eastern New York, was founded in 1661 when Arent Van Curler and eighteen associates purchased from the Mohawk a tract of flatlands on the Mohawk River, thirteen miles northwest of Fort Orange (*see* Albany). Peter Stuyvesant confirmed the grant in 1662, and in 1664 the lands were surveyed and laid out. The settlement consisted of four lots, each having a frontage of 400 feet. Although its location on the Mohawk, the only natural east-west passage through the Appalachian barrier, pointed to its growth as a trading center, Schenectady (because of the Dutch West India Company's monopoly) was forbidden to engage in the fur trade and so developed first as an agricultural community. One of the devastations that harried the Mohawk Valley from about 1689 until 1763, as England and France struggled for control of North American trade and territory, occurred in 1690. On Feb. 9 one of three raiding parties of French regulars and Indians, sent out by Gov. Louis Frontenac, attacked Schenectady and burned it to the ground. More than sixty houses and a church were destroyed. A number of inhabitants were killed or taken prisoner. The terrified survivors fled to Albany. The village was rebuilt and slowly continued to grow. It became the center of a prosperous farming community, land in the vicinity being so fertile as to commonly sell for £45 per acre.

During the Revolution the district committee in Schenectady was very active. Complete records are extant that show the election of members, the sending of representatives to confer with the Albany committee, arrest of Tories, guarding of the western passage, and efforts to placate the Mohawk.

In the 19th century Schenectady became known as the Gateway to the West, as pioneers, using the roads that fanned out from the city, pushed westward into the Mohawk Valley. Schenectady's location on the Erie Canal section of the New York State Barge Canal, which was opened in 1825, added to the city's importance as a transshipment point. In 1831 the first railroad in New York State, the Mohawk and Hudson, was established, between Albany and Schenectady. As railroads spread throughout the state, the demand for locomotives led to the establishment of a large locomotive works in Schenectady in 1848. This factory and the large plant established there by the General Electric Company in 1892 were largely responsible for Schenectady's spectacular growth; from 1860 to 1900 the city's population tripled, and from 1900 to 1920 it tripled again. Electrical equipment and locomotives continue as Schenectady's most important products. Union College is located in the city, which had a population of 77,859 in 1970.

[Nelson Greene, *History of the Mohawk Valley.*]

A. C. FLICK

SCHLOSSER, FORT, ATTACK ON (July 5, 1813). A British detail consisting of about forty officers and men of the militia, under the command of Lt. Col. Thomas Clark, crossed the Niagara River in three boats, arriving at Fort Schlosser, on the east bank of the Niagara River in New York, a little after daybreak. Surprising the small guard at the public storehouse, they captured and removed to Canada a large amount of arms, ammunition, equipment, provisions, two bateaux, and a gunboat. As they were embarking from Fort Schlosser with the booty, about fifteen men came to the beach and fired twenty shots of musketry, but there were no casualties.

[E. Cruikshank, *Documentary History of the Campaign Upon the Niagara Frontier in the Year 1813.*]

ROBERT W. BINGHAM

SCHOENBRUNN, meaning "beautiful spring," was a mission of the Moravian Brethren established by David Zeisberger and five families of Delaware Indians in 1772 near present-day New Philadelphia, Ohio. John Heckewelder and other missionaries joined him, and several little missions were organized along the Tuscarawas River for Christian Delaware and Mahican from Pennsylvania. During the Revolution the inhabitants of Schoenbrunn, who were pacifists, were forced to abandon the town and move to Lichtenau, Ohio. In 1779 a new Schoenbrunn was set up across the river from the old site, but it was destroyed in 1782, when bloody struggles between Indians and white frontiersmen took place (*see* Gnadenhutten). Schoenbrunn Village State Memorial, a restoration of the village to its original appearance, was established there in 1923.

[Edmund DeSchweinitz, *Life and Times of David Zeisberger;* E. O. Randall and D. J. Ryan, *History of Ohio,* vol. II.]

EUGENE H. ROSEBOOM

SCHOMBURGK LINE, a survey made from 1841 to 1843 by Sir Robert Hermann Schomburgk, English-German geographer, in an attempt to establish a boundary between British Guiana and Venezuela. Venezuela repudiated the survey, and the boundary remained an open question until President Grover Cleveland in 1895 forced the parties to submit to arbitration. The Schomburgk survey was of primary importance in the negotiations, which were concluded in 1899.

[George L. Burr, "The Search for the Venezuela-Guiana Boundary," *American Historical Review,* vol. 4.]

JIM DAN HILL

SCHOOL, DISTRICT, a small country school organized to serve the needs of a particular neighborhood rather than a whole township. The original form of public school in the American colonies was the town school, in New England and New York, and the private or charity (church) school in the South. As the population increased, roads and transportation improved, and Indians and wild animals became less of a danger, the population scattered over the area of the towns. Most New England towns contained several villages as well as a widely distributed farm population. The school was supported in whole or in part by a town tax. Those who voted for and paid the tax required that the school be accessible to their children; the moving school, in which the teacher went to the pupils, was developed; this arrangement was followed by the divided school, in which the school went for a portion of the year to a village. When these short school terms were made permanent, the school district was formed. This was made legal in Massachusetts in 1789. Later, Massachusetts gave the power of school support and school control to these districts, and still later (1827) made mandatory the formation of such districts by the towns.

Problems in the early district schools were numerous. Short terms, poorly equipped and poorly paid teachers, sometimes unruly schoolchildren, bad hygienic conditions, a multiplicity of textbooks, too many or too few pupils, an impossibly long program of recitations for the teacher, and lack of discipline were the leading drawbacks of the district system. Yet the district school was probably the only basis on which democracy could build up a public school system.

While the district school system of the early 19th century has been called the low point in American education, it at least made possible the development of a school system controlled and supported by the public that patronized it. It was against the evils of the system that Horace Mann in Massachusetts (1837–38) and Henry Barnard in Connecticut (1838–42) and in Rhode Island (1843–49) labored in their educational reforms. However, the district school system was carried from New England into nearly all the new states west of the Alleghenies. Thomas Jefferson advocated it, along with the town political organization, as the basis of a free society. The district system after the middle of the 19th century was modified in most western states when either the township system or the county system, or both, were superimposed on the district system. In the mid-1800's the union or county school appeared in New York (1853), in Massachusetts (1869), and in Connecticut (1889). By the close of the 19th century, good roads made possible the consolidated school, which has gradually replaced the one-room, ungraded district school throughout most of the country.

[L. Cremin, *American Education: The Colonial Experience, 1607–1783;* E. P. Cubberley, *State and County Education Organization;* G. H. Martin, *The Evolution of the Massachusetts State School System;* H. Updegraff, *The Origin of the Moving School in Massachusetts.*]

PAUL MONROE

SCHOOLBOOKS, EARLY. Because education was the handmaiden to religion in colonial America, catechisms, the Old Testament, the New Testament, and the Psalter were the most commonly used books of elementary instruction, although a few small texts and hornbooks of English origin were imported. Various primers were adapted to American schools, but among Calvinists and Lutherans *The New-England Primer* (1690), "the little Bible of New England," was preeminent as the guide to rudiments of spelling and religion until 1800. Thomas Dilworth's *New Guide to the English Tongue* (1740), a British work, dominated spelling and reading instruction until Noah Webster's *A Grammatical Institute of the English Language.* The *Institute,* which comprised a speller (1783), a grammar (1784), and a reader (1785), was revolutionary born and flamingly patriotic. Its author insisted on a native literature in the American language, with spelling that matched American pronunciation. Webster's *Spelling Book* enjoyed phenomenal success until the early 1900's; with Webster's dictionaries, published first in 1806 and 1828, it standardized spelling and pronunciation in America. Other early books to attain wide circulation were Ezekiel Cheever's *Latin Accidence* (1650), Jedidiah Morse's *Geography Made Easy* (1784), Nicholaus Pike's *Arithmetic* (1788), Caleb Bingham's *American Preceptor* (1794), Lindley Murray's *Grammar of the English Language* (1795), and Charles A. Goodrich's *History of the U.S.* (1822). As the public school system expanded in the mid-1800's, publications multiplied, but in each subject the books followed similar patterns until about 1900. In the teaching of grammar, more than elsewhere, methodology and books changed. Until 1825 memorization of rules and exceptions was universal; between 1825 and 1850 parsing became popular; between 1850 and 1890 structural analysis lent a bridge-building interest to syntactical study; after 1890 a strong tendency set in to eliminate formal grammar instruction and to substitute "good English." Since World War I functional grammar has won many adherents, although a conservative majority has urged a return to formal instruction combining parsing and analysis. English composition as a separate subject was introduced in the 1840's, but it was not until 1851 that the first textbook, G. P. Quackenbos' *First Lessons in Composition,* was published. Although practiced in conjunction with catechetical and conversational instruction, oral composition did not achieve a separate place in the curriculum until 1880; it did not attain its present importance until 1920. History texts tended to stress political and military events and, with the aid of sharp criticisms of monarchy and royalty, to extol American representative democracy. Civics was taught as a part of the work in history or reading. Although books of reading selections varied little in type, two series became especially popular. From 1827 until 1860 Samuel Griswold Goodrich used a friendly narrator and extensive pictorial illustrations as teaching devices in his enormously popular *Peter Parley* series of books for children. William Holmes McGuffey's *Eclectic Readers* (1836) captivated the whole Middle West and provided a foundation for cultural pursuits on the frontier. In general it may be said that the contents of textbooks remained haphazard in choice and arrangement until about 1825, when the principles of Johann Heinrich Pestalozzi redirected educational activity toward observation, investigation, and discussion and away from memorization and rote recitation.

[A. M. Earle, *Child-Life in Colonial Days;* Clifton Johnson, *Old-Time Schools and Schoolbooks;* G. E. Littlefield, *Early Schools and Schoolbooks of New England.*]

HARRY R. WARFEL

SCHOOL LANDS. When Congress created new states out of the public domain it reserved to itself the management and disposal of the public land within their boundaries. Chief among the government's means of disposal of these lands were land grants to the states to aid in the development of elementary schools. Beginning with the Ordinance of 1785, Congress granted one section in each township of thirty-six sections for school purposes to the new states as they were admitted into the Union; in 1848 the grant was increased to two sections in each township; and in 1896 it was again increased, to four sections in each township. Twelve states received one section, thirteen received two sections, and four received four sections. More than 100 million acres were granted to the states.

The pressure of public opinion prevented these lands from being held for high prices and induced the legislatures to take early action for their disposal. Ohio, the first state in which the land grant policy was put into practice (1803), tried a number of experiments in managing its school lands, among them being short-term leases, perpetual leases for 12 cents per acre, ninety-nine-year leases at 6 percent of appraised valuation, and one-year leases and sale at a minimum price of $5 per acre. Some states, like Ohio, held the lands and proceeds from them as trustees for the townships, while others, like Indiana, turned them over to the townships. Local management generally led to favoritism, careless administration, and reckless use of the funds derived from the sale. State management frequently played into the hands of large speculator groups as in Wisconsin, where individuals acquired as much as 57,000 acres of school lands. Wisconsin and Nebraska loaned their school-land funds to individuals, taking mortgages on the lands of these persons as security, and when payments were delayed were forced to foreclose. The more common procedure was to require that the school funds be invested in state bonds paying 6 percent interest. Despite the haste in selling, the mismanagement of the funds, and the actual diversion of receipts by some of the states, the lands did aid materially in making possible elementary schools in communities where the tax base was insufficient to permit the establishment of schools or where school taxes were opposed.

Management of school lands in the newer states of the Far West was more successful than it was in Ohio, Illinois, or Wisconsin, partly because Congress attempted to prescribe more fully the conditions under which the lands should be sold and partly because the states have been more prudent in their administration of them. Such states as Minnesota, North Dakota, and Washington have accumulated large funds from their school lands, the income from which makes up a sub-

stantial part of the state contribution to the public schools. (*See also* Land Grants for Education.)

[Paul W. Gates, *History of Public Land Law Development.*]

PAUL W. GATES

SCHOOLS, PRIVATE. The private, nonpublic, or independent school does not receive governmental support and is not under direct governmental control. Some are under religious auspices, some under secular boards, while others are operated for profit.

Private instruction was available in Boston by 1630, even before publicly supported schools were opened. There were several noteworthy secondary private schools in the 17th century: the Collegiate School of New York (1638), regarded as the oldest private day school in America; the Roxbury (Mass.) Latin School (1645); the Hopkins Grammar School (New Haven, Conn., 1660); and the William Penn Charter School (Philadelphia, 1689). The continuous existence of these schools testifies to their ability to retain their quality.

During the 18th century, private schools pioneered in the teaching of modern and practical subjects, from astronomy to trigonometry. Open evenings, they provided opportunities for advanced education and economic mobility. Of great influence were the Dummer (1763), Phillips Andover (1778), Phillips Exeter (1778), and Deerfield (1799) academies. The Zion Parnassus Academy (1785) in North Carolina also prepared teachers.

Religious schools were opened by the Quakers, Episcopalians, and Lutherans in the various colonies. A group of Jews opened a school in New York City (1731), and Roman Catholic schools were under way later in the 18th century.

The Free (later Public) School Society opened and operated private schools (1806–53) that were taken over by the New York City Board of Education. Other significant developments were the growth of Presbyterian parochial schools and the spread of the Catholic parochial school system, especially after the Third Plenary Council at Baltimore (1884); the establishment of private normal schools, especially those of Samuel R. Hall (1823, first normal school in America) and James G. Carter (1827); the opening of Round Hill (1823), A. Bronson Alcott's Temple (1834), and John Dewey's Laboratory (1896) schools, all noted for progressive ideas and practices; the first kindergarten (1856); female academies and seminaries; and the Gilman Country Day School, Baltimore (1897).

The Magna Charta of the private school was the U.S. Supreme Court decision in *Pierce* v. *Society of Sisters* (1925), which upheld the constitutionality of private and parochial schools, declaring that the child is not the mere creature of the state. Although guaranteed constitutional existence, the parochial schools experienced great financial difficulty after 1945, partially as a result of judicial bans on public support, and many Roman Catholic institutions were forced to close.

In the fall of 1972, according to the U.S. Office of Education, 5,170,000 pupils (kindergarten to grade 12) were in nonpublic schools out of a total pupil population of 51,310,000. The largest group attended Roman Catholic schools, which numbered 11,829 with a total enrollment of 4,029,183 and a teaching staff of 188,000 (1971–72).

[W. W. Brickman, *Educational Systems in the United States;* J. H. Fichter, *Parochial School: A Sociological Study;* O. F. Kraushaar, *American Nonpublic Schools: Patterns of Diversity;* J. S. McLachlan, *American Boarding Schools: A Historical Study.*]

WILLIAM W. BRICKMAN

SCHOOLS, PUBLIC. *See* **Education.**

SCHOOLTEACHERS, EARLY. Teachers were scarce in early colonial days. In 1624 Gov. William Bradford of Plymouth Colony wrote: "Indeed, we have no common school for want of a fit person or hitherto means to obtain one." Efforts were made in New England to avoid employing schoolmasters who "have manifested themselves unsound in the faith, or scandalous in their lives." In general the parish pastor reviewed the candidate's qualifications, but by the beginning of the 19th century the schools had passed from the care of the church to that of the state.

The simple rudiments were taught at mother's knee; gifted women sometimes drew their own and neighbors' children into a little circle, or girls of sixteen or older conducted dame schools. The colonial schoolmaster seldom received as much as a third of the sum paid a pastor. His qualifications were few; often he was required to possess no more than "the knack to continue in the schoolroom the discipline of the kitchen, and to be a good mender of quill pens." Ignorance, incompetence, ill temper, intemperance, boorishness, and laziness were commonly mentioned as characteristics of teachers, yet among the wielders of the ferule were many men and women whose idealism fostered intellectual ambitions in callow frontier lads.

Four classes of teachers existed: preachers who conducted parish or grammar schools (*see* Latin Schools); young college graduates who taught school while preparing for professional careers in law, medicine, and divinity; indentured servants who earned their freedom by teaching; and men and women who dedicated their lives to education and remained for many years in charge of common and grammar schools. One of the most famous of the latter class was Ezekiel Cheever, author of *Accidence, A Short Introduction to the Latin Tongue,* a famous colonial book. At twenty-three he began a twelve-year service in New Haven, Conn.; he then taught at Ipswich, Mass., for eleven years and at Charlestown, Mass., for nine; and at fifty-six he was called to Boston, where he remained as head of the Boston Latin School until his death in 1708.

Girls were generally excluded from colonial public schools; but private schools made progress in educating women. After the Revolution girls were admitted to a few academies, but in the main received advanced education at such schools as Sarah Pierce's at Litchfield, Conn. (1792). Some of the graduates of these seminaries were pioneers in establishing women's colleges. With the founding of normal schools, open to women and chiefly concerned at first with the training of elementary-school teachers, women replaced men as teachers in the lower schools and gradually advanced into higher institutions.

[R. G. Boone, *Education in the United States;* E. S. Slosson, *The American Spirit in Education;* W. H. Small, *Early New England Schools.*]

HARRY R. WARFEL

SCHOONER, a sailing vessel that, in its pure form, originated at Gloucester, Mass., in 1713–14. It is a fore-and-aft-rigged craft, originally small (50 to 100 tons), with two masts, designed for coastwise trade, but developed in the 1880's and 1890's into vessels of 2,000 to 3,000 tons, having four, five, and even six masts. Only one seven-master was attempted (1901–02), the *Thomas W. Lawson,* 368 feet long and 5,200 tons.

The use of schooners began to decline gradually, beginning in the mid-1800's with the advent of steam-powered vessels, but the schooner has always stood as the favorite and distinctive rig of American waters.

[Winthrop L. Marvin, *The American Merchant Marine;* S. E. Morison, *Maritime History of Massachusetts.*]

WILLIAM LINCOLN BROWN

SCHUYLER, FORT. *See* **Stanwix, Fort.**

SCHWENKFELDERS, followers of Kaspar Schwenkfeld, a 16th-century German religious reformer. Persecuted as sectarians, they emigrated to Pennsylvania in 1734. In 1968 there were six churches with 2,500 members; headquarters are at Pennsburg, Pa.

[H. E. Kriebel, *Schwenkfelders in Pennsylvania.*]
AUGUSTUS H. SHEARER

SCIENCE, POPULARIZATION OF. American scientists have engaged in the popularization of science in three distinct periods. In the 19th century, beginning principally in the 1820's, they utilized popular science in justifying professionalization. In the 20th century, from 1921 to 1930, they popularized science as part of a campaign to raise funds to support basic research. And from 1944 to 1950, they directed popular science to a political audience in lobbying for civilian control of atomic research and for federal money for a science foundation.

During these periods, the popularization of science consisted of the description for a lay public of the character and values of the scientific enterprise, with the intention of persuading the public to grant scientists professional autonomy, financial support, and intellectual freedom. Popularization is therefore distinguished from the vulgarization of science, which is simply the reportage of the intellectual advances of science in a manner comprehensible and intriguing to persons without technical training. Popularization is one means of legitimating the organized pursuit of knowledge by an elite community in a society in which privilege is suspect.

In the decades 1820–50, the nascent American scientific community was professionalizing itself. Scientists sought the authority to determine who could be called a scientist, the right to decide what problems they wished to investigate, the freedom to do research and to theorize without moral or political restrictions, and the privilege of distributing their own financial support. Professionalization also withdrew knowledge from the public domain into technical specialties in which it was intellectually inaccessible to nonprofessionals. In an effort to justify this specialization, scientific leaders like Edward Hitchcock, a geologist, prophesized utilitarian benefits to flow from the new state of science.

The professional status of the scientists was threatened afterward primarily by the evolution controversy, during which many popularizations of Charles Darwin's theory of evolution were written to protect the scientists' independence. While modernists were persuaded, fundamentalists were not. The efforts of fundamentalists to curtail the scientists' authority to pronounce on man's origins led to the Scopes trial of 1925.

The most important concerted popularization movement before World War II occurred in the 1920's, when a group of scientific leaders, including Robert A. Millikan, a Nobel Prize-winning physicist, and George Ellery Hale, an astronomer, attempted to convince the public and industrialists that financial support of basic science would bring economic progress and preserve social and political democracy. They aided Edward Wyllis Scripps, the newspaper magnate, and Edwin E. Slosson, a chemist and journalist, in founding the Science Service in 1921. This agency provided authenticated news about science and expressed the scientists' ideological message. It also published school periodicals and broadcast radio programs about science. In 1925 the Hale-Millikan group enlisted the aid of Herbert Hoover in a campaign to solicit funds for a national research endowment. Failure to convince anyone except their friends to contribute and the Great Depression defeated the campaign in 1930.

The atomic scientists' movement of 1944–46 and the indirectly related effort to establish a national science foundation, 1945–50, were the most successful popularization movements. The atomic scientists' movement originated in 1944 at the Metallurgical Laboratory at the University of Chicago, which was part of the Manhattan Project to build the atomic bomb. Scientists were concerned about two basic problems: Who was to conduct postwar atomic research in the United States? Was postwar international atomic research to be conducted by an open scientific community or by secret, national groups? Led by scientists like Eugene Rabinowitch, a biophysicist, and Leo Szilard, a physicist, the scientists opened a campaign to educate the federal government on the dangers of secret, military-controlled, domestic atomic research and on the necessity of internationally controlled atomic weapons. Their educational and lobbying efforts brought the creation of the civilian Atomic Energy Commission in 1946. Many of the scientists of this movement also acted to secure federal patronage of basic scientific research. Led particularly by Vannevar Bush and James B. Conant, who headed the national government's defense research offices during World War II, scientists lobbied from 1945 to 1950 to obtain the National Science Foundation (created in 1950). This campaign involved careful education of congressmen on the traditional theme of popularization—that disinterested, unfettered pure science leads to utilitarian benefits for the whole nation.

[George H. Daniels, *American Science in the Age of Jackson;* J. L. Penick, Jr., and others, eds., *The Politics of American Science, 1939 to the Present;* Alice Kimball Smith, *A Peril and a Hope, the Scientists' Movement in America, 1945–47;* Ronald C. Tobey, *The American Ideology of National Science, 1919–1930.*]

RONALD C. TOBEY

SCIENTIFIC AMERICAN, a magazine of popular science, owed its early success to the great appeal applied science had for 19th-century Americans. Rufus Porter, a peripatetic musician, painter, inventor, and publisher of mechanics' magazines, designed the first issue—which came out on Aug. 28, 1845—as a family newspaper. But instead of politics, he interspersed poetry, religion, and news curiosities amidst features on advancements in the mechanic arts. His creative vision of a cheap weekly newspaper, suitable for family reading but so full of valuable technical information that it would not be thrown away, was essentially the editorial policy for the next century. But Porter was a man of wandering disposition, and within the first year of publication he sold his interests to Alfred E. Beach, whose father published the *New York Sun,* and Orson D. Munn, of Monson, Mass.

Under the firm name of Munn and Company, Beach and Munn dropped poetry and religion from the paper, altered its format, and introduced a varied set of prize schemes to increase circulation, which by 1853 had reached 30,000 copies. They also opened a patent agency whose interests dovetailed with those of the newspaper. Inventors who employed the company's services were rewarded by publication of their invention in *Scientific American,* a device that also increased circulation. Because of that relationship, many publicized inventions were of dubious value, but the paper's wide popularity insured coverage of the 19th century's most dramatic innovations. Electromagnetism was one of the paper's early interests and Thomas A. Edison, also a client of the patent agency, one of its favorite subjects.

The editors of *Scientific American* emphasized progress and practicality. Porter had originally subtitled the paper "Advocate of Industry and Enterprise." In the same vein, Munn, Beach, and their descendants, who controlled the periodical for over a hundred years, energetically promoted the development of new technologies, especially in the fields of electricity, urban transit, weaponry, the automobile, and aviation. Through a variety of advice columns, the editors implicitly suggested that any reader might win fame and fortune by mechanical skill. The "Handy Man's Workshop" column in the "Automobile" number of 1909, for example, showed how to convert a horse-drawn buggy into an automobile for less than $300.

But the increasing complexity of modern technology simultaneously diminished the importance of the individual inventor and called for more sophisticated analysis of the industrial applications of science. The *Scientific American Supplement,* initiated in 1876 to provide information "more technical and special in nature," was the first of a series of steps in the transformation of *Scientific American* from a mechanics' newspaper into a magazine of popular science. The patent agency was separated from the publishing company in the 1890's, and in a major editorial shift in 1921, the *Supplement* was dropped while the paper was made into a monthly magazine, with feature articles by outside specialists. An even more significant alteration occurred in 1947, when Munn and Company sold the magazine to the newly formed Scientific American Publishing Company. The enormous expansion of scientific research and development during World War II revealed the importance not only of basic science, but also of its social and political implications. Under the editorship of Gerard Piel, *Scientific American* was broadened to encompass the physical, biological, and social sciences—basic and applied—and was glamorized by the liberal use of charts and photographs in a glossy format. In its new format the magazine aimed at a readership of educated laymen, which the editor defined to include scientists interested in developments outside their own fields. It found wide acceptance and by 1975 had a monthly circulation of 640,000 copies.

[Albert G. Ingalls, "A Century of Scientific American," *Scientific American,* vol. 173 (December 1945); F. L. Mott, *A History of American Magazines,* vol. II; "Orson Desaix Munn," *Scientific American,* vol. 96 (Mar. 9, 1907); "Rufus Porter, Founder of the Scientific American," *Scientific American,* vol. 51 (Sept. 6, 1884).]

BRUCE SINCLAIR

SCIENTIFIC EDUCATION. Science has been part of American higher education since the colonial period. Viewed first as an ally of religion, science came to be valued in the early 19th century in utilitarian terms. As Alexis de Tocqueville observed, "In

SCIENTIFIC INFORMATION RETRIEVAL

America, the purely practical part of science is admirably understood." New educational institutions embodied this spirit: mechanics' institutes, academies, and military schools brought the rudiments of science and engineering to a wide audience. The lyceum movement popularized science for the public. Natural philosophy, already part of the traditional college curriculum, was supplemented in some of the newer colleges with applied science courses. Other schools, such as the U.S. Military Academy at West Point (after 1816) and Rensselaer Polytechnic Institute (founded 1824), began to produce a small but important cadre of professional engineers. The faculties of the older colleges included such outstanding scientists as Benjamin Silliman and Joseph Henry. Eventually scientific schools, still primarily engineering, were established at Harvard (1847) and Yale (1860). At the time of the Civil War the craft tradition still dominated engineering, but the bulk of the active research scientists were products of liberal arts colleges and medical schools.

The expansion of scientific education after the Civil War was given special impetus by the Morrill Act (1862), which established the land-grant colleges, and the beginning of graduate education. By 1974 federal support had created seventy-one land-grant institutions devoted to the application of science to national needs. The rise of the graduate school, heralded by Johns Hopkins University (founded 1876), began the transformation of the American university into a research institution. Increasingly the education of scientists involved advanced study, basic research, and specialization. Undergraduate education in science was strengthened by the increased competence of instructors, the expansion of facilities, the revision of the curriculum, and the proliferation of departments. The professionalization of science was the major achievement of 19th-century scientific education.

The phenomenal growth of scientific education in the 20th century resulted from the increasing demands of a technological society, the expansion of college enrollments, and, most important, a public policy that led to large-scale support for research and training. During World War II science was recognized as a major intellectual resource, and in the postwar years federal funding shaped the direction and growth of scientific education. Stimulated by the cold war and Soviet accomplishments in space science, federal support was channeled to universities through such agencies as the National Science Foundation, the Atomic Energy Commission, the Department of Defense, the National Institutes of Health, and the

National Aeronautics and Space Administration. Most of the research funds went to science and engineering, causing an enormous expansion of research activity and a rapid increase in the number of scientists. As universities grew to depend on government funds, alterations in federal priorities in the 1960's had immediate repercussions among the 40 percent of American scientists in academic institutions. By the last quarter of the 20th century scientific education had become an important social force.

[C. V. Kidd, *American Universities and Federal Research;* Frederick Rudolph, *The American College and University.*]

ROBERT C. DAVIS

SCIENTIFIC INFORMATION RETRIEVAL is generally meant to cover the entire problem of recovering from recorded scientific and engineering knowledge those particular pieces of information that may be required for particular purposes at particular times. In this context it usually includes a wide range of techniques and devices used to collect, index, store, retrieve, and disseminate specialized information resulting from scientific research and development.

Scholars and researchers in all fields find it increasingly difficult to keep abreast of the published literature in their subjects or related areas of specialization. This problem is particularly acute for science and technology, in which the volume of publications doubles approximately every ten years and information often ages rapidly because of new scientific discoveries.

The expression "information retrieval" was coined in the United States in 1950, and the major developments in this area came about as a result of the tremendous expansion in research and development during and after World War II, which produced a veritable flood of published material. U.S. federal agencies, in particular, invested large sums of money in developing new systems for coping with this problem. The impetus toward more inclusive techniques of handling information was also increased as a result of rapid engineering advances, particularly in the development of electronic computers and improved communication techniques. The earliest large-scale information systems were designed in America to meet the specialized needs of the space, atomic energy, defense, and intelligence programs.

Scientific information retrieval systems can take many different forms. It can include such conventional practices as library cataloging and classification, but the trend since the 1950's has been toward development of mechanical or electronic devices to replace these manual methods. Probably the earliest large-scale system using punched cards was that developed by the Central Intelligence Agency in 1954 for their Intellofax system. In this operation, intelligence documents were microphotographed and mounted in apertures on IBM punched cards. Access to the documents was through codes punched into the cards to indicate subject, area, source, security classification, and other pertinent data.

The National Aeronautics and Space Administration was one of the first to develop a retrospective literature search system, using magnetic tape and an IBM 7010 electronic computer. This system was operational in 1963 and included both report and journal literature covering space and related sciences. By the 1970's nearly every major U.S. federal agency with significant responsibility in scientific research or development had developed a modern computer-based system for handling information.

In scientific information systems, efforts have been made to deliver immediately the exact information needed directly from the system's own memory, rather than to provide references to documents that must then be acquired and read. The major impediments to this approach have been the cost of encoding the full text of documents into machine-readable form and the limitations of electronic memory devices. Perhaps even more serious are problems of a linguistic nature, as may be seen in the continued controversy over the comparative merits of assigning descriptive labels from controlled vocabularies against the free use of the language in the documents themselves.

Regardless of the complexity or sophistication of the information retrieval system employed, the fundamental task is to provide the best match between the user's query and the data supplied by the system. It is necessary to describe both the query and the contents of the file, in order to match one against the other and to have criteria on which to judge the relevance of each record to the elements of meaning in the records.

Information retrieval studies were dominated first by a concern for the comparative efficacy of various indexing vocabularies and their compatibility with devices used in retrieval. An obvious criterion of excellence of a system is its ability to retrieve from its total store those documents that are relevant to the query. But relevance does not inhere in the documents—it is a complex and subtle relationship between the meanings in the documents and the users of

the system. Thus, later studies attempted to measure the effects of a wide range of variables that may determine a system's performance. Their results indicated that in the mid-1970's the state of the art was not such as to make it possible to design highly exact systems, nor even to measure system effectiveness with any degree of precision. The limitations introduced by human decisionmaking seem to outweigh other determinants of system performance, and research is expected to occupy itself largely with these factors for a long time to come.

[Lauren B. Doyle, *Information Processing and Retrieval;* Robert Fairthorne, *Towards Information Retrieval;* John Sharp, *Some Fundamentals of Information Retrieval;* B. C. Vickery, *Techniques of Information Retrieval.*]

JOHN SHERROD

SCIENTIFIC MANAGEMENT, a term adopted in 1911 to identify the system of manufacturing management developed and promoted by Frederick Winslow Taylor of Philadelphia. Many later elaborations and offshoots of the central doctrine have been given separate names, but the original term is still in common use to describe the whole movement in the 20th century toward systematic coordination and control of machines, materials, and workers in manufacturing operations. Subdisciplines, such as time and motion study, production planning, and inventory control, were included in Taylor's doctrine; later elaborations have included statistical quality control, operations research, and systems analysis.

The economic advantages, both to owners and to employees of industrial firms, of this extensive rationalization of production have been clearly demonstrated. Industrial productivity, measured in dollar value of product per man-hour of human labor, has risen steadily with increasing mechanization and control of factory production. On the other hand, the human problems inherent in the factory system, chief of which is an individual worker's psychological need to participate in decisions affecting his work and to find purpose or significance in it, have not been satisfactorily resolved.

The entire movement toward greater industrial efficiency represents a logical extension of the factory system, introduced in its modern form in England near the end of the 18th century. A vigorous "shop management" movement appeared in the United States just before 1900. Taylor's particular system included the rationalization of both machines and people. It grew out of many years of investigations and experiments pursued by Taylor successively in the works of the Midvale Steel Company and the Bethlehem Steel Company.

In rationalizing machines, a long series of experiments in the Midvale machine shops resulted in techniques for insuring the maximum production of, for example, a lathe through a proper adjustment of machine variables such as speed, feed, and shape of cutting tool. At Bethlehem, in collaboration with Maunsel White, a metallurgist, Taylor developed an improved alloy for cutting tools, aptly named "high-speed steel" (1900). Armed with objective information on machine capabilities, Taylor was able to refurbish existing shops and often to show astonishing gains in production. In addition to the improved performance of individual machines, a marked increase in shop efficiency was obtained through planned routing of work, improved procedures for issuing materials and tools, systematic maintenance, and cost accounting routines to monitor the detailed effects of changed procedures.

Taylor's approach to the rationalization of human labor was not essentially different from his work with machines. Through observation and study of workers, he determined "scientifically" (that is, systematically) how a particular human task might be done most quickly. He then selected the worker best suited for the task and made sure that the worker was thoroughly instructed in what to do and how to do it. A piece-rate system, which included penalties for low performance and moderate bonuses for high performance, was devised to insure a desired level of production. The explicit assumption that Taylor made was that all workers had a tendency to "soldier"—that is, to loaf on the job. His implicit assumptions were two: that people work only for the money they earn and that they will not be influenced by those with whom they work. Much of organized labor's resistance to the Taylor system can be traced to the crudity of Taylor's conception of human motives. Nevertheless, since Taylor's assumptions were shared by many if not most employees and engineers, no fundamental revision of the basis or methods of scientific management was even considered until many years after his death in 1915.

From 1927 to 1932, Elton Mayo, of the Harvard Graduate School of Business Administration, conducted a series of inquiries in the Hawthorne plant of the Western Electric Company that became known as the Hawthorne Experiment. Its results challenged fundamental assumptions regarding the performance of workers by demonstrating the importance of group associations and of workers' having a voice in decisions affecting their work. The experiments were undertaken originally to determine the effects of factors in the physical environment, such as lighting and rest periods, on the productivity of assembly-line personnel. It was found that a much more powerful controlling variable in productivity was the attitude of employees to their jobs. Although the conclusions of the Hawthorne Experiment have had a prominent place in subsequent doctrines of scientific management, it is a curious fact that the central message—workers will respond to genuine interest in having their cooperation and help—has been effectively muted by the apparent need for a system that insures full and rigid control by management of all aspects of work routines. Elaborate procedures for listening to employees' complaints and suggestions have been devised, but workers easily recognize the difference between being asked about a problem and having some effective input to its solution.

In addition to its early effects on industrial productivity, the Taylor system triggered a remarkable popular "efficiency" craze that by 1912 reached into schools, churches, and homes. Dozens of articles in large-circulation magazines brought to a wide audience the notion that efficiency was in itself a positive good. The idea of efficiency was also embraced by the conservation movement of the Progressive era, and Teachers College of Columbia University took the lead in pursuing the means to "educational efficiency."

The effect of Taylor's system of scientific management on the whole economic and social fabric of the United States in the 20th century cannot be overestimated. It caught the popular mood and imagination with its reduction of complex problems to a set of simple, easily remembered rules. Particularly in the public schools, its legacy has been a preoccupation with financial and administrative problems, with emphasis on measurable rather than qualitative results. The important increases in industrial productivity owe as much to implicit general principles as to specific methods. Taylor and his followers, such as Henry L. Gantt and Frank B. and Lillian E. Gilbreth, were able to demonstrate to a generation of engineers and businessmen that problems of industrial production could be systematically studied and analyzed, and that improvements in productivity were possible. In economic terms, American industries under scientific management have been spectacularly successful both at home and abroad.

[Hugh G. J. Aitken, *Taylorism at Watertown Arsenal;* Raymond E. Callahan, *Education and the Cult of Ef-*

ficiency; Samuel Haber, *Efficiency and Uplift: Scientific Management in the Progressive Era;* Carl Heyel, *The Encyclopedia of Management;* Elton Mayo, *The Social Problems of an Industrial Civilization;* Milton J. Nadworthy, *Scientific Management and the Unions.*]

EUGENE S. FERGUSON

SCIENTIFIC PERIODICALS. Two factors led to the creation of journals devoted to publishing scientific studies in Europe during the 17th century: the growth of the periodical press (including newspapers) and the increase of scientific activity in centers of learning. Most historians accept the *Journal des sçavans,* begun in France in January 1665 and published as a scientific journal until 1792 (plus one volume in 1797), as the first periodical concentrating on science. In May 1665 Henry Oldenburg issued the first number of the *Philosophical Transactions of the Royal Society of London,* which continues as a distinguished scientific journal. By 1700, thirty scientific and medical periodicals had appeared in Europe. The 18th century showed a sharp increase in numbers of scientific journals: one authority counts over 700 by 1800, with about 400 titles in German and 50 in English. Several reasons explain this increase—cheaper printing costs, greater numbers of scientific societies to serve as sponsors, better communication within Europe, and curiosity about the world outside Europe as symbolized by the great exploring expeditions of the French, English, and Russians. Toward the end of the 18th century, journals began to reflect the specialization within science, and the French *Annales de chimie* (1789–   ), the German *Journal der Physik* (1790–   ; title changed to *Annalen der Physik* in 1799), and the English *Curtis's Botanical Magazine* (1787–   ) appeared. The last of these is also notable for the impact of its scientific illustration, especially in the use of color plates.

At first, colonial Americans found European journals, especially the Royal Society's *Philosophical Transactions,* an adequate medium for publication of their scientific work, but conditions eventually favored the establishment of their own periodicals. The delay in publication caused by slow transatlantic travel cost Americans priority in reporting discoveries in fields being worked on simultaneously by European savants. The problem became especially acute when disputes arose over whether an American or a European worker had first named a new species of plant or animal. Also, the ideology of independence during the era of the American Revolution and subsequent cultural nationalism spurred efforts to create independent American periodicals. And American science itself expanded to the point where it could sustain journals of its own, as evidenced by the appearance in the second half of the 18th century of durable institutions such as the American Philosophical Society in Philadelphia, the American Academy of Arts and Sciences in Boston, the State University Regents in New York (noted for its support of meteorological research), the Connecticut Academy of Arts and Sciences, and city and college museums. Within the region that became the United States, the *Transactions of the American Philosophical Society* (1769–   ) constituted the first long-lived periodical that devoted a large part of its contents to science. In 1780 the American Academy began its *Memoirs,* and in 1787 the New York Regents started issuing its *Reports.* These early publications, editorially and financially controlled by their sponsoring institutions, were not the only outlet for printing American scientific writing. Many agricultural magazines and some physicians' journals, such as the *Medical Repository* (1797–1824) in New York, also accepted original scientific papers, especially those with applications to farming or medicine.

The earliest periodical in the United States devoted exclusively to science was Dr. Archibald Bruce's *American Mineralogical Journal* (1810–14), a one-volume venture of four annual issues that terminated with its editor's death. More important was the establishment of the *American Journal of Science* (1818–   ). Its first two editors, Benjamin Silliman and James Dwight Dana, were professors at Yale, and the college indirectly supported the journal through their salaries. The journal's readers and contributors were from all over the nation rather than just from Yale. Silliman and Dana were both mineralogists, but the journal did not specialize in geochemistry until well into the 20th century; in its early years it had even carried occasional scholarly pieces on the arts. The format of the *American Journal of Science* from its beginning resembled that of present-day scientific periodicals. On its pages were review articles on recent developments in science, detailed reports of experiments and fieldwork, book reviews, news of people in the profession, and abstracts of articles published in other journals.

As in the 18th century, American scientific societies founded before the Civil War began printing a profusion of proceedings, reports, memoirs, journals, transactions, and bulletins soon after their establishment. Especially noteworthy for this activity were the Academy of Natural Sciences of Philadelphia (founded 1812), the Lyceum of Natural History of New York City (1817; later the New York Academy of Sciences), the Franklin Institute (1824) in Philadelphia, the Albany Institute (1824), the Boston Society of Natural History (1830; merged eventually into the city Museum of Science), the Association of American Geologists (1840; the American Association for the Advancement of Science from 1848), the Smithsonian Institution (1846), and the Chicago and the Saint Louis academies of science (both 1856). The trend toward original scientific papers appearing in medical or agricultural journals continued and even expanded to embrace trade and business journals before subsiding in the face of increasing specialization among scientific and technical professions. In the 19th century, the growth of scientific periodicals was curbed somewhat by the appearance of another agent active in scientific publication—the government. The reports of state geological and natural history surveys were usually published with public money as separate monographs, and the results of federal surveys of the trans-Mississippi West appeared in documents that were part of the federal executive or congressional series.

Scientific literature in the 19th century increased enough in volume to warrant the founding of the *Annual of Scientific Discovery* (1850–71), the first sustained American journal devoted to abstracting scientific material published elsewhere. The antebellum era also saw the beginning of a few specialized periodicals that printed material relevant for only one branch of science, such as the *Mining Magazine* (1853–61) of New York, the *American Entomological Society Proceedings* (1861– ; title changed in 1867 to *American Entomological Society Transactions*), the *American Journal of Conchology* (1865–71), and the *American Ethnological Society Transactions* (1845–53). However, long-lived specialized journals required a national professional society for editorial and financial backing. These organizations began mostly in the 1880's and 1890's, and with them began the enormous proliferation of scientific journals that still marked publishing in the 1970's. The Gilded Age also saw the professionalization of the social sciences: journals of national scope were established in anthropology, economics, and sociology. Also, as scientific papers began to be written in more technical language during the 19th century, enterprising editors saw the need for periodicals that summarized scientific progress in ordinary prose for a general readership. *Scientific American* (1845–) and *Popular Science Monthly*

(1872–) both functioned to reach this wider audience. These magazines were financed as commercial ventures; the professional, specialized journals that came to dominate scientific publication during the Gilded Age were underwritten by scientific societies and, as higher education burgeoned in the United States, by universities.

One authority estimated that by 1895 approximately 8,800 scientific journals had appeared throughout the world, counting both defunct undertakings and those being published at that time. This growth accelerated during the 20th century: the cumulative figures were 25,000 in 1920; 50,000 in 1950; and 75,000 in 1970. As of 1962 between 26,000 and 35,000 of these journals were still being published, a plurality (17 percent) of them in the United States. One response to this flood of information was an increase in abstracting journals, with periodicals for each discipline created to keep its practitioners abreast of developments in their field. The abstracting journals also came to serve as bibliographic guides to scientific literature. Another response to the growth of scientific publications in the 20th century was the differentiation of function between scientific journals. Increasingly, individual disciplines each supported a placement newsletter, a review journal, an abstracting periodical, one or more magazines concentrating on practical applications of discoveries within the field, and journals for specialized branches (organic, physical, analytic, industrial, and agricultural chemistry, for example). For scientists and lay people curious about developments in many fields, general-purpose magazines such as *Science* (1883– ; after 1900 an official publication of the American Association for the Advancement of Science) continued to offer a sampler of overview articles on scientific breakthroughs, detailed research reports, political news as it bears on science, information on a wide variety of jobs, and reviews of new books.

Scientific periodicals are useful to American historians for two reasons. First, the journals reflect other events and ideas in the cultural setting. In the 19th century, for example, scientific magazines were filled with information on technological and economic developments and on the exploration of the oceans and of the continental West. The history of scientific journals is tied to the history of higher education in particular and of the growth of intellectual life in general. In this regard, it is noteworthy that the format of scientific journals is similar to that of other learned journals and that the history of publications in history and literature often parallels that in science. Scientific prose and illustrations in journals usually reflected prevailing styles of the day, with the conventions of romantic art and writing evident in antebellum scientific periodicals. Advances in numbers and sophistication of scientific publications are correlated with urbanization and with developments in printing technology. Scientific journals also adopted, consciously or not, many of the ideas prevalent in American society, including its seamier aspects, such as racism.

The other historical use of scientific journals is in studying the history of science in this country. On occasion, a particular journal becomes identified as an important publishing outlet for adherents of a certain theory, as was the case with neo-Lamarckism in the early *American Naturalist* (1867–   ) and diastrophism in the early years of the *Journal of Geology* (1893–   ). Sometimes the rise and virtual disappearance of a whole branch of science can be traced through journals, as with phrenology and eugenics. In the 20th century, journals are useful indices of scientists' increased concern for the political, technological, and ecological impact of their discoveries; the *Bulletin of the Atomic Scientists* (1946–   ) is noted for its attention to such problems. Scientific periodicals aided in professionalizing the discipline by setting standards for acceptable research and theories; journals that defied the consensus of American scientists on controversial issues were often as short-lived as the *Monthly American Journal of Geology and Natural Science* (1831–32), which published Constantine S. Rafinesque's heretical ideas on the variability of species. The scientific periodical press recorded the growth of American science—its institutions and ideas, its triumphs and shortcomings—and as such chronicled a vital part of American intellectual life since the very beginnings of the nation.

[Ralph S. Bates, *Scientific Societies in the United States;* Edward S. Dana et al., *A Century of Science in America;* Bernard Houghton, *Scientific Periodicals: Their Historical Development, Characteristics and Control;* David Knight, *Sources for the History of Science 1660–1914;* Frank L. Mott, *A History of American Magazines, 1741–1930;* George Sarton, *A Guide to the History of Science.*]

MICHELE L. ALDRICH

SCIENTIFIC SOCIETIES emerged concomitant with an increasing interest in science in the 17th century. Americans, with a tendency toward forming associations, recognized the relationship between scientific advance and the creation of such organizations.

Highly visible and self-selecting European societies, especially the Royal Society of Great Britain (1660) and the Paris Academy of Sciences (1666), served as models for the Americans. Nearly a century passed after Increase Mather's short-lived Boston Philosophical Society (1683) before two ongoing groups, the American Philosophical Society (1743) in Philadelphia and the American Academy of Arts and Sciences (1780) in Boston, were founded.

Like their predecessors, these groups were dedicated to a broad understanding of natural philosophy. Membership tended toward a local, leisured, upperclass constituency, buttressed by local academicians. Within two generations persons whose interest in science was more than avocational or amateur led a movement for more narrowly defined scientific organizations. Typically middle-class with occupational motivations, this group founded new scientific societies in the second quarter of the 19th century that informally served educational functions and permitted like-minded investigators to exchange knowledge. Most successful were groups that stressed the natural sciences, such as the Academy of Natural Sciences of Philadelphia (1812), the Lyceum of Natural History of New York City (1817; later the New York Academy of Sciences), and the Boston Society of Natural History (1830). All of these organizations held regular meetings for local membership, established a network of correspondents for exchange of specimens, created research collections, and published significant research results. Although not professional in the modern sense, such organizations had identified goals characteristic of their late 19th-century successors.

By the 1840's limited effectiveness and local constraints led to several efforts to found a national scientific organization. The specialized and highly integrated Association of American Geologists and Naturalists (AAGN), founded in 1840, was the first to establish a national constituency. In 1848 the AAGN became the multidisciplinary American Association for the Advancement of Science (AAAS). Its leadership, deliberately diverse, included geologists, physicists, mathematicians, and biologists. All agreed that the establishment of standards for scientific research and of scientific ethics had high priority, although they frequently disagreed on details. Moreover, these full-time scientists wanted better recruitment and training for potential scientists and supported plans for a national university at Albany, N.Y. But advanced scientific training was not available until after the Civil War, when reformed programs were initiated at Harvard University and new graduate institutions like Johns Hopkins University, Clark University, and the University of Chicago. The AAAS through the 1850's was, in fact, the only forum for discussing mutual concerns for the growing number of scientific practitioners in Boston, Albany, New York, Philadelphia, and Charleston, S.C. Such geographic separation of active researchers required a national organization able to enhance communication among scientists and to present scientific concepts to the public.

Basically the pre–Civil War organizations pinpointed problems: inconsistent standards in publication, insufficient support for research, and inadequate scientific training. None was successful in overcoming them, in part because each area of science had issues peculiar to itself. The sectional meetings of the AAAS inadvertently contributed an arena for discussions that led to the development of specialized professional societies. The young organizations tended to reflect academic disciplines as well as the traditional technical and scientific arts. In fact, applied fields, such as engineering, had groups that slightly predated the new societies. The professional societies in science reinforced the increasing specialization of practitioners who shared a limited body of knowledge with some depth, university and governmental employees who required better research facilities, and research scholars who accepted a national tendency toward centralization and bureaucracy. Established gradually, the new specialized societies in such areas as physics, chemistry, and geology, as well as in economics and anthropology, were part of national science by the turn of the century. Most established a national headquarters and regularly published proceedings, bulletins, or journals. Networks of collegiate clubs and local societies echoed the efforts of the national organizations. By World War I, subspecialties, as well, had groups that met annually and published members' papers.

The older societies, eclipsed by the vigorous competition for membership, redefined their goals and extended their functions. Many of the local and regional groups, such as the Boston Society of Natural History, turned to popularization, offering public lectures and extending museum holdings. National groups also sought to renew their public identity (the AAAS assumed publication of *Science,* for example) while they continued to advocate governmental support for science (especially the National Academy of Sciences, founded in 1863).

The results of professionalization and specialization were a clearer identification of scientific stan-dards and more efficiently shared information. Yet the exclusive nature of these groups meant, in some cases, fewer opportunities for women and for some minorities. Sometimes these people were explicitly excluded, but more often omission was *de facto* because of limited academic possibilities. As one result, some of those excluded formed alternative societies.

The multiplicity of organizations, each with its own specialized knowledge, boundaries, and formal institutional structure, created a need to coordinate transmission across discipline boundaries and into applied fields. The AAAS and the National Academy of Sciences did not fill these functions, although the AAAS began a policy of affiliating specialized societies. In 1916, during World War I, the National Research Council, formed by the National Academy of Sciences, supervised manpower and fund allocation. After the war the council continued to offer recommendations and attempted to balance support for basic research and applied projects. The American Council of Learned Societies (1919) and the Social Science Research Council (1923) similarly coordinated diverse but parallel professional groups. Other such groups were established after World War II.

Although it is impossible to quantify the effect of scientific societies, their functions of standardization, communication, and coordination meet a need expressed by practitioners. Many scientists combine areas of specialization and join more than one organization, some on the national and others on the local level. The professionalization of science was made possible through institutions—especially scientific societies—that created a sense of common respect, a vehicle for united action, a group capable of enforcing ethical and procedural standards, and a concern for the public awareness of, and support for, science. (*See also* Scientific Periodicals.)

[Ralph S. Bates, *Scientific Societies in the United States;* George Daniels, "The Process of Professionalization in American Science: The Emergent Period, 1820–1860," *ISIS,* vol. 58 (1967); Sally Gregory Kohlstedt, *The Formation of the National Scientific Community, The American Association for the Advancement of Science, 1848–1860;* Max Meisel, *A Bibliography of American Natural History: The Pioneer Century, 1769–1865;* Alexandra Oleson and Sanborn Brown, eds., *The Pursuit of Knowledge in the Early American Republic: American Scientific Societies From the Colonial Times to the Civil War.*]
SALLY GREGORY KOHLSTEDT

SCIOTO COMPANY, a speculative land-buying syndicate organized to purchase territory in the Ohio Valley. It was established in July 1787 when the Rev.

Manasseh Cutler, who was attempting to purchase 1.5 million acres of land for the Ohio Company, was approached by a group of New York speculators, headed by William Duer, secretary of the Board of Treasury. The group offered Cutler enough money for a down payment on his land if he would secure for them, while concealing their names, an option from Congress on the great tract of land lying north and west of the Ohio Company's proposed purchase and extending to the Scioto River on the west. As later surveyed, the tract contained 4,901,480 acres. Payment was to be made in six installments at 66⅔ cents per acre, the first payment due six months after the boundary had been surveyed. A number of New York and Massachusetts speculators divided the thirty shares among themselves, with Duer, Royal Flint, and Andrew Craigie acting as trustees and Richard Platt as treasurer. Joel Barlow was sent to France as their agent, and with William Playfair, an unscrupulous Englishman, Barlow organized the Compagnie de Scioto to sell the Scioto lands. Although sales were active at first, little cash came in and the French company presently collapsed. The financial panic of 1792 swept away the fortunes of the leading American partners, and the Scioto Company defaulted on its contract with the government. Thus the 500 or more Frenchmen who had purchased what they thought were deeds to land owned by the company had in fact acquired only options to buy the homesites. Congress, recognizing their plight, awarded them land elsewhere in Ohio. Gallipolis, Ohio, was founded by those Frenchmen who chose to remain in the area.

[R. A. Billington, *Westward Expansion: History of the American Frontier;* Francis S. Philbrick, *The Rise of the West, 1754–1830.*]

EUGENE H. ROSEBOOM

SCIOTO GAZETTE, a newspaper established in Chillicothe, Ohio, by Nathaniel Willis on Apr. 25, 1800. Later in the year it absorbed *Freeman's Journal,* successor to the *Centinel of the North-Western Territory,* which was the first newspaper in the Old Northwest. Published continuously with little change of name, the *Scioto Gazette* was originally Democratic-Republican, later Whig, and eventually Republican in politics. The last edition of the *Scioto Gazette* was published in December 1939; on Jan. 2, 1940, it became the *Chillicothe Gazette.*

[O. C. Hooper, *History of Ohio Journalism, 1793–1933.*]

EUGENE H. ROSEBOOM

SCIOTO TRAIL, frontier route that followed the Sandusky and Scioto valleys almost due south from Sandusky Bay to the Ohio River and southward through Kentucky to Cumberland Gap, in Tennessee. A branch ran southeast from the Scioto River along the divide west of the Hocking River to the mouth of the Great Kanawha River, which it followed into Virginia. The main trail was used both for the fur trade and as a warpath by northern Indians to reach the Cherokee and Catawba country, and during the American Revolution for raids in Kentucky by the Ohio tribes. Part of the trail near Cumberland Gap, known as the Warriors' Path, was used for Daniel Boone's Wilderness Road.

[A. B. Hulbert, *Historic Highways of America,* vol. II.]

EUGENE H. ROSEBOOM

SCOPES TRIAL. The fundamentalist movement, which arose in the United States about 1910, led to the passage of laws in Tennessee, Mississippi, and Arkansas forbidding the teaching of the theory of evolution in the public schools and colleges of the state. In 1925, in Tennessee, a twenty-five-year-old high school teacher, John Thomas Scopes, was tried for violating the state's "monkey law" (the Butler Act of Mar. 21, 1925). The case began with an argument between Scopes and three friends, on May 5, 1925, in a drugstore in Dayton. They decided to engineer a test case to settle the law's constitutionality and incidentally to "put Dayton on the map."

The Monkey Trial, as it was popularly known, began on July 10 and aroused enormous interest. William Jennings Bryan, political leader and ardent fundamentalist, served as a volunteer lawyer for the prosecution, while Scopes had as defenders several eminent attorneys, including Clarence S. Darrow. Judge John T. Raulston tried to run a fair and orderly trial, but this proved hard in the circus atmosphere that sprang up in the normally quiet, conservative town. Dayton swarmed with evangelists, eccentrics, and traveling showmen, some of whom exhibited tame chimpanzees.

The defense planned to attack the law on three main constitutional grounds: first, that it violated the First and Fourteenth amendments to the Constitution by writing into the law a religious doctrine, namely fundamentalist creationism; second, that it was unreasonable in that it forbade the teaching of a well-established fact of nature; and third, that it was vague, because it did not say whether it meant "teach" in the sense of "set forth" or "explain" or in the sense of "advocate" or "recommend." To prove the second point, the defense brought to Dayton a dozen scientists to testify to the overwhelming evidence for evolution. The prosecution, however, succeeded in having such testimony excluded as irrelevant, so the scientists remained merely spectators.

Toward the end of the trial, Darrow called Bryan as an expert witness on the Bible. Fearing for the floor of the old courthouse because of the number of spectators, Judge Raulston had moved the trial out on the lawn. In an hour and a half of grilling, Darrow showed that Bryan, although a man of many attractive qualities, knew nothing about many subjects on which he had pontificated and could not understand scientific reasoning. On the next day, Raulston expunged the Darrow-Bryan debate from the record and called in the jury. Darrow hinted that he wanted a guilty verdict to make possible an appeal. The jury obliged, and Scopes was fined $100.

When the case was appealed, the Tennessee Supreme Court set aside the verdict because the judge had committed a legal blunder in levying the fine. At the court's suggestion, the prosecution nol-prossed the bizarre case. Scopes, who admitted that he had never taught evolution at all (he had been too busy coaching the football team), became a geologist. Bryan died in his sleep five days after the trial. The Butler Act was repealed in 1967, and shortly thereafter the two remaining laws prohibiting the teaching of evolution were found unconstitutional.

[L. Sprague de Camp, *The Great Monkey Trial;* Ray Ginger, *Six Days or Forever?*]

L. SPRAGUE DE CAMP

SCOTCH-IRISH, a people, in the American colonies and the United States, emanating from the Scottish Protestants who were transplanted to Ulster, Ireland, chiefly during the 17th century, and from their descendants. The migrations from Scotland to Ulster, begun during the years from 1607 to 1609 under the sponsorship of James I, continued intermittently throughout the century. By the close of the 17th century, adverse economic conditions and political and religious disabilities arose, creating in them a desire to leave Ireland. Their farms were owned by absent English landlords who demanded high rentals; parliamentary regulation, 1665–80, seriously impaired their cattle-raising industry; the Woolens Act of 1699, which forbade the exportation of wool from Ireland, rendered sheep raising unprofitable; an act of Parliament in 1704, excluding Presbyterians from holding civil and military offices, denied them a voice in gov-

ernment; and the government taxed them to support the Anglican church, in which they did not worship. Consequently, thousands of these people from Ulster, with their Scotch heritage, their experience in colonization, and their Presbyterian faith, emigrated to America.

The Scotch-Irish began to arrive in the American colonies as early as the middle of the 17th century, if not before, and continued to settle in small numbers until about 1715. This influx was greatly accelerated after 1717, because of efforts of English landlords to increase rentals on Ulster farms held under long-term leases that were expiring in that year. Thereafter, a steady stream of Scotch-Irish poured into American ports, as many as 10,000 reputedly arriving in Pennsylvania within a single year. The total number of these immigrants to America has never been definitely ascertained, but various studies indicate that in 1790 probably 6 percent of the total U.S. population, or approximately 225,000 people, were Scotch-Irish or of Scotch-Irish extraction.

On their arrival in America, they scattered themselves widely and established clusters of settlement in every colony. Their tendency was to penetrate to the frontiers, however, following the main channels of migration to the fertile lands along the streams and in the valleys of the mountains of the backcountry. While Scotch-Irish immigrants arrived in nearly every port along the Atlantic seaboard, Baltimore and Philadelphia were the chief ports of entry. From Baltimore many of these settlers followed the Potomac River westward to the Shenandoah Valley and turned southward into the back counties of Maryland, Virginia, and the Carolinas or went westward to the Monongahela country in southwestern Pennsylvania; others went northward along the Susquehanna River and into the valleys between the mountain ranges in Pennsylvania. From Philadelphia, many followed the Delaware River to the north or went westward to the frontier. Thus, while Scotch-Irish settlers were found in every colony, the frontier regions of Pennsylvania and the southern colonies received the greater contingents. Approximately 65,000 Scotch-Irish settled in the piedmont of North Carolina between 1739 and the Revolution. As the frontiers moved westward across the continent, the Scotch-Irish and their descendants, usually among the vanguard of settlers, migrated to the newer regions. While they may now be found in every state in the Union, they settled in greater numbers in Tennessee, Kentucky, Missouri, Ohio, Indiana, and Illinois.

Scotch-Irish contributions to the development of

the United States have been great. Rugged and daring, they made fine settlers on the more extended frontiers; their educated ministers gave an effective intellectual leadership and stimulated the founding of many institutions of higher learning; and their qualities for leadership and their inclination for politics produced from among them fine political leaders in every generation.

[R. J. Dickson, *Ulster Emigration to Colonial America, 1718–1775;* Ian C. Graham, *Colonists From Scotland;* E. R. Green, ed., *Essays in Scotch-Irish History;* James G. Leyburn, *The Scotch-Irish.*]

R. J. FERGUSON

SCOTT, FORT, on the Marmaton River in Bourbon County, Kans., was established in 1842 as an intermediate post on the military road from Fort Leavenworth, Kans., to Fort Gibson, Okla., which had been constructed to facilitate the protection of the Southwest from hostile Indians. Fort Scott, which was named for Gen. Winfield Scott, was abandoned as a post during 1853–54. In 1855 the federal government sold the fort's substantial frame buildings at public auction to some settlers, and shortly thereafter the present city of Fort Scott came into existence. The city, which had a population of 8,697 in 1970, is located in an agricultural area and is a center of dairy farming. Coal, gas, oil, and limestone are among the region's natural resources. Fort Scott National Historic Site was established in 1965.

[T. F. Robley, *History of Bourbon County, Kansas.*]

RALPH P. BIEBER

SCOTT-PILLOW QUARREL. Maj. Gen. Gideon J. Pillow, commanding Gen. Winfield Scott's Third Division in the Mexican War, was a political appointee of President James K. Polk. In 1847, after the Battle of Contreras (Aug. 19–20) and the Battle of Chapultepec (Sept. 12–13), Pillow claimed, in his official report, undeserved credit for the victories. Scott asked that the report be revised, which Pillow did, but not to Scott's satisfaction. Then Pillow caused publication in the *New Orleans Delta* of an anonymous and vainglorious account of his military prowess, exasperating Scott. Arrested for insubordination and disrespect, in 1848 Pillow appeared before the same court that, on the basis of Pillow's appeal of Scott's charges against him, was investigating Scott's conduct. Both were exonerated, but Pillow was discredited by the army.

[Justin H. Smith, *The War With Mexico;* C. W. Elliott, *Winfield Scott, The Soldier and the Man.*]

CHARLES WINSLOW ELLIOTT

SCOTTSBORO CASE. In April 1931 in Scottsboro, Ala., eight of nine black teenagers were convicted and sentenced to death for allegedly raping two white women. (The ninth was sentenced to life imprisonment.) From 1931 to 1937, during a series of appeals and new trials, the case grew to an international cause célèbre as the International Labor Defense (ILD) and the Communist Party of the U.S.A. spearheaded efforts to free the "Scottsboro boys." In 1932 the U.S. Supreme Court concluded that the defendants had been denied adequate counsel (*Powell* v. *Alabama*), and the following year Alabama Judge James Edwin Horton ordered a new trial because of insufficient evidence. In 1935 the Supreme Court again ruled in favor of the defendants by overturning convictions on the ground that Alabama had systematically excluded blacks from jury service (*Norris* v. *Alabama*).

But public opinion in Alabama had solidified against the Scottsboro youths and their backers, and each successful appeal was followed by retrial and reconviction. Finally, in 1937, defense attorney Samuel Leibowitz and the nonpartisan Scottsboro Defense Committee arranged a compromise whereby four of the nine defendants were released and the remaining five were given sentences ranging from twenty years to life. Four of the five defendants were released on parole from 1943 to 1950. The fifth escaped prison in 1948 and successfully fled to Michigan. In 1966 Judge Horton revealed theretofore confidential information that conclusively proved the innocence of the nine defendants.

[Dan T. Carter, *Scottsboro: A Tragedy of the American South.*]

DAN T. CARTER

SCOUTING ON THE PLAINS. Fur trappers and hunters who penetrated the West before the advent of civilization acquired a remarkable knowledge of the geography and Indian tribes of the country that fitted them to be scouts and guides in the later military campaigns on the Plains. Such celebrated scouts as Kit Carson, Jim Bridger, Bill Williams, Charlie Reynolds, Billy Comstock, and Sharp Grover were former fur trappers, while others, including Billy Dixon and William F. ("Buffalo Bill") Cody, were buffalo hunters.

For all the skill of these white frontiersmen, the army would have been seriously handicapped had it not been for friendly Indian scouts. Thus, Osage guides led Gen. George Armstrong Custer's march in the Washita campaign of 1868; the Pawnee battalion under Frank North and Luther North took Gen.

SCRIPPS INSTITUTION OF OCEANOGRAPHY

Eugene Asa Carr to the Cheyenne village at Summit Springs in 1869, Gen. R. S. Mackenzie to Dull Knife's camp on the Crazy Woman in 1876, and did much scouting and fighting elsewhere. Tonkawa, Delaware, Seminole, and other scouts guided Gen. Nelson A. Miles, Mackenzie, and other officers in the Indian Territory uprising of 1874 (*see* Red River Indian War); Shoshone, Crow, and Arikara warriors did the trailing and much of the fighting for the commands of Custer, Gen. George Crook, and Miles in the Sitting Bull Sioux war of 1876–77; and Cheyenne and Sioux performed important services in the Ghost Dance uprising of their own people in 1890–91.

In the Southwest, friendly Apache, Mohave, Papago, and other Indian scouts actually bore the brunt of many campaigns against hostile Apache, notably in the Geronimo wars of 1881–83 and 1885–86. Scouting on the Plains required rare qualities of endurance, courage, and wisdom. A military commander could be said to have been no more successful than the excellence of his body of scouts permitted.

[George Bird Grinnell, *Two Great Scouts and the Pawnee Battalion;* Paul I. Wellman, *Death on the Prairie.*]
PAUL I. WELLMAN

SCRIPPS INSTITUTION OF OCEANOGRAPHY. In the early 1890's William E. Ritter, instructor in biology at the University of California and organizer of the university's first laboratory instruction in zoology, conceived the project of a systematic biological survey of the part of the Pacific Ocean adjacent to the California coast. Explorations of coastal waters by Ritter and his colleagues culminated in 1900 in university approval of Ritter's proposal for creation of a permanent seaside station at San Pedro. The site was shifted in 1903 to San Diego, chiefly because of the interest of Fred Baker, a San Diego physician, and, through him, newspaper publisher Edward W. Scripps and his sister Ellen Scripps. The Marine Biological Association of San Diego was organized that same year to secure "the foundation and endowment of a scientific institution to be known as the San Diego Marine Biological Institution." The present site in northern La Jolla was acquired in 1907, and Ritter became the first permanent resident director in 1909. Affiliation with the University of California remained tenuous until 1912, when the institution became the Scripps Institution for Biological Research of the University of California. Gifts from E. W. and especially Ellen Scripps remained the chief source of support until World War II.

Ritter's successor in 1924, T. Wayland Vaughan, put new emphasis on physical oceanography. In 1925 the institution was renamed the Scripps Institution of Oceanography. The first doctoral degree in oceanography for work at Scripps was granted in 1930. Vaughan's successor from 1936 to 1948, Norwegian oceanographer Harald U. Sverdrup, initiated an intensive program of research cruises. World War II brought extensive involvement in war-related research. Under Sverdrup's successors, the institution continued to expand with increasing federal sponsorship of oceanographic research; the 25 staff members of 1936 became 800 by 1966. Through the efforts of Director Roger Revelle the Scripps Institution became the nucleus of the San Diego campus of the university, first opened to undergraduates in 1964. Of the institution's many research programs, none has attracted more public attention since 1967 than the deep-sea drilling project, with its impressive confirmations of continental drift and the theories of sea-floor spreading.

[Helen Raitt and Beatrice Moulton, *Scripps Institution of Oceanography: First Fifty Years;* Scripps Institution of Oceanography, *Annual Reports.*]
CURTIS WILSON

SCULPTURE. The beginnings of American sculpture are found in the 17th-century gravestones of New England, produced by artisan stonecarvers, with their Protestant imagery of death. Gravestone carving continued to flourish in the 18th century throughout the colonies, but the images became less preoccupied with death. The increased wealth of the 18th century brought about a demand for fine wood carving for elegant Chippendale furniture and for elaborate decorative architectural carving. The Skillins family of Boston and Samuel McIntire of Salem excelled in this type of work, as did William Rush of Philadelphia. These men also carved handsome figureheads for the burgeoning American merchant fleet. Rush carried the native school of wood carving to its zenith, as may be seen in his figure *George Washington* (1814, Philadelphia Museum of Art).

After the revolutionary war Americans turned to foreign sculptors to produce marble images of their great men, thereby downgrading the native school of carvers. The most prestigious of the foreign sculptors was the Frenchman Jean-Antoine Houdon. His marble statue of George Washington (1788, Virginia State Capitol, Richmond) is a good example of the kind of neoclassic sculpture that influenced several generations of American sculptors. By the second quarter of the 19th century America produced its own native school of sculptors, led by Horatio Greenough, Hiram Powers, and Thomas Crawford.

Greenough, a Bostonian, left in 1825 for Italy, where he spent most of the rest of his life. He thereby became one of the first expatriate American sculptors. These expatriates could not find at home the art schools, the models, the artisan assistants, the fine marble, or the artistic climate Italy offered in abundance. In Florence, Greenough created his Zeus-like marble statue *George Washington* (1832–41, Smithsonian Institution). Powers, a mechanic from Cincinnati, took up sculpture and went to Italy in 1837, never to return to the United States. Countless Americans visited his famous studio in Florence to have busts made of themselves in his undramatic naturalistic style. Powers' most popular piece was the celebrated full-length, life-size marble *Greek Slave* (1843, Yale University Art Gallery); it was as famous in Europe as in the United States. Crawford began as a wood carver and tombstone cutter in New York City. He studied and chose to continue to work in Italy. He created the sculptures for the pediment of the Senate wing of the U.S. Capitol (1855) in his studio in Rome.

Henry Kirke Brown also went to Italy, but in 1846 he returned to America, rejecting Italianate neoclassicism for a style based on naturalism—as in his bronze equestrian statue *George Washington* (1853–56, New York City). With Brown the age of bronze sculpture began in America. Clark Mills was a former plasterer with no formal training in sculpture. He had never created anything more ambitious than a few portrait busts when he was commissioned to make what became a tour de force in bronze equestrian statuary: the *Andrew Jackson* (1848–53, Washington, D.C.), an excellent example of 19th-century American ingenuity in technology. During the same period, in the area of Albany, N.Y., the former carpenter Erastus Dow Palmer produced a thoroughly American counterpart to Powers' *Greek Slave* in his marble *White Captive* (1857, Metropolitan Museum of Art). Another sculptor with little formal training was John Rogers. A former engineer, he began modeling small, naturalistic genre groups about 1860. Thousands of these groups were cast, and Rogers attained great popularity among the middle class.

Another generation followed the first to Italy—men such as the Bostonian William Wetmore Story, who gave up a career in law to create heroic marble figures. Most acclaimed was his *Cleopatra* (1858, Metropolitan Museum of Art). Story's studio was a center

of the artistic and intellectual life in Rome. From Baltimore young William Rinehart came to Rome in 1858 where he, too, created marble images of antique subjects (*Clytie,* 1872, Metropolitan Museum of Art) and naturalistic portraits of prominent Americans. Randolph Rogers epitomized the romantic neoclassicism in his statue of *Nydia, The Blind Girl of Pompeii* (1859, Metropolitan Museum of Art), which was so popular that nearly 100 replicas were commissioned in the years that followed. Rogers also produced several multifigured war memorials, which became big business for American sculptors in the years between the Civil War and World War I.

Bronze portrait statuary was created in large amounts in the "era of the galvanized hero," particularly by John Quincy Adams Ward, a student of Brown. His *Henry Ward Beecher* (1891, Brooklyn, N.Y.) and *President James A. Garfield* (1887, Washington, D.C.) possess the unromanticized, undramatic naturalism that was then in vogue. Ward became the dean of American sculptors in the last quarter of the 19th century and was one of the founders of the National Sculpture Society. Thomas Ball was another practitioner of this rather prosaic naturalism in portrait statuary.

With the rise of the generation led by Augustus Saint-Gaudens and Daniel Chester French the aesthetics of naturalism was revitalized. Italy was largely rejected as a place to study, and the new style came out of the École des Beaux Arts in Paris. Nowhere is this better demonstrated than at the World's Columbian Exposition (Chicago, 1893), where Saint-Gaudens, French, Olin L. Warner, Frederick W. MacMonnies, Philip Martiny, Karl Bitter, and Hermon A. MacNeil collaborated with numerous architects to give the exposition that neobaroque exuberance that characterizes the Beaux Arts style. Saint-Gaudens and French dominated this golden age; the former is best known for his vigorous portraiture—as in his bronze *Abraham Lincoln* (1887, Chicago) and his equestrian *General William T. Sherman* (1903, New York City). His most successful attempt at symbolic imagery was the sibyl-like *Adams Memorial* (1886–91, Washington, D.C.). But it was French who gave the era its sculptured personifications of such idealized concepts as the Republic, death, political and civic virtues, and industry. French's career began auspiciously with the bronze *Minuteman* (1874, Concord, Mass.) and closed half a century later with his marble, seated *Abraham Lincoln* (1922), part of the Lincoln Memorial in Washington, D.C.

SCURVY

In the years preceding World War I there was a confrontation of artistic ideologies: the conservatives, represented by the academic tradition and the advocates of the eclectic Beaux Arts style, entrenched themselves against the aesthetic assault of those who pursued the experiments of the modern movement. Paul Manship and Paul Jennewein represented a compromise that drew on the past but incorporated some abstraction. American sculptors did not give themselves over to total annihilation of natural form the way some of their European counterparts did, and men such as Robert Laurent, William Zorach, and John B. Flannagan developed an aesthetic around the simplification and stylization of natural form plus the technique of direct carving in wood and stone.

After World War II American sculpture moved dramatically toward abstract and nonobjective form. David Smith introduced welded metal, and Alexander Calder developed his well-known mobiles and stabiles; both men were greatly influenced by constructivism. Others owed more to abstract expressionism: Seymour Lipton, Herbert Ferber, and Theodore J. Roszak, whose work may be seen at the Museum of Modern Art in New York City.

The generation of the 1960's and 1970's brought American sculpture into a direct confrontation with reality as it incorporated actual everyday objects into its art—as in George Segal's *Girl in Doorway* (1965) and Marisol's *Women With Dog* (1964), both at the Whitney Museum of American Art in New York City. "Junk sculpture," or assembled discarded objects, is represented by Louise Nevelson and Richard Stankiewicz, while "light sculptures"—using neon and fluorescent tubes—have been created by Dan Flavin and Chryssa.

[Wayne Craven, *Sculpture in America, From the Colonial Period to the Present;* Albert T. Gardner, *American Sculpture, A Catalogue of the Collection of the Metropolitan Museum of Art,* and *Yankee Stonecutters: The First American School of Sculpture, 1800–1850;* Sam Hunter, *Modern American Painting and Sculpture;* Beatrice Proske, *Brookgreen Gardens, Sculpture;* Michel Seuphor, *The Sculpture of This Century,* and *Dictionary of Modern Sculpture;* Loredo Taft, *History of American Sculpture.*]

WAYNE CRAVEN

SCURVY. One of the earliest colonial references to scurvy, a deficiency disease caused by a lack of vitamin C (ascorbic acid) in the diet, occurred in 1631 when John Winthrop, writing to his wife in England who was preparing to join him in Massachusetts, cautioned her: "Remember to bringe juice of lemons to sea with thee, for thee and thy company to eate with your meate as sauce." In 1674 John Josselyn published a warning to New England voyagers to provide themselves with the "juice of Lemons well put up to cure, or prevent the scurvy." Scurvy, once the scourge of sailors on long voyages, afflicted the crew of Sebastián Vizcaíno when he explored the coast of California (1602–03); and it decimated the companions of California's first physician, Don Pedro Prat (1769). Scurvy ravaged the passengers who came to California by boat during the gold rush (1848–53), and the ships' captains admitted to an indignant health officer that the shipowners would not permit them to stop on the way to take fresh vegetables on board. Scurvy continued to flourish even though the simple remedy for its control was known. The first in the United States to describe night blindness (1842) as one of the symptoms of scurvy was Edward Coale, who noted that, because so many men of the frigate *Columbia* could not see after sundown, deck work had to be discontinued. Modern methods of food preservation and distribution and improved eating habits have made a diet rich in vitamin C accessible to most people, and scurvy has ceased to be a major American public health problem.

[Alfred Fabian Hess, *Scurvy, Past and Present.*]

VICTOR ROBINSON

SEABOARD AIR LINE RAILROAD. *See* **Railroads, Sketches.**

SEABOARD COAST LINE. *See* **Railroads, Sketches.**

SEA FENCIBLES, the first organization of the U.S. Army charged exclusively with coast defense. By an act of Congress on July 26, 1813, ten separate companies were organized to be employed "as well on land as on water for the defense of the ports and harbors." Each company consisted of a captain, first lieutenant, second lieutenant, third lieutenant, boatswain, six gunners, six quarter-gunners, and ninety privates; in aggregate, there were 1,070 men. Their most notable service was at the defense of Fort McHenry, Sept. 13, 1814, where the companies of captains M. Simmones Bunbury and William H. Addison formed part of the garrison, which also included the Baltimore Fencibles, one of several volunteer companies of the same class of troops. The Sea Fencibles were discharged on June 15, 1815.

[Francis B. Heitman, *A Historical Register and Dictionary of the United States Army.*]

DON RUSSELL

SEALERS, TOWN, are officers chosen by the New England town meeting for annual terms to test and certify the accuracy of weights, scales, and measures. Their services are frequently called for in disputes involving the weight of hay, coal, livestock, and so forth. Payment is usually by fee.

[J. S. Garland, *New England Town Law.*]

W. A. ROBINSON

SEALING in subarctic waters of the North Atlantic began in connection with whaling early in the 17th century and developed into a separate occupation late in the 18th century. The hunting of the small hair seal became an important commercial activity in the late 18th and early 19th centuries, the greatest annual kill occurring in 1831, when 687,000 seals were taken. Hair seals, which include the harp and hooded seal, are found all the way from near the White Sea to Greenland, Newfoundland, and Labrador. Their numbers, as a result of reckless exploitation, have steadily declined. The worldwide harp seal population, which at the beginning of the 20th century was estimated at 10 million, by 1967 numbered only 3 million. In 1970 Canada and Norway, prompted especially by public outcries over the killing of baby "whitecoat" seals, agreed to restrict the killing of seals in the waters off Newfoundland and Labrador, as of 1971, to 245,000 three- or four-year-old male seals each year, leaving the mature bulls for breeding purposes and the cows and their pups. The seals of Antarctic waters, mainly the southern elephant and South American fur seal, were nearly exterminated during the 19th century by hunters but began to recover when regulations were introduced in 1881. In 1972 twelve nations signed a treaty giving complete protection to some varieties of seals and restricting the killing of others.

American sealing interests have centered largely on the northern fur seal herd of the Pribilof Islands—Saint Paul and Saint George—in the Bering Sea. The herd is not stationary, the seal being migratory, its movements determined by the temperature of sea water; but the Pribilofs contain the rookeries to which the herd returns from far south every spring. There

the young are born and grow strong enough to endure the winter migration, which takes them to the latitudes of California and Mexico.

The northern fur seal was first sighted on Vitus Bering's second Alaska voyage, in 1741, and was described by Georg Wilhelm Steller, the German naturalist of the expedition, but it was not until 1786 that its breeding grounds on the Pribilofs were discovered. For more than half a century thereafter the ruthless slaughter practiced by the Russian fur traders of Alaska threatened the complete destruction of the herd, but it was saved when the killing of seals began to be restricted by the monopolistic Russian-American Company by 1835. Under that company's wise management the herd increased, though with some fluctuations, and when the United States bought Alaska in 1867 it numbered about 3 million seals.

Alaska at that time was by many considered worthless. But the tiny seal islands were a valuable estate. The government in 1870 leased them for twenty years to the Alaska Commercial Company for $55,000 per year. In addition the company agreed to pay $2.62½ for every sealskin shipped from the islands and an additional $.55 per gallon for all seal oil made. A new contract in 1890 provided for $60,000 in rental, $2.00 per skin, and $7.62½ for every seal killed. The company was licensed to kill 100,000 male seals over one year old.

The latter provision was too generous and in consequence the herd declined. Scientists at a later time maintained that the killing of males under three years of age injuriously affects the proper proportion between breeding males and females. Although the government obtained expert opinion from time to time and limited the kill accordingly, the experts were sometimes too liberal. This, plus the Alaska Company's need to make its annual operations for the year show a good profit, resulted in a continuing decrease in the herd.

Even more serious a threat to the survival of the herd was the rapid rise, beginning in the 1880's, in activity of pelagic, or deep-sea, sealers. Land killing could be regulated; but because several different nationalities—the Americans, Canadians, Mexicans, Russians, and Japanese—preyed upon the herd at sea, sometimes killing more than 100,000 seals in a single year, saving even a remnant of the herd became a grave problem.

In 1886 the United States seized several Canadian pelagic vessels, and in defense of this action Secretary of State James G. Blaine put forth the theory that the Bering Sea was a *mare clausum,* which the U.S. government had a right to police. Although many seals were killed in the Pacific also, the killing of female seals in the Bering Sea during the period when they were responsible for feeding their young resulted in the greatest destruction because an equal number of pups on the island rookeries also would die.

Blaine's theory was tested and temporarily upheld by an Alaskan court, but in 1893 an arbitration tribunal at Paris pronounced it untenable and required that damages be paid the owners of the vessels. Although the tribunal also imposed some regulations on pelagic sealing, they were insufficient and it seemed as if the northern fur seal herd would become extinct. Finally, in 1911, a treaty was signed by Great Britain, Russia, Japan, and the United States outlawing pelagic sealing. The government also tightened its regulations about killing seals. When the 1911 treaty was terminated by Japan in 1941, the United States and Canada signed an agreement continuing the ban on pelagic sealing. A 1957 pact signed by the United States, Canada, Japan, and the Soviet Union extended the prohibition. As a result of this and other sound conservation practices the herd, which by about 1911 had reached a low of 125,000 seals, is approaching its former abundance.

[Charles Melville Scammon, *The Marine Mammals of the Northwestern Coast of North America.*]

JOSEPH SCHAFER

SEAL OF THE CONFEDERATE STATES OF AMERICA, the official embossed emblem of the Confederacy. It was commissioned by the Confederate congress on Apr. 30, 1863, and decreed to depict Thomas Crawford's equestrian statue of George Washington in Richmond, Va., with the date Feb. 22, 1862 (Jefferson Davis' inauguration day), and the motto *Deo Vindice.* The seal was cut in solid silver by Joseph Shepherd Wyon of London. It was about 4 inches in diameter, cost about $600, and, with its ivory handle, weighed about 4 pounds. It reached Richmond in September 1864 but was never affixed to any document. The seal was lost during the evacuation of Richmond at the end of the Civil War, but it was recovered and is now displayed in Richmond's Museum of the Confederacy.

JOHN C. FITZPATRICK

SEAL OF THE UNITED STATES, or the **Great Seal,** is the official embossed emblem that validates a U.S. government document. Work on the design of a seal was begun by a committee appointed by the Continental Congress on July 4, 1776. Although the need for a seal with which to authenticate official documents was clear, the committee, after six weeks' work, could suggest only a weird jumble of impossible heraldic detail and biblical legend. It took Congress six years more to obtain a satisfactory design. The obverse of the seal finally adopted (a depiction of the American eagle) was the design of Charles Thomson, secretary of the Continental Congress. William Barton's idea (the pyramid and the Eternal Eye of God, symbols of the Freemasons) was selected for the reverse. The Great Seal is pictured on the U.S. one-dollar bill, the obverse being on the right of the back of the bill and the reverse on the left. The seal is kept by the secretary of state and is affixed by him to such documents as foreign treaties and presidential proclamations on the signed order of the president and, since the issuance of an executive order in 1952, on certain other categories of documents without a presidential warrant. A circle of special white paper with a serrated edge is attached to the document, and the seal is impressed through both by a metal die. From 1825 to 1871 a special wax impression (about 5 inches in diameter), enclosed in a gold or silver box, was attached to treaties by silken cords. Although recut six times for various reasons, the appearance of the Great Seal is still precisely as decreed by the Continental Congress on June 20, 1782.

[Gaillard Hunt, *History of the Seal of the United States.*]

JOHN C. FITZPATRICK

SEAMEN'S ACT OF 1915, also known as the **Furuseth Act** because it embodied reforms advocated by Andrew Furuseth and as the **La Follette Seaman's Act** because of the strong support it received from Sen. Robert M. La Follette, was approved Mar. 4, 1915. It applied to crews of vessels registered in the United States and to those of foreign countries while in United States ports. It was designed to improve living and working conditions on board ship, to attract American citizens to the sea, and to provide greater safety for all on board vessels. Among its more important provisions were those abolishing imprisonment for desertion; reducing penalties for disobedience and for neglecting to join or quitting a vessel; restricting the payment of seamen's wage allotments to certain relatives; regulating hours of work at sea and in port; fixing minimum scale and quality of daily food; regulating the payment of wages; requiring a certain number and type of lifeboats; increasing the number of able seamen to 65 percent of the total crew exclusive of officers and ordinary seamen; and requiring 75 percent of the members of each ship department to understand the language spoken by the officers.

HOBART S. PERRY

SEA OTTER TRADE. Europeans and Americans first came to the North Pacific coast of America in the late 18th century in pursuit of sea otter skins. While beaver trapping was drawing fur traders from the Atlantic seaboard into the interior of North America, the sea otter trade caused mariners to push into the North Pacific, where they established bases from which they ran the coast from the Aleutian Islands to Baja (Lower) California. In China sea otter furs were exchanged at good profit for prized Oriental goods.

Russia and Spain were the pioneer nations to engage in the sea otter trade. After Vitus Bering's expeditions in the early 18th century, *promyshlenniki* (fur traders) pushed eastward, and in 1784 they established the first permanent Russian settlement in America, on Kodiak Island. In the same year Spain organized a sea otter trade between California and China. The great fur rush to the Northwest coast was caused by published accounts of Capt. James Cook's last Pacific voyage, 1776–79. English and American vessels led the drive, but within a decade the former had practically withdrawn. At the opening of the 19th century American and Russian traders entered the California sea otter fields, where in the face of strong opposition they poached throughout the Spanish period. After 1821 the liberal commercial policy of independent Mexico stimulated the California sea otter trade, and many Americans became Mexican citizens in order to participate in the business.

The number of skins obtained in the prosperous sea otter trade can only be estimated. From 1804 to 1807 it was reported that almost 60,000 furs were taken by American vessels, while the period 1808 to 1812 yielded nearly 50,000. The greatest number of skins known to have been taken from the California coast in any one year was about 10,000 in 1811. By 1818 the number had decreased to 4,500.

The sea otter trade came to an end when ruthless hunting, intensified by the introduction of firearms, had nearly exterminated the animals. At the beginning of the 20th century the sea otter was so rare that its pelts were the most valuable of all furs, bringing as much as $1,000 each. In general, the fur areas were exhausted in the order in which they were opened,

and at approximately the following dates: Kamchatka and the westernmost Aleutians, 1790; Kodiak, 1805; Sitka to Nootka Sound, 1820; and California, 1840.

A treaty signed in 1910 by the United States, Great Britain, Russia, and Japan banned the hunting of sea otter, but its protection was thought to have come too late until the 1930's, when several sea otter colonies were discovered in the Aleutians and along the California coast. The entire population of sea otter in the mid-1970's numbered about 50,000.

[H. H. Bancroft, *History of California,* and *History of the Northwest Coast;* C. J. DuFour, E. O. Essig, Adele Ogden, *The Russians in California;* F. A. Golder, *Russian Expansion on the Pacific, 1641–1850.*]

ADELE OGDEN

SEA POWER. Some 2,500 years ago, Thucydides (an Athenian admiral turned historian), in describing the qualities that carried Athenian sea power to its zenith, gave what might be called the classic description of the role of sea power in a nation's affairs. Sea power, he said, rests on the profits from domestic industry, enhanced by oversea trade. To sustain such power, a government must afford a strong military fleet, served by all classes of the people. He warned that the soundest use for that fleet lies not in warfare but in securing and maintaining order among significant trading ports, as well as policing the sea routes that link them. Thucydides called war the enemy of commercial prosperity. Hence, no responsible sea power should seek it or prolong it. When forced into war, the prudent sea power will adhere to three priorities: protect the home base; keep the fleet relatively strong; use the fleet only for inducing the enemy to peace. To insure those priorities, he concluded, no sea power should ever attempt territorial or economic aggrandizement during war.

For twenty-five centuries Western history has testified to the wisdom of Thucydides' prescription. Even before Thucydides died, the illusion of easy prize money seduced Athens' assembly, with disastrous results. Then, within a century, Alexander of Macedon used Thucydides' formula to build on the Aegean foundation a Middle Eastern economic sphere extending from Egypt and the Danube to the Indus River. Later Carthage rejected Thucydides' prescription, to its sorrow. Then Pompey taught Rome to build a Mediterranean empire on the cornerstone of Thucydides' policy. Through the medieval centuries Genoa and Venice exercised remarkable power whenever some leader hit upon Thucydides' pattern of sea power.

247

In the 16th century, after ocean commerce overshadowed Mediterranean trade, Sir Francis Bacon reminded England's Elizabeth I that whatever nation has the power to use the sea can take as little (or as much) of any war as it may choose. Within two centuries Britain's William Pitt the Elder distilled into a clear policy the lessons about sea power that statesmen had learned since Thucydides' time. Throughout the Seven Years War (1756–63) the British government used sea power to blockade French naval bases, control the English Channel, and sustain oversea commerce. All the while Pitt withheld British armies from continental warfare. Instead he subsidized Prussian armies (with seaborne income) until they defeated France.

Unfortunately Pitt's policy proved hard to follow. When colonial Americans demanded a fuller share in Britain's wealth, Pitt's successors reversed his policy. During the American Revolution, Britain committed armies to North America and refused to blockade French naval ports. Wearied by six costly years of war, Great Britain gave up the war when George Washington cooperated with a French fleet to trap the British forces at Yorktown. Again, in the War of 1812, the British placed their hopes in an army too far inland for support by a blue-water navy. Despite effective blockade of its Atlantic ports the U.S. government generated enough naval energy, along the Great Lakes–Saint Lawrence frontier, to earn a welcome stalemate and a negotiated peace.

For a full century after 1815 the United States developed its sea power after Pitt's (and Thucydides') model. The small U.S. fleet supported worldwide ocean trade and fisheries, while technological change progressively reduced the British navy's scope. By 1914 Britain had withdrawn virtually all of its fleet to home waters, leaving the United States as the preeminent, non-European naval power. During this period Adm. Alfred Thayer Mahan laid down the basis for a U.S. policy toward sea power, which was as rational as Pitt's or Thucydides'. Mahan's theory that naval power and control of the seas are decisive in international politics was widely accepted throughout the world. Unfortunately, Mahan did not communicate readily with the dynamic individualists emerging in 1914 as U.S. naval leaders. During the ensuing decade, quantum changes in naval practice seemed to confirm their convictions that new naval matériel made ancient policy invalid.

Developments after World War I suggest that no 20th-century nation has adhered consistently to the classic uses of sea power. In the Atlantic theaters during World War I and World War II both U.S. and British policies mirrored Sir Winston Churchill's assumption that 20th-century technology invalidates lessons of the past. In both wars the Allies committed large armies to combat in Europe. Yet, when hostile submarines and aircraft disrupted their traditional use of the sea, neither the United States nor Britain—nor even the North Atlantic Treaty Organization (NATO) after 1945—evolved a 20th-century version of Pitt's plan.

In its role as a Pacific naval power the United States followed the classic rules of sea power during World War II. Operating from close-supporting mobile sea bases, elements from all U.S. armed forces advanced amphibiously along the island approaches to Japan. Yet only twenty years later, when the United States intervened in Vietnam, it foresook transpacific sea-based operations and relied almost totally on land-based forces. As the British had during the American Revolution, Americans in Vietnam found themselves hobbled by an urgent need to protect the large volume of supplies required for a full-scale land army. Their remaining energies merely contained the enemy, which could not win militarily but used attrition to attain a negotiated peace.

[Alfred T. Mahan, *The Influence of Sea Power Upon History, 1660–1782,* and *Naval Strategy;* E. B. Potter and Chester W. Nimitz, *Sea Power;* Clark G. Reynolds, *Command of the Sea.*]

W. H. RUSSELL

SEARCH, RIGHT OF. *See* **Search and Seizure, Unreasonable; Visit and Search.**

SEARCH AND SEIZURE, UNREASONABLE. The American colonists' hostility to general warrants, which authorized the apprehension of unnamed persons and indiscriminate search of their papers, and writs of assistance, which empowered customs officials to search, at their will, wherever they suspected uncustomed goods to be, is reflected in the Fourth Amendment to the U.S. Constitution, which prohibits ''unreasonable searches and seizures'' and requires that warrants be issued upon ''probable cause, supported by oath or affirmation, and particularly describing the place to be searched, and the person or things to be seized.''

Unless exceptional circumstances exist, such as the need to act swiftly to prevent the destruction of evidence, an officer may not search simply because he has "probable cause," or reasonable grounds, to do so; he must obtain a search warrant, a written authorization by a judicial officer. An arrest may be made without a warrant, even though it is practicable to obtain one. "Incident to the arrest," the person may then be searched without a warrant, as may the area "within his immediate control," in order to protect the arresting officer against attack by hidden weapons or to prevent the destruction of evidence. In the 1968 so-called stop-and-frisk cases, the U.S. Supreme Court held that an officer who lacks adequate grounds to make an arrest or search may nevertheless briefly detain a person in a public place and frisk him—that is, conduct a carefully limited search of the outer clothing of such a person to discover weapons.

The U.S. Supreme Court, in *Mapp* v. *Ohio* (1961), held that the Fourth Amendment is enforceable against the states through the due process clause of the Fourteenth Amendment and requires the exclusion of illegally seized evidence in state, as well as federal, prosecutions. This decision overturned *Wolf* v. *Colorado* (1949). By 1975 the continued vitality of this doctrine, known as the "exclusionary rule," appeared to be in serious jeopardy. It had been criticized by numerous legal commentators and law enforcement officials and, in 1971, by Chief Justice Warren E. Burger as not worth the high price it extracts from society—the release of many guilty criminals.

[Jacob Landynski, *Search and Seizure and the Supreme Court;* Wayne LaFave, " 'Street Encounters' and the Constitution," *Michigan Law Review,* vol. 67 (1968); Dallin Oaks, "Studying the Exclusionary Rule in Search and Seizure," *University of Chicago Law Review,* vol. 37 (1970).]
YALE KAMISAR

SEATTLE WORLD'S FAIR was opened by President John F. Kennedy by remote control from Palm Beach, Fla., on Apr. 21, 1962. Set on a 74-acre site and linked by a 1.2-mile monorail to the main business district of Seattle, Century 21, as it was officially known, was dominated by the 600-foot "space needle" and featured twenty national and eighty-three commercial exhibitions. Noted attractions included the House of Science and Fine Arts exhibits. Financed largely by public capital, the exposition drew 9,609,969 paying visitors and closed—having made a profit—on Oct. 21, 1962. The six-building science complex remained, forming the nucleus of a new civic center.

[Murray Morgan, *Century 21.*]
JOEL HONIG

SECEDED STATES, CONGRESSIONAL REPRESENTATION OF. With the exception of five representatives from the northwestern counties of Virginia, none of the states that seceded from the Union during the Civil War was represented in the House of Representatives after May 1861. Individuals elected by rump conventions and legislatures in North Carolina and northern Virginia (the Alexandria government) applied for admission, but they were denied their seats. Under President Abraham Lincoln's direction, loyal governments were organized in 1864 in Tennessee, Arkansas, and Louisiana, each of which sent senators and representatives to Washington, but both houses of Congress refused to seat the aspiring legislators. Two senators, elected by the loyal part of the Virginia legislature, were admitted by the Senate in July 1861. Andrew Johnson, however, was the only regularly elected senator from one of the seceded states (Tennessee) who retained his seat in the Senate. He continued his senatorial duties until he was appointed military governor of Tennessee in March 1862. Thus Virginia and Tennessee were the only Confederate states that had even partial representation in Congress during the war.

[W. A. Dunning, *Reconstruction, Political and Economic;* J. C. McGregor, *The Disruption of Virginia.*]
RICHARD E. YATES

SECESSION, ORDINANCE OF, was the enactment in legal form by which eleven southern states withdrew from the Union in 1860–61. According to the compact theory of union, sovereign states had entered the partnership by ratifying the Constitution of the United States. Secession, therefore, was achieved by a repeal of the act of ratification. This was accomplished in each state by a convention, elected for the purpose, as the instrumentality of government most nearly expressive of the sovereign will of the people.

[D. L. Dumond, *The Secessionist Movement, 1860–1861.*]
C. MILDRED THOMPSON

SECESSION, RIGHT OF. The southern states of the American Union were advancing no new theory when they appealed to and exercised the right of secession in 1860–61. Publicists and statesmen had championed the right from the beginning of American independence. The right of a people to establish, alter, or abolish their government and to institute a new one if their safety and happiness demanded it was a fundamental principle of the American Revolution (*see* Declaration of Independence). This idea was the basis of the threat of both Vermont (*see* Haldimand Negotiations) and Kentucky (*see* Spanish Conspiracy; Western Separatism) during the 1780's to separate from the Confederation and set up independent governments, or to ally with some foreign power.

More specifically the right of secession was based on the doctrine of state sovereignty and the compact theory of the Union. James Madison stated this theory very clearly when he wrote: "Our governmental system is established by compact, not between the Government of the United States and the State Governments but between the states as sovereign communities, stipulating each with the other. . . ."

The first serious threat of secession came in 1798 when the Democratic-Republicans, smarting under Federalist legislation, talked of separation. John L. Taylor, a prominent North Carolina judge, openly advocated secession, but the more moderate views of Thomas Jefferson prevailed, and Virginia and Kentucky adopted their resolutions condemning the legislation as unconstitutional, null and void, and proclaiming the right of the states to interpose or nullify such acts. Jefferson's purpose was to appeal to the people in the election of 1800, rather than to apply either nullification or secession.

After Jefferson's presidential victory in 1801 the New England Federalists sought a remedy against Democratic domination. Sen. Timothy Pickering of Massachusetts said that "the principles of our Revolution point to the remedy—a separation." The purchase of Louisiana further antagonized the Federalists, and the Essex Junto planned a new confederacy composed of New England and New York, "exempt from the corrupt . . . influence and oppression of the aristocratic democrats of the South." Alexander Hamilton blocked their efforts, but Rep. Josiah Quincy of Massachusetts still maintained in 1811 that the admission of Louisiana would dissolve the Union. The disgruntled Federalists of New England resorted to treasonable action in opposing "Mr. Madison's war," and in 1814 met in the Hartford Convention behind closed doors and in utmost secrecy. There is little doubt that their object was the dissolution of the Union and the formation of a New England confederacy if their program of constitutional reform failed. Fortunately the news of the peace treaty prevented action.

The next rumblings of discontent were heard in the southern states. Threats of separation were made over both the Missouri question (*see* Missouri Compro-

mise) and the Indian controversy (*see Cherokee Nation* v. *Georgia*), and the tariff issue brought these threats to the very threshold of action. South Carolina nullified the tariff acts of 1828 and 1832 and signified its intention of seceding if the federal government attempted coercion (*see* Nullification).

Slavery in the territories caused both North and South to threaten to secede. John Quincy Adams thought the free states would secede if Texas were annexed, and the southern leaders threatened separation if slavery were excluded from the Mexican cession. This controversy culminated in the assembling of the Nashville Convention of 1850 and of state conventions in several southern states. These conventions reluctantly accepted the Compromise of 1850 and secession was halted. The abolitionists called a convention of all the free states to meet at Cleveland in 1857 to consider separation, but the depression prevented the meeting.

The threat of secession was the last resort of the minority to protect its interests under the Constitution, and was constantly present from the Revolution to the Civil War.

[Alpheus Thomas Mason, ed., *The States Rights Debate: Anti-Federalism and the Constitution;* Paul C. Nagel, *One Nation Indivisible: The Union in American Thought, 1776–1861.*]

FLETCHER M. GREEN

SECESSION OF SOUTHERN STATES. On Abraham Lincoln's election to the presidency, the governor of South Carolina, William H. Gist, recommended and the legislature called a state convention (that being the method by which the Constitution of 1787 was ratified), which met amidst great excitement on Dec. 20, 1860. By a unanimous vote the convention passed an ordinance dissolving "the union now subsisting between South Carolina and other States." The convention issued a Declaration of Immediate Causes, expressing the states' rights view of the Union, and appointed commissioners to other southern states and to Washington, D.C. This action seemed precipitate by many who favored further efforts to secure constitutional rights (through an all-southern convention, appeals to the North, or compromise through Congress). But South Carolina had assurances that other states would follow, and many thought that better terms might be made out of the Union than in it. Overriding minorities, six other states by conventions passed ordinances of secession early in 1861: Mississippi, Jan. 9 (84 to 15); Florida, Jan. 10 (62 to 7); Alabama, Jan. 11 (61 to 39);

Georgia, Jan. 19 (164 to 133); Louisiana, Jan. 26 (113 to 17); and Texas (over the opposition of Gov. Sam Houston), Feb. 1 (166 to 8), thus completing the secession of the lower South. Nearly all who voted against secession did so because they doubted its expediency, not the right.

President James Buchanan, believing secession unconstitutional but considering himself without authority to coerce, and anxious not to give the upper South cause for secession, was determined not to risk war by an overt act in protecting federal property (such as forts, arsenals, and post offices) and sustaining the operation of federal laws. The South Carolina commissioners, sent to negotiate with Buchanan for the peaceful division of property and debts, demanded that Maj. Robert Anderson, then occupying Fort Sumter in Charleston harbor, evacuate that post, inasmuch as continued federal occupancy was inconsistent with the sovereignty of South Carolina. This he refused to do. Meanwhile Congress, despite an address from some southern members saying that "All hope of relief in the Union, through the agency of committees, Congressional legislation, or constitutional amendments, is extinguished," was sifting compromise proposals. Of these the Crittenden Compromise, involving the extension of the Missouri Compromise line, was the more hopeful, but it failed to get the support of the Republican leaders, as did Kentucky Sen. John J. Crittenden's suggestion for a national referendum. More certain was the failure (because opposed by the extremists on either side) of the Washington Peace Conference (Border Slave State Convention) that, two months later, presented proposals similar to Crittenden's.

With compromise failing and with Buchanan taking a firmer attitude as he became less hopeful of peace and union (he sent the *Star of the West* to reinforce Sumter), representatives from the seceded states met at Montgomery on Feb. 4, 1861, to organize a new nation. Lincoln's inaugural promise "to hold, occupy, and possess the property and places belonging to the government," coupled with his assertion that "Physically speaking, we cannot separate," seemed none the less threatening by his assurance, "The government will not assail you." Peaceful secession seemed remote after Lincoln's fateful decision to relieve Fort Sumter, the firing on the fort on Apr. 12, and Lincoln's call for volunteers three days later. This practical state of war compelled the states of the upper South to make a reluctant choice between the Confederacy and the Union.

Earlier in April the Virginia convention voted against secession (88 to 45), preferring a conference of the border states and further discussions with Lincoln. But two days after the call for volunteers the convention, Apr. 17, adopted the ordinance of secession (88 to 55), which was ratified by popular vote on May 23, although the convention had entered into a military league with the Confederacy on Apr. 24. In Arkansas opinion was very evenly divided (a popular referendum had been set for Aug. 5), but the governor rejected Lincoln's call for militia, and on May 6 the convention passed the secession ordinance (65 to 5). Tennessee, like Virginia, had large nonslaveholding sections where many people for geographic, economic, or social reasons did not feel that their interests would be served by the Confederacy. The legislature on Jan. 19 provided for a popular vote for delegates to a convention and for the convention itself, which was rejected (Feb. 9) by a vote of 68,282 to 59,449. After the firing on Fort Sumter and the threat of coercion, the legislature ratified a league with the Confederacy (May 7) and authorized the governor to raise a force of 55,000 men. On June 8 the people voted for secession (104,913 to 47,238). The opposition to secession in western Virginia led to the formation of a separate state; a like movement in eastern Tennessee proved abortive. The unanimous vote for secession by the convention of North Carolina, the last state to secede (May 20), was clearly the result of Lincoln's proclamation. The border slave states of Kentucky, Maryland, Delaware, and Missouri did not secede, and Kentucky's attempted neutrality failed.

[William Barney, *The Road to Secession;* Steven A. Channing, *Crisis of Fear: Secession in South Carolina;* Avery O. Craven, *The Coming of the Civil War;* D. L. Dumond, *The Secessionist Movement, 1860–61;* Kenneth Stampp, *And the War Came.*]

R. H. WOODY

SECRET PROTOCOL OF 1917. During the conversations preceding the signing of the Lansing-Ishii Agreement of Nov. 2, 1917, Secretary of State Robert Lansing had striven to include in the agreement the following statement: "The Governments of the United States and Japan will not take advantage of the present conditions to seek special rights or privileges in China which would abridge the rights of subjects or citizens of other friendly states." This was precisely what the Japanese negotiator did not wish to accept, because it was Japan's real policy to take advantage of the conditions that existed in China in order to secure a special position there. With the express approval of President Woodrow Wilson, this formula was relegated to a secret protocol signed on Oct. 31. But the language of the secret protocol sounds more like an epitaph for the formula than a confirmation of it, because it records that: ''Upon careful examination of the question, it was agreed that the clause above quoted being superfluous in the relations of the two Governments and liable to create erroneous impressions in the minds of the public, should be eliminated from the declaration. It was, however, well understood that the principle enunciated in the clause which was thus suppressed was in perfect accord with the declared policy of the two Governments in regard to China.'' The protocol was kept secret until 1935.

[Department of State, *Papers Relating to the Foreign Relations of the United States: The Lansing Papers, 1914–1920.*]

SAMUEL FLAGG BEMIS

SECRET SERVICE, UNITED STATES, was created on July 5, 1865, as a bureau of the Department of the Treasury, to suppress rampant counterfeiting. It was estimated during the Civil War that one-third of the currency in circulation was counterfeit. Because there were approximately 1,600 state banks designing and printing their own notes and each note bore a different design, it was difficult to distinguish one of the 4,000 varieties of counterfeit notes from the 7,000 varieties of genuine notes. It was hoped that the adoption of a national currency in 1863 would resolve the problem. But it, too, was soon counterfeited extensively, so that it became necessary for the government to take enforcement measures.

In addition to the suppression of counterfeiting, the Secret Service was often requested to conduct investigations later assigned to other government agencies. These investigations included such matters as mail frauds, bank and train robberies, bounty claims, illicit traffic in whiskey, Ku Klux Klan activities, and counterespionage (during the Spanish-American War and World War I). The Secret Service continues to suppress forgery and fraudulent negotiation or redemption of government checks, bonds, and other obligations or securities of the United States.

Since its inception, the Secret Service has greatly expanded. After the assassination of President William McKinley in Buffalo, N.Y., in 1901, it was assigned to protect President Theodore Roosevelt, although legislation authorizing presidential protection by the Secret Service was not enacted until 1906. In 1913 such protection was also authorized for the president-elect, and in 1917 for members of the presi-

dent's immediate family. An act of Congress in 1951 authorized the Secret Service to protect the vice-president. Protection was also later extended to the vice-president-elect, a former president and his wife during his lifetime, the widow of a former president until her death or remarriage, and minor children of a former president until they reach sixteen years of age. Protection for major presidential and vice-presidential candidates was authorized in 1968; recipients of such protection are designated by the secretary of the Treasury after consultation with an advisory committee.

On Mar. 19, 1970, President Richard M. Nixon signed legislation establishing the Executive Protective Service, a uniformed division of the Secret Service. This increased the size and responsibilities of the former White House Police Force. The Executive Protective Service protects the White House and foreign missions in the metropolitan area of the District of Columbia. In January 1971 Congress enacted legislation authorizing the Secret Service to protect a visiting head of a foreign state or foreign government and, at the direction of the president, other distinguished foreign visitors to the United States and official representatives of the United States performing special missions abroad.

[Harry E. Neal, *The Story of the Secret Service.*]

JAMES J. ROWLEY

SECRET SOCIETIES existed in rudimentary form among primitive peoples and have appeared in all lands and ages, but they have been especially numerous and active in the United States. Organized, in most instances, for the social and moral welfare of their members and to promote good fellowship and patriotism, secret societies have apparently met a deep-seated psychological need in the American people. In addition they have done a great amount of charitable and educational work that has been of advantage to the general community. Freemasonry, the ritual and philosophy of which have influenced many similar organizations, was introduced from Great Britain about 1730; the Independent Order of Oddfellows was brought over from the same country in 1819. A roster of indigenous societies would reach encyclopedic proportions. A few well-known ones are the Knights of Pythias, founded in 1864; the Benevolent and Protective Order of Elks, 1868; the Knights of Columbus, 1882; and the Loyal Order of Moose, 1888.

For a decade following 1826 there was a strong popular prejudice against secret orders. While directed primarily against the Masons, this prejudice was even directed against college fraternities, which during this period were under popular disfavor and which were the subjects of an extensive literature of exposure and denunciation in the press. The movement soon subsided; Masonry quickly revived; new societies were formed; and ritual and secrecy were effectively used to promote a wide variety of causes—temperance, liquor control, agricultural improvement, life insurance, and the betterment of the underprivileged. Local societies occasionally showed vigilante proclivities, pursuing alleged evildoers with tar and feathers, birch rods, or even more lethal weapons.

The subversive and revolutionary secret society, so common in European countries, has had an unfruitful field in America, although the prerevolutionary activity of the Sons of Liberty, the disloyal operations of the Knights of the Golden Circle during the Civil War, and the Molly Maguires in the post–Civil War period are somewhat analogous. Antiforeign and anti-Catholic prejudice produced the secret Know-Nothing party in the 1850's, and history repeated itself seventy years later in the similar activities of the revived Ku Klux Klan. For the most part American secret societies have avoided direct participation in politics, but the mere existence of large and cohesive bodies of brethren has made them a factor to be considered by politicians.

[Arkon Daraul, *A History of Secret Societies.*]
W. A. ROBINSON

SECTIONALISM. The United States is by no means a homogeneous entity in regard to such characteristics as physiography, geography, topography, ecology, and climate. Understanding the nation comes more easily when one thinks of it in terms of regions: the Appalachian Mountains, the Mississippi watershed, the Great Plains, the Rocky Mountains, the Far West. The United States is filled with economic diversity as well. The economy of the tidewater South is not the same as that of the Ozark Mountains; the economy of the upper Great Plains is strikingly different from that of the American Southwest; New England's economic status and problems sharply contrast with those in areas around the Great Lakes. Political interests of Americans living in these and other regions of the United States have been affected by the physical and economic characteristics of the separate regions. Despite the fact that the nation has gained a degree of political cohesion because of the presence of national

political parties, regional influence on leaders and members of those parties has had great impact; political sectionalism has been the result. Of the many factors contributing to sectionalism, the economic interests of the people in a given region or regions are the most important.

The spirit of sectionalism and its manifestations have been present throughout American history, and every major region of the nation has strongly espoused its sectional interests at one time or another. Charles Pinckney's statement "When I say Southern, I mean Maryland, and the states to the southward of her" was made when the Constitutional Convention was bogged down over the question of the economic interests of the South. Although less cohesive than the South, the middle states at that time expressed united concern for the protection of their grain exports. New England sectionalism appeared during the War of 1812, when citizens of that region generally criticized "Mr. Madison's war." Pioneers who drove the frontier westward quickly developed loyalties to their new regions, soon advancing the economic and political interests of their section.

During the first half of the 19th century the United States consisted of three large and rather ill-defined regions: the North (the area north of the Ohio River and the Mason-Dixon Line); the South (the region below that boundary); and the West (the large area west of the Appalachian Mountains). To a large extent the history of the United States from 1800 to 1865 is the history of the relationship of those three regions. The positions and interactions of the people and leaders of these regions on a number of economic issues revealed militant sectionalism.

The question of how the United States should dispose of its vast public lands divided the nation. Northerners and southerners generally believed that the western lands should be sold to the highest bidder, gaining revenue for the U.S. Treasury. Westerners were not yet advocating that the land be given away (as they did after the Civil War), but they did favor a policy of charging settlers only a minimum amount of money for the land. Trade between North and West was advanced when somewhat better transportation facilities were developed, and both sections' economies improved as the West supplied the North with food and the North shipped the West needed manufactured goods. When states and private enterprise did not provide enough means of transportation between the two regions, northerners and westerners demanded that the national government construct additional internal improvements at national expense.

The South did not stand to gain by the building of national canals and roads, and it objected to national money being spent on such projects. As the North developed more industry it demanded that Congress pass a protective tariff; the South remained primarily an agricultural region, trading cotton and tobacco in European and world markets, and it preferred that the nation adopt low tariff rates. The West was divided on the tariff: the Northwest favored a high tariff, while the Southwest desired low rates.

Thus, no two sections had identical interests, and the West was divided within itself on the tariff question. Under the circumstances, the sections engaged in much political maneuvering to obtain the economic advantages each desired for itself. The tariff dispute brought a crisis in 1832, when South Carolina took the extreme action of nullifying a tariff law passed by Congress. A compromise resolved the disagreement, but the events were a portent of future sectional conflict.

The question of the expansion of slavery into the western territories overshadowed all other sectional concerns in the twenty years prior to the Civil War. Northerners hoped to prohibit the spread of slavery, while southerners believed they had the right to take their slaves wherever they migrated. The economic and political implications of the slavery dispute were great, and soon these subjects became intertwined with sectional prestige and honor. The annexation of Texas, the Wilmot Proviso, the Mexican War, and the admission of California as a state all became primarily sectional issues, on which leaders of both North and South staked their political future. The two sections were driven farther apart in the decade of the 1850's, until war became the only means by which to settle their differences. The Civil War was the ultimate consequence of extreme sectionalism. Although the Civil War abolished slavery and held together a badly divided nation, sectionalism did not die at Appomattox. During the Reconstruction era political and economic interests dominated the actions of many of the nation's leaders, both northern and southern. These activities intensified sectional feelings, creating bitterness that lasted well into the 20th century.

After Reconstruction various regions manifested sectionalism from time to time, but the region most closely associated with that concept remained the South. The development of what became known as the Solid South, the relegation of the freed black to a position of inferiority, and the status of the South as an economic appendage of the North were all manifestations of a nation not yet free of severe sectional differences. By mid-20th century the Solid South was breaking up; southern states began to cast electoral votes for Republican presidential candidates, and state Republican parties became more competitive with the dominant Democrats. At the same time blacks demanded and received some of the rights of American citizens, and white southerners learned to live with the new status of black southerners. The southern economy continued to be greatly influenced by northern corporations, but southern companies were established and in some instances competed with the outsiders. In any case, the southern economy prospered because of the presence and growth of industry, the South's standard of living rose, and southerners had increased purchasing power. All these factors combined to diminish the concept of sectionalism in the South, although it continued to be a political and economic factor between rural and urban areas around the nation.

[Monroe Billington, *The American South: A Brief History;* Avery O. Craven, *The Growth of Southern Nationalism, 1848–1861;* David Brion Davis, *The Slave Power Conspiracy and the Paranoid Style;* William B. Hesseltine, "Regions, Classes and Sections in American History," *Journal of Land and Public Utility Economics,* vol. 20 (1944), and "Sectionalism and Regionalism in American History," *Journal of Southern History,* vol. 26 (1960); Kenneth M. Stampp, *The Era of Reconstruction, 1865–1877;* Charles S. Sydnor, *The Development of Southern Sectionalism, 1819–1848;* George Brown Tindall, *The Emergence of the New South, 1913–1945;* Frederick Jackson Turner, *Rise of the New West, 1819–1829, The United States, 1830–1850: The Nation and Its Sections,* and *The Significance of Sections in American History;* C. Vann Woodward, *Origins of the New South, 1877–1913.*]

MONROE BILLINGTON

SECURITIES AND EXCHANGE COMMISSION. *See* **Federal Agencies; New Deal.**

SEDGWICK, FORT, was established in northeast Colorado by the U.S. Army in August 1864 at the junction of Lodge Pole Creek with the South Platte River. The fort was built to maintain control over the Sioux, Cheyenne, and Arapaho of the region during the Civil War. It was abandoned in 1871.

[H. H. Bancroft, *History of Nevada, Colorado and Wyoming.*]

CARL L. CANNON

SEDITION ACTS. Two national sedition acts had been passed in the United States by the mid-1970's.

The first, passed by the Federalist-dominated Congress of 1798, was intended to halt Democratic-Republican attacks on the government and to ferret out pro-French sympathizers in case of war with France (*see* Franco-American Misunderstanding). Two complementary alien acts allowed the government to deport French and pro-French foreigners who were generally supporters of the Democratic-Republican party. The second sedition act, passed during World War I, was aimed at subversives, such as pacifists or "Bolsheviks" who interfered with the war effort.

The Sedition Act of 1798 reestablished the English common law on seditious libel, but with some important changes. The new law accepted the idea of jury determination of sedition and also allowed truth to be considered in defense. Whether or not the act violated the First Amendment's intention of abolishing seditious libel was not established at the time, but certainly the partisan use of the act added weight to the Democratic-Republican conviction that it did so. The act expired in 1801, and during President Thomas Jefferson's tenure in office all persons convicted under the act were pardoned; Congress eventually voted to repay all fines levied against the convicted. Although the act expired before its constitutionality could be tested, it was generally assumed to be unconstitutional, and in 1964 the Supreme Court flatly declared it inconsistent with the First Amendment in *New York Times Company* v. *Sullivan.*

The Sedition Act of 1918 made it a felony to interfere in the war effort; to insult the government, the Constitution, or the armed forces; and "by word or act [to] support or favor the cause of the German Empire or its allies in the present war, or by word or act [to] oppose the cause of the United States." The most vital difference between this act and that of 1798 was the emphasis in 1918 on criticism of the government and its symbols as opposed to the listing of individual officers in the 1798 act. The most significant statement of judicial opposition to the Sedition Act of 1918 is contained in the dissenting opinions of justices Oliver Wendell Holmes and Louis D. Brandeis in *Abrams* v. *United States* (1919). The national hysteria produced by the war, climaxing in the Red scare and the Palmer raids (mass arrests of political and labor agitators, under the auspices of Attorney General A. Mitchell Palmer), ran its course by the early 1920's, and the Sedition Act was repealed in 1921. Similar acts passed by the states resulted in litigation reaching the Supreme Court. The most notable decision in this area was *Gitlow* v. *New York* (1925), in

which the Court began extending the strictures of the First Amendment to the states.

Although the Alien Registration Act of 1940, better known as the Smith Act, is not called a sedition act, it had that as a major purpose. Rather than forbidding criticism of government officers, the Smith Act prohibits advocacy of forceful overthrow of the government and makes it a crime to belong to an organization subsequently found to be guilty of advocating forceful removal of the government. Interpretations of such laws as these are generally determined by whether one sees them as necessary to national security or as threats to freedom of speech and press.

[Zechariah Chaffee, Jr., *Freedom of Speech;* Leonard W. Levy, *Legacy of Suppression.*]

JOSEPH A. DOWLING

SEGREGATION, in American history, refers to attempts by the white, Anglo-Saxon majority to separate and keep apart from themselves certain minority groups such as Afro-Americans, Indians, immigrants, and Mexican-Americans. During the colonial period and early years of the United States, white Americans generally kept themselves apart from the Indians whose lands they preempted. This action became official government policy shortly after the Civil War, when Indians were separated from whites by a reservation system. European and Oriental immigrants were crowded into the ghettos of the larger urban centers of the nation, and the Mexican-Americans of the Southwest were similarly segregated from whites. Segregation has existed throughout the nation's history and in all regions, but it has been most closely associated with the South and the efforts of southern whites to relegate blacks to a position of inferiority. Segregation of the white and black races was a recognized element in the pre–Civil War slave system; and after slavery was abolished, white southerners were determined to continue racial separation (*see* Bourbons). Examples of black integration into white society existed in the Reconstruction South, but many more instances of segregation occurred, and after a brief period of uncertainty regarding the relative relationship of the two races, segregated conditions crystallized, placing the black citizen at a disadvantage in social, political, educational, and economic spheres.

Several southern states early passed laws forbidding blacks to ride in first-class passenger railway cars, and numerous local ordinances requiring racial segregation in most public facilities followed. The enactment of these laws stimulated the U.S. Congress to pass the Civil Rights Act of 1875, to assure equal accommodations in public conveyances, inns, theaters, and other places of public entertainment. In 1883 the Supreme Court ruled this act unconstitutional, declaring that states could not abridge the privileges of American citizens but pointedly excluding individuals and private corporations from this restriction. When blacks complained that railroads discriminated against them, the Interstate Commerce Commission ruled that the railroads must provide equal facilities for members of both races. Even though facilities for blacks were never equal, the Supreme Court upheld the validity of a separate-but-equal transportation law in the *Plessy* v. *Ferguson* (1896) decision. The separate-but-equal concept spread to other areas, particularly education, in the years that followed, and it went without successful challenge for nearly sixty years. In the meantime, southerners had circumscribed many areas of contact between the races. City governments and state legislatures adopted ordinances prohibiting certain activities by blacks. Unwritten laws, regulations, customs, traditions, and practices restricting the freedom of blacks in all parts of the country also developed. From 1900 to the beginning of World War II, the injustices and inequities of racial discrimination were present in the South in almost every area of human activity. Transportation and residential restrictions were commonplace. Public parks, golf courses, swimming pools, and beaches were segregated. Marriage between the races was made illegal in most southern states. Most southern hotels, restaurants, and theaters refused the patronage of blacks, while movie houses reserved separate sections or balconies for them. Sports and recreational activities were segregated, and hospitals, prisons, asylums, funeral homes, morgues, and cemeteries provided separate facilities.

Segregation was not limited to the South. A few thousand free blacks lived in the North and West during the time of slavery, and discriminatory practices toward them were not uncommon. As the black population in the North and West grew after the abolition of slavery, restrictions increased. This was especially true during and after World War I, when great numbers of southern blacks moved northward and westward in search of economic opportunity. Some northern and western states passed statutes prohibiting intermarriage. Separate schools were often permitted and sometimes required. *De facto* segregation occurred in residential housing and restrictive covenants were commonplace in many neighborhoods; as a result, blacks crowded into the ghettos of the northern and western cities. Prejudicial attitudes of north-

erners and westerners forced blacks into subservient positions in many areas of life, especially public accommodations, even though by law blacks were equal.

Another great surge of black migration out of the South occurred during World War II, and while the migrants sometimes improved their economic status, they experienced *de facto* segregation in the North and West. Blacks were unhappy with these restrictions to their freedom, especially since they were helping the nation fight a war to free the world's enslaved peoples. They demanded that both *de jure* and *de facto* segregation throughout the United States be abolished. The federal government responded to one of these demands when President Harry Truman ordered the desegregation of the armed forces, after which racial discrimination was officially abolished in all three branches of the military. Since segregated facilities in education were transparently unequal, blacks also attacked this line of inequality. Even before World War II, blacks had initiated steps to break down the states' biracial school systems. In 1938 the Supreme Court had ruled in the *Gaines* case that Missouri must provide legal training in the state for blacks equal to that for whites. Shortly after the war, similar lawsuits in Oklahoma and Texas were successful, and black graduate and professional students were permitted to attend those states' public-supported universities. Lawsuits against public school systems followed. In 1954, in *Brown* v. *Board of Education of Topeka,* the Supreme Court rejected the separate-but-equal fiction, declaring that separate school facilities were inherently unequal and in violation of the equal protection clause of the Fourteenth Amendment. Desegregation of schools proceeded at a relatively slow pace, and in 1969 the Supreme Court ruled that school segregation must end "at once." Controversies over implementation existed in the 1970's, although much progress had been made in the twenty years after the *Brown* decision.

Blacks also pressed for other concessions rightfully theirs: equal employment opportunities, nondiscriminatory accommodations in private and public facilities, fair housing conditions, and the franchise (*see* Primary, White). Beginning in 1957 the U.S. Congress passed a series of civil rights acts, the first since Reconstruction. Included among them were bills establishing the Fair Employment Practices Commission and the Civil Rights Commission, both of which directed their efforts to redressing the grievances of minority groups. The post–World War II "civil rights revolution" revealed the progress and problems in the nation's attempt to abolish racial segregation.

[Charles S. Johnson, *Patterns of Negro Segregation;* Milton R. Konvitz and T. Leskes, *A Century of Civil Rights;* Charles S. Mangum, Jr., *The Legal Status of the Negro;* Charles E. Silberman, *Crisis in Black and White;* C. Vann Woodward, *The Strange Career of Jim Crow.*]

MONROE BILLINGTON

SEIGNIORAGE. Medieval coining authorities, who were sometimes quite minor seigneurs, could extract a small profit, known as seigniorage, beyond charges for actual mint expenses. In 1792 the U.S. Congress established "free coinage"—that is, the minting of unlimited quantities of coins from gold and silver sold to the Treasury free of seigniorage. The reaction of the prosilver forces to the drastic fall in the price of silver in the late 19th century brought about the more modern meaning of the term, in which advocates of increased silver coinage defined the very wide gap between the face value of silver dollars and even subsidiary coins, on the one hand, and the legislated price of silver (far above its market value), on the other, as seigniorage. They implied thereby that the government, too, profited from increased silver coinage, since it was able to buy a dollar's worth of goods and services with silver that cost only 50 cents or so.

[A. Nussbaum, *A History of the Dollar.*]

MARTIN WOLFE

SELDEN PATENT, the first and most bitterly contested of all the automobile patents. The original application for a patent on a vehicle propelled by an internal combustion engine was filed in 1879 by George B. Selden, a lawyer of Rochester, N.Y., but was kept pending while Selden attempted to interest capital in his ideas, and the patent (No. 549,160) was not issued until 1895. First purchased by the Pope Manufacturing Company, the rights, through several shifts in control, were brought into the possession of the Electric Vehicle Company. In 1900 this concern began a vigorous enforcement of its patent rights by filing suit against the Winton Motor Carriage Company. The case dragged along for three years, only to be abandoned when Winton and nine other companies organized themselves into the Association of Licensed Automobile Manufacturers and agreed to pay royalties.

Henry Ford refused to take part in the agreement, and in 1903 an infringement suit was filed against him. Outstanding legal talent was engaged for both

sides of the controversy, and the amazing case was spun out for eight years, amassing thirty-six large volumes of testimony. A principal argument made by the defense was that the Selden patent contemplated use of the Brayton two-cycle motor (invented by George Brayton in 1872 and improved by Selden), and not the Otto four-cycle engine then being used in practically all cars. This argument was strengthened by a contemptuous entry in Selden's diary characterizing the Otto motor as "another of those damned Dutch engines." The lower court upheld the claim of infringement, but the court of appeals, which ruled in Ford's favor (1911), stated that although the patent was valid, it was not being infringed by manufacture of vehicles using the Otto-type motor.

[James Rood Doolittle, *The Romance of the Automobile Industry.*]

RICHARD W. TUPPER

SELECTIVE SERVICE. *See* **Draft.**

SELECTMEN, executive officers chosen, since earliest times, at town meetings in all New England states except Rhode Island. Their performances are interwoven with the literature and history of the region. The usual number of selectmen has been three, although five to nine are chosen in some large communities. Annual election has been the prevailing rule, and the terms are usually of three-year duration. The selectmen constitute an executive committee for the town and handle its administrative affairs. In the earlier period they were vested with police and educational functions now usually transferred to other authorities. Their general functions are determined by state law and, while varying in different states, usually involve the preparation of the warrant for annual or special meetings, supervision of local highways, valuation and assessment of property, election control, issuance of licenses, and poor relief. Special duties not otherwise provided for may be authorized by the town meeting. The office has served as a training school for local political leadership and administration.

[J. S. Garland, *New England Town Law;* J. F. Sly, *Town Government in Massachusetts.*]

W. A. ROBINSON

SELF-SERVICE STORES. Self-service is a retailing method whereby the labor of the customer in selecting goods is substituted for that of a store clerk. In many instances self-service operation includes the customer bringing the goods to be bought to a checkout stand or cashier's booth, where payment is made and purchases are packaged, if necessary. Although self-service was used to some degree in country stores during the 19th century, its significant use was first noted in southern California grocery stores in 1912. The man frequently cited as the originator of self-service grocery stores is Clarence Saunders, who established a chain of Piggly Wiggly Stores in Memphis, Tenn., in 1916. Credited with originating the use of checkout counters and turnstiles, Saunders had 2,700 stores in forty-one states by 1928. The evolution of self-service stores is a complex cultural and socioeconomic phenomenon. It is believed to have arisen because of the high cost of labor in a labor-scarce economy, the difficulty in promoting economy in distribution by mechanization, the development of prepackaged merchandise, and the occasionally poor quality of clerk service, which made self-service preferable to many customers.

The major application of the self-service method was in food stores. During the 1920's large food stores developed in the western United States and employed varying degrees of self-service. In 1930 Michael Cullen, a former employee of a major food chain, combined the self-service and cash-and-carry methods with other existing retailing techniques, adding as well some new ideas of his own, when he established his King Cullen market in suburban New York City. From the establishment of this store is dated the emergence of the supermarket, one of the most important innovations in the history of food distribution. In 1932 the Big Bear market was established in New Jersey. Both markets were very large and emphasized self-service and low prices; both were immediate successes. By 1934 an estimated 100 supermarkets, similar to these, were in operation. During the period 1930–35, the principal appeal of these stores was their low prices. Retail food-store gross profit margins were estimated at 30 percent before 1930; the early supermarkets had margins of 10 to 14 percent. By the 1950's margins had risen to 18 percent, and during the period 1967–74 they had risen to about 21 percent. But these early supermarkets were more than simply stores divested of frills to minimize costs: they utilized a new marketing concept that involved the substitution of higher volume and turnover for low volume and high profit margins. Socioeconomic changes, such as increased use of automobiles and refrigerators, expansion in the size of markets, and long-term in-

creases in personal incomes, allowed the supermarket entrepreneurs to succeed with their innovation and thus to compensate for the lowered profit margins.

Initially the major chains ignored this new marketing concept, but in 1936–37 the Great Atlantic and Pacific Tea Company (A&P) and some other large chains began converting to supermarkets. As a result, the number of supermarkets increased from 1,200 in 1936 to more than 8,000 by 1941, by which time they accounted for about 26 percent of total grocery store sales. Following a lull during World War II, supermarkets expanded rapidly. Between 1950 and 1960, the number of supermarkets more than doubled, and the supermarkets' share of all U.S. grocery store sales increased from 40 percent to 69 percent. By 1974 there were about 43,000 large food markets, with annual sales in excess of $500,000, in operation, which accounted for 79 percent of all U.S. grocery store sales. During the period 1966–74 food chains, which operated many of the supermarkets, earned about 1 percent or less net income after taxes per sales dollar.

The supermarket has been defined by various criteria by different authorities. Common elements are that a supermarket is a complete, departmentalized grocery store in which at least the grocery department is a self-service operation. As of 1974, such grocery stores needed a sales revenue of $1,000,000 or more per year to be considered supermarkets. Food markets with annual sales in the range $500,000 to $1,000,000 are referred to as superettes.

Following the success of self-service in food stores, the practice was adopted by many kinds of stores handling a wide variety of merchandise and operating independently or as chains. F. W. Woolworth began self-service operations with a 1952 experiment. By the 1960's general merchandise firms, such as S. S. Kresge, and drug companies, such as Walgreen, were converting existing stores to self-service and all their new stores used this marketing innovation. Department store firms such as R. H. Macy and Company and Gimbel Brothers had at least converted their budget basement departments to self-service. Since the 1930's self-service has experienced widespread adoption and is currently practiced in varying degrees by almost all types of retail stores.

[Ralph Cassady, Jr., *Competition and Price Making in Food Retailing;* Frank J. Charvat, *Supermarketing;* Edward C. Hampe, Jr., and Merle Wittenberg, *The Lifeline of America: Development of the Food Industry;* George A. Prendergast, *A Comparative Statistical Analysis of the Growth of Fifteen U.S. Food Distribution Firms, 1948–1967,* University of Michigan, Microfilm.]

GEORGE A. PRENDERGAST

SEMICONDUCTORS, a class of solids whose electrical conductivity is between that of an insulator and a conductor. The most important use of semiconductors is in transistors. The semiconductor industry has experienced a remarkable growth since the first public disclosure of the transistor in 1948. The cost per transistor declined steadily from an original level of several dollars to about one cent in large-scale integrated circuits manufactured in the mid-1970's. A further concept in semiconductor electronics led to the invention of charge-coupled devices, which are thought to have a potential impact as great as the transistor and its derivative, integrated electronics.

The historical roots of the semiconductor industry may be traced to the creation of a new quantum theory of matter by an international group of physicists during the late 1920's. This culminated in Sir Alan Herries Wilson's theoretical model of semiconductors, published in 1931. The purity of semiconductor materials, including germanium and silicon, was greatly increased during the late 1930's and early 1940's as a consequence of efforts to fabricate more reliable crystal detectors for radar receivers. After World War II an interdisciplinary group was formed at the Bell Telephone Laboratories to continue fundamental research on solid-state phenomena and devices. A long-range goal was the replacement of mechanical switching devices and the bulky and inefficient vacuum tubes used in existing communication systems. This group discovered the transistor and launched the semiconductor age.

The original point-contact transistor was quickly superseded by the junction, or bipolar, transistor invented by William B. Shockley in 1948. Early commercial applications included hearing aids and the all-transistor radio, which came on the market in 1955. The greater speed and reliability needed for computers and missile-control circuits led to the development of silicon-based microelectronic technology in the early 1960's. An important new field-effect, or unipolar, transistor was developed by researchers at Bell Laboratories and at Radio Corporation of America (RCA) by 1962. The new fabrication technique, which became the basis for a variety of metal-oxide semiconductor (MOS) devices, led to greater component densities than could be achieved with the older bipolar devices. Commercial products that rely on the metal-oxide semiconductor include the pocket calculator and electronic timepieces. The basic MOS structure could also be used in the charge-coupled devices under development in the mid-1970's as a major innovation in semiconductors. Proposed applications included miniature television cameras and solid-state data-storage devices.

[Gilbert F. Amelio, "Charge-Coupled Devices," *Scientific American* (February 1974); William C. Hittinger, "Metal-Oxide-Semiconductor Technology," *Scientific American* (August 1973); Charles Weiner, "How the Transistor Emerged," *IEEE Spectrum* (January 1973).]

JAMES E. BRITTAIN

SEMINOLE, one of the Five Civilized Tribes, lived chiefly in Florida and Oklahoma in the 20th century. They were originally of Muskhogean stock and spoke Muskogee or Hitchiti. In the early 18th century they were associated with the Lower Creek on the Chattahoochee River in Georgia, but they began to move into Florida after 1700. By 1775 they had become known as the Seminole, which means "separatist" or "wild people." Their numbers were later augmented by Upper Creek, members of conquered tribes, and a considerable number of fugitive black slaves from Georgia. Although the Seminole were town dwellers, they derived their living from farming, supplemented by hunting and trading; they developed a complex social organization in which military prowess played a major role.

During the Spanish domination of Florida the relative weakness of Spanish control allowed the Seminole to develop without interference. From 1763 to 1783, while Florida was in British hands, the tribe was for the most part on good terms with the authorities, and during the American Revolution it was pro-British. The end of the Revolution brought the Seminole into conflict with their Georgia neighbors over the Indian policy of giving refuge to runaway slaves. During the War of 1812 a number of Seminole raids on the Georgia border and retaliatory expeditions from the United States took place, culminating in the first Seminole War (1816–18) and Andrew Jackson's punitive expedition in 1818. The acquisition of Florida by the United States through the Adams-Onís Treaty of 1819 brought the Seminole under American control.

Eventually subdued by U.S. forces, the tribe signed the Treaty of Camp Moultrie (1823), agreeing to its removal from tribal lands in Florida to a reserve in the West. The treaty was repudiated by a large portion of the tribe, led by Micanopy and Jumper, and border raids continued. The influx of white settlers into Florida brought renewed pressure for removal; and the treaties of Payne's Landing (1832) and Fort Gibson (1833) were negotiated with a few Seminole chiefs stipulating that the tribe should move to Creek lands in the West. Again a major part of the tribe resisted, and a series of attacks led by Osceola escalated into the second Seminole War (1835–42). At the end of that war most of the hostile Seminole were removed to the Creek lands west of the Mississippi. Until 1860 the Seminole's relations with the United States continued to be troubled by dissatisfaction with their new lands and conflict with slaveholders over runaway slaves. During the Civil War the Seminole were divided in sentiment, but most tended to support the Union, participating in the Union victory at Honey Springs in July 1863.

The Seminole Treaty of 1866 provided for a new reservation of 200,000 acres (creating what is now Seminole County, Okla.) and a grant of $235,362 and marked the beginning of a period of relative' peace and stability for the tribe. In 1901 the Seminole became U.S. citizens, and by 1902 land allotments in severalty had been made to all Seminole citizens. Tribal government was extinguished in 1906. Oil production began on a large scale in Seminole country in 1923 and 1924, providing an impetus to economic development. In 1967 a federal claims court upheld a 1964 verdict of the Indian Claims Commission that the Seminole had been illegally deprived of some 32 million acres in Florida, paving the way for compensation. By 1970 there were some 5,055 Seminole living in Oklahoma and Florida.

[Grant Foreman, *The Five Civilized Tribes;* Harry Henslick, "The Seminole Treaty of 1866," *The Chronicles of Oklahoma,* vol. 48; Edwin C. McReynolds, *The Seminoles;* John K. Mahon, *History of the Second Seminole War, 1835–1842.*]

DOROTHY TWOHIG

SEMINOLE WARS. In 1816 the United States built Fort Scott near the confluence of the Flint and Chattahoochee rivers on the border between Georgia and Florida, which was then under Spanish control. Across the Flint was a Mikasuki settlement called Fowlstown. Neamathla, the chief there, used the village as a base from which to stage raids into the southeastern United States and as a collecting point for loot and runaway slaves. He was, through long conditioning, violently anti–United States. There was no united confederation of Indians in Florida, only the Mikasuki, the Seminole, and some splinter groups who cooperated unsystematically.

Neamathla's hostility caused Brig Gen. Edmund P. Gaines, commanding at Fort Scott, to send 250 men under Col. David Twiggs to Fowlton. The result was a small battle on Nov. 21, 1817, the opening ac-

tion of the first Seminole War (1817–18). After that battle the Mikasuki retreated eastward toward the Suwannee River, where they could achieve loose cooperation with the Alachua band across the river.

In January 1818 President James Monroe's administration sent Maj. Gen. Andrew Jackson to Florida "to conduct the war in the manner he may judge best." Jackson reached Fort Scott on Mar. 9, 1818. His force quickly built up to 1,500 white men and 2,000 Creek Indians. With it he followed the Indians eastward, destroying their villages. By early April he had broken all Indian resistance west of the Suwannee River. He next turned his force against the scattered points held by the Spanish in that area, all of which he conquered.

Monroe quickly returned Jackson's conquests to Spain, but the first Seminole War had convinced the Spanish government that it would be in its interest to deed Florida to the United States before it was lost through conquest. The transfer was completed in 1821, and without their being consulted the Florida Indians, including the Seminole, went with the peninsula. Then, in 1830, Congress passed the Indian Removal Act, to transplant all the eastern Indians somewhere west of the Mississippi River. When applied to the Florida Indians, the Removal Act brought on the second Seminole War (1835–42).

On Dec. 28, 1835, Osceola, the guiding spirit of resistance to removal, directed the murder of Indian agent Wiley Thompson at Fort King and, simultaneously, the massacre of two companies commanded by Maj. Francis L. Dade. The Indians then rapidly devastated northeastern Florida and won two sharp victories over the white men.

Jackson, by then president, sent Maj. Gen. Winfield Scott, a hero of the War of 1812, to replace Brig. Gen. Duncan L. Clinch. Scott tried to use classical military methods, but the Indians countered with guerrilla tactics that rendered his campaign all but futile. Jackson, relieving Scott in May 1836, temporarily invested the governor of Florida Territory, Richard K. Call, with the command and in December assigned Maj. Gen. Thomas S. Jesup to Florida.

Jesup was the pivotal figure in the war. He had scant respect for Indians, and after they breached the faith a few times, he abandoned the conventions of so-called civilized war. He estranged the blacks from their Indian allies, experimented with bloodhounds, forced captives on pain of death to betray their friends, and violated flags of truce and promises of safe conduct. Under a flag of truce he seized the charismatic Osceola in October 1837. The largest pitched battle was fought near Lake Okeechobee on Christmas Day 1837, with Gen. Zachary Taylor in immediate command. By the time Jesup was relieved in May 1838 about 100 Indians had been killed and 2,900 captured.

During the next four years the leadership on both sides changed frequently. There was no central Indian command, but Wild Cat, Sam Jones, Tiger Tail, and Halleck Tustenuggee emerged as forceful leaders. U.S. operations were more centrally directed under the successive commands of Taylor, Walker K. Armistead, and William J. Worth. All three had to learn to use only Indian tactics. By 1842, when there were no more than 300 Seminole left in Florida, Worth recommended that the government end its attempts to force them to leave. After some delay, the War Department directed him to implement his recommendation. Accordingly, the few remaining Indians formally agreed in mid-August 1842 to confine themselves to the area south of Pease Creek and west of Lake Okeechobee. Their agreement with Worth, in no way a treaty, brought an end to seven years of war.

Florida became a state in 1845, and since conditions on the border continued to be sensitive, it sought to expel the Seminole completely. To placate the state, the federal government began to build roads into the Indian preserve and to curtail white trade with the Indians. Military patrols and survey parties found their way south of Pease Creek. One such patrol, under Lt. George L. Hartsuff, vandalized some property deep in Indian country. That property happened to belong to the foremost Seminole leader, Billy Bowlegs. This heedless act set off the explosion that ever-increasing encroachments had prepared. Bowlegs, leading thirty-five warriors, attacked Hartsuff's detachment at dawn on Dec. 20, 1855, inflicting six casualties. Nearby white people scurried for the forts, and the third Seminole War (1855–58) was under way.

At the start of the third war there were perhaps 360 Seminole in Florida, 120 of them warriors. The United States enlarged its regular force to 800 and summoned into service 1,300 Florida volunteers. This force in time was placed under the command of Brig. Gen. William S. Harney, a hardened Indian fighter with experience in Florida tactics. Since the Indians did their best to avoid pitched battles, Harney sent his detachments into the remotest haunts to ferret them out. That method finally brought the chiefs to a conference at Fort Myers on Mar. 15, 1858. There 165 persons, including Billy Bowlegs, surrendered and were shipped west. Bowlegs returned to Florida

in December 1858 and helped to persuade another 75 to migrate. This left roughly 125 Florida Seminole, who were never thereafter forced or persuaded to leave their homeland.

[Charles H. Coe, *Red Patriots: The Story of the Seminoles;* James W. Covington, *The Story of Southwestern Florida,* vol. I; Edwin C. McReynolds, *The Seminoles;* John K. Mahon, *History of the Second Seminole War;* James Parton, *Life of Andrew Jackson,* vol. II.]

JOHN K. MAHON

SENATE. *See* **Congress, United States.**

SENATE CONFIRMATION. *See* **Confirmation by the Senate.**

SENATORIAL COURTESY. *See* **Courtesy of the Senate.**

SENATORS, ELECTION OF. Until 1866 the state legislatures determined their own procedure for electing U.S. senators, in some cases the chambers voting separately, in others in joint session. Frequent deadlocks and other unsatisfactory conditions led Congress in that year to prescribe a uniform procedure, under which both branches first voted separately by roll call and in case of disagreement were required to meet in joint session and continue voting daily until a candidate secured a majority. In the meantime there was a growing demand for popular election as uniform procedure failed to create a satisfactory system. By use of the direct primary for nominating senatorial candidates and exaction of pledges from state legislators to support the popular choice, the old system of election was being rapidly nullified when, in 1913, it was formally transferred to the electorate by the Seventeenth Amendment.

[G. H. Haynes, *The Election of Senators;* Allen Johnson and W. A. Robinson, *Readings in Recent American Constitutional History.*]

W. A. ROBINSON

SENECA. *See* **Iroquois.**

SENECA FALLS CONVENTION, the first modern woman's rights convention, called through the initiative of Lucretia Mott and Elizabeth Cady Stanton, was held in the Wesleyan Methodist Church at Seneca

Falls, N.Y., July 19–20, 1848. At the gathering Stanton read a "Declaration of Sentiments," listing the many discriminations existing against women, and the convention adopted a series of eleven resolutions, one of them calling for woman suffrage. This convention launched the organized modern woman's rights movement.

[Inez Haynes Irwin, *Angels and Amazons;* E. C. Stanton, S. B. Anthony, and M. J. Gage, *The History of Woman Suffrage.*]

MARY WILHELMINE WILLIAMS

SEPARATION OF POWERS. *See* **Powers, Separation of.**

SEPARATIST MOVEMENT. *See* **Western Separatism.**

SEPARATISTS, or **Independents,** were radical Puritans who, in the late 16th century, advocated thoroughgoing reform within the Church of England. Dissatisfied with the slow pace of official reform, they set up churches outside the established order. Robert Browne gathered the first Separatist church at Norfolk, England, in 1581; later Separatists were dubbed "Brownists," but the groups did not constitute an organized movement. As with the congregation of the church at Scrooby, England, in 1602, a Separatist church resulted whenever a number of earnest Puritans concluded that the true biblical polity had to be achieved "without tarying for anie." In the main, Separatists proposed a congregational or independent form of church polity, wherein each church was to be autonomous, founded upon a formal covenant, electing its own officers and restricting the membership to "visible saints." Separation was held a major offense by the regular Puritans as well as by Anglicans and royal authorities; yet the Puritans who settled Massachusetts Bay in 1620 already believed that Congregationalism rather than Presbyterianism was the polity of the New Testament, and when founding churches at Salem and Boston, 1629 and 1630, sought advice from the Separatists at Plymouth. In England during the 1640's the minority wing of the Puritan party maintained Congregationalism against the majority in the Westminster Assembly and the Parliament, and were known as Independents, but the multitude of sects that arose out of the disorders of the time also took unto themselves the title of Independents, so that the term came to be a vague designation for opponents of Presbyterianism. Orthodox New England Puritans, although practicing a Congregational discipline, always denied that they were either Separatists or Independents.

[Henry M. Dexter, *The Congregationalism of the Last Three Hundred Years;* Perry Miller, *Orthodoxy in Massachusetts;* Williston Walker, *The Creeds and Platforms of Congregationalism.*]

PERRY MILLER

SEQUOIA, a genus of coniferous trees, comprising the species *Sequoia sempervirens* (the redwood) and *Sequoia gigantea* (the big tree). Both species average 275 feet in height, with trunks from 15 to 35 feet in diameter. They are the largest of all American forest trees. The redwood is found in the Pacific Coast region, from California to Oregon; the big tree is known only on the west slope of the Sierra Nevada in California. Their wood is soft, light, and of a reddish color that darkens on exposure. Once believed to be the oldest living thing, they probably first became known to the white man in 1833, when Capt. Joseph Walker's expedition sighted them. A. T. Dowd is credited with discovering the Calaveras grove in 1852.

In less than a decade loggers began extensive cutting of the sequoia, and cutting continued into the 20th century, although on a lesser scale. The Sequoia National Park in the Sierra Nevadas was established on Sept. 25, 1890, to protect the groves of *sequoia gigantea.* The General Sherman tree in the park is 272 feet high and one of the oldest living things in the world (more than 3,500 years).

[C. S. Sargent, *The Silva of North America.*]

JOHN FRANCIS, JR.

SEQUOYAH, PROPOSED STATE OF, was to include the lands of the Indian Territory. Consideration of such a state was precipitated by an act of Congress setting Mar. 4, 1906, as the date on which governments of the Five Civilized Tribes were to end.

Although there was some support for joint statehood with Oklahoma Territory, a number of influential Indians were opposed. Conventions were held at Eufaula on Nov. 28, 1902, and May 21, 1903, at which a group of Indians including chiefs of the Five Tribes expressed their opposition to a single state encompassing both Indian and Oklahoma territories. The Creek national council met on Dec. 15, 1903, and also declared its opposition.

A conference of Creek was held at Muskogee on July 14, 1905, at which further opposition to joint statehood was given voice. On Aug. 7 a mass meeting was held at Muskogee in order to select delegates to a convention scheduled for Aug. 21. At this convention, attended by 182 Indian and white delegates, it was decided that a constitution would be drafted for—and Congress be requested to admit—the Indian Territory as a separate state with the name Sequoyah.

A constitution was prepared, submitted on Sept. 8, and ratified by a vote of the people of Indian Territory, but Congress refused to consider the admission of Sequoyah to the Union. The movement is significant because its leaders became leaders of the Oklahoma constitutional convention the following year.

[Grant Foreman, *History of Oklahoma;* Roy Gittinger, *The Formation of the State of Oklahoma.*]

SEQUOYA'S SYLLABARY, the Cherokee alphabet, developed early in the 19th century by Sequoya, a half-breed Cherokee also known as George Gist. Using symbols adapted from English, Greek, and Hebrew letters, Sequoya's syllabary consists of eighty-six characters. He submitted it to the leaders of the Cherokee nation in 1821, who approved it, and several months later thousands of Cherokee were able to read and write their own language. Sections of the Bible were translated into Cherokee in 1824, and the *Cherokee Phoenix,* a weekly newspaper published in English and Cherokee and edited by Elias Boudinot, began in 1828.

[Grant Foreman, *Sequoyah.*]

SESQUICENTENNIAL INTERNATIONAL EXPOSITION was held in League Island Park and environs, Philadelphia, from June 1 to Dec. 1, 1926. It was designed to celebrate 150 years of American independence and to show the progress of the American people in many fields since the centennial celebration of 1876. Two notable features were the reproduction of High Street, Philadelphia's main street of 1776, and the Pennsylvania State Building. The architecture was classical and conventional. Sixteen foreign nations participated in the exposition, the total cost of which was almost $19 million. The subsequent deficit was not the most important feature of one of America's most unsuccessful expositions.

FRANK MONAGHAN

SETTLEMENT WORK. *See* **Social Settlements.**

SEVEN CITIES OF CIBOLA. *See* **Cibola.**

SEVEN DAYS' BATTLES (June 25–July 1, 1862) were the succession of battles in which Gen. Robert E. Lee's army forced that under Union Gen. George B. McClellan to abandon its threatening position east of Richmond and retreat to the James River.

McClellan had pushed his right wing, 30,000 strong under Gen. Fitz-John Porter, northward across the Chickahominy River, hoping that Union Gen. Irvin McDowell's corps would join it from Fredericksburg. Aware that Porter was separated from McClellan's main force of 75,000, Lee ordered Confederate Gen. Thomas J. ("Stonewall") Jackson, with 18,500 men from the Shenandoah Valley, to fall on Porter's right and rear. Simultaneously Lee with 40,000 of his 68,000 troops, crossing the Chickahominy north of Richmond, would assail Porter in front.

Skirmishing took place on June 25 as the Union forces moved into position. The following day Lee attacked at Mechanicsville (June 26) but, since Jackson had not arrived, he was repulsed. Porter withdrew to Gaines' Mill, where on June 27 the Confederate forces, including Jackson's command, drove him across the Chickahominy. The Union base on the Pamunkey River was now exposed, but McClellan transferred it by water to Harrison's Landing on the James, and marched his army thither. On June 29 his covering troops repulsed Confederate attacks at Savage's Station. Discovering that his adversary was retiring on the James, Lee hurried columns to Frayser's Farm. Here his desperate assaults on June 30 failed to interrupt McClellan's retreat, while at White Oak Swamp, Jackson was equally unsuccessful in crushing his rear guard. McClellan, continuing his retirement, occupied Malvern Hill, where on July 1 Lee's final attack suffered decisive repulse. McClellan then fortified his army at Harrison's Landing. Casualties over the seven days of fighting were heavy: Confederate losses were 3,286 killed, 15,909 wounded, 940 captured or missing; Union losses were 1,734 killed, 8,062 wounded, 6,053 captured or missing.

[Douglas S. Freeman, *R. E. Lee,* vol. II; R. U. Johnson and C. C. Buel, eds., *Battles and Leaders of the Civil War,* vol. II.]

JOSEPH MILLS HANSON

"SEVEN PILLARS," the seven men who entered into the covenant founding the first church at New Haven colony, Aug. 22, 1639. They were John Davenport, the minister; Theophilus Eaton, a wealthy merchant; Robert Newman; Mathew Gilbert; Thomas Fugill; John Ponderson; and Jeremy Dixon. Since the leaders of the New Haven colony had moved beyond

Massachusetts Bay, in part because they thought even that community too lax and worldly by their standards, they took exceptional care that the founders of their church should be men of indubitable righteousness. The seven gave themselves an extremely severe examination and applied equally rigorous criteria to later candidates for membership.

[Isabel MacBeath Calder, *The New Haven Colony.*]

PERRY MILLER

SEVEN PINES. *See* **Fair Oaks, Battle of.**

SEVEN RANGES SURVEY. Since Connecticut had not ceded the Western Reserve in what is now the northeast corner of Ohio, and since the Pennsylvania boundary had not been run north of the Ohio River, the first surveys under the Ordinance of 1785—the Seven Ranges—were made south of the Geographer's Line (*see* Public Lands, Survey of). Not for fifteen years were lines run north of this base. The survey was begun Sept. 23, 1785. But hostile Indians, disease, bad weather, and other hazards interposed such obstacles that only four ranges were surveyed along the outside lines of the townships by Feb. 21, 1787, even with a military escort during the last nine months of the survey. The ranges were placed on sale later in the year. Because section lines had not been surveyed but merely marked on township plats, difficulties developed, particularly where the windings of the Ohio River were little known. Also, no allowance was required to be made for the convergence of meridians, while crude instruments, a difficult terrain, and poor pay—$2 per mile—caused other irregularities. Geographer Thomas Hutchins numbered the sections in a township from south to north, beginning at the southeast corner, thus giving the first row numbers from 1 to 6, the second from 7 to 12, and so on. The Seven Ranges formed a triangle with a western boundary ninety-one miles in length, a northern one of forty-two miles, and the Ohio River as the third side.

[W. E. Peters, *Ohio Lands and Their History*; C. E. Sherman, Original Ohio Land Subdivisions, in *Ohio Cooperative Topographic Survey, Final Report,* vol. III.]

EUGENE H. ROSEBOOM

SEVENTEENTH AMENDMENT. Demand for the popular election of U.S. senators appeared in the 1830's, but the prestige and general effectiveness of the upper chamber were then such that little headway was made until after the Civil War. Popular belief that the Senate had deteriorated, recurrent cases of buying election from venal legislatures, corporate influence in selecting candidates, and other unsatisfactory features of the existing system gave a tremendous impetus to the movement. A proposed amendment to the Constitution, making direct election possible, passed the House several times, but it was not until 1912 that the Senate finally accepted the inevitable. Ratification followed, and the amendment became effective May 31, 1913. (*See also* Senators, Election of.)

[George H. Haynes, *The Senate of the United States: Its History and Practice.*]

W. A. ROBINSON

SEVENTH-DAY ADVENTISTS. *See* **Adventist Churches.**

SEVEN YEARS WAR. *See* **French and Indian War.**

SEVERN, BATTLE OF THE (Mar. 25, 1655), an engagement between Puritan settlers of Providence (present-day Annapolis, two miles from the mouth of the Severn River), in Maryland, and the forces of the colony's Protestant governor, William Stone, acting for Cecilius Calvert, Lord Baltimore. About 125 men fought on each side, the Puritans assisted by two armed ships in the Severn. Both parties lost about fifty men, but Stone was defeated and taken prisoner, and four of his men were executed. For three years the Puritans practically controlled the colony.

[W. B. Norris, *Annapolis: Its Colonial and Naval Story.*]

WALTER B. NORRIS

"SEWARD'S FOLLY." *See* **Alaska.**

SEWING MACHINE. After almost one hundred years of trials, failures, and partial successes in Europe, the sewing machine in its practical form evolved as a mid-19th-century American invention. Elias Howe, Jr., usually credited as the inventor, was not the first patentee of an American sewing machine. John J. Greenough, Benjamin W. Bean, and several others patented ideas for sewing machines in the early 1840's, before Howe was granted the first patent for the two-thread, lockstitch sewing machine in 1846. Howe's machine was far from adaptable for commercial production, and he met little success in America at the time. The machine only stitched straight seams for the length of the baster plate, which then had to be reset. Taking his machine to England, Howe was unable to adapt it to British manufacturing needs, and he finally sold the patent rights in that country to William Thomas, a corset manufacturer. On his return home he found that several other inventors had entered the field. John Bachelder had patented a continuous-feed, vertical-needle machine in 1849; Isaac M. Singer had used earlier ideas with his heart-shaped cam to move the needle and received a patent in 1851; A. B. Wilson patented the stationary rotary bobbin in 1852 and the four-motion feed in 1854. The principal technical problems had been solved, but no single manufacturer could make a practical machine without being sued for infringement of patent by another. In 1856 Orlando B. Potter, lawyer and president of the Grover and Baker Sewing Machine Company, suggested the idea of pooling the patents. This was accomplished, but each company maintained itself separately, and there was competition in the manufacturing and improving of the various machines. The four members of the "Sewing-Machine combination" were Elias Howe, Jr.; Wheeler and Wilson Manufacturing Company; I. M. Singer and Company; and Grover and Baker Sewing Machine Company. All four members had to agree on which companies would be licensed to build sewing machines, and a fee of $15 per machine was charged. Howe received $5.00 of this amount; a portion was held in reserve for possible litigation costs; and the money left was divided equally among the four parties. In 1860 the fee was dropped to $7 and Howe's share to $1. In 1867 Howe's renewed patent expired, and only the three companies were left. The combination remained active until 1877, when all the major patents expired. Although the combination had been accused of retarding the development of the sewing machine, hundreds of thousands of good machines were produced in the decades of the 1850's and 1860's. The machines were used by manufacturers for shirts, dresses, aprons, cloaks, collars, and many other items. Details such as pleating and tucking could be produced by machine very quickly and were popularly added to many costumes. By 1900 tents, awnings, sails, books, umbrellas, mattresses, hose, trunks, shoes, and flags were all stitched by machine.

The sewing machine was the first widely advertised consumer product. Because of the high initial cost of the machine, the Singer company introduced the hire-purchase plan, and installment buying placed a sewing machine in almost every home. Competition for

this ready market encouraged more and more manufacturers to enter the field. At the height of this competition in the 1870's, there were well over 200 American sewing machine companies. But foreign competition began to invade the field in the 20th century. The high cost of skilled labor in America made it very difficult to compete. Nevertheless, ingenious sewing machines continue to be produced, including those that "sew" without thread, but most of the machines produced in the United States are highly specialized manufacturing machines.

[Grace R. Cooper, *The Sewing Machine: Its Invention and Development.*]

GRACE R. COOPER

SEXUAL ATTITUDES. In general the first American settlers, for the most part members of puritanical sects, were more hostile to sex, particularly outside the marital relationship, than was the norm among their European contemporaries. Originally the New England settlers tried to base their sex code on the Bible, but this practice was abandoned when it was realized that some sexual transgressions, such as rape, were not punished in the Bible. They then enacted much more restrictive codes, which tended to make sexual transgressions, including fornication, criminal as well as religious offenses. The Congregational church, for example, required public confession of fornication by married couples who had a child within seven months after nuptials; church records are full of references to sexual misconduct and the resulting punishment. Court records also contain numerous references indicating that there were probably more indictments for illicit sexual relations in 17th-century Massachusetts than for crimes against property.

For a brief time sexual activities such as adultery and bestiality received the death penalty, and in the case of the latter crime all the animals involved were destroyed. Later, capital punishment tended to be replaced by whipping, branding, and the wearing of special clothes or symbols. In the southern colonies fornication was originally punished by fine or whipping as well as public penance in a church. Adultery tended to be looked upon as twice as sinful as fornication and received a double penalty. In all the colonies prosecution of the parents for bastardy was a standard practice, but this was more to save the parish from having to assume the support of the offspring than for the sexual activity involved. There were numerous laws against miscegenation.

One colonial custom that has received considerable

attention is bundling. The practice existed in most colonies but most conspicuously in New England. Engaged couples were permitted to ''bundle'' in the same bed although usually they kept on some or all their clothes and often a board was placed between them. Various other restraints were imposed to frustrate completion of the sexual act.

In the 18th century the number of recorded incidents of sexual crimes declined as respect for privacy grew and as the general traditions of English common law on sexual activities were incorporated into American law. Americans relied on Europe for publications dealing with sexual information; one of the most widely circulated sex manuals was an English work called *Aristotle's Masterpiece*. It was an anonymously written hodgepodge of superstition and information that went through numerous American editions. In spite of its contradictory advice, it tended to recognize that sex was a natural function and recognized the existence of the female orgasm. The Americans of the time seem to have had rather relaxed attitudes about sex, even by European standards. Some of the bawdier works of Benjamin Franklin may be offered as evidence.

During the 19th century the more or less free and open acceptance of sex, which encouraged widespread discussion of sex and dissemination of birth control information, ran into a countercurrent based on new and supposedly scientific assumptions about sex, many of which later proved to be erroneous. The chief exponent of these ideas was an 18th-century Swiss physician, Simon-André Tissot. He believed that all sexual activity was dangerous because it caused blood to rush to the brain, thereby starving the nerves and increasing the likelihood of insanity. In his classic work *L'Onanisme* (1760), he argued that the worst kind of sexual activity was the solitary orgasm, and his association of masturbation with insanity became a major theme in American ideas about sex in the 19th century. Benjamin Rush introduced similar ideas to America, and they were advocated by a number of medical practitioners until well into the 20th century. Particularly influential in this respect was the American reformer Sylvester Graham. In his anxiety to demonstrate that biblical sexual ethics had been based on sound physiological principles, Graham arrived at the conclusion that all sexual activity, in or out of marriage, was dangerous and debilitating. He went so far as to claim that the constant and pressing desire to engage in sexual intercourse was itself an indication of an unhealthy condition. Such stern moralizing resulted in a growing hostility and fear of

any sexual activity that did not result in procreation. Sex, at least in the minds of many Americans, changed from a normal to an abnormal function. Elizabeth Osgood Goodrich Willard, for example, believed that a sexual orgasm was more debilitating than a whole day's work, and while such debilitating labor might be justified when children resulted, any nonprocreative sex could only lead to disease and corruption. All types of nonprocreative sex from coitus interruptus to homosexuality were classed with masturbation. This undercurrent of fear toward open sexuality contributed greatly to antipornography and antiprostitution campaigns in the last part of the 19th century. Some of the American utopian movements also reflected these pseudoscientific ideas, although there has been little research into this connection. The coitus reservatus practiced by the Oneida community was justified as an energy-saving device, while the polygamy of the Mormons was seen by some of the Mormons as essential in order to make every emission of semen count as productive.

Although the antisex movement was influential, it was not necessarily the dominant trend in America in spite of the efforts of Anthony Comstock and other moral crusaders to make it so. Most Americans retained an interest in sexuality that helped make them more receptive to research findings about sex than was the case in England. It was no accident that Havelock Ellis published the English edition of his works in the United States before he did in England. Since 1900 there has been a long line of American investigators into sex. Notable among them was Alfred C. Kinsey and his team of researchers at the University of Indiana. Several American colleges and universities have institutes or centers devoted to research and study of sexual behavior; one of the more influential was that run by William H. Masters and Virginia E. Johnson at Saint Louis. Ultimately research into sexual processes undermined the erroneous ideas of Tissot and Graham. Unfortunately, many of the laws about sex were put on the books in the late 19th century, when the fear of sexuality had reached its height; these laws were not challenged in the courts and revised by the legislatures until the late 20th century.

Tied in with the 19th-century aversion to sex was the fear of venereal disease. This fear, which had always been present in America, had been justified by Cotton Mather as God's punishment for man's sins. Anxieties about venereal disease also reached a height in the last part of the 19th century when the varied forms of third-stage syphilis came to be known. This fear of the consequences of venereal disease was one of the reasons the American medical community joined with women's groups and religious leaders to eliminate regulated prostitution. Fears of venereal diseases declined only with the advent of safe medical cures.

By the end of World War I, much of the new findings about sex were being disseminated to a wider audience. Women were becoming emancipated not only in the economic and political sense but in their ability to control their physiological processes, particularly through birth control devices. As contraceptives became more effective and widespread and as abortions became legally available in the 1970's, women were able to express their own sexuality more freely than before. The overall result is that American attitudes toward sex became less fearful and many of the bugbears of previous ages were laid to rest.

[Vern L. Bullough, *The Subordinate Sex*, and *Sexual Variance in Society and History;* Norman E. Himes, *Medical History of Contraception;* Geoffrey May, *Social Control of Sex Expression;* S. W. Nissenbaum, *Careful Love: Sylvester Graham and the Emergence of Victorian Sexual Theory in America* (unpublished Ph.D. dissertation, University of California, Los Angeles); Milton Rugoff, *Prudery and Passion.*]

VERN L. BULLOUGH

SEYBERT, FORT, MASSACRE AT (Apr. 28, 1758). During the French and Indian War a score or more defenses were built and maintained by Col. George Washington in and about the valley of the South Branch of the Potomac River. A party of Indians led by Killbuck, a Delaware chieftain also known as Gelelemend, attacked Fort Seybert (in present-day Pendleton County, W.Va.), murdered seventeen of its occupants, and carried others into captivity. On the previous day this same party had attacked nearby Fort Upper Tract and killed all twenty-two occupants.

[Oran F. Morton, *History of Pendleton County, West Virginia;* Alexander S. Withers, *Chronicles of Border Warfare.*]

C. H. AMBLER

SHACKAMAXON, TREATY OF, is traditionally known as the Great Treaty, and much doubt still remains about its details. But there is no doubt that William Penn met the Delaware in 1682 at Shackamaxon (now Kensington), the chief village of the Delaware, and entered into negotiations with them for friendly relations and good feeling. On June 23, 1683, several agreements were signed with the Indian chiefs granting to Penn and his heirs land in southeastern Pennsylvania (in present-day Bucks County). All of these were duly witnessed by both whites and Indians. The leading representative of the Indians was Tamanen (Tammany). No valid reason exists for rejecting the traditional story of Penn's meeting the Indians seated under a large elm. This event has been made familiar by Benjamin West's painting, *Penn's Treaty With the Indians* (1772, Pennsylvania Academy of the Fine Arts, Philadelphia), and Voltaire's allusion as "the only treaty never sworn to and never broken." Penn described the seating arrangements of a meeting with the Indians in a letter to the Free Society of Traders in England written on Aug. 16, 1683.

[Wayland F. Dunaway, *History of Pennsylvania;* Howard M. Jenkins, ed., *Pennsylvania, Colonial and Federal,* vol. I.]

J. PAUL SELSAM

SHADES OF DEATH, the name given the densely wooded northern part of the Great Swamp lying some twelve miles southeast of Wilkes-Barre, Pa., toward Easton, and shown on maps before 1778. It acquired added significance from being the refuge of many survivors fleeing from the Wyoming massacre (1778).

FRANCES DORRANCE

SHADRACH FUGITIVE SLAVE CASE. While being held for examination under the Fugitive Slave Act in 1851, a slave named Shadrach was allowed to walk out of a federal court in Boston and escape into Canada. The incident added to the growing controversy between antislavery and proslavery forces.

[W. H. Siebert, *The Underground Railroad in Massachusetts.*]

WILBUR H. SIEBERT

SHAKER RELIGION, INDIAN, a nativistic cult started by the prophet John Slocum, a Squaxin Indian of Puget Sound, in 1881. Slocum was believed to have died and to have been resurrected twice. He claimed that he had been to heaven and had returned to preach a new doctrine, much of which he had actually learned from white missionaries. Slocum preached that God had told him to tell the Indians that they must give up their evil ways, including the drinking of alcohol, and be absolutely nonviolent. The religion manifests elements of Roman Catholic and Presbyterian doctrine, combined with elements of the old Indian religions. Ceremonies feature the ringing of bells and nervous twitchings of the body, which are interpreted as a sign of spiritual power. The cult spread to other Indians of the Northwest and California and is still active.

[Homer G. Barnett, *Indian Shakers.*]
KENNETH M. STEWART

SHAKERS, members of the United Society of Believers in Christ's Second Coming. The movement was founded by Ann Lee Standerin, or Stanley, on the basis of revelations to her that the Second Coming would be in the form of a woman and that she was that woman. When she and her followers moved from England to the New World in 1774 and established themselves at what was to become Watervliet, N.Y., in 1776, they adopted a communal rule of life for their society. The movement was deeply influenced by the popular millennianism of the time. Believing themselves to be the vanguard of the new age, the Shakers sought to be an intercessory remnant that would call all men to blessedness. Their well-known practice of celibacy was related to their millennial beliefs: there was no need to procreate, since the end was near. They acquired children for their communities through adoption. Although the Shakers shared many beliefs with the Quakers and other Evangelical groups, they were distinctive in their adherence to spiritualism and the important place they gave to seances in their worship. The morality of the sect was simple: they believed that the practice of the twelve virtues and four moral principles was enough to raise man from the animal to the spiritual state. The name Shaker came from a ritual form of dancing that often became quite frenzied. The Shakers reached their largest membership (6,000) before the Civil War and have declined continually since that time. By 1974 no brothers and only twelve Shaker sisters were left. Most people know of the sect through its furniture, which was classical in its functional simplicity and noted for its fine workmanship.

[Edwards D. Andrews, *The People Called Shakers.*]
GLENN T. MILLER

SHALAM, LAND OF, was a communistic, agrarian, humanitarian, and vegetarian colony established on about 1,000 acres of irrigated land near Doña Ana, N.Mex., by Andrew M. Howland, a Boston philanthropist, under the influence of John B. Newbrough, a dentist and religious mystic who had written *Oahspe: A New Bible* (1882). The colony, incorporated in

1885 under the name First Church of the Tae, was composed mainly of orphan children. Howland sank his fortune into excellent buildings, stock, and equipment, but financial failure wrecked the colony, which finally broke up in 1901.

[G. B. Anderson, "The Land of Shalam," *Out West,* vol. 25 (1960).]
P. M. BALDWIN

SHANTY TOWNS as an American social phenomenon first appeared during the lag in reemployment after World War I (*see* Depression of 1920), rising on dump heaps or wastelands within or at the edges of large industrial cities. Such communities also existed during the Great Depression, when they received the indulgence if not the approval of officials. The shanties were constructed and occupied by single men who had fitted into an economy of abundance as transient workers. Forced to stay in one place, they built crude homes of any free material available, such as boxes, waste lumber, and tin cans. Some occupied abandoned boilers, boxcars, and caves. They continued to take odd jobs when they could be found, living on the scant wages with the extra aid of social agencies.

CHARLES J. FINGER

SHARECROPPER is a farm tenant who pays rent with a portion (usually half) of the crop he raises and who brings little to the agricultural operation besides his labor and that of his family. Although sharecropping had largely disappeared by the 1970's, it was once prevalent in the South. A product of Reconstruction, it was partially a response to the scarcity of liquid capital in the South following the Civil War. But its primary purpose was to establish a stable, low-cost work force that would replace slave labor, and it thus represented the bottom rung in the southern tenancy ladder.

Working usually under close supervision, the sharecropper often lacked title to his harvest, a factor that distinguished him from a share tenant. The landlord usually furnished working stock, tools, half the necessary fertilizer, housing, fuel, and seed, varying the amounts according to the land area that the cropper and his family could cultivate.

Most sharecroppers depended on credit, which they got from independent merchants or, more frequently, from landlord-operated commissaries. Interest rates ranged from 10 to 60 percent. The security on these loans was a lien against the tenant's forthcoming crop. At harvest, the landlord established the crop's worth, subtracted what was owed him, and remitted the remainder to the tenant. The cropper's cash return was almost always low and was often swallowed up by his debt.

Concerned by the extent of sharecropping and other forms of tenancy, Congress in 1937 passed the Bankhead-Jones Farm Tenant Act, sponsored by Alabama Sen. John H. Bankhead and Texas Rep. Marvin Jones, to help renters of all types acquire their farms by empowering the Farm Security Administration to lend money to tenants who desired to purchase land. Government-aided purchase programs, the mechanization of southern agriculture, and the lure of urban employment caused the number of sharecroppers to drop from 776,278 in 1930 to 121,037 in 1959, the last year that the federal agricultural census identified croppers as a separate group.

[Calvin L. Beale, "The Negro in American Agriculture," in John P. Davis, ed., *The American Negro Reference Book;* David Eugene Conrad, *The Forgotten Farmers;* Oscar Zeichner, "The Transition From Slave to Free Agricultural Labor in the Southern States," *Agricultural History,* vol. 13 (1939).]

DAVID E. BREWSTER

SHARE-THE-WEALTH MOVEMENTS. At the lowest point of the Great Depression, the winter of 1932–33, two impressions were stamped on the popular mind by the publicity concerning technocracy. They were, first, a prophecy of impending doom and, second, a promise of potential utopia. "The nation stands at the threshold of what is simultaneously opportunity and disaster," announced Howard Scott, the foremost technocrat. These two ideas, together with the acute distress of the unemployed, the insecurity of the middle class, and the deepening plight of the aged, formed the common basis of appeal for the great mass organizations that sprang into existence in the South and West between 1933 and 1936. Among those declaring their purpose to be the redistribution of wealth were Francis E. Townsend's plan; Louisiana Sen. Huey P. Long's Share-Our-Wealth Clubs; the National Union for Social Justice party, started by Father Charles E. Coughlin, Townsend, and Rev. Gerald L. K. Smith, and having as its first presidential candidate the North Dakota agrarian Rep. William Lemke; and Upton Sinclair's End Poverty in California (EPIC).

Differing widely in their proposals, these organizations joined in disclaiming any desire to destroy the capitalist order, and all, except the EPIC, depended fundamentally on a core of inflationist doctrine. Fol-

lowing American middle-class traditions of utopianism, mingled with religious zeal, they adopted such new techniques as national radio hookups, skilled publicity methods of pressure politics, huge mass meetings or "conventions" that were characterized by frenzied emotionalism, and blind trust in spectacular individual leaders rather than in the slow education of a party. Moving in and out of alliance with the New Deal and with one another, according to the whims or mutual jealousies of their leaders, they ran the gamut of reform tactics: the whirlwind drive for power of an individual leader, the attempt to capture an old party, the trial of the third party method, disciplined backing of congressional candidates of either old party who pledged support of "the plan," and finally sporadic drives to perfect schemes within single states. Revealed in all these movements was the anxious disillusionment, the distress, the experimental frame of mind of the lower middle class, and the complete unreality of party divisions in the United States.

C. VANN WOODWARD

SHARPSBURG. *See* **Antietam, Battle of.**

SHARPSHOOTER, the term for a highly skilled marksman, comes from the German *Scharfschütze* and is found in use as early as 1802 in describing members of certain formations of Tyrolean marksmen in Austrian service. The name was also applied to French marksmen of the Napoleonic period. In the American Revolution such units as David Morgan's regiment of riflemen and in the War of 1812 Andrew Jackson's Kentucky and Tennessee riflemen followed the principle of expert marksmanship, although the term "sharpshooter" was not applied. In other American infantry units throughout the period of muzzle-loading weapons, the best marksmen were armed with the more accurate rifle in place of the standard smoothbore musket and were used to pick off officers and other leaders in the enemy's ranks. Enemy artillerymen were especially vulnerable. When the Sharps breechloading rifle was introduced (1857), troops armed with this weapon were called sharpshooters. In the Civil War two volunteer regiments of sharpshooters were raised (1861) for the Union army. These differed from other volunteer units in that they were made up of companies drawn from several states with federally appointed officers. Both regiments fought with distinction through most of the campaigns in the East.

SHARPS RIFLE

In 1884 sharpshooter became a grade of qualification for rifle practice in the army. Since 1907, army and navy rifle qualification standards rank sharpshooters above marksmen and below expert riflemen.

By World War I the term "sniper" began to replace "sharpshooter" to indicate specially trained and equipped personnel who would shoot at selected targets from concealed positions, and in this form the tradition of the sharpshooter was continued in World War I, the Korean War, and the Vietnam War.

[John K. Mahon and Romana M. Danysh, *Infantry: Part I.*]

JOHN E. JESSUP, JR.

SHARPS RIFLE, one of the earliest successful breechloaders, was invented by Christian Sharps about 1848. It was manufactured at Hartford, Conn., by the Robbins, Kendall and Lawrence Company until 1856, when the manufacture was continued by the Sharps Rifle Company, also at Hartford. The Sharps rifle first attracted wide attention during the Kansas Border War (1855–56), when some 900 of them, often called "Beecher's Bibles," were used by the Free-State party. About half of these were supplied by officers of the New England Emigrant Aid Company. These rifles gave the free-state side a moral, if not a military, superiority throughout the conflict. They probably saved Lawrence, Kans., from attack during the Wakarusa War (1855) and were undoubtedly a factor in provoking the proslavery men to acts of violence. Later they were used by James Montgomery, leader of the free-state men, in the border war and by John Brown at Harpers Ferry. The Sharps rifle was considered for adoption by the U.S. Army in 1856, and although not finally adopted, some 80,000 were used by the Union army during the Civil War. It had a high reputation for range and accuracy.

[W. H. Iseley, "The Sharps Rifle Episode in Kansas History," *American Historical Review,* vol. XII.]

SAMUEL A. JOHNSON

SHAWMUT, the Indian name of the peninsula on which the town of Boston was planted. The name fell into disuse very early, long before urban growth effaced the three hills (Tremont) and the narrow isthmus, frequently awash, which joined it to the mainland at the south.

[N. B. Shurtleff, *Topographical and Historical Description of Boston.*]

C. K. SHIPTON

SHAWNEE, a southern tribe of the Algonquin, are first recognized as inhabiting the Cumberland basin in what is now Tennessee with an outlying colony on the Savannah River in South Carolina. The latter group was the first to abandon its southern hunting grounds, in a migration lasting from about 1677 to 1707 and caused by friction with the nearby Catawba who were favored by the whites. Their new homes were in the valleys of the Susquehanna and Delaware rivers, but congestion soon caused them to remove to the waters of the upper Ohio Valley in a migration lasting from about 1720 to the years of the French and Indian War (1754–63). The Shawnee on the Cumberland began retreating north as the result of friction with the Cherokee and Chickasaw about 1710 and began to merge with their brethren from the east in a group of villages on the Ohio River from what is now Tarentum, Pa., to the mouth of the Scioto in Ohio—hunting in the forests on both sides of the river.

The Shawnee were the spearhead of resistance to advancing settlement in that period of frontier warfare lasting from 1755 to 1795, supporting and being supported first by the French and then by the English. By 1795 their homes were in the valley of the upper Miami, and the Treaty of Greenville of that year forced them to retreat to Indiana. A movement for confederated Indian regeneration and resistance to further white expansion developed under the leadership of the Shawnee brothers, Tecumseh and Tenskwatawa (the Shawnee Prophet), but met disaster in the Battle of Tippecanoe in 1811. The loss to the Indians of British support, as the result of the War of 1812, hastened the rapid dispersion of the Shawnee. The main body is now incorporated with the Cherokee in Oklahoma.

[C. C. Trowbridge, *Shawnese Traditions;* Glenn Tucker, *Tecumseh: Vision of Glory.*]

R. C. DOWNES

SHAWNEE AND DELAWARE MIGRATION to the Ohio Valley from the Susquehanna and Delaware river valleys, which took place from about 1720 to 1753, was important in the period leading up to the French and Indian War. It not only brought Indian life and power to a French area that had been uninhabited, but it also diminished English influence through the loss of those tribes. Moreover, in the Ohio region the eastern Shawnee merged with their western brethren who had migrated from the Cumberland Valley.

The migration was caused by the encroachment of whites; by such aggravations as the Walking Purchase of 1737, in which the Delaware were forced to relinquish about 1,200 square miles in eastern Pennsylvania; by the decline of hunting and knowledge of better hunting grounds in the West; by the probability that the Iroquois would not be able to keep them out of the new grounds; and by encouragement from both French and English traders. In the competition for the furs of the new region the English got the lion's share. But the fact that the English trade was accompanied by uncontrolled rum selling and unpunished fraud caused many Shawnee and Delaware to prefer the French, with whom their leaders were in touch from the beginning of the migration. They were well-disposed toward French expansion, which culminated in the French occupation of the Forks of the Ohio (1754) and the erection of Fort Duquesne that same year. The English, first through the Pennsylvania colonial government and later through the Iroquois overlords of the Shawnee and Delaware, sought in vain to bring the migrants back to English protection. Although the Iroquois scolded their dependents, they went no farther, and the failure of the Pennsylvania government to establish an Indian department impressed the Indians with the inability of the English to make their traders behave.

During the French and Indian War when the western Shawnee and Delaware, supporting the French, sought to wipe out the interior Pennsylvania settlements, the status of those remaining in the East was imperiled. The reassertion of English supremacy caused most of these to join the western tribesmen. After 1763 all were again under English influence.

[R. C. Downes, *Indian Relations in the Ohio Valley.*]

RANDOLPH C. DOWNES

SHAWNEE PROPHET, founder of a nativistic religion that had a strong influence among the Indians of the Great Lakes region in the early 19th century. The prophet, Tenskwatawa ("The Open Door"), was the brother of the Shawnee chief Tecumseh. His doctrine was similar to, and probably influenced by, that of the earlier Delaware Prophet, and it predicted the return of aboriginal conditions through supernatural means. The prophet advocated a reform ethic that combined old ways and new: Indians were to abandon alcohol, cease intermarrying with whites, and live peacefully with one another. His vision in 1805 inspired Tecumseh to attempt to unify the Indians to halt the white invaders. Followers of the prophet rapidly increased until on Nov. 7, 1811, during an absence of Tecumseh, the prophet led an unsuccessful

attack on Gov. William Henry Harrison's troops at Tippecanoe, in Indiana Territory.

[Edward Eggleston, *Tecumseh and the Shawnee Prophet;* James Mooney, *The Ghost Dance Religion and the Sioux Outbreak of 1890;* Glenn Tucker, *Tecumseh: Vision of Glory.*]

KENNETH M. STEWART

SHAWOMET, in eastern Rhode Island, was purchased in 1642 from the Indians by Samuel Gorton, a contentious religious leader, and his followers. Soon after they built at Shawomet they became involved in a controversy over ownership of the land with the Indians and with Massachusetts Bay, and that colony sent an armed force that captured the settlement in September 1643 and took Gorton and his chief men prisoners to Boston. On his release in March 1644, Gorton returned to Narragansett Bay, obtained from the Narraganset an act of submission to the king, and took this to England, where his rights to Shawomet were upheld and Massachusetts Bay was forced to withdraw. After returning to Shawomet in May 1648, Gorton renamed the settlement Warwick in honor of the Earl of Warwick, who had given him a letter of safe conduct. (*See also* Gortonites.)

[O. P. Fuller, *History of Warwick, R.I.*]

HOWARD M. CHAPIN

SHAW'S EXPEDITION of 1809, as reported in his reminiscences, was one of the earliest attempts to reach New Mexico from Missouri. Col. John Shaw claimed that in the spring of 1809, with two companions, he left Cape Girardeau, Mo., and reached the neighborhood of the Colorado mountains. It is not certain that he intended to reach Santa Fe, and the inaccuracy of his statements in some instances throws doubt on others. There is no contemporary evidence to support his contention except his own memoirs in the Wisconsin State Historical Society.

[W. J. Ghent, *Early Far West.*]

CARL L. CANNON

SHAYS'S REBELLION (August 1786–February 1787), in western and central Massachusetts, was the outstanding manifestation of the discontent widespread throughout New England during the economic depression following the Revolution. Many small property holders in Massachusetts were losing their possessions through seizures for overdue debts and delinquent taxes; many faced imprisonment for debt.

SHEEP

Town meetings and county conventions petitioned for lightening of taxes (disproportionately burdensome to the poorer classes and western sections); sought suspension, abolition, or reform of certain courts and revision of the state constitution; and especially urged the issue of paper money, but were stubbornly opposed on most points by the legislature. Lacking, in many cases, property qualifications for voting and thus unable to look for relief through the ballot, the malcontents, beginning at Northampton, Aug. 29, resorted to massed efforts to intimidate and close the courts to prevent action against debtors. Fearful they might be indicted for treason or sedition by the state supreme court at Springfield, in late September they appeared there in armed force. Daniel Shays, revolutionary veteran and local officeholder of Pelham, emerged as leader, demanding that the court refrain from indictments and otherwise restrict its business. A clash with neighborhood militia under Maj. Gen. William Shepard was avoided when both bands agreed to disperse. The court adjourned.

In January the insurgents returned to Springfield for supplies from the Confederation arsenal there, a move foreseen by state and federal authorities. Federal preparations for arsenal defense were masked by announcement that requisitioning of forces was necessitated by menacing Indians on the frontier. Adequate government funds were not forthcoming for either federal or state troops, but Gen. Benjamin Lincoln secured for the latter some $20,000 from private individuals. Shepard's forces repulsed the Shaysites' attack on the arsenal (Jan. 25); Lincoln's men dispersed a nearby insurgent force under Luke Day. Marching to Petersham through a blinding snowstorm, Lincoln surprised and captured most of the remaining insurgents early in February, and the rebellion soon collapsed. Shays escaped to Vermont; eventually, with about a dozen others condemned to death, he was pardoned. James Bowdoin, governor during the insurrection, was defeated at the next election; reforms in line with the Shaysites' demands were soon made, and amnesty granted with few exceptions. Alarmed by "this unprovoked insurrection" of "wicked and ambitious men," some conservatives despaired of republican institutions. Far greater numbers viewed the rebellion as proof of need for a stronger general government, capable of suppressing such uprisings, or, better still, preventing them by improving economic conditions throughout the United States. Thus, indirectly, the rebellion strengthened the movement culminating in the adoption of the U.S. Constitution.

[Merrill Jensen, *The New Nation: A History of the United States During the Confederation, 1781–1789*; G. R. Minot, *The History of the Insurrections in Massachusetts*; J. P. Warren, "The Confederation and the Shays Rebellion," *American Historical Review* (October 1905).]
                                                    LOUISE B. DUNBAR

SHEEP were introduced into the Americas by European colonists—into Mexico by the Spanish, into Virginia (1609) and Massachusetts (1629) by the English, into New York (1625) by the Dutch, and into New Jersey (1634) by the Swedes. These animals were unimproved.

In colonial times sheep were raised as a part of self-sufficient agriculture to supply wool for homespun clothing and not for commercial purposes. Because of wolves, improper care, and English competition, the number of sheep remained relatively few and the quality and quantity of the wool poor. The industry improved somewhat during the Revolution but slumped after peace and the resumption of British trade.

The first decades of the 19th century witnessed a marked change. Two events of importance occurred: the introduction of merino sheep and the exclusion of English competitors from the American market by the various nonintercourse acts and the War of 1812. The first merinos were imported in 1801–02 from France and from Spain. With the passage of the Embargo Act (1807), native mills increased, wool prices skyrocketed, and the demand for fine-wool sheep became insatiable. A merino craze followed. Merino wool sold for $2 a pound, and the early importers sold sheep for $1,000 a head. In the midst of this craze the Napoleonic armies broke the Spanish restrictions on the exportation of merinos, and between 1808 and 1811 approximately 24,000 merinos were imported into the United States. Sheep raising entered its commercial phase.

After 1815 British woolen importations again depressed the industry. The growth of the factory system and the tariff of 1828 revived it. Woolen manufactures doubled in a decade, the price of wool went up, and eastern flocks increased tremendously. In the 1830's, 60 percent of American sheep were in New England and the middle Atlantic states. After 1840, because of westward migration, improved transportation facilities, easy access to cheap western land, and an increase in the prices of foodstuffs, the center of sheep raising shifted westward. By 1850 it was in the Ohio Valley.

The Civil War produced a second merino craze.

After the war the sheep raised in the United States underwent improvement through importations of European breeds and selective breeding. Sheep raising continued to expand west to the Rocky Mountains and Pacific Coast states. Farmers in this region at first concentrated on wool production, while those of the East, under the stimulus of growing urban markets, turned to mutton production. English mutton breeds were introduced, including the Leicester and Shropshire. After 1890 sheep growers of the West began to place more emphasis on dual-purpose sheep, and mutton production and lamb feeding developed in this area as well.

The importance of the West in the raising of sheep continued into the 20th century, and by 1935, 60 percent of all the sheep in the United States were in the western states. The total number of sheep raised throughout the country reached a peak that same year of 51.8 million. By 1973 the number of sheep had declined to 17.7 million. Of these, only 48 percent were raised in the western states, representing a shift away from the region.

[L. G. Connor, "A Brief History of the Sheep Industry in the United States," *American Historical Association Annual Report* (1918); E. N. Wentworth, *America's Sheep Trails*; C. W. Wright, *Wool-Growing and the Tariff*.]
ROBERT G. DUNBAR

SHEEP WARS, range battles fought in the American West between cattle and sheep ranchers. Although some of the confrontations were undoubtedly caused merely by disputes over land and water rights, the main causes for the wars resulted from the fact that the grazing habits of sheep destroyed the range, sometimes making the lands unusable to cattle herds for months. Moreover, sheep polluted watering places used by cattle.

Spanish colonists introduced the sheep industry to the American West in the early 17th century, when they occupied New Mexico, Arizona, Texas, and California, but not until long after the intrusion of the Anglo-Americans were there causes for range wars. After passage of the Homestead Act of 1862, the free prairie range, upon which the cattlemen depended, rapidly diminished.

By 1875 clashes between cattlemen and sheepmen were regular occurrences along the New Mexico–Texas boundary. New Mexican sheepmen drove their flocks onto the range of Charles Goodnight, which was along the Canadian River in northeastern New Mexico. Goodnight's cowhands, in retaliation, drove more than 400 sheep into the Canadian River where

they drowned. A New Mexican court later ruled in favor of the sheepmen. In 1876 Goodnight and the sheepmen agreed to divide the Staked Plain range. The sheepmen were allowed the range of the Canadian River valley, and Goodnight's cattle were allowed to graze undisturbed in the Palo Duro Canyon area of northwestern Texas.

Other range controversies ended in bloodshed. In Colorado, Nevada, Idaho, Wyoming, and Montana many cowboys and shepherds were killed in the bitter wars, along with thousands of sheep. During the 1880's and 1890's sheepmen controlled the Arizona range from Ashfork northwest to Seligman, and they threatened to drive the cowmen from other choice ranges. This led to the Graham-Tewksbury feud, in which twenty-six cattlemen and six sheepmen lost their lives. Cattlemen in Wyoming attacked shepherds and drove more than 10,000 sheep into the mountains where they perished. In another clash, near North Rock Springs, the cowmen drove 12,000 sheep over a cliff. The sheep wars subsided only when the disputed areas were occupied by landowners and with the fencing of the open range.

[J. Evetts Haley, *Charles Goodnight*; E. P. Snow, "Sheepmen and Cattlemen," *Outlook*, vol. 73.]
C. C. RISTER

SHEFFIELD SCIENTIFIC SCHOOL had its origin in the creation at Yale College in 1846 of unsalaried professorships in agricultural chemistry and practical chemistry through the efforts of John Pitkin Norton (who was appointed to the agricultural chemistry professorship) and Benjamin Silliman, Jr. (appointed to the practical chemistry professorship). The School of Applied Chemistry under the new Department of Philosophy and the Arts was opened in 1847 in a house for which Norton and Silliman paid $150 to Yale and equipped largely at their own expense. Silliman was obliged to accept a salaried position in Kentucky in 1849, where he remained until 1854. The strain of carrying the school alone contributed to Norton's death in 1852, when only thirty years of age.

Norton's pioneering work was carried on by John Addison Porter, professor of chemistry at Yale (1852–64) and son-in-law of Joseph E. Sheffield, wealthy railroad builder and philanthropist. Sheffield shared the belief of the founders in the importance of science for the development of America. He became the principal benefactor of the school, his gifts ultimately amounting to $1.1 million. Renamed the

SHELBY'S MEXICAN EXPEDITION

Yale Scientific School in 1854, when it was combined with the School of Engineering established in 1852, it became the Sheffield Scientific School in 1861, with a separate board of trustees established in 1871.

In 1852 Yale offered the bachelor of philosophy degree to students of the Scientific School at Norton's suggestion; in 1861 the doctor of philosophy degree was granted, the first Ph.D. in America. In 1863 the Scientific School became the Connecticut beneficiary under the U.S. land grant act (Morrill Act, 1862). This money helped finance expansion of the faculty, and in 1860 a general course was established for undergraduates called the Select Course in Scientific and Literary Studies. It omitted classical studies, in which Yale College persisted, and offered science, mathematics, history, English, geography, economics, political science, and, later, social science. In 1870 the school instituted a program in biological science preparatory to medical studies, in addition to offering specific programs for teachers of science; explorers; scientific investigators; agricultural, manufacturing, and pharmaceutical chemists; metallurgists and assayers; civil, mechanical, and mining engineers; agriculturists; naturalists; and students desiring a general scientific background. Of the 7,247 students who had received the bachelor of philosophy degree by 1921 (when it was no longer exclusively given by the Scientific School), 2,106 were in the select course and 3,690 in engineering.

From the beginning the school appointed only the most highly qualified professors to the faculty, and many distinguished men rendered long devoted service. Not only were they excellent teachers, but they were also productive scholars providing outstanding and definitive studies and widely used textbooks in their various fields. To faculty achievements were soon added the achievements of the school's graduates. The school returned to its original status as a graduate department in 1945. Its faculty, under the general administration of the graduate school, presently gives instruction and guidance to graduate students in mathematics and the sciences who are candidates for the degree of master of philosophy or doctor of philosophy.

[R. H. Chittenden, *History of the Sheffield Scientific School*.]

ELIZABETH H. THOMSON

SHELBY'S MEXICAN EXPEDITION (1865). After the downfall of the Confederacy in 1865, Gen. Joseph O. Shelby, one of the ablest southern cavalry commanders, called on his men to follow him into Mexico rather than surrender. There the men voted to enlist in the army of Emperor Maximilian, then precariously maintaining his throne.

With 1,000 men, including many Confederate notables, such as generals E. Kirby-Smith, John B. Magruder, T. C. Hindman, C. M. Wilcox, and governors Pendleton Murrah of Texas, Charles S. Morehead of Kentucky, and Henry W. Allen of Louisiana, Shelby crossed the Rio Grande to Piedras Negras in northeastern Mexico from Eagle Pass, Tex., burying the Confederate flag in the river on July 4, 1865. At Piedras Negras four cannon were exchanged for gold to buy supplies, and Shelby's expedition began fighting its way across northern Mexico toward Monterrey, being impeded by guerrillas supporting Benito Juárez, the Mexican Republican leader who was fighting Maximilian.

At Monterrey, the expedition broke up into several sections, parts going to Canada, British Honduras, the Mexican state of Sonora, and even joining the French army in Mexico. Shelby, with the remnant of his men, marched to Mexico City. The vacillating Maximilian refused the offer of Shelby's sword, fearing the displeasure of the United States, and the Confederates attempted to establish a colony on land given them by the Empress Carlota. The overthrow of Maximilian and his execution, June 19, 1867, made the colony untenable, and most of the Confederate exiles returned to the United States or went elsewhere.

[John N. Edwards, *Shelby's Expedition to Mexico*.]

PAUL I. WELLMAN

SHENANDOAH, the last armed cruiser to carry the Confederate flag and, next to the *Alabama*, the most destructive to Union shipping. Originally an Indiaman named the *Sea King*, it was purchased in England in September 1864, and sailed to Madeira, where Capt. James Waddell equipped it as an armed cruiser and named it the *Shenandoah*. The cruiser was a fast, well-armed vessel of 790 tons register, powered with steam and sail. From Madeira it began a cruise to the Pacific Ocean, by way of the Cape of Good Hope and Australia, to strike at the New England whaling fleet in the north Pacific. The *Shenandoah* captured nearly forty prizes valued at about $1.4 million. On Aug. 2, 1865, Waddell learned from a British ship that the war had ended. He then sailed for Liverpool by way of Cape Horn, reaching the English port in November 1865. The British government transferred the cruiser to the United States, by whom it was sold to the sultan of Zanzibar. Later it was lost at sea. (*See also* Alabama Claims.)

[Cornelius E. Hunt, *The Shenandoah;* Virgil Carrington Jones, *The Civil War at Sea.*]

RICHARD E. YATES

SHENANDOAH CAMPAIGN (1864). Coincident with Gen. Ulysses S. Grant's advance (*see* Wilderness, Battles of the), Union forces in western Virginia, under Gen. Franz Sigel, moved eastward to clear the Shenandoah Valley and cut Gen. Robert E. Lee's supply communications. After engagements at Cloyd's Mountain (May 9), New Market (May 15), and Piedmont (June 5), the Union columns under Gen. David Hunter, Sigel's successor, were united for an advance on Lynchburg. To meet this threat, Lee detached Gen. Jubal A. Early's corps with instructions to defeat Hunter, move down the valley into Maryland, and threaten Washington, D.C. Early drove Hunter into the mountains, crossed the Potomac, defeated Union Gen. Lew Wallace at Monocacy, Md., on July 4–5, and on July 11 halted before the defenses of Washington. Too weak to do more than threaten, he withdrew into the valley. Prompted by Union division of force and uncertainty of leadership, Early, late in July, again crossed into Maryland, interrupted railroad traffic, destroyed vast supplies, burned Chambersburg, Pa. (July 30), and then safely withdrew.

Alarmed by Early's successes, Grant consolidated all Union troops in the valley under Gen. Philip H. Sheridan, whose force greatly outnumbered Early's. A month of maneuver followed. On Sept. 19 Sheridan, with a three-to-one superiority, defeated Early at Opequon and at Fisher's Hill. Instead of destroying his opponent, Sheridan spent several weeks burning crops, provisions, factories, and farm property, after which he took position along Cedar Creek. Cavalry raids (*see* Tom's Brook, Engagement at) and foraging expeditions occupied the ensuing weeks. On Oct. 19 Early attacked during Sheridan's absence and was at first successful (*see* Cedar Creek, Battle of), but for lack of numbers and because of Sheridan's energetic leadership, the Confederate army was again defeated, and it again retreated up the valley. By mid-December 1864 both Early and Sheridan had been recalled to Virginia.

Early had saved Lynchburg, threatened Washington, interrupted important communication lines, collected immense supplies, diverted a large force from Grant's army, and preserved Lee's western line of supply. Sheridan, in spite of his great superiority, had gained little from a military point of view. He did not leave the valley and never seriously interfered with Lee's defense of Richmond (*see* Petersburg, Siege of).

[R. U. Johnson and C. C. Buel, eds., *Battles and Leaders of the Civil War,* vol. IV.]

THOMAS ROBSON HAY

SHENANDOAH HUNTING PATH. *See* **Virginia Path.**

SHENANDOAH VALLEY, that part of the great valley between the Allegheny and the Blue Ridge mountains extending from the Potomac River at Harpers Ferry south to the watershed of the James River a few miles southwest of Lexington, Va. There are three parts of the Shenandoah Valley: the lower, extending from the Potomac forty miles south, settled chiefly by English immigrants from tidewater Virginia; the middle, from near Strasburg to the vicinity of Harrisonburg, settled almost wholly by Germans; and the upper, from Harrisonburg to the waters of the James, originally more wooded than the middle and lower valley. This last was the part chosen by the Scotch-Irish immigrants, most of whom came down from Pennsylvania.

There were travelers into the valley at least fifty years before Gov. Alexander Spotswood's expedition of the Knights of the Golden Horseshoe in 1716, and the larger movement of Germans led by Jost Hite in 1732, and of Scotch-Irish led by John Lewis in the same year. Settlers were known near Shepherdstown, in what is now northeastern West Virginia, in 1717; Adam Miller had settled in the present Page County by 1726; and there were settlers near Luray in 1727.

The lower valley became the seat of slavery and tobacco, the settlers adhering to the church of England; while the middle valley, marked by large barns and rolling meadows, was settled by quiet, home-loving "Valley Dutch" people who were Lutheran. The upper valley, whose inhabitants were Presbyterian in religion and Scotch-Irish in politics, was known for its fierce democracy, its exploring hunger for land, and its Indian wars. The lower valley was linked closely with tidewater Virginia geographically and socially; George Washington served in the House of Burgesses as delegate from Frederick County before he represented Fairfax. The middle valley, including Augusta County, extended to "the Great South Sea, including California," and held its county court at times near Fort Duquesne, the present city of Pittsburgh.

[Samuel Kercheval, *History of the Valley of Virginia.*]
JAMES ELLIOTT WALMSLEY

SHERIDAN'S RIDE. During the Shenandoah campaign of 1864, Confederate Gen. Jubal A. Early attacked Union Gen. Philip H. Sheridan's army at dawn on Oct. 19 along Cedar Creek, near Strasburg, Va. Two Union corps, awakened from sleep, were quickly thrown into panic. Other troops rallied and resisted the Confederate advance, although they were slowly forced back. Sheridan, returning from a visit to Washington, D.C., had stopped at Winchester on the night of the 18th. Awakened next morning by the distant sound of artillery firing, he left for the front and soon began to meet the routed commands, who told him that all was lost. He reached the battlefield about 10:30 A.M., and his presence quickly restored confidence. By midafternoon the Confederates were in retreat, losing heavily in artillery and supplies. A poem written several months later by Thomas Buchanan Read, with its refrain, "And Sheridan twenty miles away" (in reality, the distance was less than fifteen), fixed his ride in the public mind as one of the heroic events of the war.

[*Personal Memoirs of P. H. Sheridan;* R. U. Johnson and C. C. Buel, eds., *Battles and Leaders of the Civil War,* vol. IV.]

ALVIN F. HARLOW

SHERIDAN-WARREN CONTROVERSY, beginning in 1865, grew out of Union Gen. Philip H. Sheridan's dissatisfaction with Gen. Gouverneur K. Warren's handling of his troops at the Battle of Five Forks (Apr. 1, 1865). In spite of conflicting orders, Warren won a valuable victory, but to his astonishment and that of his subordinates and others, Sheridan relieved him of his command. Warren made repeated requests for a board of inquiry, but it was not until 1879 that one was ordered. Warren was fully exonerated, the court criticizing the manner of his relief.

[E. G. Taylor, *Gouverneur Kemble Warren: The Life and Letters of an American Soldier, 1830–1882.*]

THOMAS ROBSON HAY

SHERMAN ANTITRUST ACT, enacted July 2, 1890, was the first federal law directed against industrial combination and monopoly. Once considered a great landmark in the relations between government and business, it was more certainly an example of the ambivalence that has characterized the American people and government as they have sought to enjoy the benefits of big business while distrusting its methods and economic power.

In the twenty-five years following the panic of 1873, the United States experienced the first wave of industrial combination. Consolidation took many forms, but the most publicized was the "trust" device. With the 1880's an antimonopoly movement pledged to the destruction of the trusts had taken political form in several states, and by 1890 fifteen states had enacted antitrust statutes. These efforts proving ineffective, there was a growing demand for federal action, led by small entrepreneurs complaining of the unfair trade practices of monopolistic firms. In response to this demand, Congress, by a large bipartisan majority, passed the Sherman Antitrust Act. Fortuitously associated with the name of Sen. John Sherman of Ohio, its prime authors were the leading Republican members of the Senate Judiciary Committee—George F. Edmunds of Vermont and George F. Hoar of Massachusetts.

The key provision of the act was incorporated in the first of its eight sections: "Every contract, combination in the form of trust or otherwise, or conspiracy, in restraint of trade or commerce among the several states, or with foreign nations, is hereby declared to be illegal." In the Judiciary Committee it had been decided not to attempt to define a "combination" or "trust," not to include intrastate commerce, and not to widen the prohibition to include combinations in restraint of production as well as trade. Although some writers have seen this delimitation as proof of a determination by its authors to conciliate big business and deceive the public, the act in fact represented caution, not conspiracy. Anxious to encourage economic growth while curbing monopoly, the authors of the Sherman Act sought to fashion a law that would find clear justification in the commerce clause of the Constitution and make clear the authority of the federal judiciary to enforce the common-law prohibition against illegal combinations "in restraint of trade."

The subsequent history of the act is a story of periodic bursts of attention and long-term declining importance. During the 1890's the Justice Department sought few indictments under the act, and when it was stirred to action, as in the attempt to break up the sugar trust, the Supreme Court interpreted the act so strictly as to render its prohibitions meaningless. The only successful prosecutions under the Sherman Act in the 1890's were those waged against labor unions, such as *United States* v. *Debs* (1894). The presidency of Theodore Roosevelt witnessed an effort to revive the act as an instrument of federal regulation of big business, but the effort was largely unsuccessful. The few trusts that were ordered dissolved soon reappeared in another guise, and Roosevelt was himself prepared to distinguish between "good" and "bad" trusts. That distinction later received judicial sanction in a Supreme Court opinion of 1911 (*United States* v. *American Tobacco Company*) that only combinations in "unreasonable" restraint of trade were subject to the penalties of the Sherman Act. With the administration of Woodrow Wilson, the Clayton and Federal Trade Commission acts were passed (1914); when later presidents engaged in bouts of trustbusting, they used primarily these instruments and the cease-and-desist orders of the regulatory commissions. Since the administration of Franklin D. Roosevelt and the New Deal, the Sherman Antitrust Act has played only a comparatively minor role in the relations of big business and the federal government.

Although insufficient to the task assigned, the act was noteworthy as a pioneer measure in the field of federal regulatory legislation. It remains of continuing historical significance as an illustration of the ambivalent attitude of the American public and Congress toward the problem of industrial combination.

[Hans B. Thorelli, *The Federal Antitrust Policy: Origination of an American Tradition.*]

RICHARD E. WELCH, JR.

SHERMAN SILVER PURCHASE ACT. In 1890 a certain group of congressmen was anxious to enact the McKinley tariff bill, and the advocates of silver currency were urging the enactment of a bill providing for the free coinage of silver. While the silver advocates had a majority in the Senate, powerful enough to force the House into line, they were advisedly fearful that President Benjamin Harrison would veto a free coinage bill, even if it were attached as a rider to a tariff bill that he otherwise favored. As a practical solution to this dilemma the "silver" senators determined to adopt not a free coinage measure but the nearest possible approach to it. A compromise bill, the Sherman Silver Purchase Act, named for Sen. John Sherman of Ohio, became law on July 14, 1890. The act provided for the issuance of legal tender notes sufficient in amount to pay for 4.5 million ounces of silver bullion each month at the prevailing market price. Then enough silver dollars were to be coined from the bullion purchased to redeem all the outstanding Treasury notes issued in this manner.

The notes were made full legal tender except where otherwise expressly stipulated in the contract, and were made redeemable on demand either in gold or silver coin at the discretion of the secretary of the Treasury, although the act went on to declare it to be "the established policy of the United States to maintain the two metals on a parity with each other upon the present legal ratio or such ratio as may be established by law."

With the passage of the Sherman Act there were three kinds of currency, substantial in amount, which the federal government had to keep at par with gold: greenbacks, silver certificates, and Treasury notes. The direct effect of the Sherman Act was twofold: first, it increased the circulation of redeemable paper currency in the form of Treasury notes by $156 million, and second, it accentuated the drain on the government's gold reserves by requiring the Treasury notes to be redeemed in gold as long as the Treasury had gold in its possession. The financial crackup in Argentina and the resultant liquidation in Great Britain, involving the failure of the banking house of Baring Brothers and Company, eventually forced an exportation of gold from the United States to Great Britain, and this exodus, coupled with an extraordinary stringency in the money market induced by unusually heavy demand for funds evoked by the industrial activity in the West and South, created a situation bordering on panic in the latter part of 1890.

Some respite from this taut financial situation was gained by the extraordinary grain crop of 1891 in the United States and the European crop shortage, as a consequence of which the exports of gold were transformed into imports, which in turn made bank reserves ample and the money market easy. But this respite was short-lived. The arbitrary issues of Treasury notes again began to undermine public confidence. The Treasury's already precarious position ensuing from a policy of increased governmental expenditures, the marked growth of U.S. indebtedness to foreign nations, and the reduction in custom receipts brought about by the McKinley Tariff was aggravated by the additional drain on the Treasury's resources that the redemption of the Treasury notes entailed. The cumulative effect of the foregoing factors culminated in the panic of 1893, which was characterized by a fear of the abandonment of the gold standard because of the depletion of the government's gold reserve. The panic was checked in the autumn of 1893 by the repeal of the Sherman Act.

[W. Jett Lauck, *The Causes of the Panic of 1893.*]

FRANK PARKER

SHERMAN'S MARCH TO THE SEA. With a vivid and daring imagination and against Gen. Ulysses S. Grant's judgment, Gen. William Tecumseh Sherman conceived the plan of marching across Georgia from Atlanta to Savannah. His purpose was to destroy the food supplies of a region on which Gen. Robert E. Lee largely depended and to break the will of the people to continue the war. On Nov. 15, 1864, he burned Atlanta, preparatory to setting out on his march the next day. With four army corps and 5,000 cavalrymen, in all numbering 62,000 men, he pointed his course toward Milledgeville, then the state capital, Sandersville, Louisville, Millen, and Savannah. Gen. Oliver O. Howard commanded his right wing; Gen. Henry W. Slocum, his left, which Sherman himself accompanied; and Hugh J. Kilpatrick led the cavalry force. The army was spread out sufficiently to cover a course sixty miles wide through the state.

Cutting all communications, Sherman lived off the country through which he marched. His regularly organized raiding parties ranged widely, returning at the end of each day heavily laden with food, livestock, vehicles of various kinds, and a great deal of nondescript property secured through pillage. Within a week the left wing reached Milledgeville but not in time to capture the fleeing state officials. In keeping with the general picnic spirit of the march, the soldiers held there a mock session of the legislature, in which they repealed the secession ordinance. On Dec. 10 the army drove in the pickets before Savannah and, after a ten-day siege, forced the Confederates to flee across the Savannah River into South Carolina. Union troops occupied Savannah on Dec. 21, and Sherman sent his famous message to President Abraham Lincoln giving him the city for a Christmas present. Since Confederate Gen. John B. Hood had retreated into Tennessee at the outset of the march, Sherman had no opposition except for the ineffectual raiding of Gen. Joe Wheeler. Sherman estimated that he had inflicted damages amounting to $100 million—four-fifths of which was "simple waste and destruction."

[H. Hitchcock, *Marching With Sherman;* J. F. Rhodes, *History of the Civil War, 1861–1865.*]

E. MERTON COULTER

SHILOH, BATTLE OF (Apr. 6–7, 1862). Gen. Ulysses S. Grant's capture of Fort Henry (Feb. 6) in northwestern Tennessee and Fort Donelson (Feb. 15–16) twelve miles away opened the Cumberland and Tennessee rivers to Union water traffic and pierced the center of the Confederate far-flung defensive line, so that Columbus, Ky., had to be evacuated. Union Gen. Don Carlos Buell was able to occupy Nashville with the Army of the Ohio, and Gen. Henry W. Halleck on Mar. 1 could order Gen. Charles F. Smith with 30,000 troops of the Army of the Tennessee by water up that river to concentrate at Shiloh (or Pittsburg Landing) twenty-five miles north of the Confederates under Gen. Albert S. Johnston at Corinth, Miss. Grant arrived and assumed command on Mar. 16. Buell's 25,000 troops were to join by marching overland from Nashville preparatory to a vigorous combined thrust southward as the next logical step in the campaign for the conquest of the Mississippi Valley.

On Apr. 3 Johnston moved out of Corinth, 50,000 strong, to strike Grant's force before the junction could be effected. On Apr. 6, after a slow massed march, undetected by Grant, Johnston made a sudden surprise attack early in the morning against the unfortified and incompletely covered Union position. Vigorous Confederate attacks drove in Grant's outlying units, shattered the hastily formed lines in all-day fighting, which was costly for both sides, and pushed the Union troops against the river.

Grant personally was absent when the massed assault struck. He hurried to the scene, approved arrangements that Gen. James B. McPherson had made in his stead, coordinated the defense, concentrated rear units, and—Buell arriving by night—counterattacked next morning. The Confederates were disrupted and confused by their own violent attacks and the death of Johnston. Grant's stroke, with the fresh troops of Buell and Gen. Lew Wallace, aided by portions of Gen. William Tecumseh Sherman's and Gen. John A. McClernand's commands, swept them from the field toward Corinth.

[Allan Nevins, *The War for the Union,* vol. II; Kenneth P. Williams, *Lincoln Finds a General.*]

ELBRIDGE COLBY

SHIMONOSEKI EXPEDITION (1864). The opening up of Japan to foreign intercourse and particularly the treaties of 1858 with foreign powers, made in the name of the shogun, aroused the opposition of the Japanese nobles who capitalized on popular hostility to foreigners as a means of overthrowing the shogun and setting up another regime under the emperor. After the nobles subjected foreign nationals to insults and even murder, the lord of the Choshiu clan, whose holdings were near the Shimonoseki Strait, fired on French, Dutch, and American ships in the strait in June and July. The U.S.S. *Wyoming,* in Yokohama, sailed to Shimonoseki Strait and sank two of the Choshiu craft. Meanwhile, British ships bombarded the city of Kagoshima. U.S. Secretary of State William H. Seward permitted a small American chartered steamer to take part with nine British, four Dutch, and three French warships in a punitive bombardment of Shimonoseki in September, thereby weakening the antiforeign elements. An indemnity of $3 million was extracted from Japan, but the United States returned its share ($750,000) in 1883.

[Payson J. Treat, *Diplomatic Relations Between the United States and Japan, 1853–1895.*]

SAMUEL FLAGG BEMIS

SHINPLASTERS, a term that has been applied in the United States at various times to privately issued fractional paper currencies or to those issued by other than the regularly constituted authorities, and, less frequently, to all fractional paper money. The term, which originated during the Revolution, is used here in the narrower sense. It is, of course, impossible to know just how much of such currency has been issued or at just what times because of a lack of any official data on the subject. Since the establishment of the federal government it seems likely that the three or four years prior to the passage of the Coinage Act of 1853, when much of the fractional silver disappeared from circulation, and in 1862, before the postage stamp currency and fractional paper notes were used, represent the two instances in which shinplasters circulated most widely. It is probable that more than $15 million of such currency was issued in the latter period.

[N. Carothers, *Fractional Money.*]

FREDERICK A. BRADFORD

SHIPBUILDING was one of the leading industries before the American Revolution, especially in New England. There were two important reasons for the prosperity of the industry. First, the English Navigation Acts, which prohibited the carrying of goods between England and the colonies in foreign ships, classified colonial-built ships as English built. The other reason was economic. With an abundant supply of oak and pine growing almost to the water's edge, a vessel could be built in America for about 30 percent less than in England, where timber, increasingly scarce, had to be carried great distances to the shipyards. British shipowners snapped up these American bargains, and on the eve of the Revolution a third of the vessels in British registry were American built.

That lucrative situation ended with independence in 1783 and would not be revived until 1849, when Britain abolished the Navigation Acts.

The next American shipbuilding boom came between the mid-1840's and the mid-1850's, when a series of outside stimuli, ranging from Irish rainfall to California gold, produced the so-called Golden Age of American shipbuilding. During that decade American shipping almost overtook the British in quantity and far surpassed it in quality. For those ready to pay the price, excellent crack packets and clippers could be built on New York's East River or around Boston harbor. Good substantial cargo carriers could be built more cheaply along the Maine coast, particularly at Bath, Casco Bay, and the central coast. The American Civil War brought this era to a close.

An entirely new picture emerged after the Civil War. With Britain turning out compound-engine freighters in large quantities, American square-riggers were gradually squeezed out of most of the deep-sea trades, except for Maine's excellent Down Easters. Because cheaper coal and iron were available to foreign shipbuilders, the old 30 percent cost differential in favor of American vessels now turned into a 30 percent differential advantage for the foreign iron (and later steel) steamships. The American merchant marine also declined as the U.S. government failed to follow other maritime nations in adequately subsidizing its shipping. In addition, the government failed to build up its navy for a period of twenty years after the Civil War. The shipbuilding industry could not overcome these handicaps, even though there was an increasing demand for ships to carry the growing commerce along the coast and on the Great Lakes.

World War I marked the beginning of an extraordinary period of American shipbuilding activity. Total tonnage was only 225,122 tons in 1915, but was over 12 million tons between 1917 and 1922. This notable increase in tonnage enlarged the merchant marine of the United States so greatly that there was little demand for new tonnage after the boom ended. Naval construction was reduced by the international disarmaments agreements in the 1920's, and in 1929 amounted to only 128,976 tons, the lowest amount since 1830.

World War II saw tremendous construction programs, in which the navy spent $19 billion, building everything from landing craft up to superdreadnoughts and carriers. The Maritime Commission spent $13 billion constructing 5,777 ships, including 2,708 of the standardized 10-knot Liberty ships; 414 of the faster 16.5-knot Victory ships, also of around

10,000 deadweight tons; 541 of the C-2s, C-3s, and other so-called tailor-made ships of the long-range program; and 702 tankers.

The end of the war brought another postwar shipbuilding slump. In 1956 only two freighters and six tankers were under construction. The postwar construction, however, did produce some distinctive new types of ships. The liner *United States,* built in 1952, established a record as the fastest afloat. The use of nuclear power was initiated by the submarine *Nautilus,* which was followed by several other nuclear-powered submarines. Nuclear reactors also powered the giant carrier *Enterprise* and the passenger liner *Savannah.*

The Merchant Marine Act of 1970 came as a blessing to the dwindling shipbuilding industry. It authorized construction subsidies to a wide range of vessels, especially the bulk and bulk-oil carriers. Although the act's programs were later cut back in budget reducing moves, numerous large contracts were let. In 1973 U.S. shipbuilders had approximately 3.2 million gross registered tons under construction or contract.

[E. G. Fassett, *The Shipbuilding Business in the United States of America;* L. C. Kendall, *The Business of Shipping.*]

ROBERT G. ALBION

SHIPPING, OCEAN. America from the beginning has had a particular interest in ocean shipping. The stormy 3,000 miles of the north Atlantic separating it from Europe has long been the most important of all sea lanes, both in the number of ships plying it and in the value of their cargoes. Those ships, whether they flew the American flag or the flag of another country, have represented all the major types of cargo carriers. A peculiarity of ocean shipping has been its international nature: the ships of one maritime nation have differed little from those of another, and the same has been true of the ritual and hierarchy of their officers and crews. The styles of ships go relatively unchanged for long periods, broken only very occasionally by a sudden revolution.

From early colonial times to about 1870 there was little change in the ordinary cargo ships (passenger liners have been a different matter). The conventional major carrier in those early years was the three-masted square-rigged ship, or bark. The earlier ones, like the *Mayflower,* had abnormally high poops and forecastles, which gradually gave way during the 18th century to relatively flush decks. But basically they were much the same, about 100 feet long and 30 feet wide, measuring about 300 tons, with hulls of oak and masts of pine or fir; they carried crews of about thirty men. Off the transatlantic main line, smaller vessels were used: two-masted square-rigged brigs for runs to the Mediterranean or the West Indies and still smaller fore- and aft-rigged schooners or sloops for coastal and other short runs. Ownership of such ships was divided into sixty-four shares; sometimes a single person owned all shares, sometimes the shares were divided among dozens of people. One important innovation in the early 19th century was the creation in 1818 of the American Black Ball Line, sailing on fixed schedules between New York City and Liverpool with passengers, mail, and fine freight, but still using conventional ships. This new line pattern, highly profitable, expanded, but chiefly from New York.

The coming of steam gradually led to a new pattern. Robert Fulton's *Clermont* first plied the Hudson River in 1807, and in 1838 regular transatlantic service by steam-driven ships began. The early engines used so much fuel that governments were forced to subsidize steamers; consequently ordinary cargoes still continued to go by square-riggers, now somewhat larger.

A quiet revolution occurred about 1870 with the compound engine, which, by using the steam twice (and later three or four times), cut costs, so that a freighter could profitably carry such heavy cargoes as grain, coal, and sugar. These new freighters gradually drove the square-riggers from their older runs. Measuring only a few thousand tons, with iron (and later steel) hulls, some served on regular line runs, but most of them were operated as tramp steamers, picking up cargoes wherever they could find them. The American shipbuilders, who had done well with the wooden square-riggers, now could not compete with the cheaper British building costs of the new freighters. Only in the protected coastal waters did American-built ships prevail.

The smaller freighters were particularly badly hit by German submarines in World War I, but their design became the basis for the type of ship that restored America to top merchant marine position after the war. The thousands of Liberty and Victory ships built in U.S. shipyards during World War II were essentially the same type, although by that time they were fueled by oil rather than coal.

By the 1920's the oil tanker was a prominent part of ocean shipping, and the older type of freighters became known as dry cargo ships. The rapid development of the automobile stimulated a worldwide demand for oil. The U.S. World War II emergency program produced numerous 16,000-ton T-2 tankers, which became the standard for a while. Many tankers were owned by the major oil companies, and because of high American crew wages, many were registered in the merchant marines of Panama and Liberia.

An important innovation of the 1960's was the introduction of containerization. At a time when labor costs became the crucial factor in most merchant marines, shippers began to seek cheaper methods of loading and unloading ships. The previous cargo ships, first under sail and then under steam, had open holds into which longshoremen loaded the individual bags, boxes, and bales that made up a cargo, a time-honored and time-consuming process. The shippers remedied this by assembling the cargo beforehand and sending it aboard in a single container. One early step was the so-called "sea train," where loaded freight cars could be run aboard on tracks and run off at the other end. Later came other "roll on–roll off" devices for the same purpose. Then came big metal containers; a large ship might have a thousand of them hoisted aboard. But even with these devices, the ship had to put into port to load or unload. To save more time, the LASH (lighter-aboard-ship) system was inaugurated, whereby scores of self-operating little lighters could be hoisted over the side to run into port while the mother ship kept on without loss of time (a ship's stay in port could cost several thousand dollars a day).

The most dramatic innovation during the 1960's was the vastly increased tonnage of tankers and bulk carriers. The T-2 tanker of World War II measured 16,000 tons. Tonnage increased gradually after that; about 1970 the designation "very large crude carrier" (VLCC) was applied to ships of 150,000 tons or more. By the autumn of 1972 six ships measuring more than 250,000 tons were under construction and one of nearly 500,000 tons was planned.

Two factors brought on this amazing expansion. The first was the closing of the Suez Canal in the Arab-Israeli war of 1967. Some tankers from the Persian Gulf had already been getting rather large for the canal, and now there was no choice except to go around the Cape of Good Hope. It was found that the larger the ship, the less the cost per barrel of oil. Also, the longer Good Hope route meant higher tanker earnings, stimulating new construction. The second factor was American concern at the same time about its overseas supplies of raw materials. U.S. oil reserves were dropping, and the old self-sufficiency in iron ore was dwindling, with substitute ore supplies

necessary from Venezuela and northeastern Canada. Bulk carriers were developed in considerable numbers. More efficient utilization of ships was also tried. The tanker trade was traditionally a one-way affair, returning in ballast. Now some tankers carried oil one way and ore or bulk grain the other.

One serious consideration in the increased tanker size was the matter of finding where to land the oil; few ports could provide the necessary draft. Offshore loading into pipe facilities seemed one answer. Coastal communities, moreover, were concerned with the danger of oil spills, especially after a number of serious accidents had shown what extensive damage could result.

With the help of a subsidy act passed in 1970, the United States was beginning to build some new types of oceangoing ships, but it still lagged behind other countries, discounting the fact that nearly half the vessels in the Liberian merchant marine were American-owned.

[Lane C. Kendall, *The Business of Shipping;* B. Landstrom, *The Ship: An Illustrated History;* Samuel G. Lawrence, *U.S. Merchant Shipping, Policies, and Politics;* Alan Villiers, *Men, Ships and the Sea.*]

ROBERT G. ALBION

SHIPPING ACT OF 1916 created the U.S. Shipping Board empowered to construct or buy vessels for use in commerce or as naval and military auxiliaries and to operate them or lease or sell them to American citizens. In time of emergency the transfer or sale of American-flag ships to foreign registry or ownership was restricted and the president was given power to conscript vessels. Various practices, including deferred rebates, were declared unfair and prohibited to ocean common carriers. (*See also* Emergency Fleet Corporation.)

FRANK A. SOUTHARD, JR.

SHIPPING BOARD, UNITED STATES, created by the Shipping Act of 1916, controlled the Emergency (later Merchant) Fleet Corporation, established in 1917, and carried out World War I and postwar merchant marine policy. It was superseded in 1933 by the U.S. Shipping Board Bureau of the Department of Commerce, which in 1936 gave way to the U.S. Maritime Commission. (*See also* Merchant Marine.)

[United States Shipping Board, *Annual Reports.*]

FRANK A. SOUTHARD, JR.

SHIPS OF THE LINE, or line-of-battle ships, were the 18th- and early 19th-century counterparts of modern first-class battleships, ships fit to engage the most formidable enemy ships in battle line. As planned for the U.S. Navy, they were about 190 feet long, of about 2,600 tons displacement, mounted at least 74 guns on three decks, though the largest, the *Pennsylvania,* mounted 120 guns. The first U.S. ship of this type, the *America,* was launched at Portsmouth, N.H., Nov. 5, 1782, and was given to the French. Congress authorized six "seventy-fours" in 1799, but none was built. In 1813 Congress authorized four more, which were completed. The *New Orleans,* built at Sackets Harbor on Lake Ontario, was never launched; the *Franklin* was converted into a steamer in 1854; the *Washington* was broken up in 1843; and the *Independence* served as a naval receiving ship until its sale in 1913.

In 1816 Congress authorized nine more ships of the line: *Columbus, Ohio, Pennsylvania, Vermont, Virginia, Delaware, Alabama, New York,* and *North Carolina.* The *Virginia* and *New York* were never completed. The *Pennsylvania, Columbus,* and *Delaware* were burned at the Norfolk Navy Yard on Apr. 20, 1861. The *Vermont, North Carolina,* and *Ohio* were long used as receiving ships at navy yards; and the *Alabama* (renamed the *New Hampshire* in 1864 and the *Granite State* in 1904) was used as a training ship by the New York Naval Militia until 1921. None of these ships was ever engaged in battle. The introduction of steam, explosive shells, and armor plate rendered them obsolete before they could be used in actual warfare.

[Louis H. Bolander, "Ships-of-the-line of the Old Navy," *U.S. Naval Institute Proceedings* (October 1938); G. F. Emmons, *The Navy of the United States, From the Commencement, 1775 to 1783.*]

LOUIS H. BOLANDER

SHIRT-SLEEVE DIPLOMACY. Concerning a note written by Secretary of State Walter Q. Gresham in 1895 to the British government during the seal fisheries controversy, a British editor, alleging its crudeness and tactlessness, remarked caustically that the secretary would appear to have written it in his shirt sleeves. American secretaries of state and diplomats had for years been accused by Europeans (and by some Americans as well) of ineptitude, unnecessary bluntness, even truculence at times—the result of appointing inexperienced men to such positions. Many Americans professed to accept the British editor's quip as a compliment, as picturing a diplomacy less verbose and more frank and honest than the old sort.

[David Starr Jordan, *Democracy and World Relations.*]

ALVIN F. HARLOW

SHIVAREE, derived from the French word *charivari,* meaning mock music made on pots and pans, designates in America, particularly in the Middle West, an old custom, of serenading newly wedded couples with a variety of noisemaking devices, the object being to exact a "treat." Refusal to serve the serenaders with refreshments resulted in some form of hazing. The shivaree, like the barn dance, was a popular form of rural entertainment. In New England the custom was referred to as a serenade or callathump.

W. J. BURKE

SHOE MANUFACTURING. *See* **Boot and Shoe Manufacturing.**

SHOOTING MATCH reached its apex of popularity in the backwoods of the South during the early 19th century. The prize was at times a turkey or a cow. For a cow valued at $20, contestants paid the owner 25 cents a shot, eighty shots to be purchased. Any entrant could buy any number of shots. The best shot took the hide and tallow; second and third best shots, a hindquarter each, and so on. A shooting match was likely to be an all-day festival, women quilting and providing food, and everybody dancing through the night.

[David Crockett, *Tour to the North and East.*]

J. FRANK DOBIE

SHOP COMMITTEE, or works council movement, was a phase of intensified efforts of employers shortly before and during World War I to allay labor unrest and reduce industrial friction. The distinctive feature of the shop committee was joint representation of employers and employees on a single body; additional features generally found in this type of organization were restriction of jurisdiction to one establishment and of powers to the settlement of grievances.

The War Labor Board was an active sponsor of shop committees and secured their establishment in over 600 plants. During the 1920's the movement gradually died down, and the committees were either abandoned or else transformed into employee-representation plans or company unions.

[C. E. French, *The Shop Commitee in the United States.*]

MYRON W. WATKINS

"SHOT HEARD ROUND THE WORLD," a line from Ralph Waldo Emerson's *Concord Hymn,* a poem written for the dedication in 1837 of the monument at Concord Bridge in Massachusetts. The line is also carved on the base of Daniel Chester French's statue *The Minute Man of Concord,* erected at Concord in 1875. The line has been accepted by Americans as expressing the patriotism of the colonists who, risking everything in an immediate crisis, began the war that led to American independence. The first stanza of the *Concord Hymn* is as follows:

By the rude bridge that arched the flood,
Their flag to April's breeze unfurled,
Here once the embattled farmers stood,
And fired the shot heard round the world.

ALLEN FRENCH

SHOWBOATS. William Chapman, an English actor, had a small floating theater built at Pittsburgh in 1828 and, with his family of six as the entire company, toured the Ohio and Mississippi rivers until his death in 1839. His widow then managed the boat until 1847, when she sold it to Sol Smith, a popular midwestern comedian of the period. Other showboats appeared on the Ohio-Mississippi river system before the Civil War, including two circus craft, those of Spalding and Rogers and Dan Rice's Floating Palace. John Robinson's circus also traveled the rivers through one season as a boat show. Meanwhile, Henry Butler had in 1836 placed a boat on the Erie Canal system—by day a "museum" with a few stuffed animals and wax figures, by night a theater. A fleet of three boats on the Pennsylvania canals, lashed alongside each other at night with the sides removed, became one auditorium, where a vaudeville performance was given. The Civil War damaged the showboat business, but it revived again in the 1870's. Capt. A. B. French launched the boat *French's New Sensation* for four years before selling it. The Menke brothers, noted river showmen, later owned it and the *Golden Rod.* In 1890 Capt. C. F. Breidenbaugh launched the *Theatorium,* the finest boat yet seen on the rivers. W. P. Newman's Great American Water Circus, which carried forty horses and fourteen parade wagons, appeared on the Ohio in 1901. Two big barges side by side with hulls filled with earth and a canvas top overhead, supplied the ring. In 1925 there were fourteen showboats on the midwestern rivers and one touring Chesapeake Bay and the North Carolina sounds. The last showboat to tour on a regular basis in the United States was the *Golden Rod* (1943).

[Philip Graham, *Showboats: The History of an American Institution;* Wesley W. Stout, "Tonight on the River Landing," *Saturday Evening Post* (Oct. 31, 1925).]
ALVIN F. HARLOW

SHREVEPORT RATE CASE, or *Houston, E. and W. T. R. Company* v. *United States,* 234 U.S. 342 (1914), a landmark in the extension of the power of the federal government to regulate commerce within the individual states. The case grew out of a complaint by jobbing interests of Shreveport, La., against the authority of the Texas Railroad Commission to fix rates on freight shipments wholly within the state of Texas, where rates were lower than those on comparable shipments between Louisiana and Texas. In 1911 the Railway Commission of Louisiana, acting at the direction of the Louisiana legislature, placed the complaint before the Interstate Commerce Commission, which decided against the discriminatory rates. The case was appealed to the federal courts, and in a momentous decision the Supreme Court held that Congress through such an agency as the Interstate Commerce Commission may step in and override rates prescribed by a state within its borders, if such rates impose an "undue burden" on interstate commerce as a whole, or if they unduly discriminate against persons and localities shipping in interstate commerce.

S. H. ACHESON

SIBERIAN EXPEDITION (1918–20), the invasion and occupation of eastern Siberia by Allied forces. The reasons behind the invasion have been disputed, but it is generally believed that the main purpose was to keep Siberia out of German hands, thereby preventing Germany from making use of its vast natural resources. Its immediate purpose was to rescue the Czechoslovak Legion, a unit of nationalist Czechs that had been formed to fight the Germans and had attached itself to the Russian army. The legion had found itself isolated in Russia after the collapse of the czarist government. The new revolutionary government in Russia, which had taken Russia out of the war with the signing of the Treaty of Brest-Litovsk on Mar. 3, 1918, regarded the Siberian expedition as an unwarranted involvement by the Allies in its internal affairs. The U.S. government at first seemed to concur in that estimate; when Japanese and British troops landed at Vladivostok on Apr. 9, 1918, President Woodrow Wilson protested strongly.

At the time of the Allied invasion, the Bolshevik government had granted the Czechoslovak Legion the use of the Trans-Siberian railroad in its effort to reach Vladivostok. Once at that port city, it was the plan of the Czechs to sail for France and resume their fight against Germany on the western front. Strung out in groups, with a vanguard already at Vladivostok, the Czechs were persuaded, principally by the French, to turn and head westward for Archangel (Arkhangelsk) in northwestern Russia. Archangel would afford swifter transport to the western front. When collisions with the Bolshevik forces resulted, Wilson reluctantly allowed U.S. troops to land in order to help rescue the struggling Czechs and to restrain the Japanese, who were suspected of having territorial designs on eastern Siberia.

The Czechs, caught in the turbulence of Russia's continuing civil war and goaded on by France, complicated the issue by deciding to fight actively with the anti-Bolshevik White Army forces, which were led by Adm. Aleksandr Vasilievich Kolchak. Meanwhile, Maj. Gen. William S. Graves sailed from San Francisco with a contingent on Sept. 2, 1918, to join the U.S. regular Twenty-seventh and Thirty-first infantry regiments from Manila in the Philippines. Having a force of about 10,000, including experienced railroad men, Graves assumed responsibility for the Trans-Siberian east of Lake Baikal. From the rise and fall of Kolchak as would-be dictator of Siberia between Nov. 18, 1918, and Dec. 27, 1919, Graves scrupulously refrained from endorsing either the Whites or the Reds. Skirmishes that did take place, resulting in the deaths of thirty-six U.S. soldiers, were against Russian bandits for the most part, rather than against either czarist or Bolshevik forces.

Finally, the Czechs bought peace with the Bolsheviks by delivering Kolchak into their hands. The Czechoslovak Legion was then allowed to resume evacuation from Russia. Thus, in January 1920 Graves was ordered to recall his men to Vladivostok. In April 1920 the last Americans sailed for home, thereby ending one of the more bizarre episodes of World War I.

[W. S. Graves, *America's Siberian Adventure*; George F. Kennan, *The Decision to Intervene*; B. M. Unterberger, *America's Siberian Expedition.*]

DONALD W. HUNT

SIBLEY EXPEDITION TO DAKOTA. *See* **Dakota Expeditions of Sibley and Sully.**

SIBLEY EXPEDITION TO THE RIO GRANDE. *See* **Rio Grande, Sibley's Operations on.**

SICILIAN CAMPAIGN. In accordance with a decision made at the Casablanca Conference in January 1943, combined British and American ground, naval, and air forces under Lt. Gen. Dwight D. Eisenhower invaded Sicily on July 10, 1943, and conquered the island in thirty-eight days. Lt. Gen. Bernard L. Montgomery's British Eighth Army, including Canadian troops, landed on the eastern coast of Sicily; Lt. Gen. George S. Patton's Seventh U.S. Army came ashore on the southern coast. They were opposed by Gen. Alfredo Guzzoni's Sixth Army of 200,000 Italian troops, plus 30,000 Germans. Bad weather endangered the amphibious landings and widely dispersed airborne landings by parachute and glider, but the invasion was successful against moderate resistance. The most violent reaction was a counterattack at Gela, which was quickly contained.

With a beachhead well in hand, Montgomery advanced through Syracuse and Augusta to Catania, in order to seize Messina, the decisive objective. Patton was to protect his flank, but he obtained permission from Gen. Harold Alexander, the Allied ground commander, to extend westward toward Palermo. Patton's drive gained power and momentum, and on July 22 he took the city. Montgomery was halted before Catania by a strong defensive line anchored on Mount Etna.

At a conference at Feltre, Austria, on July 19, Adolf Hitler and Benito Mussolini decided to commit more German troops to Sicily. Six days later, in Rome, Mussolini was deposed from power, kidnapped, and imprisoned. Marshal Pietro Badoglio, the new head of the Italian government, assured Hitler he would continue the alliance, but he soon sought to surrender. Suspicious of eventual Italian capitulation, Hitler began to favor evacuating Sicily in order to avoid having his forces trapped on the island. Lt. Gen. Hans-Valentine Hube, the German commander in Sicily, began to displace Guzzoni and take control of the fighting, and by August the Axis effort in the northeastern corner of Sicily became a distinct delaying action designed to preserve conditions for an orderly withdrawal to the mainland.

With Patton having reached Palermo and the northern shore of Sicily, Alexander gave him permission, on July 25, to advance on Messina. Thus began converging advances and a contest between Montgomery and Patton to take Messina first. Patton launched three small amphibious end runs to help his forces forward; Montgomery, after taking Catania on Aug. 5, instituted a single amphibious operation.

On Aug. 8, Hitler decided to evacuate Sicily. The

withdrawal started Aug. 11. Meticulously planned and organized, with detailed timetables for troop movements to ferries at Messina, the operation successfully transported about 125,000 men, plus their equipment, to the mainland.

On Aug. 17, Patton entered Messina, and the campaign ended. Patton's triumph was marred by subsequent public knowledge that on two occasions he had slapped two soldiers who had been hospitalized for combat exhaustion. The unfavorable publicity almost brought his military career to a close.

[Martin Blumenson, *Sicily: Whose Victory?*]

MARTIN BLUMENSON

SIC SEMPER TYRANNIS ("Thus always to tyrants"), the motto of Virginia since 1776. It was recommended by George Mason, its probable originator. When President Abraham Lincoln was fatally shot on Apr. 14, 1865, in Ford's Theater in Washington, D.C., his assassin, John Wilkes Booth, shouted *"Sic semper tyrannis!* The South is avenged!"

IRVING DILLIARD

SIDELING HILL, a ridge rising to an elevation of 2,195 feet, approximately seventeen miles west of Fort Loudon, Pa. It was the site of an attack by the Black Boys in March 1765 on a convoy of eastern goods on its way to the Indian country beyond Fort Pitt.

In order to open the Illinois Country to military occupation and trade, the British government dispatched George Croghan, a famous trader, to take presents of ammunition, dry goods, and liquor to the Indians. At Fort Pitt this shipment was augmented by a large consignment from the firm of Baynton, Wharton and Morgan. Incensed at a series of Indian raids during and after Pontiac's War (1763) and convinced that the much-needed supplies being brought by Croghan would precipitate another period of Indian raiding, the people of the Conococheague Valley determined to prevent the delivery of the goods, particularly arms that might be used against them. When his appeals to Croghan to turn back went unheeded, Col. James Smith collected ten members of the Black Boys, a vigilante group, and ambushed the pack train on Sideling Hill; the attackers burned those goods they did not take. The Black Boys continued to patrol the road and permitted no goods to pass without their inspection.

[Albert T. Volwiler, *George Croghan and the Westward Movement.*]

R. J. FERGUSON

SIEGFRIED LINE, the name given by Allied troops to fortifications erected before World War II along Germany's western frontier. The name probably was derived either from a German defensive position of World War I, the *Siegfriedstellung,* or from the Siegfried legend celebrated in Richard Wagner's operas; it was popularized by a British music hall tune, "We're Going to Hang Out the Washing on the Siegfried Line." Known to the Germans as the Westwall, it was begun in 1938 as a short belt of fortifications in the Saar region opposite France's Maginot Line, but later was extended to the Swiss and Dutch frontiers. No thin line of *gros ouvrages* like the Maginot Line, the Siegfried Line was a band approximately three miles deep of more than 3,000 mutually supporting concrete pillboxes, troop shelters, and command posts. Where no natural antitank obstacles existed, a belt of pyramidal concrete projections called "dragon's teeth" barred access across the terrain. Touted by German propagandists as impregnable, the line contributed to German success in bluffing France and Great Britain at Munich in 1938.

The line was neglected following German victory over France in 1940 and appeared to German field commanders to have little utility; but as Allied armies approached in September 1944, Adolf Hitler decreed that it be held. The U.S. V Corps opposite the Belgian Ardennes and the VII Corps south of Aachen quickly penetrated the line, only to be contained by German reserves. An attempt to outflank the line with an airborne attack in the Netherlands failed. A penetration in October by the XIX Corps north of Aachen precipitated no deep advance, so that not until early spring of 1945, after German strength had been dissipated in a futile counteroffensive (the Battle of the Bulge), was the line pierced along its full length.

[Charles B. MacDonald, *The Siegfried Line Campaign,* and *The Mighty Endeavor.*]

CHARLES B. MACDONALD

SIGNAL CORPS, U.S. ARMY, was created by Congress on June 21, 1860. Albert James Myer, the first signal officer, is regarded as the father of the corps. For over a century the term "Signal Corps" (and, for a time, "Signal Service") referred to both a separate unit within the War Department (and its successor, the Department of the Army) and the units having primary responsibility for army signal communications.

The Signal Corps, which first used Myer's wigwag system of visual signaling, in 1862 introduced the Beardslee magnetoelectric tactical telegraph machine.

This soon led to a conflict with the U.S. Military Telegraph and to Myer's replacement for a time. The Military Telegraph ended with the Civil War, and, as the years passed, the corps became responsible for army photography; established a pigeon service; and adapted to its uses the conventional electric telegraph, heliograph, and telephone, as well as radio, radar, and the communications satellite. From 1870 to 1891 the Signal Corps provided the United States with its first national weather service, which in 1891 became the Weather Bureau, and from 1908 to 1918 directed the army's first aeronautical program using heavier-than-air craft.

In 1962 the Signal Corps lost responsibility for training, research and development, procurement, and other functions, and on Mar. 1, 1964, the chief signal officer (then David Gibbs) became the chief of communications-electronics (CC-E) because it was believed that the term "signal" did not reflect the sophisticated new communications techniques. The functions of the office were broadened, and staff and command functions were separated by establishing the U.S. Army Strategic Communications Command (USASTRATCOM) under the chief of staff but with the CC-E responsible for staff supervision. In 1973, with new functions added, USASTRATCOM became the U.S. Army Communications Command (USACC). On Sept. 16, 1967, the CC-E became the assistant chief of staff for communications-electronics (ACSC-E), a position filled by a major general of the Signal Corps until elimination of the position in a major staff reorganization and transfer of functions in 1974. Throughout all these changes, which eliminated the Signal Corps as a bureau, the Signal Corps continued as an indispensable branch of the army, its members wearing the crossed-flags and torch insignia, a stylized representation of Myer's old wigwag equipment.

[M. Deutrich, compiler, *Preliminary Inventory of the Records of the Chief Signal Officer*, Record Group III, National Archives; P. J. Scheips, "Albert James Myer, Founder of the Army Signal Corps," Ph.D. diss., The American University; D. Terrett, G. R. Thompson, D. R. Harris, and P. M. Oakes, *The Signal Corps: The Emergency, The Test, and The Outcome*, United States Army in World War II: The Technical Services.]

PAUL J. SCHEIPS

SIGN LANGUAGE, a method of gesture communication in general use among Indians of the Great Plains area, developed because of the nomadic existence of the interior tribes that, following the buffalo, frequently met other tribes with alien tongues.

Largely manual, it became a remarkable *lingua franca,* so universal that a Blackfoot from the Canadian border could freely exchange ideas with a Comanche from the Staked Plain although neither understood the other's spoken language.

Signs originally were pantomimic but many have been conventionalized. Thus the sign for "wolf"—the upraised hand with the first two fingers pointing up, the thumb and other fingers touching tips—may mean the animal, a member of the Pawnee or "wolf" tribe, or the abstract idea of sagacity, a quality ascribed to the coyote. Basic simplicity made the sign language not difficult to learn and many white men were proficient in it.

[W. P. Clark, *The Indian Sign Language.*]

PAUL I. WELLMAN

SILHOUETTES, or black profile portraits cut out of paper or painted on cards, were used as wall decorations during the first half-century of the republic. Well-known silhouettists included William M. S. Doyle and Henry Williams, both of whom worked in Boston, and William Bache, who was an itinerant. Another itinerant was the boy silhouettist Master Hubard, who cut profiles in 20 seconds. Auguste Edouart, a French visitor to America, cut full-length silhouettes. William Henry Brown, who was born in Charleston, S.C., likewise cut full-length silhouettes, and he published a *Portrait Gallery of Distinguished American Citizens* in 1855.

[E. S. Bolton, *Wax Portraits and Silhouettes;* A. Van L. Carrick, *Shades of Our Ancestors.*]

THEODORE BOLTON

SILK CULTURE AND MANUFACTURE. Sericulture, with its lure of high returns for apparently low labor and capital inputs, attracted American farmers from the foundation of the colonies through the 19th century. Efforts at silkworm raising, most prolonged in Georgia in the 18th century and in Connecticut during the early national period, failed mainly because the amounts and levels of skill required in silkworm breeding and cocoon reeling were underestimated. Silk growing was generally abandoned after the Chinese mulberry tree (*Morus multicaulis*) craze of the 1830's collapsed by 1845.

Small mills that manufactured sewing silk, ribbons, and trimmings from imported raw silk appeared in New England after 1810. Silk throwing (yarn making) reached the factory stage by the 1840's, when the industry was centered in Philadelphia, New York

City, and the Connecticut River valley. The invention of the sewing machine increased demand for sewing silks after 1850.

Following the Civil War major growth was spurred by the imposition of luxury tariffs on imported silk products (1861, 1864) and the completion of a direct transpacific and transcontinental route (1869). Simultaneously the industry relocated to northern New Jersey, particularly Paterson, which offered cheap female labor and proximity to New York markets. Power-loom silk weaving after 1870 brought the factory production of broad goods. The continuing sophistication of automatic machinery and pressures from New Jersey labor unions persuaded the silk throwers and spinners to move in search of cheap labor to the mining towns of Pennsylvania in the 1880's. Weaving mills followed. By the 1920's Pennsylvania and New Jersey contained three-quarters of the nation's silk industry; the former supplanted the latter as the leading silk-producing state before 1919, but Paterson retained its superiority in fine and fancy goods.

By means of the tariff, labor-saving technology, high-quality Japanese raw silk, and long production runs of simple weaves for mass markets, American silk manufacturers developed an industry whose growth caused a rise in annual raw silk imports from $3 million in 1870 to $427 million in 1929. After 1900 the demand for hosiery yarns became particularly important.

Increased production of synthetic fibers after the 1930's and the interruption of silk imports from Japan and China during World War II shrank the industry. Its annual raw-silk consumption fell from a peak of 81 million pounds in 1930 to 48 million in 1940, 11 million in 1950, 7 million in 1960, and 2 million in 1970.

[Shichiro Matsui, *The History of the Silk Industry in the United States;* Paul W. Gates, *The Farmer's Age: Agriculture, 1815–1860;* U.S. Bureau of the Census, *Historical Statistics of the United States: Colonial Times to 1957.*]

DAVID J. JEREMY

SILL, FORT, a military reservation in southwestern Oklahoma, is the site of the U.S. Army Artillery and Guided Missile Center and School. It was established as Camp Wichita on Jan. 8, 1869, near the foot of the Wichita Mountains in what is now Comanche County by Gen. Philip H. Sheridan. It was renamed Fort Sill on July 2, honoring Brig. Gen. Joshua W. Sill, U.S. Army Volunteers. During the Indian Wars it was a center for negotiations with a number of tribes, in-

cluding the Comanche, Kiowa, and Wichita, and served as a base for numerous campaigns. Remnants of Geronimo's Apache were held there as prisoners of war from 1869 to 1877. Among early commanding officers were William Tecumseh Sherman and George A. Custer. In 1871 Sherman arrested the Indian chiefs Satanta, Satank, and Big Tree and confined them at the fort.

The School of Fire for Field Artillery was established at Fort Sill in 1911. Also established at the fort was the School of Musketry, forerunner of the Infantry School, Fort Benning, Ga., and, after World War II, the Army Aviation School, subsequently moved to Fort Rucker, Ala. During World War I, Camp Doniphan was located on the reservation.

[Wilbur S. Nye, *Carbine and Lance: The Story of Old Fort Sill.*]

CHARLES B. MACDONALD

SILVER AS MONEY. *See* **Bimetallism; Bland-Allison Act; Free Silver; Money; Pittman Act; Sherman Silver Purchase Act; Silver Legislation; Trade Dollar.**

SILVER DEMOCRATS, a term used at various times after 1878 to refer to those members of the Democratic party who were active advocates of free coinage of silver at the 16 to 1 ratio. More general use of the term "Silver Democrats" followed the inauguration of President Grover Cleveland in 1893 and his calling of a special session of Congress to repeal the Sherman Silver Purchase Act of 1890, which required the U.S. Treasury to buy virtually all silver mined in the United States. This repeal split the party wide open, with Silver Democrats in opposition to the administration, which in turn used every means at its command to force Democrats in Congress to support the administration's plan. From 1893 until the national convention of July 1896, the Silver Democrats were a large faction of the party at odds with the official leadership. That convention was a test of strength between the administration and the Silver Democrats, and had the latter lost, undoubtedly many of them would have joined the other free-coinage factions in support of a fusion candidate. But their complete victory at the convention made the Silver Democrats the regulars beyond question, and the term tended to fall into disuse. This result was encouraged also by the decline of free coinage as a political issue. Nevertheless, the platform of 1900 was a Silver Democratic document, and only in 1904 was free coinage repudiated by the party's candidate, Alton B. Parker.

[J. F. Rhodes, *History of the United States*.]

ELMER ELLIS

SILVER DOLLAR. *See* **Money.**

SILVER GRAYS, a name given to a conservative minority of New York's Whig party in 1850. Approving of the conciliatory policies of President Millard Fillmore, the faction bolted the party's state convention of 1850 when the radical antislavery attitude of Sen. William H. Seward was endorsed. The faction was called the Silver Grays because of the color of the hair of Francis Granger, one of the bolters. A few weeks later the Silver Grays called a convention of their own.

[A. C. Flick, ed., *History of the State of New York*, vol. VI.]

A. C. FLICK

SILVER LEAGUE, a term applied to various pro-silver propaganda organizations of the late 19th century. More precisely, it referred to the American Bimetallic League, which was organized in 1892 and which, under the leadership of A. J. Warner, was the most active agitator of the silver cause. In 1895 it consolidated with its principal competitor, the National Bimetallic Union, which was under the direction of Edwin B. Light. The new organization, the American Bimetallic Union, was exceedingly active in 1896 in spreading the free-coinage doctrine and in attempting to bring about a union of all silver factions in national politics.

ELMER ELLIS

SILVER LEGISLATION refers to U.S. statutes regulating silver coinage and/or affecting the interests of silver miners as a class. Both types of legislation have loomed large in American history.

It was the intention of the founders of the nation to establish a genuine bimetallism, that is, a monetary system in which both gold and silver were legal tender. It has been generally accepted by historians that this policy was based on the theory—offered by Alexander Hamilton, the first secretary of the Treasury, in his *Mint Report*—that under bimetallism there is a more plentiful supply of money. Another reason for bimetallism was the fact that the principle of sub-

sidiary silver coinage (that is, the use of silver alloys for coins of smaller denomination than the currency unit) was unknown to science or to history, and bimetallism was a necessity if small units of silver were to be coined.

The bimetallic system was a failure. Revision of the legal ratio between the values of gold and silver in 1834 and 1837 created an adequate gold coinage but drove out the limited silver coinage in circulation, since the free-market value of silver was higher than its monetary value. From 1834 on, American silver coins as standard money ceased to play a part in the life of the nation. The establishment by Congress of subsidiary silver coinage in 1853 confirmed this situation legally. But the 1853 statute accidentally left the silver dollar as a standard coin, although the market value of silver continued to make its coinage impossible. In a revision of the statutes in 1873 the unknown piece was dropped (*see* Crime of 1873).

In 1873 the world market ratio of silver to gold fell below 16 to 1 for the first time in history. This decline coincided with the opening of rich silver mines in the West, with the post–Civil War deflation, and with a deep depression that sorely afflicted the country (*see* Panic of 1873). The consequence was a political movement, promoted by the silver interests and embraced by agrarian and proinflation elements for the restoration of bimetallism. Eventually there developed in the Senate and less definitely in the House a nonpartisan "silver bloc," led by members from the sparsely populated western states in which mine owners gained great political influence.

In the 1870's, 1890's, and 1930's, the efforts of this pressure group, reinforced by the popular clamor for inflation, almost achieved bimetallism and succeeded in extracting from Congress legislation giving a cash subsidy of some sort to the producers of silver. For example, the Bland-Allison Act of 1878 (passed over President Rutherford B. Hayes's veto) required the U.S. Treasury to buy $2 million to $4 million worth of silver a month. The Sherman Silver Purchase Act of 1890 (signed by President Benjamin Harrison but repealed at the insistence of President Grover Cleveland in 1893) mandated Treasury purchases of 4.5 million ounces of silver a month, an amount roughly equivalent to the total estimated U.S. production in 1890.

The Silver Purchase Act of 1934 followed an unprecedented decline in the price of silver during the depression that began in 1929. A flood of proposals for subsidies to silver miners was urged on Congress. The futile 1933 World Economic Conference at

London enacted, under pressure from U.S. participants, an agreement for stabilizing silver prices, under cover of which, by presidential proclamation, the United States paid from 64.64 cents to 77 cents per ounce for domestic silver, which had a market value of 45 cents. Unable to achieve bimetallism at 16 to 1 (the market ratio was 70 to 1), the silver interests finally forced the passage of the Silver Purchase Act. It provided for the nationalization of domestic stocks of silver and for the purchase of silver by the Treasury until the price should reach $1.2929 per ounce or the value of the amount held should equal one-third of the value of the government's gold holdings. The immediate effect of the legislation was a speculative rise in the market price of silver to 81 cents an ounce, which destroyed the currency systems of China and Mexico.

In 1939 the president's powers to debase the gold standard and buy silver were renewed, and Congress was allowed to set the price for domestic silver. It was pegged initially at 71 cents an ounce, 36 cents above the market price.

In World War II a shortage of silver developed, and the price rose rapidly. Under the leadership of Sen. Patrick McCarran of Nevada measures were blocked that would have provided government silver for defense production, for industrial use in nonwar industries, and for use by U.S. allies. Finally, in 1943, the Green Act provided that U.S. industries might buy silver from the Treasury at the price originally paid for it, and large amounts of silver, all of which was returned, were lent to U.S. allies.

In the 1960's, when strong industrial demand for silver created another worldwide shortage, the metal was virtually eliminated from the U.S. monetary system. The Silver Purchase Act was repealed in 1963. Two years later, under the Coinage Act of 1965, silver was eliminated from two subsidiary coins (the quarter and dime) and its content in the half-dollar was reduced from 90 percent to 40 percent. By another act of Congress, U.S. Treasury certificates could no longer be redeemed in silver after June 28, 1968.

[F. A. Bradford, *Money and Banking;* N. Carothers, *Fractional Money;* Milton Friedman and Anna Jacobson, *A Monetary History of the United States, 1867–1960;* Allen Weinstein, *Prelude to Populism: Origins of the Silver Issue, 1867–1878.*]

NEIL CAROTHERS

SILVER, PEWTER, AND OTHER METAL-WORK. The history of American silver work is easily traced, for there were hundreds of early silversmiths and their documented pieces are plentiful.

Works in pewter are likewise extant in quantity, but documented pieces in the other metals are less available.

Silver. Known work in silver dates to the 17th-century output of the partnership of John Hull and Robert Sanderson in Boston, working from about 1652 to about 1683. The synonymous use of the terms "goldsmith" and "silversmith" in England and America during the 17th and 18th centuries witnessed to the fact that silversmiths worked in both metals, as they had done at least since the 13th century. It was then that England's apprenticeship system was established by the Worshipful Company of Goldsmiths of the City of London.

The apprenticeship system was transported to the colonies, where accordingly apprentices served their masters from the age of fourteen to the age of twenty-one, at which time they became eligible to practice their craft. City ordinances in Boston (1660) and New York City (1675) set down that no person could open shop who was not of age and had not served a full seven-year apprenticeship. His indenture prepared the silversmith to be a highly skilled artisan in the use of a considerable variety of tools. One early 18th-century inventory of a silversmith's tools lists nearly 400 items, including 65 hammers, 74 punches, and 8 pairs of tongs—all being of various lengths, shapes, and weights.

Working silver in the 17th and 18th centuries began with melted coins assayed to the sterling standard (925 parts silver to which 75 parts of copper were added for hardness); the metal was then cast into ingots from which were hammered disks or sheets. These disks were the base for raising objects, such as tankards and teapots, over stakes or anvils of different shapes using forming hammers. As the silver work hardened from repeated hammering, it had to be annealed, or heated, by bringing it to a dull red and then quenching it in a diluted sulfuric acid bath. Spouts, covers, and handles were made separately and applied, while handle tips, thumbpieces, and other small parts were cast. Moldings were made by drawing silver strips through shaped openings in a steel plate. Planishing with a flat-faced hammer removed hammer marks. At this stage all parts were assembled and soldered in preparation for decoration by chasing (removing no metal) or engraving (removing metal). Prior to the final polishing and burnishing, the maker's mark was struck on the piece, denoting its quality.

In England guilds required, in addition to the maker's mark, marks for place of origin, assay, and date.

SILVER, PEWTER, AND OTHER METALWORK

There were no American guilds during the 17th and 18th centuries, but the metal was usually assayed to the sterling standard. Baltimore (ca. 1814–29) was the only city to make this standard law after much petitioning had failed in other cities. American marks were usually the maker's initials; by 1725 the surname alone or full name was also used. In the 19th century the place of origin was sometimes added. From 1820 to 1860 American silver was usually marked "coin" or "pure silver coin" (900 parts pure), but after 1860 the common mark was "sterling." The Stamping Act of 1906 made sterling the measure of purity in American silver.

Most of the procedures in making silver objects were changed by the wide availability of sheet silver by the 1790's. Stamped borders and moldings were manufactured by 1810, and by 1860 the process was almost totally industrialized. Specialization was born and with it the engravers, chasers, stampers, and spinners. The Gorham firm was one of the first to adopt new stamping and spinning methods.

Centers of the craft were Boston, Philadelphia, and New York City in the 17th and 18th centuries and later Baltimore and Providence. Most provincial cities had silversmiths by the end of the 18th century. Ornamental work in silver was less common in America than on the Continent or in England. The emphasis in America was primarily utilitarian in both domestic and religious pieces. Drinking vessels such as beakers, mugs, tankards, and goblets were popular, as were items for the tea table and dining table. Not as common were clothing ornaments and small boxes.

American silver designs were distinctive parallels of English precedents. Although less ostentatious, American works were always of fine quality, as in the exemplary pieces by Paul Revere and Jacob Hurd of Boston, Myer Myers of New York City, and Joseph Richardson, Sr., of Philadelphia. These standards were maintained in the 19th century by the works of Obadiah Rich of Boston; the Forbes of New York City; Fletcher and Gardiner, and Chaudron and Rasch of Philadelphia; and Samuel Kirk of Baltimore. Later 19th-century firms producing fine examples of the art were Tiffany, Gorham, Whiting, and Kirk.

Pewter. Despite the great amounts of silverware produced in the 18th century, most tableware of the period was either wooden or pewter. There are fewer examples of prerevolutionary pewter than of silver, however. England's embargo on unwrought pewter was the main cause. Another cause is the innate softness of the metal; regular use, rough cleaning, and excesses in temperature were enough to wear away most pewter utensils in two years.

Pewter making began as early as 1630 in the Massachusetts Bay area. There were no guilds to assay American pewter, and makers were almost wholly dependent on damaged or discarded English pieces. Nonetheless the quality of the metal was high, if not always the workmanship. Originally the metal was tin-based, with varying amounts of lead added, but the English guilds later permitted the use of several alloys in pewter making.

Similarity in design of silver and pewter objects does not mean that silversmiths worked in both metals. Moreover, while the basic tools of the silversmith were the hammer, anvil, punch, and vise, the pewterer used mostly the mold and lathe. Techniques in forming pewter objects ranged from the simple procedures of button making to the critically delicate assembling of a tulip-shaped tankard. First, molds of brass or bronze were checked for tightness of fit; then their surfaces were coated, usually with carbon from a burning candle or pine taper, to keep the casting separate from the mold. Casting began with a reservoir of molten pewter, which when raised to the proper temperature was poured into the mold. After cooling, excess metal was either melted or snipped from the casting and the rough edges filed. Small holes were filled with molten pewter, and then the body was skimmed and burnished on a lathe. Parts and appendages were then fitted, fluxed, and soldered or fused with pewter with such skill in the latter procedure that several parts would appear to have been struck as a single piece. The maker's touch was then impressed on the object. Touches usually included the maker's surname or initials and place of origin, often with eagles or geometric shapes added.

So widespread was pewter in America during the 17th and 18th centuries that itinerant pewterers were common, and even isolated villages had at least one spoon molder and mender. Major cities for artisans were Hartford, Philadelphia, and New York City. Noteworthy pewterers were John Bassett of New York City and Samuel Danforth of Hartford. More than five generations of Danforths and their trainees were prolific from prerevolutionary times to the end of the britannia period (ca. 1860's), and their wares were known from New York to Georgia. Other superior works came from William Will of Philadelphia and Henry Will of New York City.

Styles of American pewterware were not as ornate or diverse as those of European origin. Perhaps the prohibitive cost and exacting task of making molds limited experimentation. As noted above, molds were essential in the craft during the 18th century and were bequeathed from generations of pewterers, as is clear in the works of the Danforths. A further restriction may have been that the techniques of casting did not facilitate elaborate ornamentation. American pewter, although emulating popular silver designs, was essentially utilitarian. Aside from tableware and serving pieces of all kinds, other diverse objects included baby bottles, candlesticks, inkstands, furniture hardware, and communion flagons.

As with the craft of silversmithing, manufacturing methods began to displace the American pewterer and his casting techniques by the second decade of the 19th century. Pewter's softness was at last surpassed by britannia metal, also known as white metal. It did not have to be annealed, did not work-harden, contained no lead, and would polish to a sheen comparable to that of silver.

Britannia was widely used by the English guilds in the 18th century. Its use in the colonies dates from 1814 in Salem, Mass., but it was not until the second quarter of the 19th century that stamping and spinning methods, new tools, the ready availability of raw materials, and increasing amounts of capital made britannia successful enough to compete with silver. The metal was easily rolled to uniform thickness for manufacturing, thus making it more accessible to the middle class. This increased demand encouraged mass production of single parts by specialists in making handles, spouts, and lids.

The first departure from the old casting methods was stamping. For this process two heavy steel blocks or dies were used—one fixed, upon which a sheet of britannia was placed, and the other raised and dropped upon the first, thus stamping out a part. Once formed the parts were then soldered and finished by the specialists. In 1829 William Porter of Connecticut perfected single-drop stamping, and it was only five years later that he patented the spinning technique. The lathe had always been a tool in the making of pewterware and britannia; spinning, however, was completed entirely on the lathe. Desired shapes of each part were cut into wooden chucks, which were then fastened to the headstock of the lathe; a disk of britannia was pressed between the head and tail stocks, with increasing pressure being applied on the disk by a long piece of wood or metal until it was fitted to the form of the chuck. The shells thus formed were soldered together along with cast spouts and handles.

Manufacturing, specialization, and the assembly line dominated pewter making, so that by the mid-1800's the craftsman and his single shop had been overwhelmed. The Taunton Britannia Company of Massachusetts, the Meridan Britannia Company of Connecticut, and Sellow and Company of Cincinnati were among the ninety-one companies listed in the 1890 U.S. census.

Objects of britannia before 1825 included plates, mugs, tankards, and porringers. Thereafter tastes required teapots, coffeepots, lamps, and candlesticks. These objects were not made with expensive molds and slower casting methods and were therefore duplicated in mass to respond to increased demand, often resulting in poor quality of design, especially after 1825. Teapots, for example, were often made of either two tops or two bottoms fitted together. Nonetheless, excellent works were produced by the Sellow mills and by such craftsmen as Henry Hopper of New York City, Roswell Gleason of Dorchester, Mass., and George Richardson of Providence.

Industrialization made obsolete the artisan and his methods; so, too, britannia had fallen from fashion by the late 1860's because of the advent in 1845 of electroplating, a process of electrolysis whereby a thin film of silver is affixed to a base metal. Electroplating made silverware available to the middle class.

Other Metals. Unlike the documentation of silver and pewter work, that of work in other metals is difficult, as there are only cursory 18th-century accounts of work in iron, brass, and copper. Tradesmen in these metals included coppersmiths, braziers, founders, blacksmiths, gunsmiths, and whitesmiths, who produced items for domestic and agricultural use and for other trades and industries of the age.

Existing pieces are numerous, but marked examples are rare. Attributions to American craftsmanship are usually made on stylistic grounds. Documentation shows that much of the work in these fields was imported, and English rule rigidly controlled colonial manufacture. Workshops were quietly operated in outpost areas, fulfilling the needs for metalwork by the whole rural population, far from the eyes of town authorities. After the Revolution, with freedom of commerce the new way of life, crafts flourished until the Industrial Revolution took its toll. Base metal wares, when marked at all, are encountered only rarely in the 18th century.

Ironworks were established early in Falling Creek, Va. (1619–24), and on the Saugus River in Lynn, Mass. (1643). Copper mills were established by the mid-18th century. Before the Revolution, England encouraged mining in the colonies but frowned on the manufacturing of finished objects in iron, brass, or copper, thus further inhibiting accurate study of the early history of trades in these metals. It is clear, however, that these trades were gradually phased out by the industrialization of America.

[Martha Gandy Fales, *Early American Silver for the Cautious Collector;* Graham Hood, *American Silver: A History of Style, 1650–1900;* Henry J. Kauffman, *American Copper and Brass;* Ledie L. Laughlin, *Pewter in America;* Charles F. Montgomery, *A History of American Pewter;* John Marshall Phillips, *American Silver.*]

JONATHAN TRACE

SILVER PROSPECTING AND MINING. Silver sometimes occurs in ore as native silver in lodes or veins that run to great depths underground. The outcroppings of such ores identify the lode to the prospector. This silver can be recovered by crushing the ore in a stamp mill, passing it over copper plates coated with mercury, and separating the amalgam by driving off the mercury with heat. Most silver ores are more complex. Silver is usually chemically combined with gold, lead, copper, or other metals, and the identification of these ores is much more difficult than those containing native silver. The complex ores also require more intricate metallurgical processes for separation.

Silver mining in the United States began at an early period. The Spanish had worked small mines during their occupation of New Mexico, California, and Texas. Small amounts of silver also were recovered by mining in New Hampshire after 1828 and in Virginia and Tennessee after 1832. Large-scale silver mining had its beginning in Nevada after 1859, when Peter O'Riley and Patrick McLaughlin, prospecting the area eastward from the California gold fields, staked the Ophir, or Comstock, lode. They were looking for gold, but their happy discovery developed into a bonanza mine that yielded more silver than gold. The Comstock ores were so rich that within two decades more than $300 million worth of silver and gold had been extracted.

The Comstock experience of goldseekers finding silver became a pattern repeated in various parts of the American West in the years that followed. At Georgetown, Colo., an original gold placer camp developed as the center of a silver-producing district after the opening of the Belmont lode in 1864. Also in Colorado, the gold camp of Oro City was almost a ghost town when ores of carbonate of lead with a rich silver content were discovered in 1877 and the greatest of Colorado silver cities, Leadville, was born.

Again, gold prospectors accidentally discovered the Bunker Hill and Sullivan mines in the Coeur d'Alene district of Idaho.

Concentrating mills and smelters, necessary for treating complex silver ores, were not available in the United States until 1866–68. Thomas H. Selby at San Francisco; W. S. Keyes at Eureka, Nev.; A. W. Nason at Oreana, Nev.; and Nathaniel P. Hill at Blackhawk, Colo., were pioneers of the smelting industry in the United States. Recovered metals such as lead and copper became increasingly significant byproducts of the silver smelters.

The prosperity of the silver mining industry in the United States during the 19th century was intimately related to the currency policy of the federal government, particularly after the demonetization of silver in 1873. Many of the largest producing silver mines in the country, including those at Leadville, Aspen, and Silver Cliff in Colorado, those of the Silver Reef district in Utah, the Idaho mines, and the mines in the Butte district in Montana, were opened after 1873. During the quarter of a century that followed, while the nation debated the questions of silver purchases and coinage, the huge quantities of silver produced by these mines depressed the price, already reduced by demonetization. With the repeal of the Sherman Silver Purchase Act in 1893, the domestic silver market fell to levels so low that many mines suspended operations.

The industry recovered sufficiently to make the years 1911–18 the peak years in volume of production; an annual average of 69,735,000 fine ounces of silver were produced during those years. Then continuing low prices for silver and high production costs limited activity in mining. After 1920 the Coeur d'Alene district of Idaho was the leading silver-producing region in the country. In 1970 Idaho produced 42 percent of the 45,006,000 fine ounces of silver mined in the United States; most of the other silver came from mines in Arizona, Utah, and Montana.

[W. R. Crane, *Gold and Silver;* Rodman Wilson Paul, *Mining Frontiers of the Far West, 1848–1880;* Thomas Arthur Rickard, *History of American Mining;* U.S. Bureau of Mines, *Minerals Yearbook* (1971).]

CARL UBBELOHDE

SILVER REPUBLICAN PARTY, an organization formed by the delegates who bolted the Republican convention of 1896 after its adoption of the gold plank, which advocated gold only, rather than gold and silver, as the basis of the U.S. monetary system.

The Silver Republicans later issued an endorsement of the Democratic presidential candidate, William Jennings Bryan, and called upon all Republicans who believed in bimetallism to support him. In the West the Silver Republicans formed state organizations, which usually fused with the Democrats or Populists in local politics. In 1900 the party met in its first and only national convention. The leaders hoped to secure a common ticket with the Democrats, but they failed when the Democrats refused to accept a Silver Republican as the vice-presidential candidate. Thereafter, the rank and file of the Silver Republicans favored a separate vice-presidential nomination, but their leaders prevented this by postponing action. The national committee later accepted the Democratic nominee. In March 1901 the party's members in Congress joined in an address urging all supporters to unite with the Democratic party.

[Elmer Ellis, "The Silver Republicans in the Election of 1896," *Mississippi Valley Historical Review,* vol. 18 (1932).]

ELMER ELLIS

SINGING SCHOOLS were to be found in every part of the United States at some time, but they were especially common in the rural districts of the South and West during the greater part of the 19th century. A singing school was usually conducted by an itinerant teacher of music, who collected a small fee from each student enrolled. A session commonly continued from two to four weeks, with a meeting held each evening. Nominally formed to teach singing, the singing school was actually largely a social institution. Books with either "round notes" or "shape notes" were used. In the latter the note could be determined by its shape, without any regard to its position on the staff. Each evening was spent in group singing interspersed from time to time with instruction from the teacher. As a social and often a matrimonial agency, the singing school was quite successful, but it is doubtful that many of the so-called students learned much about music. Yet the schools did serve to stimulate an interest in music and no doubt gave some helpful knowledge.

[W. J. Baltzel, "A Picture of Community Music Work Eighty Years Ago," *The Musician,* vol. 22.]

EDWARD EVERETT DALE

SINGLE TAX, the name for a levy proposed by Henry George in his *Progress and Poverty,* published in 1879. In place of all other taxes George advocated a single tax that would appropriate for government use all of the economic rent on land. His proposal was intended as much more than a mere fiscal device. It was set forth as a vehicle for social reform.

On the ground that land was a gift of nature, not a product of human effort, George condemned private ownership of land, which he considered the cause of economic and social ills. Land values, he held, were attributable to social or community factors. The state, therefore, and not the individual, should be the beneficiary of these values and any increases therein. George wrote:

What I, therefore propose as the simple yet sovereign remedy, which will raise wages, increase the earnings of capital, extirpate pauperism, abolish poverty, give remunerative employment to whoever wishes it, afford free scope to human powers, lessen crime, elevate morals, and taste, and intelligence, purify government, and carry civilization to yet nobler heights, is—to appropriate rent by taxation."

Henry George was undoubtedly influenced in his views by his years in California, where he had observed the speculation in land and the rapid rise in land values following the gold rush of 1849. He was not content merely to expound his views in writing. He endeavored to secure their adoption through government action and twice ran (unsuccessfully) for mayor of New York City, in 1886 and 1897.

The single-tax program has had but limited acceptance in the United States despite vigorous attempts to promote it through political campaigns, legislative action, and general publicity. The single-tax cause was aided by large financial contributions from philanthropist Joseph Fels. In California in the early 20th century, the question of adoption of the single-tax plan was before the voters on seven occasions; each time it was rejected. Agitation for the single tax, or for a partial application of it, was also carried on in such other widely separated states as Oregon, Washington, Colorado, Missouri, New York, Pennsylvania, and Texas.

[M. H. Hunter, *Outlines of Public Finance.*]

MARVEL M. STOCKWELL

SINGLETON PEACE PLAN. In the winter and spring of 1865, James Washington Singleton, a native of Virginia, was the bearer of confidential messages between President Abraham Lincoln and Confederate authorities. These messages dealt at first with the achievement of peace and later with respect to the return of the South to the Union. Singleton's mission was ended by Lincoln's death.

[M. P. Andrews, *Virginia, The Old Dominion.*]
MATTHEW PAGE ANDREWS

SINKING FUND, NATIONAL. As secretary of the Treasury, Alexander Hamilton agreed that a national debt was a national benefit in the early years of the Republic; a national obligation would serve as a cement of union and a spur to industry. Even so, he insisted, creation of public debt should be accompanied by means of extinguishment. Under the Funding Act of 1790, Congress established a sinking fund administered by high government officers. It was supplied by surplus revenue from customs duties and $2 million of borrowed money. Hamilton checked the panic of 1792 by purchasing securities at market rate, below par, for the sinking fund.

On recommendation of Albert Gallatin, Thomas Jefferson's secretary of the Treasury, the sinking fund was reorganized in 1802. A definite annual appropriation, $8 million, was used to retire maturing bonds and buy in the market. The obligations acquired were destroyed, not retained at interest as in Hamilton's scheme. The years 1801–12 brought America prosperity as chief neutral carrier during the Napoleonic Wars. Gallatin reduced the public debt by $40 million; the remaining $45 million would probably have been promptly expunged had it not been for the War of 1812, which ran up the debt to $119.5 million by 1815. However, Treasury prosperity followed because of increased imports and mounting land sales. Large appropriations were made to the sinking fund. In 1837, from a Treasury surplus of more than $42 million, $28 million was distributed to the states before depression stopped a last installment.

The decade 1848 to 1857 boomed as a result of Mexican War expenditures, railroad expansion, gold discoveries, and increased imports. To return accumulating surpluses to circulation, Congress authorized the purchase of bonds in the market above par; $40 million was paid in premiums. The panic of 1857 resulted in three years of deficits in which the debt increased by $36 million. In spite of a sharply rising debt during the Civil War, Congress ordered a 1 percent repurchase, an empty gesture while heavy deficits persisted. In the prosperous 1920's appropriations to the sinking fund grew from $261 to $388 million. The Great Depression ushered in an era of deficit spending, prolonged by World War II and the Korean and Vietnam wars. Instead of being subjected to stat-

utory reduction, the public debt constantly increased; the debt ceiling was regularly raised by Congress, and refunding was systematized.

[H. Lewis Kimmel, *Federal Budget and Fiscal Policy;* Paul Studenski and Herman E. Krooss, *Financial History of the United States.*]
BROADUS MITCHELL

SINO-JAPANESE WAR. The conflict between China and Japan in 1894–95 concerned the United States only indirectly: U.S. Asiatic policy had not yet been crystallized by Secretary of State John Milton Hay's enunciation of the Open Door policy in 1899. A treaty with Korea, however, pledged the United States to exert its good offices in the event of a dispute with foreign powers, and efforts were consequently made to induce Japan and China to withdraw their troops from Korea. At the same time the United States rejected British overtures for foreign intervention to avert the war, but during the subsequent hostilities, the United States warned Japan that if it did not follow a moderate policy "other Powers having interests in that quarter may demand a settlement not favorable to Japan's future security and well-being." As the war proceeded the United States extended its good offices in favor of peace and was instrumental in bringing Japan and China together for the final peace negotiations.

[Tyler Dennett, *Americans in Eastern Asia.*]
FOSTER RHEA DULLES

SIOUX. *See* **Dakota.**

SIOUX-CHIPPEWA WAR. For nearly two centuries, prior to 1858, the Sioux and the Chippewa, of different linguistic stocks, battled for control of the northern Wisconsin and Minnesota hunting grounds, as the latter tribe moved slowly westward along the Great Lakes. By the aid of firearms secured from French traders, the Chippewa disastrously defeated a Sioux-Fox alliance near Saint Croix Falls, Wis., and then destroyed the Sioux villages at Sandy Lake and Mille Lacs, Minn. The withdrawal of the Sioux to southern Minnesota and their receipt of firearms after 1750 produced a territorial stalemate, and the intertribal war became a series of retaliatory raids like the Battle of Crow Wing, punctuated by truces. The government vainly laid down a boundary line between the two in 1825.

The establishment of the Indian agency at Fort

Snelling in 1819, readily accessible from the Mississippi and Saint Croix rivers, constantly drew the Chippewa deep into Sioux territory, and so conflicts were inevitable. In 1827 Sioux treacherously murdered Chippewa just outside the fort. The battles of Rum River and Stillwater in 1839 resulted from a Chippewa ambush, and the Lake Pokegama Sioux raid of 1841 produced the Kaposia battle of 1842. A Sioux-Chippewa council had been held July 10–11, 1850, called by Gov. Alexander Ramsey of Minnesota Territory to renew an 1843 peace treaty between the Sioux and Chippewa, but it did not end the hostilities. The sharp fight near Shakopee, Minn., May 27, 1858, closed the long and bloody series of ambushes and scalp raids with a final stalemate.

The Chippewa had waged war against the Sioux because of their need to get furs and food. As a consequence of Chippewa pressure, the Sioux began to move westward into the Plains in large numbers, abandoning their villages and farms, drawn by the Plains cultural pattern that centered around horses and buffalo hunting. With the departure of the Sioux the Chippewa began to occupy lake and river sites in northern Minnesota and northern Wisconsin and came to control the territory around the headwaters of the Mississippi River. The Santee (or Eastern) Sioux, however, remained in Minnesota, around the Minnesota River south of the present Minneapolis–Saint Paul area, and were successful in opposing further Chippewa inroads into their territory.

[Harold Hickerson, *The Southwestern Chippewa: An Ethnohistorical Study;* Roy W. Meyer, *History of the Santee Sioux;* Louis H. Roddis, *The Indian Wars of Minnesota.*]

WILLOUGHBY M. BABCOCK
KENNETH M. STEWART

SIOUX CLAIMS COMMISSION. Following the Minnesota Sioux uprising, Congress by law on Feb. 16, 1863, abrogated all Minnesota Sioux treaties; declared forfeit their lands and annuities; appropriated $200,000 from such funds for damages to whites; and established a claims commission, which, after hearings, awarded 2,635 claimants $1,370,374, an amount duly paid by appropriation.

[William W. Folwell, *A History of Minnesota,* vol. II.]

WILLOUGHBY M. BABCOCK

SIOUX COUNCIL (July 27–Aug. 3, 1889). During the 1880's there was ever-increasing pressure on the federal government for the reduction of the so-called Great Sioux Reservation, an area roughly extending from Nebraska's northern line to the 46th parallel and from the Missouri River to 104 degrees west longitude. Several attempts to negotiate with the Sioux by commission failed. A law was passed by Congress on Mar. 2, 1889, providing for the setting aside of certain areas for six reservation groups in Dakota Territory and for the opening of the balance for sale to whites at $1.25 per acre, the amounts received to be credited to Indian funds. Before the law became operative, it required the consent of three-fourths of the adult male Sioux. A commission, made up of Gen. George Crook, Charles Foster, and William Warner, after visiting several of the smaller agencies concerned, began its most important council at Standing Rock, on July 27. John Grass, chief spokesman for the Standing Rock Sioux, objected to the government's failure to observe the Treaty of Laramie (1868), particularly in respect to payments, schools, and so forth, and was dissatisfied with the low price offered for the land. In successive sessions the commissioners explained the provisions of the act and, by minor concessions, met the objections. Indian agent James McLaughlin in secret conferences finally persuaded Grass and Chief Gall to accept the act, and the formal signing followed on Aug. 3. Sitting Bull, who had not been informed of the date of the council at which the signing of the agreement took place, was thus unable to exercise any last-minute influence against the cession of the Sioux lands. The compensation for the land sold was estimated at upward of $7 million.

WILLOUGHBY M. BABCOCK

SIOUX TREATIES. Negotiations and treaties with the Sioux covered a period of some eighty-five years, from 1805 to 1889, and a geographical area extending from Fort Snelling (Minn.) and Portage des Sioux (Mo.) on the Mississippi to Fort Laramie in Wyoming. The terms of these treaties reflect in a general way the growth of American power as settlement crossed the upper Mississippi and advanced into the Great Plains country (*see* Westward Movement).

On Sept. 23, 1805, Lt. Zebulon M. Pike, at Pike's Island (Minn.), purchased from the Minnesota Sioux for $2,000 in goods a tract roughly nine miles square at the mouth of the Minnesota River for a military post (the later Fort Snelling), to inaugurate the series of treaties. Termination of the War of 1812 necessitated peace treaties with England's Indian allies, and between 1815 and 1817 a series of peace agreements acknowledging the sovereignty of the United States were negotiated by Gen. William Clark and others at Portage des Sioux and Saint Louis with various Siouan tribes.

The extension of fur trading operations up the Missouri River by William Ashley and the movement of troops up that stream under Gen. Henry Atkinson (*see* Yellowstone River Expeditions) produced friction with the Sioux and other tribes of the Missouri, some fighting, and then, in 1825, several treaties, such as that of Fort Lookout (S.D.), providing for peaceful relations and the admission of traders to the country. The same year witnessed the great treaty council of Prairie du Chien (Wis.), where on Aug. 19 the Sioux and other warring tribes, by treaty under governmental supervision, agreed upon mutual boundary lines and the maintenance of intertribal peace. The treaty of July 15, 1830, negotiated also at Prairie du Chien, was concerned with peace measures between the Sauk and Fox and the Minnesota Sioux and allied groups, but attempted to attain such results by setting up a block of neutral territory between tribal enemies.

By the Treaty of Washington of Sept. 29, 1837, the Sioux began the sale of their Minnesota lands and the assignment of treaty funds to settle debts to traders. By the time the agreements of Traverse des Sioux and Mendota of 1851 and Washington in 1858 had been completed, they retained only a ten-mile-wide strip in that state. The Sioux uprising in Minnesota (1862) had its Dakota phases, and eventually the great treaties of Fort Laramie in 1868 attempted to end the Indian wars by setting up a vast Sioux reserve west of the Missouri River and promising certain annuities and payments. The Indians were to withdraw opposition to the building of railroads through their country.

The act of Mar. 3, 1871 (*see* Indian Policy, National), prohibited further treatymaking with Indian tribes, but in order to secure Indian acceptance of laws applicable to them, periodic councils for ratification were held, of which those in the summer of 1889 with the Sioux are typical. Although similar to treaty councils, the Indians in these assemblies acted as individuals, not as agents for semi-independent tribal entities.

[Roy W. Meyer, *History of the Santee Sioux: United States Indian Policy on Trial;* Loring Benson Priest, *Uncle Sam's Stepchildren: The Reformation of United States Indian Policy, 1865–1887;* Francis Paul Prucha, S.J., *American Indian Policy in the Formative Years: The Indian Trade and Intercourse Acts, 1790–1834.*]

WILLOUGHBY M. BABCOCK

SIOUX UPRISING IN MINNESOTA (1862). Following the cession of nearly 1 million acres of their

land, the Santee Sioux in 1862 were crowded onto a reservation along the upper Minnesota River without any hunting areas, resulting in the semistarvation of many of the Indians. In July about 5,000 starving Indians assembled at the Upper Agency at Yellow Medicine, Minn., to receive the government's annual payment of $72,000 on their debt to the Indians for their lands. When the gold shipment did not arrive on Aug. 1 as expected, rumors spread that the federal government had exhausted its Treasury on the Civil War. Anger mounted when the Indian agent at the Lower Agency at Redwood refused to give the Indians food from the government's stores. On Aug. 17 four young Sioux murdered five settlers near Acton, Minn., and on the following day the Sioux, fearful of retaliation and angered by the many years of abuse, rose in full force and attacked the Redwood agency, killing twenty white men. For two weeks Sioux raiding bands swept through southwestern Minnesota. Despite the loss of twenty-four soldiers from Fort Ridgely, ambushed at the Redwood Ferry on Aug. 18, government troops successfully defended Fort Ridgely and New Ulm (Aug. 19–26) against Little Crow's warriors, permitting the movement up from Fort Snelling of about 1,400 troops under Col. Henry H. Sibley. The soldiers' victory at Wood Lake on Sept. 23, following their Birch Coulee triumph on Sept. 2–3, crushed the uprising, except for sporadic incidents like the killing of Amos Dustin and his family in 1863. Sibley's and Gen. Alfred Sully's expeditions (1862–64) in the Dakotas opened the frontier for further white settlement. Thirty-eight Sioux were executed at Mankato on Dec. 26, 1862. More than 800 settlers had been killed.

[Willoughby M. Babcock, "Minnesota's Indian War," *Minnesota History,* vol. 38.]

WILLOUGHBY M. BABCOCK

SIOUX WARS. The first clash between the Sioux and American troops occurred in 1854, near Fort Laramie, Wyo., when Lieutenant J. L. Grattan and eighteen men were killed. In retaliation, Gen. W. S. Harney in 1855 attacked a camp of Brulé Sioux near Ash Hollow, Neb., and killed about a hundred. Following the battle, the Brulé chief, Spotted Tail, was imprisoned, and the Sioux country was peaceful for a while. With the beginning of the Civil War, regular army troops were withdrawn from the Plains area, to be replaced by state and territorial militiamen in attempting to keep the Indians peaceful.

In Minnesota the Eastern (or Santee) Sioux had ceded much of their land, reserving for themselves territory along the Minnesota River under the provisions of the 1851 Treaty of Traverse des Sioux. White settlers soon began to press in upon the Sioux holdings, and white traders cheated the Sioux, until in August of 1862 there was a Sioux uprising in Minnesota under the leadership of Little Crow. The revolt was crushed in September, after which some of the dispersed Sioux sought refuge in Canada, while others joined the Teton Sioux in the plains of South Dakota.

The Teton were not generally hostile to the whites until 1865, when they joined with the Arapaho and Cheyenne in attacking emigrants on the Bozeman Trail to the Montana goldfields. In 1865 the Teton under Chief Red Cloud defeated an army unit at the Upper Platte Bridge, destroying this important link on the trail to the West.

With the end of the Civil War, regular federal troops were rushed to the Plains in an attempt to pacify the Indians, but the Sioux were aroused by the government's intention to erect forts along the Bozeman Trail. Red Cloud's War (1866–67) followed, during which the Sioux attacked wagon trains, halted traffic on the trail, and laid siege to the forts. On Dec. 21, 1866, Capt. William J. Fetterman and eighty troopers were annihilated by Red Cloud's warriors. In 1868 the government agreed to abandon the trail and forts and Red Cloud signed a treaty of peace at Fort Laramie.

The treaty had guaranteed the possession in perpetuity of the Black Hills by the Sioux, but in 1874 there was a rush of gold prospectors into the area. The consequence was the Black Hills War in 1876, in which Gen. George Armstrong Custer and his troops were killed at the Battle of the Little Bighorn on June 25. The Sioux separated after the battle, and Gen. George Crook defeated American Horse's band at Slim Buttes on Sept. 9. Sitting Bull was pursued to Canada by Gen. Nelson A. Miles. Crazy Horse and his Oglala fought on until they were induced by hunger to surrender on Jan. 7, 1877.

Relative peace then prevailed until the final Sioux uprising, sometimes called the Messiah War, which attended the religious excitement of the Ghost Dance in 1890. On Dec. 15 Chief Sitting Bull was killed by Indian police who had been sent to arrest him, and the pacification of the Sioux was completed on Dec. 29 with the massacre of some 300 Sioux at the so-called Battle of Wounded Knee.

[Kenneth Carley, ed., *The Sioux Uprising of 1862;* George E. Hyde, *A Sioux Chronicle;* Roy W. Meyer, *History of the Santee Sioux;* James C. Olson, *Red Cloud and the Sioux Problem;* Robert M. Utley, *The Last Days of the*

Sioux Nation; Stanley Vestal, *Sitting Bull, Champion of the Sioux.*]

KENNETH M. STEWART

SIT-DOWN STRIKES. *See* **Strikes.**

SIX NATIONS. *See* **Iroquois.**

SIX-SHOOTER. *See* **Colt Six-Shooter.**

SIXTEENTH AMENDMENT, the amendment to the U.S. Constitution authorizing Congress to impose a federal income tax. When the Supreme Court invalidated, in 1895, the income tax of 1894 in *Pollock* v. *Farmers Loan and Trust Company,* the decision aroused widespread disapproval on the grounds that as long as tariff duties and excises constituted the main source of federal revenue, those best able to pay were escaping a fair share of the tax burden. It was also argued that federal outlays were bound to increase in the future, that emergencies like war could require vast federal expenditures, and that additional taxing power was therefore needed. In view of the limitation imposed by the Supreme Court, a constitutional amendment empowering Congress to lay income taxes without apportionment among the states was the only way out of an impasse. In 1908 the Democratic platform endorsed such an amendment, and it was widely supported by the progressive wing of the Republican party. President William Howard Taft eventually recommended submission of an amendment to the states, and the necessary resolution passed both houses of Congress by overwhelming majorities in July 1909. The necessary ratifications were forthcoming, and the amendment was declared effective Feb. 25, 1913.

[E. R. A. Seligman, *The Income Tax;* A. C. McLaughlin, *Constitutional History of the United States.*]

W. A. ROBINSON

SIXTEEN TO ONE. *See* **Bimetallism.**

SKIING. Although the American Indians used snowshoes to move swiftly and easily across snow-covered terrain, the first people in America to ski in any numbers were 19th-century Scandinavian immigrants. In 1856 the Norwegian John ("Snowshoe") Thompson drew attention to skiing when he began carrying the mail over the Sierra Nevada from Placerville, Calif., to Genoa, Nev., on skis. He covered ninety miles in three days and returned in two days. His oak skis were 10 feet long and weighed 25 pounds, and he used a single large pole. Thompson continued his treks until 1869, when the transcontinental railroad was completed.

California gold miners took up ski racing in the 1860's, plunging straight downhill at speeds reportedly over 80 miles per hour. The first ski club in the United States was organized at La Porte, Calif., in 1867. In the 1880's and 1890's the Norwegian rage for ski jumping spread to America, principally among midwestern Norwegian immigrants.

Skiing became popular among college students shortly after Fred Harris, a Dartmouth College undergraduate, organized the Dartmouth Outing Club in 1909. The club put on the first collegiate winter carnival at the Hanover, N.H., campus in 1911. In 1913 Dartmouth participated in the first intercollegiate ski meet in North America at McGill University in Montreal. Competition was in jumping and cross-country racing. By 1923, 250,000 pairs of skis were being manufactured annually in the United States. Skis became shorter and lighter; two poles supplanted one pole; and secure leather bindings were developed.

In the 1920's the development of European alpine skiing styles—fast turns on steep slopes—began transforming skiing in America. Dartmouth imported Austrian ski coaches, and in 1925 slalom was introduced at the Dartmouth carnival. In 1929 the first American ski school opened at Franconia, N.H., and in that year the Boston and Maine Railroad ran a special train for skiers from Boston to Franconia.

With the development of the ski lift in the 1930's, alpine skiing prevailed. The first rope tow in the United States was installed at Woodstock, Vt., in 1934. Ski trains from Boston and New York City unloaded thousands of skiers in the villages of Vermont and New Hampshire. The 1932 Winter Olympics, held at Lake Placid, N.Y., were broadcast on radio, stoking the ski fever in the United States. The opening of the Sun Valley, Idaho, resort in 1936 set the pattern to be followed by later ski resorts. At Sun Valley, skiing was infused with glamour, prestige, and luxury. By the decade's end skiing had been transformed from a collegiate pastime into almost a mass movement.

During World War II many of America's best skiers joined the Eighty-seventh Mountain Infantry Regiment; the regiment was expanded into the Tenth Mountain Division, which saw action in Italy. At the end of the war army surplus ski equipment, inexpensive and of good quality, was put up for public sale; it introduced many newcomers to the sport.

In the 1940's and 1950's alpine technique became increasingly complicated and dependent on expensive equipment and lessons. Elaborate release bindings superseded cables. Metal skis, developed by Howard Head of Baltimore in the 1950's, superseded wooden skis. Packed, groomed slopes replaced powdery fields, and in some places, snow was artificially made. Prices of equipment and at resorts soared, as did the number of skiers. In the winter of 1959–60 alone, more new lifts were opened than had existed in 1950. At the same time ski racing became a popular spectator sport. In 1960, Squaw Valley, Calif., was host to the Winter Olympics, where ski racing was televised live for the first time in America. In 1961 the first U.S. professional ski race took place.

In the early 1960's the commercialization of skiing led some people, many of them disenchanted alpine skiers, to take up ski touring, or cross-country skiing, through the woods and fields. Aided by new lightweight, flexible, Scandinavian skis and inspired by the environmental movement and a growing awareness of the need for outdoor exercise, these skiers first appeared in New England college towns, and by the late 1960's ski touring had spread across the country. In 1968, 20,000 inexpensive, wooden skis were imported from Scandinavia; by the early 1970's the figure was over a half-million pairs annually. The number of ski tourers approached that of the alpine skiers, estimated at between 2 million and 4 million in the mid-1970's. More new skiers were taking up touring, and alpine resort developers found themselves increasingly at odds with environmentalists over the future of the mountains.

[*Ski Magazine* editors, *America's Ski Book;* L. Tapley, *Ski Touring in New England.*]

Lance Tapley

SKINNERS. *See* **Cowboys and Skinners.**

SKYJACKING. *See* **Hijacking, Aerial.**

SKYSCRAPERS. The skyscraper may be defined as a multistory elevator office building, usually of skeleton frame construction. The first skyscrapers were built in the United States in the last quarter of the 19th century, but since that time the form has been borrowed by many countries throughout the world.

The skyscraper's beginnings can be traced back to

such structures as the Equitable Life Building (Gilman, Kendall, and Post, 1868–70), the Western Union Building (George B. Post, 1873–75), and the Tribune Building (Richard M. Hunt, 1874–75), all in New York City. They were among the first buildings to use elevators to make accessible office space on higher floors.

Skeleton frame construction, which made buildings of more than ten stories economically feasible, was perfected in Chicago by William LeBaron Jenney in the Home Life Insurance Building (1883–85) and by Holabird and Roche in the Tacoma Building (1887–89). In the Wainwright Building (Saint Louis, 1890–91) Adler and Sullivan clad the metal frame with a functional design that expressed not only its structural system but also its use as a tall office building; they thus produced one of the finest examples of early skyscraper architecture.

In the East architects were moving in a different direction. The Ames Building by Shepley, Rutan, and Coolidge (Boston, 1889) represented the Romanesque mode as revived by H. H. Richardson. The New York Life Insurance Building by McKim, Mead and White (Kansas City, 1890) employed Italian Renaissance motifs. Bruce Price, in the American Surety Building (New York, 1894–95), conceived of the skyscraper as a classic column divided into base, shaft, and capital. The tower concept had many followers, as exemplified by the Singer Tower (Ernest Flagg, 1906–08), the Woolworth Building Tower (Cass Gilbert, 1913), the Chrysler Tower (William Van Alen, 1929), and the Empire State Building (Shreve, Lamb and Harmon, 1930).

The Empire State Building was, for decades, the world's tallest building until the opening in 1970 of the twin-towered World Trade Center in New York City. That, in turn, was soon superseded as the tallest building by the Sears Tower in Chicago.

New York City's Rockefeller Center (Reinhard and Hofmeister; Hood, Godley and Fouilhoux; Corbett, Harrison and MacMurray, 1928–40) marked the beginning of a trend toward open large-scale planning. The tendency toward modest development and landscaped environment was continued in such works as Lever House by Skidmore, Owings and Merrill (New York, 1952) and the Seagram Building by Ludwig Mies Van Der Rohe and Philip Johnson (New York, 1958). By the early 1970's, as urban congestion increasingly came to be perceived as a major problem, a number of cities were offering tax and other incentives to developers to plan for open space around tall office buildings.

[Carl W. Condit, *American Building Art: The 19th Century*, and *The Rise of the Skyscraper;* Henry Russell Hitchcock, *Architecture 19th and 20th Centuries.*]
WINSTON WEISMAN

SLADE'S GIRLS was a term applied to the young women sent to the West as teachers in the middle of the 19th century by the Board of National Popular Education. This organization was founded in 1847 under home missionary impulses; former Gov. William Slade of Vermont was its general agent. By 1857 the board had sent more than 400 women from New England and New York to western states and territories.
COLIN B. GOODYKOONTZ

SLANG, AMERICAN. Slang is ingenious and frequently amusing language of a highly picturesque and often metaphorical nature, generally of temporary popularity and of wide colloquial dispersion. It differs from cant, a term of depreciation describing insincere repetition of meaningless or hollow phrases, particularly by religious sectaries; from jargon, the vocabulary of a science, art, trade, sect, or specialized group intelligible only to initiates; from argot, the language of criminals and members of the underworld; from vulgarism, a word outside the pale of accepted speech; from colloquialism, an expression permissible in conversation but not in formal writing; and from standard language, the vocabulary that with its idiomatic usage has gained general acceptance in the writings of representative authors. These gradations are frequently difficult to distinguish, for language is a living entity, coming to birth and dying with vicissitudes similar to those of human beings. Not all picturesque language is slang: *like greased lightning* is picturesque, but is sound English; *blockhead* is acceptable English, but *pothead* is slang. *Nice, bunkum, to show off, to put it over, to chisel, bootlegger, racketeer, movie,* and *OK* have risen from slang into standard English.

Slang originates from an individual's effort to replace a faded, stale, or worn-out expression with a pungent, descriptive, and often satiric term. Little slang was invented in America before the great westward movement began after the War of 1812. Freed from the conventionality of the eastern settlements, the pioneers expressed their exuberant optimism and individualism in dazzling extravagances. David ("Davy") Crockett, whose books in the 1830's amused the East with western tall tales and tall talk, described himself as "fresh from the backwoods, half-horse, half-alligator, a little touched with the

299

snapping turtle; can wade the Mississippi, leap the Ohio, ride upon a streak of lightning, and slip without a scratch down a honey locust; can whip my weight in wildcats.'' The humorous literature of the Old Southwest introduced such terms as *sockdolager, hornswoggle, rambunctious, skedaddle, shebang, some punkins, galoot, go the whole hog, pie-eyed, stewed, woozy.* Mark Twain's books are rich repositories of the slang of the mid-19th century Middle West and Far West.

The improved communication systems of the 20th century have shortened the amount of time slang terms need to reach wide acceptance, and have caused the regional character of slang to decline. In the 1920's and 1930's, slang of national currency was created or disseminated by motion pictures and radio and by nationally syndicated comic strips and gossip columns. Mass circulation magazines, such as *Life, Look,* and *Time,* adopted a breezy, informal style in their presentation of the news and in their human-interest features; they did not hesitate to incorporate slang into their style; often, in fact, they coined terms. A sample of slang terms of the period: *flapper, speakeasy, whoopee, high-hat, belly laugh, blessed event, dumb Dora, schnozzle, the cat's pajamas,* and *punch-drunk.*

Slang of the early 1940's, reflecting a nation at war, was drawn mostly from the military. The coming of television in the late 1940's and early 1950's added a still more potent mass medium to assist in the quick dissemination of slang. Advertising slogans and catch phrases were widely picked up and modified (''where the yellow went''; ''a Ford in your future''; and, later, ''I can't believe I ate the whole thing''). The world of popular music—especially jazz (itself a slang word)—had always given America a rich source of slang (*on the ball, in the groove, hep, hepcat, jive, cool*), and the *beat* generation (whose adherents are *beatniks*) picked up many of those terms. The space age added such terms as *in orbit, blast-off, countdown,* and *A-okay.*

In the 1960's, *beatniks* were replaced by *hippies* (and even *yippies*). *In the groove* became *groovy; hep* became *hip; cool* retained its function as the ultimate accolade. Other terms of approval were *neat, far out, out of sight, heavy,* and *bad.* Terms of opprobrium were *straight, square, hung up,* and—the ultimate—*gross.* The world of drug users (*pushers, junkies, potheads, acid heads, speed freaks*)—to the consternation of the *straight world*—offered such terms as *strung out, spaced out, turned on* (which originally had a sexual connotation), and *freaked out.*

Slang terms, like standard terms, undergo shifts in meaning, usually becoming more inclusive as usage increases. An example is the term *rip-off.* Originally a rip-off was a theft. Then the meaning was extended to a burglary, and further extended to any swindle. Finally, a giant rip-off became virtually anything of which the speaker disapproved.

Teachers of English decry the use of slang on the ground that ''alert minds create slang; lazy minds repeat slang.'' By the 1970's the lines of demarcation between slang, standard language, colloquialisms, and vulgarisms had become so hazy that traditional critics of slang would find it difficult to establish their battleground. Most critics limited their criticism to those fad words that sweep the country, are vastly overused, and quickly become boring to the listener or reader.

[Daniel J. Boorstin, *The Americans: The National Experience;* Henry L. Mencken, *The American Language;* Harold Wentworth and Stuart Berg Flexner, *Dictionary of American Slang With a Supplement.*]

HARRY R. WARFEL
DONALD W. HUNT

SLANG, MILITARY. Military slang—constantly changing, often short-lived, and usually of inexact origin—has long been a rich part of armed forces vocabulary. Many words once considered slang and many from the French or British military traditions have developed into accepted and official military language. Slang within military organizations often reflects official phrases or abbreviations, specialized military equipment or conditions, and not infrequently criticism or sarcasm, sometimes profane, from the ranks.

Army Slang. During the Civil War numerous slang phrases and words became popular, some reflecting earlier origins, including ''AWOL'' (''absent without leave''), which is still used; ''pup tent''; and ''dog tag.'' The words ''contraband,'' a name for recently freed and usually homeless slaves; ''bust,'' meaning a reduction in rank; and ''hooker,'' the name given to prostitutes serving the troops in Washington, D.C., under the command of Gen. Joseph Hooker, came into use at that time.

The Indian wars witnessed a continuation of Civil War slang, such as ''galvanized Yankees,'' describing Confederate prisoners opting for frontier service as federals rather than imprisonment, and the addition of such phrases as ''Soapsuds Row,'' for the line of laundry quarters on frontier posts. A soldier's closest friend and confidant was his ''bunkie,'' derived from the practice of two men sharing bunks. "Over the hill," also popular during World War I, originated during this period as another phrase to describe desertion. The combination saloon, brothel, and gambling center that was usually located just off the military reservation at western posts for the benefit of troopers was known as the "hog ranch." Black soldiers, introduced into the regular army in 1866, were nicknamed "buffalo soldiers," a title accepted with pride by the black cavalrymen of the Ninth and Tenth regiments. The common explanation for the nickname is that the Indians saw the similarity between the black soldier's hair and that of the buffalo, an animal they revered greatly. The Indians themselves became known as "hostiles."

During World War I "doughboy" emerged as the name for soldiers; in World War II the meaning was narrowed to include only infantrymen. "Foxhole," a word introduced in World War I, increased in popularity in World War II, as did "black market," a phrase that soon entered popular civilian usage.

In both world wars military acronyms became slang. Such acronyms included AEF for the American Expeditionary Forces under Gen. John J. Pershing's command in World War I and SHAEF, the Supreme Headquarters, Allied Expeditionary Force, in World War II. The acronym "GI," which originally stood for "galvanized iron," as in a GI bucket of World War I, came to mean "government issue" in World War II and eventually any member of the army. Common words often assumed new meanings: "scrounger," for example, defined a person who could acquire military supplies by other than official means; and "liberating" became a euphemism for looting.

"Chicom" described the Chinese Communists in the Korean War, which also saw such widely publicized names for scenes of battle as "Pork Chop Hill," "Iron Triangle," and "Bowling Alley."

During the Vietnam War acronyms blended with code words and were used both officially and as slang; examples include "roadrunner" for armed convoys, "bushmaster" for ambush patrols, and "dust-off" for medical evacuation helicopters. The enemy was often known as "Charlie," a name derived from "Victor Charlie," the pronunciation of the abbreviation "VC" for Vietcong in the U.S. Army's phonetic alphabet. Much geographical slang developed in Vietnam, including "Thunder Road" for Highway 13 north of Saigon and "Snoopy's Nose" for a curve in a river in the Mekong Delta. "Catcher's Mitt," "Elephant's Ear," and "Key-hole" were designations for areas around Saigon that frequently appeared on operations maps.

JOHN ALBRIGHT

Navy Slang. The slang of American naval officers and enlisted men must be distinguished from the technical jargon of the U.S. Navy. The purpose of this jargon is serious and precise communication; navy slang, on the other hand, is usually disposed to be jesting and often deliberately obfuscates meaning. A naval slang term is most frequently a nickname for an authorized term, a salty variant for an accepted word or expression. American naval slang is usually different from that of other seafarers, such as merchantmen and whalemen. A distinguishing characteristic of American naval slang is that it is often long-lived, whereas general slang is usually soon worn-out with overuse. Naval slang belongs to an oral tradition. Printed records of it from the remote past are found chiefly in long-forgotten man-of-war narratives by enlisted men and in a few books by established American writers, such as Herman Melville's *White-Jacket* (1850).

John Adams, in composing the "Articles of War" for the federal navy, followed almost literally the British Admiralty code. The famous American frigates of 1797 were constructed with an eye to English ship design, and their long guns and carronades were modeled after English and Scottish cannon; it was therefore natural that much of the slang of British tars should become that of American navy men, although the latter may have rejected some locutions, as they did the sea-song "Cheer'ly Men," which they scorned as an effete English chantey. Many Briticisms were retained, such as "loblolly boy" (the naval surgeon's attendant in sick bay), a term that appears in Tobias Smollett's *Roderick Random* (1748); was abbreviated in 19th-century American Watch, Quarter, and Station Bills as "L.L.B."; and is referred to in L. R. Hamersly's *Naval Encyclopaedia* (1881) as "bay-man or nurse." The early salty, colloquial language in the U.S. Navy was largely imported. When the navy turned from square riggers to ironclads, a new, authentically American slang did not develop, chiefly because from the Civil War until 1910, when a national apprentice program was fully developed, most sailors aboard American warships were foreign mercenaries who spoke little English.

American naval slang was remarkably revitalized during World War I and, especially, World War II, becoming an extensive colloquial language, original, vigorous, and expressive. New classes of warships

SLAUGHTERHOUSE CASES

with sophisticated weapons systems, new technical terms of mechanization, and a greatly enlarged and diversified body of personnel, drawn from all walks of life, led to a slang that has become a distinctly American linguistic phenomenon. The "black shoe," or surface navy; the "brown shoe," or naval aviation wing; and the "gyrene" arm, or marines (sometimes jocosely called "jar heads" by sailors, who in turn are called "deck apes"), have each developed a service slang of its own, although many words and terms are shared in common. The "boomers" of the nuclear-powered navy use a new technical language, with resultant colorful slang coinages. Acronyms have led to hundreds of slang locutions, such as the humorous "sink us" for CINCUS (commander in chief of the U.S. fleet, whose acronym was soon altered to COMINCH).

The U.S. Naval Academy is the source of a substantial slang vocabulary, which midshipmen acquire while in school and take with them after graduation to new duty stations ashore and afloat. Much of this slang, as printed in the annual handbook *Reef Points,* seems fresh, humorous, and singularly inventive to each incoming class of "mids," but part of this service-school slang is ancient and traditional, with some expressions recorded in 1898 still in active use in the 1970's.

WILSON HEFLIN

Air Force Slang. The slang used by U.S. Air Force members has roots in both civilian flying and in military life. Some words originated soon after the powered airplane itself; the term "pilot" prevailed early over "driver" and others, although "driver" reappeared in light conversation in the 1960's, competing with "jockey" or simply "jock." To "taxi" an airplane was also known in 1911 British training schools as "waltzing" or "rolling." The verb "strafe" emerged during World War I, apparently from the German expression *Gott strafe England* ("God strike England"). American crewmen in that war called antiaircraft fire "archie"; the next generation used "flak" (from the German for "antiaircraft gun") and "ack-ack." The term "bail out" was no longer considered slang after World War II and was replaced by the phrase "punch out." To crash in an airplane was to "buy the farm" or to "augur in."

Many aircraft had unofficial designations, apart from their publicly known nicknames. The P-47 Thunderbolt was affectionately known as the "Jug." The C-47 was the "Gooney Bird," or simply "Goon," throughout its long career from World War

II through Vietnam. The A-1 prop craft of Southeast Asia became the "Spad," after the World War I craft of that name; the later A-7 became the "Sluf" (for "short, little, ugly fellow"). The F-105 was the "Thud," and the hills lining its path into Hanoi became "Thud Ridge." The squat rescue helicopter used in Southeast Asia was known as the "Jolly Green Giant," taken from commercial advertising, and the night gunship as "Spooky."

Places, too, were given special names by airmen. "Happy Valley" meant the German Ruhr to bomber crews of 1944, while crewmen in Vietnam used the term for the region surrounding one American base. The "Mae West" life preserver appeared early in World War II, and the term has endured for decades despite changes in design; less enduring was the "Gibson Girl," long-range survival radio. The expression "Hangar Queen"—the constantly out-of-commission plane, robbed of parts, or "cannibalized," for benefit of its sisters—has been in use since World War I.

U.S. Air Force men in the 1960's did not obfuscate; they "blew smoke." Instead of attacking a problem with persistence, they "bird-dogged" it. When they succeeded, they "hacked the program" or put on "a good show" (from the British). To fail was to "bomb out" or, more traditionally, to "wash out." Flamboyant pilots, usually young, were "hot dogs," "hot rocks," or "space cadets"; less obnoxious flyers were "tigers." Nonflying officers were "ground pounders" (in World War I, "kiwis"). Individuals in higher headquarters were "weenies." From the Vietnam War came the "roach coach" (the flightline snack bar on wheels), the "ramp tramp" (the flightline coordinator and his vehicle), and the "Sams" (surface-to-air missiles). Infantrymen in Vietnam, often uncommunicative because of fatigue, were always the "grunts." It appeared that the most likely of these expressions to endure were the ones flavored with humor, along with those for which formal equivalents were either nonexistent or cumbersome.

RAY L. BOWERS

[Gershom Bradford, *A Glossary of Sea Terms;* Elbridge Colby, *Army Talk;* Woodward A. Heflin, ed., *The United States Air Force Dictionary;* H. L. Mencken and R. I. McDavid, *The American Language;* Harold Wentworth and S. B. Flexner, *Dictionary of American Slang.*]

SLAUGHTERHOUSE CASES, 16 Wallace 36 (1873), are considered as the Supreme Court's first interpretation of the due process clause of the Fourteenth Amendment and the most important decision of that Court since the Dred Scott case. In 1869 the carpetbag legislature of Louisiana, probably under corrupt influences, granted a monopoly of the slaughtering business within the city limits of New Orleans in favor of a single corporation, thereby depriving some 1,000 persons of their occupation. This monopoly was challenged in the courts mainly as a violation of the Fourteenth Amendment, particularly with reference to the privileges and immunities clause, the denial by the state of equal protection of the laws, and a deprivation of property under the due process clause. Justice Samuel Miller, delivering the majority opinion of the Court, declared that the "one pervading purpose" of the Fourteenth Amendment was the protection of the newly freed slaves and not that of transferring the control over the entire domain of civil rights from the states to the federal government. This decision was in flagrant violation of the intent of the Radical Republican framers of the amendment, who had desired to bring about federal protection of corporations and other businesses from discriminatory state legislation, as well as to achieve social guarantees for blacks. The Slaughterhouse Cases are significant as a temporary reversal of the strong trend, since the Civil War, toward centralization of power in the federal government.

[C. Warren, *The Supreme Court in U.S. History.*]

HARVEY WISH

SLAVE INSURRECTIONS. Rebellion and conspiracy to rebel were the forms of protest that the victims of American slavery most often took against those who enslaved them. They involved careful planning, collective action, and the willingness to stake one's life on a cause that had little chance of success. As an attack on the ultimate in undemocratic practices, these unsuccessful attempts and the labors of their leaders can be viewed as being in the tradition of the ideals of the Declaration of Independence and as promoting the concept of individual freedom and human dignity. The oppression against which they fought and the odds against their success were far greater than those encountered by the patriots who made the American Revolution.

Until well into the 20th century, historians tended to play down unrest among slaves and to picture insurrections as seldom occurring in the United States. This mythology both reflected and was needed to support slavery and the Jim Crow practices that followed emancipation. Post–World War II historians find that

the evidence warrants a different interpretation. More than 250 cases have been identified that can be classified as insurrections, and periodic expressions of fear among whites of slave revolts can be documented. Further evidence exists in the slave codes and the records of punishment. It is difficult to be definitive on this matter, because of the obvious policy of silence regarding such events, the bias of the records maintained by those supporting slavery, the difficulty of distinguishing between personal crimes and organized revolts, and the quick spread of rumors. However, there is now general agreement that dissatisfaction with their condition was characteristic among slaves and that insurrection was more frequent than earlier historians had acknowledged. A unique record of slave convictions in the state of Virginia for the period 1780–1864 gives support to the revisionist. Of a total of 1,418 convictions, 91 were for insurrection and 346 for murder. When this is added to the several recorded examples of plots and revolts in the state in the 17th and early 18th centuries, the record for that state alone is impressive.

The first slave revolt in territory that became the United States took place in 1526 in a Spanish settlement near the mouth of the Pee Dee River in what is now South Carolina. Several slaves rebelled and fled to live with Indians of the area. The following year the colonists left the area without having recaptured the slaves. Insurrection in the British colonies began with the development of slavery and continued into the American Revolution. The most serious of the period occurred in New York and in South Carolina. In 1712 a slave conspiracy in New York City led to the death of nine whites and the wounding of five or six others. Six of the rebels killed themselves to avoid capture. Of those taken into custody twenty-one were executed in a variety of ways. Some were hanged, others burned, one broken on the wheel, and one hanged in chains as an example to other would-be insurrectionists. In 1739 an uprising known as Cato's Revolt took place at Stono, S.C., near Charleston. Blacks seized guns and ammunition and fought the militia before being defeated. Approximately twenty-five whites and fifty blacks were killed. In 1741 a conspiracy among slaves and white servants in New York City led to the execution of thirty-one blacks and four whites.

The successful slave revolt in Haiti during the French Revolution led to a series of plots in the South. Others followed up to the Civil War. Of these Gabriel's Revolt, the plot of Denmark Vesey, and Nat Turner's Revolt were the most significant.

303

In 1800 Gabriel Prosser and Jack Bowler planned a revolt to involve thousands of slaves in the Richmond area. Authorities became aware that something was under way, and James Monroe, then governor of Virginia, ordered that precautions be taken. In spite of this the leaders planned to proceed on Saturday, Aug. 20. On that day there occurred what a contemporary described as "the most terrible thunder accompanied with an enormous rain, that I ever witnessed in the state." Nevertheless, over a thousand armed slaves gathered only to find that a bridge over which they had to pass had been washed away. On the same day an informer gave specifics of the plot to authorities. Many arrests were made, including Prosser and Bowler. Thirty-six slaves, including the leaders, were executed.

In 1822 Denmark Vesey, a black who had purchased his freedom in 1800, planned an uprising in the area of Charleston. With able assistance from such leaders as Peter Poyas and Mingo Harth many slaves over a large area were involved. The plan was to attack Charleston on the second Sunday in July, Sunday being a day on which it was customary for many blacks to be in the city and July being a time when many whites were vacationing outside the city. Weapons were made and information secured as to the location where arms and ammunition were stored. However, betrayal led Vesey to move the date ahead one month; but before action could be taken, further information led to the arrest of the leaders. Vesey and thirty-four others were found guilty and hanged.

In 1831 Nat Turner led a revolt in Southampton County, Va. Slaves killed over seventy whites and caused panic over a wide area. Soldiers defeated the rebels, and Turner and others were executed.

Some generalizations can be made about these insurrections. They involved mainly slaves, with only occasional participation by free blacks and rare involvement of whites. They were stimulated by factors and events external to the local situation—such as the revolution in Haiti—and each uprising brought a new crop of repressive laws. The measure of the importance of these revolts is not determined by their failure to free slaves but by the information they provide about slaves and their reactions to the institution of slavery.

[Herbert Aptheker, *American Negro Slave Revolts;* Nicholas Halasz, *The Rattling Chains;* Marion D. Kilson, "Toward Freedom: An Analysis of Slave Revolts in the United States," *Phylon,* vol. 25 (1964).]

HENRY N. DREWRY

SLAVE REPRESENTATION. *See* **Compromises of the U.S. Constitution.**

SLAVERY. Africans, or Negroes, as they were also called by European slave traders, were first brought to the British continental colonies in August 1619 when a Dutch frigate sold twenty black captives to settlers in Jamestown, Va. It is not certain whether these black bondsmen were indentured servants or slaves, but it seems clear that from the time of their arrival in British America, blacks were treated as inferiors to all whites, indentured or free.

By the year 1640 some blacks in Virginia were actually being held in perpetual bondage as *de facto* slaves and some of their children had inherited the same obligation, while others remained contracted servants or had been set free by their masters. After that date the bonds of black servitude tightened in the colony. The rising costs of free and indentured labor added to the availability of cheap African labor that could be compelled to serve for life, and Anglo-Saxon color prejudices led to the transformation between 1640 and 1660 of informal black slavery into black chattel bondage sanctioned by law. By the 1660's Virginia had enacted a series of laws giving statutory recognition to the institution of slavery and consigning blacks to a special and inferior status in society.

As slavery evolved in Virginia, it appeared in the other British colonies. By the end of the 17th century it had gained legal recognition throughout British America and had become the presumed status of all blacks. Along the southern seaboard, where environmental conditions were suitable for the production of staple crops, such as tobacco, rice, and cotton, slavery took firm root. The institution never took strong hold in the middle Atlantic and New England settlements. Less temperate climates, rockier terrain, and a predominantly commercial economy supplemented by subsistence agriculture prevented settlers from duplicating on northern soil the lucrative plantation economy developing in the South. Nevertheless, huge profits were reaped by those northerners, particularly merchants in Massachusetts and Rhode Island, who were involved in the Atlantic slave trade.

In all of the colonies, despite various social and ecological differences, enslaved blacks suffered a gradual erosion of their status; by about 1700 they had reached their complete debasement, being regarded as human property. Each region, out of fear, antimiscegenationist sentiments, and racial prejudice, passed in the course of the 18th century elaborate sets of slave codes to regulate slave activity and to protect white society against black uprisings. Slaves were denied the right to marry, own property, bear arms, or defend themselves against assault. So that baptized slaves and children fathered by white men could not escape enslavement, colonial legislatures ruled that conversion to Christianity had no effect upon a person's condition, bond or free, and that status was determined by the race of the mother.

As imperfections in the system were corrected and as slave importations from Africa and the Caribbean increased in the 18th century, the slave population in the English colonies grew to large proportions, expanding from 20,000 in 1700 to 500,000 by the time of the American Revolution. The majority of the slaves were concentrated in those colonies along the southern seaboard in which tobacco, rice, indigo, and cotton were the important crops. South Carolina had a slave population in 1765 of 90,000 out of a total population of 130,000, and Virginia had a population of 120,000 slaves out of a total of 290,000 in 1756. The numbers of slaves never attained such levels in the North, where only in New York and Rhode Island, because of their extensive agricultural enterprises, were sizable groups of blacks concentrated.

Because of its tenuous base north of the Potomac River, the institution of slavery was unable to survive the attack directed against it there during the revolutionary war era. Strong abolitionist impulses inspired by the Quakers, the libertarian ideals of the war for independence, black freedom petitions, and the marginal importance of slavery to the North's economy produced between 1780 and 1804 a number of state court decisions and laws gradually abolishing slavery in New England and the middle Atlantic states. The institution remained basically untouched in the South, which was heavily dependent upon slave labor. Despite the antislavery pronouncements of some liberal southern statesmen, such as Thomas Jefferson, emancipation of the slaves was widely regarded as an impractical and irresponsible act that was detrimental to the economy and harmful to the blacks who allegedly benefited from their masters' paternalistic care.

To avoid disruptive conflict with the South and thereby hold together the newly formed republic, the framers of the U.S. Constitution agreed at the Constitutional Convention, held in Philadelphia in September 1787, to several compromises favorable to southern interests. The Constitution included a provision by which, for purposes of congressional apportionment, a slave was to be counted as three-fifths of a person; an extension of the slave trade until 1808; and a fugitive slave clause, which ensured the return of runaway slaves to their masters. Although the Constitution proved to be a conservative compact between northern commercialists and the southern aristocracy, the passage by Congress in 1787 of the Northwest Ordinance, which prevented the expansion of slavery into the midwestern territories, and the closing in 1808 of the African slave trade greatly restricted the future development of American slavery and deeply affected its character.

Congressional barriers against western expansion and exclusion from the international slave trade did not result, as some emancipationists had hoped, in the natural death of southern slavery. The institution had become by the late 1780's a viable economic system so intricately woven into the social fabric of southern life that black emancipation was never seriously considered. Growing demands in the world and domestic markets for cotton and the invention of the cotton gin in 1793 by Eli Whitney, which revolutionized the production of southern cotton, made slavery at the turn of the century an even more profitable enterprise, believed to be absolutely essential to the southern economy and society.

Because of its heightened commercial value and improved means of production, cotton soon became the staple crop throughout much of the South, spreading from the southeastern states, which until about 1800 had grown most of the nation's cotton, into the virgin lands acquired through the Louisiana Purchase of 1803. By the 1830's the fertile Gulf Coast states of Mississippi, Alabama, and Louisiana dominated an American cotton industry that was producing three-fourths of the world's supply.

With the rise of the southern cotton kingdom came increased demands by the planters for slave labor. For a brief period continued imports from Africa had been relied upon, but after the 1808 prohibition, planters were forced to turn to the domestic slave trade then being developed by states in the upper South, such as Virginia and Maryland, which had an excess supply of slaves. During the four decades preceding the Civil War, the domestic slave trade accounted for the transfer of about 200,000 slaves from the soil-exhausted Chesapeake Bay region to the alluvial Black Belt area, where cotton had become "king." Despite its volume, the domestic slave trade failed to supply planters in the lower South with the number of slaves needed on their extensive cotton fields. Since Congress could not be persuaded to reopen the trade with Africa, the planters had no choice but to increase their slave force by natural reproduction.

Out of economic necessity, American slaveowners generally created on their plantations material conditions conducive to the natural production of a large indigenous slave population. Of all the slave systems in the New World, it was only in North America that the slave population grew naturally to large proportions. Existing on the fringes of the Atlantic basin slave trade, the United States probably imported not more than about 430,000 slaves from Africa, less than 5 percent of the estimated total involuntary immigration of blacks to the Western Hemisphere. The growth of the slave population from 750,000 in 1790 to over 4 million in 1860, an increase of about 30 percent each decade, was attributable almost entirely to natural reproduction.

American slaveholders put their vast black work force to effective use, utilizing it in various capacities, not all of which was agriculturally based. Almost half a million slaves were employed in nonagricultural pursuits in the cities, towns, and labor camps of the antebellum South. Because of the special skills many slaves had acquired and the low costs of unfree labor, there was, throughout much of the antebellum era, a great demand among southern urbanites and industrialists for slave artisans and factory workers.

The farm or plantation remained nonetheless the slave's typical environment. In 1860 more than half of North America's 4 million slaves lived in the countryside on plantations worked by 20 or more slaves, but the bulk of the slave population was owned by a distinctly small segment of southern society. On the eve of the Civil War there were only 385,000 slaveholders in a free white population of 1.5 million families. Therefore only one-quarter of southern whites had a vested economic interest in slavery. But aspirations of one day belonging to the planter class, deeply ingrained racial prejudices, and psychological gratification derived from their superiority over the degraded blacks caused nonslaveholders to support an economic system that conflicted with their own class interests.

By the 1830's, virtually all opposition among southern whites to the institution of slavery had disappeared. Public reactions to mounting abolitionism in the North and increasing fears of slave insurrections in their own states silenced or drove into exile any remaining southern advocates of emancipation. To stifle all dissent, the South constructed an elaborate ideological and militant defense of slavery. Headed by George Fitzhugh, the proslavery ideologue of Virginia, southern apologists, including politicians, clergymen, social scientists, and natural scientists, popularized arguments that slavery was a positive good, divinely ordained, and that blacks were inherently inferior to whites.

Convinced of black inferiority and of the sanctity of slavery, southerners of all classes were prepared to protect the system by force if necessary. Service on the slave patrols and militia units instituted throughout the South to crush any internal or external threats was considered a civic duty and contributed to the emergence of a martial spirit in the region that verged on fanaticism and gave more authoritarian and coercive features to the slave system itself. Yet, absolute control of slave activity was never achieved. Unlike the modern concentration camp, which possessed the sophisticated means to induce widespread infantilism among its inmate population, the plantation, even under the harshest of conditions, was not so totalitarian a system that it was able to reduce its black work force to obsequious childlike dependents.

From dawn to dusk and sometimes long after dark during the harvest season, the slaves toiled under the supervision of either their masters, hired overseers, or trusted slaves called drivers; both brutal force and a complex system of rewards were used to get them to work efficiently. The daily routine of extended hours at forced labor was rarely interrupted except for a brief meal in the afternoon, and work in the fields only came to a full halt on Sundays and special holidays, such as Christmas. Consequently, it was usually only at night that the slaves enjoyed any respite from their labor. But as much as their lives were regimented by the plantation, the slaves often developed personalities strong enough to withstand the full psychological brunt of slavery's negative impact.

A communal spirit developed in the slave quarters, where the slaves were free of the constant scrutiny of their masters. The semiautonomous black culture created there out of both fragmentary African traditions and the American experience was among the chief factors protecting black personalities against adverse psychological change. The slave community, with its own hierarchy of male and female leaders, strong family ties, folklore, and spiritual beliefs, provided the slaves with the psychic ability to endure their oppression and the mental capacity to envision a better future, if not for themselves, for their children.

Those slaves who were fully socialized to the slave system probably longed for a heavenly reward in the afterlife and passively accepted their subjugation, but many others who were less submissive sought to make the most out of their immediate conditions through subtle and overt forms of resistance.

A particular set of impersonal factors, including geography, demography, and political stability, generally prevented the development in the United States of physical and social conditions conducive to slave uprisings. Unlike the situation in the Caribbean and Latin America, where the large ratio of slaves to their masters, political unrest, and the rugged terrain of the interior facilitated slave insurrections, conditions in North America militated against them. So formidable were the obstacles to rebellion in the United States that, for the most part, slaves could not think realistically of collective violence.

"Day-to-day resistance," expressed in malingering, work slowdowns, sabotage, arson, self-mutilation, and the feigning of illness or incompetence, was a more common form of the Afro-American slaves' opposition to the slave system. Black culture was also used as a subtle instrument of protest by the slaves. Masked in inoffensive language, slave sermons, spirituals, and folklore often contained subversive themes and messages that contributed to the cultivation in the slave quarters of a tradition of resistance to white oppression.

More overt examples of slave unrest are represented in the numerous attempts by slaves to run away to the free states in the North or to Canada. As perilous as such undertakings were, thousands of slaves tried to secure their freedom by fleeing from the South. Numerous slaves succeeded in their flight for freedom, mainly with the assistance of free blacks working as "agents" for the "Underground Railroad," such as Harriet Tubman. The most dramatic, but also rarest, form of slave protest was open rebellion. Historians have been able to identify some 250 instances of slave conspiracies and revolts in North America, the most noted of which were the Gabriel Prosser plot of 1800 in Henrico County, Va.; the Denmark Vesey conspiracy of 1822 in Charleston, S.C.; and the Nat Turner rebellion of 1831 in Southampton County, Va.

Except for the very rare occasion when rebel slaves managed to escape into the wilderness and form maroon societies, the rebellions were ruthlessly crushed and their leaders brutally executed. Repressive laws usually followed to terrorize the slave and free black population of the South into total submission. To protect the slave system against northern-based attacks, southern politicians, led by John C. Calhoun of South Carolina, upheld the principle of states' rights in Congress and sought to maintain a balance in the Senate between free and slave states. These efforts were intensified during and after the Missouri Compromise of 1820, which resulted in the admission of Missouri to the Union as a slave state. Through the diplomacy of Speaker of the House Henry Clay, the compromise preserved the delicate balance of power then existing between the free and slave states but served notice to the South of the growing opposition in other sections of the country to the issue of slavery and its expansion.

With the extension of America's borders to the Pacific in the 1840's, northern industrialists and farmers, for economic, political, and constitutional reasons, took a stand against the expansion of slavery into the newly acquired territories west of the Louisiana Purchase. Growing sectional strife over the issue reached a climax in the 1850's. The admission of Texas to the Union in 1845 as a slave state and the problem of slavery in the territories won from Mexico in 1848 led to a long and disruptive constitutional debate. Senators Stephen A. Douglas of Illinois and Henry Clay of Kentucky produced an omnibus bill, known as the Compromise of 1850, which temporarily settled the dispute and succeeded in preventing the threatened secession of the South from the Union. In the end, the compromise only provided an uneasy truce between the two sections. The illusory peace it created rapidly disintegrated under a wave of new disputes stemming from the slavery issue.

Tempers inflamed by the passage of the stringent Fugitive Slave Act (a proslavery provision of the Compromise of 1850), Harriet Beecher Stowe's novel *Uncle Tom's Cabin* (1852), the Kansas-Nebraska Act and conflict of 1854, and the Dred Scott Supreme Court decision of 1857 brought the nation to the brink of war. When white abolitionist John Brown and his interracial band attacked the federal arsenal at Harpers Ferry, Va. (now West Virginia), in 1859 to incite a general slave insurrection and Republican Abraham Lincoln of Illinois was elected president in 1860, most whites in the South were convinced that the only way to preserve southern civilization was to secede from the Union. In late 1860 and early 1861, seven Deep South states proceeded to secede from the Union, and on Apr. 12, 1861, South Carolina troops fired upon Fort Sumter, beginning the Civil War.

When Lincoln dispatched federal troops to repress the rebels, he had no intention of freeing the slaves.

His sole aim was restoration of the Union. Still, slavery was the fundamental cause of the conflict, and the issue of emancipation could not be indefinitely avoided by the president. Union generals in the field quickly recognized that freeing of the slaves would cripple the southern war effort and attract thousands of freed blacks to the side of the North. Fearful, however, of driving the loyal slave states of Maryland, Delaware, Missouri, and Kentucky into the Confederate camp, Lincoln resisted freeing the slaves and even prevented for a time the enlistment of free blacks into the Union army.

Initially, most northerners supported Lincoln's limited war aims and his opposition to black troops, but military expediency and growing moral concern soon transformed the conflict into a crusade to free the slaves as well as to save the Union. Abolitionists and Radical Republicans gradually convinced Congress and much of the general public of the need to abolish slavery, which was seen as the cornerstone of the Confederacy. Under mounting pressures from these groups and because of military necessity, Lincoln reluctantly altered his position on black soldiers and emancipation. In the spring and summer of 1862, Lincoln signed legislation abolishing slavery in the District of Columbia, banning slavery in the territories, and freeing slaves who escaped to northern lines. These actions were followed in the fall by decisions to authorize the enlistment of black volunteers into the army and to issue a preliminary emancipation proclamation.

By the terms of the preliminary announcement, issued by Lincoln in September 1862, all slaves in those states still in rebellion on Jan. 1, 1863, would be freed. Slaves in the loyal border states and in areas occupied by Union forces were excluded from the ruling, revealing the president's continued ambivalence toward general emancipation. Had the Confederates surrendered within a period of 100 days, the South might have been able, under the provisions of Lincoln's proclamation, to retain its slaves. But no concession short of independence was acceptable to southerners. The Confederacy refused to surrender, forcing the president to issue the Emancipation Proclamation on its scheduled date. Presented to the nation as a necessary war measure, the edict legally freed over 3 million slaves held in rebel territory and enabled freedmen to serve in the Union army. Issuance of the proclamation was acclaimed at home and abroad as a great humanitarian act, but the document was flawed. It left in bondage some 800,000 slaves in the border states and in areas controlled by the federal government. They were not freed until the adoption in December 1865 of the Thirteenth Amendment, which formally brought to an end nearly 250 years of black slavery in America.

[Herbert Aptheker, *American Negro Slave Revolts;* John W. Blassingame, *The Slave Community;* Philip Curtin, *The Atlantic Slave Trade;* Melvin Drimmer, ed., *Black History;* Robert William Fogel and Stanley L. Engerman, *Time on the Cross;* Winthrop Jordan, *White Over Black;* John Hope Franklin, *From Slavery to Freedom;* Eugene Genovese, *Roll, Jordan, Roll;* August Meier and Elliot Rudwick, *From Plantation to Ghetto;* Benjamin Quarles, *The Negro in the Making of America;* Kenneth Stampp, *The Peculiar Institution;* Allen Weinstein and Frank Otto Gatell, *American Negro Slavery.*]

WILLIAM R. SCOTT

SLAVES, FUGITIVE. *See* **Fugitive Slave Acts.**

SLAVE SHIPS. The earliest slave ships were converted merchantmen, but later, special vessels were built, based on troop transports and equipped with air scuttles, ports, and open gratings. The first definitely authenticated American ship to carry slaves was the *Desire,* sailing out of Salem, Mass., in 1638. Like most of the early slavers, it was small: 120 tons burthen and 79 feet long. The *White Horse,* sailing out of New Amsterdam (New York) in 1654, was 120 feet long and 25.5 feet wide and could carry 400 slaves. Many of these vessels were heavily armed both for self-defense and for highjacking other slavers. The *Hannibal,* an English slaver of 1693, was 450 tons and mounted 36 guns, which it was frequently forced to use; it carried 700 slaves. Of the smaller slavers, the most common was the Snow class: approximately 140 tons, square-sterned, 20 feet beam, 5 feet between decks. Even with such small holds as this, many slavers rigged a shelf in the middle called a "slave deck," which extended 6 feet from each side to hold additional slaves. Sometimes a second slave deck was also used, leaving only 20 inches of headroom, so that the slaves were unable even to sit upright during the entire voyage.

When the slave trade was made illegal in 1808, traders turned to fast ships to outrun the British frigates guarding the African coast. Many were topsail schooners or brigs. With such vessels, every consideration was sacrificed for speed, and the accommodations for the slaves were even worse than on earlier vessels. The *Diligente,* an American clipper sailing in 1839, was characterized by long straight lines, sheer very slight, its yards greater in length than half its deck, and with tremendous head spars. Such a ship could do 19 knots in a good wind. Another clipper was the *Nightingale* of Salem (1860), 1,000 tons and carrying 2,000 slaves. The last American slaver was probably the *Huntress* of New York, which landed a cargo of slaves in Cuba in 1864.

[H. I. Chapelle, *The Baltimore Clipper;* George Francis Dow, *Slave Ships and Slaving.*]

DANIEL MANNIX

SLAVE STATES were those states where, prior to the Civil War, slaveholding was sanctioned by law. This was the case in all the states in 1776. Under the influence of the American Revolution, slavery disappeared from those areas north of Delaware and Maryland. Pennsylvania moved against it in 1780, Massachusetts abolished it by court action in 1783, and Connecticut and Rhode Island passed laws prohibiting slavery in 1784. New York in 1785 and New Jersey in 1786 passed manumission acts that were followed by more effective legislation in 1799 and 1804. The Northwest Ordinance (1787) prohibited the establishment of slavery in any state formed in that territory. But the trend did not continue. The Compromise of 1820 had been worked out to define the territory from which slave states might develop, and by 1845 nine new slave states had entered the Union. Efforts to add additional slave states and to prevent the spread of slavery led to fighting in Kansas and became a major national issue in the 1850's. On the eve of the Civil War the slave states were Alabama, Arkansas, Delaware, Florida, Georgia, Kentucky, Louisiana, Maryland, Mississippi, Missouri, North Carolina, South Carolina, Tennessee, Texas, and Virginia.

HENRY N. DREWRY

SLAVE TRADE. African slaves were first brought to the New World shortly after its discovery by Christopher Columbus (there are records of them in Haiti in 1501), but the slave trade proper did not begin until 1517. It was largely the inspiration of Bartolomé de Las Casas, later the bishop of Chiapas, Mexico, who had seen that the Indian slaves "died like fish in a bucket," as one indignant Spaniard remarked, while "these Negroes prospered so much . . . [they] would never die, for as yet none have been known to perish from infirmity." In an effort to save the Indians, Las Casas suggested the wholesale importation of black slaves, a suggestion he was later bitterly to regret. In

response to his plea, Charles V of Spain issued the Asiento, a contract giving the holder a monopoly on importing slaves to the Spanish dominions; Charles gave it to a favorite courtier. For the next two centuries the Asiento was to be a much coveted prize in European wars and treaties.

Portugal claimed the west coast of Africa as a result of expeditions sent out by Prince Henry the Navigator and at first controlled the export of slaves. Many of the words associated with the trade came from the Portuguese, such as "palaver" (a conference), "barracoon" (a slave pen), "bozal" (a newly captured black), "panyaring" (kidnapping), and "pickaninny" (a child). Portugal's hegemony was soon challenged by French, Dutch, Swedish, Danish, Prussian, and English slavers, but Portugal managed to retain control of the area south of the Bight of Benin and did until 1974. The various slaving companies erected a series of great forts, built on the design of medieval castles, along the coast of Africa. The castles, some of which are still standing, served the double purpose of acting as barracoons for the slaves and as protection against native attacks.

The slaving territory extended roughly from the Senegal River to Angola. The Bight of Benin provided so many slaves that it became known as the Slave Coast, mainly because it included the mouths of the Niger River, to which slaves were shipped down from the interior by canoe in large numbers. Some of the African tribes particularly associated with the trade were the Mandingo, Ashanti, Yoruba, Ewe, and Ibo.

Slavery was a recognized institution in Africa but consisted mainly of domestic slaves, for the continent was not industrialized and so had no market for large crops raised by slave labor. Some of the Mandingo nobles owned a thousand slaves. The local kings sold their surplus slaves, as well as criminals, debtors, and prisoners of war, to the European traders. In times of famine, parents often sold their children. These sources did not meet the constantly growing demand, and soon slave-catching raids were organized by the coastal tribes, using firearms supplied by the slavers. Even tribes reluctant to cooperate with the Europeans were forced to do so, because without firearms they would have been enslaved by their neighbors.

England, as the outstanding sea power, gradually came to control the trade. The first English slaver was John Hawkins, one of the most famous Elizabethan sea dogs. Hawkins engaged in a series of raids, beginning in 1560, on native communities along the coast, selling his captives in Spanish possessions in defiance of the Asiento. Queen Elizabeth called the business "detestable," but once aware of Hawkins' profits she became a shareholder in his subsequent voyages. Francis Drake as a young man also took part in the trade.

At first the English colonies in North America depended on European indentured servants for labor. When the supply of such individuals began to run short, the colonists turned to slaves. The first black slaves were landed in Jamestown, Va., in 1619. They were regarded as indentured servants, but by the middle of the 17th century slaves had come to be considered human chattels. All the colonies had slaves, but as the plantation system developed in the South, the slaves became concentrated there. Slavery was abolished in the northern colonies, principally as an inducement to white laborers to emigrate, but the New England colonies continued to take an active part in the slave trade itself, providing ships and crews and selling the slaves south of the Mason-Dixon Line. The trade expanded rapidly after 1650. It is thought that only 900,000 slaves were exported to the colonies during the whole of the 17th century, but by 1750, 100,000 slaves a year were arriving. There was an increasing demand for sugar, tobacco, rice, and later cotton, crops that could be supplied most profitably by slave labor.

In 1662 the Royal Adventure Trading Company (reincorporated as the Royal African Company in 1663) was founded in England and bought up all the castles along the coast, thinking this would give it a monopoly of the trade. By this time the tribal kings were as deeply involved in the trade as the Europeans, so the castles with their elaborate system of defense had become an anachronism. The company went bankrupt in 1750.

By the 18th century, the actual slave catching was done mainly by such warlike inland tribes as the Ashanti and the Dahomey, with the coastal tribes acting as middlemen. The slaves usually came from 200 to 300 miles inland, often much further. Mungo Park traveled 500 miles with a slave coffle (slave gang). To prevent escape, two slaves were often yoked together by means of a stick with a fork at each end into which the slaves' necks were fastened. The coffle was then marched to the coast, where the slaves were kept in a barracoon usually presided over by a European called a factor. When enough slaves had been collected, they were ferried out by canoe to the ships waiting off shore. The task of ferrying was generally conducted by the Krumen, a tribe of fishermen that came to specialize in this work.

In 1713 the Treaty of Utrecht gave England the Asiento and a virtual monopoly of the trade north of the equator. There followed a great boom in the slave trade. Liverpool was largely built on money made from the trade. So many slaves were exported that the Africans were convinced that white men were cannibals who existed solely on human flesh, as they could think of no other explanation for the enormous demand.

The American colonies developed triangular trade in the mid-18th century. A captain would load up with trade goods and rum and sail to Africa, where the goods would be exchanged for slaves. He would then land his slaves in the West Indies and take on a cargo of molasses, which he would transport to New England to be made into rum. In this way a captain was never forced to sail with an empty hold and could make a profit on each leg of the voyage. The base of the triangle, the run across the middle of the Atlantic, became known as the Middle Passage. At first slavers attempted to make some provisions for the welfare of their human cargo, such as "loose packing" (not overcrowding the slaves), arguing that the fewer the slaves who died, the greater the profits. Later most slavers became convinced that it was more profitable to pack slaves into every available square foot of space and make a run for it, a practice called "tight packing." With good winds the voyage could be made with little loss of life in two months, but with contrary winds most of the human cargo would be lost.

Since the slaves were packed "spoon fashion" with "no more space than a man would have in his coffin," it was necessary to bring small groups, heavily shackled, on deck for short periods and force them to "dance" to restore their blood circulation. Nets had to be rigged along the ship's sides to prevent the slaves from leaping overboard and drowning themselves. Many refused to eat and had to be force-fed by a device called the "speculum ores," which resembled a funnel and was forced down the slave's throat. Then "slabber sauce," made of palm oil, horse beans, and flour, was poured down the funnel. Many died of the flux (dysentery), smallpox, and what the slavers called "fixed melancholy," or simply despair. A few captains were more merciful, such as Hugh Crow, who was awarded a bounty by the Anti-Slave Society for making a series of runs without losing a single slave; John Newton, who later became a clergyman; and Billy Boates, who was actually able to arm his slaves to beat off the attacks of privateers.

By the end of the 18th century there began to be

strong moral opposition to the slave trade, although many considered it an economic necessity and the only method of providing manpower. In America, the fight against the trade was led by such men as John Woolman and Anthony Benezet. In England, the antislavery forces were led by Thomas Clarkson and William Wilberforce. Great Britain abolished the trade in 1807, and the United States did the same in 1808. The other European and South American countries gradually followed suit, either from pressure exerted on them by Great Britain or from honest conviction.

The trade continued to increase despite the prohibition. The invention of the cotton gin in 1793 and the development of the power loom, which created an unlimited demand for cotton, resulted in fresh demands for slaves. The value of a prime field hand rose from $500 to $1,500. Theodore Canot, a famous slave smuggler, left records of his voyages showing that on a single successful trip he made a net profit of $41,439. Two or three such voyages could make a man wealthy for life. The slavers started using fast ships—the forerunners of the clipper ship—which were rarely caught by the old-fashioned frigates sent by the British to patrol the African coast. As slavery was still legal in Africa, the native rulers continued to erect barracoons along the coast and await cruising slavers, which would signal, usually by flags, that they were in the market for a certain number of slaves. The slaves would be ferried out and loaded in only two or three hours; the slaver would then hoist all sails and run for the West Indies. Unless a frigate was able to catch a slaver with sails furled in the act of loading, capture was highly unlikely, although after the British had managed to capture a few slavers and used them as patrol vessels, the odds were more even.

A tangle of legal restrictions was imposed on the slaving squadron. Many nations, including the United States, refused to allow any ship flying their respective flags to be searched by the British even though it could be proved that the ship was using the flag illegally. As a result, slavers carried with them a number of different flags and appropriate papers to frustrate the frigates. To be condemned as a slaver, a ship had to be carrying slaves when boarded. This resulted in slavers tying their captives to the anchor chain and then, if in danger of capture, dropping the anchor over the side, dragging the slaves with it. Even if this was done in full view of the pursuing frigate, the ship could not be seized if no slaves remained onboard.

Slavers were declared pirates by both the United States and Great Britain under the treaty of 1820 and could be hanged, although this sentence was in fact not carried out until a later period. In 1839 the Equipment Clause was passed, authorizing a frigate's captain to seize a ship if it was obviously fitted out as a slaver with slave decks, large amounts of extra water casks, shackles, and grilled hatches. The Webster-Ashburton Treaty of 1842, between Great Britain and the United States, provided for American warships to cruise along the coast with the British vessels so that if a suspected slaver was flying American colors, the American warship could pursue it. This joint cruising was largely a failure. Few American frigates were ever sent, and most of those did not take their duty seriously. Some of them were under the command of southern officers who sympathized with the slavers, but a few American captains, such as Commodore Andrew Foote, did make an honest effort to suppress the trade and succeeded in making some captures.

In 1840 Capt. Joseph Dennan of the British navy, tired of seeing the barracoons packed with slaves along the coast, finally burned them after freeing the captives. The African monarchs angrily protested, but Parliament supported Dennan, although a few years before he would have been court-martialed for such an act. As a result, the barracoons had to be relocated far inland, which made loading the slaves onto ships much more difficult. Brazil was notorious for openly practicing the trade even though it had declared against it, and so in 1849 British Adm. Barrington Reynolds sailed into the port of Rio de Janeiro and burned all the slavers that he could find lying at anchor. To the populace's furious protests, Don Paulino, the Brazilian foreign minister, could only reply, "When a powerful nation like Great Britain is evidently in earnest, what can Brazil do?" To avoid the slaving squadron, some slavers dared to make the long and dangerous cruise around the Cape of Good Hope and load with slaves in East African ports, especially Zanzibar. A few thousand slaves were shipped in this way until the British sent paddlewheel frigates to stop the practice.

Meanwhile, slaves continued to be run into southern ports. In 1860 Capt. Nathaniel Gordon of the *Erie* was captured with a cargo of slaves. At President Abraham Lincoln's command, Gordon was hanged in New York, although troops had to be called out to prevent mobs from rescuing him.

With the abolition of slavery in the United States and the end of the Civil War, the trade largely came to an end. A few cargoes were probably run to Brazil in the 1870's and possibly even in the early 1880's, but to all intents and purposes, the trade was finished. In 1867 the slaving squadron was withdrawn.

Some 15 million blacks were exported from Africa during the 300 years of the slave trade. The number who died in native wars growing out of the slave trade was at least three times that figure. For Europeans and Americans, the trade provided much of the capital that financed the Industrial Revolution and supplied the labor that developed the American South and Southwest. For Africans, it was a disaster. It bled dry great sections of the continent, leaving communities so weak that they could not harvest crops; encouraged local wars; and discouraged development of the continent's resources, because the trade was so enormously profitable nothing else could compete with it.

[Theodore Canot, *Adventures of a Slave Trader;* Captain Colomb, *Slave-Catching in the Indian Ocean;* Basil Davidson, *Black Mother;* Elizabeth Donnan, ed., *Documents Illustrative of the History of the Slave Trade to America;* W. E. B. Du Bois, *The Suppression of the Slave Trade;* Christopher Lloyd, *The Navy and the Slave Trade;* Daniel Mannix and Malcolm Cowley, *Black Cargoes.*]

DANIEL MANNIX

SLAVOCRACY, in its broader sense, refers to the persons or interests in the antebellum South representing slavery and using their influence to preserve and expand that institution. In spite of the abolition of slavery in some northern states soon after the American Revolution, the slavocracy was successful in securing the recognition of slavery in the Constitution, in continuing the slave trade for some years, and in adding nine slave states to the Union by 1845. Its influence can be seen in the absence of any effort by the federal government to move against slavery in the states until late 1862; even then the action taken in the Emancipation Proclamation was only against slavery in those states still in rebellion against the United States.

In its more restricted sense, the term ''slavocracy'' was used in the North during the 1850's to designate a group of southern expansionists supposedly united in a plot to extend the area of American slavery into the territories and possibly to Mexico, Cuba, and Central America. Apparently no such united movement actually existed, although southern imperialists were interested in extending slave territory and were supported by representatives in Congress from the slaveholding South.

[Eugene Genovese, *The World the Slaveholders Made;* Loren Miller, *The Petitioners.*]

HENRY N. DREWRY

SLEEPING CARS. *See* **Pullmans.**

SLEEPY HOLLOW. About three-quarters of a mile north of Tarrytown, N.Y., lies Sleepy Hollow, famous for its old Dutch church (1699) and for its association with the writings of Washington Irving. The area was named for a narrow ravine through which flows the Pocantico River. Sleepy Hollow is the site of Irving's classic tale of Ichabod Crane, who fled wildly across the bridge to escape the ''headless horseman.'' Irving visited the Sleepy Hollow region in his youth, probably for the first time in 1798, and he now lies buried in the cemetery behind the Dutch church. Romantic memories of Sleepy Hollow recur in Irving's essays (for example, *Wolfert's Roost*) and attain their most complete and delightful expression in ''The Legend of Sleepy Hollow,'' originally published in number VI of *The Sketch Book,* on Dec. 29, 1819.

STANLEY T. WILLIAMS

SLIDELL'S MISSION TO MEXICO. John Slidell, a Democratic congressman from Louisiana, was sent to Mexico by President James K. Polk in November 1845 to secure a boundary adjustment between the United States and Mexico. His flexible instructions included authorization to commit the U.S. government to pay liberal bonuses in return for relinquishment by Mexico of claims to certain territory. For example, $5 million might be offered for the cession of New Mexico; $20 million for a line to the Pacific yielding San Francisco to the United States; and $25 million for a line to Monterey.

Notwithstanding previous pledges, the Mexican government did not receive Slidell officially. After the formal rejection of his proposal, on Dec. 21, 1845, Slidell withdrew to Jalapa, where he remained until April 1846, fulfilling the auxiliary purpose of his mission, to act as an observer, and striving ''to place [the United States] in the strongest moral position before our own people and the world by exhausting every means of conciliation.'' Failure of the mission presaged war with Mexico.

[Louis Martin Sears, *John Slidell.*]

LOUIS MARTIN SEARS

SLIM BUTTES, BATTLE OF (Sept. 9, 1876). After the Sioux victory at the Battle of Little Bighorn (June

25–26), troops under Gen. George Crook and other commanders pursued and scattered the Indians. His rations nearly exhausted, Crook finally abandoned pursuit and marched for the Black Hills settlements. At Grand River, a party of 150 cavalrymen on the strongest horses was sent ahead for supplies, and twenty miles south, at Slim Buttes, they discovered a Sioux village of fifty lodges, containing 100 warriors under American Horse. At daybreak on Sept. 9, the cavalrymen rushed the village and captured it. A messenger was sent to Crook, who brought up the main body of troops by noon, and American Horse, mortally wounded and trapped in a cave, surrendered. Crazy Horse, arriving tardily with a large force consisting primarily of Oglala Sioux, attacked but was repulsed, and Crook's troops reached the Black Hills safely.

[Cyrus Townsend Brady, *Indian Fights and Fighters;* Charles King, *Campaigning With Crook.*]

JOSEPH MILLS HANSON

SLOCUM, GENERAL. See **Disasters.**

SLOGANS, CAMPAIGN. The purpose of campaign slogans, particularly in presidential campaigns, is usually to distract attention from the real issues and to center it on emotional aspects of the current scene. The idea emphasized by the slogan may be quite irrelevant, but it may nevertheless be extremely effective in developing group loyalty among the supporters of a candidate or a common bond of contempt for the opposition. Examples are: "Tippecanoe and Tyler Too" (1840); "Fifty-four Forty or Fight" (1844); "A House Divided Against Itself Cannot Stand" (1860); "Full Dinner Pail" (1896); "The Big Stick" (1904); "He Kept Us Out of War" (1916); "The Forgotten Man" (1932); "A New Deal" (1936); "The New Frontier" (1960); and "A Clear Choice" (1972).

The informal nicknames of candidates have frequently acquired a currency not easily distinguishable from that of the slogans: "Old Hickory"; "Honest Abe"; "The Great Commoner"; "Cautious Cal"; and "Ike." Similarly, certain tunes adopted for campaign songs have become intimately associated with candidates, such as: "There'll Be a Hot Time in the Old Town Tonight" (Theodore Roosevelt, 1904); "I Didn't Raise My Boy to Be a Soldier" (Woodrow Wilson, 1916); "The Sidewalks of New York" (Alfred E. Smith, 1928); and "Happy Days Are Here Again" (Franklin D. Roosevelt, 1932).

[Joseph B. Bishop, *Presidential Nominations and Elections;* Carl Scherf, "Slang, Slogan and Song in American Politics," *Social Studies* (December 1934).]

W. BROOKE GRAVES

SLOOP, a naval vessel, generally square-rigged and three-masted and carrying all its guns on the open spar deck. In the War of 1812 U.S. sloops such as the *Wasp* won many famous actions. More heavily armed wooden-screw sloops, such as the *Hartford, Niagara, Brooklyn,* and *San Jacinto,* saw action in the Civil War.

[Howard I. Chappelle, *The History of the American Sailing Navy.*]

WALTER B. NORRIS

SLUMS are seriously blighted residential districts that contribute to the social disorganization of their inhabitants. Slums have appeared in most cities, particularly in those of rapid growth and increasing heterogeneity. Except for scattered tenements that became overcrowded, the slow-growing cities in the American colonies escaped the blighting effects of slums until their increased size in some cases made the primitive sanitary facilities unwholesome. Poverty and other hardships abounded, but it was not until 1832, when the ravages of cholera exacted a heavy toll among the inhabitants of congested urban districts, that a few observant citizens in New York, Philadelphia, and Boston became aware of the existence there of wretched slums. In smaller towns these afflictions could still be attributed to an angry deity, but in New York a health survey by Dr. John H. Griscom prompted the formation in 1842 of the Association for Improving the Conditions of the Poor. Yet many members regarded it as only one of over a hundred charities, and the early attempts of its leaders to expose the evils of congestion had little effect, despite such reports as one in 1853 that pointed out the crowding of 18,456 persons into 3,742 cellars. The draft riots of 1863 revealed for the first time the extent of alienation that had developed in the slums. As a result the Citizens' Association made its appearance and appointed a council of hygiene and public health, which conducted an investigation that prompted the adoption of the first tenement house law in 1867.

Although the existence of slums was recognized, the causes and character of their growth were so poorly understood that successive housing reforms were vitiated. The rapid influx of poor Irish and German immigrants in the 1840's and 1850's inundated the older districts of Albany, New Orleans, and some other, smaller cities, as well as New York, Philadelphia, Baltimore, and Boston. Many substantial old houses and some warehouses, too, were hastily converted into multiple residences with minimal sanitary facilities, and flimsy annexes were added, often covering the last square inch of available land. When the early housing codes in New York City endeavored to preserve some open space and, later, to ban dark rooms, the builders added additional floors and provided airshafts that carried foul odors and sounds into every apartment. The increased density thus provided made it profitable to replace the less-substantial houses of an earlier day with solid rows of five- and six-story tenements that extended over wide districts and attracted only the poorest residents. A mounting influx of newcomers in the last decades of the century dumped thousands of Germans, Jews, Poles, Russians, and Italians into the vast expanse of tenements, where they competed for control of ethnic colonies and strove to ameliorate the slum environment by the introduction of their native customs.

Ethnic colonies appeared in most northern cities and in New Orleans in the South by midcentury, when over half the urban population was of foreign birth or parentage. Some, particularly in the German and Jewish colonies, which included many migrants who had urban experience abroad, successfully developed ethnic neighborhoods or ghettos that maintained wholesome communities and made vital cultural contributions to the growing cities. But as the streams of immigrants shifted and successive waves of eastern Europeans and Italians crowded their Irish and German predecessors out of the old districts, the ravages of time combined with the blight of poverty and the tensions of a new invasion to transform struggling ghettos into wretched slums.

The public awareness of the slums, induced by revealing accounts, such as those of Jacob Riis in New York and Jane Addams in Chicago, helped to support the social settlements in their endeavor to assist the residents of blighted districts develop wholesome communities. Together the settlement workers and neighborhood leaders pressed for increased civic provisions for health and safety and for the public enforcement of building codes, as well as for playgrounds and schools and finally for public housing. But their accomplishments were often dissipated and forgotten as the more promising and successful residents moved away or an influx of dissident newcomers brought a renewed struggle for local identity and survival. Each fresh invasion not only added new complications, contributing to social disorganization, but also deteriorated the housing stock. A federal survey in 1893 found the worst slum districts largely concentrated in New York and Chicago, but later studies found them widely present in most older cities of the Northeast.

The sudden drop in the tide of immigrants during World War I brought a sharp decline in the density of many old ethnic districts. In several heavy-industry cities in the North, where the wartime demand for labor had prompted efforts to import blacks from the South, a new invasion of the oldest slum districts commenced, producing violent race riots in a few cities. The migration from the South dropped off after the armistice, when the influx from southern and eastern Europe resumed until checked by the exclusion acts of the 1920's. The problems of the slums appeared to subside during the prosperous 1920's, in part because of the drastic reduction in the number of new immigrants, a situation that continued in the early years of the depression that followed. As unemployment and poverty spread, the influx of newcomers, and consequently the densities of the slum populations, declined. Moreover, the new federal relief measures brought the first public housing projects, among other welfare benefits, to some of the worst slum districts.

But the respite was short-lived in most cities. World War II stimulated a movement of blacks from the South that continued in the postwar years. The settlement of these blacks in old immigrant districts spurred the migration of former residents to the outskirts and suburbs, creating inner-city black ghettos that added the new dimensions of color and prejudice to the problems of the slums. As the migration continued, the expansion of these areas threatened both the downtown business districts and the nearby residential neighborhoods to which some of the older immigrant groups had removed. As the tension increased, focusing attention on the slums, the pressure for federal action mounted, spurring an expansion of the public housing program as a means of eradicating the slums. Unfortunately the demolition of old tenements had the effect of scattering their inhabitants, and in the face of a continued influx of blacks and a new influx of Puerto Ricans the search for new housing was intensified. Efforts to locate the new projects in outlying wards met stiff neighborhood resistance; the result was a concentration of the low-cost units in high-rise blocks that in some cities exceeded the worst densities of the old slums. And when key locations near the business district were cleared for commercial or high-rental developments, the charge of black removal added to the mounting tensions, which finally erupted in a contagion of inner-city riots of unprecedented violence in the 1960's. The rioting eventually subsided, and the introduction of new model-city participatory programs for the redevelopment of blighted districts offered federal assistance for their rejuvenation. The federal effort fostered the newly developing sense of black pride, which brought a surge for black power that helped to determine the character of some new housing projects in inner-city areas. Their combined efforts proved insufficient, however, to counteract the blighting effects of poverty, unemployment, and race prejudice. Frustrated by the limited accomplishments, the federal government terminated the model-city projects and merged its subsidies in a block-grant system that turned responsibility for the fate of the slums back to the cities.

[Charles Abrams, *The City Is the Frontier;* Roy Lubove, *The Progressives and the Slums;* Jacob Riis, *How the Other Half Lives.*]

BLAKE MCKELVEY

SMALL BUSINESS ADMINISTRATION. *See* Federal Agencies.

SMALLPOX in its classic form is an acute, highly contagious disease with an average fatality rate for untreated cases of about one in six to one in four. Survivors are often permanently disfigured or disabled. First clearly described by medieval Arab writers, smallpox was by the 17th century a common disease of children in Europe. Brought to the Americas by explorers and settlers, it destroyed many Indian tribes. It became epidemic several times in the British colonies in the 1600's and occasioned the first colonial medical publication, Thomas Thacher's *A Brief Rule to Guide the Common-People of New-England How to Order Themselves and Theirs in the Small Pocks, or Measels* (Boston, 1678). To prevent the introduction and spread of the disease, the New England colonies created an elaborate system of quarantine and isolation during the 18th century.

About 1700, reports began reaching England about the practice, called inoculation, of inserting matter from a pustule of a smallpox patient into superficial incisions in the arms of persons who had not had the disease. The person so inoculated generally had a comparatively mild case of smallpox. Like natural

smallpox, inoculated smallpox conferred lifelong immunity. After reading an account in the Royal Society's *Philosophical Transactions,* Cotton Mather persuaded Dr. Zabdiel Boylston to try it in 1721, when smallpox next became epidemic in Boston. A violent controversy ensued as Mather and Boylston were accused of spreading the disease. Statistics showed, however, that the case fatality rate for inoculated smallpox was much lower than for natural. In Boston in 1721 there were 5,759 cases of natural smallpox, with 842 deaths (nearly 8 percent of the total population), and 287 inoculated cases, with only 6 deaths. Subsequent experiences were generally more favorable, so that inoculation became widely accepted, especially among those who expected to be exposed to the disease. Inoculation entailed some risk, and, if unregulated, could expose the community to the hazard of contagion. Several colonies passed laws prohibiting inoculation except during epidemics or in isolated hospitals. Many communities were thus able to avoid smallpox altogether for years. In the Middle Colonies, by contrast, inoculation was freely allowed, and in Philadelphia smallpox spread widely at frequent intervals, just as in British towns of comparable size. After the first year of the Revolution, American recruits were regularly inoculated, which made smallpox a minor threat to the effectiveness of the army. Although inoculation could not eliminate smallpox—it was, after all, a form of the disease itself—it could, when properly regulated and publicly supported, contribute significantly to reducing the death rate.

In 1798 the English physician Edward Jenner introduced vaccination—that is, the inoculation of cowpox, a naturally occurring disease among dairy cattle and dairy workers—using techniques virtually identical to those used for the inoculation of smallpox (now known also as variolation). Vaccination, according to Jenner, was never fatal, did not spread naturally, and offered permanent protection against smallpox. Since then vaccinia has replaced cowpox virus as the usual inoculum and Jenner's conclusions have been found to be not strictly true; in particular, periodic revaccination is necessary for full protection. Compared to variolation, however, Jennerian vaccination was an immeasurable advance—probably the greatest single advance in preventive medicine ever achieved. Despite inevitable opposition, misuse, and errors, it was rapidly accepted around the world.

Soon after Jenner's announcement it was reported in the United States in medical publications and in newspapers. Several physicians sought to import vaccine; with one minor exception, the first to do so successfully was Benjamin Waterhouse, who vaccinated his son Daniel on July 8, 1800. At first Waterhouse sought outrageous profits from his temporary monopoly, but soon other physicians received vaccine from England independently; thereafter Waterhouse actively promoted its use. Vaccine institutes were promptly organized to treat the poor free, the first under James Smith in Baltimore in 1802. Smith later received an appointment as U.S. agent of vaccination under an 1813 act of Congress.

Vaccination was not universal in the 19th century. During the Civil War the Union army experienced some 19,000 cases and 7,000 deaths from smallpox. Preservation of live vaccine virus was difficult, and the vaccine sometimes became contaminated with other pathogenic microorganisms. The introduction of animal vaccine produced in calves in 1870 and of glycerinated lymph somewhat later helped to obviate these difficulties. As health departments began urging compulsory vaccination, especially after the pandemic of 1870–75, antivaccination societies were founded. Alleging the dangers of the introduction of other diseases, the infringement of personal liberty, and the ineffectiveness of vaccination, the antivaccinationists were supported by patent medicine interests, homeopaths, and others who opposed government regulation of drugs or of medical practice. As a result, the United States, of the twenty-six countries reporting smallpox morbidity to the League of Nations in 1921–30, had the highest attack rate of any nation except India. The great majority of cases in the United States were a relatively mild form known as alastrim, with a case fatality rate of less than 1 percent. Nevertheless, during an outbreak of classic smallpox in 1924–25 imported from Canada, some 1,270 deaths occurred. The use of vaccination increased substantially during the 1930's and World War II, and the incidence of smallpox since then has been extremely small. In the 1960's, as deaths from the occasional rare complications of vaccination in many countries outnumbered those from smallpox itself, the question was seriously raised whether vaccination should be continued as a standard routine. In 1967 occurrences of smallpox were reported to the World Health Organization (WHO) from forty-three countries; in thirty it was considered endemic. In that year the WHO began a program of intense surveillance and vaccination aimed at eradicating the disease. During 1974 smallpox was reported in only nine countries; in only three—India, Bangladesh, and Ethiopia—was the disease considered endemic, and

the prospect of complete eradication within another two or three years appeared bright.

[John B. Blake, *Benjamin Waterhouse and the Introduction of Vaccination: A Reappraisal*, and *Public Health in the Town of Boston 1630–1822*, Harvard Historical Studies, vol. LXXII; A. W. Hedrich, "Changes in the Incidence and Fatality of Smallpox in Recent Decades," *Public Health Reports*, vol. 51 (1936); A. J. Rhodes and C. E. Van Rooyen, *Textbook of Virology*; World Health Organization, "Smallpox in 1974," *WHO Chronicle*, vol. 29 (April 1975).]

JOHN B. BLAKE

SMELTERS. Smelting is a method of separating gold, silver, and other metals from their ores with fire and heat intense enough to melt the ores. A Spanish law (Aug. 22, 1584) required a government smelter to be established in every mining district in the New World and required all miners to bring their gold and lead-silver to a government furnace. Ruins of crude smelters have been found in southern California.

In 1750 coal was first used as a fuel for smelting. Beginning in 1830, anthracite coal was used, and by 1860 smelters had attained practically their present form. But the era of improved metallurgical and chemical processes had scarcely begun. Colorado's gold sulfide ores defied recovery until a professor of chemistry, Nathaniel P. Hill, after conducting experiments at Swansea, Wales, and Freiberg, Germany, built the Boston and Colorado smelter at Blackhawk, Colo., in 1867. Its successor, built at Argo (near Denver) in 1878 and managed by Richard Pearce, who had collaborated with Hill on improving smelter design, began the smelting of copper ores in reverberatory furnaces. Until 1900 the Argo smelter was the only one to smelt gold and silver ores to matte exclusively in reverberatories. Discovery of lead carbonates at Leadville, Colo., resulted in the construction of a dozen large smelters there.

A major change in smelter design in the late 1800's was the introduction of much larger furnaces. The Blackhawk smelter had only one small calcining and one small reverberatory furnace. In 1888 Meyer Guggenheim, who had bought two mines at Leadville the year before, decided that he would make more profit if he smelted his own ores. Accordingly he built the Philadelphia smelter at Pueblo, Colo., with six great furnaces, each with a capacity of 60 tons of ore daily. In 1893 the largest smelters in the United States were at Denver, Pueblo, and Salt Lake City. The Washoe smelter of the Anaconda Copper Mining Company at Anaconda, Mont., had a smokestack 300 feet high with a 30-foot inside diameter. Leading up the hillside to the base of this stack were 1,234 feet of flue 60 feet wide.

Toward the close of the 19th century cutthroat competition between the smelters led to combination. On Apr. 4, 1899, the American Smelting and Refining Company brought together eighteen of the country's largest smelting companies. In 1901 the firm of Meyer Guggenheim and his sons, the largest of the independents, joined the trust under terms that ensured them control of American Smelting.

[W. Davis, *The Story of Copper;* G. Williams, *William Guggenheim.*]

PERCY S. FRITZ

SMITH, FORT, an early frontier military post, was established in 1817 by Maj. Stephen H. Long on what is now the Arkansas-Oklahoma border, at the confluence of the Arkansas and Poteau rivers. It was named for Col. Thomas A. Smith of the U.S. Army. The original walls were made of pickets with blockhouses at the corners. Inside the enclosure were barracks and officers' quarters. Founded to protect frontier settlements from Indian attacks, by the 1840's the fort became a significant point for pioneers bound for Santa Fe. It was also an important border post during the Civil War.

[J. B. Thoburn, *History of Oklahoma.*]

EDWARD EVERETT DALE

SMITH, FORT, COUNCIL OF, met early in September 1865 to make peace with the Five Civilized Tribes and other smaller tribes of Indian Territory that had allied themselves with the Confederacy during the Civil War. The commissioners representing the federal government were important civil or military officials, while the Indian representatives included the ablest leaders of the various tribes. The work of the council was complicated by the fact that the Cherokee had two groups of delegates. One of these, led by John Ross, represented the faction that had repudiated, in 1863, the former treaty with the Confederacy and declared allegiance to the United States. The other was led by Stand Watie, head of the southern branch of the tribe. The Indians were told that by joining the Confederacy they had made themselves liable to a forfeiture of all the rights guaranteed them in former treaties with the United States. They were given the general terms of new treaties they would be required to sign to receive the favor and protection of the United States. The various tribes then signed an agreement formally establishing peace and amity with

the United States and further agreed to send commissioners to Washington, D.C., the following year to negotiate these new treaties.

[A. H. Abel, *The American Indian Under Reconstruction;* M. L. Wardell, *A Political History of the Cherokees.*]

EDWARD EVERETT DALE

SMITH, FORT C. F., named for Gen. Charles Ferguson Smith, was established Aug. 12, 1866, by Lt. Col. N. C. Kinney at the Bighorn River crossing of the Bozeman Trail, in southern Montana, ninety-one miles north of Fort Phil Kearny. It was built of logs and adobe.

During most of its existence, the fort was besieged by hostile Sioux, since the opening of the Bozeman Trail and the establishment of military posts to protect it violated a treaty concluded in 1851. On Aug. 1, 1867, Indians attacked haymakers and their soldier escort in a meadow three miles northeast of the fort (*see* Wagon Box Fight). By agreement with the Sioux, the fort was abandoned early in August 1868, at the conclusion of Red Cloud's War.

[G. R. Hebard and E. A. Brininstool, *The Bozeman Trail.*]

PAUL I. WELLMAN

SMITH ACT (June 28, 1940) provides for the registration and fingerprinting of aliens living in the United States and declares it unlawful to advocate or teach the forceful overthrow of any government in the United States or to belong to any group advocating or teaching such action. Passage of the act reflected American anxiety over Germany's rapid conquest of Western Europe at the beginning of World War II and over Communist-inspired strikes intended to injure American defense production. The act has been strongly criticized on the ground that it interferes with freedom of speech, guaranteed by the First Amendment. In a famous case, *Dennis* v. *United States,* concerning the conviction of eleven Communists under the act, the Supreme Court in 1951 upheld its constitutionality. In 1957, however, in *Yates* v. *United States,* the Court held that the teaching or advocacy of the overthrow of the U.S. government that was not accompanied by any subversive action was constitutionally protected free speech not punishable under the Smith Act.

[Edward S. Corwin, "Bowing Out 'Clear and Present Danger,'" *Notre Dame Lawyer,* vol. 27; Wallace Mendelson, "Clear and Present Danger: From Schenck to Dennis," *Columbia Law Review,* vol. 52.]

CHARLES S. CAMPBELL

SMITH EXPLORATIONS. Jedediah Strong Smith, fur trader and explorer, joined William Henry Ashley's expedition in 1822 to establish the Rocky Mountain Fur Company. The expedition began at Saint Louis and ascended the Missouri River. In the spring of 1824 Smith headed the first party of Americans to travel through South Pass (Wyoming), which later became the gateway for westward migration. In the summer of 1826 Smith led a party from the Great Salt Lake in Utah to southern California—the first group of Americans to reach the Spanish settlements by an overland route (*see* Cajon Pass). In June 1827 he and two companions returned to the Great Salt Lake by the central route—the first white men to cross the Sierra Nevada and the Great Salt Desert from west to east. Shortly afterward he set out again for California, with eighteen men, ten of whom were massacred by Mohave on the Colorado River. In 1827–28 he traveled up the Pacific coast, opening up a new route to Fort Vancouver on the Columbia River. Smith lost all but three of his men by massacre on the Umpqua River in Oregon. In 1829 he explored the Snake River country, and the following year he returned overland to Saint Louis. In the spring of 1831 he set out with a wagon train for Santa Fe, N.Mex., and while seeking water for his party was killed by the Comanche on the Cimarron River in southwestern Kansas on May 27.

[H. C. Dale, *The Ashley-Smith Explorations and the Discovery of the Central Route to the Pacific;* Maurice S. Sullivan, *The Travels of Jedediah Smith.*]

JOHN G. NEIHARDT

SMITH-HUGHES ACT (1917), a landmark in the advance of federal centralization as well as in vocational education, created the Federal Board for Vocational Education for the promotion of training in agriculture, trades and industries, commerce, and home economics in the secondary schools and provided funds to prepare teachers of vocational subjects. Funded by federal grants-in-aid to be matched by state or local contributions, or both, the act required that state boards submit their plans for vocational education to the board for approval, thus providing for greater federal control than had previously existed in aid to education. Supplementary acts have extended the original activities to vocational counseling and rehabilitation and research in guidance and placement.

[W. P. Sears, *The Roots of Vocational Education.*]

HARVEY WISH

SMITH-LEVER ACT (1914) provided for an elaborate system of agricultural extension work conducted through a field force of specialists with the assistance of federal grants-in-aid based on equal state contributions. Students not attending college received instruction and demonstration work in agriculture and home economics from county agents and thus enjoyed indirectly the benefits of the agricultural colleges and experimental stations. Like other forms of grants-in-aid, the Smith-Lever Act provided for an element of federal control of local activities. This was the first time that federal standards were a factor in aid to education.

[W. H. Shepardson, *Agricultural Education in the United States.*]

HARVEY WISH

SMITHSONIAN INSTITUTION, an establishment dedicated to research, education, and national service to science, the arts, and humanities. Headquartered in Washington, D.C., it was chartered by Congress in 1846 pursuant to the will of the Englishman James Smithson (1765–1829). In 1826 Smithson, who was the illegitimate son of Sir Hugh Smithson, Duke of Northumberland, and Elizabeth Keate Macie, descended from Henry VII, bequeathed his fortune, amounting to about $550,000 (a considerable sum for those days), to "the United States of America, to found at Washington, under the name of the Smithsonian Institution, an Establishment for the increase and diffusion of knowledge among men." Smithson's motivations for this unusual bequest are conjectural, but several influences may have been involved: Disillusionment due to the circumstances of his birth, which, in Britain, barred him from certain privileges and inheritances; his keen interest in science (he was an Oxford graduate, a competent chemist, and a member of the Royal Society); his faith in America, generated perhaps from his friendship with Americans traveling in Europe, although he himself never visited the United States; and perhaps the general revolutionary temper of the times, which impelled him to do something original for the benefit of mankind and make his name remembered long after, as he said, "the names of the Northumberlands and Percys are extinct and forgotten."

When, after much debate, Congress accepted the gift, there began a long argument as to what form the institution should take in order to conform most clearly with Smithson's broad prescription. The format that finally evolved and was enacted (Aug. 10, 1846) was due in large part to John Quincy Adams, who was then back in Congress following his presidency and whose articulate championing of science and education was most effective.

The Smithsonian derives its support both from appropriations from Congress and from private endowments, of which Smithson's gift was the nucleus. It is considered an independent establishment in the role of a ward of the U.S. government, the trustee. It is governed by a board of regents made up of the vice-president and chief justice of the United States (ex officio) and three U.S. senators, three representatives, and six citizens named by Congress. The regents elect one of their number as chancellor and choose a secretary, who is the executive officer, or director, of the institution. Since its founding the Smithsonian has had only eight secretaries: Joseph Henry, professor and physicist at the College of New Jersey (now Princeton), noted for his research in electromagnetism, who served from 1846 until his death in 1878; Spencer Fullerton Baird, biologist, secretary from 1878 until his death in 1887; Samuel Pierpont Langley, astronomer and aviation pioneer, from 1887 to 1906; Charles Doolittle Walcott, from 1907 to 1927; Charles Greeley Abbot, astrophysicist, from 1928 to 1944; Alexander Wetmore, biologist, from 1945 to 1952; Leonard Carmichael, psychologist, from 1953 to 1964; and S. Dillon Ripley, zoologist, after 1964.

Henry's original program for the Smithsonian and its plan of organization were based on his interpretation of how best to "increase" and "diffuse" knowledge in order "to carry out the design of the testator." To increase knowledge he proposed to "stimulate men of talent to make original researches, by offering rewards for memoirs containing new truths" and "to appropriate a portion of income for particular researches, under the direction of suitable persons." To diffuse knowledge it was proposed to "publish a series of periodical reports on the progress of different branches of knowledge" and "to publish occasionally separate treatises on subjects of general interest." These objectives have continued to guide the activities of the institution. But this simplicity of design did not last long, and the institution began to proliferate as Congress began assigning the institution jobs to do and "bureaus" to administer. Over the years it has assembled under its wings a group of museums and art galleries and other branches that have made it perhaps the largest museum and cultural complex in the world. The Smithsonian occupies seven buildings flanking the Mall between Fifth and Fourteenth streets and other buildings in several other parts of the city and in a number of places outside Washington, including New York City, Cambridge, Mass., and the Canal Zone.

The following are the bureaus and agencies under the Smithsonian's administration (located in Wash-ington unless otherwise noted). The National Museum of Natural History, which with the National Museum of History and Technology constitutes the National Museum, is the oldest of the Smithsonian's branches and the center of its vast natural history collections and their study. The National Museum of History and Technology was separated from the National Museum of Natural History in 1965 when its new building was completed and dedicated. The Smithsonian Astrophysical Observatory (1890), in Cambridge, Mass., is a research branch founded by Langley. The International Exchange Service was initiated in 1850 by Baird and Henry to facilitate the international exchange of scientific and other scholarly publications. The National Zoological Park, one of the most eminent zoos in the United States, was founded by Langley in 1889. The National Collection of Fine Arts (1846) and the National Portrait Gallery (1962) have, since 1968, jointly occupied the renovated Old Patent Office Building. The Freer Gallery of Art, opened in 1923, is a center for the collection, display, and study of Oriental art; it was the gift of Charles Lang Freer, Detroit industrialist and art collector. The Radiation Biology Laboratory (established in 1929 as the Division of Radiation and Organisms) is located in Rockville, Md. The Smithsonian Tropical Research Institute, formerly the Canal Zone Biological Area (established in 1940), is on Barro Colorado Island, Panama. The National Air and Space Museum is dedicated to the history and display of America's aeronautical and astronautical accomplishments. Its new building opened in 1976. The Science Information Exchange, Inc., under the aegis of the Smithsonian since 1954, is a center for prepublication information about research that is planned or in progress in the United States and in some other countries.

Several additional adjuncts of the Smithsonian Institution include the Anacostia (D.C.) Neighborhood Museum (1967); the Cooper-Hewitt Museum of Decorative Arts and Design (1967), in New York City; the Archives of American Art, a bureau of the Smithsonian since 1970, in New York; the Renwick Gallery (1972); the Joseph H. Hirshhorn Museum and Sculpture Garden (1974); and the Center for the Study of Man (1968).

There are also three agencies technically under the aegis of the Smithsonian but administered by separate boards of trustees: the National Gallery of Art (established 1941); the John F. Kennedy Center for the Performing Arts (opened 1971); and the Woodrow Wilson International Center for Scholars (1968).

The Smithsonian museums, embracing all fields of

science, technology, and the arts, are famous for their many unique objects on display. In addition to such showpieces as Charles Lindbergh's *Spirit of St. Louis*, the First Ladies' inaugural ball gowns, the Hope Diamond, Benjamin Franklin's printing press, the original ''star-spangled banner,'' and the giant model of the blue whale, the dozens of exhibit halls throughout the museums display much of man's knowledge of the earth and human civilization and culture. There are also vast study collections, numbering in the millions of objects and specimens, that form the basis of the research conducted not only by the large staff of Smithsonian scientists but also by students and researchers in history, technology, and the physical and natural sciences. The institution is equally famous for its worldwide exploration programs, which were initiated by Henry and Baird.

The first Smithsonian publication, *Ancient Monuments of the Mississippi Valley,* was issued in 1848, and since that time there have appeared under the Smithsonian imprint (now called the Smithsonian Press) thousands of books, pamphlets, catalogs, bulletins, and periodicals in all branches of science, art, and technology. Most of them are scholarly publications, but a few are popular in nature. Smithsonian publications—some financed by government funds and some by the institution's private funds—are widely distributed to libraries, research institutions, and students. Since 1970, in conjunction with a subsidiary organization, the Smithsonian Associates, the institution has published a popular magazine, *Smithsonian.*

Since the early 1960's the Smithsonian has expanded its activities, particularly in the field of public education, in an effort to identify the institution more closely with the academic world and with modern educational and research trends.

[G. Brown Goode, *The Smithsonian Institution, 1846–1896: The History of Its First Half Century;* P. H. Oehser, *Sons of Science: The Story of the Smithsonian Institution and Its Leaders,* and *The Smithsonian Institution;* W. P. True, *The Smithsonian Institution,* Smithsonian Scientific Series, vol. 1.]

PAUL H. OEHSER

SMOKY HILL TRAIL, a route from the Missouri Valley to Denver that came into importance with the Pikes Peak gold rush in the late 1850's. John C. Frémont had traversed part of it in 1844. The trail, which was about 600 miles long, led westward up the Kansas (Kaw) River and the Smoky Hill fork to its source, thence westerly to and along Big Sandy

Creek, and then to and down Cherry Creek to its mouth at Denver. A party of goldseekers broke the trail in the fall of 1858. Others who followed suffered because water and food were lacking along the way, and instances of cannibalism were reported. The route soon acquired the grim nickname ''Starvation Trail.'' Such difficulties discouraged use of the trail, although it was the shortest to the gold country. In 1860 Leavenworth, Kans., employed Green Russell, discoverer of gold in Colorado, to survey and mark the trail in an effort to divert emigration over it and through the sponsoring city, but this had little effect. The Butterfield Overland Dispatch was established on the trail in 1865 and later competed with Holladay's Overland Mail, established in 1866. Minor variations of route developed. The stage service was displaced when the Kansas Pacific Railroad completed its track from Kansas City, Mo., to Denver in 1870. Highways U.S. 40 and Interstate 40 now follow rather closely the old Smoky Hill Trail.

LEROY R. HAFEN

SMOOT-HAWLEY TARIFF. *See* **Tariff.**

SMUGGLING, COLONIAL. The extent of smuggling and its effect on the imperial relationship offer one of the most perplexing problems of colonial history. That smuggling existed there can be no doubt. Parliament was surprisingly negligent in providing for the enforcement of the Navigation Acts. It established regulations in 1651, 1660, and 1663 governing exportations and importations, but it was not until 1673 that officials were appointed to enforce them, and these officials were not given the powers granted customs officers in England until 1696. The 1696 act established admiralty courts, with jurisdiction in cases involving violations of the trade laws. Such courts, which had no juries, prosecuted trade offenses more strenuously than ordinary courts, in which public opinion was more lenient toward smugglers. The colonial charters complicated problems of enforcement already made complex by natural geographic conditions. The lengthy coastline, with numerous sheltered coves, afforded tempting opportunities for clandestine activities. Accounts of tobacco packed in flour barrels and foreign wine masquerading as New England rum, of the connivance of officials, forgery of certificates, and tarring and feathering of informers all show that violations occurred.

A quantitative analysis of colonial trade throws a

clearer light on the extent of smuggling. Although obviously no statistical records of surreptitious activities exist, official records showing the great volume of tobacco and other enumerated products moving in legal channels and the quantities of European manufactures coming to the colonies from England as the laws prescribed demonstrate that the bulk of the trade with Europe was legitimate. Any other assumption would greatly exaggerate colonial productive and consumptive capacities. Violations of the Molasses Act (1733) were a different matter. The amount of rum produced in the northern colonies demonstrates that a flourishing illicit trade existed with the Dutch, French, and Spanish West Indies. It is more difficult to estimate the extent of smuggling during the revolutionary period, but the probabilities seem to be that it was held in check by increased enforcement activities.

Many elements were required to precipitate the American Revolution, and smuggling did more than add spice to the formula. The very fact that the European clauses of the laws were reasonably well enforced left the colonists with an unfavorable balance of trade in the Old World. The monopolistic advantages enjoyed by the English factors kept southern planters in a state of continual indebtedness, which served to intensify any irritation aroused by other causes. After the Molasses Act, illicit trade with the non-British West Indies was an economic necessity. The treasonable aspect of such trade with the French colonies during the French and Indian War (1754–63) aroused British resentment, and subsequent attempts to restrain the trade such as the American Revenue Act of 1764, popularly known as the Sugar Act, awakened such active opposition in the colonies as to warrant John Adams' remark that "molasses was an essential ingredient in American independence."

Equally important, the other commercial reforms that Britain initiated at the same time attempted too much. The new duties in America imposed by such measures as the Townshend Acts (1767) and the decreased drawbacks on goods that the colonists were obliged to acquire in England either tended to increase smuggling or added economic grievances to political irritation. The Tea Act of 1773, by which the East India Company was granted the right to sell its tea directly to its agents in the colonies, aroused smugglers, whose profits were threatened by the company's lower-priced legally imported tea, and angered law-abiding colonial tea merchants, who were also undersold by the company. The demand for bonds even when shipping nonenumerated articles, the bur-

densome restrictions on the coasting trade, and, most irritating of all, arbitrary adherence to the letter of the law injured even the "fair trader" and added to the colonists' bitterness. At first the colonial merchants expressed their resentment, but such attempts at peaceful coercion soon led to such acts of "riot and rebellion" as the Boston Tea Party (Dec. 16, 1773).

[C. M. Andrews, *The Colonial Period;* G. L. Beer, *British Colonial Policy, 1754–1763;* L. A. Harper, *English Navigation Acts;* V. D. Harrington, *The New York Merchant on the Eve of the Revolution;* A. M. Schlesinger, *Colonial Merchants and the American Revolution.*]

LAWRENCE A. HARPER

SMUGGLING OF SLAVES. The importation of slaves into the United States was not made illegal until 1808, because of a constitutional provision that forbade congressional interference with the slave trade until that year. By then, however, most of the states had already passed laws prohibiting the trade. Subsequent federal laws included the act of Apr. 20, 1818, which provided for fines, imprisonment, and forfeiture of the vessel used for slave trading, and the act of May 15, 1820, which defined slave trading as piracy and provided for the death penalty for anyone convicted of engaging in it. Although cruisers and revenue cutters were authorized by the federal government to capture slave traders, their efforts to stem the trade were largely unsuccessful because U.S. naval forces of the time were insufficient to patrol American and African coastal waters adequately. Federal courts were directed to try offenders, but juries, especially in the South, were often reluctant to convict smugglers. These national measures generally emphasized the punishment of smugglers rather than the prevention of smuggling. The traffic became a very profitable business, supported by northern capital and dovetailing with the domestic slave trade in the South. Illicit cargoes of blacks were either infiltrated into the South through secluded rivers and inlets or baldly unloaded at ports of entry where public apathy or the connivance of local authorities permitted the business. Between 1808 and 1860 more than 250,000 blacks were thus imported. Cargoes of captured bootleg slaves were occasionally returned to be colonized in Sierra Leone or Liberia. More frequently, however, they were sold at auction in the southern slave market to cover the costs of capture and prosecution, thus paradoxically defeating the original purpose of the laws. Sometimes the seized slaves were turned over to the state governor's agents, who committed them under bond to a planter, often the one from whom they had been captured, who thereupon simply forfeited the normal bond and retained the slaves.

International cooperation to suppress the slave traffic was generally ignored or rejected by the United States until 1842, although the Treaty of Ghent (1815) contained a statement condemning the trade. In the Webster-Ashburton Treaty of 1842 the United States agreed to send a squadron with eighty guns to the African coast, but subsequently failed to provide its full quota. More effective was the belated Anglo-American treaty of June 7, 1862, which granted a limited mutual right to search merchant vessels for smuggled slaves and which established three international courts (at Sierra Leone, Cape of Good Hope, and New York) to try the smugglers. The boundaries of the territory in which the mutual right of search existed were greatly extended by another treaty between the United States and Great Britain, signed on Feb. 17, 1863. By 1864 slave trading had come to almost a complete halt as a result of the Union blockade during the Civil War. Finally, in 1865, the Thirteenth Amendment, by abolishing domestic slavery, at the same time gave the final blow to the slave trade.

[W. E. B. Du Bois, *The Suppression of the African Slave Trade*.]

MARTIN P. CLAUSSEN

SNAGBOATS, twin-hull steamboats designed especially for use in removing snags from western rivers. Operating during low water, when snags were visible above or immediately below the surface, the heavy iron-plated beam connecting the two hulls, below the water line, was run under the snag to loosen it from its moorings, after which it was hauled aboard and disposed of. As steamboat traffic increased, snag losses were heavy, mounting to $1,362,500 between 1822 and 1827. Congress was petitioned to take care of this menace in 1820, but no action was taken until 1828, when Capt. Henry Miller Shreve, the most prominent of the snagboat operators, was appointed superintendent of western river improvements. Between 1829 and 1841 Shreve removed most of the snags from the Ohio and Mississippi. Other men continued his work, the need for which constantly decreased with the disappearance of timber from the river banks as settlement expanded.

[J. Fair Hardin, "The First Great Western River Captain: A Sketch of the Career of Captain Henry Miller Shreve," and Caroline S. Pfaff, "Henry Miller Shreve: A Biography," both in *Louisiana Historical Quarterly*, vol. 10.]

WALTER PRICHARD

SNAKE RIVER, formerly the Lewis, a 1,038-mile stream that rises in Shoshone Lake in Yellowstone National Park in northwest Wyoming, loops about southwestern Idaho, forms part of the Idaho-Oregon and the Idaho-Washington boundaries, and cuts across southeast Washington to empty into the Columbia River. Meriwether Lewis and William Clark followed the Snake from the mouth of the Clearwater in Idaho to the Columbia in 1805. John Jacob Astor's expedition to Astoria in northwest Oregon in 1811 attempted to float down the turbulent river and suffered great hardships. The Rocky Mountain Fur Company and the Hudson's Bay Company battled each other in the fur-trapping business up and down the stream through the early 19th century. From Fort Hall, Idaho, the Oregon Trail paralleled the river closely for some 400 miles. In the 20th century numerous irrigation canals and hydroelectric power projects were established along the Snake.

[C. J. Brosnan, *History of the State of Idaho*.]

ALVIN F. HARLOW

SNAP CONVENTION, the name given to a New York state convention called by supporters of Sen. David B. Hill for president on Feb. 22, 1892, to control the election of delegates to the Chicago Democratic national convention. The state gathering was nicknamed the "Snap Convention" because it was held at an unusually early date. To oppose the solid Hill delegation, the "Anti-Snappers" called a convention and sent a protesting delegation to Chicago. Hill's action was strongly resented by supporters of Grover Cleveland's renomination.

[Allan Nevins, *Grover Cleveland, A Study in Courage*.]

A. C. FLICK

SNELLING, FORT, was established in 1819 by Col. Henry Leavenworth as part of a general plan of frontier defense. Its site in southeastern Minnesota, at the junction of the Mississippi and Minnesota rivers, was originally selected in 1805 by Lt. Zebulon M. Pike. It was first called Fort Saint Anthony, but in 1825 its name was changed to Fort Snelling in honor of Col. Josiah Snelling, who had become commandant in 1820 and had erected permanent buildings and fortifications. The fort was headquarters for the Indian agency, of which Maj. Lawrence Taliaferro had charge for twenty years. It also served to protect the headquarters of the American Fur Company, located across the Minnesota River at Mendota, and the pioneer settlers of Minnesota. The fort was never the scene of a hostile demonstration. It lost much of its importance when other northwestern forts were established and was abandoned in 1858, but it was reoccupied in 1861. A museum of Minnesota history was later established in the Round Tower of the fort; the tower is the oldest structure still standing (1976) in the state.

[W. W. Folwell, *History of Minnesota,* vol. I; M. L. Hansen, *Old Fort Snelling.*]

T. C. BLEGEN

SNOWSHOES. Archaeological specimens of snowshoes are known both in the Old World and the New World. They seem to have reached their highest form of development among the Indians of Canada and the northern United States. The French traders and immigrants adopted them, as did the adventurous trappers and traders in New England and the North Atlantic states. These shoes facilitated winter travel and made possible winter attacks on outposts, as in the case of Schenectady, N.Y. (1690), and York, Maine (1692).

[D. S. Davidson, "Snowshoes," *Memoirs, American Philosophical Society* (1937).]

CLARK WISSLER

SNUG HARBOR. *See* **Sailors' Snug Harbor.**

SOAP AND DETERGENT INDUSTRY. Traditionally soap has been manufactured from alkali (lye) and animal fats (tallow), although vegetable products such as palm oil and coconut oil can be substituted for the tallow. American colonists had both major ingredients of soap in abundance, and so soapmaking began in America during the earliest colonial days. Tallow came as a by-product of slaughtering animals for meat, or from whaling. Farmers produced alkali as a by-product of clearing their land, and until the 19th century wood ashes served as the major source of lye. The soap manufacturing process was simple, and most farmers could thus make their own soap at home.

The major uses for soap were in the home for washing clothes and for toilet soap and in textile manufacturing, particularly for fulling, cleansing, and scouring woolen stuffs. Soap usage dramatically increased with the rise of cities and of industry. Because colonial America was rural, soapmaking remained widely dispersed, and no large producers emerged. But by the eve of the American Revolution the colonies had developed a minor export market; in

1770 they sent more than 86,000 pounds of soap worth £2,165 to the West Indies. The revolution interrupted this trade, and it never recovered.

The growth of cities and the textile industry in the early 19th century stimulated the rise of soapmaking firms. By 1840 Cincinnati, then the largest meatpacking center in the United States, had become the leading soapmaking city as well. The city boasted at least seventeen soap factories, including Procter and Gamble (established 1837), which was destined to become the nation's dominant firm. A major change in soap manufacture occurred in the 1840's with the substitution of soda ash, a lye made through a chemical process (which used as its ingredients sulfuric acid, salt, and limestone) for lye made from wood ashes. But before the Civil War soap factories remained small. Almost all soapmakers also produced tallow candles, which for many was the major business. The firms made soap in enormous slabs, and these were sold to grocers, who sliced the product like cheese for individual consumers. There were no brands, and no advertising was directed at consumers.

The period between the end of the Civil War and 1900 brought major changes to the soap industry. The market for candles diminished sharply, and soapmakers discontinued that business. At the same time competition rose. Many soapmakers began to brand their products and to introduce new varieties of toilet soap made with such exotic ingredients as palm oil and coconut oil. Advertising, at first modest but constantly growing, became the major innovation. In 1893 Procter and Gamble spent $125,000 to promote Ivory soap, and by 1905 the sales budget for that product alone exceeded $400,000. Advertising proved amazingly effective. Surveys have shown that nine out of ten shoppers buy nationally promoted brands even though they may cost 40 to 45 percent more than unadvertised soaps of equal quality. In 1900 soapmakers concentrated their advertising in newspapers but also advertised in streetcars and trains. Quick to recognize the communications revolution, the soap industry pioneered in radio advertising, particularly by developing daytime serial dramas; Procter and Gamble originated "Ma Perkins," one of the earliest, most successful, and most long-lived soap operas, to advertise its Oxydol soap in 1933. By 1962 major soap firms spent approximately $250 million per year for advertising, of which 90 percent was television advertising. In 1966 three out of the top five television advertisers were soapmakers, and Procter and Gamble was television's biggest sponsor, spending $161 million.

Advertising put large soapmakers at a competitive advantage, and by the late 1920's three firms had come to dominate the industry: Colgate-Palmolive-Peet, incorporated as such in 1928 in New York State, though originally founded by William Colgate in 1807; Lever Brothers, an English company that developed a full line of heavily advertised soaps in the 19th century and in 1897 and 1899 purchased factories in Boston and Philadelphia; and Procter and Gamble.

The 1930's marked the start of a revolution: synthetic detergent—not a soap, but a chemical synthesis that substituted fatty alcohols for animal fats. Detergents were developed in Germany during World War I to alleviate a tallow shortage. Detergents are superior to soap in certain industrial processes (the making of textile finishes, for example); they work better in hard water; and they eliminate the soap curd responsible for bathtub rings. Procter and Gamble introduced a pioneer detergent, Dreft, in 1933. The advertising of Dreft was aimed at the dishwashing market because it was too light for laundering clothes. It succeeded, especially in hard water regions, but World War II interrupted detergent marketing.

In 1940 the "big three"—Colgate, Lever, and Procter and Gamble—controlled about 75 percent of the market. They produced a wide variety of products, such as shampoos, dishwashing detergents, liquid cleaners, and toilet soap, but the most important part of their business was heavy-duty laundry soap, which accounted for about two-thirds of sales. Procter and Gamble had about 34 percent of the market; Lever was a close second with 30 percent; and Colgate trailed with 11 percent. In 1946 Procter and Gamble radically shifted the balance in its favor when it introduced Tide, the first heavy-duty laundry detergent. By 1949 Tide had captured 25 percent of the laundry market, and by 1956, even though Lever and Colgate had developed detergents of their own, Procter and Gamble held 57 percent of the market, as compared with 17 percent for Lever and 11 percent for Colgate. Despite Procter and Gamble's triumph, the big three still fought each other strongly. By 1966 Lever had regained strength, controlling about 27 percent of the market, as compared with 47 percent for Procter and Gamble and 12 percent for Colgate. By 1972 detergents had almost eliminated soap from the laundry market, but toilet soap remained unchallenged by detergents. In the 1970's bans on detergents by some local governments, which feared contamination of their water supplies, had little impact on the composition or sales of laundry products,

and the demand for soap remained small. In 1972 there were slightly more than 602 soap and detergent companies, and these employed more than 31,500 people and shipped products valued at $3.4 billion. The small firms produced a multitude of specialized cleansers for home and industry. In the highly important fields of toilet soaps and laundry soaps and detergents, the big three remained dominant together, controlling about 80 percent of the total market.

[Spencer Claw, "The Soap Wars: A Strategic Analysis," *Fortune*, vol. 67 (1963); Alfred Lief, *"It Floats": The Story of Procter and Gamble;* Charles Wilson, *The History of Unilever.*]

STEPHEN SALSBURY

SOCIAL COMPACT. *See* **Compact Theory.**

SOCIAL DEMOCRATIC PARTY. The Social Democracy of America as an organization was formed at Chicago, June 15–18, 1897, of sections of the American Railway Union, the Socialist Labor party clubs, and various religious and trade-union groups. The "colonization" plan advocated by Eugene V. Debs provided that the Socialists concentrate their forces on a western state, such as Colorado, in which unemployment was to be abolished, cooperative industry fostered, and a Socialist government voted into office. This scheme of colonization was repudiated in June 1898, during the Social Democracy's first national convention, by a group of Socialists led by Debs himself, Victor L. Berger, and Jesse Cox. This group, made up of thirty-three delegates who were committed to political activism rather than colonization, quickly formed the Social Democratic party of America. Later that year the Social Democrats were able to send two members to the Massachusetts legislature and to elect the mayor of Haverhill, Mass.; during the presidential election of 1900 their candidate, Debs, polled 87,814 votes. The subsequent fusion in 1901 of anti–De Leonites in the Socialist Labor party and the Social Democratic party led to a new party designation, the Socialist party of America.

[N. Fine, *History of Farmer and Labor Parties in the U.S.*]

HARVEY WISH

SOCIAL GOSPEL, a late 19th- and early 20th-century American Protestant reform movement attempting to apply the principles of Christianity to the social and economic problems that resulted from increased industrialization, urbanization, and immigration following the Civil War. The movement had its origins in Unitarianism's emphasis on the social side of Christianity during the early 1800's, but it did not become a major force until the 1880's. At that time, the rise of labor organizations and the resulting labor disturbances brought the accusation from labor that the church was more sympathetic to capital than to labor. This stirred liberal church leaders to a study of the implications of the teachings of Jesus on social and economic questions. Among the early leaders in the movement were Washington Gladden, Richard Theodore Ely, Charles Monroe Sheldon, Walter Rauschenbusch, and Shailer Mathews. Their teachings and writings, which advocated the abolition of child labor, a shorter work week, improved factory conditions, and a living wage for all workers, as well as prison reform and changes in the free-enterprise system, exercised widespread influence. They aroused a lively social consciousness within the major denominations that led to the establishment of various kinds of social-service agencies and the adoption of liberal social programs.

[Washington Gladden, *Tools and Man: Property and Industry Under the Christian Law,* and *Applied Christianity;* Shailer Mathews, *The Church and the Changing Order;* Walter Rauschenbusch, *Christianity and the Social Crisis.*]

WILLIAM W. SWEET

SOCIALIST LABOR PARTY. Out of several American branches of the Socialist First International (1864) emerged the Social Democratic Workingmen's party of North America (July 4, 1874), which in 1877 was transformed into the Socialist Labor party. Extensive industrial dissatisfaction stimulated its growth.

The history of the party cannot be divorced from the career of Daniel De Leon. De Leon had lectured on Latin-American diplomacy at Columbia between 1883 and 1889 and before joining the Socialist Labor party in 1890 had been associated with the Knights of Labor and with Edward Bellamy's Nationalist movement. In 1892 he became editor of the Socialist Labor party weekly, *The People,* and thereafter until his death in 1914 was the party's leading publicist.

Among the central ideas of the party have been its emphasis on industrial unionism as against craft unionism, its advocacy of both militant political action and the strike, and its insistence on party discipline. Its ideology has been Marxist throughout, and V. I. Lenin thought highly of De Leon as a theoretician.

In its early days the Socialist Labor party seemed to show much promise in terms of numbers and electoral strength. But factional struggles and the formation of the ideologically less rigid Socialist party of America (1901) weakened it. Although it nominated a candidate for the presidency of the United States in every election from 1892 until 1968, its vote remained small: in 1900 Joseph H. Maloney obtained 39,739 votes, and in 1936 John W. Aiken reached a low point of 12,777; in 1960 Eric Hass received 48,000, and in 1968 Henning Blomen was awarded the all-time high, 52,588.

[H. W. Laidler, *Social Economic Movements.*]
MULFORD Q. SIBLEY

SOCIALIST MOVEMENT. Socialism is an outlook or a social philosophy that advocates that the major instruments of production, distribution, and exchange should be owned and administered by society for the welfare of all rather than for the benefit of a few. Basically, socialism would abolish private property in major producers' goods or capital while usually retaining it in consumers' goods. The gap between lowest and highest personal incomes would be drastically reduced, and there would be an expansion of "free" goods and services (Socialists often advocate not only free parks and schools but also free public transport, health services, and legal services). There have been many schools of Socialist thought, the varying perspectives often turning on differences in strategy and on interpretation of ultimate goals.

In American history the Socialist movement began during the early part of the 19th century, when communitarian experiments, gaining their inspiration from such Europeans as Charles Fourier, Étienne Cabet, and Robert Owen, were established. Brook Farm, founded in 1841 and associated with several of the Transcendentalists, was Socialist in spirit. The Oneida Community in New York State, founded by John Humphrey Noyes in 1848, might also be described as reflecting one variety of socialism, although it went further in the direction of communism than socialism in general.

After the publication of Karl Marx's and Friedrich Engels' *Communist Manifesto* (1848), a new type of socialism appeared, generally called Marxism. Analyzing the dynamics of industrial society, Marx and Engels foresaw the day when industrial capitalism would disintegrate and socialism would arise in its place. Generally speaking, Marx and Engels believed that socialism was likely to develop first in the most highly industrialized societies, where accelerating class consciousness would play an important role.

SOCIALIST PARTY OF AMERICA

After the Civil War the influence of Marxian socialism began to be felt in the United States. Along with native American Socialist currents, it challenged the framework of American capitalism. The hard times of the 1870's and 1880's stimulated the development of the movement. In 1877 the Socialist Labor party was established. Edward Bellamy's followers in the Nationalist movement a decade later were fundamentally Socialist, and many Populists (organized in 1892) had somewhat the same point of view. In 1897 the Social Democracy of America was launched by Eugene V. Debs. Out of it emerged the Social Democratic party in 1898—which, with other groups, established the Socialist party of America in 1901.

From 1901 to World War I the Socialist party waxed in strength. By 1912 it had enrolled 118,000 members. Its leader, Debs, was favorably received both in industrial areas and among many farmers (as in Oklahoma). In 1920, while in prison for opposing World War I, Debs received 919,799 votes for the presidency. The party began to disintegrate after the Bolshevik revolution in Russia in 1917. Dissidents formed the Communist party and the Communist Labor party; in 1920 another splinter group established the Proletarian party. Debs's successor as leader of the Socialist party, Norman Thomas, ran for the presidency six times (1928, 1932, 1936, 1940, 1944, and 1948), but only once, in 1932, did he win a substantial vote (881,951).

By the 1950's the formal Socialist movement in the United States had been reduced greatly. The Socialist party ceased to run candidates for the presidency after 1956. Although other groups called Socialist continued to exist and to nominate candidates, their electoral strength was small: in the 1968 presidential election the Socialist Labor party won 52,588 votes and the Socialist Workers party (Trotskyite), only 41,300.

Scholars have long been concerned to explain the decline of American socialism, but they have differed among themselves in their emphases. Causes often listed to account for the disintegration of the movement have been the relatively high standard of living enjoyed by American workers, making socialism less attractive to those who were supposed to be its vanguard according to Marx; a labor movement that has been relatively unsophisticated politically; the development of the New Deal, which some Socialists thought of as moving toward their goals; and the many internal feuds that weakened the movement, particularly after 1917.

[Donald D. Egbert, Stow Persons, and T. D. Seymour Bassett, eds., *Socialism and American Life*; H. W. Laidler, *A History of Socialist Thought*; James Weinstein, *The Decline of Socialism in America, 1912–1925*.]

MULFORD Q. SIBLEY

SOCIALIST PARTY OF AMERICA was formed in July 1901 by a union of Eugene V. Debs and Victor L. Berger's Social Democratic party and Morris Hillquit's wing of the Socialist Labor party. The Socialist party gave to American radicalism, normally fragmented and divided, a unique era of organizational unity. Only the tiny Socialist Labor party and, later, the Industrial Workers of the World remained outside. The Socialist party incorporated surviving elements of western populism; until 1918 the highest percentage of its popular vote came in states west of Mississippi (Oklahoma boasted the largest state organization). The party was also well entrenched in the labor movement: the Socialist candidate captured almost one-third of the vote for the presidency of the American Federation of Labor in 1912. In that year, too, the Socialists reached the high point of their electoral success: Eugene V. Debs, running for the U.S. presidency, gained 6 percent of the vote; and some 1,200 Socialists were elected to public office, including seventy-nine mayors.

The party's growth stopped after 1912, but the following years can be characterized as a time of consolidation rather than as a time of decline. For once departing from its policy of inclusiveness, the party in 1913 cast out the syndicalist wing led by William D. Haywood. By eliminating the one group not committed to political action, the Socialist party became more cohesive without altering the balance between the right and left wings. World War I severely tested, but did not undermine, the Socialist movement. Unlike its western European counterparts the American party adhered to the stand of the Second International against war. The enunciation of that position at the Saint Louis convention of April 1917 did drive out prominent prowar members, but it did not split the party. Wartime persecution hurt the movement: Debs and many others went to prison; vigilante action and the barring of Socialist literature from the mails weakened outlying bodies, especially in the western states. These setbacks were more than counterbalanced by the rapid growth of the party's foreign-language federations and by the tapping of antiwar sentiment, as was evident in the party's strong showing in wartime elections.

The Bolshevik revolution in Russia (1917) was the turning point. The problem was not the event itself—this was universally hailed by American Socialists—but whether it provided a model for the United States. The left wing, and especially the foreign-language federations, believed that it did, and they were sustained by instructions coming from the Third Communist International in 1919. The party leaders thought otherwise: they did not think that the United States was ripe for revolution, nor were they willing to reconstitute the party along Leninist lines. With the left wing about to take over, the established leadership in May 1919 suddenly expelled seven foreign-language federations and the entire Michigan party and invalidated the recent elections to the national executive committee.

A decisive break with the past had occurred. Not only was American radicalism permanently split between Communists and Socialists, but the latter had lost their authenticity as a movement of radical action. By 1928 Socialist membership was not a tenth of the 1919 level, and although it experienced some revival during the 1930's, the party never regained either its popular base or the electoral appeal of earlier years. Having lost its left wing, moreover, the Socialist party evolved into an essentially reformist movement whose appeal was largely to the urban middle class. The new national leadership after the death of Debs in 1926 symbolized the change: Norman Thomas was a Princeton graduate, a former Presbyterian minister who had come to socialism via pacifism and the appeal of conscience. After 1956 the Socialist party ceased to nominate presidential candidates and increasingly viewed itself as an educational rather than a political force. In 1972 the Social Democratic Federation, a moderate wing that had split away in 1936, was reunited with the Socialist party; at the end of 1972 the name was changed to Social Democrats USA. In the 1972 presidential election, the united party supported George McGovern and took as its principal job the rallying of the liberal and labor vote for the Democrats. With a claimed membership of roughly 20,000, the Social Democrats in 1974 pledged to work with the Democratic party and the trade union movement toward Socialist goals and "to transform the Democratic Party into the Social Democratic Party."

[David A. Shannon, *The Socialist Party of America;* James Weinstein, *The Decline of Socialism in America.*]

DAVID BRODY

SOCIAL LEGISLATION seeks to protect the living standards of citizens when they are threatened by unemployment, sickness, disability, accident, old age, and other circumstances. Until the 1930's such protection was left to private, religious, and charitable institutions in the United States, or to state and local authorities. The general welfare clause of Article I, Section 8, of the Constitution was interpreted narrowly by the federal government, which did little for social welfare. In the 17th and 18th centuries Americans regarded poverty as a sort of crime, resulting usually from personal negligence or drink. This popular belief was buttressed by puritanism, the inheritance of the attitudes embodied in the English Poor Law, and middle-class desires to limit taxation and to reinforce the work ethic.

In the 19th century industrialization brought rapid economic growth and urbanization, but greater poverty and unemployment. Various states built workhouses and almshouses, following such examples as New York's County Poor House Act of 1824. Often thrown together were the poor, the temporarily unemployed, the sick, orphans, the insane and feeble-minded, the blind, and deaf mutes, with little distinction on the basis of sex, age, and condition. Private charity societies resisted such a policy—notably the New York Association for Improving the Condition of the Poor, founded in 1843, which began a system of visits to homes by social workers and emphasized rehabilitation and work rather than relief and institutionalization. In 1863 Massachusetts tried to systematize various state efforts by creating a unified state board of charities. Other states followed suit, and in the late 19th century the Charity Organization Society became a national lobby for social legislation: housing and tenement laws, prison reforms, health laws, and protection of child labor.

The states did pass laws to help special cases. The indigent blind were first aided by Indiana state law in 1840, and first given annual pensions by Ohio in 1898. The first state school for the feebleminded was established in Boston in 1848. Dorothea Dix fought for humane treatment of the insane and influenced various states. A federal bill, the Twelve-and-a-Quarter Million Acres Bill, to set aside public lands to finance the relief of the insane, deaf, and blind, was vetoed in 1854 by President Franklin Pierce as unconstitutional. Only for the deaf did the federal arm intervene: in 1864 Congress funded the Columbia Institute for the Deaf and Dumb (now Gallaudet College) in Washington, D.C.

Beginning in the 1790's the federal government had given aid to war veterans and merchant seamen and had treated American Indians as its wards. It left control over immigrants mainly to the states until 1882 (the Passenger Act of 1819 regulated health). It had no federal prisons for its own offenders until 1890. Congress did create the Children's Bureau (now part of the Department of Health, Education, and Welfare) in 1912, and the Maternity and Infancy Act of 1921 led many states to found child welfare divisions. Most states protected child and women's labor by 1930, though with great local variations.

The two chief periods of federal social legislation were the 1930's and 1960's. The Social Security Act of 1935, part of President Franklin D. Roosevelt's New Deal, is the keystone of the modern American welfare state. Previously, workers were protected by state compensation laws from accidents at work (the Supreme Court upheld three such laws in 1917), and some categories of workers also had federal protection (railroad workers, for example). Old-age protection was largely nonexistent before 1935, although Alaska had passed old-age legislation in 1915. Unemployment was covered by only one state (Wisconsin, 1932). Indeed, some trade·unions opposed state unemployment insurance, and the American Federation of Labor voted the idea down in 1931. The Social Security Act (1935) provided for social insurance (federal old-age pensions and survivors' benefits, and federal-state unemployment insurance); categorical assistance (specific federal grants-in-aid through the states for the aged, needy blind, and dependent children); and health and welfare services (federal aid to the states to maintain services for crippled children and orphans, vocational rehabilitation of the disabled, and public health). The Social Security Board, which administered the act, was absorbed into the Department of Health, Education, and Welfare in 1953. The act has been amended many times (significantly in 1965) and its scope and coverage broadened. Federal measures—the Coal Mines and Safety Act of 1969 and the Occupational Safety and Health Act of 1970—extended coverage to occupational diseases and took notice of the demand for relaxation of work controls over youths and women. The feminist movement of the 1970's tended to resent earlier paternalism towards women's work.

After World War II the Employment Act of 1946 gave the federal government the responsibility of maintaining full employment. And social legislation of the late 1940's, 1950's, and 1960's dealt with housing, education, and civil rights; the War on Poverty of the 1960's; and social security extensions for medical protection in 1965. Local authorities were given federal funds to buy up slum property and build housing under the Housing Act of 1949, but the true beginning of urban renewal came with the Housing Act of 1954. Housing acts of 1961 and 1962, under the administration of President John F. Kennedy, tried to take into account the wishes of that part of the population most in need of improved housing—usually poor and often black. In 1965 President Lyndon B. Johnson succeeded in achieving cabinet status for the new, unified Department of Housing and Urban Development. The next year the Demonstration Cities Act aimed to steer policy away from mere slum clearance to rehabilitation of existing structures. While this Model Cities program tried to preserve neighborhoods, rent supplements were designed to scatter poor families in better-class housing.

The population boom brought pressure for federal aid to education, in the National Defense Education Act of 1958 and the Elementary and Secondary Education Act of 1965. Students were also helped by work grants under the War on Poverty program. The major breakthrough in civil rights, with the Civil Rights Act of 1964 and the Voting Rights Act of 1965, encouraged minorities, particularly black Americans, to partake more fully of the benefits of American society. Modeled largely on New Deal ideas, Johnson's Economic Opportunity Act of 1964 offered youth programs (the Job Corps and college work-study programs); small business loans; the VISTA program, a sort of domestic Peace Corps; and a controversial plan for the participation of the underprivileged in antipoverty activities. Community action programs (CAP) were funded to fight local poverty through local groups, such as neighborhood councils (and even street gangs, as with the Blackstone Rangers in Chicago). Sometimes the federal government bypassed state authorities and dealt directly with local people, as in the Headstart program of support for school boards to begin training preschool children. Politics, and fear that the poor would become a political force, led to the abandonment of most participatory schemes. Nevertheless, a strong welfare rights movement sprang up in 1967–68, as poor Americans became more politically aware.

In the 1960's public assistance rolls grew enormously, and the public welfare system became bureaucratic and complex. Simpler methods of countering poverty were offered, such as the negative income tax and the guaranteed income plan, the mere mention of which would have been rejected in earlier decades. Congress took no action, however, during the first administration of President Richard M. Nixon, 1969–73. The greatest gap in the American welfare system remained in the health sphere, though social security amendments of 1960 (Medicaid) and 1965

(Medicare) began to provide medical security for those over sixty-five years of age. The 1970's seemed to presage a public reaction against further social legislation and a reversion to the earlier, more punitive approach to social welfare.

[F. F. Piven and R. A. Cloward, *Regulating the Poor: The Functions of Public Welfare*; R. E. Smith and D. Zietz, *American Social Welfare Institutions.*]

PETER D'A. JONES

SOCIAL SECURITY. The social security system in the United States began Aug. 14, 1935, when the Social Security Act was signed by President Franklin D. Roosevelt. The term "social security" probably originated in the United States, where it is used to designate a number of public programs designed to provide protection against loss of income resulting from death, old age, retirement, unemployment, and sickness. Programs of this nature were developed first in the industrialized nations of Europe in the latter part of the 19th century.

The American Social Security system was a product of the depression of the early 1930's, which disclosed that the states, localities, and private charities were unable to cope with prolonged, mass economic and social distress. Temporary federal programs of public works and relief were instituted, but the nation was stirred to seek more ordered and permanent ways of providing safeguards against the hazards of dependency. The Committee on Economic Security, appointed by the president in 1934, after extensive study, made recommendations that Congress considered exhaustively in formulating the Social Security Act of 1935.

The basic program of this act was contained in Title II, which authorized a system of "old-age benefits." It was designed to assure a "basic floor of protection against loss of income" through a compulsory government system of insurance that provides benefits related to wage loss. Based on social insurance principles, the system places more weight on presumptive social need and less on individual equity than does private insurance. Title II was amended in 1939 to extend benefits to survivors upon the death of the wage earner and to certain dependents. In 1954 coverage was extended to farm operators and most farm and domestic workers, and in 1956 to most of the self-employed and to the armed forces. Further amendment in 1956 extended coverage to totally disabled workers fifty years of age and over, and, in 1958, to their dependents. By 1972 almost all the gainfully employed except some government workers were

covered. Similarly, the benefit formula in Title II has been amended from time to time to provide larger benefits, largely because of increasing living costs. For retirees just coming on the rolls in 1972, the benefit averaged $161 a month for a single person and $270 a month for a husband and wife. It was estimated that about 28 million beneficiaries of all types would be receiving a monthly cash benefit by December 1972, totaling some $3.4 billion. As benefit costs have risen, successive social security tax adjustments have been made to meet them. By a 1972 revision, effective beginning in 1973, the employer-employee tax rate for the cash benefit was set at 4.6 percent each (6.9 percent for the self-employed) of the first $10,000 of covered earnings. Net annual income to the combined Old Age, Survivors Insurance (OASI) trust funds amounted to about $37.7 billion for the year 1972.

Titles I and III of the original Social Security Act, designed to supplement the OASDI program of Title II, provided for federal grants to the states to help finance public assistance for the needy aged, families with dependent children, the blind, and, beginning in 1950, the permanently and totally disabled. These are "needs test" programs, sometimes called "welfare," for people who do not qualify for social security (social insurance) or whose payments under that program have been too small to provide benefits adequate to meet basic needs. In 1972 about 14 million persons—about one-half children—were receiving public assistance at an annual expenditure of about $11.2 billion of federal-state-local funds. Amendments in 1972 transferred, as of Jan. 1, 1974, the administration of the adult categories of public assistance (the aged, blind, and disabled) from the states to the federal government and guaranteed a minimum monthly income of $130 to a single person and $195 to a married couple with no other income. Assistance to families with dependent children remained within the administrative jurisdiction of the states.

Title IV of the original act provided federal grants for child welfare services, maternal and child health services, and services for crippled children, but the health provisions were greatly enlarged by the amendments passed in 1965—two related contributory health insurance plans were established for almost all persons aged sixty-five and over: a basic compulsory program of hospital insurance and a voluntary elective program of supplementary medical services. The compulsory program pays a large part of the cost of inpatient hospital services for defined periods of time. After a three-day hospital stay it also pays a substantial part of the cost of up to 100 days of care in a participating, extended-care facility, as well as for up to 100 home health visits. Additional protection is provided for the costs of inpatient services at a tuberculosis or a psychiatric hospital. The program is financed through its own trust fund based on an earnings-tax applied to employees, employers, and the self-employed. Persons who choose to enroll voluntarily for the supplemental medical insurance program become eligible for 80 percent (after a $50 deduction per year) of the costs allowed for physicians and for other specified medical and health services, such as X ray, ambulance use, and physical therapy. Those who enroll for this service pay an additional premium, which is matched by an equal amount from federal general revenues. A separate trust fund has also been established for this supplementary medical insurance. State welfare agencies may buy participation in this program for service to public assistance recipients.

The administration of the Social Security system was originally placed under the direction of a bipartisan board called the Social Security Board. Subsequent reorganizations eliminated the board, established the Social Security Administration in its place, and placed it under the Department of Health, Education, and Welfare. Unemployment insurance, originally under the board, was transferred to the Department of Labor. The federal aspects of public assistance, formerly under the Social Security Administration, were transferred to the Social and Rehabilitation Service of the Department of Health, Education, and Welfare.

[Arthur J. Altmeyer, *The Formative Years of Social Security;* J. Douglas Brown, *An American Philosophy of Social Security;* William Haber and Wilbur J. Cohen, eds., *Social Security Programs, Problems and Policies: Selected Readings;* Social Security Administration, *Social Security Programs in the United States.*]

WILLIAM L. MITCHELL

SOCIAL SETTLEMENTS, neighborhood social-service centers established to aid urban dwellers. Rapid industrialization, frenzied urbanization, and great waves of immigration in the late 19th and early 20th centuries gave rise to a wide variety of social problems. Labor unrest during the 1870's and 1880's, colonies of immigrants who were bewildered by unfamiliar customs and a strange language and were isolated in congested tenements, unemployment, dangerous and unhealthy working conditions, exploitative labor practices, and the progressive lowering of

the standard of living were rich soil for unscrupulous politicians. The settlement-house movement, which arose in response to these problems, sought to improve urban working and living conditions, to encourage social, economic, and political reform, and to provide a sense of community and caring for poor or disadvantaged city residents. In 1886 Stanton Coit and Charles B. Stover, following the example of Toynbee Hall, London (1884), established the first American settlement house, the Neighborhood Guild (later University Settlement) in New York City "to cultivate friendly relations between the educated and uneducated and thus to uplift the latter."

Many others followed: College Settlement, New York, 1889 (Vida Dutton Scudder and Jean G. Fine); Hull House, Chicago, 1889 (Jane Addams and Ellen Gates Starr); East Side House, New York, 1891; Northwestern University Settlement, 1891 (Harriet Vittum); South End House, Boston, 1892 (Robert Archey Woods); Henry Street Settlement, New York, 1893 (Lillian D. Wald). Economic distress brought a rapid increase in the number of settlements established after 1893, including Hudson Guild, New York, 1895 (John L. Elliot); University of Chicago Settlement, 1894 (Mary McDowell); Chicago Commons, 1894 (Graham Taylor); Hiram House, Cleveland, 1896 (George A. Bellamy); and Greenwich House, New York, 1902 (Mary Kingsbury Simkhovitch). After World War I there was a decline in the number of houses founded, as government and private agencies assumed much of the work of the settlements. As of 1930 there were approximately 460 houses, most of which were church-supported. The Catholic church founded about twenty settlements, and Jewish agencies were responsible for twenty-eight. The Young Men's Christian Association and other national agencies carried on similar work. The mid-1970's saw a resurgence in the founding of settlement houses. Approximately 340 houses were affiliated with a national federation of neighborhood centers, established in 1911, and there were 100 unaffiliated houses.

Among the greatest services of the settlements was the role they played in the Americanization of immigrants. In addition, they have sponsored group study of music, art, literature, and handicrafts; provided free health clinics, job training, child care, visiting nurses, classes in cooking and child care, playgrounds, summer camps, and employment bureaus; revived national festivals; and helped inspire the little theater movement. Social settlements also provided crucial leadership in the battle to secure housing reforms and clean government and helped to win enactment of laws providing for juvenile courts, workmen's compensation, and the regulation of child labor.

[Allen F. Davis, *Spearheads for Reform: The Social Settlements and the Progressive Movement, 1890–1914;* John C. Farrell, *Beloved Lady: A History of Jane Addams' Ideas on Reform and Peace;* Helen Hall, *Unfinished Business.*]
HAROLD E. DAVIS

SOCIAL WORK. The profession of social work in the United States developed early in the 20th century among persons employed in local and state charitable organizations. Although governmental auspices predominated in institutions, hospitals, and prisons, innovative ideas tended to come from such settlement houses as Henry Street in New York and Hull House in Chicago, as well as from such charity organization societies houses in Boston, New York, and Baltimore. By World War I paid workers were displacing wealthy volunteers in many agencies. Professional associations emphasized communication between members, ethics, quality in education and performance, research and writing, and improved working conditions. Six such organizations merged in 1955 to form the National Association of Social Workers (NASW).

Social work education started in New York City in 1898 with an agency-sponsored summer school. Collegiate auspices (Simmons College and Harvard) were achieved in Boston in 1904, and by 1930 two-year graduate programs were becoming standard. In 1975 eighty-one universities in the United States offered masters degrees and thirty-one offered doctoral degrees in social work. Nevertheless, staff needs were so great in a rapidly expanding field that membership in NASW, previously limited to those with masters degrees, was opened to graduates of 135 accredited undergraduate programs.

Emphasis in the profession has always been divided between effecting "retail" individual social adjustments and "wholesale" solutions through institutional change. The latter approach reached a high point in 1912 when Theodore Roosevelt, then candidate for the U.S. presidency, incorporated large sections of a social work report on standards of living and labor in the Progressive (Bull Moose) platform. Following World War I, with reform in eclipse, enthusiasm for Freudian psychology shifted the emphasis of social work toward adjustment of individuals. This trend was confirmed in the schools during the New Deal, when many reform-minded teachers were drawn into administration of the Social Security Act

and other new programs. In the post–World War II era the National Mental Health Act financed a further sharp, unbalanced increase in the psychiatric aspect of social work with the institution of the War on Poverty and other programs of the 1960's.

Notable early leaders of social work include Mary Richmond (1861–1928), Jane Addams (1860–1935), Richard Cabot (1868–1939), and Harry Hopkins (1890–1946). The influential magazine *The Survey,* until its demise in 1952, was a principal interpreter of social work concerns.

[Arthur E. Fink, C. Wilson Anderson, and Merrill B. Conover, *The Field of Social Work;* Robert Morris, *The Encyclopedia of Social Work;* Ralph E. Pumphrey and Muriel W. Pumphrey, *The Heritage of American Social Work.*]
RALPH E. PUMPHREY

SOCIETY FOR THE PREVENTION OF CRUELTY TO ANIMALS. *See* **Animal Protective Societies.**

SOCIETY FOR THE PREVENTION OF CRUELTY TO CHILDREN. In April 1874 the American Society for the Prevention of Cruelty to Animals rescued and obtained the protection of the state for Mary Ellen Wilson, a mistreated child. In April of 1875, as a direct result of this case, the first child protective agency, the New York Society for the Prevention of Cruelty to Children, was incorporated.

During the ensuing quarter century more than 150 similar societies were formed across the country. The primary objective of such agencies is the protection of abused and neglected children. Upon receipt of a complaint alleging child neglect or abuse, the child protective agency investigates and offers indicated services to correct unwholesome home conditions and, in appropriate situations, secures protection of the child by legal proceedings. Child protective services are accepted as a responsibility of every community and, under public or private auspices, are to be found in every state.

THOMAS BECKER

SOCIETY FOR THE PROPAGATION OF THE GOSPEL IN FOREIGN PARTS, sometimes called the Venerable Society, was founded in 1701 and conducted the foreign mission work of the Anglican church in the American colonies and other English possessions overseas. Between 1702 and 1785, when it withdrew from the mission field in the United States, it assisted 202 central stations at an expenditure of £227,454, sent out 309 ordained missionaries, and distributed thousands of Bibles, prayer books, and other religious works. It also sent out school-teachers, medical missionaries, and libraries. In many colonies the first schools and the first libraries were founded by the society. In 1775 it was helping to support seventy-seven missionaries in the continental colonies, but as the Revolution progressed most of them were forced to retire. The Society for the Propagation of the Gospel is still engaged in missionary activity in various parts of the world.

[C. F. Pascoe, *Two Hundred Years of the S.P.G., 1701–1900.*]

HUGH T. LEFLER

SOCIETY OF CINCINNATI. *See* **Cincinnati, Society of.**

SOCIETY OF COLONIAL WARS, composed of the General Society and constituent state societies (thirty in 1975), was established in 1892 to perpetuate the memory of events of colonial history from the settlement of Jamestown, Va. (1607), to the Battle of Lexington (1775), by membership, preservation of records, commemorations, and memorials. Membership is open to male lineal descendants, in male and female lines, of men who, in colonial and British military, naval, and civil positions, assisted in the establishment, defense, and preservation of the American colonies.

[Wallace Evan Davies, *Patriotism on Parade: The Story of Veterans' and Hereditary Organizations in America, 1783–1900.*]

FRANCES DORRANCE

SODA FOUNTAINS, apparatus for generating and dispensing soda waters. They were developed following a demand created when a Philadelphia perfumer began to serve soda water with fruit juices soon after 1800. In 1834, in New York City, John Mathews started to manufacture machinery to make carbonated beverages. Improvements soon appeared and about 1858 the marble fountain was invented and patented in Massachusetts. An American soda fountain was exhibited in Paris in 1867, and a popular concession at the Centennial Exposition at Philadelphia in 1876 marked it as a national institution. In 1970 more than half of the approximately 50,000 drugstores in the United States had soda fountains.

[Paul Dickson, *The Great American Ice Cream Book.*]

VICTOR S. CLARK

SOD HOUSE, a dwelling made of dirt, constructed by settlers on the Great Plains in the 19th century in areas where timber and stone were not available. The Plains Indians had long made their permanent winter homes from sod, and as the white man settled the area beyond the Missouri River he adapted the Indian habitation to his needs. In the early days of settlement in many counties 90 percent of the people at one time or another lived in sod houses. Some of the sod houses were built half above ground and half underground, with the upper part made of sod and the lower part made of bare earth.

In building a sod house the settler plowed half an acre of ground. The thick strips of turf were cut into three-foot bricks with a spade and were then hauled to the building location and piled up like bricks to form a wall. The first layer was laid side by side around the base except where the door was to be. The cracks were then filled with dirt and two more layers were placed on top. The joints were broken, as in bricklaying. Every third course was laid crosswise to bind the sods together. A doorframe and two window frames were set in the wall and sods were laid around them. Sometimes hickory withes were driven down into the walls for reinforcement.

The gables were built of sod or frame according to what the builder could afford. Poorer settlers were forced to build very crude roofs. They set a forked pole in each end of the cabin for support for the ridge pole and used poles for the rafters and brush covered with a layer of prairie hay for the sheeting. Over this they often placed a layer of sod. Those who could afford it sometimes used lumber sheeting covered with a light layer of sod. The cracks were filled with fine clay. In a short time growths of sunflowers and grass appeared on the roof. Sometimes the inside of the sod house was plastered with ashes and clay, and often the outside was hewn smooth. The dirt floor was sprinkled in dry weather to keep down the dust. In wet weather the water-soaked roof dripped constantly, making puddles on the floor. The whole structure was built for less than $5.00. These little cabins often housed a dozen people. Because of the three-foot walls the houses were warm in winter and cool in summer, but they were poorly ventilated and dark. As soon as they could afford lumber the family built and moved into a frame structure, leaving the old house to the stock.

[Cass G. Barnes, *The Sod House;* Everett Dick, *The Sod House Frontier.*]

EVERETT DICK

SOFT DRINK INDUSTRY in the United States dates from the introduction early in the 1800's of carbonated soda water from Europe, where it had long been prized for the medicinal properties of the soda (sodium carbonate) in the liquid. Because of a widespread belief by Americans in the therapeutic value of natural mineral waters, the synthetic product was readily accepted. By the 1820's equipment for producing and dispensing carbonated soda water had been installed in apothecary shops throughout the country.

During the 1830's the soda was eliminated from carbonated soda water—the result being a drink taken for refreshment rather than for medicinal purposes. The demand for plain carbonated water—which kept the name "soda water"—was considerably intensified a few years later by the addition of various flavorings, sometimes blended with cream, to the drinks sold by the apothecaries. The final step in this evolution came in 1874, when the proprietor of a soda fountain in Philadelphia combined ice cream and soda water to "invent" the ice cream soda. The array of carbonated drinks did much to make the ubiquitous corner drugstore with its soda fountain a symbol of the American way of life.

The possibility of selling flavored carbonated drinks in bottles early attracted the attention of American businessmen. The available methods of production, however, posed a number of difficulties. Carbonating equipment was relatively inefficient; bottles were obtainable only in limited sizes and shapes and, being handblown, were expensive; washing the used bottles returned to the plants for refilling, adding the flavoring, and filling and capping the bottles were all separate hand operations. Despite these limitations, in 1899 the industry produced nearly 39 million cases of bottled drinks (12 bottles per capita), worth $23 million. This was an impressive record; yet the best estimate suggests that at the turn of the century more than 70 percent of the soft drinks consumed in the United States were sold at the soda fountain.

Whereas the growth of the bottling industry was comparatively slow during the 19th century, the opposite was true after 1900. In part the growth was the result of a series of innovations that greatly increased the efficiency of bottling operations. These included the introduction during the 1890's of automatic glass blowing machinery that assured the industry a supply of high-quality low-cost bottles. A parallel development of power-driven equipment removed the necessity of hand washing returned bottles, while the prob-

lem of a satisfactory closure was largely solved by the development of a cork-lined disk that could be securely crimped to the top of the bottle by machine. Thus when compressed carbon dioxide in cylinders became available, about 1910, it was possible to link a continuous flow of carbonated water with equipment that automatically added the flavoring and filled and capped the bottles. The final step toward complete automation came with the introduction of the bottle conveyor belt during the 1920's.

Another feature of the industry's development during the 20th century came as companies, such as Coca-Cola, Pepsi-Cola, Hires, and Dr. Pepper—organized originally to supply local markets with their concentrated syrups—began franchising bottlers throughout the country to produce and distribute the finished drinks. Growing competition at the national (and international) level led these companies to adopt vigorous advertising and marketing programs that not only stimulated sales, but made "Coke" and "Pepsi" household words throughout most of the world.

The promotion of branded drinks, combined with the automation of bottling plants, played a key role in the growth of the industry, which in 1967 turned out 1.76 billion cases of bottled soft drinks (211 bottles per capita) valued at approximately $3 billion.

[John J. Riley, *A History of the American Soft Drink Industry: 1807–1957.*]

HAROLD F. WILLIAMSON

SOFT MONEY is the opposite of hard money, which is based on specie. The term originated about 1876 when the Greenback party was formed by debtor farmers and others from the Republican and Democratic ranks who sought to raise agricultural prices by means of an inflated currency. Greenbackers, at their national convention in 1877, adopted a platform that opposed the resumption of specie payments, authorized by the Resumption Act of 1875 to begin in 1879, and the issuance of notes by national banks and called for the free coinage of silver on a par with gold. They thought that the currency should be a government paper one, not redeemable in specie, but convertible on demand into federal interest-bearing notes that would serve as legal tender for the payment of debts and taxes. Later the Populists held similar views.

[D. R. Dewey, *Financial History of the United States.*]

JAMES D. MAGEE

SOIL

SOIL is a mixture of fragmented and partly or wholly weathered rocks and minerals, organic matter, water, and air, in greatly varying proportions. It has more or less distinct layers, or horizons, developed under the influence of climate and living organisms. The first step in the development of soil is the formation of parent material, accumulated largely through rock weathering. This material contains important and varying amounts of water, oxygen, and carbon dioxide. True soil results when organic matter is added, the primary source of which is the vegetation that develops on the parent material. Soil is further modified by the actions of microorganisms.

Man has learned by trial and error to maintain soil productivity by such methods as the use of manures and lime, crop rotation, irrigation, terracing, and similar techniques. Similarly, he noted that soils differ in such varied respects as color and texture and that the types of crops best grown in a particular area vary with the nature of the soil.

Agricultural chemistry, beginning in the 18th century in England, France, and Germany, brought new concepts of soil. In the 1840's the German scientist Justus von Liebig expressed ideas that led to the concept of soil as a more or less static storage bin of plant nutrients; this theory failed to show the dynamic nature of soil in its relationships to plants. In the 1870's a school of soil science developed in Russia under the leadership of V. V. Dokuchaiev, followed by N. M. Sibirtsev, K. D. Glinka, and K. K. Gedrioz, who turned from the laboratory to field studies of soil. They argued that each soil had its individual character and its own geographic extension as the product of a particular environment. The Russians then erected a system of soil classification in which the various types of soil might be placed. By the turn of the century some Americans—notably E. W. Hilgard in California, C. G. Hopkins in Illinois, and F. H. King in Wisconsin—had emphasized the regional character of soil science. About 1900 Milton Whitney and, a few years later, C. F. Marbut, both of the U.S. Department of Agriculture, began to survey the soils of the United States and developed a system of soil classification for the nation. The soil surveys were continued until almost all the agricultural land of the United States had been covered.

Although local and regional differences exist among them, soils can be classified into six broad belts. While covering the world, all are represented in the United States except the dwarf shrub and more covered tundra soils of the frigid climates. The pod-zolic soils dominate a broad belt in the higher latitudes of the Northern Hemisphere and some smaller areas in the southern half of the world. They are the forested soils of humid, temperate climates. Latosolic soils dominate equatorial belts of Africa and South America and are found in the southeastern parts of Asia and North America. They are the forested and savanna-covered soils of humid and wet-dry tropical and subtropical climates. Chernozemic soils have been formed under prairie or grass vegetation in humid to semiarid and temperate to tropical climate. These soils in the temperate zones are among the most naturally fertile in the world, and within the United States include the Corn Belt and major wheat-producing regions. Desertic soils have been formed under mixed shrub and grass vegetation or under shrubs in arid climates ranging from hot to cold. They are prominent in the great deserts of Africa, Asia, and Australia and in the smaller ones of North America and South America. The soils of mountains, or lithosols, are stony and include one or more of the other major soils, depending on climate and vegetation.

Before the fertility of any soil can be truly determined, its supply of certain elements necessary for plant growth must be measured. Once the measurement has been made, missing elements may be added. In the mid-19th century chemists centered attention on the elements required in large amounts for plant growth. These include nitrogen, potassium, calcium, and phosphorus. Others needed include sulfur, iron, zinc, boron, copper, manganese, and certain trace elements, as well as organic matter and living organisms of one type or another. Thus, bacteria of certain types must be present for legumes to obtain nitrogen from the air and fix it in the soil. The lack of nitrogen, one of the most serious problems of soil management, was solved during World War I when Fritz Haber, a German chemist, developed a means to form ammonia, an outstanding source of nitrogen, from the elemented nitrogen of the air and the hydrogen from natural gas or petroleum refining.

Soil, whatever its type or its content of plant nutrients, is subject to change. This change may either increase or decrease its ability to support plant, and thus animal, life. The continued cropping of soil, removing the plants that are grown, may lead to inability of the soil to support useful plant life. The cultivation of row plants and soil tillage away from the natural contours of the land may also lead to soil deterioration and to erosion. When the land is left bare, either through exhaustion, drought, or other disaster, it is most subject to water and wind erosion.

Erosion is older than agriculture. The water-scoured canyons and wind-carved monuments of the American West and the shifting sand dunes of desert areas around the world testify to this. Yet overgrazing and exploitative cropping have accelerated and induced erosion in almost every part of the world. It has been argued that it was silting of irrigation canals combined with erosion from overgrazing and row-crop farming that brought the great Mesopotamian civilizations to an end. China and North Africa have seen similar disasters in centuries long gone by.

The problem of erosion becomes particularly acute when sloping lands are cleared and cultivated. Of the 460 million acres in the United States suitable for crops, only 100 million are flat alluvial land. When the first English colonists settled at Jamestown in 1607, they faced heavily forested lands, broken here and there by Indian maize fields. But, with ax and plow, Europeans, at an ever accelerating rate, cleared the land of trees and planted tobacco and grain year after year in the same fields. In the 18th century there were references to worn-out land, and by 1800 much farm acreage along the coast had been abandoned. Even earlier Jared Eliot, a Connecticut minister and physician, had seen the connection between muddy water running from bare, sloping fields and the loss of fertility. He incorporated his observations in a book of essays published in 1748.

Thomas Jefferson invented a sidehill plow for turning the soil on the contour. Another gentleman farmer of Virginia, John Taylor, wrote and was widely read after the Revolution on the need to care for the soil. John Lorain of Pennsylvania was pointing out at about the same time that under natural conditions the soil gained as much as it lost. But civilized man upset the balance by clearing land and exposing it to washing rains. Perhaps the best known of this group of pre–Civil War reformers was Edmund Ruffin of Virginia. Clean-cultivated row crops, corn and cotton, according to Ruffin, were the greatest direct cause of erosion. He urged liming the soil and planting clover or cowpeas as a cover crop. His writings and demonstrations were credited with restoring the fertility and stopping erosion on large areas of southern land.

After the Civil War farmers moved west, plowing the prairies and the plains. While new areas thus became subject to erosion, interest in the problem seemed to decline, although conservationists tried to keep it in the public eye. In 1927 H. H. Bennett of the U.S. Department of Agriculture pointed out in a bulletin, *Soil Erosion a National Menace*, that the situation should be of concern to the entire nation. Congress then appropriated funds for soil erosion research.

The depression of the early 1930's and the dust storms of 1934 and 1935 led to programs to encourage conservation. The Soil Erosion Service and the Civilian Conservation Corps began soil conservation programs in 1933 with funds appropriated for work relief. The dust storms then influenced Congress in 1935 to establish a long-range program in the Department of Agriculture under the Soil Conservation Service. Within a few years the service was giving assistance to farmers who were organized into soil conservation associations. These associations, governed by local committees, determined the practices to be adopted in cooperation with the Soil Conservation Service. These included contour cultivation, strip farming, terracing, drainage, and, later, installing small water facilities. By 1973 more than 90 percent of the nation's farmland was included in soil conservation districts. In 1936 Congress added a new and controversial dimension to soil conservation legislation with the Soil Conservation and Domestic Allotment Act, which linked saving the soil to raising farm incomes and prices. The act provided for payments to farmers for shifting from soil-depleting crops (generally the major crops) to soil-conserving crops. Farmers were also paid on a cost-sharing basis for the application of soil-conserving practices to their lands. The need for this program gradually decreased in importance as new programs were introduced. Broadened to include water and wildlife conservation and renamed the Rural Environmental Assistance Program in 1971, it remained controversial. By the mid-1970's, although some land was still being eroded by water during major floods and by wind during periods of drought, large-scale damage by erosion to the nation's farmland was almost at an end.

[Roy L. Donahue, John C. Shickluna, and Lynn S. Robertson, *Soils: The Introduction to Soils and Plant Environment;* D. Harper Simms, *The Soil Conservation Service;* U.S. Department of Agriculture, *Yearbook* (1938, 1957, 1958).]

WAYNE D. RASMUSSEN

"SOLD DOWN THE RIVER," an expression that refers to the punishment meted out to unruly slaves in the border slave states in antebellum days. The belief was prevalent that labor on Louisiana sugar plantations and the great cotton estates of the lower South was exceedingly severe; and the mere threat of being "sold down the river" usually changed the conduct of unruly slaves.

[F. Bancroft, *Slave Trading in the Old South.*]
WALTER PRICHARD

SOLDIERS AND SAILORS CONVENTIONS (1866), political gatherings held during the political campaign waged by President Andrew Johnson and his conservative supporters against the Radical Republicans as they sought to influence the outcome of fall elections. Attempting to show themselves as national in scope and thus the true party of the Union, Johnson and his supporters met at the National Union Convention in Philadelphia, on Aug. 14. Former Union and Confederate officers, many prominent Copperheads, and a large number of moderate southern Democrats who favored Johnson's Reconstruction policies participated in the gathering, which became known as the Arm-in-Arm Convention.

At a second meeting on Sept. 17, conservative federal veterans, led by generals Thomas Ewing, Jr., Gordon Granger, George Armstrong Custer, John Alexander McClernand of Illinois, and J. B. Steedman of Ohio, urged support of the president's policies of conciliation and immediate restoration of the seceded states to the Union. Gen. John Ellis Wood, who presided, denounced the abolitionists as "revengeful partisans with a raging thirst for blood and plunder." Many leaders joined in a round robin attacking Edwin M. Stanton, secretary of war.

The Radicals countered by calling northern and southern supporters of congressional Reconstruction policies to a gathering at Philadelphia on Sept. 3. A second group, mostly former military men, met at Pittsburgh in the Soldiers and Sailors Convention (Sept. 25). Gen. Jacob Dolson Cox, of Ohio, was permanent president. The convention's resolutions, drafted by Benjamin Franklin Butler, "the hero of Fort Fisher," endorsed the Fourteenth Amendment as "wise, prudent and just" and denounced the Johnson policies.

[G. F. Milton, *The Age of Hate.*]
GEORGE FORT MILTON

SOLDIERS' HOMES. The United States Naval Home, in Philadelphia, Pa., was the first home for disabled veterans. Authorized in 1811 but not completed and occupied until 1831, the home was for "disabled and decrepit Navy officers, seamen and Marines." In 1975 the home had a capacity of approximately 350. Applicants must have served during wartime in the navy, marine corps, or coast guard and be disabled. Each member of the navy and marine corps contributes twenty cents per month for the support of the home, which also receives fines imposed on navy personnel.

The U.S. Soldiers' and Airmens' Home, in Washington, D.C., with a capacity of approximately 3,000, was authorized by a bill approved Mar. 3, 1851, introduced by Jefferson Davis, then a senator from Mississippi. In addition to a place of residence, medical treatment and nursing and hospital care are available, as required. Enlisted members and warrant officers of the regular army and air force who have had twenty years of service, or having had less than twenty years of service are war veterans and disabled, are eligible. Enlisted members and warrant officers of the regular army and air force contribute ten cents per month for the support of the home. Courts-martial fines, unclaimed estates of deceased members, and a portion of the post funds of the army and air force are also received by the home. Accommodations are available for women veterans. President Abraham Lincoln used this home as his summer residence from 1862 to 1864.

The National Home for Disabled Volunteer Soldiers—an agency to provide a place of residence, complete medical treatment, and hospital care—was created by Congress by an act of Mar. 3, 1865, as amended by an act of Mar. 21, 1866. The first home under its auspices was established at Augusta, Maine, and soon thereafter others were opened at Dayton, Ohio; Milwaukee, Wis.; and Hampton, Va. By 1930 seven more branches had been established, bringing the total capacity to approximately 25,000. In 1923 accommodations were provided for women veterans. In 1930 the National Home, the Veterans Bureau, and the Pension Bureau of the Department of the Interior were consolidated into the Veterans Administration. By 1975 additional domiciliary care had been provided for by the Veterans Administration at eighteen field stations, with a capacity of approximately 11,000, including four at which women veterans were admitted.

Thirty states and the District of Columbia operated soldiers' homes in 1975. All provided residential and nursing care, and some provided hospital care. The states receive a subsidy from the Veterans Administration for the care of veterans who are eligible for care by the Veterans Administration and for the construction of nursing homes and the improvement of existing buildings. Some of the homes admit husbands and wives, widows, and mothers of veterans. At many of the homes personal income in excess of a certain amount is required to be paid to the home.

Thirteen southern states maintained homes for Confederate veterans. These homes, which received no federal support, were closed in the 1920's and 1930's. The states of Missouri and Oklahoma maintained separate homes for Union and Confederate veterans.

[George E. Ijams and Philip B. Matz, "History of the Medical and Domiciliary Care of Veterans," *Military Surgeon,* vol. 76 (1935); Charles H. Stockton, *Origin, History, Laws and Regulations, U.S. Naval Asylum.*]
CARL S. MCCARTHY

SOLID SOUTH, a term used to refer to the South of the United States in the context of the political domination of the southern states by southern Democrats after the Reconstruction era. After being controlled by Republicans and blacks during Reconstruction, southerners turned to the Democrats for political leadership. A one-party system developed when Republicans proved to be weak in numbers and power and when blacks were wholly or partially disfranchised. From 1877 until 1974 Democratic candidates won more than 90 percent of all elections in the southern states. Although the Solid South was properly characterized as Democratic, the Democratic party there was far from being a united organization, especially in the 20th century. Bifactional political arrangements within the dominant party resembled a two-party system in some southern states. Other southern states developed multifactionalism. This factionalism revealed that the South was far from "solid," even though it was overwhelmingly Democratic.

The major reason for the development of the so-called Solid South was the white politician's determination to control the black voter. Whites were unhappy during Reconstruction, when the black man was politically active, and they were determined to suppress black political involvement afterward. Southern Democrats instituted literacy tests, poll taxes, property qualifications, and other devices as deterrents to the participation of blacks in the political process. When blacks and Republicans fused with dissident Democrats to form the southern Populist parties in the 1890's, fears of the consequences of a black political voice surfaced again, and southern Democrats instituted new measures in the early 1900's to restrict black voting. In the 1950's southern

blacks began to vote in increasing numbers, especially after the U.S. Congress passed a series of acts aimed at restoring their civil rights. The Voting Rights Act of 1965 was particularly important. By 1970 nearly 3.5 million southern blacks were registered to vote, constituting 66.3 percent of all voting-age blacks in the South. Approximately two-thirds of these registered southern blacks voted in the 1972 elections, and so the principal factor in the development of the Solid South was all but removed.

Even though the Republican party in the South was weak after the Reconstruction era, it did exist. While most southern Republicans were content to preside over skeletal organizations and to accept patronage from Republican administrations in the nation's capital, some worked to make the party a competitor to the dominant Democratic organization. Their efforts were greatly aided by social and economic changes in the South in the 20th century, including a rising standard of living, urban growth, federal expenditures in the region, the pressure of the national party system, the national Democratic party's stand on race, and the increasing black vote. Furthermore, the conservative southern Democrats began to acknowledge that their political philosophy was closer to mainstream Republicanism, since they generally favored low taxes, limited welfare programs, and more power in the hands of state governments. Also they had sympathy for business and a dislike for organized labor. After about 1950 southern Republicanism grew at a more rapid rate. It manifested itself in presidential campaigns most noticeably. In 1952 the Republican presidential candidate won the electoral votes of four of the eleven southern states; in 1956, five; in 1960, three; in 1964, five; and in 1968, five. In 1972 President Richard M. Nixon won the electoral votes of all eleven southern states in an unprecedented and complete reversal of history. State and local Republican candidates also began to win office. In 1973, 7 of the South's 22 U.S. senators and 34 of its 108 U.S. representatives were Republicans. Six states had recently elected Republican governors, and in 1973 every state legislature had a contingent of Republicans. Hundreds and hundreds of Republicans held lesser offices throughout the region. By 1973 state Republican parties were viable competitors to the Democrats in Tennessee, Virginia, and Florida, and conditions were such that Republicanism was likely to grow in strength in the remaining southern states. The Solid South was disappearing.

[Dewey W. Grantham, Jr., *The Democratic South;* George Brown Tindall, *The Disruption of the Solid South.*]
MONROE BILLINGTON

SOLID STATE PHYSICS

SOLID STATE PHYSICS. *See* **Physics, Solid State.**

SOMERS ISLES. *See* **Bermuda Islands.**

SOMERS **MUTINY.** The U.S. brig *Somers* was en route from the African coast to New York when, on Nov. 26, 1842, the purser's steward reported to Comdr. A. S. Mackenzie that Acting-Midshipman Philip Spencer had attempted to induce him to aid in seizing the ship and murder the officers and turn pirate. Two seamen were also named as Spencer's accomplices. The three men were held prisoner, and a court of inquiry was convened, which adjudged them guilty. Mackenzie caused them to be hanged on Dec. 1. Subsequently Mackenzie was tried by court-martial for his act, but was acquitted.

[J. F. Cooper, *Proceedings of the Naval Court-Martial in the Case of Alexander Slidell Mackenzie.*]

LOUIS H. BOLANDER

SOMERS' VOYAGE TO VIRGINIA. In 1609 the Virginia Company, having secured a new charter and subscriptions to a large joint stock fund, placed Sir George Somers in command of the largest expedition ever attempted prior to 1630 for purposes of English settlement in America. Somers sailed from Plymouth on June 2, with "eight good shippes and one Pinnace," 600 "land men," and a possible total of 800 prospective colonists of all sorts. Seven weeks out of port, on a course that ran southwestward to a point west of the Canary Islands and then ran directly westward toward Virginia, the *Sea Adventure*, carrying Somers, Sir Thomas Gates, and Capt. Christopher Newport, the three men most important to the execution of the company's plans, was separated from its consorts in a severe storm. It foundered off Bermuda on July 28, but all passengers were saved. In two small vessels constructed of Bermuda cedar Somers eventually brought his company to Jamestown, arriving on May 24, 1610. The remainder of the fleet had reached Virginia safely the preceding summer. The settlement of Bermuda by a group of Virginia adventurers in 1612 was a direct outgrowth of Somers' experiences there.

[C. M. Andrews, *Colonial Period of American History*, vol. I; W. F. Craven, *Introduction to the History of Bermuda.*]

WESLEY FRANK CRAVEN

SOMME OFFENSIVE (Aug. 8–Nov. 11, 1918). The first Americans to serve on the western front in World

War I were some 2,500 medics and engineers with the British in the Battle of Cambrai, which started in the Somme River area in northern France on Nov. 20, 1917. These detachments were still present for the second Battle of the Somme commencing on Mar. 21, 1918, the first of five great luckless efforts by the Germans to win the war before the American Expeditionary Forces were ready at the strength planned by Gen. John J. Pershing. By May 1918, the British were systematically training behind their lines U.S. divisions, each at 27,152 men, more than twice the size of the division standard of the other combatant nations. Thus, some Americans were at hand during the German-precipitated crises of the summer in the British sector. The 131st Infantry of the Thirty-third National Guard Division from Illinois fought in the Fourth Army under Gen. Sir Henry Rawlinson, helping capture Hamel on July 4. During the reduction of the Amiens salient, the 131st on Aug. 9 lost nearly 1,000 at Chipilly Ridge and Gressaire Wood, pressing on to help take Etinchem Spur on Aug. 13.

As the British planned their share of French Gen. Ferdinand Foch's grand offensive, which produced the armistice, Pershing lent Rawlinson the Second Corps of George W. Read. The Second Corps had two National Guard divisions, fresh veterans from the August Ypres-Lys operations: the Twenty-seventh from New York and the Thirtieth from Tennessee and the Carolinas.

Read's corps entered the British line east of Péronne. In Rawlinson's attack of Sept. 29, the corps broke through the Hindenburg Line at the Bellicourt Canal Tunnel, an incredible fortification partially inspiring the later Maginot Line. Alternating attacks with the Australian corps of Sir John Monash, Oct. 9–21, Read's divisions captured Brancourt-le-Grand, Premont, and Vaux-Andigny; crossed the Selle River; took Ribeauville, Mazinghien, and Rejet-de-Beaulieu; and nearly reached the Sambre River—a hard-fought advance of eleven and a half miles, costing 3,414 killed and 14,526 wounded.

[J. M. Hanson, *The Stars and Stripes*; J. J. Pershing, *My Experiences in the World War*; T. S. Stamps and V. J. Esposito, *A Short Military History of World War I.*]

JOSEPH MILLS HANSON
R. W. DALY

SONS OF LIBERTY (American Revolution), radical organizations formed in the American colonies after Parliament's passage of the Stamp Act in 1765. Societies sprang up simultaneously in scattered communities, an indication that although leadership was an important factor in agitating American independence, there existed among the people a considerable degree of discontent over parliamentary interference in colonial affairs. New York and Boston had two of the largest and most active Sons of Liberty chapters.

The organizations constituted the extralegal enforcement arm of the movement for colonial self-government. Members circulated patriotic petitions, tarred and feathered violators of patriotic decrees, and intimidated British officials and their families. They stimulated a consciousness of colonial grievances by propaganda. They conducted funerals of patriots killed in street brawls; promoted picnics, dinners, and rallies; drank toasts to the honor of historic leaders of liberty; denounced British tyranny; and hanged unpopular officials in effigy. Upon discovering that British authorities were unable to suppress them, the Sons of Liberty issued semiofficial decrees of authority and impudently summoned royal officials to "liberty trees" to explain their conduct to the people.

[Roger Champagne, "The Military Association of the Sons of Liberty," *New York Historical Society Quarterly*, vol. 41; E. S. Morgan and H. M. Morgan, *The Stamp Act Crisis*.]

LLOYD C. M. HARE

SONS OF LIBERTY (Civil War), a secret organization of Copperheads, strongest in the Northwest, was formed in 1864 by the reorganization of the Order of American Knights, with C. L. Vallandigham of Ohio, then in exile in Canada, as supreme commander. The 300,000 members were sworn to oppose unconstitutional acts of the federal government and to support states' rights principles. They opposed the draft and discouraged enlistments. Confederate agents in Canada attempted unsuccessfully to promote a so-called Northwest Conspiracy, which involved using the Sons of Liberty to form a Northwestern Confederacy. Six members of the organization were arrested and tried for treason at Indianapolis in September and October 1864. Three were condemned to death but never executed.

[E. J. Benton, *The Movement for Peace Without a Victory During the Civil War*.]

CHARLES H. COLEMAN

SONS OF THE AMERICAN REVOLUTION, NATIONAL SOCIETY OF THE, a patriotic hereditary organization. The Sons of Revolutionary Sires was organized in San Francisco, Oct. 22, 1875, and on Apr. 30, 1889, combined with certain members of the

Society of the Sons of the Revolution to organize in New York City the Sons of the American Revolution. Membership is restricted to lineal descendants of those who saw actual military or naval service during the revolutionary war. The society was incorporated in 1906.

[W. Seward Webb, *Historical Notes of the Organization of Societies of Sons of the American Revolution*.]

ALVIN F. HARLOW

SONS OF THE REVOLUTION, SOCIETY OF THE, patriotic and hereditary, was organized in New York City, Feb. 22, 1876, and reorganized on Dec. 4, 1883. Its membership consists of male lineal descendants of those who actively participated in procuring American independence during the revolutionary war. The society became active in preserving and marking historic spots, especially in the vicinity of New York City. The New York City chapter, an autonomous state society, restored and has its headquarters in Fraunces Tavern, where George Washington bade farewell to his officers in 1783.

[E. H. Hall, *History of the Movement for the Union of the Societies of the Sons of the American Revolution and Sons of the Revolution*.]

ALVIN F. HARLOW

SONS OF THE SOUTH, sometimes called Blue Lodges, Social Bands, and Friends Society, was a secret society formed in 1854 and devoted to making Kansas a slave state. Its members, who were mostly Missourians and were organized in bands, encouraged southern emigration to Kansas, protected proslavery settlers there, and in numerous other ways, sometimes illegally and violently, tried to counteract the efforts of northern emigrant aid societies to make Kansas a free state.

HENRY T. SHANKS

SOO CANAL. *See* **Sault Sainte Marie Canals.**

SOO LINE. *See* **Railroads, Sketches.**

SOONERS were those persons who illegally entered certain lands in the Indian Territory prior to the date set by the U.S. government for the opening of the lands to settlement. The term was first used in connection with the settlement of the so-called Oklahoma

Lands in 1889. A proclamation issued by President Benjamin Harrison authorized settlement of these lands as of noon, Apr. 22, and forbade any person to enter them earlier. Those who did so came to be called Sooners. The term was also used at later openings of Indian Territory lands to settlement.

[J. S. Buchanan and E. E. Dale, *A History of Oklahoma;* J. B. Thoburn, *History of Oklahoma,* vol. II.]

EDWARD EVERETT DALE

SORGHUM. In the 1840's sorghum seeds were imported from Liberia and grown in the United States, with a view to manufacturing sugar commercially from the plant's juice. All such attempts proved futile, however, since glucose is the only saccharine matter in the plant. Col. Isaac Hedges of Missouri was the greatest promoter of the product. During the Civil War, when southern molasses was unavailable in the North, sorghum became a popular product in the upper Mississippi Valley. The sorghum stalks, while standing in the field, were stripped of their leaves by farmers using large wooden knives. The stalks were then cut and hauled to a local mill and run between rollers to extract the juice, which was then boiled to the proper consistency in large vats. Great quantities of this "long sweetening" were made and used as a substitute for sugar on the prairie frontier.

[Wm. M. Ledbetter, "Isaac Hedges' Vision of a Sorghum Industry in Missouri," *Missouri Historical Review,* vol. 21.]

EVERETT DICK

SOUND DUES. By "immemorial prescription" Denmark claimed the right to collect dues on ships passing through the Sound, between Denmark and Sweden. American vessels paid the dues until 1854, when Secretary of State William L. Marcy informed Denmark that, as the United States had not helped establish the size of the payments and had never received any benefit from them, it intended to stop paying them. Denmark, in 1855, invited an international congress to meet in Copenhagen to discuss the problem. The United States refused to send delegates. The congress met, however, and in February 1856 decided to replace the dues with a one-time payment to Denmark of 35,000,000 rix-dollars. The amount each nation was to pay was based on its proportion of the total trade through the Sound. Although the United States had not taken part in the congress, it agreed by treaty (1857) to pay its share, 717,829 rix-dollars ($393,011). Denmark agreed to maintain

lighthouses, buoys, and other improvements of the Sound.

[S. P. Fogdall, *Danish-American Diplomacy, 1776–1920;* C. E. Hill, *The Danish Sound Dues and the Command of the Baltic.*]

S. P. FOGDALL

SOUTH, ANTEBELLUM. If, as has been said, the South is today a history in search of a country, such an assertion would not have been true during most of the antebellum period. The considerable interest in the history of the South developed in the post–Civil War period, when there was a golden age to remember and its passing to lament. The revolutionary war stimulated some historical writing, but otherwise there was relatively little attention given to the history of a society not yet fully sectionally conscious. During the years of early settlement the indefinite boundaries of its several colonies, established by the whims of English monarchs, were of no great moment; reference to the Chesapeake country, the Carolina-Georgia lowlands, and the backcountry inland from these two areas defined the life experiences of the settlers much more realistically. As economic and political focuses developed in the 18th century—such centers as Saint Marys and Annapolis, Md.; Jamestown and Williamsburg, Va.; New Bern, Edenton, and Charleston in the Carolinas; and, later, Nashville, Natchez, and New Orleans—colony and state entities became administratively and jurisdictionally functional and served to give separate identities to populations within them.

The Old South never achieved a single outstanding urban focus; New York handled at least as much of the South's trade as did Charleston, New Orleans, or Baltimore, which in 1860 was its largest city. On the eve of the Civil War the South was still overwhelmingly rural, and its towns and small cities were gracious plantation capitals dominated more by planters than by merchants. It had by that time developed a planter gentry that exercised an economic and political influence in each southern state, as well as in the nation, out of all proportion to its numbers. By 1850 planters were being separately enumerated in the U.S. census. Behind the great planters, possessing thousands of acres and hundreds of slaves, ranged a larger number of small planters and an even larger number of white yeoman farmers. Behind these came poor whites, free blacks, black slaves, and scattered Indian groups. By 1860 the Old South had achieved a heterogeneity that linked into an organic whole the parts of its massive and varied geographical areas from Maryland to eastern Texas and moved it toward a political and cultural unity.

In this area there developed and spread a distinctive institution—the plantation—not present in the European or African traditions of the settlers or in any other part of continental North America. It shared certain characteristics with the English manor, Old Testament Hebrew patriarchal society, the classical Greek state, and the Roman latifundium, but it had a distinct mode of its own. It produced agricultural staples for sale, not for local consumption. It was the driving force behind the settlement of the land and of the westward expansion of southern civilization. Plantations largely determined the settlement, distribution, and tasks of labor not only on the estates themselves but also in the farm areas symbiotic to them. They accommodated the relationships between people of diverse race, nationality, and culture and, in doing so, provided order, stability, and continuity; and they set the stage for the identification of the white people of the area as southerners and for the class and racial stratification of the whole population.

Southern civilization had its inception in the 1607 settlement of Englishmen at Jamestown, Va., and modified English traditions and institutions continued to dominate southern society into the late 20th century. Of the South's white population in 1860—about 60 percent of the total—no less than two-thirds was of English stock; persons of Scottish and Scotch-Irish descent made up about one-fifth; and the balance of the white population was made up of smaller percentages of French, Spanish, German, and Celtic-Irish descendants. The southern black population—about 40 percent—accounted for about nine-tenths of the black population of the United States.

The London (later, Virginia) Company initiated what was originally intended to be a trading factory at Jamestown, after the precedent of Italian and English trading factories in the Baltic and the Levant, but trade with the native Indians proved unprofitable. The economic motive explicit in the enterprise was realized after 1619 in the production of tobacco, an addictive drug with a market elastic enough to pay the cost of production in Virginia and of transportation to England and yet yield a profit. Entrepreneurial tobacco plantation agriculture began an independent development in Virginia and Maryland in the early 17th century; the rice and indigo plantations of South Carolina and the sugar plantations of Louisiana were African and/or West Indian transplants in the early 18th century.

Like the tobacco plantation, the rice, indigo, and sugar plantations were territorially delimited; they did not undergo any significant westward expansion, as did cotton plantations. Following the invention of the cotton gin in 1793 and the surging demand for raw cotton in England incident to the Industrial Revolution, it was the cotton planters who mobilized the tremendous energy necessary to cross southern state boundaries, and by 1860 they had carried the institution of the plantation all the way to eastern Texas. South Carolina, the leading cotton-producing state, was the focus of secessionist activities.

An analysis of the bases of the civilization of the Old South falls conveniently into three contexts: the regional, the sectional, and the cultural. The regional South is delineated in demographic, ecological, and economic terms; the sectional South, in political and ideologic terms; and the cultural South, in terms of its way of life. The plantation was the active institutional determinant in all three respects.

The South as region or as subregion was originally differentiated from the rest of North America as a specialized territorial division of labor along with eastern Mexico, central America, northern and northeastern South America, and the islands of the West Indies for the production of tropical and subtropical agricultural staples for the markets of Europe. Because of the relative cheapness of water transportation, plantation America hugged the islands and coastlands of the Atlantic, the Caribbean, the Gulf of Mexico, and the rivers that emptied into those waters. The area now called the South, with outlets along the Atlantic coast and the Gulf of Mexico, was the northern part, or subregion, of the larger plantation region. It was, and is, the only region of the United States that fronts the sea on two sides, and it has a total shoreline of nearly 3,000 miles, greater than the rest of the United States, North and West, combined.

Those parts of the New World where colonial wares profitably could be produced were areas of what H. J. Niebor, in his *Slavery as an Industrial System* (1910), calls "open resources," areas where there was more land than there was labor to till it and where men of capital and enterprise competed with each other for such workers as could be made available. It was in response to this situation that white indentured servitude, Indian slavery, and, far more important, black slavery were introduced. In consequence, the society became biracial, with blacks and whites in the plantation areas intermixed on the same land. There was a concentration of white yeoman farmers and squatters in the more inaccessible and less fertile areas.

In the course of bringing land into new, and presumably higher, economic uses, the plantation became a political institution, a little state or subdivision of the state, within which a monopoly of authority was exercised by the planter. On the unruly southern frontier the planter, himself often lawless, established law on his own plantation, privileged to reward and punish even by the occasional exercise of the power of life and death, especially in the early years. By virtue of his authority he pursued a sort of military agriculture, employing a hierarchically ordered, regimented labor, imported and distributed as a utility. The people thus imported—black Africans—interbred with some of the whites in authority over them, especially where there was an imbalance of the sexes. The concept of race, already present in the Atlantic slave trade, became much more than a physical anthropological expression, for it was elaborated into a set of symbols and dogmas to set the races apart and keep both the mixed and the unmixed portions of the nonwhite population within the ranks of the laboring caste. It thus became a political idea, and although most of the mixed population—almost half a million people—had by 1860 become free blacks, they were not yet free men. Between 1830 and 1860 the subject of the free black surpassed the subject of slavery as the most discussed problem of the Old South, but it was caste, as well as slavery, together with the idea of race implicit in them, that set the South off against the North in a sectional bipolarity.

"I shall recognize as tests of sectionalism all those methods by which a given area resists national uniformity," wrote Frederick Jackson Turner in *The Significance of Sections in American History*. In these terms the South became "the South" as a section rather than a region or subregion. The northern part of plantation America became part of a political entity, the United States, to which other parts of the Gulf-Caribbean-Atlantic region did not belong; and from the years of the American Revolution on, there was a mounting conflict of interest between the South and the other sections of the Union. During the Constitutional Convention, in the words of Charles C. Pinckney of South Carolina, "a real distinction between northern and southern interests arising from the character of their means of livelihood" became apparent. It was to become more apparent when events such as the War of 1812, the nullification controversy, the Nat Turner slave rebellion in 1831, the war with Mexico (1846–48), the failure of compromise efforts, and John Brown's raid at Harpers Ferry (1859) fanned the flames of sectional opposition. It was as if an institutional fault line extending westward from the Mason-Dixon line broke the continuity of northern and southern social systems. The plantation had intruded an alien social stratum into the southern system, which threw all other institutions out of line with their northern counterparts. Revolutionary abolitionists in the North began an attack on the evils of slavery and the dark purposes of "the slave power" that broadened into a condemnation of the South generally. Southerners responded with equal intemperance. In the processes of attack and counterattack the interests and customs of each society, and especially of the South, came to be regarded by the members of each as essential to survival and thus to be defended at all costs.

Such considerations introduce the South as a culture area, as ethnologists tend to think of culture, characterized by those intangible aspects of a civilization that are felt rather than satisfactorily apprehended intellectually and expressed verbally. Southern culture is manifest in a climate of conventional understandings that are difficult to fix in terms easily understood by nonsoutherners. A map of plantation societies around the world, past and present, shows the South to have been the largest such society the world has ever known. Millions of people grew up and lived in this system of society and knew no other, or very little of any other, having little opportunity for comparison and contrast with other cultures. The southern region in the larger world community and the individual plantation in the forest were highly isolated, and the resultant culture was a product of isolation. The culture of the Old South was a way of life, a distinctive style of living, taken for granted and requiring no analysis or explanation. A young woman visiting in New York was "surprised to hear of 'plantation customs' said to exist" in the South. Thus, it is not surprising that the storytellers of the Old South could, like Jane Austen, apply themselves to the telling of the tale itself "by agreeing with society and being at peace with it." The resulting literature emphasized manners and chivalry and was generally romantic.

In terms of Matthew Arnold's idea of culture as the cultivation of "what is best and noblest in us," those attributes of a civilization that can be pointed to, praised, and refined, the Old South exhibited itself in the literary societies of its colleges and universities, the achievements of its scientists, its oratory, its literary periodicals, its architecture, its literature, its statesmen, and its theologians. There were eminent southern men of achievement in all such areas. Southern ethnocentrism has perhaps overpraised both them and the society that produced them, but such overpraise is a sin of ethnocentrism generally. The ingredients of a high civilization were present in the lives of the plain folk of the South—such as gardens, balladry, folk sermons, and culinary art—yet few creative masterpieces of an enduring nature were inspired by them.

The regional, sectional, and cultural aspects of the Old South came together to form a social system at the center of which was the institution of the plantation supported by a series of satellite institutions. The "plantation system" and "the South" became almost synonymous, and although not every southerner lived within the physical bounds of a plantation, perhaps all properly called southerners lived within the plantation system. The plantation took on a familial form, modifying the family within itself as well as the families of all classes symbiotic to it, whether deriving from Europe or from Africa. There was little place for free public schools until near the end of the pre–Civil War period, but academies were fairly numerous, and state and denominational colleges drew students from among the sons of the smaller planters as well as the affluent ones. These educational institutions, as well as military schools, functioned within the plantation system to indoctrinate and to support it. Protestant, Roman Catholic, Jewish, and even such black religious organizations as there were came to be part of the system and to serve it by seeking to transfer attention from the ills of this world to salvation in the next. The county developed as a primary social, as well as governmental, unit, with the plantation often functioning as an informal, but effective, subdivision. The states, too, came under control of planter oligarchies. All lived under the laws sponsored by plantation interests, even where the institution was not physically present and where the system tapered off, somewhat diluted, toward piedmont and mountain areas. It was a system that gave southerners the sense of belonging to an ordered civilization and led to the first use of the word "sociology" in America, notably by Henry Hughes and George Fitzhugh in the 1850's. Sociology, according to Fitzhugh, was the descriptive social science of the South, just as its enemy, political science, was that of the North.

[U. B. Phillips, *Life and Labor in the Old South;* David Potter, *The South and the Sectional Conflict;* Wendell Holmes Stephenson, *A Basic History of the Old South;* Edgar T. Thompson, *Plantation Societies, Race Relations, and the South.*]

EDGAR T. THOMPSON

SOUTH AMERICA, COMMERCE WITH. Colonial Period to World War I. U.S. commerce with South America originated in the intercourse of the thirteen colonies with ports in the Spanish Indies. Shortly after the United States acknowledged the independence of the Spanish-American republics, it began to negotiate treaties of commerce with them (*see* Latin-American Republics, Recognition of). The treaty signed on Oct. 3, 1824, between Colombia and the United States regulated trade between that country and northern South America for many years.

During the period from 1825 to 1850 large quantities of cotton goods were exported from the United States to Colombia, Chile, and Brazil. South America sent to the United States hides, wool, sugar, guano, and copper. During the year ending June 30, 1850, the United States imported $15,856,701 of produce from South American countries, while it exported to them goods amounting to $7,050,767. After 1850, because of the Civil War and the increasing competition from European countries, the export trade of the United States with South American nations declined. Although in 1867 the United States made purchases of coffee and rubber from Brazil and of sugar, spices, fruits, chemicals, and woods from other nations of South America amounting to $88,408,119, yet its sales of manufactured goods to these countries amounted to scarcely one-third of the total of its purchases from them.

Meantime, a brief experiment was made with reciprocity. The McKinley Tariff Act of Oct. 1, 1890, authorized the president to reimpose the duties on sugar, molasses, coffee, tea, and hides, which were on the free list, whenever he deemed that the duties imposed on products of the United States by nations exporting those articles were "reciprocally unjust or unequal." Secretary of State James G. Blaine accordingly negotiated reciprocity agreements with Brazil, Guatemala, Honduras, Nicaragua, El Salvador, and the Dominican Republic. These reciprocity agreements were all ended by the Wilson-Gorman Tariff in 1894.

During the years from 1900 to 1914 a marked development took place in the commerce of the United States with South American nations. In particular, there was an increase in the volume of imports from Argentina, Brazil, Chile, Peru, Colombia, and Venezuela. Imports into the United States from Argentina increased from $105,078,714 in 1900 to $273,821,496 in 1914. The United States was the second largest importer from Chile, while the amount of its exports to that country was exceeded only by those of England and of Germany.

During World War I leading nations of South America sent larger shares of their products to the United States and purchased more manufactured goods in this country. Imports into the United States from South America in 1916 were nearly 100 percent in excess of those in 1914, while exports from the United States to that continent showed a gain of 140 percent during the two-year period, 1914–16. By 1917 the United States enjoyed about one-half of the total trade of South America.

The years immediately following World War I were distinguished by a great expansion of commercial life in South America. In 1913 Colombia and Venezuela purchased $10 million of goods from the United States; in 1927 they purchased $90 million. After the construction of the Panama Canal (1904–14), the trade of the United States with countries on the west coast of South America increased considerably. The chief exceptions to this tendency were countries in the basin of Río de la Plata, where the staple products were the same as those of the United States. Import duties levied by the U.S. tariff on wheat as well as the stringent application of sanitary regulations to meat provoked resentment in Argentina, which made that country turn more and more toward English marts and markets.

WILLIAM SPENCE ROBERTSON

World War II and After. During World War II and immediately thereafter South America was the most important source of U.S. imports and the second most important market for U.S. exports. But in the late 1940's the South American share of U.S. trade began to decline steadily as Europe and Japan rapidly recovered from the devastation of the war and together with Canada became the major U.S. trading partners. U.S. imports originating in South America as a proportion of total U.S. imports dropped from 22 percent in 1950 to about 6 percent during the early 1970's, while the South American market fell from about 15 percent of total U.S. exports to 7 percent during the same period. Yet in 1973 the region was still the fourth largest market for U.S. goods and the fourth largest U.S. supplier.

The United States provided about half of South America's imports around 1950, but only about one-third in 1970. During those two decades the U.S. market for South American products declined in similar fashion. Nevertheless, although South America reoriented its trade to Europe and Japan, the United States remained South America's most important single trading partner by far.

U.S. imports from South America remained fairly stable from the early 1950's to the mid-1960's, ranging between $2.2 billion and $2.5 billion. Sub-

sequently there was a marked increase, only in part due to price increases, and imports reached $4.4 billion in 1973. The value of U.S. exports to the region fluctuated greatly after World War II but showed a steady increase after the mid-1960's, reaching $4.8 billion in 1973. Until the end of the 1960's, U.S. imports exceeded U.S. exports in most years by an average of almost $400 million a year. These deficits of the U.S. trade balance were the result of large U.S. imports of petroleum from Venezuela. (Excluding Venezuela, the U.S. trade balance with South America has usually shown a surplus, with U.S. exports exceeding U.S. imports.) After 1968, as the region's industrialization accelerated, South American demand for U.S. products increased more sharply than its exports to the United States. In 1973 the surplus of the U.S. trade balance with South America reached $400 million, or $1.2 billion excluding Venezuela. South American trade formed a triangular pattern, the region being a net exporter to Europe and Japan and a net importer from the United States.

By the late 1960's Brazil surpassed Venezuela as the largest market for U.S. exports to South America, importing nearly $2 billion from the United States in 1973, nearly double Venezuela's purchases. As U.S. suppliers, however, the importance of these two countries is reversed: U.S. imports originating from Venezuela were more than double those from Brazil in 1973.

Argentina—the country with the highest standard of living in South America and, after Brazil, the region's largest in terms of population, national income, and degree of industrialization—has had a relatively weak commercial relationship with the United States. From World War II until 1975 its trade with the United States was consistently exceeded by that of Venezuela and Brazil and in some years also by Colombia, Peru, and Chile, economically much less developed countries than Argentina. The United States provided between 20 and 25 percent of total Argentine imports. Only 19 percent of Argentina's exports went to the United States in 1950, the lowest proportion of any South American country in that year. In subsequent years Argentina reoriented its trade away from the United States, toward Europe and Japan, even more than most South American countries, and only 9 percent of its exports went to the United States in the early 1970's. A sharp drop in the proportion of Chilean exports going to the United States took place in 1971 and 1972 during the leftist regime of President Salvador Allende Gossens. Uruguay is also a special case because its foreign trade collapsed during the late 1950's, primarily as a result of both domestic production problems and the precipitous fall in the demand for its products, particularly wool. Its export share to the United States dwindled from 51 percent in 1950 to less than 5 percent in 1971.

About 75 percent of U.S. exports to South America has traditionally consisted of manufactured goods, but the kinds of manufactured goods exported changed during the post–World War II period from primarily finished consumer products to primarily machinery, equipment, industrial raw materials, and supplies. This change coincided with the acceleration of industrialization based on import substitution in the major South American countries. The production of most of the manufactured consumer goods that had been formerly imported from the United States began in Argentina, Brazil, Chile, and Uruguay and then developed in Colombia, Peru, and Venezuela. This industrialization process required imports of investment goods for the establishment and operation of South America's new factories. In 1970 the United States supplied between 33 and 50 percent of the manufactured imports of South American countries.

The U.S. aid program instituted by President John F. Kennedy under the Alliance for Progress in 1961 indirectly helped U.S. export to the region by requiring the recipient countries to purchase aid-financed products and services from the United States. Tie-in aid was discontinued by President Richard M. Nixon in 1972, when aid loans and grants to Latin America had declined to $345 million from about $730 million in 1968. Yet South American countries continued to spend the major part of U.S. aid funds on imports from the United States. Because the emphasis of U.S. aid shifted from donations to loans during the mid-1960's, a significant part of South America's imports from the United States was financed through increasing indebtedness. The external public debt of South American countries became a serious burden on their economies during the 1960's, surpassing $15 billion in 1971, nearly five times the earnings from their exports to the United States in that year. Interest payments on their external public debt amounted to nearly one-third of their 1971 exports to the United States.

Natural resource products have been the traditional U.S. imports from South America. Between World War I and World War II coffee and petroleum were the most important single imports. After World War II, crude oil and petroleum products began to outweigh coffee in the value of U.S. imports from South

America. It is estimated that their import value amounted to about $2 billion in 1972, nearly all the petroleum imports originating in Venezuela. More than one-third of this amount came to the United States via the Netherlands Antilles, where much Venezuelan crude oil was refined after the 1950's. The value, but not the quantity, of petroleum imports from South America quadrupled in 1974 because of the sharp price increases imposed by the Organization of Petroleum Exporting Countries (OPEC), of which Venezuela and Ecuador were members. Crude oil imports from Ecuador did not become significant until 1973.

Brazil and Colombia provided by far the largest share of U.S. coffee imports immediately after World War II, supplying almost 1 million metric tons a year, or about 90 percent of U.S. consumption. U.S. coffee imports from South America declined thereafter, as Africa became an important U.S. supplier. By the end of the 1960's South America was shipping to the United States about 650 thousand metric tons yearly, which amounted to roughly two-thirds of the U.S. market.

Copper has been the third most important U.S. import from South America, with most copper imports coming from Chile, which shipped to the United States over 200 million metric tons of refined copper and about 50 million metric tons of the unrefined product ("blister" copper) a year during the early 1950's. By 1960 nearly all U.S. copper imports from Chile were in unrefined form, as Chile shifted its refined copper exports to Western Europe. During the second half of the 1960's Chilean refining capacity increased, and U.S. imports of refined copper resumed. During the 1950's Peru became another South American source of U.S. copper imports. Peruvian production increased rapidly during the 1960's, primarily in the form of concentrates, but exports to the United States remained far below those of Chile. Until the early 1970's most copper output in Chile and Peru was produced by U.S. subsidiaries, which, except for one in Peru, were subsequently expropriated by the respective governments. In 1973 South America supplied almost half of U.S. imports or almost 10 percent of U.S. copper consumption, but some of it was reexported to Western Europe and Japan.

After World War II, South American iron ore production increased rapidly and, aside from sugar, was the only other commodity of which the export value to the United States began to exceed $100 million. Venezuela, Brazil, Chile, and Peru supplied over 22 million metric tons of iron ore for the U.S. market by 1960, but after that time most of the increase in South American production for export was sold to Japan. In 1973 Venezuela, Brazil, and Peru supplied almost 40 percent of U.S. iron ore imports, or 12 percent of U.S. consumption.

Other important U.S. imports from South America have been sugar, primarily from Brazil and Peru; bananas, primarily from Ecuador; cocoa from Brazil and Ecuador; fishmeal from Peru; tin from Bolivia; manganese from Brazil; tungsten from Peru and Brazil; zinc ores from Peru; and processed meats from Argentina. As late as 1970 the U.S. import value from the region for any of these products, except sugar, still remained below $100 million, although these imports from South America accounted for significant proportions of U.S. consumption. The elimination of the U.S. import quota for sugar in 1974 benefited South American exports.

Of all South American countries, Argentina's exports of temperate zone agricultural products have competed most directly with U.S. production, which may explain the relatively low level of United States–Argentine trade. As U.S. consumption of beef began to outstrip domestic production after World War II, the United States imported increasing quantities of beef, Argentina's most important export commodity beginning in the mid-1950's. Although U.S. imports of fresh and frozen beef reached $1 billion in 1973, none of it came from any South American country because of the strict enforcement of U.S. sanitary regulations.

The Treaty of Montevideo of 1960, in which Mexico joined South American countries to form the Latin American Free Trade Association (LAFTA), has not affected the region's commerce with the United States. Neither has the Andean Common Market, a more successful subregional arrangement between Bolivia, Chile, Colombia, Ecuador, Peru, and Venezuela, established at the end of the 1960's. These schemes probably stimulated trade in manufactures, which also became more important in the region's exports to the United States. Manufactured products accounted for about 5 percent of South American exports to the United States in 1950 and about 12 percent in 1970. Exports of manufactures continued to rise, reaching 20 percent of Argentine exports, 12 percent of Brazilian, and 13 percent of Colombian exports in 1972. A significant part of this increase was the result of the expanded role of U.S. and other foreign investments in South American manufacturing production.

By 1970 the industrialization of South American countries had become increasingly dependent on the import of U.S. technology and capital and had led to a large foreign indebtedness. Subsequently the prices of the region's raw material exports increased more than the prices of its imports, and the value of South American exports grew faster than its external debt to the United States as shortages of raw materials made themselves felt during the economic boom of 1973 in industrial countries. As a result of the ensuing economic recession in the United States and other developed countries, South America's raw material prices had weakened again by the end of 1974. Nevertheless, the first half of the 1970's brought into sharp focus what was already apparent: a growing economic interdependence had become a fact of United States–South American relations.

JOSEPH GRUNWALD

[Donald Baerrensen, Martin Carnoy, and Joseph Grunwald, *Latin American Trade Patterns;* Martin Carnoy, Miguel Wionczek, and Joseph Grunwald, *Latin American Economic Integration and U.S. Policy;* Joseph Grunwald and Philip Musgrove, *Natural Resources and the Economic Development of Latin America;* William Spence Robertson, *Hispanic-American Relations With the United States;* United Nations, *Handbook of International Trade and Development Statistics.*]

SOUTHAMPTON, Long Island, the oldest English town in the state of New York, was settled in the summer of 1640. The original inhabitants came from Lynn, Mass., and the emigration was an early example of the resettlement of New England natives that eventually carried New England influence to the Pacific.

The Dutch claimed all of Long Island and had peopled the west end, but the English, in settling Southampton, Southold, and Easthampton, established a claim to the east end. The English settlers, under the leadership of Edward Howell, received title to the land from the Earl of Stirling, who had been granted Long Island in 1635 by Charles I, and from the local Indian tribes. Southampton's early connections were almost wholly with Connecticut, but after the English conquest of New Amsterdam, it took its place among the other small communities of the proprietary colony of the Duke of York, which soon became the royal colony of New York. Located on the south shore of Long Island, the village of Southampton has developed into a summer resort. Its population in 1970 was 4,904.

[J. T. Adams, *History of the Town of Southampton.*]
JAMES TRUSLOW ADAMS

SOUTHAMPTON INSURRECTION. *See* **Nat Turner's Rebellion.**

SOUTH CAROLINA was first settled by Europeans in 1526 when Vásquez de Ayllón led an expedition of Spaniards from Hispaniola to San Miguel de Gualdape on Winyah Bay. Jean Ribault tried to plant a colony of French Huguenots at Port Royal in 1562. The English, who were sent out by eight lords proprietors to take up their grant under the charters of 1663 and 1665, began the continuous settlement of South Carolina at Albemarle Point on the Ashley River in April 1670.

The Fundamental Constitutions, drawn up by John Locke and Anthony Ashley Cooper, Earl of Shaftesbury, in 1669 were never adopted by the colonists, since the feudal system they provided for was unsuited to the wilderness of South Carolina. The Anglicans from Barbados, the Dissenters from England, and the Huguenots from France ultimately compromised their religious differences in 1706 by accepting an act establishing the Church of England. Rice, produced by the labor of black slaves, became the first great staple. In December 1719 the proprietary government was overthrown, and in September 1729, Parliament compensated the lords proprietors.

The reorganization of the government under royal authority by Gov. Robert Johnson (1730–35) and the successful growing of indigo by Eliza Lucas Pinckney (1744) ushered in the golden years that made South Carolina on the eve of the American Revolution the most prosperous of the English mainland colonies. The fear of the Indians had been removed by Col. James Grant's victory over the Cherokee at the Battle of Etchohih on June 10, 1761; the fear of the Spaniards, by the cession of Florida to England by the Treaty of Paris of 1763.

The merchants and the planters, who wished to be protected in their newly won riches and to be respected for the place they had achieved in society, engineered the revolutionary activity in South Carolina. After Lord William Campbell, the last royal governor, had fled on Sept. 15, 1775, the patriots, led by Christopher Gadsden, Henry Laurens, and John Rutledge, meeting in the provincial congress, drew up a temporary constitution on Mar. 26, 1776, and a more permanent one on Mar. 19, 1778, which disestablished the Anglican church. After the British took Charleston on May 12, 1780, the backcountry, which had been filled up in the 1750's and 1760's by settlers of Scotch-Irish descent from the north, rallied behind the partisan leaders Francis Marion, Thomas Sumter, and Andrew Pickens and held the British at bay until Gen. Nathanael Greene's Continental army could drive the British army back upon its last base at Charleston.

The low-country elite recognized the backcountry's contribution to the winning of the Revolution by consenting in 1786 to the removal of the capital from Charleston to Columbia and in 1790 to a new constitution that established two sets of state officials, one in Charleston and one in Columbia. Almost as a protection against these concessions and as a means of paying off the huge state debt, the low-country elite led the movement to ratify the Constitution of the United States.

With the sudden expansion of cotton production in the sea islands after the invention of the cotton gin in 1793, the state underwent fundamental changes. Any chance for the elimination of slavery disappeared as the institution spread with cotton rapidly into the backcountry. The backcountry farmer became a cotton planter, united in interest with the low-country rice planter. The two sections moved in 1803 to reopen the slave trade, which had been cut off in 1787, and agreed in 1808 by an amendment to the state constitution to divide equally the representation in the general assembly.

The year 1808 was the most important dividing line in the history of the state. The U.S. Congress brought an end to the foreign slave trade on Jan. 1, 1808. President Thomas Jefferson's embargo struck a mortal blow at foreign commerce, which had carried new ideas as well as cargoes to Charleston. With this economic disruption, the merchant class quickly declined in influence. South Carolina College, which had accepted its first class in 1805, produced new leaders for the state, trained to support the planter elite. Those who opposed slavery, particularly the Quakers, began to move to the Old Northwest. After the passage of a law in 1820 making it almost impossible to free slaves and after Rep. Charles Pinckney's denial during the Missouri controversy that free blacks could be citizens of a state, the antebellum mind of South Carolina was set. John C. Calhoun became the most articulate defender of a state's right to shape its own society.

The threats of slave insurrections in Charleston in 1822 and in Georgetown in 1829 and the rapid decline in the price of cotton during that decade placed the state on the defensive. Calhoun's *Exposition* of 1828, written secretly, and the Ordinance of Nullification of Nov. 24, 1832, declaring void the tariffs of 1828 and 1832, were the first protective gestures; the Ordinance of Secession of Dec. 20, 1860, was thought to be the ultimate protection.

The Civil War, which began at Fort Sumter on Apr. 12, 1861, ended disastrously with the burning of Columbia on Feb. 17, 1865. The state signaled its contrition by ratifying the Thirteenth Amendment on Nov. 13, 1865, but balked at accepting the Fourteenth Amendment. After a reconstruction that brought the freedmen for the first time to a constitutional convention in January 1868, the state ratified the Fourteenth Amendment on July 9, 1868. The new constitution of 1868 provided for more democratic forms of government, black suffrage, and free public education. Yet the bittersweet memories of the glory followed by the destruction, nurtured by the United Daughters of the Confederacy, organized in the 1890's, suffused the mind of the white population. When the nation permitted Wade Hampton to oust Daniel Chamberlain from the governorship in 1877 and Benjamin R. Tillman to remake the state constitution in 1895, driving blacks from the polls, white South Carolinians mistook permissiveness for truth. From 1902, when the last black left his seat in the state legislature, until 1970, when blacks reappeared in that body, a segregated society existed.

The poverty of the Great Depression united white and black South Carolina in overwhelming support of the New Deal. But South Carolina's economy took on renewed life only with the advent of World War II. The new prosperity rested on the presence of army, air, and naval installations; the rapid industrialization of the state; and the redevelopment of the port of Charleston. The textile industry, which antedated the Civil War, remained the major industry, although good water supplies and untapped labor reserves induced many blue-chip companies to open plants in small towns throughout the state.

South Carolina bankers and industrialists responded to the dynamic political leadership of such governors as Ernest F. Hollings (1959–63), Donald S. Russell (1963–65), Robert E. McNair (1965–71), and John C. West (1971–75), who not only revitalized the State Development Board and improved education but also urged acceptance of the Civil Rights Acts of the 1960's. The blacks themselves, after the Rock Hill lunch-counter sit-in of 1960, forced the white leadership to take their aspirations seriously. A historian of the future might well say that the decade of the 1960's was a more important dividing line in the history of the state than 1808.

[Lewis P. Jones, *Books and Articles on South Carolina History;* I. A. Newby, *Black Carolinians: A History of Blacks in South Carolina From 1895 to 1968;* George C. Rogers, Jr., *A South Carolina Chronology;* David Duncan Wallace, *South Carolina, A Short History, 1520–1948;* Peter Wood, *Black Majority: Negroes in Colonial South Carolina From 1670 Through the Stono Rebellion.*]

GEORGE C. ROGERS, JR.

SOUTH CAROLINA, PROPOSED NOBILITY IN. The Fundamental Constitutions of Carolina, drawn up in 1669, established both a government agreeable to Charles II of England and a safeguard against a "numerous democracy." The constitutions reserved two-fifths of the land for a hereditary nobility, whose estates were to be inalienable and indivisible. Some proprietors of the colony established estates, and twenty-six landgraves (members of the second-highest rank of nobility) and thirteen caciques also acquired estates and seats in the governor's council. A title of landgrave or cacique passed through three generations and carried with it a barony, or tract of land, of 12,000 acres. Although no manors or manorial jurisdictions were created or exercised, social and political privileges were enjoyed. These proprietary efforts to transfer English feudal law and practice to America produced a half-century of conflict, until South Carolina became a royal colony in 1719.

[Edward McCrady, *South Carolina Under Proprietary Government.*]

O. C. SKIPPER

SOUTH CAROLINA, SPANISH EXPEDITIONS AGAINST. French attempts to gain a foothold along the southern Atlantic coast prompted Spain to capture Fort Caroline (Florida) and to found Saint Augustine in 1565. In the same year Spaniards from Cuba burned Jean Ribault's abandoned Charlesfort at Parris Island (*see* Port Royal). Spaniards from Saint Augustine fortified the island and held the region from 1566 to 1586.

British settlement of South Carolina began in 1670. In August of that year Spanish vessels from Saint Augustine appeared before Charleston but retired without attacking. South Carolinians began trading with the Spanish Indians, and in 1686 the Spanish, in retaliation, destroyed Stuart's Town, a Scotch settlement near Port Royal, and raided to the north. Spanish Indians, retaliating for attacks in 1702 on Saint Augustine and on the region around and to the east of Tallahassee were crushed by South Carolina traders and Indians. An expedition led by South Carolina Gov. James Moore ravaged the Tallahassee region and the area east of it in December-January 1703–04. In 1706 a Franco-Spanish naval attack on Charleston failed disastrously. South Carolinians generally believed that the Spanish inspired the Yamasee War, but that belief seems groundless, although the Spanish did harbor the defeated Yamasee. Forces from Saint Augustine, seeking to avenge a Georgia–South Carolina attack on Florida in 1740, were defeated by a force led by Georgia's founder, James Oglethorpe, in 1742 at Bloody Marsh, Ga. The Spanish then abandoned their planned attack on South Carolina.

[V. M. Crane, *Southern Frontier;* E. McCrady, *South Carolina Under Proprietary Government,* and *South Carolina as a Royal Province.*]

D. D. WALLACE

SOUTH CAROLINA, STATE BANK OF,

was a commercial state-owned institution located in Charleston, with branches in Columbia, Camden, and Abbeville. It was established in 1812 and remained in operation until 1868. The state deposited its funds in the bank, accepted its notes and limited its debt-contracting power. The size, the security, and the distribution of its loans among the state's electoral districts were regulated by statute. The bank made loans to the state without interest, managed the state's debt, and from its profits retired a large part of that debt.

Beginning in the late 1830's Christopher G. Memminger, as head of the state house of representatives' finance committee, attempted to dissociate the state from banking activities. James H. Hammond, who became governor of South Carolina in 1842, charged the bank with favoritism and with possessing dangerous power, and he succeeded in imposing charter revisions beneficial to the state.

[D. D. Wallace, *History of South Carolina,* vol. II.]

O. C. SKIPPER

SOUTH CAROLINA CANAL,

between the Santee and Cooper rivers, was proposed in 1786 by U.S. Rep. John Rutledge. One hundred shares of stock of indefinite value were subscribed, the state legislature granted a charter, and operations were begun in 1792. In 1795–96 a lottery was resorted to in order to provide additional funds. The canal, dug mostly by blacks, was 35 feet wide at the surface and 4 feet deep. It was completed in 1800. In 1858, after railroads were established, the canal was abandoned.

[U. B. Phillips, *Transportation in the Eastern Cotton Belt.*]

CHARLES B. SWANEY

SOUTH CAROLINA INTERSTATE AND WEST INDIAN EXPOSITION,

held at Charleston from Dec. 1, 1901, to June 1, 1902, was designed to promote closer commercial relations between the United States and the seventy principal West Indian islands. The exposition cost $1.25 million and covered 160 acres; there were 20 acres of midway attractions. Although the fair included a complete display of West Indian resources and products, the emphasis was chiefly upon American manufactures and exports.

FRANK MONAGHAN

SOUTH CAROLINA RAILROAD.

The South Carolina Canal and Railroad Company, organized in 1827 by a group of Charleston merchants and business people for the prime purpose of reviving the economy of that city, constructed a railroad line from Charleston to Hamburg (a village across the Savannah River from Augusta, Ga.). Completed in October 1833, the line was 136 miles long, making it the longest in the United States at that time.

In 1843 the South Carolina Canal and Railroad Company merged with the Louisville, Cincinnati and Charleston Railroad Company to form the South Carolina Railroad Company. The year before, the Louisville, Cincinnati and Charleston had completed a line from Branchville, a station on the Charleston-Hamburg road, to Columbia, as a part of an ambitious but futile scheme to build a trunk line from Charleston to Cincinnati. This branch of sixty-six miles became the property of the new company. In 1848 a branch of thirty-seven miles was constructed from Kingville, on the Branchville-Columbia line, to Camden. The Charleston-Hamburg road and the two branches constituted the total mileage of the railroad.

The company remained intact until 1878, when it was forced into bankruptcy and sold to a group of New York entrepreneurs. The new company was known as the South Carolina Railway Company. In 1894 the railroad was again sold as a result of bankruptcy and became the South Carolina and Georgia Railroad Company. In 1899 the Southern Railway Company acquired control of the firm, and in 1975 it was still providing freight service on the three lines.

[S. M. Derrick, *Centennial History of South Carolina Railroad.*]

S. M. DERRICK

SOUTH DAKOTA,

the southern half of what was Dakota Territory, is separated into several distinct regions. The southeastern part of the present state is corn belt, and the northeastern, lake country. West of the Missouri River the topography tilts and the rainfall diminishes; this is the land of the cattleman and the wheat rancher. On the extreme western edge of the state are the Black Hills, sacred to the Sioux and the highest mountains east of the Rockies.

The state received its name from the Dakota Sioux who inhabited all sections of it by the mid-18th century; their descendants are located on nine reservations. This was the home of Red Cloud, Crazy Horse, Sitting Bull, Spotted Tail, and other great Indian leaders. All the state west of the Missouri River was part of the great Sioux reservation created by the Treaty of 1868, later broken up by cessions in 1877 and 1889 and the heavy influx of white settlers engendered by the Dawes General Allotment Act of 1887.

South Dakota, which was admitted to the Union as a state on Nov. 2, 1889, is predominantly agricultural in its economy and outlook. While there was a discernible shift in population to urban areas after World War II, farming and ranching remained of primary importance. In the west the gold mining industry has receded until only one major mine, the Homestake at Lead, remains. It is the largest operating gold mine in the Western Hemisphere and a product of the great Black Hills gold rush of 1876.

Numerous ethnic groups make up the state's population. Predominant are the Norwegians, Germans, and Russians who came in the late 19th century. There are also strong concentrations of Czechs, Irish, Finns, and French.

Politically, South Dakota has been dominated by the Republican party during most of its history. Yet, the innate conservatism of the farmers and ranchers has given way to agrarian radicalism on occasion. The state was one of the leaders in the Populist movement in the 1880's and 1890's and in state socialism during the Progressive era. The Democratic party subsequently made severe inroads into Republican control, and a two-party system emerged.

Tourism and pheasant hunting are among the major industries of the state, and recreation, based on the series of major dams on the Missouri River, may be a wave of the future. For a state used to drought and normally short of water, it is surprising to find that it has more shoreline on major bodies today than any other state in the Union. South Dakota's population in 1970 was 666,257.

[George Kingsbury, *History of Dakota Territory;* Howard R. Lamar, *Dakota Territory, 1861–1889;* Doane Robinson, *History of South Dakota;* Herbert Schell, *History of South Dakota.*]

JOSEPH H. CASH

SOUTHEAST ASIA TREATY ORGANIZATION (SEATO) was formed by a treaty signed on Sept. 8, 1954, at Manila, by the United States, Great Britain, France, Australia, New Zealand, the Philippines, Pakistan, and Thailand, with headquarters at Bangkok. Cambodia, Laos, and the Republic of Vietnam, protocol states, were represented by observers. Hong Kong and Taiwan (Formosa) were excluded from the treaty. India, Burma, Ceylon, and Indonesia declined to join.

The treaty forming the organization calls for collective action to resist armed attacks and to counter subversion from without against the territorial integrity and the political stability of any of the eight member nations. The provisions of the Manila pact are consistent with those of the United Nations. Complementing other security treaties made in the area and at the time of the signing of the SEATO pact, the signators also subscribed to the Pacific Charter, a statement of ideals and intentions.

SEATO is a flexible alliance, which has responded to the changing defense needs in Southeast Asia. It renounces force as an instrument of policy, subscribing to its use only as a defense against aggression. SEATO does not have a fixed life span, but its continuance is implied as long as the threat of Communist aggression exists in the area.

For the United States, the avowed importance of the treaty was that it could be used to meet either internal or external aggression. An "understanding" was added by the United States stating that provisions of the treaty "apply only to Communist aggression" but that "in the event of other aggression or armed attack" the United States will consult the other signators to the treaty about what action should be taken. Great Britain was released of sole responsibility for keeping peace in the area; France signed the treaty as the only guarantee to the political independence and territorial integrity of Cambodia, Laos, and South Vietnam.

SEATO activities have been concerned not only with defense against subversion and aggression from outside but also with the promotion of social, economic, and cultural developments among its member nations. Although not militarily involved, SEATO, while opposing the invasion of the Republic of Vietnam by North Vietnam, did what it could to provide economic assistance in the form of direct grants and commodity import assistance, for example.

France and Pakistan gradually reduced their activities as members of SEATO, and neither participated in the 1972 meeting of the SEATO council. On Nov.

8, 1972, Pakistan announced its decision to withdraw from SEATO, an act permitted in the Treaty of Manila, and the withdrawal became effective one year later. (With respect to Vietnam, the United States acted on the assumption that a member could act unilaterally under the terms of the treaty.)

Despite the indifference of France to its membership in SEATO, the note of denunciation of Pakistan, and the warming of the political climate in Southeast Asia, SEATO remained in the mid-1970's a possible means of immediate opposition to any sudden revival of Communist aggression in the region and exercised a stabilizing influence in the area.

THOMAS ROBSON HAY

SOUTHERN BOUNDARY, SURVEY OF THE. On Mar. 29, 1798, after long delay, work was begun on determining by survey the border between the southern United States and the Spanish colonies of East Florida and West Florida. Participating in the project were Andrew Ellicott, U.S. commissioner; Thomas Freeman, surveyor (who was soon suspended by Ellicott); and Stephen Minor and Sir William Dunbar, Spanish commissioners. The line surveyed extended from the Mississippi River eastward along the thirty-first parallel to its intersection with the Chattahoochee River (*see* Dunbar's Line); the line then followed that river southward to its junction with the Flint, and from there it ran southeast directly to the head of Saint Marys River and down that stream to the Atlantic Ocean (*see* Pinckney's Treaty). Accompanied by military escort, the survey party cut through virgin forest and dense canebrake; forded swamps, bayous, and rivers; fought off Indian attacks; and was delayed by Spanish procrastination. Transporting supplies, baggage, and instruments over the rough terrain and combating disease and sickness impeded the surveyors' efforts. The work itself was laborious and frequently interrupted, and over two years were required for its completion.

[B. A. Hinsdale, "The Southern Boundary of the United States," *American Historical Association Report* (1893).]
THOMAS ROBSON HAY

SOUTHERN CAMPAIGNS of the American Revolution (1780–81) were a vigorous effort by the British, who had suffered setbacks in the North, to stamp out rebellion in the Carolinas and Georgia. On Dec. 26, 1779, Sir Henry Clinton and Gen. Charles Cornwallis sailed from New York with 8,000 men, landing at Savannah. They quickly surrounded the forces under Gen. Benjamin Lincoln, American commander in the South, in Charleston and compelled his surrender on May 12, 1780. The only American regiment not in Charleston was destroyed at Waxhaw Creek on May 29, leaving no organized American force in the three southernmost states. But partisan leaders such as Thomas Sumter, Francis Marion, and Andrew Pickens raised troops of patriots and engaged in guerrilla warfare. Gen. George Washington sent 2,000 men under Gen. Johann Kalb to the aid of South Carolina. However, Kalb was superseded by Horatio Gates, who promptly lost most of his army at the Battle of Camden (Aug. 16), and again the Carolinas seemed conquered. Cornwallis detached Maj. Patrick Ferguson with 1,200 men to recruit in the highlands, but this force was annihilated at Kings Mountain on Oct. 7, and another detachment under Col. Banastre Tarleton was destroyed at the Battle of Cowpens (Jan. 17, 1781). Nathanael Greene had succeeded Gates in December 1780. With Gen. Daniel Morgan's aid, he lured Cornwallis into North Carolina and dealt him a crippling blow at Guilford Courthouse on Mar. 15, 1781. After that defeat, the British commander retired to Wilmington, N.C., and then marched into Virginia. Benedict Arnold had been sent into Virginia with 1,600 British troops by Sir Henry Clinton, and Baron von Steuben was detailed on the American side to watch him, but Arnold initiated no major actions. Greene, ignoring Cornwallis, returned to South Carolina, and although he theoretically lost engagements at Hobkirk's Hill (Apr. 25), Ninety-Six (May 22–June 19), and Eutaw Springs (Sept. 8), he so weakened the British forces that by Dec. 10, 1781, he had won his objective and driven the only remaining British army in the Deep South into a state of siege at Charleston. Meanwhile, Cornwallis had been cornered by a joint American-French force, and he surrendered at Yorktown, Va., on Oct. 19, 1781.

[John R. Alden, *The Revolution in the South, 1763–1789*; Burke Davis, *The Campaign That Won America: The Story of Yorktown.*]
ALVIN F. HARLOW

SOUTHERN CHRISTIAN LEADERSHIP CONFERENCE. An outgrowth of the Montgomery [Ala.] Improvement Association (which was founded in 1955 and led by Martin Luther King, Jr.), the Southern Christian Leadership Conference (SCLC), based in Atlanta, was formed in 1957 as a "non-sectarian coordinating agency" for "nonviolent direct mass action." The first major civil rights organization to orig-

SOUTHERN COMMERCIAL CONVENTIONS

inate in the South, the SCLC was a Southwide umbrella of loosely affiliated organizations, mostly of black Baptist churches, that sought "full civil rights and total integration of the Negro into American life." Amorphous in organization, SCLC's principal force was symbolic, especially through its president, King. By filling the ideological and generational vacuum between the more conservative National Association for the Advancement of Colored People (1909) and National Urban League (1910), on the one hand, and the more radical Congress of Racial Equality (1942) and Student Nonviolent Coordinating Committee (1960), on the other, SCLC added prestige, respectability, and money to the civil rights movement, especially between the time of King's winning of the Nobel Peace Prize in 1964 and his assassination in 1968.

[Kenneth B. Clark, "The Civil Rights Movement: Momentum and Organization," in Talcott Parsons and Kenneth B. Clark, eds., *The Negro American;* August Meier, "On the Role of Martin Luther King," *New Politics,* vol. 4 (1965).]

HUGH DAVIS GRAHAM

SOUTHERN COMMERCIAL CONVENTIONS, convocations in the third quarter of the 19th century intended to promote the economic development of the South. The most notable gatherings were the sessions of the so-called Southern Commercial Convention, which met successively at Baltimore, Memphis, Charleston, New Orleans, Richmond, Savannah, Knoxville, Montgomery, and Vicksburg between December 1852 and May 1859.

The original object of the Southern Commercial Convention was to devise remedies for southern "decline." The South was not keeping pace with the North in population, manufacturing, railroad building, shipping, and other lines of economic development. This disparity deeply troubled the proud southerners, and many of them also felt that the industrial and commercial dependence of their section resulted in southern earnings being drained away and used to build up the North further. In addition, the superior population and wealth of the free states were giving them an advantage in the bitter struggle over slavery. The convention examined a wide variety of proposed remedies, such as building a railroad to the Pacific by a southern route, promoting trade with Latin America, attracting a greater share of the European import trade, and encouraging southern manufactures by paying bounties or by imposing discriminatory taxes on northern-made articles.

Although convention sessions were in effect mass meetings, the earlier ones were representative of all parts of the South and all shades of opinion. As time went by and the convention failed to produce tangible results, moderate men ceased to attend, and the sessions came to be dominated by the secessionists of the lower South, who contended that the Union was an obstacle to southern economic development. Finally, a question was injected that threatened seriously to divide the secessionists themselves, namely the desirability of reopening the foreign slave trade. Secessionist leaders at that point brought the convention to an end. The net result of the gatherings was the promotion of southern sectionalism.

Similar to the Southern Commercial Convention, and forerunners of it, were the "direct-trade" conventions held in Augusta and Charleston (1837–39) and in Richmond and Norfolk (1838), and the Southwestern Convention held in Memphis (1845).

[R. R. Russel, *Economic Aspects of Southern Sectionalism, 1840–1861;* H. W. Wender, *Southern Commercial Conventions, 1837–1859.*]

R. R. RUSSEL

SOUTHERN CULT, or Southeastern ceremonial complex, was associated mainly with prehistoric Mississippian cultures in the Eastern Woodlands between about A.D. 900 and the historic period. The roots of the cult may extend back to the inception of subsistence patterns relying on the unpredictable yields of domesticated plants. Although the early history and the inspiration for the elaboration of this highly developed religious cult remain largely unknown, its florescence is well documented in later southern sites.

The series of rituals, objects, and iconographic elements integrated into the ceremonial complex was a blend of indigenous and Middle American religious themes connected with the harvest and renewal. Among the common iconographic elements are a weeping or forked eye, the spider, a cross within a sunburst circle, the feathered rattlesnake, human skull-and-bone motifs, a hand holding an eye or cross in the palm, and a batonlike mace. These elements were carved, embossed, or engraved on a variety of materials, including shell, polished stone, pottery, and copper. Eagle, serpent, and feline god-animal motifs also occur as major symbols in the ceremonial art. Among the array of finely made objects associated with the cult are monolithic stone axes; batonlike maces; ceremonial stone knives; well-sculptured stone pipes; copper headdresses and earspools; copper, stone, and shell plaques; and decorated, pol-

352

ished stone bowls. Copper plaques, shell gorgets, and whole conch shells have been found decorated with human figures dressed in elaborate costumes and carrying batons and trophy heads. It is these human representations and the god-animal themes that indicate most strongly some form of Middle American affiliation.

Major cult centers were established at a number of Mississippian towns, including Moundville (Alabama), Etowah (Georgia), and Spiro (Oklahoma). Because many of the objects and design motifs were recovered from burial mounds, the ceremonial complex has often been considered a cult connected with death and death symbols. However, the complex may have served primarily as an integrating institution during the development and spread of the Mississippian cultures. It seems certain from the many representations of human sacrifice in a variety of mediums that this ritual was an integral part of cult activities.

[A. J. Waring, Jr., and Preston Holder, "A Prehistoric Ceremonial Complex in the Southeastern United States," *American Anthropologist,* vol. 47 (1945).]

GUY GIBBON

SOUTHERN EXPOSITION, first opened at Louisville, Ky., in the summer of 1883, was successfully revived each year through 1887. The one principal exhibit covered fifteen acres. After the first year the educational exhibits disappeared, and industry and amusement clearly dominated the exposition, which was designed to "save the city of Louisville from falling into the commercial lethargy overcoming other and larger cities."

FRANK MONAGHAN

SOUTHERN LITERARY MESSENGER, a magazine published at Richmond, Va., from 1834 to 1864 that was devoted especially to literature and the fine arts. Its most famous editor was Edgar Allan Poe. Usually, the magazine reflected the views of the southern country gentleman who owned slaves. It was outspoken in 1842 against Great Britain's search of American ships suspected of carrying African slaves. From January 1846 through October 1847, while Benjamin Blake Minor was editor and proprietor, the magazine was known by the more ambitious title *Southern and Western Literary Messenger and Review.* Other editors were Thomas W. White, John Reuben Thompson, George William Bagby, and Frank H. Alfriend. It ceased publication in 1864

because of the fighting around Richmond during the Civil War.

[David Kelly Jackson, *The Contributors and Contributions to the Southern Literary Messenger.*]

FRANK MARTIN LEMON

SOUTHERN OVERLAND MAIL, also known as the **Butterfield Overland Mail,** was the first land mail route from the East to California. Overland service was authorized after a long struggle in Congress. The act of Mar. 3, 1857, provided for a semiweekly service on a twenty-five-day schedule at $600,000 per year. Postmaster General Aaron V. Brown, a native of Tennessee, chose a southern route, running from Saint Louis and Memphis to San Francisco by way of Fort Smith, Ark., El Paso, Tex., and Tucson, Ariz. John Butterfield, W. G. Fargo, and others were the contractors. After a year's preparation, service began Sept. 15, 1858, with four-horse coaches; the passenger fare was $100 to $200 each way. The schedule was successfully maintained until the outbreak of the Civil War, when the line was moved to a more northerly route (*see* Overland Mail and Stagecoaches).

[L. R. Hafen, *The Overland Mail, 1849–1869.*]

LEROY R. HAFEN

SOUTHERN PACIFIC RAILROAD. *See* **Railroads, Sketches.**

SOUTHERN RAILROAD ROUTE. A southern route of travel from New Mexico to California via the Gila River (through southern New Mexico and Arizona) was well known prior to the Mexican War. But during the war, when Gen. Stephen W. Kearny made his well-known expedition of 1846 from Leavenworth, Kans., to San Diego, Calif., he reported that the southern travel route was also suitable for a railroad line. Kearny was accompanied by Lt. W. H. Emory, whose notes and sketches were the basis for the proposal. The Gadsden Purchase (1853) guaranteed a right-of-way entirely within the United States. Also in 1853, Congress appropriated $150,000 for Pacific railway surveys, and one of these was made soon thereafter over the southern approach. Surveying east of El Paso was done by Capt. John Pope, and surveying farther west was conducted by Lt. John G. Parke.

[J. R. Perkins, *Trails, Rails, and War;* Lewis H. Haney, *A Congressional History of Railways in the United States, 1850–1887.*]

C. C. RISTER

SOUTHERN RAILWAY. *See* **Railroads, Sketches.**

SOUTHERN RIGHTS MOVEMENT. Although as old as the Union itself, the movement for southern rights during the antebellum period is particularly associated with aggressive efforts during the late 1840's and the 1850's to solidify the South for the protection of its interests, expressed chiefly in the institution of slavery. The movement took various forms and was sponsored by men of varying beliefs. Influenced by John C. Calhoun, southern congressmen in Washington issued addresses to the southern people in 1848 and again in 1850, urging "unity among ourselves"; at the same time various southern state legislatures resolved "to act with resolution, firmness and unity of purpose." Southern commercial conventions worked for economic independence, while certain politicians were interested in the formation of a sectional political party. William L. Yancey organized the League of United Southerners in 1858 and later favored committees of safety that, at the proper moment, could "precipitate the cotton states into a revolution." Among the lesser lights were a group of self-styled secessionists per se who had always advocated a southern Confederacy in preference to any possible means of protection within the Union. It was this group that became the nucleus of the movement for southern independence after the election of Abraham Lincoln in 1860.

[J. T. Carpenter, *The South as a Conscious Minority*.]
JESSE T. CARPENTER

SOUTHERN UNIONISTS. Of the fifteen slave states at the time of the Civil War, the border states of Missouri, Kentucky, Virginia, Maryland, and Delaware were the greatest strongholds of unionism. Their desire to remain in the Union is evident, for if war came they saw themselves made the battlefield; and with their economic and social connections north and south, they could better weigh the advantages of a united country. In all these states except Virginia, they were able to prevent secession, and even that part of Virginia joining free territory broke away and formed the state of West Virginia. In the Confederacy itself there were many people who remained loyal to the Union or who soon returned to their former loyalty. They lived mostly in the upcountry, especially in the mountains or in the pine barrens and other less fertile regions. East Tennessee was the outstanding storm center of unionism within the Confederacy.

Fundamental love for country, opposition to the antebellum and wartime leadership of the slaveholders, and, as the war progressed, dislike of conscription and of Confederate revenue measures—all combined to make people Unionists. It has been estimated that almost 300,000 southerners fought in the Union armies.

[C. C. Anderson, *Fighting by Southern Federals*; T. Speed, *The Union Cause in Kentucky, 1860–1865*; G. L. Tatum, *Disloyalty in the Confederacy*.]
E. MERTON COULTER

SOUTH IMPROVEMENT COMPANY, a firm utilized by John D. Rockefeller and associates in their first attempt (1871–72) to secure a monopoly of the petroleum industry by means of exclusive rebates from the railroads serving the oil-producing region of Pennsylvania. Resistance from producers, public indignation, and annulment of the firm's charter defeated the monopoly scheme.

[Henry D. Lloyd, *Wealth Against Commonwealth*.]
CHESTER McA. DESTLER

SOUTHOLD, Long Island, N.Y., was purchased and settled by migrants from the New Haven colony in the summer of 1640. Southold became part of Connecticut on Oct. 9, 1662, when a charter uniting New Haven with the older Connecticut colony was promulgated. But Southold (against its residents' will) was obliged to submit to the Duke of York's less libertarian government in 1665.

[E. R. Lambert, *History of the Colony of New Haven*.]
MORTON PENNYPACKER

SOUTH PASS, the most celebrated of the passes in the Rocky Mountains, because through it ran the great emigrant trail to Oregon and California. It is located in Wyoming at the southern end of the Wind River Mountains. The approach to the pass is so gradual that, in the words of explorer John C. Frémont, "the traveller, without being reminded of any change by toilsome ascents, suddenly finds himself on the waters which flow to the Pacific Ocean." There are claims that John Colter discovered the South Pass in 1807 or 1808 and that Robert Stuart and the returning Astorians crossed it in 1812, but both claims are disputed. It is certain that the effective discovery was made in 1824 by Thomas Fitzpatrick, a fur trader. Capt. Benjamin L. E. Bonneville first took wagons over the pass in 1832, and a few years later it became the mountain gateway on the Oregon Trail.

[Hiram M. Chittenden, *The American Fur Trade of the Far West;* E. W. Gilbert, *The Exploration of Western America, 1800–1850.*]

DAN E. CLARK

SOUTH PLATTE ROUTE, a branch of the Oregon (or Overland) Trail, leading to Denver. Leaving the main trail at Julesburg, Colo., where the Oregon Trail crossed the South Platte River and headed northwest toward Fort Laramie, Wyo., the branch route followed the right bank of the South Platte River all the way to Denver. An important stage and freight route, it was attacked by Cheyenne war parties early in 1865. Julesburg was looted twice and burned the second time, and ranches up and down the river were destroyed. As a result, traffic on the South Platte route was suspended for a considerable period.

[George Bird Grinnell, *The Fighting Cheyennes.*]

PAUL I. WELLMAN

SOUTH SEA EXPEDITION. *See* **Wilkes Exploring Expedition.**

SOUTHWEST may be roughly defined as the southwestern quarter of the United States, although any distinct delimitation of the area is necessarily arbitrary. So considered, it includes Oklahoma, Texas, New Mexico, Arizona, the southern half of California, and the southern portions of Kansas and Colorado. With the exception of most of Kansas and Oklahoma, which formed part of the Louisiana Purchase, all of the Southwest was a part of the possessions of Spain, and later of Mexico, well into the 19th century and so has, historically, a background that is distinctly Spanish. Kansas is a "marginal state," since its history is partially bound up with that of the Southwest and in part with that of the central prairie states. Oklahoma and Texas each has a history essentially its own. Oklahoma was for more than half a century a great Indian territory, forbidden to settlement by whites. The Five Civilized Tribes, occupying much of it, formed small commonwealths or republics, each with its own government and laws. Texas, settled largely by Anglo-Americans, won its independence from Mexico in 1836. After nearly ten years' existence as a republic, it was annexed by the United States in 1845. The remainder of this southwestern region, except for the small strip of land acquired

from Mexico in 1853 in the Gadsden Purchase, became a part of the United States in 1848 with the signing of the Treaty of Guadalupe Hidalgo with Mexico.

The influence of the Southwest on the political history of the United States began early in the 19th century. The Louisiana Purchase boundary line, which had been the subject of much controversy, was drawn in 1819, leaving Texas to Spain (*see* Adams-Onís Treaty). Later, the question of the annexation of Texas became an important political issue. After annexation, the dispute over the Texas-Mexico boundary helped to precipitate the Mexican War (1846–48). Disputes over the organization of the new territory acquired from Mexico by this war ended in the much-debated Compromise of 1850, under which California entered the Union as a free state but slavery was not restricted in the newly created New Mexico and Utah territories. Four years later came the Kansas-Nebraska Act, allowing the residents of these territories to decide for themselves whether to become free or slave states, and the violent controversies following it attracted the attention of the entire nation.

Significant as the Southwest has been in the political history of the United States, its importance in U.S. economic history is even more apparent. The discovery of gold in California and Colorado in the 19th century brought about one of the most picturesque movements in all American history. The settlement of the Pacific coastal region and the increased production of gold stimulated industry, caused the building of the Pacific railways, and created demands for a canal between the Pacific and Atlantic.

Texas, which had early developed as a great cattle-raising area, sent a stream of cattle northward from 1866 to 1890 to stock ranges on the central and northern Plains; thus, it was the chief factor in the formation of the "cow country" that spanned much of the American West. The production of petroleum and natural gas in California and in the great midcontinent field lying largely in Oklahoma and Texas has been of great significance in the economic life of the nation. The fruit-growing industry of southern California, Arizona, and the lower Rio Grande valley of Texas has also been of great importance to the country as a whole. The production of wheat and cotton in this area adds materially to the nation's crops of these two staples. Manufacture and distribution of motion pictures have long centered in southern California, and the industry's influence on the people of the United States can hardly be estimated. Since World War II the Southwest has also become a major center for the aerospace and electronics industries.

Culturally the Southwest has not been without some importance. It has produced many writers and a regional literature of considerable significance.

[R. N. Richardson and C. C. Rister, *The Greater Southwest;* C. C. Rister, *The Southern Plainsmen.*]

EDWARD EVERETT DALE

SOUTHWEST, OLD. In contrast with the historical concept of the territorial limits of the Old Northwest, the Old Southwest was never so exact. The term was first applied to the region embraced by the present states of Tennessee and Kentucky, but it was extended to include also Alabama and Mississippi and sometimes even Louisiana and Arkansas. In colonial times it came within the limits of Virginia, North Carolina, South Carolina, and Georgia, but no attempt was ever made to extend an active government over this region. The Proclamation of 1763 reserved the Old Southwest "under the sovereignty, protection, and dominance of the king" and forbade further land grants west of the Appalachians by colonial governments.

Colonial adventurers and land speculators paid little attention to this proclamation. In 1769 various emigrants, mostly from Virginia, established a settlement along the Watauga River, the first settlement in what is now Tennessee; three years later they set up a government. In 1774, Richard Henderson was instrumental in organizing the Louisa Company, soon renamed the Transylvania Company, which established a settlement at Boonesborough in a region later to become part of Kentucky. Near the end of the Revolution, Nashborough (now Nashville) in the Cumberland Valley of Tennessee was founded. Virginia stamped out the Henderson venture, but other settlements were promoted, which led to the organization of the state of Kentucky in 1792. Watauga grew into the state of Franklin, which North Carolina suppressed, but the settlements there, with those in the Nashborough region, developed into the state of Tennessee, admitted to the Union in 1796.

After the treaty of peace in 1783, fixing the western limits of the United States at the Mississippi, a movement sprang up among the small states to force the states with western lands to cede them to the central government. Virginia refused to cede the Kentucky region but later gave it permission to become a state; North Carolina in 1789 gave up the Tennessee region to the federal government; South Carolina ceded its dubious claim to a twelve-mile-wide strip south of Tennessee; but Georgia refused to make terms that Congress would accept. Claims to the Georgia western lands were varied and confused. The federal government denied the validity of the Georgia claims, and Spain declared all lands south of 32°28′ its own, reinforcing this claim by continuing to occupy the Natchez region (in present-day Mississippi). To add to the complication, powerful tribes of Indians (Creek, Cherokee, Choctaw, and Chickasaw) held actual control of most of the region. In 1795 Georgia sought profit from the confusion by selling most of it to four Yazoo companies (*see* Yazoo Fraud). The first federal control over any part of the Old Southwest came with the organization of the Southwest Territory in 1790.

[Archibald Henderson, *The Conquest of the Old Southwest;* Constance L. Skinner, *Pioneers of the Old Southwest, The Chronicle of America series.*]

E. MERTON COULTER

SOUTHWEST BOUNDARY. *See* **Adams-Onís Treaty; Louisiana Purchase, Boundaries of; Mexican Boundary.**

SOUTHWESTERN OIL FIELDS. Large-scale production of petroleum in the southwestern states—including Arkansas, Louisiana, Kansas, Oklahoma, Texas, and New Mexico—is essentially a 20th-century phenomenon. Between 1859 and 1900 the major domestic sources of crude oil in the United States were in the Northeast—in New York, Pennsylvania, Ohio, and West Virginia. Most of their flow was refined into kerosine. But during the 20th century the center of American oil production shifted to the Southwest, to the midcontinent fields, and the Gulf area, as technological changes created major new national markets for gasoline, fuel oil, and natural gas.

Initial expansion of southwestern oil fields came in the two decades before World War I, when Kansas, Oklahoma, and Texas first became important producers. In 1901 two energetic Texas oil prospectors, Anthony Lucas and Patillo Higgins, made one of the great finds at Spindletop, Tex., inaugurating large-scale exploitation in the Lone Star State. In succeeding years petroleum became one of its major economic resources. Serious exploration in nearby Oklahoma began when prospectors there brought in rich fields near Bartlesville (1904) and the Glenn (1905) and Cushing (1912) pools. Many of these new sources of crude oil were particularly well suited for refining into gasoline, for which the rapidly increasing number of automobiles was creating a seemingly insatiable demand. The exploitation of southwestern oil fields was undertaken by thousands of independent producers, as well as by major integrated oil corporations.

Between World War I and World War II the Southwest firmly established itself as the major oil-producing region in the United States, supplying about two-thirds of the nation's total production. Spurred by burgeoning demands for gasoline and fuel oil in the 1920's, oil drillers uncovered great new reserves in Oklahoma, Texas, and Louisiana. They also made notable finds in Arkansas, Kansas, and New Mexico, which contributed to an almost threefold increase of crude-oil production between 1919 and 1929. Indeed, discovery of the rich Oklahoma City fields and the vast reserves in eastern Texas from 1927 to 1935 resulted in such a glut of petroleum as to plunge the already ailing industry—beset by the world depression—into economic chaos. Only the unprecedented demands for oil during World War II revitalized southwestern oil production, which increased output significantly to supply war needs.

During the three decades after World War II the southwestern oil fields almost doubled their production of crude petroleum. At the same time, natural gas, a by-product, became a major new form of energy, used widely in homes, offices, and factories, providing an additional source of wealth for the Southwest. Texas retained its position as the greatest oil-producing state in the Union, supplying fully one-half of the nation's oil. Louisiana emerged as a close rival, while the landlocked states of Kansas, Oklahoma, Arkansas, and New Mexico continued to provide smaller, but significant, sources of supply. A major new development during that period was extensive offshore drilling in the Gulf of Mexico, which came to supply an increasing percentage of total national production.

Exploitation of the southwestern oil fields was accompanied by considerable government regulation, much of which was supervised by state, rather than federal, authorities. A prime goal of the industry and of government agencies has been conservation of oil and, at the same time, stabilization of production and prices. As early as 1915 Oklahoma established a corporation commission to regulate oil production by assigning quotas to each operator and by enforcing conservation laws. Other southwestern states eventually followed the example of Oklahoma. In 1931, during the Great Depression, the governors of Oklahoma and Texas went so far as to call out the National Guard to close the oil fields in order to enforce rigid production

limitations. As a result of this experience the southwestern states in 1935 formed the Interstate Oil Compact to coordinate their respective policies. During the next four decades the Interstate Oil Compact Commission did much to stabilize production and to decrease waste. Composed of a representative from each oil-producing state, the commission allocated production quotas for states and, ultimately, individual operators. The southwestern oil fields thus have been developed by private individuals and corporations, but under close government supervision.

[Gerald D. Nash, *United States Oil Policy, 1890–1964;* Carl Coke Rister, *Oil—Titan of the Southwest.*]

GERALD D. NASH

SOUTHWEST FUR COMPANY. As part of his scheme to dominate the American fur trade, John Jacob Astor, chief proprietor of the American Fur Company and the Pacific Fur Company, organized the Southwest Fur Company, which in 1811 bought out the British-owned Michilimackinac (Mackinaw) Company at Mackinac. This move was designed to give Astor control of the fur trade of the Great Lakes and the upper Mississippi, for his associates agreed to sell their stock in the Southwest Company to him in five years.

Unfortunately his partners were British subjects and directors of the North West Company of Canada. In the War of 1812 the North West's traders occupied the trading forts of the Southwest Fur Company. After the war Astor dissolved the Southwest Company, regained its scattered properties, merged them with the American Fur Company as its Northern Department, and placed an American, Ramsay Crooks, in command.

[Hiram Martin Chittenden, *The American Fur Trade of the Far West;* Washington Irving, *Astoria.*]

BLISS ISELY

SOUTHWEST POINT, a promontory located where the Clinch and Holston rivers form the Tennessee. It was crossed by the Cumberland Road and was the western outpost of the state of Franklin, organized briefly in the 1780's by settlers in the Tennessee region, which was then part of North Carolina. The settlement of Kingston, now part of the Knoxville metropolitan area, was established at Southwest Point. In 1792 U.S. troops were stationed there to protect settlers on the road to Nashville and in the surrounding territory. The land, formally ceded by the

SOUTHWEST TERRITORY

Cherokee in the Tellico treaty, Oct. 27, 1805, was tentatively designated as the state capital.

[James Phelan, *History of Tennessee*.]

THOMAS ROBSON HAY

SOUTHWEST TERRITORY, the short title applied to the region set up in 1790 and officially denominated the "Territory of the United States, south of the River Ohio." It consisted in fact of only the future state of Tennessee, although in theory it also embraced the twelve-mile strip that South Carolina had ceded and, possibly, the Georgia western lands. Actual federal governance was applied only to Tennessee. The government of this territory was similar to that set up for the Northwest Territory, except that it was bound by certain conditions set by North Carolina in its cession of 1789. William Blount was appointed governor and superintendent of Indian affairs, and he served in this capacity for the entire life of the territory. When Tennessee became a state in 1796, the territorial government fell into abeyance, but it was essentially reinstated in 1798, when the Mississippi Territory was established.

[F. L. Paxson, *History of the American Frontier, 1763–1893*.]

E. MERTON COULTER

SOVEREIGNS OF INDUSTRY, a cooperative movement active in the 1870's that was concerned with the distribution of the necessities of life. It grew out of the Patrons of Husbandry and at one time numbered 40,000 members. It maintained a number of cooperative stores, some of which followed the principles established by the Rochdale Society of Equitable Pioneers in England. At one time the Sovereigns of Industry absorbed some trade unions. The organization began to decline after 1875.

[J. R. Commons and others, *History of Labor in the United States*.]

CARL L. CANNON

SOVEREIGNTY, DOCTRINE OF, is a legal concept that attempts to explain the final location and source of political authority in the modern state. Sovereignty may be defined as that supreme authority which is externally independent and internally paramount (T. E. Holland), and a sovereign nation as a political community without a political superior (Abraham Lincoln).

There are two aspects of sovereignty. One is *de facto*, subject to the test of its actual use as shown by the exercise of authority, and the other is *de jure*, or its legal justification. While the subject of much controversy among lawyers and political theorists, sovereignty on the one hand is usually considered to be indivisible. On the other hand, the administration or use of sovereign powers may be delegated to various subordinate administrative authorities. In accordance with this theory, sovereignty lies in the people of the United States, who have created a national government and delegated to it certain sovereign powers. But "The powers not delegated to the United States by the Constitution, nor prohibited by it to the States, are reserved to the States respectively, or to the people" (Amendment X of the U.S. Constitution). Therefore, the fifty American states are not sovereign, but are subject to the sovereignty of the people of the entire nation as such.

[T. E. Holland, *Jurisprudence*; C. E. Merriam, *American Political Theories*.]

WILLIAM STARR MYERS

SOW CASE, a lawsuit adjudicated in 1643–44 that became famous in Massachusetts history because of its far-reaching consequences. The case arose out of a controversy between a poor woman named Sherman and a well-to-do shopkeeper, Keayne, over the ownership of a sow. Lower courts decided in favor of Keayne, but Sherman, encouraged by popular sympathy, appealed to the General Court, or legislature. In that body, the majority of assistants, or magistrates, supported Keayne; the deputies supported Sherman. Although up to that time the assistants and deputies had sat in one body, the former claimed a negative voice on the actions of the latter. The assistants' attempt to exercise that negative in the sow case against the sympathies of the deputies brought the conflict to a crisis, the outcome of which was the division of the General Court into two houses.

[C. M. Andrews, *The Colonial Period of American History*, vol. I.]

VIOLA F. BARNES

SPANISH-AMERICAN RELATIONS. Generally, the relations between the United States and Spain were marked by mutual antagonism until the end of the 19th century. The American colonists shared in the belief of the "Black Legend" about Spain, which portrayed it as a fanatical, bloodthirsty, and tyrannical power, and inherited the sense of rivalry between Protestant Britain and Catholic Spain, a rivalry that was extended to the New World as Britain established dominion over an area that Spain considered its monopoly. When the American colonists sought independence, Spain was confronted with a dilemma. While desirous of using the event to strike at England and recover the substantial territories lost by the Treaty of Utrecht (1713) and the Peace of Paris (1763), Spain was anxious of the effect the American Revolution would have on its colonies. Although Spain declared war on England in 1779 after attempts at peaceful mediation for the price of Gibraltar for itself had failed, it did not promptly recognize American independence; and even though it granted loans and subsidies to the rebels, Spain's military efforts were principally aimed at recovering Florida and its island possessions in the Mediterranean.

The issues between Spain and the new American republic included the question of boundaries, relations with the border Indians, the right of navigation of the Mississippi, and trade. To resolve these, the Spanish envoy, Diégo de Gardoqui, negotiated with American Secretary of State John Jay. Although the talks did not bear final fruit, they were responsible for the inclusion in the Constitution of the clause requiring a two-thirds majority of senators for treaty ratification. Commissions sent to Spain for the purpose of settling the outstanding issues were no more successful. What changed the situation was the French Revolution and its wars and Spain's change of ally from Britain to France. The desire of Spain to protect itself better across the seas made it yield on the litigated points, and news of the ratification on June 24, 1795, of Jay's Treaty with Great Britain increased the conciliatory mood of the Spanish government. In Pinckney's Treaty (Oct. 27, 1795), also known as the Treaty of San Lorenzo, Spain recognized the thirty-first parallel as the boundary to the south, the free navigation of the Mississippi by U.S. citizens, and the privilege of deposit. The principle of neutral rights was affirmed, and each side agreed to restrain the Indians within their borders from attacking the territory of the other.

Pinckney's Treaty and the fact that Louisiana Province proved to be a heavy burden led to Spain's retrocession of Louisiana to France by the Treaty of San Ildefonso (Oct. 1, 1800). France then sold Louisiana to the United States in 1803. Spain protested the legality of the sale but had to yield to the fact. Soon the purchase of Louisiana led to disputes between Spain and the United States over boundaries. The United States contended that the Rio Grande was the western boundary, thus including Texas in the purchase, and

that the Perdido River was the eastern boundary, thus including a sizable part of West Florida. Spain naturally disputed both claims. The immediate aim of the United States was the acquisition of the Floridas. President Thomas Jefferson took the first step of inducing Congress to pass the Mobile Act on Feb. 24, 1804. He then sent James Monroe as special plenipotentiary to assist Charles Pinckney in Madrid to secure the outright recognition of the title of the United States to West Florida and the cession of East Florida. The United States would either renounce its pecuniary claims against Spain or buy the Floridas directly. Jefferson also intrigued with Napoleon I and Charles Maurice de Talleyrand-Périgord to put pressure on Spain. None of these strategies availed, and continued Spanish spoliations on American neutral shipping brought Spain and the United States close to war.

When Napoleon foisted his brother Joseph on the Spanish throne in 1808 and a civil war erupted in the peninsula, the United States suspended diplomatic relations with Spain until a more stable government was established. During this period Spanish authority was gravely weakened in the New World. President James Madison made use of a revolt in the Baton Rouge district in 1810 to order the occupation of the area up to the Perdido River, although American forces actually stopped at the Pearl. The United States also used the War of 1812 to seize Mobile, Ala. At the end of the war (1815) a third of West Florida and all of East Florida were still in Spanish hands; demands for annexation were soon heard again.

Spanish appeals to save the Floridas, if not to recover Louisiana, went unanswered by the European powers, exhausted after the recent conflicts. Against this background Secretary of State John Quincy Adams and the Spanish minister, Luis de Onís, began their talks on the Louisiana boundaries late in 1817. It was not difficult to reach a *quid pro quo* understanding: the United States would withdraw pecuniary claims against Spain in exchange for the Floridas. Gen. Andrew Jackson's invasion of the Floridas in 1818, with the ostensible aim of wiping out the bases of Indian raids into American territory, although an affront to Spanish honor, emphasized the futility of saving the Floridas. On the western side of Louisiana, the boundary line was drawn largely along the west banks of the Sabine, Red, and Arkansas rivers; thence north to the forty-second parallel; and westward all the way to the Pacific Ocean. Historians have aptly renamed the Adams-Onís Treaty the Transcontinental Treaty and consider it the most important diplomatic achievement in U.S. history. Signed on Feb. 22,

1819, the treaty was not fully ratified until 1821, in part because of Spanish attempts to secure a pledge from the U.S. government not to assist the rebellious Latin-American colonies. The United States granted recognition to the new Latin-American republics in March 1822, and the Monroe Doctrine was proclaimed in December 1823. Actually, Spain's hopes of subduing the revolutionary movements in its colonies were largely frustrated by British policy rather than the Monroe Doctrine, whose significance was not of the moment. Nor was its significance clear for the future, for during the American Civil War, Spain intervened in Santo Domingo and Peru.

Cuba was the next preoccupation of Spanish-American diplomacy. The desirability of acquiring Cuba, the "pearl of the Antilles," became part of the idea of Manifest Destiny. Attempts to acquire Cuba by purchase or other means culminated in the sensational Ostend Manifesto of 1854. The Civil War diverted American attention from Cuba, but interest was rekindled during the Cuban wars of independence. There were two such insurrectionary wars in the second half of the 19th century. The first, in 1868–78, was the more prolonged and sanguinary, but it came at a time when Americans were weary after the Civil War and national attention was turned inward. President Ulysses S. Grant's administration refused to grant belligerent status to the insurgents and acted circumspectly during the *Virginius* incident. Had the national mood been otherwise, the *Virginius* affair could easily have been converted into a *casus belli*. Spain declined the mediation of the United States and terminated the Cuban conflict with promises of wide-ranging reforms.

Fighting erupted anew in Cuba in 1895, in part because of difficulties arising from recent tariff changes in the United States. This time the United States was economically and psychologically prepared for pursuing an adventurous foreign policy. There were the vocal adherents of Alfred Thayer Mahan's naval theories and of a new version of Manifest Destiny; and there was the influence of "yellow journalism," particularly of the William Randolph Hearst and Joseph Pulitzer newspapers, which prevailed over the antiwar interests of business. Spain's procrastination with the Cuban problem and the hardships caused by the militarily and strategically logical "reconcentration" policy introduced by the Spanish commander Gen. Valeriano Weyler provided grist for the interventionist mill. The last straws were the leak of the tactless contents of a private correspondence of the Spanish minister, Dupuy de Lôme (Feb. 9, 1898),

and the sinking of the *Maine* in Havana harbor on Feb. 15, 1898. In the United States blame for the *Maine* tragedy was widely attributed to Spain, although it is impossible to conceive that Spain would have intentionally caused it. President William McKinley submitted the Cuban question to Congress on Apr. 11, 1898, which, of course, given the prevailing American sentiment, meant war. Little attention was paid by Congress to the fact that the Spanish government had made most of the concessions demanded in the instructions from Washington to the American minister in Madrid. On Apr. 19 a joint declaration of Congress included the independence of Cuba as part of the ultimatum to Spain; when this was not accepted, Congress declared a state of war to have been in existence since Apr. 21.

The Spanish-American War was "short" in that it only lasted three months, but it was not "glorious," inasmuch as it involved two very unequal powers. By the Treaty of Paris of Dec. 10, 1898, the United States obtained Puerto Rico, Guam, and the Philippines and established a protectorate over Cuba. The loss of the remnants of the Spanish empire did not long embitter Spanish-American relations, for Spain had realized that the end was only a matter of time.

When the Spanish civil war broke out in 1936, the United States applied the new neutrality legislation, depriving the legitimate Spanish republican government of the right to purchase arms and ammunition. On Apr. 1, 1939, the United States recognized the regime of Francisco Franco. During World War II the Allies were able to keep wavering Spain neutral, which was of great value during the landings in North Africa. At the end of the war, the United States led in the effort to deny Spain's admission to the United Nations and to recall the chiefs of diplomatic missions from Madrid, as well as to encourage the establishment of a democratic regime in Spain. In the thick of the cold war and at the time of the Truman Doctrine (1947), this attitude began to change but not enough to include Spain in either the Marshall Plan (1948) or the North Atlantic Treaty Organization (1949). It took the outbreak of the Korean War (1950) to bring about a change, when questions of security overrode those of ideology. In November 1950 full diplomatic relations were resumed with Spain. More far-reaching was the signing of the Pact of Madrid on Sept. 26, 1953, which allowed the United States to build air and naval bases in Spain for ten years. In 1963, despite grave difficulties at reaching a new understanding, the agreement was renewed for another five years. Although the economic and military aid given to Spain had been reduced, the latter was able to change the nature of the pact to a quasi-alliance. The Pact of Madrid was renewed in 1975, but its future is uncertain.

[Samuel Flagg Bemis, *Pinckney's Treaty;* Philip C. Brooks, *Diplomacy and the Borderlands: The Adams-Onís Treaty of 1819;* French Ensor Chadwick, *The Relations of the United States and Spain;* Ernest R. May, *Imperial Democracy;* Richard P. Traina, *American Diplomacy and the Spanish Civil War;* Arthur P. Whitaker, *The Spanish-American Frontier, 1783–1795,* and *Spain and the Defense of the West: Ally and Liability;* Juan F. Yela Utrilla, *España ante la independencia de los Estados Unidos.*]

VICENTE R. PILAPIL

SPANISH-AMERICAN WAR. The sinking of the battleship *Maine* in Havana harbor on Feb. 15, 1898, provided a dramatic *casus belli* for the Spanish-American War, but underlying causes included U.S. economic interests ($50 million invested in Cuba; $100 million in annual trade, mostly sugar) as well as genuine humanitarian concern over long-continued Spanish misrule. Rebellion in Cuba had erupted violently in 1895, and although by 1897 a more liberal Spanish government had adopted a conciliatory attitude, U.S. public opinion, inflamed by strident "yellow journalism," would not be placated by anything short of full independence for Cuba.

The *Maine* had been sent to Havana ostensibly on a courtesy visit but actually as protection for American citizens. A U.S. Navy court of inquiry concluded on Mar. 21 that the ship had been sunk by an external explosion. Madrid agreed to arbitrate the matter but would not promise independence for Cuba. On Apr. 11, President William McKinley asked Congress for authority to intervene. Congress, on Apr. 19, passed a joint resolution declaring Cuba independent, demanding the withdrawal of Spanish forces, directing the use of armed force to put the resolution into effect, and pledging that the United States would not annex Cuba. On Apr. 25 Congress declared that a state of war had existed since Apr. 21.

The North Atlantic Squadron, concentrated at Key West, Fla., was ordered on Apr. 22 to blockade Cuba. The squadron, commanded by Rear Adm. William T. Sampson, consisted of five modern battleships and two armored cruisers, after the *Oregon* completed its celebrated sixty-six-day run around Cape Horn and joined the squadron. The Spanish home fleet under Adm. Pascual Cervera had sortied from Cadiz on Apr. 8, and although he had only four cruisers and two destroyers, the approach of this "armada" provoked near panic along the U.S. East

Coast, causing Sampson to detach a flying squadron under Commodore Winfield Scott Schley to intercept Cervera.

Spanish troop strength in Cuba totaled 150,000 regulars and 40,000 irregulars and volunteers. The Cuban insurgents numbered perhaps 50,000. Initial U.S. strategy was to blockade Cuba while the insurgents continued the fight against the Spanish, with the expectation of an eventual occupation of Cuba by an American army. At the war's beginning, the strength of the U.S. Regular Army under Maj. Gen. Nelson A. Miles was only 26,000. The legality of using the National Guard, numbering something more than 100,000, for expeditionary service was questionable. Therefore, resort was made to the volunteer system used in the Mexican War and Civil War. The mobilization act of Apr. 22 provided for a wartime army of 125,000 volunteers (later raised to 200,000) and an increase in the regular army to 65,000. Thousands of volunteers and recruits converged on ill-prepared southern camps; there was a shortage of weapons, equipment, and supplies; and sanitary conditions and food were scandalous.

In the Western Pacific, Commodore George Dewey had been alerted by Acting Secretary of the Navy Theodore Roosevelt to prepare his Asiatic Squadron for operations in the Philippines. On Apr. 27 Dewey sailed from Hong Kong with four light cruisers, two gunboats, and a revenue cutter—and, as a passenger, Emilio Aguinaldo, an exiled Filipino insurrectionist. Dewey entered Manila Bay in the early morning hours on May 1. Rear Adm. Patricio Montojo had one modern light cruiser and six small antiquated ships, a force so weak that he elected to fight at anchor under protection of Manila's shore batteries. Dewey closed to 5,000 yards and shot Montojo's squadron out of the water, but he had insufficient strength to land and capture Manila itself. Until U.S. Army forces could arrive, the Spanish garrison had to be kept occupied by Aguinaldo's guerrilla operations.

In the Atlantic, Cervera managed to elude both Sampson and Schley and to slip into Santiago on Cuba's southeast coast. Schley took station off Santiago on May 28 and was joined four days later by Sampson. To support these operations a marine battalion on June 10 seized nearby Guantánamo to serve as an advance base. Sampson, reluctant to enter the harbor because of mines and land batteries, asked for U.S. Army help. Maj. Gen. William R. Shafter, at Tampa, Fla., received orders on May 31 to embark his V Corps. Despite poor facilities, he had 17,000 men, mostly regulars, ready to sail by June 14 and by

June 20 was standing outside Santiago. Sampson wanted Shafter to reduce the harbor defenses; Shafter was insistent that the city be taken first and decided on a landing at Daiquiri, east of Santiago. On June 22, after a heavy shelling of the beach area, the V Corps began going ashore. It was a confused and vulnerable landing, but the Spanish did nothing to interfere. Once ashore, Shafter was joined by insurgent leader Calixto Garcia and about 5,000 revolutionaries.

Between Daiquiri and Santiago were the San Juan heights. Shafter's plan was to send Brig. Gen. Henry W. Lawton's division north to seize the village of El Caney and then to attack frontally with Brig. Gen. Jacob F. Kent's division on the left and Maj. Gen. Joseph Wheeler's dismounted cavalry on the right. The attack began at dawn on July 1. Shafter, sixty-three years of age and weighing more than 300 pounds, was soon prostrated by the heat. Lawton was delayed at El Caney by stubborn enemy resistance and failed to come up on Wheeler's flank. Wheeler, one-time Confederate cavalryman, sent his dismounted troopers, including the black Ninth and Tenth cavalries and the volunteer Rough Riders, under command of Lt. Col. Theodore Roosevelt (he had left the navy to seek a more active role in the war), against Kettle Hill. Kent's infantry regiments charged up San Juan Hill covered by Gatling-gun fire. The Spanish withdrew to an inner defense line, and as the day ended, the Americans had their ridge line but at a cost of 1,700 casualties.

Shafter, not anxious to go against the Spanish second line, asked Sampson to come into Santiago Bay and attack the city, but for Sampson there was still the matter of the harbor defenses. He took his flagship eastward on July 3 to meet with Shafter, and while they argued, Cervera inadvertently resolved the impasse by coming out of the port on orders of the Spanish captain general. His greatly inferior squadron was annihilated by Schley, and on July 16 the Spaniards signed terms of unconditional surrender for the 23,500 troops in and around the city.

On July 21 Miles sailed from Guantánamo in personal charge of an expedition to Puerto Rico. He landed near Ponce on July 25 and against virtually no opposition began a march to San Juan, which was interrupted on Aug. 12 by the signing of a peace protocol.

At the end of July, the VIII Corps, some 15,000 men, mostly volunteers, under Maj. Gen. Wesley Merritt, had reached the Philippines. En route, the escort cruiser *Charleston* had stopped at Guam and accepted the surrender of the island from the Spanish

governor, who had not heard of the war. Because of an unrepaired cable Dewey and Merritt themselves did not hear immediately of the peace protocol, and on Aug. 13 an assault against Manila was made. The Spanish surrendered after token resistance.

In Cuba tropical diseases reached epidemic proportions, and a number of senior officers proposed immediate evacuation. This was embarrassing for the army, but it also hastened the removal of thousands of fever patients to a camp at Montauk Point, Long Island, and gave impetus to the successful campaign against yellow fever by the U.S. Medical Corps.

The peace treaty signed in Paris on Dec. 10, 1898, established Cuba as an independent state, ceded Puerto Rico and Guam to the United States, and provided for the payment of $20 million to Spain for the Philippines. Almost overnight the United States had acquired an overseas empire and, in the eyes of Europe, had become a world power. The immediate cost of the war was $250 million and about 3,000 American lives, of whom only about 300 were battle deaths. A disgruntled Aguinaldo, expecting independence for the Philippines, declared a provisional republic, which led to the Philippine insurrection that lasted until 1902.

[R. A. Alger, *The Spanish-American War;* F. E. Chadwick, *The Relations of the United States and Spain: The Spanish-American War;* G. A. Cosmas, *An Army for Empire;* F. Freidel, *The Splendid Little War;* H. W. Wilson, *The Downfall of Spain.*]

EDWIN H. SIMMONS

SPANISH-AMERICAN WAR, NAVY IN. Shortly before the Spanish-American War, growing American interest in a modern, powerful navy had resulted in increased appropriations and a vigorous program of ship construction, especially of battleships and cruisers. The Spanish-American War lasted only about ninety days, yet it marked the generally successful combat trial of the then new American navy. Following by eight years the appearance of Alfred Thayer Mahan's *The Influence of Sea Power Upon History,* the conflict illustrated principles and techniques of war that were sometimes adhered to, sometimes violated.

The main combat areas of the war were Spanish possessions in the Philippines and Caribbean. In both theaters American naval ascendancy was first established, although by different means, to assure sea control before undertaking amphibious and military operations. On May 1, in the Battle of Manila Bay, which involved secondary cruiser forces in a secondary area, Commodore George Dewey easily defeated an antiquated Spanish squadron acting as a fixed fortress fleet. In the Atlantic-Caribbean areas, war strategy and command decisions proved more complex and difficult.

In late April the Navy Department unwisely yielded to the clamor of influential, but ill-informed, East Coast citizens for coastal protection and subsequently divided naval objectives and forces. Rear Adm. William T. Sampson, with new battleships, established a blockade off Havana, the assumed Cuban strategic center. At Norfolk, Va., an intended mobile fortress fleet under Commodore Winfield Scott Schley was readied to defend against almost impossible coastal raids by the main Spanish fleet.

In early May, on learning that Spanish Adm. Pascual Cervera had left the Cape Verde Islands, Sampson lifted most of his blockade and steamed east on the erroneous assumption that his opponent would first make port at San Juan, Puerto Rico, and then continue to his assumed ultimate destination, Havana. But Cervera, given freedom of command decision, chose a different route and ultimate port than he would have in peacetime. Thus, there was no confrontation of naval forces off Puerto Rico. Cervera slipped into the nearest Cuban port, Santiago, which was then not under American surveillance. Ten days later, after confusion and delay, Schley located Cervera and established a blockade, later joined by Sampson. Soon the Americans landed marines and soldiers and began their military campaign against Santiago. As the city's fall became imminent, Cervera was directed to sortie, if possible to Havana. But in the naval battle of July 3 his fleet was overwhelmed and beached, a significant prelude to further successful American operations against Cuba and, later, Puerto Rico.

There were many important naval lessons learned in the war, from which the Americans profited. Their gunnery required swift technological improvement, which Lt. Comdr. William S. Sims soon provided. Engineering research and development were stimulated by the establishment of the Naval Engineering Experiment Station. Because it took sixty-six days for the *Oregon* to sail from San Francisco, around Cape Horn, to Key West, Fla., and join the fleet, pressure was exerted for a canal route through Central America. The necessity for overseas bases for logistic support became evident. The Spanish-American War also added strong impetus to the growing demand for an American navy second to none.

ELLERY H. CLARK, JR.

SPANISH AND SPANISH-AMERICAN INFLUENCE. Spanish influence in the United States was significant from the beginning of New World exploration, for envy of Spain was a major motive in the English colonization of North America. Spain's preeminence in the 16th century was attributed to its monopoly of the wealth of the Indies. The disappointment of the English at the initial failure of their colonies to yield comparable returns largely explains the "salutary neglect" that permitted these colonies to develop nearly autonomous political and economic institutions. Later, when their growing productivity revived British interest, it was to Spain that the British government turned to find a working model of colonial administration: the Consejo de Indias and the Casa de Contratación were paralleled in the Council for Foreign Plantations and the Council for Trade of 1660. These advisory committees of the Privy Council, combined in 1696 as the Board of Trade, formulated the policies that tightened mercantilist controls and thereby prodded the American colonies toward revolution.

Spain's intervention in the revolutionary war as a French ally was also significant. Spanish authorities in New Orleans aided Oliver Pollock, the agent of Virginia, in financing the campaigns of George Rogers Clark. Fernando de Leyba, Spanish commander at Saint Louis, provided Clark with a military diversion in 1780 by repulsing a British-Indian attack on Saint Louis. His forces then pursued the attackers to the shores of Lake Michigan and captured their base at Fort Saint Joseph. Meanwhile Bernardo de Gálvez, governor of Louisiana, launched a campaign in 1778 that drove the British from the Floridas.

Spain had also—without meaning to—created a geographic situation that very greatly facilitated the expansion of the United States. Charles III, who ruled from 1759 to 1788, had undertaken a massive advance of the Spanish frontier in North America to set up a defense-in-depth for the viceroyalty of New Spain. Louisiana was taken over from France in 1762; California was occupied in 1769; and the Floridas were annexed by the Peace of Paris in 1783. At that moment, therefore, Spain held all lands to the south and west of the United States—territories so vast and empty that Charles III's feeble successors and, later, the Republic of Mexico were able neither to colonize nor defend them. All of them fell, one by one, to the United States: the Louisiana Territory was acquired in 1803 through the intervention of France, in violation of the promises made to Spain by Napoleon I in the Treaty of San Ildefonso in 1800; West Florida was

SPANISH AND SPANISH-AMERICAN INFLUENCE

taken over by a proclamation of President James Madison, on Oct. 27, 1810, after settlers from the United States had overthrown Spanish authority and offered the area for annexation; and Spain then yielded East Florida, too, under pressure, in the Adams-Onís Treaty, on Feb. 22, 1819, and in the same treaty ceded to the United States its claim to Louisiana and to all lands north of the forty-second parallel—that is, to the Oregon country.

Spanish policy also predetermined the boundary ultimately set between Mexico and the United States in the Treaty of Guadalupe Hidalgo (Feb. 2, 1848). In the 18th century Spain had strung a line of presidios along the Rio Grande and westward across Sonora to protect settled areas from raids by nomadic Indians further north. This presidial line became the effective boundary of Mexican population, with detached salients in Texas, New Mexico, and California and was so recognized in the final settlement of the Mexican War.

The emergence of an independent Spanish America, rich, weak, and divided, led to adoption of the "two spheres" concept as the basis of U.S. foreign policy. In 1823 John Quincy Adams, then secretary of state, was handed a British proposal that the two countries should join hands to protect Spanish America and, to show good faith, should bind themselves not to attack it. Adams saw this as a British plot to prevent the further expansion of the United States, and on his advice, the Monroe Doctrine was issued with no such self-denying clause. Under this doctrine, the United States, while seeming to hold Europe at bay, proceeded itself to annex more than half the territory of Mexico. Panama was aided in seceding from Colombia, and the Canal Zone was acquired in 1903. In the same era, "dollar diplomacy" burgeoned in Central America and the Caribbean.

The deep resentment felt by the Spanish-Americans, reported by scholars, travelers, and the press, influenced public opinion in the United States, and by 1910 there were increasing demands for an end to dollar diplomacy. Woodrow Wilson attempted to allay Spanish-American fear when he promised at Mobile, Ala., on Oct. 27, 1913, "that the United States will never again seek an additional foot of territory by conquest." Again, in 1924, when the administration of Calvin Coolidge hectored Mexico over its seizure of U.S. properties, there was an outburst of newspaper criticism at this return to the "big stick" policy, and the U.S. Senate by unanimous vote (Jan. 27, 1927) called for arbitration of the difficul-

ties. This marked a turning point. The withdrawal of U.S. forces, the move to transform the Monroe Doctrine into a multilateral agreement, the Good Neighbor policy, the Alliance for Progress, and continuing efforts to improve inter-American relations can all be viewed as responses to Spanish-American mistrust of the United States.

Apart from the rich larder of American Indian food plants, for the most part given to the United States and the world by Spain, and the adoption of the Spanish peso as the basis for the U.S. dollar in 1791, the first intimate contact with Spanish-American culture occurred in Texas. There Anglo-Americans encountered the Spanish-Mexican system of managing range cattle. They found it highly developed and well adapted to the expanses of subhumid grasslands, and so they adopted it wholesale. It produced one of the truly epic figures in the story of the West: the cowboy of the prairies, with his distinctive vocabulary, costume, and way of life. Anglo-American speech was enriched. Many new words were adopted outright: *bronco, corral, remuda, rodeo, sombrero.* Some were but slightly changed: *desesperado* into "desperado," *estampida* into "stampede," *la reata* into "lariat," and *vamos* into "vamoose." Some were altered almost beyond recognition: *¿con quién?* to "coon can," *juzgado* to "hoosegow," *mostrenco* to "mustang," and *vaquero* to "buckaroo." Incidentally, the Spaniards also, very unwillingly, provided the horses that transformed prairie Indians into the magnificent buffalo hunters and warriors of the Plains.

The next significant Spanish-American influence came in California. Experienced Mexicans, mainly from Sonora, gave to the raw Anglo-Americans their first instruction in placer mining (the very word "placer" is of Spanish origin). Chileans introduced a well-organized group mining operation. More telling was the decision of the convention at Monterey that formed the first state constitution in 1849 to retain the community property provision of Spanish-Roman law, giving wives equal rights with their husbands, because they thought it more just to women than English common law. Other states, New Mexico, Texas, and Arizona among them, also show such heritages of Spanish law. Significant too was the influence of the Spanish missions in California and those strewn throughout the Southwest. Not only did they bring to the Indians religion and a language many of them still speak, but as residential training schools, they provided a model for the Indian reservation—not inaptly described as a mission without a missionary. The large Spanish and Mexican land grants had an important effect on California agriculture. With the application of the corporate form of organization, finance, and management, some of the grants and other extensive estates modeled on them developed into the specialized one-crop "agricultural factories" that have proved so highly productive that they have supplanted a number of small family farms across the country. Unfortunately, this type of agriculture requires a mass of migratory labor, and the Mexican *braceros* formed the bulk of this labor force in the Southwest. Many were forced into it by lack of education and skill and by discrimination, which denied them access to better jobs at higher wages.

In the census of 1970 there were some 10 million residents of Spanish ancestry in the United States. There is in addition a constant stream of visitors from Latin America and a rather brisk exchange of students and teachers. A considerable number of group activities are being carried on: inter-American conferences of scholars and specialists, university student organizations for cultural exchange, as well as many privately organized clubs and study groups in the general society. There is, finally, a heritage of beautiful names, of Spanish architecture and house furnishings, of outdoor living, of patio and barbecue, all of it bearing witness to the continuing influence of Spain and Spanish America.

[R. N. Burr, *Our Troubled Hemisphere*; L. Hanke, *Do the Americas Have a Common History?*; G. H. Stuart, *Latin America and the United States*.]

EDWIN A. BEILHARZ

SPANISH CAPTURE OF BRITISH POSTS on the Mississippi River and along the Gulf coast during 1779–81 was the final stage in Spain's participation in the American Revolution. Between 1776 and 1779 Spain had secretly supported the war against Great Britain, in order to weaken its imperial rival. Money and war materials were sent through intermediary merchants (*see* Spanish Supplies From New Orleans; Pollock's Aid to the Revolution), and American privateers with prizes were protected in Spanish ports. On June 21, 1779, Spain formally joined France in hostilities against Great Britain. It did not, however, explicitly guarantee the independence of the United States, because of the fear, as expressed by the Spanish foreign minister, José Moxino y Redondo, Count of Floridablanca, that a successful republican insurrection in North America might inspire Spain's own colonies to revolt and might create a new power, the United States, to threaten the Spanish empire.

Spain's military operations in America were conducted along the Anglo-Spanish frontier on the Mississippi River and the Gulf of Mexico. Under the leadership of Bernardo de Gálvez, governor of the province of Louisiana, the posts at Fort Manchac, Baton Rouge, and Natchez were easily taken from the British late in 1779. Fort Charlotte (Mobile) was captured Mar. 17, 1780, and Fort George (Pensacola) surrendered May 9, 1781, after a long naval siege combined with a land attack. Thus Spain restored its control of East Florida and West Florida, although its claim of control also of navigation on the Mississippi was not upheld in the Definitive Treaty of Peace of 1783.

[J. W. Caughey, *Bernardo de Gálvez in Louisiana, 1776–1783*.]

MARTIN P. CLAUSSEN

SPANISH CONSPIRACY, a series of more or less closely related intrigues between Spain and certain Americans living in what was then the western United States; the intrigues began in 1786 and continued for a score of years thereafter. The main purpose of Spain was to defend Louisiana and Florida by promoting the secession of the West from the United States. To achieve that purpose, the Spanish employed bribery, manipulated commerce on the Mississippi River (over which Spain retained some control until 1803), and exploited sectional antagonism between East and West. Before the United States obtained the right of free navigation of the Mississippi by Pinckney's Treaty (1795), some of the American conspirators were probably sincere in their profession of secessionist aims; but after 1795 their sole purpose (and at all times their main purpose) seems to have been to advance their own personal interests by obtaining from Spain money, commercial privileges, support for colonization schemes, and other advantages.

The first intrigue, a short-lived one begun in 1786 by Diego de Gardoqui (Spanish minister to the United States) and James White (a prominent North Carolina landowner), was related to the Muscle Shoals speculation, in which leaders of the breakaway state of Franklin attempted to settle the Muscle Shoals (Ala.) region. The central figure in the Spanish intrigues, however, was James Wilkinson, and their focal point was in Kentucky. In 1786 great indignation was aroused in the West by the decision of Congress not to press the United States' claim to the free navigation of the Mississippi; and in 1787 Wilkinson, who had won a prominent place in Kentucky politics, went to New Orleans to try his hand at direct negotiation with the

SPANISH DOLLAR

Spanish officials of Louisiana. The upshot was that he won some commercial privileges for the western people and more for himself, took an oath of allegiance to the Spanish crown, and became the principal agent of Spain in its secessionist intrigue; he was awarded a pension of $2,000 a year (later raised to $4,000), which was paid to him at intervals for many years after he became an officer in the U.S. Army (1791). Benjamin Sebastian, Harry Innes, and a few other influential Kentuckians joined in the intrigue, but they often worked at cross-purposes with Wilkinson, Spain, and each other. The existence of the conspiracy was widely suspected almost from the beginning; some partial revelations of it were made in the 1790's; and many of the details were exposed in 1806 by the *Western World* (a Kentucky newspaper) and in 1809 by Daniel Clark's *Proofs of the Corruption of . . . Wilkinson* (see Burr Conspiracy). Nevertheless, full legal proof was lacking. Wilkinson retained his commission in the army and continued to enjoy the apparent confidence of presidents Thomas Jefferson and James Madison, as he had that of presidents George Washington and John Adams. The exposure did, however, put an end to the conspiracy, which had long since become a farce. The secessionist plan was never put into action. What few advantages the conspiracy yielded were reaped by the Americans—at Spain's expense.

[Thomas R. Hay and M. R. Werner, *The Admirable Trumpeter: A Biography of General James Wilkinson*.]

A. P. WHITAKER

SPANISH DOLLAR, first coined in 1728 to replace the old piece of eight, circulated throughout the commercial world and became recognized and accepted as a reliable medium of exchange. It served as the metallic basis of the monetary system of the British colonies prior to the American Revolution. Because of its wide acceptance and familiarity, Congress adopted it in 1786 as the basis of the U.S. coinage system, the first American silver dollars containing approximately the same silver content as their Spanish counterparts.

[Davis Rich Dewey, *Financial History of the United States*.]

WALTER PRICHARD

SPANISH-INDIAN RELATIONS (1783–1803). During 1782–83, Spain formulated a plan to handle its dealings with Indians east of the Mississippi through Lt. Gov. Gilbert Antoine de Saint Maxent, who was also to monopolize the Indian trade. To pro-

vide the necessary merchandise, direct trade between Louisiana and France was permitted by a cedula of Jan. 22, 1782, but Maxent failed to fulfill his contract. Louisiana Gov. Esteban Miró had to buy gifts for the Creek who attended the "congress" in Pensacola at which Miró negotiated the treaty of May 31–June 1, 1784. By this treaty the Creek accepted Spanish protection and promised to deal only with Spanish traders. Their chief, Alexander McGillivray, became Spanish commissary at a salary of $50 per month. At another "congress" at Mobile in July the Choctaw and Chickasaw similarly came under Spanish protection.

Through McGillivray's influence Panton, Leslie and Company obtained the Creek trade through Pensacola, with the privilege of importing goods from England. Other traders, who obtained the trade of the Choctaw and Chickasaw through Mobile, were unable to please the Indians, and to check the Americans, who were undermining Spanish influence, Panton, Leslie and Company was given the Mobile trade in 1788. Thereafter, the company was one of the mainstays of Spanish-Indian policy.

Without consulting his protectors, McGillivray sent the Creek against the Georgians in 1786. Miró nevertheless supplied guns and ammunition until stopped in 1787 by orders from Spain. Munitions were furnished again in 1789 to offset the influence of the British-backed adventurer William Augustus Bowles, who attempted to drive the Spanish out of Florida. Insufficient support from Spain, however, was a major factor in causing McGillivray to agree to the Treaty of New York in 1790, in which he declared allegiance to the United States. Miró's successor, Francisco Luis Hector, Baron de Carondelet, with William Panton's help and the offer of a larger pension, won McGillivray back as a Spanish ally in 1792; McGillivray died the next year.

Meanwhile, Carondelet was working to create a confederation of all the southern Indians and to establish Spanish domination west of the Alleghenies. His subordinate, Manuel Gayoso de Lemos, built a fort at Nogales (Walnut Hills) in 1792, and in October 1793, Gayoso negotiated the Treaty of Nogales, establishing the Indian confederation. The next year Fort Confederation was built on the Tombigbee River, and Fort San Fernando was erected at Chickasaw Bluffs in 1795. Carondelet was then stopped by the Treaty of San Lorenzo (or Pinckney's Treaty) in 1795. He tried to evade it but was able only to delay the final results. Early in 1798 all Spanish garrisons retired below the thirty-first parallel.

Spain and the United States had scarcely resolved their differences when Bowles, returning in 1799, threw the Lower Creek into confusion. Through the cooperation of the agents of both nations he was captured in 1803.

[John Caughey, *McGillivray of the Creeks*; A. P. Whitaker, *The Spanish-American Frontier, 1783–1795*, and *The Mississippi Question, 1795–1803*.]

DUVON CLOUGH CORBITT

SPANISH-MISSOURI FUR COMPANY, a firm organized May 5, 1794, as the "Spanish Commercial Company for the Exploration of the Country West of the Misuri." The articles of agreement were signed by Laurent Durocher, Antoine Reihle, Joseph Robidou, Hyacinthe St. Cyr, Charles Sanguinette, Louis Chauvin, Louis Dubreuil, Joseph Motard, Benito Vasquez, and Jacques Clamorgan; Clamorgan was the chief director. The Spanish government granted the company exclusive trading rights along the upper Missouri above the Ponca Indian villages, and the firm sent three expeditions up the river: the first in June 1794, the second in April 1795, and the third in July or August 1795. The first two expeditions were commanded by Jean Baptiste Truteau and the third by James Mackay.

The business of the company was not successful; most of the merchants of Saint Louis would not deal with it, and many of the firm's own members became suspicious of and dissatisfied with Clamorgan and gradually disassociated themselves. Clamorgan succeeded in interesting Andrew Todd in the company, and it was with money advanced by Todd that the last expedition was outfitted. Clamorgan, Loisel and Company apparently took over the business of the Commercial Company.

In addition to trading and establishing contact with Indian nations hitherto unknown to whites, the company attempted to discover a route to the Pacific Ocean. To encourage this endeavor, the king of Spain offered to pay $3,000 to the first Spaniard to reach, by way of the Missouri River, the Russian settlements that had been established on the shores of the northern Pacific.

[Louis Houck, *Spanish Regime in Missouri*.]

STELLA M. DRUMM

SPANISH POSTS ON THE MISSISSIPPI, SURRENDER OF. *See* **Guion's Expedition; Southern Boundary, Survey of the.**

SPANISH SUCCESSION, WAR OF THE. *See* **Queen Anne's War.**

SPANISH SUPPLIES FROM NEW ORLEANS (1776–79). When armed hostilities between Great Britain and the American colonies began in 1775, trade between Britain and the colonies was suspended, and British fleets blockaded Atlantic ports to prevent American importation of munitions and other supplies from foreign countries. The colonists turned to the Spanish-controlled port of New Orleans as a source of needed supplies. Spain was a traditional enemy of Britain and was eagerly watching developments in America in the hope of recovering territory and prestige lost to the British in the French and Indian War. Spain also resented the trade between British West Florida and Louisiana and was fearful of the increasing British influence over the Indians west of the Alleghenies, an influence that endangered Spanish control of Louisiana.

The Spanish government was nevertheless exceedingly careful to avoid war with Britain, and the governor of Louisiana reflected this caution in his dealings with American agents sent to New Orleans in 1776. However, through the influence of Oliver Pollock, an American trader and financier living in New Orleans, these agents were permitted to purchase guns, gunpowder, blankets, and medicines, especially quinine, from Spanish sources in that port. The supplies were rowed up the Mississippi in boats carrying the Spanish flag, to prevent their seizure by British authorities at West Florida posts above New Orleans (*see* Gibson-Linn Episode).

Bernardo de Gálvez, who became governor of Louisiana in 1777, was bolder than his predecessor in assisting American agents in New Orleans, since he was unperturbed by the prospect of war with Britain as a result of pro-American acts. Through Gálvez's assistance, the traffic in supplies up the Mississippi from New Orleans continued at a brisk pace, and from this traffic the Americans procured the sorely needed matériel that enabled George Rogers Clark to defeat the British in the Old Northwest in 1778 and 1779 (*see* Clark's Northwest Campaign).

The chief obstacle to this Spanish-American trade was the lack of colonial funds to purchase supplies available in New Orleans, since the treasuries of the Continental and state governments were chronically empty. Pollock extended his credit to the limit to finance the trade, and he went bankrupt when the revolutionary governments concerned were tardy in repaying advances made by him in their behalf. When France joined the United States in the war against Britain in 1778 (*see* Franco-American Alliance), French fleets landed supplies at Atlantic ports, thus reducing American dependence on the New Orleans trade. After Spain entered the war against Britain in 1779, secrecy was no longer necessary in up-the-river traffic.

[Alcée Fortier, *History of Louisiana;* Charles Gayarré, *History of Louisiana;* James A. James, *Oliver Pollock,* and "Spanish Influence in the West During the American Revolution," *Mississippi Valley Historical Review,* vol. 4.]

WALTER PRICHARD

SPANISH TRAIL, an important overland route between Santa Fe, N.Mex., and Los Angeles. It dates from 1775–76, during the period of Spanish control of the Southwest. Two Franciscan monks first traversed most of the trail, Father Francisco Garcés traveling its westerly section in 1775–76, and Father Silvestre Velez de Escalante its eastern portion in 1776. Jedediah Smith, an American trader and explorer, came up the western half of the trail, but the first American to cover its full length was William Wolfskill, a Kentuckian, who led a company of trappers over it in 1830–31. After Wolfskill's trip, annual expeditions of traders used the trail, which was sufficiently far north to avoid most Apache raiding parties and which offered a route across the desert on which water could be found. The trail was later an important immigrant route, and the Mountain Meadows massacre (of California-bound settlers) took place on it in 1857.

The Spanish Trail led from Santa Fe up the Chama River through Durango (in what is now Colorado) and then followed the Dolores River. It crossed the Grand and Green rivers, passed through the mountains up the Sevier Valley, followed the line of the Santa Clara and Virgin rivers southwest, cut across the desert to the Mojave River, and then crossed the mountains to Los Angeles.

[George Douglas Brewerton, *Overland With Kit Carson,* Stallo Vinton, ed.]

PAUL I. WELLMAN

SPARS. *See* **Women in the Military Services.**

SPEAKEASY, also known as a "blind pig" or a "blind tiger," is an illicit or unlicensed establishment dispensing alcoholic beverages. The speakeasy had been part of the American scene for at least thirty years before the passage of the Volstead Act (1919), but it reached its heyday during the Prohibition era. At the height of their popularity (1924–33), speakeasies were generally either bars or restaurants, to which admission was gained by personal introduction or by presenting a card, although often without any formality. In social class they ranged from smart restaurants to underworld dens, but were uniformly influential in establishing a single drinking standard for both men and women. Before Prohibition most women would not frequent a public bar.

[S. Walker, *The Night Club Era.*]

STANLEY R. PILLSBURY

SPEAKER OF THE HOUSE OF REPRESENTATIVES. Although the concept of the speaker of the House was borrowed from the British House of Commons and some colonial assemblies, the speakership of the U.S. House of Representatives has developed into a uniquely original institution. The speaker is the first officer named in the U.S. Constitution: "The House of Representatives shall chuse their Speaker and other Officers . . ." (Article I, Section 2). There is no requirement that the speaker be a House member, or even an American citizen, but in 1789 the House chose a member, Frederick A. C. Muhlenberg, as its first speaker, and the tradition of choosing from its membership has continued. Through the personal impact of its many competent occupants, the speakership has come to be regarded as second only in power and importance to the presidency. Standing behind the vice-president in succession to the presidency, several speakers have been only one step away from the highest office in the land—for example, Sam Rayburn, when the administration of Harry S. Truman was without a vice-president (1945–49); and Carl Albert, after the resignation of Vice-President Spiro T. Agnew (1973), and again after the resignation of President Richard M. Nixon (1974). In diplomatic protocol the speaker ranks third—behind the president and vice-president, but ahead of the chief justice of the Supreme Court—for purposes of seating at official and social functions. The speaker is given a salary in addition to that received as a member of the House and a substantial expense account.

The speaker of the House plays a variety of roles. His first duty is to preside over the House of Representatives. Every two years, at the beginning of each new Congress, the House must elect its speaker before it can conduct its business; although the speaker is elected by the votes of a majority of all House members, in practice the House merely ratifies the choice of the majority party membership. He interprets the rules of the House, and his rulings can be overturned by a majority of the House, although from 1931 to 1975 not a single ruling was reversed. He preserves order, enforces the rules, refers bills and resolutions to the appropriate committees, and prevents dilatory tactics from paralyzing House action. He chooses the member who will preside as chairman of the Committee of the Whole, where the House conducts much of its important business. The speaker has a unique relationship with the president. In private conversations and in more formal meetings, he presents the views of the House members to the president and in turn reports the views of the president to House members informally.

Until the early 20th century, the speakership was a highly partisan office, used by the majority to work its will. The tradition then developed of a scrupulously fair presiding officer who considers it one of his highest duties carefully to protect the rights of every minority member under the rules of the House. But in his role as leader of his political party in the House, there is no pretense of nonpartisanship. The speaker has great influence in placing his party's members on committees. (Until the House internal revolution in 1910, the speaker for years had named all committee chairmen and appointed all committee members for both majority and minority parties.) He negotiates many internal matters with the minority leader, such as the membership ratio between parties on committees, and he names members of conference committees to negotiate differences with the Senate. Another important power is his right to name several hundred members of special boards and commissions. The speaker is also influential in determining which bills the House will consider.

The speaker's power over the political fortunes of his party's House members is substantial, particularly for new members. His favor can greatly advance a newcomer's career in the House; his disfavor usually has a retarding, even a blighting, effect. The speaker can aid a candidate through letters of endorsement, speeches in the candidate's home district, disbursement of campaign funds, and intervention with local party leaders. The speaker usually wields significant power in the selection of his party's presidential and, at times, vice-presidential candidates. On numerous occasions he has served as presiding officer and keynote speaker of his party's national conventions. Nev-

ertheless, the office of speaker of the House has not been a stepping-stone to the presidency; as of 1976 James K. Polk was the only former speaker ever elected president.

Time-consuming, but a source of power in the House, are the speaker's many housekeeping responsibilities. Under law and House rules, he has control over the south, or House, end of the Capitol building and grounds, and the House office buildings. The assignment of offices, and of storage and parking space, provides him with additional valuable patronage. (*For a complete list of speakers of the House, see the table following the article* Congress, United States.)

[Congressional Quarterly, *Guide to the Congress of the United States;* Mary P. Follett, *The Speaker of the House of Representatives.*]

D. B. HARDEMAN

SPECIE CIRCULAR. In pursuance of the policy of President Andrew Jackson's administration of making specie the chief form of money in circulation, several circulars were issued by the Treasury Department. The first of these, issued on Nov. 5, 1834, ordered collectors of customs and receivers of public money not to accept, after Jan. 1, 1835, any form of money not described in a congressional resolution of Apr. 30, 1816. The order was designed specifically to exclude the drafts of branches of the Bank of the United States. On Apr. 6, 1835, a second circular was issued, directing collectors and receivers to accept, after March 1836, only gold and silver for all payments of less than $10.

These actions were preliminary to the issuance of the specie circular of July 11, 1836. This document, addressed to the receivers of public money and to the deposit ("pet") banks for U.S. government funds, directed that, after Aug. 15, 1836, nothing but gold or silver should be accepted as payment for public land. Until Dec. 15, 1836, however, "actual settlers or *bona fide* residents in the State" where the sales were made could, as before, use paper money in paying for up to 320 acres of government land. By curbing land speculation, the specie circular of 1836 probably hastened the panic of 1837.

[Davis Rich Dewey, *Financial History of the United States.*]

ERIK MCKINLEY ERIKSSON

SPECIE PAYMENTS, SUSPENSION AND RESUMPTION OF. Under a system of specie payments it is required by law or custom that fiduciary money, usually in the form of bank notes or government paper money issues, be redeemed at par and upon request of the issuing bank or the Treasury in metallic coin. Since the Founding Fathers remembered with distaste the paper-money inflation of the Revolution and the excesses of some of the states during the Confederation, the decision for a specie standard of value was implicit in the constitutional grant of power to Congress "to coin Money" and "regulate the Value thereof" and in the prohibition that the states refrain from emitting bills of credit or making anything but gold or silver a legal tender.

The maintenance of specie payments in the United States was difficult from the outset. Alexander Hamilton had recommended in 1791, and Congress adopted in 1792, a bimetallic standard of value, under which the dollar was defined in terms of both silver and gold. By adopting the then prevailing market ratio of 15 to 1 as the mint ratio, Hamilton hoped to keep both metals in monetary circulation. Unfortunately, soon after coinage began, the international market price of silver began to fall and gold was hoarded or exported to Europe. It even proved difficult to keep the newly coined silver dollars in circulation, because they were accepted at a higher value in the Spanish possessions. Therefore, the nation for many years was only nominally on a specie standard, particularly in the less-developed regions where a barter system prevailed. In 1834 an attempt was made to bring gold back into monetary circulation by reducing the gold content of the dollar from 24.7 to 23.2 grains while maintaining the silver dollar at 371.25 grains. This meant a new mint ratio of silver to gold of 16 to 1. This ratio undervalued silver, since the international market ratio of the time was about 15.75 to 1. Consequently, silver tended to disappear from circulation, while an increasing number of gold coins were minted and used. Essentially, after 1834 and until 1934, the dominant standard of value in the United States was gold coin.

A basic difficulty in maintaining specie payments during the 19th century was America's usually unfavorable balance of trade. The tendency for specie to be exported in payment for goods was exacerbated in times of war and economic crisis. Also, until 1864, when the National Banking System was established, it was difficult to control the paper bank-note issues of the state-chartered banks. The Supreme Court had decided that the constitutional prohibition against the state issue of bills of credit did not apply to state-chartered banks, which proceeded to issue bank notes far in excess of their ability to maintain specie payments.

In wartime, moreover, the federal government was under great pressure to meet its needs for revenue through the issue of irredeemable paper money.

In 1814–15, specie payments were suspended by most of the banks and by the U.S. Treasury in some sections of the country. The unregulated credit expansion of the banks, combined with the wartime issue of Treasury notes, was responsible. Coin payments were resumed in February 1817. Another great credit expansion fostered by the policies of the second Bank of the United States culminated in the panic of 1819 and a severe depression during which most banks in the South and West refused to pay specie.

The years 1830–37 were marked by solid economic development as well as by feverish speculation in land. This eventually led to the panic of 1837 and a nationwide suspension of specie payments. Factors involved in the suspension included a doubling of bank circulation between 1830 and 1837; Andrew Jackson's Specie Circular of July 11, 1836, which halted the land boom; and the distribution of a government surplus, which removed much hard money from the less-developed regions of the country. Perhaps of more importance was the cessation of European investment, followed by large exports of specie. Partial resumption was achieved prematurely in 1838. Continuing outflows of metallic coin brought another suspension in 1839. Finally specie payments resumed in 1842.

The cycle repeated itself in the 1850's. Railroad and industrial expansion was fueled by heavy domestic and foreign investment. State bank-note issues increased and speculation was prevalent. In 1857 capital imports from Europe slackened and the flow of California gold decreased. Money became tight. On Aug. 24 the failure of the Ohio Life Insurance and Trust Company precipitated a panic in New York City that spread to the rest of the country. Specie payments were suspended. They were resumed six months later.

The most serious deviation from the specie standard occurred in the years 1862–79. The departure from gold payments by the banks and the government on Dec. 30, 1861, was forced by the domestic hoarding and export of specie, which had gathered momentum as the domestic military situation deteriorated and as a war with England seemed imminent. Another cause was the failure of Secretary of the Treasury Salmon P. Chase to recommend drastic increases in taxes and his use of demand Treasury notes, a form of paper money.

In February 1862 the government began issuing

U.S. notes, better known as "greenbacks." These notes were legal tender and by 1865 had been issued to the amount of $431 million. While the issuance of the greenbacks had not caused the suspension of specie payments, the failure of Secretary of the Treasury Hugh McCulloch's contraction program after the Civil War made resumption very difficult. Contraction of the greenbacks was strongly resisted by powerful economic groups because of its deflationary impact. The obvious solution would have been a devaluation of the gold content of the dollar.

The tactic of letting the country's economy grow up to the currency supply was adopted instead. On Jan. 14, 1875, Congress passed the Resumption Act, which provided that coin payments be resumed on Jan. 1, 1879.

Despite the Free Silver agitation of the late 19th century, the United States adhered to the gold standard. Attempts by western and southern agrarians to restore silver to its ancient monetary function were rebuffed by the ruling conservative administrations. Such measures as the Bland-Allison Act of 1878 and the Sherman Silver Purchase Act of 1890 simply provided a subsidy to the silver mine owners of the West. The defeat of William Jennings Bryan in 1896 effectively squelched the silver movement, and the Gold Standard Act of 1900 legally placed the nation's money on the monometallic basis, which had been *de facto* since 1879.

Difficulties in maintaining gold payments were encountered in 1893 and 1907. The basic problem was the maintenance of an adequate reserve for redemption of fiduciary money in the face of domestic hoarding and a persistent export of gold. The panic of 1907 was caused by unsound bank investments.

A deviation from the gold standard occurred shortly after the United States entered World War I. Large gold exports seemed to threaten the base of the monetary and credit structure. On Sept. 7 and Oct. 12, 1917, President Woodrow Wilson placed an embargo on exports of coin and bullion. These restrictions were removed in June 1919.

The economic cataclysm of the 1930's marked the end of a legitimately defined specie standard of value in the United States. The 1929 stock market crash was followed by more than 5,000 bank failures in three years. The international nature of the crisis was signaled by England's abandonment of the gold standard in September 1931. Gold began to be hoarded, and the specie basis of the system was further threatened by gold exports. In the two weeks preceding the inauguration of President Franklin D. Roosevelt on Mar.

4, 1933, the Federal Reserve banks lost more than $400 million in gold, bringing the reserve down almost to the legal minimum. Several states had already declared banking "holidays" when Roosevelt, on Mar. 6, issued an executive order closing all banks for four days and prohibiting them from exporting, paying out, or allowing the withdrawal of specie. By the end of March most banks had been allowed to reopen, but specie payments were not resumed. By further executive orders issued in April 1933 the break with the gold standard was made more complete. No person or institution was permitted to hold gold or gold certificates. An embargo was placed on all international transactions in gold except under license issued by the secretary of the Treasury. By a joint resolution on June 5, Congress declared void the "gold clause" in government bonds and private obligations. For the first time the United States had deliberately abandoned the gold standard *de jure*.

After fluctuating in value in international money markets for nearly two years, the dollar was finally stabilized under the terms of the Gold Reserve Act and a presidential order in January 1934. The new dollar was defined as 13.71 grains of fine gold, which marked a devaluation to 59.06 percent of its former value. On this basis Secretary Henry Morgenthau announced the Treasury's willingness to buy and sell gold at the new rate of $35 per ounce. It now became possible to obtain gold bullion for making international payments, but domestically the country continued on an irredeemable paper standard, which made gold holdings by citizens illegal.

This "bastardized" gold standard endured for thirty-seven years. Operating under a favorable balance of payments, the United States amassed a gold reserve amounting to more than $24 billion in 1949. After that time, deficits in the international balance reduced the gold stock until it amounted to only about $10 billion by 1971. The continuing deterioration of the balance of payments and the threat to the gold stock impelled President Richard Nixon on Aug. 15, 1971, to order that the Treasury cease all purchases and sales of gold. As of 1975 the dollar was not maintained either at home or abroad at any fixed value in terms of gold; it is uncertain whether gold will regain a place in the monetary system of the nation.

[Bray Hammond, *Banks and Politics in America From the Revolution to the Civil War;* Broadus Mitchell, *Depression Decade;* Robert P. Sharkey, *Money, Class, and Party;* Paul Studenski and Herman E. Krooss, *Financial History of the United States;* Peter Temin, *The Jacksonian Economy;* Irwin Unger, *The Greenback Era.*]

ROBERT P. SHARKEY

SPECIFIC DUTIES. *See* **Duties, Ad Valorem and Specific.**

SPELLING BEE, or **Spelling Match,** a teaching device traditionally employed in American schools. Its widespread use resulted from educators' overemphasizing the importance of spelling proficiency, which they erroneously assumed to be an indication of general intellectual capacity. During the 19th century, as often as twice a day, and usually at least once a week, students spelled out loud, competing for the honor of being the best speller in the class. Rivalry led to the division of classes into two parties, or teams. The game took the form of a competitive examination, in which candidates attempted to spell such words as were submitted by an examiner. Prizes were awarded to the successful contestants. Various rules marked the game; generally a single failure eliminated a contestant from a match. Since amusement went hand in hand with improvement, the sternest moralist could not object to this game. By the 1840's middle western communities held spelling matches as part of an evening's entertainment, and the widespread popularity of the game began in the West. The term "spelling bee" was first used in Edward Eggleston's *The Hoosier Schoolmaster* (1871), although Caroline M. Kirkland in *Western Clearings* (1845) described the contest as the "spelling school." In 1875 the game was first employed in London schools. The spelling match became very popular in American urban school systems in the 1930's, when local and national contests were sponsored by radio stations and educational organizations. The game's popularity declined with the advent of the progressive education movement and the subsequent deemphasis of the teaching of spelling and of rote learning in general.

[Warren Burton, *The District School as It Was.*]
HARRY R. WARFEL

SPENCER RIFLE, a self-loading, repeating weapon patented by Christopher M. Spencer in 1860 and shortly thereafter adopted by the U.S. Army. It was the first effective and widely used magazine repeater; 106,667 pieces, in rifle and carbine form, were bought by the U.S. government from Jan. 1, 1861, to June 30, 1866, for $2,861,024.38. Many Civil War officers declared the rifle to have been the best weapon of its time. The magazine capacity was seven rimfire cartridges of .52 caliber. Sixteen shots per minute could be fired. Eight Spencer patents were obtained during the years 1860–73. The weapon had a weakness in its tendency to explode shells carried in the magazine.

[H. B. C. Pollard, *A History of Firearms.*]
CARL P. RUSSELL

SPERMACETI TRUST, an organization formed in an effort to monopolize the manufacture and sale in America of candles made from sperm whale oil. Production of sperm candles in America began in Rhode Island about 1750. In 1761 Richard Cranch and Company proposed the formation of a "union," or trust, for all the colonies and enlisted all manufacturers save one in Newport and some in Philadelphia. The nine members of the United Company of Spermaceti Candlers, most of them located in New England, agreed on a maximum buying price for whale "head-matter," on commissions for factors, and on selling prices for candles, and the members pledged themselves to do all in their power by fair and honorable means to prevent any increase in competition. They also began to build up a whaling fleet of their own. The sperm-candlemaking process had been kept a trade secret, but by 1772 the Nantucket Islanders had learned it and began to open their own factories. The steady spread of knowledge of the manufacturing process and the founding of other factories gradually broke the power of the trust.

[Alexander Starbuck, *History of American Whale Fishing.*]
ALVIN F. HARLOW

SPIES. Only once has America ever entered a war with an adequate espionage service in actual operation; that war was the Revolution. Many months before the Battle of Lexington (April 1775), Paul Revere and a group of patriots, mostly his fellow "mechanics," had begun to keep British Gen. Thomas Gage's troops under secret observation and had set up a secret courier service in Boston and the surrounding countryside. It was this group that kept the patriot leaders continually informed and gave early warning of the proposed march to Lexington and Concord. Unfortunately, it failed to detect the leading British secret agent, who was performing similar services for Gage—Benjamin Church, a member of the Massachusetts Provincial Congress and, in 1755, Gen. George Washington's medical director.

Unfortunately, the espionage service of Revere's group covered only parts of New England and was allowed to lapse when New York became the theater of operations in 1776. Although Washington could easily have established a secret service before occupying New York, and especially while actually in occupation there, he failed to do so. When he had been driven to Harlem by the British, and the need for spies had become pressing, Washington sent out Nathan Hale—a brave and devoted man, but completely untrained and without code, cipher, a system of "safe houses," or communication lines. One carrier pigeon could have brought Washington the information he needed (which Hale had collected but could not send). It would probably also have saved Hale's life, for he would not then have been forced to carry the incriminating papers found on his person when he was captured and executed by the British in September 1776. After this needless tragedy, Washington did at last set up an intelligence network in Manhattan, New Jersey, and Long Island, which did admirable service throughout the rest of the war, losing surprisingly few of its very active spies. The Culpers kept up a continuous flow of information from Manhattan and Long Island, using a secret ink invented by Sir James Jay, a physician and the brother of John Jay.

When it became obvious that British Gen. William Howe might move to Philadelphia, Washington did not repeat his New York blunder but saw to it that a well-organized American spy net was waiting for the British when they marched in. After preliminary work by Gen. Thomas Mifflin, Maj. John Clark maintained a flow of copious and accurate information from the city for Washington's benefit. For Howe's benefit, Clark was also able to supply some ingeniously falsified "official" documents from American headquarters written by Washington himself. On one occasion an amused American agent heard a British staff officer commenting on the assured accuracy of certain documents, which, he boasted, had come directly from Washington's headquarters—as indeed they had. Washington's headquarters were themselves penetrated by Ann Bates, a young Tory matron working for Sir Henry Clinton.

As the Civil War approached, the federal government repeated its previous blunder by neglecting to prepare an espionage system in advance. In the meantime, Capt. Thomas Jordan, a Virginian on duty in the War Department, set up a ring of Confederate spies in Washington, D.C., with code, cipher, and courier service, which he handed over to Rose O'Neal Greenhow. Her lax security soon destroyed the ring, but not before it had supplied Confederate Gen. Pierre Beauregard with Union Gen. Irvin McDowell's exact marching orders for Bull Run.

The first Union efforts at espionage in 1861, under Allan Pinkerton, Lafayette Baker, and William Alvin Lloyd, a private spy employed by President Abraham Lincoln, were mainly failures, but as the war continued Union intelligence became very skillful. Elizabeth Van Lew, a Union loyalist living in Richmond, began spying for the Union as soon as the war started and built up a large network in Richmond, which was later taken into the much larger system directed by Gen. George Henry Sharpe for Gen. Ulysses S. Grant's forces. During the siege of Richmond, Van Lew was able to send a Richmond newspaper regularly and a bouquet of flowers frequently through Confederate lines for Grant's breakfast table.

"Sheridan's Scouts," commanded by Union Maj. H. H. Young, kept its men continually in the Confederate ranks and even in Gen. Jubal A. Early's headquarters. Gen. Philip H. Sheridan himself said he owed the victory at Winchester, Va., to information from a Quaker schoolmistress inside the town. James A. Campbell, one of Sheridan's scouts, found the courier who located her. Union Gen. G. M. Dodge operated a network of nearly 100 secret agents throughout the Confederacy during most of the war.

The Spanish-American War was too short to permit the development of an adequate intelligence system. Lt. Andrew Summers Rowan's secret visit to the Cuban revolutionary Gen. Calixto García Íñiguez in 1898 was a brilliant feat, but the fact that the War Department did not know where to find an important ally is dismal evidence of the sad state of its secret service.

A modern military intelligence division had been organized some years before World War I, and the navy by this time had created the Office of Naval Intelligence. These were largely devoted to analyses of "overt" information, coming through attachés and published sources. Before the war was over, however, there was a large and effective spy system in Europe, and the army was making remarkable advances in breaking codes and ciphers.

As World War II approached, the armed forces began to enlarge their intelligence services, mainly by calling in specially qualified reserve officers. A new espionage service was organized, but it was obvious that operations would have to be larger than the United States had ever organized before. Instead of allowing the army and navy to enlarge upon the work they were already doing, President Franklin D. Roosevelt set up the Office of Strategic Services (OSS). Like all improvised services, the OSS made some serious blunders, but it did a great deal of useful espionage and sabotage. Its success in persuading the German commanders in Italy to lay down their arms in defiance of the Nazi government was alone sufficient to justify its existence. Its successor, the Central Intelligence Agency (CIA), has since continued its work on a permanent basis. The control of German sabotage attempts was much improved over that of World War I, and numerous German spies and saboteurs were promptly captured and executed by the military authorities—for example, the spies landed secretly by submarine in Florida and on Long Island (N.Y.). On the Western Front, the detachment of German troops disguised in American uniforms infiltrated into the American lines were also detected, captured, and used either to assist the Americans or executed.

[John Bakeless, *Spies for the Confederacy*, and *Turncoats, Traitors, and Heroes*; Lafayette C. Baker, *History of the U.S. Secret Service*; W. G. Beymer, *On Hazardous Service*; James D. Bulloch, *Secret Service of the Confederate States in Europe*; Allen Dulles, *Secret Surrender*; Lewis Einstein, *Divided Loyalties*; T. M. Johnson, *Our Secret War*.]

JOHN BAKELESS

SPIRIT LAKE MASSACRE. During 1856 five cabins were built by white settlers at the Okoboji lakes and one at Spirit Lake, in the state of Iowa. The winter of 1856–57 was bitterly cold, and Indians and settlers alike suffered from hunger and exposure. On Mar. 7, 1857, a small band of Sioux under Inkpaduta held a war dance on the lakes, and the following day they attacked Rowland Gardner's cabin, killing Gardner, his wife, and three of their children; one child, Abbie, aged fourteen, was taken captive. For the next four days the other cabins were attacked. Thirty-two men, women, and children were killed and four women were taken captive. After an unsuccessful attack on Springfield, Minn., Inkpaduta fled westward. Two of the captive women were killed; one was released through the mediation of friendly Indians; and Abbie Gardner (who wrote a harrowing account of her experience) was finally ransomed. A relief expedition under Maj. William Williams set out from Fort Dodge on Mar. 24, but succeeded only in burying the dead. A detachment from Fort Ridgely in Minnesota also failed to overtake Inkpaduta.

[T. Teakle, *The Spirit Lake Massacre*.]

WILLIAM J. PETERSEN

SPIRIT OF ST. LOUIS. See Lindbergh's Atlantic Flight.

SPIRIT OF '76, a famous painting by Archibald M. Willard, a carriage painter in Wellington, Ohio. The original sketch, made in 1874 or 1875, was intended only as a humorous presentation of a Fourth of July celebration and was entitled *Yankee Doodle*. The patriotic spirit that swept the country prior to the centennial celebration at Philadelphia was responsible for the change from a comic picture to the final, serious painting. Willard modeled the central character of the painting after his own father, a Baptist minister; for the fifer he took his friend Hugh Mosher, a former soldier; and for the drummer-boy he took the thirteen-year-old son of Col. John H. Devereux. The painting, of heroic size, was prominently exhibited at the Centennial Exposition, and it attracted such wide attention that after the close of the exposition it was exhibited at Boston, Washington, D.C., Chicago, San Francisco, and a number of other cities. In 1880 it was purchased by Col. Devereux and presented by him to his native town of Marblehead, Mass., where it now hangs in the town hall (known as Abbot Hall) and is viewed annually by thousands of tourists.

The painting is a direct appeal to patriotism in times of national emergency. The poses and facial expressions of the characters—the drummer-boy looking with confidence to the old man; the latter beating his drum and exhibiting the fire of youth in his eyes as he steps sturdily forward; the man of middle age, wounded but giving the cadence with his fife; all three advancing while battle clouds loom—these seem to imply that in any crisis; whether martial or civil, citizens of all ages should rise in defense of liberty. Although there have been many political caricatures of the painting, it has often been used as a moving appeal to the public spirit.

ALLEN FRENCH

SPOILS SYSTEM. "To the victor belong the spoils of the enemy" is the motto of the spoilsmen, proclaimed in 1832 by Sen. William L. Marcy of New York. In essence, the spoils system is an arrangement in which loyalty and service to a political party is the primary criterion for appointment to public office. Under the system, following an election, incumbent officeholders are summarily removed and replaced by those faithful to the victorious party. These dismissals are defended by the premise that rotation in office is an integral part of the democratic process. The theory is that one person is as capable as another in performing the duties of public office. One of the most criticized excesses of the spoils system is the assessment of a portion of the salary of politically appointed officeholders by the party to help it cover its expenses, particularly those of the political campaign. The spoils system provides the opportunity for party leaders to create a functional political machine to do their bidding. It makes a career in public service difficult and thus discourages many of the better-qualified citizens from seeking public office.

The spoils system was hardly a new phenomenon when the U.S. Constitution went into effect in 1789. The marketing of public offices predates the Roman Empire and has throughout history affected the development of political institutions in all parts of the world. But it is under a two-party system, such as has prevailed in the United States, that the spoils system is most prosperous.

Despite President George Washington's statement that government jobs should be filled by "those who seem to have the greatest fitness for public office," during his second administration, after the rise of the party system, he appointed people on the basis of loyalty to the Federalist party. His successor, John Adams, on leaving office in 1801, made his famous "midnight appointments," including John Marshall's appointment as chief justice of the Supreme Court. When Thomas Jefferson became president, he found himself engulfed by Federalists, who dominated the government. Consequently, he replaced many Federalists with fellow Democratic-Republicans while professing to make fitness for office the only qualification for appointment.

Andrew Jackson, who assumed office in 1829, developed and justified the spoils system. Jackson's contribution to the spoils system was that he was the first to articulate, legitimize, and establish it in the American political context. Ironically, Jackson himself was elected largely by accusing his predecessor, John Quincy Adams, of patronage practices during his administration.

Historians have tended to overemphasize the role of Jackson in introducing the spoils system into national politics. Despite all the publicity he gave to the spoils system, Jackson actually removed very few officeholders. It is estimated that during his tenure of office (1829–36) only one-tenth to one-third of all federal officeholders were replaced. Jackson believed in the theory of rotation in office, and he reasoned that political patronage could give the common man the opportunity to participate in government. He was dismayed that one social class, the "aristocracy," had monopolized public office since the birth of the Republic. The worst that can be said of Jackson is that

his administration helped to perpetuate an extant political practice. He is hardly more to blame than Jefferson for its introduction. Each removed about the same proportion of officeholders, and each made appointments on a partisan basis.

The spoils system grew by leaps and bounds after the close of the Jacksonian era. Thereafter, each successive administration engaged in wholesale removals of political opponents in favor of the loyal supporters of the victorious candidate. When Abraham Lincoln became president in 1860, he removed over 75 percent of the incumbent officeholders he inherited from his predecessors, the most sweeping use of the spoils system to date.

The unrestrained use of the spoils system continued until after the Civil War, characterized by the scandals and corruption of the Grant era. It was not until the assassination of President James A. Garfield in 1881 by a demented officeseeker who personally blamed the president for his rejection that efforts to reform the system met with any success. In 1883 Congress enacted the Pendleton Act, which created the Civil Service Commission and a merit system for appointments to lower federal offices. Since then, successive presidents have, with few exceptions, extended the Civil Service classification list, so that by the mid-1970's more than 90 percent of all nonelective federal positions were included. Eligibility for these offices is determined by competitive examinations. Nevertheless, there are still thousands of officeholders who are not on the classification list whose jobs are considered political spoils for the victorious party.

[Lee Benson, *The Concept of Jacksonian Democracy*; John M. Dobson, *Politics in the Gilded Age: A New Perspective on Reform*; Ari A. Hoogenboom, *Outlawing the Spoils: A History of the Civil Service Reform Movement, 1865–1883*; Martin Tolchin and Susan Tolchin, *To the Victor . . . : Political Patronage From the Clubhouse to the White House.*]

DONALD HERZBERG

SPOKANE HOUSE, a trading post built by the North West Company, a British fur-trading company, in 1810–11 at Spokane Falls, about ten miles north of the present-day city of Spokane, Wash. The center of the Columbia, Kootenay, and Flathead rivers fur trade, it was later taken over by the Hudson's Bay Company. It was abandoned in 1826 for Fort Colville.

[E. Voorhis, *Historic Forts and Trading Posts.*]

CARL L. CANNON

SPOLIATION CLAIMS. *See* **French Spoliation Claims.**

SPORTS. *See individual articles on* **Baseball, Basketball, Golf, Football, Hockey, Horse Racing, Olympic Games, Prizefighting, Skiing, Tennis, Yacht Racing.**

SPOTSWOOD'S EXPEDITION. *See* **Knights of the Golden Horseshoe.**

SPOTSWOOD'S IRON FURNACES were erected by Gov. Alexander Spotswood of Virginia soon after 1716 at Germanna on an extensive land grant about twenty miles above the falls of the Rappahannock River. He began the work with German miners and ironworkers who had been brought to Virginia by a Swiss promoter and left stranded there. Before long, however, he was using black slaves in all except a few skilled positions. The original enterprise was a charcoal-fired smelting furnace that cast sow (or pig) iron from local rock ores and had a capacity of 20 tons a week. Spotswood later built an air furnace at Massaponax, fifteen miles distant, which remelted sows to cast hollowware, chimney backs, andirons, mortars, and other utensils in local demand. Spotswood also had an interest in a third smelting furnace at Fredericksville, a now extinct town thirty miles southwest of Fredericksburg. British as well as colonial capital was engaged in Spotswood's undertakings. Ships brought English coal for remelting iron, limestone for flux, and clay for furnace linings to Spotswood's wharf, and they took aboard his surplus pig iron for the British market. These iron works were very prosperous shortly before the Revolution but soon thereafter records of their operation cease.

[Kathleen Bruce, *Virginia Iron Manufacture in the Slave Era;* William Byrd, *A Progress to the Mines in the Year 1732.*]

VICTOR S. CLARK

SPOTSYLVANIA COURTHOUSE, BATTLE OF (May 8–21, 1864). Union Gen. Gouverneur Warren's Fifth Corps, leading Gen. Ulysses S. Grant's southward march from the Wilderness in Virginia, was stopped northwest of Spotsylvania Courthouse by Confederate Gen. Joseph Kershaw's division, leading Gen. Richard Anderson's corps. Union Gen. John Sedgwick's Sixth Corps joined Warren's left, and late in the afternoon these corps assaulted Anderson but were repulsed. On May 9 the corps of Confederate generals Richard Ewell and Ambrose Hill extended Anderson's line northeast to McCoul's House and, from there, south to Spotsylvania Courthouse; the Confederate troops were entrenched along a front four miles long. Union Gen. Winfield Scott Hancock's Second Corps joined the Fifth and Sixth corps, while Union Gen. Ambrose Burnside's Ninth Corps, marching from Fredericksburg, approached Hill's corps at Spotsylvania. At McCoul's House, Ewell's corps occupied a salient separating Burnside from the three corps of the Union right. On May 10 the latter three corps assaulted Anderson and Ewell and were repulsed. On May 12 Hancock attacked and captured Ewell's salient but was driven back to the outside of the entrenchments. Hancock was reinforced by Burnside and by Gen. Horatio Wright (who assumed command of the Sixth Corps after Sedgwick was killed on May 9), and the opposing armies engaged in hand-to-hand combat all day at this the "Bloody Angle." About midnight Ewell retired to an inner line. Thereafter for some days Grant gradually withdrew his right and pushed his left southward, and on May 20 he marched toward Hanover Courthouse. At the North Anna River, however, Lee again blocked him. Grant's losses at Spotsylvania were 17,000; Lee's, 8,000.

[D. S. Freeman, *R. E. Lee;* Matthew F. Steele, *American Campaigns,* vol. I.]

JOSEPH MILLS HANSON

SPRINGBOK ADMIRALTY CASE elaborated the doctrine of continuous voyage. The *Springbok,* English owned both as to vessel and cargo, was captured by a Union cruiser on June 29, 1862. The neutral port of Nassau was its destination.

The American admiralty courts held that the character of the cargo and the manifests indicated that the merchandise was never intended to be broken up for distribution and use on Nassau, but in reality was intended for immediate transshipment through the Union blockade on a vessel better designed for that perilous voyage. The courts further held that the ultimate destination of the cargo and not of the ship should govern and that the *Springbok* should be released but the cargo confiscated.

The British Foreign Office accepted this decision. Its principle was often invoked against American cargoes (1914–17) intended for Germany via a neutral port.

[John Bassett Moore, *International Law Digest.*]

JIM DAN HILL

SPRINGER V. *UNITED STATES*, 102 U.S. 586 (1881), a case in which the Supreme Court unanimously upheld the validity of a federal income tax. On the basis of precedents it declared that direct taxes, within the meaning of the Constitution, were capitation and real estate taxes. An income tax was not a direct tax, the Court held, and could therefore be levied on individuals without apportionment among the several states.

W. A. ROBINSON

SPRINGFIELD, BATTLE OF (June 23, 1780). When Sir Henry Clinton, commander of British forces in New York, heard rumors of mutiny in George Washington's army at Morristown, N.J., he invaded New Jersey with over 5,000 men (and simultaneously threatened West Point). At Springfield, Maj. Gen. Nathanael Greene, with 1,000 troops, contested Clinton's advance. So vigorous was Greene's defense of the bridge before that town that Clinton proceeded no farther and, after burning the village, returned to Staten Island, in New York.

[Thomas Fleming, *The Forgotten Victory;* Leonard H. Ludin, *Cockpit of the Revolution.*]

C. A. TITUS

SPRING HILL, ENGAGEMENT AT (Nov. 29, 1864). On Nov. 28 the forces of Confederate Gen. John B. Hood and Union Gen. John Schofield faced each other at Columbia, Tenn. (*see* Hood's Tennessee Campaign). During the night Hood moved northward to get across Schofield's line of retreat. Gen. James Wilson, commanding Schofield's cavalry, reported Hood's movement and urged a prompt retreat to Nashville, but Schofield delayed. Hood's troops gained position about Spring Hill, along the line of retreat. After dark on Nov. 29, Schofield's troops marched hurriedly northward within earshot of Hood's army. For some reason, never clearly established, no attack was ordered. By daylight on Nov. 30 Schofield had passed safely northward, and Hood's best opportunity to decisively defeat him had passed. The Battle of Franklin followed.

[Thomas Robson Hay, *Hood's Tennessee Campaign.*]

THOMAS ROBSON HAY

SPRINGS, underground sources of fresh water that frequently determined the location of homes and even villages in pioneer days. Except in the lowlands along the coast, a settler's cabin was almost invariably located close to a spring. So were all forts and blockhouses—although since the spring was usually in a low spot, it was almost inevitably outside the palisade and was therefore a hazard. The heroism of the women of Bryan's Station, Ky., who at dawn on a morning in 1782, when the garrison had become aware that a force of Indians lay in the surrounding woods, went to the spring at some distance down the slope and brought a supply of water, is commemorated by a stone wall monument around the spring and by a plaque. The distilleries of western Pennsylvania and Kentucky all chose large, never-failing springs of pure limestone water as their places of location, and the larger and more famous of these distilleries cherished their springs with particular care ever afterward. The hundreds of place names containing the word "spring"—Springfield, Springville, Springdale, Spring Hill, Spring Valley, Spring Run, Springs, Rock Springs, Green Springs, and many others—indicate the importance of the spring in the mind of the early settler. Many large cities cover the sites of springs that in some cases aided in their founding. There were once many springs on Manhattan Island, some of which still flow through hidden conduits into sewers. Mineral springs gave birth to some of the first vacation resorts in the United States. In the drier portions of the West, the rare freshwater spring or water hole assumed even greater importance, inasmuch as many springs in such areas were apt to be bitter, strongly alkaline, and unpotable. Trails and roads detoured in order to pass good springs, stage and express stations were established at these freshwater sources, and wagon trains and emigrants made them night stopping places.

ALVIN F. HARLOW

SPRING WELLS, TREATY OF, was made near Detroit on Sept. 8, 1815, between the United States and seven Indian tribes of the Northwest. With the Chippewa, Ottawa, and Potawatomi the treaty restored prewar relations, as had been specified by the Treaty of Ghent (ending the War of 1812); with the Seneca, Delaware, Miami, and Shawnee, the new pact confirmed a treaty made at Greenville, Ohio, the preceding year, and granted an amnesty for Indian misdeeds since that time. William Henry Harrison was the head of the U.S. delegation that negotiated the treaty. At the same time the British, at Malden (in what is now Michigan), were holding a similar council with some of the same tribes for a similar purpose, and considerable friction resulted between Harrison and the British officials.

[*American State Papers, Indian Affairs,* vol. II, pp. 15–25; C. J. Kappler, ed., *Indian Affairs, Laws and Treaties,* vol. II, pp. 117–119.]

R. S. COTTERILL

"SPURLOS VERSENKT," a German phrase, meaning "sunk without a trace being left," used by Count Luxburg, the German chargé d'affaires at Buenos Aires, Argentina, in telegrams of May 19 and July 9, 1917, to the foreign office in Berlin. Luxburg advised that Argentine ships be spared by German submarines or else "sunk without a trace being left." These telegrams and many others, which were sent through the Swedish legation in Buenos Aires, were made public in the United States on Sept. 8, 1917, and in consequence the count was expelled by the Argentine government.

BERNADOTTE E. SCHMITT

"SQUARE DEAL," a picturesque phrase used with political significance by Theodore Roosevelt while he was president to symbolize his personal attitude toward current topics of the period. He first used the phrase in Kansas while on a tour of the western states as he explained the principles later to be embodied in the platform of the Progressive party. The "square deal" included Roosevelt's ideals of citizenship, the dignity of labor, nobility of parenthood, great wealth, success, and the essence of Christian character. Later it was applied to industry. The phrase was extremely popular in 1906.

[Theodore Roosevelt, *A Square Deal.*]

FRANK MARTIN LEMON

SQUATTER SOVEREIGNTY. *See* **Popular Sovereignty.**

SQUATTERS' SOCIETIES. *See* **Claim Associations.**

SQUAW CAMPAIGN (February 1778). Gen. Edward Hand, who had been sent by Gen. George Washington to defend the western frontier, ordered out the militia of Westmoreland County, Pa., to seize some military stores at Sandusky (in what is now northern Ohio). The troops, hindered by wet weather

from reaching their objective, fell on two small camps of Indians composed mainly of Delaware women and children. One or two squaws were killed and two captured, who were later sent back to their tribe. The expedition proved a failure.

[R. G. Thwaites and L. P. Kellogg, *Frontier Defense on the Upper Ohio.*]

LOUISE PHELPS KELLOGG

SQUIER TREATY (Sept. 3, 1849) was signed by Ephraim George Squier, diplomatic agent of President Zachary Taylor, with Nicaragua. It gave the United States exclusive rights to a transisthmian canal route through Nicaragua. It differed in detail from its unapproved predecessor, the Hise Treaty (June 21, 1849), but was only a degree less challenging to England in that it recognized Nicaraguan sovereignty over the territory of the Mosquito Indians, then under British control. Although disapproved and discarded in favor of the Clayton-Bulwer Treaty (1850) with England, Squier's treaty was nevertheless symptomatic of the new, though premature, American determination not only to have a canal, but to make good the Monroe Doctrine. It was one of a series of incidents that focused Anglo-American rivalry in the Caribbean on Nicaragua. (*See also* Panama Canal.)

[Samuel Flagg Bemis, *The American Secretaries of State and Their Diplomacy,* vol. VI.]

RICHARD W. VAN ALSTYNE

"SQUIRREL HUNTERS," a term referring to a southern Ohio militia hastily gathered in 1862 when Cincinnati was in imminent danger of attack by Confederate troops (*see* Kentucky, Invasion of). Gov. David Tod called for help, asking the men to bring their own arms. The response was largely from rural districts, and the equipment that of men accustomed to squirrel hunting.

[N. E. Jones, *The Squirrel Hunters.*]

HARLOW LINDLEY

STABILIZATION FUND. *See* **Gold Standard.**

STAFFORD V. WALLACE, 258 U.S. 495 (1922). The Packers and Stockyards Act of 1921 gave to the secretary of agriculture the authority to regulate the operations of the livestock dealers and commission men. In a case that T. F. Stafford and others brought against Secretary of Agriculture Henry C. Wallace, the act was challenged on the ground that such businesses were not in interstate commerce, but were purely local in character. In the decision handed down by the Supreme Court on May 1, 1922, Chief Justice William Howard Taft declared that the stockyards and commission houses "are but the throat through which the current [of interstate commerce] flows," and that such regulation was a proper exercise of federal power under the Constitution.

[R. A. Clemen, *The American Livestock and Meat Industry.*]

ERNEST S. OSGOOD

STAGE, FISHING, a high wooden platform built on the shore for drying fish. Less specifically, the term is also used for the place on which the land operations—cleaning, curing, and oil extraction—connected with fishing were carried on. The most famous American stages were those along the Newfoundland, Nova Scotia, and New England coasts. A picture of one taken from an old woodcut may be found in D. W. Prowse, *History of Newfoundland.*

ROBERT E. MOODY

STAGECOACH LINES OF THE SOUTHWEST.
The California gold discovery of 1848 and the consequent rush of the Forty-niners made necessary transcontinental stagecoach lines. In the summer of 1849 stage service was provided between Independence, Mo., and Santa Fe, N.Mex.; and two years later another was instituted between Independence and Salt Lake City. Coaches over the central route made monthly runs. But a more satisfactory service was provided in 1857 between San Antonio, Tex., and San Diego, Calif., via the Gila Trail (1,475 miles) when semimonthly coaches were used on an approximate thirty-day schedule.

Within the next decade thousands of miles of stage lines were in use. John Butterfield and his associates began the Southern Overland Mail in September 1858 over the long "oxbow" route from Saint Louis to San Francisco via Fort Smith, Ark., across the Choctaw Nation, the frontier of Texas, and thence by El Paso, Tucson, and San Diego (2,795 miles). Memphis was made one of the eastern termini when a branch line made connection with the other at Fort Smith. A Colorado gold discovery (1858) also made possible another line, the Leavenworth and Pikes Peak Company. Ben Holladay entered the field (1862) with his extensive operations and purchased the interests of Russell, Majors, and Waddell in the

Central Overland California and Pikes Peak Express Company (which had previously taken over the Leavenworth and Pikes Peak Company). One of his lines extended from Atchison, Kans., to Denver (687 miles); another from Denver to Salt Lake City, passing over the Rocky Mountains at Bridger's Pass; and a triweekly line from Salt Lake City to the Dalles in northern Oregon (950 miles). A branch line connected Virginia City, Mont., with the main line at Fort Hall. Because of losses incurred during Indian uprisings in 1864–65, he sold his interests in 1866 to Wells, Fargo and Company.

[LeRoy Hafen, *The Overland Mail;* C. C. Rister, *Southern Plainsmen.*]

C. C. RISTER

STAGECOACH ROBBERIES occurred in eastern and middle western America, but the dramatic character of western holdups, together with the large amounts of booty secured, make them more important historically. Of these the California robberies stand out because of the movement of gold ore through the express companies who used stagecoaches to transport it. The first robbery of importance was in 1852 when Reelfoot Williams' gang took $7,500 from the express strong box. The work was carried on by "Rattlesnake Dick" Barter whose gang robbed the Wells, Fargo mule team of $80,000 in gold dust in 1855 and Rhode and Lusk's express of $26,000 in 1856. He was succeeded by Tom Bell, "gentleman highwayman." In 1856 the Bell gang tried to take $100,000 in gold from the Marysville stage, but were fought off almost singlehanded by the armed messenger. Following this attempt Bell was captured and hanged. In fifteen years of operation ending in 1869 Wells, Fargo and Company had suffered 313 stage robberies. A second era of stage holdups followed the discovery of gold in the Black Hills of South Dakota. The Wall-Blackburn gang operated in 1877 and 1878. Since the treasure on some of the coaches amounted to as much as $140,000, there were frequent attempts but not many successful large robberies, as the stage lines supplied the best guards that could be found.

[J. Brown and A. M. Willard, *Black Hills Trails;* A. F. Harlow, *Old Waybills.*]

CARL L. CANNON

STAGECOACH TRAVEL. The first successful stagecoach lines in America were established in the northern colonies in the two decades before the Revolution, most of them running to nearby places from the three largest cities, Boston, New York, and Philadelphia. The only lines connecting large cities were those between Boston and Providence, between New York and Philadelphia, and between Philadelphia and Baltimore. In each instance a short land journey was substituted for a long water passage. No stagecoaches ran south of Annapolis in colonial times.

These lines were halted by the Revolution, but most of them were again in motion before the treaty of peace was signed. They were aided financially and clothed with greater public interest when, in 1785, Congress first provided for the carrying of mail by stagecoach to those areas where the mail had grown too heavy for horse and rider. Slowly the mail stage network widened, the U.S. Post Office encouraging and frequently, through its mail contracts, giving financial assistance to proprietors who established lines through new territory. Such assistance resulted in 1803 in the first line connecting the central Atlantic states with the Carolinas and Georgia. The Ohio Valley was first penetrated by a line established to Pittsburgh in 1804. Rapid development of stagecoach facilities west of the Alleghenies did not take place until the Jacksonian era when Post Office subsidies increased greatly. The mileage of mail stage lines tripled between 1828 and 1838, the latter date representing approximately the peak of staging activity east of the Mississippi River.

As lines were thrust westward with the advancing frontier, service on the older roads in the East grew more rapid and more frequent, and additional local routes were established until there were few villages that did not have a stagecoach arriving and departing several times a week. On the busier roads stagecoach companies ran both "limited" mail coaches, taking but a few passengers through rapidly at higher fares, and "accommodation" coaches that traveled more slowly, stopped more frequently along the way, and allowed the full resting time at night. Landlords of taverns where the stages stopped were usually partners in the line, a community of interest along the road being thus established. Stages of rival lines stopped at rival taverns. Eventually, large stagecoach companies controlled the paying lines in certain areas, and these companies in turn formed working agreements with each other. The Post Office, because of its interest in efficiency and smooth connecting arrangements, generally tolerated these large combinations of interest. (*See also* Post Roads.)

After railroads invaded the heaviest routes of travel the stage lines became extensions of advancing railheads or feeders from fertile tributary areas. The amount of staging did not necessarily decline at once, for the railroads encouraged travel and shipping and often furnished the stages with more business than they had previously known. Ultimately, however, when the railroads had completed their trunk lines and built branches into the more profitable tributary regions, the stagecoaches were forced back to a marginal fringe that it did not pay the railroads to develop. In mountainous regions in both East and West they lingered, serving isolated valleys and villages until the coming of the motor bus.

[Ralph Moody, *Stagecoach West;* Oscar O. Winther, *Transportation Frontier: Trans-Mississippi West, 1865–1890,* and *Via Western Express and Stagecoach.*]

OLIVER W. HOLMES

STAKED PLAIN, or **Llano Estacado,** is the name applied to the high level part of northwest Texas and eastern New Mexico that lies above the Cap Rock escarpment. It is bounded on the north by the Canadian River and on the west by the Mescalero Ridge. Francisco Vásquez de Coronado led the first expedition of white men across it (1541), and later other Spaniards visited it. It was so named, perhaps, because one such expedition drove stakes at intervals by which to retrace their route. Another explanation is that the numerous stalks of the yucca plant, which grows in abundance in the area, suggested a "plain of stakes" to the Spanish explorers. The Comanche occupied the region until about 1880, and the whites did not consider it worth wresting from them. Within the decade 1880–90 the buffalo was extinguished, the Comanche were expelled, the Fort Worth and Denver Railroad was built across the plain, and the huge XIT Ranch was being formed by the Capitol Syndicate out of the 3 million acres that were granted to it by the state of Texas. The plain soon became cattle country, and later a dry farming and oil and natural-gas producing region.

[Fred W. Allsop, *Albert Pike;* J. E. Haley, *The XIT Ranch.*]

L. W. NEWTON

STALWARTS, a term applied to certain conservative Republican leaders led by Sen. Roscoe Conkling of New York. They opposed the southern policy and the civil-service reform program of Rutherford B. Hayes's administration and dubbed his adherents "Halfbreeds." Although the Stalwarts were unsuccessful in securing Ulysses S. Grant's nomination for a third presidential term in 1880, one of their henchmen, Chester A. Arthur, was awarded the vice-presidential nomination. After Conkling's retirement from politics in the 1880's the designation soon passed out of use.

[E. P. Oberholtzer, *A History of the United States Since the Civil War,* vol. III.]

ASA E. MARTIN

STAMP ACT. By 1763 British and colonial arms had driven French power from Canada. The extension of the British colonial empire raised new and serious problems. The conquest of Canada brought under British rule disaffected French and hostile Indians. In 1763 Indians led by Pontiac, fearing British rule and colonial encroachment on their land, fell on the frontier settlements in a devastating attack. It was clear that garrisons were needed on the long border to guard the colonists against Indian attack and the Indians against predatory whites. It was equally clear that the control of frontier affairs could no longer be left to the separate colonies with their conflicting interests. Frontier problems became more than ever a matter of common concern to be met and solved by the British government as the central authority.

The garrisoning of the border meant a heavy expense, and at once the financial question became a decisive factor. The estimates fixed £320,000 as the cost of supporting an American army of 10,000 men for defense in the mainland colonies and the West Indies. Where should this financial burden fall? The French war had doubled the British national debt, bringing it to the sum of £130,000,000 with a yearly interest charge of £4,500,000. In addition to the support of a colonial military force, increased estimates were necessary to maintain British naval supremacy. So heavy was the strain on the British taxpayer that the ministry decided to call on the colonies to share the expense of the American army. This decision once made, another decisive question arose. Should the colonial share be levied by the several colonial representative bodies or by the British Parliament? In the past, Parliament had not taxed the colonies for revenue purposes. In time of imperial wars, royal requisitions were sent to the colonies to raise and pay troops to cooperate with the British forces. But the realities of the French and Indian War plainly showed that the requisition system was inefficient and unfair. A general lack of vigorous cooperation impaired military operation. The military burden was not equitably distributed, a few colonies responded loyally, some half-heartedly, others far short of their abilities. This conduct led during the war to proposals to tax the colonies by act of Parliament. The Indian uprising under Pontiac further revealed that the colonies could not be depended on for adequate frontier defense, nor would they share the burden equitably.

These facts decided the British ministry to resort to the levy of a parliamentary tax on the colonies. The first step was the passage of the Sugar Act of 1764. The old severe duties on colonial trade with the foreign West Indies were reduced in the hope that it would yield some revenue, probably £45,000. This was held to be less than the colonial share, and Sir George Grenville, chancellor of the Exchequer, proposed a stamp tax on the colonies. He deferred the plan a year to give the colonies an opportunity to suggest means more to their liking. They protested strongly against a stamp act and suggested nothing more than taxation by the colonial assemblies as of old. Grenville conferred with the colonial agents in London, among them Benjamin Franklin of Pennsylvania and Jared Ingersoll of Connecticut. The agents pleaded for the old method of raising revenue in the colonies. To this Grenville countered by asking if the colonies could agree on the quotas each should raise and whether it was certain every colony would raise its quotas. In the light of past experience, the agents had no answer to these questions. And so Parliament proceeded to pass the Stamp Act of 1765 with a heavy majority. The use of stamps was required on all legal and commercial papers, pamphlets, newspapers, almanacs, cards, and dice. The law provided for a Stamp Office in London, an inspector for each of the colonial districts, and a stamp distributor for each colony. The estimated yield from stamps ranged from £60,000 to £100,000, collected in both mainland colonies and the West Indies. The combined revenues of the Sugar and Stamp acts, £105,000 to £145,000, would meet less than half the cost of the American garrison forces.

Few in England realized the significance of the stamp tax. Parliament, in harmony with the rule not to receive petitions against revenue bills, did not heed the colonial protests. The ministers and Parliament felt that the law was a fair solution of a pressing problem. Even the colonial agents failed to understand the colonial temper. Franklin nominated a stamp distributor for Pennsylvania and Ingersoll accepted the post for Connecticut. News of the Stamp Act blew up a colonial storm. Parliamentary taxation for revenue was an innovation that threatened the very foundation of colonial self-government and outraged the precious right of Englishmen to be taxed only by their consent. Colonial opposition nullified the Stamp Act in 1766.

[John R. Alden, *General Gage in America;* Lawrence H. Gipson, *The Coming of the Revolution, 1763–1775;* Edmund S. Morgan and Helen M. Morgan, *The Stamp Act Crisis;* John Shy, *Toward Lexington: The Role of the British Army in the Coming of the American Revolution.*]

WINFRED T. ROOT

STAMP ACT CONGRESS (1765). The Stamp Act and other recent British statutes menaced self-rule in all the colonies and thus furnished a principle of union. The House of Representatives of Massachusetts, appreciating the value of united effort, issued in June a call to all the colonies to send delegates to New York City. Nine colonies responded, and a total of twenty-seven delegates met in the City Hall from Oct. 7 to Oct. 25. They framed resolutions of colonial rights and grievances and petitioned king and Parliament to repeal the objectionable legislation. They held that taxing the colonies without their consent violated one of the most precious rights of Englishmen. Since distance precluded colonial representation in the British Parliament, they could be taxed only by their local assemblies (*see* Colonial Assemblies) in which they were represented. The congress is significant in that parliamentary threats to colonial self-control fostered the movement that slowly brought to maturity the spirit and agencies of national unity.

[C. H. Van Tyne, *Causes of the War of Independence.*]

WINFRED T. ROOT

STAMP ACT RIOT. On Nov. 1, 1765, as a part of the agitation against the Stamp Act that had gone into effect that day, the Sons of Liberty erected a sham gallows on the Common in New York City and hung there effigies of Lt. Gov. Cadwallader Colden with the devil whispering in his ear. They marched to Fort George where the stamps were being kept, threw bricks and stones at it, and taunted the soldiers. They seized the lieutenant governor's coach and burned it, together with the gallows and effigies, in front of the fort. Next they broke into another British official's house, gutted it, and burned the furnishings in the street. Their secretly promulgated threats of vengeance effectually blocked the use of the stamps.

[Martha J. Lamb, *History of New York City.*]

ALVIN F. HARLOW

STAMPEDES were the most dramatic, hazardous, and disastrous events of roundups and cattle drives.

Oxen, horses, buffalo, all might stampede, but the frantic flight that the rancheros called *estampida* was especially characteristic of longhorns. A great herd peacefully bedded down might, with the instantaneity of forked lightning, be on its feet, and then with hoofs, hocks, and horns knocking together, the ground shaking from the impact, thunder away in headlong flight. The only way to check them was to circle the leaders and thus swing the mass into a "mill." Causes of stampedes were many—the whir of a rattlesnake near the head of some snoring steer, the flirt of a polecat's tail, the jump of a rabbit, the smell of a lobo, the flash of a match by some careless cowboy lighting a cigarette, any unexpected sound such as the shaking of an empty saddle by a horse. Cowboy songs were not so much to soothe cattle as to afford a barrier against surprises. But the best preventives were bellies full of grass and water.

Western artists like Frederic Remington, Charles M. Russell, and Frank Reaugh have pictured the stampede. Popular ballads like "Lasca" and "When Work's All Done This Fall" have dramatized it. One of the most powerful stories ever written on any western subject—*Longrope's Last Guard,* by Russell—translates it fully. Yet, human fatalities from stampedes were rare. The worst results of the stampedes were to the cattle themselves—animals trampled to death, horns and legs broken, and more "tallow run off" in a night than could be restored by a month of grazing.

[J. Evetts Haley, *Charles Goodnight, Cowman and Plainsman;* W. M. Raine and W. C. Barnes, *Cattle;* C. M. Russell, *Trails Plowed Under.*]

J. FRANK DOBIE

STANDARD OIL COMPANY, an Ohio corporation, was incorporated on Jan. 10, 1870, with a capital of $1 million, the original stockholders being John D. Rockefeller (2,667 shares); William Rockefeller (1,333 shares); Henry M. Flagler (1,333 shares); Samuel Andrews (1,333 shares); Stephen V. Harkness (1,334 shares); O. B. Jennings (1,000 shares); and the firm of Rockefeller, Andrews and Flagler (1,000 shares). It took the place of the previous firm of Rockefeller, Andrews and Flagler (formed 1867), whose refineries were the largest in Cleveland and probably the largest in the world at that time. Important extensions were immediately made. Thanks partly to these refineries, partly to superior efficiency, and partly to the threat of the South Improvement Company, Standard Oil early in 1872 swallowed practically all rival refineries in the Cleveland area. The roster of stockholders on Jan. 1, 1872, was slightly increased, and the capital raised to $2.5 million. Coincidentally with the conquest of Cleveland, Standard Oil began reaching out to other cities. In 1872 it bought the oil transporting and refining firm of J. A. Bostwick and Company in New York; the Long Island Oil Company; and a controlling share of the Devoe Manufacturing Company on Long Island. In 1873 it bought pipelines, the largest refinery in the oil regions, and a half interest in a Louisville refinery. The acquisition of the principal refineries of Pittsburgh and Philadelphia was carried out in 1874–76, while in 1877 Standard Oil defeated the Pennsylvania Railroad and the Empire Transportation Company in a major struggle, taking possession of the pipelines and refineries of the latter. Another war with the Tidewater Pipeline resulted in a working agreement that drastically limited the latter's operations. By 1879 Standard Oil, with its subsidiary and associated companies, controlled from 90 percent to 95 percent of the refining capacity of the United States, immense pipeline and storage-tank systems, and powerful marketing organizations at home and abroad. Under John D. Rockefeller's leadership it was the first company in the world to organize the whole of a huge, complex, and extremely rich industry. In 1875 the stock of Standard Oil was increased to a total of $3.5 million, the million dollars of new stock being taken by Charles Pratt and Company; Warden, Frew and Company; and Harkness. In 1879 there were thirty-seven stockholders, of whom Rockefeller, with 8,894 shares, held nearly three times as much as any other man.

While Standard Oil of Ohio remained legally a small company with no manufacturing operations outside its state, practically it was the nucleus of an almost nationwide industrial organization, the richest and most powerful in the country. Its articles of incorporation had not authorized it to hold stock in other companies nor to be a partner in any firm. It had met this difficulty by acquiring stocks not in the name of Standard Oil of Ohio, but in that of some one prominent stockholder as trustee. Flagler, William Rockefeller, Bostwick, and various others served from 1873 to 1879 as trustees. Then in 1879 the situation was given more systematic treatment. All the stocks acquired by Standard Oil and held by various trustees, and all the properties outside Ohio in which Standard Oil had an interest, were transferred to three minor employees (George H. Vilas, Myron R. Keith, George F. Chester) as trustees. They held the stocks and properties for the exclusive use and benefit of Standard Oil's stockholders and distributed dividends in specified proportions. But while this arrangement was satisfactory from a legal point of view, it did not provide sufficient administrative centralization. On Jan. 2, 1882, therefore, a new arrangement, the Standard Oil Trust Agreement, set up the first trust in the sense of a monopoly in American history. All stock and properties, including that of the Standard Oil proper as well as of interests outside Ohio, were transferred to a board of nine trustees, consisting of the principal owners and managers, with John D. Rockefeller as head. For each share of stock of Standard Oil of Ohio, twenty trust certificates of a par value of $100 each were to be issued. The total of the trust certificates was therefore $70 million, considerably less than the actual value of the properties. Standard Oil's huge network of refineries, pipes, tanks, and marketing systems was thus given a secret, but for the time being satisfactory, legal organization, while administration was centralized in nine able men with John D. Rockefeller at their head.

This situation lasted until 1892, Standard Oil constantly growing in wealth and power. Then, as the result of a decree by the Ohio courts, the Standard Oil Trust dissolved, and the separate establishments and plants were reorganized into twenty constituent companies. But by informal arrangement, unity of action was maintained among these twenty corporations until they were gathered into a holding company (Standard Oil of New Jersey) in 1899. Then in 1911 a decree of the U.S. Supreme Court forced a more complete dissolution (*see Standard Oil Company of New Jersey* v. *United States*). Rockefeller remained nominal head of Standard Oil until 1911, but after 1895 he had surrendered more and more of the actual authority to his associates, with John D. Archbold as their chief.

[Ralph W. Hidy and Muriel E. Hidy, *Pioneering in Big Business, 1882–1911;* Allan Nevins, *Study in Power: John D. Rockefeller;* Harold F. Williamson, *The American Petroleum Industry.*]

ALLAN NEVINS

STANDARD OIL COMPANY OF NEW JERSEY V. UNITED STATES, 221 U.S. 1 (1911), originated in 1906 when the federal government filed a suit against more than seventy corporations and individuals alleging that they were conspiring "to restrain the trade and commerce in petroleum . . . in refined oil, and in other products of petroleum" in violation of the Sherman Antitrust Act of 1890. In 1909 the U.S. Circuit Court for the Eastern District of Missouri upheld the charge. The court's decree held that the combining of the stocks of various companies in the hands of the Standard Oil Company of New Jersey in 1899 constituted "a combination in restraint of trade and also an attempt to monopolize and a monopolization under Sec. 2 of the Antitrust Act." The New Jersey corporation was forbidden to control thirty-seven subsidiary companies or to vote their stock. In other words, thirty-eight ostensibly independent companies were to be formed. On May 15, 1911, the decree was upheld by the Supreme Court, which declared that applications of the antitrust law should "be determined by the light of reason."

This decision, confirming the dissolution of the so-called Standard Oil Trust, has often been erroneously confused with a 1907 decree by District Judge Kenesaw M. Landis, fining the Standard Oil Company of Indiana a total of $29,240,000 for receiving "an unlawful secret rate" from a railroad in violation of the Elkins Act of 1903. This decree, reversed in 1908 by the Seventh Circuit Court of Appeals, was not reviewed by the Supreme Court.

ERIK MCKINLEY ERIKSSON

STANDARDS, NATIONAL BUREAU OF. *See* **National Bureau of Standards.**

STANDARDS OF LIVING are most often measured by per capita national income, although some scholars prefer the related measure, per capita consumption of goods and services. On the basis of per capita income, the American standard of living has been among the highest in the world since the early 18th century. Long-term changes in the standard of living were probably modest before the 1840's, but have been pronounced since. Between 1840 and 1970 per capita income, after allowance for price changes, increased sevenfold. The rate of change has varied from year to year, being affected by business cycles and Kuznets cycles (fluctuations of about 20 years' duration), developed by Simon Kuznets, and has been slightly higher on the average in the 20th century than in the 19th century. Japan and many Western European countries have experienced roughly comparable rates of improvement in per capita income in the 20th century, although few of these countries have approached the U.S. level.

Standards of living have varied from region to region in the United States. Incomes of families in the Midwest and, especially, the South have tended to be lower than those of families in the Northeast and Far West. This reflects the concentration of farming, traditionally a low-income industry, in the former

regions. (The measured differences may exaggerate standard of living differences, because some components of income on farms are inadequately reflected in national income.) Regional differences, after widening between the middle and end of the 19th century (because of the effects of the Civil War), have narrowed drastically in the 20th century. This development has been the result of the industrialization of the Midwest and the South and the relative improvement in agricultural incomes.

The distribution of income by size has been roughly the same in the United States as in most Western European nations for which data are available. Just before the Civil War the richest 5 percent of U.S. families probably had about eight times as much income per family as the remaining 95 percent. There does not seem to have been any major change until after the 1920's, when the degree of inequality diminished somewhat, the rich losing and the poor gaining, in relative terms. By the 1950's the richest 5 percent had about five times the income per family of the remaining 95 percent. From then to the mid-1970's the distribution was rather stable, those in the middle-income groups gaining slightly at the expense of both rich and poor.

[Lance E. Davis, Richard A. Easterlin, William N. Parker, and others, *American Economic Growth, An Economist's History of the United States.*]

ROBERT E. GALLMAN

STANDARD TIME. *See* **Railroads.**

STANDING ORDER. From the earliest settlements until the end of the 18th century, New England was dominated by a close association of the clergy, the magistrates, and the well-to-do, which consciously controlled political, economic, social, and intellectual life. This control rested on popular acceptance, a limited suffrage, and the special legal position of the Congregational church, and was so firmly established as to win the name of the Standing Order. Its members were aristocratic and intensely conservative, and failed to hold out against the growing democracy of the early 19th century.

[H. Adams, *History of the United States.*]

HERBERT W. HILL

"STANDPATTERS," a term that came into political parlance in connection with the cleavage in the Republican party during President William Howard

Taft's administration over the Payne-Aldrich tariff, the Ballinger-Pinchot affair, and Cannonism. The insurgent Republicans, styling themselves "progressives," called the conservatives "standpatters" and denounced them as satisfied with the present social order, as being against reform, and as devoted to the vested interests. This factional difference contributed to the election of a Democratic House of Representatives in 1910 and led to the Republican split of 1912.

[J. A. Woodburn, *Political Parties and Party Problems in the United States.*]

GLENN H. BENTON

STANSBURY EXPLORATION (1849–50), led by Capt. Howard Stansbury of the U.S. Army, had for its object a survey of the valley of the Great Salt Lake, an inspection of the Mormon colony, and an examination of a new route through the mountains. These were all accomplished in the face of difficulties, and Stansbury's illustrated report (1852) and accompanying atlases make it one of the most interesting and valuable explorations ever made under government auspices.

[H. Stansbury, *Expedition to Valley of Great Salt Lake.*]

CARL L. CANNON

STANTON, FORT, was established by the U.S. Army in Lincoln County, N.Mex., in 1856 to hold the Apache in check. In 1871 the Mescalero Apache were placed on a reservation in the southeastern part of the county. Charges and countercharges of theft were made by Indians and whites. The fort was abandoned Aug. 17, 1896.

[C. C. Rister, *Southwestern Frontier.*]

CARL L. CANNON

STANWIX, FORT. In 1758 the old fort at the Oneida (upstate New York) carrying place, which had been destroyed by Gen. Daniel Webb after the French captured Oswego in 1756, was rebuilt and named Stanwix after its builder, Gen. John Stanwix. Its strategic location between the upper Mohawk River and Wood Creek made it an important point of defense during the colonial period and a center of Indian trade and treaties. After the conclusion of peace with the French in 1763, the fort was used by Sir William Johnson, superintendent of Indian affairs, as the site of a meeting in November 1768 at which the Iroquois signed the first Treaty of Fort Stanwix. The fort was allowed

to fall into disrepair, and at the beginning of the Revolution was found to be untenable. It was rebuilt and for a time called Fort Schuyler in honor of Gen. Philip J. Schuyler. It was there that in 1777 British Gen. Barry St. Leger was held back on his way to Albany by soldiers under Gen. Benedict Arnold. After being severely damaged by fire and flood in 1781, the fort was rebuilt, renamed Fort Stanwix, and in 1784 used for the negotiation of the second Treaty of Fort Stanwix. Immigrants from New England swarmed into the region, and a village, the present city of Rome, was founded on the site of the fort.

[J. A. Scott, *Fort Stanwix and Oriskany.*]

A. C. FLICK

STANWIX, FORT, TREATY OF (1768). The elimination of French authority from North America in 1763 after the French and Indian War led to English settlement in the tramontane regions and exacerbated relations with the Indians. The proclamation of 1763, establishing the Appalachians as the dividing line between white settlements and Indian lands, was only a temporary expedient, and London officials sought to reduce tensions on the frontier by establishing a more tenable line of demarcation. Colonial land speculators, who had an interest in any new boundary, lobbied to hasten the conclusion of treaties with the tribes, but it was not until early 1768 that two Indian superintendents, Sir William Johnson and John Stuart, received instructions to proceed with negotiations.

Johnson met with the Iroquois and their allies at Fort Stanwix on the Mohawk River in upstate New York in October and November 1768. Ostensibly on their own initiative, but probably at Johnson's urging, the Iroquois ceded far more land than the British government had sought to obtain. The new boundary ran south from Fort Stanwix to the Delaware River, where it turned in a southwesterly direction to the Allegheny, and followed that river and the Ohio to the confluence with the Tennessee. The Iroquois agreed to surrender all claim to lands east and south of this line. Within the area of the cession, moreover, certain land speculators received a direct grant of land, known as Indiana and previously claimed by Virginia, along the upper Ohio River. The inclusion of the area between the Kanawha and Tennessee rivers, clearly beneficial to Virginia land interests, was undoubtedly an attempt to gain the acquiescence of that colony in the Indiana grant. By accepting so large a cession, Johnson had violated his instructions, and the Board of Trade condemned his actions in April 1769.

The Treaty of Fort Stanwix had far-reaching repercussions. It forced the revision of an agreement made with the Cherokee by Stuart at Hard Labor, S.C., in October 1768, for the two boundaries conflicted. The inclusion of a private grant within the terms of the treaty created a precedent that led other speculators to seek similar concessions. The Iroquois, moreover, had disposed of lands on which other tribes, notably the Shawnee and Delaware, lived and hunted. The resentment felt by these Indians increased as white settlement pressed against them, and Lord Dunmore's War, a localized conflict between Virginians and the Shawnee, broke out in 1774. Hence, the Treaty of Fort Stanwix increased, rather than ameliorated, tensions in the West.

[James T. Flexner, *Mohawk Baronet: Sir William Johnson of New York;* Barbara Graymont, *The Iroquois in the American Revolution;* Jack Sosin, *Whitehall and the Wilderness: The Middle West in British Colonial Policy, 1760–1775.*]

JEROME C. REDDY

STANWIX, FORT, TREATY OF (1784). The powerful Iroquois had been greatly weakened by the vigorous campaigns of Gen. John Sullivan and Col. Daniel Brodhead during the revolutionary war, and their leaders recognized the futility of further resistance to the white advance. Consequently at Fort Stanwix on Oct. 22, 1784, they ceded a small tract of land in western New York, and all that part of Pennsylvania north and west of the Indian boundary line established by the 1768 Treaty of Fort Stanwix (constituting about one-fourth of the area of the state). They also relinquished their claim to land west of the Ohio River—a claim that was disputed by other tribes.

[Charles C. Royce, *Indian Land Cessions in the United States.*]

DAN E. CLARK

STAPLES, COLONIAL. The continental British-American colonies had three important staple crops— tobacco, rice, and indigo. Tobacco was a major crop in Virginia, Maryland, and parts of North Carolina. It also was an enumerated commodity and found its chief market in England and Scotland where it was graded, processed, and shipped to the various markets of the world. Rice was mainly grown on the lowlands of South Carolina and Georgia. It found its chief market in England, the West Indies, and in southern Europe. As England could not use the entire rice crop, it was permitted to be marketed in Europe south of Cape Finisterre in northwest Spain. Indigo was produced only in South Carolina and some of the West Indies, because it requires a rich soil and special treatment. The growing of indigo was encouraged by British bounties, and the crop was marketed almost entirely in England.

In the British West Indies, especially in Barbados, sugar was an important staple crop. This product, like the other staples, was enumerated and was shipped largely to England, where it was refined and marketed throughout the British Empire and Europe. Molasses was an important by-product of this industry and was used directly by the rum distilling industry in England and America.

The staple industries had several things in common. Each tended to become a plantation-type crop where the labor was almost exclusively done by slaves. Such single-crop farming tended to develop irregular production, absentee landlords, and dependence on foreign financing and foreign markets. All, except indigo, were bulky and required extensive shipping to carry them to England.

[George Louis Beer, *The Old Colonial System.*]

O. M. DICKERSON

STARE DECISIS is conventionally described as the principle of deciding judicial controversies and cases on the basis of precedent. Traditionally, it has been described as a principle of the common-law legal systems that distinguishes them from civil-law systems. In American and British legal circles, adherence to precedent is frequently cited as an attribute ensuring stability not only in the legal system but in the political system as well. Both the cross-cultural and the Anglo-American assumptions concerning the significance and impact of adherence to *stare decisis* have been subjected to serious logical and empirical challenges. For example, despite a substantial body of opinion (ranging from Alexis de Tocqueville to contemporary leaders of the bar) supporting the assumption that *stare decisis* ensures legal and political stability, legal realists and empiricists have openly attacked it. Karl N. Llewellyn summed up the realists' objection succinctly: "The doctrine of precedent is two-headed . . . Janus-faced. . . . There is one doctrine for getting rid of precedents deemed troublesome and one doctrine for making use of precedents that seem helpful." The continuing controversy over the scope and significance of *stare decisis* has served to focus greater analytical and empirical attention on the total constellation of factors that may influence judicial decisionmaking.

[Walter P. Armstrong, "Mr. Justice Douglas and *Stare Decisis*," *American Bar Association Journal*, vol. 35 (1949); Karl N. Llewellyn, *The Common Law Tradition: Deciding Appeals*; Robert Rantoul, Jr., "Oration at Scituate," in Perry Miller, ed., *The Legal Mind in America*; Alexis de Tocqueville, *Democracy in America*.]

JOHN R. SCHMIDHAUSER

STAR OF THE WEST, an unarmed merchant vessel that President James Buchanan, influenced by Unionist cabinet members, secretly dispatched on Jan. 5, 1861, with troops and supplies to reinforce Maj. Robert Anderson at Fort Sumter, S.C. Reaching Charleston harbor on Jan. 9, the vessel was fired on by the batteries on Morris Island and Fort Moultrie. Neither Anderson nor the vessel's commander returned the fire, and the *Star of the West* withdrew. It was captured by Confederate forces on Apr. 20, 1861.

[F. E. Chadwick, *Causes of the Civil War;* S. W. Crawford, *Genesis of the Civil War*.]

FLETCHER M. GREEN

STAR ROUTE FRAUDS. Star routes were roads, principally in the West, where mail was carried, under private contracts, by wagons or horses. Extensive frauds in the Post Office Department caused great financial losses to the government. Departmental officials, contractors, subcontractors, and a former senator were in conspiracy. This "gang" demanded more congressional appropriations for starting new and useless routes; fraudulent and padded petitions supported their demands for money to expedite old routes; worthless bonds and securities were imposed on the department; and contractors exacted fines and profits from subcontractors. One $90,000 contract was let on the affidavit of one contractor. Another route with $761 income annually was expedited in speed and number of trips at a cost of $50,000, although for thirty-nine days no papers or letters were carried over that road. Analysis of the specifications of John M. Peck, one contractor, showed requirements that each horse had to travel twenty hours daily and the rider forty hours daily. Congressional investigations, special agents, Pinkerton detectives, and attorneys brought about more than twenty-five indictments. Trials in 1882 and 1883 proved frauds on ninety-three routes, but no convictions resulted. The government was defrauded of about $4 million.

LOUIS PELZER

STARS, FALLING OF THE (Nov. 12–13, 1833), was the most sublime heavenly phenomenon in American history. A meteor shower, visible over a large portion of the United States, occurs every November and peaks every 133 years. During the "falling of the stars" in November 1833, the meteors descended as numerous as snowflakes in the most severe storm and with lightning speed. At Niagara Falls a luminous table appeared above the falls emitting streams of fire. At Fort Leavenworth, Kans., soldiers could read ordinary print at the darkest hour of night. Sailors far out on the Atlantic Ocean and trappers in the Rocky Mountains also reported the spectacular display. Many religious people interpreted the phenomenon as a sign of the end of the world. The meteoric storm continued until it was rendered invisible by the light of day. The meteor shower of November 1966 occurred at dawn and was visible only in the western United States.

EVERETT DICK

STARS AND BARS. *See* **Confederate Flag.**

STARS AND STRIPES. *See* **Flag of the United States.**

"STAR-SPANGLED BANNER" was inspired by the British attack on Fort McHenry in the War of 1812. On the night of the attack, Francis Scott Key, a young Baltimore lawyer, together with a group of friends had gone to the British admiral to seek the release of a prominent physician who had been captured. Because of plans for the attack, Key and his companions were detained on ship in the harbor and spent the night of Sept. 13–14, 1814, watching the British bombard the fort. Key felt sure that the attack had been successful, but when dawn disclosed the American flag still flying, Key's emotions were so stirred that he wrote the words of the "Star-Spangled Banner" on the back of an envelope. He adapted them to a then popular drinking song, "To Anacreon in Heaven," probably written by British composer John Stafford Smith. The original version was printed as a handbill the next day; a week later it appeared in a Baltimore newspaper. Later Key made a complete draft. The song soon became in fact the national anthem, but it was not until 1931 that Congress officially recognized it as such. Despite its prominence there are few people who know more than the first stanza of the "Star-

STARVED ROCK

Spangled Banner,'' and many have found the melody
difficult to sing. Numerous attempts have been made
to simplify the music, but none has been generally accepted. The actual ''star-spangled banner'' that flew
over Fort McHenry is on display in the Smithsonian
Institution.

[John Tasker Howard, *Our American Music.*]
E. H. O'NEILL

STARVED ROCK, which rises abruptly 140 feet
above the river level, is located on the south side of
the Illinois River nearly opposite the town of Utica,
Ill., in Starved Rock State Park. Three sides of the
rock, the top surface of which approximates an acre,
are almost sheer; on the fourth side the ascent is difficult. Near the rock Louis Jolliet and Jacques Marquette found the Great Village of the Illinois in 1673;
on it Robert Cavelier, Sieur de La Salle, and Henry de
Tonti erected Fort Saint Louis in 1682–83.

Known to French explorers simply as *le rocher,*
Starved Rock received its present name from a tradition to the effect that about 1770 a band of Illinois Indians was besieged on its summit by tribal enemies,
starved into submission, and then exterminated. No
evidence to support the tradition is known to exist,
but the story is popularly believed and cherished.

[Francis Parkman, *LaSalle and the Discovery of the
Great West.*]
PAUL M. ANGLE

STARVING TIME, the term used to refer to the food
shortage at Jamestown in the winter of 1609–10.
There was a similar shortage of food at Plymouth in
the spring of 1622. The Jamestown starving time was
relieved by the arrival of a ship from England, that at
Plymouth by the arrival of a fishing vessel via
Virginia.

[L. G. Tyler, *England in America;* William Bradford,
History of Plymouth Plantation.]
MATTHEW PAGE ANDREWS

STATE, DEPARTMENT OF. U.S. foreign relations
were handled under the Articles of Confederation directly by Congress until the creation of a department
of foreign affairs and the office of secretary for
foreign affairs on Jan. 10, 1781. The cabinet-level
Department of Foreign Affairs was created on July
27, 1789, by the First Congress during its first session
under the Constitution (Mar. 4 to Sept. 29, 1789).
Foreign Affairs was one of three executive depart-

ments established during the session, the others being
War and Treasury. Because of the need to provide for
the administration of ''home affairs,'' and the reluc-
tance of Congress to add a fourth department,
Congress on Sept. 15, 1789, changed the name of the
Department of Foreign Affairs to the Department of
State and changed the title of secretary for foreign af-
fairs to secretary of state.

Until the establishment of the Department of the Interior in 1849, and even afterward in some respects,
the secretary of state handled both foreign affairs and
home affairs, including responsibility for the Patent
Office and the censuses. By the mid-1970's the secretary of state administered a large department of government, acted as principal adviser to the president on
foreign affairs, and himself handled many on-site diplomatic negotiations personally. The many trips
abroad of Secretary Henry Kissinger illustrate the
modern demands of the office. The secretary of state
is the senior member of the president's cabinet and
was first in the presidential succession after the vice-
president until 1947, when the speaker of the House,
as an elected rather than an appointed official, was
added to the succession.

The number of staff members in the Department of
State grew very slowly during its first decades.
Thomas Jefferson, appointed the first secretary of
state on Sept. 26, 1789, had a staff of five clerks; two
U.S. diplomatic agents were stationed abroad, and
only four foreign governments had representatives in
the United States. By 1820 the number of personnel
had reached fifteen, but the work of the department
continued to be severely hampered, particularly since
all copies of documents had to be made by hand. Secretary of State John M. Clayton wrote in 1850 that he
hoped his successor would have enough clerical assistance to reduce the drudgery then associated with the
office. Until 1853, when the Office of Assistant Secretary of State was created, the senior official under
the secretary was the chief clerk. Shortly after the
Civil War these unsatisfactory arrangements were
substantially improved, and by 1870 there were two
assistant secretaries and a total of thirty-one officers.
By the time of the expansion of the U.S. role in world
affairs toward the end of the 19th century, the State
Department had begun to take on more suitable dimensions. Even so, in 1938 there were still only 766
Foreign Service officers (as compared with 1,360 in
1948 and 3,379 in 1968). The total State Department
personnel, including other personnel categories, such
as Foreign Service reserve, Foreign Service staff,
civil service employees, and foreign nationals, in-

creased from 5,692 in 1938 to 20,327 in 1948 and 25,495 in 1968.

The growth in personnel necessitated some attention to career patterns. Until the landmark Rogers (Foreign Service) Act of May 24, 1924, there were no formal and specific requirements for entry into the U.S. Foreign Service at each level, nor did the service have any real organizational structure in a modern sense. Even senior appointments were made in a casual way. Change had begun in 1906 with President Theodore Roosevelt's executive order providing that apointments at the lower consulate grades were to be made only after examination. In 1909, by a similar order, President William Howard Taft extended the merit system to the appointment and promotion of diplomatic service personnel below the grades of minister and ambassador. Even so, because of the small salaries, none but the sons of the wealthy could actually afford making diplomacy a career. The Rogers Act amalgamated consular and diplomatic personnel and established a system of difficult written and oral qualifying examinations. Adequate salaries were introduced, and promotion, by statute, was made on the basis of merit—promotion up or selection out. As a consequence of these reforms (and later modifications, such as the Foreign Service Act of 1946) a true career service came into being. Nevertheless, in 1940 only half the ambassadors and ministers were career men.

The Rogers Act and subsequent amendments did not solve all the personnel problems. Between 1927 and 1935, for example, the United States had in effect four or more foreign services operating abroad. In 1927 the Department of Commerce formed a separate foreign commerce service. In 1930 the Department of Agriculture established a smaller foreign agricultural service. In 1935 the Bureau of Mines created an even smaller service employing mineral specialists. All these changes had the authorization of Congress. The Treasury Department also created a foreign service. The foreign services of the Commerce and Agriculture departments and the Bureau of Mines were merged into the U.S. Foreign Service in 1939 and 1943, respectively. But the Treasury Department kept its separate foreign service, and in 1954 the Department of Agriculture created a new foreign agricultural service, with more than sixty foreign posts. By the early 1960's only 7,200 of the 30,000 U.S. federal civilian employees abroad worked for the State Department. For this reason President John F. Kennedy on May 29, 1961, issued an order that the chief of a diplomatic mission abroad was in charge of the whole mission, a position reaffirmed by President Richard M. Nixon on Sept. 18, 1969. Nixon's order gave the chiefs of mission "affirmative responsibility for the direction, coordination, and supervision of all activities of the United States Government in their respective countries." Thus foreign affairs personnel abroad came, in principle, under the Department of State.

Coordination at home between the State Department and other agencies involved in foreign affairs was also a problem of considerable magnitude. One of the major reasons for the establishment (and later refinements) of the National Security Council (NSC) under the president was to ensure a unified foreign policy formulation and implementation. Under President Harry S. Truman the NSC first began operations on a strictly advisory basis, and its executive secretary was a State Department official. Changes under President Dwight D. Eisenhower increased its functions, while the tendency under Kennedy was to concentrate full control in the White House. President Lyndon B. Johnson restored more participation by the State Department. Under Nixon a further refinement established "Interdepartmental Groups in the NSC system," each chaired by the appropriate assistant secretary of the department of state, with each group having representatives of the assistant to the president for national security affairs, the secretary of defense, the director of the Central Intelligence Agency, and the chairman of the Joint Chiefs of Staff. Senior to the other "interdepartmental groups" was the NSC Under Secretaries Committee, chaired by the under secretary of state and including the deputy secretary of defense, the director of the Central Intelligence Agency, and the chairman of the Joint Chiefs of Staff, to handle "operational matters pertaining to interdepartmental activities . . . overseas."

As the Department of State grew in size the problem of coordination within it (as compared with other agencies) also grew. In 1870 the department had only sixteen separate units; by 1931, thirty-six; by 1948, 113; and the problem has continued to grow. The number of top management employees also increased. On Dec. 31, 1971, the principal officers of the Department of State, excluding the secretary, included an under secretary, an under secretary for political affairs, a deputy under secretary for economic affairs, a deputy under secretary for administration, a counselor, and four other senior officials, plus twenty others who held the rank or equivalent rank of assistant secretary. There were also 121 chiefs of U.S. diplomatic missions reporting to these officials. In addition, there were special missions to the United Nations, Organization of American States, North Atlantic Treaty Organization, Organization for Economic Cooperation and Development, International Atomic Energy Agency, European Office of the United Nations, and European Communities. These changes in size, complexity, and administrative problems reflected the world role of the United States after World War II.

[Dean Acheson, *Present at the Creation.*]
FREDERICK H. HARTMANN

STATE BANKING. *See* **Banking.**

STATE BANK OF INDIANA was created in 1834 as a closely organized federation of banks under control of a central board at Indianapolis. The central board had power to fix the rate of dividend, make inspections, control issues, and order receiverships. Each of the ten branches originally established was mutually liable for the debts of the whole system, and a minimum fund was required to be reserved from profits as a surplus. The state owned one-half of the stock and elected the president and some members of the central board.

Because of the soundness of basic principles and conservative management, the State Bank of Indiana was one of the few successful state banks of the period. By limitation of its charter it went into a two-year liquidation period in 1857 and expired in 1859. It had withstood the panics of 1837 and 1857, paid high dividends, and turned over to the common-school fund several million dollars.

[L. C. Helderman, *National and State Banks: A Study of Their Origins.*]
LEONARD C. HELDERMAN

STATE BOUNDARY DISPUTES. *See* **Boundary Disputes Between the States.**

STATE CHAIRMAN, the title given to the individual serving as the executive director of a political party on a statewide level. He or she is usually elected by the state central or state executive committee for a given period. In a few states the chairman is elected in the party primary by the electorate, by the party candidates, or by the state convention. The elected officials of a political party, the county chairmen, financial contributors, and even opposing factions of a party greatly influence the nomination and election of the state chairman.

The state chairman's duties are fund raising, organizing and administering the party, helping in the selection and nomination of candidates, and preparing the party for elections. Frequently state chairmen themselves later become candidates for some office or are appointed to a position of importance because of their efforts as state chairman.

RONALD F. STINNETT

STATE CONSTITUTIONS. In the American federal union each of the United States has operated at all times under a written constitution of its own. For eleven of the original states this was a matter of necessity, not of choice. The royal provinces and proprietary colonies had been governed under charters that were not at all suited to independence. Only the two largely self-governing colonies were willing to retain their charters long after the Revolution—Connecticut until 1818 and Rhode Island until 1842. By 1780 each of the other states had adopted a new constitution, and four acted even before independence was formally declared. Several of the earliest constitutions were hastily drawn and soon replaced, but others served for years with only minor changes. Indeed, the Massachusetts constitution of 1780, although extensively revised, still remains in force, the oldest in America. It was also the first to be framed by a convention elected especially for that purpose and referred to the voters for their approval. In all other states the first revolutionary constitutions were the work of provincial congresses or assemblies. Among their members were many men who were soon to distinguish themselves in national affairs: John Rutledge in South Carolina, James Iredell in North Carolina, George Mason, Patrick Henry, and James Madison in Virginia, Benjamin Franklin in Pennsylvania, John Jay and Gouverneur Morris in New York, and John Adams in Massachusetts.

The revolutionary constitutions varied greatly in form and substance. Pennsylvania's was the most radical. It created a plural executive, a unicameral legislature, and a council of censors to investigate the government every seven years. Maryland's was probably the most conservative, if only for the high property qualifications it set for officeholders—£500 for representatives, £1,000 for senators, and £5,000 for governor. In all but a few states the legislative power was supreme. Only in New York and Massachusetts, among the states with new constitutions, was the governor elected by the people and given broad powers. Even in Connecticut and Rhode Island, where the governor had long been popularly elected under the colonial charters, the executive branch was dominated by the legislature. The judiciary was no less subordinate. In all but four states judges were elected by the legislature and served more or less at its pleasure. In New York, on the other hand, judges were not only appointed, four of them served on a council of revision with the governor to review all bills about to be enacted into law.

By 1787, when the new federal constitution was being drawn, its framers were able to draw on the states' own rich and varied constitutional experience. In some matters they rejected state constitutional precedents altogether. They were determined, above all, to strike a more even balance between the legislative, executive, and judicial departments than the states had been able to achieve. In separating the three departments and making them structurally independent of each other, the framers were no doubt influenced by the writings of Polybius, John Locke, and Charles de Secondat, Baron de Montesquieu, but the doctrinal precedents closest at hand were the constitutional prescriptions, although not the practice, in Virginia, Maryland, Georgia, Massachusetts, and, after 1784, New Hampshire. In most states both the executive and judicial departments were too weak to furnish a suitable model, but the framers did draw on the experience in three states. The president was to be elected only indirectly by the voters in much the same way state senators were elected in Maryland, although in his case the electors were for a time twice removed from popular vote. He was also given the same broad powers enjoyed by the governor of New York to "take care" that the laws are faithfully carried out, to pardon and reprieve offenses against the law, to inform the legislature at every session about the state of public affairs and recommend bills for it to enact, and to call it into special session. The president was also given the same veto over legislation granted the governor under the Massachusetts constitution. Similarly, federal judges were made appointive in the same way as state judges in Maryland, Massachusetts, and New Hampshire, by the chief executive with the consent of an advisory body to serve during good behavior. Finally, the Bill of Rights, which was added to the federal constitution in 1791, merely followed the example first set by Virginia in 1776.

The fifty state constitutions that are in effect vary greatly in age, length, and form. Only nineteen states, as of 1973, still operated under the constitution with which they entered the Union, and even these were extensively revised. Nine states, all but one in the South, have had at least five constitutions, and one, Louisiana, no less than ten. Three states have constitutions that date back to the 18th century—Massachusetts (1780), New Hampshire (1784), and Vermont (1793). Nine other state constitutions were adopted before 1860. Seventeen others, on the other hand, were adopted in the 20th century, and of these, twelve since World War II. Nearly half, twenty-one, were adopted between 1860 and 1899, when new constitutions had to be framed both for the new western territories and the states of the defeated Confederacy. The state constitutions presently in force vary even more in length. Those which are briefest tend to be either the earliest or the latest. The southern constitutions, on the other hand, are by far the longest, because they are loaded down with detailed provisions more appropriate to a statutory code. Their average length is twice that of the western states and more than three times that of the New England and midwestern states. Louisiana's, indeed, is in a class by itself: its more than a quarter of a million words make it ten times longer than the average of the other forty-nine states and thirty-five times longer than the federal constitution.

Only in their basic organization do all fifty constitutions follow a common pattern. In every state except Vermont a preamble declares the constitution to have been ordained by the people or, in Tennessee, by their delegates and representatives. Unlike the federal constitution, all but a few abound with references to the Deity, and a few still allude to an original social compact and to natural rights. In every state the legislative, executive, and judicial powers are vested in separate and distinct departments. In most states the legislative power is defined quite expansively. Only eleven states, in fact, vest their state legislature expressly with the police power. Hawaii and Oklahoma extend the legislative power to "all rightful subjects of legislation," and New Mexico and Oregon to "all powers necessary to the legislature of a free state." Three others provide that the legislature's authority is not restricted either because certain powers have been enumerated, as in Alaska and Oklahoma, or because others previously conferred have been omitted, as in Virginia. Yet in every state the legislature is effectively barred from exercising such sweeping power either by detailed restriction on its use or by an equally expansive guarantee of personal rights. In no less than thirty-five states political power is declared to be inherent in, or derived from, the people, and in thirty states unenumerated rights are reserved to the people. The same doctrine of popular sovereignty is implied in every other state constitution. In construing their state's constitution, moreover, state courts have usually taken a restrictive view of state legislative power and a broad view of personal, especially property, rights, which the legislature is bound to accept. It is ironic, although perhaps no longer relevant, that the power on which the practice rests—judicial review—is not explicitly provided in any state constitution.

In most states the constitution has become so detailed and rigid as to require frequent change. In every state, amendments or revisions may be proposed either by the legislature itself or by an elective convention called especially for that purpose. Increasingly, legislatures and conventions have come to rely on appointive commissions to study the constitution and to recommend proposals for its revision. Fourteen states, all but five west of the Mississippi, also permit the voters to initiate constitutional amendments. Specific amendments are usually proposed by the legislature or the voters; more thoroughgoing revision, by constitutional conventions or commissions. In Delaware, proposals to amend or revise the constitution become effective as soon as the legislature or convention has taken final action. In every other state, proposed changes must be referred to the voters for their approval. In the two centuries since 1776, at least 226 constitutional conventions have been held, 136 constitutions framed and adopted, and well over 5,000 amendments approved, most of them by popular vote. Indeed, Americans can be said to have had more experience in making constitutions than any other people in history.

[Cynthia E. Brown, *State Constitutions Conventions From Independence to the Completion of the Present Union, 1776–1959: A Bibliography*; Robert B. Dishman, *State Constitutions: The Shape of the Document*; Legislative Drafting Research Fund, *Constitutions of the United States—National and State*, and *Index Digest of State Constitutions*; Allan Nevins, *The American States During and After the Revolution, 1775–1789*; Albert L. Strum, *Thirty Years of State Constitution-Making, 1938–68*.]

ROBERT B. DISHMAN

STATE DEBTS. *See* **Debts, State.**

STATE EMBLEMS, NICKNAMES, MOTTOS, AND SONGS must be adopted officially by action of the legislative bodies of the respective states to which they belong before one properly may designate them as such. The table on pages 393–395 lists the state birds, flowers, trees, nicknames, mottos, and songs, although some states have also adopted state gems, state animals, state fish, and so on. Translations of state mottos in languages other than English (Latin,

French, Italian, Greek, Spanish, and, in the instance of Washington, Chinook) are also given.

STATE FAIRS. The state fair has its roots in Europe, where market fairs have been popular for centuries. It was not until the early 19th century that formal agricultural shows and fairs were held in America, featuring, among other activities, sheepshearing, plowing competitions, and livestock exhibits. Elkanah Watson, often called the "father of the agricultural fairs," founded the Berkshire Agricultural Society in Massachusetts in 1811 to hold cattle shows, and in so doing set up a model for later agricultural shows and societies. The holding of fairs and awarding of prizes to encourage agricultural improvements led to a nationwide wave of livestock shows and agricultural fairs in the next decade.

Most fairs and farming societies fell on hard times from 1825 to 1840. But the rapid growth of America's cities created a need for improved technology to help feed the expanding nonfarming sector of the population, and, with assistance from state governments, America's fairs returned, this time to stay. The first annual state fair was held in Syracuse, N.Y., in 1841. Michigan followed in 1848; Pennsylvania, Ohio, and Wisconsin in 1851; Indiana in 1852; Illinois in 1853; and Iowa and California in 1854.

Even though railroads often provided free transportation, it was a struggle for most farmers to ship their livestock and farm products to a distant fair. So, many of the early state fairs traveled to the farmers, changing sites from year to year. By 1900 most state fairs had fixed locations and permanent facilities, usually near urban centers.

Fair week became a major holiday somewhat like Christmas or the Fourth of July; and amusements became an integral part of the activities. In 1895 the Wisconsin State Fair paid $3,000 to sponsor a special horse race. In the 20th century horse racing often gave way to automobile racing, daredevil stunt shows, and rodeos, while carnivals and musical shows completed the amusements. In 1973, Texas held what was then the largest state fair, with over 3 million people attending.

[Fred Kniffen, "The American Agricultural Fair," *Annals of the Association of American Geographers*, vol. 39 (1949); S. W. Matthews, "America Goes to the Fair," *National Geographic Magazine*, vol. 106 (1954); W. C. Neely, *The Agricultural Fair*; E. D. Ross, "The Iowa State Fair," *Palimpsest*, vol. 35 (1954).]

WAYNE D. RASMUSSEN
PAUL STONE

STATE	BIRD	FLOWER	TREE	NICKNAME(S)	MOTTO	SONG
Alabama	Yellowhammer	Camellia	Southern pine	Cotton State; Heart of Dixie; Yellowhammer State	*Audemus jura nostra defendere* ("We dare defend our rights")	*Alabama*
Alaska	Willow ptarmigan	Forget-me-not	Sitka spruce	Land of the Midnight Sun; The Last Frontier	North to the Future (unofficial)	*Alaska's Flag*
Arizona	Cactus wren	Saguaro cactus	Paloverde	Grand Canyon State	*Ditat Deus* ("God enriches")	*Arizona*
Arkansas	Mockingbird	Apple blossom	Short-leaf pine	Land of Opportunity	*Regnat populus* ("The people rule")	*Arkansas*
California	Valley quail	Golden poppy	Redwood	Golden State	*Eureka* ("I have found it")	*I Love You, California*
Colorado	Lark bunting	Columbine	Blue spruce	Centennial State	*Nil sine numine* ("Nothing without Providence")	*Where the Columbines Grow*
Connecticut	American robin	Mountain laurel	White oak	Constitution State; Nutmeg State	*Qui transtulit sustinet* ("He who transplanted still sustains")	(none)
Delaware	Blue hen chicken	Peach blossom	American holly	Diamond State; First State	Liberty and Independence	*Our Delaware*
Florida	Mockingbird	Orange blossom	Sabal palm	Sunshine State; Peninsula State	In God We Trust	*Old Folks at Home*
Georgia	Brown thrasher	Cherokee rose	Live oak	Empire State of the South; Peach State	Wisdom, Justice, Moderation	*Georgia*
Hawaii	Hawaiian goose (nene)	Hibiscus (Pua Aloha)	Candlenut (Kukui)	Aloha State; Paradise of the Pacific	*Ua mau ke ea o ka aina i ka pono* ("The life of the land is perpetuated in righteousness")	*Hawaii Ponoi*
Idaho	Mountain bluebird	Syringa	White pine	Gem State	*Esto perpetua* ("May she endure forever")	*Here We Have Idaho*
Illinois	Cardinal	Butterfly violet	White oak	Prairie State	State Sovereignty, National Union	*Illinois*
Indiana	Cardinal	Peony	Tulip tree	Hoosier State	Crossroads of America	*On the Banks of the Wabash Far Away*
Iowa	Eastern goldfinch	Carolina wild rose	Oak	Hawkeye State	Our Liberties We Prize and Our Rights We Will Maintain	*The Song of Iowa*
Kansas	Western meadowlark	Sunflower	Cottonwood	Jayhawker State; Sunflower State	*Ad astra per aspera* ("To the stars through difficulties")	*Home on the Range*

STATE	BIRD	FLOWER	TREE	NICKNAME(S)	MOTTO	SONG
Kentucky	Cardinal	Goldenrod	Tulip poplar	Blue Grass State	United We Stand, Divided We Fall	*My Old Kentucky Home*
Louisiana	Pelican	Magnolia	Bald cypress	Creole State; Pelican State	Union, Justice, and Confidence	*Song of Louisiana*
Maine	Chickadee	Pine cone and tassel	White pine	Lumber State; Pine Tree State	*Dirigo* ("I direct")	*State of Maine Song*
Maryland	Baltimore oriole	Black-eyed Susan	White oak	Old Line State	*Fatti maschii, parole femine* ("Manly deeds, womanly words")	*Maryland! My Maryland!*
Massachusetts	Chickadee	Mayflower	American elm	Bay State; Old Bay State; Old Colony State	*Ense petit placidam sub libertate quietem* ("By the sword she seeks peace under liberty")	*All Hail to Massachusetts*
Michigan	Robin	Apple blossom	White pine	Wolverine State	*Si quaeris peninsulam amoenam circumspice* ("If you seek a pleasant peninsula, look about you")	*Michigan, My Michigan* (unofficial)
Minnesota	Loon	Pink and white lady's slipper	Red or Norway pine	Gopher State; North Star State	*L'Etoile du Nord* ("The North Star")	*Hail! Minnesota*
Mississippi	Mockingbird	Magnolia	Magnolia	Magnolia State	*Virtute et armis* ("By Valor and Arms")	*Go, Mississippi*
Missouri	Bluebird	Hawthorn	Dogwood	Show Me State	*Salus populi suprema lex esto* ("Let the welfare of the people be the supreme law")	*Missouri Waltz*
Montana	Western meadowlark	Bitterroot	Ponderosa pine	Treasure State	*Oro y plata* ("Gold and silver")	*Montana*
Nebraska	Western meadowlark	Goldenrod	American elm	Cornhusker State	Equality Before the Law	*Beautiful Nebraska*
Nevada	Mountain bluebird	Sagebrush	Single-leaf pinon	Sagebrush State; Silver State	All For Our Country	*Home Means Nevada*
New Hampshire	Purple finch	Purple lilac	White birch	Granite State	Live Free or Die	*Old New Hampshire*
New Jersey	Eastern goldfinch	Purple violet	Red oak	Garden State	Liberty and Prosperity	(none)
New Mexico	Roadrunner	Yucca	Pinon (nut pine)	Land of Enchantment; Sunshine State	*Crescit eundo* ("It grows as it goes")	*O Fair New Mexico*
New York	Eastern bluebird	Rose	Sugar maple	Empire State	*Excelsior* ("Ever upward")	(none)

STATE	BIRD	FLOWER	TREE	NICKNAME(S)	MOTTO	SONG
North Carolina	Cardinal	Dogwood	Pine	Old North State; Tar Heel State	*Esse quam videri* ("To be, rather than to seem")	*The Old North State*
North Dakota	Western meadowlark	Prairie rose	American elm	Flickertail State; Sioux State	Liberty and Union, Now and Forever, One and Inseparable	*North Dakota Hymn*
Ohio	Cardinal	Scarlet carnation	Buckeye	Buckeye State	With God All Things Are Possible	*Beautiful Ohio*
Oklahoma	Scissor-tailed flycatcher	Mistletoe	Redbud	Sooner State	*Labor omnia vincit* ("Labor conquers all things")	*Oklahoma!*
Oregon	Western meadowlark	Oregon grape	Douglas fir	Beaver State	The Union	*Oregon, My Oregon*
Pennsylvania	Ruffed grouse	Mountain laurel	Eastern hemlock	Keystone State	Virtue, Liberty, and Independence	(none)
Rhode Island	Rhode Island red	Violet	Red maple	Little Rhody	Hope	*Rhode Island*
South Carolina	Carolina wren	Carolina jessamine	Palmetto	Palmetto State	*Animis opibusque parati* ("Prepared in mind and resources") and *Dum spiro spero* ("While I breathe, I hope")	*Carolina*
South Dakota	Ring-necked pheasant	Pasqueflower	Black Hills spruce	Coyote State; Sunshine State	Under God the People Rule	*Hail, South Dakota*
Tennessee	Mockingbird	Iris	Tulip poplar	Volunteer State	Agriculture and Commerce	*Tennessee Waltz*
Texas	Mockingbird	Bluebonnet	Pecan	Lone Star State	Friendship	*Texas, Our Texas*
Utah	Sea gull	Sego lily	Blue spruce	Beehive State	Industry	*Utah, We Love Thee*
Vermont	Hermit thrush	Red clover	Sugar maple	Green Mountain State	Freedom and Unity	*Hail, Vermont*
Virginia	Cardinal	American dogwood	American dogwood	Old Dominion	*Sic semper tyrannis* ("Thus always to tyrants")	*Carry Me Back to Old Virginia*
Washington	Willow goldfinch	Rhododendron	Western hemlock	Evergreen State; Chinook State	*Al-ki* ("By and by")	*Washington, My Home*
West Virginia	Cardinal	Rosebay rhododendron	Sugar maple	Mountain State	*Montani semper liberi* ("Mountaineers are always free men")	*The West Virginia Hills* and *West Virginia, My Home, Sweet Home*
Wisconsin	Robin	Butterfly violet	Sugar maple	Badger State	Forward	*On, Wisconsin!*
Wyoming	Western meadowlark	Indian paintbrush	Cottonwood	Equality State	Equal Rights	*Wyoming*

STATE GOVERNMENT

STATE GOVERNMENT. When the American federal system of government emerged in the late 18th century, incorporating several otherwise independent states in a nationalized, interdependent confederation, it was a unique development in political history; but it was also a logical consequence of American history to that time.

During the 17th and early 18th centuries, British interests in the New World evolved from commercial trading companies into proprietary settlements and then into royal colonies with separate and different governments headed by governors appointed by the king. This same period was one of intense political ferment in Great Britain, embracing the Puritan Revolution and the Glorious Revolution, the emergence of such historic reforms as the Bill of Rights (assuring parliamentary authority over royal absolutism), and the progressive writings of such political philosophers as Thomas Hobbes and John Locke. Since the period of world history from Machiavelli to Locke is considered the birth era of modern political thought, it is obvious that the movement was not confined to England alone. By the middle of the 18th century, British political idealism had reached beyond its national borders to influence such thinkers as Charles de Secondat, Baron de Montesquieu, in France and James Otis in the American colonies. Indeed, the thirteen British colonies in America had themselves produced some rather remarkable political philosophy, and leaders of that movement increasingly found themselves at sharp odds with public officials back in the mother country.

Chiefly, the progressive colonial leaders in America resented the centralization of governmental power and decisions in London, whence, they felt, arose abusive conditions ranging from corrupt governors and other royal appointees to "taxation without representation." Especially during the 1760's and early 1770's, their grievances were aggravated by new abuses from both Parliament and the crown. So it was that various leaders from the thirteen differing colonies found a commonality of interest in their grievances against England. In 1774 colonial leaders convened the First Continental Congress to petition the king for redress; but when his response dissatisfied them, the Second Continental Congress was convened in May 1776 and moved inexorably toward a declaration of independence from Great Britain. The Declaration of Independence proclaimed each and all of the colonies to be "free and independent states," wedded by a mutual pledge of lives, fortunes, and sacred honor in "support of this Declaration." At the same session, the Congress appointed a committee to draft articles joining the new states in a permanent confederation.

As it turned out, it took thirteen years to reach lasting agreement on a federal system of government, and there is not yet any end to the various ways that system can be interpreted. The first plan for confederation was highly controversial and was adopted by Congress only after a year and a half of intense debate and extensive revisions. Then it did not go into effect until 1781, more than three years later, because it took that long for all thirteen states to ratify it.

Considering the remarkable innovation that was being essayed by those new states—attempting to act in unity as a new nation while carefully protecting the governmental integrity of each separate member—it should not be surprising that they had a difficult time devising a system both satisfactory and workable. Early proposals seemed to advocate a minimum of change from colonial situations, and ultimately their timidity worked against them. The Second Continental Congress had asked that each state prepare a new constitution. Connecticut and Rhode Island simply erased provisions about their allegiance to the king from their colonial charters and used them as state constitutions. The new constitutions adopted by the other eleven states made few obvious changes in the lives of their people. Where necessary, they democratized electoral procedures and established permanent representative assemblies.

Many states borrowed from Montesquieu his theory of the "separation of powers," but most deferred too far to the antiexecutive bias that persisted among former colonists, following the popular antipathy toward kings. Those states gave their legislative assemblies power to select both governors and judges, thereby canceling the ideal of balancing the powers of the various branches of government.

The Articles of Confederation deferred too far to the bias for predominantly localized control. They provided for neither a federal executive nor a federal judiciary, and they gave Congress no way of enforcing its will. In other words, the Confederation was essentially an international league, yet the member states were unable to function as independent sovereignties. Within six years, another constitutional convention was called to work out "a more perfect union." The result was the present Constitution, providing a federal government with three branches—executive, legislative, and judicial—whose separate powers are balanced so as to check one another. Nevertheless, the Constitution was not ratified until two

396

years later, in 1789, after the Bill of Rights (the first ten constitutional amendments) had been added. Significantly, the last of those amendments specified, "The powers not delegated to the United States by the Constitution, nor prohibited by it to the States, are reserved to the States respectively, or to the people."

While the Constitution successfully provided a stable framework for intergovernmental relations in a federal system, it left a great deal of room for argument and adjustment. In fact, the fundamental constitutional question of national-state predominance, a controversial issue dating from the first proposals for confederation, has continued through two centuries and has yet to be conclusively resolved. The very first Congress narrowly defeated a proposal to force the federal government to depend on county tax collectors to pass on its revenues. Then in 1798, Thomas Jefferson and James Madison wrote the Virginia and Kentucky Resolutions, contending that states were not bound to submit to federal acts that they considered unconstitutional. (This was considered the first notable expression of the principle of states' rights.)

Other challenges became more serious. New England leaders discussed secession from the Union in protest against the War of 1812 and the Embargo Act; South Carolina attempted to nullify the Tariff Act of 1832; some northern states wanted to nullify the Fugitive Slave Act of 1850; and in 1860–61 eleven southern states took the extreme step of withdrawing from the Union. Finally the national government asserted itself by force: the military defeat of the Confederacy dictated that the Union itself was sovereign and not a creature of the several states.

Moreover, the ascendancy of the national government was furthered by other developments during the first half of the 20th century: the initiation of the federal income tax (by far the largest revenue-producing tax yet devised), the national emergencies of two world wars, and the crippling depression between those wars. Recurring crises, both economic and military, have apparently sustained the trend; and they have not been the only influences. As the Commission on Intergovernmental Relations said in its first report to the president in 1955:

Equally insistent pressures have been brought about by intensified industrialization and population shifts from rural to urban areas, new advances in transportation and communications; and, flowing from these developments, greatly accelerated mobility of people and interchange of ideas. . . . We are doing today as a nation many things that we once did as individuals, as local communities, or as states. . . .

The national government and the states should be regarded not as competitors for authority but as two levels of government cooperating with or complementing each other in meeting the growing demands on both. . . . As an instrument of positive government, [federalism] possesses—at least for a nation as large and diverse as ours—a clear advantage over a strongly centralized government. In helping to bolster the principle of consent; in facilitating wide participation in government; in furnishing training grounds for leaders; in maintaining the habit of local initiative; in providing laboratories for research and experimentation in the art of government; in fostering competition among lower levels of government; in serving as outlets for local grievances and for political aspirations—in all these and many other ways, the existence of many relatively independent and responsible governments strengthens rather than weakens our capacity for government.

In the 1970's, despite those setbacks in confrontations with the national government, American state government remained a dynamic, growing, flexible, constantly changing, and insistently vital and viable institution. Indeed, many of the changes they underwent rendered them stronger and more agile and more effective. Most important in the general transformation of state government has been the ascendance of executive authority over state legislatures. Drafters of early state constitutions, still reacting against the primary role of colonial governors as agents of the king, provided for the dominance of state government by legislatures. (This was also expressed in the national constitution and in local governments with strong city councils and weak mayors.)

The strong legislature–weak governor tradition lasted well into the 19th century, before some efforts were made to cut back on legislative powers. Then, early in the 20th century, a movement began to strengthen the executive powers of governors, providing them with staff assistance, lengthening their terms of office, increasing their salaries, granting them veto powers, letting them succeed themselves, giving them new powers of appointment, and other benefits that varied from state to state. This trend responded to the abuse of power recorded in many state legislatures, to their growing ineffectiveness, and to the need for streamlining governmental processes. Its result has been to allow governors a greater share in stamping the character of their administrations (which in effect allows voters a clearer choice in the directions they want their state governments to move) and to cut through some of the bureaucratic fog that shrouds too many governmental operations.

Another development that helped to dispel that fog

was the adoption of various forms of civil service to staff state administrations. This trend transferred much power from patronage to professionalism, although in some cases it has led to more, instead of less, bureaucracy. Other reforms that have promoted better state government have been extensive revisions of state constitutions, including revitalization of many governmental processes, and new fluency in interstate and municipality-state relations.

In fact, one of the most promising developments in the history of American federalism appears to be the device of interstate compacts. With such diversity of size, character, needs, and roles among the states, interstate cooperation has often been difficult. But since 1900 states have found it increasingly practical to depend on interstate compacts to devise their own solutions to their own problems rather than appealing for federal legislation or adjudication to settle matters. Some of the more notable achievements in this area include creation of the Port of New York Authority (1921), now the Port Authority of New York and New Jersey; the Southern Regional Education Board (1948–49); the Compact for Education (1965); and the Southern Growth Policies Board (1971). True, as of the mid-1970's there remained some interstate problems that did not submit to such remedy—for example, the California-Arizona dispute over the Colorado River. But the interstate compact seemed likely to become an even more important instrument as America was forced into solutions of many metropolitan problems that involved more than one state. Since some estimates say that in 1975 nearly one out of every four Americans lived in an area that was then, or might soon be, an "interstate" area, it was obvious that these compacts might become increasingly important in the last quarter of the 20th century.

To the original thirteen states, thirty-seven were added, including the former territories of Alaska and Hawaii. Despite the greatly increased mobility of Americans and despite the instantaneously national scope of U.S. mass communications, the states remain diverse in their characters. There is diversity in size and population. There is diversity in the comparative wealth of their governments and of their people. There is diversity in their urban-rural population patterns and in their industrial-agricultural mix. There is diversity in their heritages, most obviously in the southern states. If there is any single institution that is responsible for retaining and nourishing the great quality of pluralism in American life, it is probably the institution of statehood, legitimized by state government.

While American state governments may have shifted somewhat from the intergovernmental position they held when Daniel Elazar described them as "keystones of the American governmental arch," they remained in the 1970's one of the most important and most competent institutions of American life. They were interposed between federal and local governments in the execution of many varied kinds of programs. Their budget increases in the 1950's and 1960's were the greatest in their history and in some cases were greater than any other level of government. Like other levels of government, they continued to expand their spheres of influence, becoming every year more involved in almost all functions and services performed for American citizens—not only in such traditional fields as education, highway construction, and social welfare but in vital new areas like mental health, environmental protection, population control and dispersal, and land-use planning. And state governments found and devised an increasing number of opportunities to serve as experimental laboratories in which they could test a variety of approaches to common or similar problems. The beneficiaries of this latter service, possibly the most enduring of their contributions to American life, might include not only governments of the other states, but the national government as well. Down through American history, the national government has often discovered its best course by following the lead of certain innovative state governments, in matters ranging from taxation to women's suffrage and to prison reform.

State governments also have their weaknesses. For example, the majority of states have constitutional or statutory requirements for a balanced budget and various limitations on debt, but many have not established firm enough restraints on spending. In 1975 New York City precipitated a crisis for New York State; the causes were numerous, but fundamentally both the city and the state had engaged in the questionable and risky practice of accumulating debt to discharge current obligations. Imposing taxes at the state level is one of the most unpopular responsibilities faced by governors and legislators, but it is a necessary concomitant of public services to be provided by the states. Fiscal mismanagement is a correctable weakness, and the citizens of those states suffering financial crises have numerous examples of state governments that are and have been managed soundly. At least it is easier to bring under control the laxity in state and local governments than it is to bring a sense of fiscal responsibility to the national government, and ultimately the kind of government that the United States has reflects the will of the citizens.

[William Anderson, *The Nation and the States: Rivals or Partners?;* Council of State Government, *The Book of States: 1974–75;* Lane W. Lancaster and A. C. Breckenridge, eds., *Readings in American State Government;* Dan W. Lufkin, *Many Sovereign States;* James T. Patterson, *The New Deal and the States: Federalism in Transition;* Neal R. Pierce, *The Megastates of America;* Terry Sanford, *Storm Over the States;* Frank Trippett, *The States —United They Fell;* Joseph F. Zimmerman, ed., *Readings in State and Local Government.*]

TERRY SANFORD

STATE GOVERNMENTS, COUNCIL OF THE. *See* **Council for New England.**

STATE LAWS, UNIFORM. In the 18th and 19th centuries the exercise of state sovereignty resulted in the development of a checkerboard of separate and often conflicting state legal systems. A valid divorce in one state, for example, was occasionally a nullity in another. Toward the end of the 19th century such factors as improved transportation and the increase in commerce persuaded lawmakers that it would be desirable to make some laws uniform throughout the states.

There are three fundamental methods of adopting laws so as to achieve the desired uniformity: (1) Congress in the exercise of one of its constitutional powers may pass a law that applies to the states uniformly; (2) state legislatures may adopt identical laws; and (3) representatives of state governments may negotiate an agreement that in turn is adopted by the respective legislatures.

Although only the latter two methods provide for uniform state laws, it is important to recognize that Congress plays a significant role in developing uniformity by merely exercising its constitutional powers to legislate in substantive areas where its failure to do so would permit idiosyncratic state regulation. Longstanding judicial doctrine holds that where Congress has the power to act, its laws preempt or supersede conflicting state laws on the subject.

In 1892, when state representatives first met at what was to become the annual National Conference of Commissioners on Uniform State Laws, they faced two monumental tasks. First, they had to draft legislation acceptable to themselves as representatives. Second, to be successful, they had to convince at least some of the state legislatures that the particular uniform act was wise state policy. Unlike federal laws,

uniform acts are not thrust into existence by a superior governmental entity. Each state is free to adopt or reject such acts. Consequently, it is not surprising that there has never been a uniform act that has met with unanimous success. The powerful arguments of economic or social "necessity," theoretical "rightness," and the convenience of uniformity of culture and attitude are countered by arguments that certain local situations are unique or that a particular area is already covered adequately. What is surprising, in view of the disparity of geographical representation and the sheer numbers of sovereign states (and the District of Columbia, Puerto Rico, and the Virgin Islands), is the degree of success the conference has had.

The Negotiable Instruments Act and its successor, the Uniform Commercial Code (UCC), have been the most significant of the uniform acts. As of 1975, the UCC was law in all states except Louisiana, and its provisions were the legal framework of most business dealings in the United States. There were over 150 uniform acts, many of which met moderate to great success with state legislatures. Some were not adopted by any states. For example, conflicting laws governing marriage and divorce still allowed for "unknowing bigamists."

Part of the success of the conference is that it constitutes an ever-present machinery to set the wheels of uniformity in motion. Since 1892 the conference has convened every year except 1945. Through its president it makes a yearly report to the American Bar Association, which in turn passes on the efficacy of new acts and provisions. In short, there is a constituent assembly that can respond in timely fashion to needs for uniformity as well as publicize its utility.

The commissioners, generally three from each state, are appointed by the respective governors, who over the years have made a practice of selecting leading lawyers, judges, and law professors.

[American Bar Association, *Reports* (annual); Allison Dunham, "A History of the National Conference of Commissioners on Uniform State Laws," *Law and Contemporary Problems,* vol. 30 (1965); National Conference of Commissioners on Uniform State Laws, "Uniformity in the Law," *Montana Law Journal,* vol. 19 (1958).]

HAROLD W. CHASE
ERIC L. CHASE

STATE-MAKING PROCESS. The American federal system with its peculiar relationship of power and function between the state and the national government is one of the more notable contributions of the

United States to the science and theory of government. In a real sense the original thirteen states had entered the nation-building process as independent nations when they drafted the Articles of Confederation, the nation's first constitution, and when they labored to produce the present constitution at the Constitutional Convention of 1789. A major question to be resolved was the manner and method by which other territories that were held or later were to be acquired by the United States might become states in the Union. At intervals throughout American history major legal and political policy debates have arisen over the state-making process, although they have been somewhat muted since the noncontiguous territories of Alaska and Hawaii acquired statehood in 1958 and 1959, respectively.

The original thirteen states had all been colonies of Great Britain, and following their successful war for independence, they formed the original United States of America. The Constitution of the United States went into effect in 1789 after its ratification by conventions in eleven of the states. North Carolina and Rhode Island followed suit soon after. Vermont may possibly be considered one of the original states, since its people formed a constitution and declared themselves independent of Great Britain in 1777. It was admitted into the Union in 1791 by act of Congress. Kentucky, originally a part of Virginia, was formed into a county of that state in 1776. The people of this district asked Virginia to consent to the creation of a new state. The consent was given in 1789, and Kentucky was admitted as a state in 1792. North Carolina originally included the territory comprising what is now Tennessee, which it transferred to the Union in 1784. Tennessee was admitted as a state in 1796. All these creations of states and admissions to the Union were authorized by acts of Congress.

The territory of the United States was extended to the Mississippi River in 1783 by the Definitive Treaty of Peace with Great Britain. National territory was widely expanded by outright purchase, as in the case of Louisiana, Florida, and Alaska. Cessions from Mexico also added major land areas that were later to become states of the Union.

Texas was an independent nation from 1836 to 1845, after winning its independence from Mexico. It was annexed to the Union by joint resolution of Congress in 1845. Hawaii had also been an independent nation, but before becoming a state it had functioned as an incorporated territory for many years. Maine separated from Massachusetts in 1820, and in 1863 during the Civil War, West Virginia separated from Virginia. The remainder of the states were carved out of the public lands that came to the United States as the result of various cessions and annexations.

Immediately following the American Revolution the Continental Congress took the first steps in organizing the western lands. Congress wanted to prepare the inhabitants for local self-government and to organize the territories for their final admission into the Union as states. The famous Northwest Ordinance, or Ordinance for the Government of the Territory of the United States Northwest of the River Ohio, was passed on July 13, 1787. It contained three very important provisions: first, there was a grant to the inhabitants of the territory of those fundamental political and personal rights that are presumed to be the basis of American liberty; second, there was a statement of a plan for the immediate government of a territory; and third, there was a statement of the policy of the federal government on the final status of such a territory. This ordinance was the basis upon which all public lands and foreign possessions of the United States were administered during the succeeding century.

For the immediate government of an organized territory all powers were vested in a governor, a secretary, and a court of three judges, all of whom were to be appointed by the Continental Congress. At first there was to be no legislature, but the territorial officials had the authority to adopt and promulgate such laws of already existing states as suited the needs of the territory. While these laws were to be reported to Congress, they were allowed to go into effect immediately unless disallowed by that body. This concentration of executive and legislative power in the same hands was a violation of fundamental American ideas of free government but was justified on the grounds of temporary expediency. A more complete government was to be set up as soon as there were 5,000 free male inhabitants in any one of the territories. There was to be a legislative body consisting of a house of representatives chosen by the people of the territory on a certain arbitrary numerical basis of apportionment and an upper house or council of five members chosen by Congress upon nomination by the lower house of the legislature. The governor and legislature, under a delegation of power by act of Congress, were to pass all laws needed for local government, but there was no provision for a veto by the governor. A further provision required that the two houses of the legislature in joint session should elect a delegate to Congress who would have a seat in that body with a right to participate in debate but no vote. This plan, as contained in the Northwest Ordinance, formed the basis on which the system of government for the future states of the United States was built. Ohio, the first state to be founded under the Northwest Ordinance, was admitted to the Union in 1803. The First Congress under the Constitution passed an act on May 26, 1790, that provided that a like plan of government should be created for the Southwest Territory, which lay south of the Ohio River.

As soon as an organized territory had maintained self-government under these conditions and had grown in population to a position sufficient to justify, in the varying public opinion of the times, its admission as a state, Congress passed a specific act under which the people of the territory could choose delegates to a territorial constitutional convention. The general procedure was for this convention to draw up a constitution for the prospective state, usually modeled on the constitutions of the original or other early states of the Union. Upon adjournment of the convention, this constitution was submitted to the people of the territory for their ratification and was generally accepted by them. The prospective state then applied to Congress for admission to full status in the Union. Congress usually passed the necessary enabling act; after acceptance by the people and government of the territory, a new state was then formally admitted into the Union. When finally admitted, each new state acquired complete equality with all the other states and a like possession of all reserved powers not specifically delegated to the national government according to the provisions of the Constitution.

Over the years new problems of social and political importance have arisen, which have on various occasions caused Congress to impose certain restrictions on the states. These have taken the form of mandatory requirements of provisions in their constitutions before Congress would pass an enabling act for their admission. Actually, this procedure began in the Northwest Ordinance, which forever prohibited slavery within territories soon to be organized. Also, when the southern states were ''readmitted'' to the Union in the years following the Civil War, Congress required their constitutions to include provisions for the abolition and future prohibition of slavery.

Another illustration of congressional restriction is to be found in the admission of Utah to the Union. Congress refused to pass the enabling act until Utah included in its constitution a provision prohibiting polygamy, then practiced by the Mormons. Utah complied and was admitted in 1896. In 1910 Congress gave the territories of New Mexico and Arizona permission to frame constitutions and apply for admission to the Union. The territories completed this procedure within the next year, but because the proposed Arizona constitution contained a provision for the popular recall of judges, admission of the territories was refused. For political reasons the case of New Mexico was included with that of Arizona. In 1912 Arizona amended its constitution to exclude the clause to which there was objection, and both states were admitted to the Union. After admission, acting on the theory that once admitted, a state is equal to all others, Arizona promptly restored the provision for recalling its judges, and it is still in effect.

A significant exception to the rule that after a territory becomes a state it is equal to all others and may not be bound by prior restrictions set by Congress was made by the U.S. Supreme Court when it held that conditions imposed on the disposition of federal lands ceded to states and other matters under federal jurisdiction are enforceable. Alaska is also a special case in this regard. Because of its vast area, sparse population, difficult climate and topography, Indian and Eskimo problems, and past history of federal subsidies, the Alaska Statehood Act and the accompanying Alaska Omnibus Act made unique and detailed provisions for continuing federal rights and responsibilities in this state, unparalleled in the others.

The admission of the first noncontiguous territories to statehood, Alaska and Hawaii, reveals some of the objections to converting such territories to states. One objection was that the process of Americanization had not gone far enough, especially in Hawaii, where there are many citizens of Oriental ancestry. In addition, the armed forces had objected to statehood for Alaska and Hawaii because they thought such a change in status would subject their bases and installations to civilian control.

[W. H. Bennett, *American Theories of Federalism;* J. W. Fesler, *The Fifty States and Their Local Governments;* C. J. Friedrick, *Trends in Federalism in Theory and Practice;* W. B. Graves, *American Intergovernmental Relations: Their Origins, Historical Development and Current Status;* W. F. Willoughby, *Territories and Dependencies of the United States.*]

DONALD E. BOLES

STATES, RELATIONS BETWEEN THE. The U.S. Constitution provides the basic principles governing relations between the states, subject ultimately to judicial and political interpretation. Article IV, Section 1, provides, "Full Faith and Credit shall be given in each State to the public Acts, Records, and judicial proceedings of every other State." Divorce proceedings and regulation of businesses provide examples where such a general constitutional rule proves difficult in application. Recognizing this, the Constitution provides Congress with certain powers to set up governing rules relating to proof and "effect."

Article IV, Section 2, provides for citizens to be entitled to "all Privileges and Immunities of Citizens in the several States." It aims at protecting individuals from unequal application of the law regardless of their state of origin. This same protective section also provides for interstate extradition of fugitives from the justice of another state. The courts have interpreted the clause to be very inclusive of what punishable offense may be the basis for extradition of the fugitive. However, governors have sometimes exercised political or equitable judgments on the guilt of the fugitive and the seriousness of the alleged crime, in deciding whether to accede to another governor's request. The privileges and immunities clause has been subject to much judicial interpretation. A full body of law has developed around it, particularly concerning business civil transactions.

The clause that has given rise to the most interesting body of interstate relations is Article I, Section 10, which prohibits a state from entering "into any Treaty, Alliance, or Confederation" and prevents any "Agreement or Compact with another State" without consent of Congress.

From 1783 to 1920 thirty-six compacts were entered into. From 1921 to 1955 there were an additional sixty-five compacts agreed to by the states. Between 1956 and 1966 an additional forty compacts were established. In 1974 the Council of State Governments *Directory of Interstate Agencies* listed fifty-seven compacts with staff and identifiable locations. The missions included regulation of a natural resource or protection of the environment (the Atlantic States Marine Fisheries Commission); administration of a metropolitan-area function (the Port Authority of New York and New Jersey); administration of a river basin or flood area (the Connecticut River Valley Flood Control Commission and the Kansas-Oklahoma Arkansas River Commission); regional sharing of state services (the Southern Regional Education Board); and settling boundary disputes (an early purpose of the constitutional provision).

Regulation, planning, conservation, and sharing services have all been effectively implemented through compacts, sometimes with as few as two states (the Arkansas River Compact Administration) and sometimes embracing nearly all. Although it has been suggested that at least in one case, the Southern Regional Education Board, the purpose of a compact had questionable initial motives (perpetuating segregation in higher education), even here the compact has ended by allowing member states to take advantage of educational specialties each has had to offer students from the other states.

In some cases compacts have been initiated to avoid federal action in a particular field. Yet in the case of the Interstate Compact to Conserve Oil and Gas, the compact came into being because the Supreme Court had overturned the National Industrial Recovery Act provisions controlling oil markets and establishing production quotas. In the 1960's and 1970's the more familiar pattern was for the state compact to serve as a device to avoid some specific congressional act, as in the conflict over the 1971 proposal for an interstate environment compact, supported by many governors but opposed by the environmental lobby.

The Interstate Compact to Conserve Oil and Gas represents one of only two cases where Congress has limited its consent to an interstate compact. (The other case was a limitation of fifteen years on the Atlantic States Marine Fisheries Compact, a provision repealed in 1950.) Originally reviewed by Congress every two years, the oil and gas compact is now considered every four years, especially in light of any possible antitrust law violations concerning price-fixing.

Other forms of "federalism without Washington" have included the cooperative adoption of uniform laws through the National Conference of Commissioners on Uniform State Laws. The umbrella organization, the Council of State Governments, was organized in 1935 for interstate cooperation. However, elective and administrative officials of the various states convened as early as 1878, at the National Convention of Insurance Commissioners. Many more such organizations come into being each year to exchange experiences, draft uniform or model state legislation, resolve jurisdictional disputes, or even agree on proposed legislation that Congress may be asked to enact "governing" them, very much with their consent. The Hill-Burton Act (1946) was largely developed by state health officials, and the National Association of State Highway Officials has much to say about what are ostensibly federal regulations governing transportation administration. Here come into place what Michael W. Reisman and Gary J. Simson have categorized as public intelligence, promotion, prescription, invocation, application, termination, and appraisal functions exercised cooperatively, in their article ''Interstate Agreements in the Federal System'' (*Rutgers Law Review*, vol. 27, Fall 1973).

While the interstate compact, the uniform state laws, and the various associations of state elected and appointed officials individually seem a relatively small part of the national decisionmaking process, these interstate modes of cooperation form a significant part of the national pattern of governance.

[Weldon V. Barton, *Interstate Compacts in the Political Process;* Daniel J. Elazar and others, *Cooperation and Conflict. Readings in American Federalism;* W. Brooke Graves, *American Intergovernmental Relations;* Morton Grodzins, *The American System, A New View of Government in the United States;* Richard H. Leach and Redding S. Sugg, Jr., *The Administration of Interstate Compacts.*]

E. LESTER LEVINE

STATE SOVEREIGNTY as a doctrine appeared shortly after 1776. James Wilson, congressman and lawyer, stated the following at the Convention of 1787:

Among the first sentiments expressed in the first Congress one was that Virginia is no more, that Pennsylvania is no more, etc. We are now one nation of brethren. We must bury all local interests and distinctions. This language continued for some time. No sooner were the State governments formed than their jealousy and ambition began to display themselves. Each endeavored to cut a slice from the common loaf, to add to his morsel, till at length the confederation became frittered down to the impotent condition in which it now stands.

So intolerable had the evils of particularism become by 1787 that Henry Knox wrote:

The State systems are the accursed things which will prevent our becoming a nation. The democracy might be managed, nay, it would be a remedy itself after being sufficiently fermented; but the vile State governments are sources of pollution, which will contaminate the American name for ages—machines that must produce ill, but cannot produce good.

There was sound reason for the display of state loyalty in 1787. State governments were known and trusted; they had carried the people through the war with Great Britain, while the impotent Congress of the Confederation had been unable to achieve the objects for which it was created. It followed that not

only did men distrust a national government, but they also failed to understand that two jurisdictions largely coordinate could work toward a similar end. They imagined that coordination meant antithesis and feared lest the surrender of a portion of the power wielded by the states would end in the destruction of personal liberty. It could therefore be argued that the national government must rest in part on the states.

The part the states should play in the American political system was the subject of prolonged debate in the Convention of 1787. Alexander Hamilton, who wanted the states reduced to ''corporations for local purposes,'' was poles apart from members who argued for the complete sovereignty of the states. As he listened to the debate, William Samuel Johnson of Connecticut remarked that ''the controversy must be endless whilst gentlemen differ in the grounds of their arguments; those on one side considering the states as districts of people composing one political society; those on the other considering them as so many political societies.'' Finally, a compromise was reached whereby the states were secured against encroachment by the national government through their equal representation in the Senate (*see* Connecticut Compromise).

The problem of sovereignty remained unsolved when the government under the Constitution was inaugurated in 1789. The prevalent opinion was that somehow sovereignty had been divided between the states and the Union. This view was staunchly maintained by James Madison and was enunciated by the Supreme Court in *Chisholm* v. *Georgia* (1793). Until the 1830's and 1840's, when the theory of John C. Calhoun became influential, the characteristic American doctrine was that in the United States the sovereignty had been divided into several portions without the destruction of its life principle.

Calhoun, in insisting that sovereignty in the United States is indivisible, returned to the issues debated in the federal convention. He declared that to the people of the several states sovereignty devolved upon the separation from Great Britain, and it was through the exercise of this sovereignty that the state constitutions as well as the Constitution of the United States were created. In other words, the Constitution of the United States was ordained and established by the people of the several states, acting as so many sovereign political communities, and not by the people of the United States, acting as one people, though within the states.

The accepted statement of the states' rights doctrine was set forth by Calhoun in his *Disquisition on*

STATES' RIGHTS

Government and his *Discourse on the Constitution and Government of the United States*. The influence of Calhoun is without question; his political theories became the dogma of the states' rights party and found expression in the constitution of the Confederate States.

The nationalist theory of the Union was defended by Daniel Webster, who insisted that the Constitution is an agreement among individuals to form a national government. "It is established," he said, "by the people of the United States. It does not say by the people of the several States. It is as all the people of the United States that they established the Constitution." Between the party of Calhoun and that of Webster the division of opinion was identical with that observed by Johnson in the federal convention. State sovereignty was made to rest on the idea that the people of the United States constitute a number of political societies among whom a treaty or agreement was made to form a national government. The Constitution was not, as the nationalists maintained, a fundamental law ordained and established by the whole people of the United States. The controversy remained for the clash of arms to settle, but the victory of Ulysses S. Grant at Appomattox in 1865 settled the question in favor of the defenders of nationalism.

[C. E. Merriam, *History of American Political Theories.*]
WILLIAM S. CARPENTER

STATES' RIGHTS. Advocates of the principle of states' rights believe that considerable governmental authority should be located in the separate and collective states of the United States. The concept of states' rights arose as an extension of colonial rights, which Americans had claimed when they were still under the British crown. This idea underlay the American Revolution, and it was present during the Confederation period. When the Constitutional Convention met in 1787, states' rights proponents pressed to include their ideas in the Constitution, but there was also the desire for a strong national government, with minimal power residing with the states. Adopted at that convention was a federal system, a reasonably satisfactory compromise reconciling state and national power. In 1791 the Tenth Amendment was added to the Constitution, which spelled out the states' rights doctrine: "The powers not delegated to the United States by the Constitution, nor prohibited by it to the States, are reserved to the States respectively, or to the people." A large part of American history from that time until 1865 was the story of the push and pull

of the national and state governments in their attempts to define their relationships to each other and to protect their respective powers. In 1798 the promulgation of the Kentucky and Virginia Resolutions, which protested acts passed by the national Congress, were manifestations of states' rights. The Hartford Convention of 1814, called by New Englanders who disagreed with President James Madison's wartime policies, was another example of states' rightism.

Although various individual states and groups of states from time to time appealed to the principle of states' rights for their political and economic protection, the South is the section of the country most often associated with the doctrine. In the first half of the 19th century, when disputes arose over the tariff, the national bank, public land policies, internal improvement, and the like, southern leaders used arguments based on states' rights in their attempts to protect their economic interests. They usually lost these battles to maintain their economic power, and their appeals to a constitutional principle went unheeded. Overriding all the other disputes was the question of the extension of slavery into the American territories. Southern states fell back on the states' rights principle once again when northerners argued that slavery should not expand. Various events of the 1850's, including the Compromise of 1850, the Kansas-Nebraska controversy, the formation of the Republican party, civil strife in Kansas, the Dred Scott decision, and John Brown's raid, and the election of Abraham Lincoln as president in 1860 were closely related to the slavery and states' rights controversies and led directly to the Civil War. That war established the supremacy of the national government and relegated the states to lesser political and economic positions. Disputes arose from time to time about the relationship of the national and state governments, and invariably the national government emerged the victor. In the first half of the 20th century, southern politicians continued to speak about states' rights, but this was often nothing more than oratory designed to please southern voters.

After midcentury, when the power, size, and authority of the national government became greater and more complex, many Americans began to have misgivings about the shortcomings of a massive government essentially run by bureaucrats. Those politicians who talked about states' rights often found they had more receptive audiences than previously. Controversies over the administration of welfare programs and other social services gave states' rights advocates issues that they could exploit. More important, the cry for states' rights was often a thinly disguised but firm stand against racial integration in regard to education, public accommodations, politics and voting, housing, and jobs, areas that states' righters insisted were within the sphere of the states. But the revival of states' rights arguments in the third quarter of the 20th century had little basic impact on the general locus of political power. The national government continued to be more powerful, the states remaining in secondary roles. The attempts of the Founding Fathers to divide sovereignty between national and state governments laid the basis for many controversies throughout the nation's history, but on the whole the structure of government that they established functioned well. Save for the Civil War, disputes had been compromised peacefully. Even as the national government gained more power within the limits of the Constitution after the mid-20th century, there appeared to be no prospect of a serious revolt over the diminishing rights of the states. (*See also* Federal-State Relations.)

[Avery O. Craven, *Civil War in the Making, 1815–1860;* William W. Freehling, *Prelude to Civil War: The Nullification Controversy in South Carolina, 1816–1836;* Arthur Meier Schlesinger, ''The State Rights Fetish,'' *New Viewpoints in American History;* Charles S. Sydnor, *The Development of Southern Sectionalism, 1819–1848.*]

MONROE BILLINGTON

STATES' RIGHTS IN THE CONFEDERACY. The doctrine of states' rights, which was developed in the South as the defense mechanism of a minority section within the Union, was productive of disastrous results when it was applied by extremists to the Confederate government during the Civil War. Led by Gov. Joseph E. Brown of Georgia, Gov. Zebulon B. Vance of North Carolina, and Vice-President Alexander H. Stephens, they attacked conscription as unconstitutional and impeded its operation even after favorable decisions by the courts. The army was crippled by the insistence on the right of states to appoint officers, and by the policy of some states withholding men and arms from the Confederate government and themselves maintaining troops. On similar grounds the states' rights faction opposed suspension of the writ of habeas corpus, so that the government was able to employ this valuable military weapon for periods aggregating less than a year and a half. Under the theory of states' rights the impressment of supplies for the army was broken down; likewise the laws were repealed that had given the government a monopoly in foreign trade by means of which it had exported cotton and brought in war supplies through the blockade.

States' rights hampered the Confederate government at every turn and in the end contributed to its downfall.

[Louise B. Hill, *State Socialism in the Confederate States of America;* Frank L. Owsley, *State Rights in the Confederacy.*]

LOUISE BILES HILL

STATUE OF LIBERTY, properly *Liberty Enlightening the World,* is located on Liberty (formerly Bedloe's) Island in New York Harbor. It was conceived by the French sculptor Frédéric August Bartholdi and cost approximately 1 million francs, a sum raised by conscription. A gift to the United States from the people of France, the colossal copper figure was shipped in sections in 1885 and unveiled on Oct. 28, 1886. President Grover Cleveland accepted it in a belated commemoration of a century of American independence. From the pedestal to the top of the upraised torch, the height is 152 feet; the overall height is 302 feet. The Statue of Liberty has served as the symbol of welcome to millions of immigrants.

IRVING DILLIARD

STATUTES AT LARGE, UNITED STATES, a chronological publication of the laws enacted in each session of Congress, beginning in 1789. This series is cited as ''Stat.,'' with the volume number preceding and the page number following—for example, 40 Stat. 603 for the Sherman Antitrust Act of 1890.

These volumes also contained presidential executive orders until the *Federal Register* began publication on Mar. 14, 1936. They also included treaties until the publication *Treaties and Other International Agreements* began on Jan. 27, 1950.

The *Statutes at Large* is legal evidence of the laws passed by Congress. They are first officially published as ''slip laws.'' The *United States Code* updates the laws in force by subject.

[M. Price and H. Bitner, *Effective Legal Research.*]

CLEMENT E. VOSE

STATUTES OF LIMITATIONS. All of the states of the United States have statutes limiting the time within which a person having a cause for court action is permitted to bring suit for the recovery of his rights. As time passes, witnesses die, papers are destroyed, and the conditions of transactions are forgotten. Such laws prevent the enforcement of stale claims that might earlier have been successfully defended. Thus legal titles and the possession of property are made more secure, and much malicious and frivolous litigation is prevented.

EARL E. WARNER

STATUTORY LAW, as distinguished from constitutional law and the common law, is that which is laid down by a legislature. Both the U.S. Congress and state legislatures enact statutes either by bill or by joint resolution, and these make up the statutory law. Federal statutes take precedence over state statutes, and state statutes are superior to the common law. Statutory law is inferior to constitutional law, and courts exercise the power of judicial review when they declare statutes unconstitutional. Statutory law is codified under titles describing the areas of action to which they appertain, and these titles are grouped together in the codes. Both the federal code and the various state codes are also issued in what are termed "annotated codes," which reflect the decisions of the courts regarding the statutes. Some annotated codes are published by the public authorities; others are published by private sources.

Enforcement of statutory law lies with the administrative branch of the government, and in the execution of the statutes recourse is often had to administrative rules and regulations that have the effect of law as long as they lie within the limits set by the statutes.

[J. C. Gray, *The Nature and Sources of Law;* H. L. A. Hart, *The Concept of Law;* H. Walker, *Law Making in the United States.*]

PAUL DOLAN

STAY AND VALUATION ACTS. As a result of the panic of 1819, many citizens of the new western states were unable to meet obligations they had incurred during the time of expansion and prosperity of the previous years. Foreclosures and forced sales at ruinous prices became common. In addition to establishing inflationist banking schemes operated by the state, the states of Illinois, Missouri, Kentucky, and Tennessee adopted stay and valuation laws.

A stay law provided for a moratorium or extension of time for meeting a debt obligation. The extensions ranged from three months to two and one-half years. The stay law usually applied an unpleasant alternative to the case of a creditor who would not agree to the valuation laws. Property sold at forced sales was bringing only a small fraction of its normal value. In order to protect the frontier debtors from such heavy losses, valuation laws provided for the appointing of a local board to set a fair value on property offered in satisfaction of debt, usually a price much above that which would be secured at forced sale. If the creditor would not accept this overvalued property in satisfaction of his debt, he was forced to defer collection for the duration of the period provided by the accompanying stay law.

The state courts were accused of sympathy with creditors when they declared both varieties of relief laws unconstitutional. Missouri attempted to curtail the power of its courts, and Kentucky was plunged into chaotic conditions when its legislature voted the state supreme court out of existence and established a new, prorelief court in its place (*see* Old Court–New Court Struggle).

[W. J. Hamilton, "The Relief Movement in Missouri, 1820–22," *Missouri Historical Review,* vol. 22; N. S. Shaler, *History of Kentucky.*]

W. J. HAMILTON

STEAMBOATING ON WESTERN WATERS was inaugurated by the *New Orleans* in 1811. Scarcely a dozen steamboats were built by 1817, but in the next two years over sixty were launched for traffic on the Mississippi, the Missouri, and the Ohio rivers. By 1834 there were 230 steamboats, aggregating 39,000 tons, on western waters. Of the 684 steam craft constructed by the close of 1835, the Pittsburgh district contributed 304, the Cincinnati district 221, and the Louisville area 103. So phenomenal was the growth that steam tonnage on western waters soon exceeded steam tonnage in the British merchant marine. The cost of running the 1,190 steamboats on western waters in 1846 was estimated at $41,154,194. At that time fully 10,126,160 tons of freight valued at $432,621,240 were transported annually. This was nearly double the U.S. foreign commerce. Pittsburgh, Cincinnati, and Louisville were great Ohio ports, while New Orleans dominated the lower Mississippi. In 1854 New Orleans and Saint Louis ranked second and third respectively in enrolled steam tonnage in the United States. Six years later Saint Louis recorded 1,524 steamboat arrivals from the upper Mississippi, 767 from the lower Mississippi, 544 from the Illinois, 277 from the Ohio, 269 from the Missouri, 35 from the Cumberland, 31 from the Tennessee, and 7 from the Arkansas.

The first steamboat navigated the Missouri in 1819, the Tennessee in 1821, the upper Mississippi in 1823, and the Illinois in 1828. Before the Civil War, more than forty tributaries of the Mississippi system had been navigated by steamboat. Captain-ownership was followed by the formation of powerful corporations, such as the Cincinnati and Louisville Mail Line, the Anchor Line on the lower Mississippi, the Northern Line on the upper Mississippi, and the Union Packet Line on the Missouri. The attempts of tramp boats or new lines to enter a profitable trade led to cutthroat competition and ruinous rates. River towns collected staggering wharfage fees but failed to provide adequate terminal facilities. Expensive litigation, unbusinesslike methods, uncertain rates, and the limited season of navigation were additional handicaps. The Civil War ruined steamboating on the lower Mississippi and contributed to the decline on the Ohio River, already locked in a death struggle with the railroads. Corporations were reestablished on the lower Mississippi after the Civil War, and Saint Louis advertised lines to the Arkansas, the Red, the Ouachita, the Tennessee, and other rivers. But the halcyon days were soon gone; not even the race of the *Natchez* and the *Robert E. Lee* in 1870 could revive them (*see* Steamboat Racing). The Mississippi was paralleled by rails and trussed with bridges that were frequently hazardous to navigation. The railroad reached Saint Joseph on the Missouri in 1859, Council Bluffs in 1867, and Bismarck in 1872. Most river improvements came after steamboating had virtually died. After World War I the gradually increasing tonnage on the Ohio and Mississippi was carried by barges and towboats, while passengers were transported on land by trains, buses, and private automobiles. The few surviving steamboats served mostly to provide excursions for tourists.

[C. H. Ambler, *Transportation in the Ohio Valley;* H. M. Chittenden, *Early Steamboat Navigation on the Missouri River;* E. W. Gould, *Fifty Years on the Mississippi;* W. J. Petersen, *Steamboating on the Upper Mississippi.*]

WILLIAM J. PETERSEN

STEAMBOAT MONOPOLIES were granted by states on a number of rivers. The procedure on the Hudson River was typical. The successful trip of Robert Fulton's *Clermont* from New York to Albany in 1807 secured for his company a monopoly on the Hudson for twenty years. Others who desired to operate steamboats were required to secure a license from the Fulton company.

There were three reasons for the monopoly's failure. First, team boats were constructed. They were twin boats with a wheel placed between them so it would be protected from floating ice. Eight horses walked in a circle on a heavy plank platform that rested on the two boats. No licenses were required to

run such boats. Second, the controversy between New York and New Jersey led to disputes. New York courts declared that New York State could control navigation on the Hudson River just as it could slavery or the transportation of infectious goods. The New Jersey courts denied the contention of the New York courts. The controversy led Chancellor James Kent of the New York Supreme Court to advise that the case be carried to the U.S. Supreme Court. In the case of *Gibbons* v. *Ogden* (1824), Daniel Webster, the foremost lawyer of his time, and Attorney General William Wirt supported the antimonopolists. Webster argued that it was the right of any steamship, when properly registered, to go anywhere on any U.S. river. Respondent attorneys Thomas J. Oakley and Thomas A. Emmet argued the right of a state to grant monopolies. The decision of Chief Justice John Marshall destroyed all monopolistic rights enjoyed by the Fulton company. This decision determined the outcome in all pending steamship monopoly cases. In one, *Heirs of Livingston and Fulton* v. *Reuben Nichols and Steamboat Constitution*, the U.S. District Court for the Eastern District of Louisiana declared against the steamship monopoly on the Mississippi River in Louisiana.

[James Alton James, *Readings in American History;* Charles Warren, *The Supreme Court in American History.*]

CHARLES B. SWANEY

STEAMBOAT RACING reached its zenith in 1870 when the *Robert E. Lee* raced from New Orleans to Saint Louis in three days, eighteen hours, and fourteen minutes, defeating the *Natchez* by over three hours. All America was agog, telegraphic reports were flashed to Europe, and more than $1 million in bets is said to have changed hands. Although editorials denounced the practice as dangerous, fast boats were popular with travelers and shippers. Moreover, few explosions occurred while boats were racing, for engineers were more alert. Many races were against time, captains endeavoring to break records between ports. By 1840, when steamboats were attaining a high standard in marine architecture, the average speed was about six miles per hour upstream, and ten to twelve miles per hour downstream. Fast boats could average better than ten miles per hour upstream. Thus, in 1844 the *J. M. White* ran from New Orleans to Saint Louis in three days and twenty-three hours, a record that stood for years. In 1815 the *Enterprise* churned from New Orleans to Louisville in twenty-five days; by 1853 the *Eclipse* had reduced this time to four days, nine hours, and thirty minutes.

In 1854 the *Cataract* raced from Saint Louis to La Salle, Ill., in twenty-three hours and forty-five minutes. The *James H. Lucas* ran from Saint Louis to Saint Joseph on the Missouri in 1856 in two days, twelve hours, and fifty-two minutes; and the *Hawkeye State* sped from Saint Louis to Saint Paul in 1868 in two days and twenty hours. On a short run from Saint Louis to Alton in 1853 the *Altoona* made twenty-five miles in one hour and thirty-five minutes.

[E. W. Gould, *Fifty Years on the Mississippi.*]
WILLIAM J. PETERSEN

STEAMBOATS. The idea of steam-powered boats intrigued men before the days of James Rumsey, John Fitch, and Robert Fulton. Practical steamboat experiments began with the double-acting engine in 1782; both Rumsey and Fitch operated their boats two years before George Washington's inauguration (1789). Successful commercial navigation is usually dated from the voyage of Fulton's *Clermont* in 1807. Thereafter, steamships were launched for deep-sea passage and for the swift streams of the tidewater and Mississippi Valley, whose tortuous curves and shallow sandbar-studded waters required high-powered, light draft boats. The first steamboat on western waters, the *New Orleans,* was built from Fulton-Livingston patents in 1811. It was a 300-ton, two-masted side-wheeler with boiler, engine, and vertical stationary cylinder placed in its open hold. The bow was reserved for freight—the cabins were aft of the machinery. In 1813 Daniel French launched the 25-ton *Comet,* a stern-wheeler featuring vibrating cylinders. The *New Orleans* and *Comet* served as models until 1816, when Henry M. Shreve built his second steamboat, the 403-ton *Washington,* although his earlier craft, the *Enterprise,* had been the first steamboat to ascend the Mississippi and Ohio rivers from New Orleans to Louisville, Ky. Shreve contributed three ideas to the *Washington:* he placed the machinery and cabin on the main deck; used horizontal cylinders with vibrations to the pitmans; and employed a double high-pressure engine. He also introduced the second deck, which became standard on all western steamboats thereafter. Subsequent marine architecture simply improved on these features.

A generation passed before the floating palaces of the Mark Twain era evolved. Steamboats increased in tonnage; they boasted ornate cabins and private staterooms, bars and barber shops, bands and orchestras, and steam whistles and calliopes. Steam was used to work the capstan, handle the spars, or swing the stage. An auxiliary engine, or doctor, pumped water into the boiler. Coal gradually replaced wood, and the electric searchlight was substituted for the wood torch. Spacious decks with promenades were built high above the main deck—the texas (for the crew) and the pilot house being placed high above all. In 1843 the second *J. M. White* was launched at Pittsburgh. It was 250 feet long, with a 31-foot beam and an 8.5-foot hold, and had seven boilers, 30-inch cylinders, and a 10-foot stroke. In 1878 the third *J. M. White* was built at Louisville at a cost of more than $200,000. It was 325 feet long, with a 50-foot beam and an 11.5-foot hold. It had ten boilers 34 feet long, and its cylinders were 43 inches in diameter with an 11-foot stroke. The main cabin was 260 feet long. It could carry 8,500 bales of cotton. The record load of 9,226 bales of cotton was carried by the *Henry Frank* in 1881. It would have taken a season of hard work for the *New Orleans* to carry this amount.

[E. W. Gould, *Fifty Years on the Mississippi;* W. J. Petersen, *Steamboating on the Upper Mississippi.*]
WILLIAM J. PETERSEN

STEAM POWER AND ENGINES. The first useful steam engine was developed in England by Thomas Newcomen and was put into operation by 1712. By 1730 the engine was not uncommon in western Europe, and in 1755 the first steam engine began operation in the American colonies, at a copper mine in Belleville, N.J. This engine, built by the British firm of Joseph Hornblower, was followed by another in Philadelphia, built in 1773 by Christopher Colles. Three years later a third engine was at work, raising water for New York City waterworks. The Newcomen engines were large, expensive, and cumbersome. Except for draining valuable mines or providing water for large cities, they were not economically attractive in America, where waterpower suitable for manufactures was reasonably plentiful along the eastern seaboard.

Providing power for transportation was a greater problem. The Newcomen engine was too bulky for such purposes, but after the improvements made by James Watt beginning in 1764, it occurred to many that the steam engine might be applied to propelling boats. Beginning in 1785 more than a dozen American inventors tried to build steamboats, including Jehosaphat Starr, Apollos Kinsley, Isaac Briggs, William Longstreet, Elijah Ormsbee, John Stevens, Daniel French, Samuel Morey, James Rumsey, and Nathan Read. They were all handicapped by having to build their own engines (the export of which was forbidden by England) with inadequate machine-shop facilities and limited knowledge of steam technology. The most successful inventor was John Fitch, who established regular steamboat service between Philadelphia and New Jersey in 1790.

The complexity of applying steam power to navigation led some of these inventors to turn to the simpler problems of supplying stationary power. The Soho works in New Jersey, which had helped Stevens on his steamboat, began in 1799 to build two large engines for a new waterworks in Philadelphia. The head of the shops, Nicholas J. Roosevelt, was later a partner of Robert Fulton in operating the first commercially successful steamboat (1807). Robert Livingston, a partner of Fulton and brother-in-law of Stevens, was also associated with Benjamin Henry Latrobe, a British physician-architect with a knowledge of steam engines, and a number of workmen who had built and operated engines in England. Some of the most prominent emigrant British engineers were James Smallman, John Nancarrow, and Charles Stoudinger; their knowledge, along with that of other British engineers, was the single most important source of new technological information for American inventors and engine builders.

In 1802 Oliver Evans of Philadelphia became the first American to make steam engines for the general market. He was followed by Smallman in 1804, and with the addition of Daniel Large and others, that city soon became the center of engine building. New York City, where Robert McQueen and James Allaire had been patronized by Fulton, became another center of engine manufacture. During the War of 1812 the building and use of engines spread to the western states. The first engine built in Pittsburgh (for a steamboat) was completed in 1811. The following year Evans opened a Pittsburgh branch of his Philadelphia Mars Iron Works. With the addition of such pioneer builders as Thomas Copeland, James Arthurs, Mahlon Rogers, and Mark Stackhouse, Pittsburgh too became a center of steam engineering. The first engine shop in Kentucky was opened in Louisville in 1816 by Thomas Bakewell and David Prentice. Work in Cincinnati, Ohio, began soon afterward, and by 1826 that city had five steam-engine factories. This western activity was brought about in part by the widespread use of steamboats on the western waters, the demand for engines on southern sugar plantations, the easy accessibility of iron and coal around Pittsburgh, and, initially, the dislocations of eastern trade caused by the War of 1812.

By 1838 steam power was widely accepted all over the United States. In that year 3,010 steam engines were counted in a federal census. Of these, 350 were used on locomotives, 800 on steamboats, and 1,860 were stationary. This last category included those that ran mills of all descriptions, were at work on farms and plantations, and raised water for cities. Pennsylvania accounted for the largest number (383) of stationary engines, Louisiana was second with 274, and Massachusetts had 165. Except for Louisiana, where the engines were typically used on large sugar plantations to grind cane, most of these were located in cities. Of the 383 engines in Pennsylvania, 133 were at work in Pittsburgh and 174 in Philadelphia; of the 165 engines in Massachusetts, 114 were in or around Boston. The steam engine had a profound effect on the nature of cities. Formerly centers only of trade, culture, and government, they now became centers of manufacturing and, consequently, the home of a large class of factory operatives. As long as factories and mills had depended on waterpower, such a development in cities had been impossible.

By the middle of the 19th century, virtually every American city contained shops producing steam engines and had a large number of the machines at work. Imported engines were not important in the trade, although American engines were regularly exported. Northern-made engines in the South were used not only on plantations but also in other extractive processes carried out in rice mills, cottonseed oil mills, cotton gins and presses, and the saline wells of western Virginia. Most important, these engines found increasing use in cotton textile mills scattered throughout the region. Southern cities, notably Charleston, S.C., and Richmond, Va., became manufacturing centers in their own right, basing their activity to a considerable extent on steam.

As the first machine necessarily made of iron, the steam engine had a critical influence on the development of the iron industry. Previously, most iron had been used in a wrought form. Most engine parts were cast, however, and the improvements in casting technique forced by engine development were available for use in making other machines as well. In addition, rolling mills began to multiply only when boiler plate came into demand from engine builders. These boiler-plate makers in turn became the first to construct iron boats. The harnessing of steam engines to railroad locomotion, of course, increased the demand for rails as well as engines. In a circle of improvement, steam engines were used to drive rolling mills, provide blast for furnaces, and run drilling machines, lathes, and other iron-working machines, all of which made it easier to produce and work iron and led to improved steam engines. The demand for coal, both for iron furnaces and steam boilers, was also greatly stimulated.

There were essentially three types of steam engines used in the country before the introduction of the turbine late in the 19th century. The first engines were of the Newcomen type. After the introduction of Watt's improvements in this engine, no more of the old style were built. Watt's atmospheric engine was widely popular for both stationary use and for the eastern steamboats, such as Fulton's *Clermont*. It was largely superseded by the high-pressure engine of Evans. The piston of the Newcomen-type engine was actuated by introducing steam under it, condensing the steam with cold water, then allowing the weight of the atmosphere (about 15 pounds per square inch) to push the piston down. Watt's key improvement was to provide a separate condenser, which would conserve heat and make the piston ''double-acting'' by introducing steam alternately on both sides of the piston. Evans' further improvement consisted in using the force of the steam itself (at 100–200 pounds per square inch) to drive the piston directly, allowing it to escape into the atmosphere uncondensed. The power of the Watt engine could usually be increased only by enlarging the cylinder. With Evans' Columbian engine, only the steam pressure need be increased. Because it provided more power in a smaller space, his engine quickly became standard on western steamboats and eventually on locomotives.

Subsequent efforts at improvement went in two directions: first, toward further refinements of the reciprocating engine, especially by such improved valve actions as that of George Corliss of Rhode Island, and second, toward a rotary engine. Hundreds of patents were taken out for such devices before the successes of such late 19th-century inventors as Charles Gordon Curtis in developing the steam turbine. In the 20th century steam power has remained of primary importance only in the generation of electricity in power plants, although its potential use in automobiles periodically receives attention.

[G. Bathe, *Oliver Evans;* H. W. Dickinson, *Robert Fulton, Engineer and Artist;* T. Hamlin, *Benjamin Henry Latrobe;* C. Pursell, *Early Stationary Steam Engines in America.*]

CARROLL PURSELL

STEDMAN, FORT, ASSAULT ON (Mar. 25, 1865). South of the Appomattox River in Virginia,

John B. Gordon's corps held the left of the Confederate defenses before Petersburg. In his front the Union army's Fort Stedman was 200 yards distant. Strongly reinforced, Gordon assaulted the works before dawn with about 11,000 men. The garrison was surprised and the fort captured easily. But further advance was smothered by the fire of adjacent Union batteries, while heavy counterattacks soon developed. By 8 A.M. the Confederates were driven to their own lines; about 2,000 Confederates were taken prisoner, and many were killed and wounded.

[Douglas S. Freeman, *R. E. Lee,* vol. IV.]

JOSEPH MILLS HANSON

STEEL. *See* **Iron and Steel Industry.**

STEELE'S BAYOU EXPEDITION. During Gen. Ulysses S. Grant's advance on Vicksburg, Miss., in 1863, flanking expeditions were set afoot to get into the rear of the city. One of these was an effort by Gen. William Tecumseh Sherman and Adm. David D. Porter with gunboats (Mar. 14–27) to reach the Sunflower and Yazoo rivers by way of Steele's Bayou, which flows into the Mississippi a few miles above the Yazoo. Falling streams and Confederate obstructions foiled the movement.

[R. U. Johnson and C. C. Buel, eds., *Battles and Leaders of the Civil War,* vol. III.]

ALVIN F. HARLOW

STEEL STRIKES. Strikes in the basic steel industry fall into three periods: historic unsuccessful recognition struggles culminating in the 1937 ''Little Steel'' strike; a period of frequent strikes that followed National War Labor Board control and ended with the long 1959 strike; and the period between 1960 and 1975, which was free from strikes.

Before the 1935 National Labor Relations Act, with its provision for certification elections, the union-recognition issue was resolved not by ballot but by brute force. The Homestead strike of 1892 was followed by other landmark violent strikes, in 1901, 1909, and 1919. In 1919 the U.S. Steel Corporation defeated a massive organizing attempt by twenty-four unions led by the American Federation of Labor (AFL). After driving out the Amalgamated Iron and Steel Workers in 1909, U.S. Steel maintained an open-shop policy until the recognition of the Steel Workers' Organizing Committee of the Congress of Industrial Organizations (CIO) in the John L. Lewis–

Myron C. Taylor discussions of 1937. The rest of the steel companies, known collectively as "Little Steel," delayed recognition of the union in 1937 by defeating the steelworkers in the last of the violent and bitter struggles. Union demonstrators at the Republic Steel Corporation plant in Chicago were fired on by the police, and ten were killed; two others were killed by special deputies at Republic's plant in Massillon, Ohio.

Free collective bargaining between the Steelworkers Union and the industry essentially began in 1946. Between 1946 and 1959 the union had the contractual right to strike ten times and struck five. Most of these strikes lasted about one month (1946, 1949, 1956). The 1952 strike was of two months' duration and the 1959 strike went on for more than three months. These were all peaceful and orderly strikes in which the companies made no attempt to operate the mills.

The struggle for recognition was over. Collective bargaining in steel was industrywide, with negotiation ultimately between the union and a coordinating committee of large companies. When the union struck it shut down the industry. This typically brought some form of government intervention in what were regarded as national emergency situations. The 1952 strike created a constitutional crisis in which the Supreme Court ruled that President Harry S. Truman's seizure of the mills was unconstitutional. The 116-day 1959 strike was ended by the Supreme Court, which upheld a national emergency injunction.

The 1959 struggle marked a turning point. Crisis bargaining gave way to joint study under the auspices of the Human Relations Committee. In this new relationship subcommittees worked constructively on many issues. Political upheaval in the union in 1965 ended formal joint study. Complex and difficult negotiations on three levels—the plant, the corporation, and the industry—took place in 1965, 1968, and 1971. In an unprecedented breakthrough, the parties agreed in 1973 to a no-strike pledge for their 1974 negotiations with submission of unresolved issues to arbitration.

[J. H. Fitch, *The Steel Workers;* Walter Galenson, *The CIO Challenge to the AFL: A History of the American Labor Movement, 1935–1941;* John A. Garraty, "U.S. Steel Versus Labor: The Early Years," *Labor History,* vol. 1 (1960); E. Robert Livernash et al., *Collective Bargaining in the Basic Steel Industry.*]

E. ROBERT LIVERNASH

STEEL TRAP. In *Book 14, Orders and Wills of York County, 1709–1716* (Williamsburg, Va.), Capt. Dan-

iel Taylor's inventory of personal property includes "steele traps." This is probably the earliest record of the steel trap in America. By the middle of the 18th century it was in use wherever Europeans traded for furs with the Indian. The records of the British trade are especially revealing in this respect, and there are a few dated traps of this period in American collections. The *Sir William Johnson Papers* contain a requisition of 1764 for 5,000 beaver traps valued at ten shillings each. British and French traps were carried far into the interior and by 1797 were in use on the Lower Red River. In October 1804 the party led by Meriwether Lewis and William Clark found steel traps in use by the Mandan, who explained that they had been obtained from the French.

The British traders of Canada and the Pacific Northwest imported from England or manufactured locally a trap of distinctive design, which found use in India as well as in America. The Hudson's Bay Company factors recognized the American-made trap as superior to the British product and obtained it whenever they were able. By 1853 the Newhouse trap made by the Oneida Community was recognized throughout America as standard for design and quality, although it had competitors. One of the best collections of traps in the United States is at the Bucks County Historical Society, Doylestown, Pa.

[J. S. Campion, *On the Frontier;* A. R. Harding, *Steel Traps.*]

CARL P. RUSSELL

STEERING COMMITTEES are committees frequently found in legislatures and generally concerned with such matters as the scheduling of legislation. In the U.S. Congress they are party committees, and as such perform a number of functions. In some cases they may be involved in the formulation of party tactics and positions for particular bills. In the Senate, both parties established such committees in the late 19th century, and each prepared a legislative schedule when its party was the majority party. In the late 1940's both parties assigned such scheduling duties to their newly created policy committees. The Republican steering committee was displaced, but the Democrats reconstituted their steering committee as a committee on committees, responsible for assigning party members to the standing committees. In the House, both parties established such committees in the 20th century to assist the leaders in the formulation of strategy. For a short time in the 1920's the Republican Steering Committee dominated the House. In 1949 it was renamed the Policy Committee to act as an advisory body for the Republican leaders. The House Democrats established such a committee in the 1930's, but it has met only infrequently and has had no great impact on party decisions. In 1975 it assumed the committee-assignment function formerly exercised by the Democratic members of the Ways and Means Committee and attempted to play a more active role in party decisionmaking.

[Charles O. Jones, *Party and Policy-Making;* Randall B. Ripley, *Party Leaders in the House of Representatives,* and *Power in the Senate.*]

DALE VINYARD

STEPHENSON, FORT, DEFENSE OF (Aug. 1–2, 1813). When British Gen. Henry A. Proctor failed to dislodge Gen. William Henry Harrison from Fort Meigs on the Maumee River in northwestern Ohio, first in a siege ending May 9, 1813, and again in July, he withdrew down the Maumee. He then proceeded up the Sandusky River to Fort Stephenson (now Fremont, Ohio). Maj. George Croghan, the commander, twenty-one years old, had about 160 men and one cannon. Disregarding Harrison's orders to evacuate if attacked in force, he resisted the assaults of some 1,200 British and Indians equipped with light artillery, inflicting heavy losses on them while his own losses were one killed and seven wounded. Proctor withdrew on Aug. 3 and made no further attempt to invade Ohio.

[E. O. Randall and D. J. Ryan, *History of Ohio,* vol. III.]

EUGENE H. ROSEBOOM

STERLING IRON WORKS, one of the oldest iron and steel producing plants in the United States, is located in the Ramapo Mountains at Sterlington, Orange County, N.Y. It dates from 1738, when Cornelius Board, who discovered the ore in 1730, built the first furnace. Purchased in 1740 by Henry Townsend, the tract remained in that family until 1864 when the Sterling Iron and Railway Company acquired it. The superiority of Sterling iron made this the preferred source of munitions during the Revolution. Anchors and farm implements were manufactured here from the middle of the 18th century until 1891.

[Macgrane Coxe, *The Sterling Furnace and the West Point Chain.*]

PAULINE K. ANGELL

STEUBEN, FORT, built on the present site of Steubenville, Ohio, and named for Baron Friedrich Wilhelm von Steuben, was an early American fortification against the Indians. Its immediate purpose was protection for the surveyors of the Seven Ranges west of the Ohio River. Begun in 1786 by Col. John Francis Hamtramck, it was completed the next year and was garrisoned by U.S. troops, 1786–87. It consisted of four blockhouses set diagonally on the corners with lines of pickets forming the sides. Apparently it burned to the ground in 1790.

[Joseph B. Doyle, *20th Century History of Steubenville and Jefferson County, Ohio.*]

FRANCIS PHELPS WEISENBURGER

STEVENS' INDIAN TREATIES. Gov. Isaac I. Stevens of Washington Territory was also superintendent of Indian affairs for his territory. From Nov. 29, 1854, and continuing until Dec. 21, 1855, he negotiated a number of important treaties with the Indian tribes north of the Columbia River and west of the Cascade Mountains. Joel Palmer, the superintendent of Indian affairs for Oregon, cooperated with Stevens in the joint negotiation of some of the most important of these treaties, and the general policy for the treaties followed the one worked out by Palmer in Oregon. This plan was to concentrate the Indians on a few reservations, pay for their lands with useful goods, and instruct them in farming. The Medicine Creek Treaty, signed Dec. 26, 1854, by sixty-two chiefs and headmen representing the Puget Sound tribes, accepted the reservation policy. In 1855 three added treaties with the Canoe of the sound region were signed.

The great council for the interior was opened in the Walla Walla Valley in May 1855, and the treaty was proclaimed June 12, 1855. It accepted the reservation policy for the powerful tribes of the interior. The outbreak of a series of Indian wars and friction between the Indian agents and federal military officers delayed the ratification of the Walla Walla treaties by the federal government until Mar. 8, 1859.

[Charles H. Carey, *A General History of Oregon Prior to 1861.*]

ROBERT MOULTON GATKE

STEVENS' RAILROAD SURVEY. Isaac I. Stevens of Massachusetts was appointed as governor of the newly created Washington Territory and given two important added duties, that of superintendent of Indian affairs for the Pacific Northwest and director of the survey to find a route for a northern railway to the Pacific coast. Stevens was a trained army engineer and excellently qualified for his job. Capt. George B.

McClellan, assigned to assist in the active direction of the survey, was to explore the Cascade Mountains for a practicable pass. Stevens' personal command, while on the overland trip to the coast, explored the passes in the Rocky and Bitterroot mountains. The Marias Pass in northwestern Montana, later used by the Great Northern Railroad, was missed by Stevens' exploring parties, although they were searching especially for it because Indians had told them of its existence.

The location of a suitable pass into the Puget Sound region (across the Cascades) proved the most difficult problem of the survey. McClellan was instructed to explore the Naches Pass but failed because he was too easily convinced it was impassable. A. W. Tinkham received orders at Walla Walla to attempt passage of the Snoqualmie Pass, and with the aid of two Indian guides made the trip through it and discovered grades practicable for a railway. Between Oct. 7, 1853, and Feb. 1, 1854, Tinkham covered some 1,164 miles of new country. McClellan long stubbornly contested the practicability of the route discovered by Tinkham, but it was accepted by Stevens.

[George W. Fuller, *A History of the Pacific Northwest.*]
ROBERT MOULTON GATKE

STILLWATER, BATTLE OF. *See* **Freeman's Farm, Battles of.**

STILLWATER CONVENTION. When Wisconsin was admitted to the Union in 1848, a large part of what is now eastern Minnesota was excluded from the new state. A demand for a territorial government by the people of this unorganized area led to a public meeting on Aug. 4, 1848, and a convention on Aug. 26, both held at Stillwater. Sixty-one delegates, including most of the prominent men in the Minnesota country, signed memorials to Congress and to the president recommending the "early organization of the Territory of Minnesota." To further that purpose, the convention named Henry H. Sibley a delegate to "visit Washington and represent the interests of the proposed territory." In October, acting on the assumption that the territory of Wisconsin was still in existence, the people of the excluded area elected Sibley as delegate to Congress, and in January 1849, to his great surprise, he was seated. Congress authorized the creation of Minnesota Territory that same year.

[William Anderson and A. J. Lobb, *A History of the Constitution of Minnesota;* W. W. Folwell, *A History of Minnesota,* vol. I.]
T. C. BLEGEN

STOCK EXCHANGES. *See* **Exchanges.**

STOCK MARKET. *See* **Exchanges.**

STOCKS, a device for punishing petty offenders, consisting of a frame in which the culprit's hands, or hands and feet, were confined while he was kept in a sitting posture. Required by law in some of the American colonies, they were to be found in practically every English town in which a court or magistrate dispensed justice. The theory behind the use of the stocks was that the public exposure humiliated offenders known to the villagers and gave honest citizens an opportunity to become acquainted with the faces of vagrants. When the offense was one that displeased the public, the onlookers adjusted the punishment by throwing things at the culprit, by pulling the stool from beneath him, or by tipping him over backwards so that he hung head down. There was also much malicious baiting of the victims; as late as the beginning of the 19th century American gentlemen sometimes amused themselves in this manner.

C. K. SHIPTON

STOCK TICKER, a printing telegraph system by which records of stock transactions are sent from an exchange as they occur and are printed at once on a tape at each place where a ticker is located. It was introduced into the New York Stock Exchange in 1867. On Black Friday (Sept. 24, 1869), the day Jay Gould and others tried to corner the U.S. gold supply, Thomas Edison watched the frenzied activity from the Western Union telegraphic booth at the New York Stock Exchange. Seeing how the tickers were unable to keep up, Edison decided to improve the stock ticker; the patent on the improved machine was sold to the Gold and Stock Telegraph Company for $40,000. Since Edison's improvements, the stock ticker has been greatly improved in speed. In 1930 a ticker printing 500 characters a minute was introduced, and in 1964 a ticker printing 900 characters a minute and able to record the transactions of 10 million shares per day came into use. Further improvements include the reproduction of the tape on a screen, so that the information is visible to a number of people at the same time, and the joining of the ticker to a computer (1965), so that a transaction can appear almost instantaneously on the tape after its completion.

[J. E. Meeker, *The Work of the Stock Exchange.*]

STOCKTON-KEARNY QUARREL. On July 23, 1846, Commodore Robert F. Stockton relieved Commodore John D. Sloat as commander of the U.S. naval force fighting the Mexicans on the Pacific coast. Stockton agressively extended Sloat's conquest to the south, precipitating revolt among the Californians. When Gen. Stephen W. Kearny, under orders to take possession of California and to set up a temporary civil government, arrived at San Diego in December, he found Stockton unwilling to relinquish his command. Strained relations existed until the middle of January 1847, when Stockton passed the governorship over to John C. Frémont, who was in turn succeeded by Kearny early in March.

[H. H. Bancroft, *History of California;* R. G. Cleland, *California: The American Period.*]

ROBERT J. PARKER

STOCKYARDS. Travelers along the Cumberland Road and other highways leading into the West of the 1820's and 1830's were accustomed to the familiar sight of droves of cattle fattened on the frontier farms of the Middle West on their way to the markets of the eastern seaboard cities. The extension of the railroads into the West in the two succeeding decades changed all this, so that by the outbreak of the Civil War, livestock had become one of the chief freight items of the western roads. This change in the marketing of livestock resulted in new business methods. At the various western termini, accommodations for holding livestock, commission firms to handle the consignments for the shipper, and packing plants to process a portion of the shipments appeared as component parts of a great business community.

The early stockyards in these terminal cities were either private yards or yards owned and operated by the railroads. As the traffic increased, need for a consolidated yard became clear to all. On Dec. 25, 1865, the Union Stock Yards, founded by John B. Sherman, were opened in Chicago. Under a charter granted by the Illinois legislature, a company known as the Union Stockyard and Transit Company was formed with a capital of $1 million. The railroads running into Chicago took most of the stock, and on the board of directors were to be found officials of most of the roads. As the trade in western cattle grew, yards were opened in other cities: Kansas City in 1871, Saint Louis in 1872, Cincinnati in 1874, Omaha in 1884, and Saint Paul and Denver in 1886.

The rise of Chicago to a position of supremacy was due to its favorable location, the convergence of nine important railroad lines there, the advantage of an early start given it by the concentration of supplies for the Union armies during the Civil War, and the enterprise of its citizens in furnishing those factors indispensable for the efficient marketing of livestock: commission houses, stockyards, and packing plants. With the concentration of the packing business in Chicago—Nelson Morris in 1859, Armour in 1867, and Swift in 1875—and the mounting flood of cattle pouring in from the western ranges, Chicago became the greatest livestock center in the world. By the early 1970's Omaha had become the largest livestock market in the world, and Chicago's Union Stock Yards were closed in 1971.

In and around the yards in the various cities, there grew up distinctive communities. The great packing companies built their plants nearby and around them sprawled the "packing towns" made famous in Upton Sinclair's 1906 novel *The Jungle.* In the yards were to be found a lusty crowd of commission men, cattle and horse buyers, railroad men, reporters of stock news, cattlemen and their cowboys from the western ranges, and stock detectives representing western livestock associations. They formed a vigorous, distinctive, and colorful group in the business community of the West. (*See also* Livestock Industry; Meat-Packing.)

[R. A. Clemen, *The American Livestock and Meat Industry;* Harold M. Mayer and Richard C. Wade, *Chicago: Growth of a Metropolis.*]

ERNEST S. OSGOOD

STODDERT, FORT, a stockaded work constructed by Capt. Bartholomew Shaumberg in July 1799 near the junction of the Alabama and Tombigbee rivers, about fifty miles above Mobile. Named for the first secretary of the navy, Benjamin Stoddert, it became a thriving settlement and military post, as well as a port of entry, the seat of a court of admiralty, and the revenue headquarters of the district of Mobile. The fort acted as a check on ambitious frontiersmen anxious to take Spanish Mobile (*see* Kemper Raid). Aaron Burr was kept prisoner at Fort Stoddert in 1807, and the first newspaper within the present limits of Alabama was published at the fort. With the taking of Mobile in the War of 1812, Fort Stoddert lost its importance and was abandoned.

[Peter Hamilton, *Colonial Mobile.*]

JAMES W. SILVER

STONE FLEETS, consisted of small sailing vessels loaded with stone, which the Navy Department purchased during the Civil War in Baltimore, New York, New Bedford, New London, and other northern ports and sank at the entrances of southern harbors in the hope of closing the channels to blockade runners. Three such vessels were sunk in Ocracoke Inlet, N.C., Nov. 18, 1861; sixteen in the main entrance to Charleston harbor, Dec. 20, 1861; and twenty in Maffitt's Channel, another entrance to Charleston harbor, Jan. 26, 1862. The work accomplished nothing since marine worms ate away the ships' timbers and the stones sank in the mud.

[J. R. Spears, *The Story of the New England Whalers.*]
LOUIS H. BOLANDER

STONE RIVER, BATTLE OF. *See* **Murfreesboro, Battle of.**

STONEWALL, a Confederate ironclad ram, was built in France, sold to Denmark, and purchased from that country by Confederate agents. The vessel was 172 feet long and 33 feet in breadth of beam. Under the command of Capt. Thomas J. Page, the *Stonewall* sailed from Copenhagen Jan. 7, 1865, and, after a futile attempt to draw two U.S. warships into combat on Mar. 24, crossed the Atlantic to Cuba. After the war ended, it was delivered to the United States and subsequently sold to Japan.

[J. Thomas Scharf, *History of the Confederate States Navy.*]

RICHARD E. YATES

STONEY CREEK, BATTLE OF (June 6, 1813). Generals John Chandler and William H. Winder, with about 1,400 Americans, encamped on June 5 at Stoney Creek at the western end of Lake Ontario, near the British camp at Burlington Heights. The following morning, shortly before daybreak, British Gen. John Vincent, with about 700 British regulars, attacked the Americans, and heavy casualties were suffered on both sides. The two American commanders, eighteen other officers, and eighty men, as well as ordnance, were captured. Fearing a renewal of the attack, the American army withdrew (*see* Niagara Campaigns).

[Louis L. Babcock, *The War of 1812 on the Niagara Frontier.*]

ROBERT W. BINGHAM

STONINGTON, BOMBARDMENT OF. On Aug. 9, 1814, four British vessels, detached from the squadron under Commodore Thomas Hardy blockading New London, Conn., appeared off the borough of Stonington, Conn., and gave warning of one hour for the removal of noncombatants before bombarding the town. Although the attack continued at intervals until noon on Aug. 12, no buildings were destroyed (though many were damaged), no persons were killed, and only a few were wounded. The citizens, assisted by the militia of the vicinity, offered effective resistance and prevented any attempt to make a landing. The action was probably intended as a preliminary to a British attack on New London.

[J. W. Barber, *Connecticut Historical Collections;* R. A. Wheeler, *History of the Town of Stonington.*]

GEORGE MATTHEW DUTCHER

STONY POINT, CAPTURE OF (July 16, 1779). Stony Point, a rocky peninsula on the west bank of the Hudson River, was connected with Verplancks Point on the east shore by Kings Ferry, a link between two main roads leading from New England to Pennsylvania. On May 31, 1779, the British occupied the two points and began to fortify them strongly. Gen. George Washington himself carefully reconnoitered Stony Point. Deciding that a surprise of the position was practicable, he chose Gen. Anthony Wayne and the American Light Infantry, a picked corps of about 1,300 men, for the attack. "I'll storm Hell if you'll plan it," Wayne is reported to have told him. The attack took place at midnight. While a small detachment in the center fired noisily to divert the attention of the defenders, two silent columns, their empty muskets surmounted by bayonets, swarmed over the fortifications to kill and wound 123 men and to take more than 540 prisoners. Although Washington abandoned the works on July 18, the expedition had done much for the morale of his army.

[H. B. Dawson, *The Assault on Stony Point.*]
EDWARD P. ALEXANDER

STORE BOATS. Each year from about 1800 to the time of the Civil War numerous flatboats, fitted out as store or trading boats, descended the Ohio and Tennessee rivers with the spring floods. The part of the craft dedicated to trade was outfitted with shelves and counters. Since they served as the department stores of the rivers, they held large stocks of groceries, liquors, dry goods, and hardware. They carried a calico flag to indicate their character and responded to a hail from dwellers on the banks, or tied up near a plantation or hamlet too small to afford a store. Their arrival was announced by a blast on a tin horn, and the inhabitants with money to spend or goods to barter flocked to the landing. Enterprising traders made the voyage every year, and the immigrant often made his way to his new home on the boats, selling goods as he drifted.

[Leland D. Baldwin, *Keelboat Age on Western Waters.*]
LELAND D. BALDWIN

STORES, GENERAL, have been characterized by their great variety of goods and services. From colonial times through much of the 19th century they constituted the typical retail unit; but in 1967 they made up less than 50,000 of the 1,763,324 retail units in the United States. In their heyday general stores, owned and operated by individuals or partners, quickly followed peddlers into newly occupied regions, even though prospective customers still grew much of their own foodstuffs and made much of their own clothing. Bad roads and scattered population also reduced the likely volume of sales. To survive in such limited markets, storekeepers sold and bartered great varieties of merchandise to customers, marketed crops taken in trade, operated local post offices, provided credit and elementary banking services, and served as social agents. Because such persons necessarily had to be familiar with all kinds of economic activities, they could and often did ultimately turn to banking, manufacturing, processing of farm crops, or other specialized business services. General stores thus met an economic need at an early and often long-enduring stage of their communities, and they also served as training schools for people who would ultimately concentrate on one specialized economic activity within the community.

[Lewis E. Atherton, *The Frontier Merchant in Mid-America;* Fred M. Jones, *Middlemen in the Domestic Trade of the United States, 1800–1860.*]
LEWIS E. ATHERTON

STOURBRIDGE LION, the first steam locomotive to run on a track in America. The Delaware and Hudson Canal Company built a railroad line between its mines at Carbondale, Pa., and its canal terminus at Honesdale, Pa., and had four locomotives built in England. The 9-horsepower *Stourbridge Lion* was tested at Honesdale on Aug. 8, 1829. It weighed 7 tons, whereas the company had specified only 3, and the company's engineer bravely drove it over trestles that trembled under its weight. That first trip was its last; it was discarded as being too heavy for any bridge. What became of the other three engines is unknown.

ALVIN F. HARLOW

STRANGITE KINGDOM. The death in June 1844 of Joseph Smith, founder and prophet of Mormonism, left a numerous religious sect bereft of a leader. A struggle over the vacant succession ensued, and among the aspiring prophets who attracted a considerable following was James J. Strang. With the aid of "angelic visitations," Strang developed the holy city of Voree, near modern Burlington, Wis., in the years 1844–49, and attracted a considerable following of Mormons scattered throughout the country.

Before long, Strang's attention was diverted to the Beaver Islands in Lake Michigan, where in 1849 the city of Saint James was founded as his new holy city. A year later (July 1850) the Kingdom of God on Earth was formally proclaimed, with Strang as God's vicegerent who should establish his rule in this world. Strang was an able orator and a man of much native shrewdness who for six years dominated the several thousand people who composed his kingdom. At length he was murdered by disgruntled conspirators (June 1856), and his followers were plundered and driven into exile by a frontier mob. A tiny body of zealots remained faithful to the Strangite faith.

[M. M. Quaife, *The Kingdom of St. James.*]
M. M. QUAIFE

STRATEGIC ARMS LIMITATION TALKS (SALT). In 1968 President Lyndon B. Johnson and Leonid I. Brezhnev, Soviet Communist party chairman, agreed to open the Strategic Arms Limitation Talks. By this time three basic problems that had stalled previous major Soviet-American disarmament agreements had been eliminated. First, the détente that followed the Cuban missile crisis of 1962 improved the political climate greatly over the days of Joseph Stalin and Joseph R. McCarthy. Second, the thorny issue of on-site inspections was made irrelevant by the development of the spy satellite. Also, America's nuclear superiority over the Soviet Union was eroding because of a massive nuclear building program undertaken by the Soviets after the Cuban crisis, eliminating the problem created by the fact that the United States was unwilling to give up its nuclear lead while the Soviets refused to negotiate except on terms of equality. So, in 1968, Johnson offered to open SALT with the clear implication that the United States would accept Soviet nuclear parity.

Unfortunately, the 1968 talks never came off. First, the Soviet Union invaded Czechoslovakia. Then Richard M. Nixon, Johnson's probable successor, attacked the president for considering abandonment of America's nuclear superiority. With Johnson already discredited by his Vietnam policy, Nixon's attack forced postponement of the talks.

After Nixon's election, Presidential Assistant Henry A. Kissinger undertook a study that showed the Soviet Union would indeed soon achieve nuclear parity. Nixon now talked of nuclear "sufficiency" rather than superiority. Still the president took a hard line. He insisted that the Soviet Union prove its good faith in Vietnam and the Middle East before convening SALT. He applied even more pressure by pushing a new, albeit limited, antiballistic missile (ABM) program through Congress and by quietly accelerating deployment of sophisticated independently targeted multiple warheads.

SALT opened in November 1969. The official delegates met in Helsinki, and later in Vienna. But the real negotiations were carried on in secret meetings between Kissinger and Soviet ambassador Anatoly Dobrynin, culminating in the SALT I agreement hammered out at the Moscow summit of 1972. SALT I limited each side to two ABM sites, outlawed mobile land missiles, prohibited interference with spy satellites, and restricted the number of strategic missiles each country could have. The Soviets were permitted 1,618 land-based missiles and 62 submarines with 710 launchers. The United States could deploy 1,000 land-based missiles and 44 submarines with 710 launchers. Although the Soviet Union was allowed more missiles, none of them was yet equipped with multiple warheads, whereas 700 American missiles already had them.

SALT I was widely cheered, but it had two significant gaps. It lacked controls on manned bombers and on multiple warheads. At the Vladivostok summit of 1974, President Gerald R. Ford announced that he and Brezhnev had already reached a tentative SALT II agreement limiting all strategic weapons. They promised to restrict their arsenals to 2,400 strategic missiles each, 1,320 of which could have multiple warheads. Although Soviet missiles carried larger payloads, this advantage was to be offset by two provisions. The United States was permitted 525 bombers to the Soviet's 160, and America's planes and missiles already stationed with the North Atlantic Treaty Organization in Europe were not to be counted against its quota of 2,400.

SALT II received far more criticism than SALT I. Conflicts over the inclusion of the Soviet "Backfire" bomber and America's "cruise missiles" in the quotas of strategic launchers that were permitted each side threatened to undermine the negotiations, while accusations that the Soviets were cheating on the agreement added to the furor. At the end of 1975 the issue was still in doubt.

[Marvin Kalb and Bernard Kalb, *Kissinger;* Harland B. Moulton, *From Superiority to Parity: The United States and the Strategic Arms Race, 1961–1971;* Chalmers Roberts, *The Nuclear Years: The Arms Race and Arms Control, 1945–1970.*]

JERALD A. COMBS

STRATFORD HALL, in Westmoreland County, Va., about a mile from the Potomac River, was built by Thomas Lee in the 1720's. It consisted of a great house with secondary structures and gardens. The central mansion was H-shaped—the two wings, each topped by four grouped chimneys, were connected by a great hall. Home of the Lees until sold in 1822, it suffered neglect and by its second century stood bleak and gaunt. In 1929 it was acquired by the Robert E. Lee Foundation and restored.

[Ethel Armes, *Stratford Hall, The Great House of the Lees.*]

LEONARD C. HELDERMAN

STRAUDER V. WEST VIRGINIA, 100 U.S. 303 (1880), a case in which the Supreme Court declared that a West Virginia statute restricting jury service to whites violated the Fourteenth Amendment because it denied blacks equal protection of the law. The Court also upheld the Civil Rights Act (1866) provision for removal of cases to the federal courts when equal rights were denied in state courts.

[Charles Warren, *The Supreme Court in United States History.*]

RANSOM E. NOBLE, JR.

STRAWBERRY BANK. David Thomson's settlement on the Piscataqua River (*see* New Hampshire) was taken over in 1630 by the Laconia Company (based on a grant received Nov. 17, 1629), which sent two ships under Walter Neale. He carried on some fishing and trading and explored as far as the White Mountains. Capt. John Mason, the most active member of the company, secured in 1631 more colonists who moved the settlement to the west bank of the upper harbor and named it "Strawbery Banke" for the many wild strawberries found growing there. The company sent, in all, about eighty persons, spent £3,000, failed, and divided its assets in 1634, leaving Mason to work alone until his death in 1635. Deserted by his heirs, and outstripped by the settlement at

Dover Point (founded by Edward Hilton under a grant from Plymouth Colony), the slowly growing Strawberry Bank formed its own government and elected Francis Williams governor, until 1641. It then placed itself under Massachusetts, which claimed the region, reserving for its Anglican inhabitants the right to vote. Under the new rule, with more security and protection, the town grew; town meetings provided for ferries, roads, a highway to Boston, and a fort. In 1652 it was allowed to elect representatives to the Massachusetts General Court, and in 1653 it changed its name to Portsmouth.

[Ralph May, *Early Portsmouth History*.]
HERBERT W. HILL

STREET RAILWAYS. The first street railway in America was laid on Bowery and Fourth Avenue, from Prince Street to Murray Hill, New York City, in 1832–33. A portion of it was put into operation in June 1833. The horse-drawn cars had bodies like stagecoaches, and there was room for two passengers on the dickey, or driver's seat. This road met much opposition because its rails were slotted so deeply that they damaged the wheels of other vehicles. It was a financial failure, and not until 1836 was another car line attempted, this one in Boston. Thereafter, little was done to provide street railways until about 1850; between that date and 1855, six new lines were built in various cities. In 1855 the Boston line installed a rail with a slot only seven-eighths of an inch deep, and in the following year, the modern type of streetcar rail was designed for a Philadelphia line, which greatly accelerated the development of the business. Between 1855 and 1860 thirty new lines were built; between 1860 and 1880 eighty more came into being. By 1890 there were 769 such railways in the principal cities of the United States.

As cities grew larger and distances greater, horses became too slow for the longer lines. Beginning in the 1870's, steam cars were tried in some cities, but they were highly objectionable. The cable car, with a continuous cable running in a slot under the surface—the cars attaching themselves to it by a clutch or grip—next became the most popular form of rapid transit. The first such line was completed in San Francisco in 1873, and was found well adapted to the steep hills of that city. During the next fifteen years most of the larger cities had one or more cable lines, but such systems were very costly—about $100,000 per mile. Electric cars, introduced between 1880 and 1890, rapidly superseded all other systems (*see* Railways,

Electric). In 1912 there were 41,065 miles of electric railways in the United States, but the rapid development of the automobile and then the motor bus was already beginning to threaten their existence. By 1920 street railways in most places were losing money heavily. Fares—which had always been five cents for almost any length of ride—were being raised practically everywhere save in New York City, but this only increased competition. After 1930 the railway lines began to disappear more and more rapidly and to be replaced by motor buses. By the early 1960's street railways had almost completely vanished from American cities, save in New Orleans and San Francisco.

ALVIN F. HARLOW

STRICT CONSTRUCTION. *See* **Constitution of the United States.**

STRIKES are organized work stoppages by employees and may be classified by purpose. The organization strike is designed to pressure the employer to recognize the union as the collective voice of the employees. The economic strike is designed to improve the economic returns to the workers through higher wages or fewer hours. The sympathy strike is designed to bring pressure on an employer, government body, or group of consumers to grant the demands of a group of workers other than the strikers. In the sitdown strike the strikers occupy the work premises to assure that no substitute workers are brought in. The jurisdictional strike is intended to persuade an employer to recognize and deal with the strikers in preference to another group of organized workers. The wildcat strike is a work stoppage in violation of an existing collective agreement prohibiting strikes between the parent union and the employer. The grievance strike is held to protest an alleged failure of the employer to carry out the terms of the agreement or to settle a dispute not covered by the "prohibition to strike" clause of the contract.

Most early strikes in the United States did not involve a labor union or organization. The workers merely got together on a temporary basis to present their demands or to take joint action to protect their interests. Such workers organizations as did exist had been formed not for economic reasons but for philanthropic purposes. They were mutual aid societies, providing various sick and death benefits for their members.

In 1805 a Philadelphia court ruled, in the Philadelphia Cordwainers' case, that a strike is "a conspiracy of workmen to raise their wages" and therefore criminal. In 1809 a New York court decided that a strike, regardless of its objective, was necessarily an unlawful conspiracy intended to injure the employer and his business. In 1835 a court of final jurisdiction in New York sustained the common-law doctrine that all combinations to raise wages were illegal.

The Supreme Court of Massachusetts heard the case of *Commonwealth* v. *Hunt* in 1842. This case was considered by many to be the first break in the early judicial rulings. The court ruled that it was not unlawful for laborers to go on strike to gain a closed shop. Illegality would depend on the means used. This case led to judging the legality of work stoppages on the basis of their purpose and the means used by the strikers to gain their ends. After the decision in *Commonwealth* v. *Hunt,* workers were still prosecuted for conspiracy, but these cases usually involved acts of violence.

Labor organizations were not yet free to strike; the injunction was used against them. The railway strike of 1877 served as the earliest precedent for the use of the injunction in labor controversies. The first use of an injunction in a labor dispute that was confirmed by the Supreme Court was in the Pullman strike of 1894. In *In re Debs* (1895) the Court ruled against Eugene V. Debs, president of the American Railway Union. In *Loewe* v. *Lawler* (1908), known as the Danbury Hatters case, the Court ruled that a secondary boycott by a union (in this case, the boycott of shops in other states carrying a specific manufacturer's goods) was illegal. This attempt to compel the manufacturer to unionize was considered a conspiracy in restraint of interstate commerce within the meaning of the Sherman Antitrust Act (July 2, 1890). It was the first time the act was used against labor.

Congress, in the Clayton Antitrust Act of 1914, attempted to remove labor from the jurisdiction of the antitrust laws. Section VI of the Clayton Antitrust Act specifies that the labor of a human being is not a commodity or article of commerce. Nothing contained in the antitrust laws could be construed as forbidding the existence and operation of labor, agricultural, or horticultural organizations instituted for mutual help or similar purposes.

In 1921 it became evident that the courts believed a common-law right to strike existed that they were obligated to protect, and they would refuse to enjoin strikes for legitimate objectives. This general principle was stated by Chief Justice William Howard Taft in *American Foundries* v. *Tri-City Council* (1921).

The Norris–La Guardia Act of 1932 forbade the use of injunctions in labor disputes and repudiated antiunion (yellow-dog) contracts as a basis for equal and equitable rights. Section IV of this act protected the right to strike by specifying actions that were not subject to injunctions. Although the Railway Labor Act of 1926 had protected the right of labor to organize and bargain collectively, there had been no legislative protection of the right to strike, nor was such protection afforded by the amended Railway Labor Act of 1934.

The National Labor Relations (Wagner-Connery) Act of 1935 contained language similar to that found in Section 7(a) of the National Industrial Recovery Act of 1933. It also expressly provided that "nothing in this Act shall be construed so as to interfere with or impede or diminish in any way the right to strike."

The Strikebreakers Act of June 24, 1936, made it a felony to transport strikebreakers in interstate commerce. In *National Labor Relations Board* v. *Fan Steel Corporation* (1939) it was ruled that sit-down strikes were illegal. The National Labor Relations Board devised the theory that employees who strike for purely economic reasons may be replaced, but that those whose strike is caused or prolonged by unfair labor practices on the part of the employer may not be replaced or discharged, at least in the absence of unlawful strike activity.

After World War II, reaction to the fear that unions were growing too powerful led in 1947 to passage of the Taft-Hartley Act, which prohibited strikes under a number of circumstances: (1) to force a self-employed person to join a labor or employer organization; (2) to force an employer to join an employer or labor organization; (3) to force an employer or other person to cease using the products or services of another employer (in effect forbidding all secondary boycotts); (4) to force an employer, other than the employer of the striking employees, to bargain with an uncertified union; and (5) to force an employer to bargain with one union when another union has been certified or to force an employer to assign particular work to employees in one labor organization or trade craft or class rather than another.

The most important effect of the Wagner and Taft-Hartley acts was that they provided a legal means to establish union recognition. The bloodiest strikes by far were those over union recognition. Now the employer was not free either to extend or to withhold recognition at his option. The acts provided a juridical process to determine rights of representation.

Some contracts provide for legal strikes despite the

existence of a labor agreement. For example, many agreements in the automobile industry permit strikes in disputes over production standards. When the company maintains that it can refuse to bargain over rates of production, the union may refuse to give a no-strike pledge in disputes over this issue.

John Dunlop noted in the 1960's that there has been a secular decline in the number of strikes and lockouts and a marked decline of violence in industrial strife. Part of the reason for fewer strikes is that some types of strikes, organizing efforts, jurisdictional disputes, and secondary boycotts have become subject to public machinery designed to resolve the dispute or prohibit the work stoppage. Strikes or lockouts usually occur over the terms of reopened or expiring agreements; they accounted for approximately 80 percent of the work time lost in the 1960's and 1970's. These disputes, Dunlop believes, probably offer the greatest scope for the development of new procedures by private parties. Joint mediation, joint study committees, and improved mediation by outsiders may be the way most future labor disputes are resolved.

Dunlop distinguishes four major functions of strikes by established unions: to change the structure of bargaining; to change the relations between the principal negotiators and their constituents in union and management; to change the budget allotment or policy of a government agency; or to change a bargaining position of the other side. He advances several reasons for the secular decline of strikes: the capacity to shut down operations in many industries has been reduced; the costs of the stoppage to both parties have been increased by the reaction of customers through inventories and substitutions; the expansion of government employment in sensitive sectors has made strikes less effective; more sophisticated methods of resolving issues in negotiations have come into play, making traditional bargaining procedures, including strikes and lockouts, less useful; and negotiation and mediation skills and resources have become more highly developed.

A typical example of a strike designed to change the structure of bargaining was the strike in 1962–63 of New York Typographical Union No. 6 under the leadership of Bertram A. Powers. It had been customary for the publishers to deal with the weakest union, the Newspaper Guild; reach agreement on a contract; and then hold all the other unions, who had much more power than the Newspaper Guild, to the terms accepted by the guild. The strike by Powers and the typographers was an attempt to break up this leadership by the Newspaper Guild. It was successful in

persuading publishers that hereafter they might have to negotiate first with a strong union like that of the typographers, because it refused to be bound by terms accepted by a weaker union.

[Foster Rhea Dulles, *Labor in America;* John T. Dunlop and Neil W. Chamberlain, *Frontiers of Collective Bargaining;* Sumner H. Schlichter, James J. Healy, and E. Robert Livernash, *The Impact of Collective Bargaining on Management.*]

WILLIAM GOMBERG

STRIP. *See* **Cherokee Strip.**

STUART'S RIDE. As Gen. Robert E. Lee prepared to resist Union Gen. George B. McClellan's attempt to capture Richmond in 1862 (*see* Seven Days' Battles), it was necessary to know the exact position of the Union right (*see* Jackson's Valley Campaign). On June 13 Confederate Gen. J. E. B. Stuart's cavalry accomplished this. Then, Stuart decided to ride around McClellan's army, because he thought such a movement would be unexpected. On June 14 Stuart was behind McClellan; on June 15 the cavalry rode into Richmond with 165 prisoners, having traveled more than 100 miles and having lost only one man. As a result of Stuart's ride McClellan changed his supply base to the James River; Lee was supplied with the information he required. The moral value of the ride was tremendous; from a military viewpoint its value was questionable.

[John W. Thomason, *Jeb Stuart.*]

THOMAS ROBSON HAY

STUDENT NONVIOLENT COORDINATING COMMITTEE (SNCC) was founded in April 1960, to coordinate the southern black college-student nonviolent direct-action protests against lunch-counter segregation that had arisen earlier in the year. As this phase of the southern black protest movement subsided toward the end of the year, with the dropping of the color bar at many chain and department store dining facilities in Texas and the upper South, SNCC changed from a committee coordinating campus-based groups to a staff organization that initiated its own projects in local communities. SNCC played a central role in the desegregation and voter registration campaigns that followed in the Deep South. Operating in the most oppressive areas, its dedicated workers became celebrated for their courage in the face of white intimidation. Despite noteworthy accomplishments, the millenarian SNCC people became disillusioned with their failure radically to reshape southern society in a few short years. In the radical vanguard of the black protest movement, by 1966 they adopted an ideology of black separatism and revolutionary violence—a transformation accompanied by the rapid decline and ultimate disappearance of the organization. Yet SNCC had made a key contribution to the important social changes that had occurred in the South.

AUGUST MEIER

STUDENTS, EXCHANGE. *See* **Exchange Students.**

STUDENTS FOR A DEMOCRATIC SOCIETY. SDS was the main organizational expression of the campus-based radical movement known as the New Left in the 1960's. An almost moribund organization of about 300 students at the start of the decade, it grew to the point where probably well over 50,000 people took part in the activities of local SDS chapters in 1968–69.

SDS originated as the student department of the League for Industrial Democracy, a mildly social-democratic educational service. In the 1950's, under the name Student League for Industrial Democracy, the campus affiliate had consisted of a dwindling number of campus discussion groups. When student political activism began to revive, starting with sit-ins at segregated lunch counters in the South in 1960, SDS began to orient itself toward the new movement. Gradually there began to form a core of articulate student leaders who were interested in such issues as civil rights and nuclear disarmament and in the relations between them. Under the leadership of Tom Hayden and Al Haber of the University of Michigan, SDS in 1962 issued the ''Port Huron Statement,'' a sixty-four-page document that proclaimed independence from traditional radical and liberal formulas and that became a manifesto for student activists of the new generation.

SDS's own membership grew slowly until the escalation of American military intervention in Vietnam in 1965. SDS sponsored the first national demonstration against the war, a march on Washington in April 1965, which drew upward of 20,000 mostly young people. From then on, although it ceased playing a leading role in the antiwar movement, its growth was rapid. It also became progressively more radical

in the late 1960's, cutting its ties to the League for Industrial Democracy in 1965. By the end of the decade, SDS at the national level was an avowedly revolutionary organization. Its influence within the student movement came largely through its insistence that the alienation felt by many young people had its roots in the same social system that carried on the Vietnam War and oppressed racial minorities in the United States. At many schools, notably at Columbia University in 1968 and Harvard University in 1969, SDS chapters led disruptive protests against university ties with the military and other issues.

The momentum of events in the late 1960's caused many in SDS to believe that a social revolution was not far away, and this feeling in turn exacerbated factional divisions. At its annual convention in June 1969, SDS split into two groups, one (led by members of the Progressive Labor party) advocating a worker-student alliance and the other (led in part by people who later formed the ''Weather Underground'') placing main emphasis on support for Third World and black revolutionaries. The former group still existed under the name SDS in 1974, but its following was only a tiny fraction of that commanded by SDS in the late 1960's.

[Thomas Powers, *Diana;* Kirkpatrick Sale, *SDS;* Massimo Teodori, ed., *The New Left.*]

JAMES P. O'BRIEN

STUMP SPEAKERS. Andrew Jackson's heavy popular vote in the national election of 1824, when he ran against—and was defeated by—John Quincy Adams, first apprised the eastern seaboard of the potential power, as well as peculiar prejudices, of the backwoods voters beyond the Alleghenies. Local politicians had already gauged the fierce, often cantankerous, dislikes of the independent pioneers: their distrust of the townsman, his money power, his suave manners and effete learning, and his easy, ''degenerate'' life. Campaigning among the scattered settlements, the successful candidate for town, county, or state office, mounting a stump in a clearing, stressed the things that would appeal to his farmer, woodsman, village-storekeeper hearers. His oratory was of the florid, bombastic variety, wherein freedom, the flag, and the right to do and acquire as one pleased were mixed with violent denunciations of bankers, manufacturers, and Philadelphia lawyers. It was a guarantee of victory if he could impugn his opponent as eastern educated, foppish, and in sympathy with the rich. Promises were freely made, and liquor was as freely, though a trifle more discreetly, dispensed.

The candidate dressed for the part and professed the democratic dogma that he was but the humble equal of the roughest-dressed of the horny-handed nobles before him. Thus was the pattern set for all later appeals to the rural vote; and stumping retained its usage long after the decaying tree stumps of the pioneer settlements gave way first to the platform under the trees and, in the 20th century, to the private train and the automobile equipped with loudspeakers. Stumping became a national phenomenon in the gaudy presidential campaign of 1840, when William Henry Harrison himself, though descended from Virginia aristocrats, played the part of a rough westerner in coonskin cap and spoke from stumps as well as platforms in his tour through the former Northwest Territory.

CHARLES J. FINGER

STURGES V. CROWNINSHIELD, 4 Wheaton 122 (1819), examined at length the respective powers of state and federal governments over bankruptcy and what constitutes that "impairment of the obligation of contract" that the Constitution forbids. Ruling on the constitutionality of a New York State bankruptcy law, the Supreme Court maintained that state bankruptcy laws were permitted since congressional legislation was lacking. The Court concluded that the power of Congress to enact "uniform laws on the subject of bankruptcies" was supreme but not exclusive until Congress, by legislation, makes it so and that the obligation of contracts lies in the law that makes the contract binding at the time it is made, and provides the remedy in case of breach. But the New York law was declared invalid because it applied retroactively to contracts made prior to its enactment.

[Charles Warren, *The Supreme Court in United States History*.]

HARVEY PINNEY

SUBLETTE'S CUTOFF, a dry branch of the Oregon Trail between South Pass and Bear River, Wyo., fifty-three miles shorter than the better-watered Fort Bridger route. Part of the cutoff was used in 1832 for pack mules by William L. Sublette, hair-trigger fur man and congressional aspirant. Capt. Benjamin L. E. Bonneville's wagon train followed the route in 1832. Others took the same general course. Father Pierre-Jean De Smet, crossing South Pass (1841) ahead of the Oregon migration, found two trails, one bearing south, the other west across the desert. One became the Oregon Trail. The other—Sublette's—

was also called Meek's, Greenwood's, or Hedspeth's cut off. Both were traveled extensively until 1869.

[H. M. Chittenden, *The American Fur Trade;* Washington Irving, *Adventures of Captain Bonneville*.]

JAY MONAGHAN

SUBMARINES. The first operating submarine was tested by the Dutch inventor Cornelis Drebbel (1620–24), but not until early in the 18th century were a significant number of submersibles conceived and tested. The first submarine used in combat was built in 1775 by David Bushnell, a Yale student. His one-man wooden craft, the *Turtle,* failed in its submerged attack on the British ship *Eagle* in New York harbor (1776). Later, Robert Fulton, a famous American artist and inventor, built the *Nautilus* (1801) out of wood covered by iron plates. Although successful in submerged tests against wooden ships, the *Nautilus* failed to interest the government of France, England, or the United States. Bushnell produced another submarine for the War of 1812 against England, but as with the *Turtle,* his craft was unsuccessful.

The Civil War saw the next significant American effort at submarine warfare. Eager to break a strangling Union blockade of its ports, the Confederacy undertook the construction of various submarines. Horace L. Hunley financed the building of the *Pioneer* (1862) by James McClintock and Baxter Watson, but it never entered combat. A second vessel was lost en route to the fighting. The first submarine to sink a ship was the hand-powered *Hunley.* Designed by Barriens and built by Hunley and McClintock, this cigar-shaped boat was made of boiler plate and manned by a crew of nine. It took the lives of thirty-five volunteers in five trial runs and became known as the Peripatetic Coffin. The *Hunley* was therefore ordered to operate as a surface vessel. On the night of Feb. 17, 1864, it drove its spar torpedo into the Union *Housatonic* anchored at the entrance to Charleston harbor, S.C., and both vessels sank. The Union's one attempt to construct a submarine proved abortive; the main effort went into semisubmersibles and monitors.

Submarine development in the 19th century was advanced by England, France, Sweden, Russia, and Spain. Modern undersea craft in America evolved from the pioneering work of John P. Holland, an Irish immigrant, and Simon Lake. Holland built six submarines (1875–97), one of which, the *Plunger,* won the U.S. government's competition for a practical submarine design in 1893. It was never completed.

His most famous craft, the 53-foot *Holland,* was built at his own expense and became the U.S. Navy's first submarine. It was launched in 1897 and was accepted by the navy on Apr. 11, 1900. Lake, Holland's chief competitor, was interested in submarines mainly as salvage and exploration vehicles. His *Argonaut* (1897) had wheels for the submarine to roll over the ocean floor. Lake's company built seven submarines for Russia (1901–06) and twenty-seven for the United States, with the first completed in 1911.

England and Germany had a delayed interest in submarines. The first English orders, for five Holland-designed craft, did not come until 1901; the first German vessel, the 139-foot U-1, was not completed until 1905. At the outset of World War I there were submarines in the fleets of all the major navies. They had grown in size until the standard submarine was about 200 feet long and displaced several hundred tons on the surface. Most undersea activity in World War I was by German craft. They sank more than 5,000 merchant and fishing ships during the conflict. After the war, the U.S. Navy constructed the *Argonaut* (1928), a long-range submarine. Subsequently, the navy built a series of classes leading to the successful Gato and Balao classes of submarine of World War II.

Germany again used submarines to good advantage during World War II, although its extensive attacks against merchant shipping failed in the end because of a devastating Allied antisubmarine campaign. In the Pacific, U.S. submarines sank 1,314 naval and merchant ships (1941–45). Two wartime developments—radar (using radio waves to search through the air to detect ships and aircraft) and the snorkel (breathing tubes enabling submarines to draw in air for their diesels and crew from just under the surface)—made a major impact on submarine combat.

After World War II the United States was quick to adapt advanced German submarine technology. Some fifty-one war-built diesel submarines were converted to the improved GUPPY-configuration (1946–62), and the world's first nuclear-powered submarine, the U.S.S. *Nautilus,* was launched in 1954. With a 3,000-ton displacement and 320 feet long, the *Nautilus* cruised 60,000 miles on its initial fuel and traversed the Arctic Ocean under the ice cap, crossing the North Pole on Aug. 3, 1958. This last feat has been duplicated by the American nuclear submarines *Skate* (1958) and *Sargo* (1960). Seven contemporary submarines were built to conventional hull designs, including one for launching guided missiles. The U.S. Navy then married the advanced Albacore "tear

drop" hull with a nuclear propulsion plant to produce the Skipjack (1956–57) class of very fast submarines, capable of underwater speeds exceeding 30 knots. This design was later used in the Thresher (1958–61), Sturgeon (1962–65), and Los Angeles (under construction in 1975) classes.

The majority of U.S. nuclear submarines are primarily intended to destroy enemy submarines; the remainder are the fleet ballistic-missile submarines armed with strategic Polaris or Poseidon missiles for use against cities and other fixed, land targets. Beginning with the *George Washington,* the navy commissioned forty-one Polaris-Poseidon submarines between 1959 and 1967. Of these, thirty-one were of the Lafayette class and were being converted to fire the Poseidon missile with a 2,500-mile range. Displacing between 5,900 and 7,320 tons each, these vessels were a vital part of the U.S. nuclear deterrent force. The Trident undersea long-range missile system (ULMS) was under development in the mid-1970's as an improved (6,000-mile range) and more survivable successor to the Polaris-Poseidon force.

Thus, in 200 years of American history, submarines progressed from one-man, hand-operated craft to 140-man, nuclear-propelled warships and evolved into what may be the most important of all strategic weapons. This importance is derived from the survivability of the Polaris-Poseidon system and because of the submarines' ability to avoid detection. The credibility of the U.S. sea-based nuclear deterrent is thus assured, helping to prevent global warfare.

[R. H. Barnes, *United States Submarines;* F. T. Cable, *Birth and Development of the American Submarine;* E. P. Hoyt, *From the Turtle to the Nautilus;* S. Lake, *The Submarine in War and Peace;* N. Polmar, *Atomic Submarines;* T. Roscoe, *United States Submarine Operations in World War II.*]

KEN W. SAYERS

SUBMARINES AND INTERNATIONAL LAW. From the advent of the first functional submarine built by Robert Fulton during the 18th century, attention has been focused on the wartime regulation of subsurface weapons. This problem was officially addressed for the first time at the Hague Peace Conference of 1899 with the Russian proposal to prohibit the use of submarines in naval warfare. No agreement could be reached, and the measure was defeated. Most future conferences encountered the same perplexing bottleneck, a lack of consensus among the participants. The smaller nations, siding with the nonmaritime powers, believed that the submarine was a useful defensive weapon, and, for the most part, the major naval powers viewed the submarine as a threat to their control of the sea. The rejections of the many proposals to abolish the submarine have in actuality affirmed its acceptance as a legitimate weapon of war.

In general, since no special customary law has developed governing the conduct of war by submarines, undersea craft must follow the normally accepted rules of war. As with surface ships, they may attack valid military targets without warning. This *modus operandi* has seldom been subject to criticism, although great controversy has been generated as to the submarine's role against merchant ships.

Traditionally, before a belligerent merchant ship could be sunk, a warning had to be given, and the victim's crew and ship's papers positioned in a place of safety. The legal status of merchantmen became cloudy when they were armed and sailed in convoys, and when their intelligence-gathering capabilities were considered.

The question of the legality of submarine operations against merchant shipping was brought into focus during World War I by the German use of submarines for commerce raiding in retaliation for British mining operations. Great Britain reacted by arming its merchant ships, instructing its captains to open fire in self-defense "notwithstanding the submarine may not have committed a definite hostile act. . . ." The submarine was thus placed in jeopardy because of its limited means of attack and defense. In the last act of the reprisals, Germany resorted to unrestricted submarine warfare within specified war zones.

After the war attempts were made once again to regulate the use of the submarine. The necessary consensus was not reached at the Washington Conference (1921–22) or at the Geneva Three-Power Naval Conference (1927), but the London Naval Treaty of 1930 recognized, at least by implication, the lawful combat status of submarines. Article XXII set forth the following regulations: (1) submarines must conform to the same rules as other warships in their actions against merchant ships and (2) except in the case of persistent refusal to stop or of active resistance, a merchant vessel may not be sunk before all its personnel and papers are in a place of safety. This portion of the treaty was to "remain in force without limit of time" and was agreed to by the United States, Great Britain, Japan, France, and Italy. The London Protocol of 1936 restated Article XXII, and by September 1941, thirty-nine additional states had ratified the treaty. An untenable paradox was created whereby it was impossible under existing interna-

tional law for a submarine to carry out the type of warfare for which it was best suited—effective commerce warfare.

As in 1917, Germany in 1939 again attempted to restrict submarine operations against neutral merchant ships, setting up danger zones within which only certain merchant ships would be sunk, that is, neutral ships in convoy and all ships sailing without lights, refusing to stop when requested, or using their radios. In answer to the German submarine challenge, Britain in May 1940 ordered unrestricted attacks against enemy shipping off southern Norway and in the Skagerrak between Norway and Denmark. After the United States entered the war in 1942, Germany issued the order to sink any merchant ships its submarine commanders saw fit without warning, even outside the danger zones.

After the war, Adm. Karl Doenitz, who had served first as head of the German submarine service and then as the commander in chief of the navy, was brought to trial by the International Military Tribunal at Nuremberg (1945). He was indicted for "waging unrestricted submarine warfare contrary to the London Protocol of 1936." Since the Allies had shown little more restraint in conducting their own submarine operations, Doenitz, although found guilty of violating the protocol in sinking "neutral merchant vessels" in operating areas, was not punished for this offense. Thus, the principle that threats to national interests supersede rules of war and international law was reaffirmed.

[W. T. Mallison, Jr., *International Law Studies 1966.*]
MARVIN L. DUKE

SUBMARINES AND TORPEDOES, CIVIL WAR. The Confederacy employed the only real submarine in combat during the Civil War when the *Hunley,* a hand-propelled ironclad vessel with a spar explosive attached to its bow, attacked the Union corvette *Housatonic* in Charleston harbor, S.C., in February 1864. Both vessels sank. The Union built one submarine, the *Alligator,* which sank while under tow off Cape Hatteras, N.C.

Torpedoes—now called mines—were used principally by the Confederacy to protect its rivers and harbors. Although the first Union ironclad, the *Cairo,* was sunk by a mine in December 1862 inland on the Yazoo River in Mississippi, mine warfare was employed mainly along the coast. By 1863 more sophisticated Confederate mines made Union ships reluctant to penetrate farther than the river mouths. Usually employed defensively, mines were normally anchored to streambeds and detonated on contact or were fired manually or electronically from a concealed position on land. Mines also were used sparingly offensively. Those sent floating downstream toward the enemy generally were ineffective. At Charleston, in October 1863, a cigar-shaped ironclad ram equipped with a spar torpedo (mine), of a class of semisubmersibles known as Davids, attacked and severely damaged the *New Ironsides,* the largest Union ironclad afloat.

Still, the Davids and other mine-equipped boats never seriously threatened the Union blockade. Nets and log booms placed around Union ships and anchorages, coupled with the use of picket boats farther out, effectively countered the offensive mines. At Mobile Bay, Ala., in August 1864, when Adm. David G. Farragut issued his famous order "Damn the torpedoes," only one ship was sunk, because most of the mines had become inactive from age. Altogether the Union lost twenty-nine ships to mines, more than were sunk by Confederate warships. Only one Confederate ship, the *Albemarle,* was sunk by a Union mine.

[Milton F. Perry, *Infernal Machines: The Story of Confederate Submarine and Mine Warfare.*]

GEORGE L. MACGARRIGLE

SUBSIDIES. The United States has been exceedingly liberal in granting subsidies to various commercial enterprises, despite frequent doubts concerning the constitutionality of such action. Throughout U.S. national history, state and privately owned transportation improvements have been freely subsidized. Between 1825 and 1829 Congress voted to subscribe $235,000 to the Louisville and Portland Canal, $1 million to the Chesapeake and Ohio Canal, $225,000 to the Chesapeake and Delaware Canal, and $80,000 to the Dismal Swamp Canal. At about the same time land grants were made to aid in the construction of three canals to connect the Great Lakes with the Ohio and Mississippi rivers; one of these waterways, the Illinois and Michigan Canal, was still receiving assistance from the state of Illinois in the mid-1970's. The Sault Sainte Marie Canal (*see* Saint Marys Falls Ship Canal) also received a large land donation from Congress. Railroad promoters also sought federal subsidies, and between 1850 and 1871 more than 131 million acres of public lands were given to them. The first transcontinental railroads, the Union Pacific and the Central Pacific, received 20 million acres of public lands and a loan of $53 million.

Mail subsidies to the merchant marine were generously granted during the years 1845–58, 1864–77, 1891, and after World War I, but in each case they failed to establish a shipping industry comparable to that of Great Britain. The subsidies given to aviation have been more successful. Between 1926 and 1933, $87 million in mail subsidies were given to various air transport companies, and although excessive in amount and accompanied by corruption, they were largely responsible for the present far-flung air service. Airplane manufacturers not only profited from this boon to commercial flying; they also received many lucrative contracts for the sale of their planes to the War and Navy departments.

Newspapers have also enjoyed government subsidies. In the 19th century many newspapers were largely financed by government advertising, and a change in administration meant a goodly number of the old party organs would be forced to suspend because of the loss of patronage. Cheap postage rates on fourth-class matter have also served as a subsidy to newspapers and periodicals.

Under the Newlands Reclamation Act of 1902 the U.S. government has spent billions of dollars on reclamation projects. Farmers benefiting from government-supplied water were expected to pay reasonable charges, but poor planning raised costs so high that farmers could not meet the charges and substantial parts of both interest and principal have been written off. Irrigation projects necessitate the construction of dams and reservoirs, many of which provide electric power. This power has been sold at low rates to distributing companies, which have thus been saved from undertaking expensive construction work. Electric power companies further benefited by the government land policy, which, until Theodore Roosevelt's administration, permitted them to preempt power sites at little cost.

The establishment in 1932 of the Reconstruction Finance Corporation and in 1933 of the Public Works Administration with their "pump priming" programs marked a new era in government subsidies to business and local governments. Not only were loans made to banks, railroads, and industrial corporations at low rates, but outright grants were offered to state and local governments for permanent improvements such as sewage-disposal plants, waterworks, parks, public schools, municipal buildings, and settlement houses. Federal subsidies and grants-in-aid have assisted agricultural colleges, vocational training schools, state road construction, state forests, and parks.

Tariffs, although not strictly speaking subsidies,

have the effect of subsidies, because they artificially increase the income of producers of protected goods. The very first tariff gave some protection to American manufactures, and that protection was progressively increased until 1833, when the free-trade elements succeeded in forcing a compromise that brought rates down to a lower level. But at no time has the policy of indirectly subsidizing business by tariff protection been abandoned. The farmers who have been more hurt than helped by tariffs obtained their subsidy in 1933 in the Agricultural Adjustment Act, which provided for benefit payments to farmers who cooperated with the government in the adjustment program. Payments to "farmers" to reduce their output of basic crops kept on increasing until in 1970 nine individuals or corporations each received over a million dollars; the largest payment was $4.4 million. Between $3 billion and $4 billion annually was being paid to larger farmers, to a considerable degree to corporate—conglomerate agribusiness—farmers. These government subsidies tended to eliminate the small farmer and sharecropper and to concentrate the production of basic crops in the hands of the more efficient larger owners.

Most industries and businesses and major population groups have received generous subsidies, directly or indirectly, since 1933. Mining industries, especially the oil companies, benefited enormously from the generous depletion allowance that reduced their taxes on income. The cattle and sheep industries in the eleven far western states benefit through the privilege of grazing their livestock within Bureau of Land Management districts and national forests at less than commercial rates. Cane and beet sugar producers have profited from a series of protectionist rates alternating with outright subsidies. Middle- and low-income families and the construction industry and the building trades have been subsidized by public housing programs. Federal regulations have at times required government agencies to use only certain American-made or -raised goods.

[C. Goodrich, *Government Promotion of American Canals and Railroads, 1800–1890;* J. E. Saugstad, *Shipping and Shipbuilding Subsidies: Subsidy and Subsidylike Programs of the U.S. Government.*]

PAUL W. GATES

SUBSISTENCE HOMESTEADS played an important role in the earlier stages of the nation's industrialization, since workers frequently supplemented their wages by cultivating small plots of land to supply the food required by their families. The practice declined with increasing urbanization, although it was encouraged by some employers—such as George M. Pullman and Henry Ford—who located industrial plants in communities where subsistence farming was or could be undertaken. In 1933 the National Industrial Recovery Act, as part of its sweeping attack on economic depression, provided $25 million "to aid in the redistribution of the overbalance of population in industrial centers by establishing subsistence homesteads." The Federal Subsistence Homestead Corporation proceeded to build communities of new homes located on tracts of one to five tillable acres, offering them at low rentals to the eligible unemployed. Production facilities appropriate to the skills of the populations were also provided in most cases. One of the most successful communities was Arthurdale, W. Va., where employment in native crafts was emphasized. An effort to provide employment for garment workers from New York City in a cooperatively managed plant at Jersey Homesteads was less successful. The program was of little significance as relief or recovery policy, and interest declined with improved economic conditions; it was terminated in 1942.

[Russell Lord and Paul H. Johnstone, eds., *Subsistence Homesteads; A Place on Earth, A Critical Appraisal of Subsistence Homesteads.*]

CLARENCE H. DANHOF

SUBSTITUTES, CIVIL WAR. No conscription in the North during the Civil War was absolute. There was always the opportunity for the drafted man to hire a substitute, if he could afford it. This was first allowed in the militia draft of 1862 on the theory that, so long as each name drawn from the wheel produced a man, it made no difference whether the drafted person or one hired to take his place appeared for muster. The Conscription Act of Mar. 3, 1863, definitely legalized this method of draft evasion, and each later amendment perpetuated it. Until the act of Feb. 24, 1864, the conscript could take his choice between hiring a substitute or paying the government $300 as commutation of service. Thereafter, substitution alone was permitted, except for conscientious objectors. Furthermore, exemption by furnishing a substitute extended only until the next succeeding draft, when the principal again became liable (*see* Bounty Jumper). At once the prices of substitutes rose far above the $300 to which the commutation clause had held them. For this reason legal draft evasion became the prerogative of only the unusually well-to-do. In the last two years of the war 118,010 substitutes were enlisted, as contrasted with 52,067 conscripts.

The Confederacy also allowed a limited substitution system from the early days of the war. The first Confederate Conscription Act (Apr. 16, 1862) permitted substitutes from men not legally liable to service to the extent of one man a month in each company. Frauds in the supplying of such substitutes approximated those in the North, as did also the cost of such service (in comparative values). The second Conscription Act (Sept. 17, 1862) made men previously furnishing substitutes again liable to service, thus causing much dissension and legal action. The whole system was abolished by the end of the year 1863. The number of substitutes has never been accurately compiled.

[F. A. Shannon, *Organization and Administration of the Union Army;* A. B. Moore, *Conscription and Conflict in the Confederacy.*]

FRED A. SHANNON

SUBTREASURIES arose from the problem of the care of the federal government's funds. After President Andrew Jackson had the government's deposits removed from the second Bank of the United States (*see* Removal of Deposits), they were placed in so-called "pet banks." This system did not prove to be satisfactory, and an act, approved July 4, 1840, set up an independent treasury. Until June 30, 1843, part of the payments to the government might be other than specie. The law was repealed Aug. 13, 1841, but was reenacted in August 1846, with the intent that receipts and expenditures were to be in specie or Treasury notes. Subtreasuries were established at New York, Philadelphia, Charleston, New Orleans, Saint Louis, and Boston; and later at Chicago, San Francisco, and Cincinnati. The gravest trouble came because government surpluses caused a shortage in the money markets. The situation was helped after the establishment in 1863–64 of the national banks, which were made government depositories. Secretary of the Treasury Leslie M. Shaw, from 1902 to 1907, used many devices to smooth the effect of Treasury operations on the money market. The Federal Reserve Act of 1913 provided that the Federal Reserve banks might act as fiscal agents for the government. This made the subtreasuries unnecessary. But political pressure caused them to be temporarily retained. The last one was abolished Feb. 10, 1921.

[D. R. Dewey, *Financial History of the United States.*]

JAMES D. MAGEE

SUBURBAN GROWTH. Urban sites in North America have typically been settled in quick succession in a series of distinct clusters, each risking its future growth on access to a unique feature of the commonly advantageous location. This polycentric pattern was apparent, for example, in the string of villages that the first English colonists established on the sheltered periphery of Massachusetts Bay. It appeared again, across the continent and across centuries, in the rivalry of adjacent towns at the mouth of San Francisco Bay and in the Los Angeles Basin.

The term "suburban growth," seen against this pattern, designates two processes rather than one. It describes both the radial expansion of one or more clusters at an urban site (so that the areas at the fringe may be described as suburbs) and the integration of previously distinct settlements into a unified economic and social system. This second process is easily obscured by the rapid expansion of the areas of continuous urban land use in the 20th century. Even in the 1970's small towns in the Northeast, protected from adjacent cities by substantial open spaces, were being suburbanized in much the same way as the Plymouth Colony was suburbanized by Boston in the 17th century and Brooklyn by New York City in the 19th century.

The expansion of the radius of cities has been the product of self-conscious and often explicated, although rarely coordinated or centrally managed, decisions. From the middle of the 19th century Americans have seen the opening of new urban land through the improvement of transportation and the consequent deconcentration of population clusters as a way both of satisfying consumer demands and of solving nagging collective problems attributed to density and to contact with the poor or dangerous classes of society. Only after World War II, with the acceleration of expansion, has a countercritique emerged indicting rather than lauding suburban growth.

Expansionary decisions have determined much of the form and character of the core cities. If new and accessible land were not constantly introduced into the market, densities would be higher, established cities would be rebuilt at a faster rate, and residential neighborhoods would be a shifting mosaic of old and new homes. Perhaps most important, the social differentiation of both neighborhoods and political units would be reduced.

Until the middle of the 19th century, the suburban areas of cities—whether newly settled or newly integrated into the urban economy—were commonly poorer than the central city that dominated the region. Elements of this pattern persist. The outermost fringes of virtually every urban area in the nation include a substantial number of low-income residents, whose fate is usually to be displaced by the next wave of settlement. Cities with a population of less than 500,000 characteristically demonstrate higher per capita incomes than their adjacent suburbs.

The older pattern has been reversed in the largest cities in the nation. They are denser at their centers and more capital-intensive in their land use than small cities. As a result, only in their outer rings do they usually allow for the spacious single-family dwellings commonly desired by middle- and upper-income Americans rearing families. Through the 19th and into the 20th century most of these cities were able to consolidate their outer rings into unified political units. After about 1920, large city annexation was sharply reduced as the suburban areas became more politically organized.

The requirements of technical coordination continued to be met by special-purpose authorities, such as metropolitan planning and port and transportation authorities and intersuburban school and sewer districts, but the general political boundaries of the central cities themselves were fixed. The new rigidity of local political boundaries in these major cities underlies the characteristic (and only partially correct) image that suburbs are rich and cities poor. It also underlies the political and fiscal dilemmas of great cities, supporting the major infrastructure of a metropolitan economy and society, yet starved for tax revenues to service their population.

[Marion Clawson, *Suburban Land Conversion in the United States: An Economic and Governmental Process;* Kenneth T. Jackson, "Metropolitan Government Versus Political Autonomy: Politics on the Crabgrass Frontier," in Kenneth T. Jackson and Stanley K. Schultz, eds., *Cities in American History;* Leo F. Schnore, *The Urban Scene.*]

S. J. MANDELBAUM

SUBVERSION. Subversive activities of totalitarian inspiration aroused widespread congressional concern in the 1930's and led to the creation, at the suggestion of Vice-President John Nance Garner, of the Special Committee on Un-American Activities in 1938. Opposed by the administration of Franklin D. Roosevelt because it concentrated on Communists rather than on Nazis and Fascists, the committee was backed by public opinion and in 1945 became a standing committee of the House of Representatives.

In 1946 defected Soviet code clerk Igor Gouzenko revealed the existence of widespread Soviet espionage in Canada and led indirectly to the arrest and conviction of Klaus Fuchs, Julius and Ethel Rosenberg, and others. The following year, alarmed at the extent of Communist penetration of government and its cold war implications, the administration of Harry S. Truman promulgated Executive Order 9835 to screen government employees for subversive connections and authorize their discharge if "reasonable grounds" for a finding of disloyalty existed. A loyalty review board was set up within the Civil Service Commission, and the program was extended to bar from "sensitive positions" persons whose presence there was "prejudicial to the national security."

Testimony before the House Committee on Un-American Activities in 1948 by confessed former Soviet espionage agents Elizabeth Bentley and Whittaker Chambers revealed extensive policy and espionage penetration of the federal government at high echelons. Of the fifty or so persons named by Chambers or Bentley as spies or contacts, a majority took the Fifth Amendment. Such high officials as presidential adviser Lauchlin Currie; former Assistant Secretary of the Treasury Harry D. White; and Alger Hiss, former secretary-general of the UN Charter Conference in San Francisco, vigorously denied the charges.

The House committee had suffered from amateurish and somewhat irresponsible leadership in the past. Invigorated by the presence of Rep. Richard M. Nixon and Rep. Karl E. Mundt, it conducted a vigorous and trenchant investigation of the diametrical conflicts of testimony between Chambers and Hiss that led ultimately to the conviction of the latter for perjury in connection with espionage.

Public fear of Communist activities reached its high-water mark in the late 1940's and early 1950's. The Senate Internal Security Subcommittee held an inquest into the recent fall of mainland China to Communist forces and publicized adverse findings against prominent Foreign Service officers. After the 1952 Republican electoral victory, Sen. Joseph R. McCarthy became chairman of the Senate Committee on Government Operations and used this position for relentless and indiscriminate attacks on suspected Communists and officials allegedly "soft on communism." The suspicion grew that he was using the investigative committee as an instrumentality for the aggrandizement of power to an extent unprecedented since the Reconstruction era. McCarthy asserted that Congress was entitled to unlimited access to all presidential papers and appealed to "two million Federal employees . . . to give us any information which they have about graft, corruption, communism, treason. . . .''

President Dwight D. Eisenhower considered that McCarthy's course jeopardized the national consensus on which his administration rested, but he wished to avoid a head-on collision. McCarthy was charged with misconduct in the Senate, subjected to a telecast investigation by a special subcommittee in 1954, and condemned by a Senate majority on Dec. 2, 1954.

The McCarthy affair brought congressional probes of communism into a disrepute from which they never fully recovered, despite such historically valuable inquiries as the Senate Internal Security Subcommittee hearings on the seizure of power by Fidel Castro in Cuba in 1959 and on efforts at continental subversion by the Castro regime.

[Earl Latham, *The Communist Controversy in Washington.*]

NATHANIEL WEYL

SUBVERSIVE ACTIVITIES CONTROL BOARD. *See* Federal Agencies.

SUBWAYS. Street congestion in the larger American cities was becoming intolerable in the late 19th century. Elevated railroads were built in three of the largest cities, New York, Chicago, and Boston, but were unsatisfactory because of noise, unsightliness, and depreciation of adjacent property values. Subways had been discussed in New York City in 1860, but the idea was dropped because of enormous cost. Between 1895 and 1900 Boston removed 1.7 miles of trolley-car tracks from crowded streets and placed them underground. Later these tunnels were extended and integrated with the city's system.

By 1900, when New York City's first contract for a subway was let, a billion passengers a year were riding crowded, slow streetcars. As the city grew and spread out, faster movement was necessary. The first subway line was opened by the Interborough Rapid Transit Company on Broadway in 1904. An extension to Brooklyn followed, and a tunnel under the East River was completed in 1908. By 1930 the Interborough operated 224 miles of subway and 139 miles of elevated line. The Brooklyn Rapid Transit Corporation developed a network of lines in Brooklyn and entered Manhattan by three tunnels under the East River, the last completed in 1924. The Hudson and

Manhattan Tubes, completed in 1911, connected Manhattan with Jersey City, Hoboken, and Newark, N.J.

Philadelphia opened its first subway in 1907. After 1920 Newark, Saint Louis, and Los Angeles placed short sections of their surface-car lines underground. Between 1900 and 1910 a system of freight subways was built under downtown Chicago, but in the 1930's it was superseded by the motor truck. New York's private companies were supplemented by a city-owned system that completed its Eighth Avenue line in 1932. Most of the elevated lines in Manhattan were gradually abandoned, and the private companies and city system were merged under a transit authority in 1940. A Second Avenue subway and an additional East River tunnel, planned for many years, had construction halted in 1975 because the city was short of funds.

Between 1938 and 1943 a short subway was built in Chicago to supplement the elevated lines. Two new subways planned to replace the Loop and other elevated roads were held in abeyance in the mid-1970's because of the heavy deficits of the Chicago Transit Authority. The Bay Area Rapid Transit (BART) system in the San Francisco area, opened in 1973–74, comprises 75 miles of line, of which 16 are in tunnels under the city connected to the aboveground East Bay trackage by a four-mile tunnel under San Francisco Bay. In 1976 the first stage of a comprehensive metropolitan transit system, 4.5 miles of subway, was scheduled to open in Washington, D.C. The systems of the 1970's featured quiet, air-conditioned, and automated cars. More modern equipment was rapidly replacing older cars on New York's system, which in the 1970's was the most extensive and heavily patronized in the world.

[Interborough Rapid Transit Company, *The New York Subway: Its Construction and Equipment*; James R. Walker, *Fifty Years of Rapid Transit, 1864–1917*; Edward E. White and Muriel F. White, *Famous Subways and Tunnels of the World.*]

ERNEST W. WILLIAMS

SUEZ CRISIS (October-November 1956). In July 1956, following Egypt's trade agreement with the Soviet Union, the United States and Great Britain withdrew an offer to aid in the construction of the Aswan High Dam on the Nile River. Egypt retaliated by nationalizing the Universal Suez Canal Company, an international corporation (whose major stockholders were British and French) that long had operated the Suez Canal. Britain and France, who were largely dependent on oil supplies brought through the canal, reacted to the seizure by proposing that the United States endorse their employment of military force to recover control of the canal. To the consternation of prime ministers Guy Mollet of France and Anthony Eden of Britain, U.S. Secretary of State John Foster Dulles emphatically refused to countenance armed intervention. There then ensued three months of inconclusive international conferences and unsuccessful negotiations. The crisis came to a head on Oct. 29 when Israel, fearing further raids by Egypt, invaded the Gaza Strip and the Sinai peninsula, inflicting a stinging defeat on the Egyptian forces. The Israeli military operation was followed two days later by preconcerted British and French attacks on Egypt. Since President Dwight D. Eisenhower viewed the Anglo-French intervention, as well as the Israeli invasion, as indefensible, there was a major rift in the Western alliance. The United States, backed by the Soviet Union, was instrumental in a call by the United Nations for an immediate cease-fire. This was arranged (Nov. 2) and an international peace force was dispatched to the Near East, where it remained until May 1967.

JACOB E. COOKE

"SUFFERING TRADERS," a group of men trading to the western Indian tribes who lost horses, goods, and in some instances their lives to Indians on foray during Pontiac's War (1763). Their sufferings were set forth as a basis for compensation in the form of a land grant at the Treaty of Fort Stanwix in 1768. To strengthen the claim another was combined with it: that of an earlier group, including the trader and later Indian agent George Croghan, which had suffered similar losses (1749–54). The claimants received a grant of land from the Iroquois Confederation, the fate of which was bound up with that of the Indiana Company.

[A. T. Volwiler, George Croghan.]
SAMUEL C. WILLIAMS

SUFFOLK, OPERATIONS AT (1863). In February 1863 Confederate Gen. James Longstreet's corps was detached from Gen. Robert E. Lee's army to the vicinity of Petersburg, Va., for better subsistence and to provide against any sudden Union movement in that locality. Longstreet's command was divided, two divisions being stationed near Petersburg, Longstreet going with the other two divisions into southeastern

Virginia to collect much needed forage and provisions. It was his first independent command. While carrying on his foraging mission, he allowed himself to become involved in a fruitless siege of the Union headquarters at Suffolk (April 1863), which so long delayed him that he was unable to rejoin Lee until after the Battle of Chancellorsville (May 1–4). Although he accomplished nothing of consequence, Longstreet's absence greatly jeopardized Lee's safety.

[D. S. Freeman, R. E. Lee.]
THOMAS ROBSON HAY

SUFFOLK BANKING SYSTEM. When the Suffolk Bank in Boston was chartered by the state of Massachusetts (1818), it agreed to redeem the notes of any New England bank at par if the issuing bank would keep with it a permanent deposit of $2,000 or upward, depending on the amount of the bank's capital, and, in addition, deposit sufficient funds to redeem any of its notes that might reach Boston through the ordinary channels of trade. It was calculated that the use of the $2,000 permanent deposit would compensate the Suffolk Bank for its services. Country bankers were enraged, for the plan threatened to reduce note circulation and the profit of their banks. But the Suffolk Bank persisted, collecting notes of country banks and presenting them for redemption in specie. By 1824 other Boston banks joined with the Suffolk Bank, making the plan effective throughout New England. Specie redemption so elevated the standing of all New England bank notes that they gradually were accepted at par throughout the country. This specie-redemption plan was later incorporated into the National Bank Act of 1863.

[Davis R. Dewey, State Banking Before the Civil War.]
FRANK PARKER

SUFFOLK RESOLVES (Sept. 9, 1774). Of the many meetings held in Massachusetts in 1774 to protest the Coercion Acts, the best known was that of delegates from Boston and other towns in Suffolk County, held at Dedham on Sept. 6 and adjourned to Milton on Sept. 9. There Joseph Warren presented the resolves, which vigorously denounced the actions of England; refused obedience to the recent acts, or to officials created under them; urged weekly militia musters, nonpayment of taxes, and nonintercourse with Great Britain; and suggested the need of a provincial congress to meet at Concord in October. The resolves were passed unanimously and taken by Paul Revere to the Continental Congress at Philadelphia, which by endorsing them on Sept. 17 moved another step toward independence.

[Richard Frothingham, *Joseph Warren;* A. B. Hart, *Commonwealth History of Massachusetts.*]

HERBERT W. HILL

SUFFRAGE. *See* **Franchise; Voting; Woman's Rights Movement.**

SUFFRAGE, AFRO-AMERICAN. Since emancipation most Americans of African descent have encountered difficulties in exercising the right to vote. More than a century after the adoption of the Fifteenth Amendment in 1870 some limitations still existed. It is significant that protection of suffrage for blacks required specific legislation; the measures that supported voting rights for other citizens did not suffice. By the 1970's, except for two brief periods, one in the 1860's and 1870's and the other in the 1960's and 1970's, the limitations on black voting had been so successful as to make the denial of suffrage for blacks characteristic of the American political scene.

Restrictions on suffrage have not been limited to blacks. In the early history of the United States various religious groups—mainly Jews, Quakers, and Catholics—were prevented from voting. Debtors, illiterates, and persons with "bad" moral character were excluded. Women were unable to vote until 1920. In addition, property qualifications existed in the early years and opposition to voting by Orientals was not rare. Of all these restrictions of suffrage, those for blacks were most concentrated, most severe, and most long-lasting.

Voting was not initially a constitutionally protected right. The Constitution provides that "the Times, Places and Manner of holding Elections for Senators and Representatives, shall be prescribed in each State by the Legislature thereof." Only with the passage of the Fourteenth (1868) and Fifteenth (1870) amendments did the federal government establish a meaningful right to vote. At the same time it guaranteed that right to blacks.

Voting requirements and access to suffrage were written into state constitutions or passed by state legislatures during the Revolution. In some cases free blacks were excluded; in others they were not. Blacks voted in New Hampshire, Massachusetts, New York, Pennsylvania, Maryland, and North Carolina. Blacks

also voted in Maine, Vermont, and Tennessee, which became states soon after ratification of the Constitution. A movement to reduce the status of free blacks that got under way early in the 19th century (at the same time as the movement to extend democracy for free whites) resulted in the loss of suffrage for many. Disfranchisement took place in Maryland in 1810, in Tennessee in 1834, in North Carolina in 1835, and in Pennsylvania in 1838. By 1840 over 90 percent of the free blacks in the United States lived in states that excluded them from or put limitations on suffrage.

After the Thirteenth Amendment (1865) had ended slavery, the Fourteenth Amendment sought to nationalize citizenship and remove it from the caprice of states. Support for these amendments came from persons genuinely concerned with extending citizens' rights to blacks and from those seeking to make political capital that would insure continued Republican party control of the federal government. The Fourteenth Amendment made blacks citizens of the United States and the state in which they lived, prohibited the enforcement by states of laws that would abridge the privileges of citizens, and required each state to provide equal protection of the law for all. A further section provided for the reduction of representation in Congress if male inhabitants of a state were denied the right to vote. Framers of this amendment saw in it the opportunity to attract the votes of blacks in support of the Republican party—the party of Lincoln and emancipation—or, if blacks were excluded from voting in the South, to reduce the congressional representation, presumably from the Democratic party, in proportion to the number of Afro-American males denied the vote. To establish voting firmly as a right, the Fifteenth Amendment provides that "the right of citizens of the United States to vote shall not be denied or abridged by the United States or by any State on account of race, color, or previous condition of servitude." Important as these amendments are as a base for black suffrage, they came into existence under the cloud of partisan political expediency.

Blacks voted in numbers throughout the South during Reconstruction and the years immediately following. However, extralegal efforts to destroy their political influence began immediately. Secret societies of southern whites—the Ku Klux Klan was the most powerful—effectively used threats, intimidation, and violence to discourage blacks from voting. Various corrupt practices, including the stuffing of ballot boxes and the manipulation of the counting of votes, reduced the effectiveness of those blacks who were able to cast their ballots. In addition, the general amnesty of 1872 restored voting rights to all but about 600 Confederate officers. With large numbers of whites voting the Democratic ticket and with blacks prevented from voting or not having their votes counted, Democrats regained control of all southern states by 1877. Immediately steps were taken to create a legal framework to destroy black suffrage. The end of Reconstruction ushered in the second period of disfranchisement, which by the early years of the 20th century all but wiped out the black vote.

Southern states used several methods of disfranchisement—gerrymandering, the development of complicated registration and voting procedures, and a series of state constitutional changes, among them. In Mississippi, where in 1890 a majority of the population was black, a revised constitution imposed a poll tax of $2 and barred all who could not read and interpret any part of the state constitution to the satisfaction of the registrar. Similar action followed in South Carolina in 1895 with the added requirement that voters own property worth $300. In 1898 Louisiana added a "grandfather clause" making it unnecessary for a person to meet the educational and property qualifications if his father or grandfather had been qualified to vote on Jan. 1, 1867. By the start of World War I North Carolina, Alabama, Virginia, Georgia, and Oklahoma had joined the ranks of states disfranchising blacks. Typical of the effectiveness of these actions was the reduction of registered black voters in Louisiana from 130,344 to 5,320 and in Alabama from 181,471 to 3,000 as a result of changes in the states' constitutions. "White primaries" excluded blacks who remained on the voter lists from the nomination process in the Democratic party in states where the Democratic nomination meant election. White southern leaders did not deny that disfranchisement was their aim. At a Virginia constitutional convention Carter Glass declared that the delegates were elected "to discriminate to the very extremity of permissible action under the limitations of the Federal Constitution with a view to the elimination of every Negro voter who can be gotten rid of, legally, without materially impairing the numerical strength of the white electorate." In North Carolina gubernatorial candidate Charles B. Aycock announced "universal manhood suffrage and Negro disfranchisement" as one of his goals.

Improvement in the area of voting took place after 1914 mainly through action by the Supreme Court, the movement by blacks to states having no official limitation on suffrage, and federal legislation to protect voting rights. In *Guinn and Beal* v. *United States*

(1915), the Court declared unconstitutional the grandfather clause in the Oklahoma constitution. White primaries were voided by the Court in a series of cases, including *Nixon* v. *Herndon* (1927), *Nixon* v. *Condon* (1932), *Grovey* v. *Townsend* (1935), and *Smith* v. *Allwright* (1944). In *Gomillion* v. *Lightfoot* (1960) the Court struck down an Alabama effort to gerrymander out of existence the effective black vote in the city of Tuskegee. These decisions provided minor relief for the majority of disfranchised blacks. Except for the ruling on the grandfather clause, they served only to protect the vote of those already registered. No judicial remedies were provided for disfranchisement by literacy tests, by the variety of extralegal arrangements or, until 1966, by the poll tax. (The Twenty-fourth Amendment, adopted in 1964, prohibited use of the poll tax as a requirement for voting in federal elections. The Supreme Court invalidated the poll tax as a requirement for voting in state elections in *Harper* v. *Virginia Board of Elections* in 1966.)

The migration of blacks from the South, which began in the 19th century, grew to sizable proportions during World War I. By that time northern and western states had no legal restrictions on blacks voting. Most important in terms of voting effectiveness was the concentration of the migrants in a few urban areas where their weight could be felt. Northern politicians gave increased attention to black votes, and black elected officials began to appear for the first time since Reconstruction. Oscar De Priest was elected alderman in Chicago before being voted into the House of Representatives in 1928. By 1932 blacks had been elected to legislatures in New York, New Jersey, Pennsylvania, Ohio, Kentucky, West Virginia, Illinois, Indiana, and California. The chance that the weight of numbers could be felt through voting was increased when the Supreme Court in *Baker* v. *Carr* (1962) ordered reapportionment of state legislatures to better reflect population patterns within the states.

Despite the Supreme Court decisions and the migration of southern blacks, further action was needed to insure voting rights for the majority of blacks who still lived in the South. Precisely because of the difficulty in voting, blacks were unable to put the usual pressure on elected state and federal officials for legislative remedies. The alternative to which blacks turned in the 1950's and 1960's was protest demonstrations. Voting rights were among the objectives of civil rights activists throughout the South. The federal government responded with a series of laws intended to enforce the Fourteenth and Fifteenth amendments.

The first of these passed in 1957, the year after the Montgomery, Ala., bus boycott. It created the Commission on Civil Rights and gave power to the federal government to initiate action to protect the right to vote of citizens. To the surprise of no one, the commission found that blacks were being regularly and systematically prevented from voting in many parts of the South. As a result of the findings, the Justice Department brought suits in Alabama, Georgia, and Louisiana. In 1960 a second act was passed to prevent evasive actions by registrars and to strengthen some aspects of the 1957 act, and in 1962 Congress submitted the Twenty-fourth Amendment, outlawing the poll tax as a requirement for voting in federal elections, to the states. This legislation prompted increased voter-registration efforts among southern blacks and increased efforts on the part of some whites to prevent registration. Evasive tactics were adopted by elected and appointed officials, and violence and intimidation were used. In Mississippi in 1964 three civil rights workers were murdered and twenty-four black churches were burned or bombed.

Even after the passage of the Civil Rights Act of 1964, which was intended to eliminate existing loopholes in the area of voting, southern officials found ways to prevent blacks from voting. Their actions led to further demonstrations by blacks; the most significant was in Selma, Ala., in 1965. Dallas County, in which Selma is located, and the four nearby counties included 87,972 blacks and 47,285 whites in their population. Of these, 904 blacks and 24,037 whites were registered to vote. Loundes and Wilcox counties, with black populations of 12,500 and 14,500, had no black voters. In Selma 64 percent of the eligible white voters, but less than 1 percent of the eligible black voters, were registered. Delay and evasion on the part of the registrar for Dallas County led blacks to plan a march to the state capitol in Montgomery to petition the governor for assistance. The marchers were attacked by local and state police, beaten, and gassed. In the following days three persons assisting in the demonstrations were killed. Reaction to the violence stimulated the drive that led to passage of the Voting Rights Act of 1965. The new law suspended literacy tests and other devices in states and counties that used them and in which less than 50 percent of those of voting age had voted in 1964. It also authorized sending federal registrars to areas where local officials refused to obey the law.

The findings of the Commission on Civil Rights show the result of actions taken to protect the voting rights of blacks. In 1956 only 5 percent were registered in the 100 of the approximately 900 counties in Alabama, Florida, Georgia, Louisiana, Mississippi, North Carolina, South Carolina, and Tennessee that contained about one-third of the black population of those states. In 1962 registered black voters had risen to only 8.4 percent, or from 37,000 to 56,000. For the South as a whole the proportion of voting-age blacks who were registered rose from 28 percent in 1960 to 39 percent or 2.2 million in 1964. Two years later there were 2.7 million black voters in the South. In Mississippi, registered blacks numbered 28,000 in mid-1965; the number rose to 122,000 by January 1966.

The effect of judicial and legislative actions has been to remove, for all practical purposes, legal opposition to voting by blacks, although equality in suffrage had still not been attained in the mid-1970's. Some areas found ways to make black votes meaningless. One county in Alabama raised the filing fee in primaries from $50 to $500. In another, the term of a post being sought by a black was extended. Other rule changes were made. Efforts to combat these through additional federal legislation were unsuccessful when a bill providing further voting protections failed in the Senate in 1966 in spite of the fact that only about 50 percent of voting-age blacks were registered at that time.

The major problems of suffrage for blacks in the mid-1970's involved failures to implement existing legislation and extralegal actions aimed at reducing the number of blacks able to vote or at reducing the effectiveness of those who get to the polls.

[William Gillett, *The Right to Vote: Politics and the Passage of the 15th Amendment;* Harry Holloway, *The Politics of the Southern Negro;* V. O. Key, *Southern Politics in State and Nation;* Rayford Logan, *The Betrayal of the Negro: From Rutherford B. Hayes to Woodrow Wilson.*]

HENRY N. DREWRY

SUFFRAGE, COLONIAL. Neither the extent nor the exercise of suffrage in colonial America can be described precisely. Voting qualifications were fixed by each colony, and in many the requirements were changed during the colonial period. The generally accepted philosophy was the English concept that only those with "a stake in society" should vote. Translated into English law as early as 1430, this philosophy confined voting for Parliament to freeholders whose land was worth at least 40 shillings a year in rental value. American practice generally mirrored English theory, each colony establishing some property qualification for voting for the lower house of the

SUFFRAGE, EXCLUSION FROM THE

provincial legislature. The upper house was almost always appointive.

The definition of freeholder in the colonies varied from colony to colony. In New York, a freehold was an estate worth £40 or bearing 40 shillings rent; by 1760, it was the same in Rhode Island, having been reduced from an earlier high of £400 and £10 rent; in New Hampshire, the figure was £50. In Connecticut and, after 1691, Massachusetts a freehold was an estate bearing 40 shillings annual rent. Other colonies fixed acreage rather than money definitions for the term "freehold": 100 acres in New Jersey; 100 acres of unimproved or 25 acres of improved land in Virginia; 50 acres in the Carolinas, Georgia, Maryland, Pennsylvania, and Delaware. In at least two colonies, New York and Virginia, long-term leaseholders qualified as freeholders for voting purposes, and in Rhode Island, the eldest son of a freeholder could vote even if he had no property himself.

Many colonies had alternatives to landholding as a suffrage qualification, usually the possession of other property but sometimes mere taxpaying. In Massachusetts after 1691, any property worth £40 sufficed; in Connecticut, it was £40 of personal property; in Maryland, a £40 "visibile estate"; and in Pennsylvania, £50 of real or personal property. In South Carolina, any freeman who paid 20 shillings in taxes could vote.

An added complication was the numerous separate qualifications established for dwellers in towns and boroughs, usually lower and more liberal than the general provincial franchise. Virginia town dwellers could vote by virtue of possession of a house and lot, and in North Carolina, all taxpaying tenants and homeowners in towns and boroughs were voters. In Annapolis, Md., the franchise was extended to anyone owning a £20 estate or a house or who had served five years at a trade in the town. In New York, all "freemen" of Albany and New York City qualified, and freemanship was liberally conferred on virtually everyone who completed an apprenticeship or practiced a trade in those cities. New England town qualifications were bewilderingly varied, the net effect being to admit virtually all the adult male inhabitants to the franchise.

Limitations of race, sex, age, and residence were more often the result of custom than of law. Generally, Jews and Roman Catholics were barred, usually by their inability to take the English test oaths with regard to the Anglican church. Maryland and New York specifically barred Catholics by statute, and New York excluded Jews by law in 1737. These prohibitions were not always enforced. Jews appear on New York City voting lists in 1768 and 1769, and Catholics voted in Virginia in 1741 and 1751. Women were excluded by statute only in four colonies, but there is rare evidence that any ever voted anywhere. The age qualification was almost universally twenty-one, but in Massachusetts, suffrage was confined to twenty-four-year-olds in the 17th century and sometimes extended to nineteen-year-olds in the 18th century. Pennsylvania's two-year residence requirement was the most stringent; other colonies usually demanded six months or a year. Slaves and indentured servants were invariably denied the franchise, and in the Carolinas, Georgia, and Virginia, freed blacks as well. Indians did vote at times in Massachusetts.

The number of adult males who qualified as voters under these requirements can only be estimated, in the absence of complete or accurate lists of property owners and taxpayers. Probably 50 to 75 percent of the adult male population could qualify as freeholders, and in some colonies up to 80 or 90 percent as freeholders or freemen. The relative ease of obtaining land in America and the high rate of wages opened the door fairly wide to those persons who sought the franchise, and surprisingly large numbers of voters participated in elections when issues arose that affected their interests. Suffrage limitations do not appear to have been a grievance in any of the popular protest movements that developed during the colonial period. On the other hand, this rather broadly based electorate usually voted into office a narrowly based leadership and deferred to its judgment in running the colonies' political affairs.

[Cortlandt F. Bishop, *History of Elections in the American Colonies;* Richard P. McCormick, *The History of Voting in New Jersey;* Albert E. McKinley, *The Suffrage Franchise in the Thirteen English Colonies in America;* Chilton Williamson, *American Suffrage From Property to Democracy, 1760–1860.*]

MILTON M. KLEIN

SUFFRAGE, EXCLUSION FROM THE. It is generally estimated that because of state property and taxpaying qualifications, fewer than one-fourth of all white adult males were eligible to vote in 1787–89, the time the U.S. Constitution was being ratified. The history of the suffrage in the United States since then has been one of steady expansion, partly through constitutional amendments and partly through legislation. The states had largely abandoned the property qualifications for voting by 1850. The Fifteenth Amendment, ratified in 1870, forbade denial of the right to vote "on account of race, color, or previous condition of servitude." The Nineteenth Amendment, which was adopted in 1920, prohibited denial of the right to vote on account of sex. The poll tax was outlawed for federal elections by the Twenty-fourth Amendment (1964) and for state elections by a Supreme Court decision (*Harper* v. *Virginia Board of Elections,* 383 U.S. 663, 1966). The Twenty-sixth Amendment, ratified in 1971, lowered the age limit for all federal and state voting to eighteen. Various obstacles to Afro-American suffrage were progressively eliminated by Supreme Court decisions—for example, the white primary in 1944 (*Smith* v. *Allwright,* 321 U.S. 649) and the "reasonable interpretation" of the Constitution test in 1965 (*Louisiana* v. *United States,* 380 U.S. 145)—and by federal legislation, notably the Voting Rights Act of 1965, which outlawed literacy, educational, "good character," and voucher devices aimed at keeping black suffrage to a minimum. Lengthy local residential qualifications for voting eligibility were declared unconstitutional by the Supreme Court in 1972 (*Dunn* v. *Blumstein,* 31 Lawyers Edition, U.S. Supreme Court Reports, Second Series 274). Unequal voting power resulting from malapportionment was held unconstitutional in a notable series of Court decisions beginning with *Baker* v. *Carr,* 369 U.S. 186 (1962). Thus, by 1972 all persons over eighteen, of whatever sex, color, or race, were legally entitled to vote. The remaining obstacles to voting were largely administrative in character and related to such matters as registration procedures and the times, places, and manner of holding elections.

[Richard Claude, *The Supreme Court and the Electoral Process.*]

DAVID FELLMAN

SUGAR ACTS. Throughout the American colonial period the British Empire was dependent on its West India islands for sugar. The rich sugar planters, residing in England, became politically powerful, and in 1733 secured the enactment of the Molasses Act. Under this law foreign molasses, imported into any British colony, was subject to an import duty of six pence per gallon. The object was not taxation, but to give the British sugar planters a monopoly of the American molasses market. The law was opposed by the New England merchants, especially in Massachusetts and Rhode Island, on the ground that the resultant increased price of rum would injure both the fishing industry and the trade to Africa. The protests were ineffective, and the dire results failed to de-

velop. Opposition to the law died down, especially as there was little systematic effort to enforce it. The sugar planters discovered that the Molasses Act was of little value to them, and what they most needed was a larger market in Europe, which they got through a rebate of the import duties on sugar exported to the Continent. In time the British rum distilleries absorbed the British molasses, while there was no market for that from the growing French sugar industry. This situation made French molasses cheap, and there developed a well-organized colonial evasion of the import duty.

In 1764 George Grenville, chancellor of the Exchequer, had enacted a new sugar act, by which he undertook to end the smuggling trade in foreign molasses and at the same time secure a revenue. The duty on foreign molasses was lowered from six to three pence a gallon, the duties on foreign refined sugar were raised, and an increased export bounty on British refined sugar bound for the colonies was granted. The net result was to give the British sugar planters an effective monopoly of the American sugar market; smuggling of foreign sugar became unprofitable; and the old illicit trade in foreign molasses was disturbed. Americans had been importing large quantities of foreign molasses on which they paid, by collusion, total sums that averaged somewhere between half a penny and a penny a gallon. Most of this money went into the pockets of the customs officials instead of the treasury. Under the act of 1764, the three pence was more than the traffic would bear, if the law was enforced. There were violent protests at first; two years later the duty was lowered to one penny a gallon, applied alike to foreign and British imports, and the protests on the molasses duty came to an end. At this lower rate it was an important revenue producer and yielded annually from 1767 to 1775 an average of £12,194 per year.

Other phases of the Sugar Act of 1764 were far more irritating than was the lowered duty on molasses. One was a new duty on wine imported from Madeira, which prior to this time had come in duty free and was the main source of profit for the fish and food ships returning from the Mediterranean. This part of the Sugar Act led to few direct protests, but did produce some spectacular attempts at evasion, such as the wine-running episode in Boston involving a ship belonging to Capt. Daniel Malcolm, in February 1768. The provisions that produced the most irritation were new bonding regulations compelling ship masters to give bond, even when loaded with nonenumerated goods (*see* Enumerated Commodities). The worst feature was a provision that bond had to be given before any article enumerated or nonenumerated was put on board. Under American conditions it was impossible for a shipmaster to give a new bond at a customhouse before he took on board every new consignment of freight. The universal practice was to load first, then clear and give bond. Under the Sugar Act any ship caught with any article on board before bond covering that article had been given was subject to seizure and confiscation. The customs commissioners made this provision a source of private profit to themselves. The most notorious seizures for technical violations of the bonding provision included John Hancock's sloop *Liberty* (June 10, 1768) and the *Ann* belonging to Henry Laurens of South Carolina.

[F. W. Pittman, *Development of the British West Indies, 1700–1763.*]

O. M. DICKERSON

SUGARCANE, which was brought to the New World by Christopher Columbus, was first cultivated successfully in Louisiana around the middle of the 18th century. Although efforts to make sugar from the cane juice succeeded in Louisiana as early as 1760 and in Florida a few years later, until the 1790's cane was cultivated in small quantities mainly for the manufacture of syrup and rum. The spectacular success of a wealthy Louisiana planter, Jean Étienne Boré, in making sugar on a substantial scale in 1795 was followed in the next years by a rapid shift of planters from indigo to sugarcane. When the United States took possession of Louisiana in 1803, there was already a small, but thriving, sugar industry in south Louisiana.

Climatic conditions in the southern United States were not as favorable for cane culture as those of the West Indies, because of shorter growing seasons and the danger of freezes. Nevertheless, as a result of a protective tariff, the introduction of cold-resistant cane varieties, the adoption of steam power for grinding cane, and notable advances in the processes of clarification and evaporation of cane juice, the growth of the cane sugar industry was impressive in the years prior to the Civil War. Although cane was grown for syrup mainly on small farms in South Carolina, Georgia, Florida, Alabama, Mississippi, Louisiana, Arkansas, and Texas, only on the large plantations in south Louisiana and Texas was a successful sugar industry established. In 1850, on plantations worked by slaves, the southern states produced almost 114,000 tons of cane sugar, approximately one-half of the sugar consumed in the United States.

In the second quarter of the 20th century new disease-resistant cane varieties, tractor cultivation, and mechanical harvesting contributed to the expansion of sugarcane culture. Although sugar production in Texas ended in the 1920's, a thriving modern sugar industry emerged in Florida south of Lake Okeechobee. When Puerto Rico and Hawaii were acquired by the United States in 1898, sugar culture was already well established in both areas. In 1970 cane acreage harvested for sugar was 742,000 acres (267,000 in Louisiana, 172,000 in Florida, 114,000 in Hawaii, and 189,000 in Puerto Rico). In 1970 approximately 3 million tons of sugar were produced from sugarcane in the continental United States, Hawaii, and Puerto Rico. About 2.6 million gallons of syrup were produced from 7,000 acres of sugarcane in the southern states.

[J. Carlyle Sitterson, *Sugar Country: The Cane Sugar Industry in the South, 1753–1950;* U.S. Department of Agriculture, *Agricultural Statistics* (1971); John W. Vandercook, *King Cane: The Story of Sugar in Hawaii.*]

J. CARLYLE SITTERSON

SUGAR HOUSE PRISONS. There were several sugar refineries commonly called sugar houses in New York City when the American Revolution began —among them Livingston's, Rhinelander's, Cuyler's, Bayard's, and Roosevelt's. These sturdy brick and stone buildings were used by the British as prisons, where both captured American soldiers and civilians under suspicion were confined. The most notorious were Livingston's, on Liberty Street, and Rhinelander's, at Rose and Duane streets. Shocking narratives were prevalent of cruelty and privations in these prisons.

[James Grant Wilson, *Memorial History of the City of New York.*]

ALVIN F. HARLOW

SUGAR INDUSTRY. In colonial America sugar was made from maple sap for household use and for local trading. With the acquisition of Louisiana in 1803, the United States acquired a small, but rapidly growing, sugar industry. Major improvements were made in the manufacture of sugar, including the introduction in the 1820's of steam power for crushing cane and the invention in the 1840's by Norbert Rillieux, a Louisiana Creole, of a multiple-effect system for evaporating cane juice, which replaced the open kettle boilers and revolutionized sugar manufacture.

Prior to 1861, most Louisiana cane sugar was shipped to cities throughout the Mississippi Valley and the East Coast, and much of it was consumed in the form of raw sugar. Refiners in eastern cities imported raw sugar from the West Indies and, by a refining process of melting the sugar, clarifying the juice in boneblack filters, and centrifugal drying, produced a dry, white sugar.

In the 20th century further improvements occurred in sugar culture and manufacture. Just as horses and mules replaced oxen in cultivation prior to 1840, tractors replaced mule power in the 1920's and 1930's. Since World War II, mechanical harvesters have replaced much of the handcutting of cane. In the late 19th and early 20th centuries, the cultivation of sugar beets spread throughout the central and western states from the Great Lakes to California, and in both cane and beet processing, large expensive central mills dominated the manufacture of sugar.

By the 1960's the refining branch of the sugar industry was dominated by large corporations and was concentrated in coastal cities, especially New York, New Orleans, Savannah, Baltimore, Philadelphia, Boston, and San Francisco. Refiners process raw sugar from Louisiana, Florida, Hawaii, Puerto Rico, and foreign countries.

In 1970 more than 6 million tons of raw sugar (cane and beet) were produced in the United States and its possessions, and an additional 5 million tons were imported from foreign countries. Refined sugar was marketed in more than 100 varieties of grades and packaging to meet highly specialized demands. Per capita sugar consumption in the United States increased rapidly during the 20th century and by the 1970's had been stabilized at about 100 pounds per year.

[Victor S. Clark, *History of Manufactures in the United States;* J. Carlyle Sitterson, *Sugar Country: The Cane Sugar Industry in the South, 1753–1950;* U.S. Beet Sugar Association, *The Beet Sugar Story;* U.S. Department of Agriculture, *Agricultural Statistics* (1971).]

J. CARLYLE SITTERSON

SUGAR ISLANDS, a popular name in colonial times for the sugar-producing islands of the West Indies, not including the Greater Antilles. They were occupied shortly before 1650 by English and French colonists, and some of them were at first homestead settlements of small farmers. Soon, the latter were reinforced by Dutch and Portuguese sugar growers from Brazil forced out of that country by political disturbances. Capital flowed in from Holland and England to finance large plantations and changed their social organization. The islands were important in colonial commerce because the New England and c tral colonies sold them codfish, cooperage stock,

flour, and provisions in exchange for sugar and molasses. They also traded rum distilled from molasses for slaves on the Guinea coast, which they sold to island planters, thus supplementing the direct north and south trade by triangular trade across the Atlantic Ocean, to the added enrichment of colonial towns.

[Lowell J. Ragatz, *The Fall of the Planter Class in the British Caribbean;* William B. Weeden, *Economic and Social History of New England.*]

VICTOR S. CLARK

SUGAR TRUST, a term first applied to a combination of owners of sugar refineries effected in 1887, which was held to be illegal by the New York Court of Appeals (*People of the State of New York* v. *North River Sugar Refining Company*). Thereafter, the term was applied to the American Sugar Refining Company, organized in 1891 under the laws of New Jersey. The earlier trust had taken the form of a small body of trustees to whom various corporations had assigned their stock, giving the trustees authority to vote the stock as they saw fit. The later trust took the form of a distinct corporation, the certificate holders of the earlier trust becoming the stockholders of the American Sugar Refining Company, while the directors and officers of the new trust remained substantially as under the old. Thus, with merely a change in name and in technical legal form, the practical management remained the same. By March 1892 the trust had obtained a practical monopoly of the business of refining and selling sugar. The combination was prosecuted by the Department of Justice as a combination in restraint of interstate commerce, prohibited by the Sherman Antitrust Act of 1890. A majority of the Supreme Court in 1895 held that the primary business of the American Sugar Refining Company was manufacturing, not commerce; and that the Sherman Act did not prohibit combinations of manufacturers, even though the ultimate purpose was to engage in interstate commerce (*see United States* v. *E. C. Knight Company*).

[E. Jones, *The Trust Problem in the United States;* W. H. Taft, *The Antitrust Act and the Supreme Court.*]

P. ORMAN RAY

SULFUR INDUSTRY. *See* **Chemical Industry.**

SULLIVAN-CLINTON CAMPAIGN (1779) was planned by Gen. George Washington in an effort to curb the attacks of the Indians and Tories on the frontiers of New York and Pennsylvania (*see* Cherry

SULLIVAN IN RHODE ISLAND

Valley Massacre; Wyoming Massacre). Originally planned in 1778 as a westward movement along the Mohawk River, the main drive was shifted in 1779 to the Susquehanna River. The command, first offered to Gen. Horatio Gates and curtly refused, was given to Gen. John Sullivan. In order to hold the eastern tribes of the Iroquois in check, Gen. James Clinton, who was in charge of the New York wing of the army, sent Col. Goose Van Schaick in April to make a surprise attack on the Onondaga.

The major force of the campaign was mobilized in Easton, Pa. On June 18 Sullivan with about 2,500 men under generals William Maxwell, Edward Hand, and Enoch Poor moved toward Wyoming, Pa. Disappointed at not finding the supplies he expected, he delayed there for more than five weeks while, with difficulty, supplies were collected. On Aug. 11 the army reached Tioga, and the following day the greater part of the troops was pushed forward to attack the Indian town of Chemung. The Indians fled, and being pursued by Hand ambushed a part of his men, killing six. Sullivan fell back to Tioga, where Fort Sullivan was built as a base for supplies. On Aug. 22 he was joined there by Clinton, with 1,500 men, who had proceeded southwestward from Canajoharie on the Mohawk, destroying the Indian villages on the upper Susquehanna. On Aug. 26 Sullivan moved his whole force toward the territory of the Cayugua and Seneca. At Newtown, near the present city of Elmira, N.Y., the Indians and Tories made their only stand. The fatalities on both sides were not large. The Indians and Tories were driven from the field. From Newtown the army pushed forward, skirting the eastern shore of Lake Seneca, to old Genesee Castle. Forty Indian villages were burned and 160,000 bushels of corn destroyed. Failing to make a junction with Col. Daniel Brodhead, who had left Fort Pitt on Aug. 11 (see Brodhead's Allegheny Campaign), Sullivan felt the season was too far advanced to attempt the capture of Niagara as had been planned and returned to Easton.

[A. C. Flick, *The Sullivan-Clinton Campaign in 1779.*]

A. C. FLICK

SULLIVAN IN RHODE ISLAND (1778). Because of expected reinforcement by a French fleet under Comte Jean Baptiste d'Estaing, with 4,000 soldiers, Brig. Gen. John Sullivan planned a joint attack on the British at Newport, R.I. Militia reinforcements were furnished. Marie Joseph du Motier, Marquis de Lafayette, and Nathanael Greene were also sent.

D'Estaing arrived off Newport early in August 1778, after having delayed at New York. As he prepared to land his troops a British squadron appeared. D'Estaing decided to attack it, but a furious gale so damaged his ships as to cause him to go to Boston for repairs. Sullivan objected in indiscreet terms. Meanwhile, he had invested Newport, but his militia melted away. Lacking d'Estaing's support, Sullivan decided to withdraw, and the British pursued. On Aug. 29, 1778, a spirited fight took place, known as the Battle of Rhode Island, or Battle of Quaker Hill. All British attacks were repelled, but news of coming British reinforcements caused Sullivan to cross to Tiverton on the mainland. The British returned to Newport.

[F. V. Greene, *The Revolutionary War and the Military Policy of the United States.*]

THOMAS ROBSON HAY

SULLY, FORT, was built by Gen. Alfred Sully in 1863 as a station for the army in the war against the Sioux. It was first located three miles below Pierre, S.Dak., but in 1866 was relocated twenty-eight miles above Pierre where forage was more abundant for the cavalry. It was abandoned in 1891 when no longer needed for the protection of the region from hostile Indians. No battles were fought in the region. It was a regimental post.

DOANE ROBINSON

SULLY'S EXPEDITIONS. See **Dakota Expeditions of Sibley and Sully.**

SUMMER RESORTS. See **Resorts and Spas.**

SUMMIT CONFERENCES. One of the effects of World War I was to change the conduct and style of foreign policy. Whereas before 1914 Western publics and parliaments had restricted their supervision primarily to domestic concerns and had left foreign policy to the experts, the length and fantastic cost in lives of World War I—whose eruption was blamed on secret diplomacy—led to the demand for "open covenants openly arrived at." Popularly elected figures, held responsible by the electorate, were considered more trustworthy than professional diplomats in handling a nation's business and avoiding war. It also became politically profitable for premiers, prime ministers, and presidents to journey to other lands in the quest for peace.

Summit meetings involving the United States since World War II have been of two types, one held between adversaries and the other among allies, and at two levels, between chiefs of government and, just below this pinnacle, between foreign ministers; attention has naturally focused on the former. Regardless of the level at which summit meetings are held, summitry serves several purposes. The first is symbolic. A summit gathering can signal major changes in the relationships between the participants, as did Dwight D. Eisenhower's 1955 meeting with the Soviet leaders or Richard M. Nixon's 1972 journeys to Peking and Moscow. A second aim is to resolve major conflicting interests. Thus, Nixon and Premier Chou En-lai attempted to settle the Formosa problem, which impeded better Sino-American relations. Also, Nixon and the Soviet leaders signed an arms control agreement limiting the number of defensive and offensive missiles and negotiated on other key issues. The assumption is that political leaders possess authority that diplomats do not have to make decisions, although the latter usually prepare the groundwork. A third objective is for the leaders to take one another's measure. Thus, John F. Kennedy met Nikita S. Khrushchev in Vienna in 1961 to caution him not to confuse American restraint with a lack of will to uphold vital interests and therefore precipitate a confrontation through miscalculating. Summitry also serves propaganda purposes. Instead of talking to one another, each adversary seeks to persuade his respective public that he is for peace while the adversary is the warmonger who keeps tensions high and makes it impossible to resolve differences. Presumably this tactic helps the mobilization of public support for one's foreign policy. Finally, and closely related, is the incumbent party's desire to be reelected or, in a dictatorship, for the leader to consolidate his position among his colleagues and rivals.

Summitry also has certain drawbacks. A chief of government must deal with numerous foreign and domestic issues so that he can concentrate on a few issues and prepare thoroughly for negotiations only by neglecting his other responsibilities. If he does not prepare properly, the cost can be high. These consequences may even be felt by a foreign minister who deals only with external problems. Furthermore, summit conferences produce greater public expectations, which, if disappointed by a lack of results, may create cynicism and undermine the possible fruitful uses of diplomacy at more favorable moments. In addition,

summitry can backfire if one leader fails to impress his adversary, as Kennedy discovered when the crises he had sought to avoid were precipitated by Khrushchev in Berlin and later in Cuba.

On balance, two conclusions seem apparent: summit conferences will continue to be held and, if used with moderation, can yield satisfactory foreign and domestic results. If used too frequently, with a lack of preparation, they are more likely to backfire.

JOHN W. SPANIER

SUMNER, FORT, was a miliary post on the Pecos River in east central New Mexico, established in 1862, near Bosque Redondo, a reservation where 8,000 Navaho and 400 Mescalero Apache were held as prisoners of war. At a time when regular troops had been withdrawn from New Mexico because of the Civil War, the Navaho had increased their raids on the Rio Grande settlements. The renowned frontiersman Kit Carson was commissioned colonel and ordered into the field in command of a force of militiamen to round up the Navaho. He pursued a strategy of killing the Navaho sheep and destroying crops in the fields until groups of starving Navaho began to straggle in to Fort Defiance to surrender. Eventually 8,000 of them made the "Long Walk" of 300 miles to detention at Fort Sumner. The Mescalero and Navaho quarreled with each other, and in 1865 the Mescalero slipped away from the reservation. Despite the troops at Fort Sumner, the Navaho suffered from Comanche raids on their livestock. In 1868, after signing a treaty, the Navaho were permitted to return to a new reservation in their homeland in northeastern New Mexico and adjacent Arizona, and Fort Sumner was immediately abandoned.

[Lynn R. Bailey, *The Long Walk;* William A. Keleher, *Turmoil in New Mexico, 1846–68;* Lawrence G. Kelly, *Navajo Roundup;* James D. Shinkle, *Fort Sumner and the Bosque Redondo Indian Reservation.*]

KENNETH M. STEWART

SUMNER'S EXPEDITION (1857). Depredations by the Cheyenne in Kansas and Nebraska caused Col. Edwin V. Sumner to march against them from Fort Leavenworth with six companies of cavalry and three of infantry. On July 29 the cavalry advance encountered 400 warriors on Solomon Fork of the Kansas River. A pitched battle ensued, with Sumner losing eight men, killed or wounded. Leaving one company, which built Fort Floyd, to protect the wounded and sick, he fruitlessly pursued the Indians with his remaining troops. Marching 1,000 miles during the campaign, the soldiers returned to Fort Kearny in August, many barefooted or destitute of clothing.

[Thomas F. Rodenbaugh and William L. Haskin, *The Army of the United States;* Oliver L. Spaulding, *The United States Army in War and Peace.*]

JOSEPH MILLS HANSON

SUMPTUARY LAWS AND TAXES, COLONIAL. The term "sumptuary laws" is usually meant to refer to legal attempts to regulate food, clothing, morals, amusements, church attendance, and Sabbath observance. In this respect there were sumptuary laws in all of the colonies. Some of these were general statutes enacted by the colony, others were local regulations, others were applications of what was understood to be the common law applicable to local situations, and still others were the fixed customs of the people of the different colonies. Custom and practice are as much a part of the total laws of a community as are the formal statutes, although their enforcement is different. The most discussed collection of such laws is that of the blue laws of Connecticut. These were originally compiled by the Loyalist and Anglican clergyman Samuel A. Peters and published in England in his *General History of Connecticut* (1781). For many years people accepted or denounced this account of the Connecticut colonial code. In 1898 Walter F. Prince published in the *Report of the American Historical Association for 1898* a detailed analysis of the Peters laws based on careful research. He found that one-half did exist in New Haven, more than four-fifths existed in one or more of the New England colonies, others were inventions, exaggerations, misunderstandings, or the result of copying from other writers on New England history.

The laws against wearing gold decorations, lace, hatbands, ruffs, silks, and similar materials when one's station in life did not warrant such expensive clothing were confined mostly to the 17th century and were not peculiar to New England. In 1621 directions were sent to Virginia limiting the right to wear such apparel to members of the council. Enforcement was usually by fine, although in Massachusetts the wearer might have his assessed valuation raised to £300 in addition to a fine. Connecticut had no definite laws regulating dress, while in Massachusetts the regulations were very detailed. Laws against Sabbath breaking were common to all of the colonies, and, in most of them, church attendance was prescribed by law. Enforcement was probably stricter in New England than elsewhere. In all but the middle colonies every-

body was taxed to support the local church and its minister. In New England doctrinal uniformity was prescribed by law. Quakers were punished and driven from Massachusetts, and three were hanged for persistent return. Baptists were also beaten and imprisoned. Alleged witches were proscribed and several hanged, all in the latter half of the 17th century. Yet with all this reputation for harshness, there were far fewer death penalties provided by law in New England than in the English statutes of the same time.

Laws against sex immorality were similar in all the colonies, although in the South they were directed particularly against amalgamation of whites with the blacks. Seating at church in accordance with one's rank in the community was common, and students' names in the catalog of Yale were arranged in a similar way as late as 1767 and at Harvard till 1772.

[T. J. Wertenbaker, *The First Americans, 1607–1690.*]

O. M. DICKERSON

SUMTER, FORT, situated on a sandbar at the mouth of the harbor of Charleston, S.C., and commanding the sea approach to the city, draws its significance from the important part it played in the Civil War. On the night of Dec. 26, 1860, following the passage of the Ordinance of Secession (Dec. 20) by South Carolina, Maj. Robert Anderson, in command of the Union forces at Charleston, removed his garrison from Fort Moultrie, on Sullivan's Island, to Fort Sumter where he believed he would be in a better position for defense in the event of hostilities. President James Buchanan, whose term of office would expire on Mar. 4, 1861, avoided the momentous decision of whether to recall Anderson or send an expedition to reinforce him at the risk of provoking war. Upon assuming the office of president, Abraham Lincoln, Buchanan's successor, met the issue by dispatching a fleet to relieve the fort. With this fleet momentarily expected at Charleston, Gen. Pierre G. T. Beauregard, in command of the Confederate forces, offered Anderson a final opportunity to evacuate. This was not accepted, and at 4:30 on the morning of Friday, Apr. 12, the Confederate batteries opened fire on Fort Sumter. On Apr. 13, after a bombardment of thirty-four hours, Anderson surrendered; the Civil War had begun.

On Apr. 7, 1863, Fort Sumter, then garrisoned by Confederates and commanded by Col. Alfred Rhett, was attacked by a Union fleet of nine ironclads under the command of Adm. Samuel F. Du Pont. This engagement, which lasted only two hours and twenty-five minutes, was far-reaching in its effects. While it inflicted on the United States one of the greatest defeats in its naval history, it was conducted on a sufficiently large scale to bring out the strength as well as the weakness of the new type of fighting ship, and inaugurated the era of the modern steel navy.

In August 1863 the great siege of Fort Sumter, by combined Union naval and land forces, began and lasted for 567 days. During this period the fortification was subjected to three major bombardments (the first from Aug. 17 to Aug. 23), totaling 117 days of continuous fire, day and night. For 280 days it was under fire "steady and desultory." Projectiles to the number of 46,053, weighing 3,500 tons, were hurled against it. Casualties (with a normal complement of officers and men of 300) were 53 killed and 267 wounded. After the first bombardment of sixteen days the fort had been pronounced "silenced and demolished." But it was rebuilt under fire by its defenders. This occurred again after both the second and third bombardments. During this protracted and successful defense, commanding Confederate officers were successively: Col. Alfred Rhett; Maj. Stephen Elliott, Jr.; Capt. John C. Mitchell; and Capt. Thomas A. Huguenin. Maj. John Johnson was engineer officer in charge during the entire siege, and much of the credit for the defense was attributed to his skill and resourcefulness.

Fort Sumter was never surrendered by the Confederates. On Feb. 17, 1865, when the approach of Gen. William Tecumseh Sherman's army of 70,000 made the evacuation of the whole Charleston sector inevitable, the fort was closed and abandoned.

Fort Sumter National Monument was established by the U.S. government in 1948.

[Richard Current, *Lincoln and the First Shot;* DuBose Heyward and Herbert Ravenel Sass, *Fort Sumter, 1861–1865.*]

DuBose Heyward

SUN COMPASS, a nonmagnetic instrument that indicates direction by using the path of the sun as a reference line. The Ordinance of 1785 provided for a rectangular system of land survey based on astronomical lines, in place of the older plan of indiscriminate location of lands. In the early 1830's William A. Burt of Michigan, a surveyor, became convinced that the magnetic needle could not be relied upon for accuracy, and his reflections led to the invention of the sun compass (patented 1836), by whose use the true north-south meridian is determined from an observation of the sun. Burt's invention has proved of in-

calculable benefit and is still used, substantially unchanged, by most countries.

[John Burt, *History of the Solar Compass.*]

M. M. Quaife

SUN DANCE. The native religion of the Indian tribes of the Great Plains involved some of the more complex rituals and ceremonies found among North American Indians. A personal vision quest, especially for the would-be warrior, involved the development of amulets, songs, and ritual patterns. The personal element related in turn to the communal ceremonies designed to promote tribal welfare, the increments of the sacred "bundles" common to most Plains tribes being drawn from visions. Bundles were displayed, opened, and generally associated with the sacred cycles of hunting, war, tobacco planting, farming on the sedentary Plains, and, especially, world renewal. Not the least of the great communal rituals among the Plains Indians, and unquestionably one of the most dramatic, was the Sun Dance. Although the ceremonies of the dance were most often initiated by an individual, generally in the name of a relative or associate killed in battle, the more pervasive purpose of the rites was to restore order in the world, to effect for the benefit of the group the continuation of life, the world, and the human enterprise.

The Sun Dance can be broken down into a series of component traits. Of these, the Arapaho and the Southern Cheyenne had the greatest number, suggesting to some observers that the Sun Dance complex originated in the west-central Plains. But even if in peripheral regions—such as among the Kiowa, the Ute, or the Canadian (Minnesota) Dakota—the total pattern was not represented, the basic elements were present and an institution of considerable temporal depth can be suggested. Among the major features of the Sun Dance were a specially obtained central dance pole, a characteristic lodge, elements of self-torture by the dancers, the lowering of sexual restrictions, altars, priestly figures, and vows of revenge against enemies. Given the war emphasis so distinctively Plains Indian, it is of interest to note that a party went off to seek the central pole of the Sun Dance, treated it as an enemy, and counted coup on it. Women frequently played a part in bringing the sapling back to the Sun Dance site. At the dance, held in series of four-day cycles, four being the sacred number of many tribes of American Indians, dancers might skewer the flesh of their back to cords and allow themselves to be suspended from the central pole.

SUNDAY SCHOOLS

Others dragged bison skulls about, these also hooked into the flesh.

The purpose of the dance series was vengeance and renewal of the world, two interrelated concepts in Plains thought. Men found their status through war and the hunt, while through the rituals effecting communal cohesion, such as the Sun Dance, the cycle of hunting, warfare, and the human relation to the cosmos could be put into motion for another span of time.

[E. Adamson Hoebel, *The Cheyennes: Indians of the Great Plains;* Leslie Spier, "The Plains Indian Sun Dance," *American Museum of Natural History Anthropological Papers,* vol. 16, pt. 7.]

ROBERT F. SPENCER

SUNDAY SCHOOLS are generally considered to have had their origin in the movement begun by Robert Raikes, editor of the *Gloucester* (England) *Journal,* in 1780. His attention was called to the deplorable condition prevailing among the children of the Gloucester poor, many of whom, being employed in a pin factory during the week, were turned loose on Sunday, their only holiday, to engage in rough and vicious sport. Thinking that their conduct was largely due to ignorance, he conceived the plan of gathering them into schools on Sundays, where they were taught to read and were also given instruction in the catechism. The movement spread rapidly, and schools were established in other towns and cities—where John Wesley, in his wide travels, came upon them, gave them his encouragement, and soon introduced them as a feature of his societies.

The situation that gave rise to Sunday schools in America was quite unlike that which brought them into existence in England. The Sunday school was formed in the American colonies solely to give religious instruction, and from the beginning it was closely associated with the church. Some of the New England churches, such as that at Plymouth, early gave instruction to children on Sundays during the intermission between the morning and afternoon services. But this was not a uniform practice. Francis Asbury, with Wesley's encouragement, organized what was probably the first Sunday school in America, in Hanover County, Va., in 1786. Four years later the American Methodists officially adopted the Sunday school, stating that the establishment of Sunday schools in or near the places of worship was to be encouraged—the first official recognition of Sunday schools in the United States by an ecclesiastical body.

In December 1790 Bishop William White of the Protestant Episcopal church formed a Sunday school in Philadelphia; and in January 1791 he with Benjamin Rush, Mathew Carey, and others of Philadelphia organized the First Day Society, also called the Sunday School Society, an interdenominational body and the first of its kind. Sunday schools then began to appear in numerous places: Pawtucket, R.I., in 1797; New York in 1801–04; and Pittsburgh in 1809. Although endorsed and adopted by individual churches, the early Sunday school movement in the United States was more largely an interdenominational movement, and Sunday school unions or societies were numerously formed in many of the larger towns and cities during the first two decades of the 19th century. In 1817 the American Sunday School Union was organized in Philadelphia. It incorporated many of the previously formed Sunday school societies as its auxiliaries. In 1824 the union began the publication of its *Sunday School Magazine,* which marks the beginning of a vast Sunday school literature. In 1830 the Sunday School Union reported 5,901 Sunday schools, 52,663 teachers, and 349,202 scholars throughout the United States.

After 1824 the formation of state and denominational Sunday school societies followed in rapid succession: the Massachusetts Sunday School Union, made up of Congregationalists and Baptists in 1825; the Sunday School Union of the Protestant Episcopal Church in 1826; and that of the Methodist Episcopal Church in 1827. All of these bodies were active in the publication of Sunday school papers and other literature.

The first national convention of Sunday school workers was held in New York City in 1832. A great advance was made in Sunday school work in 1866 when John H. Vincent projected a uniform system of teaching. This bore fruit in the establishment of the *Berean Series* of lessons in 1870 and in the *International Series* in 1873. The Chautauqua Assembly, begun in 1874 under Vincent's leadership to bring together Sunday school teachers and workers for systematic training, was soon duplicated in many sections of the country. In 1893 there were in the United States and Canada 11,669,956 Sunday school members. In 1908 a system of graded lessons was adopted. In 1903 the Religious Education Association was formed to raise the teaching standards of Sunday schools. It has introduced a more definitely church point of view and has led to an increased efficiency.

[Marianna C. Brown, *Sunday-School Movement in America;* H. F. Cope, *The Evolution of the Sunday School;*

Edwin Wilbur Rice, *The Sunday School Movement and the American Sunday School, 1780–1917.*]

WILLIAM W. SWEET

SUPERIOR, LAKE, the largest of the Great Lakes and the largest body of fresh water in the world, was discovered probably by Étienne Brulé about 1622. It is thought that Brulé reached the lake by way of the Saint Marys River from Lake Huron. The Jesuit missionaries Isaac Jogues and Charles Rambault established a mission at the outlet of the lake in 1641. René Ménard spent the winter of 1660–61 with the Ottawa on the south shore, and in the summer of 1661 lost his life in an attempt to cross over to the Huron on Green Bay. Pierre Esprit Radisson and Médart Chouart, Sieur de Groseilliers, discovered the western end and part of the north shore the same year. Claude Jean Allouez reached the lake in the autumn of 1665 and named it Lac Tracy, after the then viceroy of New France, Alexandre de Prouville, Marquis de Tracy; he founded a mission on Chequamegon Bay and explored part of the south shore. Daniel Greysolon, Sieur Duluth, was in the country around the western end of the lake between 1678 and 1682 (*see* Duluth's Explorations). His brother, Claude Greysolon, Sieur de La Tourette, is traditionally thought to have built trading posts on the north shore between 1678 and 1686, although there is no evidence to prove that he was in America prior to 1682. In 1683 La Tourette accompanied his brother to the western Great Lakes and remained to administer posts established by his brother in the region north of Lake Superior.

Zacharie Robutel de La Noue built a post at the mouth of the Kaministikwia River in 1717 and made his way inland as far as Rainy Lake on what is now the north boundary of Minnesota. Pierre Gaultier de Varennes, Sieur de La Vérendrye, wintered at Fort Kaministikwia in 1731–32, and in the spring explored the Grand Portage route to Rainy Lake and the Lake of the Woods. In the days of the fur trade three canoe routes were used from Lake Superior to the West, by way of Grand Portage, the Kaministikwia River, and the Saint Louis River at Fond du Lac; and important posts were maintained at Sault Sainte Marie and Grand Portage, the latter being removed in 1801 by the North West Company to Fort William, at the mouth of the Kaministikwia. The search for copper mines led to the building of the first sailing ship on Lake Superior in 1737; that was the beginning of an immense commerce and the gradual spread of population particularly along the south shore.

In the 19th and 20th centuries Lake Superior became the center of an important mining region, which includes the Sudbury district (copper, nickel) in southern Ontario and the Mesabi Range (iron) in Minnesota. To provide access to the lower Great Lakes, a ship canal was built (completed 1855) along the Saint Marys River. A number of industrial, manufacturing, and port cities were established on the lake, including Duluth, Minn.; Superior, Wis.; and Sault Sainte Marie, Mich. Other important ports are Two Harbors, Minn.; Ashland, Wis.; and Marquette, Wis.

[George A. Cuthbertson, *Freshwater;* T. M. Longstreth, *The Lake Superior Country.*]

LAWRENCE J. BURPEE

SUPERMARKET. *See* **Self-Service Stores.**

SUPPLY, ARMY. *See* **Army, United States.**

SUPPLY, CAMP, a stockade post established on the Canadian River in present northwest Oklahoma by Gen. Alfred Sully in November 1868 as a base for operations against hostile Cheyenne, Kiowa, and Comanche. It was from this point that Gen. George A. Custer began his Washita campaign of 1868, and it was important in the Indian war of 1874–75 (*see* Red River Indian War). It was abandoned about 1895.

[W. S. Nye, *Carbine and Lance.*]

PAUL I. WELLMAN

SUPREME COURT, created by the Judiciary Act of 1789, originally consisted of a chief justice and five associate justices. Congress has varied the size of the Court from time to time, but since 1869 the Court has included a chief justice and eight associate justices. In 1936–37 President Franklin D. Roosevelt proposed that Congress add six more places on the Court, in an effort to secure more favorable decisions, but this attempt to "pack" the Court failed.

All justices are appointed by the president, subject to confirmation by the Senate. It is unusual for the Senate to refuse to confirm a presidential nomination; there were only three such cases in the first seventy-five years of the 20th century. President Herbert C. Hoover's nomination of Circuit Judge John J. Parker and President Richard M. Nixon's nomination of Clement F. Haynsworth, Jr., and George H. Carswell, also circuit judges, failed to win Senate ap-

443

proval. Political considerations are usually important factors in the nomination and confirmation process. A president will generally select members of his own political party, although there have been a few exceptions, and he tends to prefer men who share his basic political philosophy. The appointee's philosophy is invariably a subject of extensive inquiry and debate both in the Senate Judiciary Committee and on the floor of the Senate.

The justices of the Supreme Court hold office for life—the Constitution says "during good Behaviour"—and can be removed from office only by the impeachment process, which requires a two-thirds vote of the Senate. No Supreme Court justice has ever been impeached, although a serious attempt was made to remove Justice Samuel Chase in 1805. Most justices are well beyond middle age when first appointed to the Court, but they have enjoyed unusual longevity; in all, by 1975 there had been only a hundred men on the Court, and Warren E. Burger, who was appointed to the center chair in 1969, was only the fifteenth chief justice in the Court's history.

Six justices are necessary to constitute a quorum. The regular term of the Supreme Court begins on the first Monday in October each year and generally ends some time the following June. In unusual circumstances involving matters of urgent public concern the Court may decide to hold a special term during the summer recess.

The Court disposes of a large number of cases each year. For example, in the 1971 term 4,500 cases were filed, 3,645 cases were disposed of, oral argument was heard in 177 cases, and 129 opinions were written. A handful of cases involved suits between states, but most cases came up from the lower federal courts and the state courts. The normal procedure of the Court is to hear oral arguments from Monday through Thursday for two weeks and then to recess for two weeks. Since 1955 it holds its conferences, at which decisions are reached, on Fridays instead of Saturdays.

When cases are filed with the Court they are placed on one of three dockets: the original docket (which consists of suits between states), the appellate docket (which consists of the review of lower-court decisions), and the miscellaneous docket (which includes appeals *in forma pauperis* and applications for such extraordinary writs as habeas corpus, mandamus, and prohibition).

The Supreme Court's main business is to review appeals from the lower federal courts and from the state courts in cases raising federal issues—that is, questions of law arising under the federal Constitution, an act of Congress, or a treaty of the United States. The appellate jurisdiction of the Supreme Court is subject to regulation by Congress. According to prevailing statutes, cases reach the Court by writ of certiorari, by appeal, or by certification.

The granting of a writ of certiorari is wholly within the discretion of the Court. Under its own rules of practice the writ is granted on the vote of at least four justices, which is an exception to the general rule that all business is controlled by majority vote. The whole tendency of legislation, since the adoption of the Judiciary Act of 1925, has been to expand the classes of cases in which the Court may exercise discretion, and to narrow the range of cases the Court is obliged to take. Speaking generally, the Court grants certiorari only if the case involves a matter of considerable public importance. About 90 percent of petitions for certiorari are denied.

Cases that reach the Supreme Court by appeal are technically within the compulsory jurisdiction of the Court. At the turn of the century, however, it invented the device of dismissing an appeal if it does not involve a substantial federal question. A large majority of appeals from the highest state courts are dismissed each year for lack of a substantial federal question. It follows that, for the most part, the Court hears only those cases it believes to be in the public interest to review, since it exercises almost total control over its dockets.

Finally, several courts, mainly the federal courts of appeal and the court of claims, may choose to send a case to the Supreme Court by certifying the issues to be settled. In these instances, which are very few in number, the decision for Supreme Court review is made by the lower court. No state court may certify appeals in this fashion.

The Constitution gives the Supreme Court original jurisdiction over cases between states. The states often sue each other over a variety of issues, such as boundaries, water rights, debts, and pollution, and these cases are heard directly by the Supreme Court. Since the Court is not equipped to sit as a trial court, when it deals with an interstate dispute it appoints a distinguished lawyer or former judge to sit as a special master. The master conducts the evidentiary hearing, after which he makes recommendations on which the Court ultimately acts. In settling serious disputes between two or more states in a rational and judicial manner the Court performs an important and essential function that helps reduce inevitable tensions between the states.

JUSTICES OF THE SUPREME COURT

*(Names of chief justices are in **boldface**.)*

NAME	STATE OF RESIDENCE	YEARS IN OFFICE	NAME	STATE OF RESIDENCE	YEARS IN OFFICE
John Jay	New York	1789–95	Henry Baldwin	Pennsylvania	1830–44
John Rutledge	South Carolina	1789–91	James M. Wayne	Georgia	1835–67
William Cushing	Massachusetts	1789–1810	**Roger B. Taney**	Maryland	1836–64
James Wilson	Pennsylvania	1789–98	Philip P. Barbour	Virginia	1836–41
John Blair	Virginia	1789–96	John Catron	Tennessee	1837–65
Robert H. Harrison	Maryland	1789–90	John McKinley	Alabama	1837–52
James Iredell	North Carolina	1790–99	Peter V. Daniel	Virginia	1841–60
Thomas Johnson	Maryland	1791–93	Samuel Nelson	New York	1845–72
William Paterson	New Jersey	1793–1806	Levi Woodbury	New Hampshire	1845–51
John Rutledge [1]	South Carolina	1795	Robert C. Grier	Pennsylvania	1846–70
Samuel Chase	Maryland	1796–1811	Benjamin R. Curtis	Massachusetts	1851–57
Oliver Ellsworth	Connecticut	1796–99	John A. Campbell	Alabama	1853–61
Bushrod Washington	Virginia	1798–1829	Nathan Clifford	Maine	1858–81
Alfred Moore	North Carolina	1799–1804	Noah H. Swayne	Ohio	1862–81
John Marshall	Virginia	1801–35	Samuel F. Miller	Iowa	1862–90
William Johnson	South Carolina	1804–34	David Davis	Illinois	1862–77
Henry B. Livingston	New York	1806–23	Stephen J. Field	California	1863–97
Thomas Todd	Kentucky	1807–26	**Salmon P. Chase**	Ohio	1864–73
Joseph Story	Massachusetts	1811–45	William Strong	Pennsylvania	1870–80
Gabriel Duval	Maryland	1811–36	Joseph P. Bradley	New Jersey	1870–92
Smith Thompson	New York	1823–43	Ward Hunt	New York	1872–82
Robert Trimble	Kentucky	1826–28	**Morrison R. Waite**	Ohio	1874–88
John McLean	Ohio	1829–61	John M. Harlan	Kentucky	1877–1911

[1] Acting chief justice; rejected by Senate.

SUPREME COURT

JUSTICES OF THE SUPREME COURT (*Continued*)

NAME	STATE OF RESIDENCE	YEARS IN OFFICE	NAME	STATE OF RESIDENCE	YEARS IN OFFICE
William B. Woods	Georgia	1880–87	Louis D. Brandeis	Massachusetts	1916–39
Stanley Matthews	Ohio	1881–89	John H. Clarke	Ohio	1916–22
Horace Gray	Massachusetts	1881–1902	**William H. Taft**	Connecticut	1921–30
Samuel Blatchford	New York	1882–93	George Sutherland	Utah	1922–38
Lucius Q. C. Lamar	Mississippi	1888–93	Pierce Butler	Minnesota	1922–39
Melville W. Fuller	Illinois	1888–1910	Edward T. Sanford	Tennessee	1923–30
David J. Brewer	Kansas	1889–1910	Harlan F. Stone	New York	1925–41
Henry B. Brown	Michigan	1890–1906	**Charles E. Hughes**	New York	1930–41
George Shiras, Jr.	Pennsylvania	1892–1903	Owen J. Roberts	Pennsylvania	1930–45
Howell E. Jackson	Tennessee	1893–95	Benjamin N. Cardozo	New York	1932–38
Edward D. White	Louisiana	1894–1910	Hugo Black	Alabama	1937–71
Rufus W. Peckham	New York	1895–1910	Stanley Reed	Kentucky	1938–57
Joseph McKenna	California	1898–1925	Felix Frankfurter	Massachusetts	1939–62
Oliver W. Holmes, Jr.	Massachusetts	1902–32	William O. Douglas	Connecticut	1939–75
William R. Day	Ohio	1903–22	Frank Murphy	Michigan	1940–49
William H. Moody	Massachusetts	1906–10	**Harlan F. Stone**	New York	1941–48
Horace H. Lurton	Tennessee	1910–14	James F. Byrnes	South Carolina	1941–42
Charles E. Hughes	New York	1910–16	Robert H. Jackson	New York	1941–54
Willis Van Devanter	Wyoming	1910–37	Wiley B. Rutledge	Iowa	1943–49
Joseph R. Lamar	Georgia	1910–16	Harold H. Burton	Ohio	1945–58
Edward D. White	Louisiana	1910–21	**Fred M. Vinson**	Kentucky	1946–53
Mahlon Pitney	New Jersey	1912–22	Thomas C. Clark	Texas	1949–67
Jas. C. McReynolds	Tennessee	1914–41	Sherman Minton	Indiana	1949–56

JUSTICES OF THE SUPREME COURT (*Continued*)

NAME	STATE OF RESIDENCE	YEARS IN OFFICE	NAME	STATE OF RESIDENCE	YEARS IN OFFICE
Earl Warren	California	1953–69	Abe Fortas	Tennessee	1965–69
John Marshall Harlan	New York	1955–71	Thurgood Marshall	New York	1967–
William J. Brennan, Jr.	New Jersey	1956–	**Warren E. Burger**	Virginia	1969–
Charles E. Whittaker	Missouri	1957–62	Harry A. Blackmun	Minnesota	1970–
Potter Stewart	Ohio	1958–	Lewis F. Powell, Jr.	Virginia	1971–
Byron R. White	Colorado	1962–	William H. Rehnquist	Arizona	1971–
Arthur J. Goldberg	Illinois	1962–65			

The Court is both a judicial and a political institution. As a judicial body it deals with cases between adversary parties according to the traditional usages and rhetoric of law courts. It is political in the sense that its decisions extend far beyond the actual parties of record and thus declare fundamental policy for the whole country. Above all, having the power of judicial review, the Court may declare federal and state statutes to be unenforceable if found to be in conflict with the Constitution. Since the great power-limiting clauses of the Constitution, such as the due process and equal protection guaranties, are phrased in very broad and generous language, the Court has much room in which to maneuver. In seeking to cope with such seminal concepts as the separation of powers and the rights of the individual the Court may well be described, in the language of the British jurist James Bryce, as both "the living voice of the Constitution" and "the conscience of the people."

As the ultimate interpreter of the Constitution, the Supreme Court has had the delicate function of drawing the line between the power of the national government and that of the state governments and thus has served as the umpire of the federal system. It has also had the responsibility of drawing the lines between individual liberties and permissible social controls. In a highly pluralistic nation it has been charged with the responsibility of finding tolerable balances between its many segments. Thus, the Supreme Court has always occupied a pivotal and highly visible position

in the American political and governmental world. It has rarely been far removed from the eye of the recurrent political storms that have appeared in the course of American history. Thomas Jefferson, for example, waged political warfare against a Court drawn from his opposition, the Federalist party, and headed by a masterful adversary, Chief Justice John Marshall. During the fateful years leading to the Civil War the Court was deeply embroiled in controversies created by the existence of slavery and reached a new low in popular acceptance with its 1857 decision in the Dred Scott case. During the Reconstruction period the Court had to come to grips with the constitutional significance of a Union victory and gave great offense to the radicals, who were determined to pursue a far more drastic program than the justices were willing to accept. Later in the century a conservative Court, dominated by aging justices, frustrated the efforts of reformers to tax incomes and regulate monopolies. Between 1933 and 1937 a determined majority of five justices defeated many important New Deal statutes through a strict construction of the Constitution. On the other hand, under the leadership of Chief Justice Earl Warren in the 1950's and 1960's, the Court read the Constitution generously to extend the rights of the individual, such as the rights of free speech and of religious conscience and the rights of persons accused of crime. Whether the balance had been shifted too far in favor of persons accused of crime became a leading public issue in the United States. With the ap-

SUPREME COURT PACKING BILLS

pointment of a new chief justice and three associate justices during his first three years in office, Nixon laid the foundation for a new shift of emphasis in a more conservative direction. Particularly in the field of the rights of persons accused of crime, the Court over which Chief Justice Burger presided after 1969 tended to limit some of the decisions of the Warren Court.

[Paul A. Freund, *The Supreme Court of the United States.*]

DAVID FELLMAN

SUPREME COURT PACKING BILLS are congressional measures designed to alter the composition of the Supreme Court in order to correct alleged judicial errors or to secure desired decisions. They characteristically have taken the form of changes in the number of Supreme Court justices. Such measures are distinct from presidential court packing, broadly defined as the common effort of American presidents to consider the constitutional, political, and economic implications of their judicial appointments.

The Judiciary Act of 1789 fixed the number of justices at six; this number was successively altered to five in 1801; to six in 1802; to seven in 1807; to nine in 1837; to ten in 1863; to seven in 1866; and to nine in 1869, where it still stood in the mid-1970's despite the effort in 1937 of President Franklin D. Roosevelt to increase the number of justices to as many as fifteen. Some of these alterations were attempts to reduce the work load of the Court or to render it more efficient rather than to pack it. So it was with the increased membership provided for in 1802, 1807, 1837, and 1863.

The Judiciary Act of 1801 was an attempt to pack the federal judicial system rather than the Court itself. Having lost the election of 1800 to the Republicans, the Federalists moved to entrench themselves in the federal courts. To this end, an act was passed relieving the Supreme Court justices of circuit duty by appointing an entirely new slate of circuit court judges, positions that President John Adams, on the eve of his retirement, promptly filled with staunch Federalists. At the same time, the incoming president was to be deprived of his first appointment to the Court by a proviso reducing the size of that tribunal to five. This attempt to pack the Court with Federalists was thwarted by the Democratic-Republicans, who on Mar. 8, 1802, repealed the judiciary act of the previous year.

During the Civil War period, when the Court was at the nadir of its popularity and prestige, another packing bill was enacted. In July 1866 Congress reduced the size of the Court (then composed of ten members) to seven. A major purpose of the change was to prevent President Andrew Johnson from appointing to the high bench justices who might overrule the Radical Reconstruction program over which Congress and the new president were at loggerheads. In April 1869, with Johnson safely out of office, the number was increased to nine.

This increase allowed President Ulysses S. Grant, whom the Republican majority in Congress trusted, to appoint justices favorable to the Radical Reconstruction program and in this sense to pack the Court. The most conspicuous example involved the constitutionality of the Legal Tender Acts passed in 1862 and 1863, during the Civil War. They were invalidated in February 1870, in a four-to-three decision that was promptly reversed in 1871 when Grant's appointees to the Court voted with the former minority of three to hold the acts constitutional. If indeed this outcome was contrived, the episode (despite the weight of contrary tradition) should be viewed as an example of presidential, rather than congressional, court packing.

The most important court-packing bill in American history, if gauged by its impact on the course of judicial decisions, was rejected by Congress. This measure was the one proposed by Roosevelt. Angered by a series of decisions that had emasculated his New Deal, he submitted a plan to Congress on Feb. 5, 1937, for the reorganization of the federal court system. Among other provisions, the plan authorized the president to appoint an additional justice (or lower court judge) for each one who, having reached the age of seventy, failed to retire. The total number of Supreme Court justices was not to exceed fifteen. Never before had the role of the Supreme Court in American government been submitted to such searching scrutiny. After some five months of intensive congressional and public debate, the Senate, by a vote of seventy to twenty, rejected the president's proposal. Constitutional traditionalism and reverence for the Supreme Court played a part in the defeat. Also, the famous "switch in time that saved nine"—the almost immediate change in the opinions of Justice Owen J. Roberts and, to a lesser extent, Chief Justice Charles Evans Hughes, made possible a new Court majority and, as things turned out, a new era in American constitutional law.

After 1937, attempts were made to reverse the course of Supreme Court decisions, but neither Congress nor the president again proposed that it be done by changing the size of the Court. Instead, Congress characteristically has sought to obviate judicial cognizance of controversial questions, and successive presidents have sought to influence Supreme Court decisions by nominating justices whose jurisprudential predilections were similar to their own.

[Alfred H. Kelly and Winfred A. Harbison, *The American Constitution*; Arthur E. Sutherland, *Constitutionalism in America*.]

JACOB E. COOKE

SURGERY. *See* **Medicine and Surgery.**

SURPLUS, FEDERAL. Federal deficits have presented far more problems than federal surpluses. Nevertheless, surpluses, which were the rule until about 1930, sometimes caused problems too. From 1792 through 1930 the federal government showed a surplus in ninety-three years and a deficit in forty-six. But from 1931 through 1975 the Treasury has had a surplus in only nine years; only two surpluses (1947, 1948) were large, and neither caused a serious problem. For the most part deficits have appeared during wars or in years closely following major financial panics. Until World War II the American people expected their government to live within its revenues and even show a surplus, which it could then use to reduce the public debt.

Alexander Hamilton, while secretary of the Treasury, tended to operate at a deficit. His annual budgets averaged $6 million. Albert Gallatin, secretary of the Treasury under Thomas Jefferson and James Madison for thirteen years (1801–14), was the father of the balanced budget. He reduced the public debt substantially by piling up surpluses in ten years. The Democrats were in office most of the time until the Civil War, and they believed strongly in states' rights. This precluded Congress from siphoning off any surplus funds for federally financed public works. By 1835 the public debt was virtually extinguished. Since the Whigs wanted no tariff reduction (normally the chief revenue producer), Congress passed the Deposit Act of 1836 to distribute any surplus over $5 million on hand on Jan. 1, 1837, among the states in proportion to their electoral vote. They received over $28 million in three quarterly installments. Then the panic of 1837 struck; that surplus ended, and the nation was never again out of debt. The Treasury next showed an annual surplus in all but three years, 1844–57. By 1860 annual federal receipts were $56 million, the public debt standing at $65 million.

After eight years of deficits just before and during the Civil War, the Treasury again showed an annual surplus every year from 1866 through 1894. Mostly it used the surpluses to reduce the public debt from $2.8 billion to $1 billion. The failure of the Treasury to make many of its bond issues callable raised the cost of debt reduction. Also Congress by the Arrears Pension Act of 1879 and another pension law of 1890 gave hundreds of millions of dollars to veterans. Depression and then war with Spain in the late 1890's produced five successive years of deficits.

In the 20th century, until U.S. involvement in World War I came to an end, the Treasury had a deficit in ten years and a surplus in eight. During that period the federal government faced heavier expenditures: building the Panama Canal, enlarging the navy, governing the new possessions taken from Spain, and improving harbors and highways. Even so in 1914 federal expenditures were only about $750 million. The income tax supplanted customs duties as the chief revenue producer. Soon after the war ended and Andrew Mellon became secretary of the Treasury for a twelve-year period (1921–32), the nation had a surplus for eleven years in a row. Not only was the public debt cut from $24.3 billion in 1920 to $16.2 billion in 1930, but income taxes were reduced too. But the era of balanced budgets, annual surpluses, and falling public debt was over.

During President Franklin D. Roosevelt's twelve years in office the Treasury never had a surplus. The economics of J. M. Keynes, which advocated deficit spending to bring about economic recovery, was in vogue most of the time. In the late 1930's some economists talked of the need to balance the budget over a business cycle, the surpluses in the prosperous phases paying off the deficits in the depressed phases. Then came World War II, which at its end was costing $1 billion every four days. That ran the public debt up to $279 billion at its February 1946 peak. Following a year of economic adjustment to peace, the Treasury was able to show a surplus in every year from 1947 to 1952 except 1950. Then the Korean War brought on new deficits. On its conclusion there followed three mild surplus years in 1956, 1957, and 1960. Since then the Treasury has had a surplus only in 1969, the new reasons being the war in Vietnam, extensive social welfare expenditures, foreign aid, space programs, and at times the desire to stimulate economic growth by deficit spending. During 1971–75 there were deficits of from $3 billion to $23 billion, from 2 percent to 12 percent over annual receipts. Starting in 1972 the federal government, through revenue sharing, has distributed some of its income to state and local governments, but these were not payments from any surplus, as in 1837.

[P. Studenski and H. Krooss, *Financial History of the U.S.*; Tax Foundation, Inc., *Facts and Figures on Government Finance, 1975*; U.S. Department of Commerce, *Historical Statistics of the United States, Colonial Times to 1957*.]

DONALD L. KEMMERER

SURROGATE'S COURT or court of probate in most states is a county court having jurisdiction over the settlement of the estates of deceased persons. It receives wills for probate, issues letters of administration, supervises the management of the property, hears and allows claims against the estate, and decrees distribution in accordance with the probated will or, if no will, the laws of inheritance. In many states such a court also has jurisdiction over guardianships of minors, insane persons, habitual drunkards, and spendthrifts.

GEORGE W. GOBLE

SURVEY ACT OF 1824. Interest in national internal improvements increased after Secretary of the Treasury Albert Gallatin's Report on Roads, Canals, Harbors, and Rivers (1808). In an effort to appropriate money for such purposes, Congress passed Rep. John C. Calhoun's Bonus Bill (1816), vetoed by President James Madison, and the Toll Gate Bill (or Cumberland Road Bill), vetoed in 1822 by President James Monroe. While favoring the aims of these measures, both presidents thought an amendment to the Constitution necessary to authorize federal expenditures for the construction of roads or canals. But Rep. Henry Clay, who championed national appropriations for internal improvements, introduced the General Survey Act in 1824, which was passed by Congress in February and approved by Monroe. Clay argued that Congress had appropriated money for coast and harbor improvements but had "done nothing for the great interior of the country." The act authorized the president, with the aid of army engineers, to conduct surveys of such canal and turnpike routes as would serve an important national interest.

[Edward Frank Humphrey, *An Economic History of the United States*.]

L. W. NEWTON

SURVEYORS, EARLY. One of the first white men to appear in a frontier district was the pioneer surveyor.

In the New England colonies he preceded the settlers, ran the township lines, and laid out the lots into which the rectangular township was divided. The New England surveyor followed an orderly system in which tier after tier of townships were surveyed as additional land was required for settlement, but the surveyor was never far from settled districts. In the southern colonies surveying was done privately for speculators who were locating lands in advance of settlement or for squatters who had preceded the surveyor. There the rectangular system was not adopted, and the surveyors' lines had to conform to the squatters' improvements no matter how irregular they were.

Early surveyors operating mostly in uninhabited areas encountered many hardships and risks in the performance of their work. During the winter the heavy snow made walking difficult, food and forage were scarce, and it was difficult to cover up one's tracks to prevent pursuit by unfriendly Indians. In the summer the mosquitoes were intolerable, the heat intense, the underbrush almost impenetrable, numerous streams had to be forded, and fever and ague were likely to lay the surveyor low. The danger of attack by Indians or wild animals intimidated all but the most intrepid.

Save for the steel tape and the sun compass, surveyors in 1750 had available every basic instrument of modern surveying, including the magnetic compass, the bubble level, the telescopic sight, and the chain. But as a rule frontier surveyors were supplied with these instruments only in their crudest and most elementary form. The Mason-Dixon Line was run with wooden rods, and the Military Tract of New York was surveyed by the magnetic compass without due regard for the three degrees of declination from the true meridian. The U.S. surveys were let out on contract, the compensation depending on the nature of the land. The contract system encouraged "running" of the lines, errors in measurements and calculations, poorly marked corners, and outright fraud. When land activity was great and when surveys were being rapidly pushed, many individuals who possessed only the bare rudiments of surveying were able to secure government contracts; it was but natural that errors should be made by them.

Such early surveyors as Christopher Gist, James Harrod, Isaac Shelby, and Daniel Boone combined exploring and search for fertile land with actual surveying. As they appeared in the Indian country before it was ceded to the whites, their coming produced conflicts such as Pontiac's War (1763) and Dunmore's War (1774). To many frontiersmen whose principal occupation was exploring, buying, and selling land, knowledge of surveying was essential. Among the outstanding Americans who had early experience in surveying were George Washington, Thomas Jefferson, and Abraham Lincoln. The first official surveyor and geographer of the United States was Thomas Hutchins of New Jersey who, between 1785 and 1789, had charge of the survey of lands in the Northwest Territory, especially the Seven Ranges in eastern Ohio. On his staff was Rufus Putnam, who later surveyed the tract of the Ohio Company of Associates.

The notebooks of the early surveyors are an invaluable source for a description of the geography, flora, and soil of the public land states before they were settled.

[J. Bakeless, *Daniel Boone: Master of the Wilderness;* R. B. Buell, *Memoirs of Rufus Putnam;* M. Conover, *The General Land Office, Its History, Activities and Organization;* A. Henderson, *Conquest of the Old Southwest.*]

PAUL W. GATES

SURVEY SYSTEM, NATIONAL. *See* **Public Lands, Survey of.**

SUSAN CONSTANT, the flagship of the three vessels conveying the founders of the first successful English settlement in the New World, sailed down the Thames for Virginia on Dec. 20, 1606. The ship (100 tons) and its consorts, the *Godspeed* (40 tons) and the *Discovery* (20 tons), were under the command of Christopher Newport. Delayed off the coast by contrary winds until February, Newport followed the southern route via the West Indies. Arriving at the entrance of the Chesapeake Bay, the ships landed, Apr. 26, 1607, at the cape named Henry. After sailing well up the Powhatan (James) River in order to have better protection against attacks by Spaniards, the colonists established themselves on ''an extended plaine and spot of earth, which thrust out into the depth and middest of the channel.'' Here the *Susan Constant* and its sister ships were ''moored to the trees in six fathoms of water,'' and the site was named James-Forte or Jamestowne (May 14, 1607).

[L. G. Tyler, *Narratives of Early Virginia.*]

MATTHEW PAGE ANDREWS

SUSQUEHANNA COMPANY was a merging of a number of smaller groups of Connecticut farmers who organized at Windham, Conn., in 1753 for the purpose of settling on lands in Wyoming Valley, in northeastern Pennsylvania, basing their claim on the Connecticut Charter of 1662 (*see* Connecticut Western Lands). Leading citizens of Connecticut were shareholders in this company and included such men as Ezra Stiles, Phineas Lyman, Eliphalet Dyer, and Jedediah Elderkin. It was supported by governors Roger Wolcott and Jonathan Trumbull, although Gov. Thomas Fitch and his followers opposed the company's claims. The company leaders engaged John Lydius to effect a purchase of lands from the Six Nations, and this was done at the Albany Congress in 1754. There is reason to believe Lydius used devious means to secure the deed, and the Pennsylvania authorities bought a part of the same land from some of the same Indians at the same congress. The Susquehanna Company merged with the first and second Delaware companies, started a settlement at Wyoming in 1762 (which was wiped out by Indians in October 1763), sent Dyer to London in 1764 to obtain a charter for a separate colony, and, after the Treaty of Fort Stanwix (1768), began in 1769 to settle the lands with the establishment of the town of Wilkes-Barre. But the first Yankee-Pennamite War (1769–71) interrupted this settlement until 1772 when permanent settlement of the region by Connecticut settlers began. The company laid out townships 5 miles square throughout the forty-first parallel from a line 10 miles east of and parallel to the Susquehanna River to a line 120 miles west of the river. The jurisdiction of this territory was awarded to Pennsylvania on Dec. 30, 1782 (*see* Pennsylvania-Connecticut Boundary Dispute), and the second Yankee-Pennamite War broke out (1783), resulting in the dispossession of most of the Connecticut settlers. But under the stimulus of John Franklin's leadership a horde of half-right men invaded the upper Susquehanna from Connecticut and in 1786 made an abortive attempt to erect a separate state in the region, with Athens, Pa., as its capital. The next year Pennsylvania, urged on by land operators of Philadelphia who were tired of the conflict, passed the Confirming Act recognizing titles under the Susquehanna Company in seventeen townships that had been settled prior to 1782. This act was repealed in 1790 but reaffirmed by the Compromise Act of 1799, by which Pennsylvania claimants in the Wyoming Valley were paid off, and titles in the seventeen Connecticut townships confirmed to the Connecticut settlers on payment to Pennsylvania of a set amount per acre.

The company in its half century of existence succeeded in populating the northeastern section of Pennsylvania with Connecticut stock and in giving to the heterogeneous population of Pennsylvania a new element that has not been without its influence in the history of the commonwealth.

[J. P. Boyd, ed., *The Susquehannah Company Papers.*]
JULIAN P. BOYD

SUSQUEHANNA SETTLERS were sent from Connecticut into the valley of the Susquehanna River in Pennsylvania by the Susquehanna Company (formed 1753). An exploring party was sent out in 1755 to see if settlement were then feasible, but the French and Indian War (1754–63) made any further effort at settlement unwise until 1762. In that year a settlement was begun, but a band of Indians drove out the settlers in October 1763. In 1769 another group of settlers was sent out by the company under the leadership of Maj. John Durkee, and the town of Wilkes-Barre in the Wyoming Valley was laid out. The Yankee-Pennamite Wars, the threat of Indians, and the uncertainty of land titles were the chief obstacles faced by the settlers. They won the first Yankee-Pennamite War (1769–71) with the aid of the Paxton Boys, and a comparatively peaceful and orderly settlement began in 1772, which in 1774 was given the protection of Connecticut law. By the beginning of the Revolution there were about 2,000 taxable persons in this region living under Connecticut jurisdiction. In December 1775 an armed force of about 500 men from Northumberland County, Pa., financed by a group of Philadelphia land speculators, was met at the lower end of the Wyoming Valley and forced to retire down the river. On July 3, 1778, the Loyalists and Tories under Maj. John Butler defeated the settlers at the so-called Wyoming Massacre, causing a complete disruption of the settlement. The next year the settlement was renewed, but in 1784 the Pennsylvania local authorities brought on the second Yankee-Pennamite War, and most of the inhabitants were dispossessed. The original settlers in Wilkes-Barre and sixteen other townships were quieted in their titles by the Confirming Act of 1787, which was repealed in 1790, but reaffirmed by the Compromise Act of 1799.

The Susquehanna settlers brought with them the institutions they were familiar with in Connecticut. In particular they introduced into northern Pennsylvania free public schools half a century before the state as a whole adopted the system.

[O. J. Harvey, *History of Wilkes-Barre.*]
JULIAN P. BOYD

SUSSEX CASE. On Mar. 24, 1916, the English channel steamer *Sussex* was attacked by a German submarine. Eighty persons were killed or injured, two of the latter being Americans. The United States, regarding this action as a violation of the pledge given by the German government in the *Arabic* case (1915), stated in a note of Apr. 18 that unless Germany "should immediately declare and effect an abandonment of its present methods of submarine warfare against passenger and freight-carrying vessels," the United States would sever diplomatic relations with Germany. The German government gave the necessary assurances, but with the qualification that the United States should require Great Britain to "forthwith observe the rules of international law universally recognized before the war," that is, abandon the blockade of Germany. The United States refused to accept the German qualification and asserted that "responsibility in such matters is single, not joint; absolute, not relative." Consequently, when Germany renewed submarine warfare on Feb. 1, 1917, the United States severed relations (Feb. 3).

[Ray Stannard Baker, *Woodrow Wilson: Life and Letters,* vol. VI; Charles Seymour, *American Diplomacy During the World War.*]
BERNADOTTE E. SCHMITT

SUTLER MERCHANT was a feature of army life until after the Civil War. Because army posts frequently were located at considerable distances from towns, some arrangement had to be made to furnish troops with the simple luxuries and wants that they desired to purchase to supplement regular army rations. Consequently, a civilian was given a contract to keep a store at each army post. The post council determined what he must carry in stock, regulated his prices, and sometimes decreed that a small part of his profit must go to the post fund for social activities. In return, he received a monopoly of the post trade, army protection, and some help in collecting his bills from the soldiers. His business establishment compared favorably with the log cabin general stores of the smaller towns, and his stock of goods sometimes exceeded in value that of ordinary western stores. The later post exchange was an outgrowth of the earlier sutling arrangement.

[Marcus L. Hansen, *Old Fort Snelling, 1819–1858.*]
LEWIS E. ATHERTON

SUTRO TUNNEL. Adolph Sutro, operator of an ore stamp mill at Virginia City, Nev., conceived the idea of a tunnel into the side of Mount Davidson to intercept all the mines on the Comstock silver lode, drain them of water and gases, and make ore removal easier. His franchise specified that work must begin in 1866 and be completed in eight years, but the time was later extended because of his difficulty in raising money. He was fought by mine owners and financial interests in San Francisco, and only his indomitable will carried the project through. Ground was broken in 1869. Unable to obtain funds in America, Sutro finally found backers in England. The tunnel broke through into the Savage Mine July 8, 1878, but by that time the best days of the Comstock lode were over. The tunnel property was sold in 1889 to satisfy the English investors' bond mortgage. It was reorganized, but continued as a losing venture.

[C. B. Glasscock, *The Big Bonanza*.]
ALVIN F. HARLOW

SUTTER'S FORT, on the site of what is now Sacramento, Calif., is one of the most familiar names in American history because it was near this stronghold, and on land belonging to the German-Swiss Capt. John Augustus Sutter, that gold was discovered on Jan. 24, 1848. The fort was erected in 1841 with walls 5 feet thick and 12 feet high and room for a garrison of 100 men. Guns and other equipment were moved from the Russian Fort Ross. Here Sutter lived in baronial style, possessing at one time 4,000 oxen, 1,200 cows, 1,500 horses and mules, and 12,000 sheep. His fort was a stopping place for army officers and early California pioneers. Following the discovery of gold in California, an eruption of squatters dispossessed Sutter, and most of the movable parts of the fort were carried away. By 1852 Sutter was bankrupt.

[J. P. Zollinger, *Sutter: The Man and His Empire*.]
CARL L. CANNON

SWAMP ANGEL, the name given by Union soldiers to an 8-inch Parrott gun used in the siege of Charleston, S.C., in 1863. It was mounted on a battery constructed on piles driven into the swamp. After firing thirty-six shots, it burst on Aug. 23.

[F. T. Miller, ed., *The Photographic History of the Civil War*, vol. V.]
W. B. HATCHER

SWAMP FIGHT. *See* **Great Swamp Fight.**

SWAMPLANDS. The public land states contained great areas of swamp and overflowed lands that were neglected by the early settlers, who could not drain them. Congress, badgered by the states, which wanted to gain control of the federal lands, and wishing to aid in draining the swamp and overflowed lands, granted them to the states in which they were located. By the Swamp Land Act of 1850, 70 million acres passed into the possession of the states. Florida and Louisiana alone received 20 million and 9 million acres respectively. Great frauds were committed by the state representatives in selecting the lands, and the record of the states in disposing of them is equally bad. Few states made efforts to drain the lands. Illinois and Iowa granted their swamplands to the counties, which sold them for the benefit of schools, exchanged them for bridge construction, or offered them as military bounties in the Civil War. Michigan, Minnesota, and Florida granted large tracts to railroads. Most of the states disposed of their swamplands in unlimited amounts to capitalist groups and thereby furthered the land monopolization to which federal policy was effectively contributing.

[B. H. Hibbard, *History of the Public Land Policies*.]
PAUL W. GATES

"SWANEE RIVER," the popular title given in America to Stephen Collins Foster's "Old Folks at Home" (published 1851), one of the world's best-known songs. With simplicity in melody and harmony, Foster expresses homesick yearning over the past and far away. The verses have been translated into every European language and into many Asiatic and African tongues. Dozens of composers have woven variations about its melody. In the original draft Foster wrote, "Way down upon the Pedee River." One day in 1851 he entered his brother Morrison's office in Pittsburgh and asked for a "good name of two syllables for a Southern river." Morrison took down an atlas, passed his finger down the page until he came to Suwannee. The river, variously spelled Suwannee and Suwanee, flows through southern Georgia and Florida into the Gulf of Mexico. Foster himself never saw the river.

[Morrison Foster, *Biography, Songs and Musical Compositions of Stephen Collins Foster*.]
HARRY R. WARFEL

SWEATSHOP, an undesirable work environment characterized by job insecurity, low wages, long hours, and poor, often unhealthful, working conditions. Such work may be located in quarters provided by the employer, in which case a "shop" literally exists. But "sweated" workers frequently labor in their living quarters, so that the designation "shop" is figurative.

Work situations of this sort most commonly arise in industries of intense competition, where low capital requirements afford firms great ease of entry into and exit from the industry and where production processes require large amounts of relatively unskilled labor. Secondary earners (women and children) drawn from low-income households and primary earners (male and female) without alternative employment opportunities are the most frequent victims of sweating. Historically, the garment trades and cigar manufacturing in the years 1880–1910 provide outstanding examples of sweated trades in the United States. Competitive pressures forced wages down to levels that bore little relation to living costs. Recently arrived immigrant workers in these industries, and even the employers and subcontractors who sweated them, were relentlessly pitted against one another in their efforts to earn an income. Perhaps the best example in the 1960's and 1970's of a sweated trade would be that involving migrant farm workers.

The first extensive public exposure of sweating was made in England in 1889–90 by the Select Committee of the House of Lords on the Sweating System, although the practice undoubtedly predated these investigations by a wide margin. In the United States, the first public effort to deal with the problem took the form of a law prohibiting the production of tobacco products in living quarters (New York, 1884). This legislation and similar state laws requiring the registration and/or inspection of homework were, where sanctioned by the courts, generally ineffective. Union organization and collectively bargained standards, such as arose in the garment trades in 1910–20, were the most effective deterrents to sweating. The passage of federal minimum-wage and maximum-hour legislation in 1938 also contributed in important measure to this end everywhere except in agriculture.

[J. Seidman, *The Needle Trades.*]

H. M. GITELMAN

SWEDEN, NEW. *See* **New Sweden Colony.**

SWEDENBORGIANISM. *See* **New Jerusalem, Churches of the.**

SWEDISH IMMIGRATION. *See* **Immigration.**

SWEEPING RESOLUTION, of the Ohio General Assembly, January 1810, declared vacant all judgeships and other state offices filled by appointment by the assembly for seven-year terms on the ground that all such terms began with statehood in 1803 and had expired. It cut short the terms of officials appointed to fill vacancies after 1803 even though commissioned for seven years. The purpose was to fill the judgeships with men amenable to the will of the legislature, as impeachment proceedings had failed against two judges who had declared an act of the assembly unconstitutional. The principle of the resolution was repealed in 1812.

[W. T. Utter, "Judicial Review in Early Ohio," *Mississippi Valley Historical Review,* vol. 14.]

EUGENE H. ROSEBOOM

SWIFT V. TYSON, 16 Peters 1 (1842). The U.S. Constitution was adopted in part to establish a central government capable of regulating commercial relations between citizens of different states. Fear of the provincialism of state courts led Congress to give federal courts jurisdiction over suits between citizens of different states. In *Swift* v. *Tyson* the rule was established that in matters of commercial law where the federal court deemed a uniform rule preferable to separate state rules, it might give its own interpretation of the common law. On the basis of this decision a considerable body of national common law of commercial relations has grown up. The rule, always a matter of controversy among constitutional lawyers, was reversed in *Erie Railroad* v. *Tompkins* in April 1938.

HARVEY PINNEY

"SWING ROUND THE CIRCLE" was a tour that President Andrew Johnson and party made to Chicago (Aug. 28–Sept. 15, 1866) to participate in laying the cornerstone of a monument to Stephen A. Douglas. Using the tour to bring his moderate views on Reconstruction before the people—a congressional election was pending—Johnson was goaded into making some injudicious remarks that probably lost rather than won votes for his policies. Various factors, however, account for the unfavorable election.

[H. K. Beale, *The Critical Year;* R. W. Winston, *Andrew Johnson.*]

WILLARD H. SMITH

SWISS SETTLERS. The material on Swiss immigrants in the United States is scanty and unsatisfactory; and the immigration statistics are unreliable because the Swiss, speaking German, French, and Italian, were confused with immigrants from other lands. In the colonial period Swiss immigrants came singly and in groups; and notable settlements were established in Pennsylvania, North Carolina, and South Carolina. Similarly, group settlements were founded in the first half of the 19th century, among them being the colony in Switzerland County, Ind., shortly after 1800, and the colony of New Glarus in Green County, Wis., in 1845. From 1820 to 1924 immigration from Switzerland to the United States amounted to 278,187. Before 1881, the peak year was 1854, when nearly 8,000 arrived. The greatest influx was in the years from 1881 to 1883, with more than 10,000 arrivals.

There is a galaxy of distinguished names among the Swiss immigrants and their descendants: Albert Gallatin, secretary of the Treasury under presidents Thomas Jefferson and James Madison; William Wirt, attorney general under James Monroe and John Quincy Adams; Philip Schaff, church historian; Henry Clay Frick, steel magnate; Alexander Agassiz, curator of the Harvard Museum of Comparative Zoology; Albert J. Ochsner, surgeon; Felix Kirk Zollicoffer, Confederate general; and Christopher de Graffenried, founder of the first Swiss colony in America, at New Bern, N.C., in 1710.

[Perret Dufour, *The Swiss Settlement of Switzerland County, Indiana;* John Luchsinger, ''The Swiss Colony of New Glarus,'' *Collections of the Wisconsin State Historical Society,* vol. VIII.]

G. M. STEPHENSON

SYCAMORE SHOALS, TREATY OF (1775), was perhaps the most important treaty ever made with a southern Indian tribe. A group of North Carolinians, headed by Judge Richard Henderson, conceived a plan to acquire a vast western domain from the Cherokee. In 1769 Daniel Boone was employed to make a reconnaissance of the Kentucky country. On Aug. 27, 1774, a company was organized, the name first assumed being the Louisa Land Company (changed in January 1775 to the Transylvania Company); and Henderson soon visited the Overhill Cherokee, who deputed their great chief, Attakullaculla, to go home with Henderson and continue negotiations. The date Mar. 14, 1775, was agreed on as the time and Sycamore Shoals on the Watauga River as the place for holding the treaty. On Mar. 17 a treaty was signed that conveyed to the members of the Transylvania Company the vast domain lying between the Ken-

tucky River and the south watershed of the Cumberland River—about 17 million acres. The recited consideration was £2,000. A smaller tract was conveyed by a separate instrument called the Path Deed, because this tract connected the larger territory with the white settlements.

[S. C. Williams, *Dawn of Tennessee Valley and Tennessee History.*]

SAMUEL C. WILLIAMS

SYMMES PURCHASE. *See* **Miami Purchase.**

SYNDICALISM, or revolutionary industrial unionism, originated in France as the ideal of the Confederation Générale du Travail (1859). In the United States syndicalism has been identified with the Industrial Workers of the World (IWW), founded in 1905. The IWW supported the creation of strong, centralized unions, while the French syndicalists tended to prefer smaller unions. Both were opposed to action through existing governments.

The aim of the syndicalists was the establishment of a producers' cooperative commonwealth, in which industries would be socially owned, but managed and operated by *syndicats* or labor unions. Syndicalists emphasized the class struggle and were opposed to militarism, imperialism, and patriotism. They advocated direct action, which consisted mainly of sabotage and the general strike. Strikes were regarded as an educative and revolutionary force preparing the workers for the final overthrow of capitalism through the general strike.

Opposition to syndicalism in the United States, as expressed through antisyndicalist laws in several states, developed from the fact that the movement sought the abolition of political government, tended to condone violence, and was uncompromisingly militant. The syndicalist movement waned after World War I, with many of its former adherents joining Communist, Trotskyite, or other Socialist or trade-union groups.

[P. F. Brissenden, *The I. W. W., A Study in American Syndicalism;* Louis Levine, *Development of Syndicalism in America.*]

GORDON S. WATKINS

SYNOD OF DORT, an assembly of delegates from the principal Reformed or Calvinistic churches of the Netherlands, Germany, Switzerland, and England, was held at Dort (Dordrecht) during 1618–19. The synod condemned the doctrine of free will propounded in Holland during the previous two decades by Jacobus Arminius and his followers. It published five canons, declaring the approved Calvinist positions concerning innate depravity, irresistible grace, election, reprobation, and the perseverance of the saints. These canons thereafter furnished the standard of orthodoxy for Congregational and Presbyterian churches in England and America.

[A. W. Harrison, *The Beginnings of Arminianism.*]
PERRY MILLER

TABERNACLE, MORMON, a large turtle-shaped auditorium in Salt Lake City, built by the Mormons between 1863 and 1867. It is noted for its acoustic properties and the fact that the massive roof is a lattice truss held together by wooden pegs and strips of rawhide. Nails and bolts were not available at the time of its construction. It rests on forty-four red sandstone piers. The auditorium seats 8,000 and the general conferences of the Mormon church are held in it. It is also used for civic gatherings and concerts; several presidents of the United States have spoken from its stand.

J. F. SMITH

TABLOIDS. *See* **Newspapers.**

TACNA-ARICA CONTROVERSY. Under the Treaty of Ancón (1833), which ended the Chile-Peru War, Chile was to hold Tacna and Arica for ten years, after which a plebiscite was to determine the ultimate disposition of these formerly Peruvian provinces. It was impossible to agree on the terms of the plebiscite, and the question repeatedly brought the two powers to the verge of war until they agreed in 1922 to submit it to arbitration by the president of the United States. In 1925 President Calvin Coolidge decided that the plebiscite should be held under the direction of a commission representing the two countries and the United States. First Gen. John J. Pershing and later Gen. William Lassiter served as chairman. In June 1926 Lassiter voted with the Peruvian commissioner to terminate the plebiscitary proceedings, on the ground that the Chilean authorities had made a free vote impossible. At the suggestion of Secretary of State Frank B. Kellogg diplomatic relations between Chile and Peru were resumed in 1928. The following year a proposal made by President Herbert Hoover was ac-

cepted whereby Chile returned Tacna to Peru but retained Arica, paying a $6 million indemnity.

[W. J. Dennis, ed., *Documentary History of the Tacna-Arica Dispute.*]
DANA G. MUNRO

TAFIA, a low-grade rum, originating principally in Louisiana and the West Indies, which served as a staple of trade, and sometimes as a medium of exchange, between the Indians and the French and Spanish in the Mississippi Valley and the Floridas. Observers saw that its use was disastrous to the natives, but efforts to restrict its sale were rarely effective. Tafia's popularity survived the withdrawal of the French from North America, but with American settlement and the national preference for whiskey, its use declined.

PAUL M. ANGLE

TAFT COMMISSION, also known as the second Philippine Commission, supervised the transfer from military to civil government in the Philippine Islands. The commission of five members assumed legislative authority on Sept. 1, 1900. The president of the commission, William Howard Taft, became civil governor on July 4, 1901. The commission organized the administrative services and passed laws concerning health, education, agriculture, and public works. On Sept. 1, 1901, three Filipinos were also appointed to the commission, and each American member became an executive department head. In the reorganization that went into effect in 1907 the commission became the upper house of the Philippine legislature.

[D. C. Worcester, *The Philippines Past and Present.*]
BENJAMIN H. WILLIAMS

TAFT-HARTLEY ACT, officially known as the Labor-Management Relations Act, was enacted on Aug. 22, 1947. Sponsored by Sen. Robert A. Taft and Rep. Fred Hartley, it amended the National Labor Relations Act of 1935 (Wagner Act) in reaction to the unregulated growth of organized labor and certain alleged abuses of power by some labor leaders. A disorderly state of industrial relations was portrayed by the Republican congressional candidates in 1946, and, for the first time since 1930, Republican majorities were established in both houses of Congress, which allowed for passage of the Taft-Hartley Act by overriding the veto of Democratic President Harry S. Truman.

The depression of the early 1930's dramatized the organized power of industry in contrast to the unorganized weakness of the work force. To counter this condition, Congress enacted the National Industrial Recovery Act (NIRA) in 1933, which, coupled with the National Labor Board established by executive order that year, began a period of federal control of prices, wages, and hours. A subsequent amendment to NIRA gave employees the right to organize and bargain collectively free from the interference, restraint, or coercion of their employers. Under the act, union membership, particularly in the coal industry, expanded rapidly. The National Labor Relations Board, however, was short-lived, for in May 1935 the Supreme Court ruled NIRA unconstitutional (*see Schechter* v. *United States*). One month after that decision, Congress enacted the National Labor Relations Act, also called the Wagner Act, which gave employees the right to organize and bargain collectively free from employer interference and provided the machinery for enforcing that right. The act established a threefold process to achieve its aims. First, a three-man National Labor Relations Board was set up, with provision for a staff and field organization to administer the law; second, provision was made for board-conducted elections through which employees would select representatives for bargaining purposes; and third, the act defined five sets of employer practices designated "unfair labor practices," which the board was given the power to determine and prohibit.

Critics of the Wagner Act sued immediately to have it declared unconstitutional. In 1937 the Supreme Court declared the act constitutional (*see National Labor Relations Board* v. *Jones and Laughlin Steel Corporation*). With that issue settled, the critics changed their strategy, and began a congressional effort to have the act amended. With the problems of World War II concerning the nation, the drive for amendment was unsuccessful, and between the years 1935 and 1947, union membership expanded from three million to fifteen million. In some industries, such as coal mining, construction, railroading, and trucking, four-fifths of the employees were working under collective bargaining agreements, and union leaders wielded great power. In 1946 a wave of strikes developed, which closed steel mills, ports, automobile factories, and other industries. With the birth of the cold war era, fears of Communist-dominated unions contributed to the climate that prompted passage of the Taft-Hartley Act.

Whereas the preamble of the Wagner Act limited the blame for labor disputes obstructing commerce to employers, the Taft-Hartley Act extended the blame to the conduct of unions. The definition of unfair labor practices by employers was tightened, thereby allowing employers to speak more openly in labor controversies. The freedom of unions in the exercise of economic pressure was limited by the designation of six unfair union labor practices. Other major changes consisted of allowing the employees the right to reject organization; the closed shop agreement was outlawed; state right-to-work laws were given precedence over the Taft-Hartley provision for union shops by majority vote of the workers; unions were prohibited for the first time from engaging in secondary strikes; unions could be sued as entities; political contributions and expenditures of unions were restricted; internal union affairs were regulated and reports were required to be filed; no benefits were accorded any labor organization, under the act, unless the union officers filed affidavits showing that they were free from Communist Party affiliation or belief; and the power of "discretionary injunction" was restored to the courts. The act remained unchanged until further union restrictions were enacted in amendments to it, through passage of the Landrum-Griffin Act in 1959.

[A. Cox and D. Bok, *Labor Law, Cases and Materials.*]

DAVID MANDEL
ALFRED J. PETIT-CLAIR, JR.

TAFT-KATSURA MEMORANDUM (July 29, 1905), a so-called "agreed memorandum" exchanged between Secretary of War William Howard Taft, speaking for President Theodore Roosevelt, and Prime Minister Taro Katsura of Japan. It was negotiated on the eve of the Treaty of Portsmouth, which ended the Russo-Japanese War. The memorandum invoked Japanese-American cooperation "for the maintenance of peace in the Far East." Thus ornamented, it expressed an approval by the United States (that is to say, by the Roosevelt administration) of Japanese suzerainty over Korea and a disapproval by Japan of "any aggressive designs whatever on the Philippines." Roosevelt assured Taft afterward that his "conversation with Count Katsura was absolutely correct in every respect," thus placing his emphatic approval on this effective agreement, which remained secret until 1925.

[Ralph E. Minger, "Taft's Missions to Japan: A Study in Personal Diplomacy," *Pacific Historical Review,* vol. 30 (1961).]

SAMUEL FLAGG BEMIS

TAFT-ROOSEVELT SPLIT. At the outset of the administration of Republican President William Howard Taft (1909) political observers in Washington, D.C., noted the existence of adverse criticism of the president by men who had been closely associated with Theodore Roosevelt's reform policies. There was also disappointment among members of the House of Representatives who hoped for the support of the new president in their program of reform in the House rules. Within a year, in both House and Senate, the Republican party membership was seriously divided, a division reflected in public opinion throughout the western states following Taft's defense of the Payne-Aldrich Tariff Act. Gradually the general issue was drawn between those who supported Taft, backed by the party machine in both Senate and House and most of the states, and those who were known as Insurgents, who were led by Sen. Robert M. La Follette. On his return from Africa in June 1910 Roosevelt consulted with Taft. On the surface there was no break with Taft at this time, but on Aug. 31, in Kansas, Roosevelt delivered his ''New Nationalism'' speech, which was interpreted as an attack on Taft's conservatism. In the congressional and state elections later in the year the Republicans suffered general defeat. The following year the Insurgents organized the Republican-Progressive League, and in 1912 the Progressive-Republicans selected La Follette to contest in the primaries with Taft for the presidential nomination. La Follette's failure to win general support led seven Republican state governors, backed by a great number of former Roosevelt lieutenants, to urge Roosevelt to permit the use of his name in the preconvention canvass. This campaign was bitterly personal. Regular party leaders, including many former friends of Roosevelt, kept control of the national convention and renominated Taft. Roosevelt bolted, organized the Progressive party, and became that party's candidate for the presidency. Roosevelt and Taft were both defeated by the Democratic candidate, Woodrow Wilson.

[E. E. Robinson, *Evolution of American Political Parties*.]

EDGAR EUGENE ROBINSON

TALISHATCHEE, BATTLE OF. *See* **Creek War.**

TALKING MACHINE. *See* **Phonograph.**

TALLADEGA, BATTLE OF. *See* **Creek War.**

TALLMADGE AMENDMENT, a bill proposed on Feb. 13, 1819, by Rep. James Tallmadge of New York to amend the Missouri enabling legislation by forbidding the further introduction of slavery into Missouri and declaring that all children born of slave parents after the admission of the state should be free upon reaching the age of twenty-five. The heated debate in Congress and the agitation of the country at large marked the beginning of the sectional controversy over the expansion of slavery. The slave section was convinced of the necessity of maintaining an equality in the Senate. The House adopted the amendment but the Senate rejected it. The Missouri Compromise (1820) settled the issue.

[F. C. Shoemaker, *Missouri Struggle for Statehood, 1804–1821.*]

JOHN COLBERT COCHRANE

TALL STORIES, a term used in America to denote a comic folktale characterized by grotesque exaggeration. Although not confined to America, the tall story has flourished in the United States as nowhere else and is thoroughly characteristic of the popular psychology that resulted from the rapid expansion of the country in the 19th century. As an English traveler in 1869 observed, ''The immensity of the continent produces a kind of intoxication; there is a moral dram-drinking in the contemplation of the map. No Fourth of July orator can come up to the plain facts in the land commissioner's report.''

The subjects of the tall stories, or tall tales, were those things with which the tellers were familiar: weather, fauna, topography, and adventure. Long before the nation became ''dust-bowl conscious,'' plainsmen told of seeing prairie dogs 20 feet in the air digging madly to get back to the ground. In the southern highlands astounding tales arose, such as that of the two panthers who climbed each other into the sky and out of sight; or that of David Crockett, who used to save powder by killing raccoons with his hideous grin. Once when the animal failed to fall, Crockett discovered that he had mistaken a tree knot for a raccoon; he had, however, grinned all the bark off the knot. Tony Beaver, a West Virginia lumberman, took a day out of the calendar by arresting the rotation of the earth. A northern lumberman, Paul Bunyan, with his blue ox, Babe, snaked whole sections of land to the sawmills. Mike Fink, king of the keelboatmen, used to ride down the Mississippi River dancing Yankee Doodle on the back of an alligator. Freebold Freeboldsen, having left his team in his Nebraska field while he went for a drink, returned to find his horses eaten up by the grasshoppers, who were pitching the horses' shoes to determine which should get Freebold. Kemp Morgan, able to smell oil underground, once built an oil derrick so high that an axe falling from the crown wore out nineteen handles before it hit the ground. Pecos Bill, who according to legend dug the Rio Grande, once overpowered a Texas mountain lion, mounted him, and rode away quirting him with a rattlesnake.

Unless they were deliberately imposing on the gullibility of the tenderfoot, tall liars did not expect to be believed. Sometimes they lied as a defense against assumptions of superiority; sometimes they lied through modesty; sometimes, finding that the truth was not believed, they lied to regain their reputations for veracity; sometimes they lied with satiric intent; but mostly they lied because they were men of imagination and resource and knew how to make the time pass pleasantly. And in lying, they gave America some of its most characteristic folklore.

[Walter Blair and Franklin J. Meine, *Mike Fink, King of Mississippi Keelboatmen;* Mody C. Boatright, *Tall Tales From Texas;* Roark Bradford, *John Henry;* Esther Shepherd, *Paul Bunyan.*]

MODY C. BOATRIGHT

TAMMANY HALL. Patterned after the prerevolutionary Sons of Saint Tammany, named for Tamanend, a legendary Delaware chief, the Society of Saint Tammany or Columbian Order was founded in May 1789 by William Mooney as a patriotic, fraternal society with an elaborate Indian ritual. Its members, called "braves," were a familiar sight in the early days of the Republic as, dressed in fanciful Indian costumes and led by their thirteen sachems, they marched in Independence Day and Evacuation Day parades, retiring to their wigwam in the long room of Martling's Tavern to drink toasts to the men and causes they supported. One early sachem stated that the society "united in one patriotic band, the opulent and the industrious, the learned and the unlearned, the dignified servants of the people and the respectable plebeian, however distinguished by name, or sentiment, or by occupation."

Enthusiastically pro-French and anti-British, the Tammany Society became identified with Thomas Jefferson's Democratic-Republican party. Under the leadership of Matthew Davis, Tammany joined ranks with the Aaron Burr faction in New York City, which opposed the faction headed by De Witt Clinton. The Federalist members resigned from the society and Tammany lost all pretense of nonpartisanship. The society prospered, however, and in 1812, boasting some 1,500 members, moved into the first Tammany Hall at the corner of Frankfurt and Nassau streets. In the "labyrinth of wheels within wheels" that characterized New York politics in the early 19th century, Tammany was the essential cog in the city's Democratic wheel, and carried New York for Andrew Jackson and Martin Van Buren in the elections of 1828 and 1832.

The adoption by the state legislature in 1826 of universal white male suffrage and the arrival each year of thousands of immigrants changed the character of New York City and of its politics. Despite some early xenophobia, the Tammany leaders rejected the nativism of the Know-Nothing party, and realizing the usefulness of the newcomers, led them to the polls as soon as they were eligible to vote; in turn, the new voters looked to the local Democratic district leader as a source of jobs and assistance in dealing with the intricacies of the burgeoning city bureaucracy. As the city grew, so did the opportunities for aggrandizement in the form of franchises, contracts, and patronage for Tammany supporters. The venality of the board of aldermen—most of them Tammany men—in the 1850's earned them the title of the Forty Thieves, and it was a rare alderman who did not retire from public service a substantially richer man. Upon the election of Fernando Wood as mayor in 1854, city hall became and remained a Tammany fiefdom—except for the one-term reform administrations of William L. Strong (1894), Seth Low (1901), and John Purroy Mitchell (1913)—until the advent of Fiorello La Guardia in 1933.

With the elevation of William Marcy Tweed, an alumnus of the Forty Thieves, to grand sachem of the Tammany Society in 1863, the fraternal organization was subsumed by the political, and to all but purists the two remained inextricably fused. Under Tweed, Tammany became the prototype of the corrupt city machine, and for a time its power extended to the state capital after Tweed succeeded in electing his own candidate, John Hoffman, governor. The corruption of the Tweed Ring was all pervasive. Tweed and his associates pocketed some $9 million, padding the bills for the construction of the infamous Tweed Courthouse in City Hall Park. The estimated amounts they took in graft, outright theft, real estate mortgages, tax reductions for the rich, and sale of jobs range from $20 million to $200 million. Tweed ended his spectacular career in jail, following an exposé of the ring by the *New York Times* and *Harper's Weekly,* whose famous cartoonist, Thomas Nast, lashed out at the boss week after week, depicting him in prison stripes and Tammany as a rapacious tiger devouring the city. "Honest" John Kelly turned Tammany into an efficient, autocratic organization that for several generations dominated New York City politics from clubhouse to city hall. He spurned the outright thievery of the Tweed Ring, preferring what George Washington Plunkitt called "honest graft."

Kelly's successor as Tammany leader was Richard Croker, who was somewhat more in the Tweed mold; he took advantage of the smooth-running Kelly machine to indulge his taste for thoroughbred horses, fine wines, and high living. Through a combination of "honest graft," police corruption, and the protection of vice, Croker became a millionaire. In 1898 the consolidation of New York City with the City of Brooklyn and the towns and villages of Queens and Richmond to form Greater New York gave Tammany new opportunities. Croker was forced to resign in 1901 following the revelations of the Lexow investigation of the New York City police department that exposed a network of corruption involving police, judges, saloonkeepers, and the city's underworld. A $300 bribe got a young man a job as a police officer; $2,500 advanced him to sergeant; and $10,000 merited a captaincy, a job with a yearly salary of less than $3,000. Croker initiated the alliance between Tammany and big business, but Charles Francis Murphy, his successor, perfected it. Contractors with Tammany connections built the skyscrapers, the railroad stations, and the docks. A taciturn former saloonkeeper who had been docks commissioner during the administration of Mayor Robert A. Van Wyck, Murphy realized that the old ways were no longer appropriate. He set about developing the so-called New Tammany, which, when it found it was to its advantage, supported social legislation; sponsored a group of bright young men like Alfred E. Smith and Robert Wagner, Sr., for political office; and maintained control of the city by its old methods. Murphy died in 1924 without realizing his dream of seeing one of his young men, Al Smith, nominated for the presidency. Murphy was the last of the powerful Tammany bosses. His successors were men of little vision, whose laxity led to the Seabury investigation of the magistrates courts and of the city government.

In 1932 Mayor James J. Walker was brought up on corruption charges before Gov. Franklin D. Roosevelt but resigned before he was removed from office. In retaliation the Tammany leaders refused to support Roosevelt's bid for the Democratic nomination for president, and tried to prevent Herbert H. Lehman, Roosevelt's choice as his successor, from obtaining the gubernatorial nomination. As a result, the Roosevelt faction funneled federal patronage to New York City through the reform mayor, La Guardia (a nominal Republican). The social legislation of the New Deal helped to lessen the hold of the old-time district leaders on the poor, who now could obtain government assistance as a right instead of a favor. Absorption of most municipal jobs into civil service and adoption of more stringent immigration laws undercut the power base of the city machines. Carmine G. De Sapio briefly revived Tammany Hall in the 1950's, but the day of the old-time boss was over. New York Democratic politics was rife with reformers who were challenging the organization; De Sapio lost control of his Greenwich Village district to reformers in 1961. Shortly thereafter the New York County Democratic Committee dropped the name Tammany; and the Tammany Society, which had been forced for financial reasons to sell the last Tammany Hall on Union Square, faded from the New York scene.

[Alexander B. Callow, Jr., *The Tweed Ring;* Seymour J. Mandelbaum, *Boss Tweed's New York;* Warren Moscow, *The Last of the Big Time Bosses: The Life and Times of Carmine De Sapio and the Decline and Fall of Tammany Hall;* Jerome Mushkat, *Tammany: The Evolution of a Political Machine, 1789–1865;* M. R. Werner, *Tammany Hall.*]

CATHERINE O'DEA

TAMMANY SOCIETIES. Organizations patterned after the New York and Philadelphia Tammany societies appeared in several states about 1810. Rhode Island politics were controlled by a local Tammany society in 1810–11; an Ohio society played an active part in the factional struggles of Republicans in 1810–12. The first Ohio "wigwam" was authorized by a dispensation from Michael Leib, grand sachem of the Philadelphia society, although there is little other evidence of any central organization. The constitution and ritual were those of a patriotic fraternal order of a democratic character.

[W. T. Utter, "Saint Tammany in Ohio: A Study in Frontier Politics," *Mississippi Valley Historical Review,* vol. 15.]

EUGENE H. ROSEBOOM

TAMPICO AFFAIR. *See* **Veracruz Incident.**

TANKS, MILITARY. *See* **Armored Vehicles.**

TAOS, officially **Don Fernando de Taos,** is a town and resort on the Rio Grande in northern New Mexico, about seventy miles from Santa Fe. Within three miles of one another stand Taos Pueblo, one of the oldest existing pueblos in the United States, and Ranchos de Taos, an old Spanish town built before 1680. The pueblo, with its curious pyramidlike dwellings of three and four stories, was discovered in 1540 by some of Francisco Vásquez de Coronado's men. Juan de Oñate's expedition arrived there in 1598 and gave it its present name.

Spaniards came to Taos as missionaries early in the 17th century and later established both a village and permanent mission. With Taos as headquarters, the Indian leader Popé planned and carried out in 1680–82 a general revolt against Spanish rule that succeeded in killing or expelling all Spaniards from the province. Twelve years later Diego de Vargas reconquered the southern part of the province, but he encountered a continued and stubborn revolt among the Taos Indians until he defeated them in 1696 (see Pueblo Revolt).

The white population of Taos gradually increased after the arrival of American traders: Jean Baptiste LaLande in 1804; William Becknell and associates in the Santa Fe trade in 1822; Ewing Young and James Ohio Pattie about 1824; and Kit Carson in 1826. Chihuahua traders who sent wagons to Taos seem to have reaped enormous profits. After 1822 Americans made Taos the center of a very active fur trade.

At the turn of the 20th century Taos developed as an art colony, and many art societies, including the Harwood Foundation, were established. Taos' population in 1970 was 2,475.

[Blanche C. Grant, *When Old Trails Were New;* Eric Sloane, *Return to Taos.*]

L. W. NEWTON

TAOS TRAIL was already called the "Old" Taos Trail when Jacob Fowler traversed it in 1822. It first served as a road for Spaniards going north to the Rocky Mountains and for Plains Indians attending the annual trade fairs at Taos. Later the American fur trappers of the Rockies followed the trail south to enjoy the friendliness and hospitality of Taos. It also served as the westernmost branch of the Santa Fe Trail and was used as such until 1880. The route of the Taos Trail varied considerably. Roughly it ran north from Taos, crossed the Sangre de Cristo Range at La Veta Pass, and followed the Huerfano River to the Arkansas.

[Blanche C. Grant, *When Old Trails Were New.*]

BLISS ISELY

TAPPAN PATENT, a tract of wild land located at Tappan, N.Y., on the west side of the Hudson, was purchased on July 1, 1682, from the Indians, with the permission of the governor of New Jersey, by a group of Dutch farmers residing on Manhattan Island. In 1683 some of the shareholders settled on the land. The following year a boundary dispute arose between New York and New Jersey, and New York ordered the settlers to prove their title. The Indian deeds were produced, and on Mar. 17, 1687, a patent was issued by Gov. Thomas Dongan to the subscribers. In 1704 the land was legally apportioned, each owner apparently being confirmed in the possession of the farm he had settled.

[George Bulke, "The History of the Tappan Patent," *Rockland County Record* (1931–32).]

A. C. FLICK

TAR was made in the American colonies as a by-product of land clearing and as a regular industry, both to supply local shipyards and for export. Some colonies enacted inspection laws to guarantee its quality. Between 1687 and 1704 two groups of English promoters tried to secure from Parliament special charters to manufacture and trade in tar and other naval stores in America. Parliament denied the privileges they requested, which had a somewhat monopolistic character, but in 1705, moved by a desire to lessen the navy's dependence on Sweden for naval stores, established bounties upon those imported from the colonies including one of £4 sterling per ton on tar. Following the passage of this law and subsequent acts, annual shipments of pitch and tar from the colonies to Great Britain increased from less than 1,000 barrels to more than 82,000 barrels. One hundred years later U.S. export of these commodities to all countries averaged less than 90,000 barrels annually. Nevertheless, the commercial manufacture of tar expanded, especially in North Carolina, and during the era of wooden ships it retained an important place in manufacturing and trade statistics. In the 20th century most of the tar produced was distilled to yield carbolic oil, naphtha, and other crude products; pine wood tar was used in medicines and soap.

[Eleanor L. Lord, *Industrial Experiments in the British Colonies of North America.*]

VICTOR S. CLARK

TAR AND FEATHERS. Pouring molten tar over the body and covering it with feathers was an official punishment in England as early as the 12th century. It was never legal in the United States, but was always a mob demonstration, often directed against a violator of community opinion—as, for example, an oc-

461

casional abolitionist in the South before the Civil War. The most famous instance in American memory is that of Skipper Floyd Ireson, who, according to New England legend, was tarred and feathered by the women of Marblehead, Mass., because he refused to aid seamen in distress. A number of Loyalists were tarred and feathered at the beginning of the revolutionary war, among them Judge James Smith of the Court of Common Pleas in Dutchess County, N.Y. British soldiers in Boston tarred and feathered a "rebel" in 1775. During the Whiskey Rebellion in Pennsylvania in 1794, it is reported that more than a score of government agents were tarred and feathered. Wife beaters and immoral persons who became a scandal to the community often received this drastic treatment by way of emphatic prelude to banishment. The practice finally vanished in the late 19th century.

[H. E. Barnes, *The Story of Punishment*.]
ALVIN F. HARLOW

TARASCON, BERTHOUD AND COMPANY was composed of Louis A. Tarascon, John A. Tarascon, and James Berthoud, who had fled from France during the French Revolution. They settled in Shippingport on the Ohio, which soon thereafter became a pa of Louisville, Ky., and engaged in milling and other commercial activities during the first quarter of the 19th century. Wealthy, aristocratic, and public-spirited, they lived in a style seldom seen in frontier towns.

[Lewis Collins, *History of Kentucky*.]
OTTO A. ROTHERT

TARAWA (Nov. 20–24, 1943). As the opening blow in the American offensive through the central Pacific, the Second Marine Division, under the command of Maj. Gen. Julian C. Smith, began landing on Betio, an islet in the Tarawa atoll, on the morning of Nov. 20, 1943. Tarawa is part of the Gilbert Islands, a British colony, and had been occupied by the Japanese early in World War II. The Japanese had solidly fortified the island and, despite heavy preassault bombardment, the 4,500 defenders under Rear Adm. Keiji Shibasaki fought back stubbornly from strong underground defenses and log and concrete emplacements. Moreover, most of the assault craft grounded on the inner reef of Betio, and the marines had to wade 400–500 yards to the beach through devastating Japanese fire. By nightfall 5,000 Americans had landed, but over 1,500 were killed or wounded. Stub-

born, bloody fighting continued for the next few days, as tenacious Japanese resistance forced the marines to root out each defensive position almost on an individual basis. Air support and naval gunfire helped effectively in this effort. A final Japanese counterattack was defeated on the night of Nov. 22–23, and the last defenders were eliminated on the 24th. Tarawa cost more than 1,000 American lives, and twice as many wounded. It provided a valuable base and, in particular, a number of extremely important lessons for future amphibious assaults.

[Henry I. Shaw, Jr., Bernard C. Nalty, and Edwin T. Turnbladh, *Central Pacific Drive*, in *History of U.S. Marine Corps Operations in World War II*, vol. III.]
STANLEY L. FALK

TARIFF, a duty levied on goods coming into the ports of a nation from foreign sources (called a specific duty if levied at so much per article or unit of weight or measure; called ad valorem if levied at so much per dollar value). Tariffs may be essentially either for the purpose of raising revenue or for protecting the domestic economy; that is, a low tax may be levied that discourages importations only a little but brings in money to the treasury for helping maintain the government, or on the other hand, a high tax may block the flow of incoming goods in whole or in part and thus theoretically encourage domestic production. A policy of absolutely unhampered economic intercourse is described as free trade. This practice of levying no duties either on imports or on exports is based on the premise that each politicogeographic unit should produce what it can produce best and most cheaply. Thus without the maintenance of high-cost production and its consequent high prices, consumers, whether they be buyers of finished goods or purchasers of raw materials for processing, theoretically enjoy both quality and cheapness. As a practice and as a philosophy of the national government of the United States, levying import duties was born with the Constitution, while the stipulation was clearly made that exports should not be subject to duties.

The Democratic party, under whatever name it has been designated since the beginning of the nation, has traditionally, though not exclusively, sponsored low tariff rates. As a consequence it was long referred to as a free trade party, a term habitually applied both in Europe and in the United States to all parties and individuals advocating low duties. Sensing the inaccuracy of the term "free trade," the Democrats came eventually in the late 19th century to designate their policy as favoring "tariff for revenue only." Even that was a selective term, for it meant, whether specifically put into words or not, revenue exacted from those most able to pay or from those who bought extravagantly. Salt, sugar, coal, flour, and other essentials of human beings regardless of their incomes were exempted whenever possible. Leather for harness, coarse cloth, cheap dishes, lumber, and similar products used by the poor in their quest of livelihood were taxed lightly on the theory that even if there was no competition, domestic manufacturers might use the rates as an excuse for maintaining high prices. Luxuries, however, might bear heavier levies than protectionists would demand. Whether the rates have been high or low, revenue has been an important aspect of the U.S. tariff. With the exception of two years, 1814–15, during war with England, and a short period in the middle 1830's, when the land boom was at its height, money for the maintenance of the government until 1860 was derived overwhelmingly from the customs dues. From 1868 until the end of the first decade of the 20th century the tariff, thoroughly protectionist, was, except for a half dozen years in the 1890's, still the greatest single contributor of revenue. The two basic premises of the argument of the advocates of low tariff rates were that unrestricted trade in the short run prevented exactions of the many by the few and in the long run promoted a rising standard of living among all the people. In the years after the Civil War many noted intellectuals joined the farmers, workmen, and others in a vigorous attack on the high rates. Before the administration of Woodrow Wilson (1913–20), however, only a few abortive reductions were achieved.

The theory of a protective tariff has origins deep in American history. Colonial experience shaped some of the protectionist thought; and in the early years of the government, especially after the War of 1812, it became obvious that the development of basic domestic industries was necessary if the people wanted to escape the economic-financial subservience of colonial days. Although the first tariff laws were in part dictated by a deep concern with encouraging domestic industries, protection as such did not begin until after 1816, suffered a decline in the 1840's and 1850's, and rose to dominance with the burgeoning industry of the second half of the 19th century. The two primary arguments of the protectionists were; first, that high duties defended infant industries against competition and permitted them to grow into producers for the nation and, second, that high duties benefited the workman by giving him more days of work at higher rates of pay. Prosperity and protection

as allies were set forth in bold strokes by Alexander Hamilton in the first years of the nation's history and brilliantly portrayed by Henry Clay in the first half of the 19th century; but it was in the twenty years preceding 1900 that the full dinner pail, the smoking factory chimney, and the happy laborer were forged into a seemingly indestructible industrial montage. There were other arguments. Political, economic, and often patriotic groups declared vehemently for protection of home industries against specific low-cost foreign competition (as, at times, in the case of sugar) even though the cost to consumers was frequently much higher than the gain to the producers. Others demanded tariffs to equalize in general the disadvantages of the United States in competition with the low-cost, low-wage products of the world. And always there was the argument, emphasized again after World War II, that preservation and promotion of strategic industries and arts are essential to national survival.

Whatever the theories advanced, high tariffs were achieved largely through promises of prosperity by eminent political leaders, backed by aggressive and generous manufacturers. Effective, too, was the fact that legislators, whatever their importance, were forced to support bills providing protection of products of other regions in order to obtain privileges demanded by the economic interests of their own constituents. The bitterest criticisms of protection were that industrialists, selling in a closed market, exacted unwarranted profits from consumers; that high tariffs mothered trusts and monopolies; that "infant industries" never grew to maturity; and that the duties were a tax as clearly (as Grover Cleveland put it) as though the tax gatherer called at stated intervals and collected the tolls.

Tariff Commissions. *The Revenue Commissions.* Section 19 of the Internal Revenue Act of Mar. 3, 1865, authorized the secretary of the Treasury to appoint a commission of three persons to "inquire and report" on how much money should be raised by taxation to meet the needs of the government, the sources from which it should be drawn, and the "best and most efficient mode of raising the same." The commission was neither impartial nor nonpolitical. David A. Wells, scientist, teacher, and author, and recent but ardent convert to protection, was chairman. Stephen Colwell, former lawyer, ironmaker, and active member of the American Iron and Steel Association, was also an easterner and a protectionist. Western agrarian, Democratic, and other minority interests were represented by Samuel S. Hays, comptroller of the city of Chicago. Wells and Colwell were anxiously watched and carefully instructed by Henry C. Carey, Philadelphia's high priest of high tariff.

Colwell became within a short time merely an adviser to the industrialists about how to organize and present their demands. Wells, on the other hand, began to question a policy of protection, especially after the new tariff bill, based in part on his recommendations, was put before the House on June 25, 1866. In July leaders of the hopelessly entangled Congress substituted for the commission the new Office of Special Commissioner of the Revenue. Wells, appointed to the position, began the basic preparation for another bill, which he soon found was doomed to failure. Even the commissioner himself was drawn into the welter of confusion that was created by the interplay of selfish interests and was finally beaten into the ranks of the tariff reformers. The office came to an end on June 30, 1870.

Tariff Commission of 1882. In December 1881 President Chester A. Arthur, confronted with domestic and foreign economic disturbances and plagued with a Treasury surplus of $100 million, recommended a tariff commission. The Democrats bitterly opposed the measure, not only on the premise that the commission would be protective but also on the assumption that the congressmen were more familiar with the needs of the people than the members of a commission could be. Not a single member of the commission as appointed was an advocate of tariff reform. John L. Hayes, secretary of the Wool Manufacturers' Association, was named chairman. Despite bias the report of the commission as submitted to Congress cited facts to show that some of the high rates were injurious to the interests supposed to be benefited. Reductions in the general tariff were recommended, though sometimes, as the chairman of the commission wrote, as ''a concession to public sentiment, a bending of the top and branches to the wind of public opinion to save the trunk of the protective system.'' No basic changes were made, and the Democrats, when they returned to power in the House in December 1883 let the commission die.

Tariff Board. Sensing the difficulties that might arise in applying reciprocity provisions (limited reciprocity plans had been included in both the McKinley and the Dingley tariffs), the Republicans in the Payne-Aldrich tariff of 1909 authorized the president to employ such persons as might be required in the discharge of his duties. President William Howard Taft, using the loosely worded authority that was his, created in September the Tariff Board, with Henry C. Emery, professor of political economy at Yale, as

chairman. The board, in cooperation with the State Department, made studies of discriminatory practices on the part of foreign states and, in addition, investigated American industries in relation to cost of production, duties demanded, and duties already exacted for their benefit. But the board's life was short. The protectionists, already under heavy challenge, feared it was a new threat to their supremacy. The Democrats, suspecting anything Republican as protectionist, refused in 1912 to make appropriations for its continuance.

Tariff Commission of 1916. President Wilson in 1916 appointed what is often referred to as the first nonpartisan tariff commission. There was, he said, a world economic revolution and the changes accompanying it were so rapid that congressmen, already overwhelmed by the magnitude of their duties, had neither time nor means for the inquiry necessary to keep them informed. Headed by Frank W. Taussig until 1919, the commission survived despite accusations of partisanship and occasionally of incompetence.

The work of the commission was first used in the preparation of the incongruous Fordney-McCumber tariff of 1922. That legislation not only continued the commission but also increased its powers. The president was authorized—on recommendation of the Tariff Commission—to raise or lower duties by not more than 50 percent of the ad valorem rate on articles that threatened to capture American markets because of a higher cost of production. Although it was obvious that Europe could pay its huge debt to the United States only through the shipments of goods, the Tariff Commission under the Smoot-Hawley tariff continued its cost investigations.

Tariff Powers of the President. Always a potentially significant force in the direction of the tariff despite the jealously guarded rights of the legislators, the president in the 20th century has become a powerful factor both in shaping and in applying the tariff. The authority necessary to carry out the reciprocity provisions of the tariffs of 1890 and 1897 was carefully circumscribed, but in 1909 the president was given rather broad powers in the Payne-Aldrich bill. These powers were further enlarged in 1922, when, in the Fordney-McCumber Tariff Act he was delegated the right, after hearings and a favorable report by the Tariff Commission, to raise or lower established duties by 50 percent without further reference to Congress. Challenged by a New York importer, this action was upheld in *J. W. Hampton, Jr., and Company* v. *United States,* 276 U.S. 394 (1928). The cost equalization formula that, until the early 1930's, underlay the flexible provisions tended to increase the tariff.

The forces that have made tariff a subject of concern to the American people have varied from time to time both in nature and intensity; the purposes for levying duties have been always complex and sometimes uncertain. Generally, the history of the tariff in the nation can be divided into three great periods: from 1789 to 1860, from 1860 through the second quarter of the 20th century, and from the depression years of the 1930's into the post–World War II period.

Tariff of 1789. Controversy over tariff for revenue only and tariff for protection began with the First Congress. A bill of 1789, presented by James Madison as a simple means of raising money, emerged as a partially protective measure. Several states, particularly Massachusetts and Pennsylvania, were able to impose ad valorem duties ranging from 5 percent to 15 percent in defense of leading articles of manufacture in the new nation. Some agricultural products were included also, and specific duties with the obvious intent of promoting home output were levied on certain articles of common use, such as nails and glass.

As early as 1790 Secretary of the Treasury Hamilton had begun to collect information on the condition of and the attitude toward industry in the various states. On Dec. 5, 1791, he submitted his brilliant Report on Manufactures, but his pleas for further protection were ignored. Congress did make many changes by increasing duties on special items and by enlarging the free list of raw materials, but the general level remained much the same.

Tariff of 1816. In less than a fortnight after war was declared by the United States against Britain in 1812, Congress doubled all import duties and levied additional restrictions on all goods brought in in foreign bottoms. An embargo a year later almost destroyed the already crippled commerce. Rehabilitation began immediately after the war. All restrictions (both on tonnage and on goods) based on nationality of vessels were soon repealed—providing, of course, that all foreign discriminations were abolished also. American commerce, less restrained than it had ever been, began to flourish. But the per capita debt of the nation had more than doubled; prices were declining; and England, eager to regain its sales abroad, began dumping its surplus goods onto the markets of the United States for whatever they would bring.

The tariff problem was confused. John C. Calhoun, though warned of the penalties that must fall on agri-

culture, sponsored high duties in the hope of stimulating cotton manufacturing and cotton sales. Other nationalists, especially in the South and West, hostile toward England and resentful of the nation's dependence on Europe for munitions and military supplies of various kinds, joined the clamor for high rates. But it was the owners of the iron mills and textile plants that had grown up with such astounding rapidity during the war who cried out the loudest. "Infant industries" that had saved the nation deserved, they said, rates high enough to make their continued operation possible, even though they were obviously inefficient. To further complicate the traditional alignment on the tariff question, Daniel Webster spoke out against protection for New England, where the commercial and shipping aristocracy, though weakening, still dominated.

The bill that was finally passed in April 1816 marks the beginning of tariff for protection. Cotton and woolen goods and pig iron and hammered and rolled bars were especially favored. Estimates of the general average rate of protection have varied from 30 percent to 45 percent. The argument for higher rates continued. Clay wished to protect the "home market" for the benefit of agrarians and industrialists alike— and the profits derived were to be used for internal improvements. His "American system" envisioned increasing wages for the industrial workers and rising prices for the farmers. The situation, however, was changing. The South was becoming a bitter enemy of a tariff system that seemed to benefit only manufacturers. Deluded by false hopes of quick prosperity that would spread transportation across the Appalachians and bring pounding factories to their section, growers of foodstuffs and also of hemp, flax, and wool in western Pennsylvania, Ohio, Indiana, Illinois, Kentucky, and Missouri joined the middle Atlantic states in an incongruous protectionist alliance and in 1824 passed a new tariff that not only raised the rates of 1816 substantially but also placed duties on such untaxed products as lead, glass, hemp, silk, linens, and cutlery.

"Tariff of Abominations." The woolen manufacturers especially were dissatisfied with the protection afforded by the tariff of 1824, and the mild recession of 1825 spread discontent. In 1827 the deciding vote of Vice-President Calhoun alone defeated a bill that would have raised the ad valorem duty on the most used woolen cloth to about 70 percent. In that same year delegates from more than half the states, in a meeting at Harrisburg, Pa., spoke out dramatically for general tariff increases. Angry protests arose against what were regarded as unneeded and unwarranted levies, particularly in the South. The tariff issue, in fact, had become not only sectional but partisan as well. Andrew Jackson, smarting from the injustices of the assumed "corrupt bargain" of 1824, was determined to win enough followers to send him to the White House. His supporters are charged with constructing a tariff in such a way that its anticipated defeat would isolate New England but bring enough support in New York, Pennsylvania, and the West—when joined with the vote of the South—to elect the general. Jackson was not personally involved in the plan, and neither were at least some of the men who pushed the measure through Congress in 1828; but there was some substance to the remark of John Randolph that the bill was concerned only with the manufacture of a president.

Cottons, woolens, iron, hemp, flax, wool, molasses, sailcloth, and whatever else could be protected was protected in the new bill. The tax on raw wool, molasses, and sailcloth, along with many others, irked the New Englanders, but enough of them voted for the measure to pass it. Nobody was pleased; the phrase "tariff of abominations" was bandied about everywhere and in the South became a rallying point for nullificationists.

Compromise Tariff of 1833. The protests of 1828, coupled with the budding Treasury surplus, soon forced the protectionists to desert in part the infant industry doctrine in favor of the pauper-labor argument. Clay, hoping to quell rising criticism, pushed through Congress in 1832 a bill that removed most of the objectionable features of the "abominations" tariff and lowered general duties slightly below those of 1824. But in November 1832 South Carolina declared the act (as well as its predecessor) null and void. Jackson—with much meaningless bluster—took a firm stand. He swore he would collect the revenue; and he asked Congress for a force act authorizing the use of military power in dealing with the situation.

Clay and Calhoun worked out a compromise plan to give seeming victory to all involved. By skillful congressional manipulation they both revised the tariff and passed the force bill on the same day—Mar. 1, 1833. To please the South they enlarged the free list and stipulated that all rates above 20 percent should be lowered to that level by June 30, 1842. To placate the protectionists they provided for gradual reduction of one-tenth every two years until 1840 (the remaining six-tenths was to be removed in the last six months). The compromise tariff was replaced shortly after it expired by a hurriedly prepared measure that

reversed temporarily the downward trend of duties. But because financial and business conditions had improved, the trend turned downward again in the Walker Act of 1846, and further reductions were made in 1857.

Morrill Tariffs. The first of the Morrill tariffs, enacted Mar. 2, 1861, was precipitated by the panic of 1857, which drastically affected federal revenue. Succeeding acts in 1862, and 1865 raised the rates to undreamed-of heights. Revenue was not completely forgotten, but the need to assuage American manufacturers upon whose products heavy internal revenue taxes had been levied was far more important. The end of the Civil War and a growing Treasury surplus soon brought repeal of most of the internal revenue levies except for those on such items as liquors and tobacco. The Morrill tariffs, however, remained basically undisturbed until 1890, when they were raised. Although some modest efforts at tariff reductions began soon after the war, the moderate proposals of 1866, 1867, 1872, 1875, 1883, and other years brought no real changes.

The Democrats won the speakership of the House of Representatives in 1875 (and held it with the exception of one term, 1881–83, until 1889), but it was not until December 1883 that the southern and border states tariff-revisionist wing of the party—with the help of midwestern farmers—stripped Samuel J. Randall of Pennsylvania, Democrat and staunch friend of industry, of his power and elected John G. Carlisle of Kentucky to the speakership. Early in 1884 William R. Morrison introduced a bill to reduce the tariffs by a horizontal 20 percent, with no rates lower than those of the Morrill Act of 1861. But Randall and his forty protectionist followers representing Ohio wool growers, Louisiana sugar producers, and a handful of other small interests in the House defeated the measure. The election of President Cleveland in 1884 brought no immediate help. A depression had strengthened the protectionists, the silver issue had disturbed the political situation, and, despite remarks that "The Old Hose Won't Work" any more (bloody shirt issue in putting out the tariff reform fire), the Democratic party—to the profit of the industrialists—still lay faintly in the shadow of the political charges of treason. Moreover, Carlisle was too theoretically democratic to be ruthless; Cleveland was too adamant to be politic; and the Democrats were too divided to use their power effectively.

President Cleveland, after the Morrison bills had failed again in 1885 and 1886, decided to make the tariff alone the subject of his message to Congress in

December 1887. In July the next year a very real reform tariff prepared by Rep. Roger Q. Mills was passed in the House with only four Democratic votes in opposition. Randall had lost his power, and the decision on protection was left to the Republican Senate.

McKinley Tariff of 1890. The Republicans chose to regard the election of Benjamin Harrison to the presidency in 1888 as a mandate for higher tariffs. Rep. William McKinley's bill, pushed by sheer ruthlessness through the House by Speaker Thomas B. Reed, was reshaped in the Senate. That body, in fact, was for the next nineteen years the major force in tariff legislation. Taxes on tobacco and alcohol were reduced, but the tariff duties were raised appreciably, with protection as the primary purpose. Bounties were given sugar growers, and for the first time a reciprocity provision was included.

Wilson-Gorman Tariff of 1894. Since they had won the House in the fall elections of 1890 and the presidency and the Senate two years later, success seemed within reach of the tariff-reform Democrats, but the golden hopes of reductions soon faded. The Harrison administration had stripped the Treasury of its surplus, a paralyzing panic fell on the country in April, and Cleveland split his party into bitter factions by his determined repeal of the Sherman Silver Purchase Act in a special session of Congress in the late summer of 1893. The bill that William L. Wilson introduced in the House early in 1894 fell in the Senate into the hands of Arthur P. Gorman of Maryland, a protectionist Democrat, and was completely reshaped; 634 amendments were added by various interests. The House majority made a dramatic stand, but the Senate had its way, and Cleveland, having declared that "party perfidy and party dishonor" had been involved in its making, let the Wilson-Gorman bill become a law without his signature.

Dingley and Payne-Aldrich Tariffs. After victory in the campaign of 1896, the Republicans turned not to gold but to the tariff, and, despite swelling opposition to protection even within their own party, maintained for more than a decade the highest duties in American history up to that time. It took just thirteen days to push through the House the bill that Nelson W. Dingley introduced in March 1897. After 872 amendments and two months of argument in the Senate, the bill emerged from Congress with the highest duties ever passed. But with growing opposition from the intellectuals and increasing protests from the people and their liberal representatives, tariff was becoming politically dangerous. President Theodore Roose-

velt chose to avoid the issue altogether. By 1908, however, pressure for reduction had become so great that even the Republican party seemed in its platform to promise downward revision.

The moderate House bill that Sereno E. Payne submitted early in 1909 was quickly passed. Nelson W. Aldrich reshaped it in the Senate; a total of 847 amendments were made, almost wholly in the interest of higher duties. Despite some concessions to President Taft and brilliant opposition by the Republican insurgents, the tariff remained protectionist, and Taft ineptly praised the measure as the best ever passed.

Underwood Tariff of 1913. In tariff philosophy President Wilson represented not only the majority of his party but also the thought of the intellectuals, who had long been questioning the prevailing protectionist practice of the nation. Comprehending in part at least the currents of change that were sweeping the nation into the world, he turned his knowledge of theoretical and practical politics to the task of reshaping domestic policy in many fields. Soon after Rep. Oscar W. Underwood of Alabama revealed his tariff proposals to the special Congress in 1913, the long-familiar lobbyists, a significant force in tariff legislation, flocked into Washington. The president struck out in a biting condemnation and the "third house" departed. Approved by the Senate with few changes, the measure became effective in October, providing the first real and consistent reductions since the tariffs of 1846 and 1857. The free list was greatly enlarged, 958 rates were reduced, 307 were left unchanged, and fewer than a hundred were increased. Rates averaged roughly 26 percent; some had not been lower since the first tariff.

Unfortunately the low duties never had a chance to prove themselves because of the start of World War I. The conflict with Germany and its satellites, when the United States joined the Allies, brought not only increasing prices but also new producing plants, hurriedly and expensively built. The inevitable cry against foreign competition was certain to come up when war's end brought reconversion to peacetime needs with its accompanying costly production and its shrinking days of work, declining wages, and lessening demand for agricultural and other extractive products. New industries were also to fight for benefits.

Fordney-McCumber and Smoot-Hawley Tariffs. Pulling the nation out of its economic difficulties by increasing protection in the dozen critical years after World War I was attempted by an emergency tariff of 1921, which was designed to soothe the discontented farmers and check some beginning imports from Europe. But it was the bill introduced in the House by Joseph W. Fordney the next year and taken up in the Senate by Porter J. McCumber that sought to withdraw the nation from the economic world as others were attempting to isolate it from the political world. Equalization in an exaggerated form in part determined the details, and nationalistic ambitions gave it spirit. The farmers were again promised impossible prosperity by the levying of duties on products already in overabundance at home. The rates in general were the highest in American history, and a flexible provision by which the president could revise rates up or down by 50 percent ensured maintenance of the equal-cost-of-production principle. Conditions did not improve materially, and the only answer politics had to offer was more protection. The rates of the Smoot-Hawley Act of June 1930 set a new record in restrictive legislation and brought much-deserved criticism. More than a thousand members of the American Economic Association petitioned President Herbert Hoover to veto the bill. Other economic and financial organizations, as well as individuals, joined the rising protest that spread over the world. European nations not only spoke out boldly but also passed retaliatory laws. The depression grew worse, war-debt payments from Europe ceased, and, as a result of a combination of circumstances, world economy ground to a standstill.

Tariffs by Reciprocity Agreements. Sen. Cordell Hull of Tennessee was among the few men in Congress during the depression who insisted that national prosperity depended on freeing the commerce of the world rather than on restricting it. He became secretary of state in the administration of President Franklin D. Roosevelt and in 1934, by authority of the Reciprocal Trade Agreements Act of that year, inaugurated a series of executive agreements with foreign nations by which he in part freed trade not only for the United States but, also, by applying the most-favored-nation clause principle, for other nations as well. But there was little time for rehabilitation. World War II, with its appalling destruction, soon swept over Europe and Asia. Old nations and new were plagued by poverty. They needed everything but had no money with which to buy, and the United States, surfeited with goods, real and potential, had no place to sell. A profound change was beginning in world economy. International interdependence, particularly in trade, was becoming clear even to the most nationalistic. In the United States it was obvious also that Europe, the major prewar market of the United States, must be restored. Thus the Marshall Plan, the Point Four program, and various

other governmental and private restorative measures were instituted. Money was poured into Europe to rebuild the devastated industrial plants and restore the ravished farms. Military forces were established to protect the struggling nations, and the money necessary to support them joined other money in putting Europeans back to work.

Everywhere trade practices underwent radical changes as the economic structure was rebuilt. In the United States tariff had already ceased to be a strictly domestic and almost wholly political issue. Foreign considerations had become a major factor in the formulation of tariff policy: tariff making was losing its purely national aspects (dominated by Congress) and was becoming an international problem centered primarily around the president and his executive and diplomatic agents (the State Department was soon to be denied any substantial part in tariff making decisions). Bolstered by liberal philosophers and by economists in the tradition of Adam Smith, the conviction that trade could flourish only when it was free was slowly finding acceptance among governments.

The tragic postwar economic situation that so drastically changed world thinking concerning trade brought many reform efforts. It was obvious that a free world economy required an international mechanism for payments. Even before the war had ended a conference at Bretton Woods in New Hampshire in the summer of 1944 set up the basic machinery for a world monetary system. The two significant units were the International Monetary Fund (IMF) and the International Bank for Reconstruction—known simply as the World Bank. Labeled a failure by many individuals and groups, the two have served their purposes as a beginning experiment. But burdened with an impossible gold redemption task that the United States had unsuccessfully attempted in the 1890's, pulled in diverse and often contradictory directions by academic specialists, faced by an overvalued dollar that was impossible to change except multilaterally, and hampered by nationalistic jealousies and political resentments, these two organs became the chief centers around which gathered the disenchanted in the late 1960's to discredit the philosophy of free trade in the world.

Economic restoration after World War II rested heavily on American money and on international reform in tariff duties. The General Agreement on Tariffs and Trade (GATT), formulated by many nations in Geneva in 1947 and devoted in large part to the reduction of tariffs and the abolition of trade discriminations, was firmly established by January 1948. The United States, largely ignoring the International

Trade Organization (ITO), actively participated in the work of GATT from the beginning. Although tariff reform in the nation was still governed by the Trade Agreements Act of 1934 and its many extensions (eleven by 1958), significant reductions in U.S. duties were made in the immediate postwar years, incorporating the established principle that the president had the power to raise or lower rates, within limits, without reference to Congress. Conscious of the fact that rate reductions bring inevitable economic impositions, real or assumed, the tariff reformers provided protective safeguards against injuries to industries through "peril point" judgments and "escape clause" decisions. A peril point judgment was the rate of duty determined through study by the Tariff Commission, before negotiations were entered into, which the commission judged to be the minimum that would not injure the particular industry involved. If the president disregarded the judgment, he was required to explain his reasons to Congress. Escape clause decisions provided for relief from injuries after rate reductions had been agreed on. The president, the Congress, the Tariff Commission itself, or any interested party could invoke the escape clause on the assumption that the existing duties were imposing economic hardships on an industry or industries. The commission was required to study each complaint and recommend a course of action. The president might or might not follow the commission's recommendations, although by later amendment any rejection could be reversed by a two-thirds vote of the Congress. Despite the reluctance of the lawmakers to share their power, much had been accomplished in economic legislation by the end of the 1940's, and the tariff rates had been reduced for the most part to the levels of the Wilson administration.

In 1957 France, Belgium, West Germany (German Federal Republic), Luxembourg, Italy, and the Netherlands joined together in the European Economic Community (EEC, most often referred to as the Common Market). Great Britain, Sweden, Norway, Denmark, Austria, Switzerland, and Portugal (Finland became an associate member in 1961) formed the European Free Trade Association (EFTA) three years later. Although these memberships later shifted and similar-minded organizations were formed in South America and elsewhere, it was clear by the beginning of the 1960's that a world revolution in economic action and thought had attained a commanding stature if not maturity. The European organizations and the United States were in themselves a loose common unit that soon came to be referred to as the Atlantic Community.

1960–72. Although a rising undercurrent of bitterness was everywhere apparent in the economic relations of the somewhat united free world, the 1960's opened on an expanding economy. The Democrats, traditional liberals in trade regulations, had won the presidency under John F. Kennedy in the November elections in 1960; and already ministers were preparing for a session in Geneva to set up ground rules for the coming meeting of GATT, called "rounds" in the parlance of the new trade world. But the last extension of the Reciprocal Trade Agreements Act of 1934 was to expire in June 1962, and a new law was needed if the dream of the reformers was to be achieved.

On Jan. 25, 1962, Kennedy set forth the existing complexities in a message to Congress. There were three basic areas on which he dwelt: the economic realities and possibilities of the new Atlantic Community, which might even reach out to the developing countries; the gains to be had by unchaining international commerce from the protective tariffs, quotas, and other restrictions by which it was bound; and the political imperatives involved in creating and preserving a powerful and prosperous free world. Common economic growth was the key factor involved, he said, but economic growth depended on a relatively free exchange of goods, and a free exchange of goods depended in turn on agreements reached through orderly and accepted cooperative action on the part of the participating nations.

In the legislation he proposed, Kennedy sought power not only to make tariff revisions at home but also to bargain with authority abroad, either within GATT or individually. He advocated an "open partnership" in which all free nations, and the developing countries as well, could share by opening their markets freely. Kennedy argued that the United States had nothing to lose in pressing for open markets at home and abroad; it could lose, he emphasized, only if the Common Market, for example, should throw up a tariff wall that halted the flow of American goods. The two great Atlantic economic units would, he said, "either grow together or . . . apart." Foreign imports, he argued, could do little damage to the United States because of its tremendous industrial potential; cheap labor, he added, would always be smothered by the greater American productivity per man hour.

A bill, made up of permissions and prohibitions, was enacted as the Trade Expansion Act in late summer 1962. The president was authorized to take various actions designed to stimulate economic growth at home, promote trade and peaceful relations abroad, and prevent Communist penetration of the free world or the markets of its potential friends, mostly the developing nations. He was also given permission to make across-the-board tariff cuts of 50 percent or more on a most-favored-nation basis, to include agricultural items in the negotiations, and to reduce tariff levies up to 100 percent on a few items. Tariffs of 5 percent or less, mostly in deference to Canadian trade, could be entirely eliminated, as could the duties on certain tropical products. The chief executive was required, however, to insert certain terminal dates on all items negotiated, consult the Tariff Commission and the departments concerned, and withhold most-favored-nation status from any country dominated by communism (later relaxed in the case of Poland and Yugoslavia). He was directed also to reserve any article from negotiation that was protected by action under the escape clause and any products included in the act's national security amendment, as, for instance, petroleum.

Early in 1963 the free world began preparations for an international conference under the auspices of GATT in the hope of lowering tariff and other barriers throughout the Atlantic Community, but there were difficulties. President Charles de Gaulle of France had in January vetoed England's entrance into the Common Market. Moreover, several European leaders were not enthusiastic about Kennedy's Trade Expansion Act; and some Americans thought it a good time to have a general showdown. The free-world monetary system was under attack; America's balance-of-payments deficit was causing alarm; and American capital was pouring out to Europe to build industrial plants, which provoked both European resentments and American criticisms.

The general meeting of GATT, called the Kennedy Round, convened at Geneva on May 16, 1964. Present were more than 600 delegates from eighty-two countries. Christian A. Herter, armed with fifty-five volumes of hearings—including the Tariff Commission's advice—led the American delegation. Common understanding was lacking: it was, for instance, utterly impossible to give a uniform classification to the multitude of products from the various nations assembled. The largely English-speaking group at the conference—dominated by the United States—found itself for the first time in tariff history faced by an equally powerful European bargaining group, the representatives of the Common Market. Directed chiefly by De Gaulle, these leaders, it seemed, were as much interested in demonstrating their might as they were in developing a workable economic system. De Gaulle and his followers were convinced that

such existing institutions as the IMF and GATT were creatures of England and the United States and were more concerned with new creations, especially in the monetary field, than with mere modifications. The third group at the conference represented the developing countries, nations scattered over Asia, Africa, and Latin America. Some of them, no older than the war that had directed the forces drawing the delegates to Geneva, were painfully poor. Their leaders were convinced that all existing economic organizations had been created to aid the developed countries and hinder the developing countries—and they forewarned the powerful in the group of their future potential. In the meantime, they lodged their hopes in the United Nations.

Because the old method of settling rates item by item had become virtually impossible, the United States at the opening of the meeting immediatly proposed a 50 percent linear reduction across-the-board on a most-favored-nation basis. Opposition arose immediately. The argument was that European tariffs were much lower in general than those of the United States and that, even with a 50 percent reduction, American rates would still remain much higher. The Common Market delegates, led by France, submitted an *écrêtement*, or harmonization plan, to lower tariffs halfway from their existing levels to a fixed target level—10 percent for manufactures, 5 percent for semimanufactures, and zero for raw materials. The linear proposal eventually won out, but there was much controversy over equalizing the cuts in cases of wide differences in rates. In order to avoid petty negotiations, it was stipulated that the higher rate must be double the lower rate and that the higher rate must exceed the lower by 10 percentage points; in such cases reductions were limited to 25 percent.

Changing production patterns and shifting consumption habits had created problems in the agricultural areas and the American delegation offered few concessions. The developing countries, which concentrated on the production of tropical fruits, further complicated the agricultural problem; special industries, such as textiles in Taiwan, Hong Kong, South Korea, and other countries, evoked protests against cheap labor. Non-tariff restrictions, especially if they nullified a tariff agreement, stirred bitter dissensions—they could, in fact, destroy the hopes of the meeting. There were also protests against the American Selling Plan (ASP), which used domestic prices for determining tariff rates in the benzenoid chemical and two other minor fields. Agreements were arrived at with difficulty. One delaying factor was that many countries were reluctant to accept proposals in one area while other areas were still being negotiated. There was no generally accepted body of statistics on which to base judgments, and there was no absolute means of identification of goods, for similar names did not always mean similar goods.

For nearly four years the GATT delegates argued over reducing international tariff barriers equitably. The United States feared that high support prices, variable import levels, and export subsidies might eliminate old markets in Europe for its agricultural products. (There were reasons to believe that a general loss in sales might result even if there were no nontariff barriers, for the six nations were now surrounded by a common tariff wall.) On the other hand, France in particular and the Common Market in general cherished the dream of shifting domination of the new free-world economics to Europe.

The achievements of the international meeting were substantial. The United States won its initial argument over the method to be used in reducing rates. The escape clause was appreciably modified as the government for individual plants—not a complete industry—assumed responsibility for training and otherwise aiding workers who had lost their jobs and also for reestablishing the displaced industrialist. Tariff reductions, although disappointing in many ways, were, in view of the enormity of the opposing factors, indeed remarkable. The average rate arrived at was slightly more than 35 percent; 66 percent of the imports of the industrialized countries—except meat, cereal, and dairy products—were either freed of duty or subject to 50 percent or more reduction. On the other hand little was done concerning tariffs on such items as iron and steel, textiles, clothing, and fuel. Although the United States made some concessions, the developing countries benefited only slightly. Most nations were disappointed, but the agreement was signed on Jan. 30, 1967.

While the delegates from the United States were urging free international trade at Geneva, many factory owners and factory workers at home were pressing hard for a return to a protective tariff. Americans generally were angered by European grumbling about NATO, the IMF, and the ASP; and their anger was heightened when European leaders—such as Chancellor Willy Brandt of West Germany—spoke from their prospering nations to say that although American sacrifices were appreciated, they were, after all, for the good of the United States. The European countries were working together; Canada refused to join any group; the countries of the New World (Mexico, Central America, and South America) were in the developing stage; and it ap-

peared the United States might be standing alone. In addition the balance of trade had swung heavily against the United States in the late 1950's for several reasons: tourist expenditures abroad increased; Japan began to challenge the great export nations of the world; steel from formerly noncompetitive mills began to compete with U.S. markets; automobiles and textiles in particular, as well as other products, began to set records in American sales; and the balance of payments deficit, spurred by the high prices that inflation and the over-valued dollar had created, brought disruptions in the free-world monetary sytem that rested heavily on the American dollar and the American gold reserve.

Academic arguments that the world could not live unless its goods were freely exchanged did little to check the rising resentments that by late 1968 had prompted the introduction of 717 bills in Congress to impose quotas on imports and the exertion of many legislative efforts in the states to require American-made products in public construction projects. The difficulty was that the advocates of free trade were talking about long-time gains, whereas farmers, industrialists, and laborers were thinking of short-time losses. In the quarrel between the United States and the Common Market, equality in trade was in some degree maintained by a give-and-take bargaining that has been called tit-for-tat exchanges, and in the monetary area by *ad hoc* agreements.

By 1970 the protectionist movement had achieved its greatest intensity since the days of the Great Depression. Industrialists were thoroughly convinced that the escape clause as modified in the 1962 Trade Expansion Act was no friend of the manufacturers and that the Tariff Commission and other agencies concerned were interested only in economic philosophy. There was not a single favorable finding under the law from 1962 to 1969; and the outward flow of American capital furthered the protectionist movement.

After coming into office in January 1969, President Richard M. Nixon reduced American commitments in Vietnam, but he had only limited success in stopping inflation and reducing unemployment. Congress, urged by many groups at home and irked by French and Japanese protective actions abroad, was by late 1970 pushing hard toward restrictive legislation. On June 29, 1971, the cry went up, "Stop the flow of imports!" "Save American Jobs!" as a thousand members of the International Union of Electrical, Radio, and Machine Workers marched down Constitution Avenue in Washington, D.C., and on to Capitol Hill to take their message to the lawmakers. The message was a familiar one, and it fell on sympathetic ears in Congress. The Burke-Hartke Act, which provided that the nation should, in effect, return to the tariff rates of the Smoot-Hawley law of 1930, was passed.

On Aug. 15, 1971, Nixon, in an effort to reduce unemployment, slow inflation, better the monetary situation, and improve the balance-of-payments deficit, froze wages, prices, and rents for a period of ninety days and recommended to Congress a limited but aggressive action that included a buy-American policy for capital goods. In international trade he suspended dollar redemptions in gold and imposed a 10 percent surtax on dutiable imports. The surtax, soon removed, had no appreciable effect on the amount of goods coming into American ports, but the "Nixon Shock," despite some fears to the contrary, did tend to stabilize the critical monetary situation. At the same time foreign reaction to the Burke-Hartke Act was quick and uncompromising. Some European countries placed immediate restrictions on American goods; and in November at a meeting of 102 nations on Ibiza, a small Spanish island off the east coast of Spain, a common and biting retaliation was agreed on. An escalation clause provided for progressively harsher penalties as the time of enforcement of the offending law lengthened. Pressure for repeal of the Burke-Hartke Act soon appeared in the United States, and was backed by many groups, including labor. On Dec. 24, 1971, Congress repealed the act. At the beginning of 1972 world leaders—and particularly Secretary of State William P. Rogers—were speaking out for freer international trade, although self-interest and resentments were all too obvious.

On July 16, 1972, sixteen nations met in Brussels to draw up plans for the formation of the largest economic unit in the free world. The six nations of the Common Market were to be joined on Jan. 1, 1973, by Great Britain, Denmark, Norway, and Ireland; the admission of Sweden, Switzerland, Austria, Finland, Iceland, and Portugal to limited membership was to make up the sixteen-nation unit. (Nine of the sixteen had been members of EFTA.) The many problems to be resolved included common tariffs, internal harmonizations, and the old problem of ultimate destination. Moreover, it was necessary to set forth clearly rules of origin. When it appeared that the new trade group might foster further restrictions, the United States objected vigorously, and controversies stirred further resentments among the Europeans, already quarreling among themselves. Unity, it seemed to some, was falling apart. Norway, with only 0.5 per-

cent unemployment and one of the highest standards of living in the world, feared that its economic welfare was being threatened and voted 53.6 percent against joining the new Common Market. Inflation, sweeping over Europe and Japan, further threatened unity. Gold, with a two-tier price, was being bid higher in Europe by speculators as it grew scarcer in the United States. George P. Schultz, secretary of the Treasury, proposed on Sept. 26, 1972, at a meeting of the IMF several pointed reforms to be made in the monetary system; though approved, they brought no immediate action.

Even some of the leaders of the movement to liberate world commerce had faltered. In midsummer Karl Schiller, West Germany's economic and finance minister and perhaps Europe's staunchest defender of free trade, resigned. In the United States, Rep. Wilbur D. Mills, chairman of the powerful House Ways and Means Committee, wavering in his long-time devotion to free trade, declared that he would support higher tariffs and import quotas unless "some other countries mended their ways."

Troubles fell thick and fast on the nation during 1973–75, and international trade continued to stir up controversy. The dollar, devalued for the second time in February 1973, was further deteriorated by the subsequent currency float; and at the end of the year a gasoline shortage developed, following the oil embargo by the Arab nations in October. The economic situation worsened in 1974, and by midyear the nation was in a deep recession. Unemployment continued to increase, surpluses continued to pile up, and prices continued to climb upward. Trade regulations lost some of their immediacy, but in 1976 the principle of a relatively free international commerce remained a fundamental necessity in the minds of the leaders of the concerned nations.

[Robert E. Baldwin, *Nontariff Distortions of International Trade;* Robert E. Baldwin and others, *Trade Growth and the Balance of Payments;* James A. Barnes, *John G. Carlisle: Financial Statesman;* William Beveridge, *Tariffs: The Case Examined;* Kenneth W. Dam, *The GATT: Law and International Economic Organization;* Herbert R. Ferleger, *David A. Wells and the American Revenue System;* J. Frank Gaston, *Border Taxes and International Economic Competition;* Harry Gordon Johnson, *Aspects of the Theory of Tariffs;* Kenneth C. Mackenzie, *Tariff Making and Trade Policy in the United States and Canada;* Allan Nevins, *Grover Cleveland: A Study in Courage;* Howard Samuel Piquet, *The United States Trade Expansion Act of 1962;* Ernest H. Preeg, *Traders and Diplomats: An Analysis of the Kennedy Round;* William A. Robinson, *Thomas B. Reed: Parliamentarian;* Frank W. Taussig, *The Tariff History of the United States.*]

JAMES A. BARNES

DICTIONARY OF AMERICAN HISTORY